55.00

55.00

RHODODENDRON HYBRIDS
Second Edition

RHODODENDRON HYBRIDS
Second Edition

(Includes selected, named forms of rhododendron species)

Homer E. Salley
and
Harold E. Greer

TIMBER PRESS
Portland, Oregon

Printed in Hong Kong

ISBN 0-88192-184-X

TIMBER PRESS, INC.
9999 SW Wilshire, Suite 124
Portland, Oregon 97225

Library of Congress Cataloging-in-Publication Data

Salley, Homer E.
    Rhododendron hybrids : (includes selected, named forms of
  rhododendron species) / Homer E. Salley and Harold E. Greer. -- 2nd
  ed.
        p.   cm.
    Includes bibliographical references.
    ISBN 0-88192-184-X
    1. Rhododendron--Varieties. 2. Rhododendron--Origin.   I. Greer,
  Harold E.   II. Title.
  SB413.R47S25 1992
  635.9'3362--dc20
                                                       91-44638
                                                          CIP

TABLE OF CONTENTS

Color plates follow page 194

INTRODUCTION TO THE SECOND EDITION

In his preface to the fourth edition of *The Rhododendron*, 1876, E. S. Rand, Jr. stated "While a new edition is demanded, there is, however, little the author can add to the subject matter. While many seedlings have been produced, we have seen none superior to the old varieties. This superiority we can hardly hope for, but we may attain by judicious hybridization increased hardiness, larger foliage, and greater substance of flower." If Mr. Rand could visit a modern hybridizer's greenhouse he would see some of his hopes realized and he would understand why "another edition" is frequently needed.

Our first edition described over 4,800 named rhododendron hybrids and selected, named forms of species. It included lepidotes, elepidotes and vireyas but not azaleas. This edition does not include vireyas or azaleas which have been treated elsewhere. Published registrations of hybrids and named forms of species from 1985 through 1991 are included here in addition to those described in the first edition. Many unregistered hybrids and named forms have also been added. Hybrids of unknown parentage have been included in the body of the text, whereas before they were briefly listed in an appendix. Previously an appendix described Delp Hybrids without parentage diagrams; if known to be in distribution, Weldon Delp's creations have now been included in the main text with complete genealogy.

An important change in format has now brought together hybrids of the same or nearly the same parentage. Though all are not technically grexes since not all those grouped have exactly identical parentage, such groupings were done for the convenience of the reader, as well as for economy of space in a book which previously duplicated many very long parentage diagrams.

Our works are largely compilations of the works of others. Complete parentage of each hybrid, all given in one place, is our own unique contribution. We think the present grouping by parent (with the family tree) will be recognized as a "first" and will be utilized as a time-saving device by hybridizers, growers and propagators. Registration officials must have wondered why rhododendron hybridizers kept doing the same thing over and over. The truth is the hybridizer may not have known he was duplicating the efforts of others of the past, but he does know the results are not always the same.

With much gratitude we acknowledge here the five most significant additions to the bibliography. Walter Schmalscheidt's thorough and beautiful work covers all hybrids of Germany, including the great work of Hans Hachmann. Greer's updated guidebook to what is now available was especially useful for data on hardiness, size and season of flower. Peter Cox is a nurseryman who writes; he and his son Kenneth wrote *Encyclopedia of Rhododendron Hybrids* after they conducted a wide survey of what grows well and where. Dr. Lansing Bulgin's studbook was extremely useful in making our groupings by parent, and John Street's book caused several revisions in English hybrid parentage.

Several others made significant and lasting contributions. David Balint of Vancouver, Washington, sent voluminous materials and made numerous corrections. Sarah Salley was an enduring resource for verifying details. Myra Best, a doctoral student in English, read much of the final text. Color illustrations will show photo credits for slides by Ray Redford of England, Dr. R. Withers of Australia, Dr. Richard Gustafson, Dr. Don Kellam and many others. Harold Greer provided most of the color photographs.

To read descriptive entries given in the text, some explanations are needed:

Abbreviations: ARS American Rhododendron Society
RBG Royal Botanic Garden(s)
RHS Royal Horticultural Society
cl. Clone, an asexual reproduction true to its parent in every way.
g. Grex, a group of sister seedlings all with the same parents, but with some variations in traits.

The abbreviations used in citing color illustrations published elsewhere are shown with the Bibliography, p. 342.

GIVEN BELOW IS AN EXPLANATION OF THE PARENTAGE DIAGRAMS SHOWN ON PAGES 1–334:

```
              -lacteum 1/2              -griffithianum 1/16    > species contribu-
              -                         -                        tion to the parentage
              -                         -                        in fractions; species
              -               -Kewense -                         plus unknowns
  LIONEL'S    -               -         -                        must total one
  TRIUMPH     -               -         -
              -       -Aurora -         -fortunei 5/16          > species names in
              -       -       -                                   lower case
              -       -       -
              -Naomi  -       -thomsonii 1/8                    > hybrid names
                      -                                           capitalized
                      -
                      -
                      -fortunei
```

6 ft (1.8m) *(at 10 yrs)*	−5F (−21C) *(bud hardiness)*	M *(blooming season: Early, Midseason, Late)*	5/4 *(flower/plant ratings [1–5])*

Cornish cream flowers, opaline pink margins fading later; up to 18 large flowers in magnificent trusses. Considered by Exbury to be highest quality. Rothschild. A.M. 1954. F.C.C. 1974. Color illus. J ARS 27:4 (1973), p. 238

> *description of flowers and foliage*
> *hybridizer/awards*
> *published color citation*

Awards of the ARS: S.P.A. Superior Plant Award
A.E. Award of Excellence
C.A. Conditional Award
P.A. Preliminary Award

Awards of the RHS: A.G.M. Award of Garden Merit
F.C.C. First Class Certificate
F.C.C. Wisley Trials (After testing)
A.M. Award of Merit
A.M. Wisley Trials (After testing)

The authors welcome comments, corrections and additions for future revisions.

LIST OF PLATES

Plate 1. 'Abe Arnott' by Weber.
Plate 2. 'Abegail' by Phetteplace.
Plate 3. 'Abendsonne' by Hobbie.
Plate 4. 'Abraham Lincoln' by Parsons.
Plate 5. 'Ada Lohr' by Blough.
Plate 6. 'Adelphia' by Dexter.
Plate 7. 'Admiral Piet Hein' by C. B. van Nes.
Plate 8. 'Albatross' by Rothschild.
Plate 9. 'Alice Poore' by Dexter.
Plate 10. 'Aloha' by Phetteplace/Briggs/Paden.
Plate 11. 'Amigo' by Goheen.
Plate 12. 'Amphion' by A. Waterer.
Plate 13. 'Anica Bricogne', origin unknown.
Plate 14. 'Anna Baldsiefen' by Baldsiefen.
Plate 15. 'Anna Rose Whitney' by Whitney/T. Van Veen, Sr.
Plate 16. 'Anne Teese' by A. J. Teese.
Plate 17. 'Anne's Delight' by Whitney/Sather.
Plate 18. 'Annie Dalton' by Gable.
Plate 19. 'Antoon Van Welie' by Endtz.
Plate 20. 'Apodeno' by Aberconway.
Plate 21. 'Apricot Delight' by Van de Ven.
Plate 22. 'April Chimes' by Hillier.
Plate 23. 'Aries' by Ramsden.
Plate 24. 'Arthur J. Ivens' by Hillier.
Plate 25. 'Audacious' by Brueckner.
Plate 26. 'Aurora' by Gill/Rothschild.
Plate 27. 'Autumn Gold' by T. Van Veen, Sr.
Plate 28. 'Avalanche' by Rothschild.
Plate 29. 'Baden-Baden' by Hobbie.
Plate 30. 'Balalaika' by Hachmann.
Plate 31. 'Ballet' by Pride.
Plate 32. 'Balta' by Mezitt.
Plate 33. 'Barbara Behring' by Behring.
Plate 34. 'Barbara Wallace' by C. B. van Nes.
Plate 35. 'Bariton' by Hachmann.
Plate 36. 'Barmstedt' by Hachmann.
Plate 37. 'Bashful Betty' by J. Elliott/Fisher.
Plate 38. 'Bass River' by Dexter.
Plate 39. 'Belona' by Hachmann.
Plate 40. 'Berg's Yellow' by Berg.
Plate 41. 'Bernard Shaw' by Reuthe.
Plate 42. 'Besse Howells' by Shammarello.

Plate 43. 'Betty Anderson' by E. Anderson.
Plate 44. 'Betty Sears' by Whitney/Sather.
Plate 45. 'Betty Wormald' by M. Koster.
Plate 46. 'Betty's Bells' by Sheedy/Skei.
Plate 47. 'Billy Budd' by Hanger.
Plate 48. 'Black Sport' by Nelson/Briggs.
Plate 49. 'Blandyanum' by Standish and Noble.
Plate 50. 'Blue Bell' by C. B. van Nes.
Plate 51. 'Blue Ensign' by Slocock.
Plate 52. 'Blue Pacific' by Whitney/Sather.
Plate 53. 'Blue Star' by Gen. Harrison.
Plate 54. 'Blue Tit' by J. C. Williams.
Plate 55. 'Bluette' by Lancaster.
Plate 56. 'Bob', a hybrid from New Zealand.
Plate 57. 'Bodnant Yellow' by Aberconway.
Plate 58. 'Brandt Red' by Brandt.
Plate 59. 'Brinny' by Graves/Janeck.
Plate 60. 'Britton Hill' by Britt Smith.
Plate 61. 'Britton Hill Bugle' by Britt Smith.
Plate 62. 'Brocade' by Rothschild.
Plate 63. 'Buchanan Simpson' by Greig.
Plate 64. 'Burgundy Cherry' by Dexter/Knippenberg.
Plate 65. 'Burgundy Rose' by Lem.
Plate 66. 'Buttermint' by Mauritsen/Greer.
Plate 67. 'C.O.D.' by Dexter/Everitt.
Plate 68. 'C. P. Raffill' from R.B.G., Kew.
Plate 69. 'Cabaret' by Sather.
Plate 70. 'Cadis' by Gable.
Plate 71. 'Caerhays John' by J. C. Williams.
Plate 72. 'Caerhays Philip' by Charles Williams.
Plate 73. 'Camillo Schneider' by Hobbie.
Plate 74. 'Campy' by Shammarello.
Plate 75. 'Canadian Beauty' by Lofthouse.
Plate 76. 'Caperci Special' by Caperci.
Plate 77. 'Captain Kidd' by Henny.
Plate 78. 'Caractacus' by A. Waterer.
Plate 79. 'Carex Blush' by Rothschild.
Plate 80. 'Carita' by Rothschild.
Plate 81. 'Carlene' by Lem/Fawcett.
Plate 82. 'Carmen' by Rothschild.

Plate 83. 'Caroline Allbrook' by A. F. George.
Plate 84. 'Catalode' ('County of York') by Gable.
Plate 85. 'Catawbiense Album' by A. Waterer.
Plate 86. 'Cecil Number 8' by Dexter.
Plate 87. 'Celebrity' by Elliott.
Plate 88. 'Centennial Celebration' by Peste/Briggs.
Plate 89. 'Charlotte De Rothschild' by Rothschild.
Plate 90. 'Cheer' by Shammarello.
Plate 91. 'Chelsea' by Rothschild.
Plate 92. 'Cherry Jam' by Delp.
Plate 93. 'Cherry Red' by Dexter.
Plate 94. 'Chesapeake' by Nearing.
Plate 95. 'Chikor' by Cox.
Plate 96. 'China Doll' by A. J. Teese.
Plate 97. 'Chinmar' by Sifferman/McClure.
Plate 98. 'Clara Raustein' by Raustein.
Plate 99. 'Clementine Lemaire' by Moser.
Plate 100. 'Clove' by Rothschild.
Plate 101. 'College Pink', from Massey College, NZ.
Plate 102. 'Colonel Coen' by E. Ostbo.
Plate 103. 'Comte de Gomer' by J. Waterer.
Plate 104. 'Concorde' by A. van Nes.
Plate 105. 'Conroy' by Aberconway (not a hybrid).
Plate 106. 'Consolini's Windmill' by Consolini.
Plate 107. 'Constable' by Hanger.
Plate 108. 'Cornubia' by B. Fox.
Plate 109. 'Corona' by J. Waterer.
Plate 110. 'Coronation Day' by Crosfield.
Plate 111. 'Cotton Candy' by J. Henny/Wennekamp.
Plate 112. 'Countess of Derby' by H. White.
Plate 113. 'Coupon' by Blough.
Plate 114. 'Cowslip' by Aberconway.
Plate 115. 'Cream Crest' by Wright.
Plate 116. 'Cream Pie' by Minor/Greer.
Plate 117. 'Creole Belle' by Thompson.
Plate 118. 'Crimson Glory', from Cottage Gardens.
Plate 119. 'Dairymaid' by Slocock.
Plate 120. 'Dalkeith' by McLaughlin/Warren.
Plate 121. 'Damaris' by E. J. P. Magor.

x

LIST OF ADDITIONAL PEDIGREES

The following hybrids are pictured in the book but do not have accompanying text descriptions.

'Belona'. Synonym of 'Hachmann's Belona', q.v. Plate 39.

'Betty Sears' (*yakushimanum* × 'Corona'). Whitney/Sather. Plate 44.

'Bob' (*yakushimanum* × 'May Day'). New Zealand hybrid. Plate 56.

'Britton Hill' ('Jean Marie de Montague' × 'Red Loderi'). Britt Smith. Plate 60.

'Britton Hill Bugle' ('Karkov' × 'Red Loderi'). Britt Smith. Plate 60.

'Comte de Gomer'. Parentage unknown. J. Waterer. Plate 103.

'Duque de San Lucar' ('Marion' × 'Prof. C. S. Sargent'). Felix/Dijkhuis. Plate 148.

'Falcon Gold' (*macabeanum* × *falconeri*). G. Smith, Pukeiti, NZ. Plate 168.

'Fred Waterer' (*catawbiense* hybrid). J. Waterer, pre-1958. Plate 181.

'Friesland' ('Pink Pearl' × *catawbiense* hybrid). Endtz, pre-1958. Plate 182.

'Gumdrop'. Parentage unknown. From Hendrick's Park. Plate 213.

'Helene Strybing' (*cinnabarinum* × *maddenii?*). Reiter. Plate 225.

'James W. Seihl'. Name change from 'Gahagen', q.v. Blough. Plate 257.

'Madame Cochet'. Parentage unknown. Bertin. Plate 328.

'Marcat' ['Mars' × (*catawbiense* × *haematodes*)]. Gable. Plate 339.

'Marcy Margot' (*griersonianum* × unknown). Lelliott. Plate 341.

'Margaret Caroline'. Parentage unknown. From Australia. Plate 342.

'Marlis' ('Mars' × *yakushimanum* 'Koichiro Wada'). Hachmann, 1985. Plate 347.

'Melrose Pink' (*fortunei* hybrid). Eichelser. Plate 360.

'Midway'. Parentage unknown. Van de Ven. Plate 364.

'Moerheim Scarlet' ('Earl of Athlone' × *forrestii* Repens Group) Hobbie/Ruys. Plate 367.

'Mrs. O. B. Watson'. Parentage unknown. Watson, Portland, OR. Plate 392.

'My Valentine' (*chaetomallum* × 'Cornubia'). Cochran. Plate 398.

'N. N. Sherwood'. Parentage unknown. Sibray. Plate 399.

'Nosutchianum' (*kalmia* × *williamsianum*). Lem. Plate 406.

'Polycinn' (*polyandrum* × *cinnabarinum*). Origin unknown. Plate 441.

'Prairie Fire'. Parentage unknown. Korth. Plate 445.

'Red Prince'. Parentage and origin unknown. Plate 461.

'Rimini'. Parentage and origin unknown. Plate 468.

'Rollie Mulkie' ('A. Bedford' × orange hybrid). Mulkie. Plate 472.

'Rose Walloper' (Walloper g.). Lem. Plate 476.

'Roundabout' (Azaleodendron). Parentage and origin unknown. Plate 478.

'Salmon Grierson'. Parentage and origin unknown. Plate 486.

'Satin Glow' ('Loderi King George' × 'Cup Day'). Van de Ven. Plate 489.

'Sckookumchuck' (*yakushimanum* × 'Mars') × 'America'. Minch. Plate 492.

'Scott's Valentine' ([*johnsonteanum* × *veitchianum* Cubittii Group] × *moupinense*) × 'Rose Scott'. Hybridizer: Scott. Plate 493.

'Sloppy Joe' ('Whitney's Orange' × 'Idealist'). Thompson. Plate 506.

'Strawberry Cream' (*flavidum* × 'Lady Rosebery'). Brandt/Cox. Plate 520.

'Sydney Sunset'. Parentage unknown. From Australia. Plate 532.

'Top Dollar'. Parentage unknown. Whitney. Plate 551.

'Waterer's Rose Perfection'. Parentage unknown. Waterer. Plate 568.

'White Peter' ('Blue Peter', selfed). Mehlquist, reg. 1991. Plate 575.

'Wilsoni'. Synonym of 'Laetevirens', q.v. Origin unknown. Plate 582.

A

                    -mauve seedling--unknown 1/2
A. BEDFORD or ARTHUR BEDFORD-
                    -ponticum 1/2
6ft(1.8m) -5F(-21C) ML 4/3   Habit large, upright, vigorous;
sun-tolerant. Leaves to 6.5in(16.5cm) long, red-stemmed, glossy
dark green; held one year. Openly funnel-shaped flowers, light
mauve in tube, with darker lobes, marked deep rose madder to almost black; 16 in domed trusses.   Named for the Head Gardner to
Lionel de Rothschild.   T. Lowinsky.   A.M. 1936.   F.C.C. Wisley
Trials 1958.   Color illus. Cox pl. 1; JS p. 91; VV p. 2.

                    -campylocarpum 1/2
A. GILBERT-
                    -fortunei ssp. discolor 1/2
Pale creamy buff with saffron rose-pink.   Lowinsky. A.M. 1925.

* *
                                -catawbiense 3/8
                    -Parsons Grandiflorum-
        -America-   -unknown 5/8
AA-17-   -dark red hybrid--unknown
    -               -catawbiense
        -Ann Rutlidge-
                    -unknown
Buds a blend of grayed deep crimson and deep red; flowers vivid
red-purple, edged in grayed medium purplish red, a darker flare.
A tall plant, hardy to -25F(-32C).   W. Delp.
AA-36 Parentage as above
Plant and flower much like the above, but semi-petaloid.   Delp.
* *
* *
                    -campylocarpum 1/2
ABALONE-
                    -callimorphum 1/2
Flowers cream to soft pink. Top buds cut by frost at Exbury, in
severe winters.   Rothschild, 1933.
FLASHLIGHT   Parentage as above, except reversed
Flower buds orange-pink opening to lemon yellow, fading to pale
yellow, with a red blotch. Plant of neat habit and slow growth,
about 7ft(2.1m) at Exbury when mature.   Rothschild, 1938.
* *

ABBEYI Parentage unknown
Flowers of delicate pink, the exterior frosted and veined with
rose. G. Abbey. A.M. 1900.

        -thomsonii 1/2
ABBOT-
        -arboreum ssp. delavayi var. delavayi 1/2
Deep red flowers, blooming very early.   Rothschild, 1933.

                    -caucasicum 1/4
        -Dr. Stocker-
ABBY BOULTER-   -griffithianum 1/4
                    -unknown 1/2
Trusses of 11-13 funnel-shaped flowers, white with pink spotting
on the dorsal lobe. Elliptic leaves, 3.5in(9cm) x 1.5in(3.5cm).
Plant 6.6ft(2m) tall. V. Boulter cross; F. Boulter, reg. 1986.

                    -maximum 1/4
        -Marchioness of Lansdowne-
ABE ARNOTT-   -unknown 1/2
    -               -catawbiense 1/4
        -Lee's Dark Purple-
                    -unknown
5ft(1.5m) -5F(-21C) ML   Orchid purple flowers; a heavy blotch
on upper lobe spreads into the throat and adjacent lobes. Round
truss of 16. Narrowly elliptic leaves. E. Weber, reg. 1974.

                    -catawbiense
        -Album Elegans-
    -Loder's White-   -unknown
ABEGAIL-   -griffithianum
    -calophytum, pink form
5ft(1.5m) -5F(-21C) E 3/3   For other possible parentage information, see LODER'S WHITE.   Leaves 5.5in(14cm) x 2in(7.6cm).
Flowers 3in(7.6cm) across, pink, small dark dorsal blotch; about
14 in a spherical truss. Dr. C. Phetteplace, reg. 1979.   Col-
or illus. ARS Q 33:3 (1979), p. 170.

                    -calostrotum ssp. keleticum 1/4
        -unnamed hybrid-
ABEILLE-   -dauricum 1/4
        -unknown 1/2
20in(.5m) -22F(-30C) M Funnel-shaped flowers, vivid to strong
reddish purple, spotted red; lax trusses of 3-5. Glossy, elliptic leaves, with tiny brown scales. Plant rounded, broader than
tall.   Seed from Siberia, Vladimir Vasak collector; J. Brueckner, reg. 1986.

ABENDGLUT   Described under ELISABETH HOBBIE, q.v.

ABENDROT   Described under ELISABETH HOBBIE, q.v.

                    -catawbiense 1/4
        -John Walter-
ABENDSONNE-   -arboreum 1/4
        -dichroanthum ssp. syphocalyx 1/2
4ft(1.2m) 5F(-15C) EM Bell-shaped orangey red flowers. Plant
compact and rounded; dark green leaves held 3 years. D. Hobbie,
cross c. 1952.   Color illus. WS, 1989, p. 34.

        -Laura   -griersonianum 1/2
    - Aberconway-   -thomsonii 1/8
    -       -Barclayi-   -arboreum 1/16
ABESSA-   -Glory of Penjerrick-
    -                           -griffithianum 1/16
    -       -forrestii Repens Group 1/4
    -Elizabeth-
            -griersonianum
Scarlet flowers.   Lord Aberconway, intro. 1946.

            -yakushimanum 1/2
ABIGAIL JURY-   -dichroanthum 1/4
        -Dido-
            -decorum 1/4
Trusses of 9-10 flowers, 6-lobed, of white flushed carmine rose,
upper lobe spotted green and red.   Fawn-colored, suede-like indumentum on young foliage.   F. M. Jury, New Zealand, reg. 1982.

                    -catawbiense 1/2
ABRAHAM LINCOLN-
                    -unknown 1/2
5ft(1.5m) -25F(-32C) M 3/3   Real hardiness. Flowers strong
red, slowly fading to pink.   S. B. Parsons, before 1875.

                                    -catawbiense 1/16
                        -Parsons Grandiflorum-
            -America-   -unknown 11/16
    -Vivacious-   -dark red hybrid--unknown
    -       -   -griersonianum 1/8 -arboreum 1/32
    -       -Dr. Ross-   -Doncaster-
    -           -Borde Hill-   -unknown
    -           -   -   -griffithianum
ABUNDANT-   -Mrs. A.M.-
    -                       Williams-unknown
    -                           -griffithianum 3/32
    -                   -Queen Wilhelmina-
    -       -Britannia-   -unknown
    -Francesca-   -Stanley Davies--unknown
            -
            -Dexter no. 202--unknown
Abundant flowers of clear, bright red.   The Haags, intro. 1988.

                    -griffithianum 1/8
            -Mars-
        -Vulcan-   -unknown 1/8
ABUNDANT LIFE-   -griersonianum 1/4
            -Gunrei--Satsuki azalea 1/2
Unregistered azaleodendron. A. Martin, 1961.

ACADIA   Synonym for CORNWALLIS

* *
        -Pygmalion--unknown
ACCLAIM-   -haematodes
        -unnamed hybrid-   -fortunei
                    -Wellfleet-
                        -decorum
5ft(1.5m) -5F(-21C) M 3/3   Exact combination of parentage is
uncertain. Flowers of good substance, 4in(10cm) wide, of strong

purplish red with a small dark eye; 16 held in a ball-shaped
truss 6in(12.5cm) across. Plant rounded, well-branched. Dexter
before 1943; selected by J. Wister; Tyler Arboretum, reg. 1980.
Color illus. Cox pl. 2.
ACCOMAC   Parentage as above
4ft(1.2m) -5F(-21C) M 3/3 Plant rounded, moderately branched; yellow-green leaves. Openly funnel-shaped flowers 2.5in(6.4
cm) broad; strong purplish red corolla, spotted darker on dorsal
lobes, very dark in throat. Spherical trusses of 14. Dexter
cross; Tyler Arboretum, reg. 1980. Color illus. LW pl. 11.
ACCOMPLISHMENT   Parentage as above
5ft(1.5m) -15F(-26C) M 3/3   Flowers white with wide border
of strong purplish red (bicolor effect); trusses hold 15. Quite
different from others of this group. Dexter before 1943; grown
at Swarthmore College; Tyler Arboretum, reg. 1985.
ARONIMINK   Parentage as above
5ft(1.5) -5F(-21C) EM 4/3   Flowers strong purplish red, 4in.
(10cm) across, spherical trusses of 20. Vigorous plant, as wide
as tall; leaves olive. Dexter; Scott Hort. Found., reg. 1980.
AVONDALE   Parentage as above
5ft(1.85m) -5F(-21C) M 3/3   Flowers of heavy substance, fragrant, widely funnel-campanulate, 3in(7.6cm) wide, of strong red
spotted black. Globular truss 5in(12.7cm) broad, of 14 flowers.
Well-branched plant. Dexter cross; Tyler Arboretum, reg. 1980.
Color illus. HG p. 135.
DEXTER'S AGATHA   Parentage as above
4ft(1.2m) -5F(-21C) M   Purplish red flowers, 3in(7.8cm) wide,
6- or 7-lobed; spherical trusses of 10. Plant as broad as high;
olive green leaves. Dexter cross; Tyler Arboretum, reg. 1981.
DEXTER'S HARLEQUIN   Parentage as above
10ft(3m) x 9ft(2.7m)(21 yrs.) -5F(-21C) M   Flowers deep purplish pink at edges, paling to nearly white in centers, 5-7 very
wavy lobes; truss of 10-15. Glossy olive green foliage. Dexter
cross; Tyler Arboretum, reg. 1983. Color illus. (incorrectly
captioned as HALESITE) ARS Q 29:2 (1975), p. 102.
DOROTHY RUSSELL   Parentage as above
5ft(1.5m) -5F(-21C) M   A parent of BIG DADDY. Large flowers
of rose, with darker spots. Dexter; R. Schwoebel raiser. Col-
or illus. ARS J 43:4 (1989), p. 206.
KELLEY   Parentage as above ?
6ft(1.8m) 0F(-18C) M   Flowers strong purplish red with darker spotting, lower lobes medium purplish red; spherical truss of
10. Olive green foliage. Dexter cross; G. Wister, reg. 1983.
TODMORDEN   Parentage as above ?
5ft(1.5m) -10F(-23C) M 3/3   Deep purplish pink margins shading lighter, fading almost white--a bicolor effect. Spherical
truss of 8-15 flowers of 5 to 7 wavy/frilled lobes. Plant broad
as tall. C. Dexter; Scott Horticultural Foundation, reg. 1983.
WISSAHICKON   Parentage as above ?
5ft(1.5m) -10F(-23C) M   Bright rose red flowers with deeper
red throat and brownish green spotting. Heat-resistant. Autumn
bloom possible. Dexter cross. Color illus. Cox pl. 200.
* *

ACCOLADE   Described under VALLEY CREEK, q.v.

ACCOMPLISHMENT   Described under ACCLAIM, q.v.

* *
                  -thomsonii 1/4
        -Barclayi-   -arboreum 3/8
        -         -Glory of Penjerrick-
ACHILLES-   -griffithianum 1/8
        -         -arboreum
        -Werei-
                  -barbatum 1/4
Cherry red flowers, 5-lobed, 3in(7.6cm) across. Trusses hold 16
flowers. Gen. Harrison, reg. 1969.
ADAMANT   Parentage as above
Flowers deep red, unmarked, 3in(7.6cm) across, 2in(5cm) long; 15
per tight truss. Gen. Harrison, reg. 1962
* *

                       -wardii ? 1/8
                -Chlorops-
        -Lackamas Spice-   -vernicosum ? 1/8
ACIERTO-   -diaprepes 1/4
        -         -fortunei ssp. discolor 1/4
        -Bonito-   -fortunei 1/8
               -Pride of Leonardslee-
                (Luscombei)   -thomsonii 1/8
6ft(1.8m) 0F(-18C) M   Fragrant, 7-lobed flowers of light Ney-

ron rose, with geranium lake flares, in 8in(20cm) broad trusses
of 17. Upright plant, half as wide as tall; yellow-green leaves
held 3 years. D. Goheen cross; reg. 1984. Bulgin, intro. 1982.

* *
                  -smirnowii 1/8
        -unnamed-
        -       -hybrid-   -Parsons   -catawbiense
        -King-   -America- Grandiflorum-   5/32
        - Tut-   -   -unknown
        -    -   -dark red hybrid unknown
ACTIVE DUTY-   -   -catawbiense, red form
        -    -unnamed hybrid-
        -              -unknown 7/32
        -yakushimanum--Ken Janeck 1/2
Buds blend strong purplish red to strong purplish pink. Flowers
white, frilled, edges and anthers vivid purplish red; filaments
and style of deep purplish pink. Al Smith cross; Delp raiser.
SOLID IMPACT   Parentage as above
Buds vivid purplish reds. Frilled flowers of deep purplish pink
with dorsal spotting of vivid yellow-green; white filaments. Al
Smith cross; W. Delp raiser.
SPECIAL SPARKLE   parentage as above
Buds a blend of vivid purplish reds, deep purplish pink; frilled
white flowers edged in same pink, spotted with brilliant yellow-
green. Al Smith cross; Delp raiser.
* *

* *
        -Lady Alice Fitzwilliam--unknown 1/2
ACTRESS-
        -edgeworthii (bullatum) 1/2
Flowers white inside, stained red outside, and fragrant. Blooms
early. Gen. Harrison, reg. 1965.
BERT'S OWN   Parentage as above
5ft(1.5m) 15F(-9C) M   White flowers streaked in pale purplish
pink, very fragrant; trusses of only 2. J. Evans, Penjerrick,
raiser; Leonardslee intro.; Maj. E. W. M. Magor, reg. 1988.
* *

ACUBIFOLIUM(ACUBAEFOLIUM)--form of ponticum
Light lilac flowers; spotted foliage. Hardy. --E. Rand (1876).

                       -diaprepes 1/4
              -Polar Bear-
ADA AGNES ARCHER-   -auriculatum 1/4
        -                 -griersonianum 1/4
        -Vulcan's Flame-   -griffithianum 1/8
                 -Mars-
                        -unknown 1/8
3ft(.9m) -5F(-21C) VL Flowers of good substance, 5in(12.7cm)
by 3in(7.6cm), fragrant, deep purplish pink. Trusses 13in(33cm)
wide by 6in(15.2cm), hold 10 flowers. A. J. Holden, reg. 1981.

* *
                  -Dexter hybrid--unknown
        -Janet Blair-
ADA LOHR-   -unknown 9/16
        -         -catawbiense var. album Glass--Catalgla 1/4
        -Ice Cube-   -catawbiense 1/16
        -         -   -Catawbiense Album-
                  -Belle Heller-   -unknown
                        -catawbiense var. album 1/8
Large trusses of beige- to flesh-colored flowers, with a golden
blotch. Plant of medium size, compact, well-foliaged. Blough.
Best of Show Award, Great Lakes Ch., ARS, 1987.
PRISTINE   Parentage as above
White flowers, edged pink with green blotch. R. L. Blough.
* *

ADAMANT   Described under ACHILLES, q.v.

                  -fortunei 1/4
        -Mary Cowan-
ADANA-   -diaprepes 1/4
        -         -arboreum ssp. nilagiricum 1/4
        -Noyo Chief-
                  -unknown 1/4
5ft(1.5m) 5F(-15C) EM   Ball-shaped truss 6in(15cm) across, of
14-16 flowers, vermilion red with jasper red throat, 7-lobed.
Plant broader than high; leaves held 4 years; new growth bronze.
Dr. David Goheen, intro. 1980; reg. 1986.

```
        -thomsonii 1/2
ADDER-
        -diphrocalyx 1/2
Flowers of deep rose.    Rothschild, 1933.


                  -griffithianum 1/8
           -Kewense-
        -Aurora-      -fortunei 1/8
ADELAIDE-      -thomsonii 3/4
        -thomsonii
5ft(1.5m)  OF(-18C)  M  Waxy red flowers as thomsonii, five dark
nectar pouches at base.   Rothschild, intro. 1930.   A.M. 1935.


             -maximum 1/2        -griersonianum 1/8
ADELE'S PINK-             -Azor-
          -unnamed hybrid-    -fortunei ssp. discolor 1/8
                          -unknown 1/4
3ft(.9m)  -15F(-26C)  L    Deep rose pink buds.  Flowers openly
funnel-shaped, 2.5in(6.4cm) broad, medium rose shading to creamy
white in center and throat.  Domed trusses of 14-16.  W. Fetter-
hoff, reg. 1981.


* * * * * * * * * * * * * * * * * * * * * * * * * * * *
             -maximum, ivory form 1/2
ADELE'S YELLOW-
             -wardii 1/2
3ft(.9m)  -10F(-23C)  L    Buds cream and pink; flowers primrose
yellow, widely funnel-campanulate; lax truss of 14.  Plant broad
and semi-dwarf, branching well.   W. Fetterhoff, reg. 1980.
SUSAN KAY   Parentage as above
1.5ft(.45m)  -10F(-23C)  L   Plant compact, and twice as wide as
tall.  Primrose yellow flowers, with dorsal blotch of light yel-
low-green; lax trusses of 15.   W. Fetterhoff, reg. 1981.
* * * * * * * * * * * * * * * * * * * * * * * * * * * *

ADELPHIA   Parentage unknown
5ft(1.5m)  -5F(-21C)  EM   Flowers medium purplish pink at rims,
paling to white at center.   C. O. Dexter cross.


       -neriiflorum 1/2
ADJUTANT-
       -sperabile 1/2
Scarlet trusses on a very free-flowering plant, "but not as good
as either parent"--L. de R.   Rothschild, intro. 1933.


                     -souliei 1/16
             -Soulbut-
       -Vanessa-       -fortunei--Sir Charles Butler 1/16
       -             -griersonianum 1/4
    -Adonis-       -griffithianum 3/8
    -      -Sunrise-
ADLO-             -griersonianum
    -      -griffithianum
    -Loderi-
          -fortunei 1/4
Flowers pale pink.   Lord Aberconway, intro. 1950.


ADMIRABLE   Parentage unknown
Trusses of 10-12 flowers, whitish rose, a brownish green blotch.
Late season.   R. de Belder, Belgium, reg. 1968.

ADMIRAL PIET HEIN   Described under MRS. A. T. DE LA MARE, q.v.


          -dichroanthum 1/4
       -Jasper-             -fortunei ssp. discolor 1/8
       -      -Lady Bessborough-
ADOLPH             -campylocarpum Elatum Group 1/8
HEINEMAN-       -griersonianum 1/4
       -Tally Ho-
              -facetum (eriogynum) 1/4
Straw yellow flowers tipped in pink, appearing late.  Bush semi-
dwarf.   C. S. Seabrook, reg. 1965.


                -souliei 1/8
          -Soulbut-
    -Vanessa-       -fortunei--Sir Charles Butler 1/8
ADONIS-    -griersonianum 1/2
    -       -griffithianum 1/4
    -Sunrise-
          -griersonianum
Pale pink flowers.   Lord Aberconway, intro. 1942.
```

```
                  -souliei 1/16
           -Soulbut-
           -Vanessa-      -fortunei--Sir Charles Butler 1/16
    -Adonis-      -griersonianum 1/4
    -       -      -griffithianum 1/4
    -      -Sunrise-
ADOTA-             -griersonianum
    -      -griffithianum
    -      -Loderi-
    -Coreta-       -fortunei 1/8
          -arboreum ssp. zeylanicum 1/4
Red-flowered trusses.   Lord Aberconway, intro. 1946.


          -williamsianum 1/2
ADRASTIA-
          -neriiflorum 1/2
3ft(.9m)  OF(-18C)  EM   3/2   Selected from a group, but only
one form known in the U.S.  Flowers deep pink, bell-shaped  like
most williamsianum hybrids, held in clusters of 1-4.  Lord Aber-
conway, 1946.


                -williamsianum 1/4
    -Adrastia-
ADREAN-       -neriiflorum 1/4
    -beanianum 1/2
Red flowers.   Lord Aberconway, intro. 1946.


ADRIAAN KOSTER   Described under ZUIDERZEE, q.v.


                          -griersonianum 1/4
          -Mrs. Horace Fogg-        -griffithianum
          -             -Loderi Venus-
ADRIENNE ELIZABETH-             -fortunei 3/8
          -       -griffithianum 3/8
          -Loderi-
                -fortunei
6ft(1.8m) x 6ft(12 yrs)  5F(-15C)  EM   Buds deep purplish pink
opening to pale purplish pink, shading to yellowish white in the
throat, with margins strong purplish pink; a star-shaped blotch.
Britt M. Smith, reg. 1989.


                     -griersonianum 1/4
       -Grierosplendour-       -ponticum 1/8
       -          -Purple Splendour-
ADVENT-             -unknown 3/16
       -             -decorum 1/8
       -       -Decatros-       -catawbiense 1/16
       -Millard Kepner-      -Atrosanguineum-
             -yakushimanum 1/4     -unknown
5.5ft(1.65m) high x 6ft(1.8m)  -5F(-21C)  ML   Ball truss of 14
flowers with 5 wavy-edged lobes, deep purplish pink; prominent
red blotch on dorsal lobe.  Leaves dull green, slightly convex.
Shrub wider than tall.   M. E. Byrkit, reg. 1988.


          -arboreum 1/4
       -Cornubia-       -thomsonii 1/8
ADVIE-       -Shilsonii-
       -             -barbatum 1/8
       -diphrocalyx 1/2
Compact plant.  Flowers deep rose.   Rothschild, 1933.


AESTIVALE--form of cinnabarinum
Yellow flowers, tipped orange; leaves narrower than other forms.
Hutchinson.


          -ambiguum 1/2
AFFECTION-
          -cinnabarinum Blandfordiflorum Group 1/2
Pale yellow flowers with rose tips.   Sunningdale, 1951.


AFGHAN   Parentage and origin unknown
Flowers deep, blood red.  A parent of an Exbury hybrid, MICHELE.


          -fortunei ssp. discolor 1/2
AFTERGLOW-
          -hardy hybrid--unknown 1/2
Flowers pale pink and mauve.   W. C. Slocock, 1935.


          -dichroanthum 1/2
AGATE PASS JEWEL-
          -unknown 1/2
```

3ft(.9m)   5F(-15C)   L 3/3   Flowers 1.5in(3.8cm) across, pale
orange with faint green stripes inside and out; trusses of about
5.   Leaves 3.5in(9cm) x 1.5in(4cm), held 3 years.   Benj. Nelson
cross; Florence Putney, reg. 1975.

* *
        -yakushimanum 1/2
AGATEEN-   -catawbiense 1/4
        -Henriette Sargent-
                          -unknown 1/4
4ft(1.2m)(13 yrs) -10F(-23C) ML   Semi-dwarf plant, broader
than tall; leaves with plastered brown indumentum, held 3 years.
Buds of Neyron rose, opening to spinel red flowers, of good substance; trusses of 15.   Frank Arsen cross; reg. 1983.
GAY ARSEN   Parentage as above.
Flowers Neyron rose, fading lighter, dorsal blotch sap green,
openly funnel-shaped; domed trusses hold 15. Plant broader than
high; leaves held 3 years.   Arsen intro. 1974; reg. 1983.
* *

                    -sanguineum ssp. didymum 1/4
        -Arthur Osborn-
AGLARE-   -griersonianum 1/2
     -              -griersonianum
        -Rapture-
                    -arboreum ssp. zeylanicum 1/4
Flowers deep red, 12 per truss.   Gen. Harrison, 1955.

                    -sanguineum ssp. didymum 1/4
        -Arthur Osborn-
AGLEAM-   -griersonianum 1/4
     -              -griffithianum 1/4
        -Isabella-
                    -auriculatum 1/4
Bright red flowers.   Gen. Harrison, 1954.

AGLO   Described under OLGA MEZITT, q.v.

    -diaprepes 1/2
AGLOW-   -sanguineum ssp. didymum 1/4
     -Arthur Osborn-
                    -griersonianum 1/4
Flowers pink with darker center.   Gen. Harrison, 1954.

AGNES   Parentage unknown
A parent of HOMER, a 1906 cross by Seidel, and surely not AGNES
(A.M. 1943) by Lord Swathling. (Seidel might have used AGNES
BEAUFORT or AGNES MANGLES).   Large, lilac-tinged carmine flowers
with a dark spot.

    -griersonianum 1/2
AGNES-   -griffithianum 3/8
     -              -Beauty of Tremough-
     -Norman Gill-   -arboreum 1/8
                    -griffithianum
Deep pink in bud, opening lighter pink, with darker pink on the
edges and the base of the tube. Lord Swaythling. A.M. 1943.

        -griffithianum 1/2
AGNES BEAUFORT-
        -unknown 1/2
Color, etc. unknown.   Possibly intro. by Methven or Mangles.

            -Loder's White, q.v. for 2 possible
AGNES LAMONT-   parentage diagrams
            -thomsonii
Various shades of pink.   Royal Botanic Garden, Edinburgh.

            -griffithianum 1/2
AGNES MANGLES-
            -unknown 1/2
Cross by Mangles. Date unknown.

                -griffithianum 1/4
    -George Hardy-
AIDA-   -catawbiense 1/4
    -auriculatum 1/2

White flowers with dark red markings.   Rothschild, 1933.

        -griffithianum 1/2
AILEEN HENDERSON-
        -unknown 1/2
Flowers yellow to creamy white, with a brownish yellow blotch,
held in large conical trusses.   M. Koster & Sons, before 1958.

            -tephropeplum 1/2
AILSA-JEAN-
            -moupinense 1/2
Pale pink flowers.   G. M. Adams-Acton, 1942. A.M. 1946.

            -lutescens 1/2
AIRY FAIRY-
            -mucronulatum--Cornell Pink 1/2
4ft(1.2m)   OF(-18C) E 3/3 Flowers pink with deeper red spotting, widely funnel-shaped, 1.75in(4.4cm) across, trusses of 3;
floriferous. Leaves narrowly elliptic, almost deciduous. Maloney cross; Mae Granston, reg. 1976.   A.M. Wisley Trials 1984.

AJAX   Parentage unknown
Flowers of bright rose.   G. Waterer, before 1860.   A.M. 1890.

AKBAR   Described under ALBATROSS, q.v.

AKSEL OLSEN   Described under ELISABETH HOBBIE, q.v.

            -griffithianum 1/4
        -Mars-
AL JOLSON- -unknown 1/4
        -sanguineum ssp. sanguineum var. haemaleum 1/2
Compact plant with small leaves. Flowers cardinal red, campanu-
late, 2.25in(5.6cm) long by 2in(5cm); 4-8 in a loose truss.   C.
S. Seabrook, reg. 1969.

                    -griffithianum 7/32
                -Mars-
            -       -unknown 18/32   -catawbiense
        -Madras-   -Parsons Grandiflorum-
        -       -America-   -unknown
        -   -Fanfare-   -dark red hybrid--unknown
        -   -   -catawbiense 7/32
AL SMITH-   -Kettledrum-
        -           -unknown
        -       -America- (as above)
        -   -unnamed-
        -   - hybrid-   -Mars- (as above)
        -Cindy-   -Blaze-
         Lou -   -catawbiense, red form
            -           -Mars- (as above)
            -Red Brave-
                    -America- (as above)
Bud hardy to -15F(-26C).   Buds and flowers a blend of deep red,
strong red, and vivid red, dorsal spotting of deep red.   Delp.

* *
        -griersonianum 1/2
ALADDIN-
        -auriculatum 1/2
6ft(1.8m) OF(-18C) VL 3/3 Large plant, improved by pruning;
leaves 7in(17.8cm) by 2in(5cm). Much like auriculatum. Flowers
medium pink, deeper in throat, trumpet-shaped; trusses hold 14.
Heat-tolerant. J. J. Crosfield, 1930.   A.M. 1935.
TIITNESS ALADDIN   Parentage as above, except reversed
Rose-colored trusses in late season. Sir J. Horlick, reg. 1962.
* *

                    -griersonianum 1/4
            -Aladdin-
            -       -auriculatum 1/4
ALADDIN'S LIGHT-   -neriiflorum 1/8
            -       -Nereid-
            -Peach-   -dichroanthum 1/8
            Lady-
                    -fortunei ssp. discolor 1/4
Blend of shell pink and Delft rose. Late. Lancaster, reg. 1965.

```
                    -neriiflorum 3/8
          -F. C. Puddle-
    -Ethel-         -griersonianum 3/8
ALAN-    -forrestii Repens Group 1/4
    -         -neriiflorum
    -F. C. Puddle-
                    -griersonianum
```
Blood red flowers. Lord Aberconway, 1946.

* *
```
                              -dichroanthum 1/8
                    -Goldsworth-
          -Tortoiseshell Champagne-  Orange -fortunei s. discolor
ALARIC  -                   -griersonianum 1/4
HAMILTON-               -griffithianum 1/8
          -         -Loderi-
          -Albatross-       -fortunei 1/8
                    -fortunei ssp. discolor 3/8
```
8ft(2.4m) x 8ft. 5F(-15C) ML   Lax truss of 12-14 flowers, of
6-7 wavy-edged lobes, cream white with a faint pink spot. Foliage smooth, hairless, to 7.8in(20cm). I. Hamilton, reg. 1989.
MRS. INNES HAMILTON   Parentage as above
Similar to above, with flowers of pure flesh pink.   Cdr. Innes
Hamilton, reg. 1989. P.C. 1989.
* *

ALASKA   Syn. for FINLANDIA, described under APPLAUSE

* *
```
                    -griffithianum 1/4
          -Loderi-
ALBATROSS-     -fortunei 1/4
          -fortunei ssp. discolor 1/2
```
6ft(1.8m) 0F(-18C) L 4/3   A large, beautiful hybrid. Open
habit; leaves 6in(15.2cm) long, held one year. Buds deep pink,
opening slightly blush pink; fragrant huge flowers of white, reverse tinged pink. Parent of MOONWAX. Rothschild, 1930. A.M.
Wisley Trials 1953. A.G.M. 1968. Color illus. PB pl. 58.
AKBAR   Parentage as above
Tall, sturdy plant. Deep rose pink flowers with crimson streaks
in the throat; sweetly fragrant. Loose trusses of 12. Flowers
in June. Rothschild, 1933. A.M. 1952.
EXBURY ALBATROSS Parentage as above
6ft(1.8m) 0F(-18C) L 4/3   Blush pink flowers, speckled with
mahogany in throat. A fine, tall plant; large flowers and long,
broad leaves. Rothschild, 1930. F.C.C. 1935.
TOWNHILL ALBATROSS   Parentage as above
Flower fuchsine pink; white center. Lord Swathling. A.M. 1945.
* *
```
          -caucasicum 1/4
    -Viola-
ALBERT-   -unknown 1/2
    -         -catawbiense 1/4
    -Everestianum-
                    -unknown
```
Flowers delicate lilac-blue, yellow-green blotch. Seidel, 1899.
BISMARCK   Parentage as above
Pale purplish pink, reddish brown spots.   Seidel, cross 1891.
* *
* *
```
          -maximum 1/2
ALBERT CLOSE-
          -macrophyllum 1/2
```
5ft(1.5m) -10F(-23C) L 3/2   Flowers bright rose pink, heavy
chocolate-red spotting in throat; compact conical truss. Strag-
gly, open growth. Tolerates heat. Fraser and Gable, 1951.
Color illus. LW pl. 42; VV p. 22.
MAXIE   Parentage as above but may be reversed.
Pink, heavily spotted; very late season. Fraser and Gable.
GEORGE FRASER   May be a member of this grex.
Pink flowers. Plant very tall, with a weeping habit.
* *

ALBERT SCHWEITZER   Parentage unknown
6ft(1.8m) -5F(-21C) ML Large pyramidal trusses of 13-14 flowers, rose Bengal, currant red blotch.   Adr. van Nes, reg. 1962.
Silver Medal, Holland, 1960.

```
          -falconeri 1/2
ALBERTI-
          -ponticum ? 1/2
```

Synonym ALBERTUS.   Corolla purple magenta, bell-shaped. Origin
unknown.

ALBERTUS   Synonym for ALBERTI

ALBESCENS   Parentage unknown
Large white flowers, marked sulphur yellow at base; fragrant. A
parent of HARRY TAGG, BASILEOS.   Origin unknown.

ALBIFLORUM LANCINIATUM--form of hirsutum
White flowers, held in terminal clusters; leaves deeply incised.
Native of central and eastern Alps. Grown by Froebel of Zurich.

* *
```
          -campylocarpum
ALBINO-
          -Loder's White, q.v. for 2 possible parentage diagrams
```
Flowers near-white. Stephenson Clarke; exhibitor Whitaker, 1935.
SERIN   Parentage as above; cross by Collingwood Ingram.
* *

ALBION RIDGE--white form of macrophyllum
6ft(1.8m) 15F(-10C) M 3/3   Broadly funnel-shaped white flowers, 2.5in(6.4cm) across, ruffled; up to 15 per truss. Upright
plant; elliptic foliage, 6.5in(16.5cm) x 3in(7.5cm). Layered in
the wild by J. Drewry.   E. German, reg. 1976.

```
                    -brachycarpum ssp. fauriei 1/8
          -unnamed hybrid-       -wardii 1/8
ALBORADA-               -Inamorata-
    -                   -fortunei ssp. discolor 1/8
    -smirnowii 1/2
```
4ft(1.2m) x 2.3ft(.7m)(11 yrs) -10F(-23C) M   Trusses of 10-14
flowers, vivid purplish red in bud, open to pale purplish pink,
and age to ivory white. Floriferous. Brueckner, reg. 1989.

```
                    -catawbiense var. album Glass--Catalgla 1/4
          -Ice -         -catawbiense var. album 1/8
ALBULA-Cube-Belle Heller-                   -catawbiense
    -               -white catawbiense hybrid-       1/16
    -yakushimanum--Exbury form 1/2         -unknown 1/16
```
4ft(1.2m) high x 7ft(2.1m)(19 yrs) -25F(-32C) ML Ball trusses
of 17-21 flowers, funnel-shaped, of heavy substance. Light pink
buds open white, with faint yellow spotting. Plant habit dense,
spreading; leaves held 3 years.   Dr. J. Brueckner, reg. 1988.

```
          -arboreum ssp. cinnamomeum var. album 1/2
ALBUM-
          -caucasicum 1/2
```
Flowers held in compact trusses, pink in bud, opening white or
blush, with a faint ray of yellowish green. Early. Habit compact. Cunningham & Fraser of Edinburgh. A.G.M. 1969.

```
          -catawbiense 1/2
ALBUM ELEGANS-
          -unknown 1/2
```
6ft(1.8m) -20F(-29C) L 2/3   Flowers open pale lilac, fading
white, yellow-green blotch; 16 in compact truss. Vigorous plant
of open habit. Waterer, before 1847.   Color illus. VV p. 14.

```
          -catawbiense 1/2
ALBUM GRANDIFLORUM-
          -unknown 1/2
```
5ft(1.5m) -15F(-26C) ML 3/3   Pale mauve, rather frilly flowers, 3in(7.5cm) wide; brownish green flare.   Waterer, pre-1851.

```
          -catawbiense 1/2
ALBUM NOVUM-
          -unknown 1/2
```
5ft(1.5m) -20F(-29C) ML 3/3   Flowers white with a rose-lilac
tinge and greenish yellow spots.   L. van Houtte.

```
          -lutescens 1/2
ALCESTA-
          -burmanicum 1/2
```
2ft(.6m) 10F(-12C) EM   Flowers pale creamy yellow with darker
yellow blotch. New growth bronze. Lord Aberconway. A.M. 1935.

```
                   -haematodes 1/4
          -Hiraethlyn-
ALCIBIADES-          -griffithianum 1/4
          -               -neriiflorum 1/4
          -F. C. Puddle-
                   -griersonianum 1/4
Turkey red flowers.  Lord Aberconway, intro. 1941.
```

```
          -yakushimanum 1/2                    -catawbiense 1/16
ALDHAM-                    -Atrosanguineum-
       -               -Atrier-              -unknown 1/16
       -Gable's Flamingo-    -griersonianum 1/8
                   -               -decorum 1/8
                        -Dechaem-
                             -haematodes 1/8
1.5ft(.45m)  -5F(-21C)  M   Flowers 3in(7.6cm) across, 6-lobed,
pink with a rose-red throat, held in trusses of about 12.  Plant
as wide as tall; leaves 4.7in(12cm) x 1.5in(4cm).  Lewis Bagoly,
cross 1969; raiser C. Herbert; reg. 1980.
```

```
               -neriiflorum Euchaites Group 1/4
       -Portia-
ALESIA-       -strigillosum 1/4
       -meddianum 1/2
Flowers of crimson scarlet.  Lord Aberconway, intro. 1941.
```

```
ALEXANDER ADIE    Parentage unknown
Synonym JAY GOULD.  A parent of EIDAM, HOLBEIN.  Flowers dark
pink to rosy scarlet; compact trusses.  J. Waterer, before 1871.
```

```
          -catawbiense 1/2
ALEXANDER DANCER-
          -unknown 1/2
Flowers reddish magenta, centers lighter.  A. Waterer, 1865.
```

```
ALEXANDER STEFFEN   Described under BRITANNIA'S BELLS, q.v.
```

```
          -cinnabarinum Roylei Group 1/2
ALEXANDRA GORDON-
          -augustinii ssp. chasmanthum 1/2
Trusses of 7 flowers, phlox purple, flushed magnolia purple, red
spotting.  Leaves oblanceolate.  Lady Adam Gordon, reg. 1985.
```

```
          -dalhousiae 1/2
ALF BRAMLEY-
          -nuttallii var. stellatum--Kallistos 1/2
Yellow buds open white, blushed pink.  A. Bramley, reg. 1970.
```

```
* * * * * * * * * * * * * * * * * * * * * * * * * *
                   -catawbiense 1/2
ALFRED---EVERESTIANUM, selfed-
                   -unknown 1/2
5ft(1.5m)  -15F(-26C)  ML  Flowers lilac with faint green-yellow
spots; frilled.  P. Cox called it one of the most attractive hy-
brids in this color.  Seidel, 1899.  Color illus. Cox pl. 3.
ALLAH   Parentage as above
Light purplish pink, yellow markings, pale center.  Seidel.
ANTON  Parentage as above
Frilled flowers, lilac with ochre markings.  Seidel, 1906.
AUGUST  Parentage as above
Pink flowers, strong yellowish green markings.  Seidel, 1906.
BERTHA  Parentage as above
Flowers carmine pink, orange-red markings.  Seidel, cross 1892.
CAROLA  Parentage as above
Flower pure rose, yellow markings; hardy to -20F(-29C).  Seidel.
* * * * * * * * * * * * * * * * * * * * * * * * * *
```

```
ALFRED COATES    Described under AYAH, q.v.
```

```
          -edgeworthii 1/2
ALFRED MARTIN-       -ciliicalyx 1/4
          -Else Frye-
                   -unknown 1/4
5ft(1.5m)  15F(-9C)  VE  Ball truss of 5 flowers, deep yellowish
pink in bud, opening light to pale purplish pink,  dorsal blotch
of brilliant yellow; calyx of deep pink.  Plant as wide as high.
J. P. Evans cross; Mrs. Evans, reg. 1988.
```

```
ALFREDA WIACZEK   Described under P.J.M., q.v.
```

```
                   -fortunei ssp. discolor 1/4
       -Margaret Dunn-     -dichroanthum 1/8
       -            -Fabia-
ALGERIENE-          -griersonianum 3/8
       -       -haematodes 1/4
       -May Day-
                   -griersonianum
Ivory flowers, flushed pale rose at tips.   Sunningdale, 1955.
```

```
          -griffithianum 1/2
ALICE-               (or possibly seedling of PINK PEARL)
       -unknown 1/2
6ft(1.8m)  -5F(-21C)  M  4/3  Flowers frosty pink; large truss.
Vigorous upright plant. Named for Mrs. Gomer Waterer.  J. Wat-
erer cross; G. Waterer named and intro.   A.M. 1910.   Col. ill.
F p. 31; JS p. 86.
```

```
* * * * * * * * * * * * * * * * * * * * * * * * * *
               -campylocarpum Elatum Group 1/4
       -Ole Olson-
ALICE   -        -fortunei ssp. discolor 1/4
FRANKLIN-          -griffithianum 1/4
          -Loderi King George-
                   -fortunei 1/4
6ft(1.8m)  0F(-18C)  ML  3/3  Flowers medium yellow, with green
throat, about 4in(10.2cm) wide.  Resembles Loderi.   Halfdan Lem
cross; H. Larson, reg. 1962.   P.A. 1960.
MARSHALL LYONS   Parentage as above
Flowers phlox pink with deeper shades, a small red blotch.  Oval
leaves, pointed.  Plant of open habit.  M. Lyons, reg. 1972.
* * * * * * * * * * * * * * * * * * * * * * * * * *
```

```
          -fortunei 1/2
ALICE IN WONDERLAND-
          -unknown 1/2
6ft(1.8m)  -10F(-23C)  M  3/3  Flowers openly funnel-shaped, 2
in(5cm) broad, 7 wavy lobes of light purplish pink; truss of 16.
Plant upright, rounded.  C. Dexter; Tyler Arboretum, reg. 1980.
```

```
          -griffithianum 1/2
ALICE MANGLES-
          -ponticum 1/2
The first hybrid of griffithianum  to be given an award,  but no
description was found.  James Mangles.  F.C.C. 1882.
```

```
          -fortunei ssp. discolor 1/2
ALICE MARTINEAU-
          -unknown  1/2
5ft(1.5m)  -15F(-26C)  L  3/3  Flowers rosy crimson with a dark
blotch and dark throat.  Blooms very late.  W. C. Slocock.
```

```
ALICE POORE   Dexter unknown
5ft(1.5m)  -5F(-21C)  EM  Pink flowers, much like SCINTILLATION.
```

```
                        -griffithianum 1/16
                   -George Hardy-
          -Mrs. Lindsay Smith-      -catawbiense 1/16
       -Diane-               -Duchess of Edinburgh--unknown 1/4
ALICE -     -           -campylocarpum 1/8
STREET-     -unnamed hybrid-
       -               -unknown
       -wardii 1/2
4ft(1.2m)  -5F(-21C)  M  3/4  Flowers soft yellow; foliage grass
green.  Compact habit.   M. Koster, 1953.
```

```
* * * * * * * * * * * * * * * * * * * * * * * * * *
               -mucronulatum, pink form 1/4
          -unnamed hybrid-
ALICE SWIFT-       -racemosum 1/4
          -minus Carolinianum Group 1/2
4ft(1.2m) x 4ft  -20F(-29C)  E  3/3  Flowers bright clear pink;
later than P.J M.  Green foliage in winter. Yavorsky, reg. 1987.
VIRGINIA DELITO   Parentage as above
Similar to ALICE SWIFT but has large flowers of deep pink; plant
is taller, to 3.5ft(1m) in 10 years.  L. Yavorsky, reg. 1987.
* * * * * * * * * * * * * * * * * * * * * * * * * *
```

```
       -Sir John Waterer--unknown 1/2
ALINTA-       -catawbiense 1/4
       -Vesuvius-
                   -arboreum 1/4
Solferino purple flowers, 14-16 in a spherical truss.   V. Boul-
```

ter, Australia, reg. 1962.

```
            -yunnanense 1/2
ALISON   -
  JOHNSTONE-cinnabarinum ssp. xanthocodon Concatenans Group 1/2
```
5ft(1.5m) 5F(-15C) EM 4/4   Blue-green waxy foliage like con-
catenans. Needs sun. Truss of 9 flowers, delicate amber, pink-
frosted. Maj. G. Johnstone. A.M. 1945. Col. ill. Cox pl. 4.

```
        -barbatum 1/2
ALIX-
        -hookeri 1/2
```
6ft(1.8m) 10F(-12C) E Brilliant, clear crimson flowers; gaunt
habit. Barely hardy at Exbury. Rothschild, 1930. A.M. 1935.

ALL BEAUTIFUL   Parentage unknown
Flowers pink and fragrant. Kersey cross; Frederick, reg. 1976.

* *
```
          -Catalgla--catawbiense var. album Glass
    -Gosh-                     -decorum?
    -Darn-          -Caroline-
ALL -   -Mrs. H. R. Yates-     -brachycarpum?
EAST-            -unknown
    -           -Mrs. H. R. Yates (as above)
    -unnamed hybrid-
            -wardii
```
The parentage of GOSH DARN was selfed. Buds of medium to bril-
liant greenish yellow; flowers brilliant to light greenish yellow. Hardy to -15F(-26C). W. Delp.
KEYSTONE Parentage as above
Brilliant to light greenish yellow buds, opening to flowers of
light yellow-green. Medium-sized shrub. W. Delp.
* *

ALLAH   Described under ALFRED, q.v.

* *
```
          -griersonianum 1/4
    -Azor-
ALLEGRO-    -fortunei ssp. discolor 1/4
    -              -griffithianum 1/4
    -Loderi King George-
              -fortunei 1/4
```
This parentage produced a plant with pink flowers. Lancaster.
GWEN'S PINK   Parentage as above, except reversed
6ft(1.8m) 5F(-15C) L   Very fragrant flowers, 7-lobed, 4.5in.
(11.5cm) wide, light Neyron rose shading to claret rose; trusses
of 9. G. Barefield cross; M. Barefield, reg. 1983.
* *

```
            -wardii 3/16
      -Crest-          -fortunei ssp. discolor 1/16
    -      -Lady-
  -unnamed-    Bessborough-campylocarpum Elatum Gp. 1/16
  - hybrid-         -wardii       -griffithianum 3/64
  -      -Idealist-      -Kewense-
ALLEN -   -Yellow-   -Aurora-     -fortunei 5/64
HARRIS-   Creek-       -fortunei
  -         -            -griersonianum 1/16
  -            -Sarita Loder-    -griffithianum
  -                      -Loderi-
  -unknown 1/2               -fortunei
```
Flowers greenish yellow to pale yellow, margins pinkish. Plant
5ft(1.5m) at 13 years. Mrs. I. Harris, New Zealand, reg. 1987.


```
            -yakushimanum 1/2
ALLEN'S SURPRISE-
            -unknown 1/2
```
Deep pink buds open to flowers of moderate purplish pink, throat
of strong purplish pink with brown spotting. Leaves indumented.
Seed from ARS Seed Exchange; Mrs. I. Harris, reg. 1987.

ALEXANDER STEFFEN   Described under BRITANNIA'S BELLS, q.v.

ALLEY CAT   Parentage unknown
Coral pink flowers with a darker blotch. Endre Ostbo selection;
intro. by Owen Ostbo; reg. 1961. P.A. 1960.

```
            -dichroanthum 1/2
        -Fabia-
ALLURE-    -griersonianum 1/4
    -      -dichroanthum
    -Dante-
            -facetum (eriogynum) 1/4
```
Scarlet flowers. Lord Aberconway, 1942.


```
            -yakushimanum 1/2
ALMA PESTE PAUL-      -arboreum 1/4
            -Doncaster-
                  -unknown 1/4
```
2ft(.6m) high x 2.5ft(.75m) OF(-18C) ML Buds of vivid purple-
reds open to pale purplish pink flowers with deeper rays; 23 per
truss. Leaves of heavy texture, held 3 years; reddish brown indumentum. F. Peste, cross 1979; S. P. Johnston, reg. 1986.

* *
```
            -Pygmalion--unknown 3/16
        -unnamed hybrid-
      -Weldy-          -haematodes 3/16
ALMOND-   -yakushimanum, Exbury form 3/8
 CREAM-
    -       -Weldy- (as above)
    -Robert -
    Weldon-          -yakushimanum 1/8
      -Serendipity-
            -aureum (chrysanthum) 1/8
```
Buds vivid red with pale greenish yellow, open to frilled white
flowers tinged pale yellow-green, with deep purplish red throat;
white anthers. W. Delp.
YUPPIE POWER   Parentage as above
Buds light greenish yellow and pale yellow-green. Flowers pale
yellow-green with throats of light greenish yellow; dorsal spots
strong yellow-green; grayish red anthers. W. Delp.
* *


```
            -racemosum 1/2
ALMOND THACKER-      -ciliatum 1/4
            -Rosy Bell-
                  -glaucophyllum 1/4
```
Parents reversed in Leach. Deep almond-pink. Thacker, 1946.

* *
```
            -arboreum--Blood Red 1/4
        -Cornubia-       -thomsonii 1/8
ALMONDTIME-    -Shilsonii-
    -                  -barbatum 1/8
        -sutchuenense 1/2
```
Flowers of bright cerise pink with a few dark crimson dots. E.
J. P. Magor. A.M. 1925.
CORNSUTCH Parentage as above
Carmine purple flowers, with a dark blotch. Magor. A.M. 1925.
* *


```
        -fortunei 1/2
ALMOST-
    -          -dichroanthum 1/4
    -Goldsworth Orange-
              -fortunei ssp. discolor 1/4
```
Flowers rose-colored (toward orange). C. R. and V. Haag, 1986.


```
            -griffithianum 1/8
        -Mars-
    -Vulcan-    -unknown 1/8
ALOHA-    -griersonianum 1/4
    -yakushimanum, Exbury form 1/2
```
3ft(.9m) -15F(-26C) M   Domed truss of 19 flowers, vivid red
in bud, opening deep pink, fading to pale purplish pink. Leaves
wrinkled; white indumentum when young. Phetteplace, cross 1973;
Briggs, intro. 1983; D. W. Paden, reg. 1988.


```
    -Furnivall's Daughter, parentage as Mrs. Furnivall, q.v.
ALONY-   -dichroanthum
    -Fabia-
        -griersonianum
```
2.3ft(.7m) x 1.5ft(.45m)(9 yrs) -5F(-21C) ML   Flowers saucer-
shaped, held in flat trusses of 10; 5 smooth-edged lobes, vivid
reddish orange. Foliage has grayish, felt-like coating below.
Plant of dense growth habit. T. Aunsbjorn, Denmark, reg. 1989.

```
                    -arboreum 1/4
        -Sir Charles Lemon-
ALPACA-                     -unknown 1/4
        -neriiflorum 1/2
Pink flowers.  Discontinued at Exbury.   Rothschild, 1933.
```

ALPEN ROSE--older common name for ferrugineum ("rusty colored"),
now called ALPINE ROSE. A semi-dwarf plant, leaves to 1.5in(3.8
cm), dense reddish brown scales below. Small trusses of tubular
rosy crimson flowers, late season. Found on limestone cliffs in
Alps of S. Europe; introduced to England in 1752.
ALPEN ROSE--also older name for hirsutum ("hairy") formerly also
called GARLAND and ALPINE ROSE! Also of Alpine origin, and like
the above, but with smaller leaves and flowers, bristle-edged.
First cultivated rhododendron of record in the western world, in
a 1656 plant list of botanist John Tradescant's garden.--Sabuco.

* *

```
                                  -catawbiense
                    -Parsons Grandiflorum-      5/16
          -America-            -unknown 17/32
     -unnamed-        -dark red hybrid--unknown
     - hybrid-            -griffithianum 3/32
     -        -      -Mars-
  -Purple-   -Blaze-   -unknown
  - Susy -        -catawbiense var. rubrum 1/16
  -        -           -griffithianum
ALPHA-    -        -Mars- (as above)
OMEGA-    -Red Brave-
  -            -America- as above)
  -        -catawbiense
  -Sefton-
          -unknown
```
Buds grayed, deep and vivid purplish reds; flowers of strong and
deep purplish red with deep fuchsia purple; spotted in dark red.
Dr. Tom Ring cross; W. Delp raiser.
GARNET GLOW   Parentage as above
Grayed dark red, deep purplish red in bud, opening to flowers of
ruby red, deep purplish red, dark red and cardinal red. Dr. T.
Ring cross; W. Delp raiser..

* *

ALPINE DEW Parentage uncertain; may be racemosum(dwarf) x TESSA
3ft(.9m) x 4ft(1.2m)(15 yrs) -15F(-26C) M   Buds pale yellow-
green flushed pink, open to white flowers, 1.2in(3cm) wide, of 5
wavy-edged lobes; 3-5 buds in flat, multiple-budded terminal inflorescences. Plant dense, floriferous; small, dull green foliage, scaly beneath.   J. C. Cowles cross; R. King raiser; A. R.
Brooks, reg. 1990.

```
        -brachyanthum 1/2
ALPINE GEM-
        -ferrugineum 1/2
```
Flowers yellow, shaded pink.   Thacker, 1942.

ALPINE GLOW Described under AVALANCHE, q.v.

ALPINE MEADOW--leucaspis selected seedling
2ft(.6m) 5F(-15C) EM   White flowers, ivory throat, brown stamens; truss of 4. Plant compact. Dunedin Rhod. Gp., reg. 1985.

ALPINE ROSE   Described under AVALANCHE, q.v. Also, ALPEN ROSE.

```
            -lindleyi 1/4
        -unnamed hybrid-
ALPINE SNOW-            -dalhousiae 1/4
            -taggianum 1/2
```
7ft(2.1m) high x 4.5ft(1.35m)(12 yrs) 22F(-6C) E   Light yel-
lowish green buds open to funnel-campanulate flowers, 4.75in(12
cm) wide, very fragrant, of yellowish white, throat blotch reddish orange. Lax truss holds 7-11.   C. Edwards, cross c. 1969;
E. Philp, reg. 1986.

```
            -campylocarpum 1/8
        -Ethel-
   -Alan-    -orbiculare 1/8
   -   -         -neriiflorum 1/8
ALRE-   -F. C. Puddle-
   -             -griersonianum 1/8
   -forrestii Repens Group 1/2
```
Blood red flowers.   Lord Aberconway, intro. 1946.

ALSTON   Described under LUNAR QUEEN, q.v.

```
                    -catawbiense 1/4
        -unnamed hybrid-
ALTACLERENSE-            -ponticum 1/4
        -arboreum 1/2
```
From Highclere Castle. One of the first man-made rhododendron
hybrids. Grows to become a very large tree. Deep red flowers.
Gowen, 1831.   F.C.C. 1865.   Color illus. JS p. 52.

```
        -Ivery's Scarlet--unknown 1/2
ALVINDA-    -griffithianum 1/4
        -Loderi-
            -fortunei 1/4
```
Pale rose pink flowers.   Lord Aberconway, intro. 1933.

* *

```
        -Scintillation--unknown 1/2
ALWAYS ADMIRED-
        -haematodes 1/2
```
4ft(1.2m) -15F(-26C) M 4/4   Scintillation foliage. Flowers
peachy pink and yellow. Compact habit.   J. Wister, 1965.
PEACH BRANDY   Parentage as above
4ft(1.2m) -5F(-21C) M   Flowers strong pink, slight dark red
spotting, openly funnel-shaped, 3in(7.6cm) across, with 5-6 wavy
lobes; truss of 13.   Scott Horticultural Foundation cross; Tyler Arboretum, reg. 1981.
* *

```
                    -Lady Bess-  -fortunei ssp. discolor
            -Jalisco- borough  -                1/8
            -        -            -campylocarpum Elatum Gp
       -un. -        -    -dichroanthum 5/16        1/16
       -hyb.-    -Dido-
       -    -        -decorum 1/32
   -unnamed-  -unknown 1/4
   - hybrid-        -wardii 1/16
   -    -     -Crest-
   -    -unnamed-    -Lady Bessborough- (as above)
   -    hybrid-        -fortunei ssp. discolor
AMADEUS-    -King of Shrubs-    -dichroanthum
   -                  -Fabia-
   -                    -griersonianum 1/32
   -            -ponticum 1/8
   -   -Purple Splendour-
   -Sonata-        -unknown
        -dichroanthum
```
Flowers in truss of 9-12, deep and moderate yellowish pink with
a vivid yellow (pale to orange-yellow) blotch. Plant of compact
habit. Lofthouse cross; C. Wellmeir, reg. 1987.

```
            -arboreum--Blood Red 1/4
     -Cornubia-    -thomsonii 1/8
AMALFI-    -Shilsonii-
     -            -barbatum 1/8
     -calophytum 1/2
```
Carmine rose, shaded white on tube, spotted dark red with crim-
son splash at the base. Spherical trusses of 20 flowers, 2.3in.
(6cm) wide. Rothschild, 1933. A.M. 1939.

```
                -griffithianum 1/8
            -Mars-
        -Vulcan-    -unknown 5/8
AMANDA JOAN YOUNG-    -griersonianum 1/4
        -unnamed Dexter hybrid--unknown
```
2ft(.6m) -15F(-26C) M   Flowers 3in(7.6cm) wide, 6 wavy lobes,
edged strong Neyron rose, shading to pale rose center; throat of
very pale purple; dorsal spotting orange- to brilliant yellows;
ball trusses of 7-9.   A. & S. Anderson, cross 1976; reg. 1989.

```
        -dichroanthum ssp. scyphocalyx 1/2
AMARETTO-            -catawbiense 1/8
        -        -Omega-
     -Hachmann's Marina-    -unknown 1/8
                -wardii 1/4
```
4.6ft(1.4m) x 3.7ft(1.1m)(12 yrs) -15F(-23C) ML Trusses of 12
-16 flowers, campanulate, Spanish orange to salmon, tinged blood
red. Smooth, dark green, ovate foliage. Hachmann cross; Stück,
reg. 1988.   Color illus. WS, 1989, p. 119.

```
                -hemsleyanum 1/2
AMARILLO-          -fortunei ssp. discolor 1/4
    -Autumn Gold-      -dichroanthum 1/8
                  -Fabia-
                       -griersonianum 1/8
6ft(1.8m) OF(-18C) ML   Fragrant flowers, 7-lobed, bright lem-
on yellow, the reverse light Mars orange; held in an 8in(20.3cm)
truss of 13. Plant 2/3 as wide as tall.   D. Goheen, reg. 1986.
```

```
                     -campylocarpum Elatum Group 1/8
           -Penjerrick-
    -Amaura-        -griffithianum 3/8
AMASUN-  -griersonianum 1/2
   -          -griffithianum
    -Sunrise-
              -griersonianum
Pale rose flowers.   Lord Aberconway, cross 1939; intro. 1946.
```

```
                -williamsianum 1/4
       -Adrastia-
AMATA-        -neriiflorum 1/2
   -                -neriiflorum
    -F. C. Puddle-
                  -griersonianum 1/4
Red flowers.   Lord Aberconway, cross 1935; intro. 1941.
```

```
                -campylocarpum Elatum Group 1/4
    -Penjerrick-
AMAURA-        -griffithianum 1/4
   -griersonianum 1/2
Pale pink flowers.   Lord Aberconway, 1933.
```

```
AMAZEMENT   Described under PRELUDE, q.v.
```

```
                     -catawbiense 5/16
     -Mrs. C. S. Sargent-
AMAZING-             -unknown 5/16
  GRACE -                      -catawbiense var. album 3/8
    -            -Belle Heller-               -catawbiense
     -Swansdown-         -white catawbiense hyb.-
                    -catawbiense var. album        -unknown
3ft(.9m) -30F(-35C) L  3/3  Budo orchid lavender; flower phlox
pink, of heavy substance; trusses hold 12.  Broad, well-branched
plant. Pride, reg. 1979.  Color ill. ARS Q 34:3 (1980), p. 138.
```

```
                     -campylocarpum Elatum Group 1/8
           -Penjerrick-
    -Amaura-        -griffithianum 1/8
AMAZOR-  -griersonianum 1/2
   -          -griersonianum
    -Azor-
          -fortunei ssp. discolor 1/4
Pink flowers.   Lord Aberconway, cross 1934; intro. 1946.
```

```
    -racemosum, white form  1/2
AMBA-
    -burmanicum 1/2
Pale yellow flowers.   Lord Aberconway, cross 1926; intro. 1934.
```

```
       -Jan Dekens--unknown 13/16
    -
    -                            -ponticum 1/16
AMBASSADEUR-          -Michael Waterer-
   -             -Prometheus-         -unknown
    -Madame-           -Monitor--unknown
     de Bruin-        -arboreum 1/8
                  -Doncaster-
                          -unknown
Flowers of deep pink, 3in(7.6cm) wide; upper petal lighter pink.
Trusses of 20.   P. van Nes, reg. 1962.   S.M. Rotterdam 1960.
```

```
* * * * * * * * * * * * * * * * * * * * * * * * * * * *
       -fortunei 1/4
    -Fawn-      -dichroanthum 1/4
    -    -Fabia-
AMBER-         -griersonianum 1/8
  GEM -              -fortunei ssp. discolor 1/8
    -        -Lady Bessborough-
     -Jalisco-          -campylocarpum Elatum Group 1/8
      -           -dichroanthum
       -Dido-
            -decorum 1/8
3ft(.9m) -5F(-21C) ML   A superior plant with fragrant 7-lobed
```

```
flowers of heavy substance, 4.5in(11.4cm) across, Venetian pink,
shading to nasturtium orange, strong orange-red spotting.  Loose
truss of 10.  Broad plant. James cross; A. Childers, reg. 1978.
MARY TASKER   Parentage as above, except reversed
Flowers of dawn pink rimmed in Naples yellow, with a currant red
throat.   H. R. Tasker, New Zealand, reg. 1979.
SHERILL   Parentage: FAWN x JALISCO
6ft(1.8m) -10F(-23C) M  Very fragrant flowers, 6in(15cm) wide,
barium yellow, a large blotch of currant red in throat, 7-lobed.
Shrub as broad as high; ivy green leaves held 3 years.   Del W.
James cross; reg. by Mrs. James for Hendricks Park, 1980.
* * * * * * * * * * * * * * * * * * * * * * * * * * *
```

```
                     -dichroanthum 3/8
          -Dido-
AMBERGRIS-    -decorum 1/4
   -         -fortunei 1/4
    -Fawn-      -dichroanthum
          -Fabia-
                -griersonianum 1/8
Strong yellowish pink buds opening to 7-lobed flowers 3.5in(9cm)
across, of brilliant to light yellow.   Blooms in October in New
Zealand.   Mrs. J. M. Coker raiser; Mrs. J. M. Kerr, reg. 1987.
```

```
* * * * * * * * * * * * * * * * * * * * * * * * * * *
       -minus var. minus Carolinianum Group 1/2
AMBIE-                -racemosum 1/8
   -              -Conemaugh-
    -Pioneer (Gable)-        -mucronulatum 1/8
                   -unknown 1/4
3ft(.9m) -20F(-29C) M   Buds dark purplish red; flowers widely
funnel-shaped, creamy white and irregularly variegated, one lobe
of each flower all pink; 5-18 per cluster. Plant rounded, com-
pact, tightly branched to the ground.  Fetterhoff, reg. 1979.
BILLY BEAR   Parentage as above
2.5ft(.75m) -20F(-29C) M  Buds cyclamen purple; flowers widely
funnel-shaped, amaranth rose, shaded at lobe edges.  Ball-shaped
terminal clusters of 1-4 trusses, each of 2-4 flowers.  Glossy
leaves held 1 year.  W. Fetterhoff, reg. 1979.
DAVID JOHN   Parentage as above
3ft(.9m) -20F(-29C) M    Ball-shaped terminal clusters, of 2-6
trusses, each 2-5 flowered (total of 4-20 flowers).  Corolla of
mallow purple with faint red spotting.   Fetterhoff, reg. 1980.
GARY   Parentage as above
2.5ft(.75m) -20F(-29C) M  Flowers in terminal spherical clus-
ters, composed of 1-4 clusters, each of 3-5 flowers (total 3-20)
of rhodamine pink.  Plant wider than tall; yellowish green foli-
age held 1 year.  W. Fetterhoff, reg. 1980.
* * * * * * * * * * * * * * * * * * * * * * * * * * *
```

```
       -ambiguum 1/2
AMBITION-
    -lutescens 1/2
Flowers pale primrose yellow with a yellowish flare.  C. P. Raf-
fill, cross at RBG, Kew; Collingwood Ingram, reg. 1962.
```

```
                -griffithianum 1/4
    -Queen Wilhelmina-
AMBROSE-        -unknown 1/4
    -haematodes ssp. chaetomallum 1/2
Flowers rose pink.  Rothschild, 1933.
```

```
       -Rochester Pink--unknown
AMBROSE LIGHT-
    -unknown
2.6ft(.8m) x 3ft(.9m)(8 yrs) -5F(-21C) E  Compact shrub; small
leaves.  Very pale purple flowers, wavy-edged; ball trusses hold
10.  F. Arsen, reg. 1989.   Best of Show, New York, 1985, 1988.
```

```
AMELIA MARGARET--form of ambiguum
Yellow-green buds; greenish white flowers, heavily marked green.
Shrub wide as broad.  F. Waley raiser; D. Sampson, reg. 1987.
```

```
* * * * * * * * * * * * * * * * * * * * * * * * * * *
       -catawbiense 1/4
    -Parsons Grandiflorum-
AMERICA-        -unknown 3/4
    -dark red hybrid--unknown
5ft(1.5m) -20F(-29C) ML  3/2  Medium-sized, sprawling plant,
matte green foliage. Compact truss, ball-shaped, of very dark,
blue-toned red flowers. Extremely hardy.  Parent of Sumatra,
Vivacious. M. Koster, cross 1904; intro. 1920.   Color illus.
```

ARS J 43:4 1989, p. 183; Cox pl. 5; VV p. viii.
NOVA ZEMBLA   Parentage as above.
5ft(1.5m) -25F(-32C) M 4/3   Very showy red flowers, spotted
darker, in well-filled, rounded trusses. Perhaps the most commonly grown red in severe climates, either hot or cold. Foliage
and habit and better than AMERICA; flower very similar. M. Koster, 1902.   Color illus. Cox pl. 133; VV p. 3.
* *

                                        -griffithianum 1/4
                        -Queen Wilhelmina-
AMERICANA--sport of Britannia-   -unknown 3/4
                        -Stanley Davies--unknown
5ft(1.5m) -10F(-23C) ML 3/3   Sport of Britannia, occurring
at the graft union; the understock was a hybrid of fortunei ssp.
discolor. Crimson red flowers. B. Lancaster, before 1958.

AMETHYST (Noble)   Parentage unknown
Bright rose-purple. Noble, before 1850. A.M. 1931

* *
                -russatum 1/2
AMETHYST (Arends)-   -intricatum 1/8
                        -Intrifast-
            -Blue Diamond-   -fastigiatum 1/8
                        -augustinii 1/4
Two others by this name. Light lilac to lilac-blue flower; win-
ter-hardy in W. Germany. Grows to 16-20in(.4-.5m).   G. Arends,
mid-1930s.   Color illus. WS, 1989, p. 168.
AZURWOLKE (BLUE CLOUD)   Parentage as above
3ft(.9m) -10F(-23C) M   Flower trusses of 7, of medium violet.
Vigorous bush; scaly leaves. Distinctive appearance. Hachmann
cross; Stück reg. 1983. Col. ill. Cox pl. 11; WS, 1989, p. 163.
BLUE CHIP   Parentage as above
Violet-blue flowers, widely funnel-shaped, 3.5in(9cm) broad; 5-
to 7-flowered axillary clusters form rounded, terminal trusses.
Dark green foliage. Hydon Nurseries, reg. 1976.   A.M. 1978.
COBALT   Parentage: BLUE DIAMOND X russatum
Deep blue flowers on a small plant. C. Ingram, reg. 1970.
GLETSCHERNACHT (GLACIER NIGHT)(STARRY NIGHT) As AMETHYST, above
3ft(.9m) -5F(-21C) EM   Flowers an unusually deep violet-blue
with white filaments, in trusses of 7-8. Dense bush. H. Hachmann cross; Stück reg. 1983. Color illus. WS, 1989, p. 164.
HYDON MIST   Parentage as AMETHYST, above
2ft(.6m) -5F(-21C) EM   Light violet flowers, held in trusses
of 6-7, on a dwarf, compact plant. Hydon Nurseries, reg. 1976.
RUSTIC MAID   Parentage as AMETHYST, above
2.5ft(.75m) -5F(-21C) EM 4/3 Flowers of deep, vibrant lilac
blue. Collingwood Ingram, 1945.   P.C. 1972.
* *

                -fortunei ? 1/2
AMETHYST (Dexter)-
                -unknown 1/2
4ft(1.2m) -5F(-21C) M 3/3   Light purple, frilly flowers, dark
eye; vigorous grower.   Dexter cross; Westbury Rose Co., 1959.

        -aberconwayi 1/2   -arboreum 1/16
        -                  -Doncaster-
AMIGO-   -unnamed-   -unknown 1/8
        -         - hybrid-   -neriiflorum 1/16
        -         -   -Nereid-
        -Witch Doctor-   -dichroanthum 1/16
        -              -griffithianum 1/16
        -         -Mars-
        -Vulcan- -unknown
        -griersonianum 1/8
3ft(.9m) 5F(-15C) M 4/3   Buds deep pink; flowers of heavy
substance, reddish edges blend to yellow center, heavily spotted
red; 15 in truss. New growth bronze green.   Goheen, reg. 1974.

AMILCAR   Parentage unknown
Flowers deep violet purple, black spots. Standish. F.C.C. 1860.

                        -haematodes 1/8
                -Grosclaude-
                -       -facetum (eriogynum) 1/8
        -Brandt's Red-   -griffithianum 1/16
        -         -   -Queen Wilhelmina-
AMITY-   -Britannia-   -unknown 3/16
        -         -   -Stanley Davies--unknown
        -yakushimanum--Koichiro Wada 1/2

3ft(.9m) -10F(-23C) M 4/4   Flowers campanulate, 2.5in(6cm)
wide, rose opal to jasper red. Truss 5in(13cm) wide of 15 flowers. New growth silver-indumented.   J. A. Elliott, reg. 1983.

        -ambiguum 1/2
AMKEYS-
        -keysii 1/2
Orange outside, fading to yellow. E. J. P. Magor, intro. 1926.

AMMERLANDENSE   Described under BRITANNIA'S BELLS, q.v.

        -ciliatum 1/2
AMOENUM-
        -dauricum 1/2
Pink flowers. Similar to PRAECOX, but flowers are larger. Ori-
gin unknown.

        -griersonianum 1/2
AMOR-
        -thayeranum 1/2
3ft(.9m) 5F(-15C) L 3/3 White flowers flushed with irregular
pink staining, tinged pink on the outside; trusses of 10. Foliage attractive. J. B. Stevenson, 1927.   A.M. 1951.

AMOUR   Described under HAWK, q.v.

        -catawbiense 1/2
AMPHION-
        -unknown 1/2
6ft(1.8m) -15F(-26C) ML 4/3   Synonym F. L. AMES. Rose pink
flowers. Unusual glossiness on large broad leaves. A. Waterer.

        -catacosmum 1/2
AMRIE-
        -haematodes ssp. chaetomallum 1/2
Blackish crimson flowers.   J. B. Stevenson, 1951.

                        -maximum 1/4
        -Burgemeester Aarts-
AMSEL-   -L. L. Liebig--unknown 1/4
        -williamsianum 1/2
Flowers of clear rose color. Dietrich Hobbie, 1942-44.

        -griffithianum 1/2
AMY-
        -unknown 1/2
5ft(1.5m) -5F(-21C) M 3/3   A sturdy plant with medium green
leaves 6in(15cm) long. Rose pink flowers, salmon-flecked; truss
compact and upright. Heat-tolerant.   Waterer, Sons & Crisp.

AMY ANN   Parentage unknown
Rose opal flowers in late season.   The Hennys, reg. 1963.

* *
        -yakushimanum 1/2
AMY JANE-   -griffithianum 1/8
        -              -Queen Wilhelmina-
        -Earl of Athlone-   -unknown 3/8
                        -Stanley Davies--unknown
3ft(.9m)(12 yrs) 10F(-12C) M   The above cross was selfed.
Flowers of light Neyron rose, narrowly edged in rose red; domed
truss of 11. Plant rounded, as wide as tall; leaves have grayed
ornge indumentum below. Stanton cross; E. Anderson, reg. 1983.
ESTHER WAGNER   Parents: (yakushimanum x EARL OF ATHLONE) selfed
5.5ft(1.65m) 0F(-18C) M Openly funnel-shaped flowers 3.25in.
(8cm) across, 7 frilly lobes, light to pale pink, fading to pale
yellowish pink, strong purplish red (light ruby red) markings in
throat; large domed trusses of 19. E. T. Anderson, reg. 1985.
* *

                        -ponticum 3/4
                -Purple Splendour-
ANAH KRUSCHKE-   -unknown 1/4
                -ponticum
5ft(1.5m) -15F(-26C) ML 4/3 Parentage given as in Van Veen,
though registered as ponticum seedling. Dense bush; shiny foliage; heat-tolerant. Deep purple flowers, 3in(7.6cm) wide; tight
trusses of 12. F. Kruschke cross; A. Wright, Sr., intro. 1955;
T. Van Veen, reg. 1973.   Color illus. VV p. 56.

```
                      -griffithianum 1/8
            -Queen Wilhelmina-
      -Britannia-              -unknown 3/8
ANANOURI-      -Stanley Davies--unknown
      -fortunei ssp. discolor 1/2
```
3ft(.9m) -5F(-21C) ML 4/3   Leaves 7in(17.8cm) long. Flowers
of medium red; trusses of 12.   Phipps, reg. 1971. C.A. 1973.

ANCHORAGE   Described under RAY, q.v.

* *
```
                      -griffithianum 1/8
            -Queen Wilhelmina-
      -Britannia-              -unknown 3/8
ANDRÉ-        -Stanley Davies--unknown
      -yakushimanum      1/2
```
Truss of 14 flowers; buds of deep rose open pink, and fade pale
pink. De Belder cross; Res. Sta., Woody Nurs. Crops, reg. 1979.
FLIRT   Parentage: BRITANNIA x yakushimanum--Koichiro Wada.
3ft(.9m) -10F(-23C) M 4/4   Rose-red flower, white throat; as
the color fades, white throat extends to half of each lobe. Lax
truss of 14.   J. Elliott, reg. 1980.
HACHMANN'S BELONA   Parentage: yakushimanum K. Wada x BRITANNIA
Deep purplish pink flowers, spotted dark red, shade to a brighter pink center; trusses of 11-14. Leaves have dark brown indumentum below. Hachmann cross; G. Stück , reg. 1984.
MARY CHANTRY   Parentage: yakushimanum x BRITANNIA
2.5ft(.75m) OF(-18C) ML   Buds of Neyron rose open to fragrant
flowers, bright Neyron rose, shading lighter in throat; trusses
of 12. Plant as wide as tall; leaves deep yellow-green, retained 3 years. L. Brandt cross; Linda Mallard, reg. 1984.
ROSY DREAM   Parentage: yakushimanum x BRITANNIA
2ft(.6m) OF(-18C) M   Cardinal red buds open to funnel-shaped
spinel red flowers with paler throat, in domed trusses of 12-16.
Plant twice as wide as tall; leaves indumented silver, aging to
cinnamon. H. Larson, cross 1969; J. A. Davies, reg. 1986.
RUTH WICK   Parentage: BRITANNIA x yakushimanum
1.5ft(.45m) OF(-18C) M   Flowers with Neyron rose at margins,
lighter in center, funnel-shaped; round trusses of 12. Plant
broader than tall; heavily textured leaves. R. Wick, reg. 1983.
SIESTA   Parentage: BRITANNIA x yakushimanum
3ft(.9m) -15F(-26C) M 4/4   Pink buds opening soft pink, then
fading white. Foliage with light indumentum. W. Elliott.
* *

```
      -catawbiense var. album--Catanea 1/2
ANDREW EDDY-                        -griffithianum 1/4
      -The Hon. Jean Marie de Montague-
                          -unknown 1/4
```
4.5ft(1.4m)(15 yrs) -10F(-23C) M   Deep cardinal red buds open
strong purplish red; conical trusses, 6in(15cm) wide, hold about
10 flowers. Leaves held 4-5 years. A. Raustein, reg. 1986.


```
            -Scintillation--unknown 1/2
ANDREW PATON-
            -calophytum, pink form 1/2
```
3ft(.9m) x 5ft(1.5m)(14 yrs) -15F(-26C) E   Trusses of 20 white
flowers with deep red markings, including central solid blotch.
Leaves convex, glossy green. Furman cross; Swift, reg. 1988.


```
            -arboreum 1/2
ANDROCLES-
            -calophytum 1/2
```
Large trusses hold about 30 flowers, of rhodamine pink with four
lines of darker spots. Rothschild, 1933. A.M. 1948.


```
            -stewartianum, scarlet form 1/2
ANDROMEDA-
            -neriiflorum 1/2
```
Crimson scarlet flowers. Reuthe, 1941.


```
                                        -catawbiense
            -Harrisville--Newport F4-         1/2
      -unnamed hybrid-              -unknown 1/8
      -              -              -catawbiense
ANDY PORTER-          -Pink Twins-
      -                        -haematodes 1/8
      -              -smirnowii 1/4
      -unnamed hybrid-
                  -catawbiense
```
Beetroot purple buds open to flowers deep purplish pink, frilled
edging lilac purple, chartreuse spots; white anthers. W. Delp.

```
                      -fortunei--Sir Charles Butler 1/4
      -Van Nes Sensation-
      -                        -griffithianum
      -      -Halopeanum (White Pearl)-         3/8
ANGEL-                        -maximum 3/8
      -                  -griffithianum
      -Halopeanum (White Pearl)-
                        -maximum
```
White flowers, pale mauve on the outside, with red speckling on
the upper lobe. R. L. Rowarth, Australia, reg. 1972.

ANGEL--selected form of yakushimanum, by Greer
See color illus. Greer catalog, 1990, pl. 22.


```
            -maximum, white form 1/2
ANGEL BLUSH-
            -yakushimanum--Koichiro Wada 1/2
```
5ft(1.5m)(20 yrs) -15F(-26C) ML 4/4   Flowers mostly white or
blush, aging to pure white.   Others named of this cross: ANGEL
GLOW, ANGEL STAR, and ANGEL LIGHT. Dr. Mark Konrad, cross 1969.
Color illus. ARS J 43:1 (1989), p. 23.


```
                        -brachycarpum 1/4
      -Dated Yellow-              -wardii? 1/16
      -        -        -Chlorops-
      -        -unnamed hybrid-    -vernicosum? 1/16
      -                  -aureum (chrysanthum) 1/8
ANGEL-      -Catalgla--catawbiense var. album Glass 1/8
 DUST-  -Gosh -              -decorum? 1/32
      -  - Darn-        -Caroline-
      -        -Mrs. H. R. Yates-    -brachycarpum?
      -Sweet-              -unknown 1/16        1/32
      Lulu-              -neriiflorum 1/32
      -              -Nereid-
      -        -Phyllis -    -dichroanthum 1/32
      -unnamed- Ballard-fortunei ssp. discolor 1/16
         hybrid-
              -catawbiense--Clark's White 1/8
```
Grayed red/red-orange bud; corolla and anthers very pale orange-
yellow. Exterior veins strong yellowish pink. Light chartreuse
green flare, brighter dorsal spotting. White filaments. Delp.

ANGEL FALLS   Parentage unknown
White flowers, blushed light pink, 4in(10cm) wide, with a creamy
throat; 7-lobed, fragrant. Kersey cross; Frederick, reg. 1976.

ANGELIQUE   Described under ELEANOR BEE, q.v.

* *
```
            -griffithianum 1/2
ANGELO-
            -fortunei ssp. discolor 1/2
```
6ft(1.8m) -5F(-21C) L 4/3   This cross was first made at
Caerhays, in Cornwall, by J. C. Williams, who called it Cornish
Loderi, but Rothschild's ANGELO blooms later and grows taller.
(Bean, p. 833). ANGELO'S flowers blush pink outside, white with
pale green spots within. Tall truss of 12. Rothschild, 1930.
A.M. 1935; F.C.C. 1948. Color illus. PB pl. 10.
ANGELO DIADEM   Parentage as above
White flowers. M. Haworth-Booth.
ANGELO SOLENT QUEEN   Parentage as above
Flowers very pale rose fade to almost white, spotted green; fra-
grant. Small, late-blooming shrub. Rothschild. A.M. 1939.
EXBURY ANGELO   Parentage as above
Tree-like plant with leaves 9in(23cm) long. Flowers white with
green spots in the throat. Rothschild, 1930. F.C.C. 1947.
SHEFFIELD PARK ANGELO   Parentage as above
6ft(1.8m) 5F(-15C) L 3/3   Beautiful large leaves and flowers,
pure white, except for chartreuse area at base of tube.   A. G.
Soames. A.M. 1950.
SOLENT QUEEN   Parentage as above
6ft(1.8m) 5F(-15C) ML 3/3 Flowers of blush pink with a green
ray, fading to almost pure white, 5.5in(14cm) across; fragrant.
Rothschild, 1933. A.M. 1939.
SOLENT SNOW   Parentage as above
Beautiful pure white flowers, green markings. Rothschild, 1933.
SOLENT SWAN   Parentage as above
Pure white flowers, no markings. Rothschild.
* *

ANICA BRICOGNE   Parentage unknown; may contain ponticum
5ft(1.5m) -10F(-23C) ML 3/3   Dense, attractive habit; heat-
tolerant. Flower pale mauve to orchid, golden blotch. Unknown.

ANILIN   Described under ANUSCHKA, q.v.

```
        -campylocarpum 1/2
ANITA-
        -griersonianum 1/2
```
Yellow flower flushed rose; campanulate. Lord Aberconway, 1941.

ANITA DUNSTAN   Described under BEAUTIFUL DAY, q.v.

```
                        -griffithianum 1/4
            -Jean Marie de Montague-
ANITA GEHNRICH-                    -unknown 1/4
            -yakushimanum 1/2
```
3.5ft(1.m) high x 4ft(1.2m)(12 yrs) -5F(21C) M Domed truss of
14 flowers. Buds strong red, opening deep pink, fading to pale
purplish pink in throat.   Slight, brown, felted indumentum, beneath mature leaf. P. Waldman, Roslyn Nursery, reg. 1988.

```
                    -elliottii 1/8
            -Fusilier-
    -Mrs. Helen      -griersonianum 1/4
    - Weyerhaeuser-  -griersonianum
ANITA OWEN-         -Jean-
    -              -decorum 1/8
    -sanguineum ssp. sanguineum var. haemaleum  1/2
```
Tall plant; foliage small, dark green leaves. Flowers chrysan-
themum red; loose trusses of 3-6. C. S. Seabrook, reg. 1964.

ANKA HEINJE   Described under OAKTON, q.v.

```
        -keiskei 1/2
ANN CAREY-
        -spinuliferum 1/2
```
5ft(1.5m) 5F(-15C) E 3/3 Campanulate flower 1in(2.5cm) wide,
opening chartreuse, changing to coral pink. Plant as broad as
tall; leaf margins rolled.   Lem cross; Mrs. S. Anderson intro.,
reg. 1977.   P.A. 1966.   Color illus. HG p. 73.

```
            -yakushimanum 1/2
ANN ELIZABETH-
            -unknown 1/2
```
2.5ft(.75m)(12 yrs) -10F(-23C) ML   Strong purplish red buds
open to flowers of deep reddish purple, with a pale pink throat;
truss of 15. Plant upright, as wide as tall; medium olive green
foliage. John Ford, Secrest Arboretum, reg. 1984.

```
                                        -catawbiense
                    -Parsons Grandiflorum-
        -Nova Zembla-                  -unknown
        -           -dark red hybrid--unknown
    -Blinklicht-   -griffithianum
    -           -Mars-
ANN             -           -unknown
LINDSAY-                -griffithianum
    -           -Mars-
    -unnamed hybrid-     -unknown
    -yakushimanum--Koichiro Wada
```
3ft(.9m) x 5ft(1.5m) -15F(-26C) ML   Flowers in trusses of 14-
17, strong red with lobe centers and throats white; unmarked.
Petioles reddish brown. Hachmann, cross 1969; Stück, reg. 1988.
Color illus. WS, 1989, p. 119.

ANN LUETTGEN   Advanced generation hybrid including catawbiense
                and maximum, and possibly unknown hybrids.
5ft(1.5m) -15F(-26C) M   Buds deep purplish red; flowers 4in.
(10.2cm) wide, deep pink with dark purplish red dorsal spotting.
Trusses of about 17.   W. David Smith, reg. 1979.

ANN PASCOE   Described under CHANG TSO LIN, q.v.

```
                                -catawbiense 1/2
ANN RUTLIDGE (ANN RUTLEDGE) (ANNE RUTLEDGE)-
                                -unknown 1/2
```
Red flowers. A parent of AA-17, AA-36. Warren E. Stokes, reg.
1956. Color illus. ARS J 42:4 (1988), p. 186.

ANN SULLIVAN   Parentage unknown
3ft(.9m) x 5ft(1.5m)(7 yrs)   Flowers in trusses of 20, funnel-
shaped, 5-lobed, light purple with a large flare of medium yellow. N. Sullivan, Australia, reg. 1989.

```
                        -griffithianum 5/8
            -Beauty of Tremough-
    -Norman Gill-        -arboreum 1/8
ANNA-        -griffithianum
    -                   -griffithianum
    -Jean Marie de Montague-
                        -unknown 1/4
```
6ft(1.8m) OF(-18C) M 5/4 A plant of unusual foliage, heavily
textured, deeply veined. Deep reddish pink flower buds, opening
deep pink with a reddish flare in the throat (two-toned effect);
fades to pale pink. Halfdan Lem, before 1958. P.A. 1952.

```
            -fortunei ? 1/4
        -Ben Moseley-
ANNA ALMEDA-       -unknown 1/2
        -       -Moser's Maroon--unknown
        -Dusky Maid-
                -fortunei ssp. discolor 1/4
```
Buds strong purplish red and deep purplish pink, open to frilled
flowers, shading moderate to pale purplish pink, to white. Ruby
red dorsal spotting; very pale purple anthers.   W. Delp.

```
                        -racemosum 1/4
                -Conemaugh-
ANNA BALDSIEFEN---PIONEER, selfed-    -mucronulatum 1/4
                                -unknown 1/4
```
3ft(.9m) -20F(-29C) E 3/3 Heavily clothed in small foliage,
more evergreen than PIONEER.   Flowers clear phlox pink, margins
deeper; trusses hold 17. Very free-flowering. Baldsiefen, reg.
1964. A.M. Wisley Trials 1987. Col. ill. Cox pl. 6; K. p. 48.

```
            -adenopodum 1/2
ANNA CAROLINE-
GABLE    -degronianum (metternichii var. tsukusianum?) 1/2
```
Pale pink flowers appearing early. Plant has good tight form.
Hardy to -10F(-23C).   Joseph Gable.

* *
```
                                    -catawbiense 1/8
                -Parsons Grandiflorum-
        -America-               -unknown 9/16
    -unnamed-     -dark red hybrid--unknown
    - hybrid-     -griffithianum 3/16
    -       -Mars-
ANNA DELP-     -Blaze-  -unknown
    -           -catawbiense var. rubrum 1/8
    -       -Mars- (as above)
    -Red Brave-
            -America- as above)
```
5ft(1.5m) -15F(-26C) ML 4/3 Buds deep red; flowers deep red
shading to currant red, darker dorsal spots.   White filaments,
pale greenish yellow anthers. W. Fetterhoff cross; Delp raiser.
SUSY and PURPLE SUSY of same parentage, Dr. Tom Ring raiser.
* *
* *
```
        -catawbiense var. album 1/2
ANNA H. HALL-
        -yakushimanum--Koichiro Wada 1/2
```
3ft(.9m) -25F(-32C) M 4/4   Plant compact and densely foli-
aged; thin brown indumentum; new growth conspicuously indumented. White flowers from fresh pink buds, in trusses of about 15,
resembling yakushimanum.   David G. Leach, reg. 1963.
ELAINE BEHRING   Parentage: CATALGLA x yakushimanum
Moderate purplish pink flowers; dorsal lobe pale purplish pink,
with heavy medium red spotting. R. Behring, reg. 1986.
GREAT LAKES   Parentage as ANNA H. HALL, above
5ft(1.5m) -25F(-32C) M 4/4 Clear pink buds opening lighter,
fading to chalk white flowers, 15 per truss. Leach, reg. 1961.
MAY TIME   Parentage as above (Not distributed)
PINK FROSTING   Parentage as above (Not distributed)
SPRING FROLIC   Parentage as above
5ft(1.5m) -25F(-32C) E 4/5 Clear pink buds. White flowers,
like yakushimanum; very floriferous. Plant broader than high,
very dense. Elliptic foliage held 3 years; new growth farinose,
brown for several weeks. Leach, intro. 1963; reg. 1972. Col-
or illus. ARS Q 25:2 (1972), p. 100.
SIAM   Parentage as above, but pollen not from KOICHIRO WADA
5ft(1.5m) -20F(-29C) L 4/4 Bush well-branched, broader than
tall; glossy convex leaves with orange-brown indumentum beneath.
Roseine purple buds, opening light phlox pink and fading white.
Rounded trusses of 19-20.   Leach cross; intro. 1975; reg. 1982.
* *

```
          -catawbiense 1/2
ANNA PARSONS-
          -unknown 1/2
Purplish red flowers.    S. B. Parsons, before 1875.
```

```
* * * * * * * * * * * * * * * * * * * * * * * * * *
          -griersonianum 1/2        -griffithianum
          -                      -George Hardy-
ANNA ROSE WHITNEY-        -Pink -        -catawbiense 3/16
          -              - Pearl-        -arboreum 1/16
          -Countess -      -Broughtonii-
            of Derby -                -unknown 1/16
                   -                -catawbiense
                   -Cynthia-
                          -griffithianum 3/16
6ft(1.8m) -5F(-21C) ML 5/3  Impressive sight in flower: deep
rose pink flowers 4in(10.2cm) across, with light brown spotting.
Handsome foliage of fern green leaves 8in(20.3cm) x 3in(7.6cm).
Does well in sun, but prefers some shade.    Van Veen, Sr. cross;
Whitney intro. 1954.    A.M. Wisley Trials 1987.    Color illus.
Cox pl. 7; JS p. 84; VV p. 60.
LUCKY STRIKE    Parentage as above
4ft(1.2m) 10F(-12C) ML 3/3  Flowers of deep salmon pink, fun-
nel-shaped, 3in(7.6cm) wide in firm, conical trusses of 9.    Dull
green leaves, 6in(15cm) long.    Van Veen, Sr., reg. 1958.
VAN    Parentage as above
6ft(1.8m) -5F(-21C) ML 4/4    Flowers deep pink, heavily spot-
ted purplish red on dorsal lobe, 4.5in(11.5cm) across; trusses of
13-15.  Plant as wide as tall; very fine foliage. Van Veen, Sr.,
cross; Greer, reg. 1979.   Color illus. HG p. 147.
* * * * * * * * * * * * * * * * * * * * * * * * * *
```

```
ANNA STRELOW--form  of annae Laxiflorum Group  F 27706
5ft(1.5m) 10F(-12C) EM 3/3  White flowers, shading near base
to yellow white, in loose trusses of 14-16.    Col. S. R. Clarke
raiser; R. N. Stephenson Clarke, reg. 1979.    A.M. 1979.
```

```
          -keiskei--Yaku Fairy 1/2
ANNA VOJTEC-
          -unknown 1/2
Dwarf -10F(-23C) EM    Clusters of creamy white flowers  cover
a tiny rock garden plant.    Lincoln Foster raiser.
```

```
          -campanulatum 1/2
ANNABELLA-        -griffithianum 1/4
          -Loderi-
                -fortunei 1/4
White flowers, flushed light mauve.    Rothschild, 1933.
```

ANNAPOLIS ROYAL   Described under FORTUNE, q.v.

```
ANNAPURNA--form of anthopogon ssp. hypenanthum  S S & W 9090
18in(45cm)  OF(-18C)  EM  4/3    Collected in Nepal by Stainton,
Sykes, and Williams.    Light yellow, narrowly tubular flowers in
trusses of 8 or 9.   Small leaves, glossy deep green; dark brown,
scaly indumentum below.   Cox, reg. 1974.   A.M. 1974.
```

```
          -forrestii Repens Group 1/2
ANNA'S RIPLET-              -campylocarpum Elatum Group 1/4
          -Letty Edwards-
                    -fortunei 1/4
3ft(.9m)  OF(-18C)  EM  4/3    Plant habit rounded.  Many flowers
opening rose pink, changing later to soft yellow.    Halfdan Lem.
```

```
     -thomsonii 1/2
ANNE-
     -unknown 1/2
A pink-flowered shrub.    Messel.    A.M. 1928.
```

```
          -arboreum ssp. cinnamomeum var. roseum 1/2
ANNE CLARKE-
          -sutchuenense 1/2
Pink flowers, fading to white; truss of 20-22. Narrow, elliptic
foliage of dark green, with silvery gray, felted indumentum be-
neath.   R. N. S. Clarke, Borde Hill, reg. 1977.    A.M. 1977.
```

```
          -campylocarpum ssp. caloxanthum 1/2
ANNE DE ROTHSCHILD-
          -eclecteum 1/2
Orange-red buds open cream with small throat blotch, strong red;
flowers 7-lobed, filaments cream, anthers brown.  Trusses of 10
or 12.  Wynniatt cross; E. de Rothschild, reg. 1986.  A.M. 1986.
```

```
* * * * * * * * * * * * * * * * * * * * * * * * * * *
          -Lady        -fortunei ssp discolor 3/8
     -Day  - Bessborough-
     - Dream-        -campylocarpum Elatum Group 1/8
     -       -griersonianum 1/4
ANNE GEORGE-        -dichroanthum 1/8
          -       -Dido-
     -Ice Cream-    -decorum 1/8
          -fortunei ssp. discolor
5ft(1.5m)  5F(-15C)  M    Salmon pink buds open paler; in loose
trusses.  Slender foliage, soft green. A. F. George, reg. 1966.
SNOW GOOSE    Parentage as above
Funnel-shaped flowers, white in bud, opening white with a large
yellow blotch; trusses of 10.    A. F. George, reg. 1966.
* * * * * * * * * * * * * * * * * * * * * * * * * * *
```

ANNE GLASS   Syn. for MRS. CARTER GLASS, MRS. POWELL GLASS

ANNE HARDGROVE   Described under JAY McMARTIN, q.v.

```
               -griffithianum 1/8
          -Loderi-
     -Avalanche-        -fortunei 1/8
ANNE HENNY-        -calophytum 3/4
     -calophytum, pink form
Buds deep pink.  Flower campanulate, light pink fading to white,
red blotch.  Trusses dome-shaped, of 15 flowers.  Plant branches
moderately.   Cross by Anne Henny, 1951; Carl Heller, reg. 1980.
```

```
     -ciliicalyx 1/2
ANNE TEESE-
     -formosum 1/2
White flowers, flushed solferino purple; striped purple outside.
A. J. Teese, Australia, reg. 1968.    Color illus. Cox pl. 8.
```

```
     -catawbiense 1/2
ANNEDORE-
     -unknown 1/2
In Register of 1958 as a synonym of LADY ARMSTRONG, credited to
A. Waterer, 1870.  Flowers of bright, light carmine red, white
throat, ochre markings.  Offered by T. J. Hermann Seidel, 1926.
```

```
          -Marion (Cheal)--unknown 3/4
ANNELIES  -
VAN DE VEN-              -arboreum 1/4
          -Mrs. Henry Shilson-
                    -unknown
Flower red-purple with a lighter center.  Van de Ven, reg. 1974.
```

```
ANNE'S DELIGHT    Parentage unknown
3ft(.9m)  OF(-18C)  EM  4/3    Light greenish yellow flowers with
throat markings of red; trusses of 14.  Wavy, dark green leaves;
compact plant.   Whitney cross; Sather, reg. 1986.
```

```
     -wardii 1/2
ANNE'S PET-
     -unknown 1/2
3ft(.9m)  5F(-15C)  E    Deep green foliage amply furnished, held
3 years.  Buds young; flowers primrose yellow.    Whitney/Sather.
```

```
          -fortunei ssp. discolor 1/2
ANNETTE WEYERHAEUSER-        -griersonianum 1/4
          -unnamed hybrid-
                    -unknown 1/4
Truss of 12 light magenta flowers, 5-lobed.  Larson, reg. 1982.
```

ANNIE DALTON   Described under MADONNA, q.v.

```
          -Marion--unknown
ANNIE DOSSER-
          -unknown
Bright pink flowers, shading to white in center.  Trusses of 13.
D. Dosser, Australia, reg. 1982.
```

```
               -griffithianum 1/4
          -Loderi King George-
ANNIE DRING-        -fortunei 1/4
          -Corona--unknown 1/2
Flowers reddish purple, with a basal blotch of purple; truss of
14.   W. V. Joslin cross; Mrs. Lillian Hodgson, reg. 1977.
```

```
                        -griffithianum 1/8
              -George Hardy-
      -Pink Pearl-          -catawbiense 5/8
      -            -        -arboreum 1/8
ANNIE E. ENDTZ-      -Broughtonii-
      -                         -unknown 1/8
      -catawbiense, red form
```
5ft(1.5m) OF(-18C) ML 3/3 Flowers medium pink with frilled margins, trusses of 7-9. Plant spreading, vigorous; deep green leaves, 6in(15.2cm) long. Heat-tolerant. L. J. Endtz, 1939.

```
      -griffithianum 1/2
ANTHAEA-
      -unknown 1/2
```
Also called ANTHEA. James H. Mangles.

* *

```
                  -sanguineum ssp. didymum 1/4
          -Arthur Osborn-
ANTHONY-          -griersonianum 1/4
      -griffithianum 1/2
```
Deep red flowers. Gen. Harrison, 1952.
KING ARTHUR Parentage as above
Another selection by Gen. Harrison, 1956.
* *

```
          -Scintillation--unknown 5/8
ANTHONY WAYNE-             -catawbiense 1/8
      -         -Atrosanguineum-
      -Atrier-            -unknown
            -griersonianum 1/4
```
Cross by Charles Herbert.

```
                -campylocarpum 3/4
          -Lady Primrose-
ANTHONY WEBB-       -unknown 1/4
      -campylocarpum
```
Soft yellow flowers. T. C. Thacker, 1938.

```
                          -catawbiense 1/16
                    -Atrosanguineum-
            -Atrier-            -unknown 9/16
      -Mary Belle-    -griersonianum 1/8
      -        -        -decorum 1/8
ANTIGUA-      -Dechaem-
      -                -haematodes 1/8
      -Dexter's Apricot--unknown
```
5ft(1.5m) -5F(-21C) M 3/3 Flowers of azalea pink shading to Naples yellow, base of throat blood red, dorsal blotch; corolla openly funnel-shaped, 5-lobed, 3.25in(8cm) across. Lax truss of 10. Plant as wide as tall. Becales cross; Herbert, reg. 1977.

ANTJE Described under ELISABETH HOBBIE, q.v.

ANTON Described under ALFRED, q.v.

```
                    -fortunei ssp. discolor 3/8
      -Sir Frederick Moore-        -arboreum ssp. zeylanicum
ANTON -              -St. Keverne-                   1/8
 RUPERT-                  -griffithianum 1/8
      -          -elliottii 1/4
      -Kilimanjaro-    -Moser's Maroon--unknown 1/8
                -Dusky Maid-
                      -fortunei ssp. discolor
```
5ft(1.5m) OF(-18C) M 4/3 Flowers pink, shading deeper rose in the throat. E. de Rothschild, reg. 1971.

* *

```
      -arboreum 1/4
      -Gill's Triumph-
ANTONIO-          -griffithianum 1/4
      -fortunei ssp. discolor 1/2
```
Synonym EXBURY ANTONIO. Suffused rose pink, paling with age, a crimson blotch; spotted within. Rothschild, 1933. A.M. 1939.
ANTONIO OMEGA Parentage as above
Pale pink flowers. Rothschild, 1933.
* *

```
                        -griffithianum 1/8
              -George-
      -Pink Pearl- Hardy-catawbiense 5/8
ANTOON VAN WELIE-      -        -arboreum 1/8
      -                -Broughtonii-
      -catawbiense, red    -unknown 1/8
```
6ft(1.8m) -5F(-21C) ML 4/3 Huge flowers, deep pink; trusses very nice. Large, waxy leaves. Endtz. Color illus. VV p. x.

* *

```
                        -griffithianum 1/8
              -Mars-
      -         -unknown 5/16        -catawbiense 1/16
      -Sammetglut-    -Parsons Grandiflorum-
ANUSCHKA-      -Nova-              -unknown
      -        Zembla-dark red hybrid--unknown
      -yakushimanum--Koichiro Wada 1/2
```
3ft(.9m) -15F(-26C) ML Truss of 11-14 flowers, 5-lobed, spinel red, shading inwards to Neyron rose; calyx greenish pink. Leaves densely hairy. Hachmann, cross 1962; Stück, reg. 1983. Color illus. WS, 1989, p. 146.
ANILIN Parentage as above
2ft(.6m) x 4ft(1.2m) -15F(-23C) M Flowers in trusses of 14-18, lobes of deep purplish pink shaded vivid purplish red inside and out, with white throat and lobe centers. Hachmann cross; Stück, reg. 1988. Color illus. WS, 1989, p. 146.
BARMSTEDT Parentage as above
Flowers Neyron rose, fading paler, light centers; trusses of 22. New growth silvery with indumentum. Named for the nursery town: location of Hachmann's nursery. Hachmann cross; G. Stück, reg. 1983. Color illus. ARS J 39:2 (1985), p. 63; WS, 1989, p. 147.
* *

AOLA--form of valentinianum
2.5ft(.75m) 15F(-10C) E 3/2 Flowers 3in(7.6cm) wide, double and fimbriated, canary yellow. B. Lancaster, reg. 1963.

```
                -griffithianum 1/4
      -Gill's Triumph-
APACHE-          -arboreum 1/4
      -thomsonii 1/2
```
Bright rose flowers. Not grown at Exbury. Rothschild, 1933.

```
      -aperantum 1/2
APAR-
      -arboreum 1/2
```
Flowers of deep red. Lord Aberconway, cross 1938; intro. 1946.

```
                -haematodes 1/4
      -Choremia-
APEREMIA-      -arboreum 1/4
      -aperantum 1/2
```
Deep red flowers. Lord Aberconway, cross 1937; intro. 1946.

```
      -aperantum 1/2
APERME-
      -meddianum 1/2
```
Red flowers. Lord Aberconway, cross 1937; intro. 1946.

```
      -edgeworthii (bullatum) 1/2
APIS-
      -nuttallii 1/2
```
Pure white flowers, a canary yellow base. S. R. Clarke, 1936.

```
                -sperabile 1/4
      -Eupheno-
APODENO-      -griersonianum 1/4
      -dichroanthum ssp. apodectum 1/2
```
Vermilion flowers. Lord Aberconway, cross 1935; intro. 1946.

```
      -dichroanthum ssp. apodectum 1/2
APODORUM-
      -decorum 1/2
```
A parent of FIRE FLAME by Scrase-Dickins, otherwise unknown.

```
                -dichroanthum ssp. apodectum 1/2
APOTROPHIA-
      -facetum (eriogynum) 1/2
```
A small shrub with oblong-elliptical leaves, 2.75-4.75in(7-12cm) long. Flowers of good substance, tubular campanulate, of shrimp pink; surfaces of lobes marked with darker tinted areas. E. J. P. Magor cross; Maj. E. W. M. Magor, reg. 1963.

```
* * * * * * * * * * * * * * * * * * * * * * * * * *        -fortunei
           -catawbiense var. album Glass--Catalgla 1/2       APRICOT GLORY-
-                         -campylocarpum 1/16                      -Ted's Yellow (uncertain combination of fortunei,
APPLAUSE-          -unnamed hybrid-                                        wardii, dichroanthum)
-            -Adriaan-          -unknown 1/8              Apricot yellow flowers.   C. R. & V. Haag, 1987.
-         - Koster-               -griffithianum 1/32
-unnamed-       -          -George-                              -maximum 1/2
   hybrid-    -Mrs. Lindsay- Hardy-                      APRICOT GLOW-
-         Smith-       -catawbiense 1/32                     -Ostbo's Low Yellow--unknown 1/2
          -williamsianum 1/4   -Duchess of Edinburgh--unk.   5ft(1.5m) x 7ft(2.1m)(19yrs, cutting)  -10F(-23C) ML  Buds pink
5ft(1.5m)  -20F(-29C) EM 3/3  Flowers white, faint ivory shad-  at tip; funnel-shaped flowers 2in(5cm) wide, edges moderate pink
ing, openly campanulate, 5-lobed, about 2.5in(6.4cm) wide; truss  shading to pale buff center; flat trusses.  Dense plant.  Leaves
of 11.  Plant dense, broader than tall.  D. Leach, reg. 1972.  arras green, glossy, to 6.3in(16cm); held 3 years.  W. Hunnewell
FINLANDIA  Parentage as above                           cross; R. Ticknor raiser; R. Brooks, reg. 1989.
5ft(1.5m)  -20F(-29C) EM 4/5  Synonym ALASKA.  Many glisten-
ing white flowers of heavy substance, from pink buds.  Spherical              -dichroanthum 1/8
trusses of 12.  Leaves small, convex, down-turned; held 3 years.          -Goldsworth-
Rounded, well-branched plant.  Leach, reg. 1974.  Color illus.      -Tortoiseshell- Orange  -fortunei ssp. discolor 1/4
ARS J 36:1 (1982), p. 6.                                 - Wonder  -
FLAIR  Parentage as above                               -          -griersonianum 3/8
5ft(1.5m)  -15F(-26C) EM 4/3    Buds light to strong purplish  APRICOT GOLD-        -griffithianum 1/16
pink open to flowers of heavy substance, white with faint ivory  -          -Loderi-
shades.  Truss ball-shaped, 10-11 flowers.  Leaves medium green,  -    -Albatross-    -fortunei 1/16
held 3 years on a round, well-branched shrub.  Leach, reg. 1974.  -Cup Day-    -fortunei ssp. discolor
ROBIN LEACH  Parentage as above                         -          -elliottii 1/8
5ft(1.5m)  -20F(-29C) EM 4/4   Bush much wider than high, with    -Fusilier-
dense foliage; medium green, ovate leaves turn convexly, sharply       -griersonianum
downward.  Flowers 3in(7.6cm) across, open-campanulate, of white  Truss of 12-15 flowers, funnel-shaped, 3.5in(8.3cm) x 2in(5cm),
with faint red spots; full trusses of 7.   Leach, reg. 1972.  5-lobed, light orange-yellow flushed pink.  Plant 4ft(1.2m) tall
* * * * * * * * * * * * * * * * * * * * * * * * * * * *  in 14 years.  K. Van de Ven, Victoria, Australia, reg. 1987.


                -fortunei 1/2                            APRICOT ICE   Described under APRICOT DELIGHT, q.v.
APPLE BLOSSOM-          -campylocarpum 1/4
          -unnamed hybrid-                               APRICOT LADY CHAMBERLAIN  Described under LADY CHAMBERLAIN, q.v.
                -unknown (1/4)
Parentage as in Slocock catalog.  Low-growing shrub with flowers              -dichroanthum 5/16
pink, cream, and white.  Slocock.                            -unnamed hybrid-
                                                         -unnamed-          -neriiflorum 1/8
APPLE BLOSSOM (APPLEBLOSSOM)   See SANDWICH APPLEBLOSSOM  - hybrid-          -fortunei ssp. discolor 1/4
                                                         -          -unnamed hybrid-  -dichroanthum
              -catawbiense var. album Glass--Catalgla 1/4  APRICOT-          -Fabia-
        -unnamed-                                        NECTAR-          -griersonianum 1/16
APPLE  - hybrid-yakushimanum--Koichiro Wada 1/4          -          -fortunei ssp. discolor
 DUMPLING-     -lanigerum--Round Wood 1/4                -    -Lady Bessborough-
        -unnamed-                                        -Jalisco-          -campylocarpum Elatum Group 1/8
        hybrid-catawbiense, red form 1/4                 -    -dichroanthum
2ft(.6m)  -10F(-23C) ML   Pale lemon yellow flowers with green-  -Dido-
ish yellow throat, 7-lobed, fragrant, in trusses of 7.  Upright,       -decorum 1/8
well-branched plant.  H. Yates cross; Mrs. Yates, reg. 1977.  3ft(.9m)  -5F(-21C) ML 4/4  Orange-colored flowers with light
                                                         scarlet edges.  Compact plant; large leaves.  Lyons, reg. 1972.
              -neriiflorum Euchaites Group 1/4
        -Portia-                                         APRICOT ROAD   Parentage unknown
APPLEFORD-   -strigillosum 1/4                           Medium-sized, compact shrub, blooming in autumn in NZ.  Flowers
        -barbatum 1/2                                    held in trusses of 10, 7-lobed, strong red on lobes, upper lobes
Bright cardinal red flowers open in compact, dome-shaped trusses  spotted green; the throat and back of tube, pale yellow.  Mrs.
of 20.  Leaves 3 times as long as wide, narrowly oblong, slight-  I. Henry, reg. 1988.
ly revolute.  Crown Estate, Windsor, reg. 1966.   A.M. 1966.


* * * * * * * * * * * * * * * * * * * * * * * * * * * *              -Lady          -fortunei ssp. discolor 1/8
        -Marion--unknown 13/16          -griffithianum   - Bessborough-
        -(Cheal)          -Loderi-          1/64         -Jalisco-          -campylocarpum Elatum Group
-Freckle-          -Albatross-     -fortunei 1/64        -          -          -dichroanthum 7/16          1/8
- Pink -     -Cup Day-     -fortunei ssp. discolor       -Comstock-     -Dido-
-          -elliottii 1/32    1/32                       -          -          -decorum 5/16
APRICOT-     -Midnight-     -Fusilier-                   APRICOT-     - -dichroanthum
DELIGHT-     -          -griersonianum 1/32              SHERBET-     -Jasper-
-          -          -ponticum 1/16                     -          -Lady Bessborough- (as above)
-          -Purple Splendour-                            -   -dichroanthum
-unknown          -unknown                              -Dido-
Pollen parent may be APRICOT GOLD, q.v.   Funnel-shaped flowers       -decorum
3.25(8cm) wide, light yellowish pink, in a truss of 20-26.  Bush  4ft(1.2m)  5F(-15C) M 4/4  Long, oval leaves on a mound-shaped
is 39in(1m) at 10 years.  K. Van de Ven, Australia, reg. 1985.  plant.  Buffy apricot-colored flowers, with a large calyx of the
APRICOT ICE  Parentage as above                         same color.  H. Greer, intro. 1985.   Color illus. HG p. 169.
Funnel-shaped flowers 4in(10cm) across, light yellowish pink, in
trusses of 20-26.  Shrub 39in(1m).  K. Van de Ven, reg. 1985.  APRICOT SPINNER   See next page for diagram, etc.
OLINDA PRIDE  Parentage as above
Truss of 20 funnel-shaped flowers, 7-lobed, pale yellowish pink,              -minus Carolinianum Group, white form 1/2
spotted strong greenish yellow.  K. Van de Ven, reg. 1985.  APRIL BLUSH-
* * * * * * * * * * * * * * * * * * * * * * * * * * * *       -mucronulatum, pink form 1/2
                                                         2ft(.6m)  -25F(-32C) E 3/3  Flowers blush pink, fading white.
APRICOT FANTASY   Described under PINEAPPLE DELIGHT, q.v.  Plant semi-deciduous.  G. Guy Nearing, reg. 1970.
```

```
                      -George-griffithianum 3/32
           -Mrs. Lindsay- Hardy-
           - Smith    -       -catawbiense 1/32
        -Diane-           -Duchess of Edinburgh--unknown
     -        -          -campylocarpum 3/16
  -unnamed-    -unnamed hybrid-
   - hybrid-     -              -unknown 1/8
   -         -        -campylocarpum
APRICOT-    -Citronella-    -griffithianum
SPINNER-           -Kewense-
   -                        -fortunei 1/16
   -              -wardii 1/4
  -unnamed hybrid-   -dichroanthum 1/8
                -Dido-
                      -decorum 1/8
Yellow tinged with orange.   Waterer, Sons & Crisp, reg. 1975.
```

```
             -yakushimanum 1/4
     -Pirouette-        -Jan Dekens--unknown 7/32
     -        -Pink    -      -Queen    -griffithianum
APRIL -     Petticoats-Britannia-  Wilhelmina-      1/32
AFFAIR-     -                -              -unknown
   -                        -Stanley Davies--unknown
   -              -strigillosum 1/4
   -Promise of Spring-
                  -arboreum 1/4
Flowers of hot pink; wavy margins.  Early.   Lofthouse, 1982.
```

APRIL BLUSH   See previous page

```
        -hippophaeoides 1/2
APRIL CHIMES-
        -mollicomum 1/2
3ft(.9m) 0F(-18C) EM 4/3  Attractive, pointed leaves.  Flow-
ers rosy mauve.  Excellent as cut bloom.   Hillier, reg. 1969.
```

* *

```
                      -minus Carolinianum
           -P.J.M.(dbl. flower)-      Group 7/16
      -unnamed-            -dauricum, white 7/16
  -unnamed- hybrid-mucronulatum, pink 1/8
  - hybrid-
APRIL-     -dauricum, white
CLOUD-       -minus Carolinianum Group
   -unnamed hybrid-      -minus Carolinianum Group
             -P.J.M.-
                  -dauricum, white
4ft(1.2m) x 3ft(.9m)(9 yrs) -20F(-29C) EM   Light yellow-green
buds open pale yellow-green; broadly funnel-shaped, double flow-
ers 1.5in(4cm) wide in ball-shaped truss 2in(5cm) across. Peta-
loid stamens. Dense habit.  Mezitt cross; Weston, reg. 1987.
```
APRIL SNOW   Parentage as above
3ft(.9m) x 3ft(9 yrs) -18F(-28C) EM Pale yellowish green buds
open to pure white, openly funnel-shaped, double flowers 1.5in(4
cm) wide, lobe tips pointed, petaloid stamens; truss of 12. Aromatic, dense foliage; yellow petioles. E. Mezitt cross; Weston
Nurseries, reg. 1987.   Color illus. Weston 1990 catalog, cover.
* *

```
        -minus Carolinianum Group, white form 1/2
APRIL DAWN-
        -dauricum, white form 1/2
3.5ft(1.0m) x 2.5ft(.75m) -25F(-32C) EM  Flowers widely fun-
nel-shaped, slightly fragrant, 5 smooth-edged lobes, light pink.
Leaves held 2-3 years, mahogany color in autumn, scaly indu-
mentum.  G. A. L. Mehlquist, Gem Gardens, reg. 1988.
```

APRIL DREAM   Parentage unknown
Pink flowers with large red blotch. Whitney, reg. 1976.

```
                  -forrestii Repens Group
           -Elizabeth-
           -            -griersonianum
  -unnamed hybrid-          -sanguineum ssp. didymum
                      -Carmen-
APRIL-       -Little-    -forrestii Repens Group
 FIRE-       Gem  -elliottii 1/8
   -              -griffithianum 1/8
   -      -King George-
  -Gipsy King-      -unknown 1/8
            -haematodes 1/4
```

3ft(.9m) 5F(-15C) E   Scarlet, bell-shaped flowers; lustrous,
dark green foliage; mound-shaped plant. W. Elliott.

* *
```
                      -minus Carolinianum Group, white 1/8
           -unnamed hybrid-
      -unnamed-         -mucronulatum--Cornell Pink 1/8
APRIL- hybrid-dauricum F2, white
  GEM -        -dauricum, white form
      -white selection-
                  -dauricum 3/4
3ft(.9m) x 2ft(.6m) -25F(-32C) EM  Flowers slightly fragrant,
double, funnel-shaped, 5 smooth-edged lobes, pure white. Leaves
held 2-3 years; scaly indumentum.  G. Mehlquist, reg. 1988.
```
APRIL WHITE   Parentage as above
Similar to the above.   Flowers semi-double, pure white. Leaves
bright yellow in autumn. Dr. G. A. L. Mehlquist, reg. 1988.
* *

```
         -Wilgen's Ruby--unknown 1/2
APRIL GLOW-
         -williamsianum 1/2
3ft(.9m) -10F(-23C) EM 4/4   A rounded, dense-growing plant;
rosy pink flowers 3.5in(9cm) across.  New foliage reddish.  Van
Wilgen Nurseries, reg. 1968.  Gold Medal Boskoop 1966.
```

* *

```
                          -minus Carolinianum
           -P.J.M. (dbl flower)-     Group 1/8
         -unnamed-         -dauricum, white 1/8
    -unnamed- hybrid-mucronulatum, pink 1/8
    - hybrid-
APRIL-    -dauricum, white 1/4
 LOVE -              -racemosum 1/16
    -        -Pioneer -      -mucronulatum 1/16
   -unnamed- (Gable)-unknown 1/4
    hybrid-              -minus Carolinianum Group
    -              -P.J.M.-
    -unnamed hybrid-    -dauricum, white
                  -unknown
4ft(1.2m) x 3ft(.9m)(9 yrs) -20F(-29C) EM   Double flowers 1.5
in(4cm) across, widely funnel-shaped; 6-8 in trusses 2.5in(6cm)
wide. Light purplish pink flowers, frilled margins of pale yel-
low; petaloid stamens. Plant of dense habit.  E. Mezitt cross;
Weston Nurseries, reg. 1987.
```
APRIL SONG   Parentage as above
5ft(1.5m) x 5ft(9 yrs) -20F(-29C) EM Flowers widely funnel-
shaped, 2in(5cm) across, in trusses of 10. Colors are contrasting moderate purplish pink and a paler pink.   E. Mezitt cross;
Weston Nurseries, reg. 1987.
* *

```
        -minus var. chapmanii 1/2
APRIL PINK-
        -mucronulatum--Cornell Pink 1/2
4ft(1.2m) -10F(-23C) E   Deep pink, slightly fragrant; flowers
larger than Cornell Pink.  Compact growth habit.  A. E. Kehr.
```

```
                  -minus Carolinianum Group, white form
           -unnamed hybrid-                   1/4
APRIL REIGN-       -mucronulatum--Cornell Pink 1/4
         -dauricum, white form, selfed 1/2
3ft(.9m) x 2ft(.6m) -25F(-32C) EM  Widely funnel-shaped flow-
ers, double and slightly fragrant, of 5 smooth-edged lobes, pink
with lighter centers.   Leaves held 2-3 years; scaly indumentum.
G. A. L. Mehlquist, Gem Gardens, reg. 1988.
```

```
                  -minus Carolinianum Group, white 1/4
         -unnamed hybrid F2-
APRIL ROSE-       -mucronulatum--Cornell Pink 1/4
         -dauricum F2 1/2
3ft(.9m) x 2ft(.6m) -25F(-32C) M   Double flowers, widely fun-
nel-shaped, slightly fragrant; 5 smooth-edged, vivid red lobes.
Leaves held 2-3 years, reddish bronze in autumn; scaly indument-
um beneath.  G. A. L. Mehlquist, Gem Gardens, reg. 1988.
```

APRIL SHOWERS   Synonym for APRIL GLOW

APRIL SNOW   Described under APRIL CLOUD, q.v.

APRIL SONG   Described under APRIL LOVE, q.v.

APRIL WHITE   Described under APRIL GEM, q.v.

        -ponticum 1/2
APRILIS-
        -dauricum 1/2
One of the very few hybrids resulting from a cross between elep-
idote (non-scaly) and lepidote (scaly).   See also GRIERDAL, and
JOHN MARCHAND. Rose-colored flowers.   Herbert, 1843.

        -williamsianum 1/2
ARAB-
        -sperabile 1/2
Low, compact plant; pink flowers. Early.   Rothschild, 1933.

            -arboreum ssp. cinnamomeum var. album 1/2
ARBAD-
        -adenogynum 1/2
Flowers white, bold crimson spots; pink exterior.   Magor, 1926.

* *
            -arboreum ssp. cinnamomeum var. album 1/2
ARBCALO-
        -calophytum 1/2
Pink suffused, white flowers, a claret blotch.   E. J. P. Magor.
TRETAWN   Parentage as above, except reversed
Trusses of 14 white flowers shading to phlox pink in the throat,
with a blotch of Indian lake.   E. J. P. Major cross; Maj. E. W.
M. Magor, reg. 1976.   A.M. 1976.
* *

        -campylocarpum 1/2
ARBCAMP-
        -arboreum ssp. cinnamomeum var. album 1/2
Flowers creamy white.   E. J. P. Magor, cross 1915; intro. 1928.

                -wardii 1/4
        -Crest-
    -     -Lady   -fortunei ssp. discolor 1/8
ARBORFIELD-   Bessborough-
    -                  -campylocarpum Elatum Group 1/8
    -              -griffithianum 1/4
        -Loderi Julie-
                -fortunei 1/4
Lax trusses of 12 mimosa yellow flowers, campanulate, 4.5in(11.5
cm) across.   Crown Estate, Windsor, reg. 1963.   A.M. 1963.

        -arboreum, pink form 1/2
ARBSUTCH-
        -sutchuenense 1/2
Pink-flowered.   E. J. P. Magor, 1915.

        -minus Carolinianum Group 1/2
ARBUTIFOLIUM-
        -ferrugineum 1/2
Clusters of about 12 small, bell-shaped flowers of crimson pink,
slightly spotted; late. Dense, dwarf plant. Foliage small, in
winter purplish. Very hardy.   Origin unknown; before 1917.

* *
            -minus Carolinianum Group, white form 1/2
ARCTIC DAWN (Lewis)-
            -dauricum--Arctic Pearl 1/2
3ft(.9m) -15F(-26C) E 3/3   A white lepidote, blooming season
same as P.J.M. Aromatic, recurved leaves.   G. D. Lewis.
ARCTIC GLOW   Parentage as above
3ft(.9m) -15F(-26C) E 3/3   A week earlier than P.J.M. Similar to ARCTIC DAWN, except petal rims show a blush of lavender.
Ball truss of 2-3 buds, each with 3 flowers.   Lewis, reg. 1988.
* *
* *
            -maximum, white form 1/2
ARCTIC DAWN (Behring)-
            -brachycarpum (as ssp. tigerstedtii) 1/2
8.75ft(2.6m) -35F(-37C) L Very hardy. Funnel-shaped flowers,
19 per truss; pure white, red margins.   R. Behring, reg. 1984.
ARCTIC SNOW   Parentage as above
4ft(1.1m) x 4ft(8 yrs) -35F(-37C) L   Light pink buds open to
fragrant white flowers, the dorsal lobe spotted yellow. Corolla
widely funnel-shaped.   R. Behring, reg. 1983.
* *

ARCTIC GLOW   Described under ARCTIC DAWN (Lewis), q.v.

ARCTIC GOLD   Parentage unknown; elepidote
3ft(.9m) x 2.5ft(.75)(8 yrs) -20F(-29C) ML   Strong pink buds;
flowers pale yellow, with a strong greenish yellow blotch. Very
floriferous. Dense habit.   E. Mezitt cross; Weston, reg. 1988.

ARCTIC PEARL--form of dauricum, white
4ft(1.2m) -25F(-32C) E 3/3   Flowers purest white, 2in(5cm)
across, up to 5 per truss. Upright plant; small leaves. Needs
well-drained site.   Baldsiefen raiser, c. 1960; reg. 1970.

ARCTIC SNOW   Described under ARCTIC DAWN (Behring), q.v.

        -trichostomum 1/2
ARCTIC TERN-
        -ledum ? 1/2
2ft(.6m) 0F(-18C) M 3/3   Bi-generic hybrid. Produces large
clusters of white flowers, surrounded by small leaves. Called a
"superb and unusual" plant by Cox. Larson raiser; P. Cox, reg.
1982. A.M. Wisley Trials 1989.   Color ill. ARS J 44:2 (1990),
p. 102; Cox pl. 9.

            -glaucophyllum 3/4
ARDEN BELLE-   -ciliatum 1/4
        -Rosy Bell-
                -glaucophyllum
Rose pink flowers; smooth, mahogany-colored bark. Thacker, 1942.

        -racemosum 1/2
ARDEN FAIRY-
        -lutescens 1/2
Creamy pink flowers.   T. C. Thacker, 1946.

        -wardii 1/2   -griffithianum 1/8
ARDEN PRIMROSE-   -George Hardy-
        -Pink Pearl-   -catawbiense 1/8
        -             -arboreum 1/8
            -Broughtonii-
                -unknown 1/8
Pale yellow flowers.   T. C. Thacker, 1940.

    -forrestii Repens Group 1/2
ARDIS-
    -arboreum var. wearii ? 1/2
Bright red flowers.   Lord Aberconway, cross 1936; intro. 1946.

ARDRISHAIG---selected form of bureavii
Trusses of 10-11 flowers (very large truss for this species), 5-
lobed, yellowish white, upper throat densely spotted in moderate
purplish red. Leaves with rusty brown indumentum below.   P. A.
Cox, reg. 1988.   A.M. 1988.

ARDY   Described under BRITANNIA'S BELLS, q.v.

    -haematodes 1/2
ARENA-   -griersonianum 1/4
    -Matador-
        -strigillosum 1/4
Red flowers.   F. Hanger cross; RHS Garden, Wisley; intro. 1953.

    -griffithianum 1/2
ARETHUSA-
    -unknown 1/2
Delicate pink flowers.   Waterer, Sons & Crisp.

* *
        -augustinii 1/2
ARGIOLUS-
        -concinnum 1/2
Pale mauve flowers. Lord Aberconway, 1946.
DANUBE   Parentage reversed from above.   Lord Aberconway.
* *

* *
        -fortunei ssp. discolor 1/2
ARGOSY-
        -auriculatum 1/2
6ft(1.8m) -5F(-21C) VL 3/3   Sweet-scented white flowers, on
an upright plant; fast-growing, long-leaved.   Rothschild, 1933.
ARGOSY SNOW WHITE   Parentage as above
White flowers. Rothschild cross; Waterer & Crisp.   A.M. 1938.
* *

```
* * * * * * * * * * * * * * * * * * * * * * * * * *
                              -catawbiense 9/64
                      -Blandy--              -catawb.
                      - anum -        -unnamed-
              -Ascot   -      -Alta- - hybrid-
              -Brilliant-      clerense-      -ponticum
              -        -        -       -    1/64
     -J. G. Millais-        -        -arboreum 3/32
     -            -        -thomsonii 5/8
     -            -              -griffithianum 1/16
ARGYLL-          -      -George Hardy-
     -          -Pink -        -catawbiense
     -          Pearl-        -arboreum
     -thomsonii      -Broughtonii-
                              -unknown 1/16
A plant with red flowers.   Sir James N. Horlick, 1957.
RED ROVER   Parentage as above
Small flowers of deep crimson.   Whitaker.
* * * * * * * * * * * * * * * * * * * * * * * * *
```

```
        -griffithianum 1/2
ARIADNE-
        -Grand Duke of Wurtemberg--unknown 1/2
Rose flowers, heavily spotted.  Very poor habit.  G. B. van Nes.
```

```
        -fortunei ssp. discolor 1/2
ARIEL-
        -Memoir--unknown 1/2
White or pale pink flower; well-shaped plant.  Rothschild, 1933.
```

```
                                    -griffithianum 7/16
            -The Hon. Jean Marie de Montague-
            -                          -unknown 5/16
            -                    -griffithianum
ARIEL SHERMAN-            -George-
            -          -Pink - Hardy-catawbiense 3/16
            -          - Pearl-        -arboreum 1/16
            -Countess-        -Broughtonii-
             of Derby-              -unknown
            -              -catawbiense
            -Cynthia-
                      -griffithianum
3ft(.9m)(12yrs)  25F(-4C)  VL  Funnel-shaped flowers 3in(7.6cm)
wide, in domed truss of 15-17,  cardinal red, white throat, pink
spotting.  Dull green leaves held 3 years.  Moynier, reg. 1985.
```

```
        -thomsonii 1/2
ARIES-
        -neriiflorum 1/2
Medium height;  flowers blood red, bell-shaped, in flat trusses.
Sir John Ramsden, 1922.  A.M. 1932.  F.C.C. 1938.
```

```
                              -griffithianum 1/8
                  -George Hardy-
            -Pink Pearl-        -catawbiense 1/8
            -        -        -arboreum 1/8
ARISTIDE BRIAND-        -Broughtonii-
                              -unknown 5/8
            -unnamed hardy hybrid--unknown
Deep rose flowers in large trusses;  plant medium height.  Endtz.
```

ARISTOCRAT   Parentage unknown
Pink flowers with dark spots. Koster, reg. 1965.

```
              -sanguineum ssp. didymum 1/4
      -Carmen-
      -        -forrestii Repens Group 1/4
      -                    -campylocarpum 1/16
ARKLE-              -unnamed-
      -        -Adriaan- hybrid--unknown 1/8
      -        - Koster-                -griffithianum 1/32
      -                        -George-
      -Moonshine-      -Mrs. Lindsay- Hardy-catawbiense 1/32
       Supreme -        Smith -
      -              -              -Duchess of Edinburgh--
      -                                          unknown
              -wardii Litiense Group 1/4
2ft(.6m)  -5F(-21C)  M  3/4   Campanulate flowers, of waxy red.
Compact, spreading habit.  Hydon Nurseries, reg. 1972.
```

ARLENE UTZ--Advanced generation hybrid including catawbiense,
            maximum and possibly unknown hybrids

6ft(1.8m) -15F(-26C) ML   Flowers 3in(7.6cm) wide, 7-lobed, of
deep pink, edges darker; 11 per truss.   W. D. Smith, reg. 1978.

ARLEQUIN   Syn. for DEXTER'S HARLEQUIN, described under ACCLAIM

```
      -dichroanthum 1/2
ARMA-
      -forrestii Repens Group 1/2
Flowers orange-scarlet.   Lord Aberconway, 1933.
```

ARMANTINE   Synonym for CALOMINA

```
      -cinnabarinum  ssp. xanthocodon Concatenans Group 1/2
ARMIA-
      -lutescens 1/2
Yellow flowers.   J. B. Stevenson, intro. 1947.
```

```
                              -griffithianum 1/4
              -unnamed hybrid-
ARMISTICE DAY-              -unknown 3/4
              -Maxwell T. Masters--unknown
Scarlet red flowers, in trusses of 10-14.   C. B. van Nes, 1930.
Or: "Out of the same seed pod" as BRITANNIA, q.v. --J. Street.
```

```
              -catawbiense 1/4
      -Everestianum-
ARNO-              -unknown 3/4
      -unknown
A pale lilac flower with red markings.   T. J. R. Seidel, 1906.
```

ARNOLD PIPER   Described under WALLOPER, q.v.

```
                                          -griffithianum
            -unknown 9/16              -George-      1/64
            -                    -Mrs. Lindsay- Hardy-catawbiense 1/64
ARNOLD-                  - Smith -
TEESE-              -Diane-        -Duchess of
      -        -Alice -      -        Edinburgh--unknown
      -        -Street-      -        -campylocarpum 1/32
      -unnamed-      -      -unnamed hybrid-
        hybrid-      -wardii 1/4        -unknown
            -      -wardii
            -Crest-        -fortunei ssp. discolor 1/16
                  -Lady-
                  Bessborough-campylocarpum Elatum Group 1/16
Plant 7ft(2m) tall.  Light greenish yellow, bell-shaped flowers;
truss of 13-15.  Leaves 4.75in(12cm) long.  A. Teese, reg. 1985.
```

AROMA--(uncertain combination of CADIS, WHEATLEY, decorum)
Light pink flowers with much fragrance.   C. R. & V. Haag, 1983.

```
* * * * * * * * * * * * * * * * * * * * * * * * * *
                        -auriculatum 1/2
AROMANA---FLAMEHEART, selfed-      -griersonianum 1/4
                        -Azor-
                              -fortunei ssp. discolor 1/4
White flowers, very fragrant; late.   Farall Nursery, reg. 1968.
BULLSEYE   Parentage as above
Flowers 3in(7.6cm) across, 7-lobed, crimson with a red eye.   M.
Haworth-Booth, reg. 1968.
FARALL TARGET   FLAMEHEART improved by selfing.  Late-blooming.
Flowers orange-red.   M. Haworth-Booth, Farall Nurs., reg. 1968.
* * * * * * * * * * * * * * * * * * * * * * * * * *
```

ARONIMINK   Described under ACCLAIM, q.v.

```
              -Moser's Maroon--unknown
ARROW FEATHERS-
              -Marcat--unknown
Bi-color, hose-in-hose flower; white center, red-purple margins.
C. R. and V. Haag.
```

ARSEN'S PINK   Described under MARY FLEMING. q.v.

```
                      -dichroanthum
                 -Dido-
         -Warm Spring-    -decorum
         -           -     -fortunei
         -        -Fawn-      -dichroanthum
   -un. -              -Fabia-
   -hyb.-                    -griersonianum
   -    -          -      -wardii          -griffithianum
   -    -    -Idealist-         -Kewense-
   -    -    -     -     -Aurora-     -fortunei
   -   -Yellow-     -Naomi-    -thomsonii
   -    Creek-      -          -fortunei
ART  -        -          -griersonianum
CHILDERS-     -Sarita Loder-     -griffithianum
   -                -Loderi-
   -                      -fortunei
   -       -wardii
   -    -Crest-             -fortunei ssp. discolor
   -    -    -Lady Bessborough-
   -    -                  -campylocarpum Elatum Group
   -un. -                     -arboreum, white
   hyb.-           -Loder's White-
   -     -C.I.S.-         -griffithianum
   -     -     -     - dichroanthum
   -unnamed-    -Fabia-
       hybrid-           -griersonianum
       -                      -fortunei ssp. discolor
       -        -Ole Olson-
       -     -Lem's Goal-     -campylocarpum
             -     -griersonianum
             -Azor-
                 -fortunei ssp. discolor
```

(Species fractions not given: parentage is uncertain for LODER'S
 WHITE, q.v.)
6ft(1.8m) 0F(-18C) ML Spherical trusses of 14-16. Buds moderate yellow, tinged medium reddish orange. Fragrant flowers of
light yellow. Leaves dark yellowish green. A. Childers cross;
Bovees intro.; M. Childers, reg. 1988.

* *
```
                      -griffithianum 1/8
           -Queen Wilhelmina-
   -Britannia-            -unknown 3/8
ART  -       -Stanley Davies--unknown
 WICKENS-    -dichroanthum 1/4
   -Jasper-          -fortunei ssp. discolor 1/8
        -Lady Bessborough-
                      -campylocarpum Elatum Group 1/8
```
Spreading habit. Turkey red flower; late. Seabrook, reg. 1968.
ERNEST R. BALL   Parentage as above
Flowers orange-yellow, unfading darker stripes; tight trusses of
14. Open habit; foliage like Britannia. Seabrook, reg. 1967.
* *

```
      -arboreum ssp. cinnamomeum var. album 1/2
ARTEMIS-
      -griffithianum 1/2
```
A hybrid with white flowers. E. J. P. Magor, 1921.

ARTHUR BEDFORD   Synonym for A. BEDFORD

```
      -calophytum 1/2
ARTHUR HARDY-    -wardii 1/4
   -Idealist-    -fortunei 5/32
           -Naomi-          -griffithianum 1/32
           -      -Kewense-
           -Aurora-     -fortunei
                  -thomsonii 1/16
```
Rounded truss of 14-16 flowers, 7-lobed, pale yellow-green, with
small grayed purple blotch; prominent nectaries. Smooth, oblong
leaves, dark green. G. A. Hardy, reg. 1986. A.M. 1986.

```
           -decorum 1/4          -griffithianum 1/16
      -White-        -George Hardy-
      - Swan-Pink Pearl-      -catawbiense 1/16
      -        -          -arboreum 1/16
ARTHUR HORSLEY-         -Broughtonii-
      -        -fortunei 1/4    -unknown 1/16
      -Nestucca-
           -yakushimanum 1/4
```
4ft(1.2m) 5F(-15C) ML Strong purplish pink buds open to fun-
nel-shaped flowers, 6 wavy lobes, yellowish white with brilliant

yellow-green blotches; domed truss 6in(15cm) broad, holds 13-17.
Leaves moderate olive green.   D. A. Horsley, reg. 1986.

```
           -williamsianum 1/2
ARTHUR J. IVENS-
           -fortunei ssp. discolor Houlstonii Group 1/2
```
3ft(1.2m) -10F(-23C) M 3/3   A dome-shaped plant with ovate,
medium-sized leaves. Campanulate flowers, Persian rose. Slow
to flower. Arthur J. Ivens was a nursery manager at Hillier's
Nursery. Hillier. A.M. 1944.   Color illus. F p. 32.

```
           -salmon-colored seedling--unknown 3/4
ARTHUR JOHN HOLDEN-          -ponticum 1/4
           -Purple Splendour-
                      -unknown
```
2.5ft(.75m) 0F(-18C) M Flowers of good substance, red-purple,
in trusses of 14. Plant branches well, wider than tall; leaves
held 3 years. Paul Holden cross; Mrs. A. J. Holden, reg. 1981.

* *
```
           -sanguineum ssp. didymum 1/2
ARTHUR OSBORN-
           -griersonianum 1/2
```
3ft(.9m) 5F(-15C) VL 3/3 Very dark red; dark green foliage,
indumented. Needs some cool shade. RBG, Kew, 1929. A.M. 1933.
NUTMEG   Parentage as above
Hardier and sturdier than the above. Smaller, but more numerous
flowers, ruby-colored, trumpet-shaped. Farall, reg. 1969.
* *

```
           -griersonianum 1/4     -griffithianum
           -              -George-
   -Anna Rose-     -Pink - Hardy-catawbiense 3/32
   - Whitney -    - Pearl-       -arboreum 1/8
   -        -Countess-    -Broughtonii-
   -        of Derby-            -unknown 9/32
ARTHUR OSTLER-      -catawbiense
   -              -Cynthia-
   -                  -griffithianum 1/8
   -                 -griffithianum
   -    -Coombe Royal-
   -Mrs. G.W.-     -unknown
   Leak  -            -caucasicum
        -Chevalier Felix de Sauvage-     1/8
                      -unknown
```
Phlox pink buds opening lighter with paler center, prominent red
flare in the throat. Funnel-shaped flowers 3in(7.5cm) wide, in
trusses of 18. Shrub medium-sized. A. G. Ostler, reg. 1984.

```
      -maximum 1/2
ARTHUR PRIDE-
      -catawbiense 1/2
```
5ft(1.5m) -30F(-35C) L Flowers 2in(5cm) across, white center
with orchid edges and blotch of chartreuse; ball-shaped truss of
29. Natural hybrid collected in North Carolina, 1934. Pride,
reg. 1979. Color illus. ARS Q 34:3 (1980) p. 138.

* *
```
      -wardii 1/2
ARTHUR SMITH-
      -decorum 1/2
```
Large, deep yellow flowers. Lord Digby, cross 1951; named IG-
THAM YELLOW. Reuthe raiser 1952, as ARTHUR SMITH --John Street.
Color illus. JS p. 43.
RIMA   Parentage as above
Parent of BOW STREET. Creamy yellow flowers. Stevenson, 1941.
* *

```
      -souliei 1/2       -griffithianum 1/4
ARTHUR STEVENS-   -Pink Shell-
   -Coronation-      -unknown 1/8
   Day    -     -griffithianum
        -Loderi-
             -fortunei 1/8
```
Trusses full but not tight, 7-10 flowers. Pink buds open white,
blotch of oxblood red. Hillier, reg. 1976. A.M. 1976.

ARTHUR WARREN   Described under OLGA, q.v.

```
                 -griersonianum 3/4
ARTHURIA-               -griersonianum
     -Master Dick-                -arboreum 1/16
               -         -Doncaster-
               -The Don-          -unknown 1/16
                         -griffithianum 1/8
Flowers rose, darker throat; truss of 13.   Unknown.   A.M. 1952.
```

ARTIE MOON   Parentage unknown
Lavender flowers with maroon blotch.   C. Loeb, reg. 1966.

```
                         -lacteum 1/8
                 -Lacs-
     -unnamed hybrid-     -sinogrande 1/8
ARTIST-            -unknown 1/4
     -irroratum 1/2
White flowers, touched with pink.   Gen. Harrison, reg. 1964.
```

```
                    -campylocarpum Elatum Group 1/8
          -Penjerrick-
     -Amaura-          -griffithianum 1/8
ARTUS-      -griersonianum 1/2
     -      -dichroanthum 1/4
     -Fabia-
          -griersonianum
Red flowers.   Lord Aberconway, cross 1934; intro. 1941.
```

```
                    -campylocarpum Elatum Group 1/4
     -Penjerrick-
ARUNA-          -griffithianum 1/4
     -wightii 1/2
Yellow flowers.   Lord Aberconway, cross 1926; intro. 1933.
```

```
                         -catawbiense 5/16        -catawbiense
               -Blandyanum-                -unnamed hyb.-
               -         -Altaclerense-           -ponticum 1/16
ASCOT BRILLIANT-                    -arboreum 1/8
               -thomsonii 1/2
5ft(1.5m)  5F(-15C)  EM  3/2   Lax, open habit.  Blood red flow-
ers, trumpet-shaped.  Very free-flowering.  John Standish, 1861.
```

ASCREAVIE--form of maddenii L & S 1141
4ft(1.2m) 15F(-9C) L 3/3   White flowers, the reverse flushed
red-purple; truss of 3-5.   A. E. Hardy, reg. 1978.   A.M. 1978.

ASHCOMBE--form of veitchianum Cubittii Group
4ft(1.2m) 20F(-7C) ML 4/3   White flower, 4.5in(11.5cm) wide,
an orange-yellow blotch; fragrant. Loose truss holds 5.   Crown
Estate, Windsor, reg. 1962. F.C.C. 1962.   Color illus. ARS J
39:3 (1985), p. 122.

```
          -fortunei ? 1/2
ASHES OF ROSES-
          -unknown 1/2
4ft(1.2m)  -10F(-23C)  M  3/3   Pastel peach flowers.   Dexter.
```

```
* * * * * * * * * * * * * * * * * * * * * * * * * * * * * *
                 -dichroanthum 1/4
          -Astarte-          -campylocarpum Elatum Group 1/8
ASPANSIA-      -Penjerrick-
          -                    -griffithianum 1/8
          -haematodes 1/2
Brilliant red flowers; a dwarf plant of spreading habit.   Lord
Aberconway, cross 1932; intro. 1945.   A.M. 1945.
ASPANSIA RUBY      Parentage as above
Blood red flowers.   Lord Aberconway, 1932.
* * * * * * * * * * * * * * * * * * * * * * * * * * * * * *
```

ASSAYE   Described under ROBIN HOOD, q.v.

```
   -forrestii Repens Group 1/2
ASTA-
   -haematodes ssp. chaetomallum 1/2
Deep red flowers.   Lord Aberconway, 1941.
```

```
                 -dichroanthum 1/2
          -Fabia-
ASTABIA-       -griersonianum 1/4
     -          -dichroanthum
     -Astarte-          -campylocarpum Elatum Group 1/8
          -Penjerrick-
                    -griffithianum 1/8
```

Red flowers.   Lord Aberconway, 1942.

```
                 -dichroanthum 1/2
ASTARTE-          -campylocarpum Elatum Group 1/4
     -Penjerrick-
                 -griffithianum 1/4
3ft(.9m)  5F(-15C)  M  Flower apricot or salmon pink, pendulous,
in trusses of 8.   Lord Aberconway, intro. 1931.   A.M. 1931.
```

```
                    -dichroanthum 1/4
     -Astarte-          -campylocarpum Elatum Group 1/8
     -         -Penjerrick-
ASTEL-               -griffithianum 1/8
     -          -forrestii Repens Group 1/4
     -Elizabeth-
               -griersonianum 1/4
Red flowers.   Lord Aberconway, cross 1937; intro. 1946.
```

```
                 -sperabile 1/4
     -Eupheno-
     -          -griersonianum 1/4
ASTENO-          -dichroanthum 1/4
     -Astarte-          -campylocarpum Elatum Group 1/8
          -Penjerrick-
                    -griffithianum 1/8
Deep red flowers.   Lord Aberconway, cross 1937; intro. 1946.
```

```
* * * * * * * * * * * * * * * * * * * * * * * * * * * * * *
                 -caucasicum 1/4
     -Dr. Stocker-
ASTEROID-          -griffithianum 1/4
     -thomsonii 1/2
Flowers of rich, rosy pink.   Rothschild, 1933.
CRIMSON BANNER   Parentage as above
ROSY QUEEN   Parentage as above
The last two named above, were exhibited by Sunningdale, 1934.
* * * * * * * * * * * * * * * * * * * * * * * * * * * * * *
```

```
               -sanguineum ssp. didymum 1/4
     -Arthur Osborn-
ASTOS-          -griersonianum 1/4
     -          -dichroanthum 1/4
     -Astarte-          -campylocarpum Elatum Group 1/8
          -Penjerrick-
                    -griffithianum 1/8
Flowers of brilliant scarlet.   Lord Aberconway, intro. 1946.
```

```
                    -catawbiense 1/4
     -Catawbiense Grandiflorum-
ASTRAEA-                    -unknown 1/4
     -fortunei ssp. discolor 1/2
Large flowers, colored mallow to violet.   Hobbie, before 1946.
```

ASTROGLOW   Described under BALLY COTTON, q.v.

```
               -dichroanthum 1/4
     -Astarte-          -campylocarpum Elatum Group 1/8
ASTROW-      -Penjerrick-
     -hookeri 1/2     -griffithianum 1/8
Dark red flowers.   Lord Aberconway, cross 1936; intro. 1946.
```

```
               -arboreum ? 1/4
     -Werei-
ATALANTA-      -barbatum 1/4
     -thomsonii 1/2
Flowers red, with darker spots.   E. J. P. Magor, intro. 1946.
```

```
          -catawbiense 1/2
ATHENIA-
          -unknown 1/2
Blush white, yellow blotch.  Origin unknown.  Commendation 1860.
```

ATHENS   Synonym for LAST HURRAH

```
                    -catawbiense 1/4
     -Atrosanguineum-
ATKAR-               -unknown 1/2
     -                    -brachycarpum 1/4
     -Kentucky Cardinal-
                    -Essex Scarlet--unknown
Red flowers: also AS-1, AS-2, ATKAR STAR and BEST ATKAR.  Gable.
```

```
* * * * * * * * * * * * * * * * * * * * * * * * * * * *              -griersonianum 1/4
                          -catawbiense 1/8                      -Azor-
                     -Caractacus-             AUDREY GRACE-   -fortunei ssp. discolor 1/4
ATOMIC          -unnamed hybrid-     -unknown 1/8         -      -fortunei ssp. discolor 1/4
 BLAST--unnamed hybrid F2-      -fortunei ssp. discolor 1/4       -Argosy-
                  -yakushimanum 1/2                                  -auriculatum 1/4
Vivid reddish purple buds;  flowers blend vivid to light reddish   10ft(3.0m) OF(-18C) VL   Trusses of 12 white flowers, 7-lobed;
purple to moderate purplish pink; spots purplish red.  W. Delp.    red flush at base of dorsal throat blends to yellow flush around
(Plant may be extinct.)                                            it.  Petioles dull reddish purple.  G. Witherwick, reg. 1988.
MARY BEAN   Parentage as above, but not selfed
White flowers, red throat.  Medium size plant.  Hardiness -15F     * * * * * * * * * * * * * * * * * * * * * * * * * * * * * * *
(-26C).  W. Delp.                                                           -augustinii 1/2
WILLIAM BEAN    Parentage as above, but not selfed               AUGFAST-
White, red throat; plant medium-sized.  Pubescent.  Hardiness as        -fastigiatum 1/2
above.  W. Delp.                                                 3ft(.9m) OF(-18C) EM 4/4  An abundance of deep lavender blue,
WELDON'S GIFT   Parentage as ATOMIC BLAST, above                 star-shaped flowers in small trusses.  Plant dome-shaped, dense.
Buds purplish pink blush, opening to white flowers.  Delp cross; Magor, 1921.   Color illus. F p. 33; HG p. 167; JS p. 78.
H. E. Salley raiser.                                            IGHTHAM   Same parentage; exhibited by Reuthe, 1952.
* * * * * * * * * * * * * * * * * * * * * * * * * * * * * *     * * * * * * * * * * * * * * * * * * * * * * * * * * * * * * *
* * * * * * * * * * * * * * * * * * * * * * * * * * * * * *

          -catawbiense 1/4                                      AUGUST   Described under ALFRED, q.v.
     -Atrosanguineum-                                                                     -catawbiense 1/8
ATRIER-          -unknown 1/4                                                     -Charles Dickens-
     -griersonianum 1/2                                             -Dr. V. H. Rutgers-           -unknown 3/8
4ft(1.2m) -10F(-23C)  M  3/1  Lax trusses of clear red flowers.  AUGUST LAMKEN-        -Lord Roberts--unknown
Plant of open habit.  Joseph Gable, exhibited 1945.                       -williamsianum 1/2
RED HEAD   Parentage as above                                   Unusually heavy-textured flower and foliage--possibly polyploid.
5ft(1.5m) -5F(-21C)  M  3/3   Red flowers; loose trusses.  Does  Deep rose, frilled flowers, darker dorsal spotting; loose truss.
best in light shade.  Joseph Gable.                             Down-curving leaves.  One of the hardiest williamsianum hybrids.
WILLIAM MONTGOMERY   Parentage as above                         D. Hobbie, 1942-44.   Color illus. WS, 1989, p. 21.
Clear scarlet flowers.  Plant hardy to -5F(-21C).   J. Gable.
* * * * * * * * * * * * * * * * * * * * * * * * * * * * * *              -Marion (Cheal)--unknown 3/4
                                                                AUGUST MOON-      -campylocarpum 1/4
               -catawbiense 1/4                                      -Unique
     -Atrosanguineum-                                                 -unknown
ATROFLO-          -unknown 1/4                                   4ft(1.2m) OF(-18C)  E   Hybridized in Australia where it blooms
     -floccigerum 1/2                                           in August.  Large flowers, bright yellow, early.  Medium-sized
5ft(1.5m) -5F(-21C)  M  4/3   More than one form;  one may have  shrub, vigorous and compact; dense foliage.   V. J. Boulter.
smirnowii as seed parent.  Long thin foliage with thick fawn in-
mentum.  Bright rose-colored flowers of good substance.  Gable,           -ponticum 1/2
1940.  A.E. 1960.  Illus. ARS J 36:1 (1982), p. 11; Cox pl. 10.  AUGUSTE VAN GEERTE-
                                                                     -unknown 1/2
          -catawbiense 1/4                                      6ft(1.8m) OF(-18C)  EM   Purplish red flowers in large trusses.
     -Atrosanguineum-                                           Earlier than most ponticum.   van Geerte, Belgium, before 1867.
ATROR-          -sanguineum 1/4
     -          -orbiculare 1/4                                           -ponticum 1/2
     -unnamed hybrid-                                           AUNT MARTHA-
              -williamsianum 1/4                                     -unknown 1/2
Pinkish crimson flowers fading to blush pink.   J. Gable, 1945.  5ft(1.5m) -10F(-23C) ML 4/3  Flower bright red-purple, speck-
                                                               led gold in center; large trusses.   Foliage dense and leathery;
          -catawbiense 1/2                                      Vigorous, sun-tolerant plant.  Roy W. Clark, reg. 1958.
ATROSANGUINEUM-
          -sanguineum 1/2                                       AUNTY THORA   Described under SIGRID, q.v.
6ft(1.8m) -20F(-29C) ML  2/3   Rich, dark red flowers.  Plant
has good foliage and habit.   H. Waterer, 1851.                      -xanthostephanum 1/2
                                                               AUREDGE-
          -catawbiense 1/4                                           -edgeworthii 1/2
     -Atrosanguineum-                                           A hybrid by E. J. P. Magor, intro. 1938.
ATSONII-          -unknown 1/4
     -thomsonii 1/2                                                  -griersonianum 1/2
Red flowers.   Joseph Gable, exhibited 1937.                    AURIEL-          -diaprepes 1/4
                                                                    -Polar Bear-
ATTAR--form of decorum from the Hu Yu expedition                             -auriculatum 1/4
6ft(1.8m) 5F(-15C)  E  3/3   Light rose flowers, throat shaded  Pink flowers.   Sir James Horlick, 1942.
sap green; corolla funnel-campanulate, 6- to 8-lobed, 4.5in(11.5
cm) wide.   J. Barto raiser; R. Henny, reg. 1963.                            -catawbiense 1/4
                                                                    -Catawbiense Album-
                                                               AURIGA-          -unknown 1/4
               -ponticum 1/2                                         -          -wardii 1/4
ATTRACTION-                                                          -unnamed hybrid-
          -unknown 1/2                                                       -yakushimanum 1/2
Spreading habit; mauve flowers, late season.   M. Koster & Sons. 4ft(1.2m) x 3.3ft(1.0m)(15 yrs) -15F(-26C)  L   Flowers openly
                                                               campanulate, 5 smooth-edged lobes, pale greenish yellow deepen-
AUDACIOUS---from dauricum Sempervirens Group, open pollinated   ing to brilliant yellow-green at center.   Brueckner, reg. 1988.
8.3ft(2.5m) x 7.5ft(2.25m)(12 yrs)  -20F(-29C) VE  Lax truss of  Color illus. ARS J 44:2 (1990), p. 82.
3 flowers, imperial purple, 5 wavy-edged lobes, to 2.3in(5.5cm)
wide x .25in(.5cm).  Small, scaly, semi-deciduous leaves.  Plant            -griffithianum 1/4
spreading; very floriferous.  Dr. J. Brueckner cross; reg. 1989.     -Kewense-
                                                               AURORA-          -fortunei 1/4
                                                                    -thomsonii 1/2
AUDREY DEFANE   Described under MARGARET EINARSON, q.v.          6ft(1.8m) OF(-18C)  M  4/4   Soft pink flower; wide lax truss
                                                               of 10; sweetly fragrant.  A parent of Naomi, other fine hybrids.
```

Gill cross; named by Lionel de Rothschild.   A.M. 1922.

```
* * * * * * * * * * * * * * * * * * * * * * * * * * *
                                -dichroanthum  3/16
                      -Goldsworth-
            -Tortoiseshell- Orange   -fortunei ssp.
            - Wonder       -              discolor 1/8
            -              -griersonianum 3/16
        -APRICOT-                      -griffithianum 3/16
        - GOLD -              -Loderi-
        -      -      -Albatross-      -fortunei 1/32
        -      -Cup Day-        -fortunei ssp. discolor
        -            -              -elliottii 1/16
AUSTRALIAN-          -Fusilier-
  CAMEO   -                    -griersonianum
          -            -dichroanthum
          -        -Dido-
          -        -      -decorum 1/8        -griffithianum
      -Lem's Cameo-              -Beauty of-
          -                     - Tremough-arboreum 1/32
          -      -Norman Gill-
          -Anna-          -griffithianum
          -                        -griffithianum
            -Jean Marie de Montague-
                            -unknown 1/16
```
Funnel-shaped flowers, light orange-yellow flushed pink; trusses
hold 20-24. Leaves oblanceolate, 4in(10cm) x 2in(5cm). Bush 39
in(1m) tall.   K. Van de Ven, reg. 1986.
AUSTRALIAN PRIMROSE   Parentage as above
Flowers funnel-shaped, 3.25in(8cm) wide, light greenish yellow,
in trusses of 22. Shrub 39in(1m) tall. Van de Ven, reg. 1986.
AUSTRALIAN SUNSET   Parentage as above
Trusses of 20-24 funnel-shaped flowers, of strong orangey yellow
inside, moderate reddish orange outside. Van de Ven, reg. 1986.
OLINDA SUNSET   Parentage as above
Flowers in trusses of about 20-23, funnel-shaped, 7-lobed, vivid
red inside, with blotch in the throat, deep pink exterior; fades
light orange. Shrub 5.5ft(1.6m); elliptic foliage.   K. van de
Ven, cross 1978; Australian Rho. Soc., Victorian Br., reg. 1987.
* *

AUSTRALIAN CANARY   Parentage unknown
Unregistered hybrid with large trusses of yellow. Unknown.

```
              -dichroanthum 3/8
        -Fabia-
        -      -griersonianum 1/4
AUTUMN-                    -dichroanthum
      -              -Neda-
      -Clotted Cream-    -caucasicum--Cunningham's Sulphur 1/8
              -auriculatum 1/4
```
Orange flowers.   Lord Aberconway, cross 1942; intro. 1950.

```
            -Searchlight--unknown
AUTUMN BEAUTY-
            -unknown
```
Rose-colored flowers.   F. Lovegrove, Australia, reg. 1972.

AUTUMN GOLD   Described under MARGARET DUNN, q.v.

```
* * * * * * * * * * * * * * * * * * * * * * * * * * *
              -griffithianum 1/4
        -Loderi-
AVALANCHE-      -fortunei 1/4
        -calophytum 1/2
```
6ft(1.8m) 0F(-18C) E 5/4 Huge truss of pure white flowers, a
small rosy blotch at base; fragrant. Leaves 8.5in(21.6cm) x 2.5
in(6.4cm), held one year. Rothschild, 1933. A.M. 1934. F.C.C.
1938. Color illus. JS p. 92; PB pl. 18.
ALPINE GLOW   Parentage as above
6ft(1.8m) 0F(-18C) VE 5/4   Large trusses, pale pink; Rothschild, 1933. A.M. 1938. Color illus. ARS J 41:2 (1987), p. 91.
ALPINE ROSE   Parentage as above
Delicate pink, a bit deeper than ALPINE GLOW. Rothschild, 1933.
* *

```
              -griersonianum 1/2
        -Tally Ho-
AVANIA-      -facetum (eriogynum) 1/4
      -        -griersonianum
      -Rapture-
              -arboreum ssp. zeylanicum 1/4
```

Geranium red flowers, 16 per truss.   Gen. Harrison, 1955.

AVIS   Described under BARCLAYI, q.v.

```
        -azalea occidentale 1/2
AVITA-
      -              -fortunei ssp. discolor 1/4
      -Margaret Dunn-    -dichroanthum 1/8
                  -Fabia-
                    -griersonianum 1/8
```
Azaleodendron. Tangerine orange flowers.   Lester Brandt, 1951.

AVIVA ANN   Described under YAKU WARRIOR. q.v.

```
        -fortunei ssp. discolor 1/2
AVOCET-
      -fortunei 1/2
```
6ft(1.8m) -10F(-23C) L 3/3 A parent of Melrose. Large white
sweet-scented flowers, in June. Rothschild, 1933.

AVONDALE   Described under ACCLAIM, q.v.

```
        -ciliatum 1/2
AVRIL-
      -uniflorum var. imperator 1/2
```
Dwarf 5F(-15C) E   Flowers of amaranth rose, deeper in bud,
up to 2in(5cm) across by 1.5in (3.8cm), funnel-campanulate; 2 or
3 per truss. B. Mulligan, reg. 1965.

AWARD   Described under HALF PENNY, q. v.

```
* * * * * * * * * * * * * * * * * * * * * * * * * * *
              -brachycarpum 1/4
        -Skeeter-    -wardii 1/8
       - Hill -Crest-          -fortunei ssp. discolor
       -            -Lady     -              1/16
AWESOME-          Bessborough-campylocarpum Elatum Gp. 1/16
  ARRAY -                  -Pygmalion--unknown 1/16
       -            -unnamed hybrid-
       -      -Weldy-          -haematodes 1/16
       -Robert -    -yakushimanum, Exbury form 1/8
       Weldon-          -yakushimanum 1/8
              -Serendipity-
                    -aureum (chrysanthum) 1/8
```
Medium purplish red buds open to frilled flowers of pale Empire
yellow, edged with strong reddish purple. Dark ruby red dorsal
spotting; pale yellow throat, white anthers. Weldon Delp.
BOLD ELEGANCE   Parentage as above
Buds vivid fuchsia purple and pale yellow-green; frilled flowers
of pale yellow-green edged in vivid purplish red. W. Delp.
COLOR BUSTER   Parentage as above
Buds moderate and strong currant red open to frilled white flowers edged with purplish pink; light yellowish green flare; grayish spots, stigma vivid red. W. Delp.
* *

AXEL (AXSEL) OLSEN   Syn. for AKSEL OLSEN under ELISABETH HOBBIE

```
* * * * * * * * * * * * * * * * * * * * * * * * * * *
        -fortunei ssp. discolor 1/2
AYAH-
      -facetum (eriogynum) 1/2
```
6ft(1.8m) -10F(-23C) L 3/3   Several forms; some hardier and
more upright than others; all flower late. Colors are pastel
pinks, light yellow in throat. Rothschild, 1933.
ALFRED COATES Parentage as above
Rose madder flowers; trusses hold up to 13.   Cross about 1938;
raiser Coates; Royal Botanic Garden, Kew, reg. 1978.
HILL AYAH   Parentage as above
Flowers rose madder, funnel-shaped, 7-lobed, opening from cardinal red buds; 8-11 per compact truss. E. J. Magor cross; Major
E. W. M. Magor, reg. 1966.
* *

```
        -fortunei ssp. discolor 1/2
AYESHA-
      -arboreum 1/2
```
Tall but compact plant; flowers bright pink.   Rothschild, 1933.

```
           -wardii 1/4
      -Crest-              -fortunei ssp. discolor 1/8
      -  -Lady Bessborough-
      -                          -campylocarpum Elatum Group 1/8
AYTON-                            -griffithianum 1/32
      -                 -Kewense-
      -         -Aurora-          -fortunei 5/32
      -   -Naomi-     -thomsonii 1/16
      -Golden Dream-    -fortunei
               -campylocarpum 1/4
```
Trusses hold 12 flowers, of light chartreuse yellow.   Edmund de
Rothschild, reg. 1982.

```
         -ponticum 1/2
AZALEOIDES-
         -azalea, periclymenoides (nudiflorum) 1/2
```
Azaleodendron.   Flowers pale lilac with yellow center; fragrant.
Thompson of London, c. 1820.

AZAMIA   Described under RUSSAUTINII, q.v.

```
      -griersonianum 1/2
AZMA-
      -fortunei 1/2
```
6ft(1.8m) 10F(-12C) ML 3/2 Flowers soft salmon pink, up to
4in(10.2cm) wide, in rounded lax trusses.   Long narrow leaves;
upright plant.   J. B. Stevenson, intro. 1933.

```
         -griersonianum 1/4
      -Azor-
AZONEA-            -fortunei  ssp.  discolor  1/4
      -catawbiense var. album--Catanea 1/2
```
6ft(1.8m) -15F(-26C) L   Neyron rose flowers 3in(7.6cm) broad,
12 in a ball-shaped truss 6in(15.2cm) wide. Plant upright, with
moderate branching.   G. Guy Nearing, reg. 1973.

* *
```
      -griersonianum 1/2
AZOR-
      -fortunei ssp. discolor 1/2
```
5ft(1.5m) 5F(-15C) L 3/3   Several forms exist, mostly salmon
pink with ruddy brown fleckings toward the base; loose trusses.
Large shrub or small tree--some hold foliage less than one year.
Stevenson, 1927.   A.M. 1933.   Color illus. VV p. 74.
AZOR'S SISTER   Parentage as above, but a later cross
Flowers rhodamine pink, shading to red at the base, currant red
speckling on upper petal at throat.   Trusses 7in(17.8cm) broad,
dome-shaped, 9-flowered.   Stevenson, reg. 1962.   F.C.C. 1960.
C. F. WOOD   Parentage as above.   Exhibited by Preston, 1947.
LILY DACHE   Parentage as above.   Salmon pink.   J. B. Stevenson.
MRS. JOHN CRAWFORD   Parentage as above
Vigorous plant of spreading habit. Flowers rose madder, 3.5in.
(8.9cm) across, crimson throat, dark spots on upper lobes; truss
of 14. Floriferous.   Sir James Horlick, reg. 1963.
* *

```
      -griersonianum 1/2
AZRIE-
      -diaprepes 1/2
```
Flowers soft salmon pink.   J. B. Stevenson, intro. 1933.

```
      -arboreum 1/2
AZTEC-
      -irroratum 1/2
```
Flowers pink with maroon spotting.   Rothschild, intro. 1933.

```
            -dichroanthum ssp. scyphocalyx 1/4
         -Indiana-
      -          -kyawii 1/4
AZTEC GOLD-           -wardii ? 1/8
      -      -Chlorops-
      -Inca Gold-      -vernicosum ? 1/8
               -unknown 1/4
```
4ft(1.2m) 0F(-18C) EM 3/3 Glossy green foliage; coppery new
growth. Rounded trusses hold about 18 bell-shaped flowers, deep
but clear primrose yellow.   B. Lancaster, reg. 1965.

```
            -augustinii
      -unnamed Gable ? hybrid-
AZURAY-                 -unknown 1/2
      -dauricum Sempervirens Group 1/2
```
6ft(1.8m) x 3.5ft(1.0m)(13 yrs) -15F(-26C) EM   Flowers widely

funnel-shaped, of heavy substance, 5 smooth-edged lobes, of brilliant to light violet. Lax truss of 3-4.   Brueckner, reg. 1988.

AZURIKA   Described under HACHMANN'S VIOLETTA, q.v.

* *
```
                              -catawbiense
            -Parsons Grandiflorum-        1/16
      -Nova Zembla-           -unknown 9/16
   -Danamar-      -dark red hybrid--unknown
   -       -          -ponticum 3/8
AZURRO-   -Purple Splendour-
   -            -unknown
   -Purple Splendour, as above
```
4ft(1.2m) x 5ft(1.5m) -15F(-26C) L   Color similar to the well-
known Purple Splendour: deep to strong purple, inside and out;
conspicuous blotch of dark red. Better foliage and more compact
plant. H. Hachmann cross; G. Stück, reg. 1988.
RASPUTIN   Parentage as above
Similar to above, with flowers 11-14 per truss. Hachmann cross;
G. Stück, reg. 1988.
* *

AZURWOLKE   Described under AMETHYST (Arends), q.v.

                              B

```
               -arboreum 1/8
         -Doncaster-
   -The Don-      -unknown 1/8
B. B. C.-      -griffithianum 1/4
         -neriiflorum Euchaites Group 1/2
```
Red flowers. Similar to the species parent.   Rothschild, 1934.

```
         -catawbiense 1/2
B. DE BRUIN-
         -unknown 1/2
```
5ft(1.5m) -15F(-26C) ML   Synonym BAS DE BRUIN. Flowers of
dark rich scarlet or red, spotted black, fringed petals; trusses
of about 20.   Sprawling habit.   A. Waterer.

```
      -haematodes 1/2
BABA-          -griersonianum 1/4
   -Sarita Loder-     -griffithianum 1/8
            -Loderi-
                 -fortunei 1/8
```
Deep red, waxy flowers, funnel-shaped, 3in(7.6cm) across. Loose
trusses.   Ramsden cross; W. Pennington-Ramsden, reg. 1964.

BABETTE   Described under BOB BOVEE, q.v.

* *
```
                  -souliei 1/4
      -Rosy Morn-      -griffithianum 1/8
      -       -Loderi-
BABY BONNET-           -fortunei 1/8
      -       -dichroanthum 1/4
      -Dido-
           -decorum 1/4
```
Flowers peach-colored, lighter at center, dark fuchsia pink mar-
gins, 8-lobed, 12 per truss. Late midseason. Henny, reg. 1965.
HOOPSKIRT   Parentage as above
Flowers orange to peach to yellow, with basal blotch of yellow.
Rudolph Henny, cross 1944; reg. 1958.
* *

```
            -yakushimanum--Koichiro Wada 1/2
BABY DOLL-              -caucasicum 1/8
   -       -Cunningham's White-
   -Holden-        -ponticum, white form 1/8
            -catawbiense 1/4
```
2ft(.6m) -5F(-21C) EM   Cherry pink buds open near-white; 15 in
a spherical truss. B. Lancaster seed; Morris raiser; reg. 1973.

BABY MOUSE--form of campylocarpum
Flowers deep plum purple.   C. Ingram, reg. 1973.   A.M. 1973.

```
      -calophytum 1/2
BABYLON-
      -praevernum 1/2
```
6ft(1.8m) -10F(-23C) E 5/4 Plant habit dense, rounded mound;

rigid red stems, large lustrous leaves. Huge satin white flower
with chocolate blotch. Excellent hybrid.   Reuthe, 1955.

* *
             -unnamed garden hybrid--unknown 7/8
BACCARAT-   -caucasicum 1/8
             -Chevalier F. de Savage-
    -Max Sye-   -unnamed hybrid--unknown
             -unknown
Crimson flowers with large black blotch, in round trusses of 14.
Adr. van Nes; reg. 1962.   A.M. Boskoop Trial 1960.
BOSKOOP   Parentage as above
Rosy red flowers with a dark brown blotch. Rounded truss of 13.
Adr. van Nes, reg. 1962.   A.M. Boskoop Trial 1960.
* *

BACCHUS   Parentage unknown
A parent of EMELINE BUCKLEY.   Crimson flowers in a large truss.
A. Waterer, before 1915.

BACH CHOIR   Described under FRED WYNNIATT, q.v.

* *
                              -griffithianum 1/8
                  -Queen Wilhelmina-
        -Unknown Warrior-   -unknown 3/8
BACHER'S GOLD-   -Stanley Davies--unknown
      -          -dichroanthum 1/4
         -Fabia-
                  -griersonianum 1/4
5ft(1.5m) 5F(-15C) ML 3/3   The cross of a red and an orange:
large flowers, salmon pink, shading to yellow center; cream stamens, brown anthers. Large flowers. John Bacher. P.A. 1955.
GENEVA   Parentage as above
Camellia rose, campanulate flowers, lighter in the centers, 3in.
(7.6cm) across, and frilled. Bacher, reg. 1958.   P.A. 1955.
* *

BAD EILSEN   Described under ELISABETH HOBBIE, q.v.

                  -garden hybrid--unknown 1/2
BAD ZWISCHENAHN (Hobbie)-
                  -williamsianum 1/2
Very winter-hardy in northern W. Germany; flowers of light rose.
D. Hobbie.

                              -arboreum 1/8
                   -Doncaster-
         -unnamed hybrid-   -unknown 3/8
BAD ZWISCHENAHN (Bruns)-   -yakushimanum 1/4
      -                  -catawbiense 1/4
         -Catherine van Tol-
                   -unknown
3ft(.9m) OF(-18C) ML   Pink flowers, greenish yellow blotch, 8
-10 per truss. Glossy oval leaves, to 4in(10.2cm) long; silvery
new growth. Bruns cross; reg. 1985. Col. ill. WS, 1989, p. 88.

BADEN-BADEN Described under ELISABETH HOBBIE, q.v.

BAGOLY'S BEAUTY   Described under YAKU WARRIOR, q.v.

                  -thomsonii 1/4
             -unnamed hybrid-
BAGSHOT RUBY-   -unknown 1/4 (or maximum hybrid)
             -catawbiense 1/2 ?
4ft(1.2m) -10F(-23C) ML   Pollen parent may be John Waterer,
catawbiense cross. Large conical truss of 14 ruby red flowers.
Parent of PRINCESS ELIZABETH. J. Waterer, c. 1900. A.M. 1916.

BAGSHOT SANDS--form of lutescens
6ft(1.8m) 5F(-15C) EM 3/3 A slender-growing shrub. Funnel-
shaped truss, primrose yellow. Mrs. Roza Stevenson. A.M. 1953.

                  -catawbiense 1/8
         -Mrs. Milner-
    -Daisy-   -unknown 1/8
BAJAZZO-   -smirnowii 1/4
    -            -fortunei ssp. discolor 1/4
       -Oldenburg-
                  -williamsianum 1/4
3ft x 3ft(.9m) -15F(-26C) ML   Flowers in loose truss of 9-12,
6-7 lobes, deep purplish pink inside, vivid purplish red outside
and unmarked. Winter flower buds intense reddish brown.   Hans

Hachmann, cross 1957; G. Stück, reg. 1988.

                  -catawbiense 1/4
       -Omega-
BALALAIKA-   -rose-colored hybrid--unknown 1/2
       -            -dichroanthum ssp. scyphocalyx 1/4
       -unnamed hybrid-
                  -unknown
3ft(.9m) x 4ft(1.2m)(12 yrs) -15F(-26C) Rather loose truss of
6-10 flowers, narrow rim of strong purplish red to deep purplish
pink, pale yellow centers. Dense, rounded shrub.   H. Hachmann,
cross 1975; Stück, reg. 1988.   Color illus. WS, 1989, p. 121.

BALI   Described under NUANCE, q.v.

* *
       -Dexter No. 1--unknown 7/8
BALLAD-   -catawbiense 1/8
    -      -Parsons Grandiflorum-
    -America-   -unknown
       -dark red hybrid--unknown
3ft(.9m) -15F(-26C) ML 3/3 Flowers very pale purple, edging
purplish pink, bold red blotch; reverse darker. Full pyramidal
trusses of 15. Narrowly obovate leaves. Leach, reg. 1972.
MADRID   Parentage as above
5ft(1.5m) -20F(-29C) ML   Plant broader than tall; dark green
foliage. Flowers roseine purple with bold ruby red blotch, held
in trusses of 12-14. Leach, reg. 1983. Color illus. HG p. 137.
* *

                  -griffithianum 1/4
       -Alice-
BALLERINA-   -unknown 1/4
       -fortunei ssp. discolor 1/2
White flowers, yellow flare; 14 per truss.   Waterer & Crisp.

BALLET   Described under SATIN DOLL, q.v.

* *
             -yakushimanum--Koichiro Wada 1/2
BALLY COTTON-
             -aureum 1/2
Dwarf -5F(-21C) EM 3/4 Spreading plant; leaves held 3 years,
light tan indumentum. Flowers 2in(5cm) across, white, yellowish
green dorsal blotch; 7 per ball-shaped truss. Reese, reg. 1979.
ASTROGLOW Parentage as above
Dwarf -25F(-32C) E   Flowers openly funnel-shaped, Egyptian
buff (very light yellow-orange) with greenish spotting; reverse
pink to pale pink.   Truss of 10, 4in(10cm) across. Leaves with
medium amount gray-brown indumentum. B. C. Potter, reg. 1981.
GOLD SPREAD   Parentage: yakushimanum, Exbury form x aureum
7in(18cm) -25F(-32C) EM   Very dwarf plant, 5 times as wide as
high, well-branched; indumented foliage. Flowers Dresden yellow
3.5in(9cm) wide; truss of 12. B. Potter, cross 1967; reg. 1981.
MINI GOLD   Parentage: yakushimanum--Koichiro Wada x aureum
1ft(.3m) -25F(-32C) EM   Plant much broader than tall. Foliage lightly indumented; held 2-3 years. Mimosa yellow flowers.
2.4in(6cm) wide; domed trusses of 8.   Potter, reg. 1981.
SERENDIPITY   Parentage: yakushimanum x aureum
1ft(.3m) -25F(-32C) M   Plant compact and spreading. Flowers
pale primrose yellow, widely campanulate, 2.3in(6.4cm) broad, in
trusses of 9-10. B. C. Potter, reg. 1972.
SUMMIT GOLD   Parentage: yakushimanum, Exbury form x aureum
1ft(.3m) -25F(-32C) EM Bush well-branched, 3 times wider than
tall. Flowers primrose yellow; truss of 9.   Potter, reg. 1981.
* *

       -minus var. minus Carolinianum Group 3/4
BALTA-   -minus var. minus Carolinianum Group
    -P. J. M. -
       -dauricum 1/4
3ft(.9m) -25F(-32C) E 4/4   Pastel pink buds; flowers almost
white; 1 week later than P.J.M. Very floriferous; slow-growing,
3-5in(7.6-12.7cm) per year. Wide, upright plant, sun- and wind-
tolerant; small, convex, dark green leaves.   "Balta" is Latvian
word for white. E. Mezitt, Weston Nurseries.

BALTIC LACE Parentage unknown; elepidote
2ft(.6m) -20F(-29C) ML   Yellowish white flowers, up to 25 per
truss. Very floriferous; spreading, dense habit. Mezitt cross,
1980; Weston Nurseries, reg. 1988.

* *
```
    -yakushimanum 1/2
BAMBI-      -dichroanthum 1/4
    -Fabia Tangerine-
                -griersonianum 1/4
```
3ft(.9m) 5F(-15C) M   Compact habit. Flowers strong red in
bud, opening deep pink and fading to strong pink, 7-9 per truss.
P. Wiseman, cross 1951; J. Waterer, Sons, & Crisp, reg. 1986.
MOLLY MILLER   Parentage as above
3ft(.9m) 5F(-15C) M   Yellow flowers, tinged rose. Foliage of
average size; some indumentum. J. Waterer & Crisp, reg. 1972.
PERCY WISEMAN   Parentage as above, except pollen parent selfed
3ft(.9m) 5F(-15C) M   Vigorous, compact plant, wider than high.
Dark green leaves 3in(7.6cm) long; no indumentum. Flowers funnel-shaped, opening peach pink and fade cream white, pale yellow
centers, orange spots; truss of 14. Waterer & Crisp, reg. 1971.
F.C.C. Wisley Trials 1986. Color illus. Cox pl. 142; JS p. 34.
SHRIMP GIRL   Parentage as BAMBI, above
3ft(.9m) OF(-18C) M 3/4   Compact habit; good foliage. Soft
Neyron rose flowers. Slow-growing. Waterer & Crisp, reg. 1971.
TIMOTHY JAMES   Parentage as BAMBI, above
3ft.9m) -5F(-21C) M Rosy flowers speckled brown, fade to off-
pink. Foliage has red petioles. Waterer & Crisp, reg. 1971.
* *

```
                        -griffithianum 7/32
            -Queen Wilhelmina-
        -Britannia-         -unknown 1/4
    -unnamed-    -Stanley Davies--unknown
    - hybrid-yakushimanum, Exbury form 1/4
                -dichroanthum 1/8
BAMBINO-    -Dido-
    -    -    -decorum 1/8
    -    -            -griffithianum
    -Lem's-   -Beauty of Tremough-
    Cameo-  -Norman-         -arboreum 1/32
        - Gill -griffithianum
    -Anna-        -griffithianum
        -Jean Marie -
            de Montague-unknown
```
4ft(1.2m) x 6ft(1.8m) OF(-18C) M 4/4   Flowers openly funnel-
shaped and fragrant, 3.1in(8cm) wide; 6 wavy lobes of light yellowish pink with dorsal red flare, a large yellowish pink calyx;
ball trusses of 12. Well-branched. Brockenbrough, reg. 1988.

BAMBOLA   Described under LAMPION, q.v.

```
        -keiskei, dwarf form 1/2
BANANA BOAT-
    -dauricum--Arctic Pearl 1/2
```
2ft(.6m) -10F(-23C) E 3/3   Plant blooms early, like keiskei,
but flowers are more open, with much yellow. Foliage dark green
in winter; aromatic. G. D. Lewis, reg. 1988.

```
            -griersonianum 1/4
    -Matador-
    -        -strigillosum 1/4
BANDOOLA-        -arboreum 1/16
    -        -Doncaster-
    -    -The Don-    -unknown 1/16
    -Red Lamp-   -griffithianum 1/8
        -facetum 1/4
```
3ft(.9m) EM 3/3   Scarlet flower; long, slender leaf. Reuthe.

* *
```
    -catawbiense var. album 1/2
BANGKOK-    -dichroanthum 1/4
    -unnamed hybrid-    -griffithianum 1/8
            -unnamed hybrid-
                -auriculatum 1/8
```
4ft(1.2m) -20F(-29C) M 4/4 Three tender species make a hardy
hybrid. Flowers open funnel-shaped, of heavy substance, pale to
strong coral pink, center soft orange-yellow; blotch and spots
dark reddish orange. Lax truss of 13. Rounded dark green foliage 4in(10.2cm) long. D. Leach, cross 1952; reg. 1972. Color
illus. ARS J 36:1 (1982), p. 6; Cox pl. 12.
DUET   Parentage as above
5ft(1.5m) -25F(-32C) ML 4/2   A beautiful hybrid for colder
climates. Pale yellow flowers, rimmed in pink, green blotch and
spotting in throat. Plant as wide as tall. Leach, reg. 1961.
MONACO   Parentage as above
6ft(1.8) -20F(-29C) VL   Spirea red buds open Dresden yellow,

the reverse very light spirea red, bold olive-yellow blotch and
spotting. Corolla 3.25in(8.3cm) wide; flat trusses, 19 flowers.
Plant broad as tall; long leaves held 1 year. Leach, reg. 1984.
PEACH PARFAIT   Parentage as above
5ft(1.5m) -15F(-26C) VL 4/2   Buds of roseine purple, opening
near-orange with primrose yellow stripes; trusses of 13-15. Un-
gainly habit. D. G. Leach, reg. 1983. Color illus. American
Hortculturist 52:4 (1973), p. 18.
* *

```
        -auriculatum 1/2
BANSHEE-    -arboreum 1/4
    -John Tremayne-
            -griffithianum 1/4
```
Tall, well-branched; blush pink flowers late. Rothschild, 1934.

* *
```
    -campylocarpum Elatum Group 1/2
BARBARA-    -griffithianum 1/4
    -Loderi-
        -fortunei 1/4
```
Loose trusses of deep cream, flushed a soft pink.   L. de Roth-
schild, cross 1934; E. de Rothschild, intro. 1948.
PINAFORE   Similar to above, but with white flowers blushed pink
toward the edges. Rothschild, 1948.
* *
```
        -Sappho--unknown 3/4
BARBARA-
BEHRING-        -catawbiense var. album Glass--Catalgla 1/4
    -unnamed hybrid-
            -Sappho--unknown
```
1ft(.3m)(6 yrs) -25F(-32C) ML Domed trusses of 13 white flow-
ers with dark purple and strong purplish red blotch, deep purple
dorsal spots. Leathery olive green leaves. Behring, reg. 1986.

```
                    -catawbiense 1/16
            -Atrosanguineum-
        -Atrier-    -unknown 1/16
    -Mary Belle-   -griersonianum 1/8
    -        -decorum 1/8
BARBARA-    -Dechaem-
   COOK -        -haematodes 1/8
    -            -caucasicum 3/16
    -        -Jacksonii-    -caucasicum
    -Goldsworth Yellow-   -Nobleanum-
            -campylocarpum 1/4 -arboreum 1/16
```
3ft(.9m) x 3ft -15F(-26C) M Buds strong red, opening to med-
ium purplish pink flowers of 7 wavy lobes, aging to pale yellow;
deep purplish red rays in throat; truss of 6. Elliptic foliage.
J. J. Brooks, cross 1976; Mrs. P. Walton raiser; reg. 1989.

```
        -yakushimanum 1/2
BARBARA HAYES-   -venator 1/4
    -Fire Music-
        -dichroanthum 1/4
```
Campanulate flowers of deep purplish pink with a stripe of light
orange-yellow, strong yellowish pink spots. Leaves olive green;
young growth has tawny brown indumentum. I. Hayes, reg. 1987.

```
        -souliei ? 1/4
    -Virginia-
    - Scott  -unknown 3/8
BARBARA HOUSTON-    -arboreum 1/8
    -        -Doncaster-
    -Belvedere-   -unknown
        -dichroanthum 1/4
```
5ft(1.5m) 10F(-12C) L 4/3   Flowers 3in(7.6cm) wide, orange-
buff with large red spots on lower lobes, margins pink; about 9
per truss. Leaves medium-sized. H. Larson, reg. 1979.

* *
```
        -maddenii (calophyllum) 1/2
BARBARA JURY-   -maddenii ssp. crassum 1/4
    -Sirius-
        -cinnabarinum Roylei Group 1/4
```
Trusses of 5 or 6 flowers of Naples yellow, deepening on outside
of tube, flushed pink, orange-yellow within. Foliage has brown
indumentum. F. M. Jury, 1982.
CHRISTINE DENZ   Parentage as above
Truss of 5-6 flowers, carmine rose in bud opening to Naples yellow, flushed pink, with bright yellow throat. Brown scaly indu-

mentum beneath elliptic leaves.   Jury, reg. 1982.
FELICITY FAIR   Parentage as above
Trusses hold 7-8 flowers, 5-lobed, amber yellow, orange throat. Elliptic leaves, brown scaly indumentum.   Jury, reg. 1982.

* *

```
                     -Lady        -fortunei ssp. discolor 1/8
                     - Bessborough-
          -Jalisco ?-         -campylocarpum Elatum Group
          -                -dichroanthum 1/8         1/8
BARBARA REUTHE-      -Dido-
          -              -decorum 1/8
          -unknown 1/2
```

4ft(1.2m) 5F(-15C) ML 4/4 Amber yellow flowers, 7-lobed, in trusses of 8. Leaves oblong to elliptic. G. Reuthe, reg. 1985.

BARBARA TANGER Complex parentage: catawbiense, maximum, others
10ft(3m) -15F(-26C) M Strong reddish purple buds. Flowers 3.5in(8.8cm) wide, medium purplish red, deep purplish red dorsal spotting. Trusses of about 17. W. D. Smith, reg. 1979.

```
                    -griffithianum 1/4
          -Queen Wilhelmina-
BARBARA WALLACE-          -unknown 3/4
          -Helen Waterer--unknown
```

Flowers reddish pink, white center. C. B. van Nes, before 1958.

```
          -barbatum 1/2
BARBAROSSA-
          -unknown 1/2
```

Early and bright red; similar to barbatum.   Horlick, pre-1958.

```
          -dichroanthum 1/2
BARBET-
          -callimorphum 1/2
```

Creamy pink flower. Not grown now at Exbury. Rothschild, 1934.

```
          -barbatum 1/2
BARBSUTCH-
          -sutchuenense 1/2
```

Deep rose pink flowers, a crimson blotch. E. J. P. Magor, 1930.

* *

```
          -thomsonii 1/2
BARCLAYI-
          -                -arboreum 1/4
          -Glory of Penjerrick-
                            -griffithianum 1/4
```

5ft(1.5m) 15F(-9C) EM   Large flowers of intense crimson, held in open trusses. Samuel Smith, Penjerrick; intro. c. 1921.
AVIS   Parentage as above
Crimson flowers on upright plant; attractive foliage. S. Smith.
HELEN FOX   Parentage as above
5ft(1.5m) 15F(-9C) E 4/2 Leaves 5in(12.7cm) x 2in(5cm) with red streak on upper side of midrib. Deep crimson scarlet flowers, of heavy substance; trusses rounded and loose. S. Smith.
ROBERT FOX   Parentage as above
5ft(1.5m) 15F(-9C) E 4/3 Rounded truss, deep blood red flowers of waxy texture. Habit upright, open; flat oval leaves with red streak on upper side of midrib. Barclay Fox. A.M. 1921.
ROMALA   Parentage as above
First known as BARCLAYI var. ROMALA. Crimson flowers. B. Fox.
* *

```
                              -griffithianum 1/2
                    -Beauty of Tremough-
          -Norman Gill-        -arboreum 1/8
     -Anna-        -griffithianum
     -   -              -griffithianum
     -   -Jean Marie de Montague-
BAREFIELD'S-                -unknown 3/16
BEST GIRL -              -griffithianum
     -         -George Hardy-
     -   -Peter Koster-        -catawbiense 1/16
     -   -              -arboreum
     -unnamed-       -Doncaster-
       hybrid-              -unknown
          -        -griffithianum
          -Loderi-
                 -fortunei 1/8
```

6ft(1.8m) 10F(-12C) ML   Fragrant flowers of heavy substance, 4.5in(11cm) wide, red with purple staining; 15 in trusses 7.5in. (19cm) across by 8.5in(21.5cm) high. Leaves held 4 years; plant upright, branched moderately. Mary Barefield, reg. 1980.

```
                              -griffithianum 3/8
                    -Beauty of Tremough-
          -Norman Gill-        -arboreum 1/16
     -Anna-        -griffithianum
     -   -              -griffithianum
     -   -Jean Marie de Montague-
BAREFIELD'S-                -unknown 1/8
BRIDGET  -              -griffithianum
     -         -Loderi-
     -   -Lodauric-        -fortunei 1/16
     -unnamed-       -auriculatum 1/8
       hybrid-   -dichroanthum 1/8
          -Fabia-
                 -griersonianum 1/8
```

5ft(1.5m) 10F(-12C) ML   Buds of cardinal red; flowers Venetian pink, fragrant, tubular funnel-shaped, 4in(10.2cm) across; large dome-shaped trusses of 14-16. Broad plant; leaves 7in(17.8cm) x 2in(5cm). G. Barefield cross; M. Barefield, reg. 1980.

```
                    -griffithianum 3/16
          -Mars-
     -Vulcan-   -unknown 1/8
     -   -   -griersonianum 1/4
BAREFIELD'S -                -griffithianum
GRANDDAUGHTER-         -George Hardy-
     - -Mrs. Lindsay-        -catawbiense 1/16
     -Dot- Smith   -Duchess of Edinburgh--unknown 1/8
          -fortunei 1/4
```

5ft(1.5m) 10F(-12C) M   Buds Tyrian purple, flowers rhodamine pink, shading to rose red margins, 4in(10.2cm) across; 14-21 in trusses 8in(20.3cm) tall. Plant broad and well-branched; leaves held 3 years. Grady Barefield cross; Mary Barefield, reg. 1980.

* *

```
                              -griffithianum 3/8
                    -Beauty of Tremough-
          -Norman Gill-        -arboreum 1/16
     -Anna-        -griffithianum
     -   -              -griffithianum
BAREFIELD'S-   -Jean Marie de Montague-
LIZA     -                -unknown 3/8
     -         -Tudelu (Lem)--unknown
     -unnamed-       -lacteum 1/8
       hybrid-unnamed hybrid-        -griffithianum
          -Loderi-
                 -fortunei 1/16
```

6ft(1.8m) 10F(-12C) M   Buds of Neyron rose, opening to flowers of paler Neyron rose, red at margins, ruby red stain in throat, 5.5in(14cm) across. Truss 8.5in(21.5cm) wide, holds 13-16. Upright plant; bronze new growth. Mary W. Barefield, reg. 1980.
MAMMOTH PINK   Parentage as above
6ft(1.8m) 5F(-15C) VL   Plant well-branched, dark grass green leaves 9in(23cm) long, held 3 years. Cardinal red buds open to light Neyron rose with ruby blotch, 6-7 wavy lobes, scented; 13 per truss. G. Barefield cross; M. Barefield, reg. 1981.
* *

```
                              -griffithianum 3/16
                    -Queen Wilhelmina-
          -Earl of Athlone-        -unknown 5/8
     -   -Stanley Davies--unknown
BAREFIELD'S-                -griffithianum
P. LEE  -         -George-
     -   -Mrs. Lindsay Smith- Hardy-catawbiense
     -Mrs. Betty-        -   1/16
       Robertson-       -Duchess of Edinburgh--
     -                  unknown
          -unnamed-campylocarpum 1/8
            hybrid-
              -unknown
```

3ft(.9m) 10F(-12C) M   Rose red buds open to flowers of Neyron rose, tubular funnel-shaped, 3in(7.6cm) wide; 14 in high, ball-shaped trusses. Floriferous. Broad, well-branched bush; foliage held 2 years. G. Barefield cross; M. Barefield,reg. 1980.

```
                -griffithianum 9/32
          -Mars-
    -Vulcan-    -unknown 3/16
    -      -griersonianum 1/4
    -                        -griffithianum
BAREFIELD'S -            -Beauty of-
VIRGINIA ANNE-          -Norman- Tremough-arboreum 1/32
    -      -Anna- Gill -
    -      -    -    -griffithianum
  -unnamed-   -              -griffithianum
  - hybrid-   -Jean Marie de Montague-
    -                        -unknown
    -              -campylocarpum Elatum Group 1/8
             -Ole Olson-
                  -fortunei ssp. discolor 1/8
```

4ft(1.2m) 10F(-12C) M Flowers 3in(7.6cm) wide, of dark pink,
deepening in throat, exterior with darker stripes. Trusses hold
12. Plant floriferous, broad, well-branched; leaves 8in(20.3cm)
x 2.5in(6.4cm); held 3 years. M. Barefield, reg. 1980.

BARITON Described under BLUE RHAPSODY, q.v.

BARMSTEDT Described under ANUSCHKA, q.v.

```
                              -griffithianum 1/8
                        -Kewense-
                  -Aurora-      -fortunei 3/8
    -Naomi Stella Maris-      -thomsonii 1/8
    -                  -fortunei
BARNSDALE-                  -campylocarpum 1/8
    -          -unnamed hybrid-
    -          -              -fortunei ssp. discolor 1/8
  -Ilam Canary-                  -griffithianum
    -              -Loderi-
    -yellow Loderi sdl.-      -fortunei
                        -unknown 1/8
```

Flowers stone cream with a chestnut blotch, 7-lobed, in trusses
of 15. Blooms midseason. Shrub to 12ft(3.6m); foliage broadly
ovate. H. N. White cross; J. M. Hudson, New Zealand, reg. 1985.

```
          -fortunei ? 1/2
BARNSTABLE-              (Dexter hybrid)
          -unknown
```

5ft(1.5m) -5F(-21C) M 3/3 Very fragrant, light purplish pink
flowers; trusses of 10.   Briarwood Gardens form called salmon-
colored. John Wister, reg. 1980.

BARON DE BRUIN   See B. DE BRUIN

```
          -yakushimanum, Exbury form 1/2
BARON LIONEL-
          -yakushimanum 1/2
```

Not a hybrid; a selected yakushimanum. Truss of 14-17 flowers,
light orchid-pink opening to clear white, speckled with absinthe
green. L. de Rothschild cross; E. de Rothschild, reg. 1982.

```
                        -griffithianum 1/16
                  -Kewense-
              -Aurora-      -fortunei 5/16
        -Exbury-      -
BARON PHILLIPE- Naomi-      -thomsonii 1/8
DE ROTHSCHILD-      -fortunei
    -      -wardii 1/4
    -Crest-          -fortunei ssp. discolor 1/8
          -Lady Bessborough-
                  -campylocarpum Elatum Group 1/8
```

Upright, compact habit like Naomi. Bears well-formed trusses of
large, pale yellow flowers in profusion. At Exbury, withstands
cold in an exposed location. E. de Rothschild, reg. 1964.

```
          -Metternianus--degronianum ssp. heptamereum
    -Rijneveld-              (metternichii)        1/4
    -    -              -griersonianum 1/8
BARON VAN-    -unnamed hybrid-
  DEDEM -              -unknown 5/8
    -unknown
```

7ft(2.1m) x 13ft(3.9m) -5F(-21C) EM Trumpet-shaped flowers,
held in trusses of 20-28; clear pink corolla. A. Vuyk; Royal
Boskoop Horticultural Society, reg. 1988.

```
                -catawbiense 1/2
BARONESS SCHROEDER-
          -unknown  1/2
```

5ft(1.5m) -10F(-23C) ML There is also a vireya named Baroness
Henry Schroeder (F.C.C. 1883)--I.R.R. 1958.   White flowers with
a pale magenta flush and dark spotted flare; deep reddish purple
petioles; truss of 20. J. Street suggests arboreum as a parent.
J. Waterer, before 1900.   Color illus. JS p. 82.

BARRY RODGERS Described under PIROUETTE, q.v.

```
          -catawbiense 1/2
BARRYB-                    and perhaps some hybrids
          -maximum 1/2
```

6ft(1.8m) -10F(-23C) ML Flowers 2in(5cm) wide, reddish purple
with yellow green dorsal blotch, 14 per truss.   Floriferous.
Plant upright, well-branched.   W. D. Smith, reg. 1978.

```
              -thomsonii 1/4
    -Barclayi-          -arboreum 1/8
    -      -Glory of Penjerrick-
BARTIA-                  -griffithianum 1/8
    -      -neriiflorum 1/4
    -Portia-
          -strigillosum 1/4
```

Turkey red flowers, truss of 12. Lord Aberconway. A.M. 1948.

BARTO ALPINE   Lapponica hybrid
3ft(.9m) -10F(-23C) EM 3/4 Orchid-rose flowers all along the
stems. Aromatic leaves, a nutmeg-like scent in warm sun. Plant
habit dense, upright, rugged. Barto raiser; Greer, reg. 1964.

BARTO BLUE--form of augustinii
6ft(1.8m) -5F(-21C) EM 4/4   Excellent plant. Clean, clear,
beautiful blue. Barto raiser; Phetteplace, intro. 1958.

```
          -fortunei 1/2
BARTO IVORY-
          -unknown  1/2
```

6ft(1.8m) -10F(-23C) EM 4/3   Fragrant, rich ivory flowers;
Heavy foliage. Barto cross; Steinmetz raiser; Greer, reg. 1962.

```
              -fortunei ? 1/2
BARTO LAVENDER-
          -ponticum ? 1/2
```

6ft(1.8m -10F(-23C) M 3/3   Orchid-pink flowers, fragrant.
Vigorous habit; large wavy leaf. Barto cross; Greer reg. 1962.

BARTO ROSE--form of oreodoxa var. fargesii
5ft(1.5m) -10F(-23C) E 4/3 Flowers rose madder, spotted deep
purple, 7-lobed, 2.25in(5.7cm) wide. Truss of 14. Plant 3/4 as
broad as tall.   Barto raiser; Phetteplace, reg. 1963.

BAS DE BRUIN   See B. DE BRUIN

BASHFUL Described under PINK CHERUB, q.v.

```
              -souliei 1/4
    -Halcyone-              -fortunei ssp. discolor
    -      -Lady Bessborough-            1/8
BASHFUL BETTY-              -campylocarpum Elatum Gp.
    -      -sanguineum ssp. didymum 1/4      1/8
    -Carmen-
              -forrestii Repens Group 1/4
```

3ft(.9m) OF(-18C) EM 4/3 Dark rosy red flowers in great profusion. Leaves glossy dark green. Elliott cross; Fisher intro.

BASILEOS Described under HARRY TAGG, q.v.

```
          -fortunei ? 1/2
BASS RIVER-              (Dexter hybrid)
          -unknown 1/2
```

4ft(1.2m) -5F(-21C) EM 3/4   Moderate purplish pink truss of
14 flowers. Fine habit, glossy foliage. G. Wister, reg. 1982.

BASTION Described under GIBRALTAR, q.v.

```
          -griffithianum 1/4
    -Gill's Goliath-
BATTLE AXE-          -unknown 1/4
    -fortunei ssp. discolor 1/2
```

Rich pink flowers.   Rothschild, 1934.

```
                      -griffithianum 1/4
         -Dawn's Delight-
BAUBLE-                -unknown 1/4
         -campylocarpum 1/2
```
Campanulate flowers, straw yellow; lemon style, filaments. Bush
dense; small, rounded, glossy leaves. Rothschild, 1934.

* *
```
              -dichroanthum 1/4
         -Fabia-
BEACON-       -griersonianum 1/2
-                         -sanguineum ssp. didymum 1/4
         -Arthur Osborn-
                          -griersonianum
```
Brilliant scarlet flowers. Lord Aberconway, 1942.
FABOS   Parentage as above
Crimson flowers. Routho, 1952.
LITTLE TROOPER   Parentage as above, except reversed
2ft(.6m) OF(-18C) L   Compact plant, broader than tall; dull
olive green leaves. Deep, blood red flowers. Baker, reg. 1967.
* *
```
                    -dichroanthum 1/8
          -Astarte-              -campylocarpum Elatum Group 1/16
-Ouida-        -Penjerrick-
BEADA-    -               -griffithianum 1/16
-         -griersonianum 1/4
-beanianum 1/2
```
Pink flowers. Lord Aberconway, cross 1939; intro. 1942.

```
                                      -griffithianum
                         -Kewense-          1/64
              -Aurora-       -fortunei 21/64
         -Naomi-    -thomsonii 1/32
    -unnamed-    -fortunei
-unnamed   - hybrid-decorum 1/8
- hybrid F2-
BEA'S GLORY-      -orbiculare 1/4        -wardii 1/8
-                   -unnamed hybrid-
    -unnamed hybrid F2-        -dichroanthum 1/8
                    -fortunei
```
4ft(1.2m) high x 6ft(1.8m) -5F(-21C) M Truss of 12; pale yel-
low buds opening to pale yellowish green, 2 deep red dosal rays;
fragrant. B. McDonald, reg. 1988.

```
          -haematodes 1/4
     -Choremia-
BEATRICE-      -arboreum 1/4
     -meddianum 1/2
```
Pink flowers. Lord Aberconway, cross 1937; intro. 1950.

BEATRICE HYDE   Described under P.J.M., q.v.

* *
```
                    -caucasicum 1/8
             -Dr. Stocker-
       -Logan Damaris-        -griffithianum 1/8
BEATRICE KEIR-        -campylocarpum 1/4
       -lacteum 1/2
```
5ft(1.5m) OF(-18C) EM 4/3 Parentage may be reverse of above
Flowers light chartreuse green, open-campanulate, of heavy substance, in firm truss of 18-20. Bushy habit.   J. B. Stevenson
cross; Crown Estate exhibited; reg. 1974. A.M. 1974.
JOHN BARR STEVENSON Parentage as above; may be reversed
Pale greenish yellow flowers; rounded trusses, 7in(18cm) across,
of 14-16. J. B. Stevenson, reg. 1962. A.M. 1971.
* *
```
                    -catawbiense 1/4
          -Charles Dickens-
BEATRICE PIERCE-              -unknown 1/4
-                         -decorum 1/4
          -unnamed hybrid-
                    -griffithianum 1/4
```
Rose flowers with maroon center. G. Guy Nearing, 1944.

* *
```
          -burmanicum 1/2
BEATRIX ANDERSON-
          -unknown 1/2
```

Cool greenhouse plant. Yellowish green buds open paler; flowers
4in(10.2cm) wide, in loose trusses of 5.   E. B. Anderson cross;
Crown Estate, Windsor, raiser; reg. 1968.   A.M. 1968.
CREAM DELIGHT   Parentage as above
New Zealand hybrid.   Trusses of 5-11 flowers, of light greenish
yellow, spotted with green. B. W. Campbell, reg. 1977.
* *
```
          -Essex Scarlet--unknown 1/2
BEAU BRUMMEL-
          -facetum (eriogynum) 1/2
```
5ft(1.5m) -5F(-21C) L 3/3   A good, late variety with dark,
blood red, waxy flowers, speckled in black. Trusses are compact
balls of 20. Open habit. Rothschild, 1934. A.M. 1938.

* *
```
                    -caucasicum 1/4
          -Boule de Neige-          -catawbiense 1/8
BEAUFORT-            -hardy hybrid-
          -fortunei 1/2              -unknown 1/8
```
5ft(1.5m) -20F(-29C) M 3/3   Insect-resistant, compact plant.
Fragrant white flowers, tinted mauve. Trusses of 14. Compact
habit; large leaves. Joseph Gable.   Color illus. LW pl. 50.
ROCOCO   Parentage as above
5ft(1.5m) -25F(-32C) EM 3/4   May be extinct. Plant as broad
as tall; superior foliage density. Flowers fluted, ruffled, 2.5
in(5.7cm) across, lilac-pink, deeper pink rims, and yellow-green
rays; truss of 12. Joseph Gable cross; David Leach, reg. 1965.
* *
```
          -griffithianum 1/2
BEAULIEU-
          -unknown 1/2
```
Peach pink flower, whitish pink edges. Waterer, Sons & Crisp.

BEAULIEU HAWK   Described under HAWK, q.v.

BEAUT ONE   Described under MELBA, q.v.

* *
```
                    -dichroanthum 1/8
          -Goldsworth Orange-
     -Hotei-              -fortunei ssp. discolor 1/4
     -    -          -souliei 1/8
BEAUTIFUL DAY-   -unnamed hybrid-
-                -wardii 3/8
     -   -wardii
     -Crest-          -fortunei ssp. discolor
          -Lady Bessborough-
                    -campylocarpum Elatum 1/8
```
4ft(1.2m) -5F(-21C) L 4/3   Buds brick red blending to orange
buff; flowers empire yellow, narrowly striped tangerine.   Truss
of 12 large flowers, openly funnel-shaped. Leaves held 3 years.
Whitney cross; George & Anne Sather, reg. 1975.   Color illus.
ARS J. 44:1 (1990), front cover; HG p. 76.
ANITA DUNSTON   Parentage as above, except reversed
3ft(.9m) high x 2.5ft(.75m)(8yrs) OF(-18C) M   Brilliant yellow
flowers, tipped orange, funnel-shaped. Plant as broad as tall;
stiff, upright branches. W. Hill cross; B. Briggs, reg. 1986.
* *

BEAUTIFUL DREAMER   Parentage unknown
6ft(1.8m) 5F(-15C) EM 4/3   Yellow flowers lightly tinged with
orange on each lobe, fading to yellow. Truss of 12. Foliage of
medium size. Whitney cross; Sather, reg. 1976.

```
          -catawbiense 1/2
BEAUTY OF BAGSHOT-
          -unknown 1/2
```
White flowers, tinged soft mauve with dark blotch.   J. Waterer.

BEAUTY OF BENMOI Described under JEANNE CHURCH, q.v.

BEAUTY OF BERRY HILL Parentage unknown
Scarlet flowers, finely spotted.   A. Waterer.   F.C.C. 1872.

```
          -griffithianum 1/2
BEAUTY OF LITTLEWORTH-
          -campanulatum ? 1/2
```
6ft(1.8m) -5F(-21C) M 4/3 Very large truss of 16-19 flowers
of pure white, spotted reddish purple; each 5in(12.7cm) across.
New stems over 12in(30.4cm) long. Leggy habit; dark green foli-

age.   Possibly the largest specimen grows at Corsock, Scotland.
J. Mangles, before 1884.   F.C.C. 1904;   F.C.C. Wisley Trials
1953.   Color ill. ARS J 41:2 (1987), p. 91; F p. 33; JS p. 61.

* *
                              -griffithianum 1/2
BEAUTY OF TREMOUGH-
                              -arboreum (blood red form) 1/2
Rose pink, fading to pale rose. Richard Gill, Gardener to Henry
Shilson, Tremough, Cornwall. F.C.C. 1902.
BODNANT BEAUTY OF TREMOUGH   Parentage as above
Pale pink flowers, scented.   Lord Aberconway, 1948.
GILLII   Parentage as above
Flowers of soft rose. R. Gill & Son. A.M. 1919.
GILL'S TRIUMPH   Parentage as above
Strawberry red, fading to pink. R. Gill & Son. A.M 1904.
GLORY OF PENJERRICK   Parentage as above
Deep strawberry fading to pink. R. Gill & Son. A.M. 1904.
JOHN TREMAYNE   Parentage as above
Cross by Tremayne of Heligan. Originally called BEAUTY OF TRE-
MOUGH VAR. JOHN TREMAYNE.
TREETOPS   Parentage as above
Loose truss of 10 flowers, white flushed reddish purple shades,
widely funnel-campanulate. Lord Aberconway, 1981. A.M. 1981.
* *

BEAUTYBOUND   Described under GOLDEN YEARS, q.v.

                -catawbiense var. album Glass--Catalgla 1/2
BEAUTYMASTER-   -fortunei 1/4
                -Golden Star-
                                -wardii 1/2
Buds of strong purplish red and light greenish yellow open to a
pale greenish yellow star, rimmed with strong and light purplish
pinks; dorsal spots of strong yellow-green. Weldon Delp.

                        -fortunei ssp. discolor 1/2
BECKYANN--unnamed hybrid, F2-
                        -campylocarpum 1/2
4ft(1.2m) -10F(-23C) ML   Flowers of heavy substance, openly
funnel-shaped, 5-lobed, cream-color with grayed red dorsal spotting. Ball truss of 12. H. Yates cross; Mrs. Yates, reg. 1977.

* *
                    -catawbiense var. album Glass--Catalgla 1/4
         -Caltwins-   -catawbiense 1/8
                    -Pink Twins-
BEDAZZLED-   -haematodes 1/8
    -        -yakushimanum 1/4   -fortunei ssp. discolor
    -        -   -Lady   -   3/32
    -D.D.-   -Day   -Bessborough-campylocarpum Elatum
        -Gold- -Dream-   -   1/32
            Mohur-   -griersonianum 3/32
                -        -fortunei ssp. discolor
            -Margaret-   -dichroanthum 1/32
                    Dunn   -Fabia-
                            -griersonianum
Light chartreuse green and white in bud, opening pale chartreuse
yellow with dorsal spots of medium lettuce green. Anthers light
magenta rose. Weldon Delp.
ULTRASLEEK   Parentage as above
Buds pale through medium shades of Venetian pink. Frilled white
flowers, with throat a blend of pale primrose yellow and strong
guardsman red. Anthers light Neyron rose. W. Delp.
* *

* *
                            -catawbiense 1/4
            -Atrosanguineum-
BEECHWOOD PINK-   -unknown 1/4
            -fortunei 1/2
6ft(1.8m) -15F(-26C) M 4/3   Flowers bright fuchsia pink in
large trusses. Gable cross; C. Herbert, reg. 1962. A.E. 1960.
DAVID GABLE   Parentage as above
5ft(1.5m) -15F(-26C) M 4/4 Flowers fuchsine pink, 3.5in(9cm)
across, blotch of Indian red. Large, dome-shaped trusses. Good
plant habit; dark green leaves, 7in(17cm) long. J. Gable, 1962.
A. E. 1960.   Color illus. VV p. 91.
* *

                    -elliottii 3/4
        -Fusilier-
BEEFEATER-   -griersonianum 1/4
        -elliottii
5ft(1.5m) 10F(-12C)   Excessively large, poorly formed, flat-
topped trusses of 26 flowers, geranium lake red, with some pale
spots. RHS Garden, Wisley, reg. 1962. A.M. 1958. F.C.C. 1959.

BEEKMAN'S DELIGHT   Described under JOAN THOMPSON, q.v.

BEER SHEBA--form of cerasinum
3ft(.9m) -5F(-21C) EM   White flowers tinted with rose madder.
Trusses of 5. L. de Rothschild selection; reg. 1963.

BEIGE   Described under JOE GABLE, q.v.

        -Jan Dekens--unknown 13/16
    -                            -ponticum 1/16
BEL AIR-   -Michael Waterer-
    -            -Prometheus-   -unknown
    -                        -Monitor--unknown
    -Madame de Bruin-   -arboreum 1/8
                    -Doncaster-
                        -unknown
Flowers dark rose, with a pink blotch. P. van Nes; reg. 1961.
S.M. Rotterdam 1960; A.M. Boskoop 1960.

BELINDA BEEKMAN   Described under JOAN THOMPSON, q.v.

        -Essex Scarlet--unknown 1/2
BELISHA BEACON-
        -arboreum 1/2
Of medium size; tight truss of dusky scarlet. Rothschild, 1934.

        -Mrs. J. G. Millais--unknown 19/32
    -            -wardii 5/16   -griffithianum
    -            -   -George-   1/128
BELKANTO-   -unn.-   -Hardy -catawbiense
    -        -hyb.-   -Mrs. L.-   9/128
    -    -   -   -Diane- Smith -Duchess of
    -    -   -   -   Edinburgh--unknown
    -Gold- -   -Alice -   -   -campylocarpum 1/64
        dekor-   Street-   -unnamed-
        -                -   hybrid-unknown
        -            -wardii
        -            -catawbiense ?
        -        -Omega-
        -unnamed-   -rose-colored hybrid
        hybrid-   --unknown
                -wardii
3.7ft(1.1m) x 4.7ft(1.4m) -15F(-26C) ML   Flowers pale yellow,
funnel-shaped, 3in(8cm) wide, tinged pale yellowish pink; dorsal
spotting greenish yellow on bright chartreuse base. Truss of 14
to 17. Hairless, medium green leaves; compact bush. Hachmann,
cross 1977; Stück, reg. 1988. Color illus. WS, 1989, p. 120.

BELL SONG   Described under MAY SONG, q.v.

            -thomsonii 1/4
    -Shilsonii-
BELLA-   -barbatum 1/4
    -griffithianum 1/2
Pale rose flowers. Lord Aberconway, cross 1926; intro. 1936.

            -griffithianum 1/4
        -Isabella-
BELLBIRD-   -auriculatum 1/4
        -souliei 1/2
Pure white flowers; loose trusses. Capt. C. Ingram, 1964.

BELLE   Described under LADY BESSBOROUGH, q.v.

                    -catawbiense 1/2
        -Catawbiense Album-
BELLE HELLER-   -unknown 1/2
    -                    -catawbiense
    -white catawbiense hybrid-
                    -unknown
5ft(1.5m) -15F(-26C) M 4/3 Fine habit, vigorous plant; large
dark green foliage. Big white flowers, with a striking golden
flare, in large trusses. A. Shammarello, before 1958. Color

illus. Cox, pl. 13; VV p. 111.

```
                  -aberconwayi 1/2
BELLE OF LOCKINGTON-
                  -unknown 1/2
```
Trusses of 13 flowers: funnel-shaped, white, spotted with rose.
Shrub to 3ft(1.5m).   D. J. Dosser, reg. 1985.

```
                  -rigidum var. album 1/2
BELLE OF TREMEER-
                  -augustinii 1/2
```
4ft(1.2m) 5F(-15C) EM 3/3   A slender-growing natural hybrid
with clusters of pale mauve flowers. Gen. Harrison. P.C. 1969.

BELLEFONTAINE   Described under KATHERINE DALTON, q.v.

```
                       -fortunei ssp. discolor 1/4
            -Norman Shaw-
                       -catawbiense 1/8
BELLEROPHON-          -B. de Bruin-
                               -unknown 1/8
            -facetum (eriogynum) 1/2
```
Late-blooming flowers, bright crimson red in tight trusses of 10
or more. Tall plant of tidy habit. Rothschild, 1934.

```
* * * * * * * * * * * * * * * * * * * * * * * * * *
                  -catawbiense ? 1/4
       -Omega (Seidel)-
BELLINI-           -rose-colored hybrid--unknown 1/4
       -wardii (without interior red marks) 1/2
```
5ft(1.5m) -5F(-21C) ML   The first Hachmann hybrid introduced.
Very light yellow; plant compact. Hachmann cross 1963; not reg.
HACHMANN'S MARINA   Parentage as above
A parent of other Hachmann hybrids.   Flowers pure light yellow.
H. Hachmann cross; G. Stück reg. 1984.
```
* * * * * * * * * * * * * * * * * * * * * * * * *
```

BELLRINGER   Parentage unknown
3ft(.9m) OF(-18C) M Soft creamy white flowers on a well-formed plant.   Consolini.

```
          -smirnowii 1/2
BELLROSE-
                           -catawbiense 1/4
       -Mrs. Charles S. Sargent-
                           -unknown 1/4
```
5ft(1.5m) -15F(-26C) M   Olive green leaves; light indumentum.
Flowers rose pink with a dark flare. Upright trusses. Unknown.

BELLVALE   Described under P.J.M., q.v.

```
       -Red Yard--unknown Dexter hybrid 1/2
       -                     -griffithianum 1/16
BELLWETHER-       -Kewense-
       -       -Aurora-     -fortunei 5/16
       -Naomi-    -thomsonii 1/8
            -fortunei
```
4.5ft(1.35m) x 5ft(1.5m)(20 yrs) OF(-18C) M   White flowers,
tubular funnel-shaped, of heavy substance, in trusses of 9.   M.
& B. Shapiro, reg. 1989. Color illus. ARS J 42:2 (1988), p. 62.

```
              -arboreum 1/4
       -Doncaster-
BELVEDERE-       -unknown 1/4
       -dichroanthum 1/2
```
Soft pink. Grown in Pacific Northwest (US).   Rothschild, 1927.

```
              -Corona--unknown 1/4
       -Bow Bells-
BEN BRIGGS-      -williamsianum 1/4
       -              -griffithianum  1/4
            -Loderi King George-
                       -fortunei 1/4
```
3ft(.9m) OF(-18C) VE Tubular funnel-shaped flowers 3.5in(9cm)
broad, of 6 wavy-edged lobes, white tinted pink, fading to faint
greenish white;lax truss. Elliptic, concave, glossy leaves, to
2.5in(6.5cm). Broad floriferous plant.   B. Briggs, cross 1976;
W. Elliott raiser; reg. 1988.

```
                            -wardii ? 1/8
                    -Chlorops-
         -Lackamas Spice-    -vernicosum ? 1/8
BEN LANCASTER-           -diaprepes 1/4
         -              -fortunei ssp. discolor 1/4
         -Evening Glow-      -dichroanthum 1/8
                    -Fabia-
                         -griersonianum 1/8
```
4ft(1.2m) -5F(-21C) L   Mimosa yellow flowers, deepening with
age, 3.5in(8.9cm) wide, campanulate, fragrant; trusses hold 12.
Bushy habit.   B. Lancaster, reg. 1971.

```
              -fortunei ? 1/2
BEN MOSELEY-
              -unknown 1/2
```
5ft(1.5m) -20F(-29C) M 3/4   One of the best Dexters; flowers
of light purplish pink, deeper on margins. Foliage olive green.
Moseley, Vossberg, Wister; reg. 1980. Color illus. Cox pl. 15.

```
                     -ponticum 1/4
         -Purple Splendour-
BEN SHAPIRO-         -unknown 1/4
         -           -aureum 1/4
         -Nikomontanum-
                     -brachycarpum 1/4
```
7ft(2.1m) x 5ft(1.5m)(22 yrs) OF(-18C) M   Strong reddish pur-
ple buds open to very pale purple flowers, heavily spotted with
dark red to deep purplish red.   M. & B. Shapiro, reg. 1989.

```
                          -arboreum 1/16
                  -Doncaster-
              -unnamed-      -unknown 3/8
              - hybrid-      -neriiflorum 1/16
              -       -Nereid-
       -Witch Doctor-        -dichroanthum 1/16
       -            -          -griffithianum 5/16
       -            -    -Mars-
BEN VELTRI-         -Vulcan-  -unknown
       -            -         -griersonianum 1/8
       -            -griffithianum
       -Starfish-
              -unknown
```
2ft(.6m) OF(-18C) M   Buds rose red; reddish purple flowers,
spotted orange. Lax truss, 6in(15cm) wide, of 17. Broad plant;
leaves held three years.   Paul Holden, reg. 1981.

BENGAL (Hobbie)   Described under ELISABETH HOBBIE, q.v.

BENGAL (Leach)   See MADRAS

BENGAL ROSE   Described under ROSE OF CHINA, q.v.

BENGT M. SCHALIN   Described under PRELUDE, q.v.

```
       -fortunei ssp. discolor 1/2
BENITO-      -fortunei 1/4
       -Luscombei-
            -thomsonii 1/4
```
Buds pink; flowers white, with brownish rose markings on the up-
per lobe. Origin unknown. A.M. 1934.

BENMORE--form of montroseanum (mollyanum)
5ft(1.5m) 10F(-12C) E 3/3   Pink flowers with a crimson blotch
at the base. Plant of compact habit; large foliage. Known only
in cultivation.   Younger Botanic Garden, Benmore; reg. 1961.
A.M. 1957. F.C.C. 1957.

BENNAN--form of meddianum var. atrokermesinum K W 19452
Cardinal red flowers with darker markings held in trusses of 17.
Collector Kingdon Ward. Brodick Castle, reg. 1977.   A.M. 1977.

BERGIE--form of ciliatum. White flowers. H. L. Larson.

```
              -wardii 1/2
BERGIE LARSON-    -dichroanthum  1/4
         -Jasper-
              -Lady       -fortunei ssp. discolor 1/8
              Bessborough-
                    -campylocarpum 1/8
```
3ft(.9m) 10F(-12C) L 3/4   Red buds open to flowers of heavy
substance, 3in(7.6cm) wide, cadmium orange with light red spots.
Trusses 5in(12.7cm) across, 12-flowered.   Plant broad and well-

branched; leaves retained 3 years.   Larson, reg. 1979.

```
                                       -griffithianum 1/16
                          -George-
              -Mrs. Lindsay- Hardy-catawbiense 1/16
               - Smith    -
        -Mrs. Betty -            -Duchess of
        - Robertson-            Edinburgh--unknown 1/4
        -                       -campylocarpum 1/4
BERG'S YELLOW-        -unnamed-
        -              hybrid-unknown
        -                       -campylocarpum
        -            -Mary Swaythling-
        -Fred Rose-              -fortunei 1/8
              -lacteum 1/4
```
4ft(1.2m) OF(-18C) M 4/4 Very bright trusses of yellow-green
flowers, with extremely nice foliage.   Warren Berg.

```
                                   -ponticum 1/16
                          -Michael Waterer-
              -Prometheus-            -unknown  5/16
        -Madame de Bruin-        -Monitor--unknown
        -                        -arboreum 1/8
BERLIN-              -Doncaster-
        -                        -unknown
        -williamsianum 1/2
```
Large pink flowers, bell-shaped, pendant.   J. Bruns, 1964.

```
                   -catawbiense var. album 1/4
        -Anna H. Hall-
BERMUDA-             -yakushimanum--Koichiro Wada 1/4
        -       -fortunei 1/4
        -Nestucca-
              -yakushimanum 1/4
```
4ft(1.2m) -20F(-29C) ML 4/4   Rounded plant, much wider than
tall. Dome-shaped truss of 14 flowers, phlox pink spotted with
yellow-green. Indumented new growth.   D. G. Leach, reg. 1983.

```
        -decorum 1/2
BERN-
        -hybrid unknown  1/2
```
Flowers pastel mauve with lighter centers; prominent rose blotch
on upper lobes. John Bacher.   P.A. 1955.

```
                          -griffithianum 1/8
              -George Hardy-
        -Pink Pearl-            -catawbiense 1/8
        -            -            -arboreum 1/8
BERNARD CRISP-        -Broughtonii-
        -                        -unknown 5/8
              -hardy hybrid--unknown
```
Flowers of pale rose pink. Waterer, Sons & Crisp.   A.M. 1921.

```
              -arboreum ssp. zeylanicum 1/2
BERNARD GILL-
        -griffithianum--Roseum Superbum 1/2
```
Flowers soft rose red, with a few dots of deeper carmine pink.
R. Gill & Son.   A.M. 1925.

```
              -calophytum 1/2
BERNARD SHAW-
        -                        -griffithianum 1/8
        -            -George Hardy-
        -Pink Pearl-            -catawbiense 1/8
        -            -            -arboreum 1/8
        -            -Broughtonii-
                                 -unknown 1/8
```
5ft(1.5m) OF(-18C) EM 4/3   Very large, sugar pink trusses.
Big, deep green leaves. Reuthe, 1955.

```
        -maddenii (calophyllum) 3/4
BERNICE-              -cinnabarinum Blandiiflorum Group 1/4
        -Royal Flush-
              -maddenii (calophyllum)
```
Trusses of 7 flowers, 5-lobed, crimson, blush white on margins.
Leaves elliptic; brown scaly indumentum. F. M. Jury, reg. 1982.

```
* * * * * * * * * * * * * * * * * * * * * * * * * * * *
                   -dichroanthum 1/4
        -Goldsworth Orange-
BERNSTEIN-              -fortunei ssp. discolor 1/4
        -Mrs. J. G. Millais--unknown 1/2
```
5ft(1.5m) -10F(-23C) ML   Truss of 12-15 flowers, soft yellow-

---

orange, conspicuous blotch of bright orange-red. Nice foliage.
Bernstein = amber, in German.   Hachmann cross; Stück, reg 1983.
Color illus. WS, 1989, p. 121.
HACHMANN'S LIBELLE   Parentage as above
Light yellow-green, 5-lobed, about 14 flowers per truss. Stück,
reg. 1984.
```
* * * * * * * * * * * * * * * * * * * * * * * * * * * *
* * * * * * * * * * * * * * * * * * * * * * * * * *
                   -arboreum 1/4
        -Doncaster-
BERRYROSE-              -unknown 1/4
        -dichroanthum 1/2
```
3ft(.9m) OF(-18C) ML 4/2   Vivid apricot orange flowers, with
yellow centers. Rounded plant; foliage held only one year; leaf
spotted.   Rothschild. A.M. 1934.
MINTERNE BERRYROSE   Parentage as above
First known as BERRYROSE MINTERNE.   Lord Digby, exhibited 1952.
```
* * * * * * * * * * * * * * * * * * * * * * * * * * * *
                   -griersonianum 1/4
        -Diva-            -fortunei ssp. discolor 1/8
BERT LARSON-    -Ladybird-
        -            -Corona--unknown 1/8
        -strigillosum 1/2
```
5ft(1.5m) 10F(-12C) E 3/3   Blood red flowers, darker brownish
red spotting. Trusses 6in(15cm) across, of 14. Leaves retained
4 years; grayed orange indumentum beneath. Larson, reg. 1979.

BERTHA Described under ALFRED, q.v.

BERT'S OWN Described under ACTRESS, q.v.

BERYL Parentage unknown.
Dull purple flowers. Origin unknown.   A.M. 1931.

BERYL TAYLOR--form of campylocarpum LS & T 4738
1ft(.3m) -10F(-23C) EM 3/3 Compact, upright plant with small
leaves. Clusters of 4-5 campanulate, red-purple flowers.   Lord
Aberconway, reg. 1975. A.M. 1975.

```
        -spinuliferum 1/2
BERYLLINE-
        -valentinianum 1/2
```
Dense, low-growing shrub. Very showy trusses of pale gold flowers flushed rose. Small, compact trusses.   Rothschild, 1934.

BESS Described under SMYRNA, q.v.

BESSE HOWELLS Described under PINK CAMEO, q.v.

```
                                       -griffithianum 1/8
                          -Loderi King George-
              -Olympic Lady-            -fortunei 3/8
BESSIE-              -williamsianum 1/4
FARMER-    -fortunei
        -Fawn-    -dichroanthum 1/8
              -Fabia-
                   -griersonianum 1/8
```
3ft(.9m) OF(-18C) ML A compact mound. Fragrant, flat-faced
flower; pale pink buds opening pure white. Childers, reg. 1971.

BETA--form of lanigerum
Flowers rose-opal. Sir Edward Bolitho, reg. 1963.

```
        -griersonianum 1/2
BETELGEUSE-
        -Madame Colijn--unknown 1/2
```
Flowers of salmon pink. G. Reuthe, 1940.

```
                                   -thomsonii 1/8
                          -Bagshot Ruby-
              -Princess Elizabeth-            -unknown 3/8
BETSIE -              -unknown
 BALCOM-        -forrestii Repens Group 1/4
        -Elizabeth-
              -griersonianum 1/4
```
4ft(1.2m) OF(-18C) ML 3/4   Flowers openly funnel-shaped, of
5 wavy lobes, currant red. Conical truss 6in(15.2cm) broas, 13-
flowered. Plant dense, rounded, branching well; leaves bullate,
retained 3 years; new growth tinged red. McGuire, reg. 1977.

```
* * * * * * * * * * * * * * * * * * * * * * * * * * *
                    -catawbiense var. album Glass--Catalgla 1/4
          -Cataldi-
BETSY KRUSON-        -wardii 1/4
          -          -griffithianum 1/4
          -Mars-
                    -unknown 1/4
4ft(1.2m) -10F(-23C) ML 3/3  Flowers reddish purple, shading
to white in throat, small grayed yellow flare.  Conical truss of
10, 6in(15.2cm) wide.  Large leaves.   Mrs. Yates, reg. 1976.
JACK OWEN YATES    Parentage:  (Catalgla x wardii) X Mars
3ft(.9m) -10F(-23C) ML   Upright plant with arching branches.
Flowers light burgundy red paling to a white center, with 2 yel-
low flares.  Conical truss of 12-13.  Mrs. Yates, reg. 1976.
* * * * * * * * * * * * * * * * * * * * * * * * * * * *
```

BETSY TROTWOOD   Parentage unknown
A parent of MARS NOVUS, a hybrid by Seidel before 1880. Flowers
rose red.   Standish & Noble, before 1860.

```
                    -forrestii Repens Group 1/4
          -Elizabeth ?-
BETTER HALF-        -griersonianum 1/4
          -unknown 1/2
3ft(.9m) OF(-18C) EM 3/4    Attractive red trusses.  Dense,
compact foliage.  The "better half" of two seedlings once grow-
ing together as one in Whitney Gardens.   The Sathers.
```

```
* * * * * * * * * * * * * * * * * * * * * * * * * * *
     -fortunei 1/2
BETTY-
     -thomsonii 1/2
Deep pink flowers.  Loder.  A.M. 1927.
HULLABALLO    Parentage as above
Rose Bengal flowers, paler at edges, a small cardinal red blotch
in throat;  darker staining on reverse.  Loose trusses of 10-12.
Sir E. Loder cross; Hon. H. E. Boscawen, reg. 1974.  A.M. 1974.
* * * * * * * * * * * * * * * * * * * * * * * * * * * *
```

```
* * * * * * * * * * * * * * * * * * * * * * * * * * * *
                    -fortunei--Sir Charles Butler 1/4
          -Van Nes Sensation-
          -          -          -griffithianum 1/4
          -          -Halopeanum-
BETTY     -                    -maximum 1/8
 ANDERSON-          -griffithianum
          -     -Mars-
          -unnamed-    -unknown 1/4
           hybrid-
                    -Purple Splendour-
                              -ponticum 1/8
                              -unknown
5ft(1.5m) 10F(-12C) M    Buds reddish purple; flowers amethyst
violet, the reverse darker, and striped; truss of 10.  Plant up-
right, 3/4 as wide as tall.  Edwin (Ted) Anderson, reg. 1983.
BONNIE SNAZA  Parentage as above
Large lilac purple flowers, heavily spotted ruby red.  Plant 2/3
as wide as tall; well-branched.  E. Anderson, reg. 1983.
* * * * * * * * * * * * * * * * * * * * * * * * * * *
```

BETTY ARRINGTON   Parentage unknown
5ft(1.5m) -15F(-26C) VL 4/3   Good plant habit; large, showy
leaves. Fragrant flowers of rose madder, ruby red flare. Truss
of 17. Dexter cross; selected by Arrington; reg. 1972. Color
illus. HG p. 75.

BETTY BOULTER   Described under JOAN BYE, q.v.

```
     -smirnowii 1/2
BETTY BREENE-
          -Fluffy Ruffles F2, Dexter hybrid--unknown 1/2
4ft(1.2m) -25F(-32C) ML 2/4  Plant compact, well-branched, as
wide as tall; nice foliage.  Large trusses of pale pink, flushed
mauve; too few flowers caused its withdrawal.  Leach, reg. 1962.
```

BETTY GRAHAM--form of anthopogon L & S 1091
1ft(.3m) -5F(-21C) EM 3/3   Flowers narrowly tubular, of five
small joined lobes, very fragrant, of rose purplish pink, deeper
toward base. Truss of 8-10. Aromatic leaves; dense, dark brown
scales beneath. P. Cox of Glendoick, reg. 1970 A.M. 1969.

```
          -fortunei ? 1/2
BETTY HUME-
          -unknown 1/2
```

5ft(1.5m) -5F(-21C) ML 4/4 Flowers pink, ruffled, fragrant,
to 4in(10.2cm) across.   Dexter cross; Baldsiefen raiser; Efing-
er, reg. 1963. Color illus. Cox pl. 17.

```
                    -fortunei 1/4
          -Luscombei-
BETTY KING-        -thomsonii 3/4
          -thomsonii
Various clones, red to rose pink.  RIGHT ROYAL, a fine dark red.
Sir James Horlick, intro. 1942.
```

BETTY STEWART   Parentage unknown
Flowers of cherry red, spotted and suffused white, on the upper
lobes. C. B. van Nes & Sons. A.M. 1936.

```
* * * * * * * * * * * * * * * * * * * * * * * * * * * *
                    -aureum (chrysanthum) 1/4
          -unnamed hybrid-
          -          -maximum 1/4    -neriiflorum
BETTY WHITE-        -Nereid-
          -     -Phyllis Ballard-  -dichroanthum 1/16
          -unnamed hyb.-        -fortunei ssp. discolor 1/8
                    -catawbiense--Clark's White 1/4
Buds a mixture of currant red and primrose yellow; frilled flow-
ers a blend of lighter yellow and strong post office red.  Delp.
CAT'S PAJAMAS   Parentage as above
Buds blend of brilliant to light greenish yellow, strong to med-
ium orange-red.  Flowers light chartreuse green, dorsal spotting
strong lettuce green; throat brilliant greenish yellow.   Delp.
DANDY ANDY   Parentage as above
Vivid cherry red in bud, opening to pale orange-yellow, edged in
vivid red.  Flower slowly fades to white.  W. Delp.
JOYCE HARRIS   Parentage as above
5ft(1.5m) -15C(-26C)  Deep yellowish pink buds open pale pink,
edged in strong rose pink; light yellow-green throat.  W. Delp.
YELLOW DATE   Parentage as above
5ft(1.5m) -15F(-26C)  Yellow flowers; medium-sized bush.  Delp.
* * * * * * * * * * * * * * * * * * * * * * * * * * * *
```

```
* * * * * * * * * * * * * * * * * * * * * * * * * * * *
                    -griffithianum 1/4
          -George Hardy-
BETTY WORMALD-     -catawbiense 1/4
          -red hybrid--unknown 1/2
6ft(1.8m) -5F(-21C) M 4/3    Very large, almost flat, pastel
pink flowers, pale center, light purple spotting, in huge, dome-
shaped trusses.  Plant upright, spreading; large foliage.   M.
Koster, before 1922.   A.M. 1935  F.C.C. Wisley Trials 1964.
A.G.M. 1969.  Color illus. JS p. 62; VV p. 58.
MARINUS KOSTER   Parentage as above
Similar to above, with a more spreading and compact habit.  Rich
crimson buds open rose pink,  heavy brown spots on upper petals;
flowers campanulate, 5in(12.7cm) wide, in huge trusses of 10-12.
Sun-tolerant; pest-resistant.  M. Koster, 1937.   F.C.C. 1948.
Color illus. JS p. 86.
* * * * * * * * * * * * * * * * * * * * * * * * * * * *
```

```
          -campylogynum 1/2
BETTY'S BELLS-
          -racemosum 1/2
4ft(1.2m) -5F(-21C) EM 4/4  Like racemosum with buds along
stem.  Vivid pink flowers; small olive green leaves with reddish
stem.  Betty Shedy raiser; T. Skei intro.  Col. ill. HG p. 87.
```

BETTY'S PURPLE RUSSATUM   See NIGHT EDITOR

```
                    -dichroanthum 3/16
          -Dido-
     -unnamed-   -decorum 3/16  -fortunei ssp. discolor
     - hybrid-       -Lady     -                1/16
     -     -Jalisco-Bessborough-campylocarpum Elatum 1/16
BEVERLEY-     -     -dichroanthum
TASKER -     -Dido-
     -          -decorum
     -     -Sarita-griersonianum 1/8
     -     - Loder-   -griffithianum 5/64
     -Yellow-   -Loderi-
     Creek-          -fortunei 9/64
     -          -wardii 1/8          -griffithianum
     -Idealist-          -Kewense-
     -          -Aurora-     -fortunei
     -Naomi-     -thomsonii 1/32
          -fortunei
```

4ft(1.2m) 14F(-10C) M   Frilled flowers of ripe lemon yellow,
green in base of throat, 3in(7.6cm) across; pink stamens, green
pistil. Loose truss of 7-11. Floriferous, broad plant; foliage
rather glossy, medium green.   H. R. Tasker, NZ, reg. 1978.

BEVERLY HARVEY   Parentage unknown
Funnel-shaped flowers of Persian rose, in upright trusses of 12.
Trequa Coen cross; C. Fawcett, reg. 1966.

* *
                              -catawbiense 1/8
            -unnamed hybrid-   -dichroanthum 5/64
            -                -Fabia-
         -Ginny-   -griersonianum 7/64
         - Mae -   -yakushimanum 1/4
         -     -   -fortunei
         -   -Si Si-   -Lady   -ssp. discolor 3/64
         -     -   -Day -Bessborough-
         -     -Gold -Dream-   -campylocarpum
BEWILDERED-   Mohur-   -   Elatum Gp. 1/64
         -          -   -griersonianum
         -          -   -fortunei ssp. discolor
         -        -Margaret Dunn-   -dichroanthum
         -                     -Fabia-
         -                          -griersonianum
         -          -smirnowii 1/8
         -       -Oh My-
         -unnamed hybrid-   -yakushimanum
                     -aureum 1/4
Strong red-purple buds open to a mixture of medium to soft red-
purple (spirea red); white throat and flare. Dorsal spotting of
moderate olive green.   W. Delp.
DOUBLE TROUBLE   Parentage as above
Buds deep ruby red; flowers full hose-in-hose, pale purplish
pink with dorsal spotting of deep red.   W. Delp.
* *

              -racemosum 1/4
        -Racil-
BEWITCHED-   -ciliatum 1/4
        -mucronulatum--Cornell Pink 1/2
4ft(1.2m) OF(-18C) E 3/3   Upright plant; leaves 1.5in(3.8cm)
x .5in(1.3cm), persistent. Flowers 2in(5cm) wide, light purple-
pink; 2 5 per spherical truss. Guttormson, reg. 1968.

BIANCA   Parentage unknown
Different forms exist--salmon pink, delicate crimson, pure white
with yellow spots. Bull. F.C.C. 1866.

* *
            -catawbiense 3/4
       -Mrs. Milner-
BIBBER-   -unknown 1/4
       -catawbiense
Flowers carmine red with faint brown markings. T. J. R. Seidel,
cross 1900.
GRANAT   Parentage as above
Ruby red flowers, with pale marks on lighter background; frilly,
Seidel, intro. 1905.
* *

       -Moser's Maroon--unknown 1/2
BIBIANI-
       -arboreum 1/2
6ft(1.8m) 5F(-15C) E 4/4   Bright, blood red flowers in early
spring. Trusses of 14, dense and rounded. Foliage very glossy.
A vigorous plant; easy to propagate. Rothschild. A.M. 1934.

        -grande 1/2
BIG BEN-
        -unknown 1/2
Red flowers, in trusses of 23-28. J. Beekman, reg. 1980.

                        -catawbiense 1/4
            -unnamed hybrid-
        -Pinnacle-   -unknown 3/4
        -          -   -catawbiense
BIG BOY-   -unnamed hybrid-
        -                    -unknown
        -Brown Eyes--unknown
Large pink flowers, with a heavy blotch.   Hardy to -25F(-32C).
Robert Blough.

                                      -catawbiense
                  -Parsons Grandiflorum-   1/32
            -America-   -unknown 6/32
            -        -dark red hybrid--unknown
         -Cindy-   -griffithianum 3/32
       - Lou -   -Mars-
     -Source- -unnamed- -unknown
     - Bank -   hybrid-catawbiense var. rubrum 1/16
     -       -   -griffithianum
     -       -   -Mars-
BIG BUCKS-   -Captain Jack- -unknown
     -               -facetum (eriogynum) 1/8
     -                -aureum (chrysanthum) 1/8
     -    -unnamed hybrid-
     -White Dove-   -maximum 1/8
            -catawbiense var. album Glass--Catalgla 1/4
Buds of moderate and strong purplish reds open to a blending of
deep and pale purplish pinks, dark red stigma. Strong purplish
pink on the reverse. Weldon Delp.

* *
       -Dorothy Russell (Dexter)--unknown 7/8
BIG DADDY-   -catawbiense 1/8
        -Parsons Grandiflorum-
     -America-   -unknown
            -dark red hybrid--unknown
A blend of deep reds, cardinal and ruby, in bud. Flowers strong
to moderate purplish red and pink; ruby red spotting. B. Schram
cross; W. Delp raiser..
BRIAN SCHRAM   Parentage as above
Cardinal red buds open to frilled flowers of cardinal red, with
dorsal spots of ruby red; throat pale greenish yellow.   Schram
cross; W. Delp raiser.
* *

BIG DEAL (Delp)   See DELP'S BIG DEAL

BIG DEAL Parentage unknown; elepidote; low white hybrid F2
2ft(.6m) -20F(-29C) ML   Flowers pale yellow, dark greenish
yellow blotch; ball truss 8in(15cm) wide. Low, spreading, dense
habit.   E. Mezitt cross; Weston Nurseries, reg. 1988.

          -C.O.D.--white Dexter hybrid--unknown 1/2
BIG GIRL-   -fortunei ssp. discolor 1/4
        -Avocet-
          -fortunei 1/4
3ft(.9m) -10F(-23C) ML   Tubular funnel-shaped flowers of pale
purplish pink with an olive green blotch. Loose trusses, 7.5in.
(19cm) wide, hold about 11. Howard Phipps, intro. 1973.

       -catawbiense var. album--La Bar's White 1/2
BIG MAC-
       -macabeanum 1/2
Barium yellow flowers, with a dark red blotch; trusses of 11-12.
Mrs. J. Knippenberg, cross 1955; reg. 1977.

BIG MAMA   Parentage unknown
5ft(1.5m) OF(-18C) M   Very large, pink flowers.   Whitney.

* *
                -catawbiense var. album Glass--Catalgla 1/2
BIG-O---CALTWINS, F2-   -catawbiense 1/4
                 -Pink Twins-
                      -haematodes 1/4
5ft(1.5m) -15F(-26C) L   Buds of phlox purple open to lighter
flowers, fading white, with a beetroot purple blotch on upper 3
lobes. Weldon Delp.
GINNY HILEMAN   Parentage as above
Buds ruby red to magenta rose, open to frilled flowers of magno-
lia purple, with white flare; dark greenish yellow dorsal spots.
Weldon Delp.
RENEE SHIREY   Parentage as above
Buds of magnolia purple and rhodamine purple; flowers roseine to
rhodamine purple; dorsal spots of vivid yellow-green.   W. Delp.
* *

```
                                  -griffithianum 9/16
                     -Beauty of Tremough-
          -Norman Gill-                  -arboreum 1/16
       -Anna-              -griffithianum
       -                              -griffithianum
BIG RED-    -Jean Marie de Montague-
       -                        -unknown 1/8
       -                       -griffithianum
       -Loderi Pink Diamond-
                        -fortunei 1/4
```
5ft(1.5m) 5F(-15C) M 4/4   Large conical trusses of currant
red flowers; truss of 12-18. Deep green leaves, with new growth
bronze red.   Nielson cross; Mrs. J. E. Sinclair, reg. 1984.

BIG SAM   A parent of GALA.   Listed under NASELLE, q.v.

```
                     -catawbiense var. album Glass--Catalgla
          unnamed hybrid-                                1/4
       -                      -fortunei 1/4
BIG SAVAGE-                  -decorum ? 1/8
       -        -Caroline-
       -Cadis-          -brachycarpum ssp. brachycarpum ? 1/8
                -fortunei ssp. discolor 1/4
```
5.5ft(1.7m) -10F(-23C) ML Flowers lavender-pink with greenish
throat, widely funnel-shaped and 5- or 6-lobed; trusses hold 13.
Plant dense, vigorous, large glossy foliage.   Yates, reg. 1972.

BIG SAVAGE RED   Described under LEAH YATES, q.v.

```
                                        -thomsonii
                         -Bagshot Ruby-    1/16
             -Princess Elizabeth-        -unknown
       -Betsie Balcom-              -unknown 1/4
       -            -           -forrestii Repens Group 1/8
       -            -Elizabeth-
BIG SHOT-                -griersonianum 1/8
       -                      -Pygmalion--unknown
       -              -unnamed hybrid-
       -       -Weldy-              -haematodes 1/16
       -unnamed-    -yakushimanum, Exbury form 1/8
        hybrid-          -yakushimanum 1/8
             -Serendipity-
                    -aureum (chrysanthum) 1/8
```
Buds of strong purplish red and cardinal red, opening to flowers
of vivid purplish red and deep purplish pink; exterior of strong
purplish red.   Al Smith cross; W. Delp raiser.
PAINTED DOLL   Parentage as above
Buds of cardinal red open to flowers of pale purplish pink edged
with strong red; reverse strong red. Smith cross; Delp raiser.
* *
* *

```
            -catawbiense var. album Glass--Catalgla 1/2
BIG SPLASH-                  -griffithianum 1/4
            -Lady de Rothschild-
                        -Sappho--unknown 1/4
```
Buds of ruby red and magenta rose open to flowers of light pur-
plish pink and phlox purple; dorsal spots of dark red and medium
purplish red; throat pale greenish yellow. W. Delp.
HIP HIP ARRAY Parentage as above
Buds of roseine purple and strong reddish purple open to flowers
of mallow purple, edged in deep to strong purplish pinks; dorsal
spots of deep greenish yellow.   W. Delp.
* *

```
          -yakushimanum (collected wild) 1/2
BIG WIG-
          -catawbiense var. album Glass--Catalgla 1/2
```
Buds moderate to pale purplish pink.   White flowers, with light
green dorsal spots.   Weldon Delp.

```
          -catawbiense--La Bar's White 1/2
BIG WILLY-
          -williamsianum 1/2
```
5ft(1.5m) -10F(-23C) M 3/4 Very large white flowers. Shrub
has the rounded foliage of williamsianum.   Mrs. J. Knippenberg.

```
          -yakushimanum, Exbury form
BIG YAK-
          -uncertain: selfed?
```
8ft(2.4m) x 10ft(3m)(19 yrs) -10F(-23C) M   Possible hybrid of
yakushimanum.   Deep purplish pink buds open cherry red, fading
pink, to white; flowers 2.3in(6cm) broad, with red-brown dorsal

blotch. Tall trusses of 10-21. Large, dark foliage, orange indumentum. A massive plant, covered with trusses. See also SAM-
ISEN. B. Nelson cross, 1965; Mrs. Hill, reg. 1986.

```
          -caucasicum 1/2
BIJOU-
          -unknown 1/2
```
Introduced by Moser, 1914.

```
          -Mrs. J. G. Millais--unknown 1/2
BILL BOWEN-
          -catawbiense, white form--La Bar's White 1/2
```
6ft(1.8m) x 6ft(24 yrs) -22F(-30C) ML Pinkish mauve buds open
mauve-white, fading white. Funnel-shaped flowers, of heavy substance, 3.5in(9cm) wide, a large dorsal blotch of strong citron
green. Large trusses of 14-18. Wm. Fetterhoff, reg. 1987.

BILL BROWNING--form of mallotum Farrer 815
Trusses of 12 crimson flowers.   Raiser Col. S. R. Clarke; R. N.
S. Clarke, reg. 1978.   A.M. 1933.

```
                          -Parsons      -catawbiense 1/8
                -America- Grandiflorum-
                -        -            -unknown 1/2
          -Vivacious-    -dark red hybrid--unknown
          -        -      -grier. 1/16    -arboreum 1/64
          -        -Dr. Ross-   -Doncaster-
          -        -         -Borde-        -unknown
       -unnamed-             Hill-        -griffithianum
       - hybrid-              -Mrs. A.M.-         7/64
       -        -              Williams -unknown
       -        -America (as above)
BILL -    -Cindy Lou-
McKEE-         -           -griffithianum
       -        -unnamed-Mars-
       -          hybrid-  -unknown
       -                  -catawbiense var. rubrum 3/16
       -Cindy Lou (as above)
```
Buds of dark red and currant red. Flowers cardinal red and deep
red.   W. Delp.

BILL MAGNESS--form of macrophyllum
4ft(1.2m) x 4ft(8 yrs after graft) 0F(-18C) M Widely funnel-
shaped flowers, 20 per truss, yellowish white with yellow-green
blotch, yellowish green spotting. Collected wild; Britt Smith,
reg. 1987.

```
          -ciliatum var. bergii 1/2
BILL MASSEY-
          -nuttallii 1/2
```
4ft(1.2m) 20F(-7C) EM 4/3 Synonym NUTBERGER. Buds apricot-
pink, open to tubular funnel-shaped flowers, near-white; reverse
slightly pink. Very fragrant. Trusses of 5.   Drucker cross,
1973; Trillium Lane Nursery intro.; B. Vaerlen, reg. 1977.

BILLY BEAR   Described under AMBIE, q.v.

BILLY BOY   Described under VIET VET, q.v.

```
               -haematodes 1/4
          -May Day-
BILLY BUDD-       -griersonianum 1/4
          -elliottii 1/2
```
3ft(.9m) 0F(-18C) M 3/4 Flat, dense trusses of 10 to 12 waxy
red flowers. Leaves slightly wavy, with traces of tomentum. F.
Hanger cross; RHS Garden, Wisley intro. 1954.   A.M. 1957.

```
                              -arboreum 1/16
                    -Doncaster-
          -unnamed hybrid-       -unknown 1/4
          -        -        -     -neriiflorum 1/16
          -        -        -Nereid-
       -Witch Doctor-        -dichroanthum 1/16
       -        -        -griffithianum 1/16
       -        -    -Mars-
BILLY -        -Vulcan-  -unknown
STIELER-           -griersonianum 1/8
       -              -griffithianum 1/8
       -        -Mars-
       -Captain Jack-  -unknown
                -facetum (eriogynum) 1/4
```
3.5ft(1m) x 4ft(1.2m)(15 yrs) 0F(-18C) EM   Vivid red flowers

with wide rim of currant red, and deeper red spotting. Truss of
10. Leaves medium olive green, held 3 years. Plant wider than
tall, well-branched. P. Holden, reg. 1985.

```
              -wightii 1/4
         -China-
BINFIELD-       -fortunei 1/4
    -       -wardii 1/4
         -Crest-              -fortunei ssp. discolor 1/8
              -Lady Bessborough-
                             -campylocarpum Elatum Group 1/8
```
5ft(1.5m) -10F(-23C) EM 4/4   Flowers primrose yellow, slight
red stain in throat. About 17 in round trusses. Leaf 6in(15cm)
by 2.5in(6.4cm). Crown Estate, Windsor, reg. 1965.   A.M. 1964.

```
                   -fortunei 13/16
              -Kewense-
         -Aurora-        -griffithianum 1/16
    -Naomi-       -thomsonii 1/8
BIRTHDAY-        -fortunei
GREETING-
         -fortunei
```
5ft(1.5m) -5F(-21C) M 4/4   Yellow-orange flowers, diffusing
toward edges to red-purple; deep red markings in throat. Truss
of 6-7 flowers. E. de Rothschild; reg. 1979. A.M. 1979.

```
         -fortunei ssp. discolor 1/2
BISCUIT BOX-
         -elliottii 1/2
```
Flowers barium yellow, fading outward to empire yellow, outside
tinged pink; trusses of 10. Corolla openly funnel-shaped. F.
Hanger cross; RHS Garden, Wisley, reg. 1965. A.M. 1964.

```
                        -fortunei ssp. discolor 1/4
              -Lady Bessborough-
    -Jalisco-                -campylocarpum Elatum 1/4
    - Elect -
    -       -    -dichroanthum 1/8
BISHOPSGATE-      -Dido-
    -              -decorum 1/8
    -       -wardii 1/4
    -Crest-              fortunei ssp. discolor
              -Lady Bessborough-
                             -campylocarpum Elatum Group
```
5ft(1.5m) -10F(-23C) L   Openly campanulate flowers of yellow,
variably flushed red, blotched upper throat. Full rounded truss
holds 10-12. Crown Estate Commissioners, reg. 1974. P.C. 1974.

```
    -cinnabarinum Roylei Group 1/2
BISKRA-
    -ambiguum 1/2)
```
5ft(1.5m) 5F(-15C) M 4/3   An erect, slender bush growing to
15ft(4.6m), bearing distinctive trumpets of vermilion blended to
biscuit; lax trusses of 5. Other forms exist. Rothschild, 1934.
A.M. 1940. Color illus. ARS Q 27:2 (1973), p. 102.

BISMARCK   Described under ALBERT, q.v.

```
                        -griffithianum 1/16
              -George Hardy-
         -Mrs. Lindsay Smith-    -catawbiense 1/16
    -Diane-              -Duchess of Edinburgh--unknown 1/4
    -       -              -campylocarpum 3/8
BITTER-    -unnamed hybrid-
 LEMON-              -unknown
    -              -campylocarpum
    -Gladys Rose-
              -fortunei 1/4
```
Pale primrose with a red blotch. Waterer & Crisp, reg. 1975.

```
                   -ponticum 5/8
              -Purple Splendour-
    -Anah Kruschke-        -unknown 3/8
BLACK EYE-        -ponticum
    -              -ponticum
    -Purple Splendour-
              -unknown
```
5ft(1.5m) -10F(-23C) ML 4/4   Red-purple flowers, deep black
eye in upper lobe. Greer, intro. 1982.

* *
```
              -griffithianum 5/16
         -Jean Marie -
         - de Montague-unknown 7/16
BLACK MAGIC-                   -griffithianum
         -              -Queen Wilhelmina-
         -    -Britannia-              -unknown
         -Leo-        -Stanley Davies--unknown
              -elliottii 1/4
```
4ft(1.2m) -5F(-21C) ML 4/4   Unusual blackish red flowers in
late spring; abundant foliage, matte forest green. Floriferous.
Greer, intro. 1982.
HEAT WAVE   Parentage as above
5ft(1.5m) -5F(-21C) ML 4/3   Large, upright trusses of deep
blood red flowers. Strong growth habit; medium to large leaves
of deep forest green, a strong contrast to the trusses. Greer,
intro. 1982.
* *

```
              -thomsonii 1/2
BLACK PRINCE-
    -              -Moser's Maroon--unknown 1/4
         -Romany Chal, F.C.C. form-
                   -facetum 1/4
```
5ft(1.5m) OF(-18C) ML 4/2   Oxblood red flowers in trusses of
15-16. Lester Brandt, reg. 1962.

BLACK PRINCE'S RUBY   Described under OPORTO, q.v.

BLACK SPORT   Parentage unknown
5ft(1.5m) -5F(-21C) ML 3/3   Deep green foliage; unusual red-
purple flowers, held in tight trusses. Fall blooming possible.
Nelson and Briggs, intro.

BLACK SATIN   Described under P.J.M., q.v.

```
         -dichroanthum 1/2
BLACK STRAP-
         -sanguineum ssp. didymum 1/2
```
Flowers of deep blood red. Sunningdale Nurseries, 1951.

BLACKHILLS--form of lacteum
5ft(1.5m) -5F(-21C) EM 4/4   Flowers primrose yellow without
blotch or spots. S. V. Christie, reg. 1966.   F.C.C. 1965.

* *
```
         -Essex Scarlet--unknown 1/2
BLACKIE-
         -brachycarpum ? 1/2
```
4ft(1.2m) -5F(-21C) ML 3/3   Very dark red flowers, with an
unusual fruity fragrance. Joseph Gable.
KENTUCKY CARDINAL Parentage as above
4ft(1.2m) -15F(-26C) ML 2/3   Small flowers of very dark red.
Attractive dark green foliage; open habit. Gable, before 1958.
* *

```
              -Moser's Maroon--unknown 1/2
BLACKIE (Henny)-        -sanguineum ssp. didymum 1/4
         -Arthur Osborn-
                   -griersonianum 1/4
```
Cardinal red flowers. R. Henny, reg. 1961. Color illus. ARS Q
31:2 (1977), p. 103.

BLACKWATER--form of spinuliferum
4ft(1.2m) 5F(-15C) EM 3/3   Superior Turkey red tubular flowers, greenish white at base. Filaments white, anthers black.
Free of stamens. Brodick Castle, reg. 1977. A.M. 1977.

```
                   -griffithianum 1/2
         -Gauntlettii-
BLANC DE CHINE-        -unknown 1/4
    -         -griffithianum
         -Loderi-
              -fortunei 1/4
```
Flowers light pink to white. Two hybrids are named GAUNTLETTII;
one may have the same parentage as LODER'S WHITE. Ingram, 1939.

* *
```
                   -griffithianum 1/4
         -Godesberg-
BLANC-MANGE-        -unknown 1/4
    -auriculatum 1/2
```

Flowers of pure white, openly funnel-shaped, frilled at margins,
held in a well-poised truss of 18. Shrub to 15-20ft(4.5-6m) and
as broad as high.   Rothschild, 1934. A.M. 1947.
SWAN LAKE Parentage as above, except reversed
A tall plant and equally as wide, with large matte green leaves.
White flowers similar to BLANC-MANGE.   Rothschild, 1955.
* *

```
                           -neriiflorum 1/16
                    -Nereid-
               -unnamed-         -dichroanthum 1/16
          -Blazen- hybrid-
          - Sun -       -fortunei ssp. discolor 1/8
BLANCHE BROWNING-   -             -maximum 1/8
          -    -Russell Harmon-
          -                -catawbiense 3/8
          -                -cataubiense
          -Mrs. Charles S. Sargent-
                          -unknown 1/4
```
Hardy to -15F(-26C). Flowers of medium pink, edges deeper pink,
with light centers.   O. Pride cross; Dr. J. Browning raiser.

* *
```
               -cataubiense 5/8
BLANDYANUM-                    -cataubiense
               -unnamed hybrid-
          -Altaclerense-          -ponticum 1/8
                    -arboreum 1/4
```
Rosy crimson flowers, 25 in a dense truss; midseason. Elliptic
leaves with gray-felted petioles; shrub dense, rounded. Stand-
ish and Noble.   Silver Knightian Medal, 1848.
TOWARDII Parentage as above
Flowers light rose, or a rosy lilac.   Standish & Noble, 1850.
* *

BLANDFORDIAEFLORUM---form of cinnabarinum
Orange-yellow, tubular flowers. Origin unknown.   A.M. 1945.

```
          -augustinii--Tower Court
BLANEY'S BLUE-                -intricatum 1/8
          -          -Intrifast-
          -Blue Diamond-      -fastigiatum 1/8
                    -augustinii 3/4
```
5ft(1.5m) -5F(-21C) EM 4/4   Vigorous plant, masses of misty
blue flowers. Dense foliage, forest green in summer, and bronze
in winter.   Blaney cross; R. Ticknor, intro. 1978.

```
          -wardii 1/4
     -Babette-
     -     -yakushimanum--Koichiro Wada 1/4
BLANKA-         -cataubiense 1/16
     -         -Humboldt-
     -    -Hachmann's-    -unknown 3/8
     -unnamed- Ornament -         -fortunei 1/16
       hybrid-    -Direcktor E. Hjelm-
       -                -unknown
          -Furnivall's Daughter--unknown
```
2.5ft(.75m) x 3.3ft(1m) -15F(-26C) ML   Campanulate flowers in
trusses of 10-15, 6- or 7-lobed, white, tinged moderate purplish
red to dark purplish pink.   Hachmann cross; Stück, reg. 1988.

* *
```
          -russatum 1/4
     -Azurika-
BLAUBART-    -impeditum 1/4
     -         -augustinii 1/4
     -Blue Tit Magor-
               -impeditum 1/4
```
2ft(.6m) x 3ft(.9m) -10F(-23C) M   Flowers in trusses of 4-6,
light violet, with dorsal spotting of strong purple.   Hachmann,
cross 1978; Stück, reg. 1988.
BLAUMEISE Parentage as above
1.5ft(.45m) x 2ft(.6m) -10F(-23C) M   Flowers in trusses of 4-
6, with 5 wavy-edged lobes of brilliant purplish blue to light
violet throughout, unmarked.   Hachmann cross; Stück, reg. 1988.
BLUMIRIA Parentage as above
Dense habit with flowering season mid- to late May. Flowers in
trusses of 4-6, vivid purple to light violet, unmarked. Dark
green leaf, margins recurved.   Hachmann cross; Stück, reg. 1988.
* *

* *
```
          -griffithianum 1/4
     -Mars-
BLAZE-    -unknown 1/4
     -cataubiense, red form   1/2
```
4ft(1.2m) -25F(-32C) M 2/3   Funnel-shaped flowers of strong
red, rims deeper, light pink blotch; firm truss of 16-18. Foliage medium- sized; dull red, downy petioles.   Leach, reg. 1960.
YATES ALBINO Parentage as above, except reversed
4ft(1.2m) -10F(-23C) ML   Plant as broad as tall; leaves maple
green, 5.25in(13.3cm) long. Lax truss of 11 flowers, white with
spotted blotch of medium apple green.   Mrs. Yates, reg. 1976.
JACK SWIFT Parentage: (cataubiense x MARS), selfed
5ft(1.5m) x 7.5ft(23 yrs) -10F(-23C) M   Openly funnel-shaped
flowers, 5-lobed, vivid purplish red with pale yellow center; 18
per truss, 6.5in(16.5cm) across.   L. Yavorsky, reg. 1987.
* *
* *
```
               -neriiflorum 1/8
          -Nereid-
     -unnamed hybrid-    -dichroanthum 1/8
BLAZEN SUN-         -fortunei ssp. discolor 1/4
     -              -maximum 1/4
     -Russell Harmon-
               -cataubiense 1/4
```
Other spellings: BLAZING SUN, BLASEN SUN. Large trusses of
brilliant orange-red, in mid-season. Plant habit attractive;
hardy to -15F(-26C).   Leach cross; Pride raiser; named 1976.
BLONDIE Parentage as above
5ft(1.5m) -12F(-24C) ML   Pale yellow flowers; compact, slow-
growing shrub. Used as parent for other yellows.   Pride, 1969.
PEACHES AND CREAM Parentage as above
6ft(1.8m) -10F(-23C) ML   Pale pink and yellow flowers. Plant
of good habit.   Pride, 1970.
PINK MANGO Parentage as above
5ft(1.5m) -10F(-23C) ML   Good plant habit, with flowers of a
stunning coral pink. D. Leach cross; Pride raiser; intro. 1970.
Color illus. ARS Q 34:3 (1980), 143.
* *
```
          -smirnowii 1/4
     -Oh My!-
BLAZING PETALS-    -yakushimanum 1/4      -thomsonii 1/8
     -              -Bagshot Ruby-
     -Princess Elizabeth-    -unknown 3/8
               -unknown
```
Buds of ruby red and magenta rose, opening to fuchsia purple and
light purplish pink; dorsal spots of deep red.   Weldon Delp.

```
                         -facetum (eriogynum)
          -unnamed-unnamed hybrid-
     -Dopey- hybrid-         -unknown
     -    -    -    -dichroanthum
     -    -    -Fabia-
     -    -         -griersonianum
BLAZING RED-    -         -yakushimanum
     -    -unnamed hybrid-         -dichroanthum
     -         -Fabia Tangerine-
     -              -griersonianum
     -Al Smith (for parentage see AL SMITH main entry)
```
Buds of cardinal red and currant red; frilled flowers of currant
red and vivid red; dorsal spots cardinal red.   Weldon Delp.

```
                         -arboreum 1/16
               -Grand Arab-
          -unnamed hybrid-    -cataubiense 1/16
     -John Coutts-    -griffithianum 1/4
BLESSED-    -griersonianum 1/2
  EVENT -    -griersonianum
     -Sarita Loder-    -griffithianum
          -Loderi-
               -fortunei 1/8
```
Flower Tyrian rose, cherry spots; truss of 9.   Lyons, reg. 1962.

```
     -roxieanum 1/2
BLEWBURY-
     -maculiferum ssp. anhweiense 1/2
```
2ft(.6m) 0F(-18C) M 3/4   Flowers white, throat spotted reddish purple; rather tight, full truss of 19. Leaves convex like
roxieanum, lightly covered with pale brown indumentum. Crown
Estate, Windsor, reg. 1969. A.M. 1968. F.C.C. 1983.

BLIND DATE   Parentage unknown
6ft(1.8m) -5F(-21C) ML Fragrant flowers, 6-lobed, rosy pink,
shading to a yellow center with a small, rusty brown eye. Whitney cross; Sather, reg. 1975.

* *
                                    -catawbiense 1/8
                    -Parsons Grandiflorum-
            -Nova Zembla-   -unknown 5/8
BLINKLICHT-   -dark red hybrid--unknown
            -              -griffithianum 1/4
            -Mars-
                    -unknown
Trusses of 15-21 flowers, rich cardinal red, slight marks of ox-
blood red. Hairy, elliptic leaves. H. Hachmann, cross 1960; G.
Stück, reg. 1983. Color illus. WS, 1989, p. 122.
HACHMANN'S FEUERSCHEIN (Firelight) Parentage as above.
Large scarlet flowers, brown spots, white-tipped anthers; truss
of 14. Bush 5ft(1.5m) at maturity; dense foliage. Hardy to -17
F(-27C). Stück, reg. 1983. Col. ill. ARS J 39:1 (1985), p. 19.
HACHMANN'S LAGERFEUER Parentage as above
Flowers in trusses of 14-16, strong red. Stück, reg. 1984.
NICOLINE   Parentage as above
Flowers in trusses of 16-18, 5-lobed, deep red. Hachmann, cross
1960; Stück, reg. 1984.
SAMMETGLUT (Velvet Glow)   Parentage as above, except reversed
Trusses of 16-21 flowers, 5-lobed, bright cardinal red, conspic-
uous anthers of light peach. Hairy leaves. Stück, reg. 1983.
Color illus. WS, 1989, p. 139.
* *

    -haematodes 1/2
BLITZ-
    -G. A. Sims--unknown 1/2
3ft(.9m) 5F(-15C) M 3/4 Very dark red. Plant floriferous,
dense, mound-like. Admirable little hybrid. R. Clark, 1945.

* *
                            -smirnowii 1/8
                -unnamed hybrid-
                -              -yakushimanum 1/8
        -Oh Joyce-   -maximum 1/16
        -              -Midsummer-
BLIZZARD-   -Joyce-   -unknown 1/16
        -        Lyn -   -maximum 1/16
        -              -Adele's Yellow-
        -aureum (chrysanthum) 1/2   -wardii 1/16
Buds of spinel red opening to frilled white flowers, the reverse
amaranth rose. Dorsal spotting of citron green. W. Delp.
SILVER ROSE   Parentage as above
Buds of ruby red and magenta rose; flowers of pale purplish pink
edged with magenta rose. Dorsal spots of ruby red. W. Delp.
* *

                            -catawbiense 1/8
            -unnamed hybrid-   -dichroanthum 5/64
            -              -Fabia-
    -Ginny-   -griersonianum 7/64
    - Mae -yakushimanum 3/8   -fortunei ssp. discolor
    -    -Si-   -Lady -   3/64
    -    Si-   -Day -Bessborough-campylocarpum Elatum
    -      -Gold -Dream-   1/64
BLONDE-   Mohur-   -griersonianum
BOMBER-   -fortunei ssp. discolor
    -              -Margaret-   -dichroanthum
    -              Dunn -Fabia-
    -                  -griersonianum
    -          -yakushimanum
    -Serendipity-
                -aureum (chrysanthum) 1/4
Buds of chartreuse green open to pale yellow-green flowers, with
a primrose yellow flare; dorsal spots light yellow-green. Delp.

BLONDIE   Described under BLAZEN SUN, q.v.

* *
            -dichroanthum 1/2
BLOOD ORANGE-   -griersonianum 1/4
            -May Day-
                -haematodes 1/4
A hybrid from Sunningdale Nurseries, 1951. A mollis azalea also
bears this name. Caldecot & Claremont Nursery, 1934.

SEALING WAX   Parentage as above
Vermilion flowers. Sunningdale Nurseries, 1955.
* *

                    -forrestii Repens Group 1/2
BLOOD RUBY-   -haematodes 1/4
            -Mandalay-
                -venator 1/4
2ft(.6m) OF(-18C) M 3/3 Flowers rich red, in trusses of 5.
Small, rounded foliage. Brandt, 1954.

                            -griffithianum 1/8
                -Queen Wilhelmina-
            -Britannia-   -unknown 3/8
BLOODLINE-   -Stanley Davies--unknown
            -        -arboreum--Blood Red 1/4
            -Cornubia-   -thomsonii 1/8
                -Shilsonii-
                    -barbatum 1/8
6ft(1.8m) OF(-18C) M Truss of 10 flowers, tubular campanulate,
strong red. K. van de Ven cross; P. & C. Dean, reg. 1988.

* *
                    -yakushimanum 1/4
            -Tols-
BLOODLINE (Delp)-   -catawbiense 1/4
            -hyperythrum, ex Gt. Britain 1/2
Strong purplish red buds. Flower lightly tinted spirea red with
dorsal spots of same red; exterior strong purplish red and pur-
plish pink. Weldon Delp.
STARGLIDER   Parentage as above
Buds of rhodamine and light purplish pink, open white. W. Delp.
* *

BLOODSHOT   Described under TIM CRAIG, q.v.

BLUE ADMIRAL   Parentage unknown
3ft(.9m) -5F(-21C) EM 4/4 A parent of FLORENCE MANN. Plant
entirely covered with fine, dark green foliage and blue flowers.
Origin unknown.

BLUE BELL   Parentage unknown
Hybrid by C. B. van Nes, 1932.

            -intricatum 1/2
BLUE BIRD-
            -augustinii 1/2
3ft(.9m) OF(-18C) EM 4/4 Numerous flowers of electric blue.
Plant finely textured, with small foliage. Aberconway, 1930.

* *
        -Blue Ensign--unknown 3/4
BLUE BOY-   -ponticum 1/4
    -Purple Splendour-
                -unknown
5ft(1.5m) OF(-18C) L 4/3 Violet flowers of good substance,
2.5in(6.4cm) across; prominent, almost black, triangular blotch;
ball-shaped truss 6in(15.2cm) wide, 18-20 flowers. Floriferous.
Leaves held 3 years. Elsie M. Watson, reg. 1981.
BLUE HAWAII   Sibling to the above, similar but lighter in col-
or. Flowers larger, with greenish yellow blotch, orange spots.
Less dense. Elsie M. Watson, reg. 1981.
* *

BLUE CHIP   Described under AMETHYST (Arends) q.v.

BLUE CLOUD--form of augustinii ssp. chasmanthum
6ft(1.8m) OF(-18C) EM 4/3 Small-leaved as is species; flowers powder blue, 2.5in(6.4cm) wide, very profuse. Hansen, 1958.

BLUE CLOUD (Hachmann) See AZURWOLKE, described under AMETHYST.

BLUE CROWN   Described under RONKONKOMA, q.v.

            -fortunei ssp. discolor 1/2
BLUE DANUBE-   -ponticum 1/4
    -Purple Splendour-
                -unknown 1/4
6ft(1.8m) -5F(-21C) ML Truss of 22 rich lavender-blue flowers,
a faint green blotch. Blooms with BLUE PETER. Waterer, 1958.

```
* * * * * * * * * * * * * * * * * * * * * * * * * * *
              -campanulatum 1/4
        -Susan-
BLUE DAWN-       -fortunei 1/4
        -Mrs. Davies Evans--unknown 1/2
```
6ft x 6ft(1.8m)(13 yrs) 10F(-12C) ML Buds strong violet open-
ing paler, reverse and edges strong violet, dorsal lobe spotted
green. Flowers 2.7in(7cm) wide, openly funnel-shaped; truss of
23. Leaves bullate, dark yellow-green.   A. Johnson, reg. 1986.
BLUE GIRL   Parentage as above
5ft x 5ft(1.5m)(13 yrs) M Buds strong violet or reddish purple
opening paler, edges and reverse strong violet; dark red spots.
Flowers funnel-shaped; trusses of 20.   Johnson, reg. 1986.
```
* * * * * * * * * * * * * * * * * * * * * * * * * * *
* * * * * * * * * * * * * * * * * * * * * * * * * * *
              -intricatum 1/4
        -Intrifast-
BLUE DIAMOND-       -fastigiatum 1/4
        -augustinii 1/2
```
3ft(.9m) -5F(-21C) EM 4/4   One of the best "blues". A pro-
fusion of small, bright blue flowers, along the stems.   Foliage
small, bronze green in winter. Two forms exist.   Crossfield,
1935.   F.C.C. 1939.   A.G.M. 1968.   Color illus. JS p. 95; VV
p. 17, 49.
OUDIJK'S FAVORITE   Parentage as above
3ft(.9m) -10F(-23C) EM 3/3   Tight ball trusses of campanula
violet. Fa. le Feber, reg. 1965.   Flora Nova & Silver Medal,
Boskoop 1958.
```
* * * * * * * * * * * * * * * * * * * * * * * * * * *
```

BLUE ENSIGN--unknown (may be ponticum hybrid)
4ft(1.2m) -15F(-26C) M 4/3 Flowers pale lavender blue, prominent dark blotch, round trusses of 16, earlier than BLUE PETER.
Large leaves, dark matte green, as BLUE PETER, but better habit.
W. C. Slocock, 1934.   A.M. 1959. Color illus. VV p. 126.

```
        -ponticum 1/2
BLUE FROST-
        -unknown 1/2
```
6ft(1.8m) -10F(-23C) ML 2/3   Light purple flowers with white
throats, spotted in shades of orange.   Trusses of 20.   Whitney
cross; Sather, reg. 1976.

BLUE GIRL   Described under BLUE DAWN, q.v.

BLUE HAWAII Described under BLUE BOY, q.v.

```
        -hippophaeoides Fimbriatum Group 1/2
BLUE HAZE-             -russatum 1/4
        -Russautinii-
                    -augustinii 1/4
```
Dwarf plant with small blue flowers, funnel-shaped. Mid-season.
Sir John Ramsden cross; W. Pennington-Ramsden, reg. 1965.

```
        -ponticum 1/2
BLUE JAY-
        -Blue Ensign ?--unknown 1/2
```
5ft(1.5m) -10F(-23C) ML 3/4   Reg. as a ponticum seedling.
Flowers lavender-blue, 3in(7.6cm) across, pansy violet edges, a
blotch of dahlia purple. Ball trusses of 15.   Foliage dense and
glossy green; heat- and sun-tolerant.   Larson, reg. 1964.

```
* * * * * * * * * * * * * * * * * * * * * * * * * * *
              -yakushimanum--Koichiro Wada 1/4
   -Kristin-            -Corona--unknown 3/8
   -       -Bow Bells-
BLUE LADY-             -williamsianum 1/8
   -          -catawbiense var. album Glass--Catalgla 1/4
   -Calsap-
            -Sappho--unknown
```
Buds strong roseine purple, opening to white flowers edged with
strong and light purple; dorsal spots of vivid green. Al Smith
cross; Weldon Delp raiser.
LILAC HAZE   Parentage as above
Buds of vivid purple open to flowers of amethyst violet and pale
purple, a violet purple flare; dorsal spots violet purple.   Al
Smith cross; Delp raiser..
```
* * * * * * * * * * * * * * * * * * * * * * * * * * *
```

BLUE LAGOON   Described under BLUE RHAPSODY, q.v.

BLUE LIGHT--form of brachyanthum ssp. hypolepidotum

Flowers pale aureolin yellow. Foliage covered below with dense,
silvery scales.   Crown Estate, Windsor; reg. 1962.   A.M. 1951.

```
                    -intricatum 1/8
              -Intrifast-
        -Blue Diamond-       -fastigiatum 1/8
BLUE MOON-       -augustinii 3/4
        -augustinii
```
Lord Digby, 1955.

```
        -fastigiatum, F.C.C.
BLUE MOUNTAIN-       -impeditum, lavender 1/4
        -Blue Tit-
                    -augustinii 1/4
```
Truss of 1-3 flowers, broadly funnel shaped, about 5/8in(1.5cm)
across, of rich blue; prominent stamens. Small leaves with pale
and reddish scales below, non-contiguous; compact plant.   Jack
Drake cross; J. G. Lawson, reg. 1987.

```
                    -ponticum 1/4
        -Purple Splendour-
BLUE PACIFIC-       -unknown 1/4
   -       -campanulatum 1/4
        -Susan-
              -fortunei 1/4
```
5ft(1.5m) -5F(-21C) ML 4/3   Bluish purple flowers, of good
substance, a distinct deep blotch, openly funnel-shaped. Ball-
shaped truss of 12.   Prefers some shade.   Whitney, cross 1965;
A. Sather, reg. 1976.   Color illus. K p. 109.

BLUE PETER   Parentage unknown. (ponticum hybrid ?)
4.5ft(1.4m) -15F(-26C) M 4/3   Flowers light lavender-blue, a
striking purple flare, very frilly rims.   Tight conical trusses.
Plant wider than tall; grows in sun or shade.   Waterer & Crisp.
A.M. 1933.   F.C.C. 1958.   A.G.M. 1969.   Color ill. VV p. 17.

```
                    -impeditum 3/8
              -Blue Tit-
        -Sapphire-       -augustinii 5/8
BLUE POOL-       -impeditum
        -augustinii
```
A compact shrub of slow growth, 3-4ft(.9m-1.2m) in height and in
breadth. Flowers lavender-blue. Knap Hill, reg. 1967.

```
* * * * * * * * * * * * * * * * * * * * * * * * * * *
              -ponticum 1/2
        -A. Bedford-
BLUE RHAPSODY-       -unknown 1/2
   -             -ponticum
        -Purple Splendour-
              -unknown
```
5ft(1.5m) -5F(-21C) ML 4/3   Flowers 3.5in(8.9cm) wide, med-
ium purple, darker spots on throat, upper petal; white stamens.
Ball-shaped truss of 12.   Whitney cross; Sather, reg. 1976.
BARITON   Parentage as above
5ft(1.5m) x 5ft -10F(-23C) L Trusses of 14-16 flowers, exterior of strong purple, tinged strong reddish purple; interior has
deep reddish purple rims, center light purple; conspicuous dark
red blotch.   Hachmann, cross 1974; Stück, reg. 1988.
BLUE LAGOON   Parentage as above, except reversed
5ft(1.5m) -10F(-23C) ML 3/4 Smoky blue-purple flower with a
large, deep purple eye. Recurved leaves of deep forest green.
Greer cross; raisers G. Baxter, W. Thompson.
DREAM OF KINGS   Parentage as above
4ft(1.2m) 0F(-18C) ML   Lavender flowers, large purple blotch,
3.5in(8.9cm) across, openly funnel-shaped; trusses of 18. Plant
wide as tall; glossy leaves. Mrs. H. Frederick, Jr., reg. 1977.
IMPERIAL   Parentage as above
4ft(1.2m) -5F(-21C) ML 4/2   Flower buds often appear on very
young plants. Flowers of bluish purple, with a prominent black
flare. Leaves glossy green; red petioles.   Greer, intro. 1982.
KING'S FAVOR   Parentage as above
3ft(1.2m) -10F(-23C) ML Dark purple buds open imperial purple
with a golden yellow blotch; spherical trusses of 12. Plant as
broad as tall; dark green leaves.   Mrs. Frederick, reg. 1978.
NEW WINE   Parentage as above, except reversed
3ft(.9m) high x 5ft(1.5m)(12 yrs) 0F(-18C) M Strong purplish
red buds open to funnel-shaped flowers of strong purple, blotch
of speckled dark red. Trusses of 17.   D. Horsley, reg. 1988.
PLUM BEAUTIFUL   Parentage as BLUE RHAPSODY, above
5ft(1.5m) -5F(-21C) ML 4/2 Delightful plum purple with deep,
black-purple flare. Medium-sized, glossy leaves.   Greer, 1982.

Color illus. Greer Catalog, 1990, pl. 16.
PRIDE OF KINGS   Parentage as BLUE RHAPSODY, above
4ft(1.2m) -10F(-23C) M Light purple flowers with a dark brown
blotch, throat satiny royal purple; 9-10 blooms per truss. Bush
almost as broad as tall. Mrs. Frederick, reg. 1978.
* *

```
                   -impeditum 1/4
            -Blue Tit-
BLUE RIBBON-        -augustinii 3/4
            -augustinii
```
Blue flowers. See also GREEN EYE. G. H. Johnstone, 1954.

```
                   -russatum 1/4
            -Russautinii-
BLUE RIDGE-         -augustinii 3/4
            -
             - augustinii
```
4ft(1.2m) -12F(-24C) M 4/3 Flowers campanula violet, paler
in throat, in dome-shaped truss of 4-5. Plant rounded, about
as wide as high, with fragrant foliage. The Haags, reg. 1981.

```
                         -fortunei--Sir Charles Butler 1/4
            -Van Nes Sensation-
            -                   -griffithianum 1/8
BLUE RIVER-       -Halopeanum-
            -                   -maximum 1/8
            -Emperor de Maroc--unknown 1/2
```
5ft(1.5m) -5F(-21C) M 3/3 Flowers campanula violet, openly
bell-shaped, 4in(10.2cm) wide; upright trusses of 17. Bush compact; glossy dark foliage. Ruth Lyons, reg. 1962. A.E. 1961.

```
       -augustinii 1/2
BLUE SKY-
       -rubiginosum Desquamatum Group 1/2
```
Blue flowers. Lord Digby cross, 1940; intro. 1955.

* *
```
                -impeditum 3/4
         -Saint Tudy-
BLUE STAR-         -augustinii 1/4
         -impeditum
```
Mauve blue flowers, 1.25in(3.2cm) wide. Gen. Harrison, r. 1961.
SAINT MERRYN   Parentage as above
2.5ft(.75) -5F(-21C) EM 3/3   A small compact hybrid with
aster violet flowers about 1in(2.5cm) broad, in clusters of 2-4.
Plant twice as wide as tall. Gen. Harrison, reg. 1971. F.C.C.
Wisley Trials 1986. A.M. Wisley Trials 1983.
* *

BLUE STEEL--form of impeditum, selfed
1ft(.3m) -15F(-26C) EM 4/4 Densely twiggy dwarf shrub, with
silver-gray leaves .5in(1.3cm) long. Flowers light violet-blue,
clusters of 3. G. H. White raiser; J. P. C. Russell, reg. 1983.

```
       -maximum 1/2
BLUE STEM-
       -unknown 1/2
```
Tall-growing; pink flowers in June. Very hardy. Bob Carlson.

```
                            -intricatum 1/8
                   -Intrifast-
            -Blue Diamond-        -fastigiatum 1/8
BLUE THUNDER (Newcomb)-           -augustinii 1/4
                   -unknown 1/2
```
4ft x 5ft(1.4m x 1.5m)(26 yrs) -5F(-21C) EM   Flowers funnel-
shaped 1.6in(4cm) across, vivid violet with strong red-purple
throat; truss of 3-5. Small leaves reddish brown in winter; new
growth lettuce green, edged currant red. Newcomb, reg. 1987.

```
                          -catawbiense 1/4
                 -Purpureum Elegans-
          -Roslyn-              -unknown 1/2
          -      -             -catawbiense
BLUE THUNDER-        -Everestianum-
(A.W. Smith)-                   -unknown
          -       -catawbiense var. album Glass--Catalgla 1/4
          -Calsap-
                 -Sappho--unknown
```
Buds of vivid and moderate violet opening to white flowers edged
in strong and brilliant violet; dorsal spots lettuce green. Al
(A. W.) Smith cross; W. Delp raiser.

* *
```
       -impeditum 1/2
BLUE TIT-
       -augustinii 1/2
```
3ft(.9m) -5F(-21F) EM 3/4   Abundant flowers of gray-blue.
Small leaves on a compact plant; new growth bright yellow. Sun-
tolerant. Confused with AUGFAST, which is violet-blue. J. C.
Williams, 1933. Color illus. F p. 35; VV p. 30.
BLUE TIT   Same cross as above by Herbst
Flowers bright sky blue (leuchtend himmelblau). Hobbie raiser.
BLUE TIT MAGOR   Same cross as above by Magor. Flowers pale
lilac with better foliage, as observed in W. Germany by P. Cox.
SAINT BREWARD   Parentage as above
3ft(.9m) -15F(-26C) EM   Small, dense, very hardy bush, wider
than high, with flowers sea lavender violet, darker at margins.
Tight spherical truss of 26. Magor cross; Gen. Harrison, reg.
1962. F.C.C. 1962.
SAINT TUDY   Parentage as above
3ft(.9m) -5F(-21C) EM 3/3 A vigorous plant, bearing flowers
of lobelia blue. Dome-shaped trusses of 14. Magor raiser; Gen.
Harrison, reg. 1960. A.M. 1960. F.C.C. Wisley Trials 1973.
* *

BLUE WONDER   Described under RUSSAUTINII, q.v.

BLUEBELL   Parentage unknown
A. Waterer, before 1880. Large, compact trusses of shapely campanulate flowers, wide edges of light purple tinged blue, center
white, a few yellowish dorsal spots. Vigorous plant.--Descript.
from: The Florist and Pomologist, 1884, S.65. (W. Schmalscheidt)

```
       -intricatum 1/2
BLUEBIRD-
       -augustinii 1/2
```
3ft(.9m) OF(-18C) EM 4/4   Dense, small foliage on a finely
textured plant, wider than high; numerous electric blue flowers.
Needs open sun. Lord Aberconway. A.M. 1943. A.G.M. 1968.

```
              -intricatum 1/4
          -Bluebird-
BLUESTONE-        -augustinii 3/4
          -augustinii
```
Terminal clusters of deep lilac-blue flowers, appearing in early
season. Lord Aberconway, 1950.

```
       -impeditum 1/2
BLUETTE-
       -augustinii--Lackamas Blue 1/2
```
3ft(.9m) -5F(-21C) M 3/4 Abundant flowers of hyacinth blue;
truss of 8. Twiggy, globe-shaped plant; scaly leaves 1.5in(3.8
cm) x .5in(1.3cm). Needs sun. B. Lancaster, reg. 1958.

BLUMEISE   Described under BLAUBART, q.v.

```
          -Blue Peter--unknown 1/2
BLURETTIA-
          -yakushimanum--Koichiro Wada 1/2
```
Trusses of 11-14 flowers, with wavy edges of medium mallow pur-
ple, paling to much lighter centers. Leaves ovate, hairy. H.
Hachmann cross; Stück, reg. 1983. Col. ill. WS, 1989, p. 148.

```
                    -dichroanthum 1/8
              -Astarte-          -campylocarpum Elatum Group 1/16
      -Ouida-       -Penjerrick-
BLUSH-      -                   -griffithianum 1/16
      -      -griersonianum 1/4
      -aperantum 1/2
```
Pale pink flowers. Lord Aberconway, cross 1933; intro. 1944.

```
              -C. O. D. (Dexter hybrid)--unknown
BLUSH BUTTON-
              -Honeydew (Dexter hybrid)--unknown
```
5ft(1.5m) -10F(-23C) M Coral red buds open to cream flowers, 3
in(7.6cm) wide; flat trusses of 8. Plant spreads 1.5 times its
height. Mrs. Knippenberg, reg. 1976.

```
                -arboreum 1/2
BLUSHING BEAUTY-
                -unknown 1/2
```
Blush pink flowers. R. Gill & Son.

```
                       -griffithianum 1/4
              -Dawn's Delight-
BLUSHING BRIDE-           -unknown 1/4
              -fortunei ssp. discolor 1/2
Rosy carmine. Not grown now at Exbury.     Rothschild, 1934.


                            -catawbiense 1/4
            -Catawbiense Grandiflorum-
BLUTOPIA-                        -unknown 1/2
     -              -mauve seedling--unknown
        -A. Bedford-
                     -ponticum 1/4
5ft(1.5m) x 5ft  -15F(-26C)  L    Trusses of 12-15 flowers; lobes
slightly wavy, strong purple; dorsal lobes heavily spotted with
strong greenish yellow.   Hachmann cross; Stück, reg. 1988.


           -thomsonii 1/2
BOADICEA-
        fortunei ssp. discolor 1/2
A tall, upright plant with waxy crimson flowers, like thomsonii.
Free-flowering; blooms early. Rothschild, 1934.


                 -yakushimanum 1/2          -catawbiense
BOB AS---unnamed  -          -Parsons Grand- -          1/16
      hybrid F2-    -America- iflorum        -unknown 1/4
           -Cindy-         -dark red hybrid--unknown
           Lou  -            -griffithianum 1/16
                  -unnamed-Mars-
                   hybrid-    -unknown
                      -catawbiense var. rubrum 1/8
Buds of Tyrian purple opening to flowers of Neyron rose and pale
purplish pink; dorsal spots of medium orange.   W. Delp.



* * * * * * * * * * * * * * * * * * * * * * * * * * *
         -yakushimanum--Koichiro Wada 1/2
BOB BOVEE-
        -wardii 1/2
3ft(.9m)  -5F(-21C)  M  3/4    Flowers primrose yellow, with red
spot changing to green in the throat, 3in(7.6cm) wide.  Truss of
12.  Plant dense; glossy dark green leaves held 3 years.   Bovee
cross; Sorensen and Watson, reg. 1976.
BABETTE   Parentage: wardii x yakushimanum--Koichiro Wada
3ft(.9m) x 4ft(1.2m)  -10F(-23C)    Flowers in trusses of 8-11,
campanulate, pale greenish yellow with a basal blotch of strong
red.  Compact plant habit.  Hachmann cross; Stück, reg. 1988.
JULIE GRACE   Parentage: yakushimanum, Exbury form x wardii
16in(40.6cm) x 12in(30.5cm)(20 yrs)  -10F(-23C)  M   Flowers in
truss of 14, frilled edges, of pale yellowish green with strong
greenish yellow spotting.  L. B. Mraw, reg. 1988.
VOLKER   Parentage: wardii x yakushimanum
Flowers in trusses of 11, openly campanulate, pale yellow.    D.
Hobbie cross; Slocock exhibitor.   H.C. Wisley Trials 1987.
* * * * * * * * * * * * * * * * * * * * * * * * * * *
            -williamsianum 1/4
        -Adrastia-
BOB CHERRY-         -neriiflorum 1/4
        -forrestii Repens Group 1/2
Flowers of deep crimson red.   Sunningdale Nurseries, 1951.


* * * * * * * * * * * * * * * * * * * * * * * * * * *
          -minus Carolinianum Group, pink form 1/2
BOB DANIK-       -minus Carolinianum Group 1/4
        -P.J.M.-
               -dauricum 1/4
A lepidote with reddish purple flowers; medium-sized plant hardy
to -25F(-32C).    Weldon Delp.
MARGE DANIK   Parentage as above
Flowers reddish purple; medium-sized plant; hardy to -25F(-32C).
W. Delp.
SIDEKICK   Parentage as above
Buds of strong and light purples;   flowers of very pale purple,
with a strong purple exterior, orange anthers.    W. Delp.


* * * * * * * * * * * * * * * * * * * * * * * * * * *

BOB PETERS SPECIAL--seedling of fortunei
4ft(1.2m)  -15F(-26C)  M  Very fragrant flowers, light purplish
pink,  pale orange-yellow throat,  3.5in(8.9cm) across, 7 lobes.
Flat truss 7in(17.8cm) wide,  9 blooms.  New twigs yellow-green.
Plant wider than tall.   R. Carter intro.; R. Peters, reg. 1983.
```

```
* * * * * * * * * * * * * * * * * * * * * * * * * * * *
     -campylogynum 1/2
BOBBET-                         (Not a hybrid)
     -campylogynum  Cremastum  Group  1/2
2ft(.6m)  -5F(-21C)  M    Flowers greenish golden yellow, long
pedicel; large calyx.  Small obovate leaf.  Caperci, reg. 1966.
KIM   Parentage as above
1ft(.3m)  -5F(-21C)  M  4/4    Little yellow lanterns open from
pink buds, .75in(1.9cm) wide and long.  Excellent habit: compact
and wider than tall; jade green foliage. J. Caperci, reg. 1966.
A. E. 1973.    Color illus. ARS J 37:3 (1983), cover.
LITTLE AMY  Parentage as above, except reversed
1ft(.3m)  OF(-18C)  ML    Flowers orient pink .75in(1.9cm) wide,
in trusses of 6 nodding flowers.   Plant well-branched, twice as
wide as tall; aromatic foliage held 1 year. Caperci, reg. 1977.
Color illus. ARS Q 31:2 (1977), p. 102.
* * * * * * * * * * * * * * * * * * * * * * * * * * * *


          -fortunei ssp. discolor 1/2
BOBOLINK-
         -neriiflorum 1/2
5ft(1.5m)  OF(-18C)  L  3/3    A free-flowering shrub, with deep
yellow or apricot flowers.   Rothschild, 1934.


                         -augustinii ssp. chasmanthum 1/8
                  -Electra-
        -Ilam Violet-     -augustinii 3/8
        -               -russatum 1/4
BOB'S BLUE-                  -intricatum 1/8
        -              -Intrifast-
        -Blue Diamond-       -fastigiatum 1/8
                  -augustinii
3ft(.9m)  OF(-18C)  M  4/4    Violet-colored flowers, in trusses
of 3-5.   Dr. Robert C. Rhodes, reg. 1979.


     -wardii 1/2               -caucasicum 3/32
BOB'S -           -Jacksonii-       -caucasicum
YELLOW-      -Goldsworth-      -Nobleanum-
     -          - Yellow  -          -campylocarpum 5/32
     -Goldfort-          -campylocarpum
                 -fortunei 1/4
Trusses of 10 light yellow flowers, with a yellowish green flare
in the throat.   Dr. R. C. Rhodes cross; reg. 1979.


     -Catawbiense Compactum--form of catawbiense 1/2
BOCCIA-
     -williamsianum 1/2
4ft(1.2m) x 5ft(1.5m)  -15F(-26C)  ML   Flowers in loose trusses
of 6-9, 5 wavy lobes, very pale purple, veined in strong to pale
purplish pink, unmarked.  Plant of compact habit.  Hobbie, cross
c. 1942; Hachmann intro.; Stück, reg. 1988.


           -arboreum, white 1/2
BODDAERTIANUM-                 (Some records show:
(BODARTIANUM)-                  arboreum x campanulatum)
           -ponticum, white (or hybrid of same) 1/2
6ft(1.8m)  OF(-18C)  EM  3/3  Named for Boddaert, foreman to van
Houte of Ghent.  Compact, rounded trusses of 18-22.  Buds laven-
der pink open to funnel-shaped flowers, white with a crimson ray
and dark purple markings.   Van Houtte, intro. 1863,  under the
name CROIX D'ANVERS.   Color illus. JS p. 70.


                    -ciliatum 1/4
         -Cilpinense-
BODEGA CRYSTAL PINK-        -moupinense 1/4
              -mucronulatum--Cornell Pink 1/2
3.5ft(1m)  -5F(-21C)  M  4/4  Flowers openly funnel-shaped, flax
pink, red-purple spotting in trusses of 3-7.  Leaves small, el-
liptic, light green, semi-deciduous.  C. Heller, reg. 1976.


                      -griffithianum 1/16
              -George Hardy-
        -                -catawbiense 1/16
        -Hugh Koster-        -arboreum 1/32
        -            -         -Doncaster-
     -David-       -unnamed-      -unknown 3/32
BODEGA-    -        hybrid-
  RUBY-    -               -unknown
  RED-   -neriiflorum 1/4
     -          -sanguineum var. haemaleum 1/4
     -unnamed-
       hybrid-thomsonii 1/4
```

5ft(1.5m) 5F(-15C) EM   Flowers currant red, spotted black on upper lobe, of heavy substance, 5-lobed. Flat truss of 7. Narrowly elliptic leaves held 3 years.   C. Heller, reg. 1975.

```
                     -venator 1/4
            -Vanguard-
BODEGA TOREADOR-     -griersonianum 1/2
           -        -griersonianum
            -Matador-
                     -strigillosum 1/4
```
3ft(.9m) 5F(-15C) M   Flowers signal red, red spots on upper lobes, widely funnel-campanulate. Lax truss of 8. Foliage narrowly elliptic to lanceolate with tan indumentum, held 3 years; rounded, well-branched plant.   C. Heller, reg. 1975.

```
                                    -griffithianum 9/16
                           -Kewense-
                  -Aurora-         -fortunei 1/16
                  -       -
          -Yvonne Opaline-        -thomsonii 1/8
BODEGA Y QUADRA-        -griffithianum
          -             -arboreum ssp. cinnamomeum var.
          -Loder's White-               album 1/4
                        -griffithianum
```
5.5ft(1.65m) 12F(-11C) M   (See LODER'S WHITE for other possible parentage) Flowers bright pink, blending to a paler throat, a red spot; 4.25in(11cm) broad, widely funnel-campanulate. Conical truss 10in(25.4cm) broad, 9-flowered.   Heller, reg. 1977.

```
                            -catawbiense 5/64
                 -Blandyanum-           -catawbiense
          -Ascot -         -        -unnamed-
          -Brilliant-       -Alta-  - hybrid-ponticum
    -unnamed-        -     clerense-          1/64
BODIL- hybrid-      -thomsonii 1/8   -arboreum 1/32
     -       -neriiflorum 1/4
     -haematodes 1/2
```
Red flowers.   Exhibited by Acton, 1950.

BODNANT BEAUTY OF TREMOUGH   Described under BEAUTY OF TREMOUGH.

BODNANT DAY   See BUDGET FARTHING

BODNANT MAY DAY   Described under MAY DAY, q.v.

BODNANT PINK--form of arboreum ssp. cinnamomeum var. album
Introduced by Lord Aberconway.

BODNANT RED--form of campylogynum Cremastum Group
2.5ft(.75m) -10F(-23C) EM 4/4   Flowers medium chrysanthemun (grayed) red, 1in(2.5cm) wide, 5 deeply divided lobes.   Crown Estate Commissioners, raisers; reg. 1971. A.M. 1971.

BODNANT THOMWILLIAMS   Described under THOMWILLIAMS, q.v.

BODNANT YELLOW   Described under LADY CHAMBERLAIN, q.v.

* *

```
                        -catawbiense var. album 1/8
                    -                   -catawbiense
             -Lodestar-     -Catawbiense-      5/32
             -          -Belle - Album   -unknown 5/16
       -R. O. -         Heller-white cat. hyb.--unknown
      - Delp -                       -catawbiense
      -      -         -Atrosanguineum-
      -      -     -Atrier-        -unknown
      -      -Mary -    -griersonianum 1/16
      -      Belle-   -decorum 1/16
      -          -Dechaem-
BODY LANGUAGE-           -haematodes 1/16
      -                      -griffithianum
      -                 -George-          1/32
      -              -Mrs. Lindsay- Hardy-catawbiense
      -              - Smith     -
      -     -Harvest-        -Duchess of
      -     - Moon -         Edinburgh--unknown
    -unnamed-       -         -campylocarpum 1/16
       hybrid-    -unnamed hybrid-
             -                -unknown
             -Ice -catawb. v. album Glass--Catalgla 1/8
             Cube-
                -Belle Heller (as above)
```

Buds strong to moderate purplish red, opening to flowers deep to light purplish pink.   Weldon Delp.
CHARLIE G   Parentage as above
Buds a mixture of medium to light violet purples and strong reddish cyclamen purple; frilled flowers of light violet, fading to white; 3 dorsal lobes spotted deep ruby red.   W. Delp. Color illus.. ARS J 43:1 (1989), p. 3.
PURITY   Parentage as above
Buds of deep to strong purplish red, open to pale yellow flowers with dorsal spotting of strong purplish red.   W. Delp.
TIGHT END   Parentage as above
Buds strong reddish purple to mallow purple. Flowers combine deep to paler violet purples, with dorsal spotting of dark beetroot purple.   W. Delp.   Color illus. ARS J 43:1 (1989), p. 3.
* *

```
                      -maximum 1/4
           -Midsummer-
           -         -unknown 1/2           -catawbiense 1/16
BOGGLE-          -Parsons Grandiflorum-
      -          -America-          -unknown
      -          -       -dark red hybrid--unknown
      -Cindy Lou-           -griffithianum 1/16
      -             -Mars-
      -unnamed hybrid-   -unknown
                         -catawbiense var. rubrum 1/8
```
Buds strong purplish red. Flowers combine strong and vivid purplish reds and strong purplish pink.   W. Delp.

BÖHLJE'S SÄMLING   From a shoot of unknown root stock
Flowers open funnel-shaped, pure pink with heavy dark red spotted blotch, 5-lobed. Böhlje intro. 1937; W. Schmalscheidt, reg. 1985.   Color illus. WS, 1989, p. 100.

```
                  -fortunei 57/128
        -Ruby F. Bowman-        -griffithianum 21/128
        -              -Lady Bligh-
BOLD    -                       -unknown 1/8
ADVENTURE-          -fortunei
        -          -Fawn-   -dichroanthum 1/16
        -          -    -Fabia-
        -          -        -griersonianum 1/8
        -Skipper-           -griersonianum
        -        -Sarita-   -griffithianum
        -        - Loder-Loderi-
        -Indian-        -fortunei
        Penny-   -wardii 1/16    -griffithianum
          -Idealist-          -Kewense-
          -        -Aurora-  -fortunei
          -Naomi-    -thomsonii 1/64
                  -fortunei
```
3ft(.9m) 10F(-12C) M   Fragrant flowers of heavy substance in trusses of 14; 7 smooth-edged lobes; strong red buds open pale purplish pink, deep red in throat; two medium red dorsal flares. Open growth habit.   Dr. L. W. Bulgin, reg. 1988.

```
                -brachycarpum ssp. tigerstedtii 1/2
BOLD AND BREEZY-
               -eclecteum, Cox form 1/2
```
Buds ruby red and magenta, opening to flowers of vivid purplish red with deep and pale purplish pinks; dorsal spotting of strong purplish yellow.   D. Hinerman cross; W. Delp raiser.

```
             -yakushimanum 1/2
BOLD BLUSH-                     -catawbiense 1/8
          -        -Mrs. C. S. Sargent-
          -Meadowbrook-        -unknown 1/4
          -          -        -catawbiense 1/8
          -          -Everestianum-
                              -unknown
```
Buds of vivid purplish red open to flowers of pale purplish pink with margins of vivid purplish red.   W. Delp.

BOLD ELEGANCE   Described under AWESOME ARRAY, q.v.

```
                                -griffithianum 1/8
                   -Queen Wilhelmina-
          -Unknown Warrior-        -unknown 3/8
BOLD LAD-            -Stanley Davies--unknown
        -arboreum 1/2
```
Trusses of 22 red flowers, slightly spotted.   T. Lelliot cross; G. Langdon, reg. 1976.

```
                    -elliottii 1/4
            -Fusilier-
BOMBARDIER-        -griersonianum 1/4
            -griffithianum 1/2
Bright pink flowers 4.5in(10.8cm) across, 3in(7.6cm) high; about
16 to a truss.  Gen. Harrison, reg. 1961.


                              -dichroanthum ssp. scyphocalyx 1/8
            -unnamed-unnamed hybrid-
            - hybrid-            -kyawii 1/8
BOMBAY-      -catawbiense var. album Glass--Catalgla 1/2
            -            -catawbiense var. album Glass--Catalgla
            -unnamed hybrid-
                              -wardii 1/4
3ft(.9m)  -10F(-23C) EM  3/2    Flowers greenish yellow, darker
on exterior, blotch of vivid greenish yellow; domed trusses hold
12-14.  Foliage dark green; superior density.  Leach, reg. 1972.


                        -brachycarpum 1/4
            -Scott David-
            -            -catawbiense 7/16    -catawbiense
BON BON (Delp)-      -Parsons Grandiflorum-
            -      -America-            -unknown 5/16
            -AA 36-      -dark red hybrid--unknown
            -            -catawbiense
            -Ann Rutledge-
                        -unknown
Strong purplish red and strong reddish purple buds open to peta-
loid flowers of deep purplish pink, the underside veined in very
pale purple.  Medium-sized plant; hardy to -15F(-26C).  Delp.


        -souliei 1/2
BONBON-
        -maximum 1/2
Cream-colored flowers, on a medium-sized, compact shrub.  Roth-
schild, cross 1927; intro. 1934.


                    -fortunei ssp. discolor 1/4
            -unnamed hybrid-
BONFIRE-            -Mrs. R. G. Shaw--unknown 1/4
            -griersonianum 1/2
5ft(1.5m)  -5F(-21C) ML  3/3    Fiery orange-red flowers; large,
loose, conical trusses. Leaves dull green, 6in(15.2cm) x 2in (5
cm).  Best in open sun.     Waterer & Crisp, 1928.    A.M. 1933.


        -fortunei ssp. discolor 1/2
BONITO-        -fortunei 1/4
        -Luscombei-
                -thomsonii 1/4
6ft(1.8m)  -5F(-21C) ML  4/3  Flower pale blush pink, fading to
white, heavy brown spotting on the upper corolla, to 5in(12.7cm)
wide; large, rounded trusses. Dark green leaves, 7in(17.9cm) by
2.7in(7cm); upright, vigorous plant. Another similar form mark-
ed with green and yellow.  Rothschild.  A.M. 1934.


            -griffithianum 1/4
        -Mars-
BONNIE-    -unknown 1/4
        -            -catawbiense 1/4
        -unnamed hybrid-
                    -haematodes 1/4
Hardiness to -10F(-23C).  Pale buff flowers; mid-season.  Gable.


                    -wardii ? 1/8
            -Chlorops-
        -Inca Gold-      -vernicosum ? 1/8
BONNIE BABE-      -unknown 3/4
            -orange hybrid--unknown
3ft(.9m)  OF(-18C) ML  4/3     Synonym CECIL'S CHOICE.  Flowers
barium yellow with cardinal red spots; dome-shaped trusses of 10
to 14.  Plant wider than high.     J. Elliott, reg. 1983.   Color
illus. HG p. 168.


            -Scintillation--unknown 5/8
BONNIE BRAE-                    -catawbiense 1/8
            -            -Atrosanguineum-
            -Red Head (Gable)-        -unknown
                        -griersonianum 1/4
6ft(1.8m)  -5F(-21C) ML  Flower 4in(10.2cm) wide, 7-lobed, fra-
grant, orchid-pink, edges darker, yellowish green blotch;  truss
of 17.  Leaves 7in(17.8cm) x 3in(7.6cm).  Herbert, reg. 1977.
```

```
                              -campylocarpum 1/8
                -Mary Swathling-
            -Fred Rose-            -fortunei 1/8
BONNIE JEAN-        -lacteum 1/4
            -        -griersonianum 1/4
            -Matador-
                    -strigillosum 1/4
5ft(1.5m) x 4ft(1.2m)(14 yrs)  5F(-15C)  E    Spherical truss of
20 flowers, 6 to 7 wavy-edged lobes, strong red  with a dark red
blotch.  Light indumentum on young leaves.  B. Smith, reg. 1989.


            -fortunei 1/2
BONNIE MAID-
            -unknown 1/2
5ft(1.5m)  -10F(-23C) M  Saucer-shaped flower 2.75in(7cm) wide,
7-lobed, pink with red dorsal rays; trusses of 13.  Leaf  5.5in.
(14cm) x 2in(5cm).   M. Hall cross; E. J. Brown, reg. 1979.


BONNIE SNAZA   Described under BETTY ANDERSON, q.v.


        -lutescens 1/2
BO-PEEP-
        -moupinense 1/2
4ft(1.2m)  5F(-15C)  E  3/3  Flat, funnel-shaped flowers of pale
greenish yellow,  with darker yellow spotting on the back of the
tube.  Trusses of 2-3  flowers; often-multiple buds give the ap-
pearance of more.  Leaves small, glossy, light green.  Grown for
bright, early flowers; a companion plant for P.J.M., q.v.  Roth-
schild, 1934.   A.M. 1937.   Color illus. F p. 36.


                -arboreum 1/4
            -Doncaster-
BORDE HILL-        -unknown 1/2
            -            -griffithianum 1/4
            -Mrs. A. M. Williams-
                        -unknown
3ft(.9m)  5F(-15C)  ML  4/3  Waxy flowers, dark scarlet, medium-
sized, in rounded trusses.  Large, pointed leaves; upright plant
of medium density.   C. B. van Nes.    A.M. Wisley Trials 1948.


BORDE HILL MAY DAY   Described under MAY DAY, q.v.


BORDE HILL RED CAP  Described under RED CAP, q.v.


        -microgynum Gymnocarpum Group 1/2
BORDEAUX-
        -beanianum 1/2
5ft(1.5m)  5F(-15C)  EM  2/2  Synonym Burgundian.  Flowers dark
red, waxen.  A compact plant;  small, dark green, glossy foliage
with brown indumentum beneath.   E. de Rothschild, reg. 1963.


BORDERER   Described under SPARKLER, q.v.


                            -catawbiense 1/8
            -Parsons Grandiflorum-
        -America-            -unknown 3/8
BORKUM-        -dark red hybrid--unknown
        -williamsianum 1/2
Clear rose flowers.  Dietrich Hobbie, 1942-44.


* * * * * * * * * * * * * * * * * * * * * * * * * * *
                            -maximum 1/2
                -unnamed hybrid-
        -unnamed hybrid-            -yakushimanum 1/8
        -        -            -maximum, ivory form
        -        -Adele's Yellow-
BORN FREE-            -wardii 1/4
        -            -maximum
        -        -Stokes Bronze Wings-
        -unnamed hybrid-            -catawbiense 1/8
                    -Adele's Yellow (as above)
Buds of imperial-to-aster reddish purples; flowers of white with
a vivid yellow-green blotch across three dorsal lobes.  W. Delp.
DREAM MAKER   Parentage as above
Strong purplish red and pale purplish pink buds, opening to pale
yellow-green, frilled flowers  with a pale greenish yellow flare
and strong lettuce green dorsal spots.  W. Delp.
NO WONDER   Parentage as above
Buds a blend of rhodonite reds,  opening to pale yellowish white
flowers with strong yellow-green dorsal spots; medium red-orange
stigma, yellowish pink anthers on white filaments.  W. Delp.
* * * * * * * * * * * * * * * * * * * * * * * * * * *
```

BOSKOOP   Described under BACCARAT, q.v.

BOSLEY/DEXTER 1016   Parentage unknown
White flowers blushed light pink with dark brownish blotch; ruffled edges.   Dexter cross; Paul Bosley, Sr., raiser.
BOSLEY/DEXTER 1020   Parentage unknown
Flowers have medium pink edges, white centers.   Red stems on new growth.   Dexter cross; Paul Bosley, Sr., raiser.
BOSLEY/DEXTER 1040   Parentage unknown
Cherry pink with light centers, very ruffled edges.   Dexter cross; Paul Bosley, Sr. raiser.

* *
```
                     -caucasicum 1/4
        -Boule de Neige-              -catawbiense 1/8
BOSUTCH-              -unnamed hybrid-
-                                     -unknown 1/8
        -sutchuenense 1/2
```
5ft(1.5m) -5F(-21C) E 3/4   Plant of good habit; dark green foliage. White flowers, lavender-spotted, campanulate. Gable.
BOSUTCH PINK   Parentage as above
Pink flowers a week later than BOSUTCH.   Joseph Gable.
* *

```
                -Metternianus--degronianum ssp. heptamereum
        -Rijneveld-              (metternichii)        1/4
        -          -              -griersonianum 1/8
BOSWEGE-      -unnamed hybrid-
-                                  -unknown 5/8
        -red hybrid--unknown
```
Flowers held in rounded trusses of 7-9, dark pink, with a speckled blotch.   Royal Boskoop Horticultural Society, reg. 1988.


```
        -yakushimanum 1/2
BOTANY BELLE-      -dichroanthum 1/4
        -Tidbit-
               -wardii 1/4
```
15.7in(.4m) -10F(-23C) ML   Cardinal red buds open strong Neyron rose at edges, lighter at base. Flowers campanulate, 1.5in. (4cm) wide, 5 emarginate lobes. Leaves with whitish indumentum, aging to fawn. J. F. McQuire, reg. 1987.


```
                    -catawbiense 1/2
BOTHA--Everestianum, selfed-
                    -unknown 1/2
```
Flowers pale lilac-pink with ochre markings on a lighter ground; frilled.   T. J. R. Seidel, cross 1892.


```
        -caucasicum 1/2
BOULE DE NEIGE-              -catawbiense 1/4
             -unnamed hybrid-
                            -unknown 1/4
```
4ft(1.2m) -25F(-32C) M 4/4   "Ball of Snow," one of the ironclads; an old, still popular hybrid.   White flowers, in medium-sized, compact, rounded trusses. Foliage heavily textured, of a rather light green. Dense, rounded plant, vigorous and easy to grow. Oudieu, 1878. Color illus. VV p. 31.


```
                    -catawbiense 3/8
        -unnamed hybrid-
BOULE DE ROSE-              -unknown 3/8
        -                  -caucasicum 1/4
           -Boule de Neige-              -catawbiense
                          -unnamed hybrid-
                                       -unknown
```
3ft(1.2m) -25F(-32C) EM 3/2 Flowers bright rose pink, slight brownish flare on upper lobe.   Low, compact plant. Shammarello cross; David G. Leach, intro. 1957, reg. 1962.


```
                    -caucasicum 1/4
        -Boule de Neige-              -catawbiense 1/8
        -              -unnamed hybrid-
BOULODES-                            -unknown 3/8
        -                          -griffithanum 1/8
        -                -Loderi-
        -unnamed hybrid-        -fortunei 1/8
                      -unknown
```
5ft(1.5m) -15F(-26C) ML   Fragrant flowers, light pink turning white, faint yellow spots, frilled, openly funnel-shaped, 3.5in. (8.9cm) wide. Trusses ball-shaped, of 10 flowers. Plant rounded; elliptic, flat, deep green leaves. G. Nearing, reg. 1973.

BOULTER'S CREAM   Parentage unknown
Large yellow-white flowers on a very tall shrub, to 8.5ft(2.5m). F. Boulter, Australia, 1986.


```
                    -caucasicum 1/4
             -Nobleanum-
BOULTER'S ROSALEA-      -arboreum 1/2
             -      -arboreum--Blood Red
             -Cornubia-      -thomsonii 1/8
                    -Shilsonii-
                            -barbatum 1/8
```
Campanulate flowers of vivid red with paler centers, dorsal lobe spotted vivid red; trusses of 12-15. Plant 9.9ft(3m) tall. F. Boulter, reg. 1986.

* *
```
                        -catawbiense v. album--
                -unnamed- La Bar's White 1/16
         -unnamed- hybrid-fortunei 1/16
   -Vinecrest- hybrid-wardii (croceum) 1/8
        -      -wardii Litiense Group 1/4
   -                    -catawbiense 1/16
BOUNTIFUL-      -Parsons Grandiflorum-
   -      -America-      -unknown 1/4
   -      -      -dark red hybrid--unknown
   -Cindy Lou-      -griffithianum 1/16
   -      -Mars-
   -unnamed-      -unknown
        hybrid-catawbiense var. rubrum 1/8
```
Buds of ruby red and cardinal red; frilled flowers of white with blend of vivid purplish red and deep purplish pinks.   Al Smith cross; W. Delp raiser.
FAN FLARE   Parentage as above
Deep red and strong purplish red buds, open to flowers of rhodamine and phlox pinks, dorsal spotting of strong greenish yellow. Al (A. W.) Smith cross; Delp raiser.
* *

BOUNTY   Described under CALFORT, q.v.


```
        -davidsonianum 1/2
BOUQUET-      -rigidum (caeruleum var. album) 1/4
        -Peace-
             -cinnabarinum ssp. xanthocodon Concatenans Group
White flowers.   Lord Aberconway, 1950                        1/4
```


```
                -Moser's Maroon--unknown 1/4
        -Grenadier-
BOURNEMOUTH-      -elliottii 1/4
 BELLE  -      -wardii 1/4
        -Crest-      -fortunei ssp. discolor 1/8
             -Lady-
             Bessborough-campylocarpum Elatum Group 1/8
```
4ft(1.2m) 0F(-18C) M Funnel-shaped flowers in trusses of 16, edged, spotted and striped strong purplish red. May, reg. 1988.

BOURSAULT   See CATAWBIENSE BOURSAULT


```
        -Corona--unknown 1/2
BOW BELLS-
        -williamsianum 1/2
```
3ft(.9m) -5F(-21C) EM 3/4   Cup-shaped, light pink flowers, deeper on reverse; lax trusses of 4-7. Plant rounded, floriferous; medium-sized leaves, new growth bronze.   Needs some shade. Rothschild, 1934. A.M. 1935. Color illus. F p. 36; VV p. 10.

BOW STREET   Described under CAROLINE DE ZOETE, q.v.


```
        -minus var. chapmanii 1/2
BOWIE-
        -minus Carolinianum Group 1/2
```
6ft(1.8m) 0F(-18C) L 3/3 Many pink flowers, to 1.5in(3.8cm) across, a pale brownish green blotch; terminal ball-shaped clusters from 2 or 3 buds, each 10-14 flowered. Plant vigorous and compact. Skinner cross, 1953; U.S. National Arbor., reg. 1979.


```
        -brachyanthum 1/2
BRACHBOOTH-
        -boothii 1/2
```
Flowers butter yellow with a green tinge, darker spotting.   E. J. P. Magor cross, 1920; intro. 1926.

```
                -brachycarpum 1/2
BRACHDIS-
            -fortunei ssp. discolor 1/2
Flowers blush yellow, with green spotting.   Magor, intro. 1925.


                -brachycarpum 1/2
BRACHDIS (Gable)-
                -fortunei ssp. discolor 1/2
-10F(-23C)  L  4/3  Flesh-colored flowers with copper markings.
Joseph Gable cross.


                -brachyanthum 1/2
BRACHLEP-
            -lepidotum 1/2
Flowers yellow to pink.   Magor cross; intro. 1924.


                -brachycarpum 1/2
BRACHSOUL-
            -souliei 1/2
Flower spotted crimson, light rose shading to white, darker out-
side.  E. J. P. Magor cross, 1917; intro. 1927.


                -brachyanthum 1/2
BRACHYDUM-
            -flavidum 1/2
Yellow flowers.   J. Waterer, 1921.


                -brachyanthum  Wilson 6771  1/2
BRACHYDUM PRIMUM-
                -flavidum  Wilson 1773  1/2
Pale yellow flowers, tubular-shaped.    Collector, Wilson;  hy-
brid's origin unknown.   A.M. 1924.


* * * * * * * * * * * * * * * * * * * * * * * * * * * * *
            -souliei 1/2
BRADFIELD-
            -yakushimanum 1/2
White flowers,  edges flushed reddish purple, upper throat spot-
ted red-purple,  reverse more heavily flushed with same.   Crown
Estate, Windsor, reg. 1979.   P.C. 1979.
SWALLOWFIELD   Parentage as above
Flowers white, with light reddish purple blotch on upper throat,
in trusses of 6-7.  Vigorous plant, compact, broader than tall.
Crown Estate, Windsor, reg. 1981.   H.C. Wisley Trials 1981.
* * * * * * * * * * * * * * * * * * * * * * * * * * * * *


            -brachycarpum 1/2
BRAMAX-
            -maximum 1/2
White flowers.  Late-blooming; hardy to -20F(-29C).   J. Gable.


                -haematodes 1/4
            -Grosclaude-
        -                 -facetum (eriogynum) 1/4
BRANDT RED-                    -griffithianum 1/8
        -          -Queen Wilhelmina-
        -Britannia-              -unknown 3/8
                    -Stanley Davies--unknown
4ft(1.2m) OF(-18C) ML  4/3  Ruby red flowers surrounded by in-
dumented foliage.   Brandt.


* * * * * * * * * * * * * * * * * * * * * * * * * * * * *
            -pubescens 1/2
BRANDYWINE-
            -keiskei 1/2
3ft(.9m)  -10F(-23C)  EM  4/2  Small cream-colored flowers edged
rose, 2in(5cm) wide in spherical trusses.   G. G. Nearing, 1950.
CHESAPEAKE   Parentage as above
3ft(.9m)  -10F(-23C)  EM  3/2  Leaf up to 2in(5cm) long.  Flow-
ers apricot fading white, on every terminal.   Nearing, 1950.
DELAWARE   Parentage as above
3ft(.9m)  -10F(-23C)  EM  3/2   Small leaves and small flowers;
apricot fading to white.   Nearing, reg. 1958.
HOCKESSIN   Parentage as above
3ft(.9m)  -25F(-32C)  E  3/2  Flowers apricot, fading white with
clusters on all terminals.    Leaves rich green and hairy.    Much
like CHESAPEAKE, larger and more open. Nearing, intro. c. 1950.
LENAPE   Parentage as above
3ft(.9m)  -10F(-23C)  E  3/4  Well-branched, shapely plant; rich
green, hairy foliage.  Terminal clusters of small, light yellow
flowers.  Floriferous.    Nearing, intro. 1950; reg. 1958.
MONTCHANIN   Parentage as above
```

```
3ft(.9m)  -25F(-32C)  EM  2/2   Profusion of small white flowers
in terminal clusters.  Shapely plant.   Nearing, reg. 1958.
* * * * * * * * * * * * * * * * * * * * * * * * * * * * *


                -auriculatum 1/2
BRASS RUBBER-
            -griersonianum 1/2
Flowers white, irregularly suffused with red, the coloring more
concentrated in throat and on the edges; reverse red.   Leaves
lightly covered with reddish brown indumentum beneath.   Crossed
at Bodnant, 1938; Lord Aberconway, reg. 1978.   A.M. 1978.


                -brachycarpum tigerstedtii 1/2
BRATMAC-
            -macabeanum 1/2
Buds of spinel red opening to pale purplish pink flowers; dorsal
spots of ruby red, throat deep red.   W. Delp.


* * * * * * * * * * * * * * * * * * * * * * * * * * * * *
            -catawbiense var. album 1/2
BRAVO!-          -fortunei 1/4
    -unnamed hybrid-          -arboreum 1/8
                -unnamed hybrid-
                            -griffithianum 1/8
6ft(1.8m) -25F(-32C)  E  4/4   Trusses of 11-12 flowers, light
purplish pink, lighter in center,  sparse dorsal brown spotting.
D. G. Leach, reg. 1974.   Color illus. Cox pl. 20; HG p. 87.
DOLLY MADISON   Parentage as above
7ft(2.1m) -20F(-29C)  M  4/4   White flowers with reddish brown
blotch, openly campanulate 3.25in(8.3cm) across; in truss 12-13.
Leaves flat, semi-glossy; average density.   Leach, reg. 1972.
* * * * * * * * * * * * * * * * * * * * * * * * * * * * *


                -griffithianum 1/4
    -unnamed hybrid-
BRAY-           -unknown 1/4
    -      -wardii 1/4
        -Hawk-           -fortunei ssp. discolor 1/8
        -Lady Bessborough-
                        -campylocarpum Elatum Group 1/8
Deep pink buds  open soft mimosa yellow,  the upper lobes paler;
the reverse shaded pink.   Crown Estate, reg. 1961.   A.M. 1960.


                -griffithianum 1/4
        -Dawn's Delight-
BREAK OF DAY-           -unknown 1/4
            -dichroanthum 1/2
4ft(1.2m) -5F(-21C)  M  3/1   Open, uncrowded truss of 14 flow-
ers, funnel-shaped, deep orange at the base and edged in orange-
pink; unusual colors.   Rothschild, 1934.   A.M. 1936.


BRECK PINK   Parentage unknown
Pink with white centers.  Dexter hybrid; Ashville, N. C. area.


                -catawbiense var. album Glass--Catalgla 1/4
        -Gosh Darn-                    -decorum ? 1/16
BRED LINE-        -           -Caroline-
            -          -Mrs. H. R. Yates-        -brachycarpum ? 1/16
        -wardii 1/2                 -unknown 1/8
Buds pale purplish pink, vivid red, vivid purplish red,  opening
to white flowers, lightly edged in strong purplish pink.   Delp.


* * * * * * * * * * * * * * * * * * * * * * * * * * * * *
            -haematodes 1/2
BREMEN-                     -catawbiense 1/4
        -red catawbiense hybrid-
                        -unknown 1/4
2ft(.6m)  -5F(-21C)  E  4/4    A dwarf plant; leaves elliptic to
ovate, 2-3.5in(5-9cm) long.  Loose trusses of 10 or 12  rose red
flowers, campanulate; small red calyx.  G. Arends cross; Böhlje,
reg. 1963.   Color illus. WS, 1989, p. 169.
CHINA BOY   Parentage as above
Glowing red flowers.  May be less vigorous.  Böhlje, reg. 1963.
GNOM   Parentage as above
Slow-growing; leaves have scant brown, felted indumentum.  Truss
lax; 15 scarlet flowers, large calyx. Arends/Böhlje, reg. 1963.
* * * * * * * * * * * * * * * * * * * * * * * * * * * * *


                -garden hybrid--unknown 1/2
BREMEN (Hobbie)-
            -williamsianum 1/2
2.5ft(.75m) -10F(-23C)  EM  3/3   Deep rose pink flowers, held
```

in loose trusses.   D. Hobbie.   Gold Medal Boskoop 1970.

```
            -J. H. Agnew--unknown 1/2
BRENDA-
    -griersonianum 1/2
```
Plant medium-sized, good habit, compact; many pink trusses. No
longer in cultivation at Exbury.   Rothschild, 1927. P.C. 1935.

```
             -catawbiense var. album 1/2
BRENDA LEE-              -ponticum 1/4
       -Purple Splendour-
                        -unknown 1/4
```
4ft(1.2m) -20F(-29C) ML Flower openly funnel-shaped, 5 frill-
ed lobes of bishop's violet, with a paler blotch. Ball truss of
11, 7in(17.8cm) across. Plant wider than tall.   Mrs. H. Yates,
reg. 1977.

```
                        -Essex Scarlet--unknown 5/8
          -Elizabeth Hobbie-
          -              -forrestii Repens Group 1/4
BRENDON KING-                      -griffithianum 1/8
          -              -Queen Wilhelmina-
          -Earl of Athlone-        -unknown
                        -Stanley Davies--unknown
```
Compact trusses of deep blood red flowers. Leaves glossy green.
Plant low-growing.   H. W. King cross; S. M. King, reg. 1984.

BRENTOR   Described under LUNAR QUEEN, q.v.

BRIAN SCHRAM   Described under BIG DADDY, q.v.

```
          -leucaspis 1/2
BRIC-A-BRAC-
          -moupinense 1/2
```
3ft(.9m) 5F(-15C) VE 3/3 Flower snow white, faint pink markings on upper lobes; anthers chocolate, an interesting contrast.
Small, round, pubescent leaves; new growth bronze. Bark on older plants shiny, papery, peeling. Rothschild, 1934. A.M. 1945.

```
* * * * * * * * * * * * * * * * * * * * * * * * * * * * *
          -williamsianum 1/2
BRICKDUST-   -dichroanthum 1/4
          -Dido-
          -decorum 1/4
```
3ft(.9m) -5F(-21C) M 4/4   Flower 3in(7.6m) wide, rose madder
shaded to rhodonite red, 6-8 in lax trusses. Rounded leaves,
2in x 1in (5cm x 2.5cm). Vigorous plant. R. Henny, reg. 1960.
LADY APRIL   Parentage as above, except reversed
1.5ft(.45m) -10F(-23C) EM Very slow-growing, wider than tall;
new foliage bronze. White flowers, lightly flushed spinel red,
fading to translucent pink; trusses of 5.   Childers, reg. 1978.
ROSE POINT   Parentage as LADY APRIL
3ft(.9m) OF(-18C) EM 3/4   Rounded plant, dense, wider than
tall. Spirea red buds opening lighter red, 7-lobed, in trusses
of 7. Lem cross; L. Pierce raiser; J. Elliott, reg. 1980.
* *
```

```
          -yakushimanum ? 1/2
BRIDAL BOUQUET-
          -unknown 1/2
```
3ft(.9m)  OF(-18C)  M   Yellow flowers, peachy edging.  Compact
habit like a "yak" hybrid but lacks indumentum.   Whitney/Sather.

BRIDE   See THE BRIDE

BRIDGE   See THE BRIDGE

```
                -wardii Litiense Group 1/4
       -Henry R. Yates-
BRIDGE-   -unknown 3/8
  NORTH-   -caucasicum 1/4
       -Boule de Neige-   -catawbiense 1/8
                -unnamed hybrid-
                        -unknown
```
4ft(1.2m)  -5F(-21C)  ML   Flower openly funnel-shaped, 6-lobed,
of Neyron rose, fading lighter, throat spotted gold; ball-shaped
truss of 14.   C. Herbert, cross 1968; W. A. Reese, reg. 1977.

```
                -griffithianum 1/4
       -Loderi Helen-
BRIDGEPORT-      -fortunei 1/4
       -strigillosum 1/2
```

A selection named by H. L. Larson.

```
                -griffithianum 1/4
       -Dawn's Delight-
BRIGADIER-      -unknown 1/4
       -arboreum 1/2
```
Tall plant of loose habit; pale pink trusses. Rothschild, 1934.

```
          -unknown 1/2
BRIGADOON-
          -yakushimanum 1/2
```
3ft(.9m) x 4ft(1.2m)(12 yrs) OF(-18C) M Funnel-shaped flowers
of heavy substance, vivid red in bud and flower; trusses hold 8.
Dense growth habit.   H. Larson cross; F. & J. Minch, reg. 1989.

```
          -griffithianum 1/2
BRIGHT EYES-
          -diphrocalyx 1/2
```
White flowers, flushed pink.   Rothschild, 1934.

```
                    -unnamed-fortunei ssp. discolor 5/32
          -unnamed- hybrid-
          - hybrid-       -unknown 1/8
     -unnamed-   -facetum (eriogynum) 1/8
     - hybrid-   -unnamed-fortunei ssp. discolor
     -     -unnamed- hybrid-
     -          hybrid-   -unknown
     -          -griersonianum 5/16
BRIGHT-              -Lady       -fortunei ssp. dis-
FUTURE-             - Bessborough-          color
     -          -Jalisco-     -campylocarpum Elatum
     -          -Eclipse-          1/32
     -    -unnamed-   -   -dichroanthum 5/32
     -    - hybrid-   -Dido-
     -    -    -   -decorum 1/32
     -unnamed-   -   -elliottii 1/16
     hybrid-   -Fusilier-
     -          -griersonianum
     -          -dichroanthum
     -Fabia (Waterer)-
                -griersonianum
```
Orient pink flowers, upper lobes heavily marked in citron green.
John Waterer, Sons & Crisp, cross 1958; reg. 1975.

```
          -Scintillation--unknown 1/2
BRIGHT PROSPECT-      -haematodes 1/4
          -unnamed hybrid-
                    -unknown 1/4
```
6ft(1.8m) -5F(-21C) ML Openly funnel-shaped flowers, 6 lobes
deep purplish pink, backs have narrow stripes of same; blotch of
strong red spots. Trusses of 11, on a plant broader than tall.
Scott Arbor. cross; J. Wister named; Tyler Arboretum, reg. 1986.

```
          -forrestii Repens Group K W 6832  1/2
BRIGHTWELL-
          -barbatum 1/2
```
Leaves 2.5in(5.4cm) long, narrowly elliptic. Loose trusses of 6
flowers, widely funnel-campanulate, 2.25in(5.7cm) broad, currant
red.   Crown Estate, Windsor; reg. 1966.   A.M. 1966.

```
          -insigne 1/2
BRIGITTE-
          -Mrs. J. G. Millais--unknown 1/2
```
3ft(.9m) -10F(-23C)F ML   Truss of 19-23 flowers, medium ros-
eine purple shading toward center to rhodamine purple and white,
olive green blotch. Pointed, glossy foliage on a dense, compact
plant. Recommended by Cox.   Hachmann cross; Stück, reg. 1983.
Color illus. Rhododendrons, 1990 (RHS), fig. 4.

BRILLIANCY--unknown.   A parent of BRILLIANT ABBE, q.v.

```
          -thomsonii 1/2
BRILLIANT (Waterer)-
          -unknown 1/2
```
Bright red flowers.   John Waterer.

```
                -forrestii Repens Group 1/4
          -Elizabeth-
BRILLIANT-   -griersonianum 1/4
          -Labrador Tea--Ledum glandulosum? 1/2
```
2ft(.6m) OF(-18C) M True rhododendron? A ledodendron? Small
bright red, bell-shaped flowers; new growth also bright red. Of
```

open habit, slow growth. Lime- and heat-tolerant. Halfdan Lem.
Color illus. Cox pl. 22.

```
                        -kalmia latifolia 1/4
           -Brilliant-
BRILLIANT ABBÉ-         -williamsianum 1/4
           -arboreum ssp. delavayi 1/2
```
Vivid red flowers, spotted darker, in rounded truss. Foliage to
6in(15cm); thin gray-orange indumentum. Mrs. Pinney, reg. 1985.

BRILLIANT WHITE   Described under FLADA W. BLOUGH, q.v.

```
                -griffithianum 1/4
      -Loderi-
BRINCO-           -fortunei 1/4
      -thomsonii 1/2
```
Tall shrub; big trusses of rose pink flowers. Rothschild, 1955.

* *
```
                           -fortunei ssp. discolor 3/16
              -Lady    -
              -Day  -Bessborough-campylocarpum Elatum Group 1/16
        -unnamed-Dream-
        - hybrid-       -griersonianum 3/16
BRINNY-      -          -fortunei ssp. discolor
        -  -Margaret Dunn-   -dichroanthum 1/16
        -              -Fabia-
        -unnamed sdl.--unknown 1/2 -griersonianum
```
4ft(1.2m) -5F(-21C) M 3/3   Bronze buds open to straw yellow
flowers with bronze red center, campanulate, 4.5in(11.5cm) wide;
compact trusses of 8-10. A rather compact plant. Wilbur Graves
cross; Mr. & Mrs. K. Janeck, reg. 1964.
DREAM GIRL   Parentage as above
Dark, flame red buds open to flame red flowers, suffused yellow,
tubular funnel-shaped; truss of 6-7. Tall, upright plant, flowering midseason. Graves cross; Mr. & Mrs. K. Janeck, reg. 1965.
* *

BRITALIER Described under SOLITUDE, q.v.

* *
                -griffithianum 1/4
        -Queen Wilhelmina-
BRITANNIA-   -unknown 3/4
        -Stanley Davies--unknown
```
4ft(1.2m)  -5F(-21C)  ML  4/4  A well-known rhododendron that is
difficult to propagate.  Campanulate, bright scarlet flowers, in
round trusses.  Large, deeply veined leaves of light dull green;
held 3 years.  Performs well in sun, but with even lighter fol-
iage.  C. B. van Nes, 1921.  A.M. 1921.  F.C.C. Wisley Trials
1937.  A.G.M. 1968.  Color illus F p. 37.
C. B. VAN NES  Parentage as above.
5ft(1.5m)  5F(-15C)  EM  3/2  Bush symmetrical, compact, and up-
right, ample long narrow foliage.  Built-up truss of 12-14 glow-
ing scarlet flowers 3.5in(8.9cm) across.  C. B. van Nes.
DR. W. F. WERY    Parentage as above
Scarlet red flowers.  C. B. van Nes.
EARL OF ATHLONE  Parentage as above
5ft(1.5m)  OF(-18C)  EM  5/2    Very fine truss, dome-shaped and
compact, of 12-20 campanulate flowers, bright blood red.   Plant
habit open, spreading; leaves long, narrow, dark green.    C. B.
van Nes.  F.C.C. Wisley Trials 1933.
LANGLEY PARK  Parentage as above
5ft(1.5m)  -5F(-21C)  M  4/3    Deep red flowers to 2.5in(6.4cm)
broad, rather thin-textured; need some sun protection.  Truss of
12-15.  Plant bushy, wider than tall; dark green leaves 6in(15.2
cm) long, fold upward on midrib, don't yellow in sun.  van Nes.
LONDON  Parentage as above
Flowers pink, suffused with bright crimson; the exterior of deep
crimson.  C. B. van Nes.
MAY TEMPLAR    Parentage as above
Bright scarlet flowers.  C. B. van Nes.
TRILBY  Parentage as above
5ft(1.5m)  -10F(-23C)  ML  3/4    Deep crimson flowers with dark
markings; grayish green foliage contrasts with bright red stems.
Sun-tolerant.  C. B. van Nes.  Color illus. VV p. 103.
UNKNOWN WARRIOR  Parentage as above
5ft(1.5m)  5F(-15C)  E  3/3    An early-flowering red.  Flowers
light, but bright, deep rose red, 12-15 per domed truss.  Plant
sun-tolerant, vigorous, upright; pointed leaves fold at mid-rib.

C. B. van Nes.  Color illus. VV p. 53.
VAN NES GLORY   Parentage as above
Red flowers.  C. B. van Nes.
* * * * * * * * * * * * * * * * * * * * * * * * * * * * * *
* * * * * * * * * * * * * * * * * * * * * * * * * * * * * *
```
                              -griffithianum 1/8
                 -Queen Wilhelmina-
        -Britannia-   -unknown 3/8
BRITANNIA'S BELLS-   -Stanley Davies--unknown
                 -williamsianum 1/2
```
2ft(.6m)  OF(-18C)  EM   Widely bell-shaped flowers, 5-lobed, of
good substance, rose red; trusses of 7-8.   Sturdy, bushy mound-
ed plant; small to medium ovate leaves.    Lancaster, reg. 1965.
ALEXANDER STEFFEN   Parentage as above
Flowers of pink or rose.  D. Hobbie
AMMERLANDENSE   Parentage as above
4ft(1.2m)  OF(-18C)  M  3/3   Coral rose flowers.  Hobbie, 1946.
ARDY   Parentage as above
4ft(1.2m)  -10F(-23C)  EM  Compact, globular plant; ovate foli-
age.  Flowers rose pink.  Experiment Sta., Boskoop, reg. 1968.
KARIN   Parentage as above
3ft(.9m)  -15F(-26C)  EM  4/4   Shrub rounded and compact.  Large
pink flowers, saucer-shaped, fringed; truss of 8-9.   Experiment
Sta., Boskoop, reg. 1969.  Gold Medal Boskoop 1966.  A.M. 1968.
LINDA   Parentage as above
3ft(.9m)  -15F(-26C)  M  3/3   Compact, rounded shrub.  Rose red
flowers, open-campanulate.  Leaves  broadly ovate, to 3in(7.6cm)
long.   Exp. Station, Boskoop, reg. 1968.   A.M. Boskoop 1968.
WILLBRIT   Parentage as above
Truss of 6-8 flowers of heavy substance, dark pink; the interior
China rose, paler toward edges.  D. Hobbie cross; Le Faber, reg.
1965.   Gold Medal Rotterdam 1960.
* * * * * * * * * * * * * * * * * * * * * * * * * * * * * *
* * * * * * * * * * * * * * * * * * * * * * * * * * * * * *
```
                    -minus Carolinianum Group 1/2
BRITE MITE---FAISA, F2-
                    -polycladum Scintillans Group 1/2
```
Strong purple buds open to moderate purplish pink.   W. Delp.
SNOWFLAKE   Parentage as above
Purple buds open to white flowers.   W. Delp.
* * * * * * * * * * * * * * * * * * * * * * * * * * * * * *

BRITE PINK   Parentage unknown
Large, bright pink flowers.  Contrasting foliage of apple green.
A Dexter hybrid from Ashville, N. C. area.

```
           -Vervaeniana, Indian azalea ? 1/2
BROCADE-
           -williamsianum 1/2
```
3ft(.9m)  OF(-18C)  M  3/3   (Cox doubts the azalean parentage)
Azaleodendron (?).   Clusters of flowers,  vivid carmine in bud,
open to peach-pink bells.  Attractive habit.   Rothschild, 1934.

BRODICK--form of rex ssp. arizelum
5ft(1.5m)  5F(-15C)  EM  3/4   Purple flowers with almost-black
shade of crimson in the throat; about 20 in ball-shaped trusses.
Leaves thickly indumented beneath.  Brodick Castle.  A.M. 1963.

BRONZE WING   Parentage unknown
3ft(.9m)  OF(-18C)  M  3/4   Pink buds open to creamy white with
rosy edges.  Foliage deep bronze-red; compact plant.   A. Teese,
1981.  Color illus. HG p. 115.

BRONZE WINGS (Stokes)   See STOKES BRONZE WINGS

BROOKS COMSTOCK   PINK BONNET x BLAZEN SUN
Flowers red with lighter centers.  Hardy to -25F(-32C).  O. Pride
cross; D. Hinerman raiser.

```
                           -fortunei ssp. discolor 1/8
             -Lady Bessborough-
        -Jalisco -   -campylocarpum Elatum Group
        - Goshawk- -dichroanthum 1/8   1/8
BROOKSIDE-   -Dido-
        -             -decorum 1/8
        -griersonianum 1/2
```
4ft(1.2m)  -10F(-23C)  EM   Flowers yellow ochre, shaded darker,
tinged with Delft rose, from blood red buds.  Lax trusses of 11.
Leaves 7in(18cm) x 2in(5cm).   Crown Estate, Windsor; reg. 1962.
A.M. 1962.

BROOKVILLE   Described under WHEATLEY, q.v.
```

```
            -arboreum ssp. arboreum 1/2
BROUGHTONII-
            -unknown 1/2
```
6ft(1.8m) (-10F(-23C) M 3/3 Rosy crimson flowers with darker
spotting; 20-flowered, pyramidal truss.   Large, dense shrub, to
20ft(6m). Broughton, before 1853. Color illus. F p. 7.

```
                    -maximum 1/4
              -unnamed hybrid-
BROUGHTONII AUREUM-              -ponticum 1/4
                    -molle 1/2
```
4ft(1.2m) -5F(-21C) ML 3/2 Azaleodendron. Flowers of soft
yellow, spotted orange-yellow, about 2.5in(6.4cm) across; small
round truss. Foliage rough-textured, rather sparse.   Smith of
Norbiton, c. 1830. F.C.C. 1935.   Color illus. VV p. 129.

```
            -fortunei ? 1/2
BROWN EYES-
            -unknown 1/2
```
6ft(1.8m) -20F(-29C) M 4/4   A very dependable plant, where
hard winters happen. Many rose pink flowers, with a prominent
brown flare. Very good foliage. Rated among the top 5 Dexters.
Bosley, before 1958. Color illus. Cox pl. 23.

```
                         -campylocarpum 1/2
BRUCE BRECHTBILL---bud sport of UNIQUE-
                         -unknown 1/2
```
4ft(1.2m) OF(-18C) EM 4/5 Identical to UNIQUE, except pale
pink color, a very light yellow throat. Has beautiful foliage.
Brechtbill, reg. 1974.   Color illus. Cox pl. 24; HG p. 169.

```
            -leucaspis 1/2
BRUCE CAMPBELL-    -chrysodoron 1/4
              -Lovelock-
                    -unknown 1/4
```
15in(.38m) x 15.75in(.4m)(6 yrs) Campanulate flowers about 2in.
(5cm)wide, of light greenish yellow, barium yellow throat markings; truss of 5-6. Ovate leaves, 2in(5cm) long. In NZ, blooms
in early spring.   B. Campbell cross; Dunedin R. Gp., reg. 1988.

BRUCE STAFF   Described under TIM CRAIG, q.v.

```
                  -griffithianum 1/4
          -Sincerity-
BRUMAS-           -unknown 1/2
      -              -adenogynum 1/4
      -Xenosporum (detonsum)-
                         -unknown
```
Flowers pure white, purple honey pouches, very lightly spotted,
4,5in(11.5cm) across; truss of 13.   Gen. Harrison, reg. 1961.

```
* * * * * * * * * * * * * * * * * * * * * * * * * * * *
          -wardii 1/2
BRUNHILDE-    -griffithianum 1/4
          -Loderi-
                 -fortunei 1/4
```
Pale cream flowers.   J. B. Stevenson, cross 1930; intro. 1951.
ROZA STEVENSON   Parentage as above, except reversed
4ft(1.2m) -5F(-21C) EM   Flowers saucer-shaped, with 7 joined
petals, 4.5in(11.5cm) across, of deep lemon yellow, from darker
buds. Full trusses of 10-12.   Mr. & Mrs. J. B. Stevenson, reg.
1970.   Shown as MRS. ROZA HARRISON by RBG, Kew. F.C.C. 1968.
* *

```
            -fortunei ? 1/2
BRYANTVILLE-
            -unknown 1/2
```
3ft(.9m) -5F(-21C) M Flowers medium purplish pink, faint yellow-green spotting, openly funnel-shaped, 3.5in(9cm) wide; 16-
flowered, ball-shaped truss, 6in(15cm) wide. Plant broader than
high. Dexter cross; Wister named; Tyler Arboretum, reg. 1981.

```
                     -fortunei ssp. discolor 1/4
       -King of Shrubs-    -dichroanthum 1/8
       -            -Fabia-
BRYCE -                 -griersonianum 1/8
CANYON-    -wardii 1/4         -griffithianum 1/32
       -Idealist-        -Kewense-
       -     -Aurora-      -fortunei 5/32
          -Naomi-     -
              -       -thomsonii 1/16
                  -fortunei
```

3ft(.9m) OF(-18C) M Flowers carrot red, red blotch in throat,
openly funnel-shaped, 3.5in(8.3cm) wide; truss dome-shaped, 7in.
(18cm) broad, of 10-14 flowers. Floriferous, upright plant; new
foliage bronze.   Childers cross; Bovees Nursery, reg. 1982.

BUCCANEER (Slieve Donard Nursery)   See HARRY BRYCE

```
            -oreodoxa var. fargesii  (erubescens) 1/2
BUCHANAN SIMPSON-
            -unknown 1/2
```
5ft(1.5m) -5F(-21C) EM 4/3 Flowers phlox pink, 3.5in(8.9cm)
wide, throat speckled reddish olive, base of corolla yellowish;
trusses hold 8-10.   Plant compact with sturdy stems and bright
green, bullate leaves.   Mr. & Mrs. E. J. Greig, reg. 1963.

```
* * * * * * * * * * * * * * * * * * * * * * * * * * * *
                   -souliei 1/8
            -Soulbut-
       -Vanessa-     -fortunei--Sir Charles Butler 1/8
BUCKLAND-     -griersonianum 1/4
       -yakushimanum 1/2
```
Loose, open truss of 8 flowers, funnel-shaped, 3in(7.6cm) broad,
red-purple. Leaves 3.5in(9cm) by 1.25in(3.2cm), dark green. L.
S. Fortescue. H.C. 1982. A.M. Wisley Trials 1985.
MARDI GRAS   Parentage: yakushimanum--KOICHIRO WADA x VANESSA
2.5ft(.75m) OF(-18C) EM 4/4   Pale pink flowers fading into
white, margins and exterior of strong purplish pink. Ball truss
of 11-12. Plant broader than tall; reddish brown indumentum on
leaves held 3-4 years.   Bovees Nursery, reg. 1976.
TANYOSHO   Parentage: yakushimanum x VANESSA
3ft(.9m) -5F(-21C) M 4/4   Free-flowering pink trusses fade
to almost-white. Compact habit; indumented leaves.   Bovees.
* *

```
                     -griffithianum 1/2
BUCKLAND BEAUTY-          -campylocarpum Elatum Group 1/4
              -Letty Edwards-
                         -fortunei 1/4
```
Flowers yellow with slight basal red spotting on upper lobes, in
trusses of 11.   L. S. Fortescue, reg. 1977.

```
                 -wardii 1/4
       -Windsor Hawk-          -campylocarpum Elatum Group 1/8
BUCKLAND-         -Lady       -
  CREAM -         Bessborough-fortunei ssp. discolor 1/8
       -                    -griffithianum 1/4
          -Loderi Julie--Loderi selfed-
                         -fortunei 1/4
```
Yellow flowers with central inner stains of red, in trusses of 7
or 8.   L. S. Fortescue cross; Keith Wiley, reg. 1980.

BUCKLEBURY   Described under NEW HOPE, q.v.

```
            -unknown 1/2
BUD FLANAGAN-
            -ponticum 1/2
```
6ft(1.8m) -5F(-21C) ML Flowers sparkling mauve, with a large
flash of deep chestnut. Enormous truss of 18-20.   E. de Rothschild, reg. 1966. Color illus. PB pl. 20.

BUDGET FARTHING--oreodoxa var. fargesii
5ft(1.5m) -10F(-23C) E 3/3   White flowers suffused reddish
purple, 7-lobed, campanulate, 2.5in(6.4cm) wide; trusses of 8-9.
Dark green leaves, 3in(7.6cm) long. Lord Aberconway, reg. 1969.
A.M. 1969.

BUFF LADY   Described under CORAL, q.v.

```
            -griffithianum 1/4
       -Spitfire-
BUKETTA-    -unknown 1/2
       -            -Essex Scarlet--unknown
       -Frühlingszauber-
                   -forrestii Repens Group 1/4
```
3ft(.9m) -10F(-23C) M   Truss of 10-12 flowers, cardinal red,
deeper than SCARLET WONDER, faintly marked with dark ruby red.
Leaves hairy, elliptic. H. Hachmann, cross 1963; G. Stück, reg.
1983. . Color illus. WS, 1989, p. 145.

```
            -edgeworthii (bullatum) 1/2
BULBUL-
            -moupinense 1/2
```

Rather straggly, somewhat tender; flowers white, with faint yellow spotting.   Rothschild, 1934. A.M. 1949.


```
                      -elliottii 1/2                    -griffithianum 1/8
BULLDOG-                         -Queen Wilhelmina-
            -Earl of Athlone-                    -unknown 3/8
                                -Stanley Davies--unknown
Deep red flowers.  Bolitho, 1937.
```

BULLSEYE   Described under AROMANA, q.v.

* *
```
                              -griffithianum 1/2
              -Loderi King George-
BULSTRODE BEAUTY-             -fortunei 1/4
              -                -arboreum ssp. cinnamomeum
              -Loder's White-                    var. album 1/4
                              -griffithianum
```
See LODER'S WHITE for other possible parentage. White flowers.
Sir John Ramsden, 1934.
BULSTRODE BELLE   Parentage as above
White flowers.   Sir John Ramsden, 1934
* *

```
                              -griffithianum 1/4
              -unnamed hybrid-
BULSTRODE PARK-              -unknown 1/2
              -                -catawbiense 1/4
              -Sefton-
                    -unknown
```
6ft(1.5m) -5F(-21C) M 3/2   Flowers bright scarlet crimson,
waxy; trusses large, loose.   C. B. van Nes & Sons, before 1922.

BUMBLEBEE   Described under RONKONKOMA, q.v.

* *
```
              -dichroanthum 1/4
       -Fabia-
BUNTING-       -griersonianum 1/4
       -              -caucasicum 1/4
       -Dr. Stocker-
                     -griffithianum 1/4
```
Trusses of 9-11 flowers, tubular-campanulate, 3in(7.6cm) across,
Dresden yellow and spotted green.   R. Henny, reg. 1961.
WHITE ROBE   Parentage as above, except reversed
3ft(.9m) 5F(-15C) M   Plant broader than tall. Pale yellow
buds open to white flowers, 3in(7.6cm) wide, openly campanulate,
in upright trusses.   Rudolph & Leona Henny, reg. 1965.
* *

```
           -maximum 1/2
BURGEMEESTER AARTS-
           -L. L. Liebig--unknown 1/2
```
A plant of tall habit with dark red flowers.   M. Koster, 1915.

* *
```
                              -griffithianum 1/8
              -Queen Wilhelmina-
       -Britannia-              -unknown 5/8
BURGUNDY-       -Stanley Davies--unknown
       -              -ponticum 1/4
       -Purple Splendour-
                       -unknown
```
5ft(1.5m) -15F(-26C) ML 4/3   Burgundy red flowers in trusses
of 15. Good habit and foliage. Seed by Rose of England; H. Lem
intro. before 1958.
MONIQUE   Parentage as above
3ft(.9m) -5F(-21C) M   Small plant with narrow leaves, medium-
sized light purple flowers. M. R. Nelson, reg. 1972.
* *
* *
```
                    -catawbiense var. album Glass--Catalgla 1/2
BURGUNDY BUTTERFLY-                    -griffithianum 1/8
              -              -Loderi King George-
              -Exotic-                    -fortunei 1/8
              -              -Ostbo Y-3--unknown 1/4
```
Flowers off-white, with a burgundy flare. Hardy to -15F(-26C).
Plant slightly open; average foliage.   Dr. T. L. Ring.
OREGON EXPRESSIONS   Parentage as above
Flowers of pink, yellow undertones. Plant as wide as tall; good
long foliage. Hardy to -10F(-23C).   Dr. Ring.
* *

BURGUNDY CHERRY   Parentage unknown
5ft(1.5m) -5F(-23C) M Flowers 2.25in(5.5cm) wide, carmine red
with purple spotting and blotch; truss of 12. C. Dexter cross;
Mrs. Knippenberg, reg. 1960.


```
                              -ungernii 1/4
              -unnamed hybrid-
BURGUNDY ROSE-              -auriculatum 1/4
              -              -Moser's Maroon--unknown 1/4
              -Romany Chal-
                          -facetum (eriogynum) 1/4
```
6ft(1.8m) OF(-18C) L 3/3 Deep red new growth lasts 2 months.
Light pink flowers appearing same time as new growth.   H. Lem.

* *
```
              -griffithianum 1/4
       -Mars-
       -       -unknown 9/16                    -catawbiense 3/16
BURMA-              -Parsons Grandiflorum-
       -       -America-                    -unknown
       -Fanfare-       -dark red hybrid--unknown
       -              -catawbiense
              -Kettledrum-
                         -unknown
```
5ft(1.5m) -20F(-29C) ML 4/4 Plant 1.5 times as wide as tall,
well-branched; yellowish green leaves, held 2-3 years. Conical
trusses of about 17 flowers, brighter than cardinal red, heavily
spotted black.   David G. Leach, reg. 1984.
MADRAS   Parentage as above
4ft(1.2m) -15F(-26C) M Synonym BENGAL. Plant twice as broad
as high; elliptic leaves 4.75in(12cm) long. Flower cardinal red,
dorsal blotch of maroon, widely funnel-shaped, 2.75in(7cm) wide.
Leach intro. 1973, later withdrawn; reg. 1983.
* *

```
                              -dichroanthum 1/4
              -Fabia Tangerine-
BURMA ROAD-                    -griersonianum 1/4
              -              -Moser's Maroon--unknown 1/4
              -Romany Chal-
                          -facetum (eriogynum) 1/4
```
Compact, flat-topped truss of 11. Flowers 3.5in(9cm) across, of
rich yellowish apricot, suffused pale rose pink; deeper on the
reverse.   F. Hanger cross; reg. 1964. A.M. 1958.


```
              -haematodes 1/2
BURNING BUSH-
              -dichroanthum 1/2
```
A low spreading shrub, with narrow campanulate flowers of bright
tangerine red.   Rothschild, 1934.

BURNING LOVE   Described under ELISABETH HOBBIE, q.v.


```
              -auriculatum 1/2
BUSTARD-              -campylocarpum Elatum Group 1/4
       -Penjerrick-
                   -griffithianum 1/4
```
6ft(1.8m) 5F(-15C) L 3/3   Very large, white flowers, with a
crimson spot in the throat, of good substance. Truss large and
upright.   Rothschild, 1934.

BUTCHER WOOD--form of tephropeplum K W 20844
2.5ft(.75m) 5F(-15C) EM 3/4   Attractive pink flowers; very
good plant habit. Maj. A. E. Hardy, reg. 1975. A.M. 1975.

BUTHEANA--form of mucronatum
Selection of the "species" mucronatum, now considered a hybrid
of unknown origin. The name is now properly written MUCRONATUM.


```
       -fortunei--Sir Charles Butler 3/4
BUTKEW-       -griffithianum 1/4
       -Kewense-
              -fortunei
```
Pink flowers. E. J. P. Magor cross, 1918; intro. 1929.


```
              -catawbiense 1/4
       -Old Port-
BUTLER PORT-       -unknown 3/4
       -unknown
```
5ft(1.5m) -15F(-26F) M 4/2 Well-shaped trusses of fine red-
dish purple flowers; leaves held 1 year. Pride or Stokes intro.
Best of Show award, Great Lakes Ch., ARS, 1988.

```
* * * * * * * * * * * * * * * * * * * * * * * * * *
                            -dichroanthum 1/4
              -Goldsworth Orange-
      -Hotei-                  -fortunei ssp. discolor 1/8
      -       -unnamed-souliei 1/8
      -         hybrid-
BUTTER -                  -wardii 1/8
BRICKLE-                  -dichroanthum
      -       -Dido-
      -       -       -decorum 1/8
      -Lem's -         -Beauty of-griffithianum 5/32
      Cameo-   -Norman- Tremough-
      -     - Gill -         -arboreum 1/32
            -Anna-   -griffithianum
            -                     -griffithianum
                  -Jean Marie de Montague-
                               -unknown 1/16
5ft(1.5m) 5F(-15C) M   Long-lasting flower of heavy substance,
7-lobed, chrome yellow edged in buttercup yellow, reverse strong
gold, cardinal red blotch.  Truss of 12.   Lofthouse, reg. 1982.
MOONDANCER   Parentage as above
31.5in(.8m) x 4ft(1.2m) 10F(-12C) ML   Campanulate flowers, 2.6
in(6.5cm) wide, 6-7 very wavy-edged lobes,  light yellow to pale
amber, spotted deep pink; reverse strong to moderate pink; large
irregular,  yellow calyx.   Smooth elliptic leaves of medium olive
green.    J. Lofthouse, cross 1976; C. Wellmeier, reg. 1987.
NANCY EVANS   Parentage as above
3ft(.9m) 10F(-12C) M  Orange-red buds open to flowers of amber
yellow, hose-in-hose, 6 wavy lobes; truss of 19.  Plant broad as
tall, rounded; new growth brownish.   Brockenbrough, reg. 1983.
Color illus. ARS J 42:2 1988, p. 119.
STARDANCER   Parentage as above
4ft(1.2m) x 5ft(1.5m) 10F(-12C) M  Trusses of 16 flowers, cam-
panulate, 7-lobed, pale orange-yellow, striped moderate red  and
dark yellowish pink.   Lofthouse cross; C. Wellmeier, reg. 1987.
SUNRISE SERENADE   Parentage as above
5.5ft(1.65m) x 4.5ft(1.35m) OF(-18C) M    Light yellowish pink
buds open to flowers of 7 wavy lobes, pale yellowish pink, light
gold spotting; trusses of 14-18, 7in(17.8cm) wide.  Leaves re-
tained 2 years.   R. Mann raiser; Lofthouse cross, reg. 1986.
* * * * * * * * * * * * * * * * * * * * * * * * * *

                  -wardii 1/4
          -Crest-            -fortunei ssp. discolor 1/8
BUTTER YELLOW-   -Lady Bessborough-
          -                     -campylocarpum Elatum Gp. 1/8
          -Golden Yellow--unknown 1/2
5ft(1.5m) OF(-18C) M  Yellow flowers on a compact bush.  Hill.

          -xanthostephanum 1/2
BUTTERBALL-
          -triflorum 1/2
Trusses hold 3-4 open-campanulate flowers, canary yellow, light-
ly speckled  with deeper brownish yellow.  Sturdy upright plant,
4ft(1.2m) at 10 years.   E. J. Greig, reg. 1968

          -campylocarpum 1/2
BUTTERCUP-
      -A. W. Hardy Hybrid--unknown 1/2
Yellow flowers shaded apricot.   Walter C. Slocock, 1924.

BUTTERED POPCORN   Described under SPUN GOLD, q.v.

          -campylocarpum 1/2
BUTTERFLY-            -catawbiense 1/4
      -Mrs. Milner-
                  -unknown 1/4
5ft(1.5m) OF(-18C) M 3/3   Rounded trusses hold pale yellow
flowers, spotted red.   Rather compact habit,  but often appears
leggy.  Easily propagated; heat-tolerant.  Slocock.   A.M. 1940.

              -campylocarpum 1/4
      -Unique-
      -       -unknown 1/4
BUTTERMINT-            -dichroanthum 1/8
      -       -Fabia-
      -unnamed hybrid-   -griersonianum 1/8
                  -dichroanthum ssp. apodectum 1/4
3ft(.9m) -5F(-21C) M 4/3  Orange buds open to yellow flowers,
red dorsal spotting, red streaks on reverse.  Lax truss of about
15.  Plant rounded, as broad as tall.    Mauritsen cross; Greer,
reg. 1979.  Color illus. HG p. 148.
```

BUTTERSTEEP   Described under WARFIELD, q.v.

BUXOM   Described under GIPSY MAID, q.v.

C

C. B. VAN NES Described under BRITANNIA, q.v.

C. F. WOOD Described under AZOR, q.v.

```
                  -arboreum ssp. cinnamomeum var. album 1/4
      -Loder's White-
C. I. S.-         -griffithianum 1/4
      -       -dichroanthum 1/4
      -Fabia-
          -griersonianum 1/4
```
4ft(1.2m) 5F(-15C) M 4/3   See LODER'S WHITE for other pos-
sible parentage. Flowers orange-yellow changing to creamy apricot, bright orange-red throat, to 4in(10.2cm) wide; loose truss
of about 11. Floriferous, upright plant, as broad as tall; leaf
tips twist distinctively. Named for C. I. Sersanous, Past President, ARS. Henny, pre-1958. P.A. 1952. A.M. Wisley Trials
1975.   Color illus. Cox pl. 37; VV p. 57.

```
          -fortunei ? 1/2
C. O. D.-
      -unknown 1/2
```
4ft(1.2m) -5F(-21C) M   Named in honor of C. O. Dexter. Fragrant flower of white and pink, dark throat, deep yellow blotch,
pink flush on reverse. A parent of BLUSH BUTTON. C. O. Dexter,
1925-42; Samuel Everitt intro.; reg. 1958.

```
                               -griffithianum 1/8
                  Queen Wilhelmina-
          -Britannia-            -unknown 3/8
C. P. RAFFILL-     -Stanley Davies--unknown
              -griersonianum 1/2
```
5ft(1.5m) OF(-18C) L 3/3   Deep orange-red flowers in large
rounded trusses. Plant rather dense and spreading; light green
leaves 6in(15.2cm) long, reddish brown petioles.   Other forms
exist; above ratings for Kew form.   RBG, Kew, exhibited 1949.

```
          -catawbiense 1/2
C. S. SARGENT-
```
Red flowers. A parent of Sardis. A. Waterer, 1888.

CABARET   Parentage unknown; may be FABIA x MRS. FURNIVALL
4ft(1.2m) 5F(-15C) M   Cerise-edged flowers from bright cherry
pink buds. Flowers have light pink throat, bright lime markings
at base, cerise stripes from base to lobe sinuses. Leaves olive
green, hairless.   Sather, reg. 1986.

```
              -griersonianum 1/4
      -Tally Ho-
CABLE CAR-     -facetum (eriogynum) 1/4
      -fortunei 1/2
```
4ft(1.2m) 5F(-15C) ML Neyron rose flowers of heavy substance,
funnel-shaped, 5- to 7-lobed, 4.5in(10.8cm) across; 11 in ball-
shaped truss 9in(23cm) wide. Plant well-branched; leaves medium
green; held 2 years.   A. Golden, cross 1962; reg. 1974.

```
* * * * * * * * * * * * * * * * * * * * * * * * * * * *
              -decorum ? 1/4
      -Caroline-
CADIS-     -brachycarpum ? 1/4
      -fortunei ssp. discolor 1/2
```
5ft(1.5m) -15F(-26C) ML 3/4 Flowers light pink, large, very
fragrant, in flat trusses. Plant of good habit; dense, pretty
foliage of long narrow leaves. Gable, before 1958. A.E. 1959.
Color illus. Cox pl. 27; LW p. 39; VV p. 69.
DISCA   Parentage as above, except reversed
5ft(1.5m) -10F(-23C) ML 3/3   Fragrant flowers, white tinged
with pink, frilled edges, in large dome-shaped trusses. Prefers
light shade. Vigorous. Gable, 1944.   Color illus. VV p. 68.
ROBERT ALLISON   Parentage: Caroline x fortunei ssp. discolor
5ft(1.5m) -10F(-23C) ML 4/3 Pink flowers with golden throat;
fragrant, flat-topped trusses. Waxy, green foliage. Gable.
```
* * * * * * * * * * * * * * * * * * * * * * * * * * * *
          -cinnabarinum 1/2
CAERHAYS JOHN-
          -cinnabarinum ssp. xanthocodon Concatenans Group 1/2
```

Shrub medium-sized, erect; bushy habit. Funnel-shaped flowers,
waxy, deep apricot; later than Caerhays Lawrence. Not a hybrid,
but a form of the species cinnabarinum. J. C. Williams, 1967.
Color illus. Hillier Colour Dictionary p. 197.
CAERHAYS LAWRENCE   Parentage as above
Rich yellow, waxy flowers, otherwise similar to Caerhays John.
J. C. Williams, 1967.   Color illus. ARS J 37:4 (1983), p. 182.
* *

                -cinnabarinum ssp. xanthocodon Concatenans Group 1/2
CAERHAYS-
  PHILIP-cinnabarinum ssp. cinnabarinum Blandfordiiflorum Gp. 1/2
Yellow flowers 2.5in(6.4cm) across, funnel-shaped; 7 per loose
truss.   Leaves 4.5in(11.5cm) long, elliptic, with very scanty
brown indumentum. Blooms early. Raisers Charles Williams and
his Head Gardener, Charles Michael; reg. 1966. A.M. 1966.

CAERHAYS PINK--form of davidsonianum
Flowers clear pink, spotted red.   J. C. Williams.

* *
                -edgeworthii 1/2
CAERHAYS PRINCESS ALICE-
                -ciliatum 1/2
Dwarf, compact growth habit. White flowers tinged pink outside;
fragrant.   Caerhays.
PRINCESS ALICE   Parentage as above, except reversed
Sweet fragrance. Flowers long, narrow, white when fully open;
pink line down back of each lobe in bud. Veitch. F.C.C. 1862.
* *

             -fortunei 1/2
CAERNARVON-
             -unknown 1/2
3.3ft(1m) -5F(-21C) M Flowers dark pink with deeper spotting;
fragrant, funnel-shaped, 3.25in(8.3cm) across; round truss holds
14. Plant upright, stiffly branched; leaves held 2 years.   A.
Consolini cross; R. de Longchamp, W. Reese raisers; reg. 1977.

CAERULEUM--form of rigidum
6ft(1.8m) -5F(-21C) EM 4/3 A plant of neat, glaucous foliage
and masses of pure white flowers, olive markings.   Lovely Tri-
flora; draws much attention.   Origin unknown.   Sold by Cox.

              -catawbiense var. album Glass--Catalgla 1/4
     -unnamed-
     - hybrid-fortunei 1/4
CAIRO-   -degronianum ssp. heptamereum (metternichii)
     -unnamed-Eidam-   1/8
     - hybrid-   -Alexander Adie--unknown 1/8
              -williamsianum 1/4
6ft(1.8m) -20F(-29C) EM 3/3   White flowers, bright greenish
small blotch and spotting, 3.25in(8.3cm) wide; ball truss of 16.
Dark green, elliptic foliage; held 2 years.   Leach, reg. 1973.

              -dichroanthum 1/4
     -unnamed hybrid-
CALCUTTA-   -kyawii 1/4
     -catawbiense var. album Glass--Catalgla 1/2
3ft(.9m) -15F(-26C) L 2/3 Orange buds open to brilliant yellow flowers with orange edges, 5-lobed, tubular-campanulate, 1.5
in(3.8cm) wide; 13-flowered lax, pendulous trusses. Plant twice
as broad as tall; dense foliage. Leach, reg. 1972.

* *
            -calophytum 1/2
CALFORT-
        -fortunei 1/2
6ft(1.8m) -5F(-21C) M Pink buds open to white flowers, crimson markings on the reverse. Collingwood Ingram. A.M. 1932.
BOUNTY Parentage as above
Flowers off-white, reddish purple blotch, reverse flushed red-
purple at base and along veins; 15-17 per truss. Leaves narrowly elliptic, 10.5in(26cm) long. Ingram. A.M. 1967.
CANTICA Parentage as above; exhibited by Ingram, 1954.
* *

            -augustinii 1/2
CALIFORNIA BLUE-
            -unknown 1/2
4ft(1.2m) -5F(-21C) EM 4/4 Smooth fir green leaves; electric
blue flowers in profusion. Greer intro.

                -ciliicalyx 1/4
         -Else Frye-
CALIFORNIA GOLD-   -unknown 1/4
         -            -valentinianum 1/4
         -Eldorado-
                 -johnstoneanum 1/4
6ft(1.8m) 15F(-9C) VE 4/4 Flowers primrose yellow, fragrant,
tubular funnel-shaped, 3.25in(8.3cm) across, 5 wavy lobes; truss
of 6. Floriferous, well-branched plant. Foliage spinach green,
silvery scales below.   P. and R. Bowman, cross 1962; reg. 1976.

CALLAGOLD   Described under TIDBIT, q.v.

        -calophytum 1/2
CALLIGHT-
        -Neon Light--unknown 1/2
Flowers of light spirea red paling with age, maroon eye; trusses
hold 22 flowers.   K. Van de Ven, Australia, reg. 1973.

        -caucasicum 1/2
CALLIOPE-
        -unknown 1/2
Pink flowers, fading white; red-brown markings.   Seidel, 1894.

                -caucasicum 1/4
       -Dr. Stocker-
CALLIRHOE-   -griffithianum 1/4
       -arboreum, blood red form 1/2
Flowers of Neyron rose, crimson spots.   E. Magor, intro. 1928.

                -griffithianum 1/4
       -Queen Wilhelmina-
CALOMINA-   -unknown 1/4
       -calophytum 1/2
Synonym ARMANTINE. Medium to tall plant bearing trusses of pink
flowers, with a darker blotch. Blooms early. Lady Loder, 1934.

CALOSTROTUM PINK, CALOSTROTUM ROSE   See CUTIE

       -calophytum 1/2
CALROSE-
       -griersonianum 1/4
Deep rose in bud, opening to pink funnel-shaped flowers, a deep
rose stain. Large plant; good foliage.   Lord Aberconway, 1939.

* *
            -catawbiense var. album Glass--Catalgla 1/2
CALSAP-
       -Sappho--unknown 1/2 (May contain maximum)
4ft(1.2m) x 6ft(1.8m)(12 yrs) -25F(-32C) ML 4/3   Very pale
purple buds opening white; tubular funnel-shaped flowers, 5 wavy
lobes, reverse slightly flushed pale purple. Conical trusses of
18. Striking, very dark blotch of grayed reddish purple. Smooth
oblong leaf. M. Michener cross; reg. 1986. Best of Show Award
Great Lakes Ch., ARS, 1985.
DEADLY FORCE   Parentage as above
Buds very pale purple; flowers very light purple and white, dorsal spots of strong greenish yellow on 3 lobes; anthers magenta
rose, white filaments and style.   Michener cross; Delp raiser.
DEEP THOUGHTS   Parentage as above
Very pale to light purple in bud; white flowers edged with light
purples, dorsal spotting of lettuce green, magenta rose anthers
and a darker stigma, white style.   Michener cross; Delp raiser.
MONACA LAD   Parentage as above
Buds combine light and rose purples; flowers of same colors plus
white, with lettuce green dorsal spotting, magenta rose anthers,
white filaments, fuchsia stigma.   Michener cross; Delp raiser.
WHEELER DEALER   Parentage as above
Light and very pale purple in bud; white and very pale purple in
flower, with beetroot purple and dark red dorsal spotting, light
yellow-green stigma, white style.   Michener cross; Delp raiser.
RITCHIE   Parentage: (Catalgla x Sappho) selfed
Buds of vivid purple open to pale purple flowers, edged in vivid
and strong purples; beetroot purple flare, dorsal spots.   Delp.
* *

CALSTOCKER   described under EXBURY CALSTOCKER, q.v.

          -catawbiense var. album Glass--Catalgla 1/2
CALTWINS-   -catawbiense 1/4
     -Pink Twins-
                -haematodes 1/4

Cross by M. W. Michener and others.   Some clones pink or red or white; some hose-in-hose.   A parent of several Delp hybrids.

```
             -griffithianum 1/4
      -Gilian-
CALYPSO-      -thomsonii 1/4
      -smithii 1/2
```
Introduced by E. J. P. Magor in 1934.   Parentage information of Gilian obtained from Maj. E. W. M. Magor, son of E. J. P. Magor.

CALYPSO (Delp)   Described under TIM CRAIG, q.v.

```
      -campylocarpum 1/2
CAMAN-
      -beanianum 1/2
```
Red flowers.   Lord Aberconway, intro. 1946.

```
                -campylocarpum Elatum Group 1/4
      -Penjerrick-
CAMILLA-      -griffithianum 1/2
      -              -griffithianum
      -Loderi King George-
                -fortunei 1/4
```
Large white flowers.   Lord Aberconway.   A.M. 1944.

```
                         -griffithianum 1/8
                -Queen Wilhelmina-
      -Britannia-              -unknown 3/8
CAMILLO SCHNEIDER-      -Stanley Davies--unknown
      -forrestii Repens Group 1/2
```
Plant of vigorous, upright habit, very free-flowering.   Flowers waxy, glossy, strong red; lax trusses of 6.   D. Hobbie raiser. F.C.C. Wisley Trials 1986.

```
      -campylocarpum 1/2
CAMPBUT-
      -fortunei--Sir Charles Butler 1/2
```
Pale yellow flowers of 5 or 6 lobes, densely spotted with crimson.   E. J. P. Magor, 1926.

```
      -campylocarpum 1/2
CAMPDIS-
      -fortunei ssp. discolor 1/2
```
Parent of rhododendron E. J. P. MAGOR, by D. Hobbie, c. 1954.

* *
```
             -maximum 3/8
      -Fireking-      -forrestii Repens Group 1/8
      -      -Gertrud-      -Michael -ponticum 1/32
      -      Schäle-Prometheus- Waterer-
      -              -              -unknown 15/64
      -                    -Monitor--unknown
CAMPFIRE-              -griffithianum 1/16
      -      -Mars-
      -      -      -unknown      -catawbiense
      -      -Madras-      -Parsons Grand--      3/64
      -              -America- iflorum      -unknown
      -Snapper-      -Fanfare-      -dark red hybrid--unknown
      -      -      -      -catawbiense
      -              -Kettledrum-
      -unnamed-maximum      -unknown
      hybrid-
             -griersonianum 1/8
```
Buds cardinal red; flowers cardinal to vivid red.   W. Delp.
HEAP BIG INDIAN   Parentage as above
Buds a blend of dark red, cardinal red, and currant red; frilled flowers currant red to vivid red, white anthers.   Trusses of 26. Named for William Storms (Cardinal Nursery).   W. Delp.
* *

```
      -campylocarpum 1/2
CAMPIRR-
      -irroratum 1/2
```
4ft(1.2m) OF(-18C) EM   A fine old hybrid from Lamellen with pale yellow flowers and crimson spotting.   E. J. P. Magor, 1926.

* *
```
      -campylocarpum 1/2
CAMPKEW-      -griffithianum 1/4
      -Kewense-
             -fortunei 1/4
```

Creamy white flowers with crimson spots.   Magor, intro. 1925.
CITRONELLA   Parentage as above, but a different cross
3ft(.9m) OF(-18C) M 3/3   Primrose yellow flowers, with a red eye.   Glossy green foliage, somewhat rounded.   J. Waterer.
* *

```
      -campylocarpum 1/2
CAMPXEN-      -adenogynum 1/4
      -Xenosporum (detonsum)-
             -unknown 1/4
```
Flowers white or pale yellow, spotted red.   The former name for detonsum was xenosporum, now considered a hybrid of adenogynum, hence the new hybrid name XENOSPORUM.   E. J. P. Magor, 1940.

CAMPY   Parentage unknown
Glistening pink flowers contrast nicely with soft, shiny green new foliage.   Hardy to -15F(-26C).   One of the best Shammarello hybrids.

```
      -campylogynum ? 1/2
CANADA-
      -unknown 1/2
```
2ft(.6m) -5F(-21C) M 3/3   Very small, tubular, deep rose pink flowers.   Terminal inflorescense of 3-5 small trusses, each with 3-5 flowers.   Reddish edges on new foliage.   E. J. Greig cross; J. F. Caperci, reg. 1977.

* *
```
                         -griersonianum 1/4
             -Mrs. Horace Fogg-      -griffithianum 15/32
      -              -Loderi-
      -                    Venus-fortunei 1/8
CANADIAN-                    -griffithianum
DEAUTY -              -Beauty of-
      -              -Norman- Tremough-arboreum 1/32
      -              - Gill -
      -      -Anna-      -griffithianum
      -Point   -griffithianum
      Defiance-      -griffithianum
             -Marinus Koster-
                    -unknown 1/8
```
6ft(1.8m) OF(-18C) ML 4/4 Flowers pale pink at center, shading darker on edges, openly funnel-shaped, 5in(10.8cm) wide; 16 per truss.   J. Lofthouse, reg. 1971.   Color illus. Cox pl. 28.
LADY OF SPAIN   Parentage as above
4ft(1.2m) OF(-18C) EM 3/3   Funnel-shaped flowers 6in(15cm) wide, crimson fading to carmine rose; tall, conical truss of 12-15.   Plant broader than tall; glossy yellow-green leaves.   John Lofthouse, reg. 1981.
SIERRA BEAUTY   Parentage as above
5ft(1.5m) OF(-18C) ML   Red buds open to flowers of very light pink, edges and 2 dorsal rays darker; dome-shaped trusses of 18. Plant wide as high; leaves held 3 years.   Lofthouse, reg. 1983.
SIERRA SUNRISE   Parentage as above
6ft(1.8m) OF(-18C) ML 5/4 Large, handsome plant; dark green, pointed leaves curve upward from midrib.   Large ruffled flowers, pale pink to white, narrowly edged in rose pink; conical trusses about one foot tall.   Lofthouse, reg. 1975.
* *

```
                         -dichroanthum 1/8
             -Goldsworth Orange-
      -Hotei-      -fortunei ssp. discolor 1/8
      -      -      -souliei 1/8
CANADIAN-      -unnamed hybrid-
GOLD  -      -      -wardii 3/8
      -      -wardii
      -unnamed hybrid-
             -unknown 1/4
```
4ft(1.2m) 5F(-15C) EM 4/4   Golden yellow buds opening to pale sulphur yellow flowers, with a reddish maroon blotch; trusses of 9-11.   Compact plant; glossy foliage.   Lofthouse, reg. 1979.

* *
```
                         -caucasicum 1/8
             -Cunningham's White-
      -Rocket-              -ponticum, white 1/8
CANADIAN-      -catawbiense, red 1/4
LILAC  -      -catawbiense var. album Glass--Catalgla 1/4
      -unnamed-      -fortunei ssp. discolor 1/8
      hybrid-Lady-
             Bessborough-campylocarpum Elatum Group 1/8
```

15in(37cm) -25F(-32C) ML   Flower petals almost triangular,
light purple, spotted with light tan; truss of 13. A tiny plant
of creeping branches; yellow-green leaves. Behring, reg. 1983.
CANADIAN MAGENTA   Parentage as above
2ft(.6m) -25F(-32C) ML   Flower petals shaped like above, very
light cyclamen purple with darker spotting; 13 per truss. Dense
plant, as wide as tall. R. Behring, reg. 1983.
CANADIAN MAUVE   Parentage as above
Dwarf plant with dome-shaped trusses of 15 flowers, medium purplish pink; exterior striped strong reddish purple. Rugose, elliptic foliage. R. Behring, reg. 1987.
CANADIAN PINK   Parentage as above
3ft(.9m) -25F(-32C) L   Truss of about 15 flowers, light mallow
purple, cyclamen purple spotting. Plant upright, half as wide
as high; glossy foliage. R. Behring, cross 1974; reg. 1985.
* *

CANADIAN SUNSET   Described under GYPSY ROVER, q.v.

                        -campylocarpum 1/4
        -unnamed hybrid-
CANARY (Stead)-   -fortunei ssp. discolor 1/4
        -             -griffithianum 1/4
        -Loderi-
                    -fortunei 1/4
Pale yellow flowers. W. T. Stead.

                        -campylocarpum 1/4
        -unnamed hybrid-
CANARY (Koster)-   -unknown 1/4
        -caucasicum 1/2
4ft(1.2m) -10F(-23C) EM 3/3   One of the most hardy yellow
hybrids. Tight trusses of bright lemon yellow flowers. Leaves
deeply veined. M. Koster, intro. 1930.

CANARY ISLANDS   Parentage diagram below: unnamed hybrid x PEKING
                -catawbiense var. album 9/64
        -unnamed-
        - hybrid-   -fortunei ssp. discolor 3/32
        -     -unnamed-   -dichroanthum 1/64
   -un. -   hybrid-Fabia-
   -hyb.-   -griersonianum 3/64
   -    -   -catawbiense 1/64
   -    -   -Atrosanguineum-
-un. -   -   -Atrier-   -unknown 1/64
-hyb.- -Mary Belle-   -griersonianum
-    -   -   -decorum 1/32
-    -   -Dechaem-
-    -   -haematodes 1/32
-   -catawbiense var. album--Catalgla
-          -catawbiense var. album
-    -unnamed-   -wardii 1/8
-    - hybrid-Hawk-   -fortunei ssp. discolor
-Peking-   -Lady
-          Bessborough-campylocarpum Elatum Group 1/16
-             -catawbiense var. album--La Bar's White
        -unnamed-   -wardii
          hybrid-Crest-
                -Lady Bessborough (as above)
4.5ft(1.35m) -20F(-29C) M 4/5 Flowers 2.7in(7cm) wide, light
greenish yellow with dorsal lobe slightly darker yellow, a deep
red blotch, and spotting; truss of 16. Glabrous, elliptic foliage of glossy green, 4in(10cm) long. D. G. Leach, reg. 1985.

        -campylogynum Cremastum Group 1/2
CANDI-
        -racemosum 1/2
3ft(.9m) -10F(-23C) M 3/3   Leaves 1in(2.5cm) long. Flowers
bright rose, growing in clusters of up to 6, along the branches.
J. F. Caperci, reg. 1963.

        -catawbiense ? 1/2
CANDIDISSIMUM-
        -maximum ? 1/2
5ft(1.5m) -15F(-26C)? L   Dark green foliage with nice trusses
of blush white flowers. Truss 6in(15cm) wide, holding 12. Reg.
1967 without origin stated. Rand says (1876): the blush form is
tender; the S. B. Parsons plant (form? of the same name) is pure
white, and hardy.

* *
                        -catawbiense 1/4
        -unnamed hybrid-
        -             -yakushimanum 1/2
        -             -yakushimanum   -fortunei ssp.
CANDIED- -Si Si-   -Day -Lady   - discolor 3/64
 APPLE- -   -   -Dream- Bessborough-
        -   -   -Gold -   -   -campylocarpum
        -   -   Mohur-   -griersonianum Elatum 1/64
        -D.D.-   -   -fortunei ssp. discolor
        -         -Margaret-   -dichroanthum 1/64
        -            Dunn -Fabia-
        -                  -griersonianum 3/64
        -     -yakushimanum
        -Serendipity-
                -aureum (chrysanthum) 1/8
Buds of cardinal and currant red, open to frilled flowers, deep
red and strong pink, with a primrose yellow flare. Delp.
SWAN SONG   Parentage as above
Buds roseine purple and rhodamine purple. Yellowish white flowers, with a pale yellow flare and white filaments; the exterior
veined with strong purplish pink. Weldon Delp.
* *

                -Winter Favourite--unknown 1/4
        -Denise-   -chrysodoron 3/8
CANDLE GLEAM-   -Chrysomanicum-
        -                  -burmanicum 3/8
        -Chrysomanicum (as above)
Truss of 4-6 tubular funnel-shaped flowers; primrose yellow with
pink edges. Shrub to 3ft(.9m) tall.   F. Boulter, reg. 1984.

        -yakushimanum--Koichiro Wada 1/2
CANDY CANE-   -williamsianum 1/4
        -unnamed hybrid-
                -unknown 1/4
Buds of Neyron rose, opening paler, fading to blush with deeper
rose lines down the center of each lobe. Bush about 3ft(.9m) at
9 years. Pukeiti Rhododendron Trust, New Zealand, reg. 1984.

                -wardii 1/4
        -Hawk-   -fortunei ssp. discolor 1/8
        -   -Lady -
CANDY FLOSS-   Bessborough-campylocarpum ELATUM Group 1/8
        -         -griffithianum 1/4
        -Mrs. Randall-
          Davidson -campylocarpum 1/4
Campanulate flowers 3.5in(8.9cm) wide, cream suffused pink, rims
darker; lax trusses of 10. Dark green leaves, 4in(10.2cm) long;
petioles stained purple. Crown Estate, Windsor; reg. 1963.

                -Pygmalion--unknown 1/8
        -unnamed hybrid-
        -Weldy-   -haematodes 1/8
        -    -yakushimanum, Exbury form 1/4
        -             -yakushimanum 1/4   -fortunei ssp.
CANDY -   -unnamed-   -Lady   - discolor 3/64
KISSES-   - hybrid-   -Day - Bessborough-
        -    -   -Gold - Dream-   -campylocarpum
        -    -   Mohur-   -griersonianum   Elatum 1/64
        -unnamed-   -   -fortunei ssp. discolor
        - hybrid-   -Margaret Dunn-   -dichroanthum
        -                  -Fabia-   1/64
        -                      -griersonianum
        -    -yakushimanum   3/64
        -Serendipity-
                -aureum (chrysanthum) 1/8
Buds of strong red, open white. Frilled flowers, edged heavily
with spinel red and strong purplish pink. W. Delp.

        -minus Carolinianum Group--Epoch 1/2
CAN'T-   -tetraploid carolinianum 1/4
LOSE -Mini -   -fastigiatum 1/8
        Pearl-Wachtung---sport of Ramapo-
                        -minus Carolinianum Gp. 1/8
Buds of dark purplish pink opening to flowers in light shades of
purple; dorsal spots of strong purplish red, on 3 lobes.   Delp.

CANTICA   See under CALFORT.

CANTON CONSUL--form of hanceanum Nanum Group

Dwarf habit. Creamy green in bud; campanulate flowers of cream,
1in(2.5cm) wide.   Crown Estate; reg. 1962.   A.M. 1957.


```
                -williamsianum 1/2
CAPER-          -haematodes 1/4
     -Hiraethylin-
                -griffithianum 1/4
```
Flowers light azalea pink, funnel-campanulate, 4in(10.2cm) wide,
in trusses of 5-7. Compact habit.   Rudolph Henny, reg. 1964.

CAPERCI SPECIAL   Parentage unknown
2ft(.6m) -15F(-26C) EM 4/3   Tubular funnel-shaped flowers,
clear purplish pink; ball-shaped trusses of 5-7. Leaves densely
covered with brown scales beneath.   Caperci, reg. 1977.

CAPRI   See CYPRUS

CAPRICE---augustinii hybrid ?
Once considered a superior form of augustinii, selected by Hansen, but shown in the Register of 1958 as a hybrid.


```
                      -souliei 1/16
                -Soulbut-
          -Vanessa-     -fortunei--Sir Charles Butler 1/16
     -Etna-       -griersonianum
     -           -dichroanthum 1/8
CAPRIOLE-   -Fabia-
     -           -griersonianum 1/2
     -           -facetum (eriogynum) 1/4
     -Jacquetta-
                -griersonianum
```
Dark red flowers. Lord Aberconway, intro. 1942.

CAPTAIN BLOOD   Described under JULIANA, q.v.

* *
```
                -griffithianum 1/4
          -Mars-
CAPTAIN JACK-    -unknown 1/4
          -facetum (eriogynum) 1/2
```
6ft(1.8m) 5F(-15C) ML 4/3   Flowers blood red, 3.5in(8.9cm)
wide, with a waxy shine; tall truss of 15. Large leaf, unusual
roll at edges.   Henny, reg. 1962.   P.A. 1956.   Color illus.
ARS Q 29:1 (1975), p. 35.
HOTSHOT   Parentage as above, except reversed
A dwarfish plant; red flowers.   Henny, cross 1944; reg. 1962.
LAST CHANCE   Parentage as CAPTAIN JACK, above
6ft(1.8m) -5F(-21C) ML 3/3   Flowers 3.5in(9cm) across, rosy
claret, shaded orange-rose in center; trusses of 14. Emerald
green leaves.   R. Henny, reg. 1958.   P.A. 1957.
WITCHERY   Parentage as CAPTAIN JACK, above
5ft(1.5m) -5F(-21C) ML 4/3   Glowing, fiery red flowers, held
in tall trusses. Silvery tomentum on new growth.   R. Henny.
* *
* *
```
                         -thomsonii 1/8
               -Bagshot Ruby-
          -Princess Elizabeth-     -unknown 3/8
CAPTAIN KIDD-           -unknown-
          -          -haematodes 1/4
          -May Day-
                -griersonianum 1/4
```
4ft(1.2m) OF(-18C) ML   Some suggest that the pollen parent
of BAGSHOT RUBY was a maximum hybrid. Bright red, waxy flowers,
3.5in(8.9cm) across, in trusses of 14. Leaves 7in(17.8cm) long;
habit spreading and contorted. Henny, reg. 1961. P.A. 1960.


```
               -maximum 1/2
CAPTIVATION-                         -catawbiense 1/8
          -                -unnamed hybrid-
          -Altaclerense-           -ponticum 1/8
                         -arboreum 1/4
```
Rosy crimson flower, black spots. Standish & Noble, before 1850.


```
               -griffithianum 1/8
          -Kewense-
     -Aurora-     -fortunei 1/8
CARA MIA-     -thomsonii 1/4
     -      -wardii 1/4
     -Crest-                -fortunei ssp. discolor 1/8
          -Lady Bessborough-
                         -campylocarpum Elatum Group 1/8
```

Pale rose in bud, opening to cream flowers with a yellow throat,
basal crimson stain, 4.5in(11.5cm) wide; 12-15 per truss. Plant
tall and compact.   E. de Rothschild, reg. 1966.   A.M. 1966.


```
               -catawbiense 1/2
CARACTACUS-
               -unknown 1/2
```
6ft(1.8m) -25F(-32C) L 3/3 Flowers rich purplish crimson, in
fine trusses--Rand. Medium-sized leaves, deeply veined, tend to
yellow in full sun. Compact habit. A. Waterer. F.C.C. 1865.

CARDIFF   Parentage unknown
White flowers with a red dorsal blotch, spotting above it; truss
of 12. Slocock, cross c. 1964; Gable raiser; Reese, reg. 1980.


```
          -arboreum 5/8
CARDINAL-         -thomsonii 1/4
     -Barclayi-           -arboreum
               -Glory of  Penjerrick-
                         -griffithianum 1/8
```
Bright scarlet flowers. Lord Aberconway. F.C.C. 1937.


```
                    -neriiflorum 1/8
          -F. C. Puddle-
     -Ethel-           -griersonianum 1/8
CARETH-     -forrestii Repens Group 1/4
     -          -arboreum 5/16
     -Cardinal-         -thomsonii 1/8
               -Barclayi-           -arboreum
                    -Glory of  Penjerrick-
                              -griffithianum 1/16
```
Red flowers. Lord Aberconway, intro. 1946.

* *
```
          -irroratum 1/2
CAREX-
     -oreodoxa var. fargesii 1/2
```
5ft(1.3m) 0F(-18C) VE 3/3   Flowers rich pink within, darker
without, about 8 in medium-sized, neat truss. Tall, pyramidal,
bush, with grayish green foliage. Rothschild, 1932. A.M. 1932.
CAREX BLUSH   Parentage as above
Very early flowering and tall, forming a pyramidal bush. Leaves
soft grayed green, resembling fargesii. Pink buds; campanulate,
pink-tinged flowers, dark spots; truss of 8.   Rothschild, 1932.
CAREX WHITE   Parentage as above
Many moderate-sized trusses of bell-shaped flowers, pink in bud,
opening to almost pure white with maroon spots. See CAREX BLUSH
for foliage and growth habit.   Rothschild, 1932.
* *

CARIOCA   Described under MARY MAYO, q.v.

* *
```
                    -griffithianum 1/16
               -Kewense-
          -Aurora-     -fortunei 5/16
     -Naomi-     -thomsonii 1/8
CARITA-     -fortunei
     -campylocarpum 1/2
```
5ft(1.5m) 5F(-15C) M 4/4 Pink buds, opening primrose yellow.
Leaves rich green, held one year. Rothschild, 1935. A.M. 1945.
Color illus. Cox pl. 29; PB pl. 7; W p. 79.
CARITA CHARM   Parentage as above
5ft(1.5m) 5F(-15C) M 4/4   Similar to the above. Deep pink
buds opening to creamy flowers, flushed peach pink. Rothschild,
1935.   Color illus. PB pl. 6 & 7.
CARITA INCHMERY   Parentage as above
5ft(1.5m) 5F(-15C) M 4/4 Deep rose red buds open to a blend
of soft biscuit yellows, and rose or salmon; fade to opal tints.
Bush well-proportioned, rather open; rich green leaves.   Rothschild, 1935.   Color illus. F p. 37; PB pl. 7.
GOLDEN DREAM   Parentage as above
5ft(1.5m) 5F(-15C) M 4/4   Taller and more open than CARITA,
A.M. form, flowers larger. Many trusses of creamy yellow, from
dusky pink buds, cover the plant. Medium-sized, oval leaves. A
very beautiful form. Rothschild, 1935(?).   Col. ill. PB pl. 7.
* *


```
          -catawbiense 1/2
CARL METTE-
          -unknown 1/2
```
Parent of HASSAN, MRS. W. R. DYKES. Geranium red. Seidel, 1894.

```
                              -griffithianum 1/16
                    -Kewense-
                    -Aurora-         -fortunei 13/16
CARL       -Naomi Pink Beauty-      -thomsonii 1/8
PHETTEPLACE-                 -fortunei
            -fortunei, pink
```
6ft(1.8m) -10F(-23C) M 4/3 Intense pink flowers, spotted in
chocolate brown, of heavy substance, fragrant, 4in(10.2cm) wide;
round trusses of 13. Bush upright; grayish olive green foliage.
Phetteplace cross; Robert Guitteau, reg. 1975.

* *
```
                         -campylocarpum Elatum Group 1/8
              -Ole Olson-
        -Lem's Goal-         -fortunei ssp. discolor 1/4
        -            -griersonianum 1/8
CARLENE-      -Azor-
        -              -fortunei ssp. discolor
        -williamsianum 1/2
```
3ft(.9m) 5F(-15C) M 3/3 Loose bells of warm golden cream,
flushed a glowing pink at centers. Plant a bright green mound,
rounded leaves, yellow stems. Lem cross; C. Fawcett, reg 1961.
MAUREEN Parentage as above, except reversed
Very light Neyron rose, tinged yellow at base. Lem, reg. 1973.
* *

```
        -Souvenir of Anthony Waterer--unknown 1/2
CARMANIA-
        -facetum (eriogynum) 1/2
```
Hillier Manual calls it a first-class Exbury hybrid, with bright
pink flowers, blooming midseason. Also in the Rhod. Register of
1958, but not in Rothschild Rhododendrons by Phillips/Barber.
Rothschild, 1935.

CARMELITA--form of chamaethomsonii var. chamaethauma
Collected and named by Kingdon Ward (5847) from Doshong La, Himalayas. Flowers of luminous carmine, in threes. Larger foliage
than SCARLET RUNNER or SCARLET PIMPERNEL.

```
        -sanguineum ssp. didymum 1/2
CARMEN-
        -forrestii Repens Group 1/2
```
1ft(.3m) -5F(-21C) EM 4/5 Several forms of this hybrid. One
of the best dwarfs; blooms quite young. Campanulate flowers of
deep bright red, in clusters of 2-5. Bush sturdy, broad; leaves
small, dense, glossy. Rothschild, 1935.   A.M. Wisley Trials
1989. Color ill. ARS Q 28:4 (1974), p. 238; F p. 37; VV p. 41.

CARNAL Described under GOLDEN HARBINGER, q.v.

```
              -haematodes 1/4
        -May Day-
CARNIVAL-      -griersonianum 1/4
        -         -griffithianum 1/4
        -Loderi-
              -fortunei 1/4
```
Pink flowers. Lord Aberconway, intro. 1950.

* *
```
                  -diaprepes 1/4
            -Polar Bear-
CAROL AMELIA-         -auriculatum 1/4
        -              -fortunei ssp. discolor 1/4
        -Evening Glow-    -dichroanthum 1/8
                  -Fabia-
                       -griersonianum 1/8
```
4ft(1.2m) -5F(-21C) VL 4/4 Fragrant white flower 5in(12.7cm)
across, of 7 wavy lobes. Somewhat open and lax trusses of 8-10.
Plant upright and well-branched. A. John Holden, reg. 1979.
MRS. A. J. HOLDEN Parentage as above
5ft(1.5m) -5F(-21C) L Long, narrow leaves. Flowers 7-lobed,
sweetly scented, to 5.25in(13.3cm) wide, sunny yellow with light
green spotting, rimmed pink; truss of 10. Holden, reg. 1979.
* *

```
              -irroratum 1/2
CAROL GRIER-
        -unknown 1/2
```
5ft(1.5m) x 4ft(1.2m)(5yrs) Broadly funnel-campanulate flowers,
pale yellow, freckled red on 5 wavy-edged lobes, slightly fragrant; truss of 10. Upright, open habit. R. M. Bovee cross; D.
Grier raiser; M. Reeves, reg. 1988.

```
                    -forrestii Repens Group 1/4
            -Elizabeth-
CAROL HIGH-      -griersonianum 1/4
        -          -fortunei ? 1/4
            -French Creek-
                    -unknown 1/4
```
5ft(1.5m) -10F(-23C) EM Very fragrant white flowers, with
chartreuse spotting; truss 6in(15cm) wide, of 14 flowers. Plant
upright, broad; new growth bronze green. C. Herbert, reg. 1979.

```
                    -griffithianum 1/8
            -Mars-
        -Vulcan-    -unknown 1/8
CAROL JEAN-      -griersonianum 1/4
        -          -calophytum 1/4
        -Robin Hood-
                    -sutchuenense 1/4
```
Flowers carmine with a dark blotch on dorsal lobe, deeper red in
the throat; truss of 14. J. Klupenger, reg. 1977.   A.M. 1957.

CAROLA (Seidel) Described under ALFRED, q.v.

```
                  -dichroanthum 1/8
        -Astarte-         -campylocarpum Elatum Group 1/16
    -Ouida-    -Penjerrick-
CAROLA-               -griffithianum 1/16
        -    -griersonianum 1/4
        -williamsianum 1/2
```
Pink flowers. Lord Aberconway, intro. 1941.

```
              -minus Carolinianum Group 1/2
CAROLINA ROSE-
        -azalea prinophylllum (roseum) 1/2
```
3ft(.9m) -10F(-23C) M A well-branched azaleodendron, with a
profusion of small, dark pink flowers. Mrs. J. F. Knippenberg.

```
        -decorum ? 1/2
CAROLINE-
        -brachycarpum ? 1/2
```
6ft(1.8m) -15F(-26C) ML 3/4 Pale orchid pink flowers; light
fragrance enhanced by warm sun.   Highly resistant to root rot;
not easy to propagate. Nice, glossy leaves. First hybrid named
by Gable, 1956. Color illus. Cox pl. 30; LW pl. 43; VV p. 44.

* *
```
                  -yakushimanum 1/2
CAROLINE ALLBROOK-          -ponticum 1/4
                  -Purple Splendour-
                        -unknown 1/4
```
4ft(1.2m) -5F(-21C) M 4/4 Rose purple flowers, about 20 in
a truss, with cream blotching in upper center. Plant vigorous,
spreading as wide as high. A. F. George, reg. 1975. A.M. 1977.
DINTY MOORES Parentage as above
27in(.69m) -15F(-26C) M Flowers white with ruby red spots, in
trusses of 15-17. Plant as broad as high; foliage held 3 years.
Dr. R. Rhodes cross; raiser Wildfong; R. Behring, reg. 1980.
ERNEST INMAN Parentage as above
4ft(1.2m) -10F(-23C) EM Flowers lavender, fading to white at
the base. Very free-flowering and very compact plant, with dark
dense foliage. A. F. George, reg. 1976.   A.M. 1979.
LAVENDER FILIGREE Parentage as above
Flowers in trusses of 12-15, campanulate, very light purple outside, light purple inside, with a strong yellow flare on dorsal
lobe. Shrub to 5ft(1.5m). K. van de Ven, Australia, reg. 1986.
LIGHTLY LAVENDER Parentage as above
4ft(1.2m) -15F(-26C) M 3/4 Lovely, light lavender flowers in
the spring and sometimes again in the fall. Deep green foliage.
H. E. Greer, 1988. Color illus. HG p. 167.
MERVYN SETTLE Parentage as above
3ft(.9m) x 2.5ft(.75m) OF(-18C) M Truss of 19 flowers. Buds
strong purplish red, open to deep purplish pink flowers, spotted
with deep red. Fred Peste cross; S. P. Johnston, reg. 1986.
SHARON PESTE Parentage as above
2.5ft(.75m) x 3ft(.9m) OF(-18C) Openly funnel-shaped flowers,
19 per truss, 5-lobed, strong purplish pink with strong greenish
yellow spotting. Semi-dwarf, well-branched plant. Fred Peste,
cross 1976; Sharon Peste Johnston, reg. 1986.
TIGER SPLENDOUR Parentage as above, except reversed
3ft(.9m) -15F(-26C) L 3/3 Plant spreading wider than tall;
leaves very tough, moderate olive green. Trusses of 12-14 flowers. Strong purplish red buds open to light purple, a striking
dorsal blotch of strong orange-yellow.   Dr. D. Hinerman cross;

Dr H. E. Salley, raiser; reg. 1988.
WHITE FLARE   Parentage as CAROLINE ALLBROOK, above
Flowers in trusses of 20-22, funnel-shaped, 5-lobed, white, with
a light yellow flare on dorsal lobe.   Shrub 3.5ft x 3.5ft(1m)(15
yrs).   K. van de Ven, Australia, cross 1966; reg. 1987.
* *
* *

```
                    -Corona--unknown 1/4
          -Bow Bells-
CAROLINE -          -williamsianum 1/4
  DE ZOETE-                    -dichroanthum ssp. scyphocalyx 1/8
              -Socrianum-
    -unnamed-         -griffithianum 1/8
      hybrid-    -wardii 1/8
              -Rima-
                    -decorum 1/8
```
3ft(.9m) -15F(-26C) EM 4/4   Pure white, well-shaped flowers,
in trusses of about 10.   Plant of medium growth; glossy foliage,
heart-shaped.   A. F. George, Hydon Nurs., reg. 1974.   A.M. Wisley Trials 1986.   Color illus. JS p. 106.
BOW STREET   Parentage as above
3ft(.9m) OF(-18C)   Pale yellow flowers with slight pink flushing in truss of 8-10.   A. F. George, Hydon, reg. 1976.
CHEAPSIDE   Parentage as above
3ft(.9m) OF(-18C) M 4/4   Pale yellow flowers, flushed apricot
on the reverse.   A. F. George, reg. 1976.
LEGAL JOHNNY   Parentage as above
3ft(.9m) OF(-18C) M   Flowers of crushed strawberry red, creamy
yellow centers, edges of rhodonite red.   A. George, reg. 1976.
* *

```
                    -forrestii Repens Group 1/4
          -Elizabeth-
CAROLINE GEM-        -griersonianum 1/4
            -        -decorum ? 1/4
            -Caroline-
                    -brachycarpum ? 1/4
```
2.5ft(.75m) -5F(-21C) M   Empire rose buds open to carmine rose
flowers with a flush of coral, bell-shaped, up to 4in(10.2cm)
across; conical truss of 10-12.   Mrs. J. Knippenberg, reg. 1966.

* *
```
          -fortunei 1/2
CAROLINE SPENCER-
          -williamsianum 1/2
```
Bright pink flowers.   D. Hobbie, 1942-44.
HUBERT ROBERT   Parentage as above
Shell pink flowers.   G. M. Adams-Acton, 1950.
KIMBERLY   Parentage as above, except reversed
3ft(.9m) -10F(-23C) EM   3/4   Of interest all winter with moss
green foliage and bright purple bud scales.   Foliage hidden when
pastel pink flowers bloom profusely.   Flowers fade white.   Truss
open.   H. Greer, reg. 1964.   P.A. 1963.   Color ill. HG p. 86.
PSYCHE   Parentage: fortunei--Sir Charles Butler x williamsianum
Synonym WEGA.   Pink flowers.   D. Hobbie, 1950.
* *

```
                    -griffithianum 1/2
          -Halopeanum-
-Snow Queen-        -maximum 1/8
-          -         -griffithianum
CAROLINE-  -Loderi-
  WHITNER-         -fortunei 3/8
-          -         -griffithianum
-Loderi Sir Edmund-
                    -fortunei
```
Flowers of delicate pink.   Lady Loder.   A.M. 1935.

```
                              -catawbiense 3/16
                    -unnamed hybrid-
          -Boule de Rose,-        -unknown 6/16
          - selfed       -         -caucasicum 1/8
          -         -Boule de-        -catawbiense
CAROLYN DANA-         Neige -unnamed-
  LEWIS   -                    hybrid-unknown
          -                              -thomsonii
          -              -Bagshot Ruby-        1/16
          -  -Princess Elizabeth-        -unknown
          -Lanny -              -unknown
           Pride-         -smirnowii 1/8
                    -unnamed hybrid-
                              -yakushimanum 1/8
```

Buds of cardinal red and currant red, open to frilled flowers of
cardinal and currant red; cardinal red dorsal spotting;   anthers
white.   Medium-sized bush.   Hardy to -15F(-26C).   Weldon Delp.

```
          -wardii 1/2
CAROLYN GRACE-
          -unknown  1/2
```
4ft(1.2m) OF(-18C) EM 3/3   Flowers of chartreuse yellow with
green tinge, 3in(7.8cm) wide; round trusses of 7-10.   G. Grace;
reg. 1961.   A.E. 1960.   Color ill. ARS Q 29:2 (1975), p. 103.

```
                              -griffithianum 1/8
                    -George Hardy-
          -Mrs. Lindsay Smith-        -catawbiense 1/8
CAROLYN HARDY-        -Duchess of Edinburgh--unknown
          -wardii (croceum) 1/2                    1/4
```
Openly funnel-shaped flowers of light sap green, 5-lobed, 3.5in.
(8.9cm) wide ;loose trusses.   C. Ingram, reg. 1967.   A.M. 1967.

* *
```
          -minus Carolinianum Group 1/2
CAROUSEL-
          -saluenense 1/2
```
Upright, spreading plant, 29in(.73m) high x 41in(1.02m)(20 yrs).
20 years.   Flowers lavender pink with spotted throat, 1in(2.5cm)
across; trusses hold up to 10.   J. Caperci, reg. 1965.
DEBIJO   Parentage as above
2ft(.6m) -15F(-26C) EM 3/3   Trusses of 7-8 flowers, lavender
purple.   Plant spreads wider than high.   Caperci, reg. 1965.
* *

CARSE--seedling of irroratum
White-flowered; blooming early season.   P. Cox, reg. 1965.

```
          -brachycarpum 1/2
CARTE BLANCHE-        -fortunei ssp. discolor 1/8
          -        -unnamed hybrid-
          -Bonfire-        -Mrs. R. G. Shaw--unknown
                    -griersonianum 1/4        1/8
```
5ft(1.5m) -15F(-26C) LM   Striking white flowers, blushed pink
with a yellow blotch; spherical trusses.   Shapiro.

CARY ANN   Described under TRANQUILITY, q.v.

* *
```
                              -caucasicum 3/16
                    -Jacksonii-        -caucasicum
          -Goldsworth-        -Nobleanum-
CARY'S- Yellow  -              -arboreum 1/8
  CREAM-
  -              -campylocarpum 1/4
  -unnamed-brachycarpum 1/4
    hybrid-              -catawbiense 1/16
          -Mrs. P. -Atrosanguineum-
           den Ouden-        -unknown 1/8
          -              -arboreum
                    -Doncaster-
                              -unknown
```
2ft(.6m) -15F(-26C) ML   Light yellow flowers, spotted darker
yellow, in trusses of 16.   Plant well-branched;   3/4 as broad as
tall; leaves held 2 years.   E. A. Cary, reg. 1980.
CARY'S YELLOW   Parentage as above
2ft(.6m) -15F(-26C) ML   Chartreuse flowers 1.75in(4.5cm) wide,
funnel-shaped; 12 in ball-shaped, open truss. Plant as broad as
tall; dull green leaves, held 2 years.   Cary, reg. 1980.
JOSEPHINE V. CARY   Parentage as above
2ft(.6m) -15F(-26C) ML   Light orchid pink flowers with heavy
apricot spotting, funnel-shaped, 2in(5cm) across; trusses of 12.
Broad plant with dark olive green leaves.   Cary, reg. 1980.
STRAWBERRIES AND CREAM   Parentage as above
3ft(.9m) -15F(-26C) ML   Neyron rose flowers fading to empire
yellow in spherical truss of 12.   Foliage yellowish green; plant
as wide as tall.   Cary, reg. 1980.
WILLIAM P. CARY   Parentage as above
2ft(.6m) -15F(-26C) M   Pink buds open to empire yellow; truss
of 16.   Dull yellow leaves 3.5in(9cm) long.   Cary, reg. 1980.
* *

CARY'S RED   Parentage unknown
Red flowers, much like AMERICA.   Cary, reg. 1974.

CARY'S YELLOW   Described under CARY'S CREAM, q.v.

```
              -Newburyport Belle (Fowle 19)--unknown 1/2
CASANOVA-        -catawbiense var. rubrum 1/4
          -Good Hope-
                 -wardii 1/4
```
4ft(1.2m) -25F(-32C) M 4/5   Flowers 5-lobed, 2.3in(5.5cm)
across, opening pale yellow with a strong orange-yellow dorsal
blotch; the reverse flushed medium shell pink; trusses of 12-14.
Glossy, elliptical leaves.   David Leach, reg. 1985.

CASCADE SUNRISE   Parentage unknown: elepidote
8ft(2.4m)(18yrs) OF(-18C) M   Dome-shaped truss of 9-10 flowers, reddish pink in bud, opening with edges of strong purplish
pink shading through paler shades, and deep purplish pink in the
throat.   W. A. and J. Ragan, reg. 1989.

```
          -Jan Dekens--unknown 11/16        -griffithianum 7/32
       -                        -Beauty of -
CASTANETS-        -Norman Gill- Tremough-arboreum 1/32
       -     -Anna-        -griffithianum
       -       -            -griffithianum
       -Point   -Jean Marie de-
      Defiance-    Montague  -unknown
       -                     -griffithianum
       -         -George Hardy-
       -Marinus Koster-       -catawbiense 1/16
                   -red hardy hybrid--unknown
```
5ft(1.5m) OF(-18C) M 4/4   Red buds open very light pink with
large spotting of light Indian lake; fragrant. Exterior roseine
purple, radial ribs fuchsia purple. Plant as wide as high; big,
glossy leaves, yellow-green.   J. Lofthouse, reg. 1984.

```
          -barbatum, pink 1/2
CASTLE OF MEY-
          -haematodes ssp. chaetomallum 1/2
```
Named after the Scotland home of the Queen Mother. Plant bushy,
medium-sized, compact. Flowers deep red, waxy, campanulate, in
flat trusses. Leaves pale green. Rothschild, reg. 1963.

CATALGLA--catawbiense var. album Glass
6ft(1.8m) -25F(-32C) ML 3/3 Light pink buds open pure white,
in high-domed, many-flowered trusses. Parent of many very hardy
hybrids. Joseph Gable, 1959.   Color illus. LW pl. 53.

```
          -catawbiense 1/4
       -Catawbiense Album-
CATALODE-        -unknown 1/4
       -         -griffithianum 1/4
       -Loderi King George-
                  -fortunei 1/4
```
6ft(1.8m) -15F(-26C) M 3/3   Synonym COUNTY OF YORK. Flowers
of good substance, pale chartreuse in bud, opening white, olive
throat; tall trusses.   Beautiful long leaf, convex, dark green.
J. Gable, 1936.   A.E. 1960   Color illus. LW pl. 46; VV p. 64.

```
          -catawbiense var. album Glass--Catalgla 1/2
CATAMAC-
          -macabeanum 1/2
```
Buds of spirea red open to pale purplish pink flowers edged with
a blend of spirea red and pale purplish pink; dorsal spotting of
strong purplish red; ruby red throat.   Weldon Delp.

CATANEA--form of catawbiense var. album
A white, shapely form of catawbiense. Selected by Joseph Gable;
G. Guy Nearing; reg. 1972.

```
          -catawbiense 1/2
CATAWBIENSE ALBUM-
          -unknown 1/2
```
6ft(1.8m) -25F(-32C) ML 3/3   A plant of great hardiness and
vigor. Buds flushed lilac, open to pure white flowers, spotted
with greenish yellow; compact, rounded trusses. Often listed as
a form of catawbiense, rather than a hybrid. A. Waterer, before
1900. Color illus. VV p. 55.

```
          -catawbiense 1/2
CATAWBIENSE BOURSAULT-
          -unknown 1/2
```
5ft(1.5m) -25F(-32C) ML 2/3   Purple flowers, held in rounded
trusses. Plant of good sturdy habit. May be a selected form of
catawbiense. Boursault. Color illus. Cox pl. 32.

```
          -catawbiense 1/2
CATAWBIENSE GRANDIFLORUM-
          -unknown 1/2
```
6ft(1.8m) -25F(-32C) ML 2/3   Long-lasting, distinctive lilac
flowers; full rounded truss; very hardy, attractive plant.   A.
Waterer.   Color illus. F p. 73; VV p. 4.

```
          -catawbiense var. album 1/2
CATAWBIENSE GRANDIFLORUM ALBUM-
          -unknown 1/2
```
Possibly a selected seedling of CATAWBIENSE ALBUM or CATAWBIENSE
GRANDIFLORUM, both A. Waterer's.   Full rounded trusses of white
flowers. At maturity, plant 15ft(4.5m) or taller.   Very hardy,
vigorous, floriferous.   Color illus. F p. 72.

CATBY--red form of catawbiense
Buds ruby red and strong purplish red. Flowers a blend of ruby
red, strong red, vivid purplish red; 3 dorsal lobes spotted with
ruby red. A tall shrub; hardy to -25F(-32C).   Delp selection.

* *
```
                    -catawbiense 1/4
       -unnamed hybrid-
CATFORTCAMPY-        -fortunei 1/4
       -campylocarpum 1/2
```
5ft(1.5m) -5F(-21C) M 4/2   Flowers of apricot pink to coral.
Named clones: CATFORTCAMPY 2, DUPONT'S APRICOT, SALMON BAMBOO.
Joseph B. Gable.   Color illus. LW pl. 51.
CATFORTCAMPY TWO (2)   Parentage as above
5ft(1.5m) -10F(-23C) M 4/4 Hardiest and most vigorous of the
selections. Flowers soft apricot pink.   Gable.
* *

CATHAEM   See CONOCO-CHEAGUE

```
          -catawbiense 1/2
CATHARINE VAN TOL-
          -unknown 1/2
```
5ft(1.5m) -15F(-26C) ML   Rosy carmine flowers, yellowish green
spotting on paler center, to 2.6in(6.5cm) wide; round trusses of
16-20. Dark foliage.   J. C. van Tol, of Boskoop, before 1913.

```
          -rex ssp. rex 1/2
CATHERINE HOPWOOD-        -griffithianum 1/4
          -Sincerity-
                  -unknown 1/4
```
8ft(2.4m)(18 yrs) 5F(-15C) M   Truss of 15 flowers, funnel-cam-
panulate, 7-lobed, white with veins strong purplish red. Large
leaf, dark green. Gen. Harrison cross; Mrs. Hopwood, reg. 1987.

CATHERINE OLSON   Described under MARGARET EINARSON, q.v.

CATHERINE PARR   Parentage unknown
8ft(2.4m)(18yrs) -5F(-21C) L   Elepidote. Flowers openly funnel-campanulate, 4.5in(11.5cm) wide, 7 wavy lobes, medium magenta rose with central yellow rays, many red dorsal spots. Leaves
smooth, oblong, 8.5in(22cm) long; held 3 years. Plant open, upright. William A. Ragan, cross 1969; reg. 1989.

* *
```
       -Corona--unknown 5/8
CATHY-        -fortunei ssp. discolor 1/4
       -Dondis-        -arboreum 1/8
            -Doncaster-
                  -unknown
```
Flowers bright pink to white, a yellow throat.   R. Henny, 1956.
CONFECTION   Parentage as above
5ft(1.5m) OF(-18C) ML 3/3   Compact plant; large, dark green
leaves. Flowers rose madder, 3.5in(9cm) across, funnel-campanulate; upright trusses of 16. Henny, reg. 1962. P.A. 1956.
DOLL   Parentage as above
Clear bright pink flowers in high trusses. Henny, intro. 1956.
KATHY DOLL   Parentage as above
4ft(1.2m) -5F(-21C) L   Smooth, dark green foliage, with waxy
pink flowers, flattened corolla. Henny. reg. 1963.
LEONA   Parentage as above
5ft(1.5m) OF(-18C) ML 4/3 Intense rich pink flowers, lightly
spotted darker rose, very open form, 3in(7.6cm) across; trusses
dome-shaped. Plant habit open. Henny, reg. 1958.
MARY ANN   Parentage as above
Flowers pink, basal blotch on dorsal lobe. Henny, cross 1944.
* *

```
* * * * * * * * * * * * * * * * * * * * * * * * * * * * *
```
CATHY CARTER (fortunei ssp. discolor x NEREID x TALLY HO) x
       AUTUMN GOLD (Exact combination unknown)
3ft(.9m) -10F(-23C) ML   Funnel-shaped flowers 4in(10cm) wide,
7- or 8-lobed, a bicolor of carmine rose and lemon yellow; truss
of 10. Plant broader than tall.   Bernice I. Jordan, reg. 1976.
MARY TRANQUILLIA   Parentage as above
3ft(.9m) -10F(-23C) L   Flowers rimmed in Neyron rose, center
in shades of buttercup yellow, to 4in(10cm) broad; rounded truss
of 11. Upright plant, wider than high.   Jordan, reg. 1976.
```
* * * * * * * * * * * * * * * * * * * * * * * * * * * * *
```

```
                           -ponticum 3/8
              -Purple Splendour-
       -unnamed-                  -unknown 9/16
       - hybrid-                       -griffithianum 1/16
       -      -         -Queen Wilhelmina-
CATHY JO-   -Britannia-            -unknown
       -              -Stanley Davies--unknown
       -           -ponticum
       -unnamed hybrid-
                   -unknown
```
5ft(1.5m) -5F(-21C) ML 4/3   Flowers deep wine purple, dark-
er flare, flattened lobes folded back; leaves wrinkled. Disney.

CAT'S PAJAMAS   Described under BETTY WHITE, q.v.

```
       -caucasicum 1/2
CAUAPO-
       -dichroanthum ssp. apodectum 1/2
```
A hybrid with apricot colored flowers.   E. J. P. Magor, 1927.

```
       -caucasicum 1/2
CAUBUT-
       -fortunei--Sir Charles Butler 1/2
```
Flowers 7-lobed, white shading to yellow inside, spotted green.
Trusses hold about 8.   E. J. P. Magor, 1926.

```
        -caucasicum var. stramineum ? 1/2
CAUCAMP-
        -campylocarpum 1/2
```
Flowers light yellow, with red spotting.   E. J. P. Magor.

```
         -caucasicum 1/2
CAUCASICUM PICTUM-
         -unknown 1/2
```
5ft(1.5m) -10F(-23C) EM   Pink frilled flowers, with a dark
blotch; trusses of 14. Glossy dark leaves.   Ord of Manchester,
before 1853. For form of the species, see PICTUM.

```
       -caucasicum var. stramineum ? 1/2
CAUKING-                  -griffithianum 1/4
       -Mrs. Randall Davidson-
                   -campylocarpum, Hooker's form 1/4
```
Cream colored flowers, crimson spotting.   E. J. P. Magor, 1928.

```
* * * * * * * * * * * * * * * * * * * * * * * * * * * * *
```
          -Essex Scarlet--unk 1/2 (or fortunei x red catawbiense)
CAVALCADE-
          -griersonianum 1/2
5ft(1.5m) -5F(-21C) M Bright red flowers. Waterer, pre-1958.
LACKAMAS FIREBRAND   Parentage as above
3.5ft(1m) -5F(-21C) VL   Upright, bushy plant; tan indumentum.
Spherical trusses of 18 campanulate flowers, of currant red. B.
Lancaster, reg. 1967.
```
* * * * * * * * * * * * * * * * * * * * * * * * * * * * *
```

```
                     -souliei 1/16
              -Soulbut-
       -Vanessa-       -fortunei--Sir Charles Butler 1/16
       -Radiance-     -griersonianum 3/8
CAVALIER-      -griersonianum
       -facetum (eriogynum) 1/2
```
Brilliant scarlet flowers.   Lord Aberconway, intro. 1950.

```
       -Pygmalion--unknown 1/2
CAVALIER-             -griersonianum 1/4
       -Tally Ho-
             -facetum (eriogynum) 1/4
```
5ft(1.5m) 5F(-15C) ML 3/3 Large flowers of bright red, heavy
dark spotting in throat; many small trusses. Henny, reg. 1958.

CECIL NICE--form of pocophorum   (From K W 8289)
4ft(1.2m) 5F(-15C) EM 3/3   Flowers dark cardinal red, deeper markings in upper throat. Oblong leaves; heavy, brown, woolly indumentum beneath.   Anne, Countess of Rosse, Nymans; reg.
1971.   A.M. 1971.

CECIL NO. 8   Parentage unknown
Large, tight truss of pink.   Dexter hybrid, Ashville, NC, area.

CECIL S. SEABROOK   Described under TOD B. GALLOWAY, q.v.

```
                       -fortunei ssp. discolor 3/8
          -King of Shrubs-    -dichroanthum 1/8
          -          -Fabia-
CECIL SMITH-             -griersonianum 1/8
       -     -wardii 1/4
       -Crest-         -fortunei ssp. discolor
            -Lady Bessborough-
                    -campylocarpum Elatum Group 1/8
```
5ft(1.5m) 0F(-18C) M Dresden yellow flower, 4in(10.2cm) wide,
6-lobed; open, ball-shaped truss of 11. Plant as broad as tall;
ivy green leaves.   C. Smith cross; C. Phetteplace, reg. 1976.

```
                 -yakushimanum 1/2
CECILY FORTESCUE-   -wardii 1/4
            -Hawk-         -fortunei ssp. discolor 1/8
                -Lady
            Bessborough-campylocarpum Elatum Group 1/8
```
White flowers, spotted pink; truss of 12. Fortescue, reg. 1981.

```
          -fortunei 1/2
CELEBRITY-
       -unknown 1/2
```
5ft(1.5m) -10F(-23C) ML 4/3   Light pink, fragrant flowers,
spotted gold; large truss. Deeply veined foliage. Greer intro.

```
            -griffithianum 1/4
       -Alice-
CELESTE-   -unknown 1/4
       -fortunei ssp. discolor 1/2
```
6ft(1.8m) -10F(-23C) ML 4/3   Beautiful truss of fuchsia pink
flowers, on a vigorous plant. Waterer & Crisp. A.M. 1944.

CELESTIAL--fortunei or fortunei hybrid
Large flowers, shell pink. R. L. Blough.

```
              -dichroanthum 1/4
         -Fabia-
CELESTIAL BELLS-   -griersonianum 1/4
       -          -wardii 1/4
       -unnamed hybrid-
                   -souliei 1/4
```
2ft(.6m) 5F(-15C) M   Flowers of apricot yellow fade to creamy
yellow; drooping trusses of 7-8. Compact, bushy plant; foliage
4in(10cm) long, reddish petioles.   Dr. R. G. Wyrens, reg. 1965.

```
                              -griffithianum
                -Queen Wilhelmina-          1/16
          -Britannia-          -unknown 5/16
       -Purple Lace-      -Stanley Davies--unknown
       -        -          -ponticum 1/8
CENTENNIAL -          -Purple Splendour-
CELEBRATION-                -unknown
       -yakushimanum 1/2
```
4ft(1.2m) -15F(-26C) ML 4/4   Ruffled, fragrant flowers, pink
and pale orchid, sparse tan dorsal spotting; beautiful! Trusses
large, of 18 to 20. Leathery deep green foliage; upright, well-
branched plant. Selected & named by Washington State Centennial
Commission. Fred Peste cross; B. Briggs, reg. 1986. Color ill.
HG p. 74; Wayside Gardens, Spring '89 catalog, cover (a "First")

```
               -fortunei ssp. discolor 1/2
CENTURY TWENTYONE-
       -caucasicum--Cunningham's Sulphur 1/2
```
Pale sulphur yellow buds, opening to white flowers 3in(7.6cm)
wide; rounded trusses of about 15. Plant 6ft(1.8m) tall; foliage very shiny. Halfdan Lem, reg. 1962.

CERAMIC--wardii, selfed
4ft(1.2m) 0F(-18C) M 4/3   Upright trusses of 6 campanulate
flowers, pure white with a sap green throat. Henny, reg. 1962.

CERISETTE   Described under SHEILA MOORE, q.v.

CERNE   A clone of ROYAL BEAUTY grex, q.v.

CETEWAYO   Parentage unknown; may be ponticum hybrid
5ft(1.5m) -10F(-23C) ML   Very dark, almost black-purple flowers, unmarked, pale, contrasting anthers; tight trusses of about
12. Foliage dark and glossy.   A. Waterer.   A.M. 1958.

```
                -catawbiense var. album Glass--Catalgla 1/2
CEYLON-
          -fortunei 1/2
```
6ft(1.8m) -25F(-32C) M 3/4   Flowers funnel-shaped, 3.25in.
(8.3cm) across, rose purple; trusses off 12. Glossy leaves 5in.
(12.7cm) long, held 2 years.   J. Gable cross; Leach, reg. 1983.

```
                    -ciliatum 3/4
          -Countess of Haddington-
CHAFFINCH-                    -dalhousiae 1/4
          -ciliatum
```
Plant low-growing; hairy foliage. Pale pink, fragrant flowers;
numerous small trusses; early mid-season.   Rothschild, 1935.

* *
```
          -cinnabarinum 1/2
CHALICE-
          -maddenii 1/2
```
Tubular flowers, pale pink within, outside creamy white suffused
with rose. Origin unknown. A.M. 1932.
ROSE MANGLES   Parentage as above
A parent of COCK OF THE WALK. Rose pink flowers.   Mangles.
* *

```
                    -thomsonii 1/4
          -Chanticleer-
CHALLENGER-           -facetum (eriogynum) 1/4
          -           -griffithianum 1/4
          -Sunrise-
                    -griersonianum 1/4
```
Rose-colored flowers. Lord Aberconway, intro. 1950.

CHAMPAGNE   Described under TORTOISESHELL, q.v.

* *
```
                    -cinnabarinum Roylei Group 1/4
          -Lady Chamberlain-           -cinnabarinum 1/8
CHAN-                    -Royal Flush-
                              -maddenii 1/8
          -cinnabarinum ssp. xanthocodon Concatenans Group 1/2
```
Orange-yellow flowers. Lord Aberconway, 1946.
COMELY   Parentage as above
4ft(1.2m) -5F(-21C) EM   Orange-yellow flowers. Lord Aberconway, 1946.
DAYAN   Parentage as above
Truss of 8-9 flowers, 2in(5cm) wide by 2.25in(5.7cm) long; waxy
orange-yellow. E. de Rothschild, reg. 1967. A.M. 1967.
GOLDEN ORFE   Parentage as above, except reversed
4ft(1.2m) 5F(-15C) M 4/3   Flowers of drooping habit in truss
of 7, yellow with shades of nasturtium orange. Leaves medium-
sized, scaly below. Mrs. Roza Harrison, reg. 1964. A.M. 1964.
* *

CHANCELLOR'S CHOICE---selection from pseudochrysanthum
6ft(1.8m) x 5ft(1.5m)(25 yrs) OF(-18C) E   Flowers pale Neyron
rose with darker dorsal spots, wavy-edged, fragrant, fleshy, 2.5
in(6.4cm) wide; ball truss of 10-15. Glossy elliptical foliage,
held 3-4 years; dense bush. Mrs. E. Grieg; Vaartnou, reg. 1990.

```
                    -souliei 1/16
                -Soulbut-
          -Vanessa-           -fortunei--Sir Charles Butler 1/16
     -Adonis-           -griersonianum 1/4
     -           -griffithianum 1/8
CHANDON-     -Sunrise-
     -                    -griersonianum
     -           -thomsonii ssp. thomsonii 1/4
          -Chanticleer-
                    -facetum (eriogynum) 1/4
```
Pink flowers. Lord Aberconway, 1946.

```
                    -thomsonii 1/4
          -Chanticleer-
          -           -facetum (eriogynum) 1/4
CHANETA-           -griffithianum 1/8
          -     -Loderi-
          -Coreta-           -fortunei 1/8
                    -arboreum ssp. zeylanicum 1/4
```
Red flowers. Lord Aberconway, 1946.

* *
```
                         -dichroanthum ssp. apodectum 1/4
          -unnamed hybrid-
CHANG  -           -campylocarpum, Hooker's form 1/4
TSO LIN-           -wardii 1/4           -griffithianum 1/32
          -Idealist, A.M.-           -Kewense-
                         -Aurora-           -fortunei 5/32
                    -Naomi-     -thomsonii 1/16
                         -fortunei
```
Flowers cadmium orange in bud, opening to a medium lemon yellow,
darker in throat. Trusses hold about 9. Dark green leaves; no
indumentum. Lester E. Brandt, reg. 1968.
ANN PASCOE   Parentage as above
Open habit, low; leaves 4.5in x 1.5in (11.4cm x 3.8cm). Flowers
yellow, slightly flushed yellow-orange, 13 per truss. Lester E.
Brandt, reg. 1970.
* *

```
          -thomsonii 1/2
CHANTICLEER-
          -facetum (eriogynum) 1/2
```
6ft(1.8m) 15F(-9C) ML 3/2   Waxy, bright red flowers to 3in.
(7.6cm) broad, in truss of 8. Easy to grow. Parent of IVANHOE,
TALISMAN. Rothschild, 1935.

```
                              -griffithianum 1/16
               -Queen Wilhelmina-
          -Britannia-           -unknown 11/16
     -unnamed-           -Stanley Davies--unknown
CHAPEAU- hybrid-unknown
     -           -ponticum 1/4
     -Purple Splendour-
                    -unknown
```
5ft(1.5m) -5F(-21C) ML 4/3   Flowers with purple edges and
white center on all lobes; a large, deep purple blotch on upper
lobe. Foliage of matte green. Broxson-Disney, before 1983.
Color illus. HG p. 182.

CHAPEL WOOD--form of lanigerum R 03913
4ft(1.2m) 5F(-15C) EM 3/3   A handsome shrub with very tight
trusses of 40-50 flowers, medium Neyron rose. Smooth dark green
leaves, the indumentum beneath changing through white, gray, and
brown. Crown Estate, reg. 1962. A.M. 1961. F.C.C. 1967.

```
          -minus var. chapmanii 1/2
CHAPMANII WONDER-
          -dauricum var. album 1/2
```
5ft(1.5m) -15F(-26C) E 3/3   Vigorous plant; foliage similar
to P.J.M. Flowers bright lavender pink; tolerant of heat and
cold. Koichiro Wada, of Japan, before 1983.

CHARISMA--form of ciliicalyx
4ft(1.2m) 15F(-9C) EM 3/3   Truss of 2-4 flowers, rose madder
in bud, opening rose pink, deeper lines on each lobe, a yellow-
orange blotch on upper lobe. Leaves scaly. New Zealand Rhodo.
Assoc. raiser; Graham Smith, reg. 1982.

```
                              -griffithianum 1/32
                    -Kewense-
               -Aurora-     -fortunei
          -Naomi-     -thomsonii ssp. 1/16
     -Carita-     -fortunei 5/32
CHARITES-     -campylocarpum 1/4
     -     -wardii 1/4
     -Crest-           -fortunei ssp. discolor 1/8
          -Lady  -
               Bessborough-campylocarpum Elatum Group 1/8
```
Pale yellow flowers in large, well-built trusses. Plant habit,
upright and compact. E. de Rothschild, reg. 1966. P.C. 1965.

CHARLES   Described under FORTUNE, q.v.

```
                 -catawbiense 1/2
CHARLES BAGLEY-
            -unknown 1/2
6ft(1.8m) -20F(-29C) ML 2/1 Rather open and spreading habit.
Flowers cherry red, in upright trusses.  A. Waterer, 1865.


                      -campylocarpum Elatum Group 1/4
              -Letty Edwards-
CHARLES BEGG-             -fortunei 1/4
            -unknown 1/2
Flowers of Tyrian rose, paler in center.  A. Bramley, reg. 1966.


                 -catawbiense 1/2
CHARLES DICKENS-
             -unknown 1/2
6ft(1.8m) -25F(-32C) ML 2/2 Flowers of purplish crimson red,
spotted black; in conical trusses.  Dark green foliage.  Slow-
growing; difficult to propagate.  Waterer, 1865.  F.C.C. 1865.


CHARLES MICHAEL   Described under MAJOR, q.v.


               -unknown 1/2
CHARLES PHILLIPS-         -edgeworthii 1/4
               -Fragrantissimum-
                         -formosum 1/4
12ft(3.6m)  25F(-4C) VE Flat truss of 8-15 flowers, 5-lobed,
moderately fragrant, white, a pale green throat; foliage with
brown scales beneath.  C. Phillips cross; E. Connally, reg. 1986.


                 -catawbiense var. album--Catalgla 1/2
CHARLES ROBINSON-          -griffithianum 1/8
-           -Mars-
          -Vulcan-    -unknown 1/8
              -griersonianum 1/4
Deep pink flower buds; bud hardy to -25F(-32C).  O. Pride, 1977.


CHARLES THOROD   Parentage unknown
4ft(1.2m) -15F(-26C) L Purple with yellow flare.  Unknown.


CHARLES WATERER    Parentage unknown
A parent of SOUVENIR DE D. A. KOSTER.  Red flowers with lighter
center.  J. Waterer, before 1922.


          -fortunei ? 1/2
CHARLESTOWN-
           -unknown 1/2
6ft(1.8m) -5F(-21C) M    Shades of pink, chartreuse throat, 7-
lobed flowers; fragrant, 4in(10.2cm) broad.  About 16 in trusses
8in(20.3cm) across.  C. Dexter cross; S. Everitt raiser; C. Her-
bert, reg. 1976.


CHARLEY   Described under DEL, q.v.


CHARLIE G.   Described under BODY LANGUAGE, q.v.


CHARLOTTE CURRIE   Described under MAESTRO, q.v.


CHARLOTTE DE
 ROTHSCHILD    Described under SIR FREDERICK MOORE, q.v.


      -forrestii Repens Group 1/2
CHARM-       -thomsonii 1/4)
     -Shilsonii-
           -barbatum 1/4
Blood red flowers.  Lord Aberconway, 1941.


                -forrestii Repens Group 1/4
         -Charm-       -thomsonii 1/8
-           -Shilsonii-
CHARMAINE-          -barbatum 1/8
-           -haematodes 1/4
        -May Day-
              -griersonianum 1/4
Blood red flowers.  Lord Aberconway.  A.M. 1946. Color illus.
Cox, pl. 33.


         -minus var. minus Carolinianum Group, pink form 1/2
CHARME LA-
         -pemakoense Patulum Group 1/2
2.5ft(.75m) 3ft(.9m)(19yrs) -25F(-32C) M    Flowers of heavy
substance, openly funnel-shaped, 2.5in(6cm) wide, violet purple;
lax truss of 3-5.  Elliptic leaves 2in(5cm) long,  scaly on both
```

```
sides.  Floriferous.    Dr. J. Brueckner, cross 1969; reg. 1988.


CHARMER   Described under TIM CRAIG, q.v.


          -flavidum 1/2
CHARTREUSE-         -cinnabarinum Roylei Group 1/4
       -Lady Roseberry-         -cinnabarinum 1/8
              -Royal Flush, pink form-
                         -maddenii 1/8
Yellow flowers in loose trusses of 10.  Others of this grex:
FLIP (Greer) STRAWBERRY CREAM (Cox) L. E. Brandt, reg. 1961.


        -campylocarpum 1/2
CHASTE-         -Pink Bell--unknown 1/4
     -Queen o' the May-
              -griersonianum 1/4
Loose clusters of bell-shaped flowers, light primrose yellow.  A
rose form, exhibited by Lord Aberconway, 1939.  Crosfield, 1930.


* * * * * * * * * * * * * * * * * * * * * * * * * * * * * * *
            -yakushimanum
        -Tols-
CHASTITY-   -catawbiense
        -Redwing Chip--unknown
Deep red buds; flowers a frilled blend of strong and medium mag-
enta rose, with white flare and filaments,  anthers pale orangey
white, dark red stigma.  Weldon Delp.
SHARPSHOOTER  Parentage as above
Buds of cardinal red, ruby red and deep purplish red opening to
flowers of lilac, magnolia purple, strong purplish red,  with a
white flare and vivid yellow green dorsal spots.  W. Delp.
* * * * * * * * * * * * * * * * * * * * * * * * * * * * * * *
* * * * * * * * * * * * * * * * * * * * * * * * * * * * * * *
            -griffithianum 1/8
        -Loderi-
    -Albatross-    -fortunei 1/8
CHAT-       -fortunei ssp. discolor 1/4
    -wardii 1/2
5ft(1.5m) -5F(-21C) M  Flowers marigold orange changing to sap
green, 3.5in(9cm) across.  Rudolph Henny, reg. 1961.
MING   Parentage as above
Flowers 4in(10cm) wide, uranium green with reddish blotch on up-
per lobe.  R. Henny, reg. 1962.
* * * * * * * * * * * * * * * * * * * * * * * * * * * * * * *
            -Moser's Maroon--unknown 9/32
        -Impi-
CHATEAU-      -sanguineum ssp. didymum 1/4
LAFITE-    -elliottii 1/4
      -Jutland-          -fortunei ssp. discolor 1/16
-           -Norman-         -catawbiense 1/32
        -Bellerophon- Shaw -B. de Bruin-
-                        -unknown
              -facetum (eriogynum) 1/8
Small shrub, as broad as high, with deep green foliage; dark red
flowers in medium-sized trusses.  E. de Rothschild, reg. 1963.


CHATHAM   Parentage unknown; possibly fortunei hybrid
5ft(1.5m) -5F(-21C) LM   Waxy, purplish pink flowers with white
center, purplish red spotting, wavy-edged lobes, fragrant; about
12 per truss.  Plant of average compactness.  C. Dexter cross;
Scott Horticultural Foundation, reg. 1985.


* * * * * * * * * * * * * * * * * * * * * * * * * * * * * * *
            -fortunei ? 1/2
        -Ben Moseley-
-            -unknown
CHATTERBEE NO. 1-          -caucasicum 1/8
-          -Boule de Neige-       -catawbiense
        -Besse -         -hardy hybrid-
       Howells-              -unknown 3/16
-                   -catawbiense 3/16
            -unnamed red hybrid-
                    -unknown
Flower mallow purple and phlox purple with deep red flare; dor-
sal spots of deep red.  Dr. D. Hinerman cross; Delp raiser.
CHATTERBEE NO. 2   Parentage as above
Buds of deep and strong purplish reds open to flowers of strong
and light purples; flare of rose purple.  Hinerman cross; Delp.
CHATTERBEE NO. 3   Parentage as above
Buds of fuchsia purple open to flowers of strong purplish pink;
dorsal spots ruby red.  Hinerman cross; Delp raiser.
```

```
                            -sanguineum ssp. didymum 3/4
                -Arthur Osborn-
CHATTERBOX-                 -griersonianum 1/4
                -sanguineum ssp. didymum
```
Flowers currant red, funnel-campanulate, 2in(5cm) wide; 6-8 per truss. Rudolph Henny, reg. 1961.

```
                            -ponticum 1/4
            -Purple Splendour-
CHAUNCY-                    -unknown 1/4
 ALCOTT-        -dichroanthum 1/4
     -Jasper -                    -fortunei ssp. discolor 1/8
     (Exbury -Lady Bessborough-
     Special)-               -campylocarpum Elatum Group 1/8
```
5ft(1.5m) -5F(-21C) M   A spreading plant; rounded light green foliage. Flowers of porcelain rose, paler at base, 2.5in(6.4cm) wide, in trusses of 8-10. C. S. Seabrook, reg. 1967.

CHEAPSIDE Described under CAROLINE DE ZOETE, q.v.

* *
```
                                -catawbiense var. album 1/8
                            -                -catawbiense
            -Lodestar-      -Catawbiense-        3/32
            -           -Belle - Album   -unknown 3/32
            -           Heller-          -catawbiense
            -                   -white cat.-
        -R.O. Delp-             hybrid   -unknown
        -           -                    -catawbiense
        -           -           -Atrosanguineum-
        -           -     -Atrier-         -unknown
        -           -Mary -    -griersonianum 1/16
CHECKMATE-          Belle-     -decorum 1/16
        -               -Dechaem-
        -                       -haematodes 1/6
        -                           -neriiflorum 1/16
        -                       -Nereid-
        -unnamed-Phyllis Ballard-     -dichroanthum 1/16
          hybrid-              -fortunei ssp. discolor 1/8
            -catawbiense--Clark's White 1/4
```
Buds moderate purplish red, open to flowers light to pale purplish pink; dorsal spots of moderate purplish red. W. Delp.
FRECKLE FACE   Parentage as above
Buds vivid red to moderate purplish red, opening to reddish purple flowers, the reverse veined deep purplish pink. W. Delp.
PINK CAROUSEL   Parentage as above
Buds of strong purplish reds open to flowers of strong to light purplish pink. W. Delp.
PURE ELEGANCE Parentage as above
Flowers of medium to deep purplish pink; the light yellow blotch contains specks of vivid red. W. Delp.
STINGRAY Parentage as above
Blend of dark to medium ruby reds in bud; flowers deep purplish rose pink; coral red blended on 3 upper lobes; throat of strong purplish spirea red. Delp. Col. ill. ARS J 43:1 (1989), p. 2.
TOP DOG   Parentage as above
Buds deep to strong purplish red, open to flowers very pale purple with dorsal spots of deep purplish red. W. Delp.
* *
* *
```
                        -caucasicum 1/4
            -Cunningham's White-
CHEER-                  -ponticum, white 1/4
            -                   -catawbiense 1/4
            -red catawbiense hybrid-
                            -unknown 1/4
```
5ft(1.5m) -15F(-26C) EM 3/3   Shell pink flowers 2.5in(6.4cm) wide, with a conspicuous red blotch, in conical trusses. Plant rounded, compact; glossy leaves, 4in(10cm) long. Shammarello, pre-1958. Color illus. VV p. 4.
ELIE Parentage as above
6ft(1.8m) -10F(-23C) M 3/3   Flowers of a vibrant deep pink, with a red blotch; conical trusses. Shammarello, intro. 1955.
HOLDEN Parentage as above
4ft(1.2m) -15F(-26C) EM 3/4 Compact hybrid, wider than high, with lustrous dark green foliage. Flowers rose red, with small red spots. Shammarello, reg. 1958. Color illus. VV p. 124.
ROCKET   Parentage as above
5ft(1.5m) -10F(-23C) EM 3/3   Foliage quite glossy, thick, heavily veined. Frilled flowers of vibrant coral pink, blotched scarlet. Shammarello, intro. 1955. Color illus. VV p. 67.
SPRING GLORY   Parentage as above

5ft(1.5m) -15F(-26C) EM 4/2   Vigorous, compact plant; grows well in sun or shade. Flowers clear pink, deeper at the edges, large crimson blotch. Shammarello, 1955. Col. ill. HG p. 136.
SPRING PARADE Parentage as above, except reversed
4.5ft(1.35m) -20F(-29C) M 3/2   Clear scarlet red flowers in globular trusses. Plant as broad as high; dark green, recurved leaves. Shammarello, reg. 1962. Color illus. HG. p. 117.
VERNUS Parentage as CHEER, above
5ft(1.5m) -25F(-32C) VE 3/3   Very early and very hardy plant with an abundance of light pink flowers, darker at the centers. A. M. Shammarello cross; D. G. Leach raiser; reg. 1962.
* *
```
            -wardii 1/2
CHEERIO-        -souliei 1/4
        -Rosy Morn-    -griffithianum 1/8
                -Loderi-
                    -fortunei 1/8
```
Light pink to white, red markings; imbricate lobes. Henny, 1944.

```
            -williamsianum 1/2
CHEETANS-
        -souliei ? 1/2
```
White flowers, held in lax trusses. Gibson Brothers; reg. 1961. P.C. 1960

CHEIRANTHIFOLIUM--form of ponticum
A form of ponticum with very narrow, wavy leaves. Unknown.

CHELSEA Described under LADY CHAMBERLAIN, q.v.

CHELSEA CHIMES--form of coryanum K W 6311
6ft(1.8m) OF(-18C) E-M 3/3 Clear white flowers, sparse spotting in throat; trusses of 8-9. Kingdon Ward collector; Col. S. R. Clarke raiser; R. N. Stephenson Clarke exhibitor; reg. 1961. A.M. 1979.

* *
```
            -yakushimanum 1/2
            -        -Lady        -fortunei ssp. discolor 1/16
CHELSEA-             -Bessborough-
SEVENTY-    -Jalisco-        -campylocarpum 1/16
        -       -Eclipse-
        -unnamed-    -dichroanthum 1/16
        - hybrid-    -Dido-
        -       -       -decorum 1/16
        -       -elliottii 1/8
            -Fusilier-
                -griersonianum 1/8
```
3ft(.9m) OF(-18C) M 4/4   Salmon pink flowers, blending to rose pink. John Waterer, Sons and Crisp, reg. 1972.
VINTAGE ROSE Parentage as above
2ft(.6m) OF(-18C) LM   Plant broad, vigorous, compact; dark green leaves 4.1in(10.5cm) long. Flower 2.3in(6cm) wide, white, lightly tinged rose. Waterer & Crisp, reg. 1975. H.C. 1979. A.M. Wisley Trials 1989.
* *

```
            -Rose Perfection--unknown 1/2
CHERONIA-
        -orbiculare 1/2
```
Rose pink flowers. Lord Aberconway, 1933.

CHERRY BRANDY--form of cerasinum K W 6923
3ft(.9m) OF(-18C) EM 4/4   Crisp foliage; bell-shaped flowers of cherry red; trusses of 6. Named by Kingdon Ward. Countess of Rosse, Nymans. A.M. 1973. Another form, with creamy white flowers, edged cherry red, also received an A.M. 1938. Nymans. Color illus. Rhododendrons, 1988-89 (RHS), vol. 41 fig. 6.

CHERRY BRIGHT Described under THOMWILLIAMS, q.v.

```
                    -campylocarpum 1/4
        -Elsie Straver-
CHERRY CUSTARD-        -unknown 1/4
        -           -dichroanthum 1/4
        -Roman Pottery-
                -griersonianum 1/4
```
20in(.51m) OF(-18C) M   Flower buds mandarin red, open to medium saffron yellow, with coral red stripes, also on the reverse; flowers 2in(5cm) across, in flat trusses of 10-12. Plant broad, decumbent branches; leaves held 3 years. Lofthouse, reg. 1981.

```
                    -griffithianum 1/16
              -Kewense-
        -Aurora-        -fortunei 5/16
     -Naomi-      -thomsonii 1/8
CHERRY FLOAT-    -fortunei
     -unknown 1/2
```
5ft(1.5m) -5F(-21C) M 4/4 Deep ruby buds; flowers burgundy,
with phlox pink center; solid dorsal blotch, dark grayed purple.
Sun-tolerant. Lofthouse cross; E. J. Linington, reg. 1974.

```
                 -maximum 1/4
     -Fireking-       -forrestii Repens Group 1/8
        -Gertrud-                        -ponticum
CHERRY-    Schäle -       -Michael Waterer-      1/32
   JAM -        -Prometheus-        -unknown 1/4
       -               -Monitor--unknown
     -Bob As---unnamed -yakushimanum 1/4      -catawbiense
      hybrid,-    hybrid,-       -Parsons -        1/32
        selfed -    -America- Grandiflorum-unknown
              -Cindy-        -
                 Lou -      -dark red hybrid--unknown
                    -       -griffithianum 1/16
                    -Mars-
                       -unknown
```
Buds of currant red, vivid red and cardinal red, open to frilled
flowers of cardinal red and spinel red. Weldon Delp.

```
           -fortunei 1/4
     -Fawn-      -dichroanthum 1/8
        -Fabia-
CHERRY -      -griersonianum 1/4
JUBILEE-           -fortunei ssp. discolor 1/4
   -    -Lady -
     -Lem's- Bessborough-campylocarpum Elatum Group 1/6
      Goal-      -griersonianum
           -Azor-
                -fortunei ssp. discolor
```
3ft(.9m) OF(-18C) M Flowers up to 5in(13cm) across, yellow-
ish pink suffused tangerine, banded a deeper shade; truss of 9.
Open habit; leaves to 8in(20.3cm) long. A. Childers, reg. 1971.
PINK CREPE Parentage as above
6ft(1.0m) OF(-18C) ML Open habit, upright and vigorous; truss
of 7-9 flowers, 7-lobed, light purplish pink, edges and outside
strong purplish red. Childers, reg. 1972.
PINK DIVINITY Parentage as above
5ft(1.5m) OF(-18C) M Open, loose habit; leaves 7in(17.8cm)
long. Truss of 8 flowers, pale pink. Childers, reg. 1972.
* *

CHERRY RED Dexter cross. Confused with Dexter's WISSAHICKON,
but considered by some to be different. May have better habit.

CHERRY TIP--form of rex ssp. fictolacteum R 11395
5ft(1.5m) -5F(-21C) EM 3/4 Bright cherry pink buds opening
to white flowers, flushed pink, a deep crimson blotch on upper
segments. Collector, Rock; exhibitor, Lord Digby. A.M. 1953.

CHESAPEAKE Described under BRANDYWINE, q.v.

CHESTERLAND Parentage unknown
7ft(2.1m) -25F(-32C) EM 4/4 Parent of HILLSDALE. Flowers
pale pink, yellow dorsal spotting, 3.5in(8.9cm) across, funnel-
rotate, 6-lobed; truss of 12. Plant dense, slightly taller than
wide; large, glossy leaves. J. Pot cross; Leach, reg. 1964.

```
        -caucasicum 1/2
CHEVALIER FELIX DE SAUVAGE-
           -hardy hybrid--unknown 1/2
```
4.5ft(1.35m) -5F(-21C) EM 3/3 Coral rose flowers, accentu-
ated by a rich dark blotch in the center. Truss tight, 12-flow-
ered. Sauvage, c. 1870. Color illus. F p. 38; JS p. 111.

```
              -fortunei ssp. discolor 1/8
        -Lady -
        -Bessborough-campylocarpum Elatum Group 1/8
     -Jalisco-    -dichroanthum 1/8
     -      -Dido-
CHEYENNE-      -decorum 1/8
     -      -griffithianum 1/4
     -Loderi-
        -fortunei 1/4
```

5ft(1.5m) -5F(-21C) ML 4/4 Flowers deep yellow, with faint
brown markings; truss of 9. Parent of CREAM GLORY, RAZZLE DAZ-
ZLE, WHITE GOLD. Greer, reg. 1964. Color illus. HG p. 138.

* *
```
        -yakushimanum 1/2
                    -fortunei ssp. discolor 3/16
CHICKAMAUGA-      -Lady -
     -      -Day -Bessborough-campylocarpum Elatum 1/16
     -Shah -Dream-
      Jehan-      -griersonianum 3/16
          -      -fortunei ssp. discolor
          -Margaret Dunn-      -dichroanthum 1/16
              -Fabia-
                 -griersonianum
```
3ft(.9m) -15F(-26C) M Rose pink buds open to flowers light
pink on outside, white with a gold eye inside. Plant habit compact. C. P. Fawcett cross; Sweetbriar Nursery intro., 1985.
SATIN GOLD Parentage as above, except reversed
3ft(.9m) -5F(-21C) M 4/4 Soft golden yellow flowers with a
small red spot in throat. Rounded plant; fine, indumented foliage. Hybridizer uncertain; Brandt or Lawson?
* *
```
        -dichroanthum ssp. scyphocalyx 1/2
CHIEF -       -sanguineum ssp. didymum 1/8
JOSEPH-      -Rubina-      -griersonianum 3/16
     -      -      -Tally Ho-
     -unnamed hybrid-      -facetum (eriogynum) 1/16
              -dichroanthum 1/8
           -Fabia-
              -griersonianum
```
1.5ft(.45m) OF(-18C) M Low, spreading shrub, twice as wide as
tall; elliptic leaves to 4in(10.2cm) long, dark green. Flowers
bright spinel red. J. Witt, U. of Wash. Arboretum, reg. 1968.

```
                    -griffithianum 1/16
              -George Hardy-
     -Mrs. Lindsay Smith-      -catawbiense 1/16
     -      -Duchess of Edinburgh--unknown
     -Diane-      -campylocarpum 1/8
CHIEF -    -unnamed hybrid-
 KITSAP-      -unknown 1/4
     -calophytum 1/2
```
8ft(2.4m) x 3.5ft(1.05m)(20 yrs) 5F(-15C) EM Domed trusses of
15 flowers, pale greenish yellow, a deep red blotch, wavy-edged.
Leaves medium yellowish green, slight tan indumentum when young.
B. Nelson, cross 1967; A. P. Johnson, reg. 1987.

CHIEF PAULINA--form of concinnum var. pseudoyanthinum
5ft(1.5m) 5F(-15C) EM 4/3 Synonym JAMES' PURPLE. Royal
purple flowers spotted dark brown; Exbury form is redder. Small
clusters of 3-6 flowers. Foliage typical of species: dark bluish green, scaly both sides. D. James, before 1950. P.A. 1954.
Color illus. ARS Q 27:3 (1973), p. 170.

```
        -hanceanum Nanum Group 1/2
CHIFFCHAFF-
        -fletcherianum 1/2
```
2ft(.6m) OF(-18C) EM 3/3 Small, loose truss of 5-6 flowers,
lemon yellow; foliage turns red in winter. Compact plant, wider
than high. Cox, reg. 1976. A.M. 1976.

CHIFFON Parentage unknown
3ft(.9m) 5F(-15C) EM Large, saucer-shaped flowers, 7-lobed,
pink, deeper pink in throat; trusses hold 8. W. Whitney cross;
Sather, reg. 1976.

```
        -rupicola var. chryseum 1/2
CHIKOR-
        -ludlowii 1/2
```
1.5ft(.45m) OF(-18C) EM 4/4 First hybrid of ludlowii shown
to the RHS. Flowers of soft yellow; plant has twiggy stems like
a miniature tree. Foliage bronze red in winter. P. Cox, reg.
1962. A.M. 1962. F.C.C. Wisley Trials 1968. Color ill. ARS
Q 27:2 (1973), p. 102.

```
                        -dichroanthum 3/16
                  -Dido-
           -Warm Spring-        -decorum 1/8
           -             -        -fortunei 17/64
CHILDERS' -         -Fawn-        -dichroanthum
  INDIAN -                  -Fabia-
   SUMMER-                        -griersonianum 3/16
        -             -wardii 1/8           -griffithianum
        -   -Idealist-             -Kewense-            5/64
     -Yellow-        -        -Aurora-        -fortunei
       Creek-        -Naomi-        -thomsonii 1/32
             -                -fortunei
             -                -griersonianum
             -Sarita Loder-        -griffithianum
                        -Loderi-
                             -fortunei
```
8ft(2.4m)(19 yrs) 5F(-15C) M Flat truss of 9-11 flowers of 7
wavy lobes, 3in(7.5cm) wide, brilliant light yellow; plant broad
as tall; smooth leaves. A. Childers, cross c. 1962; reg. 1989.

```
      -wightii 1/2
CHINA-
      -fortunei 1/2
```
5ft(1.5m) 0F(-18C) M 4/3 Fine trusses of cream flowers with
red centers. Large leaves, deeply veined. Slocock, 1936. A.M.
1940. F.C.C. Wisley Trials 1982. Color illus. JS p. 54.

CHINA BOY   Described under BREMEN, q.v.

CHINA DOLL   See SENATOR HENRY JACKSON

```
                        -wightii 1/2
CHINA DOLL (Ex Australia)---CHINA, selfed-
                        -fortunei 1/2
```
Flowers of warm yellow. Grown by Van Veen. Hybridizer may have
been A. J. Teese.

```
            -wightii 1/4
        -China-
CHINA MOON-     -fortunei 1/4
        -          -campylocarpum 1/4
        -Moonstone-
                   -williamsianum 1/4
```
3ft(.9m) -5F(-21C) M 4/4 Bright, clear lemon yellow flowers,
without markings; floriferous. Plant habit neat and compact;
rounded moss green leaves. Eichelser.

```
            -yungningense 1/2
CHINESE BLUE-     -intricatum 1/4
          -Bluebird-
                   -augustinii 1/4
```
2ft(.6m) OF(-18C) E Compact, slow-growing plant with leaves
like BLUEBIRD but more convex; flowers a brighter blue, long red
stamens. Del W. James cross; Bovees, reg. 1982.

CHINESE SILVER--form of argyrophyllum ssp. nankingense
5ft(1.5m) OF(-18C) EM 3/5   Attractive foliage, glossy dark
green above, silvery beneath. Delicate deep pink flower. Crown
Estate, Windsor, reg. 1962. A.M. 1957.

```
      -keiskei 1/2
CHINK-
      -trichocladum 1/2
```
3ft(1.5m) -5F(-21C) EM 3/3   Pale chartreuse yellow flowers,
some darker spotting, drooping, campanulate. Lax trusses of 5.
Semi-deciduous; red winter foliage.   Crown Estate; reg. 1961.
A.M. 1961.

```
            -wightii 1/4
        -China-
CHINMAR-    -fortunei 1/4
        -          -wardii 1/4
        -Margaret Findlay-
                   -griersonianum 1/4
```
5ft(1.5m) OF(-18C) EM Light yellow, openly campanulate flower
with small red rays and spotting, 3in(7.6cm) wide, in flat truss
of 13. Bush well-branched; olive green leaves, maroon petioles.
Karl Sifferman cross; D. K. McClure, reg. 1982.

CHINTZ   Described under MRS. FURNIVALL, q.v.

```
         -ponticum 1/2
CHIONOIDES-
         -unknown 1/2  (May include maximum: the "yellow eye")
```
4ft(1.2m) -10F(-23C) ML 3/4   Flowers white, yellow centers;
many dome-shaped trusses. Broad, dense plant; attractive narrow
foliage. Tolerant of sun and cold.   J. Waterer, before 1883.
Color illus. Cox pl. 34; VV p. 51.

```
            -thomsonii 1/4
     -Barclayi-          -arboreum 1/8
CHIRON-     -Glory of Penjerrick-
     -haematodes 1/2          -griffithianum 1/8
```
Deep red flowers.   Lord Aberconway, 1946.

CHIVALRY   Described under LEDA, q.v.

CHLOROPS   Parentage uncertain
4ft(1.2m) -5F(-21C) M 3/3   Once considered a species but
known only in cultivation; may be a chance hybrid between wardii
and vernicosum. See Chamberlain, p. 430 (Notes RBG Edinb. 39:3
(1982)). Saucer-shaped flowers in trusses of 6-8, cream to pale
yellow, light purple blotch. Dense foliage, bluish olive green.

```
         -haematodes 1/2
CHOREMIA-
         -arboreum 1/2
```
5ft(1.5m) -5F(-15C) E 4/3 Waxy, bell-shaped flowers of crimson scarlet appear early. Plant much like haematodes, in habit.
Lord Aberconway, 1933. A.M. 1933. F.C.C. 1948.

```
         -wardii 3/4              -griffithianum 1/16
         -          -George Hardy-
CHOUGH-    -Mrs. Lindsay-     -catawbiense 1/16
      -Carolyn- Smith     -Duchess of Edinburgh--unknown 1/8
       Hardy -
            -wardii
```
Truss of 10-12 flowers, light greenish yellow, darker in throat;
deep purplish red blotch in upper throat. Collingwood Ingram
cross; exhibitor, G. A. Hardy; reg. 1982. A.M. 1981.

```
            -catawbiense 1/4
     -Kettledrum-
CHRIS-      -unknown 1/4
     -wardii 1/2
```
3ft(.9m) -10F(-23C) ML Flowers phlox pink in throat, shading
to primrose yellow at margins, 3in(7.6cm) wide; lax, dome-shaped
trusses hold 13-15. Upright, well-branched plant; foliage very
glossy, held 2 years. W. Fetterhoff, reg. 1981.

```
CHRIS                    -catawbiense var. album Glass--Catalgla
CROSS---CHRISTINA DELP, -           -campylocarpum    1/2
          selfed  -Mrs. W. C. Slocock-            1/4
                             -unknown 1/4
```
Buds of strong purplish red, strong reddish purple and deep pur-
plish pink open to light purples, with dorsal spots of tangerine
orange. Weldon Delp.

```
       -Tacoma--unknown 3/4
CHRISTABEL-                    -griffithianum 1/8
  TOMES  -          -Loderi (pink form)-
       -unnamed hybrid-          -fortunei 1/8
                -unknown
```
Pale cream flowers, pink markings. W. E. Glennie, reg. 1984.

```
                        -caucasicum 1/8
                  -Cunningham's White-
            -Cheer-        -ponticum 1/8
CHRISTIE-ANNE   -          -catawbiense 1/8
  BEHRING -     -red catawbiense hybrid-
        -        -discolor 1/4        -unknown 1/8
        -Disca-        -decorum? 1/8
              -Caroline-
                   -brachycarpum? 1/8
```
1.5ft(.45m) x 3ft(.9m)(8 yrs) -15F(-26C) M Flowers moderate-
ly fragrant, divided lobes, trusses of 19, moderately purplish
pink buds opening to white. Rudy Behring, reg. 1989.

```
                    -catawbiense var. album Glass--Catalgla 1/2
CHRISTINA-              -campylocarpum 1/4
 DELP   -Mrs. W. C. Slocock-
                       -unknown 1/4
```
5ft(21.5m) -25F(-32C) L 3/3   Named for hybridizer's mother.
White flowers, tipped in orchid, with a yellow eye; long stamens
recurve toward the pistil. Pyramidal trusses. Plant compact.
Weldon E. Delp, reg. 1990.   Color illus. LW pl. 94.

```
                       -catawbiense 1/4
             -Mrs. Charles S. Sargent-
CHRISTINA'S SISTER-          -unknown 1/2
         -                    -campylocarpum 1/4
             -Mrs. W. C. Slocock-
                              -unknown
```
Strong purple buds open to flowers of light purple, rimmed with
strong purple; dorsal spotting, brilliant yellow.   Weldon Delp.

CHRISTINE DENZ   Described under BARBARA JURY, q.v.

```
                                 -griffithianum
                 -lacteum 1/4 -Kewense-      1/32
         -Lionel's Triumph-   -Aurora-      -fortunei 10/64
         -                -Naomi-    -thomsonii 1/16
CHRISTINE-               -fortunei
 HILLBERG-   -wardii 1/4
         -Crest-             -fortunei ssp. discolor 1/8
             -Lady Bessborough-
                             -campylocarpum Elatum Gp. 1/8
```
Funnel-shaped flowers, in trusses of 11, 7-lobed, lemon yellow.
Shrub to 15ft(5m); oblanceolate leaves. F. Hillberg, reg. 1986.

```
             -caucasicum 1/2
CHRISTMAS CHEER-
             -unknown 1/2
```
4ft(1.2m) -10F(-23C) VE 3/4   An old hybrid of rather dense,
compact habit. Flowers pink in bud, opening blush pink, fading
to very pale pink, 2in(5cm) across. Often forced for Christmas.
Sun-tolerant.   Methven. Color illus. F front cover; Cox pl. 35.

```
                 -fortunei ssp. discolor 1/4
         -Evening Glow-   -dichroanthum 1/8
         -         -Fabia-
CHRISTY S.-          -griersonianum 1/8
         -           -ponticum 1/4
         -Purple Splendour-
                 -unknown 1/4
```
5ft(1.5m) -5F(-21C) ML 4/3   Unusual flowers of orchid rose
with touch of gold in center, and bright maroon blotch on upper
lobe. Deep green foliage.   Stockman cross; Greer, intro. 1988.
Color illus. HG p. 181.

```
     -chrysodoron 1/2
CHRYCIL-          -ciliatum 1/4
     -Cilpinense-
                 -moupinense 1/4
```
Compact dwarf; flowers lemon to yellow.   Lord Aberconway, 1947.

```
         -moupinense 1/2
CHRYPINENSE-
         -chrysodoron 1/2
```
Pale yellow flowers.   Lord Aberconway, 1946.

```
         -chrysodoron 1/2
CHRYSASPIS-
         -leucaspis 1/2
```
Yellow flowers.   Lord Aberconway.   A.M. 1942.

```
         -chrysodoron 1/2
CHRYSOMANICUM-
         -burmanicum 1/2
```
3ft(.9m) 15F(-9C) EM 3/3   Primrose yellow flowers in trusses
of 8. Compact, spreading plant.   Lord Aberconway.   A.M. 1947.

```
     -yakushimanum 1/2
CHUBBY-          -forrestii Repens Group 1/4
     -Elizabeth-
                 -griersonianum 1/4
```
Strong purplish pink flowers, 2.4in(6cm) wide; truss of 12. Fol-
iage linear-oblong, recurved edges, scattered brown indumentum.
F. May, cross 1967; reg. 1988.

CHUCKANUT SUNSET   Parentage unknown; possibly PINK PEARL or
                                        ALICE   X CREST
7ft(2.1m)(18 yrs) -5F(-21C) E Domed truss of 10 flowers, 4in.
10cm) wide, 6 wavy lobes, pale greenish yellow, red markings in
throat; flat, smooth leaves.   The Ragans, cross 1969; reg. 1989.

CHURCH LANE--yakushimanum, selfed
2ft(.6m) -15F(-26C) EM 5/5 Pink, yellow spots on upper lobe.
P. G. Valder, reg. 1972.

CHURCHILL   Described under FORTUNE, q.v.

```
     -ciliatum 1/2
CILASPIS-
     -leucaspis 1/2
```
White flowers.   E. J. P. Magor, 1931.

```
     -ciliatum 1/2
CILBOOTH-
     -boothii 1/2
```
An introduction of E. J. P. Magor, 1926.

```
     -ciliatum 1/2
CILKEISK-
     -keiskei 1/2
```
Flowers white, tinged pink.   E. J. P. Magor, 1926.

```
         -ciliatum 1/2
CILPINENSE-
         -moupinense 1/2
```
3ft(1.5m) 5F(-15C) E 4/4   Compact plant; deep forest green,
shiny leaves.   Flowers are blush pink touched with deeper pink.
Very floriferous; can be forced at Christmas.   Lord Aberconway,
1927.   A.M. 1927.   F.C.C. 1968.   Color ill. ARS Q 31:3 (1977)
p. 170; F p. 39; JS p. 84; VV p. 18.

```
     -calostrotum 1/2
CINDY-
     -ciliatum--Bergie 1/2
```
Blush pink flowers.   H. L. Larson, 1953.

```
                         -catawbiense 1/8
             -Parsons Grandiflorum-
         -America-          -unknown 1/2
         -    -dark red hybrid--unknown
CINDY LOU-          -griffithianum 1/8
         -         -Mars-
         -unnamed hybrid-   -unknown
             -catawbiense var. rubrum 1/4
```
5ft(1.5m) -15F(-26C) L 4/3 Foliage and habit as catawbiense.
Buds of moderate and cardinal red open to cardinal red; rounded
trusses.   Fetterhoff cross; Delp raiser, 1968.

CINDY LOUISE---selected form of calophytum
8ft x 8ft(2.4m)(25 yrs) -5F(-21C) VE   Trusses hold about 15
flowers, 7-lobed, dark pink in bud, opening pale purplish pink.
Upright plant, of open habit.   H. Vaartnou raiser; reg. 1989.

```
         -bureavii (A.M. 1939) 1/2
CINNAMON BEAR-
         -yakushimanum, FCC--Koichiro Wada 1/2
```
4.5ft(1.35m)(23yrs) OF(-18C) M Open campanulate flowers, 2in.
(5cm) wide, white with spinel red dorsal spotting; 20 per domed
truss. Narrow leaves to 5in(12.6cm) held 3-4 years; very heavy,
felted, cinnamon brown, hairy coating below; new growth whitish.
Well-branched.   Cecil Smith, cross 1964; S. Leopold, reg. 1989.

CINNANDRUM   Described under ROYAL FLUSH, q.v.

CINNANDRUM TANGERINE   Described under ROYAL FLUSH, q.v.

```
     -cinnabarinum 1/2
CINNCRASS-
     -maddenii ssp. crassum
```
White flowers, shading to cream at base.   E. Magor. A.M. 1935.

* *
```
     -cinnabarinum 1/2
CINNKEYS-
     -keysii 1/2
```
5ft(1.5m) 5F(-15C) ML 4/4 Clusters of tubular flowers, light
clear red in the tube, with soft yellow lobes. Shrub has oval,

glossy, grayish green leaves. Magor, 1926. A.M. 1935. Col.
illus. ARS Q 32:3 (1978), p. 170; Cox pl. 36.
MINTERNE CINNKEYS   Parentage as above
Trusses hold about 30 tubular-shaped flowers, in dense clusters,
of orange-red. Lord Digby, 1931. A.M. 1951. F.C.C. 1952.
* *

```
        -cinnabarinum 1/2
CINNMADD-
        -maddenii 1/2
```
An introduction of E. J. P. Magor.

* *
```
        -yakushimanum--Koichiro Wada 1/2
CINQUERO-
        -strigillosum 1/2
```
4ft x 4ft(1.2m) OF(-18C) M   Flower to 3in(7.6cm) wide, salmon
red with dark red nectaries; compact, rounded truss. Dark green
foliage, apiculate; fawn indumentum. Dr. D. Goheen, reg. 1989.
MICHELLE ILENA   Parentage: strigillosum x yakushimanum
4ft x 4ft(1.2m)(15yrs) 5F(-15C) E   Flowers held in flat truss
of 10, opening red, aging to deep yellowish pink. Foliage with
brown felted indumentum below. Jacob Rosenthal, reg. 1989.
* *

```
        -cinnabarinum Blandfordiiflorum Group 1/2
CINZAN-
        -cinnabarinum ssp. xanthocodon 1/2
```
4ft(1.2m) OF(-18C) M 4/3   A medium-sized, slender shrub with
pendant, apricot flowers.   A coral pink, and other forms, may
exist. J. B. Stevenson, 1951.

```
                -haematodes 1/4
        -Humming Bird-
CIRCE-          -williamsianum 1/4
-               -neriiflorum 1/4
        -F. C. Puddle-
                -griersonianum 1/4
```
Bright red flowers. Lord Aberconway, intro. 1942. A.M. 1942.

```
                -dichroanthum 1/4
        -Fabia-
CIRCUS-         -griersonianum 1/4
-               -ponticum 1/4
        -Purple Splendour-
                -unknown 1/4
```
3ft(.9m) -5F(-21C) ML 4/3   Flowers of azalea pink aging to
cadmium orange, spotting of deep Tuscan yellow, margins rhodonite red; 13 in ball-shaped truss. An upright plant, moderately
branched. G. Grace cross; L. Grothaus, intro. 1973; reg. 1981.

* *
```
                                -fortunei ssp. discolor
        -yakushimanum   -Lady                   1/16
-Si Si-         -Day  -Bessborough-campylocarpum Elatum Gp.
-       -Gold Mohur- Dream-                      1/16
-               -       -griersonianum 3/32
-               -       -fortunei ssp. discolor 1/16
CISA-           -Margaret Dunn-  -dichroanthum 1/32
-                       -Fabia-
-                               -griersonianum
-       -yakushimanum 1/2
-Serendipity-
        -aureum (chrysanthum) 1/4
```
Dwarf plant with indumented foliage; flowers open as shaded yel-
lows. Hardy to -15F(-26C). Weldon Delp.
D.D.   Parentage as above
Medium-sized plant with indumented foliage; flowers a blend of
yellows. Hardy to -15F(-26C). Delp.
* *

* *
```
        -williamsianum 1/2              -griffithianum 1/16
CITATION-                       -George Hardy-
-               -Mrs. Lindsay-                  -catawbiense 1/16
        -Diane- Smith         -Duchess of Edinburgh--unknown 1/4
                -                       -campylocarpum 1/8
                -unnamed hybrid-
                                -unknown
```
Clear red flowers, and dark green foliage; plant 1ft(.3m) high,
spreading. Leona & Rudolph Henny, reg. 1965.
MARK HENNY Parentage as above, except reversed

Dwarf plant, 1.5ft(.45m) tall. Flowers cherry red to currant
red, in trusses of 7-8. R. Henny cross; reg. 1965.
ROTHENBURG   Parentage: DIANE x williamsianum
4ft(1.2m) -10F(-23C) EM 3/4   Flowers light primrose yellow,
funnel-shaped. Large leaves, apple green, very glossy. Viktor
von Martin cross; Joh. Bruns, reg. 1972.   A.M. 1987; F.C.C.
Wisley Trials 1989.   Color illus. WS, 1989, p. 173.
* *

```
        -catawbiense var. album--Catanea 1/2
CITRINE-        -wardii 1/4
        -Crest-         -fortunei ssp. discolor 1/8
                -Lady      -
                Bessborough-campylocarpum Elatum Group 1/8
```
2.5ft(.75) -5F(-21C) M   Plant wider than tall; leaves yellow-
green, held 3 years. Fragrant flowers, funnel-shaped, 6-lobed,
light greenish yellow; trusses of 13. Raustein, reg. 1982.

CITRONELLA   Described under CAMPKEW, q.v.

CLACKAMAS WHITE--form of macrophyllum
4ft(1.2m) x 4ft -10F(-23C) M   Nearly pink buds open white, 12
per truss. M. & R. Stewart collectors; Dover Nurs., reg. 1985.

```
        -yakushimanum (Larson's No. 6) 1/2
CLAIRE-                 -griffithianum 1/4
-               -Pink Shell-            -fortunei 3/16
        -Coronation Day-        -H. M. Arderne-
        -               -griffithianum  -unknown 1/16
                -Loderi-
                        -fortunei
```
1.5ft(.45m) 5F(-15C) M Dwarf plant, wider than high, leathery
medium-sized leaves held 2 years. Flowers 4in(10.2cm) wide, 5-
lobed, very light Neyron rose fading white, held in large, conical trusses of 9. H. L. Larson cross; J. A. Davies, reg. 1983.

CLAIRE REICHELT   Described under FOXBERG, q.v.

```
                        -neriiflorum 1/8
                -Nereid-
        -Euryalus-      -dichroanthum 1/8
CLANSMAN-       -griersonianum 1/4
        -arboreum ssp. zeylanicum 1/2
```
Red flowers. Lord Aberconway, 1950.

```
        -decorum 1/2
CLARA-                  -griffithianum 1/4
        -Loderi King George-
                        -fortunei 1/4
```
4ft(1.2m) 5F(-15C) M   Pure white flowers, openly funnel-shap-
ed, 5in(12.7cm) wide, in trusses of 10-12. Bushy plant; light
green foliage. Slonecker, reg. 1962.

```
                        -griffithianum 1/8
                -Mars-
        -Vulcan-        -unknown 1/2
        -               -griersonianum 1/4
CLARA CURRY-                    -catawbiense 1/8
-               -Parsons Grandiflorum-
        -America-               -unknown
                -dark red hybrid--unknown
```
3ft(.9m) OF(-18C) M Ruby red flower, 3in(7.6cm) wide, rounded
trusses of 12-14. Plant of upright, broad habit; leaves medium
to large. New growth reddish. J. H. Hughes, reg. 1977.

```
                -decorum 1/4
        -unnamed-
        - hybrid-fortunei ssp. discolor 1/4
CLARA RAUSTEIN-         -wardii 1/8
-               -unnamed-
        -unnamed- hybrid-dichroanthum 1/8
        - hybrid-
                -fortunei 1/4
```
6ft(1.8m) -5F(-21C) M   Flowers apricot and warm yellow fading
pale yellow, 3in(7.6cm) wide; truss of 13. Plant broad, sturdy.
Raustein. reg. 1972. Color illus. ARS Q 27:3 (1973), p. 170.

```
                -haematodes 3/4
        -Choremia-
CLARA WEYERHAUSER-     -arboreum 1/4
        -haematodes
```
An unregistered selection by Lester E. Brandt.

```
                    -yakushimanum 1/4
         -unnamed-                           -griffithianum 1/16
         - hybrid-          -Queen Wilhelmina-
         -         -Britannia-               -unknown 3/16
CLARET-                     -Stanley Davies--unknown
BUMBLE-                         -fortunei ssp. discolor 1/8
         -         -Lady Bessborough-
         -         -              -campylocarpum Elatum Group 1/8
         -Jalisco-
         -              -dichroanthum 1/8
              -Dido-
                   -decorum 1/8
4ft(1.2m) 0F(-18C) ML    Flowers have plum-colored rims, and a
light plum center.  John Waterer, Sons & Crisp, reg. 1975.
```

```
                 -sanguineum ssp. didymum 1/4
           -Carmen-
CLARET CUP-      -forrestii Repens Group 1/4
           -neriiflorum 1/2
```
Dwarf plant; blooms early mid-season.   Flowers rather fleshy, 6
per truss, funnel-shaped, 5-lobed, deep red; pink calyx. Plant
8in(.2m) x 16in(.4m) at registration. J. May, reg. 1988.

```
                        -griffithianum 1/8
             -Queen Wilhelmina-
      -Earl of Athlone-          -unknown 3/8
CLARIBEL-            -Stanley Davies--unknown
      -haematodes 1/2
```
Plant 12in(30.4cm) x 12in(10yrs). Small, insect-resistant fol-
iage. Flowers currant red; loose truss. Seabrook, reg. 1965.

```
                  -sanguineum ssp. didymum 1/2
CLARICE OF LANGAU-
                  -haematodes 1/2
```
Dark red flowers in loose trusses. Low, compact bush, dense, as
haematodes. For the small garden. E. de Rothschild, reg. 1966.

CLARK'S WHITE--form of catawbiense var. album
6ft(1.8m) -25F(-32C) ML   Domed truss of 14-16 funnel-shaped
flowers, 5 smooth-edged lobes. Pure white in bud, opening white
with greenish gold spotting. Leaves elliptic, hairless, glossy.
Parent of Delp and other hybrids.   Selected by O. E. Clark, in
the 1960s; E. R. Bahnsen, reg. 1988.   Color illus. ARS Q 42:2
(1988), p. 90.

* *
```
                  -wardii 1/4
CLASS OF    -Crest-          -fortunei ssp. discolor 1/8
THIRTY-EIGHT-    -Lady  -
         -       Bessborough-campylocarpum Elatum Group 1/8
         -wardii Litiense Group 1/2
```
6ft(1.8m) 10F(-12C) E   Intro. by U. of Washington (Seattle) to
honor this class. Domed truss of 8-12 flowers, 3.5in(9cm) wide,
7 wavy-edged lobes, light chartreuse green. Glossy leaves, 6in.
(15cm); dense upright plant. W. Elliott, cross 1976; reg. 1988.
HUSKY FEVER   Parentage as above
6ft(1.8m) 10F(-12C) E Flower openly finnel-shaped, 2.7in(7cm)
wide, 5 wavy-edged lobes, light yellow green; spherical truss of
10. Open upright plant. Walter Elliott, cross 1976; reg. 1989.
* *

```
CLASSY           -catawbiense var. album Glass--Catalgla
LASSIE---unnamed hybrid,-          -decorum ? 1/8       1/2
          selfed-    -Caroline-
           -Cadis-         -brachycarpum ? 1/8
                        -fortunei ssp. discolor 1/4
```
Buds a blend of strong and light purples open to strong and very
pale purples; filaments deep purplish pink. Weldon Delp.

```
                  -Corona--unknown 5/8
         -Bow Bells-
         -              -williamsianum 1/4
CLATSOP BELLE-                              -griffithianum
         -              -Queen Wilhelmina-        1/8
         -Earl of Athlone-             -unknown
                        -Stanley Davies--unknown
```
4ft(1.2m) 0F(-18C) EM   Bell-shaped flowers, soft rose to deep
pink, slightly ruffled, 2in(5cm) wide; about 15 per loose truss.
Plant compact; olive green foliage. George Baker, reg. 1966.

```
                        -griffithianum 1/8
           -Mars-
        -Sammetglut-    -unknown 7/16          -catawbiense
CLAUDINE-       -          -Parsons Grandiflorum-
        -      -Nova Zembla-          -unknown
        -        -             -dark red hybrid--unknown
        -      -smirnowii 1/4
        -Daisy-          -catawbiense 3/16
            -Mrs. Milner-
                    -unknown
```
5ft(1.5m) x 5ft -15F(-26C) ML   Flowers in trusses of 16-19, 5
wavy-edged lobes, purplish pink with paler margins, spotting on
dorsal lobe of yellowish brown. H. Hachmann, cross 1968; Stück,
reg. 1988. Color illus. WS, 1989, p. 124.

CLEARWATER   Parentage unknown
Flowers of purplish pink. Dexter cross; G. Wister, reg. 1981.

CLEMENTINE LEMAIRE   Parentage unknown
5ft(1.5m) -15F(-26C) ML 4/3   Bright pink flowers with yellow
blotch in tight trusses; foliage deep green. Moser & Sons.

```
           -arboreum, blood red 1/2
CLEOPATRA-                      -thomsonii 1/8
         -       -unnamed hybrid-
         -unnamed hybrid-          -unknown 1/8
                    -sutchuenense 1/4
```
Flowers of deep satiny pink. E. J. P. Magor, 1931.

```
           -wardii Litiense Group 1/2
CLEWER-    -wardii 1/4
       -Crest-          -fortunei ssp. discolor 1/8
           -Lady Bessborough-
                    -campylocarpum Elatum Group 1/8
```
Primrose yellow flowers, 6- or 7-lobed, 2.25in(5.7cm) wide, in a
compact truss. Crown Estate, Windsor, reg. 1967.   P.C. 1966.

```
                              -neriiflorum 1/32
                        -Nereid-
                -Phyllis Ballard-      -dichroanthum 1/32
         -unnamed-          -fortunei ssp. discolor
    -unnamed- hybrid-catawbiense--Clark's White 1/8     7/64
    - hybrid-
    -       -pale yellow Dexter--unknown 1/4
    -           -brachycarpum 1/8
CLICKER-     -unnamed-    -wardii 3/32
    -     - hybrid-Crest-          -fortunei ssp. discolor
    -     -          -Lady
    -     -          Bessborough-campylocarpum Elatum
    -Marypat-          -catawbiense var. album 1/16
    -     -unnamed-    -wardii
    -     - hybrid-Crest-          -fortunei ssp.
    -Monte-          -Lady   - discolor
    Carlo-          Bessborough-
    -                   -campylocarpum
    -       -aureum 1/16         Elatum 3/64
    -unnamed-
    hybrid-campylocarpum 1/16
```
Buds of pale greenish yellow and deep yellowish pink, open to
yellowish white flowers with vivid yellow-green throat.   Delp.

* *
```
                  -leucaspis 1/4
           -Bric-a-brac-
CLIFF GARLAND-          -moupinense 1/4
           -mucronulatum, pure pink 1/2
```
1ft(.3m) -20F(-29C) E 4/4 Leaves, small and nearly circular.
Flowers shell pink, up to 2in(5cm) wide; 4 flowers per truss.
G. Guy Nearing, reg. 1970.
CLIFF SPANGLE   Parentage as above
1ft(.3m) -20F(-29C) E 4/4 Leaves very small, green all year.
Flower clusters of 5, deep pink, 2.5in(6.3cm) across.   Nearing;
reg. 1970.
* *
* *
```
                        -adenogynum 1/4
    -Xenosporum (detonsum)-
CLIO-          -unknown 1/4
    -   -griffithianum 1/4
    -Gilian-
        -thomsonii 1/4
```
Flowers colored carmine lake.   E. J. P. Magor, 1931.

GUY NEARING   Parentage as above
6ft(1.8m) -10F(-23C) ML Rounded plant, as wide as high; flowers reddish purple, 2in(5cm) wide; truss of 25. Nearing cross;
Raustein, reg. 1973.   Color illus. ARS Q 27:3 (1973), p. 171.
* *

```
               -ciliatum 1/4
         -Praecox-
CLODION-        -dauricum 1/4
       -
               -cinnabarinum Roylei Group 1/2
```
Flowers of dull claret red.   Adams-Acton, 1934.

```
                  -dichroanthum 1/4
            -Neda-
CLOTTED CREAM-  -Cunningham's Sulphur--caucasicum 1/4
            -auriculatum 1/2
```
Flowers of deep cream.   Lord Aberconway.   A.M. 1942.

```
           -fortunei 1/4
     -unnamed-            -decorum 1/16
     - hybrid-     -unnamed-
     -       -Madonna- hybrid-griersonianum 1/16
CLOUD-     (Gable)-                        -catawbiense
NINE-       -       -Parsons Grandiflorum     5/32
     -       -America-            -unknown 7/32
     -                     -dark red hybrid--unknown
     -            -caucasicum 1/4
     -Boule de Neige-          -catawbiense
            -unnamed hybrid-
                     -unknown
```
4ft(1.2m) -15F(-26C) M 3/4   Fragrant white flowers with fern
green blotch, 3.5in(8.9cm) wide; truss of 12. Plant as broad as
tall; leaves dull spinach green, held 3 years. Haag, reg. 1981.

```
           -catawbiense var. album 7/16
     -Great Lakes-
CLOUD -        -yakushimanum--Koichiro Wada 1/4
TWELVE-            -catawbiense 5/32
     -     -Mrs. C. S. Sargent-
     -unnamed-            -unknown 5/32
       hybrid-       -catawbiense var. album
            -Lodestar-          -catawbiense var. album
                  -Belle Heller-          -catawbiense
                     -white hybrid-
                           -unknown
```
Pure white flowers in neat, tight trusses; excellent plant habit
and foliage. Hardy to at least -20F(-29C). O. S. Pride, 1975.

```
       -sperabile 1/2
CLOVE-
       -sanguineum var. haemaleum 1/2
```
Campanulate crimson flowers. A semi-dwarf plant of dense habit.
Rothschild, 1935.

CLYNE BLUSH, CLYNE CERISE, CLYNE ELSAE, CLYNE PEARL   All described under ELSAE, q.v.

COALITION   Parentage unknown; may be GILL'S TRIUMPH x thomsonii
Bright salmon red; some forms paler. R. Gill & Son. A.M. 1924.

COALS OF FIRE--form of cerasinum K W 5830
"...trusses of five, and of an intense burning scarlet; at the
base of the corolla are five circular jet-black honey-glands,
each about the size of a shirt-button." Described and named by
Frank Kingdon Ward, 1924; quoted by W. J. Bean, Trees and Shrubs

COBALT   Described under AMETHYST (Arends), q.v.

COCCINEA--form of ferrugineum
Red form of dwarf plant, Swiss Alpine Rose. Easily propagated.
Two azaleas, one from 1835, also have this name.   Has also been
confused with very different rhododendron, NOBLEANUM COCCINEUM.

```
                  -yakushimanum 1/4
         -unnamed hybrid-     -dichroanthum 1/8
         -       -Fabia Tangerine-
COCH-Y-BONDU-                  -griersonianum 3/8
         -       -griersonianum
            -Tally Ho-
                  -facetum (eriogynum) 1/4
```
Flowers very pale sap green.   Waterer, Sons & Crisp; reg. 1975.

```
               -cinnabarinum 3/4
COCK OF THE ROCK-        -cinnabarinum
               -Rose Mangles-
                        -maddenii 1/4
```
Flowers clear orange, outside suffused ruby red on orange.   R.
Stephenson Clarke.   A.M. 1932.

```
               -yakushimanum--Koichiro Wada 1/2
COCONUT ICE-
               -aberconwayi 1/2
```
Buds camellia rose, opening white, with camellia rose edges and
red dorsal spots. Pukeiti Rhod. Trust; G. F. Smith, reg. 1984.

```
           -racemosum 1/2
CODORUS-
           -minus Carolinianum Group 1/2
```
Pink flowers resembling trailing arbutus. J. Gable, cross 1934.

```
                        -griffithianum 1/4
                  -Halopeanum-
            -Snow Queen-     -maximum 1/8
            -       -     -griffithianum
COLDSTREAM-        -Loderi-
            -            -fortunei 1/8
            -unknown 1/2
```
White flowers, suffused yellow in throat, openly funnel-shaped;
rounded trusses 7.5in(19cm) across, 10-12 flowers.   Maj. Hardy.
A.M. 1972.

```
           -fortunei ssp. discolor Houlstonii Group 1/2
COLEHURST-        -fortunei--Sir Charles Butler 1/4
     -Van Nes Sensation-     -griffithianum 1/8
                  -Halopeanum-
                        -maximum 1/8
```
6ft(1.8m) -5F(-21C) EM   Large flowers of light Neyron rose,
creamy white centers; truss of 14.   B. Boulter, AUS, reg. 1978.

```
           -williamsianum 1/2
COLINA-
     -Sir Charles Lemon--arboreum ssp. cinnamomeum var. album
```
7ft(2.1m) x 6ft(1.8m)(20 yrs) 10F(-12C) E Buds of pale coral;
white flower, 2in(5cm) x 2in.; ball truss of 14-16. Dense bush;
glossy, ovate foliage held 3-4 years.   Goheen cross; reg. 1990.

```
                  -arboreum ssp. nilagiricum? 1/2
         -Noyo Chief-
COLLEGE PINK-        -unknown 3/4
         -unknown
```
5ft(1.5m) 5F(-15C) M A parent of POSY. Rose Bengal buds open
to paler flowers, in compact trusses of 15. Fine habit and foliage. Massey College, New Zealand; G. Smith, reg. 1985.

COLLINGWOOD INGRAM--form of trichostomum Ledoides Group
2.5ft(.75m) -5F(-21C) M 4/3   Trusses of 16-20 flowers, light
fuchsia purple, 5-lobed, tubular, less than .5in wide. Leaves
about 1in(2.5cm) long, narrow, aromatic, non-scaly.   Forrest
collector; Cox raiser; Lady Anne Palmer exhibitor. F.C.C. 1976.

COLONEL COEN   Parentage unknown; possibly ponticum hybrid
5ft(1.5m) -10F(-23C) ML 4/4   Deep purple with dark spots;
dome-shaped truss. Flowers when young.   E. Ostbo, before 1958.

```
           -wardii 1/4
     -Hawk-          -fortunei ssp. discolor 1/8
COLONEL-     -Lady Bessborough-
  REMY -                  -campylocarpum Elatum Group 1/8
     -campylocarpum 1/2
```
Compact trusses of up to 13 flowers, 5-lobed, bell-shaped, very
light greenish yellow, reverse stronger color.   Edmund de Rothschild, reg. 1978.   A.M. 1978.

* *
```
           -falconeri 1/2
COLONEL ROGERS-
           -niveum 1/2
```
6ft(1.8m) 0F(-18C) EM   Tall plant, fine foliage; rose purple
flowers. Rogers cross, 1926; shown by Heneage-Vivian, 1933.
MECCA   Parentage as above
Tightly packed trusses of 42 flowers; white, light flush of cyclamen purple, small deep purple stain in throat. Mat-like
indumentum under leaves. Mrs. D. Gordon, reg. 1966. A.M. 1965.
* *

```
            -campylocarpum 1/2
COLONEL THORNEYCROFT-
            -unknown 1/2
```
Small, early hybrid; rich pink buds open to pale yellow flowers. Medium-sized trusses. Harry White, Sunningdale Nurseries, 1955.

COLOR BUSTER   Described under AWESOME ARRAY, q.v.

```
            -minus 1/2
COLTS NECK ROSE-
            -dauricum 1/2
```
6ft(1.8m)(15yrs) -25F(-32C) E   Strong purplish red buds open to wavy-edged flowers 1.4in(3.5cm) wide, strong red-purple, with dark red dorsal spots; trusses of 6-15. Elliptic foliage, scaly above, dark red in winter; compact plant.   G Lewis, reg. 1989. Color illus. ARS J 37:2 (1983), p. 70.

COLUMBIA GLORY   Parentage unknown: elepidote
5ft(1.5m)(18 yrs) OF(-18C) M   Plant wide as tall. Buds dark pink, opening white, strong purplish red wavy edges, 3in(7.5cm) across; ball truss of 16. W. & J. Ragan, cross 1969; reg. 1989.

COLUMBIA SUNSET   Described under RED SNAPPER, q.v.

COLVILLE--form of minus Carolinianum Group
4ft(1.2m) -25F(-32C) M 3/3 Flowers in clusters of 10, light red-purple, shading deeper. Leaf narrowly ovate; pitted reddish brown scales below.   Mrs. N. Colville, reg. 1984.   A.M. 1968.

COMELY   Described under CHAN, q.v.

```
            -williamsianum 1/2
COMPACTA-
            -unknown 1/2
```
3ft(.9m) -5F(-21C) ML 3/4   Buds of deep pink, opening paler. A compact plant, with rounded leaves.   D. Hobbie.

```
                        -fortunei ssp. discolor 1/4
            -Lady Bessborough-
      -Jalisco-                 -campylocarpum Elatum Group 1/4
      -          -dichroanthum 3/8
COMSTOCK-    -Dido-
      -          -decorum 1/8
      -    -dichroanthum
      -Jasper-            -fortunei ssp. discolor
            -Lady Bessborough-
                        -campylocarpum Elatum Group
```
3ft(.9m) -5F(-21C) ML 4/4 Large flower, warm orange streaked apricot and yellow; showy calyx. Dense, rounded foliage of cool forest green.   D. James cross; H. Greer, reg. 1979.

```
            -augustinii 1/2
CONCERTO-
            -searsiae 1/2
```
Purple flowers with green spotting, in umbels of 9-16. Medium-sized leaves of dark dull green.   Wilson collector; E. de Rothschild, reg. 1980.   A.M. 1979.

CONCESSIUM'S MASTER   Parentage unknown
Flowers 3in(7.5cm) wide, saucer-shaped, of rose Bengal paling at the center; tight trusses of 16. A superior form of the above? Also a very old hybrid.

CONCESSUM   Parentage unknown
5ft(1.5m) -5F(-21C) L   Long-lasting, wide-open pink flowers, deeper pink outside; prominent stamens. Pale centers give a bi-color effect.   J. Byls; Standish & Noble, offered before 1854.

```
            -ciliicalyx 1/2
CONCHITA-
            -moupinense 1/2
```
4.5ft(1.35m) 20F(-7C) E 3/3 Flower phlox pink, spotted crimson, 4in(10cm) wide, flattened, wavy-lobed; fragrant. Leaves to 4in(10cm), dark red when young.   John S. Druecker; reg. 1976.

```
                  -wightii 1/8
            -China-
      -The Master-   -fortunei 1/4
      -                  -campylocarpum  Elatum Group 1/8
CONCORD-    -Letty Edwards-
      -                  -fortunei
      -yakushimanum 1/2
```

3ft(.9m) -15F(-26C) M 3/4 White flower with a green throat; compact plant. A. F. George, Hydon Nurseries, reg. 1978.

CONCORDE   Parentage unknown; may be catawbiense hybrid
5ft(1.5m) -15F(-26C) M Flower deep carmine pink, dark blotch; large truss. Dull foliage; broad plant. A. van Nes; Stolwikj & Zomen, intro. 1970. A.M. Boskoop 1973. Gold Medal, Flora Nova.

* *
```
                        -griffithianum 1/8
            -Isabella-
      -Muy Lindo-      -auriculatum 1/8
CONDOR-      -             -decorum 1/8
      -      -unnamed hybrid-
      -Zella--unknown 1/2   -souliei 1/8
```
Flowers open from pink buds, fade to creamy white. Leaves 8.5in (22cm) long, dark green.   C. Ingram, reg. 1976.   A.M. 1976.
SARAH HARDY   Parentage as above, except reversed
White flowers, lightly flushed pink, in trusses of 11-12. Collingwood Ingram cross; G. A. Hardy intro., reg. 1982.
* *

```
            -racemosum 1/2
CONEMAUGH-
            -mucronulatum 1/2
```
5ft(1.5m) -15F(-26C) VE 3/3 Open, twiggy plant, small-leaved and semideciduous. Stellate, pinkish lavender flowers, held in a small spherical truss. Various clones exist.   Gable, 1934.

```
            -minus Carolinianum Group 1/2
CONESTOGA-
            -racemosum 1/2
```
Hardy to -20F(-29C). Pink flowers, in early season. Joe Gable cross of 1954-5, replacing his 1929's extinct CONESTOGA.

```
            -minus Carolinianum Group 1/2
CONEWAGO-
            -mucronulatum 1/2
```
5ft(1.5m) -25F(-32C) E 3/2   Flowers of lilac rose; plant of open habit, but with many branches. A very floriferous form is CONEWAGO IMPROVED. J. Gable, 1934.   Color illus. LW pl. 35.

```
            -haematodes 1/2
CONEWINGO-
            -diphrocalyx 1/2
```
Joseph Gable, intro. 1934.

CONFECTION   Described under CATHY, q.v.

* *
```
      -catawbiense var. album 1/2
      -                        -caucasicum 3/32
CONGO-                  -Jacksonii-
      -            -Goldsworth-      -caucasicum
      -            - Yellow -      -Nobleanum-
      -Goldfort-      -campylocarpum 1/8      -arboreum 1/32
            -fortunei 1/4
```
5ft(1.5m) -20F(-29C) M   White flowers from buds flushed spirea red; spherical trusses of 16. Plant much broader than high; leaves 5.5in(14cm) long, held 2 years.   D. G. Leach, reg. 1984.
LUXOR   Parentage as above
6ft(1.8m) -25F(-32C) M 4/3 Syn. MOROCCO. Buds of Neyron rose open to a moonburst of ivory (empire yellow) flowers 2.75in(7cm) wide, 5 to 7 lobes, in trusses of 15. A sturdy plant wider than tall; leaves dark green, held 3 years.   Leach, reg. 1983.
* *

```
            -caucasicum 1/4
      -Christmas Cheer-
CONNETQUOT-      -unknown 3/4
      -Pygmalion--unknown
```
1.5ft(.45m) -5F(-21C) M   Cardinal red buds to Tyrian purple flowers, in trusses of 15. Plant broader than tall; leaves held 3 years.   A. A. Raustein, reg. 1983.

```
            -kyawii 1/2
CONNIE HATTON-
            -fortunei ssp. discolor 1/2
```
6ft(1.8m) OF(-18C) VL   Fragrant dark pink flowers, paler in throat; trusses 9in(23cm) wide hold about 12. Plant upright and broad; large leaves held up to 3 years. H. A. Short, reg. 1974.

```
                                -thomsonii 1/8
                        -Bagshot Ruby-
            -Princess Elizabeth-                  -unknown 1/2
CONNIE   -                      -unknown
  STANTON-               -caucasicum 1/4
            -Boule de Neige-                -catawbiense 1/8
                           -unnamed hybrid-
                                      -unknown
```
3ft(.9m) -10F(-23C) M   Flowers watermelon pink to 3in(7.6cm)
across; shape and truss similar to Boule de Neige. Plant compact, as broad as tall. E. N. Stanton, reg. 1969.

CONNIE YATES   Described under YAKU WARRIOR, q.v.

```
                   -catawbiense, red 1/2
CONOCO-CHEAGUE-
                   -haematodes 1/2
```
4ft(1.2m) -10F(-23C) EM 3/3   Syn. CATHAEM. Rose red flowers
in lax trusses; corolloid calyx, reflexed.   Gable believed that
the haematodes from Arnold Arboretum was a hybrid; for his other
crosses he used pollen from Magor in Cornwall.   J. Gable, 1934.


```
         -cinnabarinum Roylei Group 1/2
CONROY-
         -cinnabarinum Concatenans Group 1/2
```
Bushy habit. Trumpet-shaped, waxy flowers, light orange tinged
with rose, in loose trusses. Lord Aberconway, 1937. A.M. 1950.

CONSOLINI BELLRINGER   Parentage unknown
4ft(1.2m) -10F(-23C) M   First called BELLRINGER NO. 1; later
named for Dexter's Head Gardener, who raised it. Ruffled flowers
of creamy yellow and white, in full trusses. Attractive foliage;
compact plant.   Dexter cross; T. Consolini raiser.

CONSOLINI'S WINDMILL   Paremtage unknown
Brilliant red and white bi-color. Named for a very large windmill on the site at Heritage Plantation, Sandwich, MA. Distributed by Briarwood Gardens.


```
                -wardii  1/4
        -Jervis Bay-
        -       -Lady          -fortunei ssp. discolor 1/8
CONSTABLE-      Bessborough-
        -                      -campylocarpum Elatum Group 1/8
        -wardii Litiense Group 1/2
```
4ft(1.2m) -10F(-23C) M   Open trusses of about 20 bell-shaped
flowers, greenish yellow with some reddish spotting.   F. Hanger
cross, RHS Garden, Wisley; reg. 1961. A.M. 1961.


```
                 -russatum 1/2
CONSTABLE'S PURPLE-
                 -unknown 1/2
```
3ft(.9m) -15F(-26C) EM 4/3   Dark bluish purple flowers;
foliage deep forest green in summer, bronze in winter. Greer.


```
              -campanulatum 1/2
CONSTANT NYMPH-                -ponticum 1/4
              -Purple Splendour-
                              -unknown 1/4
```
4ft(1.2m) -10C(-23C) M   White flowers, faintly blushed, in a
large, dome-shaped truss of 12-14. Plant upright and wider than
tall; dull, dark green foliage. Knap Hill, 1955.   H. C. Wisley
Trials 1969. A.M. 1971.


```
          -concinnum Pseudoyanthinum Group 1/2
CONTINA-
          -augustinii 1/2
```
5ft(1.5m) OF(-18C) M   Small trusses of vivid violet blue flow-
ers, with white stamens; floriferous at 4 years. Cox says it is
superior to many augustinii hybrids in color and hardiness.   C.
Phetteplace cross.   Color illus. Cox pl. 38.


```
          -cinnabarinum ssp. xanthocodon Concatenans Group 1/2
CONYAN-
          -concinnum var. pseudoyanthinum  1/2
```
5ft(1.5m) 5F(-15C) EM 3/4 Unusual hybrid with traits of both
parents, a yellow-green and a purple. Slender-growing, compact;
dainty, tubular flowers of delicate pink, spotted brown. CONYAN
APRICOT is creamy apricot; CONYAN PINK a soft shell pink; CONYAN
SALMON of salmon orange, flushed pink.   J. B. Stevenson, 1953.


```
                 -Pink Bell--unknown 1/4
      -Queen o' the May-
      -                 -griersonianum 3/8
COOKIE-    -fortunei 1/4
      -Fawn-   -dichroanthum 1/8
        -Fabia-
                 -griersonianum
```
4ft(1.2m) -10F(-23C) EM 4/4   Very large truss of large flow-
ers, Neyron rose, maroon spotting; fragrant. A spreading plant;
big ivy green leaves.   James cross; Hendricks Park, reg. 1980.


```
                  -campylocarpum 1/4
      -Chaste-            -Pink Bell--unknown 1/8
COOL HAVEN-    -Queen o'the May-
      -                  -griersonianum 1/8
      -wardii Litiense Group 1/2
```
Medium-sized shrub with medium leaves. Flowers in trusses of 18
-20, Dresden yellow with crimson markings and slightly fragrant.
Embley Park raiser; Hillier, reg. 1969.


```
              -griffithianum 1/2
COOMBE ROYAL-
              -unknown 1/2
```
Flowers delicate pink, brown spots. Origin unknown. A.M. 1900.

* *
```
          -edgeworthii (bullatum) 1/2
COPELIA-
          -leucaspis 1/2
```
Flowers butter yellow. Adams-Acton, 1942.
SEPTEMBER SNOW   Parentage as above, except reversed
White flowers in trusses of 4-6.   B. W. Campbell, reg. 1981.
* *


```
               -catawbiense 1/2
COPLEN'S WHITE-
               -fortunei 1/2
```
White flowers. Coplen cross; Joseph Gable, reg. 1958.

COPPER--form of cinnabarinum ssp. xanthocodon Concatenans Group
                                                       L&S 6560
3ft(.9m) 5F(-15C) EM 3/4   Flowers coral, suffused orange and
red; truss of 5-8. C. Ingram raiser; A.M. Wisley Trials 1954.


```
                 -wardii 1/4
        -Crest-          -fortunei ssp. discolor 1/8
        -       -Lady Bessborough-
COPPER -                 -campylocarpum Elatum Group 1/8
KETTLES-                      -campylocarpum 1/8
        -       -Souvenir of W. C. Slocock-
        -unnamed-            -unknown 1/8
          hybrid-dichroanthum ssp. apodectum 1/4
```
Buds open to bright copper, changing to yellow. Trusses hold 9-
11 flowers.   John Lofthouse, reg. 1979.


```
                        -souliei 1/16
              -Soulbut-
         -Vanessa-      -fortunei--Sir Charles Butler 1/16
  -Eudora-      -griersonianum 1/8
  -      -facetum (eriogynum) 1/4
CORA-           -griffithianum 1/8
  -      -Loderi-
  -Coreta-      -fortunei 1/8
          -
          -arboreum ssp. zeylanicum 1/4
```
Red flowers. Lord Aberconway, 1946.

* *
```
             -neriiflorum 1/4
       -Nereid-
CORAL-       -dichroanthum 1/4
       -fortunei ssp discolor 1/2
```
Orange-red flowers. Endre Ostbo. P.A. 1956.
BUFF LADY Parentage as above
4ft(1.2m) -5F(-21C) L 3/3   Flowers of Egyptian buff, shaded
coral pink, campanulate, 6-lobed, in a round truss of 12. Large
leaves, medium green. Rounded plant; heat-tolerant.   Seed from
Rose of England; B. Lancaster, raiser; reg. 1958.
EDWARD DUNN Parentage as above
5ft(1.5m) -5F(-21C) L 4/3   Apricot pink flowers, 3in(7.6cm)
across, in dome-shaped trusses; spreading habit, moss green foliage. Tolerates heat; best in part shade. Ostbo. P.A. 1958.

PEACH LADY   Parentage as above
4ft(1.2m) -5F(-21C) ML 3/3   Peach-colored flowers, edged in
camellia rose, with yellow eye, to 4in(10cm) wide; rounded truss
of 12. Upright plant, heat- and sun-tolerant.   Seed from Rose
of England; B. Lancaster raiser; reg. 1958.

PHYLLIS BALLARD   Parentage as above
5ft(1.5m) -5F(-21C) L 3/3   Grass green leaves with yellow
midveins and petioles.   Bronzy orange-red to coral red flowers,
in late season.   Endre Ostbo, reg. 1958.   P.A. 1956.
  Note: According to David Balint, the entire (Ostbo) cross was
  selfed to produce CORAL & PHYLLIS BALLARD but not EDWARD DUNN.
* *

```
                  -dichroanthum 1/4
           -Exbury Fabia-
           -              -griersonianum 1/4
CORAL FANTASY-          -catawbiense 1/8
           -         -red hybrid-
           -Spring -        -unknown 1/8
           Parade-             -caucasicum 1/8
              -Cunningham's White-
                              -ponticum, white 1/8
```
4ft(1.2m) x 3.5ft(1.05m) 28F(-3C) ML   Buds of light scarlet;
flowers yellowish white with vivid red throat flare, 5- 7-lobed,
2.5in(6.4cm) across. Glossy leaves, edges flat or curled.   W.
Elliott, cross 1978; reg. 1987.

```
           -mucronulatum, Cornell Pink 1/2
CORAL GLOW-
           -lutescens 1/2
```
4ft(1.2m)(cutting) -20F(-29C) E   Slightly fragrant flowers, 2
in(5cm) wide, vivid to light red-orange. Flat scaly leaves held
15 months, 4.5in(11.5cm) long; winter color mahogany. Habit upright; half as wide as tall.   Mehlquist, cross 1967; reg. 1988.

* *
```
           -elliottii 1/2
CORAL ISLAND-    -dichroanthum 1/4
           -Fabia-
               -griersonianum 1/4
```
Francis Hanger cross, 1947; RHS Garden, reg. 1958, but no longer
known at Wisley, except by the records.

SPANISH GLORY   Parentage as above
4ft(1.2m) 10F(-12C) M   Campanulate, red flowers, in trusses of
7. Open plant habit; dark green foliage. M. Sumner, reg. 1971.
* *
```
                  -thomsonii 1/4
           -Barclayi-              -arboreum 1/8
           -       -Glory of Penjerrick-
CORAL PINK-                      -griffithianum 1/8
           -      -lacteum 1/4
           -Lacs-
               -sinogrande 1/4
```
Flowers of deep coral pink, 4in(10.2cm) across, 7-lobed; trusses
hold about 16.   Gen. Harrison, reg. 1971.

* *
```
                        -fortunei ssp. discolor 1/8
           -King of Shrubs-    -dichroanthum 3/8
           -              -Fabia-
           -unnamed-              -griersonianum 1/8
           - hybrid-    -fortunei 1/8
           -      -Fawn-     -dichroanthum
CORAL QUEEN-      -Fabia-
           -              -griersonianum
           -      -dichroanthum
           -Dido-
               -decorum 1/4
```
4ft(1.2m) 0F(-18C) M 4/3   A New Zealand hybrid, with trusses
of 9 to 12 flowers, of medium rhodonite red.   Mrs. R. J. Coker,
reg. 1979.

IVAN D. WOOD   Parentage as above
3ft(.9m) 5F(-15C) ML Flowers with pale Neyron rose rims, center orange-buff, fading Naples yellow. Mrs. Coker, reg. 1979.
* *

CORAL REEF   Described under GLORIANA, q.v.

```
                  -dichroanthum 3/16
           -Dido-
       -Lem's-    -decorum 1/8              -griffithianum
       -Cameo-          -Beauty of Tremough-
       -     -    -Norman Gill-          -arboreum 1/32
       -    -Anna-        -griffithianum 5/32
CORAL-    -                  -griffithianum
SKIES-    -Jean Marie de Montague-
       -                  -unknown 1/16
       -               -dichroanthum
       -          -Fabia-
       -     -unnamed hybrid-    -griersonianum 1/16
       -unnamed-          -bureavii 1/8
         hybrid-    -wardii 1/8
               -Crest-          -fortunei ssp. discolor 1/16
                    -Lady Bessborough-
                            -campylocarpum Elatum Gp. 1/16
```
4ft(1.2m) 5F(-15C) M   Exact combination of the above unknown;
species fractions may not be correct.   Buds strong claret rose,
opening to paler hues; lobes radially striped rose on both surfaces; colors nonfading. Large trusses.   Lofthouse, reg. 1983.

```
              -yakushimanum 1/2
CORAL VELVET-
           -unknown 1/2
```
2.5ft(.75m) -15F(-26C) EM 3/3   Once considered a selected
form of yakushimanum.   Small leaves and stem thick with velvety
indumentum.   Long-lasting flowers open coral pink, fade to light
salmon, 2in(5cm) across.   Swanson & Greer, reg. 1979.

CORALIA   Described under RUTHELMA, q.v.

```
           -luteiflorum 1/2
CORALYNNE-
           -unknown 1/2
```
Seed from Scotland; grown in Australia.   Campanulate flowers, of
the bent style of the seed parent, flaming red.   Trusses of 7-8.
Shrub 4ft(1.2m) x 4ft(20 yrs).   Félice Blake raiser.   Color ill.
ARS J 1989, p.102.

```
                  -dichroanthum 1/4
           -Dante-
           -      -facetum (eriogynum) 1/4
CORDAN-          -griffithianum 1/8
           -      -Loderi-
           -Coreta-    -fortunei 1/8
               -arboreum ssp. zeylanicum 1/4
```
Flowers of deep red.   Lord Aberconway, intro. 1946.

```
                  -sanguineum ssp. didymum 1/4
           -Arthur Osborne-
CORDELIA-          -griersonianum 1/4
           -              -griffithianum 1/4
           -Loderi King George-
                  -fortunei 1/4
```
Red flowers.   Lord Aberconway, 1950.

```
                  -dichroanthum 1/4
           -Goldsworth Orange-
CORDY WAGNER-          -fortunei ssp. discolor 1/4
           -              -griffithianum 1/4
           -Loderi King George-
                  -fortunei 1/4
```
Trusses of 8-9 flowers, coral pink at edges, with rays of burnt
orange, flushed amber.   Leaves 10in(25.4cm) x 3in(7.6cm).   L.
E. Brandt, reg. 1966.

```
           -sperabile 1/4
       -Eupheno-
       -      -griersonianum 1/4
CORENO-          -griffithianum 1/8
       -      -Loderi-
       -Coreta-    -fortunei 1/8
           -arboreum ssp. zeylanicum 1/4
```
Crimson flowers.   Lord Aberconway, 1946.

```
                  -campylocarpum Elatum Group 1/4
           -Penjerrick-
CORESIA-          -griffithianum 1/2
           -              -thomsonii 1/4
           -Cornish Cross-
                  -griffithianum
```

Flowers of pale pink.   Lord Aberconway, 1933.

```
                -griffithianum 1/4
      -Loderi-
CORETA-       -fortunei 1/4
      -arboreum ssp. zeylanicum 1/2
```
Deep crimson scarlet.   Lord Aberconway.   F.C.C. 1935.

```
                -thomsonii 1/4
      -Cornish Cross-
COREUM-             -griffithianum 1/4
      -arboreum 1/2
```
Deep red flowers.   Lord Aberconway, intro. 1950.

```
                  -griffithianum 1/4
                -Mars-
CORINNE---Vulcan, selfed-    -unknown 1/4
                  -griersonianum 1/2
```
Trumpet-shaped flowers of pink, with petaloid stamens.   Halfdan
Lem cross; McClure, reg. 1958.

```
            -haematodes 1/4
      -Choremia-
CORMA-       -arboreum 1/4
      -haematodes ssp. chaetomallum 1/2
```
Dark red flowers.   Lord Aberconway, 1950.

* *
```
                              -griffithianum 9/32
                        -Loderi-
              -Albatross-        -fortunei
      -Cup Day-        -fortunei ssp. discolor 1/16
      -       -           -elliottii 1/16
      -       -Fusilier-
  -Midnight-           -griersonianum 1/16
      -       -           -ponticum 1/8
      -       -Purple Splendour-
CORMID-                 -unknown 3/16
      -                 -griffithianum
      -       -Pink Shell-           -fortunei 7/32
      -Coronation Day-       -H. M. Arderne-
      -                           -unknown
      -              -griffithianum
              -Loderi-
                  -fortunei
```
Trusses hold about 14 flowers, of light mauve, spotted deep pur-
ple, with a green center.   K. Van de Ven, reg. 1980.
MAX MARSHLAND   Parentage as above
Trusses of 19 flowers, light magenta rose with blotch of cardi-
nal red.   K. Van de Ven, reg. 1981.
SUE LISSENDEN   Parentage as above
Scarlet flowers in trusses of 19.   K. Van de Ven, reg. 1981.
YVONNE DAVIES   Parentage as above
Trusses of 17 white flowers striped light Neyron rose on reverse
with a dark red center.   Mrs. M. Davies, reg. 1980.
* *

CORNELL PINK--form of mucronulatum
5ft(1.5m) -15F(-26C) VE 3/3 Deciduous, open, upright shrub.
Before leaves appear, bright, clear pink flowers in clusters of
2-3; sometimes the ground is still snow-covered. Flowers 1.5in.
(3.8cm) across, widely funnel-shaped.   Henry T. Skinner selection; reg. 1958.   A.M. 1965.

CORNISH CRACKER Listed with DAMARIS, q.v.

* *
```
      -thomsonii 1/2
CORNISH CROSS-
      -griffithianum 1/2
```
6ft(1.8m) 10F(-12C) EM 5/3 Flowers 5in(13cm) wide, of heavy
substance, deep pink to red, fading through pink to nearly white
inside. Large loose trusses hold about 9 flowers. Upright habit; trunk of smooth maroon brown to coppery brown. Large glossy
leaves of medium green. Some forms are superior to others.   S.
Smith, Penjerrick, cross 1920; reg. 1958.   A.M. 1925.   Color
illus. F p. 29 and 40.
EXBURY CORNISH CROSS Parentage as above, except different form
of griffithianum. Flower variations in crimson, instead of the
deep pink to red of the Penjerrick CORNISH CROSS. Large plant,
open habit. Rothschild.   A.M. 1935.   Color illus. PB pl. 31.
GILIAN Same parentage as CORNISH CROSS by S. Smith

Large cardinal red flowers, lightly spotted. Magor. A.M. 1923.
PENGAER   Parentage as above (Probably the oldest of the group)
Large, handsome flowers, of crimson red.   Sir John Llewelyn, of
Swansea.   A.M. 1911.
* *
```
              -fortunei ssp. discolor 1/2
CORNISH LODERI-
              -griffithianum 1/2
```
Parent of NIMBUS. Flowers off-white. See also ANGELO.   J. C.
Williams, Caerhays Castle, reg. 1958.

CORNSUTCH   Described under ALMONDTIME, q.v.

```
          -arboreum--Blood Red 1/2
CORNUBIA-       -thomsonii 1/4
      -Shilsonii-
              -barbatum 1/4
```
6ft(1.8m) 15F(-9C) VE 4/3 A very striking early red. Large
conical trusses of blood red. Large, medium green leaves. Easily propagated plant. In mild climates, grows to a small tree.
Barclay Fox.   A.M. 1912   Color illus. VV p. 105.

```
          -fortunei 1/2
CORNWALLIS-
      -unknown 1/2
```
1.5ft(.45m) -15F(-26C) L Synonym ACADIA. Pink flowers, heavily spotted, very fragrant; up to 11 in truss 7in(17.8cm) wide.
Plant broader than tall; medium green leaves held 2 years. G.
D. Swain & D. L. Craig, Ag. Res. Sta., N.S., Canada, reg. 1977.

```
                -fortunei ssp. discolor 1/4
      -Roberte-
      -           -campylocarpum Elatum Group 1/4
COROMANDEL-             -souliei 1/8
      -       -Soulbut-
      -Vanessa-       -fortunei--Sir Charles Butler 1/8
                -griersonianum 1/4
```
A small plant with the vigor of ROBERTE (LADY BESSBOROUGH gr.);
foliage like VANESSA. Flowers bell-shaped, tangerine pink and
yellow buds opening to pale creamy yellow, 15-flowered truss.
Compact, small plant; blooms late.   Sunningdale Nursery, 1957.

CORONA   Parentage unknown
4ft(1.2m) -5F(-21C) ML 4/3 Conical trusses of about 15 rose
pink, small flowers; neat rounded trusses. Plant compact, slow-
growing, insect resistant; tolerates sun and heat. Often a parent, possibly of MARS.   J. Waterer.   A.M. 1911.   Color illus.
ARS Q 29:3 (1975), p. 170; JS p. 82.

```
                -griffithianum 1/2
      -Pink Shell-        -fortunei 3/8
      -          -H. M. Arderne-
CORONATION DAY-             -unknown 1/8
      -       -griffithianum
      -Loderi-
          -fortunei
```
6ft(1.8m) 0F(-18C) E 5/3 Very large flowers, to 5in(12.7cm)
wide, fragrant, delicate China rose, crimson basal blotch; large
loose trusses. Crosfield, 1937. A.M. 1949. Color illus. ARS
Q 26:3 (1972), p. 180.

* *
```
      -Corona--unknown 1/2
CORONET-
      -wardii 1/2
```
Exhibited by Wallace, 1937.
FRECKLE FACE   Parentage as above
PANTHER   Parentage as above
Above two selections by Collingwood Ingram, c. 1952-54.
* *

```
      -Corona--unknown 1/2
CORONIS-       -griffithianum 1/4
      -Loderi-
          -fortunei    1/4
```
Rose-colored flowers.   Lord Aberconway, 1926.

```
                  -campylocarpum Elatum Group 1/16
             -Penjerrick-
        -Amaura-          -griffithianum 5/16
   -Eros-          -griersonianum 3/8
CORROS-   -griersonianum
   -          -thomsonii 1/4
   -Cornish Cross-
                  -griffithianum
```
Red flowers. Lord Aberconway, 1946.

```
             -arboreum 1/4
        -Doncaster-
CORRY KOSTER-        -unknown 1/4
   -                 -griffithianum 1/4
        -George Hardy-
                     -catawbiense 1/4
```
5ft(1.5m) -5F(-21C) EM 3/2 Parentage uncertain but given by
Millais as above. Flowers of pale pink, heavily spotted red in
throat, frilled margins; large, rounded trusses. Upright habit;
medium green leaves stand upright. M. Koster & Sons, 1909.

```
             -haematodes 1/4
     -Choremia-
CORSA-        -arboreum 1/4
     -sanguineum ssp. sanguineum var. sanguineum 1/2
```
Blood red flowers. Lord Aberconway, 1946.

CORSOCK--form of phaeochrysum
5ft(1.5m) 5F(-15C) EM 3/3 Leaves 6.5in(16.5cm) long; brown
indumentum below. Flowers of China rose, lightly spotted; tight
truss of 18-20. No longer grown at Corsock. Forrest collector;
Gen. MacEwen raiser; F. Ingall exhibitor; reg. 1966. P.C. 1966.

```
     -decorum 1/2     -souliei 1/8
COS-      -Soulbut-
   -Vanessa-        -fortunei--Sir Charles Butler 1/8
          -griersonianum 1/4
```
5ft(1.5m) OF(-18C) EM Flesh pink buds open to ivory flowers,
with faint claret spots; open trusses. Slocock, intro. 1935.

```
                  -catawbiense 1/2
COSIMA---Everestianum, selfed-
                  -unknown 1/2
```
Frilled, rose pink flowers with yellow markings. Seidel, 1893.

```
             -caucasicum 1/4
        -Cunningham's White-
COSMOPOLITAN-          -ponticum var. album 1/4
        -Vesuvius--unknown 1/2
```
5ft(1.5m) -10F(-23C) ML 3/3 Pink flowers fade to pale pink,
with a brownish red blotch. Very nice, glossy foliage. Hagen,
Boskoop, reg. 1962. A.M. 1957. Color illus. HG p. 87.

COSTA DEL SOL   Described under JOANITA, q.v.

```
             -dichroanthum 1/4
     -Fabia-
        -griersonianum 1/4
COTILLION-          -griffithianum 1/16
   -          -Kewense-
   -   -Aurora-     -fortunei 5/16
   -Naomi-   -thomsonii 1/8
          -fortunei
```
Leaves to 8in(20.3cm) long. Large flowers, of Mars orange, out-
side jasper red, 7-lobed; truss of 9-10. R. Henny, reg. 1960.

```
                  -griffithianum 3/8
             -George Hardy-
        -Marinus Koster-          -catawbiense 1/8
COTTON CANDY-          -red hybrid--unknown 1/4
   -                 -griffithianum
        -Loderi Venus-
                     -fortunei 1/4
```
6ft(1.8m) OF(-18C) M 4/4 Tall conical truss of large pastel
pink flowers. Foliage dark green, 6in(15.2cm) long. Grows in
sun. J. Henny & Wennekamp, reg. 1961. Color illus. VV p. 104.

```
             -griffithianum 1/4
     -Loderi King George-
COUGAR-          -fortunei 1/4
   -unknown 1/2
```
5ft(1.5m) 20F(-7C) EM Synonym LODERI COUGAR. Buds cardinal

red; flowers bright Neyron rose, tubular funnel-shaped, fragrant, in a 9in(23cm) truss of 15. Flowers upright, not "floppy"
like other Loderis. Plant well-branched, as wide as tall. J.
Drewry/Gene German/Catherine Weeks, reg. 1983.

```
                          -griffithianum 1/4
             -Geoffrey Millais-
COUNTESS OF ATHLONE-          -unknown 1/2
   -                 -catawbiense 1/4
        -Catawbiense Grandiflorum-
                     -unknown
```
6ft(1.8m) -10F(-23C) ML 3/3 Purple buds open to large mauve
flowers, greenish yellow basal markings, widely funnel-shaped,
in tight conical trusses. Plant of upright habit, with glossy,
dark green foliage. "One of the few large-flowered mauve rhododendrons." --Street. C. B. van Nes, 1923. Col. ill. JS p. 60.

```
                          -griffithianum 3/8
             -George Hardy-
     -Pink Pearl-          -catawbiense 3/8
   -          -arboreum 1/8
COUNTESS OF DERBY-          -Broughtonii-
   -                 -unknown 1/8
   -          -catawbiense
     -Cynthia-
             -griffithianum
```
5ft(1.5m) -5F(-21C) ML 4/3 Synonym EUREKA MAID. Deep pink
buds open to large, widely funnel-shaped flowers, rich rose pink
fading to pale pink, reddish brown spots inside. Large trusses.
Plant open and spreading; abundant foliage of medium green. H.
White, Sunningdale, c. 1913. A.M. 1930. Color illus. VV p. 30.

```
             -ciliatum 1/2
COUNTESS OF HADDINGTON-
             -dalhousiae 1/2
```
5ft(1.5m) 20F(-7C) EM 4/4 Flower pink in bud, opening white,
flushed rose, funnel-shaped, 3in(7.6cm) broad. Very lax trusses
of 3-4. Floriferous and fragrant. Large, bright green leaves
with hairy edges. J. Parker. F.C.C. 1962.

* *
```
             -edgeworthii 1/2
COUNTESS OF SEFTON-          -ciliatum 1/4
             -Multiflorum-
                  -virgatum 1/4
```
4ft(1.2m) 10F(-12C) EM Pink buds open white, stained red, fad-
ing to pure white; fragrant; truss of 2 to 4. J. Davies, 1877.
COUNTESS OF SEXTONS   Parentage as above
5ft(1.5m) 20F(-7C) E 3/3 Flowers pink in bud, opening white,
funnel-shaped, 2.5in(6.4cm) wide; 2-3 in lax trusses. Corollas
usually split lengthwise. Bushy plant. Isaac Davies, 1877.
* *

COUNTY OF YORK   See CATALODE

COUPON   Described under FLADA W. BLOUGH, q.v.

* *
```
                  -griffithianum 1/8
             -Mars-
        -Vulcan-   -unknown 5/8
COURT JESTER-          -griersonianum 1/4
        -Sun Devil (syn. Sundancer, Whitney hybrid)--unknown
```
2ft(.6m) x 2ft(6 yrs) 5F(-15C) M Flowers vivid red with light
yellow-green center, lightly spotted yellow-green; buds currant
red. Unusual rolled calyx striped vivid red, yellow-green. Foliage narrow, dense; held 3 years. Dr. L. W. Bulgin, reg. 1988.
ELROSE COURT   Parentage as above
Similar to above. Plant wider than high; vivid red buds open to
flowers of deep pink, shading to medium yellow, moderate orange-
red spotting; trusses of 14. Bulgin, reg. 1988.
PEACH NUGGET   Parentage as above
Similar to above; unusual soft pastel peach. Bulgin intro.
SATAN'S FURY   Parentage as above
2.3ft(.7m)(7 yrs) 5F(-15C) Wavy-edged flowers 1.7in(7cm) wide,
reverse and face cardinal red, dark grayed rust brown throat and
dorsal spots; domed truss of 11. Dense plant, as broad as high;
elliptic leaves to 4in(10cm). Bulgin, cross 1980; reg. 1988.
SONIC RAY   Parentage as above

3ft(.9m)(7 yrs) 5F(-15C) M   Vivid red buds, flowers deep pink
shading to deep shell pink base on pale yellow, 7-lobed, 3.5in.
(9cm); big multi-striped calyx; upright bush. Bulgin, reg. 1988.
* *

* *
           -ciliatum 1/2
COWBELL-
       -edgeworthii (bullatum) 1/2
3ft(.9m) 15F(-9C) EM 4/4   One of the better tender hybrids,
with large, pure white flowers; fuzzy dark green foliage. Other
forms exist. Rothschild, 1935.
McNABII   Parentage as above
Similar to above with blush white flowers. Van Houtte, Belgium.
* *

           -williamsianum 1/2
COWSLIP-
        -wardii 1/2
2.5ft(.75m) OF(-18C) EM 3/3   Flower light primrose to cream,
pale pink blush, saucer- to bell-shaped; loose trusses. Plant a
compact mound; small oval leaves. Lord Aberconway. A.M. 1937.

COWTYE--form of charitopes ssp. tsangpoense K W 5844
3ft(.9m) OF(-18C) M   Purple flowers, darker spotting, tubular
campanulate, .5in(1.5cm) long; trusses of 3-5. Leaves 2in(5cm)
x 1in(2.5cm), dull dark green; plant upright, open. F. Kingdon
Ward collector; A. E. Hardy raiser. A.M. 1972.

COXE NO. 22   Parentage unknown
White flowers in great profusion. Dexter cross.

COXE NO.26   Parentage unknown
Pink buds open to large white flowers. Dexter cross.

CRACKERJACK   Described under TIDBIT, q.v.

                -dichroanthum 1/8
            -Dido-
            -    -decorum 1/8   -griffithianum
    -Lem's-   -Beauty of Tremough-
    -Cameo-   -Norman-   -arboreum 1/32
    -     - - Gill -griffithianum
CRANBERRY-   -Anna-   -griffithianum 13/32
   SWIRL -   -Jean Marie de Montague-
       -                        -unknown 1/8
       -                  -griffithianum
       -       -Pink Shell-   -fortunei 3/16
    -Coronation-   -H. M. Arderne-
       Day   -   -unknown
       -         -griffithianum
            -Loderi-
                -fortunei
3ft(.9m) x 3ft(5 yrs) 5F(-15C) M Domed trusses of 10-14 flowers of 7 wavy-edged lobes, moderate purplish red in bud, opening
deep purplish pink, aging to strong purplish pink at rims, prominent dark red throat spot; pink calyx. J. A. Davis, reg. 1989.

           -griersonianum 1/4
       -Azor-
CRANBOURNE-   -fortunei ssp. discolor 1/4
       -         -griffithianum 1/4
       -Isabella-
                -auriculatum 1/4
4ft(1.2m) -10F(-23C) M A blend of rose with a large red blotch
in the throat; reddish brown spots on upper lobe. Crown Estate,
Windsor. A. M. 1957.

       -niveum ? 1/2
CRARAE-
       -unknown 1/2
Flowers smoky purple tinged red, campanulate, 7-lobed; 1.5in(3.8
cm) wide; 20-23 per truss. Dull green leaves, 7in(17.8cm) long;
mealy white indumentum beneath. Sir George Campbell, reg. 1964.
A.M. 1965.

CRARAE CRIMSON--form of cinnabarinum Roylei Group
Received a P. C. award in 1975 as a hardy flowering plant. Sir
Ilay Campbell, raiser; C. Ingram introduced; reg. 1974.

CRASWELL   Described under YAKU WARRIOR, q.v.

           -augustinii--Barto Blue 1/2
CRATER LAKE-   -intricatum 1/4
        -Bluebird-
               -augustinii 1/4
5ft(1.5m) -5F(-21C) EM 4/3   Brilliant electric, violet blue
flowers, saucer-shaped, up to 2in(5cm) wide, ruffled edges, held
in small clusters, many per branch. Plant of upright habit,
well-branched. New growth bronze yellow, turning later to Irish
green.   Dr. Carl Phetteplace, reg. 1976. C.A. 1975. Color
illus. HG p. 182.

CRAZY JOE   Described under GAY SONG, q.v.

            -leucaspis 1/2
CREAM CASCADE-
            -lutescens 1/2
Flowers in trusses of 6, 5-lobed, pale orange-yellow with overtones of pale yellowish pink, throat markings pale yellow. Foliage lanceolate. W. Reuthe, cross 1966; C. Reuthe, reg. 1985.

CREAM CRACKER   Listed under DAMARIS, q.v.

           -rupicola var. chryseum 1/2
CREAM CREST-   -ciliatum 1/4
       -Cilpinense-
                -moupinense 1/4
3ft(.9m) OF(-18C) EM 3/4   Bright creamy yellow, cup-shaped
flowers, 1in(2.5cm) wide; 6-8 in tight trusses on a compact bush
that has vigor, good foliage and likes the sun. A. Wright, reg.
1963.   Color illus. VV p. 54; HG p. 149.

CREAM DELIGHT   Described under BEATRIX ANDERSON, q.v.

CREAM DELIGHT (Greer)   See GREER'S CREAM DELIGHT

               -Lady   -fortunei ssp. discolor 3/16
                -Bessborough-
          -Jalisco-   -campylocarpum Elatum Group 3/16
          -     -   -dichroanthum 1/4
    -Comstock-   -Dido-
    -     -   -decorum 1/8
    -     - -dichroanthum
    -   -Jasper-
CREAM-   -Lady Bessborough (as above)
GLORY-
    -        -Lady Bessborough (as above)
    -    -Jalisco-
    -    -   -   -dichroanthum
    -Cheyenne-   -Dido-
    -     -   -decorum
    -     -griffithianum 1/8
        -Loderi-
            -fortunei 1/8
4ft(1.2m) -5F(-21C) M 5/3   Flowers deep cream, of heavy substance, 4.5in(11.5cm) wide, openly funnel-campanulate, 7-lobed,
fragrant; calyx of same color. High, dome-shaped trusses hold 8
or 9. Plant rounded, about as wide as tall. Greer cross, 1965;
reg. 1979.   Color illus. HG p. 76.

            -wardii ? 1/4
       -Chlorops-
CREAM PIE-   -vernicosum ? 1/4
       -         -fortunei ssp. discolor 1/4
    -King of Shrubs-   -dichroanthum 1/8
                -Fabia-
                -griersonianum 1/8
4ft(1.2m) 5F(-15C) M 4/3 Flowers light creamy yellow. Dr.
Minor cross; Greer introduced, 1984.

CREAM TRUMPET   Described under VICTORIANUM, q.v.

CREAMY CHIFFON   Parentage unknown
4ft(1.2m) -5F(-21C) ML 4/4   A double-flowered rhododendron
with salmon orange buds opening to creamy yellow. Habit compact.
Whitney cross; B. Briggs intro.   Color illus. HG p. 179.

           -forrestii Repens Group 1/4
       -Jaipur-
CREEPING FIRE-   -meddianum 1/4
       -         -haematodes 1/4
       -May Day-
           -griersonianum 1/4

Orient red flowers in loose trusses of 8. L. Brandt, reg. 1962.

CREEPING JENNY   Described under ELIZABETH, q.v.

```
                          -Essex Scarlet--unknown 1/4
             -Frühlingszauber-
CREMINROSE-                   -forrestii Repens Group 1/4
                          -campylocarpum Elatum Group 1/4
             -Letty Edwards-
                          -fortunei 1/4
```
3.7ft(1.1m) x 6ft(1.8m)(15 yrs) ML Campanulate flowers, about
3in(7.5cm) wide, of yellowish white, tinged light to pale orient
pink, a light to brilliant greenish yellow blotch spreading into
throat; loose trusses of 6-8. Rather glossy dark leaves; erect,
compact plant. H. Hachmann, cross 1964; Stück, reg. 1988.

* *
```
                    -fortunei 1/4
          -Luscombei-
CREMORNE-           -thomsonii 1/4
          -campylocarpum 1/2
```
Well-shaped plant; medium height. Flowers medium-sized, shading
from rose to soft yellow and creamy white within. Rothschild,
1935. A.M. 1947.
TOWNHILL CREMORNE   Parentage as above
Nicely shaped, medium-sized plant with trusses of about 12 flow-
ers, Chinese yellow with rosy coral margins. Lord Swaythling,
Townhill Park. A.M. 1947.
* *


```
                   -griffithianum 3/16
            -Mars-
      -Vulcan-      -unknown 3/8
CREOLE-      -griersonianum 1/4          -griffithianum
 BELLE-                        -George Hardy-
  -          -Mrs. Lindsay-          -catawbiense
  -Harvest Moon- Smith     -Duchess of Edinburgh--unknown
   -                        -campylocarpum 1/8
            -unnamed hybrid-
                        -unknown
```
4ft(1.2m) -5F(-21C) ML 4/4 Bright pink flowers, on a well-
branched plant; forest green foliage. Thompson, 1982. Color
illus. HG p. 116.

CREST   Described under HAWK, q.v.

CRETE   Described under YAKU FRILLS, q.v.


```
              -thomsonii 1/4
      -Barclayi-          -arboreum 1/8
      -       -Glory of Penjerrick-
CRETONNE-                  -griffithianum 3/8
     -       -griffithianum
     -Loderi-
              -fortunei 1/4
```
White flowers stained rose Bengal within and without. Sir Giles
Loder. A.M. 1940.


```
                        -griffithianum 1/8
             -Queen Wilhelmina-
      -Britannia-          -unknown 3/8
CRICKET-      -Stanley Davies--unknown
      -yakushimanum--Koichiro Wada 1/2
```
3ft(.9m) -5F(-21C) M 4/4 Rosy pink flowers, fading lighter
pink; new growth silvery green to darker greens. J. Elliott.

* *
```
                  -smirnowii 1/4
          -Oh My!-
CRIMPER-      -yakushimanum 1/4
          -aureum (chrysanthum) 1/2
```
Buds of strong purplish red and very pale purple open to flowers
of very pale purple, lightly edged deep purplish pink. W. Delp.
GO FOR IT   Parentage as above
Buds of beetroot purple and strong purplish red open to flowers
of very pale purple and white, edged in strong purple. Delp.
* *

CRIMSON BANNER   Same parentage as ASTEROID, q.v.


```
                      -neriiflorum 1/4
            -F. C. Puddle-
CRIMSON BELLS-        -griersonianum 1/4
            -williamsianum 1/2
```
1.5ft(.45m) 0F(-18C) EM Crimson, bell-shaped flowers, 3in.
(7.6cm) across; trusses hold 7. Plant twice as wide as tall;
oval leaves 3in(7.6cm) long. Benjamin Lancaster, reg. 1965.

CRIMSON CLASSIC   See SAMMETGLUT


```
                      -maximum 1/4
            -Stokes Bronze Wings-
CRIMSON DELIGHT-               -catawbiense 1/4
      -          -catawbiense var. album 1/4
      -Moon-               -neriiflorum 1/16
       Mist-      -unnamed-
            -unnamed hybrid- hybrid-dichroanthum 1/16
                      -fortunei ssp. discolor 1/8
```
Buds of cardinal red, currant red and vivid red open to blend of
currant and vivid red. Weldon Delp.

CRIMSON GLORY   Parentage unknown
5ft(1.5m) -10F(-23C) ML 3/3 Crimson flowers, long-lasting.
Foliage dark green. Cottage Gardens, Eureka, intro. c. 1950.


```
            -Marion--unknown 1/2
CRIMSON GLOW-      -thomsonii 1/4
            -Shilsonii-
                  -barbatum 1/4
```
Red flowers with lighter center, slightly spotted on all lobes;
trusses of 20. K. Van de Ven, Australia, reg. 1973.


```
            -yakushimanum 1/2
CRIMSON PIPPIN-
            -sanguineum ssp. sanguineum var. haemaleum 1/2
```
2ft(.6m) -10F(-23C) M 5/4 Currant red flowers; trusses of
11. Leaves with woolly indumentum, satinwood or grayed orange.
H. L. Larson, reg. 1982.


```
            -Moser's Maroon--unknown
CRIMSON QUEEN-            -fortunei ssp. discolor 1/4
            -Azor (Harm's form)-
                        -griersonianum 1/4
```
2.5ft(.75m) -5F(-21C) M Crimson flowers, in trusses of 12.
Plant slow-growing and dense, with long, narrow leaves. Easily
propagated. B. Lancaster, reg. 1962.

CRIMSON STAIN   Described under YAKU WARRIOR, q.v.


```
                              -griffithianum 1/4
                  -Queen Wilhelmina-
            -Britannia-          -unknown 3/4
            -          -Stanley Davies--unknown
CRIMSON STAR-                        -griffithianum
            -          -Queen Wilhelmina-
            -Unknown Warrior-          -unknown
                        -Stanley Davies--unknown
```
Red flowers, from a cross of two siblings. Don Hardgrove, 1951.


```
                              -griffithianum 1/8
                  -Jean Marie de Montague-
            -Fireman-          -unknown 3/8
            - Jeff -          -haematodes 1/8
CRIMSON TIDE-      -Grosclaude-
            -               -facetum (eriogynum) 1/8
            -          -catawbiense 1/4
            -Kettledrum-
                  -unknown
```
Buds of cardinal and currant red, open to frilly flowers currant
red and cardinal red; dark red dorsal spots.   Al Smith cross;
W. Delp raiser.


```
            -Blue Peter--unknown 5/8
CRINKLES-               -arboreum 1/8
      -          -Doncaster-
      -Corry Koster-      -unknown
      -          -griffithianum 1/8
            -George Hardy-
                  -catawbiense 1/8
```
5ft(1.5m) -5F(-21C) EM Flowers reddish purple with a purple

blotch; trusses of about 21.   K. Van de Ven, reg. 1981.

```
                  -smirnowii 1/2
CRISPY---OH MY!, selfed-
                  -yakushimanum 1/2
```
Flower of mallow and phlox purples; dorsal spots deep red. Delp.

```
            -yakushimanum--Mist Maiden 1/2
CRISPY COOL-      -catawbiense 1/4
        -Cathaem-
                  -haematodes 1/4
```
Buds of currant red open to Tyrian purple and rose Bengal; dor-
sal spots of cardinal red; throat cardinal red.   W. Delp.

```
          -spinuliferum 1/2
CROSSBILL-
          -lutescens 1/2
```
5ft(1.5m) 5F(-15C) E   Slim, erect bush with striking red new
growth; tubular flowers of yellow, flushed with apricot. Early.
Other forms exist.   J. C. Williams, 1933.

```
* * * * * * * * * * * * * * * * * * * * * * * *
             -Pygmalion--unknown
     -Accomac-            -haematodes
     -      -unnamed hybrid-        -fortunei
     -                    -Wellfleet-
CROSSBOW-                       -decorum
     -                  -caucasicum
     -          -Boule de Neige-        -catawbiense
     -                    -hardy hybrid-
     -Besse Howells-              -unknown
     -          -unnamed red hybrid-   -catawbiense
                             -unknown
```
Flowers of deep purplish pink.   Weldon Delp.
CROSSFIRE   Parentage as above
Flowers of Neyron rose with ruby red dorsal spotting. W. Delp.
* *

CROSSPATCH   Parentage unknown
Pink flowers, with a red throat.   Nelson cross, McLaren intro.;
reg. 1975.

```
          -kyawii 1/2
CROSSROADS-
          -strigillosum 1/2
```
5ft(1.5m) OF(-18C) EM 4/4 Flowers of rich red; narrow leaves
covered with thick bristles.   H. L. Larson.

CROWN EQUERRY--form of niveum
5ft(1.5m) 5F(-15C) M   Purplish lilac flowers, darker at lip,
tubular-campanulate, 2in(5cm) across.   Leaves to 6.5in(16.5cm)
long; felted brown indumentum beneath.   J. B. Stevenson raiser;
Crown Estate, Windsor, reg. 1979.   F.C.C. 1979.

CROWN OF GOLD   Parentage unknown
Fragrant pink flowers striped in darker pink; chartreuse throat.
Mrs. H. Frederick, Jr., reg. 1978.

```
          -aberconwayi 1/2
CROWTHORNE-
          -souliei 1/2
```
Called a dwarf in its registration, but award description gives
height as 5.5ft(1.65m).   Upright, compact habit; glossy medium-
sized leaves.   White flowers, tinged pink with deep pink edges;
tight trusses of about 11.   Crown Estate, Windsor, reg. 1963.

CRUACHAN--form of temenium var. gilvum Chrysanthum Group R 22272
Flowers clear pure yellow, on a dwarf, spreading shrub.   Rock
collector; Mrs. K. L. Kenneth, reg. 1965.   F.C.C. 1964.

```
* * * * * * * * * * * * * * * * * * * * * * * *
             -maximum 3/4
        -Midsummer-
CRYSTAL GLO-      -unknown 1/4
        -maximum, Delp's red form
```
Light purplish pink flowers, edged with strong purplish red; a
flare of brilliant greenish yellow. Hardy to -25F(-26C). Delp.
CRYSTALAIRE   Parentage as above
Flowers white with a yellow flare. Medium-sized plant, hardy to
-25F(-32C). Delp.
* *

```
* * * * * * * * * * * * * * * * * * * * * * * * * * *
                   -catawbiense var. album Glass--Catalgla 1/8
             -Gosh-          -decorum? 1/16
        -Darn-              -Caroline-
        -      -Mrs. H.R.Yates-        -brachycarpum? 1/16
     -Keystone-              -unknown 1/8
     -      -          -Mrs.H.R.Yates (as above)
     -      -unnamed-          -unknown
CRYSTAL-      hybrid-wardii 5/32
YELLOW -                  -wardii?
     -          -Lackamas-Chlorops-
     -    -unnamed- Spice -        -vernicosum? 1/32
     -    - hybrid-        -diaprepes 1/16
     -Cecil-      -lacteum 1/8
     -          -aberconwayii 1/8
        -unnamed-      -yakushimanum 1/16
             hybrid-unnamed-      -dichroanthum 1/32
                   hybrid-Fabia-
                        -griersonianum 1/32
```
Buds brilliant and light greenish yellow opening to flowers pale
yellow-green, throat of brilliant greenish yellow. Truss of 16
flowers, each 3in(7.5cm) across.   Delp. (Plant may be extinct)
SPLASHY VISION   Parentage as above
Spirea red buds open to flowers yellowish white, edged in spirea
red; throat primrose yellow; dorsal spots of reddish orange and
dark greenish yellow.   W. Delp.
* *

CRYSTALAIRE   Described under CRYSTAL GLO, q.v.

CUFF-LINK   Parentage unknown
A plant for the cool greenhouse, with leaves medium-sized, dark
glossy green.   Trusses of 5 or 6 flowers, tubular bell-shaped,
very light yellow. Geoffrey Gorer, reg. 1978.   A.M. 1978.

CUM LAUDE   Described under VALLEY CREEK, q.v.

```
* * * * * * * * * * * * * * * * * * * * * * * * * * * *
                   -Pygmalion--unknown 1/8
             -unnamed hybrid-
        -Weldy-          -haematodes 1/8
CUMULUS-      -yakushimanum, Exbury form 1/4
        -      -yakushimanum 1/4
        -Serendipity-
                   -aureum (chrysanthum) 1/4
```
White flowers on a low plant; indumented foliage.   Bud-hardy to
-15F(-26C).   W. Delp.
MICROSPLASH   Parentage as above
Greenish white flowers with a flare chartreuse green.   W. Delp.
ROBERT WELDON   Parentage as above
Yellow flowers; indumented foliage.   Hardy to -15F(-26C); size
low.   W. Delp.
SUDS   Parentage as above
Buds of deep to strong reds, opening to flowers of pale purplish
pink, slowly fading to white; dorsal spots deep purplish red;
purplish red stigma. Size medium; hardy to -15F(-26C).   Delp.
* *

```
                   -caucasicum 1/2
CUNNINGHAM'S ALBUM COMPACTUM-
                   -unknown 1/2
```
Flowers blush pink in bud, opening white with a ray of greenish
brown markings. Sturdy, slow-growing shrub; dense, leafy habit.
Slower growth, narrower leaves (indumentum beneath) than in Cunningham's White.   Cunningham.

CUNNINGHAM'S BLUSH   Described under CUNNINGHAM'S WHITE, q.v.

CUNNINGHAM'S SULPHUR--form of caucasicum
4ft(1.2m) -5F(-21C) VE 2/2 Small pale yellow flower in round
truss of 15. Plant compact, bushy; medium green, glossy leaves.
Heat-tolerant; best in light shade.   Cunningham, early 1800s.

```
* * * * * * * * * * * * * * * * * * * * * * * * * * *
                   -caucasicum 1/2
CUNNINGHAM'S WHITE-
                   -ponticum var. album 1/2
```
4ft(1.2m) -15F(-26C) ML 2/3 Buds flushed pink open to small
white flowers, a pale yellow eye; small, upright, many-flowered
truss. Plant spreading; dark green foliage. Tolerates slightly
alkaline soil. Cunningham, 1830.   Col. ill. JS p.87; VV p. 22.
CUNNINGHAM'S BLUSH   Parentage as above

6ft(1.8m) -15F(-26C) ML Lax trusses of 10 flowers lilac pink.
J. Cunningham & J. Fraser, c. 1850.
* *
* *

```
                          -griffithianum 1/8
                -Loderi-
       -Albatross-        -fortunei 1/8
CUP DAY-        -fortunei ssp. discolor 1/4
       -            -elliottii 1/4
       -Fusilier-
                -griersonianum 1/4
```
Flowers of Tyrian rose, heavily spotted on all lobes. K. Van de
Ven, Australia, reg. 1965.
SUCCESS　Parentage as above
Flowers colored rose Bengal. K. Van de Ven, reg. 1965.
* *

```
       -yakushimanum 1/2
CUPCAKE-        -dichroanthum ssp. scyphocalyx 1/4
       -Medusa-
                -griersonianum 1/4
```
3ft(.9m) -5F(-21C) ML 4/4　Buds claret rose open to flowers
carmine rose to salmon pink in trusses of 10 to 15. Compact
habit with dark green foliage. W. Thompson intro. Color illus.
HG p. 181. (NOTE: EMMA'S CHOICE & ROY'S CHOICE, siblings of
above with yellow flowers, grown by D. Balint.)

```
       -ludlowii 1/2
CURLEW-
       -fletcherianum 1/2
```
1.5ft(.45m) -5F(-21C) EM 4/4 Bright yellow flower with upper
petals spotted, 2in(5cm) wide, openly campanulate, 5-lobed; compact trusses of 2 or 3. Plant much wider than tall. P. E. Cox,
reg. 1970. A. M. Wisley Trials 1981; F.C.C. Wisley Trials
1986. Color illus. Cox pl. 42; JS p. 70.

```
                -yakushimanum 3/8
       -Tols-
       -        -catawbiense 5/16            -catawbiense
       -                       -Parsons Grandiflorum-
CURLICUE-            -America-            -unknown 1/4
         -unnamed-        -dark red hybrid--unknown
         -Tim - hybrid-yakushimanum
       Craig-        -griffithianum 1/16
         -        -Mars-
         -Frank-        -unknown
           Moniz-America (as above)
```
Buds of deep red and currant red, opening to frilled flowers of
strong purplish red and white; dorsal spots ruby red. W. Delp.

CURRANT BELLS　Described under THOMWILLIAMS, q.v.

```
         -wightii 1/4
       -China-
CUSTARD-        -fortunei 1/4
       -decorum 1/2
```
Primrose yellow flowers, funnel-campanulate, 5- or 6-lobed, al-
most 4in(10.2cm) wide; 12-14 in racemose umbels. Plant matures
at 10ft(3m); leaves 6in(15cm) long. R. & L. Henny, reg. 1963.

```
       -calostrotum 1/2
CUTIE-
       -unknown (possibly racemosum) 1/2
```
3ft(.9m) -15F(-26C) M 3/3　Synonyms: CALOSTROTUM PINK, CAL-
OSTROTUM ROSE. Heavy blooming of small, lilac-tinted pink flowers. Compact, rounded plant; leaves 1in(2.5cm) long, slight tan
indumentum below. Mrs. Greig cross; H. Larson, reg. 1961. A.E.
1962.

```
                -neriiflorum 1/2
       -F. C. Puddle-
CYCLOPS-        -griersonianum 1/4
       -        -neriiflorum
       -Neriihaem-
                -haematodes 1/4
```
Red flowers. Lord Aberconway, 1941.

CYNOSURE　Described under ACCOLADE, q.v.

```
       -catawbiense 1/2
CYNTHIA-
       -griffithianum 1/2
```
6ft(1.8m) -10F(-23C) M 4/3　Synonym LORD PALMERSTON. Above
parentage is commonly given, but Cox has pointed out that griffithianum had not yet been introduced from the wild. Hooker introduced griffithianum from Sikkim in 1850, according to Bean,
p. 676. Showy, conical truss of rosy crimson flowers, blackish
crimson marks, 3in(7.6cm) wide. A large, vigorous, dome-shaped
bush, grows in sun or shade and may reach 9ft x 9ft(2.7m); pest-
resistant. Strong, dark green foliage. Once considered second
only to PINK PEARL in popularity. Standish & Noble, about 1856.
A.G.M. 1969. Color illus. JS p.50; VV p. 71.

CYPRUS　Described under PARTY PINK, q.v.

```
       -arboreum--Sir Charles Lemon 1/2
CYRENE-
       -lanatum 1/2
```
White flowers with a tinge of lemon. E. J. P. Magor, 1921.

CYRIL BERKELEY--form of forrestii ssp. forrestii var. tumescens
Turkey red flowers, 2.5in(6.4cm) wide, in loose trusses of 3-4.
Slow-growing; 3ft(.9m) compact bush in 10 years. Greig, Royston
Nursery, reg. 1965.

```
                -griffithianum 1/4
       -Loderi King George-
CYRIL THORNBER-        -fortunei 1/4
       -unknown
```
11.5ft(3.5m) x 8.2ft(2.5m) ML Pink-tinged buds opening to pure
white, 7-lobed flowers, with green throat on lower side, to 4in.
(10cm) wide, openly funnel-shaped; trusses hold 10-11. Blooms 3
weeks after seed parent. Broadly ovate, gray-green leaves, 6in.
(15cm) long. Lord Harewood, cross 1958; reg. 1989.

```
                      -caucasicum 3/16
              -Jacksonii-        -caucasicum
       -Goldsworth-        -Nobleanum-
       - Yellow -                -arboreum 1/16
CZECH BEAUTY-        -campylocarpum 1/4
       -unknown 1/2
```
4ft(1.2m) -10F(-23C) M　Large truss of 11 flowers, primrose
yellow, grayed orange spots, 3.5in(8.9cm) broad. Plant rounded,
broad; glossy leaves hold 3 years. L. Hindla, reg. 1979.

D

D. D. (DELP'S DREAM) Described under CISA, q.v.

```
                -catawbiense 1/4
       -John Walter-
D. HEINJE-        -arboreum 1/4
       -unknown 1/2
```
Reddish buds; June flowers of dark pink, spotted with greenish
yellow, 2.5in(6.5cm) wide; ball trusses of 13-16. Compact bush.
D. Heinje, reg. 1986. Color illus. WS, 1989, p. 113.

```
       -dichroanthum ssp. scyphocalyx 1/2
DACIA-        -neriiflorum 1/4
       -F. C. Puddle-
                -griersonianum 1/4
```
Orange-red flowers. Lord Aberconway, intro. 1941.

DAD'S KILLER　Parentage unknown
2ft(.6m) x 1ft(.3m)(3 yrs) 0F(-18C) M Flowers 4in(10cm) wide,
openly funnel-shaped, 6 wavy lobes of deep pink, throat spotting
strong claret red; domed truss of 12-16. Mauritsen, reg. 1986.

```
       -decorum 1/2        -griffithianum 1/8
DAGMAR-        -George Hardy-
       -Pink Pearl-        -catawbiense 1/8
       -        -arboreum 1/8
       -Broughtonii-
                -unknown 1/8
```
From Czechoslovakia. Flowers of an impressive delicate purplish
pink, lightly spotted green and yellow, gold in throat, frilled.
Hardy in N. Germany. B. Kavka. Color illus. Cox pl. 45.

DAFFODILLY--selection from cinnabarinum ssp. xanthocodon
10ft(3.0m)(26 yrs) 5F(-15C) M Flowers tubular campanulate, 6
per truss, light orange-yellow throughout. Leaves of dark shiny
green; golden brown scales. Mrs. R. Stevenson selection; Leon-
nardslee Gardens intro; Maj. E. W. M. Magor, reg. 1987.

```
              -haematodes 1/4
        -May Day-
DAINTY-        -griersonianum 1/2
  -            -forrestii Repens Group 1/4
        -Elizabeth-
                -griersonianum
Brilliant scarlet.  Lord Aberconway.  A.M. 1942;  F.C.C. 1944
```

```
              -williamsianum 1/2
DAINTY JEAN-
        -Helene Schiffner--unknown 1/2
1ft(.3m) OF(-18C) ML  Compact dwarf plant; white flower flush-
ed  pink outside,  quite flat,  slightly ruffled,  to 3in(7.6cm)
wide; 6 in loose trusses.   Bovee, reg. 1963.
```

```
            -campylocarpum 1/2
DAIRYMAID -
        -unknown 1/2
4ft(1.2m)  -10F(-23C) EM   A compact shrub.  Flowers cream with
pink lines on petals and red spotting in throat;  tight trusses.
Slocock, 1930.   A.M. 1934, Exbury Trial.  Color illus. F p. 22,
41, 50; PB pl. 55.
```

DAISY   Described under DELILA, q.v.

```
            -catawbiense 1/2
DAISY RAND-
        -unknown 1/2
Rose red flowers.   Samuel Parsons, 1870s.
```

```
          -dalhousiae 1/2
DALBULL-
      -edgeworthii (bullatum) 1/2
White flowers.  E. J. P. Magor, intro. 1936.
```

DALKEITH--dwarf chance seedling, possibly natural hybrid. Has
        some characteristics of Triflora, but is Uniflora.
2.5ft(.75m) OF(-18C) EM   Purple violet flowers; truss of 10-
17. Compact, densely branched plant.   C. A. McLaughlin intro;
Mrs. P. J. Warren, NZ, reg. 1977.

DALRIADA--form of degronianum
3ft(.9m) -5F(-21C) EM 3/3   A Japanese native, selected in
Scotland, grown in cold climates around the world. Bright rose-
colored flowers; attractive foliage indumented less heavily than
yakushimanum. Mrs. K. L. Kenneth, reg. 1962.   P.C. 1960.

```
* * * * * * * * * * * * * * * * * * * * * * * * * * * * *
              -caucasicum 1/4
        -Dr. Stocker-
DAMARIS       -griffithianum 1/4
        -campylocarpum 1/2
4ft(1.2m)  5F(-15C)  E  4/3   Registered as LAMELLEN DAMARIS,
1989.  Flowers in trusses of 6-10,  open campanulate, 5-lobed,
brilliant to light yellow-green, fading to pale yellow-green,
unspotted.  E. J. P. Magor, cross 1918; intro. 1926.
CREAM CRACKER  Same cross as above by Gen. Harrison, 1956.
CORNISH CRACKER  Another form from above by Harrison, 1956.
LOGAN DAMARIS   Parentage as above
4ft(1.2m)  5F(-15C) EM  4/3   Clear lemon yellow flowers, 3in.
(7.6cm) across in shapely, rather loose trusses of 10-12.  Plant
upright, vigorous; narrow, rich green leaves, 5in(12.7cm) x 2in.
(5cm).   J. B. Stevenson.   A.M. 1948.   Color illus F p. 41.
TOWNHILL DAMARIS   This form selected by Lord Swaythling, 1948.
* * * * * * * * * * * * * * * * * * * * * * * * * * * * *
```

```
                    -elliottii 3/8
              -Kilimanjaro-      -Moser's Maroon-unknown 5/16
              -            -Dusky-
        -Rubicon-           Maid-fortunei ssp. discolor 3/16
        -       -           -arboreum ssp. nilagiricum ? 1/8
DAME CECILY-      -Noyo Chief-
 PICKERILL -             -unknown
        -           -elliottii
        -Kilimanjaro-       -Moser's Maroon--unknown
              -Dusky Maid-
                    -fortunei ssp. discolor
Flowers in compact trusses, very dark red, with black spots.
Lanceolate, dark green foliage.  R. C. Gordon, reg. 1986.
```

DAME EDITH SITWELL--form of lindleyi

5ft(1.5m) 25F(-4C) E-ML 4/2   A cool greenhouse plant. Flowers white, tinged pale pink, tubular funnel-shaped, 4.3in(11cm)
across; truss of 4-5. Geoffrey Gorer, reg. 1965.   A.M. 1965.

```
                        -griffithianum
        -Irene Stead--Loderi, selfed-         3/8
        -                   -fortunei 3/8
DAME KIRI TEKANAWA-       -griffithianum
        -           -Loderi-
        -Ilam Cream-       -fortunei
                    -unknown 1/2
7ft(2.1m) x 8ft(2.4m)(16 yrs)  5F(-15C)  Oct-Nov (NZ)   Flowers
in trusses of 10-12, broadly funnel-shaped, strong purplish red
in bud, opening greenish white with a light purplish pink flush.
Oblanceolate leaves; burgundy petioles.  G. Collier, reg. 1988.
```

```
                -maximum 1/4            -catawbiense
        -Standishii-          -unnamed hybrid-       1/16
DAME NELLIE-       -Altaclerense-         -ponticum 1/16
 MELBA     -arboreum      -arboreum 5/8
6ft(1.8m) OF(-18C)  EM  3/4   Bright pink flowers with crimson
spots.  Dark green, glossy leaves.   Sir E. Loder.   A.M. 1926.
```

```
                    -caucasicum 1/8
              -Dr. Stocker-
        -Damaris-       -griffithianum 1/8
        -       -campylocarpum 1/4
DAMOPHYLE-           -adenogynum 1/8
        -      -Xenosporum (detonsum)-
        -unnamed-           -unknown 3/8
        hybrid-unknown
A shapely bush, 15ft(4.5m) at 25 years.  Campanulate white flow-
ers, held in racemose umbels of 10 to 12.  E. J. P. Magor cross;
Maj. E. W. M. Magor named; reg. 1962.
```

```
        -A. W. Bright Rose--unknown 1/2
DAMOZEL-
        -griersonianum 1/2
6ft(1.8m) OF(-18C) ML  4/4   Plant widely spreading, branching;
rather scant foliage, narrow, dark green, and thinly indumented.
Many dome-shaped trusses of about 17 funnel-shaped flowers, deep
ruby red, spotted darker red.   Rothschild, 1936  A.M. 1948 (to
a deep rose pink form).   Color illus. F p. 42.
```

```
              -forrestii Repens Group 1/4
        -Elizabeth-
        -           -griersonianum 1/4
DAN LAXDALL-               -griffithianum 1/8
        -           -Coombe Royal-
        -Mrs. G. W. Leak-       -unknown 1/4
        -                   -caucasicum 1/8
                    -Chevalier Felix-
                      de Sauvage    -unknown
3ft(.9m) OF(-18C)  ML   Buds and flowers of Neyron rose; throat
and narrow stripes on lobe centers of deeper rose.  Trusses hold
7-10.  Flowers have a "glow"  or fluorescence.   Sigrid Laxdall,
reg. 1976.   Color illus. ARS Q 30:2 (1976), p. 103.
```

DANDY ANDY   Described under BETTY WHITE, q.v.

```
* * * * * * * * * * * * * * * * * * * * * * * * * * * * *
                    -maximum 1/2
              -Midsummer-
DANDYLICIOUS-       -unknown 1/4
        -       -hyperythrum 1/4
        -Hypermax-
                -maximum
Buds a blend of purples: roseine, fuchsia, and rhodamine;  flow-
ers open white, edged lightly with vivid purplish red, flare of
Dresden yellow; anthers moderate orange-yellow.  Delp.
MAD ABOUT MAX   Parentage as above
Buds of fuchsia purple and ruby red open to flowers of pale pur-
plish pink, heavily edged in fuchsia purple;  flare of brilliant
greenish yellow; dorsal spots vivid yellow-green.   Delp.
* * * * * * * * * * * * * * * * * * * * * * * * * * * * *
```

```
                                  -catawbiense
                  -Parsons Grandiflorum-        1/16
          -America-          -unknown 1/4
   -Cindy Lou-      -dark red hybrid--unknown
   -          -                    -griffithianum 1/16
   -          -            -Mars-
DANDYRIFIC-      -unnamed hybrid-    -unknown
   -              -catawbiense var. rubrum 1/8
   -          -catawbiense var. album Glass--Catalgla 1/4
   -El Shaddai-        -catawbiense 1/8
              -Pink Twins-
                      -haematodes 1/8
```
Buds of various shades of reddish purple open to flowers of very
pale purple, edged with strong and light purples; flare of vivid
yellow-green; dorsal spots moderate yellow green.   Delp.

```
                                  -catawbiense 1/16
                  -Parsons Grandiflorum-
          -Nova Zembla-          -unknown 7/16
   -unnamed-          -dark red hybrid--unknown
   - hybrid-      -griffithianum 1/4
DANIELA-      -Mars-
   -              -unknown
   -                  -Mars (as above)
   -unnamed hybrid-
              -yakushimanum--Koichiro Wada 1/4
```
1.6ft(.5m) x 3.3ft(1.0m) -10F(-23C) ML Dense trusses of 11 to
18; flowers of deep purplish pink, shading inwards pale purplish
pink to white.   Hachmann, cross 1969; Stück, reg. 1988.

* *
```
   -dichroanthum 1/2
DANTE-
   -facetum (eriogynum) 1/2
```
Flowers described in the register as being "yellow to red-orange
or vermilion".   Lord Aberconway, 1936.
FELIS   Parentage as above
Similar to Fabia, but later and taller. Plant low, of spreading
habit; bell-shaped flowers of orange to yellow in loose trusses.
Late season. Rothschild, 1938.
LAMELLEN DANTE   Parentage as above
Trusses of 8-9 flowers, loosely held, open-campanulate, scarlet
with deep shading along edges. Throat spotting of burnt orange.
Magor cross; Maj. E. W. M. Magor, reg. 1974. P.C. 1974.
* *

DANUBE   See under ARGIOLUS.

```
   -metternichii 1/2
DAPHNE-
   -Alexander Adie--unknown 1/2
```
White flowers marked with greenish yellow. T.J.R. Seidel, 1902.

* *
```
              -arboreum 1/4
          -Red Admiral-
DAPHNE (Magor)-      -thomsonii 1/4
          -neriiflorum 1/2
```
Flowers hose-in-hose, bright crimson. Magor, 1928. A.M. 1933.
EITHNE   Parentage as above
Deep crimson scarlet flowers. E. J. P. Magor. A.M. 1937.
* *
```
          -griffithianum 1/2
DAPHNE DAFFARN-
          -unknown 1/2
```
Rounded trusses of campanulate flowers, bright rose pink shading
to white, with light red speckles. Originated before 1884.

```
          -oreotrephes 1/2
DAPHNE JEWISS-
          -davidsonianum
```
5ft(1.5m) -10F(-23C) M   Tight trusses of soft pink flowers.
Prolific bloomer. Reuthe.

```
              -arboreum 1/8
          -Red Admiral-
   -Daphne-          -thomsonii 1/8
DAPHNE-      -neriiflorum 1/4
 MAGOR-          -adenogynum 1/4
      -Xenosporum-
              -unknown 1/4
```

A plant of 10ft(3m) at 25 years, with leaves 3.25in(8.3cm) long.
Blood red flowers of good substance, large petaloid calyx; truss
of 6-8. E. J. P. Magor raiser; Maj. E. W. M. Magor, reg. 1962.

```
          -griffithianum 1/2
DAPHNE MILLAIS-
          -unknown 1/2
```
Deep pink with lighter edges. Otto Schulz, cross 1892.

DAPHNOIDES   Parentage unknown; possibly ponticum hybrid
4ft(1.2m) -15F(-26C) ML 2/4 Most unusual foliage of rolled,
glossy leaves tightly spaced on stems of a dense mound.   Prolific trusses of purple flowers.   T. Methven, cultivated 1868.
Color illus. VV p. 98.

```
              -wardii 1/4
   -unnamed-      -dichroanthum ssp. scyphocalyx 1/8
   - hybrid-Medusa-
DARIGOLD-      -griersonianum 1/4
   -          -fortunei ssp. discolor 1/4
   -Autumn Gold-      -dichroanthum 1/8
              -Fabia-
                  -griersonianum
```
Unregistered Whitney hybrid. Parent of DESERT GOLD.

DARIUS   Described under DELILA, q.v.

```
              -catawbiense 1/4
          -Kettledrum-
DARK EYES-      -unknown 3/8          -adenogynum 1/8
   -              -Xenosporum (detonsum)-
   -unnamed hybrid-          -unknown
              -griersonianum 1/4
```
5ft(1.5m) -5F(-21C) M Bright rose flowers, a dark red blotch;
truss of about 6. Rounded leaves.   G. Guy Nearing, reg. 1972.

```
              -sanguineum ssp. sanguineum var. haemaleum 1/2
DARK STRANGER-
          -williamsianum 1/2
```
Trusses of 3-4 flowers, bell-shaped, ruby red. Leaves dull dark
green, 2in(5cm) long.   Probably crossed by Col. S. R. Clarke;
raised by R. N. Stephenson Clarke; reg. 1980. A.M. 1980.

* *
```
   -griersonianum 1/2
DARLENE-          -griffithianum 1/8
   -          -unnamed hybrid-
   -Armistice Day-          -unknown 3/8
              -Maxwell T. Masters--unknown
```
Bright red flowers. Halfdan Lem, reg. 1958. P.A. 1952.
GLOW Parentage as above
Introduced by Robert M. Bovee, before 1958.
THELMA   Parentage as above
Flowers funnel-shaped, 4in(10cm) wide, 5-lobed, near geranium
lake in color; well-filled trusses. Lem, reg. 1962. P.A. 1959.
* *
```
          -Purple Lace--unknown 1/2
DARLENE ELLISON-
          -yakushimanum 1/2
```
2ft(.6m) x 3ft(.9m) OF(-18C) M   Buds of vivid purplish red,
opening to pale purplish pink flowers, with dark greenish yellow
dorsal spotting. Olive green leaves.   Fred Peste, cross 1976;
S. P. Johnston, reg. 1986.

* *
```
              -Monsieur Thiers--unknown 1/4
          -J. H. Van Nes-
DARLENE'S PINK-      -griffithianum 1/2
   -              -griffithianum
          -Loderi King George-
                  -fortunei 1/4
```
4ft(1.2m) 15F(-9C) EM Flowers of strong purplish red, 2.75in.
(7cm) across, openly funnel-campanulate, 5-6 wavy lobes; dome-
shaped trusses of 11-15. Plant taller than wide. Foliage long,
narrow; held 2-3 years.   B. Briggs cross; E. Knight, reg. 1980.
EMILY ALLISON   Parentage as above
4ft(1.2m) 10F(-12C) ML White flowers with a currant red ring
in throat, very fragrant, 7-lobed; 20 in truss 8in(20.3cm) wide.
Plant broad as tall.   H. Lem cross; J. Bailey, reg. 1983.
EULALIE WAGNER   Parentage as above

Flowers fuchsine pink, darker veins, funnel-shaped, in truss of
12, 9in(23cm) high.   Lem cross; Fawcett, reg. 1974. P.A. 1963.
KNIGHT'S PINK   Parentage as above
5ft(1.5m) 15F(-9C) E   Trusses of 14 flowers, Neyron rose with
light orchid pink throat and lobe stripes, colors fading slowly.
Plant broader than tall. B. Briggs cross; Knight, reg. 1981.
LEM'S 49   Parentage as above
Color similar to EULALIE WAGNER, above. Fragrant; trusses of
10-12 with large flowers. Frank Mossman and Cyril Ward intro.
* *
                                        -caucasicum 1/8
                      -Cunningham's White-
          -Rocket (Shammarello)-   -ponticum 1/8
DARREN -   -   -catawbiense
SCHMAHL-   -red catawbiense hyb.-   1/8
      -                            -unknown 1/8
          -brachycarpum (as ssp.tigerstedtii) 1/2
18in(.46m)(7yrs) -25F(-32C) ML Tubular funnel-shaped, frilly
flowers, light purple spotted darker, protruding pistil; 17 per
truss. Upright bush; leaves held 3 years. Behring, reg. 1990.

          -brachycarpum 1/2   -wardii ? 1/8
DATED YELLOW-   -Chlorops-
      -unnamed hybrid-   -vernicosum ? 1/8
                  -aureum 1/4
Buds light greenish yellow; flowers pale yellow-green.   Delp.

          -yakushimanum 1/2
DAVE GOHEEN-
          -calophytum 1/2
3ft(.9m) OF(-18C) E   Buds strong purplish pink, opening paler
and fading white; flowers tubular-campanulate 2.3in(6cm) across,
yellowish white edges, a cardinal red dorsal blotch, midrib rays
of pale pink; domed truss of 14-16. Dull yellowish green leaves
4in(11.4cm) long, held 3 years; felted, pale yellow indumentum.
Broad plant.   D. W. Goheen, cross 1964; L. Bulgin, reg. 1986.

                      -griffithianum 1/8
              -George Hardy-
          -          -catawbiense 1/8
      -Hugh Koster-   -arboreum 1/16
      -          -   -Doncaster-
DAVID-   -unnamed hybrid-   -unknown 3/16
      -                  -unknown
      -neriiflorum 1/2
6ft(1.8m) 5F(-15C) EM 4/3 Fine, brilliant, blood red flowers
with white anthers, frilly margins, campanulate; loosely formed
trusses. Dark green foliage. Lord Swaythling.   F.C.C. 1939;
A.M. Wisley Trials 1957.   Color illus. Cox pl. 46; VV p. 31.

* *
          -No. 2 Red (Tom Ring)--unknown 11/16
      -unnamed-   -catawbiense 3/32
      - hybrid-   -Parsons Grandiflorum-
      -      -   -America-   -unknown
      -      -Cindy-   -dark red hybrid--unknown
DAVID -   Lou -   -griffithianum 5/32
DICKEY-   -   -Mars-
      -          -unnamed-   -unknown
      -                  hybrid-catawbiense var. rubrum 1/16
      -      -Mars (as above)
      -Frank-
          Moniz-America (as above)
Buds of deep and vivid reds, opening to flowers of cardinal and
vivid reds; dorsal spots moderate reddish orange. W. Delp.
DENNIS DICKEY   Parentage as above
Buds of deep and currant reds, open to flowers a blend of cardi-
nal, currant and vivid reds; dorsal spots dark red. W. Delp.
* *
* *
          -catawbiense var. compactum 1/2
DAVID FORSYTHE-   -griffithianum 1/4
              -Mars-
                  -unknown (1/4)
5ft(1.5m) -20F(-29C) M   Buds scarlet, opening to dark scarlet flowers, 3in(7.6cm) wide; ball-shaped trusses of about 8.
Spreading. S. Baldanza raiser; reg. 1972. Col. ill. HG p. 170.
ROBERT FORSYTHE   Parentage as above
4ft(1.2m) -15F(-26C) ML A dense, broad plant with leaves 5in
(12.7cm) long, of dark green.   Deep rose flowers, with a brown
blotch. Baldanza cross, 1958; reg. 1972.
                              * * * * * * * * * * * * * * *

DAVID GABLE   Described under BEECHWOOD PINK, q.v.

                          -haematodes 1/4
              -Humming Bird-
DAVID GRANT-   -williamsianum 1/4
              -unknown 1/2
Flowers in trusses of 5, 6-lobed, cerise throughout with black
anthers.   Shrub 1ft(.3m) x 3ft(.9m).   Two seasons, spring and
fall. Jack Drake (NZ), reg. 1988.

* *
                              -catawbiense 1/4
                      -Sefton-
DAVID HARRIS---unnamed hybrid F2-   -unknown 1/2
                  -          -ponticum 1/4
                  -Purple Splendour-
                          -unknown
Buds of dark red, plum and violet purples opening to flowers
beetroot purple; dark red flare; dorsal spots dark red. Plant
size medium; hardy to -15F(-26C).   W. Delp.
FRIZZY LIZ   Parentage as above
Buds of deep red open to frilled flowers of lilac purple; dorsal
spots lilac purple, light greenish yellow.   White flare, white
throat, white anthers. W. Delp.
* *
* *
              -minus Carolinianum Group 1/2
          -                  -racemosum 1/8
DAVID JOHN-   -Conemaugh-
          -Pioneer (Gable)-   -mucronulatum 1/8
                      -unknown 1/4
3ft(.9m) -20F(-29C) M   Ball-shaped terminal flower clusters,
2-6 trusses, each 2-5 flowered, of mallow purple with faint red
spotting. W. Fetterhoff, reg. 1981.
GARY   Parentage as above
2.5ft(.75m) -20F(-29C) M   Terminal clusters of 1-4 trusses,
each of 3-5 flowers, rhodamine pink. Semi-dwarf plant, wider
than tall; leaves held 1 year. William Fetterhoff, reg. 1981.
          *

              -griersonianum 1/4
          -Karkov-   -arboreum 1/8
          -      -Red Admiral-
DAVID   -   -thomsonii 1/8
ROCKEFELLER-   -griffithianum 1/8
          -          -King George-
          -Gipsy King-   -unknown 1/8
                  -haematodes 1/4
Trusses of 10 flowers, medium rose, speckled red.   Edmund de
Rothschild, reg. 1982.

                          -griffithianum
                  -unnamed hybrid-
          -Mrs. Furnival-   -unknown
          -          -   -caucasicum
DAVID SHELTON-   -unnamed hybrid-
          -                  -unknown
          -Loder's White, q.v. for 2 possible parentages
4ft(1.2m) OF(-18C) EM   Openly funnel-shaped flowers 4in(10cm)
wide, 5 wavy lobes of white, suffused strong spinel red (fading
pale rose), edged rose pink; domed truss of 9-10. Leaves flat,
to 6in(15cm) long.   W. Elliott cross; B. F. Heuston, reg. 1986.

      -griffithianum 1/2
DAWN-
      -unknown 1/2
White flowers blushed phlox pink; 8-flowered trusses.   Waterer,
Sons & Crisp.   A.M. 1950

                  -griffithianum 1/2
DAWN'S DELIGHT-
                  -unknown 1/2
5ft(1.5m) 5F(-15C) ML 3/3 Stems show pink tinge of griffithianum. Carmine buds open to large, frilly soft pink, marked
crimson, shading to white; tall conical trusses. J. H. Mangles,
before 1884. A.M. 1911.

                      -fortunei ssp. discolor 1/4
          -Lady Bessborough-
DAY DREAM-   -campylocarpum Elatum Group 1/4
          -griersonianum 1/2
5ft(1.5m) 5F(-15C) ML 3/3 Buds rich rose, flowers the same,

turning creamy pale yellow with a glowing rose eye, then fading to creamy white; large loose trusses. Another form, BISCUIT, is hardier. Rothschild, 1936. A.M. 1940 Color ill. PB pl. 65.

DAYAN Described under CHAN, q.v.

```
               -fortunei 1/2
DAYLIGHT-                     -campylocarpum 1/4
        -Mrs. Ashley Slocock-
                             -hardy hybrid--unknown 1/4
```
Flowers pink with crimson spots, 3.5in(9cm) wide; tight trusses hold 11 flowers. Gen. Harrison, reg. 1962.

DAZZLER Parentage unknown
5ft(1.5m) OF(-18C) ML 4/3 Unusual color of reddish orange. Leaves medium-sized. Greer.

```
          -Mrs. J. G. Millais--unknown 1/2
DAZZLING- -yakushimanum 1/4
DARLING - -                       -fortunei ssp. discolor 1/16
      -Si-        -Lady
      Si-    -Day - Bessborough-campylocarpum Elatum Gp.
       -Gold -Dream-griersonianum 1/8              1/32
         Mohur-            -fortunei ssp. discolor
             -Margaret Dunn-     -dichroanthum 1/32
                          -Fabia-
                              -griersonianum
```
Buds of spirea red and pale purplish pink opening to flowers yellowish white; a flare of pale yellow green. W. Delp.

DEADLY FORCE Described under CALSAP, q.v.

DEAN HALL Parentage unknown
4ft(1.2m) x 4ft.(12 yrs) ML Flowers widely funnel-campanulate 2.7in(7cm) across, 5-7 wavy lobes of very pale Neyron rose, dorsal spotting light mustard yellow. Maurice Hall, reg. 1986.

```
             -haematodes 1/4
      -May Day-
DEBBIE-       -griersonianum 1/4
      -       -sanguineum ssp. didymum 1/4
      -Carmen-
              -forrestii Repens Group 1/4
```
2ft(.6m) OF(-18C) EM 3/4 Round and compact dwarf plant, with dense, dark green foliage. Bright blood red flowers. J. Henny, reg. 1963.

```
              -Marion--unknown
DEBBIE THOMSON-
              -unknown
```
Flowers held in trusses of 12-15, funnel-shaped, vivid reddish purple, fading to white with an orange flare on the dorsal lobe. Shrub 3ft(.9m). V. J. Boulter cross; F. Boulter, reg. 1986.

DEBIJO Described under CAROUSEL, q.v.

```
* * * * * * * * * * * * * * * * * * * * * * * * * * * * *
                  -griersonianum 1/4
      -Creeping Jenny-
      -              -forrestii Repens Group 1/4
DEBORAH-                         -griffithianum 1/8
      -              -Queen Wilhelmina-
      -Unknown Warrior-           -unknown 3/8
                      -Stanley Davies--unknown
```
Red flowers in truss of 11. Dr. E. E. Smith, Surrey, reg. 1976.
FLORENCE Parentage as above
Scarlet red flowers in truss of about 10. Dr. Smith, reg. 1976.
```
* * * * * * * * * * * * * * * * * * * * * * * * * * * * *
```

```
                     -dichroanthum
             -Fabia-
      - C.I.S. -      -griersonianum
      -      -Loder's White, q.v. for 2 possible
DEBRA TUOMALA-                   parentage diagrams
      -      -arboreum ssp. nilagricum
      -Noyo Chief-
             -unknown
```
4ft(1.2m) 15F(-9C) E Buds very light cardinal red open to flowers of 7-8 wavy lobes, light chrome yellow mottled azalea pink, in trusses of 8. Plant as wide as tall; emerald green foliage. C. Tuomala cross; E. R. German, reg. 1984.

DECALGLA Described under MRS. CARTER GLASS, q.v.

```
         -decorum 1/2
DECATROS-              -catawbiense 1/4
        -Atrosanguineum-
                      -unknown 1/4
```
Parent of MILLARD KEPNER. Pink flowers. J. Gable, cross 1932.

```
         -decorum 1/2
DECAUCK-
        -griffithianum (aucklandii) 1/2
```
White flowers. E. J. P. Magor, 1912.

```
         -decorum 1/2
DECHAEM-
        -haematodes 1/2
```
A parent of MARY BELLE and other hybrids. J. Gable.

```
                        -souliei 1/16
                -Soulbut-
         -Vanessa-      -fortunei--Sir Charles Butler 1/16
      -Radiance-
      -        -griersonianum 3/8
DECORA-     -griersonianum
      -     -griffithianum 1/4
      -Loderi-
             -fortunei 1/4
```
Pink flowers. Lord Aberconway, intro. 1946.

```
         -decorum 1/2
DECSOUL-
        -souliei 1/2
```
Rosy buds opening to almost pure white flowers. W. I. Whitaker. A.M. 1937

```
                    -dichroanthum 1/8
           -Fabia-
        -Jingle-    -griersonianum 1/8
        - Bells-        -campylocarpum Elatum Group 1/8
        -     -Ole Olson-
        -                -fortunei ssp. discolor 1/8
DEE DEE-                        -griffithianum 1/16
WEGENER-                -George-
      -        -Mrs. Lindsey- Hardy-catawbiense 1/16
      -Mrs. Betty- Smith    -
      Robertson-           -Duchess of Edinburgh--unknown
      -                    -campylocarpum 1/8
                -unnamed hybrid-
                           -unknown 1/4
```
4ft(1.2m) x 4ft 5F(-15C) M Flowers in lax trusses of 8, wavy margins, broad picotee edge of deep red shading to pale yellow. Dorsal lobe with deep red blotch. Reverse deep to strong red. Leaves moderate yellow-green. Britt M. Smith, reg. 1987.

DEEP THOUGHTS Described under CALSAP, q.v.

DEER DELL--form of glaucophyllum
3ft(.9m) OF(-18C) EM 3/2 Truss of 4-7 flowers, 5-lobed, ruby red. Scaly indumentum. J. F. McQuire, reg. 1984.

DEGAS Described under MARSHALL, q.v.

DEGRAM See ANNIE DALTON

```
* * * * * * * * * * * * * * * * * * * * * * * * * * * * *
```
(For the oldest of this group see ISPAHAN, below.)
```
      -wardii (croceum) 1/2
DEL-   -dichroanthum 1/4
      -Fabia-
           -griersonianum 1/4
```
3ft(.9m) 5F(-15C) M Rose-colored flower with blotch of greenish yellow, 4.5in(11.5cm) wide, in trusses of about 12. Del W. James cross; Dr. C. D. Thompson, reg. 1962.
CHARLEY Parentage as above
Parent of LONNY. White flowers tinted amaranth rose, turning creamy yellow, yellow blotch; sweetly fragrant, full rounded trusses. Leaves 8in(20.3cm) long. James, reg. 1962.
GOLDBUG Parentage as above
3ft(.9m) 5F(-15C) M 3/3 Very broad, compact, deep green leaves. Flowers open brick red with maroon speckling, then fade to yellow. R. Henny, reg. 1958.
ISPAHAN As above, except reversed (wardii K W 4170 ?)

Plant low and broad. Waxy flowers, orange to yellow in loose
trusses. Midseason.   Rothschild, 1941.
MITZI   Parentage as DEL, above
Crimson to orange flower, darker throat and blotch. Henny, 1958.
YELLOW JACKET   Parentage as DEL, above
Semi-dwarf.   Henny, cross 1946; reg. 1958.
* *

DEL JAMES--form of taggianum
8ft(2.4m) 20F(-7C) VE 5/2   Flowers white with yellow blotch,
rose pink in bud; loose truss of 2-5, and very fragrant. Plant
straggly but upright.   Dr. & Mrs. P. J. Bowman, reg. 1965.

DELAMERE BELLE   Described under LOCKINGTON PRIDE, q.v.

DELAWARE   Described under BRANDYWINE, q.v.

DELEILAH   See DANIELA

* *
                       -catawbiense 1/4
              -unnamed hybrid-
DELENDICH-   -unknown 1/4
              -maximum 1/2
7ft(2.1m) -25F(-32C) M Truss 6in(15.2cm) wide, up to 18 flowers, beetroot purple.   Leaves yellow-green, held 3 years on an
upright plant with stiff branches.   W. David Smith, reg. 1983.
ELIZABETH SCHOLTZ   Parentage as above
4ft(1.2m) -25F(-32C) M Dome-shaped trusses 7in(17.8Cm) wide,
spirea red. Well-branched; leaves held 3 years.   Smith, 1983.
FLORENCE RINEHIMER   Parentage as above
7ft(2.1m) -25F(32C) ML   Well-branched plant; yellowish green
leaves, held 3 years. Flowers roseine purple with dorsal spots
dark olive yellow; trusses of 16.   W. D. Smith, reg. 1983.
MARIE GIASI   Parentage as above
5ft(1.5m) -25F(-32C) M Shrub wider than tall; dark green foliage held 3 years. Ruby red buds open to deep spirea red, spotted beetroot purple, with 5 heavily ribbed lobes; trusses of 17.
W. D. Smith, reg. 1983.
* *

DELICATE SPLENDOR   Parentage unknown
Flowers in trusses of 7-10, light purplish pink, edged in strong
purplish pink.   Dexter cross; raised at Shawme Farm, then Ross
Estate; Tyler Arboreum, reg. 1981.

* *
                       -griffithianum 1/8
              -Pink Shell-   -fortunei 1/16
      -Rosabel-   -H. M. Arderne-
DELICIOUS-   -   -unknown 1/16
         -        -griersonianum 1/4
              -arboreum 1/2
Truss of 20 flowers, light carmine rose.   G. Langdon, reg. 1982.
HOT WONDER   Parentage as above
Flowers carmine with darker throat.   Langdon, reg. 1982.
* *

        -ciliatum 3/4
DELIGHT-   -ciliatum
        -Praecox-
              -dauricum 1/4
Similar to ciliatum but smaller.   R. Gill & Son. A.M. 1929.

* *
                      -catawbiense 1/4
        -Mrs. Milner-
DELILA-   -unknown 1/4
        -smirnowii 1/2
Flowers carmine red with small dark markings; frilled edges.
T. J. R. Seidel, 1902.
DAISY   Parentage as above
Bright carmine rose flowers, with yellowish green markings on a
lighter background.   T. J. R. Seidel, 1902.
DARIUS   Parentage as above
Purplish red flowers; ochre markings.   Seidel, 1902.
DESIDERIUS   Parentage as above
Frilled flower, pure dark carmine pink; greenish marks. Seidel.
DIETRICH   Parentage as above
Light purplish pink; faint yellowish brown marks. Seidel, 1902.
DONAR   Parentage as above
Frilled flowers, light carmine red with white throat and very

dark red markings.   Seidel, 1902.
ELLA   Parentage as above
5ft(1.5m) -15F(-26C) ML Carmine red flowers.   Seidel, 1915.
ERNA Parentage as above
Flowers carmine red.   Seidel.
* *

                       -dichroanthum 1/8
        -Astarte-   -campylocarpum Elatum Group 1/16
     -Ouida-   -Penjerrick-
DELIUS-   -griffithianum 1/16
      -     -griersonianum 1/4
      -elliottii 1/2
Blood red flowers shaded carmine.   Lord Aberconway. A.M. 1942.

                                  -catawbiense
                   -Atrosanguineum-   3/16
                -Atrier-   -unknown 3/16
           -Mary Belle-   -griersonianum 1/8
           -        -   -decorum 1/0
DELP'S BIG DEAL-   -Dechaem-
           -              -haematodes 1/8
           -       -catawbiense var. album Glass--Catalgla 1/4
           -Tony's -   -Catawbiense Album-   -catawbiense
              Gift -   -catawbiense
                 -Belle -   -unknown
                 Heller-   -catawbiense
                 -white catawbiense sdl.-
                                -unknown
Buds combine strong reddish purples and deep purplish pink.
Frilled flowers of white and very pale rosy purple, deep violet
edges. Strong yellowish green dorsal spots. W. Delp.

                    -Pygmalion--unknown 7/32
           -unnamed hybrid-
        -Weldy-   -haematodes 3/16
        -    -yakushimanum, Exbury form 1/4
        -              -catawbiense var. album 3/16
DELP'S -   -Lodestar-   -catawbiense var. album
   CREATION-   -   -Belle -   -catawbiense 1/16
        -     -   Heller-Madame -
        -     -   Carvalho-unknown
        -R. O. Delp-   -catawbiense
        -              -Atrosanguineum-
        -     -Atrier-   -unknown
        -Mary -   -griersonianum 1/16
        Belle-   -decorum 1/16
           -Dechaem-
                 -haematodes
Blend of strong and spinel reds in bud opening to white, tinted
lightly with strong purplish red and strong red dorsal spots,
pale greenish yellow throat.   Weldon Delp.

           -catawbiense var. album Glass--Catalgla 1/8
        -Gosh-   -decorum? 1/32
        -Darn-   -Caroline-
        -    -Mrs. H. R. Yates-   -brachycarpum? 1/32
     -Sweet-   -unknown 1/16
     - Lulu-   -neriiflorum 3/32
     -    -   -Nereid-
DELP'S -   -   -Phyllis -   -dichroanthum 3/32
SUNSHEEN-   -unnamed- Ballard-fortunei ssp. discolor 3/16
     -    hybrid-
     -         -catawbiense--Clark's White 1/8
     -    -vernicosum (18139) 1/4
     -unnamed-   -Nereid (as above)
        hybrid-unnamed hybrid-
                 -fortunei ssp. discolor
Buds strong and light orange open to flowers of light yellow and
pale greenish yellow, tinted strong reddish orange.   W. Delp.

                    -smirnowii 1/4
        -Goody Goody-
DELP'S TOUCH-   -catawbiense 1/4
  OF CLASS   -   -yakushimanum 1/4   -fortunei ssp. discolor
        -Si Si-   -Lady Bess-   3/32
           -Day - borough -campylocarpum Elatum
        -Gold -Dream-griersonianum 3/32   1/32
          Mohur-   -fortunei ssp. discolor
           -Margaret Dunn-   -dichroanthum 1/32
                 -Fabia-
                    -griersonianum

Flowers of magenta rose slowly fading to white. W. Delp.

DELTA   Parentage unknown
Flowers of phlox pink.   Boot of Boskoop, reg. 1964.

DEMI-JOHN--form of johnstoneanum
4ft(1.2m) 15F(-9C) M   Cool greenhouse plant. Fragrant white
flowers, semi-double, throat flushed medium yellowish green,
2.75in(7cm) wide; truss of 3-4.   Sir Giles Loder. A.M. 1975.

```
                            -souliei 1/4
                   -Soulbut-
        -Vanessa Pastel-       -fortunei--Sir Charles Butler 1/4
        -                      -griffithianum
                   -Norman-Beauty of Tremough-
DENALI-        - Gill -           -arboreum 1/32
     -     -Anna-     -griffithianum
     -     -            -griffithianum 7/32
     -Pink  -   -Jean Marie de Montague-
     Walloper-          -unknown 3/16
        -                   -griffithianum
        -             -George Hardy-
        -Marinus Koster-        -catawbiense 1/16
                      -red hybrid--unknown
```
7ft(2.1m) x 7ft(11 yrs) -5F(-21C) M 4/4 Many large rose pink
flowers, 4in(10cm) wide, burnt orange blotch; huge truss of 14.
Beautiful dense, deep green foliage. "Denali" is the Alaskan
Indian name for Mt. McKinley. J. Elliott, reg. 1986.

DENCOMBE   Described under SARITA LODER, q.v.

```
        -Winter Favourite--unknown 1/2
DENISE-        -chrysodoron 1/4
     -Chrysomanicum-
              -hurmanicum 1/4
```
2.5ft(.75m) 10F(-12C) E   Flowers grayed yellow, flushed with
Venetian pink. V. J. Boulter, AUS, reg. 1972.

```
        -dalhousiae 1/2
DENISONII-        -edgeworthii 1/4
       -unnamed hybrid-
              -Gibbs--unknown 1/4
```
Pure white flowers with lemon stain. Unknown. F.C.C. 1862.

DENNIS DICKEY   Described under DAVID DICKEY, q.v.

```
                        -griffithianum 1/8
                -George Hardy-
        -Peter Koster-        -catawbiense 1/8
        -          -            -arboreum 1/16
DERRELL KING-        -Doncaster-
        -      -unnamed hybrid-        -unknown 11/16
        -Blue Peter--unknown        -unknown
```
Flowers mauve, with a deep purple center, held in a dense truss.
Shrub 8ft(2.4m) at 20 years. S. M. King, reg. 1984.

```
                -wardii 1/8
        -unnamed-       -dichroanthum ssp. scyphocalyx
        - hybrid-Medusa-                      1/16
     -Darigold-       -griersonianum 1/8
     -      -        -fortunei ssp. discolor 1/8
DESERT-      -Autumn Gold-       -dichroanthum 1/16
GOLD -        -Fabia-
     -               -griersonianum
     -     -wardii 1/4       -griffithianum 1/32
     -Idealist-       -Kewense-
     -      -Aurora-       -fortunei 5/32
        -Naomi-     -thomsonii 1/16
              -fortunei
```
5ft(1.5m) OF(-18C) M 4/4 Large trusses of deep golden yellow
with small amount of red in the throat. Foliage heavy-textured,
olive green. Thompson intro. 1988. Color illus. HG p. 149.

```
        -fortunei ssp. discolor Houlstonii Group 1/2
DESERT-               -soulei 1/32
SUN -        -Soulbut-
   -     -Vanessa-       -fortunei--Sir Chas. Butler 1/32
   - -Etna-       -griersonianum 1/8
   - -   -     -dichroanthum 1/16
   -Veta- -Fabia-
   -      -griersonianum
     -venator 1/4
```

Truss of 10 red flowers, yellowish orange centers.   V. J. Boulter, Australia, reg. 1978.

DESIDERIUS   Described under DELILA, q.v.

```
        -ferrugineum 1/2
DESMIT-
     -minus Carolinianum Group 1/2
```
2ft(.6m) -15F(-26C) M 4/4 Flowers held in small pink spherical trusses. Deep green foliage. Dr. R. Ticknor cross.

```
                -dichroanthum ssp. scyphocalyx 1/4
     -Medusa-
DESNA-     -griersonianum 3/4
     -griersonianum
```
Flowers orange-red.   Lord Aberconway, intro. 1946.

```
                -griffithianum 1/4
        -Sincerity-
DESTINY-     -unknown 1/4
       -thomsonii 1/2
```
Deep coral pink flowers, 3.5in(9cm) wide; trusses hold about 12.
Gen. Harrison, reg. 1962.

```
                        -adenogynum 1/4
           -Xenosporum (detonsum)-
DETONHAEM-                -unknown 1/4
        -haematodes 1/2
```
Introduced in 1932 by E. J. P. Magor.

DETONSUM   See XENOSPORUM

```
        -fortunei ssp. discolor 1/2
DEVAGILLA-       -arboreum 1/4
       -Cornubia-       -thomsonii 1/8
              -Shilsonii-
                   -barbatum 1/8
```
Rosy pink flowers on a tall, compact hybrid.   Rothschild, 1936.

```
        -auriculatum 1/2
DEVALUATION-
         -arboreum 1/2
```
Tall but compact plant. Large white flowers, flushed with pink.
Late-blooming. Rothschild, 1936.

```
                -A. W. Hardy Hybrid--unknown 1/2
DEVONSHIRE CREAM-
              -campylocarpum 1/2
```
3ft(.9m) OF(-18C) M 3/4 Creamy yellow flowers, a deep red
blotch at base; compact, ball-shaped trusses. A very slow-growing, dense plant. Slocock, 1924. A.M. 1940.

```
        -catawbiense var. album--Catanea 1/2
DEXTANEA-
      -white Dexter hybrid--unknown 1/2
```
7ft(2.1m) -20F(-29C) M   White fragrant flowers, 3in(7.6cm)
broad; ball-shaped trusses of 10. Plant rounded, well-branched,
taller than wide. N. E. Hess cross; G. G. Nearing, reg. 1973.

DEXTER/BOSLEY 1020 and 1040   Parentage unknown
Light to dark pink. Dexter seedlings; Paul Bosley, Sr., raiser.

DEXTER'S AGATHA   Described under ACCLAIM, q.v.

DEXTER'S AMETHYST   See AMETHYST (Dexter)

DEXTER'S APPLEBLOSSOM   Parentage unknown
6ft(1.8m) -5F(-21C) ML Large flowers of white edged pink,
greenish yellow blotch; trusses of 12-15. Heritage, reg. 1977.

DEXTER'S APRICOT   Parentage unknown; haematodes x decorum?
5ft(1.5m) -OF(-18C) E   Fragrant flowers of pink, with darker
edges and yellowish green basal blotch; flat trusses hold 12-15.
Heritage Plantation, reg. 1977.

DEXTER'S BIG RED   See DEXTER'S GIANT RED

DEXTER'S BRANDY GREEN   Parentage unknown
6ft(1.8m) -5F(-21C) ML Flowers of 7 lobes, pink with a red
blotch, heavily spotted yellow-green; flat truss of 8. Foliage
large; well-branched plant. Another form exists, with flowers
cream-colored. Heritage Plantation, reg. 1977.

DEXTER'S BRICK RED Parentage unknown; haematodes x decorum?
3ft(.9m) OF(-18C) E Flowers 7-lobed, pink with a red blotch;
lax truss of 12. Low, spreading plant.   Heritage Plantation,
reg. 1977.

DEXTER'S CHAMPAGNE   Parentage unknown
5ft(1.5m) -5F(-21C) E   Flowers off-white, overlaid pink and
apricot.   N.Y. Botanical Garden; Westbury Rose Co., reg. 1958.

DEXTER'S CREAM   Parentage unknown; haematodes x decorum?
3ft(.9m) -5F(-21C) M   Flowers 6-lobed, 3.5in(9cm) wide, cream
shaded pink, with pale yellow blotch and stripes; fragrant. Lax
truss of 6-8; spreading plant. Heritage Plantation, reg. 1977.

DEXTER'S CROWN PINK   Parentage unknown
6ft(1.8m) OF(-18C) L   Vivid rose pink flowers, 6-lobed, olive
green blotch; truss of 10. Large foliage. C. Dexter called the
plant "Old Wavy Leaf".   Heritage Plantation, reg. 1977.

DEXTER'S FAVOURITE   Parentage unknown
Medium pink with bright cerise centers.   Dexter cross.

DEXTER'S GIANT RED   Parentage unknown
6ft(1.8m) -5F(-21C) L 4/3   Orange-red flowers fading reddish
pink, 4in(10cm) broad, dark red blotch, light red spotting overall; big trusses of 12-15. Large foliage. C. Dexter; Heritage
Plantation, reg. 1977.   Color illus. HG p. 118.

DEXTER'S GLOW   Parentage unknown
6ft(1.8m) -15F(-26C) L   Vibrant pink, frilled flowers with a
paler throat, dark red ring around corolla base; slightly fragrant. Lax trusses of about 10. Heritage Plantation, reg. 1977.

DEXTER'S HARLEQUIN   Described under ACCLAIM, q.v.

DEXTER'S HORIZON   Parentage unknown; may include smirnowii
5ft(1.5m) -10F(-23C) L   Flowers 6-lobed, 3.5in(9cm) wide, bi-
color with deep pink edges, white center, a yellow-green blotch;
spherical truss of 10-12.   Heritage Plantation, reg. 1977.

DEXTER'S ORANGE   Parentage unknown; may be haematodes hybrid
3ft x 6ft(.9m x 1.8m) -5F(-21C) M   Multihued flowers of deep
pink and orange, brownish orange blotch; lax truss of 8. Dense
plant; small glossy foliage. Heritage Plantation, reg. 1977.

DEXTER'S ORCHID   Parentage unknown
5ft(1.5m) -10F(-23C) M   Frilly lavender pink flowers. Dexter
cross; Vossberg intro.

DEXTER'S PEPPERMINT   Parentage unknown; possibly decorum hybrid
5ft(1.5m) -5F(-21C) ML   Very fragrant, light purplish pink
flowers with a blotch of light yellowish green.   Heritage Plantation, reg. 1977.

DEXTER'S PINK   Parentage unknown
4ft(1.2m) OF(-18C) ML Beautiful big pink flowers, frilly dark
pink edges, brown spotting, a small dark red blotch; full rounded truss. Compact bush; hardy in Cleveland, O. Vossberg intro.

DEXTER'S PINK GLORY   Parentage unknown
5ft(1.5m) OF(-18C) ML   Buds deep rosy pink; flowers 6-lobed,
to 4.5in(11.5cm) wide, fragrant, intense pink with blended central spotting of green, yellow and red; trusses of 6-8. Foliage
large. Heritage Plantation, reg. 1977.

DEXTER'S PINK SATIN   Parentage unknown
4ft(1.2m) -5F(-21C) E Pink ruffled flowers with darker edges,
a brown flare and deep red spotting; full trusses.   Dexter.

DEXTER'S PURPLE   Parentage unknown
5ft(1.2m) -15F(-26C) M   Flowers light lilac purple, purplish
red spots in center. Good foliage and habit.   Vossberg intro.
Color illus. ARS J 43:4 1989, p. 207.

DEXTER'S RAMONA   Parentage unknown; may include catawbiense
5ft(1.5m) -10F(-23C) E Large trusses of deep pink flowers, on
a well-shaped plant; glossy foliage.   Dexter cross.

DEXTER'S RED   Parentage unknown
Flowers red, with heavy chocolate brown spotting. Plant of medium size; hardy in Pennsylvania. Vossburg intro. 1959.

DEXTER'S RED VELVET   Parentage unknown
5ft(1.5m) -5F(-21C) M   Velvety textured red flowers with very
dark spotting in throat; very floriferous plant with olive green
foliage. May be best red-flowered Dexter. Knippenberg intro.

DEXTER'S SPICE   Parentage unknown
6ft(1.8m) -5F(-21C) M   Very fragrant 7-lobed flowers 4-5in(10
-12.5cm) across, wavy-edged, white with pale yellow-green dorsal
spotting; lax truss of 7. Glossy foliage; plant habit improves
with age. Very floriferous. Heritage Plantation, reg. 1977.

DEXTER'S SPRINGTIME   Parentage unknown; haematodes x decorum?
3ft(.9m) OF(-18C) E   Rose red buds to creamy white flowers,
3.5in(9cm) wide, with deep pink edges, 3 red-brown dorsal rays;
fragrant flat truss of 7-10. Heritage Plantation, reg. 1977.

DEXTER'S TWO-TONE   Parentage unknown; possibly fortunei hybrid
4ft(1.2m) -15F(-26C) M   White flowers, edged in pink.

DEXTER'S VANILLA   Parentage unknown; haematodes x decorum?
3ft(.9m) OF(-18C) M   Buds pink/white; creamy flower with deep
pink edges, red-brown dorsal blotch; corolla 7-lobed, 3.5in(9cm)
wide, fragrant; lax truss of 8. Heritage Plantation, reg. 1977.

DEXTER'S VICTORIA   Parentage unknown
5ft(1.5m) -15F(-26C) M Frilled, rich lavender flowers about 3
in(7.5cm) wide, large greenish brown blotch; truss of 15. Plant
dense, rounded; glossy leaves.   Heritage Plantation, reg. 1977.

DIADEM   See HACHMANN'S DIADEM

DIADEMA   Parentage unknown
A parent of HERME, by Seidel.

```
                -yakushimanum 1/4    -fortunei ssp. discolor
                -          -Lady   -              3/32
        -Si Si-    -Day -Bessborough-campylocarpum Elatum Group
        -     -      -Dream-                           1/16
        -     -Gold -    -griersonianum 3/64
        -       Mohur-      -fortunei ssp. discolor
  unnamed-        -Margaret-    -dichroanthum 1/64
  hybrid-          Dunn   -Fabia-
        -                     -griersonianum
        -          -yakushimanum
        -Serendipity-
DIAMOND-          -aureum 3/16
  DELIGHT-     -brachycarpum 1/8
    -unnamed-      -wardii 3/64
    - hybrid-Crest-        -fortunei ssp. discolor
    -            -Lady    -
  Marypat-          Bessborough-campylocarpum Elatum Group
    -              -catawbiense var. album 1/16
    -    -unnamed-    -wardii
    -    - hybrid-Crest-        -fortunei ssp. discolor
    -Monte-          -Lady    -
    Carlo-          Bessborough-campylocarpum Elatum
    -      -aureum
    -unnamed-
    hybrid-campylocarpum 1/16
```
DIAMOND DELIGHT = (SI SI x SERENDIPITY) X MARYPAT which is fully
expanded in the diagram above. Blend of pale yellow and medium
orange in bud, opening to pale yellow green with dorsal spotting
of strong greenish yellow and medium orange.   W. Delp.

```
            -yunnanense 1/2
DIAMOND WEDDING-
            -davidsonianum 1/2
```
White flowers, suffused purple with light orange-red spotting in
upper throat, 2.5in(6.4cm) wide; up to 24 flowers, axillary and
terminal, in firm rounded trusses. Glossy, dark green foliage.
Maj. A. E. Hardy; reg. 1978.   A.M. 1978.

```
            -yunnanense 1/2
DIANA COLVILLE-
            -unknown 1/2
```
Rose purple flowers, fading almost white at margins, rich brown
spotting in throat, 2in(5cm) wide; terminal and axillary clusters form rounded trusses of about 25. Plant 6ft(1.8m) tall,
slightly wider; leaf 3.5in(8.9cm) long, scaly brown indumentum.
Col. N. R. Colville, reg. 1968.   A.M. Wisley Trials 1972.
F.C.C. Wisley Trials 1972.

* *
```
                         -yakushimanum 1/2
DIANA PEARSON-           -Margaret--unknown 1/4
             -Glamour-
                         -griersonianum 1/4
```
Plant 2ft(.6m) x 2.5ft(.75m)(12 yrs) and vigorous. Trusses of
13 almost-white flowers. A. F. George, reg. 1981. A.M. 1980.
LUISE VEREY   Parentage as above
3ft(.9m) 0F(-18C) M Flattened pink flowers, crimson throat;
trusses of 17-18. A. F. George, reg. 1978.

* *

DIANE   Described under ZUIDERZEE, q. v.

DIANE BEEKMAN   Described under JOAN THOMPSON, q.v.

```
                -forrestii Repens Group 1/4
        -Elizabeth-
DIANE LUX-        -griersonianum 1/4
      -         -campylocarpum 1/4
        -Unique-
                -unknown 1/4
```
1.5ft(.45m) 10F(-12C) E Flowers claret rose fading Venetian
pink, widely funnel-campanulate, 2in(5cm) across, in high ball-
shaped trusses of 12; very floriferous. Plant twice as broad as
high. E. F. Drake, cross; Mrs. Vincent Lux, Jr., reg. 1981.

* *
```
                              -griffithianum 3/8
                  -George Hardy-
          -Marinus Koster-        -catawbiense 1/8
          -              -red hybrid--unknown 1/4
DIANE TITCOMB-             -griffithianum
          -         -Halopeanum-
          -Snow  -          -maximum 1/8
           Queen-   -griffithianum
                 -Loderi-
                         -fortunei 1/8
```
5ft(1.5m) -5F(-21C) M 4/4   Shrub of large foliage and fine
trusses; white flowers, edged pink. Larson, 1942. P.A. 1958.
ELIZABETH TITCOMB Parentage as above
Pink buds open to white flowers, of heavy substance, about 16 in
tall conical trusses. Strong growth habit. Larson. P.A. 1958.
JULIE TITCOMB   Parentage as above
Flowers carmine outside, blush pink within, slight crimson
spotting; large trusses of about 16. H. Larson. P.A. 1958.
* *
```
        -dichroanthum 1/2
DICHARB-
        -arboreum 1/2
```
Flowers of apricot. E. J. P. Magor, intro. 1936.

```
          -diaprepes 1/2
DICHDIAP-
          -dichroanthum 1/2
```
Introduced by E. J. P. Magor in 1938.

```
        -dichroanthum 1/2
DIDO-
        -decorum 1/2
```
3ft(.9m) 5F(-15C) ML 3/4 Orange-pink flowers, yellow center,
in lax trusses. Sturdy, compact plant. Wilding, intro. 1934.

DIETRICH   Described under DELILA, q.v.

```
                     -griffithianum 1/4
         -Glory of Leonardslee-
DIGNITY-             -unknown (1/4)
        -thomsonii 1/2
```
Rose red flowers. Lord Aberconway, 1950.

```
                  -neriiflorum 1/4
     -F. C. Puddle-
DIMITY-           -griersonianum 1/4
     -          -campylocarpum Elatum Group 1/4
     -Penjerrick-
                -griffithianum 1/4
```
Pale rose flowers. Lord Aberconway, 1946.

DING DONG   Described under REPOSE, q.v.

DINGALING   Described under EARTHSHAKER, q.v.

```
                              -haematodes 1/8
                -Humming Bird-
        -Mochica Moon-        -williamsianum 1/8
DINKY DOO-        -unknown 1/4
        -aberconwayi 1/2
```
Openly campanulate flowers, white without marks, held in trusses
of 7. Dwarf shrub, much wider than high. A. Hayes, reg. 1987.

DINTY MOORES   Described under CAROLINE ALLBROOK, q.v.

DINY DEE   Described under SPUN GOLD, q.v.

```
                  -arboreum 1/4
        -Red Argenteum-
DIOGENES-         -grande 1/4
        -calophytum 1/2
```
Very large plant; creamy pink flowers, dark blotch. Foliage and
flower resemble species parent, calophytum.   Rothschild, 1936.

```
        -neriiflorum 1/2
DIONE-              -arboreum 1/8
     -        -Cornubia-        -thomsonii 1/16
     -Cornsutch-    -Shilsonii-
     -          -         -barbatum 1/16
            -sutchuenense 1/4
```
Flowers colored carmine lake. E. J. P. Magor, 1936.

```
        -griffithianum 1/2
DIPHOLE PINK-
        -unknown 1/2
```
Flowers deep rose pink or cerise pink, faintly spotted in brown.
J. Waterer, Sons & Crisp. A.M. 1916. Color illus JS p. 55.

DIRECKTÖR E. HJELM   Second generation fortunei hybrid.
6ft(1.8m) -10F(-23C) ML Flowers dark carmine rose with bronze
blotch. D. Koster, reg. 1958.

```
                        -Queen      -griffithianum 1/16
                -Britannia- Wilhelmina-
                -         -         -unknown 5/16
        -Wilgen's Ruby-      -Stanley Davies--unknown
        -         -         -catawbiense 1/8
DIRECTEUR-         -John Walter-
 DORSMAN -         -unknown
        -        -haematodes 1/4
        -May Day-
               -griersonianum 1/4
```
A Dutch hybrid, with bright red flowers held in trusses of 6-10.
Research Sta. for Woody Nursery Crops, Boskoop, reg. 1979.

DISCA   Described under CADIS, q.v.

* *
```
          -yakushimanum 1/2
DISCRETION-      -fortunei 1/4
        -Fred  -                -fortunei ssp. discolor
        Wynniatt-    -Lady  -              1/16
              -Jalisco- Bessborough-campylocarpum Elatum Gp.
              -      -dichroanthum 1/16        1/16
                 -Dido-
                      -decorum 1/16
```
Pale purplish pink in bud, opening pale purplish pink in center,
moderate purplish pink at edges, brilliant yellow dorsal flare.
Trusses of 10-12 flowers, 7-lobed. Orange-yellow indumentum on
young foliage. Mr. & Mrs. R. J. R. Drayson, reg. 1987.
DORSET LASS   Parentage as above
Buds of strong purplish red, opening to pale orange-yellow, with
stripes and edges of deep purplish pink. Plant low and compact,
wider than high; foliage hairless. Drayson, reg. 1987.
GOSSAMER   Parentage as above
2ft(.6m) -5F(-21C) EM Deep pink and strong red in bud, opening pale yellow, lobes edged strong pink, with a flare in throat
of strong orange. Drayson, reg. 1987.
LORNA DOONE   Parentage as above
Truss of 13 flowers, 7-lobed, strong red in bud, opening to pale
yellow with deep purplish pink sinuses; fades to pale yellow;
strong greenish yellow flare in throat. Drayson, reg. 1987.
MISTRESS OF HARKWOOD   Parentage as above
Truss of 14-16 flowers, 7 very wavy-edged lobes; deep purplish
pink in bud, opening pale yellow, flushed moderate purplish pink

with dorsal flare strong greenish yellow.   Drayson, reg. 1987.
* *

DISPLAY   Parentage unknown
Rose-colored flowers, with a green blotch.   Kersey cross; Mrs.
Frederick, reg. 1976.

```
                         -dichroanthum
                 -Fabia-
      -unnamed hybrid-       -griersonianum
      -              -yakushimanum              -catawbiense
      -                          -Album Elegans-
DITTO-            -unnamed hybrid-            -unknown
      -    -Loder's-              -griffithianum
      -    - White -         -griffithianum
      -C. I. S.-     -Halopeanum-
      -                          -maximum
      -          -dichroanthum
                 -Fabia-
                    -griersonianum
```
1.5ft(.45m) OF(-18C) M See LODER'S WHITE for other possible
parentage. Flower Egyptian buff, azalea pink overlay; lax truss
of 5-7. Free-flowering. Rounded plant, almost as wide as tall;
glossy leaves held 1 year.   Childers, reg. 1982.

```
                 -fortunei ssp. discolor 1/4
      -Ladybird-
DIVA-       -Corona--unknown 1/4
      -griersonianum 1/2
```
6ft(1.8m) OF(-18C) ML 3/2   Brown indumentum shows the grier-
sonianum parentage. Medium-sized trusses of deep pink flowers,
specks of brown.   Rothschild, 1936.   A.M. 1937.

```
                                    -griffithianum 1/8
                         -George-
             -Mrs. Lindsay Smith- Hardy-catawbiense 1/16
             -                          -Duchess of Edinburgh--
      -Zuiderzee-                               unknown 1/4
      -         -                    -campylocarpum 1/8
      -         -unnamed hybrid-
DIXIE LEE-      -                    -unknown
RAY  -                               -griffithianum
      -                          -Kewense-
      -            -Aurora-         -fortunei 5/16
      -Naomi Pink Beauty-       -thomsonii 1/8
                         -fortunei
```
6ft(1.8m) 10F(-12C) EM 3/4 Flower of orchid pink, slight red
spotting, a white throat; 4.5in(11.5m) wide, 7 wavy lobes. High
dome-shaped trusses of 14-17. Floriferous. Plant wide as tall;
leaves 5in(12.7cm) long, held 3 years.   Larson, reg. 1979.

```
      -yakushimanum 1/2
DOC-
      -Corona--unknown 1/2
```
3ft(.9m) -15F(-26C) M 4/4 Flower rose pink with deeper rims,
spots on upper lobe; corolla 1.5in(3.5cm) across. Rounded truss
of 9. Plant vigorous, upright, compact.   John Waterer, Sons &
Crisp, reg. 1972.   H.C. 1978.   Color illus. JS p. 88.

```
      -fortunei 1/2
DOC TOLSTEAD-
      -unknown 1/2
```
Seed from Schumacher to Tolstead to Otto Prycl, raiser.

* *
```
                 -griffithianum 1/8
            -George Hardy-
      -Pink Pearl-       -catawbiense 3/8
      -       -       -arboreum 1/8
DOCTOR A. BLOK-       -Broughtonii-
      -                       -unknown 3/8
      -              -catawbiense
            -unnamed hybrid-
                 -unknown
```
6ft(1.8m) -5F(-21C) M 3/3 Large pink flowers with a lighter
center, pale yellow marks on upper lobe; in round truss. Plant
of good upright habit; medium green leaves 6in(15.2cm) long. L.
Endtz & Co.   A.M. 1937.   Color illus. VV p. 32.
DOCTOR ARNOLD W. ENDTZ   Parentage as above
Flowers fringed, of carmine red, tinted lilac.   L. Endtz, 1937.
* *

```
                              -dichroanthum 1/4
                 -Goldsworth Orange-
DOCTOR ANS-                -fortunei ssp. discolor 1/4
  HEYTING -
                 -Stanley Davies--unknown 1/2
```
A Dutch hybrid with flowers of deep salmon pink and an orange-
brown blotch.   Boskoop Res. Sta. for Arboriculture, reg. 1982.

DOCTOR ARNOLD W. ENDTZ   Described under DR. A. BLOK, q.v.

```
                    -oreotrephes 1/4
          -Goldstrike-        -cinnabarinum 1/8
DOCTOR   -       -Royal Flush-
  BIRDBATH-               -maddenii 1/8
          -cinnabarinum ssp. xanthocodon 1/2
```
5ft(1.5m) 10F(-12C) EM   Flowers Chinese yellow, orange shad-
ing, tubular bell-shaped; lax truss of 8. Plant branches well;
leaves very aromatic, held 3 years.   C. G. Heller, reg. 1980.

DOCTOR BOWMAN--selected arboreum lying between ssp. arboreum
               and ssp. delavayi   K W 21976
2.5ft(.75m) 10F(-12C) Dec.-Feb.   Cardinal red flowers, plum
purple nectaries at base; truss of 12. Spreading plant habit: 3
times as broad as tall; silvery indumentum.   Kingdon Ward collector, in Burma, 1956; Dr. P. Bowman, et al., raisers; E. Gor-
man, reg. 1982.   Color illus. ARS J 38:2 (1984), p. 55.

```
                              -neriiflorum 1/16
                 -unnamed-Nereid-
                 - hybrid-      -dichroanthum 1/16
          -Blondie-       -fortunei ssp. discolor 1/8
DOCTOR BRUCE-       -              -maximum 1/8
  BRADLEY  -       -Russell Harmon-
           -                       -catawbiense 1/8
           -catawbiense var. album Glass--Catalgla 1/2
```
Pale yellow flowers.   Orlando S. Pride, 1977.

```
                              -griffithianum 1/16
                 -George Hardy-
          -Pink Pearl-       -catawbiense 7/16
          -       -       -arboreum 1/16
      -Marion-       -Broughtonii-
      -       -              -unknown 7/16
DOCTOR   -              -catawbiense
C. H. FELIX-       -Catawbiense Grandiflorum-
      -                          -unknown
      -              -catawbiense
      -Prof. C. S. Sargent-
                 -unknown
```
Flowers fuchsine pink.   Felix & Dijkhuis, 1951.

```
                 -maximum 1/2              -griffithianum
                              -Queen Wilhelmina-
DOCTOR DENIS PERCELL-   -Britannia-       -unknown 3/16
      -       -       -Stanley Davies--unknown
                 -Leo-
                 -elliottii 1/4
```
7ft(2.1m)(16 yrs) -15F(-26C) ML   Truss of 16 flowers, strong
red with a deep red blotch. Rusty felt indumentum, young growth
only.   Col. & Mrs. R. H. Goodrich, reg. 1988.

```
                 -Tom Everett--unknown (Dexter hybrid)
DOCTOR ELTON TRUEBLOOD-
                 -Tom Brooks (yellow hybrid)--unknown
```
4ft(1.2m) x 4ft.(14 yrs) OF(-18C) M Flowers fragrant, 12 per
lax truss, 7-lobed, of pale purplish pink fading to cream white;
reverse pale purplish pink; 6 pale to medium yellow rays in the
throat.   Dr. E. Yelton cross; J. Todd, reg. 1987.

DOCTOR ERNST SCHÄLE   Described under GERTRUD SCHÄLE, q.v.

DOCTOR H. C. DRESSELHUYS Described under MRS. P. DEN OUDEN, q.v.

```
                 -Queen        -griffithianum
             -Britannia- Wilhelmina-        1/16
      -Linswegeanum-       -       -unknown 3/16
DOCTOR h. c. -       -       -Stanley Davies--unknown
KARL FOERSTER-       -forrestii Repens Group 1/4
      -williamsianum 1/2
```
(Dr. h. c. an honorary degree, honoris causa = for honor's sake)
Flowers deep rose pink, center paler, dark rose edges.   Hobbie,
1942-44.   Color illus. WS, 1989, p. 23.

DOCTOR H. J. LOVINK   Described under MRS. P. DEN OUDEN, q.v.

DOCTOR HENRY WADE   Described under DRUM MAJOR, q.v.

```
                    -wardii 1/4
          -Hawk-
          -    -Lady        -fortunei ssp. discolor 1/8
          -      Bessborough-
DOCTOR JOHN-                    -campylocarpum Elatum Group 1/8
   YEATES -                    -griffithianum 1/8
          -        -Loderi-
          -Ilam Cream-    -fortunei 1/8
                    -unknown 1/4
```
Truss of 15-16 flowers, magenta rose in bud, open to rhodamine
pink. Dr. J. S. Yeates cross; Mr. & Mrs. R. Perry, reg. 1981.

```
                         -maximum 1/8
               -unnamed hybrid-
          -Tahiti-             -catawbiense 1/8
          -     -unnamed-dichroanthum 1/8
DOCTOR LEWIS-      hybrid-         -fortunei ssp. discolor 1/16
   SANTINI -      -unnamed-
          -             hybrid-campylocarpum 1/16
          -catawbiense var. album Glass--Catalgla 1/2
```
6ft.(1.8m) -25F(-32C) ML   Mr. Pride called it a very hardy
plant. Pale yellow flowers; informal truss. O. S. Pride, 1975.

```
                    -Mira--unknown 1/4
          -Leopold-
DOCTOR MASTERS-    -catawbiense 1/4
          -azalea japonicum 1/2
```
5ft(1.5m) -15F(-26C) ML   4/3   Azaleodendron. Seed parent
might be PRINCE CAMILLE DE ROHAN, a caucasicum hybrid. Bright
pink in bud, opening to salmon with a yellowish tinge.   G.
Vander Meulen, 1892.

```
                    -ponticum 1/4
          -Purple Splendour-
DOCTOR NORMAN BETHUNE-        -unknown 1/4
          -fortunei 1/2
```
20ft(6.0m) x 15ft(4.5m)(12 yrs) -25F(-32C) ML   Flowers in
trusses of 12, broadly funnel-shaped, 7 wavy lobes, light purple
edging, shading to very pale purple in center, dark red blotch
in throat. Rudy Behring, reg. 1985.

* *
```
                    -ciliicalyx 1/4
          -Else Frye-
DOCTOR RICHARD ANDERSON-    -unknown 1/4
          -johnstoneanum 1/2
```
3ft(.9m) 15F(-9C) E   Large white flowers, to 4.25in(10.8cm)
wide, edges blushed pink, an orange blotch; trusses of about 6.
Stiff branches. R. Anderson cross; Dr. H. Braafladt, reg. 1979.
HUMBOLDT SUNRISE   Parentage as above
3ft(.9m) 15F(-9C) EM 4/3   Flowers Naples yellow with darker
blotch, openly funnel-shaped 3.25in(8.3cm) across in trusses of
6; heavy carnation fragrance. Plant wider than tall, leaves
with hairy margins. R. Anderson Cross; Braafladt, reg. 1979.
Color illus. ARS Q 33:1 (1979), cover.
QUALA-A-WA-LOO   Parentage as above
2.5ft(.75m) 15F(-9C) E 4/3   Plant twice as wide as tall,
glossy leaves, hairy margins, scaly below. Flowers empire
yellow with medium red blotch; small truss of 4-5. Anderson
cross; Braafladt, reg. 1979.
SUPER JAY   Parentage as above
2.5ft(.75m) 15F(-9C) E   Broader than tall, medium grass green
leaves, scaly below. Flowers fragrant, 3.5in(9cm) wide, white
with dorsal blotch of orange; small truss. Dr. Anderson cross;
Dr. Braafladt raiser; reg. 1979.
* *
* *
```
                    -caucasicum 1/4
          -Boule de Neige-          -catawbiense 1/8
DOCTOR RICHARD-        -unnamed hybrid-
   MERIAM  -               -unknown 1/8
          -vernicosum--Mt. Siga 1/2
```
4ft(1.2m) -20F(-29C) M   Clear pink flowers in loose trusses.
Plant very compact. Orlando S. Pride, 1977.
DR. WILLIAM FLEMING   Parentage as above
4ft(1.2m) -10F(-23C) M   Blooms a very pretty peach color.
Compact plant habit. O. Pride, 1975.
* *

```
                    -houlstonii (Gable's) 1/2
DOCTOR ROCK-
          -vernicosum (R 18139) 1/2
```
Openly funnel-campanulate flowers of light peach pink, 4in(10cm)
across. Better plant habit than vernicosum.   Joseph Gable.

```
                    -griersonianum 1/2
DOCTOR ROSS-             -arboreum 1/8
          -        -Doncaster-
          -Borde Hill-    -unknown 1/4
          -             -griffithianum 1/8
                    -Mrs. A. M. Williams-
                         -unknown
```
Deep maroon in bud, with flowers bright red, funnel-shaped, in
rounded trusses. Plant habit spreading; pointed, medium green
leaves 6in(15.2in) long. Rudolph Henny, reg. 1958.

```
                    -caucasicum 1/2
DOCTOR STOCKER-
          -griffithianum 1/2
```
5ft(1.5m) 0F(-18C) M 3/3 Plant wider than tall; thick, vein-
ed foliage; pest-resistant. Campanulate flowers, ivory white, 3
in(7.5cm) across.   G. Abbey raiser, gardener to Dr. Stocker, at
Avery Hill; Veitch intro. A.M. 1900.   Color illus. JS p. 94.

DOCTOR TJEBBES   Parentage unknown
6ft(1.8m) -5F(-21C) ML   Flowers roseine purple, in trusses of
14-16. Foliage dark green, to 5.5in(14cm) long.   C. A. van den
Akker, reg. 1969. A.M. Boskoop 1967.

```
                         -catawbiense 1/4
               -Charles Dickens-
DOCTOR V. H. RUTGERS-    -unknown 3/4
               -Lord Roberts--unknown
```
5ft(1.5m) -15F(-26C) ML 3/3   Flowers of bright crimson,
frilled. Plant wide-growing, dense; dark green leaves. H. den
Ouden, 1925. Color illus. VV p. 66.

DOCTOR W. F. WERY   Described under BRITANNIA, q.v.

DOCTOR WILLIAM FLEMING Described under DR. RICHARD MERIAM, q.v.

DOKER-LA--form of primuliflorum var. cephalanthoides
Not now recognized as a separate species by the RBG, Edinburgh.
A compact truss of 10-12 flowers, spirea red, paling to near
white at edges. Inside corolla tube densely hairy. Aromatic
leaves to 1in(2.5cm) long, glossy dark green; heavy indumentum.
Sir James Horlick, raiser; P. A. Cox, reg. 1980.   A.M. 1980.

DOLL   Described under CATHY, q.v.

```
                    -fortunei ssp. discolor 1/4
          -Sir Frederick-        -arboreum ssp. zeylanicum 1/8
DOLLAR  - Moore      -St. Keverne-
 PRINCESS-               -griffithianum 1/8
          -     -griersonianum 1/4
          -Tally Ho-
                    -facetum (eriogynum) 1/4
```
Trusses of very deep carmine pink. E. de Rothschild, reg. 1967.

```
                    -griffithianum 1/4
          -Dawn's Delight-
DOLLY-             -unknown 1/4
          -griersonianum 1/2
```
Pink flowers in drooping truss. Habit tall.   Rothschild, 1940.

DOLLY MADISON   Described under BRAVO!, q.v.

```
                    -dichroanthum 1/4
          -Fabia Tangerine-
DOLLY  -             -griersonianum 1/4
 MIXTURE-    -wardii 1/4
          -Crest-             -fortunei ssp. discolor 1/8
          -Lady           -
          Bessborough-campylocarpum Elatum Group 1/8
```
5ft(1.5m) 0F(-18C) M Funnel-shaped flowers, truss of 9, open-
ing deep pink, fading to pale yellow, striped deep pink. Calyx
pinkish cream. J. May, reg. 1987.

```
          -dichroanthum 1/2
DOLPHIN-
          -crinigerum 1/2
```

Salmon pink flowers, hose-in-hose, 2.5in(6.4cm) across; 12 held
in flat trusses.   Gen. Harrison, reg. 1962.

```
                               -arboreum 1/8
                -Glory of Penjerrick-
      -Barclayi-                     -griffithianum 1/4
      -            -thomsonii 1/2
DOMINO-                              -griffithianum
      -            -Glory of Leonardslee-
      -Dignity-                      -unknown 1/8
                -thomsonii
```
Red flowers. Lord Aberconway, 1950.

DON BRUNTON   Parentage unknown
Flowers in trusses of 4, rose madder in bud. opening blush white
with rose madder on back of lobes, orange flare on upper throat.
Leaves narrowly elliptic with reddish brown dense scales. Mrs.
P. Hartree, req. 1984.

DON ERNESTO   Described under THE DON, q.v.

DONA TIZIA   Described under THE DON, q.v.

DONALD WATERER   ALICE x GOMER WATERER
Deep rose pink, paler in center.   Waterer & Crisp. A.M. 1916.

DONAR   Described under DELILA, q.v.

```
           -arboreum 1/2
DONCASTER-
           -unknown 1/2
```
3ft(.9m) -5F(-21C) M 2/3   Brilliant crimson scarlet flowers,
2.5in(6.4cm) wide; rounded trusses. Plant broadly dome-shaped;
very dark green glossy leaves. Easy to grow; heat-tolerant. A
standby since the late 1800s. Often a parent. A. Waterer.

```
           -fortunei ssp. discolor 1/2
DONDIS-            -arboreum 1/4
      -Doncaster-
                  -unknown 1/4
```
A parent of CATHY, CONFECTION. Royal Botanical Garden, Kew.

DONEWELL PINK   Parentage unknown
A fine bi-color of white, edged in pink. Grown and distributed
by Holden Arboretum, Mentor, OH. Hardy to -15F(-26C). Donewell
Nursery intro.

DONNA ANITA   Described under THE DON, q.v.

DONNA FLORENZA   Described under THE DON, q.v.

* *
```
             -fortunei 1/2
DONNA HARDGROVE-            -wardii 1/4
             -unnamed hybrid-
                           -dichroanthum 1/4
```
3ft(.9m) -5F(-21C) ML   Plant round, broader than tall; leaves
held 1 year. Flowers apricot pink, flushed yellow, 2.5in(6.4cm)
wide; lax trusses of 8. Hardgrove cross; Burns, reg. 1979.
HARDGROVE'S DEEPEST YELLOW   Probably a sibling of the above.
Flowers deep yellow; truss a bit lax. Bud hardy 0F(-18C).
* *

```
             -racemosum ? 1/2
DONNA TOTTEN-
             -unknown 1/2
```
4ft(1.2m) -5F(-21C) EM 3/3   Medium-sized plant; attractive
foliage like racemosum. Flowers pink, touch of cream. Nearing.

```
               -campylocarpum 1/4
      -Unique-
DONNIE-        -unknown 1/4
      -wightii 1/2
```
Flowers cream-colored, spotted with port wine red on upper lobe;
15-flowered trusses. Sir James Horlick, reg. 1962.

```
             -haematodes ssp. chaetomallum 1/2
DONNINGTON-       -neriiflorum Euchaites Group 1/4
           -Portia-
                  -strigillosum 1/4
```
Loose trusses of 9 cardinal red flowers, 2in(5cm) wide, funnel-
campanulate. Leaves 4.5in(11.5cm) long, with loose, light brown

indumentum.   Crown Estate, Windsor, reg. 1967.   P.C. 1966.

```
                -yakushimanum 1/2
DONVALE PEARL-        -arboreum 1/4
             -unnamed hybrid-
                           -unknown 1/4
```
Trusses hold 28 flowers, bright spinel red, tubular bell-shaped.
R. J. O'Shannassy, reg. 1983.

DONVALE PINK DRIFT   Described under FIREFLY, q.v.

```
                               -griffithianum
                -Queen Wilhelmina-        1/16
                -Britannia-        -unknown 5/16
      -Lamplighter-      -Stanley Davies--unknown
DONVALE-      -               -fortunei 1/8
RUBY  -      -Madame Fr. J. Chauvin-
      -arboreum 1/2              -unknown
```
Trusses of 14-16 flowers, tubular bell-shaped, scarlet red.
Height about 3ft(.9m).   J. O'Shannassy, reg. 1984.

```
                     -facetum (eriogynum) 1/8
              -unnamed hybrid-
      -unnamed hybrid-        -unknown 1/8
      -           -        -dichroanthum 1/4
DOPEY-        -Fabia-
      -              -griersonianum 1/4
      -              -yakushimanum 1/4
      -unnamed hybrid-        -dichroanthum
             -Fabia Tangerine-
                     -griersonianum
```
3ft(.9m) 5F(-15C) M 4/4   Flowers glossy red, paling toward
margins with dark brown spots on upper lobe, campanulate, 2.5in
(6.4cm) across; 16-flowered spherical trusses. Floriferous.
Plant compact, vigorous; dull green leaves, 4in(10.2cm) long.
Waterer, & Crisp, reg. 1971. A.M. 1977. F.C.C. Wisley Trials
1979.   Color illus. Cox pl. 47; HG p. 88.

```
             -minus Carolinianum Group 1/2
DORA AMATEIS-
             -ciliatum 1/2
```
3ft(.9m) -15F(-26C) EM 4/4   White flowers lightly spotted
green, about 2in(5cm) across, in clusters of 3-6. Floriferous.
Plant twice as wide as high; deep green, dense foliage, bronze
highlights if grown in full sun; aromatic. Amateis, 1955. A.E.
no date; A.M. 1976. F.C.C. Wisley Trials 1981. Color illus.
Cox pl. 48; VV p. 16; ARS J 43:4 (1989), p. 182.

```
              -thomsonii 1/4
       -Bagshot Ruby-
DORCAS-       -unknown 1/4
       -fortunei ssp. discolor 1/2
```
Rose pink flowers; medium-sized trusses.   Rothschild, 1936.

```
       -Jay Gould--unknown 1/2
DORIA-
       -degronianum ssp. heptamereum (metternichii) 1/2
```
Flowers salmon pink with yellow markings.   T. J. R. Seidel.

```
            -griersonianum 1/2
DORINTHIA-        -haematodes 1/4
          -Hiraethlyn-
                  -griffithianum 1/4
```
3ft(.9m) 5F(-15C) M   Flowers of clear shiny red with deep wavy
lobes. Lord Aberconway, 1938. F.C.C. 1938.

DORIS BIGLER   Complex parentage including catawbiense, maximum,
               and possibly unknown hybrids
6ft(1.8m) -15F(-26C) M Small flower 2in(5cm) across, of light
purple, strong reddish purple edging and yellow blotch, 5 very
frilled lobes; 17 per truss, ball-shaped. Plant rounded; rather
glossy, olive green leaves. W. D. Smith, reg. 1979.

```
                -griffithianum 1/2
        -Loderi-
DORIS CAROLINE-        -fortunei 1/4
        -              -griffithianum
        -Lady Bligh-
                  -unknown 1/4
```
5ft(1.5m) -5F(-21C) M   Truss of 10-12 flowers, rose colored,
of 6-7 lobes. Plant upright, tall; leaves 6in(15cm) long.   R.
Henny, reg. 1961. P.A. 1960.

DORIS MOSS   Described under GWERFYL MOSS, q.v.

```
                    -griffithianum 1/4
        -Dawn's Delight-
DORMOUSE-               -unknown 1/4
        -williamsianum 1/2
```
3ft(.9m) OF(-18C) EM 3/4   Neat, compact, dome-shaped bush.
Bell-shaped flowers, delicate pink, deeper edges, in loose clusters. Oval leaf, copper-colored when young.   Rothschild, 1936.

```
            -griffithianum 1/2
DOROTHEA-
            -decorum 1/2
```
Flowers of white flushed pink, with green center. Very sweetly
fragrant. Lowinsky, 1925. A.M. 1925.

```
                                        -catawbiense 1/8
                    -Catawbiense Grandiflorum-
            -America-                    -unknown 5/8
DOROTHY AMATEIS-        -dark red hybrid--unknown
            -                    -ponticum 1/4
            -Purple Splendour-
                        -unknown
```
5ft(1.5m) -15F(-26C) ML 4/3 Large truss of rosy purple flow-
ers with a deeper purple eye. Rounded plant, wider than high;
leaves olive green 5in(12.7cm) long, held upright. E. Amateis,
raiser; W. Baldsiefen, reg. 1972.   Color illus. HG p. 150.

DOROTHY LEE   Described under JEROME KERN, q.v.

* *
```
                    -forrestii Repens Group 1/4
        -Elizabeth-
DOROTHY -               -griersonianum 1/4
 LONSDALE-             -thomsonii 1/4
        -Helen Fox-                    -arboreum 1/8
                    -Glory of Penjerrick-
                            -griffithianum 1/8
```
An Australian hybrid. Scarlet red flowers, with slight spotting
on the upper lobes. H. D. Rose, reg. 1973.
FOREST BLAZE Parentage as above
Trusses of 8-10 flowers, campanulate, guardsman red.   Height
about 7ft(2.1m). K. van de Ven, reg. 1984.
* *

```
                                -griffithianum 1/8
                    -unnamed hybrid-
        -Mrs. Furnivall-          -unknown 1/2
        -             -              -caucasicum 1/8
DOROTHY PEAKE-          -unnamed hybrid-
        -                        -unknown
        -                -ponticum 1/4
        -Purple Splendour-
                    -unknown
```
3ft(.9m) -10F(-23C) EM   Buds purplish pink; flowers yellowish
with wide edging of deep purplish pink and dark red spotting; 13
per truss. Olive green foliage. Walter Elliott cross; Mrs. A.
J. Holden, reg. 1988.


```
                -Vincent van Gogh--unknown 1/2
DOROTHY PESTE ANDERSON-                -griffithianum 1/4
                -Loderi King George-
                            -fortunei 1/4
```
4ft(1.2m) 5F(-15C) ML   Tight trusses of 24 fragrant flowers,
light solferino purple, 7-lobed. Plant as wide as tall, leaves
8in(20cm) long. Fred Peste, cross 1975; Anne Sather, reg. 1985.


```
        -campylocarpum, Hooker's form 1/2
DOROTHY ROBBINS-          -fortunei ssp. discolor 1/4
            -Margaret Dunn-      -dichroanthum 1/8
                        -Fabia-
                            -griersonianum 1/8
```
3ft(.9m) OF(-18C) M 4/4   Plant as broad as tall at 10 years.
Flowers 4in(10.2cm) wide, empire yellow. L. Brandt, reg. 1970.

DOROTHY RUSSELL Described under ACCLAIM, q.v.

```
            -wardii 3/8            -griffithianum
        -Idealist-        -Kewense-          3/128
        -       -       -Aurora-    -fortunei 13/64
    -unnamed-        -Naomi-      -thomsonii 1/32
    - hybrid-        -fortunei
    -       -        -fortunei
    -       -Fawn-      -dichroanthum 1/16
    -       -Fabia-
    -               -griersonianum 1/16
    -               -wardii
DOROTHY-    -Crest-          -fortunei ssp. discolor
YARGUS -    -       -Lady Bess--          3/32
    -       -       borough -campylocarpum Elatum 3/32
    -  -Lemon-                -George-griffithianum
    -  -Cust--          -Mrs. Lind--Hardy-
    - - ard -          -say Smith  -catawbiense
    - -       -Mrs. Betty-    -Duchess of  1/128
    -unn-    - -Robertson -       Edinburgh--unk
    hyb-  -unn-          - -campylocarpum 1/64
    -       hyb-          -unn-
    -       -wardii      hyb-unknown 1/32
    -Crest (as above)
```
3ft x 3ft(.9m) OF(-18C) ML   Flowers of heavy substance in
trusses of 10, buds of strong red opening deep pink at margins
shading to light yellow then brilliant yellow in throat. R. Yar-
gus raiser; Bruce Briggs intro.; F. Watters cross; reg. 1989.


```
                -augustinii ssp. chasmanthum 1/4
        -Electra-
                -augustinii ssp. augustinii 1/2
DORSET BLUE-                -intricatum 1/8
        -           -Intrifast-
        -Blue Diamond-      -fastigiatum 1/8
                -augustinii ssp. augustinii
```
4ft(1.2m) -5F(-21C) M   Broadly funnel-shaped flowers, 4 per
truss, of strong violet. J. May, reg. 1988.


```
                -Moser's Maroon--unknown 1/4
        -Grenadier-
DORSET CANDY-          -elliottii 1/4
        -   -wardii 1/4
            -Crest-              -fortunei ssp. discolor 1/8
                -Lady Bessborough-
                        -campylocarpum Elatum Gp. 1/8
```
4ft(1.2m) 5F(-15C) M Buds strong pink, opening pale yellowish
pink; flowers held in trusses of 14.   J. May, reg. 1988.

DORSET LASS Described under DISCRETION, q.v.

```
        -caucasicum--Cunningham's Sulphur 1/2
DORSET LEMON-
        -eclecteum 1/2
```
2ft(.6m) OF(-18C) E   Trusses of 15-18 flowers, campanulate,
light greenish yellow to pale yellowish green. May, reg. 1988.

DOSHONG LA--form of mekongense Viridescens Group
3ft(.9m) OF(-18C) ML 3/3   Rounded truss of 5 flowers, light
yellow, flushed old rose at tips. Aromatic small leaves tinged
bronze. Kingdon Ward collector; P. Cox; reg. 1972.   A.M. 1972.

```
                        -griffithianum 1/4
                -unnamed hybrid-
        -Mrs. Furnivall-      -unknown 1/4
        -           -       -caucasicum 1/8
        -           -unnamed hybrid-
DOSIDO-                  -unknown
        -               -lacteum 1/8
        -   -unnamed hybrid-      -campylocarpum 1/16
        -   -       -Mary Swaythling-
        -Unimak-              -fortunei 3/16
        -           -griffithianum
        -Loderi King George-
                    -fortunei
```
5ft(1.5m) x 5ft 10F(-12C) M Flowers held in trusses of 12-15,
phlox pink in bud, fading to white with age, dorsal spotting
barium yellow. Truss 7in(18cm) across.   J. Elliott, reg. 1986.

```
                    -griffithianum 1/8
            -George Hardy-
    -Mrs. Lindsay Smith-      -catawbiense 1/8
DOT-            -Duchess of Edinburgh--unknown 1/4
    -fortunei 1/2
```

5ft(1.5m) -10F(-23C) M 4/3   Large white flowers of unusual
satiny texture, spotted, in big trusses. Plant habit upright,
open. Lord Swaythling, intro. 1945. A.M. 1945.

DOT'S CHERRY JUBILEE   Parentage unknown
5ft(1.5m)? -5F(-21C)? ML? As in Cox: Cherry pink flowers
with deep burgundy blotch. Similar to BEN MOSELEY, but deeper
color, larger flowers. Dexter cross; Schlaikjer, before 1978.

* *
```
                        -brachycarpum 1/8
               -unnamed-       -wardii 1/16
              - hybrid-Crest-        -fortunei ssp. discolor
        -unnamed-         -Lady  -                       1/32
        - hybrid-         Bessborough-campylocarpum Elatum Gp.
        -          -maximum 1/8                          1/32
DOUBLE-     -Stokes Bronze Wings-
   DARE -                 -catawbiense 1/8
        -                   -Pygmalion--unknown 1/16
        -               -unnamed-
        -             -Weldy- hybrid-haematodes 1/16
     -Robert Weldon-   -yakushimanum, Exbury form 1/8
        -               -yakushimanum 1/8
            -Serendipity-
                   -aureum (chrysanthum) 1/8
```
Buds deep and strong reds; flowers yellowish white edged with
strong purplish red; underside of petals veined strong red;
petaloid flowers; dark red stigma. W. Delp.
X-ACTLY GREAT   Parentage as above
Buds of moderate reddish orange, deep and moderate pink; flowers
light and pale pink; dorsal spots vivid yellow-green. W. Delp.
* *

DOUBLE DATE   Parentage unknown
5ft(1.5m) -5F(-21C) M 4/3   Truss holds 10; double-flowered,
of deep purplish pink. Whitney cross; Sathers named; Mrs. W. O.
Griswold, reg. 1977.

DOUBLE DIAMOND--form of johnstoneanum, double form
Unusual, fully double flowers like creamy yellow gardenias, with
trusses of 2 or 3 flowers, each corolla 4in(10.2cm) across, 3in.
(7.6cm) long. Crown Estate, Windsor, reg. 1963. A.M. 1956.

DOUBLE DIP   Described under ANNA H. Hall, q.v.
```
            -griersonianum 3/8
            -                       -griffithianum 9/64
      -Anna Rose-          -George-
      - Whitney -       -Pink - Hardy-catawbiense 9/64
      -                  -Pearl-        -arboreum 3/64.
      -           -Countess-   -Broughtonii-
      -           of Derby-            -unknown 19/64
DOUBLE-     -          -catawbiense
   DRAKE-           -Cynthia-
      -                  -griffithianum
      -            -griersonianum
      -                         -griffithianum
      -    -Anna Rose-          -George-
      -    - Whitney -       -Pink - Hardy-catawbiense
   -unnamed-        -         -Pearl-        -arboreum
      hybrid-   -Countess-    -Broughtonii-
      -         -of Derby-              -unknown
   -unknown     -         -catawbiense
                  -Cynthia-
                      -griffithianum
```
3ft(1.2m) 10F(-12C) M   Red flowers with slight grayed orange
spotting, tubular funnel-shaped, 2in(5cm) wide, 5 frilled lobes.
Floriferous. Plant as broad as tall, rounded, arching branches;
narrow leaves. E. Drake, cross; Diane Lux, reg. 1981.


```
         -unknown 3/4
DOUBLE DUTCH-          -wardii 1/4
          -Carolyn Grace-
                    -unknown
```
2.5ft(.75m) 15F(-9C) EM   Flowers medium pink, light shell pink
throat, stripe down center of lobes, deep pink edging; 7 frilled
lobes, hose-in-hose. Plant well-branched, wide as tall, matte
olive green leaves. Ben Briggs cross; E. L. Knight, reg. 1980.

```
              -yakushimanum 1/4
         -                  -fortunei ssp. discolor 3/64
      -Si Si-        -Lady
      -          -Day -Bessborough-campylocarpum Elatum 1/64
      -     -Gold -Dream-
      -       Mohur-     -griersonianum 3/64
unnamed-     -               -fortunei ssp. discolor
  hybrid-      -Margaret Dunn-   -dichroanthum 1/64
      -                    -Fabia-
      -          -yakushimanum    -griersonianum
   -Serendipity-
DOUBLE-      -aureum 1/8
 FLOAT -                         -griffithianum 7/64
      -          -Jean Marie de Montague-
      -Fireman Jeff-          -unknown 13/64
      -               -haematodes 1/16
      -        -Grosclaude-
      -               -facetum 1/16
  Tom -                              -catawbiense
  Ring -            -Parsons Grandiflorum-      1/32
  M.D. -      -America-            -unknown
      -   -unnamed-   -dark red hybrid--unknown
      -   - hybrid-      -griffithianum
      -   -         -Mars-
   -Anna-     -Blaze-   -unknown
   Delp-      -catawbiense var. rubrum 1/32
      -       -         -griffithianum
      -         -Mars-
      -Red Brave-   -unknown          -catawbiense
      -            -Parsons Grandiflorum-
         -America-            -unknown
              -dark red hybrid--unknown
```
DOUBLE FLOAT = (SI SI x SERENDIPITY) X TOM RING, M.D. as fully
diagramed above. Blend of yellowish white and strong red in
bud, opens to blend of yellowish white and strong pink, dorsal
spots cardinal red. Flowers fully hose in hose. W. Delp.

DOUBLE TAKE   Described under YOO HOO, q.v.

DOUBLE TROUBLE   Described under BEWILDERED, q.v.


```
            -brachycarpum 1/4
      -unnamed-    -wardii 1/8
      - hybrid-Crest-     -fortunei ssp. discolor
DOUBLE VISION-     -Lady Bess- -            1/16
      -           borough  -campylocarpum Elatum
      -               -maximum 1/4           1/16
   -Stokes Bronze Wings-
            -catawbiense 1/4
```
Flowers yellowish white with a light yellowish green flare;
dorsal spots moderate red. W. Delp.


```
         -strigillosum 1/2
DOUBLE WINNER-
      -unknown 1/2
```
5ft(1.5m) OF(-18C) EM 4/4   Tight trusses of bright red.
Foliage dull, long, indumented, sometimes yellowish. H. Larson
intro. Color illus. 43:3 (1989), p. 146.

* *
```
               -wardii 1/4
      -Carolyn Grace-
DOUBLOONS-      -unknown 1/4
      -        -campylocarpum 1/4
      -Moonstone-
            -williamsianum 1/4
```
4ft(1.2m) -5F(-21C) EM 3/4 A rounded, compact plant. Creamy
yellow flowers, to 5in(12.7cm) across, widely funnel-shaped;
loose trusses of 10.   A. Wright, reg. 1963.
HONEYDEW   Parentage as above
4ft(1.2m) 5F(-15C) M 3/4   Compact plant with flowers sunny
yellow like MOONSTONE in trusses of 5-7. A. Wright, reg. 1963.
SHOW-OFF   Parentage as above, except reversed
Compact, mounded plant. Flowers cup-shaped, clear pale yellow;
lax trusses. Called "extinct"--Kraxberger. Wright, reg. 1964.
SUGAR PLUM   Parentage: MOONSTONE X CAROLYN GRACE
3ft(.9m) OF(-18C) EM 3/3   Deep pink flowers, widely funnel-
shaped to 3in(7.6cm) wide, in lax trusses of 5-8. Dense, small-
leafed plant. A. Wright, reg. 1964.
* *

```
* * * * * * * * * * * * * * * * * * * * * * * * *
          -Mrs. Davies Evans--unknown 9/16
DOUG  -    -catawbiense v. album Glass--Catalgla 1/8
KLOUGH-    -Tony's-         -catawbiense 1/16
   -    - Gift -   -Catawbiense Album-
   -Micro-   -Belle -            -unknown
     flare -   Heller-            -catawbiense
     -            -white catawbiense sdl-
     -                -maximum 1/8    -unknown
        -unnamed hybrid-
                 -vernicosum (18139) 1/8
```
Buds deep reddish purple open to frilled flowers of strong and
light purples; a white flare; dorsal spots yellow-green.   Al
Smith cross; W. Delp raiser.
PICOTEED BEAUTY   Parentage as above
Buds of violet and beetroot purple; flowers very pale purple
heavily edged imperial purple and purplish pink; dorsal spotting
light yellow-green.   Al Smith cross; W. Delp raiser.

```
* * * * * * * * * * * * * * * * * * * * * * * *
```

DOUGGIE BETTERIDGE   Described under FRED WYNNIATT, q.v.

```
                   -griffithianum 1/4
          -unnamed hybrid-
DOUGLAS McEWAN-         -unknown 3/4
          -Monsieur Thiers--unknown
```
6ft(1.8m) 0F(-18C) M 3/3   A large shrub, holding trusses of 12
rosy red flowers.   C. B. van Nes & Sons, before 1958.

```
* * * * * * * * * * * * * * * * * * * * * * * *
                         -griffithianum 1/4
          -Jean Marie de Montague-
DOUGLAS R. STEPHENS-           -unknown 3/4
          -unnamed white hybrid--unknown
```
4ft(1.2m) -10F(-23C) EM 4/4   Rose red buds open to spinel red
flowers, dark red blotch in throat; 14 in tall conical trusses.
Upright plant, broader than tall; dark green, glossy leaves, 7in.
(17.8cm) long.   Mr. & Mrs. J. Freeman Stephens, reg. 1973.
FREEMAN R. STEPHENS   Parentage as above
5ft(1.5m) -5F(-21C) M   Plant wider than tall, glossy dark
green leaves. Fragrant flower, 4in(10cm) wide, cherry red, deep
red spots; to 15 in truss 9in(23cm) high.   Stephens, reg. 1973.

```
* * * * * * * * * * * * * * * * * * * * * * * *

                 -fortunei ssp. discolor 1/4
         -King of Shrubs-    -dichroanthum 1/8
         -             -Fabia-
DOUG'S GREENEYES-            -griersonianum 3/8
         -            -Corona-unknown 1/8
         -    -unnamed hybrid-     -griffithianum 1/16
         -Flame-          -Loderi-
                 -griersonianum    -fortunei 1/16
```
8ft(2.4m) 0F(-18C) M   Flowers in loose trusses of 13-15; 7-
lobed, Neyron rose, green center. Plant tall, open; dark green
leaf 5.5in(13.3cm) long.   H. Lem cross; Britt Smith, reg. 1972.

```
            -dichroanthum 1/4
         -Dido-
DOVER ROSE-    -decorum 1/4
      -       -wardii ? 1/4
      -Chlorops-
               -vernicosum ? 1/4
```
6ft(1.8m) x 6ft(16 yrs) 0F(-18C) ML Lax truss of 10 flowers,
5 wavy-edged lobes, peach pink. M. Stewart, reg. 1987.

DRAGON   Listed with PHOEBUS, q.v.

```
         -auriculatum 1/2
DRAGONFLY-
         -facetum (eriogynum) 1/2
```
A late-flowering plant that grows to a large, dense shrub, with
long, narrow, hairy leaves. Flowers resemble auriculatum, but
carmine rather than pink or white.   Parentage as in Rothschild
Rhododendrons.   Rothschild, 1936.

```
          -wardii 1/2
DRAKE'S ORCHID-
          -fortunei ssp. discolor 1/2
```
4ft(1.2m) 10F(-12C) ML   Lavender flowers with a mimosa yellow
throat, grayed orange spotting, openly funnel-shaped, 2.5in.
(6.4cm) across, 5 to 7 frilled lobes. Upright plant with stiff
branches; glossy leaves.   E. Drake cross; Diane Lux, reg. 1981.

```
* * * * * * * * * * * * * * * * * * * * * * * * *
             -Lady       -fortunei ssp. discolor 3/8
          -Day Dream- Bessborough-
          -                     -campylocarpum Elatum Group 1/8
DREAM GIRL-      -griersonianum 3/8
          -         -fortunei ssp. discolor
          -Margaret Dunn--dichroanthum 1/8
                  -Fabia-
                      -griersonianum
```
Flowers orange buff, a blood red throat. L. E. Brandt, 1953.
GOLD MOHUR   Parentage as above
5ft(1.5m) 0F(-18C) ML 4/3   Flowers 3in(7.6cm) wide, funnel-
shaped, golden yellow, rainbow pink marking the division of each
petal; truss of 12. Leaves myrtle green.   Brandt. P.A. 1955.
GOLDEN PHEASANT   Parentage as above
4ft(1.2m) 5F(-15C) ML 3/3   Flower 4.5in(11.5cm) across, 8 per
truss, golden yellow, orange blotch. Brandt, reg. 1966.
MOHUR   Parentage as above; may be extinct.
SHAH JEHAN   Parentage as above
Compact habit, rounded leaves. Warm chrome yellow flowers, with
burnt orange spotting. Brandt, reg. 1966.

```
* * * * * * * * * * * * * * * * * * * * * * * * *
                            -catawbiense--
                    -unnamed hybrid- La Bar's White 1/16
            -unnamed        -fortunei 1/16
      -Vinecrest- hybrid-wardii (croceum) 1/8
      -          -wardii Litiense Group 1/4
DREAM  -               -Pygmalion--unknown 1/16
MACHINE-     -unnamed hybrid-
      -       -Weldy-       -haematodes 1/16
      -unnamed-   -yakushimanum, Exbury form 1/8
       hybrid-     -yakushimanum 1/8
          -Serendipity-
                  -aureum (chrysanthum) 1/8
```
Buds of jasper red and pale greenish yellow; flowers pale yel-
low-green; dorsal spots jasper red.   Al Smith cross; W. Delp
raiser.

DREAM MAKER   Described under BORN FREE, q.v.

DREAM OF KINGS   Described under BLUE RHAPSODY, q.v.

```
                -maximum 1/4
         -unnamed hybrid-
         -             -vernicosum 18139 1/4
         -              -brachycarpum 1/8
DREAMBOAT-    -unnamed--wardii 1/16
         -     - hybrid-Crest-       -fortunei ssp. discolor
         -     -            -Lady    -          1/32
         -     -            Bessborough-campylocarpum El. 1/32
         -unnamed-                    -catawbiense
          hybrid-       -Parsons Grandiflorum-      1/32
         -     -America-        -unknown 1/8
         -     -      -dark red hybrid--unknown
          -Cindy-         -griffithianum 1/32
            Lou -        -Mars-
          -unnamed hybrid-   -unknown
                       -catawbiense v. rubrum 1/16
```
Blend of strong purplish red, Tyrian purple and rose Bengal in
bud, opens to frilled flowers light purplish pink, lightly
tinted Tyrian purple. Flowers 6 to 7-lobed.   W. Delp.

DREAMLAND   Parentage: FABIA x fortunei ssp. discolor x griersonianum x facetum x yakushimanum x JALISCO, combination unknown.
4ft(1.2m) -10F(-23C) M   Data from Cox, Greer. Pale pink flowers, edged deeper pink; white calyx. Plant of excellent compact
habit; leaves held 3 years. Waterer & Crisp intro.


```
          -ciliatum 1/2
DRESDEN CHINA-      -edgeworthii (bullatum) 1/4
          -Sesterianum-
                  -formosum ? 1/4
```
White flowers.   Gen. Harrison.

DRESS PARADE   Parentage unknown
Truss of 9 flowers, light purplish pink with chartreuse throat.
Roy Kersey cross; Mrs. H. A. Frederick, Jr., reg. 1977.

```
* * * * * * * * * * * * * * * * * * * * * * * * * * *
              -griffithianum 1/4
        -Mars-
DRESS UP-     -unknown 1/4
        -          -griersonianum 1/4
        -Tally Ho-
                 -facetum (eriogynum) 1/4
```
When registered, plant was 6ft(1.8m) tall with leaves 8in(20cm)
long.   Flowers double or semi-double, Delft rose, in trusses of
10. Late midseason.   Rudolph Henny, reg. 1964.
MARTHA MAY   Parentage as above
Ten flowers per upright truss, clear red. Tall plant of medium
spread, leaves 6in(15.2cm) long, dark green.   Henny, reg. 1965.
```
* * * * * * * * * * * * * * * * * * * * * * * * * * *
* * * * * * * * * * * * * * * * * * * * * * * * * * *
          -arboreum 1/2
DRUM MAJOR-
          -griersonianum 1/2
```
5ft(1.5m) 10F(-12C) M   Red flowers in compact trusses. Open-
growing plant.   Rothschild, 1936.
DOCTOR HENRY WADE   Parentage as above
Lilac pink flowers, darker edges. Mrs. Henry Wade, reg. 1972.
EVERGLOW   Parentage as above, except reversed
Trusses of 12-14 widely funnel-campanulate flowers, currant red,
brown flecks in throat. Narrow elliptic leaves; gray indumentum
when young. Long flowering period. Blumhart cross; reg. 1984.
```
* * * * * * * * * * * * * * * * * * * * * * * * * * *

        -forrestii Repens Group 1/2
DRYAD-
        -hookeri 1/2
```
Deep red flowers.   Lord Aberconway, 1946.

```
              -souliei 1/4
        -Latona-
DRYOPE-       -dichroanthum 1/4
      -       -haematodes 1/4
        -May Day-
                 -griersonianum 1/4
```
Rose flowers, flushed coral red.   Sunningdale Nurseries, 1955.

```
                    -haematodes 1/4
              -Humming Bird-
DUCHESS FERRETI-       -williamsianum 3/4
              -williamsianum
```
Flowers in trusses of 6, 6-lobed, deep pink, areas between lobes
lighter. Leaf obovate-orbicular. E. de Rothschild, reg. 1984.

DUCHESS OF CORNWALL   Parentage unknown
A parent of ORIENT EXPRESS.   Round trusses of 18-20 flowers,
deep Neyron rose with dark red spots. Leaves with silvery plastered indumentum.   R. Gill, 1910; shown by Hillier. A.M. 1974.

DUCHESS OF EDINBURGH   Parentage unknown
Originated before 1905, according to Walter Schmalscheidt, Oldenburg, West Germany, who cares for a collection of old rhododendron hybrids, including this one. Flowers rosy red, paler at
center, small brown markings; an attractive bi-color effect.   A
parent of many hybrids. Two with this name: 1958 International
Rhododendron Register recorded the other (a vireya) and in error
listed it as a parent of elepidote hybrid MRS. LINDSAY SMITH q.v.

DUCHESS OF KENT   Parentage unknown
Flowers in trusses of 16, brilliant yellow, fading to light yellow, blotch vivid orange-yellow.   L. de Rothschild, reg.1982.

```
                 -barbatum 1/2
DUCHESS OF PORTLAND-          -caucasicum 1/4
              -Handsworth White-
                           -unknown 1/4
```
5ft(1.5m) 0F(-18C) EM   Fine foliage with brown indumentum.
Soft lavender buds opening pure white with a pale yellowish eye.
Fisher & Sibray exhibited.   A.M. 1903.

```
                           -dichroanthum 1/8
                    -Goldsworth-
                    - Orange   -fortunei ssp. discolor 1/8
              -Hotei-       -souliei 1/8
DUCHESS OF ROTHESAY-    -unnamed-
              -        hybrid-wardii 1/8
                    -decorum 1/2
```
Firm, rounded trusses of 17 flowers, 7-lobed, pale aureolin yel-

---

low, shading deeper. E. de Rothschild, reg. 1984.   A.M. 1983.

DUCHESS OF TECK   Parentage unknown
Unusual leaves, concave with a depression in the middle, waxy
and shining. Flowers lilac pink at edges, near-white in
center, with conspicuous brown spotted flare. Of compact habit.
Named for the late Dowager Queen Mary.   Waterer & Crisp intro.
1892.   A.M. 1916.

```
* * * * * * * * * * * * * * * * * * * * * * * * * * *
              -fortunei 1/2
DUCHESS OF YORK-     -catawbiense 1/4
              -Scipio-
                    -unknown 1/4
```
5ft(1.5m) 5F(-15C) M 3/3 Large fragrant flowers salmon pink,
with brownish markings on the throat. Foliage resembles that of
the species fortunei. G. Paul. A.M. 1894.
DUKE OF YORK   Parentage as above
5ft(1.5m) -10F(-23C) ML Rosy pink flower, spotted with cream.
G. Paul. A.M. 1894. Color illus. Cox pl. 49.
```
* * * * * * * * * * * * * * * * * * * * * * * * * * *
```

DUET   Described under BANGKOK, q.v.

```
* * * * * * * * * * * * * * * * * * * * * * * * * * *
              -arboreum 1/2
DUKE OF CORNWALL-
              -barbatum 1/2
```
Crimson flowers.   R. Gill & Son.   A.M. 1907.
JOHN HOLMS   Parentage as above
Scarlet flowers.   Gibson of Rhu.   A.M. 1957.
TRELAWNY   Parentage as above
Deep crimson with paler throat, darker spots. Gill. A.M. 1936.
WEREI   Parentage uncertain, but probably as above
Flowers rose pink.   Samuel Smith, Penjerrick.   A.M. 1921.
```
* * * * * * * * * * * * * * * * * * * * * * * * * * *
```

DUKE OF YORK   Described under DUCHESS OF YORK, q.v.

```
              -elliottii 1/4
        -Kiev-       -thomsonii 1/8
        -    -Robert Fox-       -arboreum 1/16
DUKESHILL-       -Glory of Penjerrick-
        -             -facetum 1/4       -griffithianum 1/16
        -Lady Digby-
                 -strigillosum 1/4
```
Flowers of scarlet red.   Crown Estate, Windsor, reg. 1973.
A.M.1973.

DUNLOE   Described under MAGIC MOMENTS, q.v.

```
                    -catawbiense var. album 1/4
              -unnamed hybrid-
DUPONT APRICOT-       -fortunei 1/4
              -campylocarpum 1/2
```
5ft(1.5m) -5F(-21C) ML   Pink flowers, with a delicate apricot
blush. Origin unknown.

```
        -ciliicalyx ? 1/2
DURHAM LIGHT-
        -unknown 1/2
```
Flowers in trusses of 5-6, funnel-shaped, primrose yellow with a
green flare, flushed pink on outside; fragrant. Compact shrub.
Duncan & Davies Nursery, NZ, reg. 1986.

```
                    -diaprepes 1/4
              -Vibrant-
              -       -wardii 1/4
DUSKY DAWN-                 -fortunei ssp. discolor 1/8
        -       -Lady Bessborough-
        -       -             -campylocarpum Elatum Group 1/8
              -Jalisco-    -dichroanthum 1/8
                    -Dido-
                           -decorum 1/8
```
Pale apricot, turning near-white.   Gen. Harrison, reg. 1973.

```
              -Moser's Maroon--unknown 1/2
DUSKY MAID-
              -fortunei ssp. discolor 1/2
```
Tall, sturdy, upright. Dark red flowers in compact trusses sim-
ilar to the seed parent, Moser's Maroon.   Rothschild, 1936.

```
* * * * * * * * * * * * * * * * * * * * * * * * * * * *
                          -Essex Scarlet--unknown 1/8
              -Cavalcade-
    -unnamed-         -griersonianum 1/8
  - hybrid-               -campylocarpum 1/8
DUSKY WOOD-      -Mary Swaythling-
-           -wardii 1/4        -fortunei 1/8
  -Crest-                -fortunei ssp. discolor 1/8
       -Lady Bessborough-
                   -campylocarpum 1/8
5ft(1.5m) 5F(-15C) M  Flowers of soft rose pink, flushed red.
John Waterer, Sons & Crisp, reg. 1975.
FOREVER AMBER   Parentage as above
An open-growing bush; flowers amber, or smoky orange, edged red.
John Waterer, Sons & Crisp cross, 1959; reg. 1975.
* * * * * * * * * * * * * * * * * * * * * * * * * * * *

         -yakushimanum 1/2
DUSTY MILLER-
         -unnamed hybrid--unknown 1/2
3ft(.9m) OF(-18C) M  Flowers of pale pink and cream on a plant
of fairly dense habit.   J. Waterer, Sons & Crisp, reg. 1975.


* * * * * * * * * * * * * * * * * * * * * * * * * * * *
                          -catawbiense var. album 1/8
                     -           -catawbiense
              -Lodestar-  -Catawbiense-    3/32
              -       -Belle - Album  -unknown 3/32
              -          Heller-        -catawbiense
              -               -white cat. hyb.-
         -R.O. Delp-                   -unknown
    -           -                       -catawbiense
    -           -         -Atrosanguineum-
    -           -      -Atrier-        -unknown
DUSTY WHIZ-      -Mary  -   -griersonianum 1/16
    -           Belle-   -decorum 1/16
    -              -Dechaem-
    -                   -haematodes 1/16
    -           -fortunei
  -Golden Star-
              -wardii 1/4
Pink buds open to orange flowers, edged red.  Delp.
LIQUID GOLD   Parentage as above
Buds combine moderate grayed red, deep shell pinks, pale yel-
low, brilliant chartreuse.  Frilled flowers, pale orange-white
tinged shell pink with a primrose yellow throat and dorsal spot-
ting of moderate yellowish green.  W. Delp.  Color illus. ARS
J 43:1 (1989), cover.
REGAL CROWN   Parentage as above
A blend of light shell pink and deep warm pinks in bud. Flowers
open pale orange-white, tinted light yellowish pink, light amber
yellow throat.  W. Delp.  Color illus. ARS J 43:1 (1989), p. 2.
STARDUST   Parentage as above
Buds brilliant greenish yellow open to pale greenish yellow flo-
wers, with dorsal spotting of medium orange.   W. Delp.
* * * * * * * * * * * * * * * * * * * * * * * * * * * *

DUTCH MARION   See MARION (Felix & Dijkhuis)

                   -dichroanthum 1/8
              -Fabia-
    -Hello Dolly-   -griersonianum 1/8
DUTCH TREAT-       -smirnowii 1/4
    -                       -caucasicum 3/16
    -           -Jacksonii-       -caucasicum
  -Goldsworth Yellow-       -Nobleanum-
                   -campylocarpum 1/4  -arboreum 1/16

Buds of crimson open to flowers rhodonite red slowly fading to
pale yellow; dorsal spotting chartreuse green.   W. Delp.

DUTCHMAN JOE   Described under P. J. M., q.v.

                   -caucasicum 3/32
              -Jacksonii-        -caucasicum
    -Goldsworth-       -Nobleanum-
    - Yellow -            -arboreum 1/32
  -Goldfort-       -campylocarpum 3/8
  -       -fortunei 1/4
DUXBURY-           -campylocarpum
    -unnamed hybrid-
```

```
6ft(1.8m) -10F(-23C) ML  Buds amber yellow and salmon open to
flowers light primrose yellow, in 7in(17.8cm) trusses of 7-11.
Plant tall, as wide as high; leaves very dark green.   L. Bagoly
cross, 1970; Mr. & Mrs. F. B. Lawson, reg. 1986.

DYING EMBERS   Described under FOXBERG, q.v.

                   -griffithianum 1/8
              -Mars-
    -Captain Jack-   -unknown 5/8
DYNASTY-           -facetum (eriogynum) 1/4
    -Sun Devil--Whitney orange hybrid--unknown
3.5ft(1.05m) x 3.5ft(8 yrs) 10F(-12C) M  Flowers held in flat
trusses of 8-10, of heavy substance,  strong red shading to dark
red at center.  Plant of dense growth habit.  Bulgin, reg. 1988.


                          E


                   -thomsonii 3/8
              -Troas-        -thomsonii
    -           -Cornish Cross-
E. H. WILDING-           -griffithianum 3/8
    -               -campylocarpum Elatum Group 1/4
         -Penjerrick-
                   -griffithianum
Flowers of blood red.   Adams-Acton, 1942.


                   -campylocarpum
              -Campdis-
E. J. P. MAGOR-   -fortunei ssp. discolor 1/4
         -williamsianum 1/2
Large flowers of bright rose.   Dietrich Hobbie, 1954.


                   -wardii 1/4
              -China-
EA TATIANA-   -fortunei 1/4
    -                   -fortunei ssp. discolor 1/4
         -Lady Bessborough-
                   -campylocarpum Elatum Group 1/4
  4ft(1.2m) x 3ft(.9m) OF(-18C) M  Flowers in large trusses of
14-16, moderately fragrant, 7-lobed, pale yellow; outside strong
pink.  Dense habit; free-flowering.  Aunsbjorn, reg. 1989.


                   -arboreum ssp. cinnamomeum roseum 1/4
         -Fair Lady-        -griffithianum 3/8
    -           -Loderi Venus-
EARL J. REED-              -fortunei 3/8
    -               -griffithianum
    -Loderi Venus-
              -fortunei
5ft(1.5m) 10F(-12C) EM  White flower, roseine purple at edges,
3.5in(8.9cm) across, 6-lobed, held in ball-shaped trusses of 13.
George Clarke, cross 1989; Edwin Anderson, intro. & reg. 1983.


                          -griffithianum 3/8
              -Queen Wilhelmina-
         -Earl of Athlone-   -unknown 5/8
EARL MOORE-       -Stanley Davies--unknown
    -                   -griffithianum
         -Jean Marie de Montague-
                   -unknown
Flowers cherry red,  in tight trusses of 10-15.  Tall plant with
long, thin, vine-like branches.   Seabrook, reg. 1967.

EARL OF ATHLONE   Described under BRITANNIA, q.v.

         -griersonianum 1/2        -griffithianum 1/16
EARL OF    -           -George Hardy-
DONOUGHMORE-      -Mrs. L. A.-        -catawbiense 1/16
         -unnamed- Dunnett -unknown 3/8
         hybrid-unknown
5ft(1.5m) -5F(-21C) M 3/3  Bright red flowers with an orange
glow.  M. Koster & Sons, 1953.  Color ill. F p. 43; JS p. 95.


* * * * * * * * * * * * * * * * * * * * * * * * * * * *
              -campylocarpum 1/2
EARL OF MORLEY-
         -arboreum ssp. cinnamomeum var. album 1/2
Flowers of glistening ivory white with crimson spots, in rounded
trusses.  A very large, slow-growing shrub or small tree of pyr-
```

amidal habit, first raised at Westonbirt c. 1910. Blooms early.
Sir Edmund Loder, before 1958.
LEONARDSLEE PRIMROSE   Parentage as above
Primrose yellow flowers, dotted on upper half with small maroon
spots. Sir Edmund Loder. A.M. 1933
* *

```
                       -catawbiense red form 1/8
              -Pink Twins-
     -Shaazam-           -haematodes 1/8
     -         -           -griffithianum 1/8
EARLENE-   -Leah Yates---Mars, selfed-
     -                    -unknown 1/8
     -yakushimanum--Koichiro Wada 1/2
```
3ft(.9m) -15F(-26C) ML   Plant rounded, semi-dwarf, as wide as
tall, leaves medium-sized. New growth with orange-brown indumentum. Flowers 2in(5cm) wide, salmon-colored, claret rose on
reverse, in ball-shaped trusses of 14. Mrs. Yates, reg. 1977.

EARLY ACCENT   Parentage: fortunei x griersonianum x Pygmalion
6ft(1.8m) x 6ft(18 yrs) -5F(-21C) M   Above information on
parentage is uncertain. Flowers strong purplish red with deep
purplish red spotting, in lax trusses of 15. Leaves moderate
olive green. A. Consolini cross. Tyler Arboretum, reg. 1985.

EARLY BRILLIANT   Described under FIREBALL, q.v.

```
                 -arboreum 1/4
        -Red Admiral-
EARLY DAYS-           -thomsonii 1/4
        -unknown 1/2
```
Trusses of 12-14 bell-shaped flowers, cardinal red. Height 5ft
(1.5m). V. J. Boulter, reg. 1983.

```
                 -ciliatum 1/4
        -Praecox-
EARLY GEM-    -dauricum 3/4
        -dauricum
```
Flowers rosy lilac. Unknown. F.C.C. 1874.

```
          -hyperythrum 1/2
EARLY SPLENDOR-
          -catawbiense var. album Glass--Catalgla 1/2
```
Large, frilly white flowers with purple spotting on upper lobe.
Usually blooms just after the last late frost. Foliage average;
plant of medium height, taller than wide. Dr. Tom Ring.

```
          -strigillosum 1/2
EARLY STIR-
          -irroratum 1/2
```
Currant red flowers. Lord Digby, 1934.

```
          -williamsianum 1/2
EARLYBIRD-
          -oreodoxa var. fargesii 1/2
```
Rose-colored flowers shading to almost white in the tube, funnel
campanulate, 3in(7.6cm) wide, in trusses of 6. Rounded leaves,
1.5in(3.8cm) across. Very early. Rudolph Henny, reg. 1960.

* *
```
          -Vineland seedling--unknown 3/4
EARTHSHAKER-     -catawbiense var. album Glass--Catalgla 1/4
          -Calsap-
               -Sappho--unknown
```
Blend of medium purplish reds in bud, opening to a frilled mix-
ture of magnolia purples and dark reds; white anthers. Al Smith
cross; W. Delp raiser.
DINGALING   Parentage as above
Deep red in bud, opens to frilled flowers, a blend of magenta
rose and dark reds. White anthers. Smith cross; Delp raiser.
GOODY GOODY GUMDROP   Parentage as above
Blend of cyclamen purples in bud, opens to mallow purple edged
with blend of light rose and phlox purple, dorsal spots of ruby
red. Al Smith cross; W. Delp raiser.
* *
* *
```
          -griersonianum 1/2
EAST KNOYLE-    -griffithianum 1/4
          -Loderi-
               -fortunei 1/4
```
Carmine red buds opening to large rose-colored flowers darker in
throat, funnel-shaped, in loose trusses. Sir J. Horlick, 1930.

NASTURTIUM   Parentage as above
Nasturtium red flowers. Horlick.
* *

EAST NORTHPORT   Parentage unknown
3ft(.9m) -15F(-26C) M   Reddish maroon flowers with a large
blotch, slightly darker. Origin unknown.

* *
```
               -williamsianum 1/2
EASTER BELLS-    -wightii 1/4
          -China-
               -fortunei 1/4
```
4ft(1.2m) 5F(-15C) EM 3/4   Medium-sized, oval leaves; plant
broader than tall. Flowers open creamy pink and fade white; lax
trusses of about 8. Benjamin Lancaster, reg. 1965.
GLAD TIDINGS   Parentage as above, except reverse
4ft(1.2m) 0F(-18C) EM 3/3   Flowers to 4in(10cm) wide, cream
tinged pink, yellow throat, red basal flare; truss of 12. Leaf
6in(15cm) long, cordate, dark green. Lancaster, reg. 1965.
* *

```
               -griffithianum 3/8
          -Loderi-
          -      -fortunei 3/8
EASTER BONNET-       -griffithianum
          -       -Loderi-
          -Mingo-       -fortunei
               -ponticum 1/4
```
Pink buds open to ivory flowers, faintly flushed pink; deep rose
pink flares in center; widely funnel-shaped flowers in truss of
8-10. Crown Estate, Windsor Great Park.

* *
```
                    -mauve seedling--unknown 5/16
          -Arthur Bedford-
EASTER BUNNY-          -ponticum 1/4
          -     -catawbiense var. album Glass--Catalgla 1/4
          -Ice Cube-               -catawbiense
          -          -Catawbiense Album-    1/16
               -Belle Heller-     -unknown
                    -catawbiense var. album 1/8
```
Buds of violet purple and lilac purple; flowers very pale purple
edged with strong and light purples, with a strong purple flare.
Dorsal spots deep greenish yellow. J. Looye cross; Delp raiser.
SOFT SENSATION   Parentage as above
Buds of lilac and magnolia purples; flowers magnolia purple and
very pale purple, slowly fading to white; a flare of ruby red;
white filaments. Jack Looye cross; W. Delp raiser.
WHIRLYBIRD   Parentage as above
Buds of strong reddish purple; flowers pale purple, edged darker.
Dorsal spotting strong greenish yellow and lilac purple. Jack
Looye cross; W, Delp raiser.
* *

```
          -aureum 1/2
EASTER CHICK-
          -dichroanthum ssp. scyphocalyx 1/2
```
Flowers pale yellow-green, spotted red; blooms early midseason.
Dwarf shrub; compact habit. B. N. Starling, reg. 1987.

```
          -minus 1/2
EASTER DAWN-
          -mucronulatum--Pink Panther 1/2
```
7ft(2.1m) -15F(-26C) E   Ball truss (2-5 buds, 3 flowers/bud),
strong reddish purple at edge, fading to light purplish pink at
center. Bright red foliage in fall. G. D. Lewis, reg. 1988.

EASTER ISLAND--alutaceum var. russotinctum F 20425
Compact trusses of 10-12 flowers, white with ruby red spotting.
Matte green leaves 4in(10.2cm) long; fawn to rusty brown indumentum beneath. George Forrest collector; Col. S. R. Clarke
raiser; R. N. Stephenson Clarke, reg. 1980. A.M. 1980.

EASTER PARADE   Described under TICKLED PINK, q.v.

EASTER ROSE   See EASTER DAWN.

```
     -minus Carolinianum Group 3/4
EBONY-    -minus Carolinianum Group
     -P.J.M.-
          -dauricum 1/4
```

1ft(.3m) -15F(-26C) EM 4/4 Light purple flowers, 1in(2.5cm)
wide, 5 wavy lobes; 4-10 in dome-shaped trusses. Floriferous.
Plant rounded, well-branched (decumbent); very small, shiny
leaves, deep maroon in winter, held 1 year.   Mezitt, reg. 1980.


```
            -decorum 1/2
ECHO-                   -fortunei ssp. discolor 1/4
     -Lady Bessborough-
                        -campylocarpum Elatum Group 1/4
```
Creamy flowers, fading white, a claret eye.   Sunningdale, 1955.

* *
```
                   -Dexter hybrid--unknown 9/16
          -Janet Blair-
          -         -unknown        -catawbiense 1/16
ECSTASY-                 -Atrosanguineum-
-                -Atrier-              -unknown
     -Mary Belle-       -griersonianum 1/8
     -          -decorum 1/8
                   -Dechaem-
                             -haematodes 1/8
```
Flowers pink and white with diffuse pigmentation.   Dr. Mark
Konrad, cross 1979.   Color illus. ARS J 43:3 1989, p. 158.
RADIANCE   Parentage as above
Flowers age to golden bronze.   Konrad cross.
SHOWTIME   Parentage as above
Flowers age to a peach color.   Konrad cross.   Color illus. ARS
J 43:3 1989, p. 158.
* *


```
          -yakushimanum 1/2
ED FARROW-            -elliottii 1/4
         -Kilimanjaro-         -Moser's Maroon--unknown 1/8
                       -Dusky Maid-
                                   -fortunei ssp. discolor 1/8
```
Buds strong red, paling to strong purplish pink, opening
purplish pink with strong red throat markings.   Late May-June.
Leaves oblanceolate. L. de Rothschild, reg. 1985.

ED KNIGHT   Described under LIVONIA LINDSLEY, q.v.

```
                   -dichroanthum 1/8
                -Fabia-
     -unnamed hybrid-      -griersonianum 1/8
ED LONG-            -unknown 1/4
       -fortunei 1/2
```
A medium-sized, compact plant; buds chartreuse green opening to
cream, with green center and blotch, to 4in(10.2cm) wide; rounded trusses.   Intro. by D. W. James, 1963.

```
               -wardii 1/4
         -Jervis Bay-
         -         -Lady         -fortunei ssp. discolor 1/8
EDDYSTONE-       Bessborough-
         -          -campylocarpum Elatum Group 1/8
         -wardii Litiense Group 1/2
```
Trusses of 14 flowers, primrose yellow with small crimson stain
in throat, openly campanulate, 2.5in(6.4cm) wide. Francis Hanger, RHS Garden, Wisley, reg. 1965.   A.M. 1964.

```
                         -catawbiense 1/8
                 -Humboldt-
     -Hachmann's Ornament-      -unknown 3/4
EDELTRAUD-       -          -fortunei 1/8
         -          -Director E. Hjelm-
     -Furnivall's Daughter--unknown     -unknown
```
4ft(1.2m) x 4ft OF(-18C) ML Flowers in dense truss of 13-16,
deep to moderate purplish pink, conspicuous blotch of very dark
purplish red.   Hans Hachmann, cross 1969; G. Stück, reg. 1988.
Color illus. WS, 1989, p. 124.

```
             -arboreum ssp. zeylanicum 1/4
     -Ilam Alarm-            -griffithianum 1/8
     -        -unnamed hybrid-
EDGAR STEAD-            -unknown 1/8
-          -thomsonii 1/4
     -Shilsonii-
              -barbatum 1/4
```
A hybrid by Stead of Australia.

EDGEMONT   Parentage unknown
Purplish pink flowers. Dexter cross; G. Wister, reg. 1980.

EDINENSE Described under CREAM TRUMPET, q.v.

```
     -fortunei ssp. discolor 1/2
EDITH-
     -hardy hybrid--unknown 1/2
```
Flowers deep rose pink with dark blotch.   Plant medium to tall;
late season. Slocock, reg. 1958.   A.M. 1931.

```
               -sanguineum var. didymoides (consanguineum) 1/2
EDITH BERKELEY-              -griffithianum 1/4
              -Loderi King George-
                                  -fortunei 1/4
```
Flowers rose madder, white stamens, no spotting, 6-lobed, 3in
(7.6cm) across. Late midseason.   Mr. & Mrs. Greig, reg. 1963.

EDITH BOSLEY   Parentage unknown
Flowers much like PURPLE SPLENDOUR but much more hardy. Bosley.

```
            -Marion (Cheal)--unknown 3/4
EDITH BOULTER-      -campylocarpum 1/4
             -Unique-
                    -unknown
```
5ft(1.5m) -5F(-21C) E 4/4 Lavender pink flowers with darker
margins, frilled; ball-shaped trusses of 15-18. V. J. Boulter,
Australia, reg. 1962.

```
                         -griffithianum 1/8
               -Coombe Royal-
          -Mrs. G. W.-          -unknown 3/4
          - Leak     -          -caucasicum 1/8
EDITH BROWN-      -Chevalier Felix-
-                de Sauvage    -hardy hybrid--unknown
     -unknown
```
Trusses of 18-24 flowers, pink with brown blotch like MRS. G. W.
LEAK, but darker.   Height to 9.8ft(3m).   Glennie, reg. 1984.

EDITH CAREY   Parentage: Luscombei, fortunei, Coombe Royal
                  (Above combination uncertain)
6ft(1.8m) OF(-18C) EM Clear rose red flowers in loose trusses
on a tall open plant. Grown in NZ. Smith & Son, pre-1931. See
Cox, p. 101.

```
                    -arboreum 1/4
               -Doncaster-
EDITH MACKWORTH PRAED-      -unknown 3/4
                     -unknown
```
5ft(1.5m) -5F(-21C) EM   Flower bright crimson or cherry
scarlet. Nice foliage. M. Koster. A.M. 1934.

```
               -catawbiense 1/4
          -English Roseum-
EDITH PRIDE-            -unknown 1/4
          -maximum 1/2
```
6ft(1.8m) -25F(-32C) VL 3/3 Pink flowers, pale yellow spot-
ting and a small white blotch; 2in(5cm) across, 5-lobed; large
ball-shaped trusses of 22. Plant well-branched, wide as tall;
narrowly elliptic leaves held 3 years.   O. S. Pride, reg. 1979.

```
               -catawbiense var. album 1/2
EDMOND AMATEIS-
              -Dexter seedling--unknown 1/2
```
6ft(1.8m) -25F(-32C) EM 4/4   White flowers with bold, twin-
rayed dorsal blotch of red; 3.5in(8.3cm) wide, rotate funnel-
shaped; spherical trusses hold up to 13. Good foliage density.
Edmond Amateis cross; David G. Leach raised, reg. 1969.

```
                    -catawbiense 1/4
               -unnamed hybrid-
EDMOND MOULIN-            -unknown 1/2
             -          -maximum 1/4
             -unnamed hybrid-
                           -unknown
```
5ft(1.5m) -25F(-32C) M   Rounded trusses 6in(15.2cm) wide, of
22 flowers, fuchsia purple with prominent blotch of grayed yellow. Plant upright, nearly as broad as high; leaves medium-
sized, dark green, held 3 years. W. David Smith, reg. 1983.

```
          -arboreum 1/2
EDMONDI-
        -barbatum 1/2
```
5ft(1.5m) -5F(-21C) EM 4/3 Large blood red trusses and elon-

gated foliage.   R. Gill, 1876.

```
                       -elliottii 1/2
             -Kilimanjaro-          -Moser's Maroon--unknown 1/8
EDMUND DE -          -Dusky Maid-
ROTHSCHILD-                         -fortunei ssp. discolor 1/8
          -            -elliottii
             -Fusilier-
                       -griersonianum 1/4
```
6ft(1.8m) 15F(-9C) ML Deep red flowers, heavily and uniformly
spotted inside, widely funnel-campanulate, 3.5in(6.9cm) wide;
large trusses hold up to 22 flowers. Upright plant, vigorous
growth habit; smooth leaves 6in(15.2cm) long. E. de Rothschild,
reg. 1963.   A.M. 1968.   Color illus. PB pl. 21.

```
                     -griffithianum 1/4
             -Alice-
EDNA MCCARTY-        -unknown 1/4
             -auriculatum 1/2
```
6ft(1.8m) -5F(-21C) L 3/2 A sterile hybrid, without stamens.
Large, fragrant white flowers; large foliage.   Endre Ostbo,
reg. 1962. P.A. 1959.

* *
```
                 -griffithianum 1/4
        -Mars-
        -       -unknown 5/8
ED'S RED-                        -catawbiense 1/8
        -         -Parsons Grandiflorum-
        -America-                -unknown
                 -dark red hybrid--unknown
```
4ft(1.2m) -15F(-26C) M   Cardinal red flowers, a light brown
blotch, in ball-shaped trusses of 20. Plant spreads equally as
broad as tall.   Harold E. Reiley, reg. 1984.
FRANK MONIZ   Parentage as above
Parent of HEATARAMA, TIM CRAIG and other Delp hybrids.
RED BRAVE   Parentage as above
5ft(1.5m) -25F(-32C) M Parent of ANNA DELP. Dark red flowers
with white stamens.   O. Pride.
VINEROUGE   Parentage as above
4ft(1.2m)(22 yrs) -15F(-26C) ML   Truss holds 20 flowers, deep
red, 5 wavy lobes. Leaves elliptic, medium green.   R. Forster
cross, 1962; Hort. Res. Inst. of Ontario, reg. 1986.
* *

             -campylocarpum Elatum Group 1/4
     -Penjerrick-
EDUSA-   -griffithianum 1/4
     -campylocarpum 1/2
```
Yellow flowers.  Lord Aberconway, intro. 1933.

EDWARD DUNN   Described under CORAL, q.v.

EDWARD LONG  Described under FAWN, q.v.

```
             -catawbiense 1/2
EDWARD S. RAND-
             -unknown 1/2
```
6ft(1.8m)  -15F(-26C)  ML  2/3    Flowers of crimson red, bronze
yellow eye; truss of 20.  Plant habit compact; foliage yellowish
green.  Resistant to root rot.   A. Waterer, 1870.

```
                   -catawbiense 1/4
          -Purpureum Elegans-
EDWIN O. WEBER-   -unknown 3/4
          -Madame Albert Moser--unknown
```
6ft(1.8m)  -5F(-21C)  ML  3/4  Flower of royal purple with large
uranium green dorsal blotch, 3.5in(8.9cm) wide;  to 28 in large
trusses.  Floriferous.  Plant moderately branched;  dark green
leaves, 6.5in(16.5cm) long, held 3 years.   E. Weber, reg. 1974.

```
               -Lady   -fortunei ssp. discolor 3/8
               -Bessborough-
        -Day Dream-   -campylocarpum Elatum Group 1/8
        -          -griersonianum 1/4
EDWIN PARKER-   -griffithianum 1/8
        -          -Loderi-
        -Albatross-   -fortunei 1/8
                   -fortunei ssp. discolor
```
6ft(1.8m)  5F(-15C)  L  Flower pink to peach, creamy pink center
on each of 5 lobes,  to 4in(10.2cm) wide, in 16-flowered trusses
9in(23cm) broad; leaves to 5in(12.7cm) long.   Henny, reg. 1968.

```
                 -catawbiense 1/2
        -Alfred---Everestianum, selfed-
EFFNER-   -unknown 1/2
       -           -catawbiense
        -Everestianum-
                   -unknown
```
5ft(1.5m)  -20F(-29C)  L  Lilac-colored  flowers with greenish
yellow and brown markings.   Seidel, 1903.

EGBERT VAN ALSTYNE   Described under REDWAX, q.v.

EGGBRECHTII    Parentage unknown
A parent of GUDRUN, HOLGER, both by Seidel.

```
          -campylogynum, white form 1/2
EGRET-
          -racemosum--White Lace 1/2
```
2ft(.6m)  -5F(-21C)  EM  4/4  Compact dwarf habit, small leaves,
medium glossy green.  Trusses of 6 white flowers, slightly ting-
ed pale green toward the calyx.  Cox, reg. 1982.   A.M. 1982.
A.M. Wisley Trials 1987.  Color illus. Cox pl. 50.

```
                 -souliei 1/4
        -Halcyone-   -fortunei ssp. discolor 3/8
        -         -Lady Bessborough-
EGYPTIAN-   -campylocarpum Elatum Group 1/8
        -              -fortunei ssp. discolor
        -Margaret Dunn-   -dichroanthum 1/8
                      -Fabia-
                            -griersonianum 1/8
```
Yellow flower overlaid salmon; brown blotch.  Sunningdale, 1955.

```
            -wardii 1/2
EHRENGOLD-
            -unknown 1/2
```
4ft(1.2m)  -10F(-23C)  ML  Rose-tinted  buds open to rounded
trusses of pale yellow, long-lasting flowers.  Foliage glossy,
recurved.  Hobbie, cross 1950-53.  Color illus. WS, 1989, p. 37.

```
          -degronianum ssp. heptamereum (metternichii) 1/2
EIDAM-
          -Alexander Adie--unknown 1/2
```
White flowers, flushed rose.   T.J.R. Seidel, cross 1903.  Color
illus. WS p. 27.

EIDER   Described under STARLIGHT, q.v.

EILEEN   Parentage uncertain.  Possibly DUCHESS OF TECK x
griffithianum, suggested by J. F. Street.
5ft(1.5m)  -10F(-23C)  L  Flowers pale and deep pink with a
yellow flare; trusses of 16.  Waterer & Crisp, before 1958.

```
                           -racemosum 1/8
                 -Conemaugh-
              -Pioneer-   -mucronulatum 1/8
EILEEN BYRNES-   -unknown 3/4
              -unknown
```
2ft(.6m) -15F(-26C)  EM     Free-flowering plant with raspberry
blossoms; semi-deciduous; small foliage.   Waterer.

```
               -griffithianum 1/4
         -Mars-
EILEEN HALL-   -unknown 1/2
         -           -Pygmalion--unknown
         -unnamed hybrid-
                       -haematodes 1/4
```
5ft(1.5m)  -15F(-26C)  M   Amaranth rose flowers with dorsal red
spotting, 3in(7.6cm) wide, in ball-shaped trusses of 10; plant
broader than tall.  M. Hall, reg. 1980.

EITHNE   Described under DAPHNE (Magor), q.v.

```
           -griffithianum 1/2
EL ALAMEIN-
           -unknown 1/2
```
5ft(1.5m)  -10F(-23C)  EM   Flowers deep blood red, conspicuous
dark brown blotches, in shapely trusses.  Kluis, intro. 1946.
```

```
                    -Beauty of-griffithianum 5/16
              -Norman- Tremough-
              -  Gill  -          -arboreum 1/16
        -Anna-       -griffithianum
        -    -                          -griffithianum
EL CAMINO-   -Jean Marie de Montague-
        -                              -unknown 3/8
        -                              -griffithianum 1/8
        -               -George Hardy-
        -Marinus Koster-               -catawbiense 1/8
                        -red hybrid--unknown
```
5ft(1.5m) -5F(-21C) M 4/4   Parentage is uncertain; may be
the same as Halfdan Lem's WALLOPER q.v.   Flowers deep pink, and
darker blotch, 5in(12.7cm) wide.   Plant stiffly branched; leaves
held 3 years.   Lem or Whitney cross; Sathers, reg. 1976.

EL CINQUE   See CINQUERO

```
              -Lady         -fortunei ssp. discolor 1/8
              -Bessborough-
        -Jalisco-          -campylocarpum Elatum Group 1/8
        -    -             -dichroanthum 3/8
EL GRECO-    -Dido-
        -          -decorum 1/8
        -       -Dawn's -griffithianum 1/8
        -Break of-Delight-
          Day   -      -unknown 1/8
                -dichroanthum
```
Flowers of saffron yellow changing to azalea pink at edges, car-
mine rose flush, 3.5in(8.9cm) across, 10 per truss.   Plant
compact, broad as tall; dull green leaves 6.5in(16.5cm) long.
RHS, Wisley, reg. 1961.   A.M. Wisley Trials 1961.

ELAINE BEHRING   Described under ANNA H. HALL, q.v.

ELAINE ROWE   Described under JOAN THOMPSON, q.v.

* *
```
              -pubescens 1/4
        -Chesapeake-
ELAM-         -keiskei 1/4
      -unknown 1/2
```
2ft(.6m) -20F(-29C) M Deep rose flowers 1.5in(3.8cm) wide, in
clusters of 3-4.   Very small leaves.   G. Guy Nearing, reg. 1963.
ELSMERE   Parentage as above
Lemon yellow flowers in clusters of 5-6.   Nearing, reg. 1963.
RAMSEY TINSEL   Parentage as above
1ft(.3m) -10F(-23C) EM Flowers ocher yellow, 1in(2.5cm) wide,
in clusters of 3-4.   Nearing, intro. 1963; reg. 1972
* *
```
                    -dichroanthum 3/16
              -Fabia-
        -unnamed hybrid-     -griersonianum 3/16
        -              -bureavii 1/4
ELBY-                         -fortunei ssp. discolor 1/8
        -            -King of Shrubs-   -dichroanthum
        -unnamed hybrid-            -Fabia-
                    -smirnowii 1/4     -griersonianum
```
4ft(1.2m) x 4ft(20 yrs) -5F(-21C) EM   Flat trusses of 6-9
flowers, buds vivid red, opening deep pink.   Plant wide as tall;
foliage glossy olive green.   Lem cross; E. F. Newcomb, reg. 1987.

```
        -valentinianum 1/2
ELDORADO-
        -johnstoneanum 1/2
```
4ft(1.2m) 15F(-9C) E 3/3   Flowers primrose yellow, medium-
sized, funnel-shaped, clusters of 3-4.   Open-growing plant.
Small, scaly, dark yellowish green leaves.   Rothschild, 1937.

* *
```
                    -griffithianum 1/8
              -Mars-
        -Vulcan-     -unknown 1/8
ELEANOR BEE-      -griersonianum 1/4
        -yakushimanum, Exbury form 1/2
```
2ft(.6m) 5F(-15C) M   Funnel-shaped flowers in flat trusses
of 14, strong purplish red from buds pale purplish pink.   Habit
spreading, dense.   Dr. L. Bulgin, Ellanhurst Gardens, reg. 1988.
ANGELIQUE   Parentage as above
Similar to above.   Wider than high; strong purplish red buds
open pale purplish pink with touches of deep purplish pink at

tips of lobes, outside deep purplish pink.   Bulgin, reg. 1988.
YAKU CORONET   Parentage as above
Similar to above.   Wider than high; buds strong red, open white
with strong purplish red picotee; outside strong purplish red
veins and margins.   Indumentum orange yellow.   Bulgin, reg. 1988.
YAKU FANTASIA   Parentage as above
Similar to above, wide as tall.   Strong purplish red buds open
to flowers strong purplish pink which persists into maturity.
Leaves held 3 years, felted medium orange.   Bulgin, reg. 1988.
YAKU SENSATION   Parentage as above
Similar to above, as wide as tall, with foliage felted light
yellowish brown.   Flower truss of 14-16 flowers of strong, per-
sistent pink; lobes frilly-edged.   Bulgin, reg. 1988.
* *

```
                    -griffithianum 1/8
              -Mars-
        -Vulcan-     -unknown 1/8
        -     -griersonianum 1/4
ELEANOR LAXDALL-    -griersonianum 1/4
        -Azor-
              -fortunei ssp. discolor 1/4
```
8ft(2.4m) x 5ft(1.5m)(25 yrs) OF(-18C) L   Flowers deep
purplish pink with moderate purplish pink margins, lighter
throat; lax trusses 6in(15cm) across.   New growth copper color.
Sigrid Laxdall, reg. 1988.

```
        -rubiginosum Desquamatum Group 1/2
ELEANORE-
        -augustinii 1/2
```
6ft(1.8m) 10F(-12C) EM 3/3   Tall plant, flowers larger than
either parent, in clusters of 4-5.   One form is lavender blue,
another blends violet and amethyst.   Rothschild, intro. 1937;
reg. 1958.   A.M. 1943.

```
        -augustinii ssp. chasmanthum 1/2
ELECTRA-
        -augustinii ssp. augustinii 1/2
```
5ft(1.5m) 5F(-15C) EM 5/4   Not really a hybrid; a cross of
two forms of the same species.   Flower one of the bluest, but
not the largest augustinii form.   Plant upright; leaves 2.5in
(6.4cm) long, medium green.   Rothschild, 1937.   A.M. 1940.

```
                    -augustinii ssp. chasmanthum 1/4
              -Electra-
ELECTRA'S SON-     -augustinii ssp. augustinii 1/4
              -unknown 1/2
```
6ft(1.8m) 10F(-12C) ML   Flowers lavender, with a yellow-green
blotch, flattened, 3in(7.6cm) broad; the exterior reddish lavender.   Terminal inflorescences of 1-4 trusses, each 2/4-flowered.
Bush well-branched; leaves to 4in(10.2cm) E. Parker, reg. 1977.

```
                    -catawbiense 5/8
              -unnamed hybrid-
        -Altaclerense-     -ponticum 1/8
ELEGANS-      -arboreum 1/4
        -catawbiense
```
Deep rose, some spotting; fine truss.   Standish & Noble, 1850.

```
        -yunnanense 1/2
ELENA-
        -cinnabarinum 1/2
```
4ft(1.2m) -5F(21C) M 4/3   Soft pink delicate flowers in
delicate clusters.   Much like LADY CHAMBERLAIN.   Unknown origin.

```
                    -caucasicum 1/4
        -Dr. Stocker-
ELFIN-       -griffithianum 1/4
        -orbiculare 1/2
```
Flowers cream-colored, flushed pink.   Sir James Horlick, 1933.

```
        -luteiflorum 1/2
ELFIN GOLD-
        -keiskei--Yaku Fairy 1/2
```
Flowers light yellow-green without markings in trusses of 5.
Compact, dwarf shrub, wider than tall.   B. Starling, reg. 1987.

ELFIN HILL Described under HERA, q.v.

ELIE   Described under CHEER, q.v.

```
              -wardii 1/4              -griffithianum 1/32
          -                      -Kewense-
      -Idealist-      -Aurora-        -fortunei 5/32
ELIE BASKER-        -Naomi-      -thomsonii 1/16
                  -        -fortunei
              -campylocarpum ssp. caloxanthum 1/2
```
4ft(1.2m) high x 5ft(1.5m) OF(-18C) EM   Lax truss of 11
flowers, light orange-yellow in bud, opening light greenish yellow with nectaries of vivid reddish orange. Phetteplace cross,
1976; D. A. Horsley, reg. 1987.

* *
                -Essex Scarlet--uncertain
ELISABETH HOBBIE-
              -forrestii Repens Group
2.5ft(.75m) -5F(-21C) EM 4/4   Deep green, elongated, rounded
leaves conceal the wood structure. Vigorous, upright, spreading
habit. Flower scarlet red, lax truss of 5-7.   Dietrich Hobbie,
1945; reg. 1958. A.M. Wisley Trial 1986, sent for trial by Cox.
Color illus. Cox pl. 52; JS p. 58; VV p. 130; WS, 1989, p. 14.
ABENDGLUT (Evening Embers) Parentage as above
Intense dark scarlet, darkest of the grex. Hobbie, intro. 1967.
ABENDROT (Evening Red) Parentage as above
Flower opens red from red bud; some autumn bloom. Glossy, dark,
compact foliage. Hobbie.
ANTJE Parentage as above
Dark blood red flower. Foliage unlike that of SCARLET WONDER.
Hobbie, 1965.
AKSEL OLSEN   Parentage as above
2ft(.6m) -10F(-23C) M 4/4   Flowers blood red (blutrot) in
loose truss; leaves very bullate. Habit rather untidy compared
to others of this cross.   D. Hobbie.
BAD EILSEN Parentage as above
2ft(.6m) -10F(-23F) M 3/4   Vigorous, compact habit. Small
leaves, heavily veined. Cardinal red flowers; lax trusses of 4-
5. Dislikes heat. Hobbie, reg. 1970. A.M. Wisley Trials 1969.
Color illus. WS, 1989, p. 13.
BADEN-BADEN Parentage as above
2ft(.6m) -15F(-26C) M 3/4   Vigorous, compact, upright habit,
over twice as wide as high. Foliage dark, glossy green. Flowers deep cherry red, waxy, bell-shaped. Sun-tolerant. Hobbie.
H.C. Wisley Trials 1972.
BENGAL   Parentage as above
3ft(.9m) -10F(-23C) M   One of the better selections of this
group. Dark red, darker than SCARLET WONDER; loose truss of 4-5
flowers. Low, compact habit. Hobbie.
BURNING LOVE Parentage as above
Red winter buds open to small red flowers.   Smooth, twisted
leaves. Hobbie.
FRIEDRICH DEUS   Parentage as above
Flowers scarlet red. Hobbie.
JUWEL Parentage as above
2.5ft(.75m) -10F(-23C) EM Truss of 3-5, dark scarlet. One of
the best of this cross. Prostrate, wide-spreading in W. Germany
and more upright in U. K. Hobbie, intro. 1960.
MANNHEIM Parentage as above
3ft(.9m) -15F(-26C) ML   Loose truss, 3-7 dark glowing red
flowers. Blooms later and is taller than others of this grex.
Many flower buds. Plant upright, broad. Hobbie, intro. 1976.
Color illus. WS, 1989, p. 17.
MOERHEIM'S JUBILEE   Parentage as above
Flowers scarlet red. Hobbie cross; Moerheim Nursery, reg. 1969.
SALUTE Parentage as above
Vigorous growing, but leggy. Dark, blood red flowers from light
brown buds that contrast with fresh green foliage.   Hobbie.
SCARLET SURPRISE Parentage as above
Glossy, bright green leaf. Much like SCARLET WONDER. Hobbie.
SCARLET WONDER Parentage as above
2ft(.6m) -15F(-26C) M 4/4   Compact, vigorous plant, twice as
wide as tall. Flowers campanulate, wavy edged, bright cardinal
red, 5-7 in loose truss. Widely distributed. Hobbie cross; Le
Feber intro. 1960; reg. 1965. Silver Gilt Medal, Rotterdam,
1960; Gold Medal Boskoop 1961. A.M. Wisley Trials 1989. Color
illus. F. p. 25; VV p. 50; WS, 1989, p. 19.
SPRING MAGIC (FRÜHLINGSZAUBER) Parentage as above
Vigorous and spreading. Deep currant red flowers; truss of 5-7.
Like ELISABETH HOBBIE, flowers more freely.   Hobbie cross; reg.
1970. A.M. Wisley Trials 1969
* *

              -griersonianum 1/2
ELISABETH INGLIS-JONES-   -haematodes 1/4
                  -May Day-
                      -griersonianum 1/4
Red flowers, in loose trusses. Sir James Horlick, reg. 1962.

                  -griffithianum 1/8
          -Mars-
      -Vulcan-   -unknown 1/4
ELISE WHIPPLE-   -griersonianum 1/4
          -              -caucasicum 1/4
          -Boule de Neige-   -catawbiense 1/8
                  -hardy hybrid-
                      -unknown
1.5ft(.45m) -5F(-21C) ML   Red buds opening to white flowers
suffused red, the reverse red, 2.5in(6.4cm) across, in flattened
trusses of 15. Plant broader than tall.   R. Kruse, reg. 1973.

                  -ponticum 1/4
    -Purple Splendour-
ELISSA-   -unknown 1/4
      -              -griffithianum 1/8
      -      -Loderi-
      -Avalanche-   -fortunei 1/8
              -calophytum 1/4
Campanulate flowers, deep purplish pink, in trusses of 18-22,
fading to very pale purple with a dark red blotch. D. J.
Dosser, reg. 1986.

ELITE   Described under P. J. M., q.v.

* *
              -forrestii Repens Group 1/2
ELIZABETH-
              -griersonianum 1/2
3ft(.9m) OF(-18C) EM 4/4 Bright red flowers 3.5in(9cm) wide,
funnel-campanulate, in lax trusses of 6-8; may have a few blooms
in autumn. Compact plant, broader than tall; dark green foliage
held 3 years. Lord Aberconway, 1929.   A.M. 1939. F.C.C. 1943.
Color illus. ARS Q 34:3 (1980), p. 194; HG p. 135; JS p. 97.
CREEPING JENNY Parentage as above, except reversed
2ft(.6m) 5F(-15C) EM 3/4 Synonym JENNY. Flowers bright red,
campanulate, in lax trusses of 5-6; compact, small-leafed plant.
Lord Aberconway.
* *

ELIZABETH BENNET--form of formosum var. inaequale C & H 301
For the cool greenhouse. White flowers, yellowish green blotch,
4.75in(12cm) wide; truss of 5 or 6. Leaves 2.75in(7cm) long,
scaly below. Mrs. E. Mackenzie raiser; reg. 1981. F.C.C. 1981.

ELIZABETH DAVID--form of burmanicum
4ft(1.2m) 15F(-10C) EM 4/3   Cool greenhouse plant. Flowers
light chartreuse yellow, with reverse slightly darker, campanulate, 2in(5cm) wide; truss of 4. Leaves, both sides with scaly
brown indumentum. Mrs. Eliz. Mackenzie; reg. 1981. A.M. 1980.

              -lacteum 1/4   -griffithianum 1/16
      -Lionel's-   -Kewense-
      - Triumph-   -Aurora-   -fortunei 5/16
      -          -Naomi-   -thomsonii 1/8
ELIZABETH DE-   -fortunei   -griffithianum
ROTHSCHILD -   -Kewense-
      -                      -Aurora-   -fortunei
      -      -Exbury Naomi-   -thomsonii
      -unnamed-   -fortunei
              hybrid-unknown 1/4
5ft(1.5m) -5F(-21C) M 4/3   Very pale yellow flowers, maroon
spotting in throat, openly funnel-shaped, 4.5in(11.5cm) broad;
rounded, well-packed trusses of about 18.   Plant upright; dark
green elliptic leaves. E. de Rothschild, reg. 1966. A.M. 1965.

              -auriculatum 1/2
ELIZABETH LOCK-
              -unknown 1/2
Leaves up to 9in(23cm) long, 3in(7.6cm) wide, dark green.
Flowers in round truss of 12-13, 5-lobed, 3in(7.6cm) wide, color
carmine rose. Shown by J. A. N. Lock. Reg. 1979. A.M. 1968.

                  -haematodes 1/2
ELIZABETH LOCKHART---sport of HUMMING BIRD-
                  -williamsianum 1/2
```
```

2.5ft(.75m) OF(-18C) EM 3/3   Flowers very dark red--darker
than haematodes.   Free-flowering. Leaves to 2in(5cm), dark
green flushed with reddish brown, petioles very dark red; young
foliage very deep, glossy red. R. D. Lockhart, reg. 1965. P.C.
1964;   H.C. 1972.   Color illus. F p. 44.

ELIZABETH LUND   Parentage unknown
Yellow flowers, with a maroon eye.   Mrs. T. Davis, reg. 1980.

ELIZABETH MOUNT   Described under MOUNT MAZAMA, q.v.

```
                  -dichroanthum 1/8
            -Tidbit-
    -unnamed-        -wardii 1/2
ELIZABETH- hybrid-caucasicum 1/4
OF GLAMIS-     -wardii
    -unnamed-         -yakushimanum 1/8
      hybrid-unnamed-    -wardii
        - hybrid-Crest-         -fortunei ssp.
                  -Lady    -  discolor 1/32
                Bessborough-campylocarpum
                           Elatum Gp. 1/32
```
Rounded truss of 12 flowers 6- to 7-lobed, light greenish yellow
deepening to brilliant greenish yellow, very small vivid red-
dish orange eye in throat. Early to late May. Compact plant.
P. A. Cox, reg. 1987.   Named with permission of H. M. Queen
Elizabeth and the Queen Mother.

ELIZABETH POORE   Parentage unknown
5ft(1.5m) -10F(-23C) M   Pinkish lavender flowers with a green
flare, from purplish red buds. Trusses of 14. Deep green foliage on a compact plant.   C. O. Dexter cross; Moseley raiser.

ELIZABETH RED FOLIAGE   Parentage unknown
3ft(.9m) OF(-18C) EM 3/4   New vegetative growth is red, and
the new leaves stay red through the seasons, although the color
tones change.   Ostbo.

ELIZABETH SCHOLTZ   Described under DELENDICH, q.v.

ELIZABETH SIDAMON-ERISTOFF   Parentage unknown
Orchid pink flowers, two conspicuous red blotches; hardy to -10F
(-23C) Howard Phipps, reg. 1970.

ELIZABETH TITCOMB   Described under DIANE TITCOMB, q.v.

ELIZABETH'S GOLD   Parentage unknown
Vivid yellow flowers, funnel-shaped, flushed green on the dorsal
lobe; trusses of 6-8.   Plant 5ft(1.5m).   A. Teese, reg. 1986.

```
              -Betsy Trotwood--unknown 5/8
    -Mars Novus-   -griffithianum 3/8
    -               -Mars-
ELLA-              -unknown
    -       -griffithianum
    -Kohinoor-
            -unknown
```
Frilled flowers, fiery dark carmine red; new foliage of red
shoots. Seidel, 1894.

```
    -smirnowii 1/2
ELLA-       -catawbiense 1/4
    -Mrs. Milner-
              -unknown 1/4
```
5ft(1.5m) -15F(-26C) ML   Carmine red flowers. Other similar
selections from this cross: DARIUS, DIETRICH, ERNA. T. J. R.
Seidel, 1915.

ELLA (Henny)   Described under TIDBIT, q.v.

ELLESTEE---form of wardii L S & T 5679.
Bright lemon yellow flowers with a deep crimson blotch. Ludlow,
Sherriff & Taylor collectors; C. Ingram, reg. 1962. A.M. 1959.

```
              -wardii 1/2
        -Carolyn Grace-
ELLIOTT'S -         -unknown 1/4
 CREAM PUFF-    -wardii
        -Crest-           -fortunei ssp. discolor 1/8
            -Lady Bessborough-
                    -campylocarpum Elatum Group 1/8
```
5ft(1.5m) x 5ft OF(-18C) E   Ball truss of 8-9 flowers, 7 wavy-

edged lobes, pale greenish yellow; moderately scented.   Leaves
olive green.   Walter Elliott, cross 1975; reg. 1987.

```
                  -souliei 1/16
          -Soulbut-
      -Vanessa-      -fortunei--Sir Charles Butler 1/16
    -Etna-      -griersonianum 1/4
    -   -      -dichroanthum 1/8
ELNA-  -Fabia-
    -         -griersonianum
    -elliottii 1/2
```
Scarlet flowers, heavy spotting.   Lord Aberconway.   A.M. 1949.

```
       -elliottii 1/2
ELRISE-      -griffithianum 1/4
    -Sunrise-
          -griersonianum 1/4
```
Red flowers.   Lord Aberconway, 1950.

```
                    -campylocarpum Elatum Group 1/16
          -Penjerrick-
      -Amaura-         -griffithianum 1/16
    -Eros-      -griersonianum 3/8
ELROS-      -griersonianum
    -elliottii 1/2
```
Salmon pink flowers with darker basal spotting; trusses hold 15.
Lord Aberconway, 1945.   A.M. 1948.

ELROSE COURT   Described under COURT JESTER, q.v.

```
                -griffithianum 1/4
      -Mrs. E.C. Stirling-
ELSA CRISP-          -unknown 3/4
    -unknown
```
5ft(1.5m) -5F(-21C) L   Flowers rose Bengal, lighter in center
with deeper margins; trusses of 14-20.   Waterer & Crisp, 1931.

ELSA REID--form of souliei
Flowers cream-colored with crimson spot in throat, 2.5in(6.4cm)
wide; trusses of 5-8. Plant upright, spreading, 5ft(1.5m) tall.
Mrs. A.C.U. Berry raiser; Bovees, reg. 1970.

* *
```
    -grande 1/2
ELSAE-
    -hodgsonii (or possibly falconeri) 1/2
```
Ivory white flowers with crimson basal blotch. Originated in
Cornwall, probably at Tregothnan. Reuthe exhibited. A.M. 1925.
CLYNE BLUSH, CLYNE CERISE, CLYNE ELSAE, CLYNE PEARL all of the
above parentage; originating at Clyne Castle, Swansea, estate of
Adm. W. Heneage-Vivian until 1952. Hybrids dated about 1933.
CLYNE ELSAE   Parentage as above
Trusses of 30 flowers, fuchsia purple, edges stained deeper.
A.M. 1940.
* *

```
        -ciliicalyx 1/2
ELSE FRYE-
        -unknown 1/2
```
4ft(1.2m) 15F(-9C) E 4/3   White flowers with chrome yellow
throat, exterior flushed rose, 4in(10.2cm) wide, very fragrant;
loose trusses of 3-6. Glossy, deeply veined, leathery leaves.
P. Bowman, reg. 1963.   Color illus. VV p. 78; Cox pl. 55.

```
        -souliei 1/2
ELSIE PHIPPS-       -campylocarpum Elatum Group 1/4
        -Penjerrick-
              -griffithianum 1/4
```
Flowers of pale yellow, flushed pink.   Lord Aberconway, 1941.

```
        -edgeworthii (bullatum) 1/2
ELSIE PURNELL-
        -calostrotum 1/2
```
Fragrant shell pink flowers, fading to white, in loose trusses.
Thatcher, reg. 1962.

* *
```
        -campylocarpum 1/2
ELSIE STRAVER-
        -unknown 1/2
```
6ft(1.8m) -5F(-21C) ML   Flowers creamy yellow, dark red blotch
in throat, campanulate; trusses of 12-16. Yellowish green,

wrinkled leaves.   Straver, reg. 1969. Gold Medal Boskoop 1966.
KING'S RANSOM   Parentage as above
Canadian hybrid. Light yellow flowers; trusses of 10-14. Dark
chocolate purple blotch.   S. Irvine cross; McCuaig, reg. 1974.
* *

```
                         -griffithianum 1/8
                  -Mars-
              -Vulcan-    -unknown 1/4
ELSIE WHIPPLE-      -griersonianum 1/4
          -            -caucasicum 1/4
          -Boule de Neige-          -catawbiense 1/8
                         -unnamed hybrid-
                                    -unknown
```
Flower white suffused strong purplish red. R. Kruse, reg. 1973.

ELSMERE   Described under ELAM, q.v.

```
                     -maximum 1/4
          -Halopeanum (White Pearl)-
ELSPETH-                 -griffithianum 1/4
     -unknown 1/2
```
Large white-flowered trusses.   R. Gill & Son, before 1927.

```
          -campylocarpum 1/2
ELSPETH-
      -hardy hybrid--unknown 1/2
```
4ft(1.2m) OF(-18C) EM 3/4   Light green leaves on a compact
plant. Bright scarlet buds open to a deep pinkish apricot, then
fade to cream; small rounded trusses.   Slocock. A.M. 1937.

```
                     -campylocarpum Elatum Group 1/16
               -Penjerrick-
        -Amaura-        -griffithianum 1/16
     -Venus-     -griersonianum 1/8
ELVUS-    -facetum (eriogynum) 1/4
     -elliottii 1/2
```
Red flowers. Lord Aberconway, intro. 1946.

```
                -dichroanthum 1/8
            -Fabia-
   -unnamed hybrid-   -griersonianum 1/8
ELYA-           -bureavii 1/4
    -yakushimanum 1/2
```
3ft(.9m) -5F(-21C) EM 4/5 Trusses of 7-8 flowers, 5-6-lobed,
Neyron rose. Leaves with orange-tan, felt-like indumentum.   H.
L. Larson, reg. 1982.

EMANUELA   Described under YAKU WARRIOR, q.v.

```
          -ciliatum 1/2
EMASCULUM-
      -dauricum 1/2
```
5ft(1.5m) -10F(-23C) VE 4/3 Pale rosy lilac flowers, funnel-
shaped, 2in(5cm) wide, 5-lobed, in truss of 2 or 3; free-flowering. Small, lightly scaly leaves. Waterer, 1958. A.M. 1976.

```
          - campylocarpum 1/2
EMBER GLOW-
      -forrestii Repens Group 1/2
```
A rounded, dwarf shrub. Blood red flowers, campanulate. Early.
Sir John Ramsden cross; Sir Wm. Pennington-Ramsden, reg. 1965.

EMBLEY BLUSH   Listed under EXMINISTER, q.v.

EMBLEY PARK   Described under EXMINISTER, q.v.

EMBLEY PINK   Described under EXMINISTER, q.v.

```
                    -griffithanum 1/4
            -unnamed hybrid-
EMELINE BUCKLEY-          -unknown 3/4
                -Bacchus--unknown
```
Flowers bright pink with dark blotch.   C. B. van Nes & Sons.

* *
```
                -wardii 1/4        -griffithianum 3/32
      -Idealist-      -Kewense-
      -      -     -Aurora-     -fortunei 15/32
      -    -Naomi-      -thomsonii 3/16
EMERALD-          -fortunei
 ISLE -           -griffithianum
      -            -Kewense-
      -     -Aurora-        -fortunei
      -Exbury-      -thomsonii
        Naomi-fortunei
```
5ft(1.5m) OF(-18C) M Bell-shaped flowers of chartreuse green,
darker in the throat. RHS Garden, Wisley.   A.M. 1956.
NEW COMET   Parentage as above
Flowers of mimosa yellow, flushed pale pink, funnel-shaped;
large, heavy, spherical truss.   RHS Garden, Wisley. A.M. 1957.
* *

EMETT ADAMS   Described under REDWAX, q.v.

```
                -caucasicum 1/4
     -Boule de Neige-          -catawbiense 3/8
     -          -hardy hybrid-
EMIL-                -unknown 3/8
     -          -catawbiense
     -Mrs. Milner-
                -unknown
```
White flowers with a soft pink touch.   Seidel, intro. 1903.

EMILY ALLISON   Described under DARLENE'S PINK, q.v.

```
              -griffithianum 1/2
EMILY MANGLES-
         -unknown 1/2
```
Flowers pink with crimson blotch. Mangles at Littleworth.

```
              -catawbiense 1/2
     -Annedore-
EMMA-         -unknown 1/2
     -          -catawbiense
     -Mrs. Milner-
                -unknown
```
Bright carmine red flowers with darker markings on a light back-
ground.   T. J. R. Seidel, intro. 1917.

```
                         -minus Carolinianum Group 1/2
               -unnamed hybrid-
EMOJENE LOUISE-          -keiskei 5/16
         -          -minus Carolinianum Group
      -unnamed hybrid-          -pubescens 1/16
            -     -Chesapeake-
            -Elam-      -keiskei
               -unknown 1/8
```
16in(.4m)(12yrs) -22F(-30C) M   Buds strong purple-pink; flow-
ers paler, 1.3in(3cm) across, white centers, yellow-green dorsal
spotting; truss of 3. Small smooth leaves, scaly below; spreading, floriferous plant.   W. Fetterhoff, cross 1975; reg. 1988.

EMPEREUR DE MAROC   Parentage unknown
Parent of BLUE RIVER. Brilliant purple flowers.   Unknown.

```
                     -decorum ? 1/4
             -Caroline-
EMPEROR WALTZ-      -brachycarpum ? 1/4
            -fortunei--Sir Charles Butler 1/2
```
8ft(2.4m)(13 yrs) -15F(-26C) L   Flowers 4in(10cm) across,
moderately fragrant, 7-lobed, very pale purple shading to light
purplish pink at edges.   Walbrecht cross; R. Brooks, reg. 1986.

EMPIRE DAY   Described under ROMANY CHAI, q.v.

EMPRESS EUGENIE   Parentage unknown
Parent of EUTHOM. Flower creamy white, finely spotted. Origin
unknown.

```
              -ponticum 1/4
     -Purple Splendour-
EMS-          -unknown
     -forrestii Repens Group 1/2
```
2.5ft(.75m) -5F(-21C) EM   Loose trusses of funnel-shaped,
dark reddish purple flowers. Habit is a compact mound. Useful
for its early season of bloom. D. Hobbie, intro. 1951.

```
          -aberconwayi 1/2
ENBORNE-
          -maculiferum ssp. anhweinse 1/2
```
3ft(.9m) -5F(-21C) M 3/3   Compact trusses of 12-14 flowers,
white flushed phlox pink, upper throat speckled pink. A dwarf
plant with reflexed leaves 3in(7.6cm) long. Crown Estate, Windsor, reg. 1967. A.M. 1966.

ENCHANTED EVENING   Parentage unknown
4ft(1.2m) 5F(-15C) ML 3/4 Dark buds open to soft salmon with
stripe of peach-orange from throat to margins of petals. Upper
lobe spotted dark lime green. Much like GOLDEN BELLE. Whitney
cross; Sather, reg. 1976.

```
          -brachycarpum--Nikko Montanum 1/2
ENCHANTRESS-
          -unknown 1/2
```
Bright rose pink buds open to very pale pink, wavy-edged flowers
with narrow rim of rose; large, yellow spotted dorsal blotch.
May be registered under different name. Shapiro.

```
          -arboreum ssp. cinnamomeum var. album 1/2
ENDEAVOUR-
          -lacteum 1/2
```
Tall shrub, early-blooming; white flowers lightly flushed pale
yellow, tubular-campanulate; full truss of 13-16. Leaves matte
dark green above, silvery brown plastered indumentum below. L.
de Rothschild cross; shown by E. de Rothschild. A.M. 1983.

ENDRE OSTBO   Described under SOULDIS, q.v.

```
          -arboreum 1/2
ENDSLEIGH PINK-
          -unknown 1/2
```
Small, pale rose flowers, lightly dotted, in neat trusses, on a
large bush. More cold-tolerant than arboreum. Origin unknown.

```
* * * * * * * * * * * * * * * * * * * * * * * * * * * * * *
                   -elliottii 1/2
          -Jutland-                  -fortunei ssp. discolor 1/16
          -        -        -Norman-
ENGLEMERE-        -Bellerophon- Shaw -        -cataubiense
          -        -elliottii   -      -B. de Bruin-     1/32
          -Royal -             -      -         -unknown 9/32
          Blood-               -facetum (eriogynum) 1/8
                   -Rubens--unknown
```
Tight rounded truss 7in(17.8cm) wide, 32 flowers, cardinal red.
Leaves 6in(15cm) long. Crown Estate, reg. 1972. A.M. 1971.
ROYAL WINDSOR   Parentage as above
3ft(.9m) -5F(-21C) M   Firm, rounded trusses of 20-22 flowers,
rich reddish purple, darker spotting in throat. Narrow leaves,
to 5.25in(13.3cm). Crown Estate, reg. 1975. A.M. 1975.
```
* * * * * * * * * * * * * * * * * * * * * * * * * * * * * *
```

```
                                  -cataubiense 1/2
ENGLISH ROSEUM--Possibly sport of ROSEUM ELEGANS-
                                  -unknown 1/2
```
6ft(1.8m) -25F(-32C) ML 3/3   Flowers of soft rosy pink, with
smooth, glossy leaves of dark green. A fast-growing hybrid,
tolerant of extremes in cold, heat, and humidity. A. Waterer.

ENID MAY   Described under PANACHE, q.v.

ENIGMA   Possible parentage: fortunei x maximum x haematodes
7ft(2.1m) x 9ft(2.7m)(32 yrs) -5F(-21C) M Strong purplish red
flowers shading to strong purplish pink with brilliant yellow-
green spotting and strong yellow-green rays in throat. Truss
7in(18cm) wide. Consolini cross; Swarthmore College, reg. 1985.

ENTICEMENT   Described under SIERRA SUNSET, q.v.

EPOCH--form of minus Carolinianum Group, white form
     Grown from colchicine-treated seed
3ft(.9m) -10F(-23C) M 3/2   A tetraploid. Flowers white,
shaded pink, frilled, good substance, saucer-shaped, up to 2.5in
(6.4cm) wide; ball-shaped trusses of 12. Plant rounded, wider
than tall; deep green foliage held 2-3 years. Dr. A. E. Kehr,
reg. 1972. Color illus. K p. 56.

```
* * * * * * * * * * * * * * * * * * * * * * * * * * * * * * *
                                            -cataubiense
                              -Parsons Grandi--        3/32
                   -Nova  - florum      -unknown
          -Hachmann's  - Zembla-dark red hybrid--unknown
          - Feuerschein-        -griffithianum 3/16
          -                   -Mars-
     -Oratorium-             -unknown 21/32
     -              -          -        -arboreum 1/16
ERATO-         -          -Doncaster-
     -         -Thunderstorm-        -unknown
     -         -                   -unknown
     -Hachmann's Feuerschein (as above)
```
5ft(1.5m) x 5ft(12 yrs) -15F(-26C) ML   Flowers in compact
truss of 14-17, buds of dark red opening to a uniform deep red,
not fading; 3 lobes spotted dark red. Hachmann, cross 1976;
Stück, reg. 1988. Color illus. WS, 1989, p. 125.
NEGRITO   Sibling of above
Similar to above. Strong red flowers, 5-lobed, yellow anthers.
Hachmann cross; Stück, reg. 1988.
TARANTELLA   Sibling of above
4ft(1.2m) x 5ft(1.5m) -15F(-26C) ML Flowers in trusses of 12-
14, funnel-shaped, 5 wavy-edged lobes, deep red shades to strong
red, dorsal lobe richly marked dark red on light ground; white
in throat. Stück, reg. 1988. Color illus. WS, 1989, p. 143.
```
* * * * * * * * * * * * * * * * * * * * * * * * * * * * * * *
```

```
          -C. O. D.--unknown Dexter hybrid 3/4
ERCHLESS-                          -griffithianum 1/8
     -              -unnamed hybrid-
     -Mrs. Furnival-             -unknown
     -              -          -caucasicum 1/8
          -unnamed hybrid-
                   -unknown
```
When registered 6ft(1.8m) tall, but age not stated. Flowers of
pale purplish pink, dark red eye, 5-lobed, frilly-edged. Open,
spreading habit. Howard Phipps, intro. 1955; reg. 1972.

```
               -dichroanthum 1/4
          -Fabia-
EREBUS-        -griersonianum 3/4
     -griersonianum
```
Flowers brilliant deep scarlet, funnel-shaped, in loose trusses.
A compact plant. Midseason bloom. Lord Aberconway, 1936.

EREDA BEEKMAN   Parentage unknown
Flowers light sap green. J. Beekman, reg. 1975.

ERIC RUDD--form of facetum (eriogynum) F 13508
Loose trusses of up to 13 flowers, 5-lobed, 2.75in(7cm) across,
color Delft rose. Leaves 6.5in(16.5cm) long, dull dark green.
George Forrest collector; Col. S. R. Clarke raiser; R. N. S.
Clarke, reg. 1981. A.M. 1980.

```
                    -dichroanthum 1/2
          -Fabia High Beeches-
ERIC STOCKTON-              -griersonianum 1/2
     -                   -griersonianum
     -Tally Ho-
               -facetum (eriogynum) 1/4
```
Leaves 6.75in(17cm) long with brown indumentum. Flowers jasper
red, darker veins, widely funnel-campanulate; trusses of 5-9.
G. H. Loder raiser; Hon. H. E. Boscawen, reg. 1967. A.M. 1967.

```
               -dichroanthum ssp. scyphocalyx 1/4
          -Medusa-
ERIDUSA-        -griersonianum 1/4
     -facetum (eriogynum) 1/2
```
Deep red flowers. Lord Aberconway, intro. 1946.

```
          -degronianum ssp. heptamereum (metternichii) 1/2
ERIKA-
          -Alexander Adie--unknown 1/2
```
Light carmine pink flowers, brown markings. Seidel, 1903.

ERIK'S CHOICE---from grande, open pollinated
14ft(4.2m) x 10ft(3.0m)(25 yrs) 5F(-15C) E Flowers in trusses
of 15-20, heavy substance, openly campanulate, 7-lobed, reddish
purple buds open purplish pink to cream. Vaartnou, reg. 1989.

```
            -griersonianum 1/4
       -Azor-
ERIOZOR-    -fortunei ssp. discolor 1/4
       -facetum (eriogynum) 1/2
Red flowers.  Lord Aberconway, 1946.
```

* *
```
                       -griffithianum 1/4
            -Queen Wilhelmina-
      -Britannia-             -unknown 3/8
ERMINE-       -Stanley Davies--unknown
      -              -fortunei--Sir Charles Butler 1/4
      -Mrs. A. T. de la Mare-        -maximum 1/8
                       -Halopeanum-
                             -griffithianum
6ft(.9m) 0F(-18C) ML 3/3  Flowers 3.5in(9cm) across, white,
unspotted, funnel-campanulate; compact, conical truss of about
11.  Plant wider than tall, a stiff growth habit; medium green
leaves 6in(15.2cm) long.  Tolerates sun.  R. Henny, reg. 1960.
HEART'S DELIGHT  Parentage as above, except reversed
Light vibrant red with deeper marking.  Well-shaped, dense plant
with dark green cover.  Alma Manenica, reg. 1983.
```
* *

```
            -fortunei 1/2
ERNEST GILL-            (Possibly fortunei x LUSCOMBEI)
            -arboreum 1/2
5ft(1.5m) 0F(-18C) EM   Flowers  bright pink, crimson basal
blotch.  R. Gill.  A.M. 1918.
```

ERNEST INMAN   Described under CAROLINE ALLBROOK, q.v.

ERNEST R. BALL   Described under ART WICKENS, q.v.

```
            -yunnanense 1/2
ERNESTINE-
            -cinnabarinum Roylei Group 1/2
Lilac pink,  trumpet-shaped flowers in great profusion.  Growth
habit tall, compact; foliage of bluish cast.   Rothschild, 1937.
```

```
            -dauricum 1/2
ERNIE DEE-
            -racemosum 1/2
1ft(.3m) 0F(-18C) EM 3/4   Slightly frilled purple flowers,
dorsal red spotting,  flattened,  to 1in(2.5cm) wide; terminal
inflorescence of 4-8; truss each 2-flowered; long-lasting, abun-
dant bloom. Plant twice as broad as high.  Caperci, reg. 1976.
```

```
                 -campylocarpum Elatum Group 1/8
         -Penjerrick-
      -Amaura-            -griffithianum 1/8
EROS-             -griersonianum 3/4
      -griersonianum
Pale pink flowers.   Lord Aberconway, 1936.
```

```
                 -dichroanthum 1/8
         -Fabia-
      -Erebus-      -griersonianum 3/8
ERSO-       -griersonianum
      -souliei 1/2
Lord Aberconway, intro. 1946.
```

```
                       -griffithianum 1/4
            -Loderi King George-
ESMERALDA-                -fortunei 1/4
            -neriiflorum 1/2
Flowers of pale pink to deep rose.   Rothschild, 1937.
```

```
            -barbatum 1/2
ESPERNZA-
            -strigillosum 1/2
Deep red flowers, tubular-campanulate,  similar to strigillosum.
Plant tall, not compact. Early.  Rothschild, 1937.
```

```
            -griersonianum 1/2
ESQUIRE-
            -unknown 1/2
4ft(1.2m) 5F(-15C) M 4/3  Buds long, pointed, opening water-
melon pink; flowers about 4in(10.2cm) across, in loose, round
trusses.  Habit upright, spreading; dark green leaves, reddish
brown petioles.  Barto raiser; Del James intro. before 1958.
```

```
            -falconeri ssp. eximium 1/2
ESSA-
            -unknown 1/2
Flowered over 20 years after the seeds germinated.  Large leaves
10in(25.4cm) long by 4in(10.2cm) wide with patchy thin  tomentum
beneath.  White flowers, faint pink stains, deep crimson blotch;
round truss of 23.  A.C. & E.F.A. Gibson, reg. 1965.  A.M. 1964.
```

```
ESSEX SCARLET   Parentage uncertain
Often a parent.  Flowers deep crimson scarlet, with almost black
blotch.  G. Paul, 1899.   A.M. 1899.
```

```
            -yakushimanum--Koichiro Wada 1/2
ESTACADA-
            -arboreum, red form 1/2
4ft(1.2m) 5F(-15C) VE      Synonym VIVID-O.  Cardinal red buds
open  to crimson to carmine rose flowers, openly campanulate,
2.5in(6.4cm) wide;  dome-shaped truss of 18-20;  plant broader
than tall;  leaves, grayed white indumentum, held 3 years; new
growth, white tomentose.  Dr. D. Goheen cross, 1967; reg. 1983.
```

```
                       -griffithianum 1/4
            -Loderi Venus-
ESTELLE GATKE-          -fortunei 1/4
            -            -griersonianum 1/4
            -Tally Ho-
                  -facetum (eriogynum) (1/4)
R. M. Gatke, intro. 1958.
```

```
                            -caucasicum 3/32
                  -Jacksonii-        -caucasicum
         -Goldsworth-        -Nobleanum-
      -Goldfort- Yellow  -              -arboreum 1/32
ESTER-       -            -campylocarpum 1/8
DUDLEY-       -fortunei 1/4
      -            -griffithianum 1/4
      -King George-
                  -unknown 1/4
Flowers yellow, deeper in throat.  H. D. Rose, AUS, reg. 1973.
```

```
            -arboreum ssp. cinnmomeum var. album 1/2
ESTEREL-
            -meddianum 1/2
Rosy pink, waxy flowers; medium-sized plant.  Rothschild, 1937.
```

```
                            -griffithianum 1/4
                  -George Hardy-
            -Pink Pearl-      -cataubiense 1/4
            -       -            -arboreum 1/8
      -Countess-       -Broughtonii-    1/8
      -of Derby-            -unknown 1/8
      -       -       -cataubiense
ESTHER GRACE-   -Cynthia-
      -            -griffithianum
      -   -decorum 1/4          -griffithianum
      -White-      -George Hardy-
       Swan-Pink Pearl-      -cataubiense
            -            -arboreum
                  -Broughtonii-
                        -unknown
5ft(1.5m) -5F(-21C) ML  White flowers with a few reddish brown
spots, quite flat, ruffled, to 4.5in(11.5cm) wide;  truss of 14.
Plant open; pointed leaves 5in(12.7cm) long.  Bovees, reg. 1972.
```

```
                  -griffithianum 3/8
            -Mars-
      -      -unknown 1/2
ESTHER PACKARD-          -griffithianum
      -            -Loderi-
      -unnamed hybrid-      -fortunei 1/8
                  -unknown
2.5ft(.75m) -5F(-21C) M   Flowers fuchsine pink, campanulate,
to 4in(10.2cm) wide; rounded trusses.  Plant low, spreading;
glossy dark green leaves.  Melvin V. Love, reg. 1964.
```

ESTHER WAGNER   Described under AMY JANE, q.v.

```
ESVELD SELECT--form of yakushimanum
4ft(1.2m) x 6ft(1.8m)(20 yrs) -10F(-23C) EM  Flowers in truss
of 10-18, campanulate, 5-lobed, appleblossom pink fading to pure
white.  New foliage with white indumentum.  D. M. van Gelderen,
selected 1970; Royal Boskoop Horticultural Society, reg. 1988.
```

```
                  -neriiflorum 1/4
     -F. C. Puddle-
ETHEL-           -griersonianum 1/4
     -forrestii Repens Group 1/2
1.5ft(.45m) 5F(-15C) EM 3/3 Blazing scarlet flowers, campan-
ulate, double calyx; truss of 3-5. Creeping, spreading habit,
very compact. Lord Aberconway, 1934. F.C.C. 1940.
```

ETHEL DUPAR   Parentage unknown
Flowers creamy yellow, with a pink blush. Whitney cross; Dupar,
reg. 1967.

```
            -minus var. chapmanii 1/2
ETHEL-MAE-
            -mucronulatum 1/2
```
4ft(1.2m) -10F(-23C) E   Terminal inflorescence of 3-4 buds,
each with 10 bell-shaped flowers of lavender pink. Plant broad,
well-branched. C. Herbert, intro. 1965; reg. 1977.

```
ETHEL V.--unnamed      -brachycarpum 1/4
  CARY   hybrid, selfed-              -catawbiense
                    -Mrs. C. S.. Sargent-        1/4
                                   -unknown 1/4
```
2ft(.6m) -20F(-29C) ML Plant broader than tall; convex leaves
with thin indumentum; new growth silver green, red stems. Flowers with orchid edge, fading white in center, reverse solid
orchid; spherical truss of about 20. E. A. Cary, reg. 1973.

```
     -campylocarpum 1/2
ETHYL-
     -orbiculare 1/2
```
A medium-sized shrub with foliage like orbiculare. Flowers of
cream, tinged pink. Early season. Rothschild, 1937.

```
                -souliei 1/8
          -Soulbut-
     -Vanessa-      -fortunei--Sir Charles Butler 1/8
ETNA-      -griersonianum 1/2
    -      -dichroanthum 1/4
     -Fabia-
           -griersonianum
```
Magenta red flowers. Lord Aberconway, intro. 1936.

```
                         -campylocarpum Elatum Group 1/16
             -Penjerrick-
      -Amaura-          -griffithianum 1/16
    -Eros-     -griersonianum 3/8
ETOS-    -griersonianum
    -thomsonii 1/2
```
Deep red flowers. Lord Aberconway, intro. 1946.

```
                 -elliottii 1/4
            -Fusilier-
ETTA BURROWS-      -griersonianum 1/4
            -strigillosum 1/2
```
6ft(1.8m) 5F(-15C) E 4/4 Plant broader than tall; fir green
leaves 9in(22.9cm) long, indumented like strigillosum. Bright
blood red flowers, 3in. (7.6cm) wide, campanulate; rounded truss
of about 30. H. L. Larson, reg. 1965. Color illus. HG p. 88.

ETZEL   Described under ALFRED, q.v.

```
     -hanceanum Nanum Group 1/2
EUAN COX-
     -ludlowii 1/2
```
1ft(.3m) OF(-18C) EM 4/3 Plant spreads much wider than tall,
leaves 1in(2.5cm) long, dull dark green. Flowers light yellow,
spotted brick-dust red, 2in(5cm) wide, in trusses of 4. E. H.
M. Cox cross; Glendoick, reg. 1981. A.M. Wisley Trials 1981.

```
     -campylocarpum 1/2
EUCAMP-
     -Empress Eugenie--unknown 1/2
```
Cream-colored flowers. E. J. P. Magor.

```
     -forrestii Repens Group 1/2
EUCHELIA-
     -unknown 1/2
```
Flowers bright deep crimson, of heavy substance. Lord Aberconway. A.M. 1935.

EUCLID   Parentage unknown

5ft(1.5m) -25F(-32C) M 2/3   Flowers in tight trusses of
rosy violet; compact-growing with nice foliage. Noble, 1850.

* *
```
                   -souliei 1/8
          -soulbut-
    -Vanessa-      -fortunei--Sir Charles Butler 1/8
EUDORA-      -griersonianum 1/4
    -facetum 1/2
```
Flowers in trusses of 11-12, campanulate, 5-lobed, of vivid pur-
plish red, lightly spotted in throat. The Second Lord Aberconway
intro 1936; Lord Aberconway exhibited. A.M. 1988.
VANITY FAIR   Parentage as above
Flowers reddish scarlet. Lord Aberconway, intro. 1941.
* *

```
             -campylocarpum 1/4
      -Unique-
EUGENE-      -unknown 1/2
    -                 -griffithianum 1/4
      -Jean Marie de Montague-
                         -unknown
```
4ft(1.2m) -5F(-21C) M 3/4 Unusually large "pine cone" flower
buds with interesting bracts. Coral red flowers, held in tight,
rounded trusses. Foliage deep green, very dense. H. E. Greer.

```
     -Empress Eugenie--unknown 1/2
EUKING-           -griffithianum 1/4
     -Mrs. Kingsmill-
                  -campylocarpum 1/4
```
Flowers of clear lemon yellow; faint red spotting. Magor, 1935.

EULALIE WAGNER   Described under DARLENE'S PINK, q.v.

* *
```
                   -souliei 1/16
             -Soulbut-
       -Vanessa-      -fortunei--Sir Charles Butler 1/16
   -Eudora-      -griersonianum 1/8
EULO-    -facetum (eriogynum) 1/4
    -      -griffithianum 1/4
     -Loderi-
           -fortunei 1/4
```
Pale pink flowers. Lord Aberconway, 1941.
NEPTUNE   Parentage as above
Flowers pale pink. Lord Aberconway, 1941.
* *
```
                -griffithianum 5/16
        -Loderi-                      -griffithianum
EUNICIE CLARIS-     -fortunei 9/16  -Kewense-
      -                    -Aurora-      -fortunei
        -Naomi Pink Beauty-      -thomsonii 1/8
                          -fortunei
```
Flowers in truss of 9-10, 7-lobed, carmine rose, frilled edges;
fragrant. Like a compact LODERI. R. C. Gordon, reg. 1984.

```
     -sperabile 1/2
EUPHENO-
     -griersonianum 1/2
```
Deep red flowers. Lord Aberconway, 1936.

```
       -arboreum 1/2
EUPHROSYNE-      -griffithianum 1/4
       -Loderi-
             -fortunei 1/4
```
Large flowers of bright carmine, speckled crimson. Rothschild.
A clone, EUPHROSYNE RUBY shown by Sir E. Loder. A.M. 1923.

```
     -arboreum 1/2
EUREKA-
     -hookeri 1/2
```
A medium-sized, compact plant. Blood red flowers; trusses of 15
to 18. Rothschild, 1937. A.M. 1939.

EUREKA MAID   See COUNTESS OF DERBY

```
     -ungernii 1/2
EUROPA-
     -kyawii 1/2
```
6ft(1.8m) 5F(-15C) L 3/3 Flowers rosy lilac, tubular, to 3in
(7.6cm) across, in rounded open trusses. Attractive foliage:

glossy, dark green leaves, prominent veining, tan indumentum.
Rothschild, 1937.   Color illus. ARS J 38:2 (1984), p. 54.

```
              -neriiflorum 1/4
        -Nereid-
EURYALUS-        -dichroanthum 1/4
        -griersonianum 1/2
```
Deep red flowers. Lord Aberconway, 1936.

```
              -arboreum ssp. cinnamomeum var. album 1/2
EURYDICE-
        -kyawii 1/2
```
A medium-sized plant with attractive foliage. Large white flow-
ers, tinged with rose and crimson.   Rothschild. A.M. 1937.

EUTERPE (Reuthe)   Described under OREOAUG, q.v.

EUTERPE (Seidel)   Described under JEWESS, q.v.

```
        -Empress Eugenie--unknown 1/2
EUTHOM-
        -thomsonii 1/2
```
Flowers light carmine shading to pink, spotted crimson.   Magor.

* *
```
              -diaprepes 1/4
        -Polar Bear-
EVA REBECCA-         -auriculatum 1/4
        -            -fortunei ssp. discolor 1/4
        -Autumn Gold-        -dichroanthum 1/8
                      -Fabia-
                      -griersonianum 1/8
```
3.5ft(1m) -5F(-21C) L Flowers orange, shading to yellow, 4in
(10.2cm) wide, openly funnel-shaped, 7-lobed, fragrant; trusses
8in(20.3cm) across, hold 8-10. Plant broader than high; foliage
7.5in(19cm) x 2in(5cm).   J. A. Holden, reg. 1979.
JANE HOLDEN   Parentage as above
4ft(1.2m) -5F(-21C) L   Lax trusses of 8-10 fragrant flowers,
empire rose, with light brick red flare. Plant wider than high,
leaves 7in(17.8cm) long. A. J. Holden reg. 1979.
* *
```
                          -caucasicum 3/16
                    -Jacksonii-
        -Goldsworth Yellow-        -caucasicum
EVA SCHMICK-              -Nobleanum-
                    -campylocarpum 1/4 -arboreum 1/16
              -wardii (a form once known as astrocalyx) 1/2
```
2.5ft(.75m) x 3ft(.9m)(9 yrs) -5F(-21C) M   Lax trusses of 6-9
flowers, pale yellow (a little deeper than GOLDSWORTH YELLOW),
a brownish red blotch in dorsal throat.   H. Schmick, reg. 1988.

EVANGELINE   See FUNDY, described under KATHERINE DALTON, q.v.

EVELYN (Henny) Described under ROSEANN, q.v.

```
                    -Essex Scarlet--unknown 3/8
        -Oudijk's Sensation-
EVELYN-              -williamsianum 1/4
      -        -smirnowii 1/4
      -Daisy-        -catawbiense 1/8
              -Mrs. Milner-
                      -unknown
```
4ft(1.2m) -15F(-26C) M   One of the hardiest of williamsianum
hybrids; slow-growing. Pink-flowered. Hachmann, intro. 1976.

```
              -yakushimanum 1/2
EVELYN SLINGER-
              -unknown 1/2
```
Strong red buds open to campanulate flowers, moderate yellowish
pink with strong red margins; trusses of 8. Long calyx, divided
irregularly.   Slieve Donard Nursery raiser. E. C. Nelson, reg.
1987.

* *
```
        -hodgsonii 1/2
EVENING-    -falconeri 1/4
        -Muriel-
              -grande 1/4
```
A hybrid by Sir Giles Loder, 1950.
HAZE   Parentage as above
Flowers light purplish mauve.   Sir Giles Loder, 1954.
MIST   Parentage as above

Flowers of dark pinkish mauve.   Sir Giles Loder, 1954.
* *

EVENING GLOW   Described under MARGARET DUNN, q.v.

```
              -griffithianum 1/4
        -Sunrise-
EVENTIDE-        -griersonianum 3/4
        -griersonianum
```
Flowers of pale rose pink.   Lord Aberconway, intro. 1941.

EVERCHOICE   Parentage unknown
A parent of ROBERT HUBER, a hybrid reg. by Charles Herbert. May
be a Dexter.

EVERETT CHRISTOPHER   Parentage unknown: unnamed hybrids
Flowers deep purple-pink (fuchsia), 2.7in(7cm) wide, wavy-edged,
of heavy substance; spherical truss of 9-12. Concave, hairless,
ovate leaves2in(5cm) long; held 3 years. Plant upright, floriferous. R.I. Agr. Exp. Sta. intro.; J. McGuire raiser; reg.1989.

```
              -catawbiense 1/2
EVERESTIANUM-
              -unknown 1/2
```
6ft(1.8m) -15F(-26C) ML 2/3 A vigorous plant, flowering profusely in sun or light shade; pest-resistant. Rosy lilac, spotted in throat, edges frilled, 2in(5cm) wide; rounded trusses of
about 15. Dark green, oval leaves. A. Waterer, before 1850.

EVERFULL   Described under FOXBURG, q.v.

```
                    -fortunei ? 1/2
EVERGLADES' HARDY MAUVE-
                    -unknown 1/2
```
A hybrid by C. O. Dexter; introduced by Samuel Everitt.

EVERGLOW   Described under DRUM MAJOR, q.v.

```
                              -fortunei ssp. discolor
                        -Lady -                  1/8
                        -Bessborough-campylocarpum Elatum Gp.
              -Jalisco-                          1/8
              -        -        -dichroanthum 3/16
        -Comstock-        -Dido-
        -        -        -decorum 1/16
        -        -        -dichroanthum
EVERYTHING-        -Jasper-        -fortunei ssp. discolor
  NICE   -        -Lady -
        -        -Bessborough-campylocarpum Elatum Gp.
        -        -campylocarpum 1/4
        -Unique-
              -unknown 1/4
```
4ft(1.2m) -5F(-21C) EM 4/4   Flowers clear pink with lighter
pink rays; the calyx rolls back its lobes as the flower ages,
making a star-shaped appearance at the center of the truss.
Compact habit. H. E. Greer, reg. 1982. Color illus. HG p. 86.

EXALTED RULER   Parentage unknown
6ft(1.8m) OF(-18C) L Flowers of light violet, with a deep maroon blotch. Large leaves; vigorous plant. Lyons, reg. 1972.

```
              -sanguineum ssp. didymum 1/2
EXBURIENSE-
              -kyawii 1/2
```
One of the latest-flowering red rhododendrons. Flowers campanu-
late, waxy, very dark red. Medium-sized, spreading plant; dark
green, rounded leaves. Rothschild, 1937.

EXBURY--form of praestans (coryphaeum)
Large leaves, 11in x 4in (28cm x 10.2cm), on a very large shrub
or small tree. Flowers white, a translucent shade of very pale
yellow, throat blotched with crimson, 2in(5cm) wide; large globular trusses of 32. E. de Rothschild, reg. 1963. A.M. 1963.

EXBURY ALBATROSS   Described under ALBATROSS, q.v.

EXBURY ANGELO   Described under ANGELO, q.v.

EXBURY ANTONIO   See ANTONIO

* *
```
             -calophytum 1/2
EXBURY CALSTOCKER-         -caucasicum 1/4
             -Dr. Stocker-
                          -griffithianum 1/4
```
6ft(1.8m) -5F(-21C) E 5/4   Flowers creamy light pink, rich
red flare in center, in huge truss of c. 23.   A tree-like rhododendron; large, thick leaves.   Rothschild.   A.M. 1948.
CALSTOCKER   The first named selection from above cross, 1935,
but not as good as the Exbury form.   Whitaker, Pylewell Park.
* *

EXBURY CORNISH CROSS   Described under CORNISH CROSS, q.v.

EXBURY FABIA   Described under FABIA, q.v.

EXBURY HAWK   Described under HAWK, q.v.

EXBURY ISABELLA   Described under ISABELLA, q.v.

EXBURY JALISCO   Described under JALISCO, q.v.

EXBURY LADY CHAMBERLAIN   Described under LADY CHAMBERLAIN, q.v.

EXBURY MATADOR   Described under MATADOR, q.v.

EXBURY MAY DAY   Described under MAY DAY, q.v.

EXBURY MERLIN   See HAWK MERLIN

EXBURY NAOMI   Described under NAOMI, q.v.

EXBURY PINK--form of souliei
5ft(1.5m) -5F(-21C) M 4/3   L. de Rothschild. F.C.C. 1936.

EXBURY RED CAP   Described under RED CAP, q.v.

EXBURY SOULDIS   Described under SOULDIS, q.v.

EXBURY SPINULOSUM   Described under SPINULOSUM, q.v.

EXCALIBUR   Described under ONE THOUSAND BUTTERFLIES, q.v.

* *
```
         -thomsonii 1/2
EXMINSTER-
         -campylocarpum 1/2
```
Flowers pink over cream.   Barclay Fox, 1923.   A.M. 1923.
EMBLEY BLUSH   Parentage as above
Cross by J. J. Crosfield; intro. 1935.
EMBLEY PARK   Parentage as above
Pale rose with yellowish tinge in tube.   Crosfield. A.M. 1936.
EMBLEY PINK   Parentage as above
Rose-colored flowers.   Crosfield.   A.M. 1930.
LEONARDSLEE PEACH   Parentage as above
Flowers of orange pink.   Sir E. Loder.
LITTLE PADDOCKS   Parentage as above
Shown by Lt. Col. J. N. Horlick, 1940.
PLEASANT   Parentage as above.   Horlick, 1855.
* *
```
         -ciliatum 1/2
EXONIENSE-
         -veitchianum 1/2
```
Creamy white flowers.   Veitch.   F.C.C. 1881.

EXOTIC   Described under MARY MAYO, q.v.

```
                -catawbiense 1/4
    -Ginny Mae-      -dichroanthum 1/8
    -          -Fabia-
    -                -griersonianum 1//8
EYE POPPER-                      -Pygmalion--unknown 1/16
    -                -unnamed hybrid-
    -        -Weldy-            -haematodes 1/16
    -Robert-      -yakushimanum, Exbury form
    -Weldon-      -yakushimanum 1/4
             -Serendipity-
                      -aureum 1/8
```
Blend of moderate reddish orange, deep yellowish pink and pale
greenish yellow in bud opening to pale yellow, edged with strong
yellowish pink; dorsal spots deep purplish red.   W. Delp.

```
             -burmanicum 1/2
EYEBRIGHT-
             -unknown 1/2
```
Trusses of 8 tubular funnel-shaped flowers, primrose yellow with
lemon yellow flare in dorsal throat; scented. Leaves have brown
scales. Compact bush; Oct. flowers, NZ.   A. Duncan, reg. 1986.

EYESTOPPER   Described under JOAN THOMPSON, q.v.

                              F

```
             -neriiflorum 1/2
F. C. PUDDLE-
             -griersonianum 1/2
```
5ft(1.5m) 5F(-15C) EM 3/3   Dull, dark green, medium-sized
leaves; habit upright. Flowers brilliant orange-scarlet. Named
for the former Curator.   Lord Aberconway, 1926.   A.M. 1932.

```
             -catawbiense 1/2
F. D. GODMAN-
             -unknown 1/2
```
5ft(1.5m) -10F(-23C) M 2/3 Flowers dark magenta red with a
black blotch; compact, rounded truss.   A. Waterer, 1888.

F. L. AMES   See AMPHION

* *
```
    -dichroanthum 1/2
FABIA-
    -griersonianum 1/2
```
3ft(.9m) 5F(-15C) M 3/4   Several have made this cross, with
various selected forms named.   Plants usually neat and compact,
with flowers carried in loose, drooping trusses. This Bodnant
form: a wide, dome-shaped bush with loose, flat trusses, funnel-
shaped scarlet flowers shaded orange in the tube, brown specked.
Lord Aberconway.   A.M. 1934.   F.C.C. 1989.   Color illus. F p.
45; Cox pl. 57.   NOTE: The above cross was also made by both
Lem and Del James.
EXBURY FABIA   Parentage as above
4ft(1.2m) 5F(-15C) ML 3/3   The largest-flowering of the Fa-
bias; apricot yellow tinged pink. A tall, spreading plant with
foliage indumented beneath.   Rothschild.
FABIA HIGH BEECHES   Parentage as above
3ft(.9m) 5F(-15C) M 3/4 A variety with orange flowers.   Col.
G. H. Loder, 1937.
FABIA TANGERINE   Parentage as above
3ft(.9m) 5F(-15C) M 3/4   Low and compact; reddish brown indu-
mentum. Flowers lighter orange color than FABIA, with a crimson
flush at tips; loose truss.   Lord Aberconway, 1934. A.M. 1940.
FABIA TOWER COURT   Parentage as above
This form is semi-dwarf, with attractive dark foliage; fragrant,
bell-shaped flowers, soft orange-pink, a deep rose flush at the
margins.   J. B. Stevenson, 1937.
MINTERNE APRICOT   Parentage as above
A selection exhibited by Lord Digby, 1952.
ROMAN POTTERY   Parentage as above
Pale orange flowers with coppery lobes.   J. J. Crosfield, 1934.
SOLVEIG   Parentage as above
Origin unknown. Incorrectly credited to RHS Garden, Wisley.
WATERER   Parentage as above
Salmon pink flowers, shaded orange; blooms later than TANGERINE.
* *

```
             -dichroanthum 1/4
    -Fabia-
FABIOLA-      -griersonianum 1/2
    -              -neriiflorum 1/4
    -F. C. Puddle-
                  -griersonianum
```
Red flowers.   Lord Aberconway, 1946.

```
                    -souliei 1/16
               -Soulbut-
           -Vanessa-       -fortunei--Sir Charles Butler 1/16
    -Adonis-       -griersonianum 1/2
    -        -             -griffithianum 1/8
FABIONIS-     -Sunrise-
    -                -griersonianum
    -        -dichroanthum 1/4
    -Fabia-
             -griersonianum
```

Pale rose flowers.   Lord Aberconway, 1946.

FABOS   Described under BEACON, q.v.

FABULOUS   Parentage unknown
4ft(1.2m) OF(-18C) E Dark pink buds open light purplish pink,
paler at center; flowers 3.5in(9cm) wide; ball truss of 7. Foliage glossy, elliptical, 3.75in(9.5cm)long, olive green; a broad
plant, blooms young. Whitney, cross 1964; A. Sather, reg. 1986.

```
                -catawbiense var. album Glass--Catalgla 1/4
     -Gosh Darn-                -decorum ? 1/16
     -              -                -Caroline-
     -          -Mrs. H. R. Yates-        -brachycarpum ? 1/16
FACE -                           -unknown 1/8
VALUE-                             -fortunei ssp. discolor 3/16
     -                  -Lady Bessborough-
     -     -Day Dream-              -campylocarpum Elatum Group
     -Gold -      -griersonianum 3/16                1/16
      Mohur-            -fortunei ssp. discolor
           -Margaret Dunn-     -dichroanthum 1/16
                          -Fabia-
                             -griersonianum
```
Buds blend a strong to moderate reddish orange; flowers primrose
yellow, edged in azalea pink, the reverse jasper red.   W. Delp.

```
               -fortunei 1/2
FAGGETTER'S FAVOURITE-
               -unknown 1/2
```
6ft(1.8m) -5F(-21C) M 5/4 Flowers flushed pink, bronze spec-
kled, in large trusses, and fragrant. Prefers some light shade.
Slocock.   A.M. Wisley Trials 1955.   Color illus. VV p. 7.

```
             -arboreum ssp. cinnamomeum var. roseum 1/2
FAIR LADY-               -griffithianum 1/4
          -Loderi Venus-
                     -fortunei 1/4
```
6ft(1.8m) OF(-18C) M 4/3 Upright truss of about 12 flowers,
rose pink with darker shading. Leaves up to 8in x 3in (20.3cm x
7.6cm). Prefers some shade.   R. Henny, reg. 1972.   P.A. 1959.

```
                  -thomsonii 1/8
             -Cornish Cross-
        -Coreum-          -griffithianum 1/8
FAIR  -      -arboreum 1/4
MAIDEN-
     -griersonianum 1/2
```
Bright red flowers.   Lord Aberconway, intro. 1942.

FAIR SKY--form of augustinii
6ft(1.8m) -5F(-21C) M 3/3 Foliage typical of species--long,
narrow, smooth, dark green, underside densely scaly. Flowers
flat-faced and square, light purplish blue, spotted yellow-green.
James Barto selected; Dr. Carl Phetteplace, reg. 1976.

FAIRVIEW   Described under FLADA W. BLOUGH, q.v.

```
                      -dichroanthum 1/4
                  -Fabia-
      -unnamed hybrid-      -griersonianum 1/4
      -                -yakushimanum 1/4
FAIRWEATHER-                    -dichroanthum
      -             -Fabia (Lem's)-
      -Hello Dolly-          -griersonianum
          -smirnowii 1/4
```
3ft(.9m) -10F(-23C) EM 4/5 Synonym SEAFOAM. Plant vigorous,
easy to grow; outstanding foliage, heavily indumented, white tomentum on new growth; leaves held 3 years. Flower light mandarin red, fading amber; ball trusses of about 16.   Brockenbrough,
reg. 1974.   Color illus. HG p. 181.

```
                -dichroanthum 1/4
      -Fabia-
FAIRY-      -griersonianum 1/2
     -          -facetum 1/4
     -Jacquetta-
                -griersonianum
```
Flowers of bright red.   Lord Aberconway, 1942.

```
             -Lady Mar--unknown 1/2
FAIRY LIGHT-
             -griersonianum 1/2
```

Fast-growing plant of medium height. Two forms exist: bright
pink, and soft salmon pink flowers.   Rothschild, 1948.

```
                        -adenogynum 1/4
            -Xenosporum (detonsum)-
FAIRY TALE-                -unknown 3/4
           -unknown
```
Flowers of pale pink, 3.5in(8.9cm) across, 7-lobed, in compact
trusses of about 13. Floriferous.   Gen. Harrison, reg. 1965.

```
                -griffithianum 1/4
          -Loderi-
FAIRY TALE-       -fortunei 1/4
           -arboreum ssp. cinnamomeum var. roseum 1/2
```
Synonym RUDY'S FAIRY TALE. The plant has fuchsine pink flowers,
4in(10.2cm) across; trusses of about 11.   Leaves 7in(17.8cm)
long. Name from American Rhododendron Hybrids. Entry in the
Register: RUDY'S FAIRYTALE.   R. Henny, reg. 1963, 1972.

```
                -keiskei--Yaku Fairy 1/2
FAIRY'S FAIRY-
                -keiskei, hardy selection 1/2
```
5in(12.7cm) x 1ft(.35m)(8 yrs) -10F(-23C) M Lax truss of 3-6
greenish yellow flowers (deeper than YAKU FAIRY), 2in(5cm) wide,
wavy-edged; scaly leaves, 1in(2.5cm) long. Shrub dense, spreading, very floriferous. Dr. J. Brueckner, cross 1981; reg. 1989.
Color illus. ARS J 44:2 (1990), p. 78.

* *
```
          -minus Carolinianum Group, pink form 1/2
FAISA-
          -polycladum Scintillans Group 1/2
```
Strong reddish purple in bud, opening to a blend of light purple
and moderate purplish pink. Hardy to -20F(-29C).   W. Delp.
MIGHTY MITE   Parentage as above
Violet and strong purple in bud open to strong and light purple
flowers; pale greenish yellow anthers.   W. Delp.
TICKLEY   Parentage as above
Strong and light purples in bud, opening to lighter flowers with
deep purplish pink stamens.   W. Delp.
* *

* *
```
                    -forrestii Repens Group 1/4
          -Elizabeth-
          -              -griersonianum 1/4
FAITH HENTY-                    -griffithianum 1/8
          -               -Queen Wilhelmina-
          -Earl of Athlone-          -unknown 3/8
                          -Stanley Davies--unknown
```
Turkey red flowers in trusses of 5-7; free-flowering and compact
plant.   J. V. Boulter, reg. 1978.
PRINCE OF McKENZIE   Parentage as above
3ft(.9m) -5F(-21C) EM Waxy, scarlet red flowers; 5 wavy lobes
in 4-6 flowered trusses, 6in(15cm) wide. Leathery leaves, held
on drooping branches. C. H. Phetteplace, reg. 1983.
* *

FAKE   See PURPLE FAKE

FALTHO   Described under SURPRISE, q.v.

FALVIA   Described under MELLOW GOLD, q.v.

```
            -dichroanthum ssp. scyphocalyx Herpesticum Group 1/4
     -Metis-
FAME-    -griersonianum 1/2
    -      -dichroanthum 1/4
    -Fabia-
         -griersonianum
```
Orange-red flowers.   Lord Aberconway, intro. 1946.

```
            -smirnowii 1/4
      -unnamed hybrid-      -fortunei ssp. discolor 1/8
FAMILY-            -Lady Bessborough-
GEM -                 -campylocarpum Elatum Group
    -yakushimanum--Koichiro Wada 1/2              1/8
```
Buds moderate red, purplish red and deep pink; 7-lobed yellow-
ish white flowers.   Al Smith cross; W. Delp raiser.

```
                    -unnamed-Pygmalion--unknown 1/16
                 -Weldy- hybrid-
              -            -          -haematodes 1/16
         -Robert Weldon-    -yakushimanum, Exbury form 1/8
FAMILY TIES-        -            -yakushimanum 1/8
         -              -Serendipity-
         -proteoides (R 147) 1/2  -aureum 1/8
```
Buds blend of vivid purplish red and medium purplish pink, open-
ing white, tinged purplish pink; deep red dorsal spots. Flowers
have three lobes. Weldon Delp.


```
              -yakushimanum, Exbury form 1/2
FAMILY TREE-                 -wardii ? 1/8
         -          -Chlorops-
         -unnamed hybrid-    -vernicosum ? 1/8
                    -aureum 1/4
```
Buds blend pale greenish yellow, strong reddish orange, yellow-
ish pink; yellowish white; frilled flowers with chartreuse
green flare, dorsal spots dark red-orange; red stigma. W. Delp.

FAN FLARE   Described under BOUNTIFUL, q.v.


```
                    -griffithianum 1/8
               -George Hardy-
    -Mrs. Lindsay Smith-      -catawbiense 1/4
FANCY-          -Duchess of Edinburgh--unknown 5/8
    -          -Mrs. J. J. Crosfield--unknown
    -Mrs. Helen Koster-          -catawbiense
         -Catawbiense Grandiflorum-
                         -unknown
```
5ft(1.5m) 0F(-18C) ML 4/3 Flowers violet to mauve; a large,
dark red dorsal blotch, fading to speckles. M. Koster & Sons.
A.M. Boskoop 1955.


```
         -unknown 1/2
FANCY FREE-
         -facetum (eriogynum) 1/2
```
Medium-sized, compact plant. Clear bright pink flowers, stained
salmon, with dark speckling. Rothschild. A.M. 1938.


```
                    -griffithianum 1/8
               -Queen Wilhelmina-
    -Britannia-          -unknown 3/8
FANDANGO-       -Stanley Davies--unknown
    -haematodes 1/2
```
Fine crimson scarlet flowers, waxy, campanulate; loose, flatten-
ed trusses. Dense plant of moderate height. Rothschild, 1938.


```
* * * * * * * * * * * * * * * * * * * * * * * * * * *
                    -catawbiense 3/8
         -Parson's Grandiflorum-
    -America-          -unknown 5/8
FANFARE-    -dark red hybrid--unknown
    -          -catawbiense
    -Kettledrum-
              -unknown
```
5ft(1.5m) -20F(-29C) ML 3/2 Flowers a nonfading bright scar-
let; domed truss. Leaves 5.25in(1.5m) long, wavy-edged, oblong.
Shade- and sun-tolerant. A. Shammarello and D. Leach, c.1962;
intro. then withdrawn; still available.
SHAM'S RUBY   Parentage as above or reversed
3ft(.9m) -20F(-29C) ML 2/2   Synonym RUBY. Flowers strong
purplish red with slight blotch of deeper tone; trusses of 16.
Plant nearly as wide as tall. Glossy, olive green leaves. Reg.
1958 as RUBY; 1976 as SHAM'S RUBY. Color illus. LW pl. 90.
* *


```
                    -catawbiense 1/4
              -Atrosanguineum-
         -Atrier-          -unknown 3/8
    -          -griersonianum 1/8
    -Mary Belle-    -decorum 1/8
    -          -Dechaem-
FANNY BELLS-          -haematodes 1/8  -catawbiense
    -              -Parsons Grandiflorum-
    -     -America-          -unknown
    -Fanfare-    -dark red hybrid--unknown
    -          -catawbiense
         -Kettledrum-
              -unknown
```
4ft(1.2m) tall x 3ft(.9m) -17F(-27C) ML   Buds deep purplish
red; flowers openly funnel-shaped, 2.3in(6cm) broad, strong pur-

plish red; domed truss of 18-24. Elliptic leaves to 5in(12.5cm)
long; floriferous shrub. H. Harrington, cross 1976; reg. 1987.

FANTASTICA   Described under YAKU WARRIOR, q.v.


```
         -Lowinsky hybrid--unknown 1/2
FANTASY-
         -griersonianum 1/2
```
Plant has a loose, spreading habit, with trusses of deep pink in
May. Rothschild, 1938.


```
              -cinnabarinum Roylei Group 1/2
FANTIN LATOUR-
              -oreotrephes 1/2
```
Mauve flowers. G. M. Adams-Acton, 1934.

FAR HORIZON--form of principis Vellereum Group
5ft(1.5m) -5F(-21C) E 3/4   Truss of up to 24 flowers, roseine purple fading to white in throat, lightly spotted magenta.
Leaves up to 4in(10.2cm) long, dull dark green with heavy silvery brown indumentum beneath. Kingdon Ward collector; Col. S.
R. Clarke raiser; R. N. S. Clarke, reg. 1978. A.M. 1979.

FARALL   Described under ROMANY CHAL, q.v.

FARALL TARGET   Described under AROMANA, q.v.


```
         -diaprepes ? 1/2
FAREWELL PARTY-
         -unknown 1/2
```
5ft(1.5m) -5F(-21C) L Leaves medium to large, glossy yellow-
green. Plant about twice as wide as high. Flowers up to 4.5in
(11.5cm) across, white with throat spotting of yellow-green, in
flat truss of 12. R. Kersey cross; Mrs. Frederick, reg. 1976.


```
         -oreodoxa var. fargesii 1/2
FARGARB-
         -arboreum, blood red form 1/2
```
Flowers violet rose of the deepest shade. E. J. P. Magor, 1928.


```
         -oreodoxa var. fargesii 1/2
FARGCALO-
         -calophytum 1/2
```
A hybrid introduced by E. J. P. Magor, 1940.


```
         -oreodoxa var. fargesii 1/2
FARGSUTCH-
         -sutchuenense 1/2
```
Flowers light pink, heavily spotted crimson.   Magor, 1933.


```
              -catawbiense 1/4
         -Everestianum-
FARNESE-          -unknown 3/4
         -Eggebrechtii--unknown
```
White flowers flushed pale lilac, light reddish brown markings.
T. J. R. Seidel, 1914.


```
         -oreodoxa var. fargesii 1/2
FAROLA-    -griffithianum 1/4
    -Loderi-
         -fortunei 1/4
```
Very pale pink flowers. Loder, 1940.


```
         -oreodoxa var. fargesii 1/2
FARTHER-
         -morii 1/2
```
Flowers white, lightly flushed orchid pink, openly campanulate,
2.5in(6.4cm) across; loose trusses of 10. Leaves 5in(12.7cm)
long. Collingwood Ingram, reg. 1970. P.C. 1969.


```
         -forrestii Repens Group 1/2
FASCINATOR-    -haematodes 1/4
    -Hiraethlyn-
         -griffithianum 1/4
```
1.5ft(.45m) 5F(-15C) EM 3/4   A low mound covered with small
leaves. Cherry red, bell-shaped flowers in profusion.   Lord
Aberconway. A.M. 1950.

```
                        -smirnowii 1/8
                -unnamed hybrid-
        -Katydid-                    -yakushimanum 1/8
        -        -       -wardii 7/32
        -        -Crest-            -fortunei ssp. discolor 7/64
FASHION-         -Lady Bess- -
   TINT -        borough- -campylocarpum Elatum Gp. 7/64
        -             -brachycarpum 1/8
        -       -unnamed-
        -       - hybrid-Crest (as above)
        -Marypat-                  -catawbiense var. album 1/16
        -           -unnamed hybrid-
                -Monte-            -Crest (as above)
                Carlo-             -aureum 1/16
                        -unnamed hybrid-
                             -campylocarpum 1/16
```

Buds of grayed reds, open to off-white flowers edged spinel red; dorsal spots bright chartreuse green, the throat paler.   Delp.

```
        -fastigiatum 1/2
FASTHIP-
    -hippophaeoides 1/2
```
Flowers very pale lavender, near-white.   E. J. P. Magor, 1926.

```
                -catawbiense 1/2
FASTUOSUM FLORE PLENO-
                -ponticum 1/2
```
6ft(1.8m) -15F(-26C) ML 3/3   Plant habit slightly open and rounded. Sun-tolerant.   Flower lavender blue with darker spotting, semi-double; rather loose truss.   Francoisi, before 1846. A.G.M. 1928.   Color illus. Cox pl. 59; F p. 7; VV p. 28.

FASTUOSUM PLENUM   See FASTUOSUM FLORE PLENO

* *
```
        -fortunei 1/2
FAWN    -dichroanthum 1/4
    -Fabia-
        -griersonianum 1/4
```
6ft(1.8m) 5F(-15C) M 4/3   Plant upright, with medium green leaves, to 8in(20.3cm). Flowers salmon pink shading orange-yellow in center, very flat, up to 5in(12.7cm) wide; open-topped trusses of about 9.   Del W. James, reg. 1958.   P.A. 1959.
EDWARD LONG   Parentage as above, except reversed
Medium-sized, compact plant with leaves 5in(12.7cm) long. Buds chartreuse green, opening to creamy flowers 4in(10.2cm) across; faint green blotch; rounded truss of 8-10. D. James, reg. 1963.
GLOWLIGHT EMBERS   Parentage: Fabia X fortunei
5ft(1.5m) -5F(-21C) M Semi-lax trusses of yellow. Hardgrove.
* *

```
                -griersonianum 1/4
        -Tally Ho-
FAYETTA-        -facetum (eriogynum) 1/4
        -              -dichroanthum 1/4
        -Golden Horn-
                -elliottii 1/4
```
Semi-dwarf plant, hardy to 5F(-15C). Flowers red, hose-in-hose. William Whitney, intro. 1956.

```
                        -souliei 1/16
                -Soulbut-
            -Vanessa-      -fortunei--Sir Chas. Butler 1/16
        -Radiance-        -griersonianum 5/8
FELICITY-        -griersonianum
        -                -neriiflorum 1/4
        -F. C. Puddle-
                        -griersonianum
```
Called a red amaranth rose in the Register.   Lord Aberconway. A.M. 1942.

FELICITY FAIR   Described under BARBARA JURY, q.v.

* *
```
        -fulgens 1/2
FELICITY MAGOR-
        -arboreum, red form 1/2
```
Deep crimson flowers, with spots of darker crimson.   E. J. P. Magor cross, 1928; Mrs. Magor, reg. 1958.
ROC   Parentage as above, except reversed
Red flowers.   J. B. Stevenson cross, 1929; intro. 1950.
* *

FELIS (FELIX) Described under DANTE, q.v.

FERELITH   Described under MRS. FURNIVALL, q.v.

```
                -souliei 1/4
        -Peregrine-     -wardii 1/8
        -       -Hawk-
FERNHILL-       -Lady        -fortunei ssp. discolor 1/16
        -           Bessborough-
        -yakushimanum 1/2       -campylocarpum Elatum 1/16
```
Trusses 7in(17.8cm) across, of 6-9 flowers, creamy white flushed pale pink. Compact plant, wider than high, with glossy foliage. Crown Estate, Windsor, reg. 1973.   A.M. Wisley Trials 1973.

FERNHILL SILVER--selection of arboreum
Flowers in trusses of 25, rose pink with darker markings. Plant attains the height of the species.   First raised at Glasnevin Botanic Garden before 1850 and distributed to the Darley family, who owned Fernhill in County Dublin.   Mrs. S. Walker and R. Walker, reg. 1985.   Color illus. p. 165 in Irish Florilegium.

FESTIVAL   Described under THERESA, q.v.

FESTIVAL (HACHMANN)   See FESTIVO

FESTIVE FEAST   Parentage unknown
Light purplish pink flowers.   Dexter cross; Wister, reg. 1980.

```
                -yakushimanum--Koichiro Wada 1/4
        -Hachmann's Polaris-     -catawbiense ? 1/8
FESTIVO-        -Omega-
        -wardii 1/2        -unknown 1/8
```
1.5ft(.45m) x 3ft(.9m) -5F(-21C) ML   Slow-growing, compact, low shrub. Flowers in loose trusses of 12 to 14, 5-lobed, pale greenish yellow with markings of grayish red.   Hachmann, cross 1971; Stück, reg. 1988.   Color illus. WS, 1989, p. 150.

```
                -minus Carolinianum Group 1/4
        -Laetevirens (Wilsoni)-
FETTERHOFF-        -ferrugineum 1/4
  SURPRISE -dauricum 1/2
```
1.5ft(.45m) x 2.5ft(.75m) -15F(-26C) ML   Lepidote with round trusses of 5 flowers, strong reddish purple in bud, opening to a vivid reddish purple, lighter at center.   W. Fetterhoff, cross 1977; reg. 1989.

```
                -griffithianum 1/4
    -King George-
FEZ-        -unknown 1/4
    -sanguineum ssp. sanguineum var. haemaleum 1/2
```
Plant habit low and dense.   Flowers waxy, crimson, and carried in loose trusses.   Midseason.   Rothschild, 1938.

* *
```
                        -catawbiense 1/8
            -unnamed hybrid-    -dichroanthum 9/64
        -               -Fabia-
        -Ginny-             -griersonianum 7/64
        - Mae - -yakushimanum 1/8       -fortunei ssp. discolor
        -    -       -          -Lady -
        -    -Si-    -Day -Bessborough-campylocarpum Elatum Gp.
        -    -Si-    -Dream-                            1/64
        -       -Gold -     -griersonianum
FIERY - Mohur-       -fortunei ssp. discolor 11/64
ORANGE-         -Margaret-
        -          Dunn  -Fabia (as above)
        -                       -neriiflorum 1/16
        -                  -Nereid-
        -       -Phyllis Ballard-      -dichroanthum
        -Dead Ringer-      -fortunei ssp. discolor
                -catawbiense--Clark's White 1/4
```
Medium red buds, opening to a blend of medium reds, chrome yellow flare, with medium red dorsal spotting, throat of brilliant greenish yellow.   W. Delp.
TRIFLE   Parentage as above
Buds of cardinal red and strong red. Large, frilled flowers of cardinal and strong reds, with light yellow flare; strong brown dorsal spots; light yellow throat.   W. Delp.
* *

```
                  -campylocarpum Elatum Group 1/16
          -Penjerrick-
     -Amaura-         -griffithianum 1/16
  -Eros-     -griersonianum 5/8
FIESTA-   -griersonianum
               -neriiflorum 1/4
  -F. C. Puddle-
          -griersonianum
Red flowers.  Lord Aberconway, intro. 1950.
```

```
                            -griffithianum 1/16
               -George Hardy-
        -Mrs. Lindsay-         -catawbiense 1/16
  -Diane- Smith      -Duchess of Edinburgh--unknown 1/4
FIFTH -              -campylocarpum 1/8
 AVENUE-    -unnamed hybrid-
  RED -             -unknown
     -haematodes 1/2
```
Flowers Neyron rose with lighter streaks, campanulate, glossy;
trusses of about 10; leaves 4in(10cm) long. A dwarf plant, to 2
ft(.6m) in sun; 3ft(.9m) in shade. R. Henny, reg. 1964.

FIFTY-FINE   See GOLDEN GALA

```
                -dichroanthum 1/8
       -Astarte-        -campylocarpum Elatum Group 1/16
       -     -Penjerrick-
  -Solon-        -griffithianum 5/16
  -   -     -griffithianum
  -   -Sunrise-
FIGARO-         -griersonianum 1/8
  -             -griffithianum
  -   -Loderi-
  -Coreta-   -fortunei 1/8
       -arboreum ssp. zeylanicum 1/4
```
Red flowers. Lord Aberconway, 1950.

```
                -catawbiense 1/4
  -Russell Harmon-
FIJI-        -maximum 1/4
  -               -dichroanthum 1/4
  -Goldsworth Orange-
          -fortunei ssp. discolor 1/4
```
4.5ft(1.35m) -20F(-29C) L 4/2   Buds dark red and yellow open
claret rose; truss of 13. Plant broader than tall, matte yellow
-green leaves.   Leach, intro. 1976; later withdrawn; reg. 1982.

FINCH--form of rubiginosum Desquamatum Group
6ft(1.8m) OF(-18C) EM 3/2 Flowers rosy lilac; compact truss.
Leaves fold in winter.   Barto selected; R. Henny, intro. 1958.

```
               -smirnowii 1/4
   -unnamed hybrid-
FINDERS-        -yakushimanum 1/4
KEEPERS-    -brachycarpum 1/4
   -unnamed-    -wardii 1/8
     hybrid-Crest-         -fortunei ssp. discolor 1/16
          -Lady Bess-
            borough  -campylocarpum Elatum Gp. 1/16
```
Buds a blend of vivid purplish reds, open to a blend of moderate
and light purplish pinks, dorsal spots of Tyrian purple; reverse
of petals rose Bengal. Weldon Delp.

FINE BRISTLES--form of pubescens
4ft(1.2m) -5F(-21C) EM 3/3   Upright, compact plant; small
leaves covered on both sides with long hairs. Deep pink buds
open to white flowers, suffused rose, all along the branches.
Crown Estate, Windsor, reg. 1962. A.M. 1955.

```
* * * * * * * * * * * * * * * * * * * * * * * * * * * *
               -ciliatum 1/4
        -Cilpinense-
FINE FEATHERS-         -moupinense 1/4
        -lutescens 1/2
```
3ft(.9m) 5F(-15C) E 3/3 Delicate flowers, white with yellow,
blushed pink. Lord Aberconway, 1946.
FINE FEATHERS PRIMROSE Parentage as above
Pale primrose yellow; early season. Lord Aberconway, 1946.
LUCIL Parentage as above
A selection named by Lord Aberconway.
* *

```
          -souliei 1/2
FINESSE-    -Corona--unknown 1/4
   -Bow Bells-
          -williamsianum 1/4
```
Flowers of Persian rose, 2.5in(6.25cm) wide, 7 in a truss.   Ru-
dolph Henny, reg. 1958.
MAMIE   Parentage as above
3.5ft(1m) -5F(-21C) M Fuchsine pink flowers, campanulate, 3in
(7.6cm) wide; truss of 7-11. Compact plant. Henny, reg. 1963.
WHIMSEY   Parentage as above
Dwarf OF(-18C) M   Flowers camellia rose in throat, shading to
Egyptian buff. Lax trusses. Henny, reg. 1958.
* *

FINLANDIA   Described under APPLAUSE, q.v.

```
          -Corona--unknown 1/4
   -Bow Bells-
FIONA-     -williamsianum 1/4
   -             -griffithianum 1/4
   -Loderi Pink Diamond-
          -fortunei 1/4
```
5ft(1.5m) OF(-18C) EM   Flowers 4in(10cm) wide, 7-lobed, pas-
tel pink, from phlox pink buds; lax trusses of 6. Large rounded
leaves on a rounded plant. L. Brandt, reg. 1962.

```
* * * * * * * * * * * * * * * * * * * * * * * * * * * *
               -griffithianum 3/8
   -Loderi King George-
FIONA-     -fortunei 1/4
WILSON-        -griffithianum
   -       -George Hardy-
   -Pink Pearl-      -catawbiense 1/8
   -        -arboreum 1/8
       -Broughtonii-
          -unknown 1/8
```
Light mallow purple flowers, in trusses of 9-10. G. Hall cross;
Lord Harewood, reg. 1979.
IRENE HALL   Parentage as above
Trusses of 11-12 flowers, white flushed pink outside, small deep
red mark at base. G. Hall cross; Lord Harewood, reg. 1979.
* *

FIRE   Parentage unknown
Rose red with dark spots. Koster of Boskoop, reg. 1965.

FIRE AND ICE   Described under FIREBALL, q.v.

```
               -fortunei ssp. discolor 1/4
   -Norman Shaw-      -catawbiense 1/8
FIRE BIRD-     -B. de Bruin-
   -               -unknown 1/8
       -griersonianum 1/2
```
6ft(1.8m) OF(-18C) ML 3/3   Large trusses of glowing salmon
red flowers, bright yellow anthers. Light green young foliage a
striking contrast against crimson bracts.   Rothschild, 1938.

```
               -griffithianum 1/4
          -Mars-
   -unnamed hybrid-   -unknown 7/16         -catawbiense
   -             -   -Parsons Grandiflorum-       1/16
FIRE  -   -America-         -unknown
CRACKER-        -dark red hybrid--unknown
   -            -griffithianum
   -   -Mars-
   -Scarlet Blast-   -unknown
       -catawbiense, red form 1/4
```
Dark red buds open to currant red flowers, lightly edged with
dark red.   Al Smith cross; W. Delp raiser.

```
               -dichroanthum ssp. apodectum 1/4
       -Apodorum-
FIRE FLAME-   -decorum 1/4
       -griersonianum 1/2
```
Bright red flowers. Scrase-Dickens, 1942.   A.M. 1942.

```
       -griersonianum 1/2
FIRE GLOW-     -griffithianum (roseum superbum ?) 1/4
       -unnamed-         -fortunei 1/8
          hybrid-H. M. Arderne-
               -unknown 1/8
```

Large-growing shrub; Turkey red flowers, faintly fragrant. Foliage wavy, twisted. Crosfield, Embley Park, 1920.   A.M. 1935.

```
              -venator 1/2
FIRE MUSIC-
              -dichroanthum 1/2
```
Fiery orange flowers.   Thacker, 1942.

* *
```
                          -griffithianum 1/8
                   -Queen Wilhelmina-
         -Britannia-                 -unknown 3/8
FIRE PRINCE-        -Stanley Davies--unknown
         -arboreum ssp. delavayi var. delavayi 1/2
```
An Australian hybrid with cardinal red flowers, lightly spotted
on upper lobe. K. Van de Ven, reg. 1973.
FIRE WALK   Parentage as above
Turkey red flowers. K. Van de Ven, reg. 1972.
FOREST FLAME Parentage as above
Trusses of 16 flowers, campanulate, currant red. Shrub 7ft(2.m)
tall. Van de Ven, reg. 1984.
RED CREST   Parentage as above
Cardinal red, faint spots on upper lobe. Van de Ven, reg. 1973.
* *

```
                      -ponticum 1/4
         -Purple Splendour-
         -                -unknown 5/16
FIRE WINE-              -fortunei ssp. discolor 1/8
         -        -Norman Shaw-        -catawbiense 1/16
         -Fire Bird-        -B. de Bruin-
         -                          -unknown
                   -griersonianum 1/4
```
3.5ft(1m) OF(-18C) ML 4/3 Unusual bright purplish red flow-
ers, darker dorsal spotting, 3in(7.6cm) wide, ruffled and frilled; large flat trusses of c.16. Plant broader than tall; narrow
grass green leaves. Greer, reg. 1979. Color illus. HG p. 147.

* *
```
              -catawbiense 5/32
                   -Blandyanum-              -catawbiense
                   -              -unnamed-
         -barbatum 1/2 -        -Alta- - hybrid-ponticum
FIREBALL-        -        clerense-              1/32
         -Ascot Brilliant-        -arboreum 1/16
                   -thomsonii 1/4
```
Glowing carmine scarlet flower, bell-shaped, with frilled edges;
rounded trusses. Very early. Richard Gill & Sons. A.M. 1925.
EARLY BRILLIANT Parentage as above, except reversed
A bright red selection by Slocock.
* *
* *
```
              -catawbiense var. Album Glass--Catalgla 1/2
FIREBALL (Delp)-       -haematodes 1/4
                   -Choremia-
                          -arboreum 1/4
```
Cardinal red flowers; tall plant. Hardy to -15F(-26C). Delp.
FIRE AND ICE Parentage as above
Cardinal red buds open flowers of strong red and empire rose;
dorsal spots pale yellow. W. Delp.
* *

```
                          -catawbiense 3/8
                   -unnamed hybrid-
FIREBOLT---Boule de Rose, selfed-        -unknown 3/8
                   -        -caucasicum 1/4
                   -Boule de-        -catawbiense
                   Neige -unnamed-
                          hybrid-unknown
```
Buds of cardinal red open to a blend of cardinal reds, with dor-
sal spotting of darker red, pale mauve pink throat. W. Delp.

FIREDANCE Parentage unknown
3ft(.9m) -5F(-21C) M 4/4 Possibly contains forrestii Repens
Group, williamsianum. Upright, fine red buds open glowing scar-
let-red. Rounded leaves. W. Whitney cross; H. Greer intro.

```
              -fortunei ssp. discolor 1/4
         -Sardis-              -catawbiense 1/8
FIREDRAKE-        -C. S. Sargent-
         -kyawii 1/2              -unknown 1/8
```
Large, bright red flowers appear late in the season on the tall,

but compact, plant.   Rothschild, 1938.

```
                          -souliei 1/16
                   -Soulbut-
              -Vanessa-        -fortunei--Sir Charles Butler
         -Radiance-        -                          1/16
         -                -griersonianum 5/8
FIREFINCH-        -griersonianum
         -        -facetum 1/4
         -Jacquetta-
              -griersonianum
```
Scarlet flowers. Lord Aberconway, 1942.

* *
```
              -spinuliferum 3/4
         -Crossbill-
FIREFLY-        -lutescens 1/4
         -scabrifolium var. spinuliferum
```
Small flowers, shaded yellow to apricot. Shrub medium-sized and
open. Rothschild, 1938.
DONVALE PINK DRIFT   Parentage as above
Trusses of 5-10 flowers, tubular funnel-shaped, bright Neyron
rose. Height about 3ft(.9m). J. O'Shannassy, reg. 1984.
* *

```
         -maximum 1/2
FIREKING-        -forrestii Repens Group 1/4
         -Gertrud Schäle-              -ponticum 1/16
         -        -Michael Waterer-
         -Prometheus-              -unknown 3/16
              -Monitor--unknown
```
Buds of currant red; flowers vivid and strong reds; a white
flare; filaments vivid red; stigma strong purplish red. Delp.

```
                   -griffithianum 1/4
         -Jean Marie de-
FIREMAN JEFF- Montague   -unknown 1/4
         -              -haematodes 1/4
         -Grosclaude-
              -facetum (eriogynum) 1/4
```
3ft(.9m) OF(-18C) M 4/4 Bright blood red flowers with large
bright red calyces; trusses of 10. Plant well-branched, broader
than high; medium green foliage held 3 years. L. Brandt cross;
J. Eichelser, reg. 1977. Color illus. HG p. 170; Cox pl. 60.

* *
```
                          -griffithianum 1/8
                   -Queen Wilhelmina-
         -Britannia-              -unknown 3/8
FIRETAIL-        -Stanley Davies--unknown
         -facetum (eriogynum) 1/2
```
6ft(1.6m) 5F(-15C) ML Flowers of deep scarlet, brown spot-
ting; compact truss of 11. Floriferous woodland plant. May be
available only in NZ. J. Crosfield. A.M. 1934. F.C.C. 1937.
TRIDENT Parentage as above
Dark red flowers. Shown by Loder, 1948.
* *

FIREWINE See FIRE WINE

FIRST LOVE Described under GOLDSTRIKE, q.v.

```
                                   -fortunei ssp.
                   -Lady    -        discolor 7/32
              -Jalisco- Bessborough-campy. Elatum Gp.
              -        -        -dichroanthum 1/32
         -unnamed-        -Dido-
         - hybrid-        -decorum 9/32
         -        -griffithianum 4/32
         -        -Loderi-
FISHER'S-        -decorum        -fortunei 4/32
FOLLY -        -wardii 1/8
         -        -Hawk-        -fortunei ssp. discolor
         -        -Lady    -
         -unnamed-    Bessborough-campylocarpum Elatum Group
         hybrid-              -griffithianum        3/32
                   -Loderi-
              -Albatross-        -fortunei
                   -fortunei ssp. discolor
```
Flower openly funnel-shaped, 4in(10cm) wide, 6, 7-lobed, yellow-
ish white, striped light greenish yellow (fading), dorsal lobes
spotted and striated in currant red. Smooth leaves, 6.7in(17cm)

long. Blooms in Oct., NZ.   Greer raiser; J. Fisher, reg. 1986.

```
                     -maximum 5/16
        -Stoke's Bronze Wings-
        -                -catawbiense 12/32
FIT AND-            -catawbiense v. album Glass--Catalgla 1/8
  TRIM -    -Tony's-                -catawbiense
     -     - Gift -    -Catawbiense Album-
     -     -      -Belle -        -unknown 1/16
  -unnamed-    Heller-              -catawbiense
    hybrid-        -white catawbiense hyb.-
        -                 -maximum    -unknown
        -       -Russell Harmon-
     -Serenata-            -catawbiense
        -        -dichroanthum 1/16
          -unnamed-       -fortunei ssp. discolor
           hybrid-unnamed-                     1/32
                 hybrid-campylocarpum 1/32
```
Buds blend pale yellowish white and pale yellowish green, open-
ing yellowish white with flare of chartreuse green. W. Delp.

```
        -racemosum 1/2
FITTIANUM-
        -unknown 1/2
```
Once considered a separate species, then thought to be a form of
dauricum, and now called a natural hybrid of racemosum.   Rose
purple flowers, very early.

```
             -racemosum 3/4
     -Fittianum-
FITTRA-      -unknown 1/4
     -racemosum
```
2.5ft(.75m) 0F(-18C) EM   A compact plant, covered with dense
trusses of about 30 vivid, deep pink, small flowers. Foliage of
medium green, small-sized. Hillier, 1938. A.M. 1949.

```
        -catawbiense var. album Glass--Catalgla 1/2
FIXATION-
        -vernicosum (18139) 1/2
```
Buds of fuchsia purple and deep purplish pink; frilled flowers
rhodamine purple; dorsal spots strong greenish yellow. W. Delp.

* *
```
           -Dexter hybrid--unknown 1/2
     -Janet Blair-
FLADA W. BLOUGH-        -unknown
        -catawbiense var. album Glass--Catalgla F2 1/2
```
Large formal trusses, of white flowers rimmed in pink. Hardy to
-25F(-32C). R. L. Blough.
BRILLIANT WHITE   Parentage as above
Large trusses of white flowers.   Blough.
COUPON   Parentage as above
Brilliant white flowers with a dark blotch. Blough.
FAIRVIEW   Parentage as above
Large formal truss of flowers with light yellow blotch. Blough.
GARRETT   Parentage as above
Large white flowers with blotch. Blough.
LOIS JEAN SEIHL   Parentage as above
Flowers with white face, violet edging and green blotch. Blough.
MARGARET BLOUGH   Parentage as above
Full creamy white truss with blotch.   Blough.
RED SAILS   Parentage as above
Large white flowers with crimson blotch.   Blough.
WESTBY   Parentage as above
Large opaque white flowers with prominent dark blotch. Blough.
* *

FLAIR   Described under APPLAUSE, q.v.
```

```
             -griffithianum 1/8
        -Loderi-
  -unnamed hybrid-   -fortunei 1/8
FLAME-   -Corona--unknown 1/4
  -griersonianum 1/2
```
A hybrid by Halfdan Lem, before 1958.

FLAME TIPS   Described under BRINNY, q.v.

```
        -auriculatum 1/2
FLAMEHEART-   -griersonianum 1/4
     -Azor-
           -fortunei   1/4
```

A parent of BULLSEYE.   Haworth-Booth, 1955.

* *
```
                     -catawbiense 3/16
           -Parsons Grandiflorum-
      -America-                -unknown 1/2
  -Fanfare-      -dark red hybrid--unknown
     -              -catawbiense
FLAMENCO-   -Kettledrum-
     -              -unknown
     -      -forrestii Repens Group 1/4
  -Gertrud-                -ponticum 1/16
   Schäle-      -Michael Waterer-
        -Prometheus-          -unknown
           -Monitor--unknown
```
1.5ft(.45m) -15F(-26C) M 3/4   Flowers 2.5in(6.4cm) wide,
crimson with spots of blood red, in flat trusses of 6-9.   Very
dense, dwarf plant, much broader than high, yellow-green leaves
held 2 years.   Leach, intro. 1968; later withdrawn; reg. 1982.
RANGOON   Parentage as above
4ft(1.2m) -15F(-26C) EM 4/3 Bush twice as wide as tall; dark
green foliage. Flowers medium to dark red, in dome-shaped truss
of 8. Dark red winter buds, leaf petioles. Leach, reg. 1973.
SINGAPORE   Parentage as above
1ft(.3m) -15F(-26C) M 4/4 Well-branched shrub twice as broad
as high. Flowers widely campanulate, medium to strong red, held
in dome-shaped trusses of 13.   D. G. Leach, reg. 1973.
SMALL WONDER   Parentage as above
3ft(.9m) -20F(-29C) EM 4/4   Flowers dark red, with lighter
small centers, in globe-shaped trusses of 7. Densely foliaged,
wider than tall. Leach, reg. 1973. Color illus. HG p. 118.
* *

FLAMING SNOW   Parentage unknown
5ft(1.5m) -10F(-23C) ML One of the hardier Dexters. Lovely,
large, long-lasting pink flowers (fade to white) with a burgundy
red blotch; large, full trusses. Likes some shade.   C. Dexter
cross; Tyler Arboretum, intro. before 1978.

```
        -Loder's White     See LODER'S WHITE for 2 possible
FLAMINGO-                   parentage diagrams
        -griersonianum
```
Vivid crimson pink buds open rich bright rose; shapely trusses.
Shown by Sir James Horlick, 1941.   Color illus. LW pl. 37.

```
        -catawbiense 1/2
FLAMME-
        -Mira--unknown 1/2
```
(Not Stevenson's MIRA, 1951) Light purplish violet flowers with
paler centers, yellow-brown markings.   T. J. R. Seidel, 1904.

* *
```
        -yakushimanum 1/2
FLANAGAN'S DAUGHTER-        -unknown 1/4
        -Bud Flanagan-
                 -ponticum 1/4
```
2.5ft(.75m) -5F(-21C) M   Trusses of 16-26 flowers, deep pur-
plish pink in bud, opening to pale purplish pink, edged deeper,
dorsal blotch dark red at edges; matures to white. Leaves with
orange-yellow indumentum below.   Mr. & Mrs. Drayson, reg. 1987.
HEIR APPARENT   Parentage as above
Tubular campanulate flowers purplish red in bud, opening to very
pale purple; very wavy edges of strong reddish and light purple;
dark red dorsal flare; truss of 21. Indumentum brownish orange.
R. Drayson, cross 1976; Mr. & Mrs. A. Drayson, reg. 1987.
* *

```
        -Mrs. R. S. Holford--unknown 1/2
FLARE-                -auriculatum 1/4
        -unnamed hybrid-
                 -griersonianum 1/4
```
5ft(1.8m) 0F(-18C) L   A late-flowering, vigorous plant, with
large trusses of bright salmon red flowers. Slocock, reg. 1958.

```
        -dichroanthum 1/4
     -Fabia-
FLASH-   -griersonianum 1/4
     -dichroanthum ssp. scyphocalyx 1/2
```
Orange-red flowers. Lord Aberconway, 1946.
```

```
                  -griffithianum 1/4
          -Mrs. Tom H. Lowinsky-          -maximum 1/8
FLASHBACK-                   -Halopeanum-
          -                             -griffithianum 1/8
          -     -catawbiense var. album Glass--Catalgla 1/4
          -Calsap-
                    -Sappho--unknown 1/4
```
Buds of spectrum violet and campanula violet open to white flo-
wers heavily edged with spectrum and campanula violets.   Delp.

```
                    -maximum, ivory white form 1/2
FLASHDANCE-                -fortunei ssp. discolor 1/4
          -Evening Glow-      -dichroanthum 1/8
                      -Fabia-
                             -griersonianum 1/8
```
Cardinal red buds open to dawn pink, pale greenish yellow
throat.   Wm. Fetterhoff cross; W. Delp raiser.

```
                -arboreum 1/2
FLASHING RED-
                -unknown 1/2
```
Flowers red with black spots; trusses of 17.   G. Langdon, Australia, reg. 1980.

FLASHLIGHT   Described under ABALONE, q.v.

```
          -Corona--unknown 1/2
FLATTERER-                   -fortunei ssp. discolor 1/4
          -Lady Bessborough-
                        -campylocarpum Elatum Group 1/4
```
5ft(1.5m) -5F(-21C) M   Some sources show parentage as CORONA
x DAYDREAM. Open-faced flowers, watermelon red, in tall trusses
of about 15. Foliage narrow, pointed. Henny, reg. P.A. 1957.

* *

```
          -brachycarpum ssp. fauriei 1/2
FLAUTANDO-                   -dichroanthum 1/4
          -Goldsworth Orange-
                        -fortunei ssp. discolor 1/4
```
3.2ft(1m) x 4.7ft(1.4m)(15 yrs) -10F(-23C) ML Narrowly funnel
-shaped flowers, rather pendant, 5-7 very wavy lobes, light yellow with azalea pink rims, reddish brown dorsal marking, outside
empire rose; bright greenish yellow calyx edged red. Leaves oblanceolate, glossy.   Hachmann, cross 1967; Stück, reg. 1988.
HACHMANN'S BANANAFLIP Parentage as above
Sibling of above. Funnel-campanulate flowers of 5-6 lobes, pale
yellow-green, dorsal blotch light greenish yellow with markings
of moderate red; loose truss of 10-13.   Stück, reg. 1988.
* *

FLAVA Synonym of VOLKER. Described under BOB BOVEE, q.v.

          -Seedling K. 30--unknown 1/2
FLAVOUR-   -dichroanthum 1/4
        -Dido-
              -decorum 1/4
```
Flowers  bell-shaped,  slightly darker than maize yellow with  a
light chartreuse throat, held in round trusses of 11.  Leaves of
medium green, about 5in(12.7cm) long.  W. C. Slocock, reg. 1962.
H.C. Wisley Trials 1960.

```
               -griffithianum 1/4
        -Loderi-
FLEECE-   -fortunei 1/2
       -          -fortunei
        -Luscombei-
                  -thomsonii 1/4
```
Loose  trusses of 7 flowers,  rhodamine pink with some deep pink
tinges and red spotting.  Adm. A. W. Heneage-Vivian cross, 1927;
Mrs. R. M. Stevenson, named 1959; reg. 1962.

```
             -thomsonii 1/2
FLEUR DE ROI-
             -campanulatum 1/2
```
Cream-colored flowers, suffused pink.   Wright, 1903.

```
                 -spinuliferum 1/2
FLEURETTE EVANS---SETA, selfed-
                 -moupinense 1/2
```
2.5ft(.75m)  5F(-15C)  E   Buds deep to strong pink (claret rose)
open pale Neyron rose, throat darker rose; flowers 1.75in(4.5cm)
broad; lax truss of 3-4.  Glossy, lanceolate foliage, 2.3in(6cm)

long, of medium olive/yellow-green; medium-sized dark red scales
below.  Bush wider than tall.  W. Moyles, cross 1972; reg. 1986.

FLEURIE--form of smithii
Turkey red flowers, tubular-campanulate, 5-lobed;  tight rounded
trusses of about 25.   Leaves, margins reflexed, up to 6in(15cm)
long, covered beneath with woolly brown indumentum.  T. J. Booth
collector; R. N. Stephenson Clark, reg. 1978.   A.M. 1978.

FLICKER   Described under GREELEY, q.v.

FLIP   Described under CHARTREUSE, q.v.

```
                              -catawbiense 1/16
                  -Parsons Grandiflorum-
          -America-   -unknown 1/4
          -        -dark red hybrid--unknown
       -Cindy Lou-   -griffithianum 1/16
       -         -   -Mars-
FLIPPER-   -unnamed hybrid-   -unknown
       -                    -catawbiense var. rubrum 1/8
       -           -dichroanthum 1/4
        -Goldsworth Orange-
                        -fortunei ssp. discolor 1/4
```
Buds of bright guardsman red, opening to crimson flowers.  Medi-
um-sized plant.  Weldon Delp, 1985.

FLIRT   Described under ANDRÉ, q.v.

```
      -keiskei 1/2
FLODA-
      -mucronulatum, pink form 1/2
```
2.5ft(.75m) x 4ft(1.2m(11 yrs)  -25F(-32C)  VE  Openly funnel-
shaped flowers 2in(5cm) wide; 5 wavy lobes, medium purplish pink
with paler edges, fading pink-striped white, light orange-yellow
blotch; flat ball truss of 3-8.   Small leaves, scaly below; red
in autumn.   P. Waldman, reg. 1988.

FLOOR SHOW  Described under PERRI CUTTEN, q.v.

FLORA DONALD  Described under GIPSY MOTH, q.v.

```
          -thomsonii 5/8
FLORA-   -campylocarpum 1/8
MARKEETA-   -Unique-
        -unnamed-   -unknown 1/8
         hybrid-   -fortunei 1/8
               -Pride of -
                 Leonardslee-thomsonii
```
4ft(1.2m)  -5F(-21C)  EM  4/5  Bush wider than tall; round glos-
sy leaves.  Coral pink buds open to ivory white flowers, flushed
coral, and rimmed in bright pink; rounded trusses of 10.   Flora
Markeeta Nursery, reg. 1968.   P.A. 1967.

```
              -nuttallii 1/2
FLORAL DANCE-
              -edgeworthii 1/2
```
Camellia rose flowers with a yellow blotch, 5 frilly lobes, fun-
nel-shaped; trusses of 4.  Ovate leaves with tan indumentum.  F.
M. Jury, reg. 1982.

FLORAL FETE  Described under MI AMOR, q.v.

```
          -forrestii Repens Group 1/2
FLORA'S BOY-   -griffithianum 1/4
          -Jean Marie de Montague-
                        -unknown 1/4
```
2ft(.6m)  5F(-15C)  EM  4/4  Flower large, bright waxy red, held
upright (First repens hybrid to do this--Greer)  Truss and plant
habit upright; small glossy leaves.   Flora Markeeta Nursery.

FLORENCE  Described under DEBORAH, q.v.

```
               -wardii 1/2
FLORENCE ARCHER-   -campylocarpum 3/8
              -Marcia-   -campylocarpum
                      -Gladys-
                            -fortunei 1/8
```
3ft(.9m)  10F(-12C)  L  Flowers of heavy substance, empire yel-
low, flushed and edged with jasper red, dorsal spotting of ab-
sinthe green; corolla of 5 wavy lobes, 3.75in(9.5cm) across.
High trusses of 8 flowers.   H. L. Larson, reg. 1979.
```

```
                   -arboreum 1/2
FLORENCE GILL-
                   -unknown 1/2
White flowers with pink margins.   R. Gill & Son, reg. 1958.


                   -rigidum 1/2
FLORENCE MANN-
              -Blue Admiral--unknown 1/2
5ft(1.5m)  0F(-18C)  EM   Plant heat-tolerant, floriferous, com-
pact.  Flowers of sea lavender violet; "The best blue for heat."
--Cox.   A. Bramley, AUS, reg. 1963.   Color illus. Cox pl. 61.


FLORENCE RINEHIMER   Described under DELENDICH, q.v.


FLORENCE SMITH   Parentage unknown
A parent of MRS. HAROLD TERRY.  Possibly same as FLORENCE SARAH
SMITH.   Pink flowers (both).   Smith of Darley Dale.


                        -oreotrephes ? 1/4
              -Oreoroyle-
FLORESCENT-            -cinnabarinum Roylei Group ? 1/4
             -cinnabarinum ssp. xanthocoden Concatenans Group 1/2
Plum-colored flowers.   Lord Aberconway, 1950.


FLORIADE   Parentage unknown
5ft(1.5m)  -5F(-21C)  ML  3/2   Possibly a hybrid of BRITANNIA.
Flowers Turkey red with a dark brown blotch;  trusses of 16-20.
Also known as FLORIDAE in North America.   Adriaan van Nes, reg.
1962.   Gold Medal Rotterdam 1960.


                   -campylocarpum 1/4
        -Moonstone-
FLOWER-            -williamsianum 1/4
 GIRL -      -wardii 1/4
        -Crest-            -fortunei ssp. discolor 1/8
             -Lady Bessborough-
                          -campylocarpum Elatum Group 1/8
3ft(.9m) -5F(-21C)  EM  3/3   Dark yellow buds open to glowing
yellow flowers;  large, rather lax trusses.   Foliage glossy
green.   Origin unknown.


                -catawbiense 1/2
FLUSHING-
             -unknown 1/2
Trusses of crimson flowers.   S. Parsons, intro. before 1875.


               -edgeworthii (bullatum) 1/2
FOLIES BERGERE-          -valentinianum 1/4
               -Parisienne-
                         -burmanicum 1/4
Flowering plant for the cool greenhouse.   Sir Giles Loder,
Leonardslee.   P.C. 1967.


FOLIUS PURPUREUS--form of ponticum
4ft(1.2m)  -10F(-23C)  L  2/4  Described in Peter Cox's Larger
Species..., p. 251, as having green foliage turning copper color
in winter.


FOLK'S WOOD--form of annae Laxiflorum Group
5ft(1.5m)  10F(-12C)  E-M  2/3   Flowers bell-shaped, 5-lobed,
pure white, held in truss of 14.  Leaves 6in x 2in (15cm x 5cm).
Major A. E. Hardy, reg. 1977.   A.M. 1977.


     -aberconwayii 1/2
FOLSCO-             -fortunei 1/4
       -Ruby F. Bowman-          -griffithianum 1/8
                      -Lady Bligh-
                                 -unknown 1/8
5ft(1.5m) x 3ft(.9m)  -5F(-21C)  M    Flowers flattened, 3in(7.6
cm) wide, centers light pink,  edges darker; spotted.  Spherical
trusses.   Upright bush; dark smooth leaves.  Goheen, reg. 1990.


           -griffithianum 1/4
        -Mars-
FORDHAM-   -unknown 1/4
        -haematodes 1/2
Hardy to at least -25F(-32C).   Floriferous; red-orange.  Blough.


           -haematodes 1/2
FORERUNNER-         -venator 1/4
             -Vanguard-
                       -griersonianum 1/4
```

Glowing scarlet flowers.   Sunnungdale Nurseries, 1951.

FOREST BLAZE   Described under DOROTHY LONSDALE, q.v.

```
                        -wardii 1/16
              -unnamed-          -neriiflorum
              - hybrid-F. C. Puddle-       1/32
                                 -griersonianum
         -Virginia-                         1/32
         -Richards-          -George-griffithianum
         -       -      -Mrs. - Hardy-        1/64
         -       -      -Lindsay-   -catawbiense
         -Vera -     -Betty -    -Duchess of   1/64
         -Elliott-   Robertson-  -Edinburgh--unknown
FOREST   -       -
FESTIVAL-        -unnamed-campylocarpum
         -       -     hybrid-         1/32
         -       -fortunei 1/4    -unknown 9/16
         -Whitney's Appleblossom-unknown
```
4ft x 4ft(1.2m)(7 yrs) 0F(-18C) ML Flowers of deep rose pink,
tubular funnel-shaped, 3in(7.5cm) wide, of heavy substance. Lax
trusses of 11-12. Flat, elliptic, dull green leaves, 7in(18cm)
long. Floriferous bush.   Walt Elliott, cross 1980; reg. 1987.

* *
```
                     -griersonianum 1/4
           -Tally Ho-
           -         -facetum (eriogynum) 1/4
FOREST FIRE-                       -griffithianum 1/8
           -          -Queen Wilhelmina-
           -Britannia-              -unknown 3/8
                      -Stanley Davies--unknown
```
Flowers red, waxy, funnel-campanulate, to 3in(7.6cm) wide, loose
truss; late season. Bushy plant. Henny cross, 1944; reg. 1958.
PARICUTIN   Parentage as above, except reversed
4ft(1.2m) -5F(-21C) ML 4/3   Bright cardinal red flowers, in
tall trusses of 23. Large foliage. "Best new hybrid, 1963"---
Seattle. L. Brandt, reg. 1968.
* *

FOREST FLAME   Described under FIRE PRINCE, q.v.

FOREVER AMBER   Described under DUSKY WOOD, q.v.

```
           -veitchianum 1/2
FORSTERIANUM-
           -edgeworthii 1/2
```
5ft(1.5m) 20F(-7C) M 4/4   Funnel-shaped large white flowers,
a yellow flare, heavily fragrant; lax truss of 3-4. Plant compact; lanceolate, hairy-edged leaves, dark rich green.   A pink
form may exist.--Cox.   Forster, before 1889.

FORT BRAGG GLOW   Described under JIM DREWRY, q.v.


```
           -griersonianum 1/2
FORT LANGLEY-
            -unknown 1/2
```
Deep red flowers in profusion. Attractive plant habit with dull
citrus green foliage. R. Clark.


```
                   -haematodes 1/4
        -May Day-
        -          -griersonianum 1/4
FORT NISQUALLY-              -griffithianum 1/8
        -            -George Hardy-
        -                       -catawbiense 1/8
        -Hugh Koster-                -arboreum
        -                      -Doncaster-    1/16
        -unnamed hybrid-     -unknown
                            -unknown 3/16
```
5ft(1.5m) -5F(-21C) ML 4/3   Vibrant red flowers; big, showy
trusses. Attractive foliage; plant of good habit. R. Clark.

* *
```
           -falconeri 1/2
FORTUNE-
        -sinogrande 1/2
```
6ft(1.6m) 5F(-15C) EM   A highly rated shrub, considered superior to its parents. Flowers bell-shaped, primrose yellow with
crimson blotch, 25-30 in trusses 9in(23cm) tall. Mature leaf is
15in(41cm) long, and holds a light coat of tan indumentum.   L.

de Rothschild.   F.C.C. 1938. Color illus. JS p. 37; PB pl. 15.
ANNAPOLIS ROYAL   Parentage as above
Trusses of 25 flowers, 11-lobed, light chartreuse green, faintly
striped in magenta.   Large leaves with woolly fawn indumentum.
Rothschild cross, 1938; L. de Rothschild, reg. 1983.
CHARLES   Parentage as above
Truss of 25 flowers, 8-lobed, very light chartreuse green with
blotch of reddish purple deep in center.   Leaves 18.4in x 7.2in
(46cm x 18cm), oblanceolate.   E. de Rothschild, reg. 1983.
CHURCHILL   Parentage as above
7ft(2.1m) 5F(-15C) M 4/4   Light primrose yellow flowers;
10 lobes in truss of up to 35, 9.5in(23cm) across.   Indumentum
brown, as falconeri.   L. de Rothschild, reg. 1972. A.M. 1971.
FORTUNE SANDRINGHAM   Parentage as above
Pale yellow-green flowers, deep red markings in throat, 9-lobed,
2.2in(5.5cm) broad; trusses of 30.   Foliage oblong-lanceolate to
lanceolate, 19.7in(55cm) long by 8.5in(22cm); fawn indumentum on
young leaves. Plant large; May blooms. L. de Rothschild, cross
c. 1930; E. de Rothschild, reg. 1988. Named by H.M. the Queen.
SIR JAMIE DARLING   Parentage as above
Trusses of 31 flowers, 8-lobed, cream with calyx of pale buff.
Leaves obovate, 15.6in x 6.8in (39cm x 17.5cm), pale buff indumentum.   J. S. Basford, cross 1961; Brodick Castle, reg. 1983.
STANLEY   Parentage as above
Truss of 28 flowers, very light sap green fading greenish white,
basal blotch of magenta on upper lobes.   Rothschild, reg. 1982.
* *

FORTUNE COOKIE   Described under VALLEY CREEK, q.v.

             -fortunei 1/2
FORTWILLIAM-
             -williamsianum 1/2
3ft(.9m) -5F(-21C) ML Flowers 4in(10cm) wide, light pink with
darker pink stripes and a yellow throat, in trusses of up to 12;
fragrant. Charles Herbert, reg. 1967.

* *
                -fortunei ssp. discolor 1/2
    -Lady Bessborough-
FOTIS-   -campylocarpum Elatum group 1/4
    -              -fortunei ssp. discolor
    -Margaret Dunn-   -dichroanthum 1/8
                   -Fabia-
                        -griersonianum 1/8
Flowers tangerine pink, fading to nankeen yellow, crimson brown
spots in throat. Sunningdale Nurseries, 1955.
HARVEST QUEEN   Parentage as above
Flower canary yellow, darker in throat. J. Russell, reg. 1972.
* *

                   -dichroanthum 3/16
            -Fabia-
    -unnamed hybrid-   -griersonianum 3/16
FOUR   -   -bureavii 1/4
CROSSES-   -fortunei ssp. discolor 1/8
    -     -King of Shrubs-   -dichroanthum
    -unnamed-   -Fabia-
     hybrid-   -griersonianum
          -smirnowii 1/4
Flower buds blood red, opening medium scarlet red, fading to a
light carrot orange; center currant red. Leaves have champagne-
colored indumentum. Cross made at N.Z. Rhododendron Asociation;
Mrs. R. Pinney raiser; reg. 1982.

FOWLE NO. 19   See NEWBURYPORT BELLE

FOWLER--maximuum, compact form (Collected wild, N. Carolina, US)
4.6ft(1.4m) tall x 8ft(2.4m)(12 yrs) -20F(-29C) VL Buds light
pink to white; flowers tubular-campanulate, .75in(2cm) broad, of
white, flushed pink; 16-18 in 3in(7.5cm) domed truss. Leaves to
4.9in(10cm), narrow, elliptic; thinly plastered tan hairs below.
Compact, dense plant. R. Fowler collector & raiser; reg. 1989.

* *
            -griersonianum 1/4
    -Matador-
FOX   -   -strigillosum 1/4
HUNTER-   -thomsonii 1/8
    -   -Shilsonii-
    -Gaul-   -barbatum 1/8
      -elliottii 1/4

Bright red flowers in trusses of 12; flowers 2.75in(7cm) wide by
2.5in(6.4cm). Gen. Harrison, reg. 1967.
JOAN SCOBIE   Parentage as above
Flowers with joined lobes, claret rose, in trusses of 15. Foli-
age elliptic, to 6in(15cm) long; traces of light brown indument-
um beneath. Gen. Harrison. A.M. 1972.
* *
* *
FOXBERG---NEWBURYPORT BELLE (FOWLE 19) F2--unknown
Flowers extremely large, white with a pink overcast. Hardy to
-25F(-32C). R. Blough.
CLAIRE REICHELT   Parentage as above
Flowers pinkish lavender with heavy burgundy blotch. Blough.
DYING EMBERS   Parentage as above
Flowers glowing pink; floriferous.   Blough.
EVERFULL   Parentage as above
Pink flowers, clear and impressive. Truss seems full, with only
half the buds opened. Blough.
MORRELLVILLE   Parentage as above
Extremely large truss of flowers with bold gold blotch. Blough.
RIVERSIDE   Parentage as above
Large truss of flowers, white with bright pink edging and yellow
centers. Blough.
* *

                         -arboreum 1/8
               -Doncaster-
     -Thunderstorm-   -unknown 3/8
FOXHUNTER-   -unknown
    -         -griersonianum 1/4
         -Tally Ho-
              -facetum (eriogynum) 1/4
Tall-growing with flowers dark scarlet, opening late.   Slocock.

FOXY--a form of fortunei
A selected form with trusses of 11-13 flowers, of amaranth rose
and lighter shades of same. John Fox, reg. 1982.

                    -fortunei 1/8
               -Luscombei-
     -Betty King-   -thomsonii 5/8
FRAGONARD-   -thomsonii
    -              -thomsonii
     -Cornish Cross-
                -griffithianum 1/4
Flowers Indian red. G. M. Adams-Acton, 1942.

         -catawbiense 1/2
FRAGRANS-
      -azalea viscosum 1/2
3-6ft(.9-1.8m) -5F(-21C) L   Plant 25-30 years old when first
introduced--Bean.   A sweet-scented azaleodendron; 12-20 flowers
1.25in(3cm) wide, per cluster, of pale mauve with centers lighter to white, purplish lilac rims. Leaves 2-4in(5-10cm), glossy;
persistent. Grows rather slowly. Plant as broad as tall; sun-
tolerant. Paxton, of Chandler & Sons, intro. 1843. (And still
available in Europe, Pacific coast, New Zealand--Cox)

FRAGRANS AFFINITY   Parentage unknown; possibly as in FRAGRANS
5ft(1.5m) -10F(-23C) L   Azaleodendron.   Flowers showy orchid
blue; strong, very dense plant. Good foliage, held better than
most azaleodendrons. H. E. Greer intro.

* *
             -edgeworthii 1/2
FRAGRANTISSIMUM-
             -formosum 1/2
3ft(.9m) 15F(-9C) EM 4/2   One of the most fragrant shrubs.
Blushed carmine buds open white, tinged pink, with creamy yellow
center; flowers 4in(10cm) wide, in lax trusses. Foliage medium-
sized, dark, glossy; a rather leggy plant. Rollisson. F.C.C.
1868. Color illus. Cox, pl. 63; JS p. 51.
PURITY   Parentage as above
White with a yellow eye. A. Waterer, before 1871. F.C.C. 1888.
SESTERIANUM   Parentage as above
Flowers creamy white. Rinz, before 1862. F.C.C. 1862.
* *
* *
                    -Dexter hybrid--unknown
          -Helen Everitt-
FRAN LABERA-   -Dexter hybrid--unknown
          -Honeydew (Dexter)--unknown

6ft(1.8m) -15F(-26C) ML Buds greenish white, opening white to cream, chartreuse throat; flowers to 4in(10.2cm) broad, 7 frilly lobes; truss of 8-11. Very strong nutmeg fragrance. Bush wider than tall. H. & S. Fuller, reg. 1978.
SALLY FULLER Parentage as above
5ft(1.5m) -20F(-29C) M   Seven-lobed flowers. very fragrant, white with slight rose flush, golden glow in throat, in trusses of 7. Plant broader than tall. Fuller, reg. 1978.
* *

FRANCES SHANNON RACOFF   Parentage unknown: elepidote
8ft(2.4m) x 10ft(3.0m)(25 yrs) -15F(-26C) M   Conical truss of 16 flowers, deep purplish pink with olive green blotch. Habit spreading, dense. Dexter cross; Winterthur Gardens, reg. 1987.

```
                    -griffithianum 1/8
          -Queen Wilhelmina-
      -Britannia-                -unknown 7/8
FRANCESCA-      -Stanley Davies--unknown
      -Dexter 202--unknown
```
8ft(2.4m) -10F(-23C) ML   Patented hybrid, no. 3709, sold by Bald Hill Nurseries, RI. Black-red flower buds open bright carmine, tubular-campanulate, 3.5in(8.9cm) wide; big truss of c.25. Large foliage. Plant habit broad, open, globular.   A. Consolini, A. Savella, reg. 1971. (The first patented rhododendron)

FRANCESCA BEEKMAN   Described under JOAN THOMPSON, q.v.

```
          -dichroanthum 1/2
FRANCIS HANGER-      -griffithianum 1/4
          -Isabella-
                -auriculatum 1/4
```
5ft(1.5m) -5F(-21C) L 2/2 Large flowers of deep yellow with tinge of pale rose at the rims; loose trusses of 7. Plant well-branched, with new foliage appearing about the time the flowers open, thus partially concealing the effect. Named for a curator at Exbury, who later was curator at Wisley. Rothschild, 1942. A.M. 1950.

FRANGO   Described under NOYO BRAVE, q.v.

```
          -griffithianum 1/4
      -Mars-
FRANK BAUM-      -unknown 1/4
      -         -dichroanthum 1/4
      -Jasper-          -fortunei ssp. discolor 1/8
          -Lady   -
          Bessborough-campylocarpum Elatum Group 1/8
```
5ft(1.5m) -5F(-21C) L 4/3   Trusses round and full; broad, cupped flowers, coral watermelon pink with gold centers. Leaves fir green, on red petioles.   Sturdy, dense and insect-resistant plant. C. S. Seabrook, reg. 1968.

```
          -ponticum 1/2
FRANK GALSWORTHY-
  (PURPLE & GOLD)-unknown 1/2
```
4ft(1.2m) -15F(-26C) ML 4/3   Dark buds, opening rich, deep reddish purple, bold flare of orange-yellow to off-white, faint greenish spotting; round truss of 15-20. Leaves 6in(15cm) long, narrow, dull green. Plant almost twice as wide as tall. Named for artist-brother of novelist John G.   A. Waterer raiser; Slocock exhibited. A.M. Wisley Trials 1960. Col. ill. JS p. 103.

```
          -fortunei ssp. discolor 1/2
      -Golden Belle-   -dichroanthum 1/4
      -         -Fabia-
FRANK -                -griersonianum 1/4
HEUSTON-      -fortunei ssp. discolor
      -Autumn Gold-   -dichroanthum
          -Fabia-
                -griersonianum
```
4ft(1.2m) OF(-18C) M   Flowers 6-lobed, light brick red edged orange buff, in 7in(17.8cm) trusses of 10 to 14. Plant spreads as broad as high; yellow-green foliage. W. Elliott, reg. 1983.

FRANK KINGDON WARD--form of glischrum ssp. rude
Flowers 7-lobed, white, with exterior stained purple, 3in(7.6cm) wide; loose truss of 16. Leaves 7in(17.8cm) long, covered with yellowish green hairs. J. F. A. Gibson, reg. 1970.   A.M. 1969.

FRANK LUDLOW--form of dalhousiae L S & T 6694
A plant for the cool greenhouse. White flowers, heavily stained

yellow, tubular-campanulate, 3.75in(9.5cm) wide; loose trusses. Leaves 5in(12.7cm) long, scaly.   Ludlow, Sherriff & Taylor collectors; Maj. A. E. Hardy, reg. 1975.   A.M. 1974.   F.C.C. 1974.

```
                    -griffithianum 1/4
          -Queen Wilhelmina-
      -Britannia-                -unknown 3/8
FRANK   -      -Stanley Davies--unknown
MARANVILLE-      -fortunei--Sir Charles Butler 1/4
      -Van Nes Sensation-      -maximum 1/8
                -Halopeanum-
                    -griffithianum
```
4ft(1.2m) x 4ft OF(-18C) EM Broadly funnel-shaped flowers to 4in(10cm) wide, vivid purple-red (rose Bengal), throat deeper, edges paler red; domed truss of 10. Smooth, elliptic, moderate olive green leaves, 5in(12.5cm) long; well-branched bush.   Dr. Ben Briggs, cross 1963; B. F. Heuston, reg. 1985.

FRANK MONIZ   Described under ED'S RED, q.v.

```
          -Margaret--unknown 1/4
  -Glamour-
FRANZ-      -griersonianum 1/4
LEHAR-      -dichroanthum 1/4
  -   -                -griffithianum 1/32
  -Jester-          -Kewense-
  -      -Aurora-      -fortunei 5/32
      -Naomi-      -thomsonii 1/16
          -fortunei
```
Blood red flowers in loose, semi-erect trusses. Plant only 18in (46cm) tall in 10 years. Late midseason.   Seabrook, reg. 1965.

```
          -ponticum 1/2
FRAU MINNA HARTL-
      -azalea--unknown 1/2
```
Azaleodendron. Double flowers of carmine rose.   Hartl, 1891.

FRECKLE FACE (Ingram) Listed with CORONET g., q.v.

FRECKLE FACE (Delp) Described under CHECKMATE, q.v.

* *
```
      -Marion (Cheal)--unknown  5/8   -griffithianum 1/32
FRECKLE-                -Loderi-
  PINK -      -Albatross-      -fortunei 1/32
      -      -      -fortunei ssp. discolor 1/16
      -Midnight-   -Cup Day-      -elliottii 1/16
      -      -Fusilier-
      -      -                -griersonianum 1/16
          -Purple   -ponticum 1/8
          Splendour-
                -unknown
```
Trusses hold 12 flowers, bell-shaped, solferino purple. Height 4ft(1.2m) when registered.   K. Van de Ven, reg. 1984.
RED THROAT   Parentage as above
Trusses of 15 flowers, campanulate, light reddish purple with a darker blotch. Shrub 4ft(1.2m).   K. Van de Ven, reg. 1984.
* *

```
          -caucasicum 3/8
      -Jacksonii-      -caucasicum
      -      -Nobleanum-
FRECKLES-                -arboreum 1/8
      -      -catawbiense 1/4
      -unnamed hybrid-
                -haematodes 1/4
```
6ft(1.8m) -10F(-23C) M Light rose pink flowers speckled brown over entire surface. Deep green foliage; vigorous plant. Hardiness rating probably lower. Joseph B. Gable.

```
          -minus var. minus 1/2
FRED CLARK-
      -yungningense (glomerulatum) 1/2
```
1.5ft(.45m) -15F(-26C) M   Mauve pink flowers, saucer-shaped, about 1.5in(3.5cm) wide, in trusses of 5-7, at terminals. Plant broader than tall, well-branched; foliage glossy, spinach green. Winter foliage greenish mahogany.   Fetterhoff, reg. 1981.

```
          -neriiflorum 1/4
      -unnamed hybrid-
FRED HAMILTON-      -griersonianum 1/4
          -dichroanthum 1/2
```

3ft(.9m) -5F(-21C) ML 4/3 Trusses of orange-yellow flowers,
lobes striped pink, spotted yellow-green; dense elliptic foliage
on a wide, well-branched bush.   Lem cross; Van Veen, reg. 1972.

         -Corona--unknown 1/2
FRED HARRIS-
         -fortunei 1/2
Clear pink flowers, 4in(10.2cm) wide, 5-7 lobes slightly reflex-
ed; conical trusses of 14.   Gen. Harrison, reg. 1962.

            -wardii 1/4
      -Prelude-
FRED HOLDEN-   -fortunei 1/4
      -Sappho--unknown 1/2
3ft(.9m) OF(-18C) EM Fragrant white flowers of good substance
with some lobes shaded pale yellow; truss of 16-19. Plant well-
branched, broader than tall, yellow-green leaves held 3 years.
P. Holden cross; Mrs. A. J. Holden, reg. 1981.

            -yakushimanum 1/4
     -unnamed hybrid-
FRED PESTE-   -Corona--unknown 1/4
      -haematodes 1/2
2.5ft(.75m) x 3ft(.9m)(14 yrs) OF(-18C) M Flowers widely funnel-campanulate, to 3in(7.6cm) wide, of non-fading cardinal red,
darker in throat; deep red spotting, heavier on dorsal lobes; 14
per flat truss. Leathery, dark olive green leaves, narrowly elliptic, 3.7in(9.5cm) long, dense golden buff indumentum.   Fred
Peste, cross 1971; S. P. Johnston, reg. 1986.

* *
         -sanguineum ssp. didymum 1/4
     -Carmen-
FRED ROBBINS-   -forrestii Repens Group 1/4
 -                 -haematodes 1/4
     -Choremia-
         -arboreum 1/4
After 9 years from seed, plant was 20in(51cm) high and about as
wide; leaves 2.25in(5.7cm) long, with silvery indumentum below.
Flowers of chrysanthemum crimson, 2.25in(5.7in) wide, with calyx
same hue; trusses of 7.   Lester E. Brandt, reg. 1965.
HONORÉ HACANSON   Parentage as above
In 9 years from seed only 1ft x 1.5ft (.3m x .45m). Flowers
cardinal red with red calyx in trusses of 8. Leaves 3.5in(9cm)
long, silvery beneath. Brandt, reg. 1965.
LITTLE NEMO   Parentage as above
Dwarf, only 8in x 15in (20cm x 38cm). Flowers Turkey red; truss
of 7; large calyx of same color. Brandt, reg. 1965.
* *

         -campylocarpum 1/4
     -Mary Swathling-
FRED ROSE-   -fortunei 1/4
     -lacteum 1/2
5ft(1.5m) -10F(-23C) M 4/3 Lemon yellow flowers with throat
lightly spotted red, widely campanulate, 2.5in(6.4cm) across;
compact rounded truss of 10. Plant habit broad as tall; leaves
dull green. F. Rose raiser; Sunningdale, reg. 1962.   H. C.
1973. Color ill. ARS Q 29:1 (1975), p. 35.   (H. Lem raised a
seedling from this cross, also naming it FRED ROSE. Plant similar but lacks spotting in the throat.---D. Balint)

* *
         -fortunei 1/2
FRED   -   -fortunei ssp. discolor 1/8
WYNNIATT-   -Lady Bessborough-
    -Jalisco-   -campylocarpum Elatum Group 1/8
    -        -dichroanthum 1/8
      -Dido-
         -decorum 1/8
4ft(1.2m) -5F(-21C) M 4/4 Flattened, lax trusses of 10 flowers, maize yellow with rose-tinged edges, 4.5in(11.5cm) across;
large calyces. Leaves 6.5in x 3in(16.5cm x 7.6cm).   Named for
the Head Gardener, Exbury. Rothschild; reg. 1964. A.M. 1963
F.C.C. 1980.
BACH CHOIR   Parentage as above
Flowers in trusses of 9-12, 7-lobed, moderate purplish pink
overlaid light yellow, more intense in center. Rothschild, reg.
1988. A.M. 1988.
DOUGGIE BETTERIDGE   Parentage as above
Flowers broadly funnel-shaped, to 4in(12cm) wide, 7-lobed, inner
surface pale primrose yellow, flushed shades of amaranth rose,

reverse deeper; 12-15 irregular stamens, anthers brown; truss of
c.15. Ovate leaves. E. de Rothschild, reg. 1986. A.M. 1986.
JEREZ   Parentage as above
Flowers pale lemon yellow. L. de Rothschild; reg. 1966.
JOYFUL   Parentage as above
Flowers of deep cream, flushed carmine pink on outer lobes with
a central red line. A tall, compact plant.   L. de Rothschild,
reg. 1967.   Exhibited at 1966 Chelsea Flower Show.
SIMITA   Parentage as above
Habit tall, compact. Flowers maize yellow with a brown eye,
slight brown spots; long petaloid calyx; flat-topped trusses of
10; late midseason. L. de Rothschild, reg. 1967.
STANWAY   Parentage as above
May be the best of the group. Flowers rich, dark yellow, tinged
pink, throat deeper, stripe down each lobe. L. de Rothschild,
reg. 1971. A.M. 1971.
TRIANON   Parentage as above
Tall, compact plant. Flowers of rose pink, with a golden yellow
throat. E. de Rothschild, reg. 1966.
* *

    -fortunei 1/2
FREDA-
    -unknown 1/2
Light pink flowers.   Paul.

FREDA ROSAGE   Described under JANET SCROGGS, q.v.

* *
         -yakushimanum 1/4
     -unnamed hybrid-
FREDERICK GEODFRIED PESTE-   -Corona--unknown 1/4
      -haematodes 1/2
20in x 30in(.5m x .8m)(14 yrs) OF(-18C) M Buds of strong red,
opening to Delft rose, fading to medium shell pink, upper lobes
spotted strong Jasper red, light salmon pink ray on each. Flowers, wavy, 2in(5cm) broad; flat trusses of c. 11. Elliptic,
olive green leaves, held 3 years; woolly grayed orange indumentum. F. Peste, cross 1971; S. P. Johnston, reg. 1986.
MARLENE PESTE   Parentage as above
3ft(.9m) x 3ft(14 yrs) OF(-18C) M Tubular funnel-shaped flowers, 5 wavy lobes, vivid non-fading red, with light to deep red
spotting; truss of 13. Glossy olive green foliage; some yellow-
orange indumentum. F. Peste cross; S. P. Johnston, reg. 1986.
* *
* *
         -catawbiense var. album 3/16
     -Lodestar-   -catawbiense var. album
 -           -Belle -   -catawbiense 3/32
    -          Heller-Madame Carvalho-
 -R.O. Delp-   -unknown 7/32
 -         -   -catawbiense
 -         -   -Atrosanguineum-
 -         -   -Atrier-   -unknown
FREE -   -Mary-   -griersonianum 1/16
REIGN-   Belle-   -decorum 1/16
 -         -Dechaem-
 -         -   -haematodes 1/16
 -         -brachycarpum 1/8
 -   -unnamed-   -wardii 1/16
 -   - hybrid-Crest-   -fortunei ssp.
 -unnamed-   -Lady Bess- - discolor 1/32
 hybrid-   borough   -campylocarpum Elatum 1/32
 -                -griffithianum 1/16
 -      -Mars-
 -unnamed- -unknown   -catawbiense
 hybrid-   -Parsons Grandiflorum-
 -America-   -unknown
 -dark red hybrid--unknown
Opens to brilliant yellow-green edged with magnolia purple, dorsal spots of brilliant yellow-green. W. Delp.
TOPPER   Parentage as above
Buds of beetroot purple and strong purplish red; flowers strong
purplish red; dorsal spots ruby red; ruby red stigma. W. Delp.
* *

FREEMAN R. STEPHENS   Described under DOUGLAS R. STEPHENS, q.v.

        -fortunei ? 1/2
FRENCH CREEK-
    -unknown 1/2
5ft(1.5m) -15F(-26C) ML   Upright plant, moderate branching;

medium-sized leaves held 3 years. Flowers to 3.5in(9cm) across,
pink fading white; large truss of 23.   C. Herbert, reg. 1977.

```
              -aberconwayi 1/2
FRESCO-            -fortunei 1/4
    -Ruby F. Bowman-        -griffithianum 1/8
                       -Lady Bligh-
                              -unknown 1/8
```
5ft(1.5m) x 3ft(.9m) OF(-18C) EM   Flat saucer-shaped flowers
of heavy substance in trusses of 9-10, strong purplish pink
margins shading to pale purplish pink.   Leaves held 3 years.
Dr. Bulgin intro.; Dr. Goheen, reg. 1989.

```
                  -maximum 1/4
       -unnamed hybrid-
                      -thomsonii 1/4
FRESH-                    -dichroanthum 1/16
  HEIR-               -Fabia-
    -          -Hello Dolly-     -griersonianum 1/16
    -Too Lips-          -smirnowii 1/8
         -            -catawbiense var. album Glass--Catalgla
         -Caltwins-          -catawbiense 1/16        1/8
                    -Pink Twins-
                             -haematodes 1/16
```
Blend of deep, moderate, and strong purplish reds in bud,
opening to blend of white, pale purplish pink and strong
purplish red; dorsal spots of brilliant greenish yellow.   Delp.

```
              -ponticum 1/4
      -Purple Splendour-
FRIDAY-             -unknown 3/4
    -unknown
```
5ft(1.5m) -5F(-21C) ML 4/3   Large flattened flowers, satiny
purple, a black velvet blotch on upper lobe. Leathery leaves of
medium matte green. An improved PURPLE SPLENDOUR?   Landauer.

FRIEDRICH DEUS   Described under ELISABETH HOBBIE, q.v.

* *
```
                  -catawbiense var. album Glass--Catalgla 1/4
       -unnamed hybrid-
FRILLED-            -Pink Dexter--unknown 3/4
CREAM -unknown
```
Flowers frilled, cream-colored. Hardy to -10F(-23C). Plant of
medium height, broader than high; nice foliage. Dr. T. L. Ring.
FRILLED WHITE   Parentage as above
Large truss of frilled white flowers. Average foliage, mod-
erately dense, taller than broad. Hardy to -15F(-26C). Ring.

* *

* *
```
                  -dichroanthum 1/8
       -Goldsworth-
    -Hotei- Orange   -fortunei ssp. discolor 1/8
    -     -unnamed hybrid-
FRILLED-                  -souliei 1/8
PETTICOATS-
    -                -wardii 3/8
    -        -Pink    -Jan Dekens--unknown 7/32
    -        -Petticoats-        -Queen       -griffithianum
    -unnamed-          -Britannia-Wilhelmina-        1/32
      hybrid-          -           -unknown
      -              -Stanley Davies--unknown
      -wardii
```
3ft(.9m) OF(-18C) M 4/3 A rounded plant, broader than tall;
glossy, yellowish green leaves 4.5in(11.5cm) long, held 3 years.
Flowers very pale chartreuse yellow, darker on reverse; 16 held
in round trusses 6in(15.2cm) wide.   John Lofthouse, reg. 1981.
GOLDEN MOMENTS   Parentage as above
4ft(1.2m) 5F(-15C) M   Flowers mimosa yellow, widely funnel-
campanulate, 6-lobed, in tall, open trusses of 15. Plant wide
as tall, leaves glossy, yellowish green. Lofthouse, reg. 1981.
YELLOW PETTICOATS Parentage as above
4ft(1.2m) OF(-18C) M Similar to HOTEI, but larger trusses and
more flowers of deep yellow, lighter at edges and unmarked; 15
per truss. Plant as wide as high. Lofthouse, reg. 1983.
* *

FRILLED WHITE   Described under FRILLED CREAM, q.v.

* *
```
                              -griffithianum 1/8
                    -George Hardy-
       -Mrs. Lindsay Smith-        -catawbiense 1/8
FRITZ -              -Duchess of Edinburgh--unknown 1/4
HENSSLER-williamsianum 1/2
```
Bright rose flowers in trusses of 8-12. D. Hobbie, 1952.
GUSTAV LÜTTGE   Parentage as above
5ft(1.5m) -10F(-23C) EM   White flowers with pale lilac tint.
Leaves rounded; loose habit.   Hobbie, intro. 1971.
* *

```
                         -catawbiense 1/4
                    -Sefton-
FRIZZY LIZ---unnamed hybrid, selfed-    -unknown 1/2
                                         -ponticum
                    -Purple Splendour-      1/4
                                      -unknown
```
Buds of deep reds open to frilled flowers, lilac purple with
white flare, dorsal spots lilac purple and light green-yellow.
White anthers.   W. Delp.

```
                     -campylocarpum Elatum Group 3/8
     -Letty Edwards-
FRONTIER-          -fortunei 1/4
    -    -wardii 1/4
    -Crest-
       -Lady      -fortunei ssp. discolor 1/8
       -Bessborough-
                   -campylocarpum Elatum Group
```
4.5ft(1.35m) OF(-18C) M 4/4   Pink, shading barium yellow
at center, 4in(10.2cm) wide, 7-lobed, lasting; truss of 14. Upright, rounded plant, as wide as tall; glossy leaves with maroon
petioles, held 3 years. J. Elliott, reg. 1977.   Color illus.
ARS J 43:3 (1989), p. 147.

```
            -yakushimanum--Koichiro Wada 1/2
FROSTED ICE-
            -aberconwayi (open-pollinated) 1/2
```
Funnel-shaped flowers, 2in(5cm) across, white with upper throat
spotted faint red; truss of 15-16. Elliptic leaves 2.4in(5cm),
deeply keeled, thin tan indumentum when young; bush 19.5in(5cm)
in 10 yrs. Seed, Pukeiti Rho. Trust, NZ.; G. Smith, reg. 1984.

```
            -Mucronatum--a hybrid with parentage unknown 1/2
FROSTY MORN-
            -Blaauw's Pink--unknown 1/2
```
Very light purple with spotting.   H. Van de Ven, reg. 1972.

* *
```
            -minus Carolinianum Group, pink form 1/2
FROSTY PINK-
    -              -racemosum 1/8
    -Pioneer (Gable)-
    -       -Conemaugh-
    -              -mucronulatum 1/8
            -unknown 1/4
```
Flowers a blend of moderate to light purplish pink. Hardy to
-25F(-32C). W. Delp.
MICROTONES   Parentage as above
A lepidote with reddish purple flowers. W. Delp.
* *

FROU FROU   Described under PERRI CUTTEN, q.v.


```
       -caucasicum 1/2
FRÜHAUF-
       -unknown 1/2
```
Ruby red German hybrid which normally flowers in April, but also used for forcing at Christmas.   F. Albertzland, Ger., 1962.

FRÜHLINGSZAUBER See SPRING MAGIC entered under ELISABETH HOBBIE


```
       -grande ? 1/2
FULBROOK-
       -unknown 1/2
```
Phlox pink flowers spotted maroon on upper lobe, bell-shaped, in
large trusses. Leaves 9.5in x 3.5in (24cm x 9cm). Mrs. Douglas
Gordon, reg. 1962.   A.M. 1961.

                              -ponticum 1/16
                    -Michael Waterer-
          -Prometheus-   -unknown 5/16
  -Madame de Bruin-   -Monitor--unknown
  -             -   -arboreum 1/8
FUEGO-   -Doncaster-
  -haematodes 1/2   -unknown
Widely campanulate flowers, luminous light red, unmarked, to 2.5
in(6.5cm) wide; lax, flattened trusses of 9-12. Leaf buds green
-gold; foliage dark olive, elliptic. Hobbie, cross 1949. Col-
or illus. WS, 1989, p. 39.

          -fulgens 1/2
FULGARB-
          -arboreum--Blood Red 1/2
Very large plant with small, compact trusses of 15 rich crimson
flowers. Very early season. E. J. P. Magor. A.M. 1937.

               -cinnabarinum Blandfordiiflorum Group 1/2
FULL HOUSE-
               -maddenii 1/2
Trumpet-shaped flowers of deep pink, flushed rose.   Johnstone.

          -wardii 1/4
     -Hawk-   -fortunei ssp. discolor 1/8
  -   -Lady Bessborough-
  -                     -campylocarpum Elatum Group 1/8
FULL-   -griffithianum 1/16
MOON-   -George Hardy-
  -       -Mrs. Lindsay-   -catawbiense 1/16
  -       - Smith   -Duchess of Edinburgh--unknown 1/4
  -Harvest-   -campylocarpum 1/8
    Moon -unnamed hybrid-
                    -unknown
4ft(1.2m) -5F(-21C) M 4/4   Flowers a deep yellow like CREST;
plant has a more compact growth habit. Foliage of shiny emerald
green, prominently veined.   John Henny, reg. 1958. P.A. 1955.
Color illus. ARS J 43:3(1989), p. 146.

FUNDY   Described under KATHERINE DALTON, q.v.

FURNIVALL'S DAUGHTER   Described under MRS. FURNIVALL, q.v.

          -oreotrephes 1/2
FURORA-
          -cinnabarinum ssp. xanthocodon Concatenans Group 1/2
Pale mauve pink flowers. Gen. Harrison, reg. 1958.

          -elliottii 1/2
FUSILIER-
          -griersonianum 1/2
5ft(1.5m) 10F(-12C) ML 4/3 Upright growth habit; large, dark
green, indumented leaves. Bright orange-red flowers; open topped, medium-sized trusses. Several forms exist.   Rothschild.
A.M. 1938.   F.C.C. 1942.

                          G

G. A. SIMS   Parentage unknown
A parent of GRIERSIMS. Flowers deep currant red, 2.5in(6.4cm)
wide, frilled edges; trusses of 16. Plant upright and spreading
with leaves 7in(17.8cm) long and glossy dark green. A. Waterer,
Jr., Knap Hill. A.M. 1938. A.M. 1972.

GABLE'S EARLY BIRD   Parentage unknown
5ft(1.5m) -10F(-23C) EM Heat-tolerant but best in light shade
and grows with open habit. Attractive lavender purple flowers
in abundance. Gable. See Cox, p. 122.

                              -catawbiense 1/8
                    -Atrosanguineum-
     -Dr. H. C. Dresselhuys-   -unknown 1/4
GABRIEL-   -   -arboreum 1/8
     -             -Doncaster-
     -smirnowii 1/2   -unknown
3ft(.9m) -15F(-26C) L Plant as broad as high, rounded, semi-
compact with medium-sized leaves. Flowers 2.75in(7cm) across,
pink with olive brown spotting, in truss of 18.   G. Swain & D.
Craig, Canada Dept. of Agri. Res. Sta., N.S., reg. 1977.

          -arboreum 1/2
GABRIELE LIEBIG-
          -ponticum 1/2
Frilled white flowers with a touch of pink and very bold reddish
brown markings. In the register as cross by Otto Schulz, 1860;
in Germany credited to Emil Liebig, before 1863.

GAHAGEN---LADY CLEMENTINE MITFORD, F2--unknown
Large trusses of purplish pink flowers. R. Blough.

                    -Loder's White, q.v. for 2 possible parentages
            -C.I.S.-   -dichroanthum
  -Big Sam-   -Fabia-
  -       -   -griersonianum
  -       -unnamed hybrid--unknown
GALA-   -dichroanthum
  -       -Dido-
  -       -   -decorum
  -       -   -griffithianum
  -Lem's Cameo-   -Beauty of-
  -       -   -Norman- Tremough-arboreum
  -       - Gill -
  -Anna-   -griffithianum
  -         -
  -         -Jean Marie de Montague-
                         -unknown
5ft x 5ft(1.5m) 10F(-12C) EM Openly funnel-shaped flowers 3.3
in(8cm) wide, of 6 wavy lobes, Neyron rose edges to pale center,
Turkey red dorsal spotting; lax ball truss of 15. Flat elliptic
leaves, parsley green, 4in(10cm) long. J. Elliott, reg. 1987.

                    -griffithianum 1/8
               -Loderi-
     -Avalanche-   -fortunei 1/8
GALACTIC-   -calophytum 1/4
     -lacteum 1/2
6ft(1.8m) -5F(-21C) EM   Early flowers, deep cream, two small
crimson rays, slightly scented, 3.5in(8.9cm) wide; very large
truss of 22. Tall, handsome plant with leaves 8in(20.3cm) long,
plastered indumentum below. E. de Rothschild, reg. 1965. A.M.
1964. F.C.C. 1970.   Color illus. PB pl. 35.

          -azalea--unknown 1/2
GALLOPER LIGHT-
          -rhododendron--unknown 1/2
5ft(1.5m) -5F(-21C) M 3/1 A deciduous azaleodendron as beautiful as GLORY OF LITTLEWORTH and more hardy. Rose pink buds
opening salmon pink, then creamy yellow; good trusses of compar-
atively large flowers. Strong foliage. A. Waterer, to L. de
Rothschild likely. Not in Exbury Register. A.M. 1927.

               -elliottii 1/4
     -Fusilier-
GANDALF'S-   -griersonianum 1/4
  FLAME -   -griffithianum 1/8
     -         -Queen Wilhelmina-
     -Britannia-   -unknown 3/8
               -Stanley Davies--unknown
5ft(1.5m) 5F(-15C) ML Open funnel-shaped flowers in trusses
of 8, color geranium lake with darker spots in throat. Young
leaves with brown indumentum.   P. Wiseman, cross 1958; D. E.
Mayers, reg. 1989.

               -wardii 1/8
     -Crest-   -fortunei ssp. discolor
  -unnamed-   -Lady   -   1/16
  - hybrid-   Bessborough-campylocarpum Elatum Gp.
  -       -   -lacteum 1/8   1/16
  -       -Lionel's-   -griffithianum
  -       Triumph-   -Kewense 5/64
  -                -   -Aurora-   -fortunei 5/64
GANDY DANCER-   -Naomi-   -thomsonii 1/32
  -                    -fortunei
  -                    -griffithianum
  -              -George Hardy-
  -    -Mrs. Lindsay-   -catawbiense 1/16
  -Diane- Smith   -Duchess of Edinburgh--unk.
  -              -campylocarpum 1/8
  -unnamed hybrid-
          -unknown 1/4

5ft(1.5m) -5F(-21C) E 4/4 Very large truss of lovely golden yellow flowers; upright plant with fine foliage. Larson cross; Clint Smith intro.

```
                    -griersonianum 1/4
        -Gladys Rillstone-
GARDIS-            -unknown 1/4
        -fortunei ssp. discolor 1/2
```
Flowers of light Neyron rose with a maroon blotch and speckles; trusses of about 14. E. de Rothschild, reg. 1982.

GARGANTUA--form of diaprepes F 11958
6ft(1.8m) OF(-18C) L 4/4 A triploid clone with thick stems. Very large, fragrant white flowers, a green basal flush. Broad, vigorous plant. G. Forrest, collector; J. B. Stevenson and the Crown Estate, Windsor, raisers. A.M. 1953. F.C.C. 1974.

```
        -griffithianum 1/2
GARNET-         -arboreum 1/4
        -Broughtonii-
                -unknown 1/4
```
5ft(1.5m) 5F(-15C) M 3/4 Flowers deep salmon rose. flushed red. Upright plant, spreading habit, quite compact; glossy dark green leaves, 5.25in(13.3cm). P. D. Williams, 1942.

GARNET GLOW Described under ALPHA OMEGA, q.v.

GARRETT Described under FLADA W. BLOUGH, q.v.

```
                    -arboreum 1/4
            -Doncaster-
GARTENDIREKTOR GLOCKER-            -unknown 1/4
            -williamsianum 1/2
```
3ft(.9m) -5F(-21C) M 3/3 Flowers deep reddish rose, edges darker, bell-shaped; truss of 8-12. Foliage dense, stiff, dark, glossy; tolerates sun. A fine hybrid. D. Hobbie, intro. 1952. Color illus. Cox pl. 65; WS, 1989, p. 24.

```
                    -campylocarpum 1/8
            -unnamed-
        -Adriaan- hybrid-unknown 1/4
        - Koster-                    -griffithianum 1/16
GARTENDIREKTOR-     -          -George-
RIEGER         -    -Mrs. Lindsay- Hardy-catawbiense 1/16
        -         Smith    -
        -                    -Duchess of Edinburgh--
        -williamsianum 1/2                 unknown
```
3ft(.9m) -5F(-21C) EM 3/4 Cream-colored flowers with a small red spot. A vigorous plant; rounded leaves like williamsianum. Floriferous. Hobbie, cross c. 1947. Color illus. ARS Q 34:2 (1980), cover; WS, 1989, p. 24.

GARY Described under DAVID JOHN, q.v.

GARY HERBERT--form of vernicosum R 18139
4ft(1.2m) -5F(-21C) M Fragrant flower of shaded salmon tones, openly funnel-shaped, 3in(7.6cm) wide, ruffled; flat truss of 7. Plant rounded, moderately branched; glossy leaves held 3 years. New growth showy; burgundy red bracts. Rock, collector, 1929; J. Gable selection; Chas. Herbert, reg. 1976.

* *
```
        -thomsonii 1/4
    -Shilsonii-
GAUL-      -barbatum 1/4
    -elliottii 1/2
```
5ft(1.5m) 1OF(-12C) EM Waxy, ruby red flowers, widely funnel-shaped; compact, spherical trusses. Early. Deep green leaves; top branches need pinching. Rothschild, 1939. A.M. 1939.
GAUL MASTODON Parentage as above
Richer red than GAUL, otherwise similar. Rothschild, 1939.
* *
```
            According to Hillier's Manual same
GAUNTLETTII     parentage as LODER'S WHITE, q.v. for 2
            possible parentage diagrams.
```
Rich pink in bud, opening blush white, speckled crimson.

Foliage dark green, glossy.   Origin uncertain; before 1934.

```
        -davidsonianum 1/2
GAVOTTE-
        -mollicomum 1/2
```
Flowers pink to mauve. G. M. Adams-Acton, 1945.

GAY ARSEN Described under AGATEEN, q.v.

* *
```
        -minus Carolinianum Group--Epoch 1/2
GAY DAY-            -minus Carolinianum Group, pink form 1/4
        -unnamed hybrid-
                -pemakoense Patulum Group 1/4
```
Buds a blend of magenta rose and pale yellow green, opening to a blend of very light and very pale purples; dorsal spotting light greenish yellow. W. Delp.
HINDSIGHT Parentage as above
Buds light and pale purplish pink open to very pale purple flowers, edged light purple; dorsal spots yellow-green. W. Delp.
SHOWOFF Parentage as above
Buds very light purple open to very pale purple flowers. Delp.
* *

```
                -Essex Scarlet--unknown 1/4
        -Beau Brummell-
GAY GORDON-            -facetum (eriogynum) 1/4
        -elliottii 1/2
```
A hybrid of medium size, loose habit, and waxy, scarlet flowers, described as "hunting coat pink."   Rothschild, 1939. Color illus. ARS J 36:1 (1982), p. 14.

GAY HOSTESS Parentage unknown
5ft(1.5m) -5F(-21C) ML Large leaves; flowers 3in(7.5cm) wide, rose pink spotted light green, the reverse paler pink. Truss of 14. R. Kersey cross; Mrs. H. A. Frederick, reg. 1976.

```
                        -catawbiense 1/8
                -Atrosanguineum-
        -Atroflo-            -unknown 5/8
GAY PRINCESS-    -floccigerum 1/4
        -unknown
```
5ft(1.5m) -5F(-21C) ML Synonym PINK PRINCESS. Plant upright, well-branched; long narrow leaves. Flower medium fuchsia purple paler on edges; throat and reverse, grayed yellow orange blotch, about 3in(7.6cm) wide; trusses of 18. C. Herbert, reg. 1979.

* *
```
        -Marion--unknown 11/16
GAY SONG-    -griersonianum 1/4          -griffithianum 1/16
        -Radium-        -Queen Wilhelmina-
            -Earl of -            -unknown
            Athlone-Stanley Davies--unknown
```
Trusses hold 14 flowers, Neyron rose, with darker rose spotting. G. Langdon, reg. 1980.
CRAZY JOE Parentage as above
Trusses of 15 cardinal red flowers. G. Langdon, reg. 1982.
MAYBE Parentage as above
Medium Neyron rose flowers in truss of 14. Langdon, reg. 1980.
* *

```
            -griffithianum 1/4
        -Azma-
GAYBLADE-    -fortunei 1/4
        -    -griffithianum 1/4
        -Mars-
            -unknown 1/4
```
3.5ft(1m) 5F(-15C) ML   Plant of compact habit. Flowers gaudy pink, in truss of 15-18. A. Wright raiser; A. Lindsley intro.; reg. 1971.

```
                -fortunei 1/2
        -Fawn-    -dichroanthum 1/8
        -    -Fabia-
GAYLE VINCENT-            -griersonianum 1/8        -griffithianum
        -                -George Hardy-            1/16
        -    -Mrs. Lindsay Smith-            -catawbiense
        -Dot-            -Duchess of            1/16
            -fortunei            Edinburgh--unknown 1/8
```
1Oft(3m) x 5ft(1.5m)(28 yrs) OF(-18C) M   Buds medium violet; 6-lobed frilly flowers, 3.5in(9cm) wide, pale purplish pink fading white, orange dorsal spotting, fragrant; ball trusses of 18.

Leaves 7in(17.5cm).   D. James, cross 1963; Childers, reg. 1988.

```
        -arboreum 1/2
GEE BEE-
        -unknown 1/2
```
Tubular campanulate flowers from rose opal buds, of blush white, with (fading) Neyron rose flushing, also on reverse; dark maroon spots; blooms late. Oblanceolate foliage to 5.5in(14cm); silvery indumentum.   Mrs. P. Gordon, NZ, reg. 1988.

```
                            -thomsonii 1/8
                    -Bagshot Ruby-
        -Princess Elizabeth-         -unknown 5/8
        -                   -
GEE WHIZ-           -unknown
        -        -catawbiense var. album Glass--Catalgla 1/4
        -Calsap-
                -Sappho--unknown
```
Medium-sized plant, hardy to -15F(-26C). Flowers mallow purple with a blotch of dark beetroot purple.   Weldon E. Delp.

```
        -Pineapple--unknown 1/2
GEISHA-
        -dichroanthum 1/2
```
Bush of low and spreading habit, with cream-colored, campanulate flowers in loose trusses.   Rothschild, cross 1932; intro. 1939.

```
* * * * * * * * * * * * * * * * * * * * * * * * * * * *
             -maximum 1/4
    -Halopeanum-
GEM-         -griffithianum 1/4
    -thomsonii 1/2
```
Flowers light blush or rose, deep pink edges.   Loder, 1926.
LEONARDSLEE BRILLIANT   Parentage as above
Flowers of deep red.   Sir Edmund Loder.
RED GLOW   Parentage as above
Bright red flowers.   Loder, 1949.
```
* * * * * * * * * * * * * * * * * * * * * * * * * * * *
                        -griffithianum 1/8
                -Dawn's Delight-
        -Bauble-            -unknown 1/8
GEMSTONE-        -campylocarpum 1/4
        -wardii 1/2
```
Medium-sized, light yellow flowers, carried in trusses of about 7. Edmund de Rothschild, reg. 1979.

GEN SCHMIDT   Described under OAKTON, q.v.

```
    -scabrifolium var. spiciferum 1/2
GENE-
    -ciliatum 1/2
```
3ft(.9m) 5F(-15C) E 4/2   Plant wider than tall; leaves about 2in(5cm) long. Rosy purple flower, funnel-shaped, 1.75in(4.5cm) long, in ball-shaped truss.   U. of Wash. Arboretum, reg. 1963.

```
        -Scintillation--unknown 5/8
GENERAL ANTHONY-
  WAYNE    -        -catawbiense 1/8
          -        -Atrosanguineum-
          -Atrier-             -unknown
                  -griersonianum 1/4
```
6ft(1.8m) -5F(-21C) ML   Plant as wide as tall, well-branched; large, glossy, rounded leaves, held 3 years. Fragrant flowers, openly funnel-shaped, 4in(10cm) wide, Neyron rose tinged with glowing orange, light green throat, with chartreuse green dorsal spots. Large conical truss of 15-17.   C. Herbert, reg. 1976.

```
        -griffithianum 1/2
GENERAL EISENHOWER-
        -unknown 1/2
```
6ft(1.8m) -10F(-23C) M 4/3   Large carmine red flowers, ruffled edges, in large trusses. Compact, sturdy, vigorous plant; big, dark green, waxy leaves.   A. Kluis, 1946.   Color illus. F p. 45; VV p. 122.

```
            -yakushimanum 1/2
GENERAL ERIC HARRISON-         -thomsonii 1/4
                    -Shilsonii-
                           -barbatum 1/4
```
Bright crimson flowers with darker red spotting.   Hydon Nurseries, reg. 1972.

```
        -catawbiense 1/2
GENERAL GRANT-
        -unknown 1/2
```
A hardy hybrid with flowers of soft rose. Intro. before 1875 by Samuel B. Parsons (1819-1906) of Long Island, N.Y.

```
GENERAL            -yakushimanum 1/2
PRACTITIONER--unnamed hybrid, selfed-
                        -unknown 1/2
```
A yakushimanum hybrid with flowers of very light sap green.   J. Waterer, Sons & Crisp, reg. 1975.

```
                    -thomsonii 1/2
GENERAL SIR JOHN DU CANE-
                    -fortunei ssp. discolor 1/2
```
To honor an officer of World War I.   A tall plant, with large lax trusses of fragrant, funnel-shaped flowers of rose madder, fading lighter, a dark crimson basal blotch.   Rothschild, 1933.

```
                        -griffithianum 1/8
                -Loderi-
        -Albatross-    -fortunei 1/8
GENE'S  -        -fortunei ssp. discolor 3/8
FAVOURITE-                -fortunei ssp. discolor
        -        -Lady Bessborough-
        -Jalisco-            -campylocarpum Elatum Group 1/8
        -        -dichroanthum 1/8
                -Dido-
                    -decorum 1/8
```
Deep pink and pale orange-yellow flowers, deep red blotch; truss of 15; rose-like scent. Elliptic leaves.   Reuthe, reg. 1985.

GENEVA   Described under BACHER'S GOLD, q.v.

```
                        -griffithianum 1/8
                -Queen Wilhelmina-
        -Britannia-            -unknown 3/8
GENGHIS KHAN-        -Stanley Davies--unknown
        -            -dichroanthum 1/4
        -Felis-
                -facetum (eriogynum) 1/4
```
4ft(1.2m) -5F(-21C) M 4/4   Flowers guardsman red, 3in(7.6cm) across; enlarged calyx of same color; rounded truss of 15. Compact plant; dense matte green foliage with silvery plastered indumentum beneath.   L. Brandt, reg. 1969. Color ill. HG p. 135.

```
        -catawbiense 1/2
GENOVEVA-
        -unknown 1/2
```
5ft(1.5m) -20F(-29C) ML   Flowers of pale lilac white, with a yellow-green blotch. A parent of MOERHEIM'S PINK.   Seidel.

GEOFFREY HALL   Parentage unknown: elepidote
Trusses of 12 flowers, 6- to 7-lobed, strong purple with a white tube, in bud, opening strong purple, with a small black-crimson blotch. Season early May.   G. Hall, reg. 1988.

```
        -edgeworthii (bullatum) 1/2
GEOFFREY JUDSON-
        -johnstoneanum 1/2
```
Creamy white flowers, a yellow blotch in throat.   G. A. Judson, reg. 1973.

```
        -griffithianum 1/2
GEOFFREY MILLAIS-
        -unknown 1/2
```
6ft(1.8m) -5F(-21C) ML   Pink buds opening to gleaming white flowers flushed pink, fragrant and frilled, in conical trusses. Large, open shrub; foliage dark green and glossy.   Otto Schulz cross, 1892; C. B. van Nes intro.   A.M. 1922.

GEORDIE SHERRIFF--form of lindleyi
5ft(1.5m) 25F(-4C) E-ML 4/2   Truss of 7 very fragrant white flowers, stained spirea red on upper lobes. Leaves dark green, with thin brown indumentum beneath. J. F. A. Gibson, reg. 1969. A.M. 1969.

```
        -arboreum 1/2
GEORGE CUNNINGHAM-
        -campanulatum ? 1/2
```
A plant with unusual flowers: exterior of flower white, interior

heavily mottled black, in neat trusses. Foliage resembles cinnamomeum. See also BODDAERTIANUM. G. Cunningham, before 1875.

GEORGE FRASER   Described under ALBERT CLOSE, q.v.

```
                   -griffithianum 3/8
          -Loderi-
          -        -fortunei 1/4
GEORGE GRACE-                    -arboreum 1/8
          -         -Doncaster-
          -Borde Hill-       -unknown 1/4
          -                        -griffithianum
                   -Mrs. A. M. Williams-
                                    -unknown
```
Flowers rhodamine pink, with the lobes slightly recurved, 4.5
in(11.5cm) across; truss of 15. R. Henny, 1943.   P.A. 1952.

```
          -griffithianum 1/2
GEORGE HARDY-
          -catawbiense 1/2
```
6ft(1.8m) 0F(-18C) ML Parentage as recorded in the Register,
but some have suggested ponticum X griffithianum. A parent of
MRS. LINDSAY SMITH, PINK PEARL. Flowers blush pink, fading to
white. Mangles, c.1922.

```
                    -diaprepes 1/4
          -Polar Bear-
GEORGE HASLAM-      -auriculatum 1/4
          -         -kyawii 1/4
          -Romarez-
                   -griersonianum 1/4
```
20ft(6m) x 16ft(4.8m)(27 yrs) 10F(-12C) L Flowers in trusses
of 12-14, deep pink to deep purplish pink, unmarked. Gen. Harrison, cross 1960; Mrs. C. G. Hopwood, reg. 1987.

GEORGE JOHNSTONE   Described under TREWITHEN ORANGE, q.v.

GEORGE M. COHAN   Described under SIGMUND ROMBERG, q.v.

```
          -yakushimanum 1/4
          -                    -Parsons    -catawbiense
          -                    -Grandiflorum-   1/16
       -unnamed-         -America-       -unknown 9/64
       - hybrid-   -unnamed-       -dark red hybrid--unknown
       -         - hybrid-     -griffithianum 3/64
       -         -     -     -Mars-
       -     -Cindy-   -Blaze- -unknown
       -       Lou-          -catawbiense, red form
GEORGE-       -                -griffithianum
RING -        -         -Mars-
       -       -Red Brave- -unknown
       -              -         -Parsons    -catawbiense
       -              -America-Grandiflorum-
       -              -            -         -unknown
       -              -            -dark red hybrid--unknown
       -       -meddianum 1/4
       -unnamed hybrid-
               -strigillosum 1/4
```
Dark red flowers, on a medium-sized plant. Hardy to -5F(-21C).
George Ring, cross; Weldon E. Delp, raiser.

```
          -griersonianum 1/2
GEORGE RITTER-
          -unknown 1/2
```
4ft(1.2m) 15F(-9C) L   Fuchsine pink flowers, crimson throat,
widely funnel-shaped, to 4.25in(10.8cm), 5-7 lobes; lax trusses
of about 6. Plant wider than tall, well-branched; spinach green
leaves, narrowly elliptic, 7.25in(18.5cm) long, held 3 years.
Else Frye cross; J. S. Drucker raiser; E. German, reg. 1976.

Note: Next entry out of alpha order.

```
          -New Yellow 6002 (Whitney) 1/2
GEORGE'S DELIGHT-     -wardii 1/4
          -Crest-         -fortunei ssp. discolor 1/8
          -Lady-
          Bessborough-campylocarpum Elatum Gp. 1/8
```
3ft(.9m) x 2.5ft(.75m) 0F(-18C) M Flowers dark pink with mar-
gins blending into soft yellow, deeper yellow in throat; reddish
orange buds. Shrub well-branched; matte green foliage. Blooms
young. Whitney, cross 1967; A. Sather, reg. 1985. Color illus.
ARS J 38:3 (1984), p. 115; Cox pl. 66.

```
                              -wardii 1/16
          -unnamed-              -neriiflorum 1/32
          - hybrid-F.C.Puddle-
          -                    -griersonianum 1/32
   -Virginia-                        -griffith.
   -Richards-              -George-
   -        -         -Mrs. Lindsay- Hardy-cataw.
-Vera -            -       - Smith
-Elliott-     -Mrs. Betty-          -Duchess of
-       -        Robertson-          Edinburgh--unk.
-       -            -       -campylocarpum 1/32
-     -fortunei 1/4     -unnamed-
GEORGE-                    hybrid-
SWEESY-                    -unknown 1/4
-                    -griffithianum 5/64
-              -George-
-            -Pink - Hardy-catawbiense 13/64
-Dr. A. Blok-Pearl-     -arboreum 1/16
-            -Broughtonii-
-            -         -unknown
-            -         -catawbiense
-unnamed hybrid-
          -unknown
```
4ft(1.2m) 5F(-15C) EM Growth habit rounded and upright, wider
than tall. Leaves medium-sized, dark green. Flowers up to 3.25
in(8.3cm) wide, open funnel-shaped, wavy margins, of soft pink
spotted golden brown; trusses of 12. W. Elliott, reg. 1981.

GEORGE TAYLOR--form of araiophyllum
5ft(1.5m) 10F(-12C) EM Flowers slightly fragrant, white with
red-purple markings and carried in loose trusses of 7-8. Leaves
dark green, brown indumentum only along midribs. RBG, Kew, reg.
1972. A.M. 1971.

GEORGE WATLING   wardii X ? or campylocarpum X ?
4ft(1.2m) 0F(-18C) M 3/3 Bright to pale primrose yellow with
a greenish touch. Glossy foliage. Greig cross; A. Cook intro.

GEORGE'S DELIGHT (Out of order: see previous column)

```
          -yakushimanum 1/2
GEORGETTE-                    -thomsonii 1/4
          -Exbury Cornish Cross-
                              -griffithianum 1/4
```
3ft(.9m) 0F(-18C) EM   Compact plant, glossy foliage, medium
dark green. Globular trusses 6in(15.2cm) high, 12-flowered.
White flowers, exterior flushed pink when young; campanulate,
2.5in(6.4cm) across. A. F. George, reg. 1972. H.C. 1977.

GEORGIA MAY   Parentage unknown
Flowers rose pink with whitish centers, maroon spots. Plant 3ft
(.9m) tall; leaves 6in(15cm) long. A. Core, reg. 1965.

GERALD LODER--form of degronianum ssp. degronianum
3ft(.9m) -5F(-21C) E 3/3 Plant compact, dense foliage, dark
green above, heavy coat brown indumentum below. Flowers erect,
10-12 per truss, white with shades of roseine purple, darker
lines down center of petals.   Shown by RBG, Wakehurst Pl., reg.
1974. A.M. 1974. Color illus. ARS J 37:4 (1983), p. 186.

```
          -praevernum 1/2
GERALDII-
          -sutchuenense 1/2
```
A large shrub bearing white flowers with a deep purple blotch;
handsome foliage. Early. Origin unknown. A.M. 1945.

```
                              -griffithianum 1/16
                         -George-
                 -Pink Pearl- Hardy-catawbiense 1/16
     -Antoon van Welie-     -       -arboreum 1/16
     -             -        -Broughtonii-
GERMANIA-         -unknown 5/16     -unknown
          -williamsianum 1/2
```
4ft(1.2m) -15F(-26C) ML Full, rounded trusses; flattened rose
pink corolla, pale in center, 5-lobed, ruffled rims deeper pink.
Cox reports no sign of williamsianum here, but good foliage and
a compact plant. D. Hobbie. Gold Medal, IGA, Munich, 1983.
Color illus. WS, 1989, p. 40.

```
* * * * * * * * * * * * * * * * * * * * * * * *
                              -ponticum 1/8
                  -Michael Waterer-
        -Prometheus-              -unknown 3/8
        -             -Monitor--unknown
GERTRUD SCHÄLE-
             -forrestii Repens Group 1/2
Large, glowing scarlet red flowers.   D. Hobbie, 1951.
DR. ERNST SCHÄLE   Parentage as above
Light scarlet flowers.  Hobbie.   Color illus. WS, 1989, p. 15.
* * * * * * * * * * * * * * * * * * * * * * * *
```

GERTRUDE BOVEE   Described under MARY MAYO, q.v.

GERTRUDE RAGAN   Parentage unknown; elepidote
5ft(1.5m) x 6ft(1.8m)(18 yrs) -5F(-21C) ML   Purple buds open
very pale purple with yellowish throat, strong reddish purple
edges, dense dorsal spotting dark purplish red; flowers 3in
(7.5cm) wide, in conical trusses of 17. W. A. Ragan, reg. 1988.

GERTRUDE SAXE   Described under LLENROC, q.v.

```
     -Doctor Torry--unknown
GESCHE-
     -unknown
```
Late-season flowers, 12-19 per truss, vivid red to purplish red,
a brownish yellow blotch. Compact habit. Heinje, reg. 1986.
Color illus. WS, 1989, p. 113.

```
* * * * * * * * * * * * * * * * * * * * * * * *
               -Moser's Maroon--unknown 1/4
        -Bibiani-
GIBRALTAR-      -arboreum 1/4
        -elliottii 1/2
```
5ft(1.5m) 10F(-12C) EM   A tall plant with a rather loose hab-
it, and very attractive foliage, of bright chestnut color when
young. Large, deep red flowers, held in large rounded trusses.
Rothschild, 1939.   Color illus. ARS J 36:1 (1982), p. 14.
BASTION   Parentage as above
Flowers dark red, with the black spotting of BIBIANI, in tight
upright trusses. Habit as GIBRALTAR. Rothschild. P.C. 1961.
RED ROCK   Parentage as above
Cardinal red flowers brighter in throat, full rounded truss of
24. Dark green leaves to 8in(20.3cm). Rothschild. A.M. 1970.
```
* * * * * * * * * * * * * * * * * * * * * * * *
```

GIBSONII   Parentage unknown
A parent of DENISONII. Flowers pure white. T. Methven, 1868.

```
                    -griffithianum 1/16
                -Loderi-
        -Albatross-      -fortunei 1/16
  -Cup Day-      -fortunei ssp. discolor 1/8
GIFT-           -ponticum 1/4
  -Purple Splendour-
                -unknown 1/4
```
3.3ft(1.m) 10F(-12C) Spring in AUS   Funnel-shaped flowers in
trusses of 10-12, 6-lobed, strong purplish red flushed in throat
deep red. D. J. Dosser, Lockington Nursery, reg. 1988.

```
     -catawbiense 1/2
GIGANTEUM-
     -unknown 1/2
```
6ft(1.8m)   -15F(-26C) EM 3/3 Should not be confused with the
species of the same name.   Very hardy plant, dark green medium-
sized leaves.   Light crimson flowers in nicely shaped trusses.
H. Waterer, before 1851.   Color illus. VV p. 99.

GIGHA--form of calostrotum
2ft(.6m) -5F(-21C) M 4/4 Gray-green leaves less than an inch
long. Flower of rose crimson instead of the usual purple, about
2in(5cm) across, saucer-shaped, 5-lobed, 2-3 per cluster. Sir
James Horlick; Hillier, reg. 1970.   A.G.M. 1969. F.C.C. 1971.

GIGI   Parentage unknown
5ft(1.5m) -5F(-21C) ML 3/4 Rose red flower, deeper spotting;
about 18 in ball-shaped trusses. PLant wider than tall, well-
branched; yellowish green leaves held 3 years. C. O. Dexter,
1925-42; S. Burns, reg. 1973.   A.E. 1973. Color illus. ARS Q
27:4 (1973), p. 238; LW pl. 17.

```
* * * * * * * * * * * * * * * * * * * * * * * *
                              -wardii 1/4
        -Crest-          -fortunei ssp. discolor 1/8
GILDED-     -Lady Bessborough-
  GOWN -              -campylocarpum Elatum Group 1/8
        -unknown 1/2
```
Orange-red buds opening light primrose yellow; trusses hold 9-10
flowers. Mrs. R. J. Coker, NZ, reg. 1979.
HONEY GLOW   Parentage as above
Trusses of 12-14 flowers, light primrose yellow, flushed very
light Neyron rose. Mrs. Coker cross; C. A. Grant, reg. 1979.
```
* * * * * * * * * * * * * * * * * * * * * * * *
```

GILIAN   Described under CORNISH CROSS, q.v.
(Incorrect parentage in the Register, 1958.)

GILLII   Described under BEAUTY OF TREMOUGH, q.v.

```
        -griffithianum 1/2
GILL'S CRIMSON-
        -unknown 1/2
```
6ft(1.8m) 5F(-15C) E 4/3 Upright, sturdy plant; bright blood
red, long-lasting flowers, in rounded trusses.   R. Gill & Son.

```
          -griffithianum 5/8
        -                     -griffithianum
GILL'S GLORIOSA-      -George Hardy-
        -Pink Pearl-      -catawbiense 1/8
        -              -arboreum 1/8
              -Broughtonii-
                   -unknown 1/8
```
Bright cerise flowers.   R. Gill & Son.   A.M. 1925

```
          -griffithianum 1/2
GILL'S GOLIATH-
        -arboreum, blood red form 1/2
```
Carmine pink.   R. Gill & Son.   A.M. 1914.

GILL'S NOBLEANUM ALBUM   Parentage unknown
Pure white flowers, green tinge at base.   R. Gill.   A.M. 1926.

GILL'S TRIUMPH   Described under BEAUTY OF TREMOUGH, q.v.

GINA   Parentage unknown
Tall plant with dark green, rounded leaves; large, deep ruby red
flowers, held in erect trusses. T. Lowinsky. A.M. 1931.

```
                         -griffithianum
              -George Hardy-      1/16
        -Pink Pearl-      -catawbiense
        -       -      -arboreum 1/16
  -Marion-      -Broughtonii-
        -       -          -unknown 7/16
        -       -          -catawbiense
GINA LOLLOBRIGIDA-   -Catawbiense Grandiflorum-
        -                    -unknown
        -          -catawbiense 7/16
        -Mrs. C. S. Sargent-
                    -unknown
```
Very hardy. Flowers of orchid purple, spotted brown, in
compact trusses of 15. Felix & Dijkhuis, Boskoop, reg. 1965.

```
        -degronianum ssp. heptamereum (metternichii) 1/2
GINNY BEALE-
        -adenopodum 1/2
```
2.5ft(.75m) -10F(-23C) M   Plant rounded, much broader than
tall, well-branched; dark green, narrow leaves, Spanish orange
indumentum below. Flowers rose, marked only by faint pink
stripes on reverse, up to 2in(5cm) across; trusses of about 16.
J. Gable cross; R. B. Davis, Jr., reg. 1979.

```
                    -griffithianum 1/8
              -Mars-
        -unnamed hybrid-      -unknown 5/8
GINNY DELP-          -yakushimanum 1/4
        -Dexter's Apple Blossom--unknown
```
A medium-sized plant, hardy to -15F(-26C). Buds roseine purple,
opening white; flowers speckled yellowish green. Weldon Delp.

GINNY GEE   Described under MARY FLEMING, q.v.

GINNY HILEMAN   Described under BIG 'O', q.v.

```
                        -catawbiense 1/4
        -unnamed hybrid-        -dichroanthum 5/32
        -               -Fabia-
GINNY-                           -griersonianum 7/32
MAE -      -yakushimanum 1/4         -fortunei ssp. discolor
    -            -Day  -                     3/32
    -Si Si-    -Day -Bessborough-campylocarpum Elatum Gp.
    -      -Dream-                               1/32
      -Gold -     -griersonianum
        -Mohur-       -fortunei ssp. discolor
            -Margaret-     -dichroanthum
                 Dunn -Fabia-
                         -griersonianum
```

Flowers very light cadmium orange with red blotch. Medium-sized
plant, hardy to -15F(-26C). Weldon E. Delp.

```
                     -catawbiense var. album Glass--Catalgla 1/4
        -Gosh Darn-                    -decorum ? 1/16
        -          -           -Caroline-
GINNY'S-      -Mrs. H. R. Yates-      -brachycarpum ? 1/16
DELIGHT-                      -unknown 1/8
       -          -fortunei 1/4
       -Donna    -           -wardii 1/8
       -Hardgrove-unnamed hybrid-
                        -dichroanthum 1/8
```

Seed parent was selfed. Strong yellowish pink buds open medium
to light yellowish pink, margins spinel red, throat light greenish yellow. Tall plant; hardy to -5F(-21C). W. Delp.

* *

```
                    -griffithianum 1/4
        -King George-
GIPSY KING-          -unknown 1/4
        -haematodes 1/2
```

3ft(.9m) 5F(-15C) M 4/3 Grows with a loose, spreading habit.
Flowers of heavy waxy substance, a rich deep red, in rather lax
trusses. Rothschild, 1939.
MEMORY   Parentage as above
Rich, dark red flowers, openly campanulate with a calyx as haem-
atodes. Rothschild. A.M. 1945.
* *

* *
```
                    -caucasicum 1/4
        -Sophia Gray-
GIPSY MAID-          -unknown 1/4
        -              -griffithianum 1/4
        -Loderi-
                -fortunei 1/4
```

Very large, open bell-shaped flowers with frilled margins, col-
ored pink, with a purple throat. Robert Wallace, 1944.
BUXOM   Parentage as above
Deep pink, with a dark throat. Sir James Horlick, reg. 1962.
* *

* *
```
                    -fortunei ssp. discolor 1/2
GIPSY MOTH-               -griffithianum 1/8
        -              -Loderi-
        -Lodauric Iceberg-      -fortunei 1/8
                    -auriculatum 1/4
```

Fragrant flowers, bright spirea red with outside deeply marked
medium magenta rose, held in large trusses. A. F. George, Hydon
Nurseries, reg. 1967. P.C. 1967.
FLORA DONALD   Parentage as above
Light orchid pink flowers, flushed phlox pink on outside. Donald Smith, UK, reg. 1972.
NORTHERN STAR   Parentage as above
5ft(1.5m) -5F(-21C) L   Large, compact plant; white flowers,
greenish throat, 7-lobed, fragrant. George, reg. 1968.
SOUTHERN CROSS   Parentage as above
5ft(1.5m) -5F(-21C) L Compact, vigorous plant. Large flowers
with bronze throat, in spherical trusses of 10-12. George, reg.
1967. A.M. Wisley Trials 1988.
STARCROSS   Parentage as above
5ft(1.5m) -5F(-21C) L 4/3 Soft rose buds; flowers blush pink
with slight bronze markings in large, compact trusses; fragrant.
George, reg. 1968.
VELDTSTAR   Parentage as above
5ft(1.5m) OF(-18C) ML Open habit; large compact trusses; pale
pink flowers, tinged red in throat. A. F. George, reg. 1968.
* *

```
            -Corona--unknown 1/4
        -Bow Bells-
GIPSY QUEEN-      -williamsianum 1/4
        -          -thomsonii 1/4
        -Robert Fox-        -arboreum 1/8
                -Glory of Penjerrick-
                        -griffithianum 1/8
```

3ft(.9m) OF(-18C) EM 4/3 Deep red flower bud scales contrast
nicely with deep green foliage. Origin unknown.

GIRARD'S PETER ALAN   See PETER ALAN

```
            -catawbiense 3/8
        -Everestianum-
GISELA-          -unknown 3/8
        -          -caucasicum 1/4
        -Boule de Neige-       -catawbiense
                -hardy hybrid-
                        -unknown
```

White flowers tinted pale lilac, with yellow green markings. T.
J. R. Seidel cross, 1905.

```
            -fortunei 5/8                  -griffithianum
        -                        -George-          1/16
        -              -Betty Wormald- Hardy-catawbiense 1/16
GIUSEPPE-      -Scandi-          -red hybrid--unknown 3/32
VERDI -    - navia-          -George Hardy (as above)
        -          -Hugh Koster-        -arboreum 1/32
        -Vineland -          -Doncaster-
        Fragrance-          -           -unknown
                -catawbiense v. album Glass--Catalgla
            -unnamed-                     1/8
            hybrid-fortunei
```

3ft(.9m) x 3ft(6 yrs) -15F(-26C) ML   Flowers held in trusses
of 15, 5- to 7-lobed, strong purplish pink with moderate yellow
flare and deep orange-yellow spotting. R. Behring, reg. 1989.

GLACIER NIGHT   See GLETSCHERNACHT,   under AMETHYST (Arend)

GLACIER QUEEN   Parentage unknown; elepidote
3ft(.9m) x 3ft(7yrs) -20F(-29C) ML   Yellowish white flowers,
strong greenish yellow blotch, wavy-edged; 10-14 in a flattened
ball truss 6in(15.2cm) across. Dense habit. Mezitt cross; Weston Nurseries, reg. 1987.

GLAD TIDINGS   Described under EASTER BELLS, q.v.

```
                -neriiflorum 1/4
        -F. C. Puddle-
GLADIATOR-          -griersonianum 3/4
        -griersonianum
```

The trusses hold deep scarlet flowers. Lord Aberconway, 1941.

* *
```
            -campylocarpum 1/2
GLADYS-
        -fortunei 1/2
```

6ft(1.8m) OF(-18C) EM 3/3 Cream-colored to pale yellow flow-
ers with crimson markings, 2in(5cm) across; small round truss
of 10. Tall, open plant; medium green leaves 5in(12.7cm) long.
Col. S. R. Clarke. One form A.M. 1926; another form A.M. 1934.
GLADYS GILLIANS   Parentage as above; exhibited by Digby, 1955.
GLADYS ROSE   Parentage as above
Creamy white with crimson blotch in throat. Clark. A.M. 1950.
GOLDEN WEST   Parentage as above, except reversed
Flowers Dresden yellow, a small red blotch, funnel-campanulate,
3in(7.6cm) across; rounded trusses of 14. Del W. James, 1958.
JUDY   Parentage: fortunei x campylocarpum
Funnel-campanulate flowers, 3.5in(9cm) wide, of primrose yellow,
a small red blotch. Del James, intro. 1956.
MARY SWAYTHLING   Parentage as above
Large truss of sulphur yellow flowers without marks.   F. Rose,
at Townhill. A.M. 1934
* *

```
                    -fortunei ssp. discolor 1/8
            -Ladybird-
        -Diva-        -Corona--unknown 1/8
GLADYS JOHNSON-   -griersonianum 1/4
        -fortunei 1/2
```

5ft(1.5m) OF(-18) ML   Large leaves; flowers up to 4in(10.2cm)
across, soft rose pink, fading lighter; rounded trusses hold 15.

Fragrant.   Johnson, reg. 1962.   P.A. 1958.

```
            -griersonianum 1/2
GLADYS RILLSTONE-
            -unknown 1/2
A parent of Exbury hybrids.
```

GLADYS ROSE   Described under GLADYS, q.v.

```
        -Margaret--unknown 1/2
GLAMOUR-
        -griersonianum 1/2
```
4ft(1.2m) 5F(-15C) M 2/2   (MARGARET may be a griffithianum
hybrid) Plant low and spreading, with deep cherry red flowers
in trusses of 10.   Rothschild, 1939.   A.M. 1946. Color illus.
PB pl. 3.

```
        -Essex Scarlet--unknown 1/2
GLAMOUR GIRL-
        -fortunei, hardy form 1/2
```
Rich pink flower with a dark eye.   Shapiro.

```
          -griersonianum 1/2      -fortunei 1/8
GLASGOW GLOW-          -Luscombei-
          -Scarlet Lady-          -thomsonii 1/8
                      -haematodes 1/4
Stirling Maxwell intro., 1953.
```

```
        -glaucophyllum 1/2
GLAUCOBOOTHII-
        -boothii 1/2
```
Flowers pinkish with brownish red spotting.   E. J. Magor, 1922.

```
        -glaucophyllum 1/2
GLAUTESCENS-
        -lutescens 1/2
```
Yellow flowers, suffused with pink.   Reuthe, 1939.

GLEAM   Described under LADY CHAMBERLAIN, q.v.

```
* * * * * * * * * * * * * * * * * * * * * * * * * * * * *
        -Marion (Cheal)--unknown 1/2
GLEN BRUCE-            -griersonianum 1/4
        -unnamed hybrid-
                      -fortunei 1/4
Trusses of 22 flowers,  medium Neyron rose with deeper rose cen-
ter.   G. Langdon, reg. 1975.
RON LANGDON   Parentage as above
Flowers in trusses of 13, medium Neyron rose, slightly spotted.
G. Langdon, reg. 1975.
SPRING FIESTA   Parentage as above
Trusses of 12 flowers, light Neyron rose.   Langdon, reg. 1976.
* * * * * * * * * * * * * * * * * * * * * * * * * * * * *
                          -haematodes 1/8
                  -May Day-
          -Glen Glow-        -griersonianum 1/8
GLEN CAMERON-         -unknown 1/2
        -              -griffithianum 1/4
        -Gill's Crimson-
                      -unknown
```
Campanulate flowers, 2.75in(7cm) wide, of strong red, in trusses
of 20-25. Calyx to 2in(5cm) long. Elliptic leaves, to 5in(13cm)
long; plant 5ft(1.5m) tall. A. B. Raper, cross 1974; reg. 1985.

```
        -sinogrande 1/2
GLEN CATOCAL-
        -macabeanum 1/2
```
Rounded truss of 28 white flowers, flushed cream, with blotch of
grayed red. Leaves 20.5in(52cm) x 10in(25cm), dark green above
with gray indumentum beneath.   J. Gibson raiser; Brodick Castle
Gardens, reg. 1976.   P.C. 1976.

GLEN CLOY--form of luteiflorum (glaucophyllum var. luteiflorum)
2ft(.6m) OF(-18C) E-M 4/3   Small shrub that may grow to 4ft
(1.2m); aromatic foliage. Flowers of Dresden yellow, 7-11 in a
truss, openly bell-shaped. Brodick, reg. 1968. F.C.C. 1966.

```
        -President Roosevelt--unknown 7/8
GLEN CRIMSON-                        -griffithianum 1/8
                      -Queen Wilhelmina-
          -Earl of Athlone-          -unknown
                      -Stanley Davies-unknown
```

An Australian hybrid with crimson flowers, in trusses of about
22. A. B. Raper, Victoria, reg. 1976.

```
              -haematodes 1/4
        -May Day-
GLEN GLOW-        -griersonianum 1/4
        -unknown 1/2
```
An Australian hybrid blooming there in October. Flowers colored
geranium lake.   A. Brandy cross; A. Raper, reg. 1964.   Color
illus. ARS J 37:2 (1983), p. 75.

GLEN ROSA--form of sidereum
6ft(1.8m) 5F(-15C) EM 3/3   Flowers of primrose yellow, crimson ring at base of throat, ventricose-campanulate, 2.5in(5.6cm)
wide, with as many as 8 lobes; about 20 per truss. Leaves about
9in(23cm) long, dull silver below.   Brodick Castle, reg. 1965.
A.M. 1965.   Color illus. ARS J 41:4 (1987), p. 183.

```
        -sanguineum ssp. didymum 1/2
GLENARN-
        -chamaethomsonii 1/2
```
Small flowers held in trusses of 4, deep cardinal red, 5-lobed.
Smooth, dark, ovate leaves, about 2.5in(6cm).   A. & F. Gibson
cross; P. Urlwin-Smith, reg. 1983.

GLENDA FARRELL   Parentage unknown
4ft(1.2m) -10F(-23C) M 4/4 Ruffled, bright orange-red flower
with dark specks, and a red blotch; fades to reddish pink. Held
in full trusses of 13. Plant well-branched, broader than tall.
Similar to GIGI.   C. Dexter cross; Tyler Arboretum, reg. 1983.

GLENDOICK--form of racemosum
4ft(1.2m) -5F(-21C) EM 4/3   Deep-colored form; dark pink
flowers all along the young shoots in April. Cox, reg. 1971.

```
        -Pacific Queen--unknown 1/2
GLENFIDDICK-
        -wardii 1/2
```
Flowers in trusses of 10, nasturtium red, shading to pale yellow
with a green ring inside the tube. L. A. Grant, AUS, reg. 1988.

GLENN'S ORANGE   See FRED HAMILTON

```
                      -diaprepes 1/4
          -Polar Bear-
GLENROSE BEAUTY-        -auriculatum 1/4
          -unknown 1/2
```
White flowers, a pale pink stripe.   W. Glennie, NZ, reg. 1980.

```
                          -griffithianum 5/16
                  -Kewense-
          -Aurora-        -fortunei 1/16
      -Naomi-        -thomsonii 1/8
GLENROSE STAR-     -fortunei
          -red seedling--unknown 1/2
```
Trusses resemble NAOMI, with flowers cherry red in bud, opening
white with red margins Habit like NAOMI. Glennie reg. 1984.

```
        -grande 1/2
GLENSHANT-
        -macabeanum 1/2
```
Leaves 10in(25.4cm) long by 4in(10.2cm) wide, silvery indumentum
beneath.   Flowers creamy white, flushed pale yellow; flat truss
of about 26.   Brodick Castle, reg. 1965.   A.M. 1964.

GLETSCHERNACHT   Described under AMETHYST (ARENDS), q.v.

GLOIRE D'ANVERS   Synonym of BODDAERTIANUM

GLOIRE DE GANDAVENSIS   Parentage unknown
Parent of some very old hybrids and still in cultivation. White
flowers, beautifully spotted.   Methven, about 1868.

```
                      -arboreum 1/8
              -Doncaster-
    -Professor F. Bettex-        -unknown 1/4
    -              -catawbiense 1/8
GLORIA-        -Atrosanguineum-
    -              -unknown
              -dichroanthum 1/4
    -Goldsworth Orange-
              -fortunei ssp. discolor 1/4
```

5ft(1.5m) -15F(-26C) ML   Loose trusses of creamy white with pink and yellow shades. J. Bruns, W. Germany. Gold Medal 1981. Color illus. Cox pl. 68; WS, 1989, p. 75.

GLORIA GANDAVENSIS   See GLOIRE DE GANDAVENSIS

* *
```
                 -dichroanthum 1/2
         -Fabia-
GLORIANA-        -griersonianum 1/4
   -                     -dichroanthum
         -Goldsworth Orange-
                         -fortunei ssp. discolor 1/4
```
Trusses of 12 flowers, brightly colored, a shade varying between claret rose and empire rose, suffused in the throat with orange. RHS Garden, Wisley. A.M. 1953.
CORAL REEF   Parentage as above
4ft(1.2m) -10F(-23C) L   Flowers salmon pink, pink margins, slightly flushed in throat, held in open, lax trusses. Francis Hanger cross; RHS Garden, Wisley. A.M. 1954.
* *

```
          -yakushimanum 1/2
GLORY OF-       -fortunei 1/4
HARKWOOD-Fred -              -fortunei ssp. discolor
   Wynniatt-     -Lady  -              1/16
              -Jalisco- Bessborough-campylocarpum Elatum 1/16
              -      -dichroanthum 1/16
                 -Dido-
                      -decorum 1/16
```
2ft(.6m) 5F(-15C) M   Deep pink buds open to flowers greenish white, edged pale purplish pink; trusses of 15-16. Oblanceolate leaves. Mrs. Dryson, Harkwood Acres, reg. 1986.

GLORY OF KESTON   Parentage unknown
A parent of PELE, q.v.

```
             -griffithianum 1/2
GLORY OF LEONARDSLEE-
             -unknown 1/2
```
Light strawberry red. A parent of DIGNITY. R. Gill & Son.

GLORY OF LITTLEWORTH   Parentage unknown
5ft(1.5m) -5F(-21C) M 5/3 Azaleodendron. Snowy white, intense orange blotch. Foliage gray-blue. Mangles. A.M 1911.

GLORY OF PENJERRICK   Described under BEAUTY OF TREMOUGH, q.v.

GLOW   Listed under DARLENE, q.v.

```
         -dichroanthum 1/2
GLOW WORM-      -souliei 1/4
     -Halcyone-        -fortunei ssp. discolor 1/8
             -Lady  -
             Bessborough-campylocarpum Elatum Group 1/8
```
Flowers of butter yellow. Sunningdale Nurseries, 1951.

GLOWING EMBER   Listed under LAVA FLOW, q.v.

```
                   -Moser's Maroon--unknown 1/4
           -Romany Chal-
GLOWING EMBERS-      -facetum (eriogynum) 1/4
           -griersonianum 1/2
```
4ft(1.2m) 5F(-15C) ML 4/3   Plant fairly compact; long, narrow, dark green leaves. Flowers of waxy texture, without stamens, of glowing orange-red. Easy to grow; sun-tolerant. John Henny, before 1958. Color illus. ARS Q 27:2 (1973), p. 103.

```
      -fortunei 1/2              -griffithianum 1/16
GLOWING-              -Queen  -
   STAR -      -Britannia-Wilhelmina-unknown 3/16
      -C. P. Raffill-
        -              -Stanley Davies--unknown
            -griersonianum 1/4
```
5ft(1.5m) -5F(-21C) EM   Flowers coral rose with a red throat, in a tight truss. Donald Hardgrove, 1954.

GLOWLIGHT   Described under FAWN, q.v.

```
       -fortunei ? 1/2
GLOXINEUM-
       -unknown 1/2
```

5ft(1.5m) -20F(-29C) M 4/3 A plant of attractive foliage but leggy growth. Flowers pink, slightly fragrant, held in large trusses.   C. O. Dexter, 1925-42; de Wilde, reg. 1958. Color illus. ARS J 43:4 (1989), p. 206.

GNOM   Described under BREMEN, q.v.

GO FOR IT   Described under CRIMPER, q.v.

GOAT FELL--form of arboreum
6ft(1.8m) 5F(-15C) E 3/4 Flowers cherry red, throat lightly spotted, tubular-campanulate, 2.25in(5.7cm) across; globular trusses of 15. Leaves about 7in(17.8cm) x 2in(5cm) wide, silver underneath. Brodick Castle, reg. 1965. A.M. 1964.

* *
```
                   -griffithianum 1/8
          -Dawn's Delight-
     -Break of Day-        -unknown 1/8
GOBLIN-        -dichroanthum 1/4
     -griersonianum 1/2
```
4ft(1.2m) 5F(-15C) M   Reaches maturity around 5ft(1.5m); foliage dark sage green, on a neat plant. Flowers of bright salmon pink, funnel-shaped, 3in(7.6cm) across, calyx large and of flower color; loose trusses of 7. Rothschild, 1939. A.M. 1939.
GOBLIN PINK   Parentage as above
Similar to GOBLIN; color soft rose, a gold throat. Rothschild.
* *

```
       -griffithianum 1/2
GODESBERG-
       -unknown 1/2
```
White flowers, with brown spotting. Otto Schulz, cross 1892; C. B. van Nes & Sons intro.

```
                      -catawbiense 1/2
     -Catawbiense Grandiflorum-
GOETHE-                 -unknown 1/2
   -           -catawbiense
     -Mrs. Milner-
              -unknown
```
Light pink flowers, pale brown markings. T. J. Seidel, 1905.

```
                -Essex Scarlet--unknown 1/4
     -Beau Brummell-
GOLCONDA-        -facetum (eriogynum) 1/4
     -dichroanthum 1/2
```
A medium-sized, compact Exbury hybrid, with bright pink flowers. Rothschild, cross 1932; intro. 1939.

* *
```
                -dichroanthum 1/4
         -Fabia-
GOLD BRAID-     -griersonianum 1/4
   -           -fortunei ssp. discolor 1/4
      -Dondis-      -arboreum 1/8
         -Doncaster-
               -unknown 1/8
```
Semi-dwarf plant. Flowers of pale pink and bright yellow; large calyx. R. Henny, cross 1942; reg. 1958.
LIPSTICK   Parentage as above
Semi-dwarf plant with deep pink flowers. R. Henny, reg. 1958.
* *

GOLD INCENSE   Described under WALT ELLIOTT, q.v.

GOLD SPREAD   Described under BALLY COTTON, q.v.

```
                   -wardii ? 1/4
          -Chlorops-
                 -vernicosum ? 1/4
GOLDEN    -                -fortunei 1/8
ANNIVERSARY-        -Golden-
   -              - West -campylocarpum 1/8
      -unnamed hybrid-      -caucasicum 1/16
         -        -Dr. Stocker-
            -Mariloo-        -griffithianum 1/16
                -lacteum 1/8
```
4ft(1.2m) 0F(-18C) M 4/4 Flowers primrose yellow with a reddish flare, bell-shaped, in rounded trusses. Leaves 5in(12.7cm) long. Benjamin Lancaster, reg. 1971.

```
                              -fortunei ssp. discolor
                    -Lady   -                    9/32
                    -Bessborough-campylocarpum Elatum
            -Jalisco-     -dichroanthum 1/8        7/32
            -        -Dido-
        -Comstock-          -decorum 1/16
        -        -dichroanthum
        -        -Jasper-        -fortunei ssp. discolor
        -                -Lady  -
        -                Bessborough-campylocarpum Elatum
    -Cream-                       -fortunei ssp. discolor
    -Glory-          -Lady    -
    -      -          -Bessborough-campylocarpum Elatum
    -      -      -Jalisco-    -dichroanthum
    -      -      -      -Dido-
GOLD  -    -Cheyenne-        -decorum
MEDAL -      -          -griffithianum 1/16
    -      -Loderi-
    -              -fortunei 1/16
    -              -fortunei ssp. discolor
    -          -Ladybird-
    -      -Diva-       -Corona--unknown 1/16
    -Seattle-   -griersonianum 1/8
      Gold  -            -fortunei ssp. discolor
        -Lady Bessborough-
                    -campylocarpum Elatum Group
```
5ft(1.5m) -5F(-21C) M 4/4   Very large golden yellow flowers,
lightly spotted, red. Vigorous plant with forest green leaves.
Greer, intro. 1988.

GOLD MOHUR   Described under DREAM GIRL, q.v.

```
                          -caucasicum 3/32
                -Jacksonii-          -caucasicum
        -Goldsworth-        -Nobleanum-
        - Yellow  -            -arboreum 1/32.
    -Goldfort-      -campylocarpum 3/16
    -      -fortunei 1/4
GOLD-          -wardii 1/8
MOON-   -Hawk-        -fortunei ssp. discolor 1/16
    -      -Lady  -
    -Full-   Bessborough-campylocarpum Elatum Group 1/16
    Moon-            -campylocarpum
        -      -unnamed hybrid-
        -Adriaan-            -unknown 1/8
        Koster-                    -griffithianum 1/32
            -          -George Hardy-
            -Mrs. Lindsay-        -catawbiense 1/32
            Smith    -Duchess of Edinburgh--unknown
```
3ft(.9m) -10F(-23C) EM   An upright plant, broader than tall,
large glossy leaves. Flower of heavy substance, 4in(10cm) wide,
7-lobed, white with throat tinged yellowish green, in trusses
of up to 11. Lewis Bagoly cross; Marie Tietjens, reg. 1976.

```
                -Scintillation--unknown 1/2
GOLDBUCKETT (GOLDEN BOUQUET)-
                    -wardii 1/2
```
4ft(1.2m) -10F(-23C) M Creamy yellow flowers, a red-brown to
ruby blotch, 5 wavy lobes; trusses of 10-14. Foliage resembles
SCINTILLATION.   H. Hachmann cross; G. Stück, reg. 1983. Gold
Medal Munich 1983.   Color illus. ARS J 39:2(1985), cover; Cox
pl. 69; WS, 1989, p. 127.

GOLDBUG   Described under DEL, q.v.

GOLDDEKOR   (wardii x ALICE STREET) x (OMEGA x wardii)
        For long parentage diagram, see BELKANTO.
Light yellow flowers with a strong dark red blotch; the exterior
slightly tinted apricot. Not very hardy. Hachmann, cross 1969.

GOLDEN ANNIVERSARY Entered out of order in previous column.

* *
```
        -keiskei--Yaku Fairy 1/2
GOLDEN BEE-
        -mekongense var. melinanthum 1/2
```
2ft(.6m) -10F(-23C) EM 5/4   A semi-dwarf, broader than tall,
small forest green leaves, held 2 years. Lax trusses of about 6
flowers, bright mimosa yellow. W. Berg, reg. 1982. C.A. 1983;
A.E. 1984.   Color illus. ARS J 38:2 (1984), p. 103.
GOLDEN PRINCESS   Parentage as above
2ft(.6m) -5F(-21C) EM 5/4   Compact, dense plant with small,

---

pointed leaves and lax trusses of yellow. Berg, 1982.
* *

GOLDEN BELLE Described under MARGARET DUNN, q.v.

* *
```
                    -haematodes 1/4
            -May Day-
            -        -griersonianum 3/8
GOLDEN COCKEREL-        -dichroanthum 1/8
            -      -Fabia-
            -Lascaux-    -griersonianum
                -wardii Litiense Group 1/4
```
3ft(.9m) 5F(-15C) M   Scarlet buds open to soft yellow flowers
spotted deeper yellow, a large double calyx; lax truss of 10-12.
A. F. George, Hydon Nurseries, reg. 1969.
GOLDEN SPUR   Parentage as above
4ft(1.2m) -10F(-23C) ML   A neat, compact plant; golden yellow
flowers from vibrant red buds. Lax trusses.   Hydon, reg. 1975.
* *

GOLDEN DAWN   Described under JOAN THOMPSON, q.v.

```
                -fortunei ssp. discolor 1/4
        -Dondis-        -arboreum 1/8
GOLDEN DAYS-    -Doncaster-
        -            -unknown 1/8
        -dichroanthum 1/2
```
4ft(1.2m) OF(-18C) EM 3/3 Flowers of maize yellow, fading to
straw yellow, edged carrot red, funnel-campanulate, 3in(7.6cm)
wide; trusses of 8-10.   Upright plant; dark green foliage.
Rudolph & Leona Henny, reg. 1959.

GOLDEN DREAM   Described under CARITA, q.v.

```
                    -dichroanthum ssp. scyphocalyx 1/8
            -Socrianum-
        -unnamed-        -griffithianum 1/8
        - hybrid-    -wardii 3/8
GOLDEN-    -Rima-
FALCON-        -decorum 1/8
    -      -wardii
    -Crest-        -fortunei ssp. discolor 1/8
        -Lady Bessborough-
                    -campylocarpum Elatum Group 1/8
```
5ft(1.5m) 5F(-15C) M   Very pale yellow flowers; truss of 10.
Plant of open habit. A. F. George, Hydon, reg. 1976.

GOLDEN FANTASY   Parentage unknown
Flowers cream, with yellow centers.   Kersey cross; Mrs. Frederick, reg. 1979.

GOLDEN FLEECE (Reuthe)   See PRINCESS ANNE

```
                -dichroanthum 1/4
        -Goldsworth Orange-
        -            -fortunei ssp. discolor 1/4
GOLDEN-            -griffithianum 5/16
FLEECE-        -Kewense-
    -      -Aurora-        -fortunei 1/16
    -Yvonne-    -thomsonii 1/8
            -griffithianum
```
5ft(1.5m) -5F(-21C) ML Large golden yellow flowers with fril-
led lobes. Slocock, reg. 1967.

```
                -dichroanthum 1/4
        -Fabia-
GOLDEN FOLLY-   -griersonianum 1/4
        -            -campylocarpum 1/4
            -Moonstone-
                -williamsianum 1/4
```
Grows to just 3ft(.9m) in 10 years, wider than high with medium-
sized leaves. Flowers bell-shaped, deep yellow, held in round
trusses. H. L. Larson, reg. 1965.

```
                -catawbiense var. album 1/4
        -Great Lakes-
GOLDEN-        -yakushimanum 1/4
GALA -        -catawbiense var. rubrum 1/4
    -Good Hope-
            -wardii 1/4
```
3.5ft(1.0m) -20F(-29C) ML 4/4   Synonym FIFTY-FINE. Flowers

of emphatic ivory, not quite yellow, broadly funnel-shaped, 2.5
in(6.4cm) across, 5-lobed, in trusses of 14. Plant well-branched, broader than tall; thick foliage, glossy olive green. For
small gardens. D. Leach, reg. 1983. Color illus. HG. p. 180.

```
                -dichroanthum ssp. scyphocalyx 1/2
GOLDEN GATE-
          -unknown 1/2
```
3ft(.9m) -5F(-21C) M 3/4 Flower edges salmon orange, throat
golden yellow, star-shaped. Compact bush. Fine dark green foliage, held 3 years. Easily propagated. Origin unknown.

```
             -rupicola var. chryseum 1/2
GOLDEN GIFT-
          -leucaspis 1/2
```
Early flowers, yellow and saucer-shaped, 1in(2.5cm) wide, 4 or 5
per truss. Plant low and spreading, 1.5ft(.45m) across when described in 1962. A. Wright, reg. 1963.

```
                        -cinnabarinum 1/4
             -unnamed hybrid-
GOLDEN GIFT-              -maddenii 1/4
             -cinnabarinum ssp. xanthocodon Concatenans Group 1/2
```
Flowers of bright orange-yellow, with pale olive green mottling
in upper throat, campanulate, 2in(5cm) wide, 5-lobed; trusses of
8. Leaves 5in(12.7cm) long. Gen. Harrison. A.M. 1970.

GOLDEN GLOVES   Parentage unknown: elepidote
2.5ft(.75m) x 2.5ft(7yrs) -20F(-29C) ML   Flowers pale yellow
with brownish orange throat which fades to deep orange yellow;
trusses of 13-16. Open habit. Mezitt cross; Weston, reg. 1988.

```
* * * * * * * * * * * * * * * * * * * * * * * * * * * * * *
             -dichroanthum 1/4
         -Fabia-
GOLDEN GLOW-    -griersonianum 1/2
       -   -griersonianum
         -Azor-
             -fortunei ssp. discolor 1/4
```
A hybrid by Benjamin F. Lancaster, reg. 1958.
UMPQUA CHIEF   Parentage as above
Vermilion flowers with large calyces. Plant of medium compact-
ness. Del W. James, before 1958.
* *

```
                        -fortunei ssp. discolor 3/16
            -King of Shrubs-    -dichroanthum 1/16
        -Cecil-        -Fabia-
        -Smith-          -griersonianum 1/16
       -   -   -wardii 1/8
GOLDEN -   -Crest-          -fortunei ssp. discolor
GODDESS-       -Lady Bessborough-
       -              -campylocarpum Elatum 1/16
       -         -lacteum 1/4      -griffithianum 1/32
       -Lionel's Triumph-        -Kewense-
               -   -Aurora-     -fortunei 5/32
                 -Naomi-    -thomsonii 1/16
                       -fortunei
```
6ft(1.8m) 5F(-15C) EM Trusses 8in(20.4cm) across, of 18 flow-
ers, of 6 wavy lobes, 4.3in(11cm) broad, empire yellow with rays
of carrot red on reverse. Smooth, oblong, spinach green leaves;
held 2 years. C. Smith, cross 1974; C. Burlingame, reg. 1986.

Out-of-order listing:
```
* * * * * * * * * * * * * * * * * * * * * * * * * * * *
             -dichroanthum 1/2
GOLDEN HORN-
          -elliottii 1/2
```
4ft(1.2m) 10F(-12C) ML 3/3 Flowers orange and deep salmon,
tubular trumpet-shaped, with a large double calyx; loose, flat-
topped trusses of 9-11. Plant compact; dark sage green foliage
with brown indumentum. Rothschild, 1939. A.M. 1945.
PERSIMMON Parentage as above
4ft(1.2m) 10F(-12C) M 3/3 Similar to the above but without
double calyx; more compact bush. Flowers waxy orange-red, dark
speckling. Rothschild, 1945. Color illus. PB pl. 11.
* *

```
                    -catawbiense var. album--Catalgla
             -unnamed hybrid-              1/8
        -Frilled-     -Pink Dexter--unknown 13/32
GOLDEN   - Cream -unknown
HARBINGER-          -fortunei, cream form 1/8
      -     -Mary -
      -     - Garrison-vernicosum (18139) 1/8
      -unnamed-              -catawbiense
        hybrid-         -Atrosanguineum-     1/32
        -       -Atrier-         -unknown
      -Mary Belle-    -griersonianum 1/16
              -      -decorum 1/16
              -Dechaem-
                  -haematodes 1/16
```
A good medium yellow, hardy to -10F(-23C). Plant compact, of
medium height; glossy foliage. Dr. T. L. Ring.
CARNAL   Parentage as above
Flowers flesh- or peach-colored. Plant of medium height with
good glossy foliage. Hardy to -10F(-23C). Dr. T. L. Ring.
* *

GOLDEN HORN   See previous column

GOLDEN HORN PERSIMMON   See PERSIMMON

GOLDEN INCENSE   See GOLD INCENSE described under WALT ELLIOTT

```
             -decorum 1/2
GOLDEN JUBILEE-
          -unknown 1/2
```
2.5ft(.75m) OF(-18C) M Flower 3.5in(9cm) wide, very fragrant,
7 lobed, light Neyron rose, in round trusses of about 9. Plant
upright, nearly as broad as high; leaves yellow-green, 7in
(17.8cm) long. R. A. Pearce cross; Elsie Watson, reg. 1983.

GOLDEN MOMENTS   Described under FRILLED PETTICOATS, q.v.

```
          -campylocarpum 1/2
GOLDEN ORB-   -wardii 1/4
       -Crest-        -fortunei ssp. discolor 1/8
             -Lady Bessborough-
                   -campylocarpum Elatum Group 1/8
```
Rounded trusses of 10-12 flowers, butter yellow. Leaves dark
green, glabrous. I. Gordon, reg. 1984.

GOLDEN ORFE   Described under CHAN, q.v.

```
* * * * * * * * * * * * * * * * * * * * * * * * * * * * * *
             -moupinense, pink form 1/2
GOLDEN ORIOLE BUSACO-
             -sulfurem 1/2
```
Synonym GOLDEN ORIOLE VENETIA. Flowers of primrose yellow suf-
fused pale reddish pink, heavily spotted on upper lobes, 1.75in
(4.5cm) across, with prominent brown anthers. J. C. Williams,
reg. 1964. A.M. 1963.
GOLDEN ORIOLE TALAVERA   Parents: moupinense, white X sulfurem
Dresden yellow flowers, spotted deep yellow on upper lobes, up
to 2in(5cm) wide, with prominent brown anthers; trusses of 3-4.
Leaves 2in(5cm) long, with deep red petioles. J. C. Williams,
Caerhays Castle, reg. 1964. A.M. 1947. F.C.C. 1963.
* *

GOLDEN ORIOLE VENETIA   See GOLDEN ORIOLE BUSACO

GOLDEN PHEASANT   Described under DREAM GIRL, q.v.

GOLDEN PIPPIN   Described under JANET SCROGGS, q.v.

GOLDEN PRINCESS   Described under GOLDEN BEE, q.v.

GOLDEN QUEEN   Described under LADY CHAMBERLAIN, q.v.

GOLDEN REUNION   Parentage unknown; elepidote
8ft(2.4m) x 10ft(3m)(15 yrs) OF(-18C) M   Ball truss 10in(25.5
cm) broad; 9-12 flowers of 8 wavy-edged lobes, light yellow with
brilliant yellow throat, to 5in(12.7cm) wide. Glossy ovate foliage; bush semi-open. Whitney cross; W. F. Watters, reg. 1988.

```
                         -fortunei ssp. discolor
                   -Lady              -              5/32
           -Jalisco- Bessborough-campylocarpum Elatum Gp
           - Elect -    -dichroanthum 11/32        3/32
        -unnamed-       -Dido-
       - hybrid-              -decorum 1/16
       -        -             -wardii 1/16
       -        -      -Crest-
       -        -unnamed-     -Lady Bessborough (above)
       -        hybrid-       -fortunei ssp. discolor
GOLDEN RUBY-       -King of-      -dichroanthum
       -        Shrubs -Fabia-
       -                       -griersonianum 1/32
       -                -ponticum 1/8
       -        -Purple Splendour-
       -Sonata-          -unknown 1/8
           -dichroanthum
3ft(.9m)  OF(-18C)  M  Plant wider than tall with flower trusses
of 9-10, moderate red in bud, opening brilliant to light yellow,
edged deep pink, finally turning to golden yellow.  Lofthouse,
cross c. 1976; G. Wellmeir, reg. 1987.


                             -catawbiense 1/4
               -Atrosanguineum-
        -unnamed hybrid-          -unknown 1/4
GOLDEN SALMON-         -griersonianum 1/2
          -as above (Probably a sibling cross)
5ft(1.5m)  -10F(-23C)  ML   Flowers of salmon with darker blotch
of radiating stripes, openly funnel-campanulate, 3.5in(8.9cm)
across, 7-lobed, of heavy substance, fragrant; lax trusses hold
10.  Plant wider than high.  G. G. Nearing, reg. 1973.


GOLDEN SPUR   Described under GOLDEN COCKEREL, q.v.


GOLDEN STAR   Described under PRELUDE, q.v.


           -yakushimanum 1/4
     -Bambi-            -dichroanthum 1/8
      -  -Fabia Tangerine-
GOLDEN-               -griersonianum 3/8
 TORCH-               -haematodes 1/8
    -        -Grosclaude-
    -unnamed hybrid-     -facetum (eriogynum) 1/8
           -griersonianum
4ft(1.2m)  OF(-18C)  ML  4/4  Compact trusses 6in(15cm) across,
globe-shaped; 13-15 flowers, soft yellow.  Upright habit, fairly
compact; leaves medium-sized, dull green, held 3 years.  Water-
er, Sons & Crisp, reg. 1972.  H.C. 1977.  A.M. Wisley Trials
1984.  Color illus. HG p. 180.


GOLDEN WEDDING   Described under ORANGE MARMALADE, q.v.


GOLDEN WEST   Described under GLADYS, q.v.


        -dichroanthum ssp. scyphocalyx 1/2
GOLDEN WIT-          -campylocarpum 1/8.
     -       -Moonstone-
     -unnamed-         -williamsianum 1/4
      hybrid-          -williamsianum
           -Adrastia-
                -neriiflorum 1/8
3ft(.9m)  OF(-18C)  M  4/4  Low plant with medium-sized foliage,
dark green.  Flowers primrose yellow spotted red, in trusses of
7-9.   J. A. Witt cross; L. Michaud, reg. 1877.  Color illus.
HG p. 76.


* * * * * * * * * * * * * * * * * * * * * * * * * *
              -catawbiense 1/4
        -Ginny Mae-    -dichroanthum 1/8
      -       -Fabia-
GOLDEN YEARS-        -griersonianum 1/8
      -             -maximum 1/4
       -Stokes Bronze Wings-
                -catawbiense 1/4
```
Buds of pale primrose yellow, and dark to medium rhodonite reds.
Flowers light greenish white, throat of brilliant yellow, rhodo-
nite red, medium yellowish green; vivid red stigma. Delp.
BEAUTYBOUND   Parentage as above
Magenta rose and ruby red in bud; flower light purplish pink and
purplish pink, edged deep purplish pink, with a yellowish white

flare and ruby red dorsal spotting. Delp.
SURRENDER   Parentage as above
Buds of moderate to strong purplish pinks, dorsal spots of deep
red, with a pale yellow flare. Delp.
* *

```
                        -griffithianum 13/128
                   -Loderi-
            -unnamed hybrid-     -fortunei 33/128
     -unnamed-           -wardii 3/16
     - hybrid-campylocarpum 1/4
GOLDENDALE-      -fortunei
     -      -Fawn-     -dichroanthum 1/16
     -      -Fabia-
     -Skipper-    -griersonianum 1/8
     -                -griersonianum
     -      -Sarita Loder-     -griffithianum
     -Indian-      -Loderi-
      Penny-            -fortunei
     -             -wardii       -griffith.
     -Idealist-          -Kewense-
     -        -Aurora-       -fortunei
     -Naomi-    -thomsonii 1/16
                -fortunei
2.5ft(.75m)  -5F(-21C)  ML  4/4  Light green foliage, of medium
size, held 3 years.  Flowers of heavy substance, butter yellow
(darker than Crest), dark red center, 3in(7.6cm) across; trusses
about 10in(25.4cm) wide, 8-14 flowers.  Chas. McNew, reg. 1974.


* * * * * * * * * * * * * * * * * * * * * * * * * *
                    -griffithianum
                -George-         1/64
               -Mrs. L.- Hardy-catawbiense
         -wardii 5/8     - Smith -        9/64
     -unnamed-       -Diane-       -Duchess of Edinburgh
      - hybrid-       -      -       --unknown 3/16
         -Alice Street-    -unnamed-campylocarpum 1/32
GOLDFEE-           hybrid-
     -         -wardii     -unknown
     -            -catawbiense ?
     -       -Omega-
     -unnamed hybrid-    -unknown rose-colored hybrid
           -wardii
2ft(.6m) x 2ft  -10F(-23C)  M  Coppery orange-yellow buds; flow-
ers funnel-campanulate, pale greenish yellow tinged light orient
pink, fading later, dorsal spots oxblood red.  Leaves dark, ell-
iptic; compact plant.  Hachmann, cross 1969; Stück, reg. 1988.
HACHMANN'S SABRINA  Parentage as above (Sibling of above)
2.7ft(.8m) x 4ft(1.2m)  -15F(-26C)  ML  Open funnel-shaped flow-
ers to 3in(7.5cm) wide, pale orient pink tinted light pink, dor-
spotting ruby red on pale greenish yellow base; trusses of 9-13.
Foliage glossy, light green; rounded plant.  Stück, reg. 1988.
* * * * * * * * * * * * * * * * * * * * * * * * * *


        -wardii 1/2
GOLDFINCH-
     -Mrs. P. D. Williams--unknown 1/2
4ft(1.2m)  -15F(-26C)  ML   Pink flowers with a beautiful golden
blotch.  R. Collyer cross; C. Ingram, exhibited 1945.


GOLDFINGER   Described under PARISIENNE, q.v.


GOLDFLIMMER---sport of catawbiense ? ponticum ?
5ft(1.5m)  -10F(-23C)  L   Neat, compact plant grown for its in-
teresting variegated foliage, as well as its ponticum-like mauve
ruffled flowers.  Better variegation than PRESIDENT ROOSEVELT,
but not as nice a flower.  Discovered by Hobbie; distributed by
Hachmann.  Color illus. WS, 1989, p. 40.


                    -caucasicum 3/16
            -Jacksonii-    -caucasicum
     -             -Nobleanum-
     -Goldsworth Yellow-        -arboreum 1/16
GOLDFORT-          -campylocarpum 1/4
     -fortunei 1/2
5ft(1.5m)  -15F(-26C)  M  4/3  A "yellow" that's more hardy than
most, but it's a light ivory yellow flower, pale greenish yellow
in center, held in rounded medium-sized trusses.  Upright, open
habit; leaves 6in(15cm) long, gold-tinged green.  Slocock, 1937.
Color illus. Cox pl. 71; VV p. 127.
```

```
                -caucasicum 1/4
        -Dr. Stocker-
GOLDILOCKS-          -griffithianum 1/4
        -campylocarpum Elatum Group 1/2
```
A plant 5ft(1.5m) tall, compact, and wind-resistant. Flowers of
Dresden yellow, 2.5in(6.4cm) across, in loose trusses of 12-14.
Michael Haworth-Booth, Farall Nurseries, reg. 1964.

```
        -xanthostephanum 1/2
GOLDILOCKS-
        -rupicola var. chryseum 1/2
```
2ft(.6m) OF(-18C) EM   Small, deep yellow flowers on a dwarf
bush of dark foliage. Plant patented.   H. Kerrigan.

```
            -campylocarpum Elatum Group 1/4
        -Letty Edwards-
GOLDJUWEL-          -fortunei 1/4
                    -wardii 1/4
        -unnamed hybrid-
                    -unknown
```
Trusses of 7-12 flowers, 6 or 7 lobes, light yellow, with a dark
red basal blotch. Leaves obovate to oval, glabrous. J. Böhlje
cross; Schmalscheidt, reg. 1984. Color illus. WS, 1989, p. 102.

* *

```
            -wardii 5/8              -griffithianum
        -                   -George-            1/64
        -           -Mrs. Lindsay- Hardy-catawbiense
    -unnamed-          - Smith    -
    - hybrid-          -           -Duchess of
    -      -Diane-     -           Edinburgh--unknown
    -      -Alice-     -           -campylocarpum 1/32
GOLDKRONE-  Street-  -unnamed hybrid-
(GOLD   -          -            -unknown 6/32
 CROWN) -          -wardii
        -          -catawbiense 9/64
        -     -Omega-
    -Hachmann's-  -unknown
        Marina  -wardii
```
4ft(1.2m) -5F(-21C) M Rounded trusses of 16 to 18 flowers, 5-
lobed, golden yellow, lightly spotted ruby or darker red. Plant
compact, rounded. H. Hachmann, cross 1969; G. Stück, reg. 1983.
P.C. 1986.   Color illus. Cox pl. 72; WS, 1989, p. 127.
GOLDRAUSCH   Parentage as above, except reversed
Orange buds opening golden yellow. Bud hardy to -8F(-22C). H.
Hachmann cross; G. Stück, reg. 1984.
GRAF LENNART   Parentage as GOLDKRONE, above
Beautiful orange-yellow buds opening pure light yellow, in lax
trusses. Floriferous. Bluish green foliage, as wardii. Hardy
to -8F(-22C). Midseason. Hachmann cross, intro. 1983.
HACHMANN'S BRASILIA   Parentage as GOLDKRONE, except reversed
3.7ft(1.1m) x 3.7ft(12 yrs) -8F(-22C) M Truss of 12-18 flow-
ers, light spinel red over yellow, the color effect orangey rose
with yellow, slight spotting of brownish yellow. Compact plant.
Hans Hachmann, cross 1969; G. Stück, reg. 1983.   Color illus.
WS, 1989, p. 129.
SANDRA   Parentage as GOLDKRONE, except reversed
Trusses of 9-11 flowers, medium Neyron rose shading lighter, and
tinted light amber yellow. Hachmann cross; Stück, reg. 1983.
* *

GOLDRAUSCH (GOLDEN ECSTASY)   Described under GOLDKRONE, q.v.

* *
```
                -oreotrephes 1/2
GOLDSTRIKE---unnamed hybrid F2-        -cinnabarinum 1/4
                -Royal Flush-
                    -maddenii 1/4
```
4ft(1.2m) OF(-18C) M 4/4   Unusual plant, up to 8 tubular-
shaped flowers per truss, golden yellow, the upper lobes buttercup yellow. Leaves medium-sized, glossy olive green. Rudolf
Henny, reg. 1962. Color illus. Cox pl. 73.
FIRST LOVE   Parentage as above
5ft(1.5m) 5F(-21C) M 4/4   Flowers pink with maroon eye; 8-
flowered trusses. Small leaves. R. Henny, reg. 1966.
* *

```
                -griffithianum 1/2
GOLDSWORTH CRIMSON-     -arboreum 1/4
                -Doncaster-
                        -unknown 1/4
```
5ft(1.5m) OF(-18C) EM 2/3 Parentage from Slocock's catalog.

Bright crimson flowers in rounded trusses. Plant spreading but
compact; dark green leaves, long and glossy.   Slocock, 1926.
A.M. Wisley Trials 1960.   F.C.C. Wisley Trials 1971.   Color
illus. JS p. 39; VV p. 24.

```
            -dichroanthum 1/2
GOLDSWORTH ORANGE-
            -fortunei ssp. discolor 1/2
```
5ft(1.5m) -5F(-21C) L 3/3 Lax truss of many flowers, funnel-
shaped, pale orange tinted pink. Leaves on red petioles. Open
plant, and spreading, heat-tolerant but flowers best in shade.
Slocock, 1938.   Color illus JS p. 105.

```
            -griffithianum 1/2
GOLDSWORTH PINK-
            -unknown 1/2
```
6ft(1.8m) -5F(-21C) M 4/3 Tall shrub with large flowers, deep
rose in bud, opening mottled rose pink fading to white; lax conical trusses. Slocock, 1933. A.M. Wisley Trials 1958. F.C.C.
Wisley Trials 1987.

```
                -caucasicum 3/8
            -Jacksonii-       -caucasicum
GOLDSWORTH YELLOW-     -Nobleanum-
            -           -arboreum 1/8
            -campylocarpum 1/2
```
5ft(1.5m) -15F(-26C) ML 2/3   Above as in Leach, p. 455.
Dense plant with yellowish green leaves, medium-sized. Apricot
buds open to buff yellow flowers of thin texture; compact truss.
Slocock. A.M. 1925. Color illus. F p. 46; JS p. 58; VV p. 125.

```
            -yakushimanum 1/2
GOLFER-
            -pseudochrysanthum, Exbury form, A.M.  1/2
```
15in(38cm) -15F(-26C) M 4/5   Neyron rose buds open to clear
pink flowers 2in(5cm) across, widely funnel-campanulate; domed
trusses of 13. Plant twice as wide as tall; leaves 3in(7.6cm)
long, margins recurved; silvery tomentum on new growth; heavy
pale gray indumentum beneath.   W. Berg, cross 1966; J. Caperci,
reg. 1980. C.A 1985.   Color illus. ARS Q 34:4 (1980), p. 206.

```
        -Antoon van Welie, q.v.
GOLIATH -Professor J. H. Zaayer, q.v.
        -Annie E. Endtz, q.v.
```
Exact combination of above parentage unknown; all are PINK PEARL
hybrids. Trusses of 15 flowers, deep pink. P. van Nes, reg.
1962. F.C.C. Boskoop 1959.

```
            -catawbiense 1/2
GOMER WATERER-
            -unknown 1/2
```
5ft(1.5m) -15F(-26C) ML 3/4   An old standby, and one of the
best-looking plants year round. Plant broadly upright, large,
glossy, dark green leaves. Buds with slight rose tinge, opening
white. J. Waterer, before 1900. A.M. 1906. Color illus. HG
p. 115; JS p. 40; VV p. 20.

```
        -Grand Marquis--unknown
GONDA-
        -unknown
```
Large shrub, with flowers in trusses of 20-22, strong pink in
bud, opening light pink and changing to pale purplish pink, with
tiny purple eye at base of tube. Leaves with silvery indumentum
beneath. Mrs. J. H. Grigg cross; Mrs. R. Pinney, reg. 1985.

```
        -Lady Harcourt--unknown 1/2
GONDOLIER-
        -griersonianum 1/2
```
Large, bright red flowers in midseason. Plant of medium size,
and loose habit. Rothschild, 1947.

```
        -Lord Milner--unknown 1/2
GOOD CHEER-
        -sutchuenense 1/2
```
A tall plant bearing compact trusses of white flowers, marked
with pink. Early season. Rothschild, 1939.

```
        -fortunei 1/2
GOOD FORTUNE-
        -unknown 1/2
```
4ft(1.2m) -15F(-26C) M   Rose-colored buds open to fragrant
flowers, white with a tinge of purplish rose. Trusses 5.5in x

4.5in (14cm x 11.5cm) hold about 10 flowers. Plant rounded, and
broader than tall.   C. Russell and Velma Haag, reg. 1981.

GOOD HOPE   Described under NILE, q.v.

```
                              -griffithianum 1/8
                    -Queen Wilhelmina-
          -Britannia-                 -unknown (5/8)
GOOD NEWS-        -Stanley Davies--unknown
        -            -Moser's Maroon--unknown
            -Romany Chal-
                      -griersonianum 1/4
```
4ft(1.2m) -5F(-21C) VL 4/4   A plant favored for its later
season of bloom. Red buds open to crimson scarlet flowers (similar to BRITANNIA), widely funnel-campanulate, to 2.5in(6.4cm)
across; lax trusses hold 12-15. Shrub compact, wider than tall.
John Henny, reg. 1974.

```
            -smirnowii 1/2
GOODY GOODY-
            -catawbiense 1/2
```
Buds of ruby red and magenta rose; flowers of magenta rose with
a chartreuse green flare; dorsal spots vivid yellow-green. Medium-sized plant; hardy to -15F(-26C). Michener cross; Delp
raiser.

GOODY GOODY GUMDROP   Described under EARTHSHAKER, q.v.

```
* * * * * * * * * * * * * * * * * * * * * * * * * * * *
                           -griffithianum 1/4
          -Mrs. Tom Lowinsky-          -griffithianum 1/8
GOOGLY EYED-              -Halopeanum-
        -                            -maximum 3/8
                            -maximum
          -Stokes Bronze Wings-
                              -catawbiense 1/4
```
White flowers with unusual dorsal spotting of dark greenish yel-
lows and moderate grayed crimson.   W. Delp.
HANG TOUGH   Parentage as above
Buds of imperial purple and light purple; flowers light purple
and moderate purplish pink; a white flare; dorsal spots of pea
green and moderate yellow-green.   W. Delp.
```
* * * * * * * * * * * * * * * * * * * * * * * * * * * *
```

```
        -ludlowii 1/2
GOOSANDER-
        -lutescens 1/2
```
2.5ft(.75m) 5F(-15C) EM 3/4   Small, dark green foliage; soft
yellow flattened flowers to 1.6in(4cm) wide, upper lobes flecked
red. Truss of 3-5. Cox, reg. 1981. A.M. Wisley Trials 1981.

```
          -Sappho--unknown 1/2
GORDON JONES-
          -yakushimanum, Exbury form 1/2
```
3ft(.9m) x 5ft(1.5m)(12 yrs) -5F(-21C) M   Strong purplish
pink buds open very pale purple, fading to white, with prominent
dark red spotting; domed truss 5.5in(14cm) wide. Oblong, glossy
foliage. R. Murcott, cross 1975; W. Brack, reg. 1989. Color
illus. ARS J 43:2 1989, p. 62.

```
                        -fortunei 1/4
            -Queen Souriya-        -campylocarpum 1/8
GORDON VALLEY SUPREME-      -unnamed-
                        -unknown     hybrid-unknown 5/8
```
Truss of 9-10 flowers, 6 to 7 wavy lobes, rhodamine pink in bud,
opening lighter, paling in center to blush white, red flare on
dorsal lobe only. Vigorous shrub. Mrs. I. Henry, reg. 1987.

```
                    -catawbiense 1/8
            -Mrs. Milner-
        -Rinaldo-          -unknown 1/8
GÜRLITZ-      -smirnowii 1/4
        -williamsianum 1/2
```
3ft(.9m) -10F(-23C) M   Deep rose pink, pendulous flowers in
truss of 7. New growth bronze. Bruns, W. Germany, reg. 1972.

```
                    -catawbiense v. album--Catalgla 1/2
GOSH        -                  -decorum? 1/8
DARN!---unnamed hyb., F2-    -Caroline-
                -Mrs. H. R. Yates-    -brachycarpum?
                          -unknown 1/4      1/8
```

Buds of light yellowish pink, pale orange yellow, and pale yellowish pink open to flowers of pale orange yellow and pale
yellowish pink; dorsal spots of strong yellowish pink. W. Delp.

GOSHAWK   See JALISCO GOSHAWK

GOSSAMER   Described under DISCRETION, q.v.

```
                              -thomsonii 1/8
                  -Bagshot Ruby-
        -Princess Elizabeth-      -unknown 3/8
        -            -unknown
GOTLOTS-      -smirnowii 1/4
        -Oh My!-
                -yakushimanum 1/4
```
Deep red and strong purplish reds in bud. Flowers pale purplish
pink, with magenta rose edges and throat, dorsal spots ruby red.
Reverse veined magenta rose.   W. Delp.

```
                                -griffithianum 1/6
                -yakushimanum 1/2    -George-
GOTTFRIED PESTE-      -Mrs. L. A. Dunnett- Hardy-catawbiense 1/16
                -Rodeo-          -unknown 1/8
                    -griersonianum 1/4
```
2.5ft(.75m) x 3ft(.9m)(7 yrs) OF(-18C) M   Buds rose red open
to flowers pale purplish pink, with deep purplish pink (Neyron
rose) edges. Trusses dome-shaped, 15 flowers. Plant well-
branched, semi-dwarf. Peste cross; S. P. Johnston, reg. 1986.

```
            -azalea--unknown 1/2
GOVENIANUM-            -catawbiense 1/4
          -unnamed hybrid-
                      -ponticum 1/4
```
5ft(1.5m) OF(-18C) L   Fragrant azaleodendron resembling FRAG-
RANS, but a richer color of soft rose.   Methven, 1868.

GOVERNOR'S MANSION   Possible Dexter hybrid
5ft(1.5m) -5F(-21C) ML   Imperial purple flowers with bronze
yellow throat in trusses of 11-15. S.E. Ch., ARS, reg. 1983.

GRACE   See GEORGE GRACE

```
                -minus var. minus Carolinianum Group, pink
          -Robby-      -mucronulatum 1/8          form 1/4
GRACE AND WILL-    -Mucram-
        -                -ambiguum 1/8
          -lutescens, F.C.C. form 1/2
```
Buds light yellow-greens and rose pink; flowers 1in(2.5cm) wide,
of yellowish white, paler yellow-greens and pink. Many rounded
trusses 3in(8cm) across, on a well-shaped plant in early season.
Narrow elliptic leaves to 3.5in(8.8cm) long. Plant 32in(.8m) at
15 years. W. Delp, cross 1975; Mrs. Sarah Salley, reg. 1990.

```
* * * * * * * * * * * * * * * * * * * * * * * * * * * *
                              -griffithianum 1/4
          -Jean Marie de Montague-
GRACE SEABROOK-              -unknown 1/4
              -strigillosum 1/2
```
5ft(1.5m) -5F(-21C) EM 5/4   Currant red at margins, shad-
ing at center to blood red, funnel-shaped, 3in(7.6cm) across, in
tight truss. Habit similar to female parent; very large dark
green leaves. Seabrook, reg. 1965. Color illus. HG p. 135.
TAURUS   Parentage as above
6ft(1.8m) -5F(-21C) EM 5/4   Magnificent shrub, vigorous, full
in shape. Leaves pointed, deep green, held 3 years. Deep red
buds in winter open to campanulate flowers 3.5in(9cm) wide, orient red petals, Turkey red to cherry red throat.   F. Mossman,
reg. 1972. C.A. 1972. A.E. 1988. Color illus. Cox pl. 182.
```
* * * * * * * * * * * * * * * * * * * * * * * * * * * *
```

```
            -lutescens 1/2
GRADUATION-
          -mekongense Viridescens Group 1/2
```
3ft(.9m) 10F(-12C) M   Flowers widely funnel-campanulate, 5-
lobed. Color varies within each truss, Naples yellow, edging
light brick red and dorsal spotting; trusses of 5. Small scaly
leaves.   Dr. C. Heller cross; Peggy Moore, reg. 1984.

GRAF LENNART (COUNT LENNART)   Described under GOLDKRONE, q.v.

```
                        -griffithianum 1/8
             -George Hardy-
        -Pink -          -catawbiense 3/8
        -Pearl-          -arboreum 1/8
GRAF ZEPPELIN-    -Broughtonii-
     -                     -unknown 3/8
     -                   -catawbiense
     -Mrs. C. S. Sargent-
                        -unknown
```
5ft(1.5m) -15F(-26C) ML 3/5   Flowers of bright clear pink,
blushing darker to edges, in rounded trusses of up to 10. Very
good-looking plant, vigorous, with outstanding foliage, glossy
and dark green.   C. B. van Nes & Sons, reg. 1958.

```
                  -catawbiense 1/4
         -Scharnhorst-
GRÄFIN KIRCHBACH-    -unknown 1/4
         -forrestii Repens Group 1/2
```
2ft(.6m) -5F(-21C) M   Round leaves with scarlet red flowers.
Joh. Bruns, reg. 1972.

```
             -ciliatum 1/4
        -Cilpinense-
GRAHAM-        -moupinense 1/4
     -unknown 1/2
```
Similar to CILPINENSE, q.v. Flowers deeper pink. New Zealand.

GRAHAM HOLMES   Parentage unknown
Red-purple flowers with small red mark in throat. Trusses of 15.
A. H. Holmes; reg. 1983.

GRAHAM THOMAS   Probably derived from campanulatum--KNAPHILL
Buds violet purple, open flowers with throat mauvette, edges cobalt blue, 6-to 7-lobed, 15 per truss. Leaves pale orange-brown
hairy below. G. S. Thomas, Knap Hill, reg. 1985.


```
        -Lady Rumbold--unknown 1/2
GRANADA-
        -griersonianum 1/2
```
A plant of medium size with trusses of red flowers, blooming in
midseason. Rothschild, 1939.

GRANAT   Described under BIBBER, q.v.

GRAND ARAB   See VESUVIUS (Waterer's)

```
                -arboreum 1/4
        -Doncaster-
GRAND FINALE-       -unknown (1/4)
        -facetum (eriogynum) 1/2
```
Vivid red flowers blooming in very late season. Haworth-Booth,
intro. 1932; reg. 1962.

GRAND GALA   Parentage unknown
4ft(1.2m) ML Flowers in trusses of 9, of 7 very broad lobes,
pale pink, exterior streaked deep pink, fading to pale yellowish
pink. E. C. Nelson, reg. 1987.

GRAND MARQUIS   Parentage unknown
An unregistered parent of LONGBEACH DREAM.   G. E. Grigg, NZ.


```
        -macabeanum 1/2
GRAND MYSTERY-
        -unknown 1/2
```
6.5ft(2m) x 9.9ft(3m)(20 yrs) Sept.-Oct. (NZ) Buds vivid red;
funnel-campanulate, 7-lobed flowers to 2.7in(7cm) broad, opening
deep pink, fading paler, a dark red basal blotch; trusses of 17.
Light brown/gray indumentum on young foliage; elliptic leaves.
Hybridizer unknown; raiser H. Marchant; S. & E. Rowe, reg. 1988.

GRAND PRÉ   Described under VATER BÜHLJE, q.v.


```
        -grande 1/2
GRAND PRIX-
        -falconeri ssp. eximium 1/2
```
Ivory-colored flowers, shaded pale carmine on reverse. Heneage-
Vivian. A.M. 1940.


```
                   -griffithianum 7/32
             -George-
        -Pink Pearl- Hardy-catawbiense 7/32
        -           -             -arboreum 3/32
    -Countess -        -Broughtonii-
    - of Derby-        -         -unknown 7/32
   -Trude-    -        -catawbiense
   -Webster-        -Cynthia-
   -         -             -griffithianum
   -         -Countess of Derby--(as above)
GRAND-                   -griffithianum
SLAM-             -George-
   -        -Pink Pearl- Hardy-catawbiense
   -   -Antoon van-    -          -arboreum
   -   - Welie    -        -Broughtonii-
   -   -           -unknown        -unknown
   -Lydia-               -fortunei ssp. discolor 1/16
   -        -Lady Bessborough-
   -   -Day  -          -campylocarpum Elatum 1/16
        -Dream-griersonianum 1/8
```
6ft(1.8m) -5F(-21C) ML 4/3 Brilliant pink flower, in a cone-
shaped truss up to 1ft(.3m) high. Large glossy green leaves,
and sturdy stems for the enormous flowers. Proper care makes it
vigorous and tidy. Greer, 1982.   Color illus. HG p. 117.


```
        -yakushimanum--Koichiro Wada ? 1/2
GRAND TETON-
        -elliottii ? 1/2
```
Above parentage is uncertain. Much like CORAL VELVET, q.v. but
taller. G. Clark.

```
        -falconeri ssp. eximium 1/2
GRANDEX-
     -sinogrande 1/2
```
Yellow flowers, flushed pink.   Lord Aberconway, 1950.

```
        -Furnivall's Daughter, parents as MRS. FURNIVALL, q.v.
GRANDEZZA-              -catawbiense
        -Roseum Elegans-
                -unknown
```
4.3ft(1.3m) x 6ft(1.8m)(15 yrs) -5F(-21C) ML   Blotched hybrid
of the MRS. FURNIVALL type: rose pink flowers with a dark red to
deep purplish red blotch over 3 dorsal lobes; trusses of 10-16.
Glossy, flat foliage. Hachmann, cross 1969; Stück, reg. 1988.

GRANDIOS   Parentage: from rootstock of ANTOON VAN WELIE, q.v.
6ft(1.8m) tall x 8ft(2.4m) -10F(-23C) ML   Lilac pink to purplish red flowers, with nearly white center and yellow markings;
truss of 12-13.   W. Schmalscheidt, discovered 1976; reg. 1988.


```
                   -elliottii 1/4
             -Fusilier-
        -unnamed hybrid-        -griersonianum 1/4
GRANDMA LARSON-            -strigillosum 1/2
        -Gina--unknown
```
7ft(2.1m) tall x 6ft(1.8m)(20 yrs) 0F(-18C) E   Ruby red buds
open to cardinal red flowers in truss 6in(15.2cm) high. Leaves
held 3 years, yellow-green. D. K. McClure, reg. 1985.


```
                   -fastigiatum 1/4
        -Watchung--sport of Ramapo-
GRANDMA MATILDA-               -minus Carolinianum Gp.
        -minus Carolinianum Group, white form 3/4
```
2ft(.6m) x 2ft(12 yrs) -10F(-23C) M   Small flowers, widely
funnel-shaped, light purple. Leaves elliptic, scaly. Yavorsky,
reg. 1987.

GRANDMA'S HAT   Parentage unknown
5ft(1.5m) x 4ft(1.2m) 0F(-18C) ML Flowers 4in(10.2cm) across,
18-20 per truss, greenish white, deep purplish red edges, dark
red blotch.   H. Lem cross; Britt M. Smith, reg. 1987.

GRANDMA'S SAUCER   Described under YELLOW SAUCER, q.v.


```
        -williamsianum 1/2
GRAYSWOOD PINK-
        -venator 1/2
```
3ft(.9m) -10F(-23C)   M   Flowers coral red, bell-shaped with
distinctive flower stalks, like venator. G. Dowry, 1949.

```
                            -griffithianum 5/8
                 -Queen Wilhelmina-
        -Britannia-                  -unknown 3/8
GREAT BRITAIN-      -Stanley Davies--unknown
        -griffithianum
A hybrid by Lord Digby, 1953.


          -rex 1/2
GREAT DANE-
          -yakushimanum 1/2
```
White flowers tinged with pink, the upper lobe heavily spotted
with bright pink; the exterior pale pink.   Jens Birck, Denmark.
Color illus. ARS J 40:3 (1986), p. 122.

```
             -catawbiense var. album Glass--Catalgla   1/2
GREAT DAY-
          -calophytum 1/2
```
5ft(1.5m) -25F(-32C) M   A very hardy hybrid; white flowers, a
deep burgundy blotch.   Very compact growth habit; leaves 10in
(25.4cm) long.   S. Baldanza cross; O. S. Pride, intro. 1977.

GREAT EASTERN   Dexter hybrid; unknown parentage
5ft(1.5m) -15F(-26C) ML 3/4 Large, fragrant, ruffled, deep purplish pink flowers, a blotch of yellow-green rays; large truss.
Glossy, light green foliage.   Scott Hort. Found., reg. 1983.

GREAT FORTUNE   Described under VALLEY CREEK, q.v.

GREAT LAKES   Described under ANNA H. Hall, q.v.

* *
     -Mrs. J. G. Millais--unknown 1/2
     -                        -fortunei ssp. discolor
GREAT-   -Lady   -   1/16
SCOTT-   -Jalisco- Bessborough-campylocarpum Elatum Group
    -      -   -   1/16
    -      -   -   -dichroanthum 1/16
    -Cheyenne-   -Dido-
    -      -   -   -decorum 1/16
    -      -   -griffithianum 1/8
    -      -Loderi-
    -           -fortunei 1/8
```
5ft(1.5m)  -5F(-21C)  M  4/3  Large flowers, pure white, in very
round, tight trusses.   Flowers 5in(12.7cm) across,  with a dark
purple maroon blotch on upper lobes.   H. E. Greer, reg. 1979.
RAZZLE DAZZLE   Parentage as above
6ft(1.8m)  -5F(-21C)  ML  4/3  Flowers in large trusses opening
pink  with a deeper picotee edge and a large deep pinkish maroon
blotch.   Greer, intro. 1982. Color illus. HG p. 136.
WHITE GOLD   Parentage as above
5ft(1.5m)  -5F(-21C)  ML  4/3   Flowers pure white with a large
dorsal flare brilliant yellow; dome-shaped truss of 12.   Greer
reg. 1979.   Color illus. HG p. 180.
* * * * * * * * * * * * * * * * * * * * * * * * *

```
          -vernicosum 1/2
GREAT SMOKY-   -fortunei 1/4
          -Hardy Giant-
                  -rex ssp. fictolacteum 1/4
```
Large conical truss of light mauve pink flowers with a prominent
reddish purple blotch.   Very vigorous plant.   V. & C. R. Haag.


* * * * * * * * * * * * * * * * * * * * * * * * *
```
             -fortunei 1/4
      -Fawn-   -dichroanthum 3/16
      -    -Fabia-
GREELEY-   -griersonianum 1/4
      -      -elliottii 1/4
      -unnamed-   -dichroanthum
       hybrid-   -Fabia-
             -Umpqua Chief-   -griersonianum
                       -      -griersonianum
                       -Azor-
                            -fortunei ssp. discolor 1/16
```
5ft(1.5m)  5F(-15C)  M  3/3    Watermelon pink flowers 4in(10cm)
across,  upper  3 lobes densely spotted; trusses of about 13.
Long, narrow leaves.   Greer, reg. 1961.
FLICKER   Parentage as above, except reversed
4ft(1.2m) -10F(-23C)  M   Delft rose flowers in large, rounded
trusses 8in(20cm) wide, with 10-12 per truss.   Plant well-

branched, wide as tall.   D. James cross;  Ray James, reg. 1980.
* * * * * * * * * * * * * * * * * * * * * * * * * *
* * * * * * * * * * * * * * * * * * * * * * * * * *
```
          -augustinii 3/4
GREEN EYE-   -impeditum 1/4
          -Saint Tudy-
                  -augustinii
```
(Not to be confused with BLUE RIBBON by Johnstone;  similar  but
not same parentage.)  Mauve blue flowers with green spots.  Gen.
Harrison, 1955.
PLAINEYE   Parentage as above
Lavender  blue  flowers,   unmarked,  in  trusses  of  4-8.  Gen.
Harrison, 1956.
PURPLE EYE   Parentage as above
Mauve blue flowers with purple spot.  Gen. Harrison, 1955.
* * * * * * * * * * * * * * * * * * * * * * * * * *

```
                          -griffithianum 1/8
                 -George Hardy-
        -Mrs. Lindsay-   -catawbiense 1/8
GREEN GODDESS- Smith   -Duchess of Edinburgh--unknown 1/4
        -              -fortunei 1/4
        -unnamed hybrid-   -dichroanthum 1/8
                     -Fabia-
                          -griersonianum 1/8
```
Chartreuse flowers with a green blotch, flattened, 3.75in(9.5cm)
across;  spherical trusses of 12.  Oval leaves 7.5in(19cm) long.
Midseason.   Marshall Lyons, reg. 1971.

```
             -wardii 1/4
        -Idealist-   -griffithianum
        -       -   -Kewense-   1/64
-unnamed-   -Aurora-   -fortunei
- hybrid-   -Naomi-   -thomsonii 1/32
        -      -Hawk-   -fortunei 5/64
        -      -wardii
GREEN   -   -fortunei ssp. discolor 3/16
HIGHLANDER-   -Lady   -
        -      -Bessborough-
        -               -campylocarpum Elatum Group
        -      -fortunei ssp. discolor
        -Lady   -
        -      -Bessborough-campylocarpum Elatum Group 3/16
        -Jalisco-
        -      -dichroanthum 1/8
             -Dido-
                  -decorum 1/8
```
5ft(1.5m)  5F(-15C)  M  3/3  Flowers of very soft yellow, deep-
ening at center, on an upright, open-growing plant.  J. Waterer,
Sons & Crisp, reg. 1975.

```
        -Marion--unknown 13/16   -griffithianum 1/64
        -                  -Loderi-
      -Freckle-   -Albatross-   -fortunei 1/64
      - Pink -   -   -fortunei ssp. discolor
        -      -Cup Day- -elliottii 1/32   1/32
GREEN- -   -   -Fusilier-
SHADE- -Midnight-   -griersonianum 1/32
        -      -   -ponticum 1/16
        -      -Purple Splendour-
        -                  -unknown
        -apricot-flowered seedling--unknown
```
Trusses of 15-17 flowers, funnel-shaped, yellowish white flushed
yellow-green.  Leaves elliptic.  K. van de Ven, reg. 1986.

GREENEYE  Described under BLUE RIBBON, q.v.

GREENFINCH  Described under ZUIDERZEE, q. v.

GREENMANTLE--form of phaeochrysum R 59229
5ft(1.5m)  5F(-15C)  EM  3/3  Round truss of 11-15 flowers, very
light greenish white with small red blotch.  Leaves 5.25in
(13.3cm) long, light coverage below of dark brown indumentum.
Col. S. R. Clarke raiser;  R. N. Clarke reg. 1977.  A.M.1977.

```
             -decorum 1/4
      -Golden Jubilee-
GREENSPRITE-   -unknown 1/4
      -    -wardii 1/4
      -Crest-   -fortunei ssp. discolor 1/8
          -Lady   -
             Bessborough-campylocarpum Elatum Group 1/8
```
```

4ft(1.2m) 10F(-12C) L   Flowers of very pale greenish white, a faint yellow-green blotch, 8 wavy lobes, about 3.5in(8.9cm) wide; spherical truss of 10. Gardenia-like fragrance. Upright plant as broad as tall; leaves held 2 years; new growth may hide some blooms. Elsie Watson, reg. 1982.

```
                              -griffithianum 5/32
                        -George-
                  -Mrs. Lindsay- Hardy-catawbiense 1/32
                  - Smith    -
            -Diane-          -Duchess of
            -     -          Edinburgh--unknown 1/8
         -unnamed-          -campylocarpum 7/16
         - hybrid-  -unnamed hybrid-
         -     -                    -unknown
GREENWELL-     -         -campylocarpum
 GLORY   -   -Gladys Rose-
         -               -fortunei 1/4
         -            -campylocarpum
  -unnamed hybrid-      -griffithianum
                  -Kewense-
                         -fortunei
```
4ft(1.2m) 5F(-15C) M   Very pale yellow flower on a deep green plant. Requires some shade. Waterer, Sons & Crisp, reg. 1975.

```
                    -Barto Ivory--fortunei ?
GREER'S CREAM DELIGHT-
                    -Barto Lavender--fortunei ? X ponticum ?
```
5ft(1.5m) -10F(-23C) ML 4/4   Large, smooth, grass green foliage; large tight trusses of creamy flowers, darker throat markings. Compact, very floriferous plant. Heat-tolerant. Greer, 1988. Color illus. HG p. 98; ARS J 39:4 (1985), back cover.

```
              -thomsonii 1/4
         -Chanticleer-
GREETING-       -facetum (eriogynum) 1/4
        -        -griffithianum 1/4
         -Loderi-
              -fortunei 1/4
```
A red-flowered hybrid. Lord Aberconway, intro. 1950.

```
         -Moser's Maroon--unknown 1/2
GRENADIER-
         -elliottii 1/2
```
6ft(1.8m) 5F(-15C) L 4/3   Large ball-shaped trusses of waxy flowers, deep rich red, black in throat. Plant very strong, and fast-growing. Large, dark green foliage. Rothschild, 1939. F.C.C. 1943. Color illus. ARS J 42:3 (1988), p. 139; PB pl. 54.

```
         -Pauline--unknown 1/2
GRENADINE-
         -griersonianum 1/2
```
4ft(1.2m) OF(-18C) ML   Compact plant of average size; needs some protection. Flowers cherry, stained orange and brown. Rothschild, 1939. A.M. 1956. F.C.C. Wisley Trials 1982.

```
                 -decorum 1/4
         -unnamed hybrid-
GRETCHEN-        -griffithianum 1/4
        -     -catawbiense 1/4
         -Kettledrum-
              -unknown 1/4
```
5ft(1.5m) -15F(-26C) ML 4/4   Plant habit and foliage both good, on a very floriferous hybrid. Pink flowers, red-throated; large dome-shaped trusses. Gretchen No. One is considered the best of this group. G. G. Nearing and J.B. Gable, 1958.

GRETCHEN GOSSLER   Described under QUEEN ELIZABETH II, q.v.

```
                 -caucasicum 1/4
         -Boule de Neige-
         -             -catawbiense 3/8
         -      -unnamed hybrid-
GRETCHEN MEDLAR-          -unknown 3/8
        -          -catawbiense
         -Henriette Sargent-
                       -unknown
```
Hybrid by Dr. Henry T. Skinner, before 1958.

```
              -neriiflorum Euchaites Group 1/4
         -Portia-
GRETIA-   -strigillosum 1/4
        -griersonianum 1/2
```
Blood red flowers 3in(7.6cm) wide, held in trusses of 14. Lord Aberconway. A.M. 1946.

* *
```
              -bureavii 1/2
GRETSEL (GRETZEL)-   -dichroanthum 1/4
              -Fabia-
                   -griersonianum 1/4
```
3ft(.9m) -5F(-21C) M 4/4   Superb dark green foliage with indumentum. Large flowers, salmon orange edging on pastel pink to shell pink; lax trusses. A very compact, shapely plant. Lem. Color illus. ARS Q 33:3 (1979), cover.
HANSEL   Parentage as above
Similar to above but flowers more orange-colored, longer leaves, and better foliage. Halfdan Lem.
* *

```
         -griersonianum 1/2
GRIERCALYX-
         -megacalyx 1/2
```
A parent of MURIEL HOLMAN. Exhibited 1941.

```
         -griersonianum 1/2
GRIERDAL-
        -dalhousiae 1/2
```
5ft(1.5m) 15F(-9C) M   According to Davidian (Vol. I, p. 15): "only one authentic hybrid between" a lepidote (scaly) and an elepidote (non-scaly). See also APRILIS and JOHN MARCHAND. Cox says GRIERDAL is the only such cross worthy of propagation. It has 5-flowered red trusses as griersonianum; plant is shape and size of dalhousiae. Walker Heneage-Vivian, intro. 1937.

```
                   -griersonianum 1/2
GRIEROCASTER       -       -arboreum 1/4
(High Beeches form)-Doncaster-
                        -unknown 1/4
```
Cross by Col. G. H. Loder at High Beeches; intro. in 1937. Same cross made by Sir Gerald Loder, intro. in 1939 from Wakehurst.

```
                   -griersonianum 1/2
GRIEROSPLENDOUR-     -ponticum 1/4
           -Purple Splendour-
                        -unknown 1/4
```
4ft(1.2m) -5F(-21C) ML 3/3   Red-purple flowers, with darker blotch, produced in profusion even on young shrubs. Plant upright, spreads when mature. Col. G. H. Loder, 1937.

```
         -G. A. Sims--unknown 1/2
GRIERSIMS-
         -griersonianum 1/2
```
Late flowers of intense scarlet. Sir John Ramsden, 1938.

```
                   -elliottii 1/4
         -Fusilier-
         -        -griersonianum 1/4
GRILSE-                -fortunei ssp. discolor 1/8
     -     -Lady     -
      -Jalisco-Bessborough-campylocarpum Elatum Group 1/8
       Eclipse-   -dichroanthum 1/8
           -Dido-
                -decorum 1/8
```
4ft(1.2m) -5F(-21C) L   Flowers of reddish rose, dark crimson spots in the throat. Crown Estate, 1948. A.M. 1957.

* *
```
              -dichroanthum 3/8
         -Fabia-
GRISELDA-   -griersonianum 3/8
        -              -fortunei ssp. discolor 1/4
         -Margaret Dunn-   -dichroanthum
                   -Fabia-
                        -griersonianum
```
Plant of medium dwarf habit, and rather slow-growing; leaves to 6in(15cm) long. Flowers orange, flushed with pink and scarlet, heavily spotted, flat, 3in(7.6cm) wide. R. Henny, before 1958.
MIRAGE   Parentage as above

Flowers flat, with a yellow throat, and shaded orange on petals.
Henny, cross 1947; reg. 1958.
* *

```
                -arboreum ssp. cinnamomeum var. album 1/2
GRISETTE-           -caucasicum 1/4
      -Dr. Stocker-
                    -griffithianum 1/4
```
6ft(1.8m) OF(-18C) EM   Pure white flowers with dark markings
in the throat. Tall, tree-forming habit.   Rothschild, 1939.

GRISTEDE   Parentage unknown
3ft(.9m) -5F(-21C) EM 4/4   Dark bluish lavender flowers and
dense foliage of small brilliant green. Greer intro.

* *
```
                    -catawbiense var. album Glass---Catalgla 1/4
          -Tony's-                         -catawbiense 1/8
        - Gift -       -Catawbiense Album-
              -Belle -                     -unknown 1/8
GROOVY NO. TWO-      Heller-               -catawbiense
          -             -white catawbiense hyb.-
          -                                -unknown
          -                  -griffithianum 3/8
          -Mrs. Tom H. Lowinsky-          -maximum 1/8
                            -Halopeanum-
                                -griffithianum
```
Flowers pale purplish pink with a flare of moderate orange and
deep purplish red. W. Delp.
PROTOCOL   Parentage as above
Buds of light purple and white open to white flowers faintly
tinted light purple, a light greenish yellow flare. W. Delp.
* *

```
                -maximum 1/2
          -Midsummer-
    -unnamed-      -unknown 3/8
    - hybrid-           -maximum
GROOVY-   -unnamed hybrid-
  PINK-               -wardii 1/8
    -           -maximum
    -Midsummer-
              -unknown
```
Buds of ruby red, strong purplish red, and Tyrian purple;
flowers white heavily edged spirea red. W. Delp.

* *
```
          -haematodes 1/2
GROSCLAUDE-
          -facetum (eriogynum) 1/2
```
3ft(.9m) 5F(-15C) M 3/4   Plant of neat, compact habit; foliage rich dark green, rusty orange indumentum. Buds of sealing
wax red open brilliant scarlet; flower waxy, campanulate, heavy-
textured; flat truss of 9-11.   Rothschild, 1941. A.M. 1945.
NOTE: eriogynum = facetum--Chamberlain
PYREX   Parentage as above
Scarlet-colored flowers. Reuthe intro. 1945.
* *

```
          -campylogynum Cremastum Group--Bodnant Red 1/2
GROUSE-
          -calostrotum--Gigha 1/2
```
1.5ft(.45m) -OF(-18C) E 5/4   Deep rose flowers, campanulate,
to 1.5in(3.8cm) wide, 5-lobed, in clusters of 2-4; elliptic
leaves about 1in(2.5cm) long. P. A. Cox, reg. 1977. A.M. 1977.


```
          -yakushimanum 1/2
GRUMPY-
          -hybrid--unknown 1/2
```
3ft(.9m) -10F(-23C) M 4/4   Plant compact, broader than tall;
medium-sized, recurved leaves of dull dark green. Orangey buds;
creamy flowers, tinged pink; globular truss of 11.   J. Waterer,
Sons & Crisp. A.M. 1979. Color illus. Cox pl. 76.

```
                    -griffithianum 1/8
          -Loderi-
    -Albatross-     -fortunei 1/8
GUARDIAN FIR-       -fortunei ssp. discolor 1/2
    -                   -fortunei ssp. discolor
    -unnamed hybrid-    -griersonianum 1/8
                -Tally Ho-
                    -facetum (eriogynum) 1/8
```

6ft(1.8m) OF(-18C) L 4/3   Plant broad as high, leaves dark
green, retained one year. Flowers 5in(12.7cm) wide, of strong
substance, of medium light pink shading to pale pink on upper
lobes, with a small red blotch; trusses of 10-11. H. Lem, reg.
1974. C.A. 1975.   Color illus. ARS Q 28:4 (1974), cover.

```
          -Ivery's Scarlet--unknown 1/2
GUARDSMAN-
          -arboreum 1/2
```
Dark red flowers. Loder.

* *
```
          -Eggebrechtii--unknown
GUDRUN-
    -Madame Linden--unknown
```
5ft(1.5m) -15F(-26C) ML   White-tinted soft purple, strongly
marked with dark brownish red. T. J. R. Seidel, 1905.
HOLGER   Parentage as above
Pale violet flowers with green spots; later than above. Seidel.
* *

GUEPIER   Described under MEROPS, q.v.

```
    -catawbiense 1/2
GUIDO-
    -unknown 1/2
```
Crimson-colored flowers. A. Waterer, before 1850.

```
                                -catawbiense
                -Parsons Grandiflorum-        5/16
          -America-               -unknown 1/2
    -unnamed-       -dark red hybrid--unknown
    - hybrid-       -griffithianum 1/8
    -Cindy-     -     -Mars-
    - Lou -   -Blaze-   -unknown
    -         -         -catawbiense, red form 1/16
GUMDROP-    -         -griffithianum
    -        -     -Mars-
    -     -Red -   -unknown
    -     -Brave-               -catawbiense
    -         -     -Parsons Grandiflorum-
    -         -America-          -unknown
    -              -dark red hybrid--unknown
    -                   -catawbiense
    -Slippery Rock---Newport F6-
                    -unknown
```
Buds deep red and strong purplish red; flowers magenta, vivid
purplish red, and deep purplish pink, a flare of vivid yellow-
green; anthers strong purple. W. Delp.


```
          -yakushimanum--Koichiro Wada 1/2
GUNBORG-   -catawbiense 1/4
    -Cynthia-
          -griffithianum 1/4
```
Light rose pink flowers with scant yellowish spotting on a white
base; ruffled pink edges. Pales with age. Midseason.   Heinje
Baumschulen, reg. 1986. Color illus. WS, 1989, p. 108.

```
          -catawbiense var. album Glass--Catalgla 1/2
GUNMETAL-        -ponticum 1/4
      -Purple Splendour-
                -unknown 1/4
```
Violet with dark purple blotch. Hardy to -25F(-32C). Blough.

GUSTAV LUTTGE   Described under FRITZ HENSSLER, q.v.

* *
```
    -Mrs. Davies Evans--unknown 11/16
    -              -yakushimanum--Koichiro Wada 1/8
GUSTO-    -Kristin-        -Corona--unknown
    -Virginia-     -Bow Bells-
    Delp -           -williamsianum 1/16
    -          -catawbiense var. album Glass--Catalgla 1/8
          -Calsap-
              -Sappho--unknown
```
Buds blend strong plum and dark violet purples. Frilled flowers
combine strong to light violet purples with a pale green flare;
dorsal spotting of lettuce green. Al Smith cross; Delp raiser.
JEEPERS CREEPERS   Parentage as above
Buds of imperial purple and light purple; frilled flowers of
light purple; dorsal spots of moderate yellow-green.   Al Smith
cross; W. Delp raiser.

MILDRED CROSS   Parentage as above
Buds of violet purple and cyclamen purple; frilled flowers light
purple, heavily edged with imperial purple; a white flare; dorsal spotting of moderate olive green.   Al Smith cross; W. Delp.
SWEET VIOLET   Parentage as above
Buds of moderate violet and vivid purple; frilled flowers of
brilliant violet; a white flare.   Al Smith cross; Delp raiser.
* *

```
                            -catawbiense 1/4
            -Mrs. C. S. Sargent-
GUY BRADOUR-                 -unknown 1/2
          -                  -ponticum 1/4
            -Purple Splendour-
                            -unknown
```
2.5ft(.75m) -15F(-26C) ML   Semi-dwarf, broader than tall with
leaves medium size.   Widely funnel-shaped flowers, 3.5in(9cm)
across, fragrant, violet with a very dark blotch, in trusses of
up to 10.   Henry R. Yates cross; Mrs. Yates, reg. 1977.

GUY NEARING   Described under CLIO, q.v.

GWEN   Parentage unknown
3ft(.9m) 5F(-15C) L   Mandarin red flowers, funnel-shaped.
Shiny, deeply veined leaves; compact habit.   New Zealand.

```
                                        -griffithianum 7/32
                       -Beauty of Tremough-
              -Norman-                  -arboreum 1/32
       -Anna- Gill -griffithianum
       -            -Jean Marie de Montague-  -griffithianum
  -Walloper-                            -unknown 11/16
GWEN-       -                           -griffithianum
BELL-       -Marinus Koster-  -George Hardy-
       -                      -catawbiense 1/16
  -unknown           -red hybrid--unknown
```
5ft(1.5m) -5F(-21C) ML 4/4   Gigantic trusses of flowers, of
medium pink with small dark eye.   Large leaves with a pleasing
bronze green color.   Halfdan Lem cross; Fisher raiser.

```
                       -wardii 1/4
GWEN           -Crest-           -fortunei ssp.
GRANT---HONEY GLOW, selfed-  -Lady    - discolor 1/8
               -              Bessborough-campylocarpum
                  -unknown 1/2       Elatum Gp. 1/8
```
Funnel-shaped flowers, 7-lobed, primrose yellow at edges, deeper
at center.   NZ season in Nov.   L. A. Grant, NZ, reg. 1988.

GWEN'S PINK   Described under ALLEGRO, q.v.

* *
```
                  -ponticum 1/4
            -Purple Splendour-
GWERFYL MOSS-           -unknown 1/2
            -           -Moser's Maroon--unknown
            -Romany Chai-
                       -griersonianum 1/4
```
Flowers of cyclamen purple, with a flash of beetroot purple; 15-
17 flowers per truss.   William Moss, Flint, Wales, reg. 1974.
DORIS MOSS   Parentage as above, except reversed
Flowers ruby red.   Wm. Moss, reg. 1975.
* *
* *
```
                  -griersonianum 1/2
GWILLT-KING  -
(GWYLLT KING)-arboreum ssp. zeylanicum 1/2
```
Large Turkey red flowers, with spotting on upper lobe.   A vigor-
ous plant.   Caton Haig, Portmeirion, Wales, 1938.   A.M. 1952.
RAPTURE   Parentage as above
Flowers porcelain rose.   Lord Aberconway, 1950.
* *

GWYNETH MASTERS   Parentage unknown
Cardinal red flowers, spotted on upper lobes; 5 dark nectaries
in throat; truss of 20-21.   Leaves 5.5in(14cm) long, with light
tan indumentum.   Mrs. G. Masters, reg. 1982.

```
                  -griffithianum 1/2
GYLLA MACGREGOR-
                  -unknown 1/2
```
Light red flowers.   M. Koster & Sons.

GYPSY PRINCESS   Described under GYPSY ROVER, q.v.

* *
```
            -yakushimanum 1/2       -griffithianum 1/8
GYPSY ROVER-           -King George-
            -Gipsy King-           -unknown 1/8
                       -haematodes 1/4
```
2ft(.6m) 5F(-15C) M   Lax truss of 8 flowers, tubular-campanu-
late flowers, strong red with deep red spotting on dorsal lobe,
in throat.   Spreading plant; young foliage has orangey indumentum.   R. Drayson, cross 1979; Mr. & Mrs. A. Drayson, reg. 1987.
CANADIAN SUNSET   Parentage as above
3ft(.9m) -5F(-21C) M 4/4   Red buds opening to salmon orange
flowers, fading to creamy yellow centers.   Bush rounded; foliage
indumented.   J. G. Lofthouse, reg. 1974.
GYPSY PRINCESS   Parentage as above
Bright red buds open to flowers deepest pink, fading to paler
pink with deeper margins, then finally palest pink and white.
Pistil bright yellow.   The Draysons (as above), reg. 1986.
MAYSPARK   Parentage as above
Trusses of 11-13 flowers, deep red in bud, opening strong red
with throat light purplish pink.   Dwarf plant.   Drayson, 1987.
MISCHIEF   Parentage as above
Buds strong red, opening lighter red and deep pink, dorsal spot-
ting grayed crimson on pale yellow.   Lanceolate leaves; sparse
orange-yellow indumentum.   Drayson.
WHISTLE PUNK   Parentage as above
3ft(.9m) -5F(-21C) E 4/4   Both plant and trusses are compact
and rounded.   Dark rose flowers fading pastel pink.   Foliage has
cream-colored indumentum.   H. Larson cross; Clint Smith intro.
WISTFUL Parentage as above
Deep purplish pink buds; campanulate flowers of same color with
paler center; matures to white, overlaid light pink.   Lanceolate
leaves; pale orange-yellow indumentum.   R. Drayson, cross 1979;
Mr. & Mrs. A. Drayson, reg. 1987.
YAKUSHI MAIDEN   Parentage as above
Truss of 11-15 flowers, strong red, dorsal spotting strong to
light purplish pink; orange-yellow indumentum.   Drayson, 1987.
* *

                                        H

```
                  -catawbiense 1/2
H. H. HUNNEWELL-
                  -unknown 1/2
```
Purple-red flowers.   A. Waterer, before 1870.

H. L. LARSON   See HJALMAR L. LARSON described under SPUN GOLD

```
                  -fortunei 1/2
H. M. ARDERNE-
                  -unknown 1/2
```
Flowers pink with a dark blotch.   G. Paul.   A.M. 1896.

```
                  -fortunei 1/2
H. T. GILL-
                  -thomsonii 1/2
```
Rose-colored flowers.   R. Gill & Son.   A.M. 1921.

```
                  -catawbiense 1/2
H. W. SARGENT-
                  -unknown 1/2
```
5ft(1.5m) -25F(-32C) ML 3/2   Very hardy; and old hybrid with
red flowers.   A. Waterer.   F.C.C. 1865.

H. WHITNER   Described under RUTHELMA, q.v.

HAAG'S CHOICE   Parentage unknown
4ft(1.2m) -10F(-23C) M   Flowers of rosy pink; dense habit.
Joseph Gable cross; raised by Velma and Russell Haag.

HACHMANN'S BANANAFLIP   Described under FLAUTANDO, q.v.

HACHMANN'S BELONA   Described under ANDRÉ, q.v.

HACHMANN'S BRASILIA   Described under GOLDKRONE, q.v.

```
                      -catawbiense 1/4
                 -Humboldt-
                          -unknown 11/16
HACHMANN'S-                                    -griffithianum
  CONSTANZE-                 -Queen Wilhelmina-           1/16
              -Britannia-               -unknown
              -Kluis -            -Stanley Davies--unknown
              Sensation-unnamed seedling--unknown
```
Trusses of 18-20 flowers, 5-lobed, magenta rose with blotch of
ruby red; calyx reddish green; leaves elliptic, hairy. H. Hachmann, cross 1959; Stück, reg. 1983.

* *
```
                            -catawbiense 1/8
                      -Humboldt-
             -Hachmann's-        -unknown 3/4
             - Ornament-                    -fortunei 1/8
HACHMANN'S DIADEM-            -Direcktor E. Hjelm-
             -                                -unknown
                   -Furnivall's Daughter--unknown
```
5.7ft(1.7m) x 4ft(1.2m)(12 yrs) -10F(-23C) ML   Light purplish
pink flower with a large, conspicuous blotch of cherry red. New
growth an attractive red. Dark, smooth, elliptic foliage. Hans
Hachmann, cross 1969; G. Stück, reg. 1984.
EDELTRAUD   Parentage as above
3.3ft(1.1m) x 4.6ft(1.4m) OF(-18C) M   Dense trusses of 13 to
16 flowers; corolla 2in(5cm) broad, deep purplish pink paling to
light pinks, a prominent blotch of dark red with deep purplish
red. Narrowly elliptic, convex leaves; edges recurved.   Hachmann, cross 1969; G. Stück, reg. 1988.
HERBSTFREUDE Parentage as above
Flowers of light pink with very pale pink centers, and a strong,
dark red blotch. Plant tends to bloom in autumn, hence the name
(lit.) "Autumn Joy".   H. Hachmann, cross 1969.
* *
```
                              -Essex Scarlet--unknown 3/8
                 -Oudijk's Sensation-
                 -                  -williamsianum 1/4
HACHMANN'S EVELYN-     -smirnowii 1/4
                 -Daisy-            -catawbiense 1/8
                      -Mrs. Milner-
                              -unknown
```
4ft(1.2m) x 4ft -15F(-26C) ML   Flowers in trusses of 9-14,
strong purplish pink, shaded vivid purplish red to deep purplish
pink, with conspicuous marks of deep red; truss of 9-14. Leaves
ovate, dull green. Hachmann, cross 1967; Stück, reg. 1988.

```
                   -wardii 5/16        -Geo. -griffith.
                             -Mrs. L.-Hardy-      1/128
           -unn.-           - Smith -       -catawbiense
           -hyb.-    -Diane-         -          17/128
           -     -      -         -Duchess of Edinb.
           -    -Alice -        -unknown 15/32
           -     Street-    -unn.--campylocarpum 1/64
    -Goldkrone-        -       hyb.-
    -            -       -         -unknown
    -            -     -wardii
    -            -          -catawbiense
HACHMANN'S-      -       -Omega-
  FELICITAS-     -Hachmann's-   -unknown (rose)
    -            Marina  -wardii
    -                       -catawbiense
    -                 -Humboldt-
    -         -Hachmann's-      -unknown
   -unnamed- Ornament -           -fortunei 1/16
     hybrid-        -Direcktor E. Hjelm-
           -                         -unknown
                -Furnivall's Daughter--unknown
```
2.7ft(.8m) x 3.7ft(1.1m) -10F(-23C) ML   Truss of 13-17 flow-
ers, pale yellow with wide edging of medium to pale pink; dorsal
blotch yellowish green. Hachmann cross; Stück, reg. 1988.

HACHMANN'S FESTIVAL   See FESTIVO

HACHMANN'S FEUERSCHEIN   Described under BLINKLICHT, q.v.

```
                 -Mary Waterer--unknown
HACHMANN'S JUNIFEUER-
                 -Moser's Maroon--unknown
```
Flowers in trusses of 14-17, 5-lobed, strong red, darker towards
edges. Shrub to 3.3ft(1m). G. Stück, reg. 1984.

```
                   -Essex Scarlet--unknown
              -Oudijk's Sensation-
HACHMANN'S KRISTINA-        -williamsianum
              -               -griffithianum
              -          -George Hardy-
              -Marinus Koster-        -catawbiense
                         -red garden hybrid--unknown
```
Trusses of 16-18 flowers, 5-lobed, light purplish pink spotted
brilliant yellow-green. Cross 1972; G. Stück, reg. 1984.

HACHMANN'S LAGERFEUER   Described under BLINKLICHT, q.v.

HACHMANN'S LIBELLE   Described under BERNSTEIN, q.v.

HACHMANN'S MARINA Described under BELLINI, q.v.
* *

HACHMANN'S MARLIS   Described under YAKU WARRIOR, q.v.

```
                      -catawbiense 1/4
            -Humboldt-
HACHMANN'S-         -unknown 1/2
ORNAMENT -              -fortunei
            -Direcktor E. Hjelm-
                       -unknown
```
Trusses of 12 flowers, 5-lobed, mallow purple spotted ruby red,
blotched a dark grayed purple; blooms late midseason. Hardy to
-8F(-22C).   Hachmann, cross 1962; G. Stück, reg. 1983.
KOKARDIA   Parentage as above
5ft(1.5m) -10F(-23C) ML Trusses of 12-17; flowers 2.5in(6.5cm)
wide, strong mauve pink flecked ruby red, a striking dark brown
blotch. Hachmann cross; Stück, reg. 1983.   Color illus. ARS J
39:2 (1985), p. 62; WS, 1989, p. 137.
* *

```
            -yakushimanum--Koichiro Wada 1/2
HACHMANN'S-      -catawbiense 1/4
  POLARIS  -Omega-
                 -unknown 1/4
```
Carmine red buds, flowers light fuchsia purple at rims, blending
to light rhodamine purple. Unusually floriferous, even as young
plant. A low, compact mound with dense foliage; leaves elliptic
and very hairy. Hardy to -17F(-27C); wind- and sun-tolerant.
H. Hachmann, cross 1963; G. Stück, reg. 1983.   Gold Medal 1980.
Color illus. WS, 1989, p. 151.

HACHMANN'S PORZELLAN   Described under SCHNEEWOLKE, q.v.

HACHMANN'S ROSABELLA   Described under YAKU WARRIOR, q.v.

* *
```
                      -insigne 1/2
HACHMANN'S ROSARKA-          -griffithianum 1/4
                      -Spitfire-
                           -unknown 1/4
```
1.5ft(.45m) x 3.3ft(1m) -12F(-24C) M   Light carmine red flow-
ers, 2.7in(7cm) wide, wavy-edged, faint dark red markings; truss
of 11-14. Compact bush. Unusually long blooming period. Hachmann cross; Stück, reg. 1984.   Color illus. WS, 1989, p. 134.
HACHMANN'S ROSELYN Sibling to above; ruby red flowers.
* *

HACHMANN'S ROSENELFE   Described under YAKU WARRIOR, q.v.

* *
```
                           -catawbiense 1/8
                 -Humboldt-
           -Kokardia-    -unknown 3/8
           -      -        - fortunei 1/8
HACHMANN'S-      -Direkctor E. Hjelm-
  ROSITA   -                -unknown
           -            -griffithianum 1/8
           -      -Mars-
           -unnamed hybrid-    -unknown
                 -yakushimanum--KOICHIRO Wada 1/4
```
Truss of 8-9 flowers, roseine purple on edges, blending to very
pale purple, wavy-edged; yellow-green dorsal spotting. Elliptic
leaves. Spreading semi-dwarf plant, compact, hardy. Hachmann,
cross 1969; Stück, reg. 1983. Color illus. WS, 1989, p. 152.
LUMINA   Sibling to above; flowers mallow purple; truss of 13.
* *

HACHMANN'S SABRINA   Described under GOLDFEE, q.v.

* *
                        -russatum 1/2
HACHMANN'S VIOLETTA-
                        -impeditum 1/2
Many trusses of 13-22 flowers each 1in(2.5cm) across, 5-lobed,
light violet, bluer than AZURIKA. Hardy to -8F(-22C).
Hachmann, cross 1963; G. Stück, reg. 1983.
AZURIKA   Parentage as above
3ft(.9m) -10F(-23C) EM   Flowers in trusses of 7-8, 5-lobed,
aster violet in color. Scaly leaves. Hachmann cross; G. Stück,
reg. 1983.   Color illus. WS, 1989, p. 163
* *
* *
                        -catawbiense 1/2
HAD---NEWPORT F4-
                        -unknown 1/2
Flowers combine moderate purple violets (spectrum to campanula).
Tall, very hardy plant. W. Delp.
HARRISVILLE   Parentage as above
Tall shrub with flowers bright purple violet, white upper lobe.
Hardy to -25F(-32C). W. Delp.
SLIPPERY ROCK   Parentage as above
Vivid purplish red buds open to flowers of medium pink, edged in
vivid purplish red, white upper lobes, brilliant greenish yellow
speckling. Medium size plant; hardy to -25F(-32C). W. Delp.
WHIRLWIND   Parentage as above
Imperial purple and vivid magenta in bud, opening vivid to
moderate cyclamen purple with white flare and ruby dorsal spots.
Hardy to -15F(-26C). W. Delp.
RUFFLED RIDGE   Parentage: NEWPORT F2
Formerly known as H-1. Buds of violet and cyclamen purple open
to very frilled flowers of imperial purple and moderate purplish
pink; a white flare and chartreuse green dorsal spotting. Delp.
NEBULA   Parentage: NEWPORT F5
Buds of beetroot purple and strong purplish red; flowers fuchsia
purple with a white flare; dorsal spots yellow-green. W. Delp.
NUBELLE   Parentage: NEWPORT F5
Buds of deep and strong purplish red open to strong purplish red
flowers; a white flare; dorsal spots vivid yellow-green. Delp.
RHODO ELITE   Parentage: NEWPORT F6
Buds of ruby red and Tyrian purple; flowers ruby red and magenta
rose with a white flare; dorsal spots brilliant greenish yellow.
W. Delp.
TOMBOY   Parentage: NEWPORT F6
Buds of magenta, fuchsia, and beetroot purples; flowers strong
reddish purple and strong purplish red with a white flare; dor-
sal spots lettuce green; white anthers; dark red stigma. Delp.
* *

                     -barbatum 1/2
HAEMBARB-
                     -haematocheilum 1/2
Flowers of bright rose pink with brown blotches.   Magor, 1915.

                                   -caucasicum 1/16
             -wardii 1/2   -Jacksonii-   -caucasicum
                           -Goldsworth-   -Nobleanum-   1/32
HAIDA GOLD-   - Yellow -   -arboreum
            -Goldfort-   -campylocarpum 1/8   1/32
                     -fortunei 1/4
3ft(.9m) OF(-18C) M 4/4   Flowers in trusses of 10, 7-lobed;
light greenish yellow contrasts with dark green leaves. R. C.
Rhodes, reg. 1985.

HAL BRUCE   Parentage unknown; elepidote
8ft(2.4m) x 5ft(1.5m)(25 yrs) -15F(-26C) M Flowers in trusses
of 7-10, 7-lobed, pale yellow, edges deep purplish pink, brownish blotch; buds strong red. Open growth habit. C. O. Dexter
cross; Winterthur Museum & Gardens, reg. 1988.

* *
             -souliei 1/2
HALCYONE-   -fortunei ssp. discolor 1/4
             -Lady Bessborough-
                      -campylocarpum Elatum Group 1/4
5ft(1.5m) -5F(-21C) M 3/3   Much like the parent souliei with
cup-shaped pink flowers held in lax trusses. Rothschild, 1940.
Color illus. PB pl. 51.   A.M. 1988.
PERDITA   Parentage as above, except may be reversed
5ft(1.5m) -5F(-21C) M 3/4 Shapely plant; foliage and flowers

like souliei. Buds of rose; cup-shaped, pale pink flowers
fading to milky white, a few red spots; lax, flat-topped truss
of 8. Rothschild, 1940.   A.M. 1948. Color illus. PB pl. 52.
SANDLING   Parentage: souliei X Lady Bessborough
5ft(1.5m) -5F(-21C) M 3/3   Narrow leaves 7in(17.8cm) long,
dark above, paler beneath. Frilled flowers, 3.5in(9cm) wide,
rhodomine pink, throat flushed amber, darker spots; compact
truss of 12. Maj. Hardy, Sandling Park, reg. 1966. A.M. 1965.
* *

HALESITE   Parentage unknown
5ft(1.5m) -10F(-23C) ML   Strong purplish red flowers, fading
lighter, with deep purplish rays in throat; 8 per truss. Dexter
cross; Scott Horticultural Foundation, reg. 1984.

HALESITE MAIDEN   Parentage unknown
5ft(1.5m) -5F(-21C) ML   Fragrant flowers, light red, in truss
of 12.   Dexter cross; Schlaikjer, reg. 1974.

* *
                            -griffithianum 5/16
                 -Beauty of Tremough-
           -Norman Gill-   -arboreum 1/16
      -Anna-   -griffithianum
HALF -   -griffithianum
PENNY-   -Jean Marie de Montague-
           -                -unknown 1/8
           -            -fortunei ssp. discolor 1/4
          -Margaret Dunn-   -dichroanthum 1/8
                     -Fabia-
                          -griersonianum 1/8
Pink buds open primrose yellow, large red blotches surround
corolla center; flowers to 6in(15.2cm) across, widely campanulate, 13 per truss. Medium-sized, compact bush, leaves to 8in.
(20.3cm) long. Late season.   D. W. James, reg. 1961.
AWARD   Parentage as above
5ft(1.5m) OF(-18C) ML 4/3 Flowers white, light yellow flare,
margins shaded pink, 4.5in(11.5cm) wide; fragrant. Ball-shaped
truss of 14. Plant as broad as high; new growth greenish copper
or bronze. James cross; Mossman raiser; C. Ward, reg. 1973.
A.M. 1988.
* *

                            -griffithianum 1/2
           -Jean Marie de Montague-
           -                -unknown 3/8
HALFDAN-   -griffithianum
   LEM -   -Loderi King George-
           -                -fortunei 1/8
        -Red -   -griffithianum
        Loderi-   -Queen Wilhelmina-
           -Earl of Athlone-   -unknown
                        -Stanley Davies-unknown
5ft(1.5m) -5F(-21C) M 5/4   Bright red flowers 3.5in(8.3cm)
wide, with darker spots on dorsal lobe; about 13 in large, tight
trusses. Deep green leaves, 8in(20.3cm) long. Vigorous plant.
Lem cross; Seattle Chapter, ARS, reg. 1974. Color illus. HG p.
118.

           -venator 1/2
HALLALI-
           -sanguineum ssp. sanguineum var. haemaleum 1/2
Trusses hold 4-7 flowers carried terminally, forming many umbels
of cardinal red with darker spotting in throat. Dull green fol-
iage, lightly felted with gray indumentum beneath. Collingwood
Ingram, reg. 1979. F.C.C. 1979.

               -williamsianum 1/4
         -Kimberly-
HALLELUJAH-   -fortunei 1/4
         -                -griffithianum 1/4
         -Jean Marie de Montague-
                          -unknown 1/4
4ft(1.2m) -15F(-26C) M 5/5   Large, dark green leaves heavily
textured with a downward bend midway in the leaf. Flowers rose
red, of good substance; large, tight truss.   May be tetraploid.
H. E. Greer, reg. 1976. A.E. 1983.   Color illus. HG p. 97.

           -griffithianum 1/2
HALOPEANUM-
           -maximum 1/2
6ft(1.8m) 5F(-15C) M 3/3   Synonym WHITE PEARL.   Flowers in

tall conical trusses, with pastel pink tint, fading to pristine white. Very vigorous plant; dark green, slightly rough-textured foliage. Halope, Belgium, 1896. A.M. 1906.

HALTON   Described under LIONEL'S TRIUMPH, q.v.

```
                    -dichroanthum 1/4
            -Fabia-
HAMMA HAMMA-        -griersonianum 1/4
            -unknown 1/2
```
5ft(1.5m) 15F(-9C) ML 3/2   Leaves medium to large, rather narrow. Cardinal red flower heavily spotted black, 2.5in(6.4cm) across, in trusses of about 18.   Roy W. Clark, reg. 1979.

```
                        -griffithianum 1/8
                -George Hardy-
    -Mrs. Lindsay Smith-            -catawbiense 1/8
HANDEL-            -Duchess of Edinburgh--unknown 1/2
    -                -campanulatum 1/4
        -unnamed hybrid-
                -unknown
```
Flowers yellow, flushed green, with green spots.   Another form with creamy white flowers. M. Koster & Sons, 1920. A.M. 1937.

* *
```
                        -Mrs. J.G. Millais--unknown
HANDSOME RIS--unnamed hybrid, selfed-
                        -catawbiense--La Bar's White
```
Buds of rhodamine and pale purplish pinks opening white with citron green spots. Weldon E. Delp.
SI BARNES   Parentage as above
Buds of strong and vivid purplish reds and deep purplish pink, open to frilled white flowers; spots of brilliant and light yellows; strong yellow stigma.   Delp.
* *

HANDSWORTH SCARLET   Described under NOBLEANUM, q.v.

```
            -caucasicum 1/2
HANDSWORTH WHITE-
            -unknown 1/2
```
A parent of DUCHESS OF PORTLAND. White flowers with pink blush. Fisher, Son & Sibray, before 1928.

HANG TOUGH   Described under GOOGLY EYED, q.v.

HANGUP   Described under YELLOW STREAKER, q.v.

```
                -racemosum 1/2
HANNAH---RIK, selfed-
                -keiskei 1/2
```
1ft(.3m) x 1.5ft(.45m) -10F(-23C) M   Flowers yellowish white or white, flushed light pink, edged deep purplish pink. Dwarf plant, compact, well-branched. L. Yavorsky, reg. 1987.

HANSEL   Described under GRETSEL, q.v.

```
            -fortunei 1/2
HAPPINESS-
            -unknown 1/2
```
Registered as a fortunei seedling in 1958.   Maitland Dougall, intro. 1939.

```
        -Pauline--unknown 1/2
HAPPY-
    -griffithianum 1/2
```
A medium-sized plant, bearing pink flowers with a darker blotch. Rothschild, 1940.

```
                        -maximum 1/4
            -Lady Clementine Mitford-
HAPPY DAY-                -unknown 1/2
    -                -fortunei ssp. discolor 1/4
        -Ladybird-
                -Corona--unknown
```
Ball-shaped trusses of phlox pink flowers, partially tubular. Plant habit compact, long leaves. Marshall Lyons, reg. 1971.

HAPPY OCCASION   Described under INDIRIDIVA, q.v.

HARDGROVE'S DEEPEST YELLOW   Described under DONNA HARDGROVE.

* *
```
            -racemosum 1/2
HARDIJZER'S BEAUTY-
            -Kurume azalea--unknown 1/2
```
3ft(.9m) -5F(-21C) EM 4/4   A semi-dwarf evergreen azaleodendron from Holland. Vigorous and sun-tolerant. Clear pink flowers open all along the stems. Small glossy foliage has purplish tinge. W. H. Hardijzer, reg. 1965. A.M. 1970. Color illus. F p. 46.
RIA HARDIJZER   Parentage as above, except Hinodegiri azalea
2.5ft(.75m) -5F(-21C) EM 4/4 Evergreen azaleodendron. Vibrant pink flowers in small trusses of 19. Compact, vigorous plant, broad as tall, small leaves tinged red. Hardijzer, reg. 1965. A.M. 1974.
* *

```
            -fortunei 1/2
HARDY GIANT-
            -rex ssp. fictolacteum 1/2
```
6ft(1.8m) -5F(-21C) ML   Leaves quite large, 9in x 3in (23cm x 7.6cm). Flowers 3.5in(8.9cm) across, creamy white, raspberry blotch; conical trusses of 14.   Mrs. Knippenberg, reg. 1967. Color illus. LW pl. 107.

* *
```
                    -ponticum 1/4
            -Purple Splendour-
HARDY SPLENDOUR-            -unknown 1/2
    -                -catawbiense 1/4
        -Purpureum Grandiflorum-
                -unknown
```
3ft(.9m) x 6ft(1.8m)(20 yrs) OF(-18C) M Flowers in trusses of 12-15, deep reddish purple shading to deep purplish red in throat with dark purple spotting.   Ben & Marion Shapiro, reg. 1989.   Color illus. ARS J 42:2 (1988), p. 63.
JANET SHAPIRO   Sibling of above
Similar to above; flowers strong purple, vivid reddish purple blotch and spotting, silvery filaments.   Shapiro, reg. 1989.
* *

```
            -racemosum 1/2
HARIET-
    -ciliatum 1/2
```
Pale pink flowers 1in(2.5cm) long, about 20 per cluster. Noble. A.M. 1957.

```
                -yakushimanum 1/2
HARKWOOD PREMIERE-            -unknown 1/4
                -Bud Flanagan-
                        -ponticum 1/4
```
Buds cerise, open lilac, fading to white with a pronounced dark red dorsal blotch; truss of 18-20. R. J. R. Drayson, reg. 1986.

```
                -yakushimanum 1/2
HARKWOOD SUPREME-    -dichroanthum 1/4
                -Fabia-
                    -griersonianum 1/4
```
Flowers tubular-campanulate, light greenish yellow in bud, opening paler, dorsal lobe spotted vivid yellow; deep orange-yellow indumentum on mature foliage. Drayson, reg. 1987. See also BAMBI.

HARLEQUIN   See DEXTER'S HARLEQUIN, described under ACCLAIM, q.v.

```
                    -dichroanthum 1/8
            -Fabia-
    -Vega-        -griersonianum 1/8
HARMONY-    -haematodes 1/4
    -        -griffithianum 1/4
        -Loderi-
            -fortunei 1/4
```
A pink-flowered hybrid by Lord Aberconway, 1950.

```
                        -griffithianum 1/8
                -Loderi-
        -Albatross-    -fortunei 1/8
HARNDEN'S-        -fortunei ssp. discolor 3/8
  WHITE  -    -wardii 1/4
        -Hawk-            -fortunei ssp. discolor
                -Lady Bessborough-
                    -campylocarpum Elatum 1/8
```
5ft(1.5m) OF(-18C) ML 4/3   Flowers off-white, 4.5in(11cm)

across; full rounded truss of 10. Growth habit upright; leaves glossy, heavily textured, and citrus green. Greer, reg. 1979.

```
                  -maximum 1/2
HAROLD AMATEIS-
                  -strigillosum 1/2
```
3ft(.9m) -10F(-23C) M   Cardinal red flowers with dark maroon throat, campanulate, 2.25in(5.7in) across; trusses of about 20. Plant broader than tall; heavy rugose leaves 6in(15cm) long. E. Amateis cross; Baldsiefen, reg. 1967.

```
                          -thomsonii 1/8
                -Cornish Cross-
      -unnamed hybrid-          -griffithianum 3/8
HAROLD-          -wardii 1/4
 HEAL -            -griffithianum
      -Loderi King George-
                  -fortunei 1/4
```
A parent of WILLY NILLY. Collingwood Ingram, 1955.

HARP WOOD--form of hodgsonii
5ft(1.5m) 10F(-12C) EM 3/4   Flowers of light cyclamen purple with darker veined markings and a darker reddish purple blotch. Maj. A. E. Hardy, reg. 1972. P.C. 1971.

HARRISVILLE   Described under HAD, q.v.

HARRY BRYCE   Parentage unknown
Vivid red flowers, darker in bud, upper lobe profusely blotched; trusses of 15. Shrub 7ft(2.1m).   E. C. Nelson, reg. 1987.

```
            -strigillosum 1/2
HARRY CARTER-
            -sutchuenense 1/2
```
5ft(1.5m) OF(-18C) E 3/3   Olive green leaves with appearance of strigillosum. Plant covered with medium pink trusses. Plant branching upright and sturdy; combines the best of both parents. Mrs. Greig, Royston Nursery; A.R. Cook intro.

```
* * * * * * * * * * * * * * * * * * * * * * * * * *
          -Albescens unknown 1/2
HARRY TAGG-
          -ciliicalyx 1/2
```
Long-lasting, frilly white flowers, faint greenish yellow stain, in trusses of 3-4, each flower 4.5in(11.5cm) wide. Fragrant. RBG, Edinburgh, reg. 1962. A.M. 1958.
BASILEOS   Parentage as above
4ft(1.2m) 25F(-4C) M Flowers white with pink flush, deep pink stripe on back of petals. Richly fragrant. Strybing Arboretum, reg. 1971.
```
* * * * * * * * * * * * * * * * * * * * * * * * * *
```

HARRY VON TILZER   Described under REDWAX, q.v.

```
      -arboreum var. kermesinum ? 1/2
      -                 -catawbiense 5/32
HARRY-      -Blandy-             -catawbiense
WHITE-    - anum-        -unnamed-
      -Ascot-    -Alta- hybrid-
      Brilliant-    clerense-      -ponticum 1/32
      -                  -arboreum 1/16
            -thomsonii 1/4
```
Scarlet or blood red flowers. Loder and Rothschild, 1922.

HARVEST MOON   Described under ZUIDERZEE, q.v.

HARVEST QUEEN   Described under FOTIS, q.v.

```
                  -thomsonii
      -Avis (Barclayi g.)-              -arboreum
HASGARD-          -Glory of Penjerrick-
      -strigillosum 1/2              -griffithianum
```
Campanulate flowers, in trusses of 10, strong red. Foliage lanceolate. Shrub 5ft(1.5m) x 4ft(1.2m).   J. A. Watts, reg. 1986.

```
                  -catawbiense 3/4
      -Carl Mette-
HASSAN-          -unknown 1/4
      -catawbiense
```
Flowers a fiery carmine red with reddish brown markings. T. J. R. Seidel, cross 1898; intro. 1906.

```
                          -griffithianum 1/8
            -Loderi King George-
      -Senorita-          -fortunei 1/8
HAWAIIAN-      -Ostbo Y3--unknown 1/4
 HOLIDAY-          -fortunei ssp. discolor 1/4
      -Autumn Gold-      -dichroanthum 1/8
                  -Fabia-
                      -griersonianum 1/8
```
5ft(1.5m) x 4ft(1.2m)(15 yrs) OF(-18C) M   Flowers of 7 wavy lobes, light purplish pink at edges shading to light yellow at center, dark red blotch; trusses of 10-12. Foliage a moderate olive green. B. M. Smith, reg. 1987.

```
* * * * * * * * * * * * * * * * * * * * * * * * * *
      -wardii 1/2
HAWK-          -fortunei ssp. discolor 1/4
      -Lady Bessborough-
                  -campylocarpum Elatum Group 1/4
```
6ft(1.8m) 5F(-15C) M 3/2   Cross was made twice in an effort to find a superior yellow. First cross used Exbury A.M. form of wardii (K W 4170). Apricot buds open daffodil yellow with a slight red eye, funnel-shaped, flowers in neat truss. Habit tall, loose, open. Rothschild, 1940. A.M. 1949.
AMOUR   Parentage as above
6ft(1.8m) 5F(-15C) M 3/2 Pale yellow flowers. Rothschild.
BEAULIEU HAWK   Parentage as above
Flowers yellow, but paler than CREST, q.v.
CREST   Parentage as above
6ft(1.8m) -5F(21C) M 5/3 Synonym HAWK CREST. A different form of wardii used in this cross from that of other HAWK clones. Bright primrose yellow flowers, slight darkening around throat, 4in(10cm) wide, in large, dome-shaped truss. Heavy bud set after well-established. Habit upright, open; leaf oval, glossy, held only 1 year. Rothschild, 1940. F.C.C. 1953. Color illus. F. p. 47; PB pl. 23.
EXBURY HAWK   Parentage as above
6ft(1.8m) 5F(-15C) M 3/2   A clear yellow but not as rich in color as others in this group. Rothschild, 1940. A.M. 1949.
HAWK CHERRY   Parentage as above ?
This author photographed this bright yellow in Savill Garden, Windsor Great Park, 4-25-88, with the no. F-24. Not recorded in Rothschild Rhododendrons.
HAWK KESTREL   Parentage as above
6ft(1.8m) 5F(-15C) M 3/2   A rich yellow. Rothschild, 1940.
HAWK MERLIN   Parentage as above
6ft(1.8m) 5F(-15C) M 3/2 Synonym EXBURY MERLIN. "Different shade of yellow" from the other clones in the HAWK grex. Rothschild.   P.C. 1950.
JERVIS BAY   Parentage as above
6ft(1.8m) 5F(-15C) M 3/2 "Best of the HAWKS", then came CREST. Still a fine yellow, deep red spot. Rothschild. A.M. 1951. Color illus. ARS J 36:4 (1982), cover.
```
* * * * * * * * * * * * * * * * * * * * * * * * * *
```

HAZE   Described under EVENING, q.v.

```
      -bureavii 1/2
HAZEL-
      -unknown 1/2
```
5ft(1.5m) -5F(-21C) EM 4/4   Light pink flowers, rimmed and striped with deep pink, slight brown spotting, 3in(7.6cm) wide; compact truss of 12-15. Upright plant; deep green foliage covered with a moderate amount of woolly, tan, indumentum. Origin unknown; H. E. Greer, reg. 1979.

HAZEL FISHER   Described under SPUN GOLD, q.v.

```
            -azalea occidentale 1/2
HAZEL SMITH-
            -Corona--unknown 1/2
```
An azaleodendron. White flowers, with a chrysanthemum crimson blotch; truss of 16-18. Bush 5ft(1.5m) x 5ft (14 years). Late midseason. Vernon Wyatt, reg. 1965.

```
            -Ben Moseley--Dexter hybrid--unknown
HEADTURNER-      -catawbiense var. album Glass--Catalgla
            -Calsap-
                  -Sappho--unknown
```
Buds of strong reddish purple and moderate purplish pink open to a blend of light purple and moderate purplish pink; dorsal spots dark red on 3 lobes; strong yellow stigma.   Weldon Delp.

HEANE WOOD--form of argyrophyllum ssp. hypoglaucum
5ft(1.5m) 5F(-15C) M 3/4 Loose trusses of 8 flowers, pink in
bud, opening white suffused with red-purple, some lighter spots
in throat. Foliage to 4.5 in(11.5cm) long; gray plastered indumentum beneath.   Major A. E. Hardy, reg. 1972.   A.M. 1972.

HEAP BIG INDIAN   Described under CAMPFIRE, q.v.

* *
```
                              -catawbiense v. album 1/8
                 -Lodestar-                 -cat. 3/32
                 -       -Belle-Catawbiense Album-
                 -       Heller-             -unk. 3/32
                 -       -          -catawbiense
        -R.O. Delp-       -wht cat hyb-
        -         -                 -unknown
        -         -                 -catawbiense
        -         -         -Atrosanguineum-
        -         -  -Atrier-        -unknown
HEART TALK-    -Mary-    -griersonianum 1/16
        -      Belle-    -decorum 1/16
        -         -Dechaem-
        -              -haematodes 1/16
        -          -Pygmalion--unknown 1/8
        -      -Weldy-
        -unnamed-    -haematodes 1/8
         hybrid-          -yakushimanum 1/8
                 -Serendipity-
                         -aureum 1/8
```
Buds moderate to strong purplish red open to pale purplish pink.
W. Delp.
SANTA'S WHISKERS   Parentage as above
White flowers with stigmas a strong reddish orange. W. Delp.
* *
```
            -yakushimanum 1/4    -fortunei ssp. discolor
    -unnamed-         -Lady Bess-              3/64
    - hybrid-     -Day - borough -campylocarpum Elatum
    -       -Gold -Dream-griersonianum         1/64
    -       Mohur-          -fortunei ssp. discolor
    -Cisa-         -Margaret Dunn-     -dichroanthum 1/64
    -    -                    -Fabia-
    -    -    -yakushimanum        -griersonianum 3/64
HEART-    -Serendipity-
THROB-         -aureum (chrysanthum) 1/8
    -              -maximum 1/4
    -       -Midsummer-
    -unnamed-       -unknown 1/8
      hybrid-          -maximum
        -Adele's Yellow-
                 -wardii 1/8
```
Buds of cardinal red and strong red; flowers white edged with
vivid purplish red and deep purplish pink; a flare of pale yellow-green; dorsal spots vivid red.   W. Delp.
PETITE FLEUR   Parentage as above
Buds of moderate and strong purplish red open to white flowers
edged with strong purplish red.   W. Delp.
* *

HEART'S DELIGHT   Described under ERMINE, q.v.

HEART'S DESIRE   See HEART'S DELIGHT under ERMINE.

HEAT WAVE   Described under BLACK MAGIC, q.v.

HEATARAMA   Described under TIM CRAIG, q.v.
```
            -unknown 1/2
HEATHER BOULTER-         -chrysodoron 1/4
            -Chrysomanicum-
                    -burmanicum 1/4
```
Trusses of 6 flowers, 2.5in(6.4cm) across, funnel-shaped, light
grayed yellow, darker spots.   V. Boulter, reg. 1984.

* *
```
                 -griffithianum 1/8
            -Queen Wilhelmina-
    -Britannia-             -unknown 5/8
HEATHER-     -Stanley Davies--unknown
 MOTH -         -yakushimanum 1/4
    -unnamed hybrid-
                 -hybrid unknown
```

Flowers very light purple, flushed darker.   Waterer, reg. 1975.
SARAH JANE   Parentage as above
Flowers light pink, deeper at edges to rose red. Waterer, 1975.
* *
```
            -caucasicum 1/2
HEATHERSIDE BEAUTY-
            -unknown 1/2
```
5ft(1.5m) -10F(-23C) E 3/3   Shrub upright and bushy. White
flowers; shapely truss. Early. Frederick Street, before 1959.
```
        -         -Catawbiense-
            -fortunei 1/2
HEAVENLY SCENT-
            -unknown 1/2
```
5ft(1.5m) 0F(-18C) EM 3/4   Large, medium pink flowers, upper
lobe faintly spotted red; high lax trusses. Delightfully fragrant. Plant habit rounded.   Whitney cross; Sathers intro.
```
            -neriiflorum 1/4
    -Neriihaem-
HEBE-         -haematodes 1/4
    -williamsianum 1/2
```
Small bush; campanulate flowers, deepest rose pink. Magor, 1927.
```
        -dichroanthum ssp. scyphocalyx Herpesticum Group 1/2
HECA-
    -campylocarpum 1/2
```
A hybrid with yellow flowers.   Lord Aberconway, intro. 1941.

* *
```
    -thomsonii 1/2
HECLA-
    -griersonianum 1/2
```
Called a good red.   Lord Aberconway, 1941.
RED DRAGON   Parentage as above, except reversed
Parent of ROWENA. Lord Aberconway, 1943.
* *

HEIDI   Parentage unknown; possibly lapponicum hybrid
3ft(.9m) 0F(-18C) EM 3/3   Small, shiny leaves with red stems
drop as white flowers appear in spring.   Del. James intro.
```
                 -griffithianum 3/16
            -Loderi-
        -Albatross-    -fortunei 3/16
    -Cup Day-       -fortunei ssp. discolor 1/8
    -    -          -elliottii 1/8
    -    -Fusilier-
HEIDI BOESCH-         -griersonianum 1/8
    -              -griffithianum
    -       -Loderi-
    -Avalanche-      -fortunei
         -calophytum 1/4
```
Flowers in trusses of 14, 7-lobed, white with strong yellowish
green flare. Shrub 3.3ft(1m). D. J. Dosser, reg. 1985.

HEINRICH PEIFFER   Described under YAKU FRILLS, q.v.

HEIR APPARENT   Described under FLANAGAN'S DAUGHTER, q.v.
```
    -decorum 1/2
HELEN-      -souliei 1/4
    -Souldis-
         -fortunei ssp. discolor 1/4
```
White flowers with a yellow throat.   Lester E. Brandt, 1952.
```
            -fortunei 1/4
        -unnamed hybrid-
HELEN CHILD-         -unknown 1/4
            -williamsianum 1/2
```
2.5ft(.75m) 10F(-12C) EM 3/4   Dark red buds open to rose pink
flowers of heavy substance, 3in(7.6cm) across, spotted pink in
throat, in 9-flowered truss.   H. L. Larson, reg. 1977.
```
                 -griffithianum 1/8
            -Queen Wilhelmina-
    -Unknown Warrior-        -unknown 1/2
HELEN-        -Stanley Davies--unknown
DEEHR-             -arboreum ssp. nilagiricum 1/8
    -       -Noyo Chief-
    -Noyo Brave-      -unknown
         -yakushimanum--Koichiro Wada 1/4
```

3ft(.9m) -5F(-21C) E   Flowers 5-lobed, crimson red, in ball-
shaped truss of 15. New foliage, medium amount of tan indumentum. Plant wider than tall.   William Moynier, reg. 1984.

```
                 -elliottii 1/2
HELEN DRUECKER-                        -griffithianum 1/8
       -                      -George Hardy-
       -Betty Wormald-                -catawbiense 1/8
                     -red garden hybrid--unknown 1/4
```
5ft(1.5m) 5F(-15C) M 4/3   Large leaves, 8in x 4in (20.3cm
x 10.2cm). Trusses hold 16 flowers, to 4.5in(11.5cm) wide, rose
madder shading darker on edges. John S. Druecker, reg. 1964.

HELEN EVERITT   Parentage: two unknown Dexter hybrids
6ft(1.8m) -15F(-26C) ML Leaves 4in x 2in (10.2cm x 5cm) Very
large flowers, 5in(12.7cm) across, overlapping lobes, pure
white, vestigial stamens; globular truss of 7-9. Very fragrant.
S. Everitt cross; H. & S. Fuller, intro. 1958; reg. 1975.

```
      -williamsianum 1/2             -griffithianum 1/16
HELEN-            -Queen Wilhelmina-
FOSEN-    -Britannia-                -unknown 5/16
     -Burgundy-        -Stanley Davies--unknown
     -                     -ponticum 1/8
          -Purple Splendour-
                     -unknown
```
Truss of 7 flowers, 5-lobed, fuchsia purple. Larson, reg. 1983.

HELEN FOX   Described under BARCLAYI, q.v.

* *
```
                        -griffithianum 1/4
                     -Loderi-
        -Irene Stead (=I.M.S.)-    -fortunei 1/4
HELEN HOLMES-                -Loderi (as above)
        -unknown 1/2
```
Truss of 12 flowers, 6-lobed, white with a prominent yellow
stigma. A. G. Holmes, reg. 1982.
HOLMESLEE TRIUMPH Parentage as above
Truss of 10 flowers, 7-lobed, rhodamine pink, upper lobe flecked
red. A. G. Holmes, reg. 1982.
* *

```
                        -caucasicum 1/8
                 -unnamed hybrid-
     -Mrs. Furnival-           -unknown 3/8
     -             -            -griffithianum 1/4
HELEN  -          -unnamed hybrid-
JOHNSON-                 -unknown
     -                       -Corona--unknown
     -              -unnamed hybrid-
     -Mrs. Donald Graham-          -griersonianum 1/8
                   -           -griffithianum
                   -Loderi-
                        -fortunei 1/8
```
5ft(1.5m) 5F(-15C) ML 3/3   Flowers carmine rose, a striking
blotch. Flower trumpet-shaped, a narrow throat opening to a
wide flare. Plant covered with lush, narrow, fir green leaves.
Endre Ostbo.   P.A. 1956.

```
        -fortunei 3/8
     -Fawn-    -dichroanthum 1/8
     -    -Fabia-
HELEN -        -griersonianum 1/8
LOUISE-          -griffithianum 1/8
     -       -Loderi-
     -Albatross-      -fortunei
               -fortunei ssp. discolor 1/4
```
A hybrid by P. Saunders.   C.A. 1972.

```
                     -racemosum 1/4
                 -unnamed hybrid-
HELEN SCOTT RICHEY-          -moupinense 1/4
                 -Cornell Pink--mucronulatum 1/2
```
2.5ft(.75m) -5F(-21C) VE 4/3 Fuchsine pink flowers lightly
spotted rose, 5-lobed, widely funnel-shaped, 1.25in(3.2cm) wide,
blooming at branch terminals holding up to 5 clusters of 2
flowers each.   Upright plant; leaves scaly below; bronze new
growth. R. W. Scott, reg. 1977.

HELEN WATERER   Parentage unknown
Red-edged flowers with white center. A parent of BARBARA

WALLACE.   J. Waterer, before 1890.

```
                    -fortunei ssp. discolor 1/4
          -unnamed hybrid-
HELEN WEBSTER-          -unknown 1/4
          -             -fortunei 1/4
          -Richard Gill-
                -thomsonii 1/4
```
Large trusses of widely bell-shaped flowers, phlox pink spotted
with orange-brown. Crown Lands. A.M. 1954.

```
          -fortunei ? 1/2
HELENE HUBER-
          -unknown 1/2
```
6ft(1.8m) -5F(-21C) ML Dark purplish pink buds opening medium
mauve pink, spotted almond shell brown, openly funnel-shaped,
3in(7.6cm) across, and very fragrant; spherical truss of 14-16.
Floriferous.   Plant upright, rounded,   Dexter cross; Swarthmore College & C. Herbert raisers; Herbert, reg. 1978.

HELENE SCHIFFNER   Parentage unknown
4ft(1.2m) -5F(-21C) M 4/4   Unusually dark buds open to pale
lilac-tinted flowers, becoming pure white with very faint yellowish to brown markings, held in upright, dome-shaped trusses.
Narrow leaves of deep mistletoe green, reddish stems.   Seidel.
F.C.C. 1893.   Color illus. VV p. 83.

```
             -decorum 1/4
     -unnamed hybrid-
HELIOS-          -fortunei ssp. discolor 1/4
     -           -fortunei 1/4
     -unnamed hybrid-          -wardii 1/8
               -unnamed hybrid-
                     -dichroanthum 1/8
```
3ft(.9m) -5F(-21C) ML Neyron rose buds opening Venetian pink,
shading to soft yellow. Flowers openly funnel-shaped, to 3.5in
(8.9cm) across; rounded trusses of 10.   Habit rounded; glossy,
green leaves held 3 years.   A. A. Raustein, reg. 1979.

```
                     -campylocarpum Elatum Gp.
HELLA'S FAVORITE---LETTY EDWARDS, selfed-            1/2
                     -fortunei 1/2
```
Flowers in balled truss of 10, vivid red in bud, opening pale
yellow. New growth greenish copper. Shrub 4ft(1.8m) x 6ft (20
yrs). Seed from U. of British Columbia; H. Vaartnou, reg. 1988.

```
               -dichroanthum 1/4
          -Fabia-
HELLO DOLLY-    -griersonianum 1/4
          -smirnowii 1/2
```
3ft(.9m) -10F(-23C) EM 3/3 Yellow flowers with warm tones of
orange and rose, 2.75in(7cm) wide; large calyx gives the effect
of a double. Plant well-branched; medium green leaves, beige
indumentum.   H. Lem cross; J. Elliott, reg. 1974. Color illus.
HG p. 138.

```
          -fortunei 1/2
HELLENIST-
          -unknown 1/2
```
Flowers pale cream, flushed pink. W. E. Glennie, reg. 1984.


```
          -fortunei 1/2
HELLOWEEN-
          -unknown 1/2
```
Flowers pale cream, flushed pink. W. E. Glennie, reg. 1984.

HELMA'S JOY---macabeanum, selfed
12ft(3.6m) x 12ft(22 yrs) 5F(-15C) VE   Flowers in trusses of
20-30, 8 smooth edged lobes, salmon orange buds open light
greenish yellow to pale yellow-green, reddish purple blotches.
Leaves held 3 years.   Brodick Castle seed; Vaartnou, reg. 1988.

```
          -catawbiense 3/8
     -Mrs. Milner-
HELMHOLTZ-     -unknown 3/8
     -          -caucasicum 1/4
     -Boule de Neige-          -catawbiense
               -hardy hybrid-
                     -unknown
```
Dark pink flowers, few markings. T. J. R. Seidel, before 1920.

```
                     -fortunei ssp. discolor 1/8
              -Lady
         -Jalisco-Bessborough-campylocarpum Elatum Group 1/8
         - Elect -      -dichroanthum 1/4
HENDRICK'S-    -Dido-
  PARK -            -decorum 1/8
      -       -fortunei 1/4
      -Fawn-         -dichroanthum
              -Fabia-
                      -griersonianum 1/8
```
6ft(1.8m) -10F(-23C) M   Very large trusses of 10-12 fragrant
flowers, Neyron rose with currant red throat. Plant upright,
well-branched; leaves 4in x 2in (10.2cm x 5cm), ivy green.
Del James cross; Hendrick's Park raiser; Ray James, reg. 1980.
Color illus. ARS J 41:2 (1987), p. 90.

```
               -catawbiense 1/2
HENRIETTE SARGENT-
               -unknown 1/2
```
5ft(1.5m) -25F(-32C) ML 2/3 Synonym HENRIETTA SARGENT. Huge
rounded truss of dark rose pink; similar to MRS. C. S. SARGENT,
but smaller, more compact, slower growing.   A. Waterer, 1891.
Color illus. VV p. 108.

```
               -dichroanthum 1/2
HENRY E. BURBRIDGE-        -campylocarpum Elatum Group 1/4
               -Letty Edwards-
                         -fortunei 1/4
```
Apricot yellow flowers.   Thacker, 1944.

```
               -wardii Litiense Group 1/2
HENRY R. YATES-
               -unknown 1/2
```
4ft(1.2m) -5F(-21C) E   Flowers 2.5in(6.4cm) across, creamy
ivory with a bold yellow flare, funnel-campanulate. Plant compact and dense; leaves to 6in(15.2cm) long. Gable, intro. 1958;
reg. 1971.   Color illus. K p. 136; LW pl. 57.

HENRY SHILSON--form of arboreum
A named, selected form with red flowers.   R. Gill, reg. 1958.

```
          -dalhousiae 1/2
HENRYANUM-
          -formosum 1/2
```
White flowers, tinged blush pink.   Shown by Henry, 1862; perhaps related to Prof. Augustine Henry of Dublin.   F.C.C. 1865.

HENRY'S RED   Parentage: catawbiense red seedling x unknown
3ft(.9m) x 2ft(.6m) -20F(-29C) ML   An ironclad hybrid; deep
red flowers, 12-15 per truss, on a bush of open habit. Mezitt
cross; Weston Nurseries, reg. 1987.


```
            -arboreum 1/2
HER MAJESTY-         -veitchianum 1/4
            -Fosterianum-
                    -edgeworthii 1/4
```
Soft crimson flowers.   Veitch.   F.C.C. 1889.

* *
```
     -haematodes 1/2
HERA-    -williamsianum 1/4
   -Jock-
         -griersonianum 1/4
```
Flowers of scarlet red.   Lord Aberconway, 1941.
ELFIN HILL   Parentage as above, except reversed
1ft(.3m) 0F(-18C) EM   Flowers of China rose to 1.75in(3.8cm)
wide, funnel-campanulate. Compact plant, as broad as tall, dark
green, oval leaves.   Vernon Wyatt, reg. 1968.
LITTLE MINX   Parentage as HERA, above
Flat dwarf plant, very slow-growing: 2in(5cm) x 6in(15cm), in 10
years. Flowers Tyrian rose, funnel-shaped; loose trusses of 6.
Wyatt, reg. 1966.
* *

HERBERT MITCHELL--form of cerasinum K W 6923
3ft(.9m) -5F(-21C) EM 4/4   Raised by the Countess of Rosse,
Nymans Garden, reg. 1973.   A.M. 1973.

HERBERT PARSONS   See PRESIDENT LINCOLN
```

---

```
            -catawbiense var. album Glass--Catalgla
   -Gosh-   -decorum?
   -Darn-   -Caroline-
  -All -   -Mrs. H. R. Yates-   -brachycarpum?
  -East-   -unknown
  -    -   -Mrs. H. R. Yates (as above)
  - -unnamed hybrid-
HERE'S-   -wardii
HOWE -   -brachycarpum
  -      -unnamed-   -wardii
  -      - hybrid-Crest-   -fortunei ssp. discolor
  -       -   -Lady -
  -Marypat-   Bessborough-campylocarpum Elatum
  -
  -                   -catawbiense var. album
  -      -unnamed hybrid-
  -Monte-   -Crest (as above)
  Carlo-   -aureum
         -unnamed hybrid-
                      -campylocarpum
```
Note:  GOSH DARN = (CATALGLA x MRS. H. R. YATES) selfed
Light greenish yellow buds open to flowers pale greenish yellow;
dorsal spots moderate orange; open flowers are flat.   W. Delp.

```
                     -griffithianum 1/8
           -Dawn's Delight-
   -Break of Day-   -unknown 1/8
HERGA-   -dichroanthum 1/4
   -              -fortunei ssp. discolor 1/4
   -Lady Bessborough-
                   -campylocarpum Elatum Group 1/4
```
Pale yellow flower with a dark throat in May.  Rothschild, 1940.

* * * * * * * * * * * * * * * * * * * * * * * * * * * * *
```
          -Kaiser Wilhelm--unknown
HERMANN-
      -Agnes--unknown
```
Bright, light carmine red flowers.   Seidel intro. c. 1916.
HOMER   Parentage as above
Parent of ROYAL PINK and others.   Intense pure pink  with faint
red-brown marks.  Two forms; one more hardy.   Seidel, 1916.
* * * * * * * * * * * * * * * * * * * * * * * * * * * * *

```
                -degronianum ssp. heptamereum (metternichii)
HERMANN NITZSCHNER-   1/2
                -catawbiense 1/2
```
Salmon pink flowers and greenish yellow markings.  Named for the
Head Gardener at Grungrabschen.   T. J. R. Seidel.

```
            -caucasicum 1/2
HERMANN SEIDEL-
            -unknown 1/2
```
Frilled flowers, light carmine red.   Seidel, before 1926.

```
                 -degronianum ssp. heptamereum (metternichii)
            -Eidam-   1/4
HERMANN SEIDEL-   -Alexander Adie--unknown 1/4
            -williamsianum 1/2
```
Bright rose flowers in umbels of 10-12.   Dietrich Hobbie, 1952.

```
   -Diadema--unknown 3/4
HERME-   -catawbiense 1/4
     -Everestianum-
                -unknown
```
Light purplish violet, with yellowish green markings. Named for
Frau Hermine Seidel.   T. J. R. Seidel, cross 1912.

```
     -dichroanthum ssp. apodectum 1/2
HERMES-   -fortunei ssp. discolor 1/4
     -Lady Bessborough-
                  -campylocarpum Elatum Group 1/4
```
Bell-shaped flowers,  chrome yellow with pink markings, in loose
trusses. Plant below average height, but spreading and compact.
Rothschild, 1940.

```
          -thomsonii 1/4
     -Gilian-
HERMIONE-   -griffithianum 1/4
     -arboreum 1/2
```
Flowers of blood red.   E. J. P. Magor, 1935.   A.M. 1941.
```

```
                -yakushimanum 1/2
HERMIONE KNIGHT-        -elliottii 1/4
            -Fusilier-
                    -griersonianum 1/4
```
Flowers strong rose red, shaded light orchid pink, fading paler
pink, cardinal red markings mainly on dorsal lobes; truss of 10.
Oblanceolate leaves, 4.3in(11cm) long; gold buff indumentum when
young. Blooms in May. E. de Rothschild, cross 1980; reg. 1988.

```
        -catawbiense 1/2
HERO-
    -Gloria Gandavensis, white form--unknown 1/2
```
Pure white with olive green markings.   T. J. R. Seidel, 1915.

```
                    -haematodes 1/8
            -May Day-
    -unnamed hybrid-        -griersonianum 1/8
HERTHA-            -wardii 1/4
    -insigne 1/2
```
Red flowers in truss of 7-8; 7 or 8 lobes. J. Bruns, reg. 1985.

```
                    -adenogynum 1/4
        -Xenosporum (detonsum)-
HESPERIA-                -unknown 3/4
        -Empress Eugenie--unknown
```
E. J. P. Magor, cross 1921.

```
            -fortunei ssp. discolor 1/4
        -Ayah-
HESPERIDES-    -facetum (eriogynum) 1/4
        -griersonianum 1/2
```
A tall, compact plant; rose pink flowers held in full trusses in
June at Exbury.   Rothschild, 1940. A.M. 1988.

```
                -campanulatum 1/4
    -Constant Nymph-            -ponticum 3/8
HESS-            -Purple Splendour-
    -                -ponticum  -unknown 3/8
    -Purple Splendour-
                -unknown
```
Crossed by Donald Waterer, 1947; Knap Hill, intro. 1975.

```
                        -dichroanthum
            -Goldsworth Orange-
    -Tortoiseshell-            -fortunei ssp. discolor 1/8
HESTIA-  Wonder    -griersonianum 1/4
    -Goliath--unknown 1/2
```
Trusses hold 11-16 flowers 3.2in(8cm) wide, cardinal red in bud,
opening Neyron rose, with bronze yellow blotch and bronze dorsal
spots. Res. Sta. for Woody Nursery Crops, Boskoop, reg. 1983.

HETHERSETT   Described under ROYAL FLUSH, q.v.

* *
```
            -brachycarpum 1/4
    -unnamed-        -wardii 1/8
    - hybrid-Crest-        -fortunei ssp. discolor 1/16
HI DRAMA-            -Lady Bess-
    -                borough  -campylocarpum Elatum Gp. 1/16
    -                -maximum 1/4
    -Stokes Bronze Wings-
                -catawbiense 1/4
```
Buds of pale purplish pink, open to white flowers with moderate
red dorsal spotting; pale yellow throat. W. Delp.
SKEETER HILL   Parentage as above
Flowers a blend of yellows. Plant of medium size, hardy to -15F
(-26C). Delp.
* *

(This entry out of alpha order.)
```
            -minus Carolinianum Group, tetraploid form 1/2
    -unnamed-
    - hybrid-fastigiatum 5/16
HI TECH-    -minus Carolinianum Group, tetraploid form
    -unnamed-                -intricatum 1/16
        hybrid-        -Intrifast-
        -Blue Diamond-        -fastigiatum
                -augustinii 1/8
```
Buds of strong purple open to strong and light purple.   Delp.

```
                    -griffithianum 7/64
        -Jean Marie de Montague-
    -Fireman Jeff-        -unknown 13/64
    -            -haematodes 1/16
    -        -Grosclaude-
    -            -facetum (eriogynum) 1/16
    -Tom-            -catawbiense 1/32
    -Ring-        -Parsons Grandi--
    -M.D.-    -America- florum    -unknown
    -    -unnamed-    -dark red hybrid--unknown
    -    - hybrid-        -griffithianum
HI-            -Mars-
LEVEL-  -Anna-    -Blaze-    -unknown
    -    Delp-        -catawbiense var. rubrum 1/32
    -        -Mars (as above)
    -    -Red Brave-    -unknown
    -            -America (as above)
    -catawbiense var. album Glass--Catalgla 1/2
```
Buds of deep and moderate reds open to flowers of deep and light
purplish pinks, dorsal spots moderate red.   Flowers fully hose-
in-hose. W. Delp.

HI TECH   Listed out of order; see previous column

```
                -williamsianum 1/4
        -Adrastia-
HIAWATHA-        -neriiflorum 1/4
        -griersonianum 1/2
```
Flowers of carmine red.   Lord Aberconway, 1941.

```
                -dichroanthum 1/4
        -Fabia-
HIGH CURLEY-    -griersonianum 1/2
    -            -griersonianum
    -unnamed hybrid-        -fortunei ssp. discolor
            -unnamed hybrid-            1/8
                -unknown 1/8
```
Flowers of light primrose yellow.   Waterer & Crisp, reg. 1975.

HIGH FLIER--form of vesiculiferum K W 10952
5ft(1.5m) 5F(-15C) EM 3/3 Loose trusses of 10-12 flowers, 5-
lobed, ruby red, outside strongly flushed magenta. Leaves to 7
in(17.8cm) long, covered with reddish-tipped, glandular hairs.
Kingdon Ward collector; Crown Estate, reg. 1968.   A.M. 1968.

* *
```
                -caucasicum 1/8
        -Dr. Stocker-
    -Damaris-        -griffithianum 1/8
HIGH GOLD-    -campylocarpum 1/4
    -    -wardii 1/4
    -Crest-        -fortunei ssp. discolor 1/8
        -Lady Bessborough-
                -campylocarpum Elatum Group 1/8
```
5ft(1.5m) -5F(-21C) M 4/4 Deep, bright, true lemon yellow.
Flowers large, open-faced, held in big trusses. Vigorous plant
with excellent branching habit; leaves bright apple green. John
Eichelser, intro. 1982.
LEMONADE   Parentage as above
6ft(1.8m) -5F(-21C) M 4/4 Bright yellow flowers, beautifully
textured. Attractive habit and foliage. Eichelser.
* *


```
            -yakushimanum 1/2
HIGH SOCIETY-
    -dichroanthum ssp. scyphocalyx 1/2
```
Flowers in truss of 14, vivid red, lobes mature to strong pink,
tube pale yellowish pink. Leaves with moderate orange-yellow
indumentum. Compact, slow-growing bush. Mrs. J. E. Keeley, NZ,
reg. 1987.

HIGH SUMMER   Described under ROMY, q.v.


```
            -yakushimanum 1/2
HIGHFIELD CREAM-
        -unknown 1/2
```
Flowers in truss of 9, mimosa yellow fading to pale cream. Mrs.
R. J. Coker, NZ, cross; Mrs. J. S. Clyne, reg. 1979.

```
                        -souliei 1/16
                  -Soulbut-
            -Vanessa-          -fortunei--Sir Charles Butler 1/16
        -Adonis-        -griersonianum
        -       -        -griffithianum 1/8
HIGHLANDER-      -Sunrise-
        -               -griersonianum 1/4
        -arboreum ssp. zeylanicum 1/2
Rose red flowers.  Lord Aberconway, 1950.
```

HIGHLIGHT   Parentage unknown
Trusses of up to 27 red flowers.   Glennie, reg. 1980.

* *
```
                        -griffithianum 1/8
                  -Queen Wilhelmina-
        -Earl of Athlone-          -unknown 3/8
HIGHNOON-             -Stanley Davies--unknown
        -       -dichroanthum 1/4
        -Fabia-
             -griersonianum 1/4
```
Bright waxy red flowers, loose truss. Plant very slow-growing;
sprawling habit. Rudolph Henny, reg. 1958.
POW WOW   Parentage as above
Bright waxy red flower; a large convex calyx. Henny, reg. 1958.
RED TAPE   Parentage as above
Clear bright red flowers.   Henny cross, 1944; reg. 1958.
SUNSET   Parentage as above
Flowers of red, with a white stripe down each lobe. Decumbent
branching; very straggly plant.   Henny, cross 1944; reg. 1958.
* *

HILARIA   Parentage unknown
Flowers deep crimson.   Magor, reg. 1963.

HILL AYAH   Described under AYAH, q.v.

HILLCREST   Parentage unknown
5ft(1.5m) -5F(-21C) ML 3/3   Strong red flowers, tight truss,
conspicuous anthers. Compact, rounded habit.   Esch and Briggs.

```
                  -forrestii Repens Group 1/4
            -Elizabeth-
HILL'S BRIGHT-      -griersonianum 1/4
   RED      -         -elliottii 1/4
          -Kilimanjaro-         -Moser's Maroon--unk. 1/8
                    -Dusky Maid-
                       -fortunei ssp. discolor 1/8
```
3ft(.9m) OF(-18C) EM 3/4   Flowers vibrant red on red stems;
leaves green with deeper veining. Hill.

```
                  -haematodes 1/2
HILL'S LOW RED-
                  -yakushimanum 1/2
```
2ft(.6m) -5F(-21C) M 4/4   Flowers dark red; leaves with very
heavy indumentum. Hill.

```
        -Chesterland--unknown 1/2
HILLSDALE-
        -fortunei 1/2
```
4ft(1.2m) -25F(-32C) M   Tall conical trusses of about 18 flowers, light Neyron rose, prominent spotting of chartreuse green.
Plant upright, rounded; leaves 5.75in(14.5cm) long, glossy dark
green, held 3 years. Plant resistant to disease and insects,
heat-tolerant. The only registered hybrid rhododendron by this
prolific hybridizer before his tragic death. Dr. H. Schroeder
cross; Stephen Schroeder, intro. 1976; reg. 1983.

HIMALAYAN CHILD   Described under HODCONERI, q.v.

HIMALAYAN STORM   Parentage unknown
5ft(1.5m) -5F(-21C) M   Large white flowers, with pinkish hue.
Origin unknown.

HINDSIGHT   Described under GAY DAY, q.v.

(Next entry entered out of order.)
HO EMMA--form of degronianum ssp. heptamereum (metternichii)
3ft(.9m) -15F(-26C) EM 4/4   Trusses of 15 flowers, 7-lobed,
white, flushed light fuchsia purple, with stronger veinal color
of deep fuchsia purple; upper throat spotted ruby red. Leaves
with felted indumentum. R. N. S. Clarke, reg. 1976. A.M. 1976.

```
                  -maximum 1/4
        -unnamed-          -dichroanthum 1/8
        - hybrid-Goldsworth Orange-
        -                  -fortunei ssp. discolor 1/8
HINDUSTAN-               -catawbiense 1/16
        -          -Parsons Grandiflorum-
        -    -America-        -unknown 9/32
        -unnamed-      -dark red hybrid--unknown
          hybrid-      -forrestii Repens Group 1/8
            -Gertrud-
             Schäle-          -ponticum 1/32
                        -Michael-
                  -Prometheus-Waterer-unknown
                        -
                  -Monitor--unknown
```
6ft(1.8m) -20F(-29C) M 4/4 Flowers of good substance, orange
-buff flushed soft pink (garden effect is orange), 3in(7.6cm)
across; dome-shaped truss of 17.   Leaves 5.25in(1.3cm) x 2.5in.
(6.4cm); plant as broad as tall.   D. G. Leach, reg. 1983.

HIP HIP ARRAY   Described under BIG SPLASH, q.v.


```
        -hippophaeoides 1/2
HIPSAL-
        -saluense 1/2
```
Flowers purplish mauve.   E. J. P. Magor, 1926.


```
            -haematodes 1/2
HIRAETHLYN-
            -griffithianum 1/2
```
Flowers are rose to deep red.   Lord Aberconway, intro. 1933.

HIS LORDSHIP--form of aberconwayi
3ft(.9m) 5F(-15C) EM 4/3   White flowers, saucer-shaped, with
red spotting.   Crown Estate, Windsor, reg. 1962.   A.M. 1945.

HISPANIOLA   Listed under INFANTA, q.v.

HJALMAR L. LARSON   Described under SPUN GOLD, q.v.

HO EMMA   Entered in previous column; out of order

HOCKESSIN   Described under BRANDYWINE, q.v.

* *
```
        -hodgsonii 1/2
HODCONERI-
        -falconeri 1/2
```
Cross by Reuthe, 1926.
HIMALAYAN CHILD   Parentage as above
Loose trusses hold 28 to-30 flowers, rhodamine purple with darker staining; small blotch of ruby red in the throat. Leaves to
11in(28cm) long, silvery brown indumentum. Grown from K W 13681
as sinogrande. Crown Estate, Windsor, reg. 1982. A.M. 1981.
* *

HOKKAIDO--form of dauricum
4ft(1.2m) -25F(-32C) EM 4/3   Very hardy, flowering species
with trusses of 2; white, faint green markings on dorsal lobe.
Leaves scaly. Blooms a month later than other strains. Intro.
to the US by W. Berg, to the UK by Cox; reg. 1979. A.M. 1979.

```
        -Alexander Adie--unknown 3/4
HOLBEIN-          -catawbiense 1/4
        -Carl Mette-
                -unknown
```
Ruby pink with faint reddish brown markings on light background;
wavy margins.   T. J. R. Seidel, cross 1906; intro. 1918.

HOLDEN   Described under CHEER, q.v.

HOLGER   Described under GUDRUN, q.v.

HOLKER HALL--form of arboreum
Flowering tree growing at Holker Hall in 1983; reg. 1958.

```
                        -griffithianum 1/4
        -Irene Stead---Loderi, selfed-
HOLMESLEE-                  -fortunei 1/4
BARNDANCE-
        -M30 seedling--unknown 1/2
```
Trusses of 9-10 flowers, 7- or 8-lobed, chartreuse green in bud,

opens white, dawn pink flush; fragrant. G. Holmes, reg. 1984.

```
                      -griffithianum 1/8
              -George Hardy-
        -Pink Pearl-           -catawbiense 3/8
HOLLANDIA-    -        -        -arboreum 1/8
        -         -Broughtonii-
        -         -        -unknown 3/8
        -                   -catawbiense
        -Charles Dickens-          (John Street calls C. D.
                  -unknown        an "arboreum hybrid")
```
6ft(1.8m) OF(-18C) ML 3/3 Plant with attractive foliage, and vibrant red flowers. L. J. Endtz, before 1958.   Color illus. F p. 48; JS p. 75.

HOLMESLEE BARNDANCE   See previous column

HOLMESLEE BRIGHT LIGHTS   Parentage unknown
Flowers of reddish purple. Graham Holmes, reg. 1979.

```
                            -griffithianum 1/8
                  -Coombe Royal-
        -Mrs. G. W. Leak-          -unknown 3/4
HOLMESLEE FLAIR-      -           -caucasicum 1/8
        -unknown     -Chevalier Felix-
                     de Sauvage    -unknown
```
Truss of 16 flowers, 5-lobed, phlox pink in bud, opens lighter, red flare and spots on upper lobe. A. G. Holmes, reg. 1982.

HOLMESLEE GREENEYES   Parentage unknown
Flowers reddish purple, fading white. A. G. Holmes, reg. 1982.

```
        -unknown       -dichroanthum
HOLMESLEE MISSIE-   -Fabia-
        -C. I. S.-    -griersonianum
            - Loder's White, q. v. for 2 possible
                            parentage diagrams
```
Flower buds cream, overlaid dawn pink, opening to Naples yellow flushed pink, red in throat. A. G. Holmes, reg. 1982.

```
                        -griffithianum 1/4
                  -Loderi-
        -Waxeye-        -fortunei 3/8
        -       -unknown 1/4
HOLMESLEE OPAL-     -fortunei--Sir Charles Butler
        -Van Nes -
        Sensation-          -maximum 1/8
              -Halopeanum-
                          -griffithianum
```
Trusses of 12-18 flowers, white with tinge of very light Neyron rose. A. G. Holmes, reg. 1982.

```
              -unknown 1/2
HOLMESLEE SUNRISE-      -decorum 1/4
        -Little Pudding-    -dichroanthum 1/8
                        -Fabia-
                          -griersonianum 1/8
```
Trusses of 7 flowers, medium spinel red, fading to cream in the upper lobe. A. G. Holmes, reg. 1982.

HOLMESLEE TRIUMPH   Described under HELEN HOLMES, q.v.

```
              -catawbiense 1/2
        -Humboldt-
HOLSTEIN-    -unknown 1/2
        -              -catawbiense
        -Catawbiense Grandiflorum-
                          -unknown
```
Flowers in trusses of 15-16, 5-lobed, lilac purple, shading paler in center, dark red blotch. Leaves oval and sparsely hairy. Hachmann cross; Stück, reg. 1983.

```
                  -fortunei ssp. discolor 1/4
        -King of Shrubs-    -dichroanthum 1/8
HOLY MOSES-          -Fabia-
        -                -griersonianum 1/8
        -Souvenir of Anthony Waterer--unknown 1/2
```
4ft(1.2m) -5F(-21C) ML 4/4   Above parentage uncertain; another parent may be smirnowii. Flowers orange and yellow bicolor. Exceptional foliage, similar to smirnowii. Halfdan Lem.

```
                -catawbiense album Glass--Catalgla 1/8
        -Gosh Darn-              -decorum ? 1/16
                -                   -Caroline-
        -unnamed-    -Mrs. H.R.Yates-    -brachycarpum ?
        - hybrid-          -unknown 1/8        3/16
        -        -unnamed-Mrs. H.R. Yates (as above)
HOLY -   hybrid-
TOLEDO-        -wardii 3/16
        -          -brachycarpum
        -   -unnamed-    -wardii
        -unnamed- hybrid-Crest-      -fortunei ssp.
          hybrid-        -Lady Bessborough-  discolor 1/32
          -          -yakushimanum  -campylocarpum Elatum
              -Serendipity-      1/8              1/32
                  -aureum (chrysanthum) 1/8
```
Buds of deep and moderate pinks, open to large frilly flowers of pale yellow green, spotted brilliant greenish yellow.   Delp.

HOMER   Described under HERMANN, q.v.

HOMESTEAD   Described under SCARLET KING, q.v.

```
        -wardii 1/2
HONEY-    -Corona--unknown 1/4
        -Bow Bells-
              -williamsianum 1/4
```
Flowers of Egyptian buff fading paler, 3.5in(8.9cm) wide. Plant 1ft(.3m) x 3ft(.9m) across; leaves 2.5in(6.4cm) broad, orbicular. Rudolph Henny, 1960; reg. 1962.

```
                  -wardii 1/4
              -Hawk-
        -   -Lady       -fortunei ssp. discolor 1/8
HONEY (Slocock)-    Bessborough-
        -          -campylocarpum Elatum Group 1/8
        -   -wightii 1/4
        -China-
              -fortunei 1/4
```
A vigorous plant, growing to 5ft(1.5m) x 5ft.   Flowers of clear yellow, opening with a pink flush, in large trusses.   Slocock. H.C. 1975.

```
            -hanceanum 1/2
HONEY BEE-
            -ludlowii 1/2
```
1ft(.3m) OF(-18C) EM 4/5 Bell-shaped flowers, creamy yellow. Bronze new growth; small foliage, dark green. Warren Berg.

HONEY DEW   Parentage unknown
Synonyms DEXTER'S HONEYDEW, HONEYDEW. A parent of BLUSH BUTTON, FRAN LABERA, MARJIE KAY HINERMAN, TRUE LOVE. Flowers colored apricot.   C. O. Dexter, before 1943.

HONEY GLOW   Described under GILDED GOWN, q.v.

HONEY WOOD--form of trichanthum
6ft(1.8m) -5F(-21C) L 2/3   Flowers in clusters of 3, widely funnel-shaped, 5-lobed, spectrum violet, outside light cyclamen purple. Elliptic leaves of medium size, both sides covered with scattered brown indumentum. Tower Court raiser; Maj. A. Hardy, reg. 1970.   P.C. 1969.   A.M. 1971.

```
                -wardii 1/4
        -Carolyn Grace-
HONEYDEW-        -unknown 1/4
        -        -campylocarpum 1/4
        -Moonstone-
                  -williamsianum 1/4
```
4ft(1.2m) 5F(-15C) M 3/4   A compact, rounded plant. Flowers sunny yellow like MOONSTONE, to 4in(10cm) wide; trusses of 5-7. Art Wright, reg. 1962.

* *
```
                  -wardii, Barto form
        -unnamed hybrid-      -A. W. Hardy Hybrid--unknown
HONEYMOON-          -Devonshire-          1/8
        -          Cream   -campylocarpum 1/8
        -wardii (as croceum) 3/4
```
4ft(1.2m) 5F(-15C) M 4/4   Compact plant; heavy, dark green foliage, held 3 years. Chartreuse green buds open to pale chartreuse yellow with dull orange blotch; about 14 per domed truss. Plant rounded, wide as tall. Whitney cross; Sathers, reg. 1976.

SECOND HONEYMOON   Parentage as above
4ft(1.2m) 5F(-15C) M 4/3   Yellow flowers with a red blotch.
Later flowering season than HONEYMOON.   W. Whitney cross.
* *

```
              -catawbiense var. album Glass--Catalgla 1/2
HONG KONG-      -wardii 1/4
         -Crest-
              -Lady      -fortunei ssp. discolor 1/8
              -Bessborough-
                    -campylocarpum Elatum Group 1/8
```
7ft(2.1m) -20F(-29C) EM 4/4   A big, vigorous plant, large
light yellow flowers, marked with a red flare in the throat, and
presented in informal, asymmetrical clusters. Plant wider than
tall; leaves glossy yellow-green. D. G. Leach, reg. 1983.

```
                    -fortunei ssp. discolor 1/8
              -Lady -
         -Jalisco-Bessborough-campylocarpum Elatum Group 1/8
         -Eclipse-     -dichroanthum 1/8
HONITON-     -Dido-
         -          -decorum 1/8
         -            -catawbiense 1/4
         -Album Elegans-
                    -unknown 1/4
```
Strong, open-growing plant; flowers cream-colored, flushed pink,
with a red eye. Knap Hill, reg. 1968.

HONORÉ HACANSON   Described under FRED ROBBINS, q.v.

```
         -keiskei--Yaku Fairy 1/2
HONSU'S BABY-
         -speciferum 1/2
```
15in(.4m) x 28in(.7m) 5F(-15C) E White flowers with pale purplish pink margins from buds strong purplish pink; conical truss
of 4. Leaves convex, scaly. Dr. H. Spady, reg. 1987. Color
illus. ARS J 44:1 (1990), p. 3.

HOOPSKIRT   Described under BABY BONNET, q.v.

```
         -lindleyi 1/2
HOPE BRAAFLADT-      -ciliatum 1/4
         -Countess of Haddington-
                    -dalhousiae 1/4
```
3ft(.9m) 20F(-7C) E 4/3   White flowers 3.25in(8.3cm) wide,
a dull lavender blotch and faint stripes, in lax trusses of 15.
Plant with willowy branches; yellow-green leaves to 3.75in (9.5
cm), golden brown scales, held 2-3 years. Braafladt, reg. 1979.

```
                    -griffithianum 3/16
              -Loderi-
         -unnamed-      -fortunei 1/8
         - hybrid-                    -griffithianum
HOPE  -        -      -Queen Wilhelmina-
FINDLAY-    -Earl of-            -unknown 3/16
         -    -Athlone-Stanley Davies--unknown
         -              -griersonianum 1/4
         -Creeping Jenny-
              -forrestii Repens Group 1/4
```
5ft(1.5m) -10F(-23C) EM   Plant vigorous, spreading, compact;
dark green, glossy leaves. Flowers currant red, funnel-shaped,
about 2.5in(6.4cm) wide, 8-10 in globular, lax truss. Windsor
Great Park. A.M. 1979.

```
              -neriiflorum 1/4
         -F. C. Puddle-
HOPEFUL-      -griersonianum 1/4
         -hookeri 1/2
```
A red-flowered hybrid. Lord Aberconway, intro. 1946.

HOPPY   Described under PINK CHERUB, q.v.

Next entry out of order.

```
                         -griffithianum 1/8
                    -Queen Wilhelmina-
              -Britannia-            -unknown 5/16
         -unnamed-      -Stanley Davies--unknown
         - hybrid-yakushimanum 1/2      -griffithianum
HORIZON -                        -George-
SNOWBIRD-      -Mrs. Lindsay Smith- Hardy-catawbiense 1/16
         -unnamed-            -Duchess of
         hybrid-yakushimanum      Edinburgh--unknown
```

3ft(.9m) x 4ft(1.2m) OF(-18C)   Flowers in trusses of 18. Buds
strong purplish pink, opening yellowish white, then snowy white;
pink filaments. Rounded bush. Dr. E. Brockenbrough, reg. 1989.

```
                         -dichroanthum 1/8
         -Goldsworth Orange-
         -Hotei-      -fortunei ssp. discolor 1/16
         -    -            -souliei 1/16
         -    -unnamed hybrid-
         -Nancy-            -wardii 1/16
         -Evans-      -dichroanthum
         -    -Dido-
         -    -      -decorum 1/16
         -    -Lem's-            -griffithianum 19/64
         -    Cameo-   -Norman-Beauty of-
HORIZON-      -  Gill - Tremough-arboreum 3/64
MONARCH-      -Anna-   -griffithianum
         -    -            -griffithianum
         -         -Jean Marie de Montague-
         -    -Anna-(as above)            -unknown 7/32
         -Point  -            -griffithianum
         Defiance-      -George-
              -Marinus Koster- Hardy-catawbiense 1/16
              -red hybrid--unknown
```
6ft(1.8m) x 6ft(7 yrs) 10F(-12C) M   Flowers held in trusses
of 15, of very heavy substance; red buds open pale greenish yellow, with small vivid red flare. E. Brockenbrough, reg. 1989.

HORIZON SNOWBIRD   See previous column

```
              -griffithianum 1/4
         -unnamed hybrid-
HORSHAM-            -unknown 3/4
         -Monsieur Thiers--unknown
```
Deep red flowers. C. B. van Nes & Sons, before 1922.

```
              -griffithianum 3/8
         -Mars-
HOT DAWN-      -unknown 3/8
         -            -yakushimanum, Exbury form 1/4
         -unnamed hybrid-   -griffithianum
              -Mars-
                    -unknown
```
4ft(1.2m) x 2.7ft(.8m)(12 yrs) -15F(-26C) ML   Vivid purplish
red flowers, 5 very wavy-edged lobes; truss of 16-22. Upright,
open bush, very floriferous. Dr. J. Brueckner, reg. 1989.

```
                    -smirnowii 1/8
              -unnamed hybrid-
         -Cherry-      -yakushimanum 3/8
         - Crisp-            -sanguineum ssp. didymum 1/16
         -    -      -Carmen-
         -    -Little Gem-      -forrestii Repens Group 1/16
HOT  -      -elliottii 1/8
DIGGETY-      -yakushimanum            -cataw.
         -    -unnamed-      -Parsons Grandiflorum-
         -    - hybrid-   -America-            -unk.
         -    -    -      -dark red hybrid--unknown
         -    -    -Cindy-            -griffithianum 1/64
         -Mitch-    Lou -      -Mars-
         -            -unnamed hyb.-   -unknown 1/8
         -                  -cataw. var. rubrum 1/32
         -            -yakushimanum
         -unnamed hybrid-            -catawbiense 5/64
                    -Henriette Sargent-
                          -unknown
```
Buds vivid red and currant red, open to flowers of same. Delp.

```
                         -catawbiense 1/16
              -Parsons -
         -America- Grandiflorum-unknown 9/32
         -unnamed-      -dark red hybrid--unknown
         - hybrid-            -griffithianum 3/32
         -    -      -Mars-
         -Cindy-    -Blaze-      -unknown
         - Lou -            -catawbiense, red form 1/16
         -    -      -Mars (as above)
HOT HANDS-    -Red Brave-
         -            -America (as above)
         -                  -dichroanthum 1/4
         -Goldsworth Orange-
                    -fortunei ssp. discolor 1/4
```

Buds of currant red and vivid red; flowers almost the same, with ruby red dorsal spots; dark red anthers and stigma. W. Delp.

HOT PANTS   See OOH-LA-LA under PIROUETTE

```
                  -sanguineum ssp. didymum 1/4
          -Carmen-
          -       -forrestii Repens Group 1/4
HOT STUFF-                        -griffithianum 1/16
          -            -Queen Wilhelmina-
          -  -Britannia-              -unknown 3/16
          -Leo-      -Stanley Davies--unknown
                -elliottii 1/4
```
2ft(.6m) 5F(-15C) M 3/4   Waxy, deep red flowers on a small plant. Leaves very dark green, highly polished. Plant of good habit; strong branches. H. E. Greer, intro. 1982.

```
                  -catawbiense var. album Glass--Catalgla 1/4
        -Fireball-        -haematodes 3/16
        -        -Choremia-
        -                   -arboreum 1/8       -griffithianum 7/64
HOT     -          -Jean Marie de Montague-
TARGET- -Fireman-              -unknown 13/64
        -   - Jeff -       -haematodes
        -      -Grosclaude-
        -      -            -facetum (eriogynum) 1/16
        -Firefox-                        -catawbiense
        -              -Parsons Grandi-       1/32
        -        -America- florum     -unknown
        -   -unnamed-      -dark red hybrid--unknown
        -   - hybrid-          -griffithianum
        -Anna-      -Mars-
        Delp-   -Blaze-   -unknown
        -         -catawbiense var. rubrum 1/32
        -           -Mars (as above
          -Red Brave-
                -America (as above)
```
Buds of cardinal red open to frilled flowers of vivid red; dorsal spots cardinal red; white filaments. W. Delp.

```
                          -catawbiense 1/8
        -Parsons Grandiflorum-
        -America-      -unknown 1/2
-Vivacious-   -dark red hybrid--unknown
-        -          -griersonianum 1/8-arboreum 1/32
-    -Dr. Ross-   -Doncaster-
-        -Borde-       -unknown
-        Hill-       -griffithianum 3/32
HOT -           -Mrs. A.M.-
TOPIC-           Williams-unknown
-                        -catawbiense
-        -Parsons Grandiflorum-
-    -America-      -unknown
-    -   -dark red hybrid--unknown
-Cindy Lou-     -griffithianum
-          -Mars-
-unnamed hybrid-  -unknown
        -catawbiense var. rubrum 1/8
```
Buds of dark red and vivid red, open to vivid red flowers edged lightly with dark red; filaments strong red. W. Delp.

HOT WONDER   Described under DELICIOUS, q.v.

```
                -dichroanthum 1/4
    -Goldsworth Orange-
HOTEI-            -fortunei ssp. discolor 1/4
    -              -souliei 1/4
    -unnamed hybrid-
              -wardii 1/4
```
3ft(.9m) 5F(-15C) M 5/4 Flower canary yellow, darker throat, open-capanulate, 2.5in(6.4cm) wide, 6-lobed; spherical trusses hold 12. Compact plant; narrowly elliptic dark green leaves to 4.75in(12cm) long. K. Sifferman cross; Ben Nelson, reg. 1969. P.A. 1964. A.M. 1974. Color illus. ARS Q 31:1 (1977), p. 35; HG p. 138; K p. 120.

HOTSHOT   Described under CAPTAIN JACK, q.v.

HUBERT ROBERT   Described under CAROLINE SPENCER, q.v.

* *
```
        -minus Carolinianum Group, white 1/2
HUDSON BAY-
        -dauricum, white 1/2
```
3ft(.9m) -20F(-29C) E   Terminal flower clusters of 3-4, each 3-flowered; white flower 1.75in(4.5cm) wide, 5 wavy lobes; plant broad, rounded, well-branched. Glossy yellow-green leaves with rusty brown scales beneath, held 2 years. D. Leach, reg. 1983.
YUKON   Parentage as above
5ft(1.5m) -20F(-29C) E 4/3   White flowers, margins flushed lilac pink, aging white; dome-shaped terminal clusters. Glossy yellowish green leaves, tan scales below. Leach, reg. 1983.
* *

```
              -forrestii Repens Group 1/2
HUGTIGHT-
        -aureum 1/2
```
2ft(.6m) OF(-18C) EM 4/4   Double peony-type flower, dark rose. Compact habit; small foliage, dark green. Larson cross; Fisher introduced.

```
                  -griffithianum 1/4
    -George Hardy-
    -          -catawbiense 1/4
HUGH KOSTER-              -arboreum 1/8
    -        -Doncaster-
    -unnamed hybrid-      -unknown 3/8
              -unknown
```
6ft(1.8m) 5F(-15C) ML 2/3 Medium-sized, fine crimson flower, lighter in center; truss rounded. Upright and spreading growth; grooved leaves. M. Koster, 1915. A.M. 1933.

```
            -unknown 3/4
HUGO CASCIOLA-          -ponticum 1/4
        -Purple Splendour-
                  -unknown
```
2.5ft(.75m) OF(-18C) M Ball-shaped trusses of 10-15 flowers, medium reddish purple, lighter margins, a large flare of Indian orange on dorsal lobe, openly funnel-shaped, 3.25in(8.3cm) across, 5-6 wavy lobes. Plant wider than tall; narrow leaves 5in(12.7cm) long, held 3 years. Paul Holden, reg. 1981.

```
            -forrestii Repens Group 1/2
HUGTIGHT-
        -aureum 1/2
```
2ft(.6m) OF(-18C) EM 4/4   Flowers of dark rose, double peony type. Very compact habit; small foliage, dark green. Larson cross; Fisher intro.

HULAGU KHAN   Described under LUMINOUS, q.v.

HULLABALLOO   Described under BETTY, q.v.

```
        -catawbiense 1/2
HUMBOLDT-
        -unknown 1/2
```
5ft(1.5m) -15F(-26C) M 4/3   Pale mauve, dark flare and dark markings. Attractive flowers. T. J. R. Seidel, 1926.

HUMBOLDT SUNRISE   Described under DR. RICHARD ANDERSON, q.v.

HUMMEL--form of rufum
4ft(1.2m) -5F(-21C) EM 3/3 Flowers white or pinkish purple. Leaves with thick brown indumentum. Unknown. A.M. (no date)

```
        -haematodes 1/2
HUMMING BIRD-
        -williamsianum 1/2
```
2.5ft(.75m) OF(-18C) EM 3/4   Flowers a deeper rich rose red than the species williamsianum, of very heavy substance, bell-shaped; lax trusses of 4-5. Plant compact, dense; leaves round, dark green, leathery. Slow-growing; needs some shade. J. C. Williams, Caerhays Castle, 1933. Color illus. F p. 48.

```
        -augustinii var. chasmanthum 1/2
HUNTER'S MOON-
        -cinnabarinum ssp. xanthocodon Concatenans Gp. 1/2
```
Flowers dull white, with greenish brown spotting, tubular, 1in. (2.5cm) x 1.5in(3.8cm); truss of 8. Gen. Harrison, reg, 1963.

HUNTING HILL   Parentage unknown
5ft(1.5m) -5F(-21C) M   Frilled flowers, deep purplish pink, shading paler to near-white in center; truss of about 13. C. O.

Dexter cross; Tyler Arboretum and G. Wister, reg. 1980.

```
              -barbatum 1/2
HUNTSMAN-
              -campylocarpum Elatum Group 1/2
A parent of the Exbury hybrid, NEHRU.   Loder.
```

```
                                         -griffithianum 7/32
                         -unnamed hybrid-
              -Mrs. Furnival-              -unknown 9/32
              -              -               -caucasicum 1/8
              -              -unnamed hybrid-
HURRICANE-                                  -unknown
              -              -griersonianum 1/4
              -              -                    -griffithianum
           -Anna Rose-                 -George-
             Whitney -           -Pink - Hardy-catawbiense 3/32
              -              -Pearl-            -arboreum 1/32
                   -Countess-      -Broughtonii-
                   -of Derby-                -unknown
                                    -catawbiense
                         -Cynthia-
                                    -griffithianum
5ft(1.5m)  5F(-15C)  M  4/4   Flowers a beautiful shade of pink,
markings deeper pink, 3in(7.6cm) across; ball-shaped truss of
15; compact plant; leaves held 3 years.  Whitney cross; Sathers,
reg. 1976.   Color illus. HG p. 75; VV p. 118.
```

```
                   -wardii 1/4
              -Crest-            -fortunei ssp. fortunei 1/8
HUSKY FEVER-    -Lady Bessborough-
              -                 -campylocarpum Elatum Group
              -wardii Litiense Group 1/2                 1/8
6ft(1.8m) x 5ft(1.5m)  10F(-12C)  E   Flowers in spherical truss
of 10, light yellow-green, 5 wavy-edged lobes.  Growth habit up-
right, rounded; oblong, dull leaves.   W. Elliott, reg. 1988.
```

```
                   -facetum (eriogynum) 1/4
         -unnamed hybrid-     -dichroanthum 1/8
         -            -Fabia-
HUSSAR-               -griersonianum 1/8
         -       -haematodes 1/4
         -May Day-
                 -griersonianum 1/4
4ft(1.2m)  5F(-15C)  M   Blood red flowers, upper lobe speckled
brown.  Plant of compact habit.   J. Waterer & Crisp, reg. 1971.
```

```
              -azalea viscosum 1/2
HYBRIDUM-
              -maximum 1/2
Azaleodendron.  Fragrant, yellow flowers, spotted and edged with
pink.  Herbert, 1817; offered by Methven, 1868-69.
```

* *

```
              -yakushimanum 1/2
HYDON BALL-       -griersonianum 1/4
         -Springbok-              -ponticum 1/8
                   -unnamed hybrid-
                             -unknown 1/8
3ft(.9m)  -OF(-18C)  M  4/4   Low compact habit, wider than tall;
leaves to 3.5in(9cm) long.  Trusses of 17 flowers, pale cream,
spotted brownish maize yellow.  George, reg. 1969.  A.M. Wisley
Trials 1977.
HYDON DAWN    Parentage as above
3ft(.9m)  5F(-15C)  M  4/4    Large compact truss of 16, rhoda-
mine pink fading paler at frilled edges, Neyron rose throat with
reddish brown spots.  Plant vigorous, compact;  leaves glossy.
A. F. George, Hydon Nurseries, reg. 1969.   F.C.C. Wisley Trials
1987.   Color illus. JS p. 77.
HYDON GLOW    Parentage as above
3ft(.9m)  OF(-18C)  M  4/4    Large, compact rounded truss of 14
flowers, rosy pink, slight spotting.  George, Hydon, reg. 1969.
HYDON HUNTER    Parentage as above
3ft(.9m)  5F(-15C)  M  4/4    Vigorous habit; leaves dark green.
Dome-shaped truss of 14 white flowers flushed light orchid pink.
George, reg. 1972.  A.M. 1976.  F.C.C. Wisley Trials 1979.
MORNING CLOUD  Parentage as above
3ft(.9m)  -5F(-21C)  M    Compact plant.  White flowers flushed
very light lavender.  George, Hydon, reg. 1972.  A.M. 1971.
MORNING MAGIC  Parentage as above
3ft(.9m)  -5F(-21C)  M   A compact plant, wider than high; dense
foliage.  White flowers, flushed Neyron rose,   orange-buff spot-
```

ting on upper lobes; trusses hold 16. George, reg. 1972.   A.M.
Wisley Trials 1982.

* *

```
                   -haematodes 1/4
              -May Day-
HYDON   -           -griersonianum 1/4
HARRIER-       -wardii 1/4
              -Jervis Bay-            -fortunei ssp. discolor 1/8
                   -Lady Bessborough-
                             -campylocarpum Elatum Gp. 1/8
5ft(1.5m)  5F(-15C)  M  Orange-scarlet flower on an open-growing
plant.  A. F. George, Hydon, reg. 1975.
```

HYDON HUNTER   Described under HYDON BALL, q.v.

HYDON MIST   Described under AMETHYST (ARENDS), q.v.

```
              -Moser's Maroon--unknown 1/2
HYDON PINK-          -dichroanthum 1/8
          -         -Dido-
          -Ice Cream-     -decorum 1/8
                    -fortunei ssp. discolor 1/4
4ft(1.2m)  OF(-18C)  ML  Flowers pinkish lavender with a crimson
throat; large compact truss of 20.   George, Hydon, reg. 1969.
```

```
                   -augustinii 3/4
HYDON RODNEY-       -russatum 1/4
          -Azamiz-
                   -augustinii
4ft(1.2m)  -5F(-21C)  EM   Flowers of vibrant violet with darker
spotting.  A. F. George, Hydon, reg. 1972.
```

```
                        -fortunei ssp. discolor 1/4
              -unnamed hybrid-
HYDON SALMON-           -unknown 1/4
              -griersonianum 1/2
5ft(1.5m)  OF(-18C)  M   Flowers a glowing salmon red, unfading,
about 2.5in(6.4cm) wide, open funnel-shaped;   full rounded truss
of 12-14.  A. F. George, Hydon, reg. 1970.   A.M. 1976.
```

```
                        -orthocladum var. microleucum 1/2
HYDON SNOWFLAKE-        -rupicola var. chryseum 1/4
              -Chikor-
                   -ludlowii 1/4
2ft(.6m)  OF(-18C)  EM    White flowers in trusses of 3.  Dwarf
plant of open habit.  A. F. George, Hydon, reg. 1978.
```

```
                   -caucasicum 1/4
        -Boule de Neige-        -catawbiense 3/8
        -              -hardy hybrid-
HYMEN-                        -unknown 3/8
        -           -catawbiense
        -Everestianum-
                        -unknown
Flowers light purplish violet,  with yellowish brown or greenish
brown markings.  T. J. R. Seidel cross, 1898; intro. 1906.
```

```
              -Mrs. R. S. Holford--unknown 1/2
HYPATIA-
              -kyawii 1/2
Red flowers on a tall plant.  Late season.  Rothschild, 1940.
```

```
                   -arboreum 5/16
        -Cardinal-                    -arboreum
        -         -          -Glory of Penjerrick-
HYPERION-    -Barclayi-              -griffithianum
        -             -thomsonii 1/8              1/16
        -forrestii Repens Group 1/2
Blood red flowers.  Little grown.  Lord Aberconway, 1941.
```

```
HYPERION (Waterer)   Parentage unknown
5ft(1.5m)  -5F(-21C)  ML  3/3   Bluish white flowers, chocolate
blotch, as SAPPHO.  Waterer, pre-1921.  Color illus. JS p. 94.
```

```
              -hyperythrum 1/2
HYPERMAX-
              -maximum 1/2
Large flowers of pale lavender with purple freckles, held in big
trusses of 14.  Plant medium-sized; hardy to -15F(-26C).   Delp.
```

```
                 -maximum 1/4
         -Stokes Bronze Wings-
HYPNOTIST-                  -catawbiense 1/4
         -Pearce's Apricot--unknown 1/2
Buds of cardinal red  open to flowers  of French rose and orient
pink, with a flare of pale yellowish pink.   W. Delp.
```

I

I. M. S.   See IRENE STEAD

```
                 -Moser's Maroon--unknown 1/4
    -Romany Chai-
IAGO-            -griersonianum 1/4
    -                     -fortunei ssp. discolor 1/4
    -Lady Bessborough-
                 -campylocarpum Elatum 1/4
Rosy crimson flowers, with darker spots.  Shrub about 5ft(1.5m),
upright.  Midseason.  Rothschild, 1941.
```

```
              -Marion--unknown 1/2
IAN WALLACE-        -griersonianum 1/4
           -Tally Ho-
                 -facetum (eriogynum) 1/4
Light red flower; throat slightly spotted.  Howells, reg. 1972.
```

```
              -griffithianum 1/4
       -Isabella-
IBERIA-        -auriculatum 1/4
       -wardii 1/2
Well-filled  trusses of 10-12 flowers,  funnel-shaped and creamy
white, with  conspicuous dark ruby crimson blotch in the throat,
widely funnel-campanulate, 2.75in(7cm) across.  Elliptic leaves
5in(12.7cm) long.  Collingwood Ingram, reg. 1962.  A.M. 1971.
```

```
    -griersonianum 1/2
IBEX-
    -pocophorum 1/2
5ft(1.5m)  5F(-15C)  EM  4/3  Flower bright crimson scarlet with
darker spots, funnel-shaped, in dome-shaped trusses.  Plant of
medium height; dark sage green leaves with brown felted indumen-
tum beneath.  Other forms have flower of rosy carmine or orange-
scarlet.  Rothschild, 1941.  A.M. 1948.
```

```
                   -griffithianum 1/16
              -Kewense-
        -Aurora-      -fortunei 1/16
     -Adelaide-   -thomsonii 3/8
IBIS-       -thomsonii
     -griersonianum 1/2
Compact plant about 5ft(1.5m) tall, bearing shapely trusses of
cherry pink flowers.  Early midseason.  Rothschild, 1941.
```

* *
```
              -campylocarpum 1/4
      -A. Gilbert-
ICARUS-        -fortunei ssp. discolor 1/4
       -dichroanthum ssp. scyphocalyx Herpesticum Group 1/2
Unusual  coloring,  with deep rose pink buds opening to biscuit-
colored, campanulate flowers shaded rose, described in some cat-
alogs as "orange"; flattened trusses.  Plant small, low-growing,
compact.  Rothschild.  A.M. 1947.
ORGANDIE  Parentage as above
Flowers  lemon yellow with pink margins and pink stain at  base.
Compact plant, nearly medium size.  Rothschild.  A.M. 1947.
```
* *

```
              -dichroanthum 1/4
       -Dido-
ICE CREAM-    -decorum 1/4
          -fortunei ssp. discolor 1/2
5ft(1.5m)  -10F(-23C) L    Vigorous plant, spreading wider than
tall, leaves 7.5in(19cm) long, medium dull green.  Flowers of
camellia rose,  with white throat  and pale olive spots on upper
petal, funnel-shaped, about 3.5in(8.9cm) wide; dome-shaped truss
of 12-14.  W. C. Slocock, reg. 1962.  A.M. Wisley Trials 1960.
```

```
              -catawbiense var. album Glass--Catalgla 1/2
ICE CRYSTALS-                     -catawbiense 1/4
           -Catalode (County of York)-      -griffithianum
                              -Loderi  -        1/8
                                 King George-fortunei 1/8
```

```
Large white truss with violet reflections; large leaves.  Hardy
to -25F(-32C).   R. L. Blough.
```

```
         -catawbiense var. album Glass--Catalgla 1/2
ICE CUBE-                         -catawbiense var. album
        -                -Catawbiense Album-              3/8
        -Belle Heller-              -unknown 1/8
                 -catawbiense var. album
4ft(1.2m)  -20F(-29C)  ML  4/3  Flowers a delightful ivory white
with a blotch of lemon yellow, funnel-shaped, 2.5in(6.4cm) wide;
conical truss.  Olive green foliage in profusion.  Shammarello,
reg. 1973.  Color illus. LW pl. 84; VV p. 35.
```

ICE FLOE   Parentage unknown
Lavender flowers aging pure white; heavy dorsal spotting, chestnut brown aging green. Larson cross; M. Wildfong, reg. 1983.

```
                     -Pygmalion--unknown 1/8
         -unnamed hybrid-
         -Weldy-       -haematodes 1/8
         -    -yakushimanum, Exbury form 1/4
ICE MILK-        -aureum (chrysanthum) 1/4
         -unnamed hybrid-
                     -maximum 1/4
Buds strong, light, and pale purplish pink.  Frilled white flow-
ers, dorsal spots cardinal red; anthers moderate red.   Delp.
```

```
         -auriculatum 1/2
ICEBERG-      -griffithianum 1/4
        -Loderi-
              -fortunei 1/4
A tall plant with long leaves  and large trusses of sweetly fra-
grant flowers, white with a green center.  Slocock.   A.M. 1950.
```

```
    -Moser's Maroon--unknown 1/2
ICENIA-              -fortunei ssp. discolor 1/4
       -Lady Bessborough-
                -campylocarpum Elatum Group 1/4
Compact trusses of pink; a medium-sized plant.  Rothschild, 1941.
```

```
            -maximum 1/4
    -Fireking-        -forrestii Repens Group 1/8
    -       -Gertrud-              -ponticum 1/32
    -        Schäle -      -Michael Waterer-
    -             -Prometheus-          -unknown 11/32
    -                  -Monitor--unk.   -catawbiense
    -                 -Parsons Grandiflorum-         1/16
ICY-         -America-                -unknown
HOT-         -           -dark red hybrid--unknown
    -      -Vivacious-     -griersonianum 1/16
    -         -       -Dr. Ross-            -arboreum 1/64
    -         -            -      -Doncaster-
    -         -           -Borde-       -unknown
    -         -            Hill-     -griffithianum
    -Sharpie-              -Mrs.A.M.-        3/64
    -                 Williams-unknown
    -                           -catawbiense
    -                -Parsons Grandiflorum-
    -         -America-               -unknown
    -         -       -dark red hybrid--unknown
    -Cindy Lou-            -griffithianum
    -                    -Mars-
    -unnamed hybrid-   -unknown
                   -catawbiense var. rubrum 1/16
Buds of cardinal red open to frilled flowers of cardinal red and
currant red; dorsal spots dark red.   Weldon Delp.
```

```
                     -catawbiense 1/16
            -Atrosanguineum-
        -Atrier-         -unknown 1/16
    -Mary Belle-    -griersonianum 1/8
    -        -       -decorum 1/8
IDA BRADOUR-   -Dechaem-
    -                 -haematodes 1/8
    -vernicosum R 18139  1/2
5ft(1.5m)  -10F(-23C)  ML  3/3  Flowers in shades of pink with a
yellow-green throat, saucer-shaped, 3in(7.6cm) wide; ball-shaped
trusses of 12-14.  Upright plant, arching branches, broader than
than high; narrow leaves.   Gable cross; Mrs. Yates, reg. 1977.
```

```
                -griffithianum 1/8
          -Dawn's Delight-
     -Dolly-                -unknown 1/8
IDAHO-      -griersonianum 1/4
     -elliottii 1/2
```
Medium-sized and erect; huge truss, brick red. Rothschild, 1941.

```
          -wardii 1/2              -griffithianum 1/16
IDEALIST-           -Kewense-
     -        -Aurora-        -fortunei 5/16
     -Naomi-      -thomsonii 1/8
                -fortunei
```
5ft(1.5m) 5F(-15C) M 4/3   Upright, vigorous plant, leaves
medium green, 4.5in(11.5cm) long. Flowers pale greenish yellow,
dark red throat, widely campanulate, 3in(7.6cm) across.   Rothschild, 1941.   A.M. 1945.   Color illus. PB pl. 4 & 5; VV p. 97.
VIENNA   Parentage as above
5ft(1.5m) 5F(-15C) M 4/3   Similar to above, but pale yellow
flowers.   Rothschild cross; selection made at Knap Hill; reg.
1964. P. C. 1962.
* *

                    -decorum? 1/8
               -Caroline-
     -unnamed hybrid-   -brachycarpum? 1/8
IDIDIT NO. ONE-   -azalea no. 638 1/4
          -azalea no. 609 1/2
```
An azaleodendron, with buds of strong and light purple, opening
to flowers of same colors; dorsal spots of deep greenish yellow.
Tall plant.  W. Delp.

```
* *
                 -griffithianum 3/8
     -Loderi King George-
     -              -fortunei 1/4
IDOL-   -griffithianum
     -       -Queen Wilhelmina-
     -Britannia-   -unknown 3/8
               -Stanley Davies--unknown
```
5ft(1.5m)  -5F(-21C)  M  4/4  Rose flower with a lighter center.
R. Henny.   P.A. 1957.
KAY   Parentage as above, except reversed
5ft(1.5m)  OF(-18C)  M  Flowers phlox pink with red spots, bell-
shaped.  Marshall Lyons, reg. 1972.
* * * * * * * * * * * * * * * * * * * * * * * * * * * *

IGHTHAM   Same parentage as AUGFAST, q.v.

```
          -wardii 1/2
IGHTHAM GOLD-
          -unknown 1/2
```
4ft(1.2m)  -10F(-23C)  VL  Flowers of light yellow-green with a
deep red blotch; trusses of 9.   Reuthe, intro. 1981; reg. 1985.
Color illus. JS p. 43.

```
          -dichroanthum 1/2
IGHTHAM PEACH-
          -unknown 1/2
```
3ft(.9m)  -10F(-23C)  M     Many flowers, in a true peach color.
Reuthe.

```
          -ponticum 1/2
IGHTHAM PURPLE-
          -unknown 1/2
```
5ft(1.5m)  -10F(-23C)  M     Very dark purple with white stamens.
Reuthe.

IGHTHAM YELLOW   See ARTHUR SMITH

```
          -catawbiense 1/2
IGNATIUS SARGENT-
          -unknown 1/2
```
5ft(1.5m)  -25F(-32C)  ML  2/2  Very hardy hybrid of open habit,
with large leaves.  Rose-colored flowers, large, slightly fra-
grant.  Waterer, before 1900.  Color illus. VV p. 99.

```
               -catawbiense var. album Glass--Catalgla 1/4
     -Ice Cube-   -catawbiense 1/16
     -        -   -Catawbiense Album-
IGLOO-   -Belle Heller-   -unknown 1/16
     -          -catawbiense album 1/8
     -yakushimanum, Exbury form 1/2
```
4.3ft(1.3m) high x 7ft(2.1m)(18 yrs)  -25F(-32C)  L   Light pink

buds open white; flowers 2in(5cm) across, of 5 wavy-edged lobes;
rather lax domed trusses of 16, 6in(15cm) wide.  Foliage oblong,
flat, held 5 years; dense habit.    Dr. J. Brueckner, reg. 1989.

```
               -griffithianum 1/4
          -unnamed hybrid-
ILAM ALARM-   -unknown 1/4
          -arboreum ssp. zeylanicum 1/2
```
6ft(1.8m)  10F(-12C)  EM  Bright red flowers, lighter in center.
E. Stead, New Zealand.

```
                    -griffithianum 1/16
               -George-
          -Pink - Hardy-catawbiense 1/16
     -unnamed-Pearl-   -arboreum 1/16
     - hybrid-   -Broughtonii-
ILAM APRICOT-   -   -unknown 5/16
     -        -arboreum ssp. zeylanicum 1/4
     -             -dichroanthum 1/4
     -unnamed hybrid-
               -unknown
```
A hybrid by Stead, possibly in the 1940s.

```
               -campylocarpum 1/4
          -unnamed hybrid-
     -             -fortunei ssp. discolor 1/4
ILAM CANARY-   -griffithianum 1/8
     -        -Loderi-
     -Loderi seedling-   -fortunei 1/8
          -unknown 1/4
```
5ft(1.5m)  OF(-18C)  EM   Large pale yellow flowers, long-last-
ing; handsome trusses.  Open plant needs some sun.   Stead, N.Z.

```
          -arboreum ? 1/2
ILAM CERISE-
          -unknown 1/2
```
6ft(1.8m)  5F(-15C)  EM  Crimson with white throat and small red
eye; crimson outside.  Very large trusses.  E. Stead, reg. 1984.

```
          -arboreum ssp. zeylanicum (NOYO CHIEF ?) 1/2
ILAM CORNUBIA-   -barbatum 1/4
          -Shilsonii-
               -thomsonii 1/4
```
6ft(1.8m)  10F(-12C)  E  Similar to CORNUBIA but a better truss,
more compact.  Early-flowering, fine red.   Stead.

```
          -griffithianum 1/4
     -Loderi-
ILAM CREAM- -fortunei 1/4
     -unknown 1/2
```
Loose trusses of 10 flowers, pink in bud,  opening pale greenish
white, suffused pink around lobes.  Edgar Stead, cross c. 1950;
L. Roland Stead, reg. 1981.  A.M 1985.

```
               -arboreum ssp. zeylanicum 1/4
          -unnamed-   -griffithianum
ILAM ORANGE- hybrid-   -George-
     -      -possibly Pink Pearl- Hardy-catawbiense
     -dichroanthum 1/2   -   -arboreum
               -Broughtonii-
                    -unknown
```
Orange-pink flowers, fading to rich yellow.  Lax trusses;  plant
compact, wider than high.  E. Stead.

```
          -formosum 1/2
ILAM PEARL-
          -unknown 1/2
```
Truss of 2-3 flowers, pure white,  Tuscan yellow at base inside,
reverse tinted cardinal red. Edgar Stead raiser;   Dunedin Rhod-
odendron Group, NZ, reg. 1981.

```
          -facetum 1/2
ILAM PINK-   -griffithianum 1/4
SPLENDOUR-Loderi-
          -fortunei 1/4
```
Truss of 10-12 flowers, Neyron rose shading lighter, with throat
of spinel red.   E. Stead cross; Mrs. R. J. Coker, reg. 1982.

ILAM RED GLOW   Described under SCARLET KING, q.v.
```

```
                   -augustinii ssp. chasmanthum 1/4
          -Electra-
ILAM VIOLET-         -augustinii 1/4
          -russatum 1/2
```
4ft(1.2m) 5F(-15C) M 4/3 Plant vigorous, upright; dark green
leaves, slightly glossy, and bronze in winter; foliage aromatic.
Compact trusses of 11 flowers, deep violet blue. W. T. Stead
raiser; sent for trials by Slocock. A.M. Wisley Trials 1983.
Color illus. VV p. 36.

```
               -dichroanthum 1/4
        -Nereid-
ILIAD-        -neriiflorum 1/4
      -kyawii 1/2
```
A small, compact plant, with deep green foliage and blood red
flower clusters. Late season. Rothschild. A.M. 1949.

```
                              -caucasicum 1/8
               -unnamed hybrid-
    -Mrs. Furnival-          -unknown 1/4
    -                        -griffithianum 1/8
ILLAHEE-        -unnamed hybrid-
    -                        -unknown
    -          -fortunei ssp. discolor 1/4
    -Evening-    -dichroanthum 1/8
    Glow  -Fabia-
               -griersonianum 1/8
```
3ft(.9m) -5F(-21C) ML 4/3 Flower 3in(7.6cm) across, lavender
pink with yellow tinged throat, orange-yellow flare, in flat
truss of 12. Leaves 6in(15cm) x 2in(5cm). A. Van Veen, reg.
1977.

```
               -Moser's Maroon--unknown 1/4
     -Romany Chal-
ILLYRIA-        -facetum (eriogynum) 1/4
     -kyawii 1/2
```
Tall plant, with large leaves; crimson flowers in late season.
Rothschild, 1941.

```
        -valentinianum 1/2
ILONA-
     -auritum 1/2
```
Many small trusses of pale golden yellow flowers. Shrub blooms
early and is not hardy. Rothschild, 1941.

```
               -maximum 1/4
          -Midsummer-
IMAGEMAKER-        -unknown 1/4
          -catawbiense var. rubrum 1/2
```
Magenta buds open to flowers of pale purplish pink and magnolia
purple. W. Delp.

IMBROS Parentage unknown
Flowers of rose Bengal. E. de Rothschild, reg. 1962.

```
     -impeditum 1/2
IMPEANUM-
     -hanceanum 1/2
```
Dwarf OF(-18C) ML One for the rock garden: almost prostrate,
seldom as much as 1ft(.3m) high. Small flowers of cobalt blue.
RBG, Kew, before 1932. F.C.C. 1934.

IMPERIAL Described under BLUE RHAPSODY, q.v.

```
     -Moser's Maroon--unknown 1/2
IMPI-
     -sanguineum ssp. didymum 1/2
```
4.5ft(1.35m) 5F(-15C) L 3/3 Medium-sized plant; deep ruddy
green leaves, red petioles. Black-red flowers in loose trusses
gleam brightly when back-lighted by afternoon sun. Rothschild.
A.M. 1945.

INA HAIR Described under JOAN THOMPSON, q.v.

```
      -wardii 1/2
INAMORATA-
      -fortunei ssp. discolor 1/2
```
The foliage resembles discolor, with long, narrow leaves in fine
rosettes, but darker, glossier; leaf tips and stalks are purple.
Flowers shaped like wardii, of soft yellow or sulphur yellow. A
tall, vigorous plant. Rothschild. A.M. 1950.
A Hobbie-raised clone of the same name is distributed in Europe,

according to Cox. Late, cream to pale yellow flowers. Perhaps
more hardy and vigorous than above. Col. ill. WS, 1989, p. 43.

INCA CHIEF Described under SCARLET BLAST, q.v.

```
               -wardii ? 1/4
     -Chlorops-
INCA GOLD-        -vernicosum ? 1/4
     -unknown 1/2
```
3ft(.9m) -5F(-21C) EM 4/4 Leaves of medium size. Flowers
3in(7.6cm) wide, barium yellow, somewhat rayed with mahogany;
trusses of 12. Benjamin Lancaster, reg. 1962. P.A. 1961.

INCHMERY Described under RED LAMP, q.v.

INDEPENDENCE DAY Parentage uncertain; possibly maximum cross
5ft(1.5m) -15F(-26C) L Long-lasting, red flowers, pale center
with dark spotting. Waterer, c. 1915.

```
          -catawbiense 1/2
INDIAN CHIEF-
          -unknown 1/2
```
Red flowers. Warren Stokes, before 1958.

* *
```
               -griersonianum 1/4
     -Sarita Loder-        -griffithianum 5/32
     -             -Loderi-
INDIAN-                    -fortunei 9/32
 PENNY-     -wardii 1/4          -griffithianum
     -Idealist-           -Kewense-
     -          -Aurora-        -fortunei
     -Naomi-     -thomsonii 1/16
               -fortunei
```
Synonym PENNY. Trusses of 12-14 flowers, light coppery aureolin
yellow. Del W. James, reg. 1958.
YELLOW CREEK Parentage as above, except reversed
6ft(1.8m) 5F(-15C) EM 4/2 Rather open habit; narrow, smooth,
light green leaves. Flowers flat, flaring to 4in(10cm) across,
of primrose yellow in lax, dome-shaped trusses of 10. D. James,
intro. 1958; reg. 1976.
* *

```
          -dichroanthum ssp. scyphocalyx 1/2
INDIANA-
     -kyawii 1/2
```
4ft(1.2m) 5F(-15C) L 3/5 Orange-red flower in medium-sized,
lax trusses. A strong- and slow-growing plant of spreading habit; foliage has edges sharply turned down. Rothschild, 1941.

* *
```
               -wardii 1/4
     -Crest-        -fortunei ssp. discolor 1/8
     -    -Lady      -
INDIRIDIVA-     -Bessborough-campylocarpum Elatum Group 1/8
     -                     -maximum 1/8
     -          -Halopeanum-
     -Snow Queen-        -griffithianum 1/4
     -          -griffithianum
          -Loderi-
               -fortunei 1/8
```
Flowers pale chartreuse yellow, deeper in throat, with dark yel-
low-green markings, widely funnel-campanulate, about 4in(10.2cm)
across, 7-lobed; rounded truss of about 10. Leaves dull green,
oblong, 6.5in(15.8m) long. Rothschild, reg. 1976. A.M. 1985.
HAPPY OCCASION Parentage as above, except reversed
An Exbury hybrid with trusses of 9-12 white flowers, centers of
yellowish green. E. de Rothschild, reg. 1980. A.M. 1985.
* *

```
          -souliei 1/2
INDOMITABLE-                -thomsonii 1/4
          -General Sir John du Cane-
                         -fortunei ssp. discolor 1/4
```
Flower similar to parent souliei; large, white, flushed pink, in
medium-sized trusses; a tall, compact plant. Rothschild, 1941.

```
                    -yakushimanum 1/4
          -Serendipity-
INDY-           -aureum 1/4                    -thomsonii 1/16
PINK-                       -Bagshot Ruby-
    -        -Princess Elizabeth-         -unknown 3/16
    -Lanny-               -unknown
     Pride-             -smirnowii 1/8
               -unnamed hybrid-
                        -yakushimanum 1/8
```
Buds of crimson and Tyrian purple opening to light and pale pur-
plish pinks; dorsal spots Tyrian purple.   Indumented foliage on
a medium-sized plant. W. E. Delp.


```
                      -griffithianum 1/4
         -Loderi King George-
INEZ MAY-             -fortunei 1/4
    -            -fortunei 3/8
      -Phyle Donegan-            -griffithianum 1/8
               -Loderi Superlative-
                        -fortunei
```
Flowers in trusses of 6-8, funnel-shaped, pale purplish pink in-
side, strong purplish pink outside, with brown spots on dorsal
lobe. Shrub 4ft(1.2m).   W. McClure, reg. 1986.


```
* * * * * * * * * * * * * * * * * * * * * * * * * * * * * * * *
                -griffithianum  1/4
        -Isabella-
INFANTA       -auriculatum 1/4
        -griersonianum 1/2
```
Flowers of light crimson deepening to rose madder at base of the
tube. Another form: huge white flowers flushed salmon pink in
throat. Collingwood Ingram, before 1956.
HISPANIOLA   Parentage as above; C. Ingram, 1958.
JUANITA   Parentage as above
Pink, flushed reddish salmon at base of throat. Ingram, 1939.
* *


```
          -catawbiense 1/2
INGEBORG-
          -unknown 1/2
```
Dark crimson flowers lighter in the throat, with umber spotting.
T. J. R. Seidel.


```
                  -Metterianus--degronianum ssp. heptamereum 1/4
          -Rijnveld-                     (metternichii)
INGENIEUR-        -           -griersonianum 1/8
 HARMSEN-   -unnamed hybrid-
          -unknown         -unknown 5/8
```
Dense rounded trusses of 8-16 funnel-shaped flowers, to 2in(5cm)
wide, light red with dark blotch.   Large lanceolate leaves; buff
indumentum when young.   Plant 9ft(3m) x 13.2ft(4m); blooming in
May.   Vuyk, cross c.1960; Royal Boskoop Hort. Soc., reg. 1988.


```
                      -griffithianum 1/8
            -Isabella-
     -Infanta-      -auriculatum 1/8
     -        -griersonianum 1/4
INGOS  -               -fortunei ssp. discolor 1/8
RUBELLUM-    -Lady    -
     -Jalisco-Bessborough-campylocarpum Elatum Group 1/8
       Goshawk-    -dichroanthum 1/8
               -Dido-
                   -decorum 1/8
```
Flowers of medium Neyron rose, fading lighter, with a dark red
blotch. Collingwood Ingram, reg. 1973.


```
      -insigne 1/2
INGRE-
      -griersonianum 1/2
```
Deep pink flowers.   Lord Aberconway, intro. 1936.


```
              -griersonianum 1/4
        -Tally Ho-
INGRID-         -facetum (eriogynum) 1/4
        -griffithianum 1/2
```
Large pink flowers held in open trusses on a tall shrub. Late-
flowering season. Rothschild, intro. 1941.


```
              -williamsianum 1/4
        -Jock-
              -griersonianum 1/4          -griffithianum
INHERITANCE-                    -George-
                        -Pink Pearl- Hardy-catawbiense
          -Antoon van Welie-    -        -arboreum
                    -          -Broughtonii-
                        -unknown      -unknown
4ft(1.2m)  -5F(-21C)  M  4/4  Tight trusses of bright pink; fol-
iage deep green.   Farwell intro.
```


```
* * * * * * * * * * * * * * * * * * * * * * * * * * * * * * * *
                            -catawbiense var. album 1/8
                 -Lodestar-              -catawbiense
          -          -Catawbiense-         3/32
          -        -Belle - Album    -unknown 3/32
          -          Heller-          -cat.
          -R.O. Delp-          -white cat. hyb.-
          -        -              -unk.
          -        -              -catawbiense
          -        -       -Atrosanguineum-
INNER SPIRIT-    -Mary -      -griersonianum 1/16
          -        Belle-     -decorum 1/16
          -          -Dechaem-
          -                -haematodes 1/15
          -        -brachycarpum 1/4
          -Lifeline-    -wardii 1/8
               -Crest-        -fortunei ssp. discolor
                  -Lady Bess-            1/16
                    borough -campylocarpum El.Gp. 1/16
```
Buds vivid purplish red and deep purplish pink, opening to pale
purplish pink flowers.   Weldon Delp.   (Plant may be extinct)
PIZZAZZ   Parentage as above
Deep ruby red buds open to roseine purple flowers, spotted med-
ium grayed red. Delp.
REMOTE CONTROL   Parentage as above
Strong, vivid, to light fuschia purples in bud; flowers purplish
pink, with deep red dorsal spotting.   Delp.
YOU BETCHA!   Parentage as above
Buds of medium reddish orange and chartreuse green, opening pale
chartreuse, darker in throat; lettuce green dorsal spots. Delp.
* *


```
       -insigne 1/4
   -Ingre-
INSUN-   -griersonianum 1/2
   -       -griffithianum 1/4
   -Sunrise-
       -griersonianum
```
Pink-flowered.   Lord Aberconway, intro. 1946.


```
             -ferrugineum 1/2
INTERMEDIUM-
             -hirsutum 1/2.
```
Dwarf -10F(-23C) L   Tight clusters of small pink flowers. A
white form also available.   Natural hybrid, about 1891.


```
                  -Essex Scarlet--unknown 1/4
        -Beau Brummell-
INTREPID-         -facetum (eriogynum) 1/4
        -kyawii 1/2
```
Tall plant; rosy red flowers; late midseason. Rothschild, 1941.


```
           -intricatum 1/2
INTRIFAST-
           -fastigiatum 1/2
```
2ft(.6m) -15F(-26C) 3/3   Small, violet blue, early-blooming
flowers; foliage bright metallic blue. Lowinsky, pre-1958.


```
              -yakushimanum 1/4
     -unnamed-                    -griffithianum 1/4
     - hybrid-    -Queen Wilhelmina-
     -        -Britannia-         -unknown 3/8
INVICTA-            -Stanley Davies--unknown
     -                -griffithianum
     -        -Loderi-
     -unnamed-    -fortunei 1/8
       hybrid-              -griffithianum
     -        -Queen Wilhelmina-
       -Britannia-          -unknown
               -Stanley Davies--unknown
```

4ft(1.2m) OF(-18C) ML   An upright plant, pale purple flowers.
John Waterer, Sons & Crisp, reg. 1975.

                    -valentinianum 1/2
IOLA-
       -edgeworthii 1/2
Clear primrose yellow flowers with a darker eye; trusses of 2-3.
Grayish green leaves, very hairy. Small, tender plant.   Roth-
schild, 1941.

                              -griffithianum 1/8
                   -Godesburg-
        -Blanc-mange-   -unknown 1/8
IOLANTHE-   -auriculatum 1/4
        -kyawii 1/2
Large cerise-colored flowers. Tall, tender, and very late-flow-
ering. Rothschild, 1941.

                         -ciliatum 1/4
        -Countess of Haddington-
IONE-   -dalhousiae 1/4
        -edgeworthii (bullatum) 1/2
Flowers open pale primrose yellow, fade to white.   Magor, 1926.

              -haematodes 1/2
IPHIGENIA-   -arboreum 1/4
        -Red Admiral-
                  -thomsonii 1/4
Red flowers. E. J. P. Magor, intro. 1934.

* *
          -yakushimanum 1/2
IRENE BAIN-   -haematodes 1/4
          -May Day-
                  -griersonianum 1/4
Pale pink flowers fading to cream, with pink frilled margins.
Dr. Yeates cross; Mrs. Irene Bain, intro. and reg. 1979.
RELAXATION   Parentage: MAY DAY x yakushimanum--Koichiro Wada
3ft(.9m) -5F(-21C) M Flowers cardinal red with dark red basal
nectaries, campanulate; lax truss of 12-15. Plant wide as tall,
with heavy indumentum, biscuit-colored. Cecil Smith, reg. 1983.
KAKDAY   Parentage as IRENE BAIN, above
Leaves with tan indumentum; flowers deep cherry red, fading to
pale pink. New Zealand Rhod. Assoc.; Mrs. R. Pinney, reg. 1982.
* *

IRENE HALL   Described under FIONA WILSON, q.v.

                   -griffithianum 1/2
IRENE STEAD---LODERI, selfed-
                   -fortunei 1/2
6ft(1.8m) OF(-18C) M 5/3   Synonym I.M.S. A shrub similar to
the LODERI group, with pink strong flowers; fragrant.   Stead,
NZ, reg. 1958. A.M. 1987.

                 -wardii 1/4
        -Jervis Bay-   -fortunei ssp. discolor 1/8
IRIS   -   -Lady bessborough-
PRIZEMAN-   -wightii 1/4   -campylocarpum Elatum Group
        -China-   1/8
                -fortunei 1/4
Flowers in trusses of 12-14, 7-lobed, primrose yellow with small
cerise blotch in the upper throat. Season May. Shrub 7ft(2.1
m) x 3ft(.9m). G. J. N. Prizeman, reg. 1988.

                      -catawbiense var. album Glass--Catalgla
        -unnamed hybrid-   1/4
        -          -wardii 1/4   -caucasicum 3/32
IRISH CREAM-   -Jacksonii-   -caucasicum
        -       -Goldsworth-   -Nobleanum-
        -       - Yellow -   -arboreum 1/32
        -Goldfort-   -campylocarpum 1/8
                   -fortunei 1/4
3ft(.9m) x 4ft(1.2m)(13 yrs) -15F(-26C) M   Flowers in trusses
of 11, 7-lobed, pale yellow-green, with brilliant yellow-green
spotting. Spreading habit. G. D. Lewis, reg. 1989.

          -yakushimanum, Exbury form 1/2
IRISH YAKU-   -griffithianum 1/4
          -Mars-
                -unknown 1/4
3ft(.9m) -10F(-23C) M   Buds of bright Neyron rose opening to
very light Neyron rose. Truss of 22 flowers, 6-lobed, openly

funnel-shaped. Plant broader than tall; leaves 6in(15cm) long,
with light brown indumentum beneath. Comerford Nursery raiser;
P. J. McGuiness, reg. 1983.

                    -Essex Scarlet--unknown 1/2
        -Oudijk's Sensation-
        -                   -williamsianum 1/4
IRMELIES-   -griffithianum 1/8
        -             -George Hardy-
        -Marinus Koster-   -catawbiense 1/8
                  -red hybrid--unknown
3ft(.9m) x 4.3ft(1.3m) -10F(-23C) M   Roseine purple buds open
to deep purplish pink funnel-campanulate flowers, spotted strong
purplish red on dorsal lobe, to 3.2in(8.5cm) wide; trusses of 10
to 11. Dark, elliptic-ovate foliage, creamy white scales below.
Very floriferous. H. Hachmann, cross 1962; G. Stück, reg. 1988.
Color illus. WS, 1989, p. 144.

               -maximum 1/4
        -Midsummer-
IRONSIDE-   -unknown 1/4
        -kyawii 1/2
Tall; late-blooming; large crimson flowers.   Rothschild, 1941.

        -irroratum 1/2
IRRIFARG-
        -oreodoxa var. fargesii 1/2
Light pink flowers, heavily spotted crimson.   Magor, 1926.

                    -catawbiense 1/4
        -unnamed hybrid-
ISAAC NEWTON-   -thomsonii 1/4
        -forrestii Repens Group 1/2
Flowers of carmine red.   Dietrich Hobbie, 1952.

        -maddenii (calophyllum) 1/2
ISABEL-
        -maddenii 1/2
Flowers of light rose. Blooms early.   Lord Aberconway, 1947.

                         -griffithianum 5/16
                -Beauty of-
             -Norman Gill- Tremough-arboreum 1/16
        -Anna-   -griffithianum
        -    -   -griffithianum
ISABEL-   -Jean Marie de Montague-
PIERCE-   -unknown 1/8
        -             -fortunei ssp. discolor 1/4
        -    -Lady   -
        -Lem's-Bessborough-campylocarpum Elatum Group 1/8
          Goal-   -griersonianum 1/8
              -Azor-
                   -fortunei ssp. discolor
6ft(1.8m) OF(-18C) M 5/4 Flowers of rich pink, paler in center, prominent brown blotch and spots in throat, narrow stripes
of deep pink from base to edges. Flower openly campanulate, 4in.
(10.2cm) wide, wavy margins; about 10 per truss. Glossy dark
leaves with a yellow midvein. Lem cross; Lawrence Pierce, reg.
1975.   Color illus. ARS Q 29:4 (1975), p. 238.

* *
        -griffithianum 1/2
ISABELLA-
        -auriculatum 1/2
Clear pink flowers.   Col. G. H. Loder, High Beeches, 1934.
(A Leonardslee form has very large, white, fragrant flowers on a
tall bush.)
EXBURY ISABELLA   Parentage as ISABELLA, above
6ft(1.8m) 5F(-15C) L 3/3   A dense plant, with large trusses
holding fragrant white flowers. Rothschild, 1948.
ISABELLA NEVADA   Parentage as ISABELLA, above
Pink flowers. Collingwood Ingram, 1936.
MARBELLA   Parentage (auriculatum x griffithianum)
Registered by Collingwood Ingram, 1972.
MARGARET FALMOUTH   Parentage as MARBELLA
White flowers with inner throat heavily marked cardinal red, 5-7
frilled lobes in trusses of 10. Leaves 9in(22.9cm) long.   G. H.
Loder raiser; Hon. H. E. & Mrs. Boscawen, reg. 1969. A.M. 1968.
* *

                    -griffithianum 1/2
ISABELLA MANGLES-
                    -unknown 1/2
5ft(1.5m) -10F(-23C) EM A tall plant with large foliage; big
trusses of light pink, trumpet-shaped flowers. Mangles, 1880.

ISABELLA NEVADA Described under ISABELLA, q.v.

              -yakushimanum--Koichiro Wada 1/2
ISADORA-   -catawbiense 1/4
      -Cynthia-
              -griffithianum 1/4
Flowers in trusses of 15-17, 5 very wavy lobes, strong to light
purplish pink inside, with reddish dorsal spots; outside strong
purplish red. Compact habit; hardy to 12F(-24C). Heinje Baumschulen, cross 1962; reg. 1986. Color illus. WS, 1989, p. 110.

ISLAND GEM--form of oreotrephes
5ft(1.5m) 10F(-12C) EM 3/4 Orchid flowers, with a reddish
blotch, in terminal inflorescence of 3 buds, each 4-flowered.
Leaves typical of species. Flowers similar in color to Exbury
form, A.M. 1937. Seed from RHS; H. A. Short raiser; reg. 1978.

      -wardii 1/2
ISME-
      -venator 1/2
Yellow flowers, with rose-colored spots, in small trusses. Med-
ium-sized, attractive plant. Rothschild, 1941.

                  -fortunei ssp. discolor 1/2
ISOBEL BAILLIE-   -griffithianum 1/8
      -              -George Hardy-
          -Betty Wormald-   -catawbiense 1/8
                          -red hybrid--unknown 1/4
Flowers ruby red, flare of red spots. Haworth-Booth, reg. 1972.

ISOM RAGAN Parentage unknown; elepidote
6ft(1.8) x 5ft(1.5m)(12 yrs) -5F(-21C) VL Flowers white with
moderate purplish pink stripe on back of lobe, 7 wavy lobes; lax
domed truss of 8. Glossy oblong leaves. W. Ragan, reg. 1989.

ISPAHAN Described under DEL, q.v.

        -Mrs. H. Stocker--unknown 1/2
ISTANBUL-
        -elliottii 1/2
A tall hybrid, with full red trusses. Late. Rothschild, 1941.

        -dichroanthum 1/2
-                        -griffithianum 1/16
ISTAR-   -Kewense-
-      -Aurora-   -fortunei 5/16
      -Naomi-   -thomsonii 1/8
            -fortunei
3ft(.9m) 0F(-18C) M 4/4 Low, compact plant. Yellow flowers
in loose trusses. Rothschild, 1941.

            -dichroanthum 1/4
        -Astarte-   -campylocarpum Elatum Group 1/8
ISTRIA-   -Penjerrick-
-                    -griffithianum 5/8
        -griffithianum
Pale pink flowers. Lord Aberconway, 1946.

ITA--form of hirtipes L S & T 3624
5ft(1.5m) 5F(-15C) EM Loose trusses of 5 flowers, 5-lobed,
funnel-shaped, phlox pink, stained and striped deeper shades.
Ludlow, Sherriff, & Taylor collectors; A. & J. F. Gibson, reg.
1966. A.M. 1965.

                -fortunei 1/4
        -Duke of York-   -catawbiense 1/8
ITALIA-   -Scipio-
-                      -unknown 1/8
        -griersonianum 1/2
Flowers salmon red, with faint red striping down the centers of
the lobes. D. Hobbie, 1954. Color illus. WS, 1989, p. 44.

                    -catawbiense var. album 1/8
            -Lodestar-   -catawbiense
            -    -Catawbiense-   1/8
            -    -Belle- Album -unknown 1/8
            -    Heller-   -catawbiense
            -          -white cat. hyb.-
        -R.O. Delp-   -unknown
        -          -   -catawbiense
        -          -   -Atrosanguineum-
        -          -Atrier-   -unknown
        -    -Mary -   -griersonianum 1/8
        -        Belle-   -decorum 1/8
IT'S SPECIAL-   -Dechaem-
        -                      -haematodes 1/8
        -                        -catawbiense
        -              -Atrosanguineum-
        -          -Atrier-   -unknown
        -    -Mary -   -griersonianum
      -unnamed- Belle-   -decorum
        hybrid-   -Dechaem-
        -                -haematodes
          -catawbiense var. album--Powell Glass 1/4
White flowers lightly edged strong purplish red and pink. Delp.

                  -catawbiense 1/4
      -B. de Bruin-
IVAN-   -unknown 1/4
      -kyawii 1/2
Plant tall, upright; large bright red flower. Rothschild, 1941.

IVAN D. WOOD Described under CORAL QUEEN, q.v.

                  -thomsonii 1/4
      -Chanticleer-
IVANHOE-   -facetum (eriogynum) 1/4
      -griersonianum 1/2
6ft(1.8m) 5F(-15C) M 3/3 Glistening, brilliant scarlet flowers, spotted with deeper red, funnel-shaped; flat-topped truss.
Plant tall, of loose habit. Blooms early to midseason. Rothschild, 1941. A.M. 1945. Color illus. PB pl. 57.

IVERY'S SCARLET Parentage unknown
6ft(1.8m) 10F(-12C) EM 3/3 Brilliant red flowers in small,
dome-shaped trusses. Growth habit upright and willowy; narrow
light green leaves, 5.5in(14cm) long. A parent of ALVINDA. Origin unknown; reg. 1958. Color illus. PB pl. 55; F p. 50.

* *
            -dichroanthum 1/4
      -Fabia-
IVIZA-   -griersonianum 1/4
-      -auriculatum 1/4
      -Bustard-   -campylocarpum Elatum 1/8
            -Penjerrick-
                    -griffithianum 1/8
Plant about 5ft(1.5m) tall. Leaves spoon-shaped, glossy green.
Coral yellow buds opening to orange salmon tubes, like FABIA, in
lax trusses. Rothschild, intro. 1941.
PHILOMENE Parentage as above
5ft(1.5m) 5F(-15C) ML 3/3 Plant medium-sized; glossy, spoon-
shaped leaves. Straw-colored flowers flushed with pink. Rothschild, 1941.
* *

IVORIANUM See IVERY'S SCARLET

              -wardii ? 1/4
      -Chlorops-
IVORY BELLS-   -vernicosum ? 1/4
          -williamsianum 1/2
3ft(.9m) -5F(-21C) EM 4/4 Chinese yellow buds opening straw
yellow; flowers flattened, to 3in(7.6cm) wide, 7-10 in graceful
trusses. Plant sturdy, compact; stiff, oval leaves. Benjamin
Lancaster, reg. 1966.

              -keiskei, Mt. Kuromi form 1/2
IVORY COAST-
              -dauricum, white form--Arctic Pearl 1/2
4ft(1.2m)(12 yrs) -20F(-29C) VE 4/4 Evergreen leaves, elliptic, scaly, 1.6in(4cm) long. Flowers 2in(5cm) wide, 5-lobed,
pale yellowish green aging to white. D. G. Leach, reg. 1985.

```
                    -catawbiense var. album Glass--Catalgla  1/2
          -              -catawbiense var. album 7/32
          -         -              -              -caucasicum 3/128
IVORY -       -Luxor-              -Jacksonii-    -caucasicum
PALACE-       -     -    -Goldsworth-      -Nobleanum-
      -       -     -Gold- Yellow  -              -arboreum
      -       -     fort-          -campylocarpum 1/32    1/128
    -unnamed-              -fortunei 1/16
      hybrid-             -catawbiense var. album
          -    -Lodestar-      -catawbiense var. album
          -    -        -Belle -        -catawbiense 1/32
          -    -            Heller-Madame -
          -R.O.-              Carvalho-unknown 1/32
          Delp-                    -catawbiense
            -              -Atrosanguineum-
            -       -Atrier-              -unknown
            -Mary -         -griersonianum 1/32
          Belle-           -decorum 1/32
                 -Dechaem-
                         -haematodes 1/32
```
Buds of pale purplish pink open to yellowish white flowers; dorsal spotting of brilliant yellowish green. W. Delp.

```
                         -griffithianum 3/16
                   -George Hardy-
          -Mrs. Lindsay-          -catawbiense 1/16
     -Diane- Smith    -Duchess of Edinburgh--unknown 1/4
     -      -            -campylocarpum 3/8
IVORY-      -unnamed hybrid-
QUEEN-                   -unknown
     -       -campylocarpum
    -Phyrne-         -griffithianum
          -Loderi-
                 -fortunei 1/8
```
4ft(1.2m) OF(-18C) EM Large, creamy white flowers with a red blotch. Glossy green foliage. Waterer & Crisp, reg. 1965.

IVORY TOWER   Described under LIMELIGHT, q.v.

IVY   Described under LADY CHAMBERLAIN, q.v.

J

J. E. HARRIS   See under SURPRISE

```
          -Ivery's Scarlet--unknown 1/2
J. EDGAR HOOVER-      -dichroanthum 1/4
          -Francis-          -griffithianum 1/8
            Hanger-Isabella-
                      -auriculatum 1/8
```
Plant of medium size; large, light green leaves. White flowers edged pink, outside rose madder to Turkey red, campanulate, to 4 in(10.2cm) across; loose trusses, but flowers upstanding. Late. C. S. Seabrook, reg. 1965.

```
                         -catawbiense 9/32
            -Blandyanum-                -catawbiense
            -         -         -unnamed-
     -Ascot -         -Alta- - hybrid-
     -Brilliant-      clerense-          -ponticum
     -       -              -arboreum 1/32
J. G. MILLIAS-      -thomsonii 1/4
     -              -griffithianum 1/8
     -      -George Hardy-
     -Pink Pearl-          -catawbiense
          -              -arboreum 3/16
            -Broughtonii-
                   -unknown 1/8
```
6ft(1.8m) 5F(-15C) E 3/2   Flowers deep blood red with heavy dark spotting; rounded trusses. Plant tall, upright, vigorous, of open habit; medium green leaves. J. Waterer, 1915.

J. H. AGNEW   Parentage unknown
A parent of the Exbury hybrid, BRENDA. Waterer.

```
          -Monsieur Thiers--unknown 1/2
J. H. VAN NES-
          -griffithianum 1/2
```
5ft(1.5m) -5F(-21C) M 3/3   Plant habit rather compact; pale green leaves. Flowers of glowing soft red, lighter in center, about 2.5in(2.6cm) across, with pointed lobes; conical, compact

trusses. C. B. van Nes, before 1958.   Color illus. VV p. 82.

```
               -nivale F 16450 1/2
J. HUTTON EDGAR-
          -unknown 1/2
```
Truss of 3 bluish purple flowers. G. Forrest collector; Col. G. H. Loder, intro. 1919; H. E. Boscawen, High Beeches, reg. 1982.

```
                         -arboreum 1/8
               -Doncaster-
     -unnamed hybrid-      -unknown 5/8
J. J. DE VINK-      -unknown
          -          -griffithianum 1/4
     -unnamed hybrid-
               -unknown
```
Trusses of 11-13 flowers, rose red with brown blotch. M. Koster & Sons. A.M. Wisley Trials 1946.

```
          -veitchianum Cubittii Group 1/2
JABBERWOCKY-
          -moupinense 1/2
```
2ft(.6m) 15F(-9C) E   Plant for the cool greenhouse. Flowers of light violet pink, dark reddish pink spots in upper throat, funnel-shaped, to 1.5in(3.8cm) wide; truss of 3.   A. F. George, Hydon, reg. 1976.   P.C. 1975.

JACK HEXT--form of spinuliferum
4ft(1.2m) 5F(-15C) EM 3/3   Currant red axillary flowers, 3's and 4's in loose terminal clusters. Elliptical leaves, sparsely scaly. New growth with soft hairs.   N. T. Holman, reg. 1974. A.M. 1971.

```
                    -arboreum 1/8
          -Doncaster-
     -Borde Hill-      -unknown 3/4
JACK LYONS-              -griffithianum 1/8
     -         -Mrs. A. M. Williams-
     -Rose Red--unknown      -unknown
```
Compact habit; large, oval, pointed leaves. Flowers crimson to cardinal red, campanulate; truss of 13.   M. Lyons, reg. 1972.

JACK OWEN YATES   Described under BETSY KRUSON, q.v.

```
          -lacteum 1/2              -griffithianum 1/8
JACK SKELTON-              -George Hardy-
          -Mrs. Lindsay Smith-          -catawbiense 1/8
                    -Duchess of Edinburgh--unknown 1/4
```
5ft(1.5m) -10F(-23C) M   Creamy white, red spots.   Unknown.

JACK SWIFT   Described under BLAZE, q.v.

```
                    -dichroanthum
               -Fabia-
          -Erebus-      -griersonianum 5/8
JACK THE RIPPER-      -griersonianum
          -              -facetum 1/4
          -Jacquetta-
                    -griersonianum
```
Blood red flowers with faint spots on upper lobes.   Lord Aberconway. A.M. 1949.

JACK VASS--form of fulvum F24314
Tubular-campanulate flowers, to 1.7in(4.5cm) across, rich creamy white base, suffused to edge with shades of purplish red, small blotch of vivid reddish orange in throat; tight rounded truss of 20. Dark, shiny green oblanceolate leaves, with cinnamon felted indumentum below. Blooms late March.   S. R. Clarke, raiser; R. N. S. Clarke, intro.; J. F. McQuire, named and reg. 1988.

```
          -macrophyllum 1/2
JACKIE ANN-
          -unknown 1/2
```
5ft(1.5m) -10F(-23C) ML 4/3   Blossoms of pink with a yellow eye; attractive cone-shaped truss.   Origin unknown, except from state of Washington.   Color illus. HG p. 74.

```
          -Loder's White, q.v. for two possible parentages
JACK'S WHITE-
          -unknwon
```
Buds light yellow-green, opening white. Flowers in trusses of 6 to 9, funnel-shaped, 6-lobed. Shrub 13.3ft(4.0m). J. W. Haverfield, Australia, reg. 1987.

```
                -caucasicum 3/4
JACKSONII-            -caucasicum
           -Nobleanum-
                      -arboreum 1/4
```
Medium-sized bush, rounded, slow growing. Flowers bright rose
pink with maroon markings and paler spots, widely funnel-shaped,
in large, well-formed trusses; early, abundant bloom. Tolerates
industrial pollution.   Herbert, 1835.   Color ill. Cox pl. 88.

```
                -williamsianum 1/2
JACKWILL-           -caucasicum 3/8
         -Jacksonii-        -caucasicum
                   -Nobleanum-
                             -arboreum 1/8
```
4ft(1.2m) -10F(-23C) EM   Dense, compact bush. Floppy truss
of 6 flowers; light rose pink, bell-shaped, 2in(5cm) wide, faint
red markings. Hobbie, before 1945. Color ill. WS, 1989, p. 26.

```
                -Moser's Maroon--unknown 1/4
          -Bibiani-
JACOBEAN-         -arboreum 1/4
          -sanguineum var. haemaleum 1/2
```
Plant about 5ft(1.5m) tall, bearing medium-sized flowers of deep
maroon. Rothschild, 1942.

```
               -griersonianum 1/2
JACOB'S RED-
               -unknown 1/2
```
A hybrid with bright scarlet flowers.   Knap Hill, reg. 1962.

```
            -facetum 1/2
JACQUELINE-                 -griffithianum 1/8
          -            -Loderi-
          -Albatross-        -fortunei 1/8
                      -fortunei ssp. discolor 1/4
```
Tall and compact. Large pink flowers; late. Rothschild, 1942.

```
* * * * * * * * * * * * * * * * * * * * * * * * * * *
                   -catawbiense 1/4
           -Sefton-
JACQUELINE LOOYE-    -unknown 1/2
           -                -ponticum 1/4
           -Purple Splendour-
                            -unknown
```
Buds of beetroot purple open to strong purplish red, a flare of
spirea red; dorsal spots dark red. Hardy to -15F(-26C). Delp.
JOYLYN   Parentage as above
Buds of cyclamen purple and strong purplish red open to frilled
flowers of cyclamen and mallow purples; dorsal spots brilliant
greenish yellow.   Delp.
K. D. HARRIS   Parentage as above
Buds of dark red and violet purple, open to frilled flowers of
beetroot purple and dark red; dark red dorsal spotting. Throat
strong red. Medium-sized plant; hardy to -15F(-26C). Delp.
MONTEGO   Parentage as above
5ft(1.5m) -15F(-26C) M   Openly funnel-shaped flowers, 3.25in.
(8.3cm) broad, violet purple with a green blotch; ball trusses
hold 18.   Plant much wider than tall; current growth near-pink.
D. G. Leach, cross 1957; reg. 1983.
SAVER   Parentage as above
Buds of vivid purple open to strong purple, a flare of deep red;
dorsal spots of deep red; throat currant red.   W. Delp.
* *

         -dichroanthum 1/2
JACQUES-   -fortunei ssp. discolor 1/8
        -    -Lady Bessborough-
        -Day -   -campylocarpum Elatum Group 1/8
        Dream-griersonianum 1/4
```
Flowers pink to orange; medium-sized bush.  Rothschild, 1942.

JACQUETTA   Described under TALLY HO, q.v.

```
          -dichroanthum 1/4
      -Fabia-
JADE-   -griersonianum 1/4
    -Corona--unknown 1/2
```
3ft(.9m)  5F(-15C)  EM  3/3    Very colorful flowers, combining
orange, pink, and later, greenish yellow; tight trusses.  Leaves
3.5in(9cm) x 2in(5cm).   Henny, intro. 1958; reg. 1964.

```
                  -bureavii 1/4
          -Gretsel-   -dichroanthum 1/4
          -       -Fabia-
JADED LADY-   -griersonianum 1/4
          -     -Fabia (as above)
          -Jade-
                -Corona--unknown 1/4
```
4ft(1.2m)  OF(-18C)  M    Fine foliage, with soft indumentum be-
low.  Plant covered with bell-shaped flowers of warm orange.  W.
& M. Thompson cross (created Ring of Fire); Greer, intro. 1989.

```
            -forrestii Repens Group 1/4
     -Jaipur-
J'AIME-   -meddianum 1/4
      -             -haematodes 1/4
      -May Day (Reuthe's)-
                         -griersonianum 1/4
```
Compact, spreading habit; leaves 3in(7.6cm) x 1.5in(3.8cm).  Lax
truss of 8-12 tubular campanulate flowers, orient red with crim-
son specks.   L. Brandt raiser; C. E. Simons, reg. 1964.

```
        -forrestii Repens Group 1/2
JAIPUR-
        -meddianum 1/2
```
3ft(.9m)  5F(-15C)  E  4/2    Flowers of heavy substance, deep
rich crimson; drooping.  Blooms young.  Rothschild, 1942.

JALIPEÑO   Described under RED PAINT, q.v.

```
* *
                    -fortunei ssp. discolor 1/4
     -Lady Bessborough-
JALISCO-   -campylocarpum Elatum Group 1/4
       -   -dichroanthum 1/4
       -Dido-
            -decorum 1/4
```
4ft(1.2m)  5F(-15C)  ML  4/3    Plant often used in hybridizing.
Straw yellow flowers,  with some dark red spotting, 3.5in(8.9cm)
across;  truss loose and drooping, of 8-10 flowers.  Broad, rich
green leaves.  Rothschild, 1942.
EXBURY JALISCO   Parentage as above
4ft(1.2m)  5F(-15C)  ML  4/4    Plant medium-sized, rich green
leaves.  Flower dusky yellow, widely funnel-campanulate.  Roth-
schild, 1942.
JALISCO ECLIPSE   Parentage as above
4ft(1.2m)  5F(-15C)  ML  4/4    Like the others.  Flowers prim-
rose yellow,  blotched and spotted crimson at the base,  crimson
streaks outside.  Rothschild, 1942.  A.M. 1948.
JALISCO ELECT   Parentage as above
4ft(1.2m)  5F(-15C)  ML  4/4    Flowers primrose yellow, paler
lobes,  brownish red spotting within.   Loose truss of about 10.
Petaloid calyx.  Rothschild, 1942.  A.M. 1948.  F.C.C. Wisley
Trials 1987.
JALISCO EMBLEM   Parentage as above
4ft(1.2m)  5F(-15C)  ML  4/3    Pale yellow flowers, with a dark
basal blotch.  Rothschild, 1948.
JALISCO GOSHAWK   Parentage as above
4ft(1.2m)  5F(-15C)  ML  4/3    Possibly best of this grex.  Flow-
ers mimosa yellow, spotted crimson.  Rothschild.  F.C.C. 1954.
JALISCO JANET   Parentage as above
4ft(1.2m)  5F(-15C)  ML  4/3  Apricot yellow.  Rothschild, 1948.
JALISCO JUBILANT   Parentage as above
4ft(1.2m)  5F(-15C)  ML  4/3  A fine late addition to this grex.
Up to 14 buttercup yellow flowers, with faint green spots in the
throat,  and a yellow calyx.  Very attractive trusses.    E. de
Rothschild.  A.M. 1966.  Color illus. ARS J 36:4 (1982), p. 139.
LINDBERG   Parentage as above
Like the rest of this group; yellow flowers.  Rothschild, 1954.
* * * * * * * * * * * * * * * * * * * * * * * * * * *

                         -griffithianum 1/8
                -Dawn's Delight-
        -Break of Day-      -unknown 1/8
JAMAICA-        -dichroanthum 1/4
        -facetum (eriogynum) 1/2
```
Low to medium-sized spreading plant, with truss of deep orange-
red campanulate flowers. Early to midseason. Rothschild, 1942.

```
* * * * * * * * * * * * * * * * * * * * * * * * * * *
             -orbiculare ? 1/2
JAMES BARTO-
             -williamsianum ? 1/2
```

5ft(1.5m) -5F(-21C) EM 3/4   Rather compact habit; tough-tex-
tured, elliptic leaves, 3in(7.6cm) long. Flowers funnel-shaped,
fuchsine pink, slightly fragrant, in loose truss of 3-5.   James
Barto cross; Clarence Prentice exhibited.   P.A. 1953.
MISSION BELLS   Parentage as above, except reversed
4ft(1.2m) -5F(-21C) M 3/4   Plant compact, sun-tolerant; foliage glossy, 4in(10cm) long. Campanulate flowers of pale pink,
slightly fragrant, lax truss of 6-8.   B. Lancaster, reg. 1958.
Color illus. VV p. 69.
* *

```
         -fortunei ssp. discolor 1/2
JAMES BURCHETT-      -catawbiense 1/4
         -unnamed hybrid-
                  -unknown 1/4
```
5ft(1.5m) -10F(-23C) L Vigorous plant, spreading 1.5 times as
wide as tall, leaves to 8in(20.3cm) long, dark green. Flower
truss 6in(15.2cm) across, compact, 15-17 flowers, white, slight
touch of pink.   Slocock, reg. 1962. A.M. Wisley Trials 1960.

```
                      -griffithianum 1/4
         -Jean Marie de Montague-
JAMES C. STEPHENS-               -unknown 3/4
         -unknown white hybrid
```
4ft(1.2m) -10F(-23C) EM   Flowers of heavy substance, spinel
red with a red blotch and spotting, openly funnel-shaped, 4.5in.
(11.5cm) wide, 5-lobed. Plant erect, broader than tall; glossy,
dark leaves 6in(15.2cm) long.   J. Freeman Stephens, reg. 1973.

JAMES COMBER--form of sanguineum ssp. sanguineum var. haemaleum
Countess of Rosse, Nymans Garden, exhibited; reg. 1973. A.M. 1973.

```
       -griersonianum 1/2
JAMES DEANS-
       -grande 1/2
```
Seven-lobed flowers in trusses of 14, of strong purplish pink,
fading to medium purplish pink. Young leaves with pale fawn indumentum. L. Jury, cross before 1957; R. G. Deans, reg. 1984.

* *
```
                 -griffithianum 3/16
               Mars
          -Vulcan-    -unknown 1/16
    -Old  -     -griersonianum 1/4
    -Copper-    -dichroanthum 1/8
JAMES-     -Fabia-
DRIVE-        -griersonianum
    -             -fortunei--Sir Charles Butler 1/4
    -Van Nes Sensation-         -maximum 1/8
                    -Halopeanum-
                         -griffithianum
```
5ft(1.5m) 5F(-15C) L   Truss of 7 flowers, light grayed orange
with darker throat and light red margins; reverse pale orange-
white. Floriferous. Plant upright, broader than tall; dull,
dark green foliage held 2 years. Walter Elliott, reg. 1981.
KNIGHT'S BEAUTY   Parentage as above
4ft(1.2m) 10F(-12C) ML   Strong purplish red flower buds
open strong purplish pink, spots on upper lobes. Compact shrub;
light green foliage. W. Elliott cross; E. Knight, reg. 1981.
* *

JAMES' PURPLE   See CHIEF PAULINA

```
       -facetum (eriogynum) 1/2
JAN BAPTISTE-
       -griffithianum 1/2
```
Coral-colored flowers.   Adams-Acton, 1934.

```
               -griffithianum 1/8
             -Mars-
    -Captain Jack-   -unknown 3/8
JAN BEE-         -facetum 1/4
    -         -arboreum ? 1/4
    -Kingianum-
         -unknown
```
3ft(1.9m) 5F(-15C) M 4/5   Tubular funnel-shaped flowers, of
heavy substance, guardsman red, spotted with dark cardinal red;
trusses of 18-20. Plant upright, broad; leaves held 3-4 years.
W. E. Berg, reg. 1981. C.A. 1982.

JAN DEKENS   Parentage unknown
5ft(1.5m) -5F(-21C) ML 3/3   A parent of PINK PETTICOATS.

Strong, vigorous plant with large, boldly curled leaves. Large
fringed flowers of vibrant bright pink, deeper on edges, rapidly
fading to pale pink. Trusses compact, upstanding.   J. Blaauw,
Boskoop, 1940.   Color illus. VV p. 41.

```
         -dichroanthum 1/4
       -Fabia-
JAN STEEN-    -griersonianum 1/4
       -              -fortunei ssp. discolor 1/4
       -Lady Bessborough-
                -campylocarpum Elatum Group 1/4
```
Flowers with cream margins, shading to pink, then to orange, and
a maroon throat blotch; upright trusses. Shrub tall, sparsely
branched. Rothschild. P.C. 1950.   Color illus. PB pl. 8.

```
    -fortunei 1/2
JANCIO-    -wardii 1/4
    -Crest-              -fortunei ssp. discolor 1/8
       -Lady Bessborough-
                -campylocarpum Elatum Group 1/8
```
Truss of 10-14 flowers of light yellow-green, darker in center,
with a small eye of currant red. E. de Rothschild, reg. 1981.

* *
```
               -lacteum 1/4
     -unnamed-              -campylocarpum 1/8
     - hybrid-Mary Swaythling-
JAN-DI-LYN-                 -fortunei 1/8
       -              -campylocarpum Elatum Group 1/4
       -Ole Olson-
                -fortunei ssp. discolor 1/4
```
5ft(1.5m) -5F(-21C) M   Flowers light cream, shading to blush
pink in throat, short trumpet-shaped, up to 4in(10cm) broad, in
compact trusses of 9.   R. G. Wyrens, reg. 1963.
MISS JACK   Parentage as above, except reversed
Compact plant of medium size; leaves 4.5in(11.5cm) long. Ivory
flowers spotted red on upper lobe, widely campanulate, 4in(10cm)
across; held in trusses of 10-12.   D. W. James, reg. 1964.
* *

JANE BANKS--form of ambiguum
5ft(1.5m) -5F(-21C) CM 3/3 Flowers in clusters of 3-7, tubular funnel-shaped, 5-lobed, chartreuse green, upper throat with
greenish spotting. Aromatic foliage of dark green.   W. L. & R.
A. Banks, reg. 1975. A.M. 1976.

JANE HARDY   Described under MI AMOR, q.v.

JANE HENNY   Described under LAKE LABISH, q.v.

JANE HOLDEN   Described under EVA REBECCA, q.v.

JANE MARTIN   Described under YAKU DUCHESS, q.v.

JANE REDFORD   Described under WELSHPOOL, q.v.

```
                    -Corona--unknown 5/8
             -unnamed hybrid-
       -Mrs. Donald-      -griersonianum 1/8
       - Graham  -     -griffithianum 1/8
JANE ROGERS-      -Loderi-
       -             -fortunei 1/8
       -Mrs. R. S. Holford--unknown
```
5ft(1.5m) -5F(-21C) ML 4/3 Clear pink flower with a vibrant
deep rose flare.   The color contrast resembles MRS. FURNIVALL.
Endre Ostbo, 1957.

JANE STENNING   CALSAP x BESSE HOWELLS
Hardiness -25F(-32C) Big red flowers; black blotch. Hinerman.

```
                  -griffithianum 3/8
             -Loderi-
    -Avalanche-    -fortunei 1/8
JANET-      -calophytum 1/4
    -         -caucasicum 1/4
    -Dr. Stocker-
             -griffithianum
```
6ft(1.8m) 5F(-15C) E 4/3   Large plant with extra large, pure
white flowers, stained deep crimson in throat; big, flat-topped
truss. Plant semi-compact; leaves to 8in(20.3cm) long.   Ranked
among the best of the tall Exbury hybrids. Rothschild, 1942.
A.M. 1950.

```
                    -Dexter hybrid--unknown
JANET BLAIR-
            -unknown
6ft(1.8m) -15F(-26C) ML 4/4  Synonym JOHN WISTER.  Parent of
many fine hybrids.  Frilled light pink flowers, paler at center,
golden bronze rays on upper lobes; large truss.  Plant vigorous,
compact, wider than tall; dense, dark foliage.   David G. Leach,
reg. 1962.  Color illus. Cox pl. 89; VV p. 82.


                           -fortunei ssp. discolor 1/4
              -Evening Glow-      -dichroanthum 1/8
             -                -Fabia-
JANET KERRIGAN-                  -griersonianum 1/8
             -                -ponticum 1/4
              -Purple Splendour-
                             -unknown 1/4
7ft(2.1m) x 7ft(15 yrs) -5F(-21C) M  Flowers in trusses of 9,
deep purplish pink, with a dark red blotch on a moderate orange
base.  Domed truss 6.5in(16.5cm) wide.  R. Kerrigan, reg. 1988.


                Complex parentage includes catawbiense,
JANET RICE     maximum, and possibly unknown hybrids.
7ft(2.1m) -15F(-26C) M    Buds of deep purplish pink, opening
to lighter purplish pink, with yellowish green spotting, openly
funnel-shaped, 3.5in(8.9cm) across; 5 frilled, pointed lobes;
rather loose, ball-shaped trusses of 10.  Plant well-branched;
glossy leaves held 2 years.  W. David Smith, reg. 1979.


* * * * * * * * * * * * * * * * * * * * * * * * * * * * *
                         -souliei ? 1/4
               -Virginia Scott-
JANET SCROGGS-           -unknown 1/4
              -           -dichroanthum 1/4
               -Jasper-
                   -Lady        -fortunei 1/8
                   -Bessborough-
                             -campylocarpum Elatum Group 1/8
6ft(1.8m) 5F(-15C) ML 4/4 Yellow flower with dorsal spotting
of dull orange, openly funnel-shaped, 2.75in(7cm) wide, 5 wavy
lobes; domed-shaped truss of 7-9.  Floriferous.   Plant broad as
tall; leaves held 3 years.  H. L. Larson, cross 1958; reg. 1979.
FREDA ROSAGE   Parentage as above
Buds of geranium lake opening to pale barium yellow, upper lobe
dark citron yellow.  Flower appears double  from the split cor-
olla.  Trusses of 13.  Larson, cross 1964; reg. 1982.
GOLDEN PIPPIN   Parentage as above
Flowers in truss of 7-9, 5- or 6-lobed, of lemon yellow, upper
lobes spotted red.  Larson, reg. 1983.
LUCILLE WILLIAMSON  Parentage as above, except reversed
Flower buds currant red, opening lighter red, interior buttercup
yellow; 7-lobed; trusses of 11.  Larson, reg. 1982.
* * * * * * * * * * * * * * * * * * * * * * * * * * * * *


JANET SHAPIRO   Described under HARDY SPLENDOUR, q.v.

                    -catawbiense 1/2
JANET WARD---sport of CYNTHIA-
                    -griffithianum 1/2
A hardy, flowering plant.  Slocock Nursery.   P.C. 1974.

                    -campanulatum 1/2
JANET WARRILOW-
               -unknown 1/2
4ft(1.2m) -5F(-21C) M  A possible hybrid or a form of campanu-
latum.  Lavender blue, a paler center.  D. Waterer, reg. 1975.

            -yellow hybrid--unknown 1/2
JANIELLE-    -campylocarpum 1/4
        -Marcia-     -campylocarpum 1/8
            -Gladys-
                  -fortunei 1/8
Pink flowers with red blotch.  Harold Greer, reg. 1961.

                   -caucasicum 3/16
               -Jacksonii-        -caucasicum
          -Goldsworth-     -Nobleanum-
JANINE    - Yellow  -              -arboreum 1/16
ALEXANDRE-         -campylocarpum 1/4
DEBRAY   -yakushimanum 1/2
Compact plant with indumented foliage.  Creamy pink flowers with
faint yellow center.  F. J. Street, reg. 1965.
```

```
                          -campylocarpum Elatum Group 1/16
              -Penjerrick-
        -Amaura-        -griffithianum 1/16
       -Venus-      -griersonianum 5/8
JANUS-     -facetum 1/4
      -griersonianum
A scarlet-flowered hybrid.   Lord Aberconway, intro. 1946.


           -lacteum 1/2
JASON-         -campylocarpum Elatum Group 1/4
      -Penjerrick-
           -griffithianum 1/4
Habit and appearance show much of lacteum.   Color between char-
treuse green and primrose yellow, fading to ivory at base; flow-
ers campanulate, 3.75in(9.5cm) across, 15-17 per truss.   Roth-
schild, 1942; reg. 1966.  A.M. 1966.


          -maximum 1/2
JASON'S MAXIM-
          -unknown 1/2
6ft(1.8m) -25F(-32C) L  Funnel-shaped flowers, white with yel-
low spotting, ball-shaped trusses of 16.  Plant very similar  to
maximum, but more compact; leaves held 3 years.  C. Bowers cross;
Planting Fields raiser;  R. F. Miller, reg. 1977.


* * * * * * * * * * * * * * * * * * * * * * * * * * * *
        -dichroanthum 1/2
JASPER-              -fortunei ssp. discolor 1/4
       -Lady Bessborough-
                    -campylocarpum Elatum Group 1/4
4ft(1.2m) -5F(-21C) M 2/3  A low, spreading plant with pale
orange flowers.  Very hardy at Exbury.  Rothschild, 1942.
JASPER PIMENTO   Parentage as above
Similar to above; flowers deep orange-red.  Rothschild, 1942.
* * * * * * * * * * * * * * * * * * * * * * * * * * * *

JAUNE--form of brachyanthum
3ft(.9m) -5F(-21C) L 2/3  Trusses of 3-4, bell-shaped, prim-
rose yellow.  Aromatic leaves 1.5in(3.8cm) long, scaly indument-
um on both sides.  C. Ingram; reg. 1966.  A.M. 1966.


JAVA  Described under SCARLET BLAST, q.v.


JAY GOULD   See ALEXANDER ADIE


         -minus Carolinianum Group 1/2
JAY MURRAY-
          -mucronulatum--Pink Panther 1/2
5ft(1.5m) x 5ft(13 yrs) -15F(-26C) EM  Flowers in ball trusses
of 4-6, 5-lobed, wavy margins, light purplish pink with brownish
orange spotting; buds moderate purplish red.  Very floriferous.
Leaves with scaly indumentum.  Dr. G. David Lewis, reg. 1987.


* * * * * * * * * * * * * * * * * * * * * * * * * * * *
                                  -griffithianum
                    -Queen Wilhelmina-      1/16
              -Britannia-          -unknown 11/16
JAY   -C. P. Raffill-    -Stanley Davies--unknown
McMARTIN-            -griersonianum 1/4
       -Moser's Maroon--unknown
6ft(1.8m) 10F(-12C) ML 4/3  Dense truss of 18 flowers, chry-
santhemum crimson,  black spots on upper lobe.   Plant straggly;
large leaves, 9in(23cm) long.  Lem cross; P. Bowman, reg. 1962.
ANNE HARDGROVE   Parentage as above
6ft(1.8m) 0F(-18C) L   Flower currant red, 5-lobed; truss of
11.  Leaves 6in(15cm) long.  Hardgrove cross; Burns, reg. 1978.
* * * * * * * * * * * * * * * * * * * * * * * * * * * *

       -griersonianum 1/2
JEAN-
     -decorum 1/2
5ft(1.5m) 10F(-12C) L   Glowing pink flowers.  Grown first in
Scotland, and now in New Zealand.  Stirling Maxwell, 1936.


              -dichroanthum 1/8
            -Fabia-
         -Jingle Bells-    -griersonianum 1/8
JEAN ELEANOR-      -         -campylocarpum Elatum Gp. 1/8
           -          -Ole Olson-
            -lacteum 1/2     -fortunei ssp. discolor 1/8
3ft x 3ft(.9m)(12 yrs) 5F(-15C) E   Open-campanulate flowers
2in(5cm) wide, light yellow-green, paler at edges, calyx 1.3in.
```

(3.2cm) long, colored like corolla. Flat truss of 17. Elliptic
leaves; light brown indumentum.   Britt M. Smith, reg. 1989.

JEAN GLENNIE   Parentage unknown
Salmon-colored flowers in loose trusses.   W. Glennie, reg. 1980.

```
                    -thomsonii 1/4
        -Barclayi-              -arboreum 1/8
        -        -Glory of Penjerrick-
JEAN    -                      -griffithianum 1/4
GOUJON-                              -griffithianum
        -                -Queen Wilhelmina-
        -Unknown Warrior-              -unknown 3/8
                    -Stanley Davies--unknown
```
Flowers vivid scarlet.   Adams-Acton, 1936.

* *
            Parentage includes catawbiense, maximum,
JEAN LEPPO   and perhaps unknown hybrids.
5ft(1.5m) -15F(-26C) M Purplish red buds opening medium pink, slight
yellow blotch, reverse strong purplish pink; flower 2.5in(6.4cm)
across, widely funnel-shaped, in trusses of 17. Plant rounded, as
broad as tall. W. D. Smith, reg. 1978.
KATHRYNA Parentage as above
6ft(1.8m) -15F(-26C) ML Purplish red with dark red blotch in trusses
of 23. Leaves 5.5in(14cm) long. Smith, reg. 1978.
* *

JEAN MARIE DE MONTAGUE   See THE HON. JEAN MARIE DE MONTAGUE

JEAN MARIE DE MONTAGUE PINK SPORT   See THE HONORABLE JEAN MARIE
   DE MONTAGUE PINK SPORT, described under THE HON. JEAN...

JEAN MARIE PINK   See PINK JEANS

```
                    -griffithianum 3/16
            -Kewense-
        -Aurora-       -fortunei 7/16
    -Naomi-    -thomsonii 1/8
JEAN    -fortunei
RHODES-             -griersonianum 1/4
    -Mrs. Horace Fogg-          -griffithianum
                -Loderi Venus-
                        -fortunei
```
Trusses of 14 flowers, Neyron rose, throat of dark chrysanthemum
crimson.   R. Rhodes cross; Mrs. L. Hodgson raiser; reg. 1979.

```
            -caucasicum 1/2
JEAN VERSCHAFFELT-
            -unknown 1/2
```
Flowers dark crimson, with a few black markings, frilled edges.
T. J. R. Seidel, before 1862.

* *
            -macabeanum 1/2
JEANNE CHURCH-   -campylocarpum 1/4
            -Unique-
                -unknown 1/4
Truss holds 21 flowers, primrose yellow with a pink flush and 3
red flares inside the base.   New Zealand Rhodo. Assoc. raiser;
Mrs. Wynne Rayner, reg. 1982.
BEAUTY OF BENMOI   Parentage as above
Flowers primrose yellow, paling to creamy white with deep maroon
blotch, fragrant, 6-lobed; trusses of 21. Compact habit; leaves
with buff indumentum. I. Gordon, reg. 1985.
SPICED HONEY Parentage as above
Trusses of 16-18 flowers, 7-lobed, apricot in bud opening
barium yellow and flushed pink on tube with deep maroon blotch.
Elliptic leaves 6in(15cm) long, with woolly gray indumentum and
yellow petioles.   G. F. Smith, reg. 1984.
* *

JEANNE YVONNE   Described under SIGRID, q.v.

```
                    -griffithianum 1/8
                -Queen Wilhelmina-
            -Britannia-        -unknown 7/8
JEANNETTE BRIGGS-       -Stanley Davies--unknown
            -unidentified seedling (W. E. Whitney)--unknown
8ft(2.4m) x 8ft(24 yrs)  10F(-12C)  ML     Openly funnel-shaped
```
flowers in trusses of 12-14, strong pink, shading to deep pink
at edges; reverse deep pink; truss 8in(20.3cm) wide. Betty Ann

Vander Wegen, cross 1962; Ben T. Briggs, reg. 1988.

JEANETTE CLARKE   Parentage unknown
Trusses of 12 funnel-shaped red flowers, darker in the throat.
Plant 5ft(1.5m), 10 years. V. J. Boulter, Australia, reg. 1984.

JEANNIE'S BLACK HEART   Parentage unknown; elepidote
2ft(.6m) x 2ft 0F(-18C) EM   Very dark (black-red) buds; dark
red flowers of heavy substance, some black spots and shading; in
flower over 1 month; lax truss of 6. Bullate leaves; pale green
tomentum when young, ages bronze; held 4 years. Minch, r. 1989.

JEEPERS CREEPERS   Described under GUSTO, q.v.

```
        -Mrs. J. G. Millais--unknown 19/32
                            -griffithianum 1/16
JELLY-                      -George-
BEAN -         -Betty    - Hardy-catawbiense 1/16
FEVER-     -Scandinavia- Wormald-red hybrid--unknown
    -         -          -George Hardy (as above)
    -unnamed-        -Hugh -
    hybrid-        Koster-        -arboreum 1/32
                    -Doncaster-
        -                  -unknown
        -catawbiense var. album--La Bar's White 1/4
```
Buds a blend of lilac, magnolia, and phlox purples open to
flowers of mallow purple, edged lighter; spots of dark greenish
yellow.   Al Smith cross; W. Delp.

JENICE COFFEY   Described under SIGRID, q.v.

* *
                        -griffithianum 1/4
                -Queen Wilhelmina-
            -Britannia-   -unknown 3/4
JENNIE DOSSER-   -Stanley Davies--unknown
            -         -griffithianum
            -Queen Wilhelmina-
            -Trilby-   -unknown
            -Stanley Davies--unknown
6ft(1.8m) -5F(-21C) L 4/3 Both parents of a common ancestry.
Light purple flowers with a deep purplish red blotch, funnel-
shaped, 4in(10.2cm) across, in tall, full trusses of about 14.
Upright plant; leaves 7in(17.8cm).   Lillie Dosser, reg. 1964.
JENNIE LEWIS   Parentage as above
5ft(1.5m) -5F(-21F) E   White flowers, tinged green, saucer-
shaped, 7-lobed, 6in(15cm) wide; rounded trusses of 10.   Plant
round with dark green leaves.   Lillie Dosser, reg. 1964.
* *

```
        -campylocarpum 1/2
JENNIFER-
        -griffithianum 1/2
```
Flowers of lemon yellow.   J. H. Johnstone.

JENNIFER HARRIS   Described under LANNY PRIDE, q.v

```
                -dichroanthum 1/4
        -Jasper-        -fortunei ssp. discolor 1/4
        -      -Lady
JENNIFER-    Bessborough-campylocarpum Elatum Group 1/4
 MARSHAL-                -campylocarpum Elatum Group
    -        -Ole Olsen-
    -Alice -        -fortunei ssp. discolor
    -Franklin-        -griffithianum 1/8
            -Loderi King George-
                    -fortunei 1/8
```
5ft(1.5m) -5F(-21C) M 4/4 Flowers 5-lobed, in trusses of 11;
deep aureolin yellow, flecked poppy orange-red.   Larson, reg.
1983.

JENNY   See CREEPING JENNY

```
    -minus Carolinianum Group, pink form  1/2
JENNY-
    -calostrotum 1/2
```
4ft(1.2m) -15F(-26C) ML 3/3 Clear pink flowers on a compact
plant spreading wider than tall.   Weldon E. Delp.

```
        -cinnabarinum Roylei Group 1/2
JENNY GORDON-
        -trichanthum 1/2
```

Trusses of 8 flowers, 5-lobed, color garnet lake. Leaves elliptic, glabrous. Lady Adam Gordon, reg. 1983.

JENNY LIND   Parentage unknown; elepidote
6ft(1.8m) high x 9ft(2.7m) -0F(-18C) ML Flowers in trusses of 15-17, 5 wavy-edged lobes, buds deep red, opening light purplish pink edged strong red, outside strong red, dorsal flare of light orange; truss 9in(23cm) wide x 7in(17.8cm).   C. S. Seabrook, cross c. 1950; B. R. Jarvis, reg. 1980; reg. published 1988.

JEREZ   Described under FRED WYNNIATT, q.v.

```
         -keiskei, Mt Kuromi form 1/2
JERICHO-
         -minus Carolinianum Group--Epoch 1/2
```
3ft(.9m) high x 4ft(1.2m)(11 yrs) -20F(-29C) M   Six flowers per truss, 5-lobed, light yellow-green in bud, open to pale yellow green, dorsal spots pale yellow. D. Leach cross; reg. 1986.

```
         -griersonianum 1/2
JERISSA-              -fortunei ssp. discolor 1/4
         -Lady Bessborough-
                     -campylocarpum Elatum Group 1/4
```
A tall shrub with good foliage of dull olive green. Pale yellow flowers with a small crimson spot, held in heavy trusses. Rothschild, 1942.   A.M. 1951.

* *
```
                 -griffithianum 1/4
         -Jean Marie de Montague-
JEROME KERN-               -unknown 1/4
         -sanguineum ssp. sanguineum var. haemaleum 1/2
```
Tall, spreading plant; broad, glossy, light green leaves. Rose Bengal flowers, funnel-shaped, 3.5in(9cm) wide, in tight trusses of 10-15.   Cecil S. Seabrook, reg. 1965.
DOROTHY LEE   Parentage as above
Semi-dwarf, with dark green leaves, 2.5in(6.4cm) long. Oxblood red flowers, tubular campanulate, held in loose trusses of 10 to 12.   Seabrook, reg. 1968.
* *

JERSEY CREAM   Described under ZUIDERZEE, q.v.

JERVIS BAY   Described under HAWK, q.v.

```
         -dichroanthum 1/2
         -                   -griffithianum 1/16
JESTER-          -Kewense-
         -    -Aurora-      -fortunei 5/16
         -Naomi-     -thomsonii 1/8
                -fortunei
```
Low and spreading; flowers yellow with pink spots. Rothschild.

```
                          -Pygmalion--unknown
                 -unnamed hybrid-
             -Weldy-              -haematodes
             -    -yakushimanum, Exbury form
          -unnamed-       -yakushimanum
          - hybrid-Serendipity-
JET SET-             -aureum (chrysanthum)
          -maximum, Jackson Center, Pa. white form
```
Buds of light chartreuse green opening to flowers pale greenish yellow; dorsal spotting chartreuse green.   W. Delp.

* *
```
         -caucasicum 1/2
JEWESS-
         -unknown 1/2
```
An old hybrid still in cultivation. Buds of light violet, open white with brown spots on upper lobe.   Emil Liebig, 1850s; sold by Standish & Noble, before 1860.
EUTERPE   Parentage as above
Pale pinkish buds, opening to pure white flowers with greenish yellow markings. T. J. R. Seidel, cross 1894.
* *

```
            -dichroanthum 1/4
         -Fabia-
JEZABEL-      -griersonianum 1/4
         -unknown
```
4ft(1.2m) -5F(-21C) M 3/3   Plant wider than tall, with elongated foliage. Flowers blood red.   Clark.

```
         -griersonianum 1/2
JIBUTI-       -arboreum 1/4
         -Gill's Triumph-
                     -griffithianum 1/4
```
Rose-colored, campanulate flowers in conical trusses. Tall, upright plant. Rothschild.   A.M 1949.

* *
```
         -lutescens 1/2
JILL-
         -unknown 1/2
```
1.5ft(.45m) -15F(-26C) M Ball-shaped terminal flower clusters of 1-4 trusses, each 2- to 4-flowered, total averages 14 flowers. Greenish yellow buds open primrose yellow, fading lighter, widely funnel-shaped, 1.5in(3.8cm) across. Plant broaderr than tall; leaves held 1 year.   Seed from Otto Prycl; W. Fetterhoff raiser; reg. 1980.
LOIS JEAN   Parentage as above
2ft(.6m) -15F(-26C) M   Primrose yellow flowers with 1/4 of each lobe shell pink. Plant wider than tall; small scaly leaves held 1 year. O. Prycl cross; Fetterhoff, reg. 1981.
* *

```
                 -griersonianum 1/4
         -Mrs. Horace Fogg-        -griffithianum 1/8
JIM DANDY-           -Loderi Venus-
         -unknown 1/2            -fortunei 1/8
```
5ft(1.5m) 0F(-18C) M 4/3 Sweetly scented white flowers with a blush of soft pastel orange, in tall, erect trusses. Plant of good habit; wider than tall. J. Elliott.

* *
```
                     -fortunei 1/4
         -Ruby F. Bowman-       -griffithianum 1/8
JIM DREWRY-           -Lady Bligh-
         -elliottii 1/2          -unknown 1/8
```
5ft(1.5m) 10F(-12C) M 4/3 Plant of slightly open but upright habit, mid-sized leaves. Flowers chrysanthemum crimson, darker spotting, funnel-shaped; truss of 27. Druecker, reg. 1971.
FORT BRAGG GLOW   Parentage as above
7ft(2.1m) x 9ft(2.7m)(15 yrs) 17F(-8C) EM Flowers 5in(12.5cm) broad, 6 wavy lobes of strong purplish red, a ruby red throat, slight deep red spotting, heavier on dorsal lobes; domed trusses of 11-14. Elliptic leaves 6in(15cm) long, medium olive. Plant rounded. J. Druecker, cross pre-1966; Mrs E. Philp, reg. 1986.
* *

```
            -neriiflorum Euchaites Group 1/2
JIMINY CRICKET-
            -microgynum Gymnocarpum Group 1/2
```
1ft(.3m) 0F(-18C) VE Dwarf plant with leaves 2in(5cm) x 1in. 2.5cm), elliptic, dark green. Flowers Turkey red, funnel-campanulate, 2.5in(6.4cm) across; rounded trusses of 13. Del W. James, reg. 1962.

```
            -wardii 3/4
         -Carolyn Grace-
JIMMY-           -unknown 1/4
         -wardii
```
6ft(1.8m) 0F(-18C) M   Plant of vigorous growth habit, good foliage. Flat, ruffled flowers, white with light flush of green in throat, 4.5in(10.8cm) across. Bovees, reg. 1963.

```
            -dichroanthum 1/4
         -Fabia-
JINGLE BELLS-     -griersonianum 1/4
         -         -campylocarpum Elatum Group 1/4
         -Ole Olson-
                     -fortunei ssp. discolor 1/4
```
3ft(.9m) 5F(-15C) M 4/4 Low-growing plant; dense foliage. Orange flowers fading yellow, with the red throat retained.   H. Lem cross; J. A. Elliott, reg. 1974. Color illus. VV p. 132.

```
         -dichroanthum 1/2
JIUSEPA-                 -fortunei ssp. discolor 1/8
         -         -Lady Bessborough-
         -Day Dream-           -campylocarpum Elatum Group 1/8
                 -griersonianum 1/4
```
Flowers a blend of biscuit and yellow, in loose trusses. Plant medium-sized and compact. Rothschild.   A.M. 1949.

```
                -campanulatum 1/4
   -Boddaertianum-
JO-            -arboreum ssp. cinnamomeum var. album 1/4
   -smithii 1/2
An introduction by E. J. P. Magor, 1920.


                 -dichroanthum 1/2
        -Jasper-                -fortunei ssp. discolor 1/8
   -      -Lady Bessborough-
JO ANN -                   -campylocarpum Elatum Group 1/8
NEWSOME-   -dichroanthum
   -Dido-
        -decorum 1/4
5ft(1.5m)  -5F(-21C)  L  4/4    Trusses of 13-14 flowers, signal
red, calyx of same color, 5-lobed.    H. L. Larson, reg. 1983.
```

JOAN   See JOAN SLINGER

* *
```
                -caucasicum 1/4
        -Nobleanum-
JOAN BYE-          -arboreum 1/4
    -         -campylocarpum 1/4
         -Unique-
                -unknown 1/4
```
Trusses hold 16 campanulate flowers, maize yellow flushed with
pink. V. J. Boulter, reg. 1963.
BETTY BOULTER   Parentage as above
Tyrian purple flowers, lightly spotted; ball-shaped trusses. V.
J. Boulter, reg. 1963.
MUNDAI   Parentage as above
Flowers magenta-colored.   Boulter, reg. 1965.
SHIRLEY SCOTT   Parentage as above
Saturn red in bud opening to barium yellow flowers in trusses of
about 16.   Boulter, reg. 1963.
* *
* *
```
        -Marion--unknown
JOAN LANGDON-
        -Sir Joseph Whitworth--(possibly ponticum hybrid)
```
Flowers lilac, blotched light olive green, in trusses of 15. G.
Langdon, reg. 1976.
MAUVE SATCHEL   Parentage as above
Trusses of 20 flowers, rose purple with lighter center, speck-
led with olive green.   Langdon, reg. 1976.
* *
```
                   -griffithianum 1/4
              -Loderi-
     -unnamed hybrid-    -fortunei 1/8
     -              -unknown 5/8
JOAN RAMSDEN-               -griffithianum
     -              -Snowdrop-
     -unnamed hybrid-        -unknown
                   -unknown
```
Pure white flowers, 3in(7.6cm) wide, held in large trusses. Sir
John Ramsden cross; Sir William Pennington-Ramsden, reg. 1965.

JOAN SCOBIE   Described under FOX HUNTER, q.v.

```
        -yakushimanum 1/2
JOAN SLINGER-
        -unknown 1/2
```
4ft(1.2m) ML Flowers in trusses of 7, campanulate, of strong
purplish pink to pure white inside. Leaves with fawn indumentum
beneath.   E. C. Nelson, reg. 1987.

* *
```
        -macabeanum 1/2
JOAN THOMPSON-
        -unknown 1/2
```
Parentage may be reversed.   Flower opens spinel red, then fades
lighter. Ruffled lobes. W. M. Spry, AUS, reg. 1968.   Color
illus. Mar. 1982, The Rhododendron. (AUS).
BEEKMAN'S DELIGHT   Parentage as above
Very pale yellow flowers with a purple blotch in the throat; 20
per truss. J. Beekman, AUS, cross; reg. 1981.
BELINDA BEEKMAN   Parentage as above
White flowers, spotted with purple. Trusses hold 17-20.   Beek-
man cross; reg. 1981.
DIANE BEEKMAN   Parentage as above
Creamy white flowers; trusses of about 16.   Beekman; reg. 1980.

ELAINE ROWE   Parentage as above
Truss of 15 flowers, 7- or 8-lobed, Neyron rose in bud, lighter
on exterior when open, inside cream with maroon flare. Foliage
with silvery gray, woolly indumentum.   G. Huthnance, reg. 1984.
EYESTOPPER   Parentage as above
Trusses of 20 flowers, primrose yellow, fading to almost white.
Huthnance, reg. 1980.
FRANCESCA BEEKMAN   Parentage as above
About 26 pale yellow flowers in each truss. Beekman, reg. 1980.
GOLDEN DAWN   Parentage as above
Flowers of primrose yellow with faint spots at base, 7-lobed, in
trusses of 12. Leaves oblong-elliptic. Huthnance, reg. 1982.
INA HAIR   Parentage as above
Flowers rose madder in bud, fading to cream, in trusses of 20.
Pukeiti Rhododendron Trust; G. F. Smith, reg. 1979.
MICHAEL BEEKMAN   Parentage as above
Red flowers aging to yellow; trusses of 20. Beekman, reg. 1980.
MILTON HOLLARD   Parentage as above
Trusses hold 22 flowers, phlox pink in bud, opening to primrose
yellow flushed pink, red spotting. B. Hollard, NZ, reg. 1979.
MRS. GEORGE HUTHNANCE   Parentage as above
Trusses of 16 flowers, primrose yellow with red flecking inside
upper lobe. Huthnance, reg. 1981.
PINK FRILLS   Parentage as above
Buds rose Bengal, open to creamy flowers with frilled margins of
rose Bengal; prominent blotch. Huthnance, reg. 1981.
THORON HOLLARD   Parentage as above
Phlox pink buds opening creamy white, striking red blotch in the
throat; outside of lobes has pink lines. B. Hollard, reg. 1979.
* *
* *
```
        -lacteum 1/2
JOANITA-
        -campylocarpum ssp. caloxanthum 1/2
```
5ft(1.5m) 0F(-18C) M   Typical crimson eye of lacteum appears
in daffodil yellow, campanulate flowers, from rich orange-yellow
buds. Distinctive broad, dark green leaves. Rothschild, 1941.
COSTA DEL SOL   Parentage as above, except reversed
Flowers of yellowish orange, flushed red in throat, openly bell-
shaped, 2.5in(6.4cm) wide; loose trusses of 14-15. Low, rounded
plant; foliage dark green, with light brown indumentum.   Rothschild, 1941. A.M. 1969 (NOTE: Reuthe also has a JOANITA, a
reverse cross of Rothschild's, which has larger yellow flowers.)
* *
```
        -Four Star Red Beauty--unknown 1/2
JOANNA -                           -maximum 1/16
STENNING-              -Russell Harmon-
     -          -unnamed-          -catawbiense 1/16
     -          - hybrid-          -neriiflorum 1/16
     -Pink Mango, F2 -     -Nereid-
     -                   -dichroanthum 1/16
        -fortunei ssp. discolor 1/4
```
Red flowers with light centers, held in spherical trusses. Very
hardy.   O. Pride cross; Dr. D. L. Hinerman raiser.

```
        -lacteum 1/2
JOCELYNE-
        -calophytum 1/2
```
Trusses hold 22 flowers, white with a tinge of cream, with a red
blotch in the throat. Plant tall; dull green foliage.   Rothschild, 1942. A.M. 1954. F.C.C. 1956. Color ill. PB pl. 22.

```
        -williamsianum 1/2
JOCK-
        -griersonianum 1/2
```
3ft(.9m) -5F(-21C) EM 3/4 Dark rosy pink flowers with orange
tint in throat, 3in(7.6cm) wide, cover the plant in small, loose
trusses. Habit dense, spreading; dark green leaves. Does best
in full sun.   Stirling Maxwell, 1939.

```
        -wardii 1/4
     -Hawk-              -fortunei ssp. discolor 5/16
     -    -Lady Bessborough-
JOCK -              -campylocarpum Elatum Group 3/16
SCOTT-         -fortunei ssp. discolor
     -         -unnamed-
     -unnamed- hybrid-unknown 1/8
       hybrid-    -Lady Bessborough (as above)
            -Lindberg-    -dichroanthum 1/16
                 -Dido-
                    -decorum 1/16
```

Flower buds apricot, opening salmon pink, a light yellow flush.
John Waterer Sons & Crisp, reg. 1974.


```
          -racemosum 1/2
JODI-
          -moupinense 1/2
```
2ft(.6m) OF(-18C) E 4/3 Leaves small, 1.5in(3.8cm) x .75in(2
cm). Flowers 1.5in(3.8cm) across, pink with a little dark spotting, blooming at branch tips in clusters of up to 6 buds, each
4-flowered. H. Lem cross; Mrs. Mae K. Granston, reg. 1977.


```
          -yakushimanum 1/2
JODIE KING-
          -unknown 1/2
```
Flowers in compact, rounded trusses, deep pink, fading with age.
Habit as yakushimanum. M. King, reg. 1984.

* *
```
          catawbiense var. album Glass--Catalgla 1/2
JOE GABLE-
          -wardii 1/2
```
5ft(1.5m) -10F(-23C) M 3/3 Plant habit dense, compact; wider
than tall. Flowers pale ivory, funnel-campanulate, to 3.5in(8.9
cm) across; trusses of 13-15.   Gable, cross 1954; reg. 1972.
BEIGE   Parentage as above
Pink buds open to ivory white flowers, with dark specks on upper
lobes.   Gable. Color illus. ARS J 36:2 (1982), cover.
MOON SHOT   Parentage as above
5ft(1.5m) -10(-23C) EM 4/4 Creamy white flowers; dark green
foliage. Gable. Color illus. LW pl. 48.
BUFFY and MILLER'S CHOICE also from the above cross.
* *

```
                    -griersonianum 1/4
          -Vulcan's Flame-    -griffithianum 3/8
          -                  -Mars-
JOE KRUSON-                    -unknown 3/8
          -        -griffithianum
          -Mars-
                    -unknown
```
3ft(.9m) -5F(-21C) M Funnel-shaped flowers, cardinal red, in
trusses of 13. Plant medium-compact, as broad as tall, revolute
pointed leaves, dark green.   H. Yates, reg. 1972.


```
                    -catawbiense 5/16
          -Catawbiense Album-
          -                  -unknown 5/16
JOE PATERNO-                   -catawbiense var. album 3/8
          -        -Belle Heller-              -catawbiense
          -Swansdown-           -hardy white hyb.-
          -                                   -unknown
                    -catawbiense var. album
```
5ft(1.5m) -20F(-29C) ML White flowers with a splash of bronze
yellow.   Orlando Pride cross; micro-propagated 1987-88.


```
          -lacteum 1/2
JOHN BARR-                              -caucasicum 1/8
STEVENSON-          -Dr. Stocker-
          -Logan Damaris-          -griffithianum 1/8
                    -campylocarpum 1/4
```
Flowers of lemon yellow.   J. B. Stevenson, reg. 1962.

JOHN BOGIE   Parentage unknown
Flowers in trusses of 6-8, tubular campanulate, 6- to 8-lobed,
blood red. Young leaves with bronze indumentum and red veins.
Mrs. A. G. Cocker, reg. 1987.


```
          -johnstoneanum  1/2
JOHN BULL-
          -edgeworthii (bullatum) 1/2
```
Pale pink flowers, flushed with cream.   First bloomed in 1957,
from seed sown in 1953.   Noble.


```
                    -griffithianum 1/8
          -Mars-
          -Vulcan-    -unknown 1/8
JOHN C. WHITE-    -griersonianum 1/4
          -fortunei, Gable's form 1/2
```
5ft(1.5m) -10F(-23C) EM Flowers openly funnel-shaped, 3.5in.
(9cm) across, 6-lobed, medium Neyron rose, edged lighter rose to
pale carrot red; domed trusses of 13. Plant broader than tall,
and well-branched; leaves 6.25in(15.8cm) long. George Ring III,

cross; Col. and Mrs. Raymond Goodrich, reg. 1980.

* *
```
                    -wardii 1/4            -griffithianum 1/32
          -Idealist-            -Kewense-
          -(selfed)-        -Aurora-      -fortunei 5/32
JOHN -            -Naomi-      -thomsonii 1/16
CALLER-          -fortunei
          -        -Lady          -fortunei ssp. discolor 1/8
          -        -Bessborough-
          -Jalisco-            -campylocarpum Elatum Group 1/8
             Orange-    -dichroanthum 1/8
                    -Dido-
                    -decorum 1/8
```
5ft(1.5m) 5F(-15C) M   Chartreuse flowers on an open plant of
strong growth habit. J. Waterer & Crisp, reg. 1975.
SAIL WING   Parentage as above
White flowers, with a blush pink tint and a yellow throat. J.
Waterer & Crisp, reg. 1975.
* *

```
                              -catawbiense 1/8
                    -Grand Arab-
          -unnamed hybrid-          -arboreum 1/8
JOHN COUTTS-          -griffithianum 1/4
          -griersonianum 1/2
```
4ft(1.2m) OF(-18C) L 4/3 Flowers glowing salmon pink, deeper
in throat, very smooth texture; large open truss.   Growth habit
dense, rather sprawly; plant completely covered by long, pointed
foliage. RBG, Kew, 1948.

* *
```
          -Blue Peter--unknown 5/8
          -                  -arboreum 1/8
JOHN DOSSER-          -Doncaster-
          -Corry Koster-          -unknown
          -                    -griffithianum 1/8
                    -George Hardy-
                              -catawbiense 1/8
```
Trusses hold 19 flowers, purple violet, paler at center, with a
black blotch.   K. Van de Ven raiser; D. Dosser, reg. 1974.
CRINKLES   Parentage as above
Flowers reddish purple, with a purple blotch; trusses hold about
21.   K. Van de Ven, reg. 1981.
* *

```
          -wardii 1/2
JOHN HARRIS-
          -macabeanum 1/2
```
Loose trusses of 14-16 flowers, pale primrose yellow with staining of maroon deep in throat, broadly campanulate, 2.5in(6.4cm)
across. Leaves elliptic-orbicular, medium green. John Harris
cross; Dr. D. F. Booth intro.; reg. 1983 A.M. 1983.

JOHN HOLMS   Described under DUKE OF CORNWALL, q.v.


```
          -cinnabarinum Roylei Group 1/2
JOHN KEATS-
          -augustinii 1/2
```
Mauve flowers, fading paler. Adams-Acton, 1942.


```
          -sperabile 1/2
JOHN MARCHAND-
          -moupinense 1/2
```
An interesting cross between the lepidote (scaly) and elepidote
(non-scaly) species. Flowers deep rose pink, open-campanulate,
2in(5cm) wide, in trusses of 3-4. Dwarf plant; broadly elliptic
leaves 1.5in(3.8cm) long, without indumentum.   John Marchand
cross; Collingwood Ingram raiser. A.M. 1966.

JOHN PAUL EVANS---nuttallii x nuttallii (another plant)
8ft(2.4m) x 6ft(1.8m) 32F(OC) EM Buds light yellow with pink
tips open to light yellow flowers, throat brilliant orangey yellow, 4in(10cm) wide; large flat trusses. Mrs. Evans, reg. 1988.

Next entry out of order:
```
                    -cinnabarinum ssp. xanthocodon 1/2
          -Daffodilly-
JOHN -          -cinnabarinum 1/4
STONE-          -augustinii var. chasmanthum 1/4
          -Hunter's-
             Moon  -cinnabarinum ssp xanthocodon
```

Flowers in trusses of 9, campanulate, 5-lobed, light yellow, fading to almost white. Shrub 10ft(3.0m) x 6.3ft(1.9m). Blooms late April. Gen. Harrison, cross c. 1970; Leonardslee intro.; E. W. M. Magor, reg. 1987.

```
                   -griffithianum 3/8
            -Mars-
            -      -unknown 7/16
JOHN PAUL II-                            -griffithianum
            -      -Jean Marie de Montague-
            -      -                      -unknown
            -unnamed-                 -caucasicum 1/16
             hybrid-  -Cunningham's-
            -      -   White      -ponticum (white form)
            -Cheer-                      1/16
                   -                -catawbiense 1/16
                       -red catawbiense-
                            hybrid   -unknown
```
4ft(1.2m) x 7ft(2.1m)(18 yrs) -25F(-32C) M   Flowers frilled, 2.7in(7cm) wide, vivid red with pale yellow dorsal lobe streaks, faint spotting of vivid yellow-green; ball truss of 15-18. Foliage 7in(18cm) long, glossy dark green, held 2-3 years. J. Minahan cross; reg. 1989. Best of Show Phila./V. Forge Ch. 1981.

JOHN R. ELCOCK--form of fortunei ssp. discolor Houlstonii Group
5ft(1.5m) -5F(-21C) M 3/3   Trusses hold 8-10 flowers, rose purple, fading to light yellow in throat, funnel-campanulate, 3.2in(8cm) wide; leaves to 3.5in(8.9cm) long, oblong-elliptic. Crown Estate, Windsor; reg. 1977. A.M. 1977.

JOHN SKRENTNY--form of arboreum
5ft(1.5m) 10F(-12C) E 4/3   Globe-shaped truss of 16 flowers, clear cherry red, bell-shaped, 2in(5cm) broad. Foliage 8in(20.3 cm) long, dark green; light fawn indumentum. John Skrentny collector; B. Lancaster, reg. 1966.

JOHN STONE   See previous column

JOHN TREMAYNE   See under BEAUTY OF TREMOUGH.

```
            -catawbiense 1/2
JOHN WALTER-
            -arboreum 1/2
```
5ft(1.5m) -10F(-23C) ML 3/3   Frilled flowers of crimson red in trusses of about 20.   Leaves slightly rough in texture, dull olive green. A vigorous grower. J. Waterer, before 1860.

```
            -catawbiense 1/2
JOHN WATERER-
            -unknown 1/2
```
Purplish red flowers. Still in cultivation.   J. Waterer, 1860.

```
               -griffithianum 1/2
JOHN WILLIS FLEMING-
               -unknown 1/2
```
Flowers of rose color.   W. H. Rogers.

JOHN WISTER   See JANET BLAIR

```
            -johnstoneanum, double form 1/2
JOHNNIE JOHNSTON-
            -tephropeplum 1/2
```
4ft(1.2m) 10F(-12C) M   Unusual, semi-double flowers, of Tyrian rose with darker staining; loose trusses. E. Bolitho, 1941. A.M. 1956.

* *
```
                    -griffithianum 1/4
            -Jean Marie de Montague-
JOHNNY BENDER-                  -unknown  1/4
            -          -dichroanthum ssp. scyphocalyx 1/4
            -Indiana-
                    -kyawii 1/4
```
4.5ft(1.35m) -5F(-21C) M 4/5   Flowers bright currant red, darker dorsal spotting, of good substance; round tight trusses. Glossy dark green leaves 6in15.2cm) long, heavily textured.   C. S. Seabrook, cross 1960; John Eichelser, reg. 1980.
MARK TWAIN   Parentage as above
A large open plant, but shapely, with very large, smooth leaves. Flowers currant red, campanulate, in tight high trusses, 8in(20 cm) across. Seabrook, reg. 1967.
* *

```
            -yakushimanum 1/2
JOHNNY ROSE-
            -unnamed hybrid--unknown 1/2
```
Light orchid pink flowers, flushed a deeper shade.   J. Waterer & Crisp, reg. 1975.

```
            -smirnowii 1/2
JOLLY RED GIANT-
            -unknown 1/2
```
5ft(1.5m) -25F(-32C) ML   A Canadian hybrid. Open trusses of light red to deep pink flowers, a yellow blotch.   L. Hancock.

```
                              -catawbiense
                  -Parsons Grandiflorum-    1/32
                  -America-         -unknown
            -Dorothy -      -dark red hybrid--unknown 13/32
      -Melanie- Amateis-          -ponticum 5/16
      - Shaw -         -Purple Splendour-
JONATHAN-                               -unknown
  SHAW -       -Purple Splendour (as above)
      -            -catawbiense var. album 1/4
      -Brenda Lee-
            -Purple Splendour (as above)
```
3.5ft(1m)(6yrs; 1.5yrs indoors) -10F(-23C) L   Flowers 3in(7.5 cm) across, vivid violet purple shades, to a strong purplish red center, prominent black flare; ball truss of 19. Lobes, foliage are wavy-edged. Dense bush. J. Leonard, cross 1981; reg. 1988.

```
            -dichroanthum 1/2
JORDAN-
            -griffithianum 1/2
```
Medium-sized plant. Pale orange flowers, with a touch of pink, opening in early mid-season.   Rothschild, 1942.

```
            -minus Carolinianum Group 1/2
JOSEPH DUNN-
            -racemosum 1/2
```
4ft(1.2m) -15F(-26C) ML   Lovely pink flowers, late midseason. Bush 4ft(1.2m) tall and 3ft(.9m) wide at 10 years; leaves 1in. (2.5cm) long, very dark green all year.   G. D. Lewis.

```
                    -maximum, white form 1/2
JOSEPH GARY FETTERHOFF-
                    -Mrs J. G. Millais--unknown 1/2
```
4ft(1.2m) x 4.5ft(1.35m)(24 yrs) -22F(-30C) ML   Buds very pale mauve. Flowers white, striking gold blotch, wavy-edged; 20 per domed truss. Smooth dark leaves.   Fetterhoff cross; reg. 1989.

```
            -ponticum 1/2
JOSEPH WHITWORTH-
            -unknown 1/2
```
6ft(1.8m) -10F(-23C) ML   Flowers deep maroon with black spotting, in full rounded trusses of 12-16.   J. Waterer, 1867.

```
            -wardii 1/2
JOSEPHINE-    -fortunei ssp. discolor 1/4
            -Ayah-
                -facetum (eriogynum) 1/4
```
Terracotta pink buds open to large, bell-shaped, cream-colored flowers, lightly spotted red in throat, and flushed pink. Plant of medium size; long, narrow, glossy leaves.   Rothschild, 1942.

JOSEPHINE EVERITT   Parentage uncertain; a fortunei hybrid?
4ft(1.2m) -10F(-23C) ML   Well-formed truss of clear pink flowers of two shades. Fragrant.   Dexter cross; Wister selection.

JOSEPHINE V. CARY   Described under CARY'S CREAM, q.v.

```
            -rupicola 1/2
JOSHUA HUDDY-
            -mucronulatum--Pink Panther 1/2
```
4ft(1.2m)(13yrs) -15F(-26C) E   Buds deep violet purple open to light purple flowers 1.75in(4.5cm) wide, wavy-edged, openly funnel-shaped; small ball truss of 6-15. Flat leaves, scaly below, to 2in(5cm); held 1.5 years. G. Lewis, cross 1974; reg. 1989.

```
* * * * * * * * * * * * * * * * * * * * * * * * * * * * * * *
               -macabeanum 1/2
JOY BELLS-      -falconeri 1/4
          -Fortune-
                    -sinogrande 1/4
N.Z. hybrid.  Cream-colored flowers, suffused chartreuse, with
a faint crimson blotch in the throat.  Mrs. W. Hayes, reg. 1979.
JOYCE     Parentage as above
Trusses hold 20-22 flowers, 7-lobed, cream suffused chartreuse,
with small crimson blotch, about 3in(7.6cm) across.  Mrs I. Mc-
Kenzie, cross 1969; J. Joyce raiser; Mrs. W. Hayes, reg. 1984.
* * * * * * * * * * * * * * * * * * * * * * * * * * * * * * *


JOY RIDE     Parentage unknown
6ft(1.8m)  10F(-12C)  EM  3/4  Pale pink flowers, with an orange
blotch, in trusses of 16.  W. Whitney cross; Sather, reg. 1976.


            -wardii 1/2
JOYANCE-
            -dichroanthum ssp. scyphocalyx 1/2
Cream flowers with pale orange spots, in small trusses.  Medium-
sized plant.  Midseason.  Rothschild, 1942.


JOYCE    Described under JOY BELLS, q.v.


JOYCE HARRIS    Described under BETTY WHITE, q.v.


                     -maximum 1/2
            -Midsummer-
JOYCE LYN-           -unknown 1/4
-            -maximum
           -Adele's Yellow-
                        -wardii 1/4
Buds of fuchsia purple and deep purplish pink  opening to white,
star-shaped flowers, edged with mallow purple and light purplish
pink; flare of Dresden yellow.  W. Delp.


JOYCE MONTAGUE    See THE HONORABLE JEAN MARIE DE MONTAGUE


               -fortunei ssp. discolor 1/2
JOYCE RICKETT-          -catawbiense 1/4
              -Madame Carvalho-
                        -unknown 1/4
White flowers with pink margins.  Hillier, 1945.



                         -campylocarpum Elatum Group 1/2
JOYCE'S JOY---LETTY EDWARDS, F2-
                         -fortunei 1/2
2ft(.6m) x 4ft(1.2m)(25 yrs)  0F(-18C)  EM  Flat trusses of 6-8
openly campanulate flowers, 2.5in(6.3cm) wide, wavy-edged, light
pink to pale salmon.  Dense, floriferous bush; glossy ovate fol-
iage to 4in(10cm), held 3 years.  H. Vaartnou cross; reg. 1989.


JOYFUL    Described under FRED WYNNIATT, q.v.


JOYLYN    Described under JACQUELINE LOOYE, q.v.


          -Blue Ensign--unknown 1/2
JUAN DE FUCA-
          -ponticum 1/2
6ft(1.8m)  10F(-12C)  L  3/3  Buds vivid purple and flowers of
lilac, with dark red spotting and blotch, 3in(7.6cm) across, in
trusses of 12; large foliage.  H. L. Larson, cross 1964; North-
west Ornamental Horticultural Society, reg. 1977.


JUANITA    Described under INFANTA, q.v.


* * * * * * * * * * * * * * * * * * * * * * * * * * * * * * *
                 -griffithianum 1/4
          -Loderi Venus-
JUBILEE-          -fortunei 1/4
 QUEEN -        -decorum 1/4
          -Rose du-          -maximum 1/8
           Barri -Standishii-          -unnamed-catawbiense
                   -Altaclerense- hybrid-          1/32
                                       -ponticum 1/32
                             -arboreum 1/16
Tips of lobes tinged rose on opening, then turning to pure white
flowers.  Lady Loder.  A.M. 1935.
MARGARET ROSE   A named clone of above grex.  Lady Loder.
* * * * * * * * * * * * * * * * * * * * * * * * * * * * * * *
```

```
              -brachycarpum 1/2       -dichroanthum 1/8
JUDANN-             -unnamed hybrid-
        -Calcutta-          -kyawii 1/16
    -unnamed-      -catawbiense var. album Glass--Catalgla
      hybrid-          -maximum 1/16          1/8
      -         -unnamed hybrid-
      -Tahiti-          -catawbiense 1/16
                   -dichroanthum
        -unnamed-      -fortunei ssp. discolor
          hybrid-unnamed-          1/32
                   hybrid-campylocarpum 1/32
Flowers Neyron rose and pale purplish pink; a vivid yellow-green
flare; dorsal spotting vivid yellow-green.  W. Delp.


               -griffithianum 1/8
          -Dorothea-
        -Rochelle-          -decorum 1/8
        -          -catawbiense 1/8
JUDITH ANNE-      -Kettledrum-
                   -unknown 1/8
        -catawbiense var. album Glass--Catalgla 1/2
Buds roseine purple open rhodamine purple and lighter, throat of
Tyrian purple, flecks of ruby red.  Medium-sized plant; hardy to
-15F(-26C).  W. Delp.


               -griffithianum 1/2
          -Gillii-
JUDITH ELLEN-      -arboreum 1/4
        -                   -griffithianum
          -Jean Marie de Montague-
                   -unknown 1/4
Funnel-shaped flowers in truss of 16, 5-lobed, of vivid purplish
red, with a darker dorsal flare.  Shrub to 5ft(1.5m)(7 yrs).  D.
J. Dosser, cross 1980; Lockington Nursery, reg. 1987.


JUDY    Described under GLADYS, q.v.


               -wardii 1/2       -griffithianum 1/32
          -Idealist-       -Kewense-
        -          -Aurora-      -fortunei
JUDY -         -Naomi-      -thomsonii 1/16
CLARKE-          -fortunei 5/32
        -      -wardii
        -Hawk-          -fortunei ssp. discolor 1/8
           -Lady          -
        -Bessborough-campylocarpum Elatum Group 1/8
Loose trusses of 8-12 flowers, 5-lobed, saucer-shaped, to 4in.
(10.2cm) across; flowers light primrose yellow, slightly deeper
in throat; calyx flushed red-purple.  Leaves elliptic-ovate, to
3.6in(9cm) long.  John Clarke, cross 1965;  Anne, Countess of
Rosse, Nymans Garden, exhibitor; reg. 1983.  A.M. 1983.


                    -griffithianum 1/4
          -Loderi King George-
JUDY HASSETT-          -fortunei 1/4
          -Phyle Donegan--unknown 1/2
Funnel-shaped flowers in trusses of 6 to 8, interior light pur-
plish pink;  pale green flare on upper lobe.  Plant 3.3ft(1.0m)
tall; oblanceolate foliage.  W. McClure, reg. 1986.


            -maximum 1/2
JUDY SPILLANE-
          -Dexter 201 (JOHN WISTER)--unknown 1/2
4ft(1.2m)  -5F(-21C)  L    Late flowers of light purplish pink,
paler in center, a prominent blotch of strong yellowish green,
openly funnel-shaped, 2.5in (6.4cm) across, fragrant; spherical
trusses of 14.  Plant rounded, dense foliage; flat olive green
leaves.  Dr. John Wister, Tyler Arboretum, reg. 1980.  Color
illus. ARS Q 32:3 (1978), p. 170.


                    -griffithianum 1/8
               -Loderi-
        -Albatross-          -fortunei 1/8
JULIA    -          -fortunei ssp. discolor 1/2
GROTHAUS-          -fortunei ssp. discolor
        -Golden Belle-      -dichroanthum 1/8
          -Fabia-
                   -griersonianum 1/8
6ft(1.8m)  0F(-18C)  L  5/4  Leaves 6in(15.2cm) long.  Flowers
fragrant, ruffled, 5in(12.7cm) wide, 7-lobed, peach, edged with
white, small brown blotch; truss of 12.  Mrs. L. Grothaus, reg.
1975.  A.E. 1988.  Color illus. ARS Q 31:1 (1977), p. 34.
```

```
* * * * * * * * * * * * * * * * * * * * * * * * * * * *
      -griersonianum 1/2
JULIANA-              -griffithianum 1/4
     -Queen Wilhelmina-
                     -unknown 1/4
Scarlet flowers.  Collingwood Ingram, 1939.
CAPTAIN BLOOD   Parentage as above
Scarlet rose flowers, slight spotting on upper lobe.  Colling-
wood Ingram.  A.M. 1947.
* * * * * * * * * * * * * * * * * * * * * * * * * * * *

                -griffithianum 1/2
JULIE---LODERI, selfed-
                -fortunei 1/2
Large white flowers, suffused sulphur, 8 per truss.   A.M. 1944.

JULIE GRACE   Described under BOB BOVEE, q.v.

                              -griffithianum 3/8
                   -George Hardy-
         -Marinus Koster-         -catawbiense 1/8
         -               -unknown 1/4
JULIE TITCOMB-                 -maximum 1/8
         -               -Halopeanum-
         -Snow Queen-             -griffithianum
         -               -Loderi-
                         -fortunei ssp. fortunei 1/8
6ft(1.8m) 0F(-18C) M  3/3 Flowers 4.5in(11.5cm) wide, carmine
outside and blush pink within; slight crimson spotting.  Large
trusses of 16 flowers.  H. L. Larson.  P.A. 1958.

JULIET     See SHAM'S JULIET under PINK CAMEO.

                    -arboreum 1/8
              -Doncaster-
      -Thunderstorm-    -unknown 3/8
JULISCHKA-        -unknown
      -yakushimanum--Koichiro WADA 1/2
4ft(1.2m) -5F(-21C) ML    Trusses of 16 to 20 flowers, 5-lobed,
deep spirea red, shading to rose Bengal and to very light Neyron
rose in throat.  Leaves lanceolate-obovate.  Hachmann cross; G.
Stück, reg. 1983.


* * * * * * * * * * * * * * * * * * * * * * * * * * * *
                    -griffithianum 1/4
             -Isabella-
JULY FRAGRANCE-       -auriculatum 1/4
             -diaprepes 1/2
5ft(1.5m) 0F(-18C) ML     Frilled flowers, white with crimson
stain at base, showing pale rose on outside, funnel-shaped, 4.3
in(11cm) across, strongly fragrant.  Loose truss of 8-10.  Hil-
lier & Sons, reg. 1968.
MIDSUMMER SNOW   Parentage as above
6ft(1.8m) 5F(-15C) L     Flowers white, green tinge in throat,
trumpet-shaped, 7-lobed; very fragrant; large, loose trusses of
8-10.  New growth bright yellowish green.  Hillier, reg. 1968.
* * * * * * * * * * * * * * * * * * * * * * * * * * * *

             -Loder's White, q.v. for 2 possible parentages
        -C.I.S.-       -dichroanthum
        -       -Fabia-
JUMPING JEFF-         -griersonianum
        -       -williamsianum
        -Jock-
              -griersonianum
3ft(.9m) x 4.5ft(1.4m)(16 yrs) 0F(-18C) M  Buds of strong pur-
plish red, open to 6- or 7-lobed flowers deep pink with red rays
on dorsal lobes; wavy-edged.  Lax trusses 6in(15.2cm) broad hold
5 to 6.  Dull olive green foliage.  G. Bell, reg. 1986.

             -decorum 3/8
        -Tumalo-                -griffithianum 3/16
  -unnamed-   -Loderi King George-
  - hybrid-             -fortunei
JUNCO-    -fortunei 5/16
     -Fawn-    -dichroanthum 1/16
        -Fabia-
        -       -griersonianum 1/16
        -    -decorum
        -Tumalo-
             -Loderi King George (as above)
```

```
5ft(1.5m) -15F(-26C) M   Very fragrant, white flowers in truss
of 6-8.  Plant well-branched, broad; ivy green leaves. Del W.
James raiser; Hendricks Park, Eugene OR, reg. 1980.

                         -griffithianum 1/16
                   -Loderi-
         -Albatross-       -fortunei 1/16
     -Marie   -               -fortunei ssp. discolor 1/4
     -Antoinette-       -fortunei ssp. discolor
JUNGFRAU-    -       -Ariel-
     -unknown       -Memoir--unknown 5/8
5ft(1.5m) 0F(-18C) ML   Named for the Swiss mountain.  Flower
throat creamy white, shading to pale Tyrian rose, 3.75in(9.5cm)
wide, in a huge conical truss of about 32.  Compact plant.  One
of the very few Exbury creations lacking complete parentage rec-
ords.  E. de Rothschild, reg. 1967.  A.M. 1966.


                    -catawbiense 1/2
JUNIFREUDE---Omega, selfed-
                    -rose-colored hybrid--unknown
2.3ft(.7m) x 4.3ft(1.3m) -15F(-26C) ML  Flowers of 5 wavy-edged
lobes, strong purplish red, shading strong purplish pink throat;
dorsal markings moderate olive green  to yellow-green; 13-16 per
truss.  Dark glossy leaves.  Hachmann cross; Stück, reg. 1988.


         -Mary Waterer--unknown
JUNIPERLE-
         -Moser's Maroon--unknown
Flowers in trusses of 12 to 15, 5-lobed, of strong purplish red,
shading lighter toward center, marked with greenish yellow.  H.
Hachmann, cross 1968; G. Stück, reg. 1984.


              -campylocarpum Elatum Group 1/8
         -Penjerrick-
   -Amaura-       -griffithianum 1/8
JUNO-    -griersonianum 1/4
   -       -neriiflorum 1/4
   -F. C. Puddle-
              -griersonianum
Pale pink flowers.  Lord Aberconway, intro. 1941.


                    -griffithianum 1/4
     -Mrs. E. C. Stirling-
JUPITER-       -unknown 1/4
     -unknown 1/2
Flowers of soft lilac rose.   J. Waterer, Sons & Crisp.


JUST DREAMIN'   Described under MELLOW GOLD, q.v.


JUST JO   Parentage unknown; elepidote
6ft(1.8m)(18 yrs) -5F(-21C) M  Deep pink buds to heavy flowers
scented minty almond, 2.8in(7cm) wide, 7 wavy lobes of light am-
ethyst purple, paler pink throat; lax trusses of 10.  Smooth ob-
long leaves to 4in(10cm); well-branched, rounded plant.  Winston
Ragan, cross 1969; W. & Joan Ragan, reg. 1988.


             -degronianum ssp. heptamereum (metternichii) 1/2
JUSTIZRATH STEIN-
             -unknown 1/2
Flowers intense salmon pink with dark markings.   Seidel, 1873.


   -elliottii 1/2
JUTLAND-           -fortunei ssp. discolor 1/8
   -       -Norman Shaw-       -catawbiense 1/16
       -Bellerophon-       -B. de Bruin-
       -               -unknown 1/16
       -facetum (eriogynum) 1/4
6ft(1.8m) 5F(-15C) L  4/2   Intense red, waxy flowers flecked
very dark red, widely campanulate; large, compact, dome-shaped
truss of 19.  Handsome foliage of dark rich green.  Rothschild,
1942.  A.M. 1942.


JUWEL   Described under ELISABETH HOBBIE, q.v.
```

K

K. D. HARRIS   Described under JACQUELINE LOOYE, q.v.

K. S. W.   See KSW (as one word)

KAISER WILHELM   Parentage unknown
A parent of HOMER. Carmine red flowers. Probably hybridized by
the Seidels, before 1890.

KAKA   Described under SCARLET KING, q.v.

KALAKALA   Parentage unknown; elepidote
7ft(2.1m) x 7ft(18 yrs) -5F(-21C) M   Deep pink buds with yellow tinge open strong purplish pink with yellowish tinge in
trusses of 8-9. Leaves held 3 years.   W. A. Ragan, reg. 1989.

```
                    -Marion--unknown 3/4
          -Edith Boulter-        -campylocarpum 1/8
          -              -Unique-
KALIMNA-                  -unknown
          -                             -griffithianum 1/8
          -              -Queen Wilhelmina-
          -Unknown Warrior-              -unknown
                    -Stanley Davies--unknown
```
5ft(1.5m) 0F(-18C) EM   Flowers medium Neyron rose to a paler
rose, light yellowish brown on upper lobe.   V. J. Boulter, reg.
192. Color illus. ARS Q 29:3 (1975), p. 170.

```
              -yakushimanum--Koichiro Wada 1/2
       -Morgenrot-        -griffithianum 1/4
       -         -Spitfire-
KALINKA-                  -unknown 1/4
       -                  -griffithianum
       -unnamed-Mars-
         hybrid-   -unknown
              -yakushimanum--Koichiro Wada
```
2.3ft(.7m) x 4.3ft(1.3m) -10F(-23C) ML Flowers of medium Ney-
ron rose, pale pink at center, rims darker, marked moderate yellow-green; truss of 12-18. Glossy leaves with brown indumentum.
Hachmann cross; Stück, reg. 1984. Color ill. WS, 1989, p. 153.

KALLISTOS--form of nuttallii var. stellatum
A parent of ALF BRAMLEY, q.v.

```
                   -cataubiense v. album Glass--Catalgla
       -unnamed hybrid-                              1/4
KANCHENJUNGA-        -fortunei 1/4
            -decorum, McLaren form 1/2
```
7ft(2.1m) x 8ft(2.4m)(13 yrs) -10F(-23C) M Very light yellow-
green buds. Flowers white with two strong yellow-green rays, of
heavy substance, 7-lobed.   Truss 8in(20.3cm) wide, of 11 to 13.
Smooth elliptic foliage.   G. Ring cross; R. Brooks, reg. 1986.

```
                   -cataubiense 3/8
            -Mrs. Milner-
       -Donar-        -unknown 3/8
KANTATE-    -smirnowii 1/4
       -         -cataubiense
       -Amphion-
              -unknown
```
3.7ft(1.1m) x 5ft(1.5m) -15F(-26C) ML   Tight trusses of 15-18
funnel-shaped flowers, wavy-edged, vivid fuchsia purple to rose
purple, throat very pale; strong yellow-green dorsal spots. Elliptic, dark leaves. Hachmann, cross 1973; Stück, reg. 1988.

KANTILENE   Described under YAKU WARRIOR,q.v.

```
       -arboreum 1/2
KAPONGA-
       -Ivery's Scarlet--unknown 1/2
```
6ft(1.8m) 10F(-12C) EM   Red-flowered New Zealand shrub; large
tree-like habit. B. Holland, reg. 1979.

```
          -Pacific Queen--unknown 1/2
KAPUNATIKI-
          -wardii 1/2
```
Funnel-shaped flowers in trusses of 11, pale greenish yellow
with throat half green and half red. Nov. blooms, in NZ. Mrs.

L. A. Grant, reg. 1988.

```
                           -fortunei ssp. discolor 3/16
                 -Ladybird-
              -Diva-        -Corona--unknown 9/16
       -Seattle Gold-  -griersonianum 1/8
KAREN -                  -fortunei ssp. discolor
TRIPLETT-      -Lady   -
       -         Bessborough-campylocarpum Elatum Group 1/8
       -late-flowering yellow--unknown
```
5ft(1.5m) -5F(-21C) M 4/4 Trusses of 10-12 flowers, aureolin
yellow, 4.5in(11.5m) wide, 6-lobed.   H. L. Larson, reg. 1982.

KARIN   Described under BRITANNIA'S BELLS, q.v.

```
       -impeditum 1/2
KARIN SELEGER-
       -dauricum 1/2
```
2.5ft(.76m) x 3.4ft(1.04m)(18 yrs) -25F(-32C) M Ball truss of
5-7 flowers, medium purple-violet, to 1.5in(3.8cm) wide, 5 wavy-
edged lobes; scaly leaves .75in(2cm) long. Plant dense, floriferous. Pollen collected in Siberia by Vasak. Dr. J. Brueckner,
cross 1971; reg. 1989.   Color illus. ARS J 44:2 (1990), p. 78.

```
       -griersonianum 1/2
KARKOV-       -arboreum 1/4
       -Red Admiral-
              -thomsonii 1/4
```
5ft(1.5m) 10F(-12C) EM 3/3 Large round truss of 16 flowers,
carmine rose lightly spotted, funnel-shaped, frilled margins.
Vigorous plant of medium size. Rothschild, 1943. A.M. 1947.

```
                               -dichroanthum 3/16
                    -Goldsworth-
       -Tortoiseshell- Orange   -fortunei ssp. discolor 1/8
       - Wonder     -griersonianum 3/16
    -Apricot-                  -griffithianum 3/32
    - Gold -          -Loderi-
    -     -      -Albatross-   -fortunei 1/32
    -     -Cup Day-   -fortunei ssp. discolor
    -     -          -elliottii 1/16
KARL-        -Fusilier-
    -                  -griersonianum
    -             -dichroanthum
    -       -Dido-
    -       -   -decorum 1/8          -griffithianum
    -Lem's Cameo-       -Beauty of Tremough-
    -       -   -Norman-         -arboreum 1/32
    -       - Gill -griffithianum
       -Anna-              -griffithianum
            -Jean Marie de Montague-
                   -unknown 1/16
```
Flowers in trusses of 12-15, light yellowish pink inside, lobes
tipped deep pink; outside deep pink. K. van de Ven, reg. 1986.

```
          -Corona--unknown 1/4
       -Bow Bells-
KARL  -     -williamsianum 1/4
HOSCHNA-      -dichroanthum 1/4
       -Jasper -           -fortunei ssp. discolor 1/8
       (Exbury form)-Lady -
              Bessborough-campylocarpum Elatum Group 1/8
```
5ft(1.5m) -5F(-21C) M   Funnel-shaped flowers, barium yellow,
2in(5cm) across, in loose trusses. Shapely habit; small glossy
leaves. C. S. Seabrook, reg. 1967.

```
          -fortunei, very hardy form 1/2 (Schroeder's)
KARMIC DEBRIS-           -forrestii Repens Group 1/8
          -     -Elizabeth-
          -Molly Ann-    -griersonianum 1/8
                   -garden hybrid--unknown 1/4
```
Light pink buds open to white, ruffle-edged flowers with a dark
center; hardy to -25F(-32C). Schroeder cross; Trautmann raiser.

```
       -souliei 1/2
KATE HURLEY-                  -griffithianum 1/32
       -         -wardii 1/4 -Kewense-
       -Idealist-    -Aurora-    -fortunei 5/32
          -Naomi-    -thomsonii 1/16
                -fortunei
```
Flowers in loose trusses of 9-10, 5-lobed, white blushed reddish

purple. Maj. A. E. Hardy raiser.   A.M. 1986.

```
                        -griffithianum 1/4
        -Mrs. E. C. Stirling-
KATE GREENAWAY-                 -unknown 3/4
        -unknown
```
Flowers soft rose, veined red, fringed.   Waterer, Sons & Crisp.

```
        -catawbiense 1/2
KATE WATERER-
        -unknown 1/2
```
5ft(1.5m) -10F(-23C) ML 2/3   Flowers rose pink with a golden
center. Plant fairly upright and compact.   J. Waterer, before
1890.   Color illus. VV p. 103.

KATHARINE FORTESCUE   Described under LUNAR QUEEN, q.v.

```
        -yakushimanum--Koichiro Wada 1/2
KÄTHE HEINJE-       -catawbiense 1/4
        -Cynthia-
                -griffithianum 1/4
```
3ft(.9m) x 4.3ft(1.3m)(22 yrs) -8F(-22C) M   Trusses of 14-16
flowers; vivid red buds open strong to light rose pink, 5 wavy-
edged lobes, small dark red spot. Plant habit compact. Heinje
Baumschulen, reg. 1986.   Color illus. WS, 1989, p. 111.

* *
```
        -fortunei 1/2
KATHERINE DALTON-
        -smirnowii 1/2
```
5ft(1.5m) -15F(-26C) M 3/4   Very large, pale lavender-pink
flowers from brighter pink buds.   Excellent plant habit; dense
foliage with scant indumentum.   Gable, intro. 1937; reg. 1958.
BELLEFONTAINE   Parentage as above
6ft(1.8m) -15F(-26C) L   Buds of rose opal opening to fragrant
flowers of Neyron rose flecked olive brown; large trusses of 10.
Plant wider than tall; foliage dark green.   Canada Agri. Dept.;
D. Craig, reg. 1977.
FUNDY   Parentage as above
6ft(1.8m) -15F(-26C) L   Plant broader than tall. Flowers 7-
lobed, fragrant, rose-colored on the edges, paler at centers; an
olive brown blotch. Trusses of 10.   Craig, reg. 1977.
* *

KATHERINE SLATER   Parentage unknown
5ft(1.5m) -10F(-23C) M Flowers lavender pink fade to white in
throat; large truss.   Open habit with good foliage.   Dexter
cross; Mezitt, intro. 1970.

```
        -lindleyi 1/2
KATHLEEN EVANS-
        -maddenii Polyandrum Group 1/2
```
Flowers in trusses of 4-6, tubular-campanulate, 5-lobed, green-
ish white in bud, opening to white, with a golden yellow blotch.
Silvery green leaves; brown scales.   Mrs. J. Evans, reg. 1986.

KATHLEEN JANE   Parentage unknown
Scarlet, spotted black; truss of 12.   J. F. Stephens, reg. 1975.

KATHMANDU--form of traillianum var. dictyotum
4ft(1.2m) OF(-18C) M 4/3   Leaves with dense, cinnamon brown
indumentum beneath. Flowers white with a crimson blotch and upper lobe spotting, openly campanulate, 2.3in(6cm) broad.   Tight
truss of 19.   Edmund de Rothschild, reg. 1966.   A.M. 1965.

```
        -spinuliferum 1/2
KATHRYN REBOUL-
        -racemosum 1/2
```
3ft(.9m) -5F(-21C) EM   Leaves small and the flowers only 1in
(2.5cm) across, pale yellow with salmon pink blushing; trusses
of 14.   Donald Hardgrove cross; Adele Reboul, reg. 1975.

KATHRYNA   Described under JEAN LEPPO, q.v.

KATHY DOLL   Described under CATHY, q.v.

KATHY VAN VEEN---sport of THE HON. JEAN MARIE DE MONTAGUE. q.v.
3ft(.9m) x 3.5ft(1.05m)(7 yrs) OF(-18C) M   Flowers of heavy
substance, 5 wavy-edged lobes, vivid red outside; nectaries and
buds strong red; colors variable. Domed trusses of 15. Leaves
held 3 years.   W. Rhein selection; Van Veen Nursery, reg. 1990.

```
                -pemakoense 1/4
        -Phalarope-
KATIE CHILDERS-     -davidsonianum 1/4
        -moupinense 1/2
```
1.25ft(.38m) x 1.25ft(9 yrs) 5F(-15C) E Flower widely funnel-
shaped, moderate purplish pink with very pale purple throat; lax
truss of 3. Plant of broad, twiggy habit; glossy leaves, scales
beneath (tan, then turning gold) A. & M.. Childers, reg. 1988.

```
        -oreotrephes 1/2
KATIE GORDON-
        -cinnabarinum Roylei Group 1/2
```
Flowers in trusses of 5-7, crimson, 5-lobed, paling on exterior
to phlox purple, flushed salmon on interior.   Lady Adam Gordon,
reg. 1985.

```
            -catawbiense var. album 1/4
    -unnamed-
    - hybrid-fortunei ssp. discolor 1/4      -ponticum 1/16
KATJA-                        -Michael Waterer-
            -Prometheus-          -unknown 5/16
    -Madame de Bruin-        -Monitor--unknown
            -             -arboreum 1/8
            -Doncaster-
                -unknown
```
4.5ft(1.35m) -10F(-23C) ML   Bright rose buds opening to vivid
pink, shading paler in throat, widely funnel-campanulate, 2in.
(5cm) wide, of heavy substance; 16 held in ball-shaped trusses.
Upright, rounded plant, as broad as tall; glossy leaves 6in(15.2
cm) long, held 2 years.   A. Raustein, reg. 1976.

* *
```
                -arboreum 1/16
            -Beauty of-
        -Norman- Tremough-griffithianum 5/16
        - Gill -
        -Anna-      -griffithianum
        -                   -griffithianum
KATRINA-    -Jean Marie de Montague-
        -                   -unknown 3/8
        -           -ponticum 1/4
        -Purple Splendour-
                -unknown
```
4.5ft(1.35m) OF(-18C) ML 4/4   Flowers magenta rose, black
blotch and spotting, openly funnel-shaped, 3in(7.6cm) across, 5
wavy lobes; spherical trusses of 10.   Plant habit open; foliage
dark green and glossy; held 3 years.   Elsie Watson, reg. 1983.
MARLEY HEDGES   Parentage as above
4ft(1.2m) high x 2ft(.6m)(18 yrs) 10F(-12C) M   Flowers 4in.
(10.cm) wide, 24 per truss, white, edged with strong red-purple,
blotch of grayish red to moderate purplish red. Very floriferous. Elsie Watson, cross 1970; reg. 1988.
* *

```
        -souliei 1/2
        -          -wardii 1/4            -griffithianum
KATY HURLEY-    -              -Kewense-
        -Idealist-    -Aurora-    -fortunei
            -Naomi-     -thomsonii
                -fortunei
```
Flowers of 9-10 in loose, open trusses, 5-lobed, white, flushed
red-purple. G. A. Hardy, reg. 1985.   A.M. 1985.

```
                -smirnowii 1/4
    -unnamed hybrid-
KATYDID-        -yakushimanum 1/4
    -      -wardii 1/4
    -Crest-          -fortunei ssp. discolor 1/8
        -Lady Bessborough-
                -campylocarpum Elatum Group 1/8
```
Plant of medium size. Flowers sap green, shading from pale to a
deeper hue. Hardy to -15F(-26C).   Weldon E. Delp.

```
        -catawbiense 1/2
KAULBACH-
        -unknown 1/2
```
White, lilac margins, yellowish brown markings.   Seidel, 1926.

KAY   Described under IDOL, q.v.

KAY KIRSTEN   Described under TRULA, q.v.

```
                    -Moser's Maroon--unknown 1/4
            -Romany Chai-
KAY LOGAN-              -griersonianum 1/4
       -               -forrestii Repens Group 1/4
            -Elizabeth-
                    -griersonianum 1/4
```
Plant large and upright; rather small leaves. Currant red, tu-
bular flowers, 2.5in(6.4cm) x 1.5in(3.8cm), crinkled, in loose
trusses. Late midseason.   C. S. Seabrook, reg. 1969.

```
                  -hybrid of unknown parentage 1/2
KAY WALTERS-
           -yakushimanum 1/2
```
2ft(.6m) high x 3ft(.9m)(21 yrs) -15F(-26C) ML   Flowers held
in truss of 15, strong purplish red, fading light purplish pink,
a brownish white blotch peppered with greenish mustard speckles.
Buds of strong purplish red.   W. Fetterhoff, reg. 1988.   Best
yakushimanum hybrid award, Great Lakes Ch. ARS, 1978.

KAYLA RAE   Described under MOUNT HOOD, q.v.

```
            -campylocarpum 1/2
KEAY SLOCOCK-
            -hardy hybrid--unknown 1/2
```
4ft(1.2m) OF(-18C) M   Flowers pale yellow, flushed salmon or
creamy white, with slight blotch.   W. C. Slocock, before 1929.

KEILLOUR CASTLE--form of ambiguum
"Hardiest yellow triflorum, the series with flowers mostly
2in(5cm) in diameter, not carried in trusses. All are extremely
free flowering in mid-spring." Catalog of Glendoick Gardens.

```
         -keiskei 1/2
KEISKARB-
         -arboreum 1/2
```
White flowers shaded to rose, with crimson blotch and two short
lines of crimson spots.   Cross by E. J. P. Magor, 1918.

KEISKRAC   See under MARY FLEMING.

KELLEY   Described under ACCLAIM, q.v.

KELLY'S KIPPS   Parentage unknown
7ft(2.1m) x 7ft(14 yrs)   -5F(-21C) EM   Flowers of heavy substance, 7-lobed, pink buds open to flowers pale purplish pink at
edges, shading to light greenish yellow at the center. W. Kelly
cross; W. A. & Joan Ragan, reg. 1989.

```
          -johnstoneanum 1/2
KEN BURNS-
          -unknown 1/2
```
Truss of 3-5 broadly funnel-shaped flowers 3.5in(9cm) wide; buds
deep biscuit, opening pale yellow-green flushed pale rose, heavy
brick red dorsal spotting. Scaly, elliptic leaves to 3in(8cm);
bush 4.7ft(1.4m) x 4.7ft(12 years). Mid-season bloom.   Unknown
raiser; Mrs. J. McLauchlan intro.; Dunedin Rho. Gp., reg. 1988.

KEN JANECK--form of yakushimanum
3ft(.9m) -15F(-26C) M 5/5 Flower fuchsine pink fading white,
upper lobe stippled fern green, openly funnel-shaped, 2.5in
(6.4cm) wide; compact trusses of 13-17. Compact plant, twice as
broad as high. Dark green foliage, heavily floccose-tomentose
beneath.   Kenneth Janeck, reg. 1965.   A.E. 1969.

```
                         -fortunei ssp. discolor 3/8
              -Lady      -
              -Bessborough-campylocarpum Elatum Group 1/8
        -Day Dream-
KENHELEN-              -griersonianum 3/8
       -                  -fortunei ssp. discolor
        -Margaret Dunn-   -dichroanthum 1/8
                     -Fabia-
                          -griersonianum
```
Flowers held in loose trusses of 8-10, 6-lobed, tubular funnel-
shaped, burnt orange in bud, opening to apricot with lemon yellow throat. Very late season. Wilbur Graves cross; Mr. & Mrs.
K. Janeck raisers; reg. 1965.

```
       -orbiculare 1/2
KENLIS-
       -meddianum 1/2
```
Trusses of 10 flowers, Neyron rose.   Headfort.   A.M. 1948.

```
              -haematodes 1/4
        -Hiraethlyn-
KENNETH-            -griffithianum 1/4
       -           -forrestii Repens Group 1/4
        -Elizabeth-
                   -griersonianum 1/4
```
Truss of 8-10 flowers, colored geranium lake.   Lord Aberconway.
A.M. 1949.

KEN'S FIND---selection of catawbiense, white form
8ft(2.4m) x 5ft(1.5m) 5F(-15C) M   Pure white buds and flowers
in trusses 5in(12.7cm) across.   Leaves held 1 year.   Ken Moore
discovered in Johnson Co., N.C.   Dr. E. R. Bahnson, reg. 1989.

KENTUCKY CARDINAL   Described under BLACKIE, q.v.

```
             -barbatum 1/2
KERNICK GEM-        -fortunei 1/4
             -Luscombei-
                      -thomsonii 1/4
```
Rich pink, dark spotting on lower petals. R. Gill. A.M. 1928.

```
              -smirnowii 1/2
KESSELRINGII-
              -ponticum 1/2
```
A natural hybrid, 1910.   Origin unknown.

```
            -catawbiense 1/2
KETTLEDRUM-
            -unknown 1/2
```
5ft(1.5m) -20F(-29C) ML Very hardy hybrid, but habit and foliage inferior. Flowers purplish crimson. Used as a parent, for
hardiness.   A. Waterer, 1877.

```
               -yakushimanum--Koichiro Wada 1/2
KEVEN (KEVIN)-         -dichroanthum 1/8
       -       -Fabia-
        -Jade-        -griersonianum 1/8
              -Corona--unknown 1/4
```
4.5ft(1.35m) OF(-18C) M 4/4   Leaves indumented, convex, 5in.
(12.7cm) long. Flowers deep pink shading to yellowish pink with
margins and exterior darker, up to 2.25in(5.7cm) across; trusses
of about 14.   R. Bovee cross; Sorensen & Watson, reg. 1975.

KEW PEARL   Parentage unknown
Parent of WARBURTON. Pink, edged in rose. RBG, Kew Gardens.

```
            -griffithianum 1/4
       -Kewense-
KEWARB-      -fortunei 1/4
       -arboreum, blood red form 1/2
```
Blood red flowers.   E. J. P. Magor, cross 1918.

* *
```
            -griffithianum 1/4
       -Kewense-
KEWDEC-      -fortunei 1/4
       -decorum 1/2
```
White flowers.   E. J. P. Magor, 1913.
KEWDEC WHITE LADY   Parentage as above
Flowers white with a tinge of green or pale crimson within, in
trusses of about 9.   E. J. P. Magor cross.   A.M. 1938.
* *
* *
```
            -griffithianum 1/2
KEWENSE-                   Same parentage as LODERI
       -fortunei 1/2
```
6ft(1.8m) OF(-18C) M   Pink in bud, blush white when open, and
fragrant. Not as large as the more famous LODERI(q.v.) but with
much vigor, and may be a little more hardy.   Perhaps the LODERI
should be called "the KEWENSE grex", since KEWENSE came 13 years
earlier?   RBG, Kew, 1888.
SNOW WHITE   Parentage as above
Pure white flowers, very open.   Lowinsky.   A.M. 1923.
* *
```
            -griffithianum 1/4
       -Kewense-
KEWXEN-      -fortunei 1/4
       -                  -adenogynum 1/4
        -Xenosporum (detonsom)-
                           -unknown 1/4
```

Violet rose flowers with ochre spotting.   E. J. P. Magor, 1927.

KEYSTONE   Described under ALL EAST, q.v.

KHASIA--form of formosum (Cox & Hutchison 320)
Truss of 3-5 flowers, 3.7in(9.5cm) broad, white, throat slightly
flushed grayed yellow; very fragrant. Scaly calyx; oblanceolate
glossy leaves, scaly beneath. Plant 8.3ft(2.5m) x 5ft(1.5m) at
20 years; blooms early May. Cox raiser; reg. 1988.   A.M. 1988.

* *
            -minus Carolinianum Group, pink form 1/2
KICKOFF-
        -mucronulatum 1/2
4ft(1.2m) x 3ft(.9m)4 yrs -15F(-26C) EM   Buds of violet and
strong purple open to light purple flowers, edged strong purple; dorsal spots greenish yellow; ball truss of 12. Wavy-edged
elliptic-obovate foliage, scaly on both surfaces.   W. E. Delp
cross; A. & S. Anderson, reg. 1989.
PURPLE PEARL   Parentage as above
Buds violet and strong purple, opening to flowers of strong and
light purple.   W. Delp.
* *

          -minus Carolinianum--Epoch 1/2
                      -minus Carolinianum, pink form 1/8
KID -   -unnamed-   -racemosum 1/32
STUFF- - hybrid-   -Conemaugh-
    -Mini-   -Pioneer (Gable)-   -mucronulatum 1/32
     Mode-   -unknown 1/16
        -               -minus Carolinianum, tetraploid form
     -unnamed hybrid-   1/8
                  -fastigiatum 1/8
Buds of moderate purplish red, open to flowers slightly frilled,
very pale purple edged light purple; anthers deep pink.   Delp.

     -elliottii 1/2
KIEV-   -thomsonii 1/4
    -Robert Fox-   -arboreum 1/8
             -Glory of Penjerrick-
                      -griffithianum 1/8
6ft(1.8m) 5F(-15C) M 3/2   White anthers contrast sharply in
this darkest of all the Exbury reds, with sooty spotting in 3 upper lobes; flower texture waxy. Trusses of about 12. A vigorous
tall, though rather lanky plant. Rothschild, 1943.   A.M. 1950.
Color illus. PB pl. 59.

KILDONAN--form of magnificum K W 9200
5ft(1.5m) 10F(-12C) VE 4/5   Leaves up to 18 x 8in(46 x 20cm)
covered below with thin, pale indumentum. Fuchsine pink flowers
tubular-campanulate, 2.75 x 2.2in(7 x 5.5cm); about 30 per compact rounded trusses. Brodick Gardens, reg. 1966 F.C.C. 1966.

        -elliottii 1/2
KILIMANJARO-   -Moser's Maroon--unknown 1/4
        -Dusky Maid-
                -fortunei ssp. discolor 1/4
5ft(1.5m) OF(-18C) ML 5/2   Very large flowers, luminous currant red, spotted chocolate inside, funnel-shaped, wavy-edged;
spherical, compact truss of 18.   Attractive deep green foliage.
Rothschild, 1943.   F.C.C. 1947.   Color illus. PB pl. 33.

KIM Described under BOBBET, q.v.

KIMBERLY Described under CAROLINE SPENCER, q.v.

* *
            -veitchianum Cubittii Group, pink form
KIMBERLY ANNE-   -ciliicalyx 1/4
           -Else Frye-
                    -unknown 1/4
6ft(1.8m) x 6ft 32F(0C) E   Deep purplish pink buds open to
flowers 3in(7.6cm) across, of 5-6 wavy-edged lobes in shades of
purplish pink, with reddish orange blotch; moderately fragrant.
Yellow-brown scales beneath broadly elliptic, flat leaves.   Dr.
J. P. Evans, cross 1968; Mrs. Evans, reg. 1989.
PAUL MOLINARI Parentage as above, but Cubittii Group not listed
3ft(.9m) x 3ft(4?yrs) 32F(0C) E   Very fragrant, white flowers
from silvery buds; large, light yellow dorsal blotch.   Elliptic
leaves with tan hairs above, brown scales beneath. Evans, cross
in 1970s; P. Molinari raiser; Mrs. J. P. Evans, reg. 1989.
* *

                -unknown 1/2
KIMBERTON-   -wardii 1/4
      -Crest-   -fortunei ssp. discolor 1/8
          -Lady
             Bessborough-campylocarpum Elatum Group 1/8
5ft(1.5m) -5F(-21C) ML   Fragrant flowers of rhodamine pink,
chartreuse green dorsal blotch, the reverse spirea red, 3.5in
(8.9cm) wide, 6 wavy lobes; truss of 12. Plant rounded; glossy
leaves held 2 years.   L. Bagoly cross; C. Herbert, reg. 1979.

               -williamsianum 1/4
      -Kimberly-
KIMBETH-   -fortunei 1/4
      -          -forrestii Repens Group 1/4
     -Elizabeth-
               -griersonianum 1/4
3ft(.9m) -5F(-21C) EM 4/4   Flowers deep Neyron rose, funnel-
shaped, 2.5in(6.4cm) wide, 5-lobed; flat trusses of 3-5. Plant
rounded, broader than tall; medium green leaves held 2 years,
new growth bronze.   Greer, reg. 1979.   Color illus. HG p. 97.

                      -fortunei ssp. discolor
            -Lady Bessborough-   3/16
       -Day -   -campylocarpum Elatum Gp.
    -Gold -Dream-griersonianum 3/16   1/16
    -Mohur-   -fortunei ssp. discolor
         -Margaret Dunn-   -dichroanthum 3/16
         -            -Fabia-
KIMBOLTON-   -griersonianum
   YELLOW -   -griffithianum 1/32
       -            -George Hardy-
       -             -Pink -   -catawbiense 1/32
       -        -unnamed-Pearl-   -arboreum 1/32
       -        - hybrid-   -Broughtonii-
       -Ilam -   -   -unknown 5/32
    Apricot-   -arboreum ssp. zeylanicum 1/8
              -              -dichroanthum
              -unnamed hybrid-
                       -unknown
Syn. TOPAZ. Flowers in trusses of 10, 6-lobed, reddish pink in
bud, opening Naples yellow with corolla lobes edged geranium
lake, fading to Naples yellow all over.   J. Yeates, reg. 1987.

KING ARTHUR   Listed under ANTHONY, q.v.

      -yakushimanum 1/2
KING BEE-
      -tsariense 1/2
2.5ft(.75m) 5F(-15C) EM   Flowers 2.25in(5.7cm) across with 5
wavy lobes, opening pale rose, fading to white, scarlet spots
and stripes of light scarlet.   Plant upright; leaves heavily
indumented below.   W. E. Berg, reg. 1983.   C.A. 1984.

                        -arboreum ssp. zeylanicum
            -Ilam Alarm-   1/8
      -Scarlet King-   -griffithianum 1/8
KING ELLIOTT-   -griersonianum 1/4
         -elliottii 1/2
Flowers currant red with darker edges; center of corolla light-
er scarlet.   E. W. E. Butler, New Zealand, reg. 1972.

      -heliolepis 1/2
KING FISHER-
       -maddenii (polyandrum) 1/2
Flowers of pale lilac, tubular-campanulate, to 3in(7.6cm) long,
in loose truss. Sir John Ramsden, Muncaster Castle, reg. 1965.

       -griffithianum 1/2
KING GEORGE-
       -unknown 1/2
Bright red, gloxinia-shaped flowers.   Otto Schulz, cross 1892;
C. V. van Nes & Sons, intro. 1896.

* *
       -Nereid
KING OF JORDAN-Tally Ho
       -fortunei ssp. discolor
3ft(.9m) -10F(-23C) ML   The exact combination of the above
parentage is uncertain. Big, dome-shaped trusses 7in(17.8cm)
high, of 10 flowers, chrome yellow, shading to dawn pink edges.
Plant rounded, broader than high. Possibly ELSE FRYE cross;
Bernice I. Jordan, reg. 1977.

KYOTO CAROL   Parentage as above
2.5ft(.75m) -10F(-23C) M Large flowers with crepe-like lobes,
geranium lake to Delft rose; dome-shaped truss of 12. Semi-
dwarf plant; reddish brown indumentum.   Jordan, reg. 1977.
* *

KING OF SHRUBS   Described under MARGARET DUNN, q.v.

```
                      -smirnowii 1/4              -catawbiense
      -unnamed hybrid-        -Parsons Grandiflorum-     1/16
KING-         -America-                    -unknown
 TUT-                 -dark red hybrid--unknown 7/16
  -                 -catawbiense, red form 1/4
      -unnamed hybrid-
                      -unknown
```
5ft(1.5m) -20F(-29C) ML 3/3   Bright, deep pink flowers with
yellowish brown blotch, 2.5in(6.4cm) across; conical trusses.
Leaves 5in(12.7cm) long.   Anthony M. Shammarello, 1958. Color
illus. LW pl. 88; VV p. xii.

```
      -dichroanthum 1/2
KINGCUP-       -auriculatum 1/4
      -Bustard-         -campylocarpum Elatum Group 1/8
              -Penjerrick-
                      -griffithianum 1/8
```
4ft(1.2m) -5F(-21C) M Waxen, tubular-shaped flowers of gleam-
ing Indian yellow, held in loose, flat-topped truss. Plant compact, rather low.   Rothschild. A.M. 1943.

KINGDOM COME--form of eclecteum var. eclecteum K W 6869
Trusses hold 5-7 flowers, white flushed very light sap green
with slight spotting of purple in upper throat. Frank Kingdon
Ward collector; Col. S. R. Clarke raiser; R. N. S. Clarke, reg.
1978. A.M. 1978.

KINGDON WARD PINK--form of edgeworthii
A fine, hardy form of this species grown at Bodnant. A.M. 1946.

```
      -arboreum 1/2
KINGIANUM-
      -unknown 1/2
```
A parent of JANET BEE. Once considered a species, it is now
regarded as an arboreum hybrid. See The Rhododendron Handbook,
1980, (RHS) under "Synonyms".

```
      -arboreum ssp. zeylanicum 1/2
KINGKING-                -griffithianum 1/4
      -Mrs. Randall Davidson-
                      -campylocarpum, Hooker's form 1/4
```
A hybrid by E. J. P. Magor, crossed 1915.

```
      -racemosum  F 19404  1/2
KINGLET-
      -Finch--rubiginosum Desquamatum Group 1/2
```
5ft(1.5m) 0F(-18C) E Racemes of 3-4 blooms along stems, fuch-
sine pink, exterior phlox pink; flowers tubular bell-shaped to
1.25in(3.2cm) across, .75in(1.9cm) long. Plant upright; dark
green leaves to 3in(7.6cm) long. Rudolph Henny, reg. 1964.

```
                      -griffithianum 1/8
              -Queen Wilhelmina-
      -Earl of Athlone-              -unknown 3/8
KING'S BUFF-        -Stanley Davies--unknown
  -                 -campylocarpum 1/4
      -Lady Primrose-
                      -unknown 1/4
```
Buff-colored flowers with dark red speckles in throat. Shrub up
to 6.5ft(2.0m).   H. W. King & Co., reg. 1985.

```
      -ponticum 1/2
KING'S CERISE-
      -griersonianum 1/2
```
Flowers in large, tight trusses, bright cerise. Shrub to 5ft
(1.5m).   H. W. King & Co., reg. 1985.

```
      -unknown 3/4
KING'S DESTINY-           -ponticum 1/4
      -Purple Splendour-
                      -unknown
```
3ft(.9m) -10F(-23C) ML   Flowers of deep lavender with darker
purple blotch and spotting, openly funnel-shaped, 4.5in(11.5cm)
across, 5-6 waxy lobes; 11-flowered tall trusses. Plant habit

well-branched, almost as wide as tall; narrowly elliptic leaves
6in(15.2cm) long.   Mrs. H. A. Frederick, Jr., reg. 1978.

```
                      -ponticum 1/2
              -Purple Splendour-
KING'S FAVOR-                -unknown 1/2
  -                 -mauve seedling--unknown
      -Arthur Bedford-
                      -ponticum
```
3ft(.9m) -10F(-23C) ML Dark purple buds open imperial purple,
a golden yellow spotted blotch; flowers openly funnel-shaped,
3.25in(8.3cm) wide with 5 frilled lobes, in ball-shaped trusses
of 12. Plant habit rounded, well-branched, broad as tall; dark
green leaves 8in x 2in (20cm x 5cm), held 2 years. Mrs. H. A.
Frederick, Jr., reg. 1978.

```
                      -catawbiense
              -Blandyanum-
      -Ascot    -           -Altaclerense, q.v.
  -J. G. Millais-Brilliant-thomsonii
KING'S  -      -campylocarpum
MILKMAID-Gladys-
      -fortunei
```
Flowers in dense trusses, creamy white, deeper yellow in throat.
Shrub to 7ft(2.1m)(20 yrs.).   S. M. King, reg. 1984.

```
      -yakushimanum 1/2
KING'S PARTY DRESS-
      -unknown 1/2
```
Flowers in tight trusses of apple blossom pink. Habit compact.
S. M. King, reg. 1985.

```
                      -griffithianum 1/8
              -George Hardy-
      -Peter Koster-         -catawbiense 1/8
  -                 -         -arboreum
KING'S PINK GLOW-         -Doncaster-     1/16
  -              -unnamed hybrid-     -unknown
      -griersonianum 1/2       -unknown 3/16
```
Flowers in large, tight trusses, deep glowing rose pink. Shrub
8ft(2.4m)(20 yrs.).   S. M. King, reg. 1984.

KING'S RANSOM   Described under ELSIE STRAVER, q.v.

```
      -insigne 1/2
KING'S RIDE-
      -yakushimanum 1/2
```
Trusses 7in(17.8cm) tall and 6in(15.2cm) across, of 17 flowers,
white, flushed phlox pink, speckled brown. Plant vigorous, compact; leaves 4.5in(11.5cm) long, dull dark green. Crown Estate
Commissioners, reg. 1972. H.C. 1975.

```
                      -dichroanthum 1/8
              -Dido-
      -Lem's-     -decorum 1/8
      -Cameo-         -Beauty of-griffithianum 5/32
  -              - Tremough-
  -      -Norman Gill-         -arboreum
KINGSTON-  -Anna-         -griffithianum 1/32
  -         -         -griffithianum
  -              -Jean Marie de Montague-
  -                      -unknown 9/16
  -Polynesian Sunset--unknown
```
6ft(1.8m) 5F(-15C) M 4/4   Plant upright, rounded, as wide as
high; glossy, dark green foliage, held 3 years; new leaves terracotta brown. Flowers carrot red fading to orange-buff, edges
rhodonite red, 3.5in(8.9cm) across, 7 wavy lobes, lax truss of
8-10. Audrey Holmeide & Alice Poot Smith, reg. 1983.

```
                      -griffithianum 1/4
      -Mrs. Kingsmill-
KINGSTON-         -campylocarpum 1/4
      -thomsonii 1/2
```
A hybrid by E. J. P. Magor.

```
      -fortunei ssp. discolor 1/2
KINGSWAY-
      -arboreum ssp. zeylanicum 1/2
```
A tall, compact, late-flowering plant. Flowers white, blushed
pink, with deep pink throat; large shapely trusses. Edmund de
Rothschild, reg. 1963. P.C. 1960.

```
          -smirnowii 1/2
KINLOSS-
          -unknown 1/2
Flowers a striking shade of cerise pink.   Knap Hill, reg. 1968.
```

KIRSTY--form of adenogynum Adenophorum Group R 59636
White flowers, suffused medium spirea red with darker spotting
in upper throat, funnel-shaped, 5-lobed, with red calyx; trusses
of 12. Dark green leaves 4.3in(11cm) long, with thick plastered
indumentum below.   Rock collector; Col. S. R. Clarke raiser;
R. N. S. Clarke exhibitor; reg. 1976. A.M. 1976.

```
                    -Moser's Maroon--unknown 3/4
          -Grenadier-
KISMET-             -elliottii 1/4
          -Pygmalion--unknown
Red-flowered hybrid by Rudolph Henny, reg. 1958.
```

KISS OF LEMON   Parentage unknown
4ft(1.2m) OF(-18C) M   Clear yellow; very heavy substance;
longer lasting than most yellows. Veined leaves. Sifferman.

```
          -catawbiense 1/2
KISSENA-
          -unknown 1/2
Purple flowers.  Parsons.
```

```
                              -arboreum ssp. zeylanicum
                    -unnamed-              -griffithianum
                    - hybrid-   -Geo. Hardy-
          -Ilam Orange-    -Pink -           -catawbiense
          -            -    Pearl-           -arboreum
          -            -          -Broughtonii-
          -unn.-       -dichroanthum         -unknown
          -hyb.-                  -campylocarpum
          -    -            -unnamed hybrid-
          -    -            -          -fortunei ssp. discolor
KIT   -   -Ilam Canary-                -griffithianum
COLLIER-      -                -Loderi-
          -              -Loderi seedling-        -fortunei
          -                        -unknown
          -                        -wardii
          -Lemon Lodge---Prelude, selfed-
                                   -fortunei
Above parentage may not all be correct.  Flowers in trusses of
8-10, pale  yellow-green, throat light greenish yellow.  NZ sea-
son Oct.-Nov.   G. Collier, reg. 1988.
```

```
          -cinnabarinum 1/2
KIT CORYNTON-
          -maddenii 1/2
Flowers of light bronze yellow,  darkening at base, with sepals
flushed jasper red.  Gen. Harrison, reg. 1972.  P.C. 1971.
```

```
          -lutescens 1/2
KITTIWAKE-
          -edgeworthii 1/2
Erect, compact plant with pale yellow flowers, faintly fragrant.
J. C. Williams, 1933.
```

* *

```
          -griersonianum 1/2
KITTY COLE-
          -unnamed white hybrid-    -fortunei ssp. discolor 1/4
                              -unknown 1/4
Rose-colored flower. Lowinsky raiser; Sir J. Horlick, reg. 1962.
SEEMLY   Parentage as above.  (Pollen from rose-colored hybrid.)
Large, rose-colored flowers in late season.  Horlick, reg. 1962.
```
* *

```
                    -yakushimanum 1/4
          -unnamed hybrid-   -dichroanthum 1/4
          -            -Dido-
KIWI MAJIC-              -decorum 1/4
          -         -Dido (as above)
          -              -Beauty of-griffithianum
          -Lem's Cameo-  -Norman- Tremough-        5/32
          -          - - Gill -        -arboreum 1/32
          -Anna-      -griffithianum
          -                  -griffithianum
          -Jean Marie de-
             Montague   -unknown 1/16
```

Flowers in trusses of 13-14, 7-lobed, deep pink in bud, opening
light pink, center brilliant yellow, overall effect at a
distance yellowish pink. Jeffrey Elliott, reg. 1988.

```
                    -neriiflorum 1/4
          -unnamed hybrid-
          -              -strigillosum 1/4
KLASSY'S PRIDE-              -griffithianum 1/8
          -          -Loderi-
          -unnamed hybrid-    -fortunei 1/8
                    -thomsonii 1/4
5ft(1.5m)  -10F(-23C)  EM   Currant red flowers, black spotting,
funnel-shaped,  2in(5cm) wide,  5 wavy lobes; 14-flowered, flat
trusses.  Plant almost as broad as tall;  leaves 5.25in(13.3cm)
long, held 3 years.   B. Nelson cross; C. G. Heller, reg. 1979.
```

```
                         -griffithianum 3/8
               -Queen Wilhelmina-
          -Britannia-        -unknown 5/8
KLUIS SENSATION-     -Stanley Davies--unknown
          -              -griffithianum
          -unnamed hybrid-
               -unknown
5ft(1.5m)  -5F(-21C)  ML  4/4  Dense, compact plant; deep green,
heavily textured leaves, edges slightly concave.  Flowers waxy
bright scarlet, funnel-shaped, 2in(5cm) across,  crinkled edges;
compact spherical truss of 17-18.  Shrub vigorous, sun-tolerant,
floriferous.  A. Kluis, 1946.   Color illus. ARS Q 28:3 (1974),
p. 170; VV p. 60; JS p. 80.
```

```
          -griffithianum 1/2
KLUIS TRIUMPH-
          -unknown 1/2
6ft(1.8m)  OF(-18C)  ML  2/3  Flowers terracotta red, lighter in
throat and along midrib, black spotting on upper petal, campanu-
late,  2.5in(6.4cm) across; 15-18 in dome-shaped trusses.  Plant
upright, vigorous,  broader than tall;  dull dark green leaves
7.25in(18.5cm) long.  Anthony Kluis, reg. 1958.  A.M. Wisley
Trials 1969.  F.C.C. Wisley Trials 1971.
```

KNAPHILL--form of campanulatum
4ft(1.2m) -5F(-21C) EM 4/3   A large shrub; obovate leaves
covered with thick, rusty brown indumentum below. Fine lavender
blue, campanulate flowers; perhaps the closest to blue of any
elepidote. Rothschild. A.M. 1925.

KNIGHT'S BEAUTY   Described under JAMES DRIVE, q.v.

```
                    -dichroanthum 1/2
          -Tidbit-
KNIGHT'S ORANGE-     -wardii 1/4
   YELLOW      -         -dichroanthum
          -Whitney's-              -griffithianum 1/16
          Orange  -    -Mrs. Lindsay-
               -Diane- Smith   -catawbiense 1/16
                    -unnamed-campylocarpum 1/6
                    hybrid-
                         -unknown 1/16
1.5ft(.45m)  15F(-9C)  ML   Flowers medium orange-yellow, strong
yellowish pink  edges and stripes down center of  lobe, openly
funnel-shaped, about 3in(7.6cm) across, 5 wavy petals; lax truss
of 10-11.  Free-flowering.  Plant twice as wide as tall;  dull
olive green leaves retained 3 years.  E. L. Knight, reg. 1981.
```

KNIGHT'S PINK   Described under DARLENE'S PINK, q.v.

Next 3 names out of order.
```
                    -Pygmalion--unknown 1/2
KNOWLE BRILLIANT-
                    -venator 1/2
Scarlet flowers.  Thacker, 1942.
```

```
                    -wardii 1/2
KNOWLE YELLOW-              -campylocarpum Elatum Group 1/4
          -Letty Edwards-
                    -fortunei 1/4
Clear yellow flowers.  Thacker, 1940.
```

KOENIG ALBERT   See KÖNIG ALBERT

* *
```
                              -maximum 1/4
                    -unnamed hybrid-
         -Masterblend-              -vernicosum (18139) 1/8
         -         -        -unnamed hybrid-
         -         -               -aureum (chrysanthum) 1/8
         -         -        -unnamed hybrid-
         -         -               -maximum
         -         -               -cataw. var. album Glass--Catalgla 1/16
         -        -Gosh -                 -decorum 1/64
         -        -Darn!-           -Caroline-
KNOCK-             -Mrs. H. R. Yates-         -brachycarpum
OUT -       -Sweet-               -unknown 3/32        5/64
 -      - Lulu-                   -neriiflorum 1/64
 -      -   -           -Nereid-
 -      -   -un.-Phyllis Ballard-    -dichroanthum 1/32
 -      -   hy.-           -fortunei ssp. discolor 3/64
 -Jenny-        -catawbiense--Clark's White 1/16
   Poo -       -brachycarpum
    -    -un.-    -wardii 1/32
    -    -hy.-Crest-        -fortunei ssp. discolor
    -    -        -Lady  -
   -un.-         Bessborough-campylocarpum Elatum 1/64
   hy.-                     -catawbiense
    -             -Parsons Grandiflorum   1/64
    -      -America-  ,           -unknown
   -Cindy-     -dark red hybrid--unknown
    Lou -        -griffithianum 1/64
      -      -Mars-
     -unnamed-     -unknown
            hybrid-catawbiense var. rubrum 1/32
```
Spirea red in bud opening to frilled flowers of phlox pink and
pale purplish pink; dorsal spots ruby red; throat ruby red and
pale greenish yellow; truss of 21. W. Delp.
LIZA SHIREY   Parentage as above
Buds of cardinal and strong reds opening to flowers of spirea
red with strong purplish red underside of petals; dorsal spots
strong purplish red. W. Delp.
OH WHOA   Parentage as above
Buds of currant red and strong purplish red open to fuchsia purple and deep purplish pink; dorsal spots ruby red. W. Delp.
* *

```
              -falconeri ssp. falconeri 1/4
         -Koenig Carola-
KOENIGDIS-          -ponticum 1/4
         -fortunei ssp. discolor 1/2
```
Flowers of a light heliotrope, one lobe spotted olive green; 8-
lobed corolla. E. J. P. Magor, 1913.

KOICHIRO WADA--form of yakushimanum
1.5ft(.45m) -15F(-26C) EM 5/5   Deep rose in bud, opening
apple blossom pink then white. Heavily indumented foliage. A
parent of many hybrids. K. Wada collector; RHS Gardens, Wisley,
raiser; reg. 1969. F.C.C. 1947. Color illus. ARS Q 35:2
(1981), p. 74; VV p. 80.

KOKARDIA   Described under HACHMANN'S ORNAMENT, q.v.

```
              -griffithianum 1/4
         -Isabella-
KOLA-         -auriculatum 1/4
         -griersonianum 1/4
         -Tally Ho-
              -facetum (eriogynum) 1/4
```
Pink flowers on well-shaped trusses. A tall plant of rather
loose habit. Late-blooming. Rothschild, 1947.

```
              -degronianum ssp heptamereum (metternichii) 1/2
KOMO-O-          -griersonianum 1/4
         -Sarita Loder-      -griffithianum 1/8
              -Loderi-
                   -fortunei 1/8
```
Coral pink; hardy to -5F(-21C). Heat tolerant. Origin unknown.

```
              -falconeri ssp. eximium  1/2
KÖNIG ALBERT-
         -unknown 1/2
```
Synonym KOENIG ALBERT. Cream-colored flowers. Origin unknown.

```
              -grande 1/2
KÖNIG ALBERT-
              -Album Hybridium--unknown 1/2
```

Rose-colored flowers.   In Seidel catalog, 1880.

```
              -Moliere--unknown 3/4
KÖNIGIN LOUISE-                        -griffithianum
         -              -George Hardy-        1/8
         -Mrs. Lindsay Smith-        -catawbiense 1/8
              -Duchess of Edinburgh--unknown
```
Distributed by M. Koster & Sons.

```
              -falconeri 1/2
KÖNIGIN CAROLA-
         -Album Hybridium--unknown 1/2
```
Flowers lavender, purple throat. Seidel, before 1878.

```
              -campylocarpum 1/2
KOSTER'S CREAM-
         -unknown 1/2
```
Flowers creamy yellow with a green blotch. M. Koster & Sons.

```
              -ponticum 1/4
         -Chionoides-
         -         -unknown 3/8           -griffithianum 1/16
KRISTEN-            -George Hardy-
   MARIE -      -Pink Pearl-        -catawbiense 3/16
         -                   -arboreum 1/8
         -Graf Zeppelin-     -Broughtonii-
         -                        -unknown
         -                   -catawbiense
              -Mrs. C. S. Sargent-
                        -unknown
```
4ft(1.2m) x 5ft(1.5m)(20 yrs) OF(-18C) ML Flowers in trusses
of 15-16, deeply cut lobes, white buds tipped strong purplish
red opening white, vivid yellow spotted flare. B. & M.
Shapiro, reg. 1989. Color ill. ARS J 42:2 Spring (1988), p. 63.

* *

```
              -yakushimanum--Koichiro Wada 1/2
KRISTIN-      -Corona--unknown 1/4
         -Bow Bells-
              -williamsianum 1/4
```
4ft(1.2m) OF(-18C) M 3/4   A parent of VIRGINIA DELP.
Pale pink flowers, red spotting, 2.5in(6.4cm) across; trusses of
14. Leaves 3in x 2in (7.6cm x 5cm). R. Bovee cross; Sorenson &
Watson, reg. 1975.
VIRGINIA ANDERSON   Parentage as above
3ft(.9m) OF(-18C) ML 3/4   Rounded plant, wider than tall.
Flowers 3in(7.6cm) across, pale purplish pink shading to white,
reverse striped purplish red; 12 per truss. Bovee cross; Sorenson & Watson, reg. 1975.
* *

```
                   -fortunei ssp. discolor 1/4
    -King of Shrubs-      -dichroanthum 1/8
    -              -Fabia-
    -                   -griersonianum 1/8
    -                        -griffithianum 7/32
KSW -              -Beauty of-
    -         -Norman-Tremough -arboreum 1/32
    -         - Gill  -
    -    -Anna--    -griffithianum
    -    -    -         -griffithianum
    -Walloper-   -Jean Marie -
    -         de Montague-unknown 3/16
    -                   -griffithianum
    -              -George Hardy-
    -Marinus Koster-        -catawbiense 1/16
              -red hybrid--unknown
```
5ft(1.5m) -5F(-21C) ML 3/4 Flowers pink with an orange tone.
Foliage is lush and full. Halfdan Lem.

* *

```
                   -griffithianum 1/8
              -Queen Wilhelmina-
         -Britannia-          -unknown 3/8
KUBLA KHAN-      -Stanley Davies--unknown
         -                   -dichroanthum 1/4
         -Goldsworth Orange-
                   -fortunei ssp. discolor 1/4
```
5ft(1.5m) -5F(-21C) ML 5/3   Mandarin red flowers, fading to
fire red; very large blotch of currant red extends to rays of
spots of same color. Calyx very large. L. Brandt, reg. 1962.
TROPICANA (Brandt)   Parentage as above

3ft(.9m) OF(-18C) L 5/3   Unique orange salmon color; light
green foliage; needs some shade. Parent of PAPRIKA SPICED, q.v.
* *
* *

          -vernicosum 1/2
KULU-   Natural hybrid from R 18139
     -unknown 1/2
6ft(1.8m) -10F(-23C) M Fragrant, Venetian pink flower, flushed deeper to French rose in the throat, openly funnel-shaped, to
4in(10.2cm) across, 7 wavy lobes; dome-shaped trusses of 7-10.
Floriferous. Showy red bracts on new growth. Plant rounded, as
wide as tall; leaves dark olive green. Rock, collected 1929;
J. Gable, intro. 1958; Caroline Gable, reg. 1979.
MOUNT SIGA   Parentage as above
5ft(1.5m) -5F(-21C) EM Orient pink, slightly deeper in throat
with faint spots of peach, 4in(10.2cm) wide, 7 wavy lobes. Also
from Rock-collected seed; Gable raiser; C. Gable reg. 1979.
* *

          -rupicola var. chryseum 1/2
KUNMING-
     -minus Carolinianum Group, white form 1/2
3ft(.9m) -15F(-26C) M Flowers barium yellow, midribs lighter,
margins aging to pale brick red, dorsal spotting of light mimosa
yellow; 9-10 floral buds form terminal clusters of 34 flowers,
each 1in(2.5cm) wide. Floriferous. Plant rounded, as broad as
tall, well-branched; closely spaced scales cover stem and underside of leaf. Leach, cross 1974; reg. 1981. (Not distributed.)

          -yakushimanum 1/2
KYLA KING-
     -unknown 1/2
Tight trusses, pale pink, with red spots in throat. Leaves
glossy green. Habit as yakushimanum.   S. M. King, reg. 1984.

KYOTO CORAL   Described under KING OF JORDAN, q.v.

                      L

L. L. LIEBIG   Parentage unknown
A parent of DURGEMEESTER AARTS. Flowers scarlet red, blackish
red markings. Emil Liebig, before 1880.

LA BAR'S WHITE--white form of catawbiense
5ft(1.5m) -20F(-29C) ML 3/3   Much like other white forms of
this species, but with light yellow markings in the throat.
La Bar's Nursery, intro. 1959; reg. 1962.

          -ciliatum 1/2
LA BELLE-   -veitchianum 1/4
     -Forsterianum-
                     -edgeworthii 1/4
A hybrid by Veitch. F.C.C. 1887.

LA MARR   Parentage unknown
A parent of the Exbury hybrid FAIRYLIGHT.

               -griffithianum 1/4
          -Mars-
     -Vulcan-   -unknown 3/8
     -          -griersonianum 1/4
LA VERNE-   -griffithianum
     -               -unnamed hybrid-
     -Mrs. Furnival-   -unknown
     -               -caucasicum 1/8
               -unnamed hybrid-
                     -unknown
3.5ft(1m) -10F(-23C) EM Buds dark rose, opening to flowers of
rose Bengal, with deep red blotch, 5-lobed, 4in(10.2cm) wide;
trusses of 9-11. Plant habit upright, broad as tall; dark green
leaves. J. Freeman Stephens, reg. 1975.

               -catawbiense 1/4
          -Catawbiense Album-
LABRADOR-   -unknown 1/4
     -yakushimanum--Mist Maiden 1/2
4ft(1.2m) -25F(-32C) ML Flowers 2in(5cm) across, white center
blends to rhodamine purple edges, brilliant yellow-green dorsal
spots, wavy-edged; truss of 24. Plant upright, slender; slight
indumentum, narrow leaves. R. Behring, cross 1972; reg. 1985.

LACKAMAS BLUE--form of augustinii

6ft(1.8m) -5F(-21C) EM 3/3 Flattened lavender blue flowers,
3.25in(8.3cm) across; truss of 3-4. Plant upright; medium green
leaves, 3in(7.6cm) long. B. Lancaster, reg. 1964.   P.A. 1963.

          -wardii ? 1/2
LACKAMAS CREAM--form of CHLOROPS-
          -vernicosum ? 1/2
3.5ft(1m) -5F(-21C) M 3/3   Flowers primrose yellow to rich
cream, rayed mahogany, 7-lobed; truss of 11. Leaves 4in(10cm) x
2in(5cm), of bluish green. Roots easily.   Benjamin Lancaster,
reg. 1963. P.A. 1962.

LACKAMAS FIREBRAND   Described under CAVALCADE, q.v.

* *
                              -griffithianum
                    -Queen Wilhelmina-   1/8
          -Earl of Athlone-   -unknown 3/8
LACKAMAS GLORY-   -Stanley Davies--unknown
          -thomsonii 1/2
3ft(.9m) -5F(-21C) M   Sturdy, slow-growing plant; dark green
lustrous leaves held 4 years. Flowers of good substance, waxen,
without stamens, campanulate, of cardinal red, 3in(7.6cm) broad;
round trusses of 10-12 long-lasting flowers. Has the persistent
calyx of thomsonii.   B. Lancaster, reg. 1963.
LACKAMAS RUBY   Parentage as above, except reversed
3ft(.9m) -5F(-21C) E   Cardinal red, bell-shaped, heavy, waxy
flowers, to 3in(7.6cm) wide; 15-17 in rounded truss. Persistent
leaves 6in(15.2cm) long, held 4 years. Lancaster, reg. 1961.
* *

          -wardii ? 1/4
     -Chlorops-
LACKAMAS GOLD-   -vernicosum ? 1/4
     -wardii 1/2
3ft(.9m) -5F(-21C) M 3/3   Compact, neat habit. Leaves medium-sized, narrow, bluish green. Flowers bell-shaped, up to 3in.
(7.6cm) across, primrose yellow; trusses of 14.   B. Lancaster,
reg. 1963. P.A. 1962.

LACKAMAS RUBY   Described under LACKAMAS GLORY, q.v.

                    -ponticum 1/4
          -Purple Splendour-
LACKAMAS SOVEREIGN-   -unknown 1/4
          -       -griersonianum 1/4
               -Tally Ho-
                    -facetum (eriogynum) 1/4
4ft(1.2m) -5F(-21C) L   Openly campanulate flowers of Tyrian
purple, 3.5in(8.9cm) wide; upright round trusses of 16. Plant
bushy, erect; leaves 6in(15.2cm) long.   Lancaster, reg. 1963.

               -wardii ? 1/4
          -Chlorops-
LACKAMAS SPICE-   -vernicosum ? 1/4
          -diaprepes 1/2
6ft(1.8m) OF(-18C) M 3/3   Flowers light yellow to creamy
white, rayed mahogany, flat bell-shaped, to 4in(10.2cm) wide;
graceful truss of 11; spicy fragrance. Plant sturdy, rounded;
leaves 7in(18cm) long. B. Lancaster, reg. 1963. P.A. 1962.

* *
          -lacteum 1/2
LACS-
     -sinogrande 1/2
Pale cream flowers, a dark crimson blotch. Magor, intro. 1936.
LACSINO Parentage as above
White flowers with a dark blotch. E. J. P. Magor.
* *

* *
               -fortunei 1/4
          -Luscombei-
LACTCOMBEI-   -thomsonii 1/4
          -lacteum 1/2
Yellow flowers, flushed pink. J. B. Stevenson, intro. 1951.
SIR GEORGE SANSOM Parentage as above
Leaves 5in(12.7cm) x 2in(5cm). Flowers pale yellow, flushed
pink, from rosy pink buds. G. Gorer, reg. 1968. A.M. 1965.
* *

```
                    -campylocarpum 1/4
              -Moonstone-
LADIES' CHOICE-      -williamsianum 1/4
              -Hawk-       -fortunei ssp. discolor 1/8
                    -Lady      -
                       Bessborough-campylocarpum Elatum Group 1/8
```
3ft(.9m) OF(-18C) M 4/4 Flowers primrose yellow with red
spots in throat, openly funnel-shaped 3in(7.6cm) across, 6 wavy
lobes; lax truss of 9-10. Plant rounded, branching well, broad
as tall; glossy spinach green leaves 3in(7.6cm) long, held 2
years. James A. Elliott, reg. 1983.

```
                            -maximum 1/4
        -Lady Clementine Mitford-
LADIFOR-                     -unknown 1/4
        -fortunei 1/2
```
Pink flowers. Joseph B. Gable, before 1958.

```
                           -yakushimanum 1/4
              -unnamed hybrid-
LADY ADAM GORDON-      -dichroanthum 1/4
              -      -wardii 1/4
              -unnamed hybrid-
                           -decorum 1/4
```
3ft(.9m) OF(-18C) M Pale shell pink flowers in trusses of 12.
A. F. George, Hydon, reg. 1976.

LADY ALICE FITZWILLIAM   Parentage unknown (possibly edgeworthii
                                          X ciliatum)
5ft(1.5m) 20F(-7C) EM 3/3   Habit like FRAGRANTISSIMUM but
bushier, more erect; leaves 3.5in(8.9cm) long, concave margins,
of dull rich green. Rosy buds open to white flowers, stained
pink in throat, funnel-shaped, to 5in(12.7cm) wide, with nutmeg
fragrance. Heat-tolerant. Fisher. F.C.C. 1881.

```
                     -maximum 1/2
LADY ANNETTE DE TRAFFORD-
                     -unknown 1/2
```
5ft(1.5m) -15F(-26C) L   Pink flowers with a dark eye. Blooms
late. A. Waterer, 1874.

LADY APRIL   Described under BRICKDUST, q.v.

```
              -catawbiense 1/2
LADY ARMSTRONG-
              -unknown 1/2
```
6ft(1.8m) -20F(-29C) ML 4/3   Very hardy old hybrid of good
growth habit. Flowers of carmine rose with white throat. A.
Waterer, before 1870.

```
                 -ciliatum 1/4
        -Rosy Bell-
LADY BERRY-      -glaucophyllum 1/4
        -           -cinnabarinum 1/4
        -Royal Flush-
                 -maddenii 1/4
```
5ft(1.5m) 5F(-15C) EM 4/4 Growth habit open and upright;
aromatic, bluish green leaves, 3in (7.6cm) long. Tubular flowers 3in(7.6m) long, 2in(5cm) across, rosy opal inside and rich
jasper red outside; pendant trusses of 8. Rothschild, 1935.
A.M. 1937. F.C.C. 1949. Color illus. ARS J 42:2 1988, p. 87.

* *
```
                 -fortunei ssp. discolor 1/2
LADY BESSBOROUGH-
                 -campylocarpum Elatum Group 1/2
```
6ft(1.8m) -5F(-21C) ML 3/3 Large loose trusses of pale yel-
low to ivory flowers, more yellow in the throat. Growth habit
open and upright. A parent of many fine hybrids. Rothschild.
F.C.C. 1933.
BELLE   Parentage as above
Flowers of very pale lemon yellow. Rothschild, 1933.
MONTREAL   Parentage as above
6ft(1.8m) 5F(-15C) M 3/2   Tall plant with pink buds opening
deep cream; flowers funnel-shaped, wavy edges. Rothschild,
1933. Color illus. F p. 49.
OLE OLSON   Parentage as above, but reversed
5ft(1.5m) OF(-18C) ML 3/3 Plant habit open, upright; medium
green leaves, 4in(10.2cm) long. Flowers pale yellow, 3.5in
(8.9cm) wide; loose truss. Gable cross; Lem intro.; reg. 1988.

OTTAWA   Parentage as LADY BESSBOROUGH above
6ft(1.8m) -5F(-21C) ML 3/3 Flower orange pink, fading white.
Habit as others in this grex. Rothschild, 1933.
ROBERTE   Parentage as LADY BESSBOROUGH
6ft(1.8m) -5F(-21C) ML 3/3 A clone given the Christian name
of Lady Bessborough. Flowers rose pink, speckled red. Rothschild. F.C.C. 1936.
* *

```
                 -griffithianum 1/2
LADY BLIGH-
                 -unknown 1/2
```
5ft(1.5m) -5F(-21C) ML 4/3   Buds open dark strawberry pink,
fading to pastel pink, making a beautiful two-toned effect; flowers widely campanulate, to 3in(7.6cm) across. Shrub spreading,
rounded, wider than tall; medium green leaves, 6in(15.2cm) long,
held 2 years. C. B. van Nes. A.M. 1934. Color illus. ARS Q
29:3 (1975), cover; VV p. 42.

```
                      -fortunei 1/4
              -Pilgrim-      -arboreum 1/8
LADY BOWES LYON-      -Gill's Triumph-
              -yakushimanum 1/2   -griffithianum 1/8
```
4ft(1.2m) -15F(-26C) M Large globe-shaped trusses of 20 flo-
wers, white, tinged rose pink darkening to phlox pink. F.
Hanger cross; RHS Garden, Wisley. A.M. 1962.

```
                 -cinnabarinum Roylei Group 1/4
   -Lady Rosebery-               -cinnabarinum 1/8
LADY-            -Royal Flush, pink form-
BYNG-                            -maddenii 1/8
   -davidsonianum 1/2
```
Rose pink flowers. Thacker, 1942.

LADY C. WALSH   See LADY CLEMENTINE WALSH

```
                 -auriculatum 1/2
LADY CATHERINE-
                 -Corona--unknown 1/2
```
Flowers flushed rose, rusty speckling within; fragrant. Late.
Sir John Ramsden, cross 1922; intro. 1936. A.M. 1936.

* *
```
                 -cinnabarinum Roylei Group 1/2
LADY CHAMBERLAIN-           -cinnabarinum 1/4
                 -Royal Flush-
                 (orange form)-maddenii 1/4
```
5ft(1.5m) 10F(-12C) ML 4/3   Plant upright, slender willowy
branches, bluish green new foliage. Flowers fleshy, bright
orange to salmon pink, tubular to long trumpet shape, 3in(7.6cm)
long by 1.5in(3.8cm) wide; 3-6 in drooping trusses. Rothschild.
F.C.C. 1931. Color illus. JS p. 93; PB pl. 36.
APRICOT LADY CHAMBERLAIN   Parentage as above
Apricot-colored flowers. Rothschild, 1930.
BODNANT YELLOW   Parentage as above
Seed parent a more yellow form of cinnabarinum. Flowers butter
yellow to orange buff with a deeper reddish flush in pendulous
clusters. A bit more hardy. Lord Aberconway. F.C.C. 1944.
CHELSEA   Parentage as above
Hanging trumpets of soft pink. Rothschild, 1930. Color illus.
HG p. 73.
EXBURY LADY CHAMBERLAIN   Parentage as above
Flowers of orange or yellow flushed with salmon, pendulous and
tubular as cinnabarinum but larger. Rothschild. F.C.C. 1931.
GLEAM   Parentage as above
6ft(1.8m) 5F(-15C) ML 4/3   Long, tubular flowers orange and
yellow, crimson-tipped petals. Upright small branches, shiny
round leaves form a narrow, columnar shrub as cinnabarinum.
Rothschild, 1930.
GOLDEN QUEEN   Parentage as above
Drooping flowers, soft yellow, flushed orange, truss of 6-7.
Erect shrub with nice foliage. Rothschild. F.C.C. 1947.
IVY   Parentage as above
Flowers salmon-colored. Rothschild, 1930.
LADY CHAMBERLAIN SEVILLE   Parentage as above
Bright orange flowers. Rothschild, 1930.
ORIFLAMME   Parentage as above
Fine orange-red flowers. Rothschild, 1930
SALMON TROUT   Parentage as above
"Color of freshly cooked salmon"--Register. Rothschild, 1930.
* *

LADY CLEMENT WALSH   See LADY CLEMENTINE WALSH

            -maximum 1/2
LADY CLEMENTINE MITFORD-
            -unknown 1/2
5ft(1.5m) -5F(-21C) ML 3/3   Flowers soft peach pink, darker
at edges, slight yellow eye. Handsome foliage, glossy green,
covered with silvery hairs when young; plant vigorous, upright,
broader than tall, free-flowering. A. Waterer, 1870. Color
illus. JS p. 81; VV p. 53.

LADY CLEMENTINE WALSH Parentage unknown (Possibly cataubiense X
                                griffithianum)
5ft(1.5m) -10F(-23C) ML   Flowers pale pink or white, spotted
green above; blush edged in pink. J. Waterer. A.M. 1902.

            -cataubiense 1/2
LADY CLERMONT-
            -unknown 1/2
Flowers rosy red or light red with a very dark blotch. A. Wat-
erer. F.C.C. 1865.

LADY CONSTANCE   Parentage unknown
Medium-sized flowers of deep rose. Unknown origin. A.M. 1923.

            -griffithianum 1/2
LADY DE ROTHSCHILD-
            -Sappho--unknown 1/2
5ft(1.5m) -5F(-21C) M 4/2   A beautiful white flower flushed
pink with a crimson blotch and faint red spotting, in large
truss. Not to be confused with the plant MRS. LIONEL DE
ROTHSCHILD, also a Waterer hybrid. A. Waterer. A.M. 1952.

            -griffithianum 1/2
LADY DECIES-
            -unknown 1/2
5ft(1.5m) OF(-18C) ML   Described in Cox as blush lilac or
light mauve with a yellow eye; flowers 4in(10cm) across, in
trusses of 20. Strong-growing, leggy. J. Waterer, before 1922.

            -facetum 1/2
LADY DIGBY-
            -strigillosum 1/2
Large shrub with shape and leaves like strigillosum; leaves indumented, 10in(25cm) long. Flowers blood red, campanulate, 8 to
a truss. Midseason. Lord Digby. A.M. 1946.

            -lindleyi 1/2
LADY DOROTHY ELLA-
            -nuttallii 1/2
Flowers broadly tubular funnel-shaped, ivory white, flushed pink
externally, with basal golden flare; very fragrant. Plant up to
about 14ft(4.2m). Duncan & Davies, reg. 1986.

                 -fortunei ssp. discolor 1/4
      -King of Shrubs-   -dichroanthum 1/8
LADY ELBERTA-   -Fabia-
      -                      -griersonianum 1/8
            -fortunei, yellow form 1/2
8ft(2.4m) x 10ft(3m)(22 yrs) OF(-18C) ML Very fragrant flowers of heavy substance with 7 wavy-edged lobes, moderate pink
shading to light yellowish pink. A. & M. Childers, reg. 1989.

            -maximum 1/2
LADY ELEANOR CATHCART-
            -arboreum 1/2
6ft(1.8m) -15F(-26C) ML 2/2   A hardy plant, heat-resistant,
somewhat compact, rounded. Flowers clear pink, a purple blotch.
Waterer, before 1850.

            -arboreum 1/2
LADY FALMOUTH-
            -unknown 1/2
Flowers rose-colored, black blotch. J. Waterer, before 1875.

LADY GALWAY   Possibly Maddenia subsection hybrid
4ft(1.2m) 15F(-9C) EM   Fragrant flowers, open from flesh-colored buds, changing to pink, then white; about 3 per truss. In
New Zealand, according to Cox. Mason intro. in Wellington.

            -cataubiense 1/2
LADY GREY EGERTON-
            -unknown 1/2
5ft(1.5m) -15F(-26C) ML 3/2   Flowers pale lilac, tight conical trusses. Very leggy. A. Waterer, before 1888.

                  -griffithianum 1/4
            -unnamed hybrid-
LADY GWENDOLINE BRODERICK-   -unknown 3/4
            -Bacchus--unknown
Flowers dark pink, heavily spotted with red; loose trusses. C.
B. van Nes, before 1922.

LADY HARCOURT   Parentage unknown
Parent of GONDOLIER. Pink, spotted with crimson. J. Waterer.

            -griffithianum 1/2
LADY HILLINGDON-
            -unknown 1/2
Pale mauve flowers with yellow markings. J. Waterer.

* *
                     -ciliatum 1/8
                -Rosy Bell-
        -Lady Berry-   -glaucophyllum 1/8
      -                  -   -cinnabarinum 1/8
LADY HOLLAND-   -Royal Flush-
      -                       -maddenii 1/8
           -maddenii ssp. crassum 1/2
6ft(1.8m) x 4ft(1.2m) 32F(OC) EM   Flowers to 5in(12.7cm) wide
in lax trusses of 8, yellowish pink, reverse strong pink. Habit
upright, well-branched. Mrs. J. P. Evans, reg. 1989.
NAN   Parentage as above
6ft(1.8m) x 6ft 15F(-9C) EM Flowers pink and white with faint
yellow throat in lax trusses 7in(17.8cm) wide. Leaves with tiny
brown scales below. Dr. Evans cross: Mrs. Evans, reg. 1989.
* *

LADY HORLICK   Described under PHRYNE, q.v.

LADY IN WAITING   Described under QUEEN ELIZABETH II, q.v.

            -diaprepes 1/2
LADY JEAN-
            -facetum (eriogynum) 1/2
A cross made by Lord Stair; intro. 1943.

                -cinnabarinum Roylei Group 1/4
        -Lady   -
LADY   -Rosebery-   -cinnabarinum 1/8
LAWRENCE-   -Royal Flush, pink form-
      -                       -maddenii 1/8
        -ambiguum 1/2
Coppery rose flowers. Thacker, 1942.

                -cataubiense 1/4
         -Cynthia-
LADY LONGMAN-   -griffithianum 1/4
      -                      -maximum 1/4
        -Lady Eleanor Cathcart-
                -arboreum 1/4
5ft(1.5m) -10F(-21C) ML Handsome, large trusses of large flowers, vivid rose on a pale ground, with a chocolate eye. Plant
heat-tolerant; leaves heavily veined. H. White, Sunningdale.

                -ponticum 1/4
      -Purple Splendor-
LADY LUCK-   -unknown 1/4
      -                       -griffithianum 1/4
      -Loderi Superlative-
                -fortunei 1/4
5ft(1.5m) OF(-18C) ML   Many large, fragrant flowers of lovely
orchid pink. Plant densely foliaged with big attractive leaves.
Distributor Greer.

                -griersonianum 1/4
         -Tally Ho-
LADY MALCOLM STEWART-   -facetum (eriogynum) 1/4
      -                       -ponticum 1/4
      -Purple Splendour-
                -unknown 1/4
Rich pink flowers. Adams-Acton, 1942.

```
                   -griffithianum 1/32
              -Kewense-
        -Aurora-         -fortunei
     -Naomi-        -thomsonii 1/16
    -Carita-        -fortunei 5/32
LADY        -campylocarpum 1/4
MALMESBURY-wardii 1/2
```
Flowers of light primrose yellow, darker in the throat, with a
deeper yellowish green eye; trusses of 12-14. E. de Rothschild,
reg. 1982.

LADY MAR   Parentage unknown
A parent of FAIRYLIGHT.


```
          -griffithianum 1/2
LADY MONTAGU-
          -thomsonii 1/2
```
6ft(1.8m)   10F(-12C) EM 4/3 A tall shrub with very large,
loose trusses; flowers large, dark rose pink, deeper outside
and of good substance. Ovate leaves. Rothschild. A.M. 1931.

* *
```
                    -maximum 1/4
        -Lady Eleanor Cathcart-
LADY OF BELFIELD-                 -arboreum 1/4
        -decorum 1/2
```
8ft x 9ft(2.4m x 2.7m)(19 yrs) -5F(-21C) L Buds deep purplish
pink open lighter pink, with dark purplish red blotch and dorsal
spots.   Flowers 2.5in(6.5cm) wide, 22 per truss. Leaves to
6in(15cm) long. Dexter cross; Tyler Arboretum, reg. 1985.
LADY OF JUNE   Parentage as above
15ft x 20ft(4.5m x 6m)(36 yrs) -5F(-21C) L Flowers strong purplish pink fading lighter, distinct greenish yellow spots; truss
of 16. Plant upright, spreading broader than tall, olive green
foliage.   Dexter cross; Dr. John Wister named; Gertrude Wister,
reg. 1980.   Color illus. LW pl. 17.
* *
* *

LADY OF SPAIN   Described under CANADIAN BEAUTY, q.v.

```
          -campylocarpum 1/2
LADY PRIMROSE-
          -unknown 1/2
```
4ft(1.2m) OF(-18C) EM 3/3 Flowers clear primrose yellow with
red spots, in a compact ball-shaped truss. Plant habit dense;
medium-sized light green leaves. Plant grows slowly and needs
shade. W. C. Slocock. A.M. Exbury Trials 1933.

```
        -souliei 1/2         -decorum ? 1/8
LADY RAE-          -Caroline-
     -Robert Allison-        -brachycarpum ? 1/8
                   -fortunei ssp. discolor 1/4
```
8ft(2.4m) -5F(-21C) M Plant habit upright, candelabra struc-
ture; leaves glossy, dark green, 8in(20.3cm) long. Flowers
saucer-shaped, color of mother of pearl, fading white in an open
truss. Joseph Gable cross; T. Coleman Andrews, reg. 1969.

```
      -yakushimanum 1/2
      -                  -lacteum 1/8      -griffithianum
LADY -         -Lionel's-     -Kewense-      3/64
ROMSEY-        -Triumph -   -Aurora-     -fortunei
      -               -Naomi-    -thomsonii 3/32
     -Elizabeth de-          -fortunei
     -Rothschild -                  -griffithianum
      -                       -Kewense-
      -                -Aurora-     -fortunei 15/64
      -Exbury Naomi-    -thomsonii
                         -fortunei
```
Trusses hold 17-20 very pale greenish white flowers, with faint
olive yellow spotting in upper throat. Edmund de Rothschild,
reg. 1982. A.M. 1982.

* *
```
       -cinnabarinum Roylei Group 1/2
LADY              -cinnabarinum 1/4
ROSEBERY-Royal Flush, pink form -
                  -maddenii 1/4
```
6ft(1.8m) 5F(-15C) M 4/3   Similar to LADY CHAMBERLAIN except
selected clones more pink than orange due to the use of the pink
form of ROYAL FLUSH as the male parent. Other named forms with
only minor variations: LADY ROSEBERY DALMENY, LADY ROSEBERY

ETNA, LADY ROSEBERY PINK DELIGHT. Plant upright, willowy habit,
taller than wide; smooth medium green leaves 3in(7.6cm) long,
scaly below. Flowers shell pink, shaded pink at base, tubular,
fleshy, in very lax trusses of 6-8. Rothschild.   A.M. 1930.
F.C.C. 1932.   Color illus. F p. 49; Cox pl. 102.
LADY ROSEBERY PINK DAWN   Parentage as above
Another selected form, introduced by Lord Digby, 1954.
* *

LADY RUMBOLD   Parentage unknown
A parent of GRENADA, an Exbury hybrid.

```
          -griersonianum 1/2
-                   -griffithianum 1/8
LADY STAIR-     -Loderi-
     -Albatross-      -fortunei 1/8
            -fortunei ssp. discolor 1/4
```
A hybrid by Lord Stair, 1939.

LADY STUART OF WORTLEY   Parentage uncertain. Possibly
                hybrid of griffithianum.
5ft(1.5m) OF(-18C) ML 3/2 Upright, open growth habit, large
leaves. Drooping trusses of big, glowing pink flowers.   M.
Koster, 1909. A.M. 1933.

```
                   -wardii 1/4
     -Prelude, A.M. form-
LADY WILCOX-         -fortunei 1/4
     -campylocarpum 1/2
```
Flowers in trusses of 10, 7-lobed, pale yellow-green, shading to
light greenish yellow deep in throat and with grayed purple
markings on dorsal lobe. E. de Rothschild, reg. 1988.

```
          -fortunei ssp. discolor 1/2
LADYBIRD-
      -Corona--unknown 1/2
```
6ft(1.8m) -10F(-23C) VL 5/3   Parent of DIVA. An extremely
vigorous plant, forming a huge bush; glossy leaves, rich green.
Very large, dome-shaped trusses of very large flowers, in soft
shades of coral pink with a darker eye, specked yellow inside.
Rothschild.   A.M. 1933.

```
          -johnstonianum 1/2
LAERDAL-
     -dalhousiae 1/2
```
Pure white flowers.   Sir Edward Bolitho, 1947.

```
          -minus Carolinianum Group 1/2
LAETEVIRENS-
       -ferrugineum 1/2
```
3ft(1.2m) -15F(-26C) L 3/3 Synonym WILSONI. Rosy pink flow-
ers in loose, small corymbs on a compact plant with narrow,
glossy leaves. Sun-tolerant.   Origin unknown.

```
     -macabeanum 1/2
LAGG-
     -magnificum 1/2
```
Flowers very light sap green, with staining deep in throat of a
light magenta rose, shading darker. Brodick Castle, reg. 1973.

```
     -smirnowii 1/2
LAJKA-          -catawbiense 1/4
     -C. S. Sargent-
              -unknown 1/4
```
5ft(1.5m) -15F(-26C) ML   Purplish violet buds open as bright
violet purple flowers with striking blotch of yellow-green. In
Czechoslovakia. Scholz, intro. 1966.

* *
```
                  -griffithianum 1/2
     -Lady Bligh-
LAKE LABISH-      -unknown 1/4
     -              -griffithianum
     -Loderi Vernus-
              -fortunei 1/4
```
5ft(1.5m) 5F(-15C) ML 4/3 Growth habit upright, open, wider
than tall; leaves 5in(12.7cm) long, medium green.   Strawberry
rose flowers, campanulate, 3.5in(8.9cm) wide; tall truss of 17.
Rudolph Henny.   P.A. 1955.
JANE HENNY   Parentage as above
6ft(1.8m) OF(-18C) ML   White flowers with soft pink shading
and mottling, pale brick red rays in throat, 4in(10cm) across,

in trusses of 13. Leaves held 3 years. Henny, reg. 1978.
NEW ROMANCE   Parentage as above
5ft(1.5m) 0F(-18C) ML   Buds of rose pink opening to white
flowers. Leaves to 5in(12.7cm) long. Henny, reg. 1966.
* *

```
                -burmanicum, Cox selection 1/2
LAKE LORRAINE-
                -cuffeanum 1/2
```
5ft x 5ft(1.5m)(15 yrs) 20F(-7C) ML   Flowers in flat trusses
of 6-8, with 5 wavy lobes, white with brilliant yellow blotch;
outside paler yellow. R. W. Scott, reg. 1989.

* *

```
                -griersonianum 1/2
LAKE OZETTE-             -griffithianum 1/4
                -Loderi Venus-
                        -fortunei 1/2
```
A cross by Clark, reg. 1958.
MRS. HORACE FOGG   Parentage as above
5ft(1.5m) 0F(-18C) ML 4/2   Pretty, compact plant; likes sun.
Very large flowers, silvery pinkish rose, stained deeper rose
red. Smooth olive green leaves. Ridgeway cross; Larson, reg.
1958. P.A. 1964. Color illus. VV p. 98.
* *

LAKESIDE--form of trichostomum Ledoides Group
Rounded compact trusses 1.12in(2.8cm) wide and .9in(2.2cm) high,
of 11 flowers about .5in(1.2cm) across, white flushed light rhodamine purple, tubular-shaped, 5-lobed. Aromatic leaves with
brown scales, narrowly oblong, about .7in(1.8cm) long. Crown
Estate Commissioners, reg. 1972. A.M. 1972.

```
                -neriiflorum 1/2
LAL KAPRA-
                -sanguineum ssp. sanguineum var. sanguineum 1/2
```
Red flowers. Sir Edward Bolitho, reg. 1962.

LALIQUE   Parentage uncertain--possibly a seedling of
                                LODERI or griffithianum
6ft(1.8m) 0F(-18C) M   New Zealand hybrid. Trusses of 14-15
flowers, white tinged pink and lilac. Open, upright plant.
Mrs. A. G. Holmes, reg. 1979. Color illus. Cox pl. 103.

```
                        -cinnabarinum Roylei Group 1/4
        -Lady Chamberlain-           -cinnabarinum 1/8
LAMBOURN-               -Royal Flush-
        -maddenii 1/2               -maddenii 5/8
```
Lax trusses of 6-7 flowers, light Persian rose with upper lobe
stained amber, reverse darker rose; tubular corolla 2.5in(6.4cm)
long by 3in(7.6cm) across. Leaves 6in(15.2in) long. Crown Estate, Windsor, reg. 1963. P.C. 1962.

* *

```
                -campanulatum 1/2
LAMELLEN-
                -griffithianum 1/2
```
5ft(1.5m) -10F(-23C) EM 4/3   Tree-like habit with flowers
light pinkish mauve; some forms near white. E. J. P. Magor,
Lamellen, 1943.
MOUNT EVEREST   Parentage as above
5ft(1.5m) -10F(-23C) E 4/3   Narrow, campanulate flowers, pure
white with brown markings, in conical trusses. Plant large,
vigorous, dense. Slocock. A.M. 1953. F.C.C. Wisley Trials
1958. A.G.M. 1969. Color illus. JS p. 43.
* *

LAMELLEN DANTE   Described under DANTE, q.v.

LAMENTOSA   Described under SCHNEEKRONE, q.v.

* *

```
                -Essex Scarlet--unknown 1/4
        -Bad Eilsen-
LAMPION-            -forrestii Repens Group 1/4
        -yakushimanum--Koichiro Wada 1/2
```
3ft(.9m) x 2.5ft(.75m) -10F(-23C) ML   Plant dense, compact.
Campanulate flowers on long pedicels, opening bright rose red to
rose pink, fading paler. Ovate-elliptic leaves; thin brown indumentum. Hachmann cross; Stück, reg. 1988. Color illus.
WS, 1989, p. 155.
BAMBOLA   Parentage as above

1.5ft(.45m) x 2.5ft(.75m) -15F(-26C) ML Flowers in loose
trusses of 3-5, strong purplish red to deep purplish pink,
strong pink in throat. Very slow-growing. Hachmann, cross
1968; Stück, reg. 1988. Color illus. WS, 1989, p. 147.
* *

```
                        -griffithianum 1/8
                -Queen Wilhelmina-
        -Britannia-            -unknown 5/8
LAMPLIGHTER-       -Stanley Davies--unknown
                            -fortunei 1/4
        -Madame Fr. J. Chauvin-
                    -unknown
```
5ft(1.5m) -5F(-21C) M 4/3   Large, sparkling light red flower,
a salmon glow; tall conical trusses of 10-12. Plant compact,
rounded; medium green foliage, 6in(15.2cm) long. M. Koster.
F.C.C. Boskoop 1955. Color illus. JS p. 69; VV p. 128.

```
                -griersonianum 1/2
LANCER-
                -hookeri 1/2
```
Blood red flowers. Lord Aberconway, 1950.

LANGLEY PARK   Described under BRITANNIA, q.v.

```
                -fortunei 1/2
LANGWORTH-
                -Sappho--unknown 1/2
```
5ft(1.5m) -10F(-23C) M Tall, vigorous plant, wider than high;
dark, dull green leaves to 8in(20.3cm) long. Large white flowers with throat streaked greenish brown, funnel-shaped, 4in
(10.2cm) wide; conical, rather lax trusses of 16. Slocock.
H.C. Wisley Trials 1960. A.M. 1962.

* *
```
                                -thomsonii 1/8
                        -Bagshot Ruby-
                -Princess Elizabeth-     -unknown 3/8
LANNY PRIDE-            -unknown
                        -smirnowii 1/4
        -unnamed hybrid-
                        yakushimanum 1/4
```
Bright guardsman red; medium-sized plant. Moyer cross; Delp
raiser.
JENNIFER HARRIS   Parentage as above
Medium-sized plant with flowers cream and pink. Moyer cross;
Delp raiser.
WENDY LYN   Parentage as above
5ft(1.5m) -15F(-26C) L 3/4 Buds a combination of currant and
vivid reds, opening to a white star-shaped flower, heavily edged
and frilled in vivid red; white filaments. Moyer cross; Delp
raiser.
* *

LANYON   See under MARSHALL

```
        -Marion--unknown 11/16            -griffithianum
LARAINE-            -Queen Wilhelmina-            1/16
LANGDON-   -Unknown Warrior-          -unknown
        -unnamed-            -Stanley Davies--unknown
        hybrid-
                -arboreum 1/4
```
Trusses of 19 flowers, medium Neyron rose. Langdon, reg. 1982.

```
                -dichroanthum 1/4
        -Astarte-            -campylocarpum Elatum Group 1/8
LARGO-         -Penjerrick-
        -            -griffithianum 1/8
        -neriiflorum Euchaites Group 1/2
```
Red-flowered hybrid. Lord Aberconway, 1946.

```
                -taggianum ? 1/2
LARTAG-
                -unknown 1/2
```
6ft(1.8m) 15F(-9C) VE 4/4   Grown for years in the Pacific
Northwest as taggianum but evidently a hybrid, from H. L. Larson. Rose pink in bud, opening pure white, small yellow blotch,
funnel-shaped, 3in(7.6cm) wide, fragrant; loose trusses of 4.
Very floriferous. Spreading, drooping bush; leaves 5in(12.7cm)
long. Dr. & Mrs. P. J. Bowman, reg. 1966.

```
            -dichroanthum 1/4
      -Fabia-
LASCAUX-      -griersonianum 1/4
      -wardii Litiense Group 1/2
```
Buds a blend of red and orange; flower fleshy, bell-shaped, barium yellow, crimson blotch. Petaloid calyx same color as flower. F. Hanger, cross 1947; RHS Garden, Wisley. A.M. 1954.

LAST CHANCE   Described under CAPTAIN JACK, q.v.

```
                  -catawbiense, white form 3/8
        -Belle Heller-            -catawbiense
LAST HURRAH-          -Madame Carvalho-
        -aureum 1/2               -unknown 1/8
```
2ft(.6m) -10F(-23C) May or Sept. 4/5 Synonym ATHENS. Flower near-white, tinged faint yellow-green, some dorsal spotting of grayed chartreuse, flat saucer-shaped, 2.75in(7cm) across, 5-lobed; ball-shaped trusses of 13. Plant well-branched, 3 times wider than tall; dark olive green leaves of heavy texture, retained 3 years. In many climates blooms almost fully in early fall. David G. Leach, intro. 1974; reg. 1981.

```
        -fortunei ssp. discolor 1/2
LAST ROSE-        -griersonianum 1/4
      -Tally Ho-
            -facetum (eriogynum) 1/4
```
Rose madder flowers held in well-rounded truss of 9; upper lobes freckled orange, staining throat with orange flush. Plant 8ft (2.4m) tall; leaves 8in(20.3cm) long. E. J. Greig, reg. 1963.

LATIFOLIA--form of ferrugineum
2ft(.6m) -15F(-26C) M 3/4 The wider-leaf form of the Swiss alpine rose, colored rose pink.

```
      -souliei 1/2
LATONA-
      -dichroanthum 1/2
```
A hybrid with flowers cream to pink. Lord Aberconway, 1933.

```
            -griersonianum 1/2
LAURA ABERCONWAY-        -thomsonii 1/4
            -Barclayi-      -arboreum 1/8
                 -Glory of -
            Penjerrick-griffithianum 1/8
```
5ft(1.5m) 10F(-12C) EM 3/2   Plant of open habit; thick, leathery, dark green leaves. Flower geranium lake, funnel-shaped, 3.5in(8.9cm) across, margins frilled; loose trusses of 8-9. Lord Aberconway, 1933. A.M. 1941. F.C.C. 1944.

```
                  -griffithianum 1/8
            -Geoffrey Millais-
      -Countess -       -unknown 1/4
LAURA- of Athlone-            -catawbiense 1/8
MARIE-        -Catawbiense Grandiflorum-
      -ponticum 1/2            -unknown
```
5ft(1.5m) -5F(-21C) M Mauve flowers openly bell-shaped, 3in (7.6cm) wide, ruffled, full rounded truss. Plant habit medium-compact; leaves 4in(10cm) long. Lancaster, reg. 1971.

LAURAGO   Described under YAKU PICOTEE, q.v.

```
            -caucasicum
      -Boule de Neige-
LAUREL-           -catawbiense
PINK -       -unnamed hybrid-
      -          -unknown
      -            -catawbiense var. album--La Bar's White
      -unnamed hybrid-        -neriiflorum
            -F. C. Puddle-
                  -griersonianum
```
4ft(1.2m) -20F(-29C) E 4/4 Parentage uncertain; reg. as BOULE DE NEIGE X catawbiense X F. C. PUDDLE. Flowers of Neyron rose, 5in(5cm) wide, 6-7 lobes, frilled, round truss of 10-12. Plant mound-shaped, wider than tall; small round leaf, 1.75in (4.5cm) long. Knippenberg cross; reg. 1966.

```
            -mucronulatum, Vossberg's Pink 1/2
LAURELWOOD SNOW BUNTING-        -leucaspis 1/4
            -Bric-a-Brac-
                  -moupinense 1/4
```
3ft(.9m) x 3.3ft(1m)(20 yrs) Flowers open rose madder then fade white, with 6 wavy-edged lobes; anthers black; pistils pink. Dense habit, spreading. Mrs. J. F. Knippenberg, reg. 1988.

```
            -minus Carolinianum Group 3/4
LAURIE-      -minus Carolinianum Group
      -P. J. M.-
            -dauricum var. sempervirens 1/4
```
3ft(.9m) -25F(-32C) EM 4/4 Light pink to white flower, sometimes semi-double; heavy blooming, later than P. J. M. Corolla has golden dorsal spotting, light purple stripes on reverse; openly funnel-shaped, 1.75in(4.5cm) wide. Terminal clusters of 33 flowers. Plant slow-growing, spreads broad as tall; glossy dark green, small foliage, aromatic when crushed, copper bronze in winter. Mezitt, reg. 1983.

* *
```
            -griersonianum 1/2
LAVA FLOW-
            -sanguineum ssp. didymum ? 1/2
```
2ft(.6m) -10F(-23C) L   Low and compact, pointed dark green leaves. Up to 10 flowers per truss, scarlet red, spotted crimson. Very late. Sunningdale, 1955.
GLOWING EMBER   Sibling and similar, but earlier-flowering.
* *

```
                  -decorum 1/4
            -unnamed hybrid-
LAVENDER CHARM-      -griffithianum 1/4
      -            -catawbiense 1/4
      -Purpureum Elegans-
                  -unknown 1/4
```
6ft(1.8m) -5F(-21C) ML   Large leaves, 7in x 2.5in (17.8cm x 6.4cm). Flowers pale pink, shadowed with lavender, a small dark blotch, the reverse much deeper; trusses of about 14. J. Gable cross; C. Herbert, reg. 1976.

LAVENDER FILIGREE   Described under CAROLINE ALLBROOK, q.v.

```
            -fortunei 1/2
LAVENDER GIRL-        -catawbiense 1/4
      -Lady Grey Egerton-
            -unknown 1/4
```
5ft(1.5m) -5F(-21C) M 3/4   Flowers of pale lavender, edges rosy mauve, fading at center with golden brown spotting on upper lobe; corolla fully expanded 2.5in(6.4cm) across, in dome-shaped trusses of 18. Fragrant and floriferous. Vigorous, wider than high; leaves slightly cupped. Slocock. A.M. 1950. F.C.C. Wisley Trials 1967. Color illus. VV p. iv.

LAVENDER PRINCESS   Parentage unknown (Possibly fortunei X)
4ft(1.2m) -15F(-26C) ML   Flower light lavender pink; compact plant, dark green foliage. Dexter cross; Bosley intro. 1965.

LAVENDER QUEEN   Described under PINK CAMEO, q.v.

* *
```
            -diaprepes 1/2
LAVENDER TIME-        -ponticum 1/4
            -Purple Splendour-
                  -unknown 1/4
```
LILAC TIME   Parentage as above
The above two hybrids by Gen. Harrison, 1956.
* *

```
                  -russatum 1/4
            -unnamed hybrid-
LAVENDULA-      -saluenense 1/4
            -rubiginosum 1/2
```
3ft(.9m) -15F(-26C) M 4/3   Compact lepidote; aromatic foliage. Large, deep lavender, very showy flowers with ruffled margins. D. Hobbie, intro. 1952. Color illus. Cox pl. 106.

LAWTON'S CHINESE RED   Parentage unknown
3ft(.9m) -5F(-21C) ML   Narrow leaves, medium size. Flowers clear red, without marks, in truss of 15. Lawton, reg. 1979.

```
                  -campylocarpum Elatum
LaWANDA WATTERS---LETTY EDWARDS, selfed-        1/2
                  -fortunei 1/2
```
5ft(1.5m) x 5ft(15 yrs) OF(-18C) EM Flowers to 4in(10cm) wide in trusses of 12-13, 7-lobed, light yellow-green; balled truss 6in(15cm) across. Dense growth habit. F. Watters, reg. 1989.

```
                                                6ft(1.8m) -20F(-29C) L 3/3  Handsome foliage: smooth, dark,
          -dichroanthum 1/2                     and glossy.  Flowers of deep purple.  Lee, before 1851.
LEABURG-        -campylocarpum Elatum Group 1/4
     -Penjerrick-
               -griffithianum 1/4                           -catawbiense 1/2
3ft(.9m) 5F(-15C) EM 4/3  Very compact plant; glossy, dark      LEE'S DARK PURPLE-
green leaves, 2.5in(6.4cm) long.  Flowers waxy, brilliant blood            -unknown 1/2
red, to 3in(7.6cm) across; flat truss.  Phetteplace, reg. 1958.   6ft(1.8m) -15F(-26C) ML 2/3  An old reliable, grown in colder
P.A. 1956.                                      areas.  Bush compact, rounded, like catawbiense in habit; fol-
                                                iage dark, slightly wavy.  Flowers royal purple, brownish marks
                                                within, in dense rounded trusses.  Lee, before 1851.  Color
LEACHII--form of maximum                        illus. ARS J 43:4 1989, p. 183.
"...a curiosity with compact growth, undulating leaves and glob-
ular flower buds  which is said to come more or less true from
seed."  P. Cox, The Larger Species of Rhododendron p. 250.                  -caucasicum 1/2
                                                LEE'S SCARLET-
                                                            -unknown 1/2
LEACH'S WHITE   See SNOW                         4ft(1.2m) -5F(-21C) VE 3/3  Flowers rosy crimson, fading to
                                                bright pink.  Earliest of all rhododendrons, flowering before
                                                Christmas in parts of Great Britain.  Lee, 1851.
* * * * * * * * * * * * * * * * * * * * * * * *
               -griffithianum 1/2
LEAH YATES--Mars, selfed-                        LEGAL JOHNNY   Described under CAROLINE DE ZOETE, q.v.
               -unknown 1/2
4ft(1.2cm) -15F(-26C) ML  Flower medium magenta, a large white
dorsal flare with 2 rays of grayed mustard spots; widely funnel-            -forrestii Repens Group 1/4
campanulate; 3in(7.6cm) across.  Plant broader than tall; dark       -Jaipur-
grass green leaves.  H. Yates cross; Mrs. Yates, reg. 1976.    LEILIE-    -meddianum 1/4
BIG SAVAGE RED   Parentage as above                    -haematodes 1/4
3ft(.9m) -20F(-29C) ML 3/3  Flowers clear pink, white dorsal       -May Day-
flare, frilled lobes, 15 per conical truss.  Yates, reg. 1978.              -griersonianum 1/4
* * * * * * * * * * * * * * * * * * * * * * * *  Semi-dwarf, 2ft x 3ft (.6m x .9m) in 16 years, compact, leaves
                                                7in(17.8cm) long, heavy brown indumentum.  Flowers orient red,
                                                2.5in(6.4cm) wide, held in trusses of 9.  Brandt, reg. 1966.
            -yakushimanum 1/2
LEANNE'S FAVOURITE-            -unknown 1/4
            -Bud Flanagan-                       LEMON BELLS   Described under LITTLE PUDDING, q.v.
                        -ponticum 1/4
Flowers in trusses of 19, funnel-shaped, 8-lobed, deep reddish
purple in bud, opening pale purplish pink.  Plant 2ft(.6m).  R.   * * * * * * * * * * * * * * * * * * * * * * * *
Drayson, cross 1976; D. M. O'Hare, reg. 1987.               -rigidum (caeruleum) 1/2
                                                LEMON BILL-
                                                          -cinnabarinum ssp. xanthocodon Concatenans Group 1/2
            -smirnowii 1/4                       Waxy, creamy white flowers with yellow markings.  Lord Aber-
     -Goody Goody-                               conway, intro. 1943.
     -           -catawbiense 5/16    -catawbiense  PEACE   Parentage as above
     -                      -Parsons Grandi-     3ft(.9m) -10F(-23C) EM 4/3  Pendulous trusses of waxy, creamy
LECTROSTATIC-        -America- florum    -unknown 9/32  white flowers, flushed pale rose.  Truss of 7-8.  Lord Abercon-
     -     -unnamed-       -dark red hybrid--unknown  way.  A.M. Wisley Trials 1946.
     -     - hybrid-            -griffithianum 3/32  * * * * * * * * * * * * * * * * * * * * * * * *
     -     -      -Mars-
     -Anna-      -Blaze-   -unknown
     Delp-          -catawbiense var. rubrum 1/16          -caucasicum 1/4
               -Mars (as above)                      -Boule de Neige-        -catawbiense 1/8
          -Red Brave-                            -                -unnamed hybrid-
               -America (as above)               LEMON CRISP-  -wardii 1/4    -unknown 1/8
Buds a blend of reds, ruby, cardinal, and Indian lake; flowers      -Crest-      -fortunei ssp. discolor 1/8
strong  purplish red edged with beetroot purple; a white flare;          -Lady Bessborough-
dorsal spots beetroot purple.  W. Delp.                          -campylocarpum Elatum Gp. 1/8
                                                Buds of salmon, pale yellowish pink, apricot  and pale greenish
                                                yellow open to frilled flowers primrose yellow; dorsal spotting
* * * * * * * * * * * * * * * * * * * * * * * *  moderate reddish brown; brilliant greenish yellow throat.  Delp.
-dichroanthum ssp. apodectum 1/2
LEDA-
  -griersonianum 1/2                                        -wardii 1/2
4ft(1.2m) 5F(-15C) ML       Medium-sized shrub; vermilion to      -Crest-           -fortunei ssp. discolor 1/8
orange-scarlet flowers.  Lord Aberconway, intro. 1933.       -   -Lady Bessborough-
CHIVALRY   Parentage as above                    -                      -campylocarpum Elatum Group 1/8
Orange salmon flowers, hose-in-hose, 3in(7.6cm) across; trusses   LEMON -               -George-griffithianum
of 8.  Gen. Harrison, reg. 1962.                 CUSTARD-       -Mrs. Lindsay-Hardy -    1/32
* * * * * * * * * * * * * * * * * * * * * * * *  -               - Smith    -    -catawbiense 1/32
                                                -    -Mrs. Betty-        -Duchess of Edinburgh--
            -sanguineum ssp. didymum 1/8         -    - Robertson-            unknown 1/8
       -Carmen-                                  -unnamed-       -unnamed-campylocarpum 1/16
  -unnamed-   -forrestii Repens Group 1/8        hybrid-        hybrid-
  - hybrid-        -haematodes 1/8               -wardii              -unknown
LEEANN-    -Choremia-                            5ft(1.5m) 10F(-12C) EM 4/4  Waxy flowers, buff yellow with no
  -            -arboreum 1/8                      markings, openly funnel-campanulate, 4in(10.2cm) across, slight-
  -        -griffithianum 1/4                     ly fragrant; lax trusses of 8-12.  Plant rounded, well-branched,
  -Gill's Crimson-                               wider than tall; dark green leaves.  Walt Elliott, reg. 1981.
            -unknown 1/4
3ft(.9m) 10F(-12C) E  Ruby red flowers, light blotch of maroon
spots, widely funnel-campanulate, 4.75in(12cm) across; lax truss            -campylocarpum 1/4
of 8.  Plant rounded, well-branched; dark green leaves held 3        -Moonstone-
years.  Carl G. Heller cross; Shirley Lent raiser; reg. 1979.  LEMON DROP-   -williamsianum 1/4
                                                          -unknown 1/2
                                                1ft(.3m) -5F(-21C) M  Compact plant, orbicular leaves.  Bril-
            -catawbiense 1/2                     liant light yellow-green flowers, 2.5in(6.4m) across.  Bovees,
LEE'S BEST PURPLE-                               reg. 1962.
            -unknown 1/2
```

```
                 -maximum 1/2
LEMON DROP-
                 -vernicosum (18139) 1/2
```
Buds of primrose yellow open to primrose yellow flowers; dorsal
spotting primrose yellow; a flare of primrose yellow. W. Delp.

```
                           -dichroanthum 1/8
                -Goldsworth-
         -Hotei- Orange -fortunei ssp. discolor 1/8
         -      -             -souliei 1/8
         -      -unnamed hybrid-
LEMON FLOAT-              -wardii 1/8
         -              -yakushimanum 1/8
         -      -White -
         -unnamed-Wedding-makinoi 1/8
          hybrid-
                 -lacteum 1/4
```
4ft(1.2m) OF(-18C) EM 4/4 Truss of 15-20 flowers, chartreuse
green. Plant low and compact with dark foliage. Sets buds when
very young. Easy to propagate. John G. Lofthouse, reg. 1979.

```
               -minus Carolinianum, yellow form 1/2
LEMON GIRL-
               -lutescens 1/2
```
3ft(.9m) -10F(-23C) EM   Terminal flower clusters, 1-3 trusses
each of 7-14 flowers, light mimosa yellow, dorsal spotting lemon
yellow, 1.25in(3.2cm) wide. Upright plant, nearly as broad as
high, with stiff branches. Louis B. Mraw, reg. 1983.

```
                    -brachycarpum 1/4
       -unnamed hybrid-    -wardii 1/8
       -        -Crest-        -fortunei ssp. discolor
LEMON-          -Lady -                  1/16
GLAZE-         Bessborough-campylocarpum Elatum Gp.
       -aureum (chrysanthum) 1/2              1/16
```
Buds of primrose yellow open to lighter primrose yellow flowers;
dorsal spotting brilliant greenish yellow. W. Delp.

```
             -wardii 1/2
LEMON GROVE-
             -unknown 1/2
```
Flowers held in trusses of 9; lobes pale greenish yellow, throat
light yellowish green, blotch brilliant greenish yellow. Shrub
medium to large. G. Reuthe, reg. 1985.

LEMON ICE   Parentage unknown
4ft(1.2m) -15F(-26C) ML 3/2 Dark slender foliage; low, open-
growing bush. White flowers with a yellowish gold blotch; much
like CHIONOIDES. Paul Bosley, Sr.

LEMON LIME   Parentage unknown
3ft(.9m) OF(-18C) M   Soft yellow blossoms on a rounded plant
with small leaves. Moderate sun tolerance. Unknown origin.

```
                       -wardii 1/2
LEMON LODGE---PRELUDE, selfed-
                       -fortunei 1/2
```
4ft(1.2m) -5F(21C) M   Huge, primrose yellow flowers, with a
few tiny spots deep in throat. Pukeiti Rhododendron Trust, NZ,
reg. 1972. Color illus. Cox pl. 107.

LEMON MARMALADE   Described under SPUN GOLD, q.v.

```
             -xanthostephanum 1/2
LEMON MIST-
             -leucaspis 1/2
```
3ft(.9m) 10F(-12C) EM 3/3 Compact bush, almost twice as wide
as tall, with narrow, medium green leaves. Bright greenish yellow flowers cover plant in early spring; corolla open funnel-
shaped, 1.5in(3.8cm) wide. R. W. Scott, reg. 1968. A.E. 1969.

LEMON PIE   Described under LILA PEDIGO, q.v.

```
                  -dichroanthum 1/8
            -Fabia-
       -Jan -     -griersonianum 1/8
       -Steen-          -fortunei ssp. discolor 1/4
LEMON -     -Lady Bessborough-
SORBET-                -campylocarpum Elatum Group 1/4
       -     -wardii 1/4
       -Crest-
            -Lady Bessborough (as above)
```

Funnel-shaped flowers in trusses of 11, 7-lobed, of pale greenish yellow, 4in(10cm) wide; April flowering. Bush to 5ft(1.5m);
smooth elliptic leaves. J. May, reg. 1987; Knoll Gardens intro.

LEMONADE   Described under HIGH GOLD, q.v.

LEM'S AURORA (catawbiense x FABIA x TALLY HO)
4ft(1.2m) -OF(-18C) M   The above parentage is uncertain. Low
and compact plant with a rainbow of colors, blending yellow, red,
and pink. Halfdan Lem cross.

* *
```
                 -dichroanthum 1/4
            -Dido-
       -     -decorum 1/4
       -                           -griffithianum 5/16
LEM'S CAMEO-       -Beauty of Tremough-
       -    -Norman-            -arboreum 1/16
       -    - Gill -
       -Anna-     -griffithianum
       -                    -griffithianum
            -Jean Marie de Montague-
                        -unknown 1/8
```
5ft(1.5m) 5F(-15C) M 5/3 An exceptional hybrid, with glowing
flowers of apricot, cream, and pink with a small scarlet dorsal
blotch; corolla widely funnel-campanulate, 3.5in(9cm) wide, 6-7
wavy lobes; large dome-shaped trusses of about 20. Floriferous.
Foliage deep shiny green in summer, bright bronzy red when new;
elliptic leaves 5in(12.7cm) long. Hard to propagate. H. Lem,
intro. 1962; reg. 1975. S.P.A. 1971. A.M. 1987. Color ill.
ARS Q 25:4 (1971), p. 230; ARS Q 29:1 (1975), cover; HG p. 168.
LEM'S 121 Parentage possibly as above; may include TALLEY HO
        and LEM'S GOAL
Similar to above, with flowers frilled, apricot and creamy pink
color combinations. New foliage bronze. Halfdan Lem.
* *

```
                                   -griffithianum
                        -Queen-            5/16
                  -Britannia- Wilhelmina -unknown
            -C. P.  -         -Stanley Davies--unknown 3/16
LEM'S-       - Raffill-
FLUORESCENT PINK-    -griersonianum 1/4
       -                   -griffithianum
            -Loderi King George-
                        -fortunei 1/4
```
Glowing pastel pink; hardy to 5F(-15C). Halfdan Lem.

```
                  -fortunei ssp. discolor 1/2
            -Ole Olson-
LEM'S GOAL-       -campylocarpum Elatum Group 1/4
       -    -griersonianum 1/4
       -Azor-
            -fortunei ssp. discolor
```
5ft(1.5m) OF(-18C) ML 3/3 Dull, light green, pointed foliage
on a plant of upright habit, not too open. Flowers soft creamy
apricot, shading darker in throat; trusses of 6-7. Halfdan Lem,
reg. 1958. P.A. 1952.

LEM'S LEGACY   Parentage unknown
6ft(1.8m) x 5ft(1.5m)(20 yrs) 5F(-15C) M   Pale orange-yellow
flowers with vivid reddish orange throat in trusses of 19-20, 7-
lobed; buds apricot-colored. Trusses 7.5in(19cm) wide by 6.3in.
(15.7cm) high.   Lem cross; Lynn Watts, reg. 1989. Best Truss
Award, Seattle Ch. 1988.

LEM'S MONARCH   Described under WALLOPER, q.v.

LEM'S ONE-TWENTY-ONE   Described under LEM'S CAMEO, q.v.

```
                      -fortunei ssp. discolor 1/4
            -King of Shrubs-   -dichroanthum 1/8
       -            -Fabia-
LEM'S SALMON-            -griersonianum 3/8
       -              -griffithianum 1/16
       -    -unnamed-Loderi-
       -Flame- hybrid-    -fortunei 1/16
       -          -Corona--unknown 1/8
            -griersonianum
```
An unregistered hybrid by Halfdan Lem.

```
                               -griffithianum
                   -Queen Wilhelmina-          5/16
         -Britannia-              -unknown 9/16
    -Burgundy-        -Stanley Davies--unknown
LEM'S  -         -             -ponticum 1/8
STORMCLOUD-    -Purple Splendour-
   -     -griffithianum    -unknown
   -Mars-
       -unknown
5ft(1.5m) -15F(-26C) ML  4/3  Large flowers of glossy red, pal-
ing at center, with a light dorsal blotch; a flattened corolla.
H. Lem cross; Britt M. Smith, reg. 1980.  Color illus. HG p. 88.
```

```
                   -fortunei ssp. discolor 3/8
         -Margaret Dunn-      -dichroanthum 3/16
         -          -Fabia-
         -              -griersonianum 3/16
LEM'S    -                      -griffithianum 5/32
TANGERINE-              -Beauty of-
         -        -Norman- Tremough-arboreum 1/32
         -  -Anna- Gill -
         -  -     -    -griffithianum
 -unnamed-    -          -griffithianum
   hybrid-  -Jean Marie de Montague-
         -            -unknown 1/16
         -          -fortunei ssp. discolor
         -King of Shrubs-      -dichroanthum
                -Fabia-
                   -griersonianum
5ft(1.5m) x 4.5ft(1.35m)(19 yrs) -5F(-21C)  M  4/3  An orange
truss, ball-shaped.  Lem cross; L. Newcomb, reg. 1987.
```

LEN BEER--form of glaucophyllum B L & M 315
3ft(.9m) OF(-18C) EM 3/2 Trusses hold 4-8 white flowers.
Beer collector; named by Kathleen Dryden in memory of L. Beer of
the Beer, Lancaster & Morris Expedition, Nepal, 1971; reg. 1978.

LENAPE Described under BRANDYWINE, q.v.

```
             -edgeworthii (bullatum) 1/4
    -White Wings-
LENCRET-         -ciliicalyx 1/4
    -ciliatum 1/2
Cream-colored flowers, fading to white.   Adams-Acton, 1942.
```

```
                   -griffithianum 1/8
         -Queen Wilhelmina-
    -Britannia-          -unknown 3/8
LEO-      -Stanley Davies--unknown
    -elliottii 1/2
5ft(1.5m) -5F(-21C) ML  5/3  Heavy, flaming red flowers set in
tight trusses of up to 25.  Blooms later than most reds.  Good
habit, with very dark green foliage.   Rothschild.   A.M. 1948.
F.C.C. 1989.   Color illus. PB pl. 28; VV p. 87.
```

```
             -Corona--unknown 1/4
    -Bow Bells-
LEO FRIEDMAN-      -williamsianum 1/4
    -strigillosum 1/2
Small, very compact plant;  small, very smooth leaves.   Flowers
of rose madder, campanulate, 1.25in(3.2cm) wide.   Early.   Cecil
S. Seabrook, reg. 1969.
```

LEONA Described under CATHY, q.v.

```
             -caucasicum 1/4
    -Boule de Neige-          -catawbiense 1/8
    -          -unnamed hybrid-
LEONA HOLMES-          -unknown 1/8
    -          -fortunei 1/4
    -unnamed hybrid-
             -vernicosum R 18139  1/4
2ft(.6m) x 3.5ft(1.05m)(18 yrs) -10F(-23C) ML      Strong pink
buds.  Flowers 7-lobed, 2.5in(6cm) wide, medium yellowish pink,
centers paler, fading to light orange; a yellow flare with 2 red
rays; truss of 10-12.  W. Fetterhoff, reg. 1986.
```

LEONA MAUD Described under SHIRLEY, q.v.

```
    -brachyanthum 1/2
LEONARD MESSEL-
    -unknown 1/2
```

Flowers held in loose trusses of 4-5, primrose yellow, lightly
flecked greenish brown, campanulate, about 1in(2.5cm) across, 5-
lobed. Elliptic leaves 2in(5cm) long, slightly fragrant, light
scaly indumentum beneath.   Kingdon Ward collector; Leonard Messel raiser; Countess of Rosse, Nymans; reg. 1966.   A.M. 1966.

```
             -griersonianum 3/4
    -Tally Ho-
LEONARDO-      -facetum (eriogynum) 1/4
    -griersonianum
Vermilion flowers.  Adams-Acton, 1937.
```

LEONARDSLEE BRILLIANT   Described under GEM, q.v.

LEONARDSLEE FLAME   Listed under RED STAR, q.v.

```
                   -ciliatum 1/4
         -unnamed hybrid-
LEONARDSLEE GEM OF THE WOODS-      -unknown 1/4
                   -virgatum 1/2
White flowers.   At Leonardslee, 1912.   A.M. 1925.
```

LEONARDSLEE GERTRUDE   Described under WHITE LADY, q.v.

```
             -maximum 1/4
    -Standishii-          -unnamed-catawbiense
    -          - hybrid-          1/16
LEONARDSLEE GILES-      -Altaclerense-      -ponticum
    -          -              1/16
    -              -arboreum 1/8
    -griffithianum 1/2
6ft(1.8m) OF(-18C)  M  4/3  Cameo pink buds opening pale pink,
fading white; campanulate flowers,  very large truss.  Vigorous,
sturdy,  large leaves; needs partial shade.  Sir E. Loder.  A.M.
1948.
```

LEONARDSLEE LEMON   See LEONARDSLEE YELLOW

LEONARDSLEE PEACH   Described under EXMINISTER, q.v.

LEONARDSLEE PRIMROSE   Described under EARL OF MORLEY, q.v.

```
             -lindleyi 1/2
LEONARDSLEE YELLOW-
             -nuttallii (sinonuttallii) 1/2
A plant for the  cool greenhouse.  Flowers soft Naples yellow in
the throat,  paling to creamy white margins, tubular funnel-cam-
panulate, 5 joined lobes 3.8in(9.5cm) across, in trusses of 3-4.
Narrowly elliptic leaves, 7in(17.8cm) long, both surfaces scaly.
G. R. Loder cross; Sir G. Loder, reg. 1964.  A.M. 1964.  F.C.C.
1980.
```

LEONARRAN Parentage unknown
A flowering plant for the cool greenhouse, with loose trusses
holding 2-3 flowers, tubular-shaped, 3in(7.5cm) long, white with
reverse flushed rose. Sir Giles Loder; reg. 1979. A.M. 1979.

LEONIE PINK   Parentage unknown
Funnel-shaped flowers, 14-18 per truss, strong purplish pink,
striped deep purplish pink with strong yellow-green blotch on
dorsal lobe.   J. Faull, reg. 1986.

* *
```
    -auriculatum 1/2
LEONORE-
    -kyawii 1/2
```
5ft(1.5m) 5F(-15C) VL Very large plant. Tall loose truss of
12 with huge, raspberry red flowers. Narrow, hairy, rich green
leaves in big rosettes. Rothschild, 1947. A.M. 1948.
RICHARD GREGORY   Parentage as above
Tubular bell-shaped flowers in loose truss of 10, pink inside,
crimson blotch, slightly fragrant. Foliage 8in(15.2cm) x 2.5cm.
(6.4cm). R. M. Gregory cross; A. M. Williams, reg. 1969.
ROYSTON FESTIVAL   Parentage as above
Trusses of 15 flowers, light Neyron rose with Delft rose center.
E. J. & Mary Greig cross; A. R. Cook, reg. 1981.
* *

```
             -mucronulatum 1/4
    -unnamed hybrid-
LEON'S RHEBA-          -racemosum 1/4
    -minus Carolinianum Group 1/2
```

5ft(1.5m) x 4ft(1.2m) -10F(23C) EM   Trusses of 6-10 flowers,
funnel-shaped, light reddish purple, shading to moderate purplish pink in center, some vivid reddish purple dorsal spotting;
center fades almost white. Scaly foliage. Yavorsky, reg. 1987.

```
            -arboreum ssp. cinnamomeum var. album 1/2
LEOPARDI-
        -unknown 1/2
```
White flowers, with a slight red tint and large red spots.   T.
Methven & Son, 1868. One of a surprising number of early British
hybrids available in the United States before 1875.

```
        -Mira--unknown 1/2
LEOPOLD-
       -catawbiense 1/2
```
(MIRA by Stevenson too recent to be used by Seidel.) Flowers of
dark purple violet marked yellow-brown.   T. J. R. Seidel, 1909.

```
                -lepidotum 1/2
LEPIDOBOOTHII-
              -boothii 1/2
```
Yellowish white flowers tinged pink and green.   E. J. P. Magor.
A.M. 1919.

```
                    -fortunei 1/4
        -Duke of York-   -catawbiense 1/8
LERIGAU-        -Scipio-
        -           -unknown 1/8
        -williamsianum 1/2
```
Large flowers, delicate rose; bronze new growth.   Hobbie, 1952.

```
                        -maximum 1/2
LESLIE K. BLOUGH---unnamed hybrid, selfed-
                            -catawbiense 1/2
```
Flowers of sparkling white. Compact, low plant. Hardy to -25F
(-32C). R. L. Blough.

```
                            -catawbiense 3/16
                -unnamed hybrid-
    -unnamed hybrid-            -haematodes 3/16
    -        -        -griffithianum 3/16
    -            -Mars-
    -               -unknown 3/16
LETTIE-                 -catawbiense
        -       -Pink Twins-
    -     -Sunset-      -haematodes
    -    - Yates-                -griffithianum
    -Ralph-     -Leah Yates--Mars, selfed-
     Pape-                    -unknown
    -           -catawbiense v. album Glass--Catalgla 1/8
        -Pink Punch-
            -fortunei 1/8
```
4ft(1.2m) x 4ft -15F(-26C) M   Flowers held in truss of 10-13;
buds of strong purplish red, opening to same color at rims, then
shading to white in the throat. Maletta Yates, reg. 1986.

```
        -campylocarpum Elatum Group 1/2
LETTY EDWARDS-
        -fortunei 1/2
```
5ft(1.5m) OF(-18C) M 3/3   Rounded, rather compact; medium
green leaves 5in(12.7cm) long. Pale pink buds open to primrose
yellow, to cream. A.M. form has clear yellow flowers and a red
throat.   Rounded trusses of 9-11. See also GLADYS. Col. S.
R. Clarke.   A.M. 1946. F.C.C. Wisley Trials 1948.

LEVERETT RICHARDS   Described under VIRGINIA RICHARDS, q.v.

LHASA--form of nuttallii (sinonuttallii) L S & E 12117
Plant for the cool greenhouse with white flowers flushed yellow.
Crown Estate Commissioners, reg. 1971.   P.C. 1971.

```
                -fortunei 1/4
        -Faggetter's Favourite-
LIBELLE-            -unknown 1/4
        -williamsianum 1/2
```
Bright rose-colored flowers.   Dietrich Hobbie, 1952.

```
            -sperabile 1/4
        -Eupheno-
LIBERTY-    -griersonianum 1/4
        -barbatum 1/2
```
red flowers.   Lord Aberconway, 1950.

LIESBETH   Parentage unknown

Flowers of solferino purple.   H. T. Hooftman, reg. 1965.

```
                -griersonianum 1/4
        -Lancer-
LIFEGUARD-      -hookeri 1/4
        -arboreum 1/2
```
A hybrid with red trusses.   Lord Aberconway, intro. 1950.

```
                    -catawbiense var. album Glass--Catalgla
        -unnamed hybrid-                              1/4
LIGHT AND-          -wardii 1/4
  LIVELY -              -maximum 1/4
        -Stokes Bronze Wings-
                    -catawbiense 1/4
```
Frilled ivory flowers with chartreuse spotting; white filaments.
W. Delp.

LIGHTLY LAVENDER   Described under CAROLINE ALLBROOK, q.v.

```
            -yakushimanum 1/2
LIKE FLUFF-         -souliei 1/8
        -       -Soulbut-
        -Vanessa-        -fortunei--Sir Chas. Butler 1/8
            -griersonianum 1/4
```
3ft(.9m) -5F(-21C) M 3/4   Nearly perfect habit. Flowers of
light pink, fading to almost white.   Bovee.

* *

```
                    -wardii 3/8         -griffithianum
                        -Kewense-      3/64
            -Idealist-   -Aurora-    -fortunei 5/64
            -       -Naomi-     -thomsonii 1/32
            -           -fortunei
        -Odee-                      -griffithianum
        -Wright-               -George-
        -       -       -Mrs. Lindsay- Hardy-catawbiense
        -   -Mrs. Betty- Smith     -           1/32
        -     Robertson -        -Duchess of
LILA PEDIGO-            -           Edinburgh--unknown
        -               -campylocarpum 3/16
        -               -unnamed-
        -   -wardii     hybrid-unknown 1/8
        -Crest-         -fortunei ssp. discolor 1/8
        -Lady Bessborough-
                    -campylocarpum Elatum Group
```
4ft(1.2m) 5F(-15C) 4/4   Chartreuse yellow flowers with light
red spotting, ruffled edges. Very free-flowering. L. Pedigo.
LEMON PIE Parentage as above, except reversed
Bright yellow flowers with some darker shading. Slow-growing
plant; glossy, dark green foliage.   George Clarke cross.
* *

LILAC HAZE   Described under BLUE LADY, q.v.

LILAC TIME   For parentage see LAVENDER TIME.

```
        -griffithianum 1/2
LILIAN-
    -Mangles hybrid--unknown 1/2
```
Red flowers fading to blush.   W. C. Slocock.

```
            -racemosum 1/2
LILIAN HARVEY-
        -Hatsugiri--Kurume azalea 1/2
```
Azaleodendron. Truss of 18 flowers, very pale lavender, lightly
flushed pinkish mauve at midribs and into throat; a speckling of
soft magenta; corolla 1.2in(3cm) wide, openly funnel-shaped with
wavy margins. Plant upright, broader than tall; small glossy
leaves. P. W. Hartijzer, reg. 1966. A.M. Wisley Trials 1983.

```
            -arboreum, red form 1/2
LILIANAE-       -thomsonii 1/4
        -Shilsonii-
            -barbatum 1/4
```
Blood red flowers shaded carmine.   Origin unknown. A.M. 1914.

```
            -grande 1/2
LILLIAN DEANS-
        -protistum var. giganteum 1/2
```
Tight trusses 10in(25.4cm) wide; rose pink buds opening to pale
cream, darker in throat. When registered plant was 9ft(2.7m)
high by 15ft(4.5m) wide; foliage 12(30.4cm) x 2in(10cm).   James

Deans raiser; R. G. Deans, reg. 1969.

```
                           -griffithianum 5/16
          -Solent Queen-
          -                -fortunei ssp. discolor 1/4
LILLIAN-                      -griffithianum
HODGSON-             -Mars-
          -       -Vulcan-   -unknown 1/16
          -       -       -griersonianum 1/4
          -Old Copper-   -dichroanthum 1/8
              -Fabia-
                  -griersonianum
```
Shell pink rims; center light orange-yellow. Rhodes, reg. 1979.

```
                           -griffithianum 1/8
                -unnamed hybrid-
          -Mrs. Furnivall-          -unknown 1/4
          -                      -caucasicum 1/8
LILLIAN MAUNEY-       -unnamed hybrid-
          -                      -unknown
              -vernicosum (Rock 18139-1) 1/2
```
5ft(1.5m) x 9ft(2.7m)(21 yrs) -10F(-23C) EM   Ball truss of 11
-13 flowers; buds vivid purplish red to deep purplish pink open
medium purplish pink, fading pale pink; striking reddish spotted
dorsal flare. R. Emmerich cross; Dr. D. Kellam, Jr., reg. 1989.

```
          -yakushimanum--Koichiro Wada 1/2
LILLIAN PESTE-
          -unnamed W. E. Whitney hybrid--unknown 1/2
```
2ft(.6m) OF(-18C) M 4/4   Dense habit. Buds dark rose pink,
opening coral pink at rims, shading to carrot red in the throat;
reverse shaded pink. Trusses of 25-30. Fred Peste, reg. 1981.

```
             -auriculatum 1/4
   -unnamed hybrid-   -griffithianum 1/4
   -          -Alice-
LILY-             -unknown 1/4
   -                      -Corona--unknown
   -              -unnamed hybrid-
   -Mrs. Donald Graham-      -griersonianum 1/8
   -              -   -griffithianum
              -Loderi-
                  -fortunei 1/8
```
A white-flowered hybrid, by Endre Ostbo.   P.A. 1952.   (Two
Ostbo hybrids originally "LILIES", received a P.A. from the ARS:
LILY (unregistered) as WHITE LILY, 1952, and LILY 3 (registered
as EDNA MCCARTY); parentage of the latter: ALICE x auriculatum)

LILY (Van de Ven)   LODERI KING GEORGE x CUP DAY or MIDNIGHT x
                    CORONATION DAY
6ft(1.8m) OF(-18C) ML   Large flowers, light purple fading to
white, pink margins, huge flare of pink spots. Leggy habit, but
a striking plant. Van de Ven, Australia.

LILY DACHE   Described under AZOR, q.v.

```
          -fortunei ssp. discolor 1/2
LILY MAID-
          -unknown 1/2
```
7ft(2.1m) 5F(-15C) L Tubular funnel-shaped flowers, fragrant,
pale pink, 3.5in(8.9cm) across, 7 frilled lobes; tall truss of
16. Leaves held 3 years. B. Nelson cross; Putney, reg. 1975.

```
                           -griffithianum 1/8
                -Queen Wilhelmina-
          -Britannia-          -unknown 3/16
          -       -Stanley Davies--unknown
       -Ermine-      -fortunei--Sir Charles Butler 1/4
       -   -Mrs. A. T.-
       -   -de la Mare-      -maximum 1/16
       -          -Halopeanum-
LILY WHITE-              -griffithianum
       -              -dichroanthum 1/8
       -       -Fabia-
       -   -Umpqua-   -griersonianum 3/16
       -   - Chief-   -griersonianum
       -unnamed-   -Azor-
         hybrid-      -fortunei ssp. discolor 1/16
       -   -fortunei
       -Fawn-   -dichroanthum
          -Fabia-
              -griersonianum
```

A medium-sized plant with flowers opening rhodonite red, slowly
fading to white.   Weldon E. Delp.

```
          -arboreum 1/2
LIMBATUM
          -unknown 1/2
```
A parent of QUAPP, a hybrid by Seidel. Flowers white, or pale
blush, edges crimson.   Standish & Noble, before 1870.

* *
```
          -catawbiense var. album 1/2
LIMELIGHT-
          -fortunei 1/4
          -unnamed hybrid-
                  -wardii 1/4
```
4ft(1.2m) -25F(-32C) ML   Pale yellow flowers with strong yel-
lowish green blotch, saucer-shaped and open like wardii, 3.5in
(8.9cm) wide; 7-lobed; 12-15 in full ball-shaped truss. Leaves
5in(12.7cm) x 2.5in(6.4cm). Bloomed after -32F(-36C). David G.
Leach, reg. 1963.
IVORY TOWER   Parentage as above
5ft(1.5m) -25F(-32C) EM 4/3   Ivory flowers, dorsal blushing
with greenish yellow stripes, 5-7 lobes; globular trusses of 13.
Plant broad as tall, leaves to 4.5in(11.5cm). Leach, reg. 1964.
* *
* *
```
                           -griffithianum 1/8
                -Queen Wilhelmina-
          -Britannia-          -unknown 3/8
LIMERICK-       -Stanley Davies--unknown
          -dichroanthum 1/8
```
A grex by the Earl of Limerick, 1948.
MARGELA   Parentage as above
Flowers of orange-brown, shading to a wide band of geranium lake
at the margins. Earl of Limerick.   A.M. 1948.
PICCANINNY   Parentage as above
Flowers orange, tinged cherry. Earl of Limerick.   A.M. 1956.
* *

LINDA   Described under BRITANNIA'S BELLS, q.v.

LINDA MARIE---from irroratum, open pollinated
8ft(2.4m) x 7ft(2.1m) 5F(-15C) EM   Flowers in trusses of 15-
18, campanulate, rosy buds opening light purplish pink; blotched
and heavily spotted maroon. Dense habit. Vaartnou, reg. 1989.

LINDBERG   Described under JALISCO, q.v.

```
          -lindleyi 1/2
LINDBULL-
          -edgeworthii (bullatum) 1/2
```
Fragrant white flowers, yellow at base. E. J. P. Magor, 1926.

```
          -lindleyi 1/2
LIND-DAL-
          -dalhousiae 1/2
```
White flowers, tinged yellow. Lord Aberconway, cross 1927.

LINDY ELLEN   Parentage unknown
Funnel-shaped flowers in trusses of 20-25, strong reddish purple
with black flare on the dorsal lobe. Bush 8ft(2.4m) x 8ft. D.
J. Dosser cross; V. Williams, reg. 1987.

* *
```
                           -griffithianum 1/8
                  -George Hardy-
          -Mrs. Lindsay Smith-      -catawbiense 1/8
          -              -Duchess of Edinburgh--unknown 1/4
LINGOS-              -fortunei ssp. discolor 1/8
          -       -Lady Bessborough-
       -Jalisco-              -campylocarpum Elatum Group 1/8
       Goshawk-   -dichroanthum 1/8
              -Dido-
                  -decorum 1/8
```
Cream-colored, shading to sulphur yellow. C. Ingram, reg. 1972.
SEA SPRAY   Parentage as above
White, a distinctive reddish brown flare. C. Ingram, reg. 1973.
* *

```
             -griffithianum 1/4
          -Loderi-
LINLEY-      -fortunei 1/4
          -unknown 1/2
```

Soft pink flowers blotched carmine at base. Messel. A.M. 1927.

```
                          -griffithianum 1/4
                 -Loderi-
LINLEY SAMBOURNE-         -fortunei 1/4
                 -unknown 1/2
```
Rich pink, blotched carmine at base.   Messel.   A.M. 1928.

```
                              -griffithianum 1/8
                 -Queen Wilhelmina-
         -Britannia-                -unknown 3/8
LINSWEGEANUM-    -Stanley Davies--unknown
         -forrestii Repens Group 1/2
```
Flowers deep scarlet red.   Dietrich Hobbie, 1946.

```
                  -wardii 1/4
         -Hawk-                -fortunei ssp. discolor 1/8
LIONEL   -    -Lady Bessborough-
FORTESCUE-                -campylocarpum Elatum Group
         -wardii--Elestee 1/2                1/8
```
Flowers medium yellow shading lighter to edges, with dark blotch
of ruby red. L. S. Fortescue, reg. 1977.

```
            -lacteum 1/2
LIONEL'S FIRST-
            -sutchuenense 1/2
```
Pale purplish pink flowers, with light purplish pink spotting,
darkening to strong purplish pink on exterior. Tall plant. L.
de Rothschild, cross c. 1920; E. de Rothschild, reg. 1985.

```
                              -catawbiense 1/8
                 -Parsons Grandiflorum-
         -America-                -unknown 3/8
LIONEL'S RED SHIELD-      -dark red hybrid--unknown
         -                -sanguineum ssp. didymum 1/4
         -Carmen-
                 -forrestii Repens Group 1/4
```
1ft(.3m) x 2.5ft(.75m)(8 yrs, cutting) -15F(-26C)   ML Currant
red flowers, 2in(5cm) wide; lax truss of 2-6. Buds almost black
red. Leaves to 2.5in(5.5cm) long, dull green. Spreading plant,
floriferous. Named by de Rothschild. J. Brueckner, reg. 1988.

```
* * * * * * * * * * * * * * * * * * * * * * * * * * * * *
            -lacteum 1/2          -griffithianum 1/16
LIONEL'S TRIUMPH-         -Kewense-
         -    -Aurora-      -fortunei 5/16
            -Naomi-    -thomsonii 1/8
                 -fortunei
```
6ft(1.8m) -5F(-21C) M 5/4   Rose pink in bud, opening to rich
Cornish cream flowers, opaline pink margins fading later; up to
18 large flowers in magnificent trusses. Considered by Exbury
to be of highest quality. Rothschild. A.M. 1954. F.C.C. 1974.
Color illus. ARS J 27:4 (1973), p. 238.
HALTON   Parentage as above
Round trusses 6in(15cm) across, holding 14 flowers of very light
sap green. Leaves 6in(15cm) x 2.75in(7cm); no indumentum.   L.
de Rothschild, reg. 1968. A.M. 1967.
```
* * * * * * * * * * * * * * * * * * * * * * * * * * * * *

LIPSTICK    Described under GOLD BRAID, q.v.

LIQUID GOLD   Described under DUSTY WHIZ, q.v.

```
   -catawbiense var. album Glass--Catalgla 1/2
   -                -decorum 1/8
LISA-   -unnamed hybrid-
   -      -   -griersonianum 1/8
   -Madonna-   -catawbiense 1/16
   -      -Parsons Grandiflorum-
      -America-   -unknown 3/16
                 -dark red hybrid--unknown
```
6ft(1.8m) -15F(-26C)  ML  3/3   White flowers, a pale sap green
blotch, 4in(10cm) across; trusses hold 18.  Elliptic leaves 8in.
(20.3cm) x 4in (10cm).  Gable, reg. 1964.  P.A. 1962.

```
                  -catawbiense 1/8
                 -Parsons Grandiflorum-
      -Nova Zembla-   -unknown 3/8
LISSABON-   -hardy red hybrid--unknown
      -williamsianum 1/2
```
3ft(.9m) -10F(-23C)  M   Flowers of deep rhodonite red, margins
cardinal red, 2.7in(7cm) broad; lax trusses of 8.  Compact bush.

V. von Martin; Bruns, reg. 1972.  Color illus. WS, 1989, p. 172.

LISSOME   Described under VALLEY CREEK, q.v.

LITTLE AMY   Described under BOBBET, q.v.

```
         -augustinii 1/2
LITTLE AUGIE-
         -unknown 1/2
```
3ft(.9m) 5F(-15C) EM  3/3   A plant of compact habit, bearing
bright blue flowers.  Barber.

* * * * * * * * * * * * * * * * * * * * * * * * * * * *
```
         -neriiflorum 1/2
LITTLE BEN-
         -forrestii Repens Group 1/2
```
2ft(.6m) 10F(-12C) EM  3/3   Low-growing, dense plant; small,
stiff, dark green leaves.  Deep scarlet, waxy, bell-shaped flow-
ers in clusters.   C. R. Scrase-Dickins.  F.C.C. 1937.
LITTLE BERT   Parentage as above, except reversed
2ft(.6m) 10F(-12C) EM  3/3   Elliptic ovate leaves, up to 3in.
(7.6cm) long, both ends rounded.  Flowers campanulate of spread-
ing lobes, scarlet crimson, hanging in clusters of 4-5; trusses
loose.  Scrase-Dickins.  A.M. 1939.  Color illus. VV p. 15.
* * * * * * * * * * * * * * * * * * * * * * * * * * * *

```
         - williamsianum 1/2
LITTLE BILL-   -griffithianum 3/8
         -      -Coombe Royal ?-
         -Lady Stuart-   -unknown (1/8)
         of Wortley -griffithianum
```
3ft(.9m) 5F(-15C) EM  2/3   Plant dome-shaped, medium compact;
narrow leaves  with reddish petioles. Trumpet-shaped flowers of
deep rose pink, held in a lax truss.   Robert Wallace, 1934.

LITTLE BIRDIE  Described under WERRINGTON, q.v.

LITTLE BOBBIE   Described under WERRINGTON, q.v.

```
                  -minus Carolinianum Gp., pink
LITTLE CREATURE---BOB DANIK F2-   -minus Carolinianum Gp.
                 -P.J.M.-   3/4
                  -dauricum 1/4
```
Buds of pale orange yellow, open to pale purplish pink and white
flowers; dorsal spotting ruby red.   W. Delp.

```
         -dichroanthum 1/4
      -Fabia-
LITTLE DRAGON- -griersonianum 1/4
      -venator 1/2
```
3ft(.9m) 5F(-15C)  M  3/3   Attractive foliage of red stemmed
leaves; fiery red flowers.  Benjamin F. Lancaster, reg. 1958.

```
         -forrestii Repens Group 1/2
LITTLE ERNIE-   -haematodes 1/4
      -May Day-
         -griersonianum 1/4
```
An upright dwarf plant with flowers of Turkey red, in trusses of
8-10.  Early.   Ernest V. Allen, reg. 1962.

```
            -sanguineum ssp. didymum 1/4
         -Carmen-
LITTLE GEM-   -forrestii Repens Group 1/4
         -elliottii K W 7725 1/2
```
2ft(.6m) 0F(-18C)  M  4/4   Flowers of dark currant red, widely
funnel-campanulate, 2in(5cm) wide, of heavy substance; lax truss
of 7-8.  Plant wider than tall, well-branched; glossy dark green
leaves, light grayish brown indumentum, held 3 years.  Whitney
cross; Sathers, reg. 1976.  P.A. 1962.   Color illus. VV p. 84.

```
         -forrestii Repens Group 1/2
LITTLE GLENDOE-
         -arboreum ssp. delavayi var. delavayi 1/2
```
2.5ft(.75m) 10F(-12C)  VE   Cardinal red flowers, campanulate,
2.5in(6.4cm) across, in trusses of 7-9. Rounded, compact plant
28in(.7m) in 14 years, broader than tall; foliage to 3in(7.6cm)
long.  L. E. Jury raiser; Ms. E. G. Johnstone, NZ, reg. 1968.

```
         -impeditum 1/2
LITTLE IMP-
         -unknown 1/2
```
3ft(.9m) 0F(-18C)  EM  3/3   More vigorous than the species  im-
```

peditum. Plant covered with bluish purple flowers. Leaves with a silvery blue cast, like some forms of this species.   Barber.

LITTLE JANET   Described under WERRINGTON, q.v.

```
            -hodgsonii 1/2
LITTLE JESSICA-
            -unknown 1/2
```
Flowers in dense, domed trusses of 29, 8-lobed, buds strong purplish red shading toward deep purplish pink, blackish red-purple blotch; opening white and unspotted. Oblanceolate leaves to 10.3in(26cm); dense tan indumentum. High Beeches, reg. 1989.

```
            -forrestii Repens Group 1/2
LITTLE JOE-        -haematodes 1/4
            -May Day-
                    -griersonianum 1/4
```
1ft(.3m) 5F(-15C) EM 3/3   Plant compact, broader than tall; elliptic dark green leaves 1.5in(3.8cm) long. Flowers bright currant red, waxy, in lax trusses of 3-4. Requires some shade; propagates easily. Lester Brandt, intro. 1951.

```
                    -ciliatum 1/8
            -unnamed hybrid-
        -Lucy Lou-            -leucaspis 3/8
LITTLE LOU-        -leucaspis
        -valentinianum 1/2
```
1ft(.3m) 5F(-15C) E   Very low and spreading, 8in(20.3cm) high and 12in(30cm) broad at 6 years; narrow leaves to 1.75in(4.5cm) long. Yellow buds opening greenish yellow, tinged apricot; flowers 1.75in(4.5cm) wide. Maurice Sumner, reg. 1964. P.A. 1963.

LITTLE MINX   Described under HERA. q.v.

LITTLE MISS MUFFET   Parentage unknown
2.5ft(.75m) x 5ft(1.5m)(22 yrs) -5F(-21C) M   Flowers of heavy substance in ball truss of 11-12; buds strong red, opening deep pink, aging yellowish pink. Leaves leathery, elliptic, 3in(7.6 cm), felt-like hairs below. Whitney cross; Watters, reg. 1989.

LITTLE NEMO   Described under FRED ROBBINS, q.v.

LITTLE PADDOCKS   Listed under EXMINISTER, q.v.

LITTLE PATTY   Described under WERRINGTON, q.v.

```
* * * * * * * * * * * * * * * * * * * * * * * * * * *
                        -griffithianum 1/16
                -Queen Wilhelmina-
            -Earl of-            -unknown 3/16
        -unnamed-Athlone-Stanley Davies--unknown
        - hybrid-      -dichroanthum 1/8
LITTLE PEEP-      -Fabia-
        -              -griersonianum 1/8
            -forrestii Repens Group 1/2
```
Blood red flowers on a prostrate dwarf.   R. Henny, reg. 1958.
LITTLE SHEBA   Parentage as above
1ft(.3m) 5F(-15C) M 3/4   Low-growing, prostrate plant; dark green leaves. Blood red flowers 2in(5cm) wide, in terminal umbels. Wind-tolerant. R. Henny, reg. 1958. P.A. 1954
```
* * * * * * * * * * * * * * * * * * * * * * * * *
```

```
        -lochiae 1/2 (vireya)
LITTLE PIONEER-
        -virgatum 1/2 (lepidote)
```
An unusual cross. Flowers in trusses of 2-3, funnel-shaped, pendulous, 5-lobed, Persian rose, deeper on tube. Terminal and axillary trusses produced. Small brown scales on young leaves. leaves. Spreading habit. O. S. Blumhardt, reg. 1984.

```
* * * * * * * * * * * * * * * * * * * * * * * * *
        -decorum 1/2
LITTLE PUDDING-  -dichroanthum 1/4
        -Fabia-
                -griersonianum 1/4
```
5ft(1.5m) 5F(-15C) ML 3/3   Slow-growing; rather asymmetrical in habit; dark green, elliptic leaves, thin indumentum beneath. Camellia rose flowers shading to coral, campanulate, 4in(10.2cm) across, 5-7 lobes; 10-13 in loose terminal umbels. R. Henny, 1958. P.A. 1953.
LEMON BELLS   Parentage as above
2.5ft(.75m) 5F(-15C) M Large flowers of pinkish yellow, bell-

shaped, 5-6 per lax truss. Leaves 6in(15cm). Henny, reg. 1958.
NEAPOLITAN   Parentage as above
Flower salmon pink outside with orangey pink base. Sunningdale.
```
* * * * * * * * * * * * * * * * * * * * * * * * * * * * *
```

LITTLE SHEBA   Described under LITTLE PEEP, q.v.

LITTLE TROOPER   Described under BEACON, q.v.

LITTLE WHITE DOVE   Described under NESTUCCA. q.v.

LITTLEWORTH FLUSH   Parentage unknown
Flowers of rose Bengal. Mangles cross; Lady Adam Gordon, reg. 1984.

LITTLEWORTH PUFFIN   Parentage unknown
Mallow purple flowers. Mangles cross; Lady Gordon, reg. 1984.

```
                -brachycarpum 1/4
        -unnamed hybrid-    -wardii 1/8
        -              -Crest-        -fortunei ssp. discolor
LIVELY-                -Lady-                    1/16
 ONE -              Bessborough-campylocarpum Elatum
        -                -catawbiense 1/8        1/16
        -    -Catawbiense Album-
        -Wizard-            -unknown 1/8
        -        -dichroanthum 1/8
            -Fabia-
                -griersonianum 1/8
```
Buds of chartreuse green and rhodonite red; flowers open to pale yellow green; throat primrose yellow.   W. Delp.

```
* * * * * * * * * * * * * * * * * * * * * * * * * * * *
                                    -griffithianum 1/2
            -Loderi King George-
LIVONIA LINDSLEY-              -fortunei 1/4
        -       -griffithianum
            -Mars-
                -unknown 1/4
```
4ft(1.2m) -5F(-21C) M 4/3 Flower orchid pink, fading slightly, in large conical trusses of 24. Plant mound-shaped; leaves 5in(12.7cm) x 2in(5cm).   A. O. Wright, Jr. & Sr., raisers; A. Lindsley, Sr., reg. 1969.
ED KNIGHT   Parentage as above, except reversed
4ft(1.2) 15F(-9C) M   Very large trusses: 19 flowers of medium magenta, frilly lobes, openly funnel-shaped. Dark green leaves held 2 years. Dr. B. Briggs cross; E. Knight, reg. 1983.
```
* * * * * * * * * * * * * * * * * * * * * * * * * * * *
* * * * * * * * * * * * * * * * * * * * * * * * * * * *
```
LIZ ANN--form of sargentianum
1.25ft(.38m) -5F(-21C) M 4/3   An excellent dwarf with small daphne-like flowers opening pastel pink, and fading lighter. J. F. Caperci raiser.
MARICEE--form of sargentianum
2ft(.6m) -5F(-21C) M 4/3   Dwarf and twiggy with shiny leaves typical of this species but faster growing and more floriferous. Flowers small, creamy white, in miniature trusses. Caperci, reg. 1962. A.M. Wisley Trials 1983.   Color illus. ARS J 37:3 (1983), p. 127.
```
* * * * * * * * * * * * * * * * * * * * * * * * * * * * *
```

LIZA SHIREY   Described under KNOCKOUT, q.v.

```
                -decorum 1/4
        -unnamed hybrid-
LIZA'S YELLOW-          -fortunei ssp. discolor 1/4
        -unknown 1/2
```
2ft(.6m) 5F(-15C) L   Trusses of 12 flowers, buttercup yellow fading to light Indian yellow at edges, fire red in the throat. Semi-dwarf plant; new growth bronze. Mary Barefield, reg. 1980.

```
* * * * * * * * * * * * * * * * * * * * * * * * * * * *
        -minus Carolinianum Group, white form 1/2
LLENROC- (Reverse spelling of Cornell)
        -mucronulatum--CORNELL PINK 1/2
```
3ft(.9m) -20F(-29C) E 4/3   Profusion of very light pink to white flowers with a yellow eye. Semi-evergreen, small leaves, green in summer, turning reddish orange in autumn. Broad, upright plant growing 7in(17.8cm) in a year.   E. Mezitt.
GERTRUDE SAXE   Parentage as above, except mucronulatum--PAUL'S
                                            HOT PINK

6ft(1.8m) x 6ft -25F(-32C) EM   Strong purplish pink flowers,
15 per truss; upright plant with small foliage. R. Murcott,
reg. 1987.
WALLY   Parentage as LLENROC, above
5ft(1.5m) -25F(-32C) E 3/2 A soft pink mass in early season.
Wide, upright plant growing 7in(17.8cm) per year. Small, dark
green, pointed leaves turn orange-yellow in autumn. Mezitt.
WICKATUNK   Parentage as LLENROC, above
Perhaps a brighter pink than others of this group. D. Lewis.
* *

LOCARNO   Parentage unknown
Flowers of rose Bengal, with dark spotting. Koster of Boskoop,
reg. 1965.

LOCH ECK--form of vernicosum
5ft(1.5m) -15F(-26C) M 3/3 A fine form of this species with
trusses of 12 flowers, 3.25in(8.3cm) wide, saucer-shaped and
pure white. Younger Botanic Garden, reg. 1965. A.M. 1964.


```
                          -dichroanthum
             -Goldsworth Orange-
         -Hotei-            -fortunei ssp. discolor
         -    -            -souliei 1/8
LOCH TAY-    -unnamed hybrid-
                            -wardii 1/8
             -caucasicum 1/2
```
4ft(1.2m) -5F(-21C) M 4/4   Flowers deep golden amber, upper
lobes with maroon red dots set in a golden calyx, also dotted
red; deep green, leathery foliage. P. A. Cox, reg. 1987. Col-
or illus. HG. p. 98.

LOCHINCH SPINBUR   Described under SPINBUR, q.v.

```
                              -griffithianum
                   -Loderi King George-       29/64
                   -                -fortunei 17/64
              -Morio-                    -griffithianum
              -    -            -Loderi-
              -    -    -Albatross-        -fortunei
    -Lockington-    -Cup-        -fortunei ssp. discolor
    - Pride -    Day-        -elliottii 1/32    1/32
    -    -            -Fusilier-
    -    -                -griersonianum 1/32
LOCKINGTON-    -                -griffithianum
    CROWN -    -Mrs. E. C. Stirling-
          -    -            -unknown 3/16
          -            -griffithianum
          -    -Pink Shell-        -fortunei
    -Coronation-        -H. M. Arderne-
       Day-            -            -unknown
          -    -griffithianum
          -Loderi-
                -fortunei
```
Funnel-shaped flowers in trusses of 17, 6-lobed, deep purplish
pink, throat blotched and flared deep purplish red. Shrub 3.5ft
(1.0m) tall; narrow elliptic foliage, 4.7in((12cm) long. Spring
flowering. Lockington Nursery, reg. 1988.


```
                     -griersonianum 3/8
          -Sarita Loder-      -griffithianum 3/16
          -            -Loderi-
LOCKINGTON-            -fortunei 3/16
    FLAME -        -Loderi (as above)
          -    -Albatross-
          -Cup-        -fortunei ssp. discolor 1/8
          Day-        -elliottii 1/8
              -Fusilier-
                  -griersonianum
```
Funnel-shaped flowers, in trusses of 17, 5-lobed, of strong red,
with darker dorsal flare. Bush 5ft(1.5m) tall; lanceolate foliage 6in(15cm) long. Flowers in spring.   D. Dosser, reg. 1988.


```
                  -Blue Peter--unknown 5/8
          -John Dosser-        -caucasicum 1/8
          -        -Corry Koster-
LOCKINGTON JANE-            -unknown
          -        -campylocarpum 1/4
          -Unique-
              -unknown
```
Truss of 15 flowers, funnel-shaped, white with spotting of red-
purple. Height 3ft(.9m); obovate leaves. Dosser, reg. 1984.

LOCKINGTON LOCKIE   Parentage unknown
Flowers in truss of 3-4, tubular-campanulate, white with a yel-
low throat. Similar to TYERMANII but better habit. D. Dosser
(Australia), reg. 1989.

* *
```
                              -griffithianum 13/32
             -Loderi King George-
             -                -fortunei 5/32
         -Morio-            -griffithianum
         -    -            -Loderi-
LOCKINGTON-    -Cup Day-    -Albatross-    -fortunei
    PRIDE -        -        -fortunei ssp. discolor 1/16
         -            -elliottii 1/16
         -        -Fusilier-
         -            -griersonianum 1/16
         -        -griffithianum
         -Mrs. E. C. Stirling-
                    -unknown 1/4
```
Trusses hold 13 flowers, light purple with a red center and red
spots on upper lobe. D. Dosser, Australia, reg. 1978.
DELAMERE BELLE   Parentage as above
Truss of 4, light rose, fading to cream. Dosser, reg. 1980.
MARG SAWERS   Parentage as above
Trusses of 18 flowers, light Neyron rose. Dosser, reg. 1978.
SNOW PEAK   Parentage as above
Flowers in trusses of 18, short funnel-shaped, 5-lobed, white
with a strong purplish red blotch. Shrub 3.3ft(1.0m) tall; El-
liptic, hairless foliage 5.2in(15cm). K. van de Ven, reg. 1988.
* *


```
            -dichroanthum 1/4
        -Fabia-
LODABIA-    -griersonianum 1/4
        -        -griffithianum 1/4
        -Loderi-
            -fortunei 1/4
```
Rose-colored flowers. Lord Aberconway, 1946.

* *
```
            -griffithianum 1/4
        -Loderi-
LODAURIC-    -fortunei 1/4
        -auriculatum 1/2
```
6ft(1.8m) OF(-18C) L 4/3 Vigorous grower, broader than tall;
light green leaves, pointed, 9in(22.9cm) long. Trumpet-shaped
white flowers, yellowish throat, 3.5in(8.9cm) wide, with a spicy
fragrance; nodding truss. G. Taylor for Sir John Ramsden, 1922.
LODAURIC ICEBERG   Parentage as above
6ft(1.8m) OF(-18C) L 4/3   Late-flowering, pure white, and
fragrant. Abundant foliage, light grass green. Slocock, 1946.
* *

LODBRIT   Described under MOUNT MAZAMA, q.v.

* *
```
            -griffithianum 1/2
LODERI-                    Cross first made at Kew, see KEWENSE
        -fortunei 1/2
```
6ft(1.8m) OF(-18C) M 5/3 A large tree-like shrub, of strong
stature. Flowers very large, lily-shaped, sweetly scented, in
enormous trusses; colors range from pastel pinks to pure white.
Register of 1958 shows 32 named clones. Beautiful foliage.
Vigorous; needs some shelter. Sir E. Loder, Leonardslee, 1901.
LODERI FAIRYLAND   Parentage as above
Pink buds open to white; fragrant. Sir E. Loder, 1901.
LODERI GAME CHICK   Parentage as above
6ft(1.8m) OF(-18C) M 5/3   Flowers pale pink, faint blotch.
Sir Edmund Loder, 1901.
LODERI JULIE   Parentage as above
Register did not credit this to Loder: possibly an omission, or
a creation by another hybridizer. Flowers cream, suffused sulphur yellow; the closest to a "yellow" LODERI. A.M. 1944.
LODERI KING GEORGE   Parentage as above
6ft(1.8m) OF(-18C) M 5/3   Considered the best white form in
this group. Pink buds open to flowers flushed pale pink, later
become white, with green basal flash; blossoms 6in(15.2cm) wide,
openly funnel-campanulate, in 9- to 10-flowered trusses; leaves
narrowly oblong, 10.5in(26cm) long. Delightfully fragrant, magnificent shrub; may become tree-sized. Needs protection from
wind, sun, subzero cold. Sir Edmund Loder, 1901. A.M. 1968.
F.C.C. 1970. Color illus. F p. 51; VV p. 26, 118.

LODERI PATIENCE   Parentage as above
White with crimson throat; fragrant.   Sir E. Loder, 1901.
LODERI PINK DIAMOND   Parentage as above
6ft(1.8m) OF(-18C) M 5/3   Flowers a pastel shell pink and
fragrant; otherwise similar to LODERI KING GEORGE.   Sir E.
Loder, 1901. F.C.C. 1914.
LODERI PINK TOPAZ   Parentage as above
6ft(1.8m) OF(-18C) M 5/3   Pink flowers, with a faint green
throat; fragrant. Sir E. Loder, 1901.
LODERI PRETTY POLLY   Parentage as above
5ft(1.5m) OF(-18C) M 5/5   Shown simply as "pink" in the Reg-
ister of 1958.   Sir Giles Loder reported it extinct; Greer's
Guidebook to Available Rhododendrons, 1988, lists it.   Sir E.
Loder, 1901.
LODERI SIR EDMUND   Parentage as above
Flowers blush pink. Sir Edmund Loder.   A.M. 1930.
LODERI SIR JOSEPH HOOKER   Parentage as above
6ft(1.8m) OF(-18C) M 5/3   Flowers of deep shell pink, conspicuous veining. Sir E. Loder, cross 1901. A.M. 1973.
LODERI SUPERLATIVE   Parentage as above
6ft(1.8m) OF(-18C) M 5/3   Giant white flowers with interior
flushed a pale yellow or pink. Fragrant.   Sir E. Loder, 1901.
LODERI VENUS   Parentage as above
6ft(1.8m) OF(-18C) M 5/3   Flowers soft pink; extremely fragrant. Sir E. Loder. Color illus. ARS Q 31:3 (1977), p. 170.
LODERI WHITE DIAMOND   Parentage as above
6ft(1.8m) OF(-18C) M 5/3 Flowers ivory white, with a blotch.
Sir Edmund Loder, 1901. F.C.C. 1914.
* *

LODERI COUGAR   See COUGAR

LODERI FAIRYLAND   Described under LODERI, q.v.
LODERI GAME CHICK
LODERI JULIE
LODERI KING GEORGE

                        -griffithianum 1/2
            -Loderi Pink Diamond-
LODERI OLGA-   -fortunei 1/2
        -                   -griffithianum
            -Loderi King George-
                            -fortunei
6ft(1.8m) -5F(-21C) M   Trusses of 10 flowers, very fragrant,
clear white, throat of Dresden yellow. L. Brandt, reg. 1968.

LODERI PATIENCE   Described under LODERI, q.v.
LODERI PINK DIAMOND
LODERI PINK TOPAZ
LODERI PRETTY POLLY

                            -griffithianum 1/2
                -Loderi King George-
LODERI PRINCESS MARINA-   -fortunei 1/2
        -                       -griffithianum
                -Loderi Sir Edmund-
                            -fortunei
6ft(1.8m) OF(-18C) M 5/3   These pale pink flowers in trusses
of 12, shade to white with pink patches.   Sir Edmund Loder.
A.M. 1948.

LODERI SIR EDMUND   Described under LODERI, q.v.
LODERI SIR JOSEPH HOOKER
LODERI SUPERLATIVE
LODERI VENUS
LODERI WHITE DIAMOND

            -arboreum ssp. cinnamomeum var. album 1/2
LODER'S WHITE-
            -griffithianum 1/2
A different parentage is given in Hillier's manual, as follows:
                                -catawbiense 1/8
                    -Album Elegans-
            -unnamed hybrid-   -unknown 1/8
LODER'S WHITE-   -griffithianum 1/2
        -                  -griffithianum
            -White Pearl-
                -maximum 1/4
5ft(1.5m) OF(-18C) M 5/4   Plant compact, broader than tall;
bright green leaves 6in(15cm) long. Truss large, conical. Buds
a delicate pink, opening to slightly fragrant white flowers with
pink edges and a tinge of yellow in the throat. Often a parent.

J. H. Mangles, before 1884.   A.M. 1911.   A.G.M. 1931. Color
illus. ARS J 39:1 (1985), p. 7; F p. 52; JS p. 74; VV p. i.

* *
            -catawbiense var. album 3/4
LODESTAR-   -catawbiense var. album
        -Belle Heller-   -catawbiense 1/8
                -white catawbiense hybrid-
                            -unknown 1/8
5ft(1.5m) -20F(-29C) ML 4/3   Flowers pale lilac fading to
white, strongly spotted dorsal blotch dark greenish yellow, full
trusses of 15; corolla widely funnel-shaped, 3.2in(8cm) wide.
Plant wider than tall, elliptic convex leaves 5in(12.7cm) long.
Leach, reg. 1964.   A.E. 1982.   Color illus. HG p. 74.
SWANSDOWN   Parentage as above
5ft(1.5m) -25F(-32C) ML 4/4   Flowers white, sometimes very
pale pink, 3in(7.6cm) wide, bold blotch strong yellow; truss of
20. Leach, reg. 1968. A.E. 1983. Color illus. K. p. 144.
* *

                -facetum 1/4
        -Jacquetta-
LODETTA-   -griersonianum 1/4
        -              -griffithianum 1/4
            -Loderi-
                -fortunei 1/4
A hybrid with scarlet rose flowers.   Lord Aberconway, 1946.

LOEB'S MOONLIGHT   Parentage unknown; may contain ponticum
5ft(1.5m) -10F(-23C) ML 3/4   Flowers rosy orchid with a yellow throat blotch. Glossy foliage. C. Loeb, reg. 1966.

                -rex ssp. arizelum 1/2
LOGAN BELLE-
            -hodgsonii 1/2
Large, compact trusses with flowers opening cream, flushed pink,
fading to cream; purple blotch. Hambro, reg. 1962. P.C. 1960.

LOGAN DAMARIS   Described under DAMARIS, q.v.

LOIS   Described under ROSE ELF, q.v.

LOIS JEAN   Described under JILL, q.v.

LOIS JEAN SEIHL   Described under FLADA W. BLOUGH, q.v.

                -arboreum 1/4
        -Cornubia-   -thomsonii 1/8
LOKI-   -Shilsonii-
    -unknown 1/2   -barbatum 1/8
Blood red flowers. Lady Loder. A.M. 1933.

                -griffithianum 1/4
        -Loderi-
LOLLIPOP-   -fortunei 1/4
            -williamsianum 1/2
2.5ft(.75m) -5F(-21C) E   Flowers rose pink, of heavy texture,
up to 4in(10cm) across, in trusses of 7-9. Plant broader than
tall. E. Ostbo raiser; Arthur O. Wright, reg. 1964.

                -williamsianum 1/2
LOLLIPOP LACE-
            -unknown 1/2
Trusses of 3 flowers, rich pink with paler, very frilly lobes,
3.75in(9.5cm) wide; a striped effect on exterior. Ovate leaves
3.25in(8.3cm) long. L. Jury cross; F. M. Jury, reg. 1982.

LONDON   Described under BRITANNIA, q.v.

            -Grand Marquis--unknown
LONGBEACH DREAM-
            -unknown
Clear white flower in truss of 21. Mrs. G. E. Grigg, reg. 1982.

            -burmanicum 1/2
LONGBOW-
            -johnstoneanum 1/2
Trusses hold 8-12 flowers, light mimosa yellow; upper lobe has a
flare of aureolin yellow. R. Scorborio, reg. 1982.

```
                    -caucasicum 1/8
            -Cunningham's White-
      -Vernus-                  -ponticum, white form 1/8
      -       -                 -catawbiense,  red form 1/8
      -    -red catawbiense-
LONGWOOD-        hybrid        -unknown 1/8
      -                          -griffithianum 1/8
      -            -Loderi King George-
      -Olympic Lady-                 -fortunei 1/8
                    -williamsianum 1/4
```
4.5ft(1.35m) 0F(-18C) M 3/3   Ruby red buds opening to lilac
pink flowers, spotted dark red in throat, roseine purple exter-
erior, openly campanulate, 2.5in(6.4cm) broad, of 6 wavy lobes;
dome-shaped truss.   Leach cross; Longwood Gardens, reg. 1976.

```
                -wardii (croceum) 1/4
      -Charley-      -dichroanthum 3/16
      -       -Fabia-
LONNY-           -griersonianum 3/16
      -          -fortunei 1/8
      -       -Fawn-      -dichroanthum
      -unnamed-   -Fabia-
        hybrid-          -griersonianum
           -               -caucasicum 1/16
           -       -Dr. Stocker-
           -Damaris-             -griffithianum 1/16
                    -campylocarpum 1/8
```
5ft(1.5m) -10F(-23C) EM Plant upright, as broad as tall with
leaves 7in(17.8cm) long. Flower funnel-shaped, chartreuse green
in throat shading to Neyron rose at edging of lobes, in trusses
10in(25.4cm) across. Del James raiser; Ray James, reg. 1980.

* *

```
                -yakushimanum 1/2
      -Tols-
      -     -catawbiense 1/4          -Pygmalion--unknown
LOOK OUT-            -unnamed hybrid-                    1/16
      -              -Weldy-          -haematodes 1/16
      -Robert Weldon-     -yakushimanum, Exbury form
                    -               -yakushimanum
                    -Serendipity-
                          -aureum (chrysanthum) 1/8
```
Buds of lilac and magnolia purple opening pure white, with beet-
root purple dorsal spots and stigma, pale orange-yellow anthers.
Indumented foliage.   W. Delp.
TICKLED PINK   Parentage as above
Cardinal red buds; frilled yellowish white flowers edged in deep
purplish and strong pinks, with cardinal red dorsal spots and a
pale yellow-green flare. W. Delp.
* *

```
                -yakushimanum 1/2
LOOKING GLASS-      -wightii 1/4
          -China-
                    -fortunei 1/4
```
5ft(1.5m) M Dark red buds open to frilled, deep pink flowers.
Shapely trusses on a handsome plant; large, forest green leaves.
H. E. Greer distributor.

```
                -maximum 1/4
      -unnamed hybrid-
      -                 -vernicosum (18139) 1/4
LOOKY-                        -smirnowii 1/8
LOOKY-              -unnamed hybrid-
      -            -                 -yakushimanum 1/8
      -            -                        -catawbiense 1/32
      -unnamed hybrid-        -Atrosanguineum-
                 -     -Atrier-         -unknown 1/32
                 -Mary -     -griersonianum 1/16
                 Belle-      -decorum 1/16
                        -Dechaem-
                             -haematodes 1/16
```
Buds of strong purplish red open to flowers pale purplish pink,
edged strong purplish red; dorsal spots moderate orange.   Delp.

LORD FAIRHAVEN   Parentage unknown
Flowers shrimp pink, suffused yellow. Knap Hill, pre-1958.

```
                    -griffithianum 1/4
            -Loderi King George-
LORD HAREWOOD-              -fortunei 1/4
            -unknown 1/2
```
Flowers white, with a rose blotch in throat; scented; 9 to 10 in
a truss. Shrub 50ft(15m) high x 27ft(8.1m)(20 yrs). June flow-
ing. Oblanceolate leaves 8in(20.2cm). Lord Harewood, reg. 1987.

```
            -griffithianum 1/2
LORD LAMBOURNE-
            -unknown 1/2
```
Red flowers.   O. Schulz, cross 1892; C. B. van Nes, intro. 1896.

LORD MILNER   Parentage unknown
A parent of the Exbury hybrid GOOD CHEER.

LORD PALMERSTON   See CYNTHIA

LORD ROBERTS   Parentage unknown
5ft(1.5m) -15F(-26C) ML 3/3   A parent of several hybrids.
Plant vigorous, rounded; foliage glossy green and crinkled.
Flowers deep red with a black blotch, 2in(5cm) across, in tight
ball-shaped trusses. Easily propagated. B. Mason, reg. 1958.
Color illus. VV, title page.

```
            -lindleyi 1/2
LORD STAIR-
            -taggianum 1/2
```
White flowers, with a pale orange stain at the base of the two
upper lobes. Lord Stair, Lochinch.   A.M. 1952.

```
                -griffithianum 1/2
LORD SWAYTHLING-
                -unknown 1/2
```
Flowers pink, Neyron rose inside with dark maroon spots.   Otto
Schulz, cross 1890; C. B. van Nes & Sons intro., 1896.

LORI EICHELSER   Described under RÊVE ROSE, q.v.

```
      -souliei 1/2
LORIEN-
      -wardii 1/2
```
Flowers a very light sap green.   Crosfield, reg. 1973.

LORNA DOONE   Described under DISCRETION, q.v.

LOST HORIZON--form of principis Vellereum Group K W 5656
5ft(1.5m) -5F(-21C) E 3/4   Flowers pink, fading to white,
flushed pink with carmine spots on interior, to 1.6in(4cm) wide;
compact, rounded trusses hold 15-22. Narrowly elliptic leaves,
dark green with fawn indumentum.   Kingdon Ward collector; Col.
S. R. Clarke raiser; R. N. S. Clarke, reg. 1976.   A.M. 1976.

```
            -dichroanthum ssp. scyphocalyx Herpesticum Group 1/4
      -Metis-
LOTIS-    -griersonianum 1/4
      -       -griffithianum 1/4
      -Loderi-
            -fortunei 1/4
```
Orange-red flowers.   Lord Aberconway, Bodnant, 1946.

```
            -Mrs. Tritton--unknown
LOUIS PASTEUR-
            -Viscount Powerscourt--unknown
```
5ft(1.5m) -5F(-21C) ML 3/1   Two-toned flowers, brilliant
light crimson margins shading to white centers, deep pink exterior; large, dense rounded trusses. Plant of spreading growth
habit. Difficult to propagate. L. J. Endtz & Co., 1923.

```
                -wardii 1/4
            -unnamed hybrid-
LOUISE KATEY-              -unknown 3/4
            -unknown
```
Campanulate flowers in trusses of 7-8, 7-lobed, off-white, with
slight rose flush on reverse; bud scales opening slightly cream-
colored. Shrub 5ft(1.5m) x 5ft.; gray-green elliptic foliage to
4.7in(12cm) long. Flowers in May. Lord Harewood, reg. 1988.

```
            -Sappho--unknown 3/4
LOU'S SACO-            -fortunei ? 1/4
      -Mrs. W. R. Coe-              (Dexter hybrid)
            -unknown
```
2ft(.6m) x 3.5ft(1.05m) -15F(-26C) M Dome truss of 12 flowers
moderate purplish pink, edged very pale purple; dorsal blotch
deep purplish red. Dense growth habit. L. B. Mraw, reg. 1989.

LOUVECIENNE--form of rigidum
6ft(1.8m) -5F(-21C) EM 4/3 Flowers of pale rose, a speckled
eye of rose Bengal, widely funnel-shaped, 3in(7.6cm) wide, in
truss of 5-7. Elliptic leaves 2in(5cm) x 1in(2.5cm). Collector
unknown; L. de Rothschild raiser; E. de Rothschild exhibitor;
reg. 1978. A.M. 1975.

```
                    -smirnowii 1/4
            -unnamed hybrid-
      -                     -yakushimanum 1/4
LOVE ME-        -brachycarpum 1/4
   TENDER-unnamed-     -wardii 1/8
          hybrid-Crest-      -fortunei ssp. discolor 1/16
                    -Lady      -
                Bessborough-campylocarpum Elatum Gp. 1/16
```
Buds of rose Bengal open to flowers rhodamine purple, edged in
roseine purple. Semi-petaloid. W. Delp.

LOVE STORY   Parentage unknown
4ft(1.2m) -5F(-21C) M Foliage narrow, medium-sized. Flowers
light peach, fading to pale yellow, with an orangey red throat;
trusses of 10. Whitney cross; The Sathers, reg. 1976.

```
        -chrysodoron 1/2
LOVELOCK-
        -unknown 1/2
```
Trusses of 5 flowers, light chartreuse green, darkening to yellow at base. Dunedin Rhododendron Group, NZ, reg. 1977.

```
                    -catawbiense var. album 3/8
            -Lodestar-          -catawbiense var. album
      -          -Belle Heller-         -catawbiense 1/16
LOVELY LADY-               -Madame  -
      -          -catawbiense var. album  Carvalho-unknown 1/16
            -catawbiense var. album Glass--Catalgla 1/2
```
Buds of violet and pale purple open to white flowers, with dor-
sal spots of strong greenish yellow and reddish orange. Delp.

```
        -neriiflorum Euchaites Group 1/2
LOVELY WILLIAM-
        -williamsianum 1/2
```
3ft(.9m) -10F(-23C) EM Deep rose pink flower. Horlick, 1940.

LOWINSKY'S WHITE   Parentage unknown
A parent of several hybrids. A large, beautiful plant with very
dark green, sharply pointed leaves. Pale pink buds open to pure
white, unspotted flowers. Blooms late to very late. T. Lowinsky, Sunningdale Nurseries, intro. before 1955.

```
                        -griffithianum 1/8
            -Queen Wilhelmina-
      -Britannia-            -unknown 3/8
LOYALTY-         -Stanley Davies--unknown
      -arboreum ssp. zeylanicum 1/2
```
Red flowers. Williams at Lanarth.

```
        -ponticum 1/2
LUCIDIUM-
        -unknown 1/2
```
5ft(1.5m) 0F(-18C) ML   Still growing in New Zealand and Australia, according to Cox. Rosy, purplish lilac flowers. Plant
of glossy dense foliage; loose, spreading habit. Waterer, 1857.

```
                        -griffithianum 1/16
                -Queen Wilhelmina-
          -Britannia-            -unknown 3/16
      -Wilgen's Ruby-      -Stanley Davies--unknown
      -          -            -catawbiense 1/8
LUCIE-        -John Walter-
BRAND-              -arboreum 1/8
      -     -forrestii Repens Group 1/4
      -Elizabeth-
          -griersonianum 1/4
```
Scarlet flowers, 1in(2.5cm) across; truss of 8-10. Wide lanceo-
late leaves, brown indumentum; plant 5ft(1.5m) x 6.5ft(2m); early. Brand & Sons, pre-1970; Royal Boskoop Hort. Soc., reg. 1988.

LUCIL Listed under FINE FEATHERS, q.v.

LUCILLE WILLIAMSON Described under JANET SCROGGS, q.v.

LUCKY BREAK Described under PANACHE, q.v.

LUCKY HIT--seedling of davidsonianum
Trusses of 6-8, small, saucer-shaped flowers, lilac rose with a
blotch of red-purple dots.   D. M. van Gelderen, Boskoop, 1969,
reg. 1969.   Gold Medal Boskoop 1966.

LUCKY STRIKE   Described under ANNA ROSE WHITNEY, q.v.

LUCY ELIZABETH--form of formosum Iteophyllum Group
4ft(1.2m) 15F(-9C) ML 4/3 A plant for the cool greenhouse.
White flower flushed chrome yellow in upper throat, funnel-shaped, 5-lobed, held in trusses of 2-3. Dark green leaves, scaly
on both surfaces. Mrs. E. McKenzie, reg. 1979. A.M. 1979.

```
            -ciliatum 1/4
      -unnamed hybrid-
LUCY LOU-       -leucaspis 3/4
      -leucaspis
```
3ft(.9m) 5F(-15C) E 3/4 Flower pure snowy white. Attractive
foliage, rounded leaves of soft green. Very floriferous. H. L.
Larson, reg. 1958.

LUCY NEAL   See GENOVEVA

```
                    -fortunei 1/4
            -Ruby F. Bowman-       -griffithianum 1/8
LUCY'S GOOD PINK-        -Lady Bligh-
      -                  -unknown 1/8
            -griersonianum 1/2
```
6ft(1.8m) -15F(-26C) L Flowers of Tyrian rose, widely funnel-
shaped, 4.75in(12cm) wide, 7-lobed; large lax trusses of 7. Upright plant, well-branched; narrowly elliptic, spinach green
leaves, held 3 years.   John S. Druecker, intro. 1966; E. R.
German, reg. 1976.

LUISE VEREY   Described under DIANA PEARSON, q.v.

LUMINA   Described under HACHMANN'S ROSITA, q.v.

* *
```
                    -cinnabarinum Roylei Group 1/4
            -Lady Rosebery-       -cinnabarinum 1/8
LUMINOUS-        -Royal Flush-
      -           (pink form)  maddenii 1/8
            -cinnabarinum ssp. xanthocoden Concatenans Group 1/2
```
A hybrid with orange-red flowers. Lord Aberconway, 1950.
HULAGU KHAN Parentage: cinnabarinum ssp. xanthocodon
                        x Lady Rosebery
6ft(1.8m)(9 yrs.) Truss of 10 pendulous flowers, bright Indian
yellow, reverse a deeper shade. Dark green leaves, scaly below.
Lester Brandt, reg. 1969.
NOTE: The two above hybrids not quite siblings, but close kin.
* *
* *
```
                    -griffithianum 1/2
LUNAR QUEEN-    -wardii 1/4
      -Hawk-           -fortunei ssp. discolor 1/8
            -Lady Bessborough-
                    -campylocarpum Elatum 1/8
```
4ft(1.2m) -5F(-21C) EM Flowers cream-colored, 4in(10.2cm)
across' and 2.5in(6.4cm) long, in trusses of 9. Gen. Harrison,
reg. 1967.
ALSTON   Parentage as above, except reversed
Large dark green leaves, ovate-lanceolate. Flowers cream white
with base stain of cream yellow; trusses hold 5-7. L. S. Fortescue, reg. 1971.
BRENTOR   Parentage as ALSTON
Flowers reddish purple, fading to cream, with basal red blotch.
Fortescue, reg. 1972.
KATHARINE FORTESCUE   Parentage as ALSTON
Trusses hold 12 flowers, light yellow paling to off-white with a
slight blotch of red in the throat. Leaves undulate, up to 5in.
(11.5cm) long. Fortescue, reg. 1970. P.C. 1975.
* *

```
        -yakushimanum 1/2
LURLINE-                -griffithianum 1/8
      -           -Queen Wilhelmina-
      -Unknown Warrior-         -unknown 3/8
            -Stanley Davies--unknown
```
2.5ft(.75m) -5F(-21C) M   Buds of dark rose madder, opening
lighter rose and fading paler, campanulate, to 2.5in(6.4cm)
wide, frilled petals; large rounded truss of about 20. Compact
plant; leaves with fawn indumentum.   P. M. Brydon, reg. 1969.

```
* * * * * * * * * * * * * * * * * * * * * * * * * * *
          -fortunei 1/2
LUSCOMBEI-
          -thomsonii 1/2
```
6ft(1.8m) OF(-18C) M   Deep rose pink flowers with a ray of
crimson, trumpet-shaped, very large, in loose trusses of 10-12.
A tall, broadly dome-shaped bush with attractive foliage. Shown
by G. Luscombe, c. 1880.   Color illus. JS p. 53.
BETTY   Parentage as above
Deep pink flowers. Sir E. Loder.   A.M. 1927.
HULLABALOO   Parentage as above
Rose Bengal with paler edges, darker staining on reverse, small
throat blotch cardinal red; loose truss of 10-12.   Sir E. Loder
cross; The Hon. H. E. Boscawen, reg. 1974.   A.M. 1974.
LUSCOMBE'S SANGUINEUM   Parentage as above
Flowers scarlet crimson. Luscombe.
PRIDE OF LEONARDSLEE   Parentage as above
6ft(1.8m) OF(-18C) EM 3/4   Considered an improved LUSCOMBEI.
Flowers of deep pink shading to mauve, in loose trusses. Plant
upright, sturdy, rounded. Sir E. Loder.
```
```
* *
```

LUSCOMBE'S SANGUINEUM    Described under LUSCOMBEI, above

```
          -dichroanthum 1/4
     -Dante-
LUSTRE-   -facetum (eriogynum) 1/4
     -griersonianum 1/2
```
Scarlet flowers.  Lord Aberconway, intro. 1941.

LUXOR   Described under CONGO, q.v.

```
     -Crober's Apricot--unknown 1/2
-                              -catawbiense 1/6
LYALL-   -Atrosanguineum-
     -Atrier-   -unknown 1/16
  -Mary -   -griersonianum 1/8
  Belle-   -decorum 1/8
          -Dechaem-
               -haematodes 1/8
```
Buds of Neyron rose open to flowers just a shade lighter; dorsal
spotting  cardinal red.   Jack Looye cross; Delp raiser.

```
               -ponticum 1/4
          -Chionoides-
LYALL FRETS-   -unknown 1/4
     -          -catawbiense v. album Glass--Catalgla 1/4
     -unnamed-   -fortunei ssp. discolor 1/8
          hybrid-Lady Bess--
               borough-campylocarpum Elatum Group 1/8
```
4ft(1.2m) x 4ft(20 yrs)  -15F(-26C) ML    Conical trusses of 12
flowers, 6-lobed, of heavy substance,  pale greenish yellow with
strong red flare and spotting, dorsal lobe.   Smooth, dull green
leaves held 3 years.  Lyall Frets cross; R. Behring, reg. 1989.

```
          -souliei 1/8
     -Soulbut-
  -Vanessa-   -fortunei--Sir Charles Butler 1/8
LYCIA-   -griersonianum 1/4
  -elliottii 1/2
```
Scarlet red.  Lord Aberconway, 1942.

```
               -griffithianum 1/16
          -George Hardy-
     -Pink Pearl-   -catawbiense 1/16
  -Antoon -   -arboreum 1/16
  -Van Welie-   -Broughtonii-
LYDIA-   -unknown   -unknown 5/16
  -               -fortunei ssp. discolor 1/8
  -          -Lady Bessborough-
  -Day Dream-   -campylocarpum Elatum Group 1/8
               -griersonianum 1/4
```
6ft(1.8m)  OF(-18C)  ML  5/3    Flowers of China rose with upper
lobe lightly marked in cardinal red,  rotate  funnel-shaped,  to
4in(10.2cm) wide; tight trusses of about 14.  Upright plant with
elliptic leaves 6in(15cm) long.   Greer, reg. 1964.   C.A. 1972.
Color illus. HG p. 97.

```
          -griffithianum 1/4
     -Alice-
LYMINGE-    -unknown 3/4
     -unknown
```

Bright pink flowers, similar to ALICE. Leaves elliptic, glossy
dark green, sparsely hairy beneath.   A. E. Hardy cross; G. A.
Hardy, reg. 1984.

```
     -unnamed hybrid--unknown (1/2)
LYMPNE-
     -elliottii 1/2
```
A red-flowered hybrid.   Maj. A. Hardy, reg. 1975.   A.M. 1975.

LYNN BOULTER   Parentage unknown
Deep to light red flowers.   F. Boulter, reg. 1984.

LYNSEY--souliei, selfed
3.5ft(2.05m) OF(-18C) M   Strong purplish pink flowers of heavy
substance, 6 wavy lobes, in large lax trusses. Foliage held one
year.   S. Hilscher, reg. 1990.

```
          -Loder's White, q.v. (2 possible diagrams)
     -C.I.S.-     -dichroanthum
LYTA WAY-     -Fabia-
     -          -griersonianum
          -macrophyllum
```
4ft(1.2m) 15F(-9C) M   Flowers carmine rose, with shading of
carmine at edges, cardinal red spotting; corolla openly funnel-
shaped, 2.5in(6.5cm) across, 5 wavy lobes; flattened trusses of
13 flowers. Plant upright, wide as high; leaves held 2 years.
Carl Tuomala, cross 1969; Eugene R. German, reg. 1984.

M

```
          -griffithianum 3/8
     -Mars-
MA CHÈRE-     -unknown 3/8
     -          -yakushimanum 1/4
     -unnamed hybrid-
          -Mars (as above)
```
1.7ft(.5m) x 2.5ft(.76m)(14 yrs) -17F(-27C) ML Deep red buds.
Flowers cardinal red with white center, 1.7in(4.5cm) wide, last-
ing to 2 weeks, fading deep pink; ball truss of 16. Dull leaves
4.5in(11.5cm) long; held 4 years.   Brueckner cross; reg. 1989.
Color illus. ARS J 44:2 (1990), p. 79.

```
     -thomsonii 1/2
MABEL-
     -unknown 1/2
```
An apricot-colored thomsonii hybrid.   R. Gill & Son.

```
     -impeditum--Blue Steel 3/4
MACAW-          -impeditum--Blue Steel
  -Night Sky-               -russatum 1/8
          -Russautinii-
               -augustinii 1/8
```
Truss of 7 flowers, 6-lobed, bluebird blue, a small white eye.
Leaf lanceolate, sparsely scaly.   J. P. C. Russell, reg. 1983.

```
     -meddianum 1/2
MACHRIE-
     -unknown 1/2
```
Moderately compact trusses hold about 15 flowers, 5-lobed, cur-
rant red. 3.5in(8.9cm) across. Calyx funnel-shaped, almost the
same color. Brodick Castle, reg. 1966.   A.M. 1965.

McNABII   Described under COWBELL, q.v.

```
     -racemosum 1/2
MACOPIN-
     -unknown 1/2
```
3ft(.9m) -20F(-29C) M Flower pale lavender, in globular clus-
ters. Glossy, dark green foliage, 2in(5cm) x 1in(2.5cm).   G.
Guy Nearing, reg. 1963.

MACULOSISSIMUM   Parentage unknown
Flowers pale lilac, much spotted.   Standish.   F.C.C. Wisley
Trials 1860.
```
                    -griffithianum 1/8
          -George Hardy-
     -Marinus Koster-     -catawbiense 1/8
MADAH JEAN-     -red hybrid--unknown
     -unknown 3/4
```
7ft(2.1m) high x 9ft(2.7m)(13 yrs) 15F(-9C) M Rose red buds
open to flowers phlox pink, edges and outside rose Bengal, spot-
```

ted Indian lake.   Pauline Newberry raiser; E. Philp, reg. 1986.

MADAME A. MOSER or
MADAME ALBERT MOSER   Parentage unknown
A parent of EDWIN O. WEBER.   Flowers pale mauve, shading white
at base, striking gold blotch on upper petal, funnel-shaped with
wavy margins; high conical trusses. Free-flowering. Plant tall
and vigorous. Moser or A. Waterer.   A.M. Wisley Trials 1954.

```
                    -catawbiense, white form 1/2
MADAME CARVALHO-
                    -unknown 1/2
```
5ft(1.5m) -15F(-26C) 2/3   Flowers white with greenish spots,
in ball-shaped trusses. Dark green foliage; leaves to 5in(12.7
cm) x 2.5in(6.4cm). Very bud-hardy. J. Waterer, 1866.   Color
illus. VV p. 101.

MADAME COLIJN   Parentage unknown
A parent of BETELGEUSE.

```
                              -ponticum 1/8
                    -Michael Waterer-
            -Prometheus-             -unknown 5/8
MADAME DE BRUIN-         -Monitor--unknown
          -              -arboreum 1/4
                    -Doncaster-
                              -unknown
```
4ft(1.2m) -10F(-23C) ML 3/2 A sturdy, vigorous shrub, taller
than wide; pointed, dark green leaf, with conspicuous pale green
midrib, 5in(12.7cm) x 2in(5cm). Cerise red flowers; ball-shaped
trusses. M. Koster, 1904.   Color illus. VV p. 39.

```
                    -fortunei 1/2
MADAME FR. J. CHAUVIN-
                    -unknown 1/2
```
5ft(1.5m) -10F(-23C) ML 4/3   Upright, compact plant; light
green foliage 7in(18cm) x 1.7in(4.4cm). Flowers rich rosy pink,
paler in throat, with a small red blotch; round trusses of 10 to
12. M. Koster, 1916.   A.M. 1933.   Color illus. VV p. 33.

```
                         -arboreum 1/4
                -Doncaster-
MADAME G. VERDE DELISLE-        -unknown 1/4
                    -griffithianum 1/2
```
Bright pink flowers. Lowinsky. A.M. 1919.

MADAME GUILLEMOT   See MONSIEUR GUILLEMOT

MADAME HUGO T. HOOFTMAN   Parentage unknown
Flowers of solferino purple. H. T. Hooftman, reg. 1966.

MADAME IDA RUBINSTEIN   Parentage unknown
6ft(1.0m) -5F(-21C) ML   Bright pink flowers, with a striking
yellow blotch. Plant habit rather open.   Moser & Fils.

```
                -caucasicum 1/2
MADAME JEANNE FRETS-
                -unknown 1/2
```
A parent of ROUGE de MAI. Early-blooming flowers of rose, with
a red blotch. C. Frets & Son.

MADAME JULES PORGES   Parentage unknown; possibly ponticum hybrid
6ft(1.8m) -10F(-23C) L   4/2   French hybrid. Flower pale mauve
with a large yellowish brown blotch. Habit straggly. Moser, c.
1900. Color illus. HG. p. 167.

MADAME LINDEN   Parentage unknown
A parent of several hybrids by Seidel. Flowers purplish violet.
J. Linden, 1873.

```
                -racemosum 1/2
MADAME LOTH-
                -Kurume azalea 1/2
```
Azaleodendron with 8-12 funnel-shaped flowers per truss, Persian
rose. W. H. Hardijzer raiser; J. van Gelderen, reg. 1965.

```
                -catawbiense 1/2
MADAME MASSON-
                -ponticum 1/2
```
5ft(1.5m) -15F(-26C) M 3/3   Large, well-shaped, dense shrub,
with shiny dark green foliage. White flowers with a golden yellow basal blotch; rather flat, separated lobes give a star-like

effect.   Bertin, 1849.   Color illus. F p. 52; VV p. 33.

```
                -campanulatum 1/2
MADAME NAUEN-
                -unknown 1/2
```
A parent of VIOLA, by Seidel.

MADAME NÉJEDLY   Parentage unknown
Flowers Bengal rose; dark spotting.   Koster, Boskoop, reg. 1965.

```
                -oreodoxa 1/2
MADAME OMEI-
                -forrestii Repens Group 1/2
```
Flowers of deep rose. Dietrich Hobbie, 1954.

MADAME POMPIDOU   Parentage unknown
Flowers salmon pink; trusses of 28.   Kordus, reg. 1972.

```
                -caucasicum 1/2
MADAME WAGNER-
                -unknown 1/2
```
5ft(1.5m) -25F(-32C) ML 3/3 Similar to VINCENT VAN GOGH and
RAINBOW, but hardier and with tighter truss.   Flowers have rose
margins and white centers.   Very old hybrid.   Confused with
PRINCESS MARY OF CAMBRIDGE, but not the same.   J. Macoy.

```
                -maddenii 1/2
MADDCHART-
                -chartophyllum var. praecox ? 1/2
```
Flowers open very pale lilac and fade white.   Magor. 1921.

MADGE BRAMLEY   Described under PHYLE DONEGAN, q.v.

```
* * * * * * * * * * * * * * * * * * * * * * * * * * * * * *
                -catawbiense var. album Glass--Catalgla 1/4
                              -catawbiense 1/8
            -Tony's-        -Catawbiense Album-
            - Gift -Belle -              -unknown 1/8
MADHATTER-      Heller-        -catawbiense
          -              -white catawbiense-
          -              hybrid      -unknown
          -Cunningham's Sulphur--caucasicum 1/2
```
Buds of pale purplish pink, opening to white flowers with purple
stamens. W. Delp.
SHEER DELIGHT   Parentage as above
Buds of vivid reddish purple; flowers strong reddish purple and
moderate purplish pink, white flare, yellow-green spots. Delp.
```
* * * * * * * * * * * * * * * * * * * * * * * * * * * * * *
```

```
                -fortunei ? 1/2
MADISON HILL-
                -unknown 1/2
```
5ft(1.5m) -5F(-21C) M   Plant rounded, wider than tall; foliage to 5.5in(14cm) long, yellowish green.   Fragrant flowers of
strong purplish pink, paler in the throat, no markings; corolla
4in(10.2cm) wide, of 5-6 wavy lobes. Spherical trusses hold 15.
C. O. Dexter cross; Gertrude Wister, reg. 1982.

MADISON SNOW--white form of dauricum (Phetteplace)
4.5ft(1.35m) x 3ft(.9m) -25F(-32C) M   Flowers of pure white,
slightly fragrant, 4 per truss; leaves with scaly indumentum.
Knight Hollow Nursery intro.; C. I. Wrzesinski, reg. 1988.

```
* * * * * * * * * * * * * * * * * * * * * * * * * * * * * *+
                              -decorum 1/4
                -unnamed hybrid-
          -              -griersonianum 1/4
MADONNA (Gable)-              -catawbiense 1/8
          -        -Parsons Grandiflorum-
          -America-              -unknown 3/8
                -dark red hybrid--unknown
```
Parent of LISA. White flower with yellow throat, fading to lav-
ender pink. Gable, 1947.
ANNIE DALTON   Parentage as above
5ft(1.5m) -15F(-26C) ML 4/2   Large, lax trusses of apricot
pink flowers, 4in(10cm) wide. Leaves 8.25in(21cm) long. Gable
cross; reg. 1960. A.E. 1960. Color illus. VV p. 16.
MARGARET VICTORIA   Parentage as above
2.5ft(.75m) -15(-26C) ML   Flowers moderate purplish pink with
dark orange-yellow spotting in dome-shaped trusses of 8-10. Upright plant, broad as tall. Gable; R. K. Peters, reg. 1983.
```
* * * * * * * * * * * * * * * * * * * * * * * * * * * * * *
```

```
                  -griffithianum 1/2
MADONNA(Messel)-
                  -Mrs. Messel--decorum 1/2
White flowers; hardy.  Messel.  A.M. 1931.
```

MADRAS   Described under BURMA, q.v.

MADRID   Described under BALLAD, q.v.

* *
```
                      -thomsonii 1/4
        -Barclayi Robert Fox-           -arboreum 1/8
MAESTRO-               -Glory of Penjerrick-
        -williamsianum 1/2             -griffithianum 1/8
```
3ft(.9m) -5F(-21C) EM   Dark red flowers, suffused with pink.
Gen. Harrison, reg. 1962.   P.C. 1969.   A.M. 1975.
CHARLOTTE CURRY   Parentage as above
Flowers deep red.   Gen. Harrison, reg. 1975.
* *

MAGGIE STOEFFEL   Parentage unknown
5ft(1.5m) OF(-18C) ML 4/4   Double flowers of light rose with
brownish crimson marks.   Whitney cross; Rutherford, reg. 1969.

* *
```
            -aberconwayi 1/2
MAGIC MOMENTS-
            -yakushimanum 1/2
```
4ft(1.2m) -10F(-23C) M 4/4   White flowers, a large, bright
maroon blotch on upper lobe; truss of 16-22. Floriferous plant;
Glossy green foliage.   John G. Lofthouse, reg. 1979.
DUNLOE   Parentage as above, except reversed
Flowers in truss of 7-9, campanulate, opening light red, fading
to pure white; reddish purple spots.   F. R. Waghorn, reg. 1983.
* *

```
                          -catawbiense 1/16
                -Atrosanguineum-
             -Atrier-            -unknown 1/16
    -Mary Belle-    -griersonianum 1/8
MAGIC-       -        -decorum 1/8
MOOD -     -Dechaem-
    -              -haenatodes 1/8
    -Honeydew (Dexter)--unknown 1/2
```
Buds of jasper red and moderate red, open to flowers of mimosa
yellow, throat of currant red; jasper red exterior.   W. Delp.

```
                    -wardii 1/4
            -unnamed hybrid-
MAGNAGLOSS-           -fortunei 1/4
            -unknown 1/2
```
5ft(1.5m) -15F(-26C) L Well-branched plant, as broad as tall;
yellow-green, glossy foliage. Flowers lilac orchid, conspicuous
blotch of grayed red; corolla funnel-shaped, 2.5in(6.4cm) wide;
ball-shaped trusses of 12.   G. Guy Nearing, reg. 1973.

```
                -fortunei ssp. discolor 1/4
      -Disca-      -decorum ? 1/8
      -    -Caroline-
      -              -brachycarpum ? 1/8
MAGNIFICAT-                        -griffithianum 1/16
      -                    -George Hardy-
      -            -Pink -          -catawbiense 3/16
      -            - Pearl-        -arboreum 1/16
      -Graf Zeppelin-    -Broughtonii-
      -                        -unknown 3/16
      -                        -catawbiense
            -Mrs. C. S. Sargent-
                        -unknown
```
7ft(2.1m) x 7ft(22 yrs) OF(-18) ML   Domed truss of 12-13 fra-
grant, wavy-edged flowers, 3.3in(8.5cm) wide. Bud strong spirea
red; flower white with rims of strong purplish pink, dorsal spot
brilliant yellow; calyx of tiny pink straps. Leaves elliptical,
flat, 6in(15.3cm) long. M. & B. Shapiro, cross 1966; reg. 1989.

MAGNIFICUM--form of cinnabarinum Roylei Group
Two other plants by this name are registered; both parentage unknown, by J. Waterer and Byls before 1839. In this one, flowers are exceptionally large, orange-red. Reuthe. A.M. 1918.

```
                    -ciliatum 1/4
          -Countess of Haddington-
MAGNIFLORUM-              -dalhousiae 1/4
          -edgeworthii 1/2
```
Exhibited by Parker, 1917.

```
                  -keiskei  1/4
        -Chink-
MAH JONG-     -trichocladum 1/4
        -valentinianum 1/2
```
2ft(.6m) -5F(-21C) E Light chartreuse green, tubular, unmark-
ed flowers in small truss of 3-5. Crown Estate, Windsor, reg.
1972. P.C. 1971.

* *
```
                            -griffithianum 1/16
                  -George Hardy-
        -Mrs. Lindsay-        -catawbiense 1/16
    -Harvest-  Smith    -Duchess of Edinburgh--unknown 1/4
    - Moon -              -campylocarpum 1/8
        -unnamed hybrid-
MAHARANI-           -unknown
            -          -campylocarpum Elatum Group 1/4
    -Letty Edwards-
            -fortunei 1/4
```
Trusses of 16 flowers, 5-lobed, grayed white tinged orchid pink,
shading inwards to ruby red, blotch about the same red. Foliage
elliptic-oval, glabrous. Hachmann cross; G. Stück, reg. 1983.
Color illus. WS, 1989, p. 137.
SIMONA   Parentage as above
Trusses of 12 flowers, very light Neyron rose, edged phlox pink,
blotched ruby red.   H. Hachmann, cross 1964; Stück, reg. 1983.
Gold Medal 1987.   Color illus. WS, 1989, p. 141.
* *

MAHMOUD   Parentage unknown
5ft(1.5m) OF(-18C) ML 3/3   Striking coloration of lavender
pink and a large, golden yellow eye.   Origin unknown.

```
                  -catawbiense var. album Glass 1/2
MAHOGANY LEAF-         -catawbiense 1/4
                -Pink Twins-
                        -haematodes 1/4
```
Flowers a mixing of lavenders and pinks with olive green spots;
white filaments.   Mitchener cross; R. Blough raiser.

MAIDEN'S BLUSH   Described under MRS. RANDALL DAVIDSON, q.v.

* *
```
    -haematodes 1/2
MAJOR-
    -thomsonii 1/2
```
Brilliant scarlet flowers set in the large thomsonii calyx. The
plant is medium-sized and rather compact.   Rothschild, 1947.
CHARLES MICHAEL   Parentage as above
A selection made by Charles Williams; exhibited 1948.
* *

```
                  -catawbiense var. album Glass--Catalgla 1/2
MAKING WAVES-          -fortunei ssp. discolor 1/4
                -Evening Glow-    -dichroanthum 1/8
                        -Fabia-
                        -griersonianum 1/8
```
Buds of claret rose opening to flowers of strong pink, with the
throat light orange.   W. Delp.

```
                      -fortunei ssp. discolor 1/4
            -Roberte-
            -          -campylocarpum Elatum Group 1/8
    -Coromandel-              -souliei 1/16
    -       -        -Soulbut-
    -       -              -fortunei--Sir Charles Butler
MALABAR-    -Vanessa-                            1/16
    -              -griersonianum 3/16
    -  -dichroanthum 5/16
    -Marmora-    -fortunei ssp. discolor
            -Margaret-    -dichroanthum
            Dunn   -Fabia-
                        -griersonianum
```
Mimosa yellow flowers, deepening in the throat.   James Russell,
Sunningdale, reg. 1972.

```
                -arboreum 1/4
        -Gill's Triumph-
MALAHAT-            -griffithianum 1/4
        -strigillosum 1/2
```
Trusses of 14 flowers, guardsman red, spotted deeper red, 2.75in
(7cm) across, 6-lobed. Leaves to 6in(15.2cm), with sparse coppery brown indumentum beneath. H. L. Larson, reg. 1983. Col-
or illus. ARS J 43: (1989), p. 31.

```
                        -thomsonii 1/8
            -Ascot Brilliant-
            -              -unknown 3/16
    -J. G. Millais-       -George-griffithianum 1/16
    -                     - Hardy-
MALCOLM-        -Pink Pearl-      -catawbiense 1/16
ALLAN -         -              -arboreum 1/16
    -                -Broughtonii-
    -neriiflorum 1/2              -unknown
```
Deep red flowers. Sir James Horlick, 1931.

```
                    -griffithianum 1/4
        -Loderi King George-
MALEMUTE-                -fortunei 1/4
        -unnamed orange hybrid by Lem--unknown 1/2
```
5ft(1.5m) 10F(-12C) EM   Buds spirea red, opening phlox pink,
darker blotch and edges, openly funnel-shaped, 5in(12.7cm) wide,
7 wavy lobes, fragrant; lax 10-flowered trusses. Floriferous.
Plant rounded, wider than tall; ivy green leaves 6in(15cm) long.
Halfdan Lem, cross 1966; J. Elliott, reg. 1978.

```
                    -auriculatum 1/4
        -unnamed hybrid-
MALETTA-             -fortunei ssp. discolor 1/4
        -            -ungernii 1/4
        -unnamed hybrid-
                    -unknown 1/4
```
5ft(1.5m) 5F(-15C) ML   Flowers cream in center, edged with
old gold, openly funnel-campanulate, 3.25in(8.3cm) wide, frilly;
pyramidal trusses hold 13 to 15. Plant rather compact; foliage
to 6in(15.2cm) long.   Henry R. Yates, intro. 1970; reg. 1972.
Color illus. LW pl. 93.

```
                -racemosum 1/4
            -Conemaugh-
MALTA---PIONEER, selfed-    -mucronulatum 1/4
    (Gable)    -unknown 1/2
```
4ft(1.2m) -25F(-32C) E 4/4 Plant rounded, broader than tall,
twiggy; red-stemmed leaves 2.5in(6.4cm) long. Flower mauve pink
flushed deeper amaranth rose, semi-double, widely funnel-shaped,
1.75in(4.5cm) across; ball-shaped trusses of 2-6. Floriferous.
David G. Leach, cross 1956; reg. 1981.

MAMIE   Described under FINESSE, q.v.

MAMIE DOUD EISENHOWER   Parentage unknown
Pure white flowers in a truss of 30.   Kordus, reg. 1972.

MAMMOTH PINK   Described under BAREFIELD'S LIZA, q.v.

```
                        -griffithianum 1/8
            -Queen Wilhelmina-
    -Britannia-             -unknown 3/8
MAN OF WAR-     -Stanley Davies--unknown
    -                   -griffithianum 1/4
        -Loderi King George-
                    -fortunei 1/4
```
A vigorous plant with large foliage, 10in(25.4cm) x 4in(10cm).
Rose red flowers with dark spots, held in conical trusses of 15.
Marshall Lyons, reg. 1972.

```
                    -griffithianum 1/8
            -Mars-
        -Vulcan-    -unknown 1/8
MANDA SUE-     -griersonianum 1/4
    -          -campylocarpum 1/4
        -Elspeth-
            -hardy hybrid--unknown 1/4
```
3ft(.9m) 0F(-18C) M 4/3 Plant of compact habit; bright green
leaves 4in(10cm) long. Flowers shell pink, with red margins and
yellowish centers, in trusses of 12-14. G. L. Baker, reg. 1971.

```
            -haematodes 1/2
MANDALAY-
            -venator 1/2
```
4ft(1.2m) -10F(-23C) EM 3/4   Plant of compact habit; foliage
deeply veined. Waxy, deep red flowers with dark spots in loose
trusses. Rothschild, 1947.

```
                -fortunei
        -unnamed hybrid-
        -              -haematodes
MANDARIN-              -Mars (griffithianum x)
        -Frazzles (Gable)-
                    -Cathaem (catawbiense x haematodes)
```
Rosy orange flowers, hose-in-hose; centers paler. Hard to
propagate. V. & C. R. Haag cross; Dr. T. Ring raiser.

```
                -campylocarpum Elatum Group 1/4
        -Letty Edwards-
MANDARIN-       -fortunei 1/4
        -griersonianum 1/2
```
Flowers of orange salmon.   Thacker, 1946.

MANDARIN   See KINABALU MANDARIN

```
        -lacteum 1/2
MANDATE-
        -thomsonii 1/2
```
Clear pink flowers, 3.5in(8.9cm) wide, in trusses of 10. Early.
Gen. Harrison, reg. 1967.

```
                        -griffithianum 1/8
                    -George-
            -Betty -Hardy -catawbiense 1/8
                -Wormald-
        -Scandinavia-    -unknown 7/32
        -       -          -griffithianum
        -       -   -George-
        -       -Hugh -Hardy -catawbiense
MANDERLEY-      Koster-             -arboreum 1/32
        -           -unnamed-Doncaster-
        -           hybrid--unknown
        -               unknown
        -       -dichroanthum 1/4
        -Fabia-
            -griersonianum 1/4
```
4ft(1.2m) -5F(-21C) M 3/4   Campanulate flowers, cardinal red
with darker spots. New foliage reddish; a medium compact plant.
Slootjes, reg. 1969.   A.M. Boskoop 1965.   A.M. Wisley Trials
1983.

```
            -griffithianum 1/2
MANGLESII-          -catawbiense 1/4
        -unnamed white hybrid-
                    -unknown 1/4
```
White flowers, spotted pink. Veitch. F.C.C. 1885.

```
                -minus Carolinianum Group 1/8
            -Conestoga-
        -Windbeam-      -racemosum 1/8
MANITAU-      -unknown 3/4
        -unknown
```
3ft(.9m) -25F(-32C) EM 4/3 Similar to WINDBEAM but more com-
pact. Small leaves, sun-resistant. Light pink flowers from top
to bottom of shrub. Origin unknown.

MANIVALDE---seedling of praestens
12ft(3.6m) x 8ft(2.4m)(25 yrs) 10F(-12C) E Truss of 20+ flowers, scented, of heavy substance, 3in(7.6cm) broad, oblique campanulate. Rosy buds, opening Neyron rose to pale Egyptian buff.
Leaves 15in(38cm) x 7in(18cm), glossy, with fawn felt-like hairs
below; held 3 years.   H. Vaartnou raiser; reg. 1989.

MANNHEIM   Described under ELISABETH HOBBIE, q.v.

```
                    -catawbiense 1/4
        -Catawbiense Boursault-
MANNIE WEBER-       -unknown 3/4
        -Madame Albert Moser--unknown
```
4ft(1.2m) -5F(-21C) ML 3/3 Flowers of imperial purple, upper
lobe spotted fern green, flat saucer-shaped, 3.5in(8.9cm) wide,
5 frilled lobes; truss holds 14. Upright plant; very dark green
leaves held 3 years.   Edwin O. Weber, reg. 1974.

```
        -tephropeplum 1/2
MANON-
    -ciliatum 1/2
```
3ft(.9m) 5F(-15C) EM 3/3   Pure white flowers. Adams-Acton,
1942.   Another MANON, "cross of SAPPHO", in Fairweather, p. 53.

* *

```
        -dichroanthum 5/16
    -Dido-
    -    -decorum 5/16
    -                            -fortunei ssp. discolor 1/16
MANOR-         -Lady        -
  HILL-       -Bessborough-campylocarpum Elatum Gp. 1/16
    -     -Jalisco-    -dichroanthum
  -unnamed-       -Dido-
    hybrid-       -decorum
        -yakushimanum 1/4
```
Very dwarf, compact habit, buttercup yellow flowers in trusses
of 8-9. Leaves dark green with sparse brown indumentum.   Crown
Estate, Windsor, reg. 1974.   A.M. 1974.
WINDLES   Parentage as above
Yellowish orange flowers in trusses of 6-8. Crown Estate, 1974.
* *

* *
```
        -falconeri 1/2
MANSELLII-
    -grande 1/2
```
Shown by Downie, 1875.
MURIEL   Parentage as above
Creamy white with a dark crimson blotch.   Loder. A.M. 1925.
* *

```
                                    -catawbiense
                    -Parsons Grandiflorum-        1/16
        -Nova Zembla-               -unknown 7/16
    -Blinklicht-       -dark red hybrid--unknown
    -       -      -griffithianum 1/4
MANUELA-     -Mars-
    -       -unknown
    -           -Mars (as above)
    -unnamed hybrid-
        -yakushimanum 1/4
```
3.2ft(1m) x 4.7ft(1.4m) -10F(-23C) ML Truss of 14-18 flowers,
strong mallow purple, paling in throat, vivid magenta midveins.
Dorsal lobe marked lettuce green on white ground. Broad, ovate
leaves; thin, pale indumentum. Hachmann; Stück, reg. 1988.

MARALYN GILLESPIE   Parentage unknown; probably a Dexter hybrid
6ft(1.8m) high x 8ft(2.4m)(11 yrs) -5F(-21C) M   Flowers in a
ball truss of 9, 7-lobed, pale purplish pink with a strong reddish purple blotch and 2 flares.   Scott Arboretum, reg. 1986.

```
        -Pauline--unknown 1/2
MARATHON-
    -elliottii 1/2
```
Plant of moderate height, spreading habit; rather tender. Flowers bright red, in late midseason.   Rothschild, 1947.

MARATHONER   See MILESTONE

MARBELLA   Described under ISABELLA, q.v.

```
        -caucasicum (citrinum)? 1/2
MARCH SUN-       -campylocarpum 1/4
    -Moonstone-
        -williamsianum 1/4
```
1.5ft(.45m) -5F(-21C) E Flowers lemon yellow with small crim-
son blotch in throat, campanulate, 2.25in(5.7cm) wide, 5-lobed;
tight truss of 12. Very compact plant; olive green leaves, 2.5
in(6.4cm) long.   Rollin G. Wyrens, reg. 1965.   P.A. 1963.

```
        -maximum 1/2
MARCHIONESS OF LANSDOWNE-
        -unknown 1/2
```
5ft(1.5m) -15F(-26C) L 3/3   Flowers of soft violet rose with
a striking dark blotch, in neat domed trusses; "a proud beauty".
Plant habit spreading, rather open. Long blooming period; heat-
tolerant. A. Waterer, before 1915. Color illus. VV p. 107.

MARCHIONESS OF TWEEDDALE   Parentage unknown
Large rosy crimson flowers; upper lobes paler with yellow spots.

Origin unknown.   A.M. 1906.

```
        -campylocarpum 3/4
MARCIA-      -campylocarpum
    -Gladys-
        -fortunei 1/4
```
4ft(1.2m) 0F(-18C) EM 4/3   Upright, slow-growing plant; med-
ium green leaves 3.5in(8.9cm) long. Flower rich primrose yellow
with small red eye, campanulate; rounded compact trusses. Needs
some shade.   Lord Swaythling. F.C.C. 1944.

```
                                    -griffithianum
                        -Queen Wilhelmina-     1/16
                -Britannia-         -unknown 5/16
        -Purple Lace-       -Stanley Davies--unknown
MARCIA JOY-     -       -ponticum 1/8
  ELLIS  -       -Purple Splendour-
        -yakushimanum 1/2      -unknown
```
3ft(.9m) x 3ft 0F(18C) M   Deep purplish pink buds open light
purplish pink, rims deeper pink; 15 per truss. Elliptic, medium
olive green leaves.   Peste, cross 1976; S. Johnston, reg. 1986.

MARDI GRAS   Described under BUCKLAND, q.v.

MARG SAWERS   Described under LOCKINGTON PRIDE, q.v.

MARGARET   Parentage unknown
A parent of several hybrids. Large trusses of widely funnel-
shaped flowers; rose-colored buds opening to white with a blackish crimson flare.   Origin unknown; possibly Lowinsky.

```
        -hybrid unknown 1/2
MARGARET ALICE-     -forrestii Repens Group 1/4
        -Elizabeth-
            -griersonianum 1/4
```
3ft(.9m) -10F(-23C) EM   Plant wider than tall, branches decum-
bent. Flowers Tyrian rose, small red streaks in throat, openly
funnel-shaped, 3.25in(8.3cm) wide, 6 waxy lobes; spherical truss
of about 8.   J. Freeman Stephens, reg. 1973.

```
        -campylocarpum 1/2
MARGARET BEAN-          -griffithianum 1/8
        -Loderi King-
    -Esmeralda- George  -fortunei 1/8
        -neriiflorum 1/4
```
Yellow flowers, fringed in pink.   RBG, Kew, 1935.

MARGARET BLOUGH   Described under FLADA W. BLOUGH, q.v.

MARGARET CUTTEN   Described under PERRI CUTTEN, q.v.

* *
```
        -fortunei ssp. discolor 1/2
MARGARET DUNN-      -dichroanthum 1/4
        -Fabia-
            -griersonianum 1/4
```
Flowers apricot pink, flushed shell pink, openly funnel-shaped,
3.5in(8.9cm) wide; loose truss of 8-9. Floriferous bush. Slim
elliptic leaves 6in(15.2cm) long. Lord Swaythling. A.M. 1946.
AUTUMN GOLD   Parentage as above
5ft(1.5m) -5F(-21C) ML 4/3   Flowers apricot salmon, shaded
pink, with an orange eye, about 10 in a truss. Light green foliage, slightly twisted. Van Veen, Sr., 1956.
EVENING GLOW   Parentage as above
5ft(1.5m) -5F(-21C) L 4/3 Flowers bright yellow with a prominent calyx; lax trusses. Compact plant habit; foliage narrow,
light green, to (12.7cm) long. Needs light shade.   Van Veen,
Sr., reg. 1958. Color illus. VV p. 19.
GOLDEN BELLE   Parentage as above
4ft(1.2m) 0F(-18C) ML 3/3 Large flowers of orange and yellow
tones, with deep pink edges, blooming in mid-season on a compact
spreading plant.   John Henny, reg. 1958.
KING OF SHRUBS   Parentage as above
4ft(1.2m) 0F(-18C) ML 4/3   One of the best orange flowers,
4in(10cm) wide, of good substance, in lax truss of 9-10. Yellow
stripes from the throat flare merge with orange at edges; mar-
gin banded rose. Plant wider than tall, open.   E. Ostbo, reg.
1958. P.A. 1950. Color illus. VV p. 62.
MARGARET DUNN TALISMAN   Parentage as above
5ft(1.5m) 0F(-18C) L 3/3 Synonym TALISMAN. Flowers funnel-
shaped, narrow, apricot colored, in flattened trusses. Medium
green leaves to 6in(15.2cm) long. Rudolph Henny, reg. 1958.

MARYKE Parentage as above
5ft(1.5m) -5F(-21C) ML 4/3 Flowers a beautiful pastel blend
of light pink and yellow, 3in(7.6cm) wide, 7-lobed; dome-shaped
trusses of 14. Plant erect, full; elliptic leaves of dull olive
green. Van Veen, Sr., reg. 1974.   Color illus. VV p. 56.
* *
* *

```
                        -griffithianum 1/8
              -Mars-
        -Vulcan-    -unknown 1/8
MARGARET EINARSON-    -griersonianum 1/2
        -    -griersonianum
              -Azor-
                    -fortunei ssp. discolor 1/4
```
2ft(.6m) 5F(-15C) L   Shrub rounded, well-branched, slightly
broader than high; boat-shaped, light green leaves; new growth
coppery bronze. Flowers glowing geranium lake with deep rose
stripes on reverse, openly funnel-shaped, 2.5in(6.4cm) wide, 6-
lobed; round trusses of 12. Mrs. Sigrid Laxdall, reg. 1977.
AUDREY DEFANE   Parentage as above
9.5ft(2.85m) x 6ft(1.8m)(25 yrs) OF(-18C) VL Flowers in ball
truss of 8; corolla openly funnel-shaped, 5 smooth-edged lobes.
Deep pink buds open to deep pink , with throat strong red, exterior has darker pink stripes. Sigrid Laxdall, reg. 1989.
CATHERINE OLSON Parentage as above
4ft(1.2m) x 5ft(1.5m)(23 yrs) 10F(-12C) VL Strong claret rose
buds opening to flowers 2.3in(5.8cm) wide; 6 wavy lobes broadly
edged in bud color, centers paler, throat light empire rose; lax
truss of 9-10. Flat elliptic leaves; coppery new growth. Mrs.
Sigrid Laxdall, cross 1961; reg. 1986.
PRESIDENT VIGDIS   Parentage as above
8.5ft(2.5m) high x 20ft(6m)(26 yrs) OF(-18C) M Trusses of 12;
buds deep purplish pink, open light purplish pink; 6 wavy lobes,
striped darker pink. Elliptic leaves, hairless. Laxdall, 1987.
ROGER CASH   Parentage as above
6ft(1.8m) x 4ft(1.2m)(28 yrs) OF(-18C) VL Deep pink buds open
strong red. Flower 2.75in(7cm) wide; domed trusses of 5-6. Elliptic, smooth leaves, 5in(12.cm) long. S. Laxdall, reg. 1988.
* *

MARGARET FALMOUTH   Described under ISABELLA, q.v.

```
              -Scintillation--unknown
MARGARET FELL-
              -white hybrid--unknown
```
8ft(2.4m) tall x 11ft(3.3m)(26 yrs) -5F(-21C) M   Buds strong
purplish pink opening pale purplish pink flowers (soon fading to
white) with a brilliant greenish yellow blotch, fragrant, 5- to
7-lobed. Scott Hort. Foundation, Swarthmore College, reg. 1985.

```
              -wardii 1/2
MARGARET FINDLAY-
              -griersonianum 1/2
```
Flowers are almost white with a red stain at the base of throat.
Sir James Horlick raiser; Crown Estate Commissioners exhibited.
P.C. 1974.

```
              -Pink Dexter--unknown 3/4
MARGARET KNIGHT-
              -    -ponticum 1/4
              -Purple Splendour-
              -    -unknown
```
3.5ft(1m) OF(-18C) M Plant of compact habit, wider than tall;
dark green leaves 5.5in(14cm) long. Flowers light violet purple
rimmed in medium violet with a blotch of ruby red, 3.5in(8.9cm)
across. Trusses of 14. Clarence Loeb, reg. 1971.

```
        -Marion (Cheal)--unknown    -griffithianum 1/16
MARGARET-              -George Hardy-
  MACK  -  -Pink Pearl-    -catawbiense 1/16
      -Annie E.-    -    -arboreum 1/16
        Endtz  -    -Broughtonii-
            -unknown (13/16)    -unknown
```
5ft(1.5m) OF(-18C) EM 4/3   Flowers soft lilac pink fading
paler to center, upper lobe scant spotting of deep rose, widely
campanulate with 5 frilled lobes. Leaves rich green, margins
slightly concave. V. J. Boulter, reg. 1965.

MARGARET MEAD--form of veitchianum
4ft(1.2m) 20F(-6C) M-L 4/3 A plant for the cool greenhouse.
White flowers flushed slightly with orange-red in upper throat,
openly funnel-shaped, 5-lobed, to 3.5in(8.9cm) wide. Dull green
leaves, scaly below. Geoffrey Gorer, reg. 1979. A.M. 1978.

MARGARET ROSE   Listed under JUBILEE QUEEN, q.v.

```
                    -Moser's Maroon--unknown 1/2
            -Purple Emperor-
MARGARET SINDORFF-    -unknown
        -    -fortunei--Sir Charles Butler
        -Van Nes Sensation-    -maximum 1/4
                    -Halopeanum-
                        -griffithianum 1/4
```
Mauve buds; light amethyst purple, broadly funnel-shaped flowers
with large dorsal flare, green fading light bronze yellow; conical truss of 12. Elliptic leaves to 5.5in(14cm); bush 4ft(1.2m)
tall. N. Sullivan, Australia, raiser; reg. 1989.

MARGARET VICTORIA   Described under MADONNA (Gable), q.v.

MARGE DANIK   Described under BOB DANIK, q.v.

MARGELA   Described under LIMERICK, q.v.

```
              -catawbiense 3/4
    -Mrs. Milner-
MARGOT-    -unknown 1/4
    -catawbiense
```
Dark purplish red with brown markings.   Seidel, cross 1910.

```
        -Mucronatum--unknown 1/2
MARGOT-
        -micranthum 1/2
```
Azaleodendron. Vivid magenta pink flowers.   C. Ingram, 1937.

```
        -smirnowii 1/2
MARGRET-
        -unknown 1/2
```
Flowers in trusses of 9-16, of salmon rose, with yellowish green
spotting. Intro. 1954; Heinje Baumschulen, reg. 1986. Color
illus. WS, 1989, p. 114.

```
        -catawbiense 1/2
MARGUERITE-
        -unknown 1/2
```
Deep pink flowers. Paul Bosley, Sr., before 1958.

```
        -late-flowering hybrid--unknown
MARHAM-
        -Mary Waterer--unknown
```
Pink with a red eye and speckled blotch. Knap Hill, reg. 1968.

```
        -President Roosevelt--unknown 3/4
MARIA VAN ZELM-    -campylocarpum 1/4
        -Lady Primrose-
              -unknown
```
Funnel-shaped flowers in truss of 12-15, moderate purplish pink.
Leaves lanceolate. Bush to 3.3ft(1m). T. Slykerman, reg. 1985.

```
                    -wardii
              -unnamed-    -neriiflorum
              - hybrid-F. C. Puddle-
        -Virginia-    -griersonianum
        -Richards-              -griff.
        -    -    -George-
    -Vera -    - Hardy-cataw.
    -Elliott-    -Mrs. Lindsay-
    -    -    - Smith    -Duchess of
MARIAN-    -Mrs. Betty-    Edinburgh--unk.
CORLEY-    Robertson-    -campylocarpum
    -    -    -unnamed-
    -    -fortunei    hybrid-unknown
    -Loder's White, q.v. (2 possible parentages)
```
4.5ft(1.4m) x 6ft(1.8m) 5F(-15C) M Flowers of heavy substance
in ball truss of 8, fragrant; buds medium purplish pink open to
yellowish pink, 7 frilled lobes; corolla 4in(10cm) wide. Plant
open; leaves to 6in(15cm), held 2 years. W. Elliott, reg. 1989.

MARIANNE HARDY   Described under REPOSE, q.v.

MARIA'S CHOICE   Described under YELLOW GOLD, q.v.

MARICEE Described under LIZ ANN, q.v.

```
                      -griffithianum 1/8
                -Loderi-
            -Albatross-      -fortunei 1/8
MARIE ANTOINETTE-      -fortunei ssp. discolor 1/2
            -        -fortunei ssp. discolor
            -Ariel-
                -Memoir--unknown 1/4
```
White flowers blushed pink and flecked yellow-green, in enormous
conical trusses.   Plant tall, upright, blooming late midseason.
Rothschild, 1945.

MARIE GIASI   Described under DELENDICH, q.v.

```
                        -fortunei 1/4
                -Queen Souriya-        -campylocarpum 1/8
MARIE IRENE-         -unnamed hybrid-
            -unknown            -unknown 5/8
```
Flowers 7-lobed, to 4.7in(12cm), opening almost flat with lobes
recurved, deep purplish pink lighter in center; dark red throat,
darker flare, dorsal spots medium ruby; truss of 12.   Narrow elliptic leaves; bush 6.5ft(2m) tall (c.15 yrs); blooms Oct.-Nov.,
NZ. Seed from ARS. A. Harris raiser; Mrs. I. Henry; reg. 1988.

```
                -yakushimanum 1/4
      -unnamed hybrid-            -dichroanthum 1/8
      -          -Fabia (red form)-
      -                    -griersonianum 1/8
MARIE -            -wardii 1/8          -griffithianum 3/64
STARKS-   -Idealist-        -Kewense-
   -      -      -    -Aurora-      -fortunei 5/64
   -      -      -Naomi-      -thomsonii 1/32
   -Odee -            -fortunei          -griffithianum
   Wright-                -George Hardy-
   -            -Mrs. Lindsay-        -catawbiense 1/32
   -Mrs. Betty- Smith    -Duchess of Edinburgh--unk.
     Robertson -          -campylocarpum 1/16
                -unnamed hybrid-
                    -unknown 1/8
```
4ft(1.2m) x 3ft(.9m) -10F(-23C) EM   Flowers 3.5in(9cm) wide,
7-lobed, light yellow-green to brilliant yellow-green, dark red
dorsal blotch; truss of 14-18, 7in(17.8cm) x 7in. E. Murray,
cross 1974; M. Starks, reg. 1985.

```
         -vernicosum 1/2
MARIE  -          -wardii 1/8
TIETJENS-   -Crest-          -fortunei ssp. discolor 1/16
   -      -      -Lady    -
   -Full-      Bessborough-campylocarpum 1/16
   Moon-                  -griffithianum 1/32
   -          -Mrs.   -George Hardy-
   -Harvest-Lindsay-          -catawbiense 1/32
     Moon  - Smith -Duchess of Edinburgh--unknown 1/8
         -            -campylocarpum 1/16
         -unnamed hybrid-
                    -unknown
```
3ft(.9m) -10F(-23C) ML Flowers soft spirea red, unmarked, 3.5
in(8.9cm) broad, 7 wavy-edged lobes; ball trusses of 7. Floriferous. Plant wider than tall; glossy leaves 6.5in(16.5cm) long.
L. Bagoly, cross 1969; Marie Tietjens raiser; reg. 1976.

```
               -degronianum ssp. heptamereum 1/8
      -First Step, F2-   (metternechii)--Metternianus
   -Tosca-      -arboreum 1/8
   -      -      -griersonianum 1/8
MARIETTA-   -Vulcan's Flame-   -griffithianum 1/16
   -               -Mars-
   -                  -unknown 1/16
   -yakushimanum--Koichiro Wada 1/2
```
13.8in(35cm) x 2.7ft(.8m) -15F(-26C) ML Deep pink buds; flow-
ers campanulate, about 2in(5cm) broad, wavy-edged, pale greenish
yellow fading paler and tinged pink, oxblood red dorsal spots.
Ovate shiny leaves, scant indumentum.   Hachmann, cross 1968;
Stück, reg. 1988. Color illus. WS, 1989, p. 156.

* *
```
            -caucasicum 1/4
      -Dr. Stocker-
MARILOO-          -griffithianum 1/4
      -lacteum 1/2
```
6ft(1.8m) 10F(-12C) EM 4/3   Named for Mrs. Lionel de Roth-
schild. Called the superior lacteum hybrid of Exbury. Flowers
bell-shaped, pale lemon yellow, flushed green; tubular campanu-

---

late on opening; the green tint fades and the tube expands. Very
large trusses, perfectly shaped; leaves about 6in(15.2cm) long.
Considered "a superlative plant."   Rothschild, 1941.   Color
illus. PB pl. 29.
MARILOO EUGENIE   Parentage as above
6ft(1.8m) 10F(-12C) EM 4/3   Similar to the above plant, with
flowers pale cream or creamy white, a few small crimson spots.
Magnificent truss of up to 17 flowers. Rothschild. A.M. 1950.
Color illus. PB pl. 30.
MARILOO GILBURY   Parentage as above.
6ft(1.8m) 10F(-12C) EM 4/3   Similar to above. Flowers pale
creamy pink with dark pink stripes on reverse of lobes. Rothschild. A.M. 1943.
* *

```
            -elliottii 1/4
      -Fusilier-
MARILYN-      -griersonianum 1/2
   -      -dichroanthum 1/4
      -Fabia-
         -griersonianum
```
A low, dwarf plant with narrow leaves, 2.5in(6.4cm) long. Large
flowers red to scarlet, orange tint.   Rudolph Henny, reg. 1965.

```
         -brachycarpum ssp. fauriei 1/2
MARIMBA-      -dichroanthum 1/4
      -Goldsworth Orange-
            -fortunei ssp. discolor 1/4
```
4ft(1.2m) -15F(-26C) ML Very hardy. Pink and yellow flowers
in trusses of 14-16. Hachmann cross; Stück, reg. 1985.

MARINE--form of augustinii
6ft(1.8m) 10F(-12C) EM 3/3   Habit typical of the species,
rather slender until mature. Flattened flowers, deep lavender
blue, spotted purple on upper petal; truss of 3.   Small leaves
medium green. J. Barto raiser; Bovees, reg. 1962. P.A. 1960.

* *
```
      -Lady      -fortunei ssp. discolor 3/16
      -Bessborough-
   -Day Dream-      -campylocarpum Elatum Group 3/16
   -      -griersonianum 1/4
MARINER-      -wardii 1/8
   -      -Hawk-
   -      -Lady      -fortunei ssp. discolor
   -Honey -      Bessborough-
   (Slocock)-      -campylocarpum Elatum Group
      -      -wightii 1/8
      -China-
         -fortunei 1/8
```
4ft(1.2m) -10F(-23C) L Truss of 15-20 flowers, unfading prim-
rose yellow with a greenish yellow blotch, ochre in bud.   A. F.
George, Hydon, reg. 1966.
MASTER MARINER   Parentage as above
Similar to above; new foliage bronze; large trusses of apricot-
colored flowers. Hydon Nurseries.
* *

```
            -dichroanthum 1/8
      -Astarte-         -campylocarpum Elatum Group 1/16
      -      -Penjerrick-
   -Solon-         -griffithianum 3/16
   -      -griffithianum
MARINKA-   -Sunrise-
   -      -griersonianum 3/8
   -      -griersonianum
   -Rapture-
      -arboreum ssp. zeylanicum 1/4
```
Pale rose flowers. Lord Aberconway, intro. 1950.

MARINUS KOSTER Described under BETTY WORMALD, q.v.

```
                  -griffithianum 1/8
            -George Hardy-
   -Pink Pearl-      -catawbiense 3/8
   -      -      -arboreum 1/8
MARION-   -Broughtonii-
   -            -unknown 3/8
   -               -catawbiense
   -Catawbiense Grandiflorum-
                  -unknown
```
Very hardy. Frilled lilac pink flowers.   Felix & Dijkhuis.

Plate 1. 'Abe Arnott' by Weber
PHOTO BY GREER

Plate 2. 'Abegail' by Phetteplace
PHOTO BY GREER

Plate 3. 'Abendsonne' by Hobbie
PHOTO BY GREER

Plate 4. 'Abraham Lincoln' by Parsons
PHOTO BY GREER

Plate 5. 'Ada Lohr' by Blough
PHOTO BY BLOUGH

Plate 6. 'Adelphia' by Dexter
PHOTO BY KELLAM

Plate 7. 'Admiral Piet Hein' by C. B. van Nes
PHOTO BY GREER

Plate 8. 'Albatross' by Rothschild
PHOTO BY GREER

Plate 9. 'Alice Poore' by Dexter
PHOTO BY LEONARD

Plate 10. 'Aloha' by Phetteplace/Briggs/Paden
PHOTO BY GREER

Plate 11. 'Amigo' by Goheen
PHOTO BY GREER

Plate 12. 'Amphion' by A. Waterer
PHOTO BY AUSTIN

Plate 13. 'Anica Bricogne', origin unknown

Plate 14. 'Anna Baldsiefen' by Baldsiefen

Plate 15. 'Anna Rose Whitney' by Whitney/T. Van Veen, Sr.

Plate 16. 'Anne Teese' by A. J. Teese

Plate 17. 'Anne's Delight' by Whitney/Sather

Plate 18. 'Annie Dalton' by Gable

Plate 19. 'Antoon Van Welie' by Endtz
PHOTO BY GREER

Plate 20. 'Apodeno' by Aberconway
PHOTO BY GREER

Plate 21. 'Apricot Delight' by Van de Ven
PHOTO BY WITHERS

Plate 22. 'April Chimes' by Hillier
PHOTO BY GREER

Plate 23. 'Aries' by Ramsden
PHOTO BY GREER

Plate 24. 'Arthur J. Ivens' by Hillier
PHOTO BY GREER

Plate 25. 'Audacious' by Brueckner
PHOTO BY BRUECKNER

Plate 26. 'Aurora' by Gill/Rothschild
PHOTO BY SALLEY

Plate 27. 'Autumn Gold' by T. Van Veen, Sr.
PHOTO BY GREER

Plate 28. 'Avalanche' by Rothschild
PHOTO BY GREER

Plate 29. 'Baden-Baden' by Hobbie
PHOTO BY GREER

Plate 30. 'Balalaika' by Hachmann
PHOTO BY BRIGGS

Plate 31. 'Ballet' by Pride
PHOTO BY BROWNING

Plate 32. 'Balta' by Mezitt
PHOTO BY GREER

Plate 33. 'Barbara Behring' by Behring
PHOTO BY BEHRING

Plate 34. 'Barbara Wallace' by C. B. van Nes
PHOTO BY GREER

Plate 35. 'Bariton' by Hachmann
PHOTO BY BRIGGS

Plate 36. 'Barmstedt' by Hachmann
PHOTO BY BRIGGS

Plate 37. 'Bashful Betty' by J. Elliott/Fisher
PHOTO BY GREER

Plate 38. 'Bass River' by Dexter
PHOTO BY LEONARD

Plate 39. 'Belona' by Hachmann
PHOTO BY BRIGGS

Plate 40. 'Berg's Yellow' by Berg
PHOTO BY GREER

Plate 41. 'Bernard Shaw' by Reuthe
PHOTO BY GREER

Plate 42. 'Besse Howells' by Shammarello
PHOTO BY GREER

Plate 43. 'Betty Anderson' by E. Anderson
PHOTO BY GREER

Plate 44. 'Betty Sears' by Whitney/Sather
PHOTO BY GREER

Plate 45. 'Betty Wormald' by M. Koster
PHOTO BY GREER

Plate 46. 'Betty's Bells' by Sheedy/Skei
PHOTO BY GREER

Plate 47. 'Billy Budd' by Hanger
PHOTO BY GREER

Plate 48. 'Black Sport' by Nelson/Briggs
PHOTO BY GREER

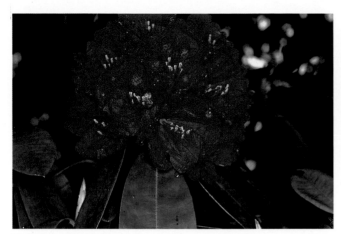

Plate 49. 'Blandyanum' by Standish and Noble
PHOTO BY GREER

Plate 50. 'Blue Bell' by C. B. van Nes
PHOTO BY GREER

Plate 51. 'Blue Ensign' by Slocock
PHOTO BY SALLEY

Plate 52. 'Blue Pacific' by Whitney/Sather
PHOTO BY GREER

Plate 53. 'Blue Star' by Gen. Harrison
PHOTO BY GREER

Plate 54. 'Blue Tit' by J. C. Williams
PHOTO BY GREER

Plate 55. 'Bluette' by Lancaster
PHOTO BY GREER

Plate 56. 'Bob', a hybrid from New Zealand
PHOTO BY GREER

Plate 57. 'Bodnant Yellow' by Aberconway
PHOTO BY SPADY

Plate 58. 'Brandt Red' by Brandt
PHOTO BY GREER

Plate 59. 'Brinny' by Graves/Janeck
PHOTO BY GREER

Plate 60. 'Britton Hill' by Britt Smith
PHOTO BY GREER

Plate 62. 'Brocade' by Rothschild
PHOTO BY GREER

Plate 61. 'Britton Hill Bugle' by Britt Smith
PHOTO BY GREER

Plate 63. 'Buchanan Simpson' by Greig
PHOTO BY GREER

Plate 64. 'Burgundy Cherry' by Dexter/Knippenberg
PHOTO BY LEONARD

Plate 65. 'Burgundy Rose' by Lem
PHOTO BY GREER

Plate 66. 'Buttermint' by Mauritsen/Greer
PHOTO BY GREER

Plate 67. 'C.O.D.' by Dexter/Everitt
PHOTO BY LEONARD

Plate 68. 'C. P. Raffill' from R.B.G., Kew
PHOTO BY GREER

Plate 69. 'Cabaret' by Sather
PHOTO BY GREER

Plate 70. 'Cadis' by Gable
PHOTO BY GREER

Plate 71. 'Caerhays John' by J. C. Williams
PHOTO BY GREER

Plate 72. 'Caerhays Philip' by Charles Williams
PHOTO BY GREER

Plate 73. 'Camillo Schneider' by Hobbie
PHOTO BY GREER

Plate 74. 'Campy' by Shammarello
PHOTO BY SALLEY

Plate 75. 'Canadian Beauty' by Lofthouse
PHOTO BY GREER

Plate 76. 'Caperci Special' by Caperci
PHOTO BY GREER

Plate 77. 'Captain Kidd' by Henny
PHOTO BY GREER

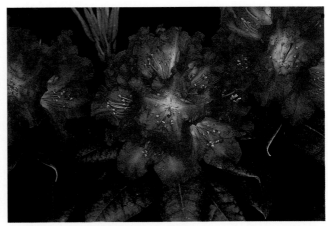

Plate 78. 'Caractacus' by A. Waterer
PHOTO BY GREER

Plate 79. 'Carex Blush' by Rothschild
PHOTO BY GREER

Plate 80. 'Carita' by Rothschild
PHOTO BY GREER

Plate 81. 'Carlene' by Lem/Fawcett
PHOTO BY GREER

Plate 82. 'Carmen' by Rothschild
PHOTO BY GREER

Plate 83. 'Caroline Allbrook' by A. F. George
PHOTO BY GREER

Plate 84. 'Catalode' ('County of York') by Gable
PHOTO BY GREER

Plate 85. 'Catawbiense Album' by A. Waterer
PHOTO BY SPADY

Plate 86. 'Cecil Number 8' by Dexter
PHOTO BY L. BEASLEY

Plate 87. 'Celebrity' by Elliott
PHOTO BY GREER

Plate 88. 'Centennial Celebration' by Peste/Briggs
PHOTO BY GREER

Plate 89. 'Charlotte De Rothschild' by Rothschild
PHOTO BY REDFORD

Plate 90. 'Cheer' by Shammarello
PHOTO BY GREER

Plate 92. 'Cherry Jam' by Delp
PHOTO BY SALLEY

Plate 91. 'Chelsea' by Rothschild
PHOTO BY GREER

Plate 93. 'Cherry Red' by Dexter
PHOTO BY GREER

Plate 94. 'Chesapeake' by Nearing
PHOTO BY GREER

Plate 95. 'Chikor' by Cox
PHOTO BY GREER

Plate 96. 'China Doll' by A. J. Teese

Plate 97. 'Chinmar' by Sifferman/McClure

Plate 98. 'Clara Raustein' by Raustein

Plate 99. 'Clementine Lemaire' by Moser

Plate 100. 'Clove' by Rothschild

Plate 101. 'College Pink', from Massey College, NZ
PHOTO BY GREER

Plate 102. 'Colonel Coen' by E. Ostbo
PHOTO BY GREER

Plate 103. 'Comte de Gomer' by J. Waterer
PHOTO BY GREER

Plate 104. 'Concorde' by A. van Nes
PHOTO BY GREER

Plate 105. 'Conroy' by Aberconway (not a hybrid)
PHOTO BY GREER

Plate 106. 'Consolini's Windmill' by Consolini
PHOTO BY SALLEY

Plate 107. 'Constable' by Hanger
PHOTO BY REDFORD

Plate 108. 'Cornubia' by B. Fox
PHOTO BY GREER

Plate 109. 'Corona' by J. Waterer
PHOTO BY GREER

Plate 110. 'Coronation Day' by Crosfield
PHOTO BY GREER

Plate 111. 'Cotton Candy' by J. Henny/Wennekamp
PHOTO BY GREER

Plate 112. 'Countess of Derby' by H. White
PHOTO BY GREER

Plate 113. 'Coupon' by Blough
PHOTO BY BLOUGH

Plate 114. 'Cowslip' by Aberconway
PHOTO BY SPADY

Plate 115. 'Cream Crest' by Wright
PHOTO BY SPADY

Plate 116. 'Cream Pie' by Minor/Greer
PHOTO BY GREER

Plate 117. 'Creole Belle' by Thompson
PHOTO BY GREER

Plate 118. 'Crimson Glory', from Cottage Gardens
PHOTO BY GREER

Plate 119. 'Dairymaid' by Slocock
PHOTO BY GREER

Plate 120. 'Dalkeith' by McLaughlin/Warren
PHOTO BY GREER

Plate 121. 'Damaris' by E. J. P. Magor
PHOTO BY GREER

Plate 122. 'Dame Nellie Melba' by E. Loder
PHOTO BY GREER

Plate 123. 'Daniela' by Hachmann
PHOTO BY BRIGGS

Plate 124. 'Dave Goheen' by Goheen/Bulgin
PHOTO BY GOHEEN

Plate 125. 'David' by Swaythling
PHOTO BY GREER

Plate 126. 'David Gable' by Gable
PHOTO BY SALLEY

Plate 127. 'Dazzler' by J. Elliott/Greer
PHOTO BY GREER

Plate 128. 'Dee Dee Wegener' by Britt Smith
PHOTO BY GREER

Plate 129. 'Denise' by V. J. Boulter
PHOTO BY GREER

Plate 130. 'Dexter/Bosley 1020' by Dexter/Bosley
PHOTO BY GUSTAFSON

Plate 131. 'Dexter's Brick Red' by Dexter
PHOTO BY KELLAM

Plate 132. 'Dexter's Champagne' by Dexter
PHOTO BY GREER

Plate 133. 'Dexter's Favorite' by Dexter
PHOTO BY L. BEASLEY

Plate 134. 'Dexter's Giant Red' by Dexter
PHOTO BY GREER

Plate 135. 'Dexter's Harlequin' by Dexter
PHOTO, ARS REGISTRAR'S FILE

Plate 136. 'Dexter's Purple' by Dexter/Vossberg
PHOTO BY GREER

Plate 137. 'Dexter's Red Velvet' by Dexter/Knippenberg
PHOTO BY KELLAM

Plate 138. 'Dexter's Springtime' by Dexter
PHOTO, ARS REGISTRAR'S FILE

Plate 139. 'Dexter's Vanilla' by Dexter
PHOTO, ARS REGISTRAR'S FILE

Plate 140. 'Ding Dong' by Sir John Bolitho
PHOTO BY GREER

Plate 141. 'Doctor Masters' by Meulen
PHOTO BY GREER

Plate 142. 'Doctor V. H. Rutgers' by H. den Ouden
PHOTO BY LEONARD

Plate 143. 'Dopey', from Waterer & Crisp
PHOTO BY GREER

Plate 144. 'Dorothy Amateis' by Amateis/Baldsiefen
PHOTO BY GREER

Plate 145. 'Dorothy Russell' by Dexter/Schwoebel
PHOTO BY GREER

Plate 146. 'Double Winner' by Larson
PHOTO BY GREER

Plate 147. 'Doug Klough' by Al Smith/Delp
PHOTO BY SALLEY

Plate 148. 'Duque de San Lucar', from Felix & Dijkhuis
PHOTO BY GREER

Plate 149. 'Early Accent' by Consolini
PHOTO BY GREER

Plate 150. 'Easter Parade' by C. Fawcett
PHOTO BY GREER

Plate 151. 'Edith Bosley' by Bosley
PHOTO BY BRIGGS

Plate 152. 'Edith Carey', from Smith & Son, NZ
PHOTO BY GREER

Plate 153. 'Eldorado' by Rothschild
PHOTO BY GREER

Plate 154. 'Elie' by Shammarello
PHOTO BY GREER

Plate 155. 'Elizabeth' by Aberconway
PHOTO BY SPADY

Plate 156. 'Elizabeth Lockhart' by Lockhart
PHOTO BY GREER

Plate 157. 'Else Frye' by Bowman
PHOTO BY GREER

Plate 158. 'Elspeth' by Slocock
PHOTO BY GREER

Plate 159. 'Elya' by Larson
PHOTO BY GREER

Plate 160. 'Emanuela' by Hachmann
PHOTO BY BRIGGS

Plate 162. 'Ethel' by Aberconway
PHOTO BY GREER

Plate 161. 'Emily Allison' by Lem/Bailey
PHOTO BY GREER

Plate 163. 'Everfull' by Blough
PHOTO BY BLOUGH

Plate 164. 'Everything Nice' by Greer
PHOTO BY GREER

Plate 165. 'Exalted Ruler' by Lyons
PHOTO BY GREER

Plate 166. 'Fabia Tangerine' by Aberconway
PHOTO BY GREER

Plate 167. 'Faggetter's Favourite' by Slocock
PHOTO BY GREER

Plate 168. 'Falcon Gold' by Graham Smith, Pukeiti, NZ
PHOTO BY GREER

Plate 169. 'Fancy' by M. Koster
PHOTO BY GREER

Plate 170. 'Fantastica' by Hachmann
PHOTO BY BRIGGS

Plate 171. 'Fittianum', origin unknown
PHOTO BY GREER

Plate 172. 'Flicker' by James
PHOTO BY GREER

Plate 173. 'Fort Bragg Glow' by Druecker/Philp
PHOTO BY GREER

Plate 174. 'Fort Nisqually' by R. Clark
PHOTO BY GREER

Plate 175. 'Fortune' by Rothschild
PHOTO BY GREER

Plate 176. 'Foxberg' by Blough
PHOTO BY BLOUGH

Plate 177. 'Fragrans Affinity' by Greer
PHOTO BY GREER

Plate 178. 'Francesca' by Consolini/Savella
PHOTO BY GREER

Plate 179. 'Frango' by Goheen
PHOTO BY GREER

Plate 180. 'Fred Peste' by Peste/Johnston
PHOTO BY GREER

Plate 181. 'Fred Waterer' by J. Waterer
PHOTO BY GREER

Plate 182. 'Friesland' by Endtz
PHOTO BY GREER

Plate 183. 'Frilled Petticoats' by Lofthouse
PHOTO BY GREER

Plate 184. 'Fulbrook' by Mrs. D. Gordon
PHOTO BY GREER

Plate 185. 'Galactic' by Rothschild
PHOTO BY GREER

Plate 186. 'Gartendirektor Glocker' by Hobbie
PHOTO BY GREER

Plate 187. 'Gary Herbert' by Gable/Herbert
PHOTO BY GREER

Plate 188. 'Gaul' by Rothschild
PHOTO BY GREER

Plate 189. 'Gauntlettii', origin unknown
PHOTO BY GREER

Plate 190. 'General Sir John Du Cane' by Rothschild
PHOTO BY REDFORD

Plate 191. 'Genghis Khan' by Brandt
PHOTO BY GREER

Plate 192. 'George Watling' by Greig/Cook
PHOTO BY GREER

Plate 193. 'George's Delight' by Whitney/Sather
PHOTO BY GREER

Plate 194. 'Gigi' by Dexter/Burns
PHOTO BY GREER

Plate 195. 'Ginny Gee' by Berg
PHOTO BY GREER

Plate 196. 'Gipsy Queen', origin unknown
PHOTO BY GREER

Plate 197. 'Glory of Littleworth' by Mangles
PHOTO BY GREER

Plate 198. 'Golden Harbinger' by T. Ring
PHOTO BY T. RING

Plate 199. 'Golden Horn Persimmon' by Rothschild
PHOTO BY REDFORD

Plate 200. 'Golden Orfe' by Roza Harrison
PHOTO BY GREER

Plate 201. 'Golden Princess' by Berg
PHOTO BY GREER

Plate 202. 'Golden Star' by Hardgrove/Burns
PHOTO BY LEONARD

Plate 204. 'Goody Goody Gumdrop' by Delp
PHOTO BY DELP

Plate 203. 'Goldflimmer' by Hobbie/Hachmann
PHOTO BY BRIGGS

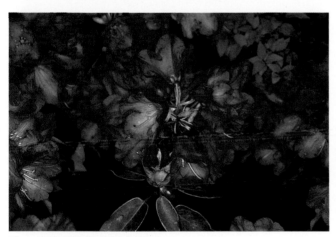

Plate 205. 'Görlitz' by J. Bruns
PHOTO BY GREER

Plate 206. 'Gosh Darn!' by Delp
PHOTO BY SALLEY

Plate 207. 'Grace and Will' by Delp/S. Salley
PHOTO BY DELP

Plate 208. 'Grand Slam' by Greer
PHOTO BY GREER

Plate 209. 'Grandma's Saucer' by C. Smith
PHOTO BY GREER

Plate 210. 'Great Eastern' by Dexter
PHOTO BY GREER

Plate 211. 'Greer's Cream Delight' by Greer
PHOTO BY GREER

Plate 212. 'Gretsel' ('Gretzel') by Lem
PHOTO BY GREER

Plate 213. 'Gumdrop', from Hendrick's Park
PHOTO BY GREER

Plate 214. 'Gunmetal' by Blough
PHOTO BY BLOUGH

Plate 215. 'Gwillt-King' by Caton Haig
PHOTO BY GREER

Plate 216. 'Hachmann's Feuerschein' by Hachmann
PHOTO BY GREER

Plate 217. 'Hachmann's Polaris' by Hachmann
PHOTO BY VALIGORSKY

Plate 218. 'Hansel' by Lem
PHOTO BY GREER

Plate 219. 'Harvest Moon' by M. Koster
PHOTO BY SPADY

Plate 220. 'Hawk Cherry' by Rothschild?
PHOTO BY SALLEY

Plate 221. 'Heavenly Scent' by Whitney/Sather
PHOTO BY GREER

Plate 222. 'Helen Child' by Larson
PHOTO BY GREER

Plate 223. 'Helen Scott Richey' by Scott
PHOTO BY GREER

Plate 224. 'Helene Schiffner' by Seidel
PHOTO BY GREER

Plate 225. 'Helene Strybing' by Reiter
PHOTO BY GREER

Plate 226. 'Helma's Joy' by Vaartnou
PHOTO BY VAARTNOU

Plate 227. 'Hendrick's Park' by James
PHOTO BY GREER

Plate 228. 'Holden' by Shammarello
PHOTO BY GREER

Plate 229. 'Hollandia' by Endtz
PHOTO BY GREER

Plate 230. 'Holy Toledo' by Delp
PHOTO BY SALLEY

Plate 231. 'Horizon Monarch' by Brockenbrough
PHOTO BY BRIGGS

Plate 232. 'Horizon Snowbird' by Brockenbrough
PHOTO BY GREER

Plate 233. 'Hot Stuff' by Greer
PHOTO BY GREER

Plate 234. 'Hotei' by Sifferman/Nelson
PHOTO BY SPADY

Plate 235. 'Hudson Bay' by Leach
PHOTO BY GREER

Plate 236. 'Hugtight' by Larson/Fisher
PHOTO BY GREER

Plate 237. 'Hunting Hill' by Dexter/G. Wister
PHOTO BY LEONARD

Plate 238. 'Hurricane' by Whitney/Sather
PHOTO BY GREER

Plate 239. 'Hydon Dawn' by A. F. George
PHOTO BY GREER

Plate 240. 'Ice Crystals' by Blough
PHOTO BY BLOUGH

Plate 241. 'Ice Cube' by Shammarello
PHOTO BY GREER

Plate 242. 'Ida Bradour' by Gable/Yates
PHOTO BY SALLEY

Plate 243. 'Ightham Yellow' by Digby/Reuthe
PHOTO BY GREER

Plate 244. 'Ignatius Sargent' by A. Waterer
PHOTO BY GREER

Plate 245. 'Ilam Canary' by E. Stead
PHOTO BY GREER

Plate 246. 'Ilam Cerise' by E. Stead
PHOTO BY GREER

Plate 247. 'Ilam Cream' by E. Stead
PHOTO BY GREER

Plate 248. 'Ilam Orange' by E. Stead
PHOTO BY GREER

Plate 249. 'Inheritance' by Farwell
PHOTO BY GREER

Plate 250. 'Irresistible Impulse' by Greer
PHOTO BY GREER

Plate 251. 'Isabel Pierce' by Lem/Pierce
PHOTO BY GREER

Plate 252. 'Ivery's Scarlet', origin unknown
PHOTO BY GREER

Plate 253. 'J. G. Millais' by J. Waterer
PHOTO BY GREER

Plate 254. 'Jackie Ann', origin unknown
PHOTO BY GREER

Plate 255. 'Jacksonii' by Herbert, 1835
PHOTO BY GREER

Plate 256. 'Jalipeño' by Goheen
PHOTO BY GREER

Plate 257. 'James W. Seihl' ('Gahagen') by Blough
PHOTO BY SALLEY

Plate 258. 'Jan Bee' by Berg
PHOTO BY GREER

Plate 259. 'Jane Rogers' by Ostbo
PHOTO BY GREER

Plate 260. 'Janet Kerrigan' by Kerrigan
PHOTO BY GREER

Plate 261. 'Jay Murray' by Lewis
PHOTO BY LEWIS

Plate 262. 'Jenny Lind' by Seabrook/Jarvis
PHOTO BY GREER

Plate 263. 'Jiminy Cricket' by James
PHOTO BY GREER

Plate 264. 'Joan Thompson' by Spry
PHOTO BY WITHERS

Plate 265. 'Joanna Stenning' by Pride/Hinerman
PHOTO BY SALLEY

Plate 266. 'Jodie King' by King
PHOTO BY GREER

Plate 267. 'Joe Paterno' by Pride
PHOTO BY GREER

Plate 268. 'John Marchand' by Marchand/Ingram
PHOTO BY GREER

Plate 269. 'Johnny Bender' by Seabrook/Eichelser
PHOTO BY GREER

Plate 270. 'Julie Titcomb' by Larson
PHOTO BY GREER

Plate 271. 'Karen Triplett' by Larson
PHOTO BY GREER

Plate 272. 'Katherine Slater' by Dexter/Mezitt
PHOTO BY L. BEASLEY

Plate 273. 'Kathy Van Veen' by Rhein/T. Van Veen
PHOTO BY GREER

Plate 274. 'Katrina' by E. Watson
PHOTO BY GREER

Plate 275. 'Katydid' by Delp
PHOTO BY DELP

Plate 276. 'Kelley' by Dexter/G. Wister
PHOTO BY GUSTAFSON

Plate 277. 'King Tut' by Shammarello
PHOTO BY SALLEY

Plate 278. 'Kingcup' by Rothschild
PHOTO BY GREER

Plate 279. 'Kinglet' by R. Henny
PHOTO BY GREER

Plate 280. 'Kingston' by Holmeide/A. P. Smith
PHOTO BY BRIGGS

Plate 281. 'Kluis Sensation' by Kluis
PHOTO BY GREER

Plate 282. 'Kluis Triumph' by Kluis
PHOTO BY GREER

Plate 283. 'Kristin' by Bovee/Sorenson & Watson
PHOTO BY GREER

Plate 284. 'Lady Alice Fitzwilliam' by Fisher
PHOTO BY GREER

Plate 285. 'Lady Bligh' by C. B. van Nes
PHOTO BY GREER

Plate 286. 'Lady Clementine Mitford' by A. Waterer
PHOTO BY GREER

Plate 287. 'Lady Primrose' by Slocock
PHOTO BY GREER

Plate 288. 'Lajka' ('Laika') by van Gelderen/Scholz
PHOTO BY GREER

Plate 289. 'Lamellen' by E. J. P. Magor
PHOTO BY GREER

Plate 290. 'Lamplighter' by M. Koster
PHOTO BY GREER

Plate 291. 'Laurago' by Goheen
PHOTO BY GREER

Plate 292. 'Lavender Girl' by Slocock
PHOTO BY GREER

Plate 293. 'Lavender Queen' by Shammarello
PHOTO BY GREER

Plate 294. 'Lavendula' by Hobbie
PHOTO BY GREER

Plate 295. 'Lee's Dark Purple' by Lee
PHOTO BY GREER

Plate 296. 'Lemon Crisp' by Delp
PHOTO BY SALLEY

Plate 297. 'Lemon Lodge', from Pukeiti Rhododendron Trust
PHOTO BY GREER

Plate 298. 'Lemon Mist' by Scott
PHOTO BY NANCY GREER

Plate 299. 'Lem's Aurora' by Lem
PHOTO BY GREER

Plate 300. 'Lem's Fluorescent Pink' by Lem
PHOTO BY GREER

Plate 301. 'Lem's Monarch' by Lem
PHOTO BY SPADY

Plate 302. 'Lem's One-Twenty-One' by Lem
PHOTO BY GREER

Plate 303. 'Leo' by Rothschild
PHOTO BY GREER

Plate 304. 'Leona Maud' by A. P. Johnson
PHOTO BY GREER

Plate 305. 'Lightly Lavender' by Greer
PHOTO BY GREER

Plate 306. 'Lily' by Van de Ven
PHOTO BY GREER

Plate 307. 'Lionel's Triumph' by Rothschild
PHOTO BY GREER

Plate 308. 'Little Joe' by Brandt
PHOTO BY GREER

Plate 309. 'Llenroc' by Mezitt
PHOTO BY GREER

Plate 310. 'Loch Tay' by Cox
PHOTO BY GREER

Plate 311. 'Lodauric Iceberg' by Slocock
PHOTO BY GREER

Plate 312. 'Loderi Julie' by E. Loder?
PHOTO BY GREER

Plate 313. 'Loderi Pink Topaz' by E. Loder
PHOTO BY GREER

Plate 314. 'Loderi Superlative' by E. Loder
PHOTO BY GREER

Plate 315. 'Loderi Venus' by E. Loder
PHOTO BY GREER

Plate 316. 'Loder's White' by Mangles/Loder
PHOTO BY GREER

Plate 317. 'Loeb's Moonlight' by Loeb
PHOTO BY GREER

Plate 318. 'Lois Jean Seihl' by Blough
PHOTO BY BLOUGH

Plate 319. 'Looking Glass' by Briggs
PHOTO BY GREER

Plate 320. 'Lord Fairhaven', from Knap Hill
PHOTO BY GREER

Plate 321. 'Lord Roberts' by Mason
PHOTO BY GREER

Plate 322. 'Lovely William' by Horlick
PHOTO BY GREER

Plate 323. 'Lucy Lou' by Larson
PHOTO BY GREER

Plate 324. 'Lunar Queen' by Gen. Harrison
PHOTO BY SPADY

Plate 325. 'Ma Chère' by Brueckner
PHOTO BY BRUECKNER

Plate 326. 'Madame A. Moser' by Moser
PHOTO BY GREER

Plate 327. 'Madame Carvalho' by J. Waterer
PHOTO BY GREER

Plate 328. 'Madame Cochet' by Bertin
PHOTO BY GREER

Plate 329. 'Madame de Bruin' by M. Koster
PHOTO BY GREER

Plate 330. 'Madame Fr. J. Chauvin' by M. Koster
PHOTO BY GREER

Plate 331. 'Madame Jules Porges' by Moser
PHOTO BY GREER

Plate 332. 'Madame Masson' by Bertin
PHOTO BY GREER

Plate 334. 'Madison Hill' by Dexter/G. Wister
PHOTO BY L. BEASLEY

Plate 333. 'Madge Bramley' by A. Bramley
PHOTO BY GREER

Plate 335. 'Magic Moments' by Lofthouse
PHOTO BY GREER

Plate 336. 'Malahat' by Larson
PHOTO BY GREER

Plate 337. 'Manitau', origin unknown
PHOTO BY GREER

Plate 338. 'Marathon' by Rothschild
PHOTO BY GREER

Plate 339. 'Marcat' by Gable
PHOTO BY GREER

Plate 340. 'Marchioness of Lansdowne' by A. Waterer
PHOTO BY GREER

Plate 341. 'Marcy Margot' by Lelliott? (from Aus.)
PHOTO BY GREER

Plate 342. 'Margaret Caroline', from Australia
PHOTO BY GREER

Plate 343. 'Margaret Mack' by V. J. Boulter
PHOTO BY GREER

Plate 344. 'Maricee' by Caperci (not a hybrid)
PHOTO BY GREER

Plate 345. 'Marion Street' by J. Street/F. Street
PHOTO BY GREER

Plate 346. 'Marjie Kay Hinerman' by Hinerman
PHOTO BY COMSTOCK

Plate 347. 'Marlis' by Hachmann
PHOTO BY BRIGGS

Plate 348. 'Mars' by Waterer, 1928
PHOTO BY GREER

Plate 349. 'Marshall' by Rothschild
PHOTO BY GREER

Plate 350. 'Martha Isaacson' by E. Ostbo
PHOTO BY GREER

Plate 351. 'Mary Belle' by Gable
PHOTO BY GREER

Plate 352. 'Mary Briggs' by Wyatt
PHOTO BY GREER

Plate 353. 'Maryke' by T. Van Veen, Sr.
PHOTO BY GREER

Plate 354. 'Maureen' by Lem
PHOTO BY GREER

Plate 355. 'Max Fetterhoff' by Fetterhoff
PHOTO BY FETTERHOFF

Plate 356. 'Maxine Childers' by Childers/Phetteplace
PHOTO BY GREER

Plate 357. 'May Morn' by Aberconway
PHOTO BY GREER

Plate 358. 'Medusa' by Aberconway
PHOTO BY GREER

Plate 359. 'Melanie Shaw' by Shaw/Leonard
PHOTO BY LEONARD

Plate 360. 'Melrose Pink' by Eichelser
PHOTO BY GREER

Plate 361. 'Merley Cream' by Dexter
PHOTO BY SCHRAM

Plate 362. 'Mi Amor' by Sumner
PHOTO BY GREER

Plate 363. 'Midsummer' from Waterer & Crisp
PHOTO BY GUSTAFSON

Plate 364. 'Midway' by Van de Ven
PHOTO BY GREER

Plate 365. 'Minnie' by Standish, 1862
PHOTO BY GREER

Plate 366. 'Moerheim' by Ruys
PHOTO BY GREER

Plate 367. 'Moerheim Scarlet' by Hobbie/Ruys
PHOTO BY GREER

Plate 368. 'Molly Ann' by Mrs. L. Freimann
PHOTO BY GREER

Plate 369. 'Molly Fordham', from Weston Nurseries
PHOTO BY GREER

Plate 370. 'Moon Shadow' by Mrs. R. J. Coker
PHOTO BY GREER

Plate 371. 'Moonglow' by Rothschild
PHOTO BY REDFORD

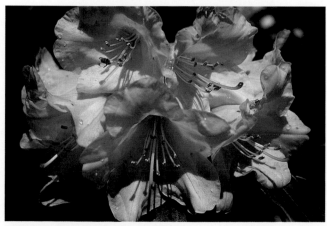

Plate 372. 'Moonshine' by Hanger
PHOTO BY GUSTAFSON

Plate 373. 'Moonshine Bright' by Hanger
PHOTO BY GREER

Plate 374. 'Moonshine Supreme' by Hanger
PHOTO BY GREER

Plate 375. 'Moonstone' by J. C. Williams
PHOTO BY GREER

Plate 376. 'Moonwax' by Lem/Newcomb
PHOTO BY GREER

Plate 377. 'Morgenrot' ('Morning Red') by Hachmann
PHOTO BY GREER

Plate 378. 'Morning Cloud' by A. F. George
PHOTO BY GREER

Plate 379. 'Morning Sunshine' by Whitney/Sather
PHOTO BY GREER

Plate 380. 'Moser's Maroon' by Moser
PHOTO BY GREER

Plate 381. 'Moth' by Aberconway
PHOTO BY GREER

Plate 382. 'Mount Everest' by Slocock
PHOTO BY GREER

Plate 383. 'Mrs. A. T. de la Mare' by C. B. van Nes
PHOTO BY GREER

Plate 384. 'Mrs. Betty Robertson' by M. Koster
PHOTO BY GREER

Plate 385. 'Mrs. C. B. van Nes' by C. B. van Nes
PHOTO BY GREER

Plate 386. 'Mrs. Calabash' by Lem
PHOTO BY GREER

Plate 387. 'Mrs. E. C. Stirling' by J. Waterer
PHOTO BY GREER

Plate 388. 'Mrs. Furnivall' by A. Waterer
PHOTO BY GREER

Plate 389. 'Mrs. Helen Koster' by M. Koster
PHOTO BY GREER

Plate 390. 'Mrs. J. G. Millais' by A. Waterer
PHOTO BY GREER

Plate 391. 'Mrs. Joan Zink' by Vaartnou
PHOTO BY VAARTNOU

Plate 393. 'Mrs. T. H. Lowinsky' by Waterer, 1917
PHOTO BY GREER

Plate 392. 'Mrs. O. B. Watson' by Watson
PHOTO BY GREER

Plate 394. 'Mrs. W. R. Coe' by Dexter
PHOTO BY LEONARD

Plate 395. 'Muncaster Mist' by Ramsden
PHOTO BY GREER

Plate 396. 'Mundai' by V. J. Boulter
PHOTO BY GREER

Plate 397. 'Murraba' by V. J. Boulter
PHOTO BY GREER

Plate 398. 'My Valentine' by Cochran
PHOTO BY GREER

Plate 399. 'N. N. Sherwood' by Sibray
PHOTO BY GREER

Plate 400. 'Naomi Nereid' by Rothschild
PHOTO BY REDFORD

Plate 401. 'Naselle' by J. Elliott
PHOTO BY GREER

Plate 402. 'Nathan Hale' by Dexter/Schlaikjer
PHOTO BY SALLEY

Plate 403. 'Neat-o' by Goheen
PHOTO BY T. VAN VEEN

Plate 404. 'Norseman' by Lem/J. Elliott
PHOTO BY GREER

Plate 406. 'Nosutchianum' by Lem
PHOTO BY GREER

Plate 405. 'Nosegay', a New Zealand Hybrid?
PHOTO BY GREER

Plate 407. 'Odee Wright' by Wright
PHOTO BY GREER

Plate 408. 'Odoratum' by Thompson, pre-1875
PHOTO BY GREER

Plate 409. 'Oh Too' by W. Elliott/Whitney/Sather
PHOTO BY GREER

Plate 410. 'Old Copper' by T. Van Veen, Sr.
PHOTO BY GREER

Plate 411. 'Olin O. Dobbs' by Dobbs/Greer
PHOTO BY GREER

Plate 412. 'Olympic Lady' by Ostbo/R. Clark
PHOTO BY GREER

Plate 413. 'Oregon Queen', a natural hybrid
PHOTO BY GREER

Plate 414. 'Osmar' by van Gelderen/de Wilde
PHOTO BY GREER

Plate 415. 'Ostbo's Low Yellow' by E. Ostbo
PHOTO BY GREER

Plate 416. 'Oudijk's Sensation' by Hobbie/Le Feber
PHOTO BY GREER

Plate 417. 'Pacific Glow' by Larson/Jack
PHOTO BY GREER

Plate 418. 'Papaya Punch' by Brockenbrough/Kesterson
PHOTO BY GREER

Plate 419. 'Paricutin' by Brandt
PHOTO BY GREER

Plate 420. 'Parker's Pink' by Dexter/Parker/Vossberg
PHOTO BY GUSTAFSON

Plate 421. 'Patricia' by Caperci (not a hybrid)
PHOTO BY GREER

Plate 422. 'Patty Bee' by Berg
PHOTO BY GREER

Plate 423. 'Paul Lincke' by Seabrook
PHOTO BY GREER

Plate 424. 'Pawhuska' by Bowhan
PHOTO BY GREER

Plate 425. 'Peach Surprise' by Greer
PHOTO BY GREER

Plate 426. 'Peekaboo' by Whitney
PHOTO BY GREER

Plate 427. 'Perfectly Pink' by Greer
PHOTO BY GREER

Plate 428. 'Peste's Pink-Yellow' by Peste/Johnston
PHOTO BY BRIGGS

Plate 429. 'Pierce's Apricot' by Pierce
PHOTO BY GREER

Plate 430. 'Pilgrim' by G. H. Johnstone
PHOTO BY GREER

Plate 431. 'Pink Cloud' by Whitney/Sather
PHOTO BY GREER

Plate 432. 'Pink Fluff' by Greer
PHOTO BY GREER

Plate 433. 'Pink Jeans' by Briggs
PHOTO BY GREER

Plate 434. 'Pink Maiden' by Girard/Trautmann
PHOTO BY TRAUTMANN

Plate 435. 'Pink Pearl' by J. Waterer
PHOTO BY SPADY

Plate 436. 'Pink Petticoats' by Lofthouse
PHOTO BY GREER

Plate 437. 'Pink Sherbet' by Larson/J. Davis
PHOTO BY GREER

Plate 438. 'Pink Snowflakes' by Scott
PHOTO BY GREER

Plate 439. 'Pirouette' by Lofthouse
PHOTO BY GREER

Plate 440. 'Plum Beautiful' by Greer
PHOTO BY GREER

Plate 441. 'Polycinn', origin unknown
PHOTO BY GREER

Plate 442. 'Popeye' by Mossman
PHOTO BY GREER

Plate 443. 'Posy' by Gordon
PHOTO BY GREER

Plate 444. 'Praecox' by Davies, 1861
PHOTO BY GREER

Plate 445. 'Prairie Fire' by Allan Korth
PHOTO BY GREER

Plate 446. 'Prince Camille de Rohan' by Verschaffelt
PHOTO BY GREER

Plate 447. 'Princess Anne' by Reuthe
PHOTO BY GREER

Plate 448. 'Professor J. H. Zaayer' by Endtz
PHOTO BY GREER

Plate 449. 'Prostigiatum' by E. J. P. Magor
PHOTO BY GREER

Plate 450. 'Ptarmigan' by Cox
PHOTO BY GREER

Plate 451. 'Purple Gem' by Gable/Nearing/Hardgrove
PHOTO BY GREER

Plate 452. 'Purple Lace', from Boskoop
PHOTO BY GREER

Plate 453. 'Quaver' by Rothschild
PHOTO BY GREER

Plate 454. 'Queen Mary', from Felix & Dijkhuis
PHOTO BY GREER

Plate 455. 'Queen Wilhelmina' by Schulz/van Nes
PHOTO BY GREER

Plate 456. 'Ragtime' by Delp
PHOTO BY SALLEY

Plate 457. 'Razzle Dazzle' by Greer
PHOTO BY GREER

Plate 458. 'Red Devil' by Fawcett
PHOTO BY GREER

Plate 459. 'Red Dog' by Delp
PHOTO BY SALLEY

Plate 460. 'Red Loderi' by Rose/Lem
PHOTO BY GREER

Plate 461. 'Red Prince', origin unknown
PHOTO BY GREER

Plate 462. 'Redwing' by Aberconway
PHOTO BY GREER

Plate 463. 'Renaissance' by Barto/Fogg
PHOTO BY GREER

Plate 464. 'Renoir' by Hanger
PHOTO BY JESSEN

Plate 465. 'Repose' by Rothschild
PHOTO BY REDFORD

Plate 466. 'Ria Hardijzer' by Hardijzer
PHOTO BY GREER

Plate 467. 'Richard Gill' by Gill
PHOTO BY GREER

Plate 468. 'Rimini', origin unknown
PHOTO BY GREER

Plate 469. 'Robert Lohr Blough' by Blough
PHOTO BY BLOUGH

Plate 470. 'Rocket' by Shammarello
PHOTO BY GREER

Plate 471. 'Rodeo' by M. Koster
PHOTO BY GREER

Plate 472. 'Rollie Mulkie' by Mulkie
PHOTO BY GREER

Plate 473. 'Rose of China' by Rose/Lancaster
PHOTO BY GREER

Plate 474. 'Rose Point' by Lem/Pierce/J. Elliott
PHOTO BY GREER

Plate 475. 'Rose Scott' by Scott
PHOTO BY GREER

Plate 476. 'Rose Walloper' by Lem
PHOTO BY GREER

Plate 477. 'Rosy Dream' by Larson/Davies
PHOTO BY GREER

Plate 478. 'Racearound' ('Roundabout') by Jim Cross
PHOTO BY GREER

Plate 479. 'Royal Flush' by J. C. Williams
PHOTO BY GREER

Plate 480. 'Rubicon' by Gordon
PHOTO BY GREER

Plate 481. 'Russellianum' by Russell, 1831
PHOTO BY GREER

Plate 482. 'Rustic Maid' by Ingram
PHOTO BY GREER

Plate 483. 'Ruth A. Weber' by Weber
PHOTO BY GREER

Plate 484. 'Saint Minver' by Gen. Harrison
PHOTO BY GREER

Plate 485. 'Saint Tudy' by Magor/Gen. Harrison
PHOTO BY GREER

Plate 486. 'Salmon Grierson', origin unknown
PHOTO BY GREER

Plate 487. 'Salmon Trout' by Rothschild
PHOTO BY GREER

Plate 488. 'Sammetglut' ('Velvet Glow') by Hachmann
PHOTO BY GREER

Plate 489. 'Satin Glow' by Van de Ven
PHOTO BY GREER

Plate 490. 'Schneebukett' by Hachmann
PHOTO BY BRIGGS

Plate 491. 'Schneekrone' by Hachmann
PHOTO BY BRIGGS

Plate 492. 'Sckookumchuck' by Minch
PHOTO BY BRIGGS

Plate 493. 'Scott's Valentine' by Scott
PHOTO BY GREER

Plate 494. 'Senator Henry Jackson' by Larson/Fisher
PHOTO BY BRIGGS

Plate 495. 'Senegal' by Leach
PHOTO BY GREER

Plate 496. 'Señorita Chère' by Greer/Boltman
PHOTO BY GREER

Plate 497. 'September Song' by Phetteplace/Greer
PHOTO BY GREER

Plate 498. 'Shamrock' by Ticknor
PHOTO BY GREER

Plate 500. 'Sierra Del Oro' by Lofthouse
PHOTO BY HATCH

Plate 499. 'Shawme Lake' by Dexter
PHOTO BY GREER

Plate 501. 'Silberwolke' ('Silver Cloud') by Hachmann
PHOTO BY GREER

Plate 502. 'Silver Jubilee' by A. F. George
PHOTO BY REDFORD

Plate 503. 'Sir Charles Lemon' by Aberconway
PHOTO BY GREER

Plate 504. 'Sir Robert Peel' by J. Waterer
PHOTO BY GREER

Plate 505. 'Skyglow' by Veitch/Dexter
PHOTO BY LEONARD

Plate 506. 'Sloppy Joe' by Thompson
PHOTO BY GREER

Plate 507. 'Snow Lady' by Rothschild
PHOTO BY SPADY

Plate 508. 'Solent Swan' by Rothschild
PHOTO BY GREER

Plate 509. 'Solidarity' by Schannen
PHOTO BY GREER

Plate 510. 'Source Bank' by Delp
PHOTO BY SALLEY

Plate 511. 'Souvenir of Anthony Waterer' by A. Waterer
PHOTO BY GREER

Plate 512. 'Souvenir of W. C. Slocock' by Slocock
PHOTO BY GREER

Plate 513. 'Sphinx' by Luenenschloss
PHOTO BY GUSTAFSON

Plate 514. 'Spring Glory' by Shammarello
PHOTO BY GREER

Plate 515. 'Spring Parade' by Shammarello
PHOTO BY GREER

Plate 516. 'Stanley Rivlin' by A. F. George
PHOTO BY REDFORD

Plate 517. 'Stanway' by Rothschild
PHOTO BY REDFORD

Plate 518. 'Star Trek' by Childers
PHOTO BY GREER

Plate 519. 'Stardust' by Fawcett
PHOTO BY GREER

Plate 520. 'Strawberry Cream' by Brandt/Cox
PHOTO BY GREER

Plate 521. 'Suave' by Liebig, 1863
PHOTO BY GREER

Plate 522. 'Sugar Pink' by Greer
PHOTO BY GREER

Plate 523. 'Summer Solace' by Leach
PHOTO BY LEACH

Plate 524. 'Sunny Day' by Whitney/Sather
PHOTO BY GREER

Plate 525. 'Sunspray' by Swenson/Greer
PHOTO BY GREER

Plate 526. 'Suomi' by Hobbie
PHOTO BY GREER

Plate 527. 'Super Jay' by Anderson/Braafladt
PHOTO BY GREER

Plate 528. 'Surrey Heath', from Waterer & Crisp
PHOTO BY GREER

Plate 529. 'Susan' by J. C. Williams
PHOTO BY GREER

Plate 530. 'Swansdown' by Leach
PHOTO BY GREER

Plate 531. 'Sweet Sixteen' by Whitney/Sather
PHOTO BY GREER

Plate 532. 'Sydney Sunset', from Australia
PHOTO BY GREER

Plate 533. 'Tasco' by Rothschild
PHOTO BY GREER

Plate 534. 'Taurus' by Mossman
PHOTO BY SPADY

Plate 535. 'Teal' by Cox
PHOTO BY GREER

Plate 536. 'Tennessee' by Leach
PHOTO BY LEACH

Plate 538. 'The Rebel' by Wapler
PHOTO BY GREER

Plate 537. 'The Master' by Slocock
PHOTO BY GREER

Plate 539. 'Thomwilliams' by E. J. P. Magor
PHOTO BY GREER

Plate 540. 'Thunderhead' by R. Clark
PHOTO BY GREER

Plate 541. 'Tickled Pink' by Fawcett
PHOTO BY GREER

Plate 542. 'Tidbit' by Henny
PHOTO BY GREER

Plate 543. 'Tiddlywinks' by Thompson
PHOTO BY GREER

Plate 544. 'Tiffany' by Baldsiefen
PHOTO BY GREER

Plate 545. 'Titian Beauty' by J. Waterer
PHOTO BY GREER

Plate 546. 'Todmorden' by Dexter
PHOTO BY GUSTAFSON

Plate 547. 'Tom Everett' by Dexter
PHOTO BY GREER

Plate 548. 'Tony' by Shammarello
PHOTO BY GREER

Plate 549. 'Top Banana' by Whitney/Sather
PHOTO BY GREER

Plate 550. 'Top Dog' by Delp
PHOTO BY DELP

Plate 551. 'Top Dollar' by Whitney/Sather
PHOTO BY GREER

Plate 552. 'Tosca' by Hanger
PHOTO BY REDFORD

Plate 553. 'Trilby' by C. B. van Nes
PHOTO BY GREER

Plate 554. 'Tripoli' by Dexter
PHOTO BY KELLAM

Plate 555. 'Turkish Delight', origin unknown
PHOTO BY GUSTAFSON

Plate 556. 'Umpqua Chief' by James
PHOTO BY GREER

Plate 557. 'Unknown Warrior' by C. B. van Nes
PHOTO BY GREER

Plate 558. 'Van Nes Sensation' by C. B. van Nes
PHOTO BY GREER

Plate 559. 'Vee Vee' by Leach
PHOTO BY LEACH

Plate 560. 'Verna Phetteplace' by Phetteplace
PHOTO BY GREER

Plate 561. 'Very Berry' by Greer
PHOTO BY GREER

Plate 562. 'Vicki Reine' by R. Clark
PHOTO BY GREER

Plate 563. 'Virginia Stewart' by Kerrigan/Stewart
PHOTO BY GREER

Plate 564. 'Viscy' by Hobbie
PHOTO BY GREER

Plate 565. 'Wally' ('Vallya') by Mezitt
PHOTO BY SPADY

Plate 566. 'Wareham' by Dexter
PHOTO BY LEONARD

Plate 567. 'Warlock' by Bledsoe
PHOTO BY GREER

Plate 568. 'Waterer's Rose Perfection' by Waterer
PHOTO BY GREER

Plate 569. 'Wedding Gown' by K. Van de Ven
PHOTO BY WITHERS

Plate 570. 'Weldon's Gift' by Delp/Salley
PHOTO BY SALLEY

Plate 571. ''Weldy' by Kehr/Delp
PHOTO BY T. RING

Plate 572. 'Westbury' by Dexter/Vossberg
PHOTO BY SALLEY

Plate 573. 'Westby' by Blough
PHOTO BY BLOUGH

Plate 574. 'Weston's Pink Diamond' by Mezitt
PHOTO BY GREER

Plate 575. 'White Peter' by Mehlquist
PHOTO BY BRIGGS

Plate 576. 'Whitney Buff' by Whitney/Sather
PHOTO BY GREER

Plate 577. 'Whitney Purple' by Whitney/Sather
PHOTO BY GREER

Plate 578. 'Wild Affair' by Greer
PHOTO BY GREER

Plate 579. 'Wilgen's Ruby' by van Wilgen
PHOTO BY GREER

Plate 580. 'Willbrit' by Hobbie
PHOTO BY GREER

Plate 581. 'Williams', origin unknown
PHOTO BY GREER

Plate 582. 'Wilsoni' ('Laetevirens'), origin unknown
PHOTO BY GREER

Plate 583. 'Windlesham Scarlet' by Frowmow
PHOTO BY GREER

Plate 584. 'Winter Snow' by Greer
PHOTO BY GREER

Plate 585. 'Wissahickon' by Dexter
PHOTO BY GREER

Plate 586. 'Woodside', from Crown Estate
PHOTO BY GREER

Plate 587. 'Years of Peace' by Mezitt
PHOTO BY SALLEY

Plate 588. 'Yellow Hammer' by J. C. Williams
PHOTO BY GREER

Plate 589. 'Yellow Pages' by Whitney
PHOTO BY BRIGGS

Plate 590. 'Yellow Petticoats' by Lofthouse
PHOTO BY GREER

Plate 591. 'Yunncinn' by E. J. P. Magor
PHOTO BY GREER

Plate 592. 'Zorba' by Goheen
PHOTO BY GOHEEN

MARION (Cheal)   Parentage unknown
Often a parent in mild climates. Tyrian rose flowers, margins
frilled and upper petal spotted orange, reverse Tyrian rose.
Cheal & Son.   A.M. 1955.

```
                                -griffithianum 1/8
                     -George Hardy-
          -Mrs. L. A. Dunnett-            -catawbiense 1/8
MARION KOSTER-                 -unknown 1/4
          -griersonianum 1/2
6ft(1.8m) -5F(-21C) L   Red flowers.  M. Koster, before 1958.
```

```
           -Slocock's Late White--unknown
MARION SHAPIRO-
           -Mrs. P. D. Williams--unknown
```
5ft(1.5m) x 6ft(1.8m)(23 yrs) OF(-18C) ML Fragrant flowers in
trusses of 13, white with prominent brilliant-to-dark greenish
yellow speckled dorsal flare.   Ben & Marion Shapiro, reg. 1989.

```
               -Stanley Davies--unknown 1/2
         -unnamed hybrid-
MARION STREET-           -red hybrid--unknown
         -yakushimanum--Koichiro Wada 1/2
```
Compact plant, with felted brown indumentum as yakushimanum;
deep pink buds opening to lighter pink flowers, white in throat,
green spotted; trusses of 14-16. J. Street cross; F. Street,
reg. 1965. A.M. 1978;   A.M. Wisley Trials 1989.   Color ill.
JS p. 39.

```
                        -griffithianum 7/16
         -Beauty of-
       -Norman- Tremough-arboreum 1/16
       - Gill -
     -Anna-      -griffithianum
     -  -              -          -griffithianum
     -    -Jean Marie de Montague-
MARJ  -                  -unknown 1/4
ANDERSON-          -griffithianum
     -          -Mars-
     -Captain Jack-   -unknown
               -facetum (eriogynum) 1/4
```
3ft(.9m) 5F(-15C) M   Flowers 3.5in(8.9cm) wide, 5-6 lobes,
fragrant, light orient pink, edging of medium Neyron rose; 11-
flowered trusses 8.5in(21.6cm) across. Leaves medium to large,
glossy dark green. G. Barefield cross; M. Barefield, reg. 1983.

```
                    -maximum 1/4
           -Nassau Red-
MARJIE KAY HINERMAN-       -unknown 3/4
           -Honey Dew (Dexter)--unknown
```
3ft(.9m) -25F(-32C) ML 4/5 Foliage conceals wood structure;
leaves 6in(15.5cm) x 2in(5cm), glossy, medium green, and held 3
years; plant broader than tall. Dome-shaped trusses 8in(20.5cm)
high, hold 12 flowers, fragrant, very pale purple, white interior, yellow blotch. Dr. D. L. Hinerman, cross 1975; reg. 1988.

```
                 -dichroanthum 1/8
          -Fabia-
     -Iviza-      -griersonianum 1/8
     -    -          -auriculatum 1/8
MARJORIE-    -Bustard-           -campylocarpum Elatum Group 1/16
 BAIRD -           -Penjerrick-
     -                -griffithianum 1/16
     -campylocarpum 1/2
```
Deep yellow flowers with a maroon blotch, tubular-campanulate.
Plant 6ft(1.8m) in 10 years; leaves 5.5in(14cm) long.   Larson,
reg. 1965.

MARK HENNY   Described under CITATION, q.v.

MARK TWAIN   Described under JOHNNY BENDER, q.v.

* *
```
               -catawbiense 1/4
         -Caractacus-
MARKA-           -unknown 1/4
     -decorum 1/2
```
4ft(1.2m) -10F(-23C) L   A Czechoslovakian hybrid with pink
flowers, red to purple blotch, spotted brown, in truss of 7-13.
Plant broad, bushy. Kavka, c. 1962.
PANENKA Parentage as above
Similar to above with pink buds opening to pink flowers, blotch-
ed ruby red in round trusses of 12-15.   Kavka, c. 1962.
NOTE: This group reported by Cox, 1988.
* *

MARKEETA--form of open pollinated adenopodum
5ft(1.5m) -5F(-21C) EM 3/4 Flowers of very light Neyron rose
fading almost white, tan spotting, widely funnel-campanulate,
3in(7.6cm) across, 5 wavy lobes; conical truss of 16-18. Plant
broad as tall; narrow concave leaves, 7in(17.8cm) long, fawn indumentum, grayed white tomentum on new growth. Leaves held 3-4
years. Dr. David Goheen, reg. 1983.

* *
```
                    -griffithianum 9/16
        -Loderi Venus-
MARKEETA'S-       -fortunei 1/4         -griffithianum
 PRIZE  -        -Beauty of Tremough-
     -    -Norman Gill-          -arboreum 1/16
     -Anna-        -griffithianum
     -                  -griffithianum
          -Jean Marie de Montague-
                    -unknown 1/8
```
5ft(1.5m) -5F(-21C) M 5/4 Plant broader than tall; leathery
dark green leaves to 6in(15.2cm) long. Scarlet red flowers 5in
(12.7cm) wide; truss of 12. Flora Markeeta Nursery, reg. 1967.
Color illus. HG p. 118.
MARKEETA'S FLAME   Parentage as above
5ft(1.5m) -5F(-21C) M 4/4   Much like MARKEETA'S PRIZE. Deep
fir green leaves, red leaf stems. Flowers Neyron rose with dorsal spotting of rose red, openly funnel-shaped, 5in(12.7cm)
across, 5 wavy lobes; ball-shaped truss of 10-12. Mrs. H. Beck
cross; Allen Korth, reg. 1978.
QUEEN NEFERTITI   Parentage as above, except reversed
5ft(1.5m) OF(-18C) M 3/4   Ball-shaped truss 8.5in(21.6cm)
wide of 12 flowers, light Neyron rose, darker edging and reverse. Plant wide as tall. Mrs. Beck cross; Korth, reg. 1977.
* *

```
          -catawbiense 1/2
MARKFRAF-
     -unknown 1/2
```
Flowers of dark violet, with brownish yellow to greenish yellow
markings; frilled edges.   T. J. R. Seidel, intro. 1910.

MARLENE PESTE   Described under FREDERICK GEODFRIED PESTE, q.v.

```
               -fortunei 1/2
        -Fawn-      -dichroanthum 1/8
     -    -Fabia-
MARLENE-      -griersonianum 1/8      -griffithianum 1/16
  SAYE -               -George Hardy-
     -  -Mrs. Lindsay Smith-         -catawbiense 1/16
     -Dot-          -Duchess of Edinburgh--unknown 1/8
          -fortunei
```
10ft(3m) x 6ft(1.8m)(28 yrs) OF(-18C) M   Very fragrant flow-
ers, 4.5in((11.5cm) wide, 7-lobed, in tall conical truss of 15;
truss 10in(25cm) broad. Light pink buds open white, with deep
greenish yellow dorsal spots. James cross; Childers, reg. 1989.

```
                              -fortunei 1/4
          -Direktör E. Hjelm--fortunei hybrid F2-
MARLENE VUYK-                   -unknown 3/4
          -unknown
```
Broadly funnel-shaped flowers to 2.4in(6cm) broad, deep purplish
pink; truss of 12-15. Hairless leaves to 9.8in(25cm) long. May
blooms. A. Vuyk, c. 1960; Royal Boskoop Hort. Soc., reg. 1988.

MARLEY HEDGES   Described under KATRINA, q.v.

```
          -dichroanthum 5/8
MARMORA-       -fortunei ssp. discolor 1/4
     -Margaret-     -dichroanthum
     Dunn -Fabia-
               -griersonianum 1/8
```
A parent of MALABAR. Flowers bright orange-yellow flushed rose
at edges. Sunningdale, 1955.

```
          -arboreum 1/4
     -Red Admiral-
MAROZE-        -thomsonii 1/4
     -meddianum 1/2
```
Tubular-shaped, waxy red flowers.   J. B. Stevenson intro. 1937.

                    -thomsonii 1/2
MARQUIS OF LOTHIAN-
                    -griffithianum 1/2
Trusses hold 7-10 flowers colored crimson and carmine rose with
a darker flush. William Martin, cross before 1880; Dunedin Rhododendron Group, NZ, reg. 1977.

            -griffithianum 1/2
MARS-
            -unknown 1/2
4ft(1.2m) -15F(-26C) ML 4/3 Flower true deep red, unspotted,
waxen, widely bell-shaped with white stamens, in neat rounded
trusses. Plant rather slow-growing and compact; narrow, ribbed,
dark green leaves. Not as hardy as NOVA ZEMBLA, but a fine red
for many cold areas. Needs afternoon shade. Waterer. A.M.
1928. F.C.C. Wisley Trials 1935. Color illus. VV p. 76.

                -griffithianum 3/8
            -Mars-
MARS-   -unknown 1/4
BARS-   -thomsonii 1/4
    -Barclayi Robert Fox-   -arboreum 1/8
                    -Glory of Penjerrick-
                                    -griffithianum
6ft(1.8m) x 3ft(.9m)(12 yrs) 10F(-12C) E Flowers in truss of
15, wavy margins, dark red with black spots. Leaves grayish
olive green. P. G. Valder cross; J. C. Brotherton, reg. 1986.

            -Betsy Trotwood--unknown 3/4
MARS NOVUS- -griffithianum 1/4
            -Mars-
                 -unknown
A parent of several hybrids. Flowers fiery scarlet red, lighter
in center. Seidel, before 1880.

* *
            -haematodes 1/2
MARSHALL-
            -elliottii 1/2
Low, spreading plant; dark green leaves with slight fawn indu-
mentum. Waxy, bright scarlet, funnel-shaped flowers in medium-
sized trusses. Midseason. Rothschild, 1947.
DEGAS Parentage as above, except reversed
Compact trusses of 9 bell-shaped flowers, currant red with very
dark spotting. Plant broader than tall, medium-sized leaves.
F. Hanger cross; RHS Garden, Wisley, reg. 1962. H.C. 1961.
LANYON Parentage as MARSHALL, above
Exhibited by Col. Bolitho, Cornwall.
* *

MARSHALL LYONS Described under ALICE FRANKLIN, q.v.

                        -griffithianum 1/8
                    -Loderi-
        -unnamed hybrid-   -fortunei 1/8
MARSHMALLOW-   -unknown 3/4
                -unknown
Truss of 10 flowers, orchid pink with a faint red-purple flare.
Leaves 6in(15.2cm) long. Mrs. R. J. Coker, reg. 1982.

MARTHA ISAACSON Described under MARY HARMON, q.v.

MARTHA MAY Described under DRESS UP, q.v.

                            -yakushimanum--Koichiro Wada
MARTHA PESTE---LILLIAN PESTE, selfed-   1/2
                        -Whitney hybrid--unknown 1/2
2.5ft(.75m) high x 3ft(.9m)(8 yrs) OF(-18C) ML   Flowers in
truss of 13, pale yellowish pink from buds of strong pink; flowers tinged and streaked strong pink. Leaves heavily indumented in moderate yellow. Peste cross; S. P. Johnston, reg. 1986.

MARTHA PHIPPS Parentage unknown
6ft(1.8m) -10F(-23C) ML   Leaves long, narrow. Pale yellow
flowers, flushed pink with mandarin orange inside edges, to 4in.
(10cm) across. Compact truss of 10. Phipps, reg. 1973.

            -forrestii Repens Group 1/2
MARTHA ROBBINS-
            -sperabile 1/2
1.5ft(.45m) OF(-18C) EM 5/4 A delightful plant. Bright red
flowers, 2.25in(5.7cm) wide, in truss of 4; floriferous. Plant

twice as wide as high; foliage like repens, slightly larger,
more vigorous; leaves glossy, dark green. L. Brandt, reg. 1971.

                -burmanicum 1/2
MARTHA WRIGHT-   -edgeworthii 1/4
            -Fragrantissimum-
                        -formosum 1/4
5ft(1.5m) 15F(-9C) EM Flowers creamy white, yellow in center,
fragrant; flat trusses of 4.   Mr. & Mrs. Maurice Sumner, reg.
1968.   Award as the best new hybrid in California, 1963.

MARTIN HOPE SUTTON   Parentage unknown
Parent of NUNEHAM PARK. Rich rose scarlet. A. Waterer, 1915.

                        -fortunei 1/4
            -unnamed hybrid-
MARTIN VAN HOF-   -unknown 3/4
            -unknown
12ft(3.6m) x 10ft(3.0m)(20 yrs) ML Flowers of heavy substance
in domed truss of 8-10, of 7 wavy lobes, very pale purple with a
dark red blotch in throat. Leaves held 3 years. R.I. Agricul-
tural Exp. Sta. intro.; J. McGuire, reg. 1989.

            -racemosum 1/2
MARTINE-
    -evergreen azalea--unknown 1/2
2.5ft(.75m) -5F(-21C) EM 4/3 An azaleodendron similar to RIA
HARDIJZER. Clear fuchsine pink flower, darker spotting on upper
lobe, 1.25in(3.2cm) wide, funnel shaped; flowers in 5-10 lateral
trusses of 2-4, forming a compact pseudo-terminal truss. Shiny
foliage. W. Hardijzer, reg. 1965.

            -Blue Peter--unknown 13/16
MARTIN'S PRIDE-   -ponticum 1/8
            -Purple Splendour-
        -unnamed-   -unknown
        hybrid-   -griffithianum
        -          -Queen Wilhelmina-   1/16
            -Trilby-   -unknown
                -Stanley Davies--unknown
6ft(1.8m) OF(-18C) ML Flowers strong reddish purple, lightly
spotted yellow-brown, openly funnel-shaped, 3in(7.6cm) across;
rounded trusses of 12-16. Floriferous. Plant as broad as tall;
deep green leaves. Martin Wapler cross; Del Loucks, reg. 1977.

MARVELLOUS H. E. Greer, reg. 1962. Extinct.

MARY ANN Described under CATHY, q.v.

MARY BEAN Described under ATOMIC BLAST, q.v.

                        -catawbiense 1/8
            -Atrosanguineum-
        -Atrier-   -unknown 1/8
MARY BELLE-   -griersonianum 1/4
        -          -decorum 1/4
        -Dechaem-
            -haematodes 1/4
5ft(1.5m) -15F(-26C) M 4/4 Flowers opening light salmon pink
from deeper buds, fading golden peach, basal blotch of cardinal
red. Flowers of much substance, 4in(10.2cm) wide, very ruffled
rims; flat trusses of 10. Gable, reg. 1964. P.A. 1962. Ill.
LW pl. 54; VV p. 106. (Gable's nickname for plant: "you-know")

            -haematodes 1/2
MARY BRIGGS-   -forrestii Repens Group 1/4
        -Elizabeth-
            -griersonianum 1/4
Compact plant 8in(20.3cm) high by 16in(40.6cm) wide at 10 years.
Blood red flowers, funnel-campanulate, 2in(5in) wide, in compact
trusses of 8-10. Dark green, elliptic foliage, 3in(7.6cm) long.
Midseason. Vernon Wyatt, reg. 1968.

MARY CHANTRY Described under ANDRÉ, q.v.

            -fortunei 1/2
MARY COWAN-
            -diaprepes 1/2
A parent of VISTOSO, q.v.   Ben Lancaster.

MARY D. BLACK Described under PINK FLOSS, q.v.

```
                -griffithianum 1/4
          -Angelo-
MARY DRENNEN-      -fortunei ssp. discolor 1/4
          -wardii 1/2
```
5ft(1.5m) -5F(-21C) L 4/4 Seven-lobed flower, light aureolin
yellow, 4.9in(12.5cm) wide; truss of 11-12. Leaves 8in(20.3cm)
long. Whitney cross; H. L. Larson, reg. 1983.

* *
```
          -racemosum 1/2
MARY FLEMING-
          -keiskei 1/2
```
2.5ft(.75m) -15F(-26C) E 4/4 Shapely plant, 4ft(1.2m) in 20
years; leaves narrow, pointed, bronze in winter. Flowers bisque
yellow; streaked, blotched salmon; abundant clusters. Nearing,
reg. 1972. A.E. 1973. Color illus. ARS Q 28:3 (1974), p.170.
KEISKRAC Parentage as above (Earliest of this group)
Pink-flowered hybrid by E. J. P. Magor, Cornwall, 1926.
YELLOW SPRING Parentage as above, except reversed
1ft(.3m) -5F(-21C) EM 3/3 Leaves of dark yellowish green,
scaly beneath. Flower 1in(2.5cm) wide, 5-lobed, strong Neyron
rose edges shading to yellow-white; terminal inflorescence of 8-
10, each 3-5 flowered trusses. C. Herbert, reg. 1976.
VINESTAR Parentage (keiskei x racemosum)
Flowers pale canary yellow, flecked orange-brown. Horticultural
Research Institute of Ontario, Canada, reg. 1977. A.M. Wisley
Trials 1989.
ARSEN'S PINK Parentage as VINESTAR
2ft(.6m) -15F(-26C) E 3/3 Profuse small pink flowers; easy
to grow. Compact dwarf. Arsen.
GINNY GEE Parentage (keiskei--Yaku Fairy x racemosum, dwarf)
2ft(.6m) -15F(-26C) EM 5/5 Broader than tall, branches creeping and stiff, small leaves. Flowers 1in(2.5cm) wide, dark pink
through shell pink, white-striped; groups of 11 buds, 4-5 flowers each. W. Berg, reg. 1979. S.P.A. 1985. Color illus. ARS
J 38:2 (1984), p. 103; also 44:1 (1990), p. 3.
RIK Parentage as MARY FLEMING, above
2.5ft(.75m) high x 4ft(1.2m)(15 yrs) -15F(-26C) E Blooms just
after P.J.M. Yellowish white flowers, edged deep purplish pink,
fading to white with age. Fine winter color with deep red stems
and foliage. Leon Yavorsky, reg. 1987.
TOM KOENIG Parentage as MARY FLEMING, above
3ft(.9m) 10F(-23C) EM 3/3 Narrow leaves, to 2in(5cm) long.
Pale pink flowers in dense clusters like racemosum, but larger.
G. Guy Nearing cross; T. W. Koenig, reg. 1970.

* *
```
          -fortunei, cream form 1/2
MARY GARRISON-
          -vernicosum R 18139 1/2
```
4ft(1.2m) -10F(-23C) EM 4/4 Openly campanulate flowers, a
blend of salmon yellow and brownish red, fading creamy yellow.
Difficult to propagate, but a good parent of yellows. J. Gable.
Color illus. LW pl. 55.

```
          -neriiflorum Euchaites Group 1/2
MARY GREIG-
          -souliei 1/2
```
Flowers rose madder, 2.5in(6.4cm) wide. Mrs. Greig, reg. 1962.

* *
```
                          -Corona--unknown 1/8
                    -unnamed hybrid-
                    -             -griersonianum 1/8
            -Mrs. Donald-   -griffithianum 1/8
            - Graham    -Loderi-
MARY HARMON-            -fortunei 1/8
          -azalea occidentale 1/2
```
An azaleodendron, with funnel-shaped flowers 2in(5cm) across,
striped pink on outside, fragrant; 15-flowered trusses. Endre
Ostbo, reg. 1962. A. E. 1958.
MARTHA ISAACSON Parentage as above
5ft(1.5m) -5F(-21C) ML A fragrant azaleodendron with unusual
foliage; sun-tolerant. Leaves tinged deep maroon, good contrast
to white flowers striped in pink. Ostbo pre-1958. P.A. 1956.
* *
```
          -yakushimanum 1/2           -griffithianum 1/16
MARY JANE-                    -Queen Wilhelmina-
          -        -Britannia-          -unknown 3/16
          -Leo-          -Stanley Davies--unknown
          -elliottii 1/4
```

3ft(.9m) OF(-18C) M Flowers of carmine rose, in ball-shaped
trusses of 12. Semi-dwarf plant, leaves with deep fawn indumentum; retained 2-3 years. Mrs. Le Vern Freidman, reg. 1974.
VALLERIE KAY Parentage as above
1ft(.3m) OF(-18C) M Bright carmine pink flowers, fading to
lighter, frilled lobes; ball-shaped truss of 20. Plant broad as
tall, leaves with fawn indumentum; new growth mouse gray. Mrs.
Freidman, reg. 1974.
VERNA CARTER Parentage as above
3ft(.9m) OF(-18C) M Pale pink buds open to white flowers, 5
wavy and frilled lobes in ball-shaped trusses of 12. Plant wide
as tall, medium green leaves with fawn indumentum; new growth
mouse gray. Mrs. Freidman, reg. 1974.
* *
```
                          -catawbiense 3/16
                    -Kettledrum-
            -Sham's Ruby-          -unknown 11/16
            -             -Parsons    -catawbiense
            -             -America- Grandiflorum-
MARY JANE MEANS-          -                   -unknown
            -             -dark red hybrid--unknown
            -                        -griffithianum
            -             -Queen Wilhelmina-          1/8
            -Unknown Warrior-          -unknown
                          -Stanley Davies--unknown
```
2ft(.6m) x 3ft(.9m)(7 yrs) -5F(-21C) M Flowers in trusses of
18-22, strong purplish red buds open to strong purplish red with
vivid purplish red spotting. R. L. Means, M.D., reg. 1989.

```
                -dwarf white hybrid--unknown 3/4
MARY KITTEL-                    -catawbiense 1/8
          -             -Atrosanguineum-
          -Mrs. P. den Ouden-          -unknown
          -             -          -arboreum 1/8
          -             -Doncaster-
                          -unknown
```
3ft(.9m) -10F(-21C) M Low, compact, slow-growing plant, form-
ing a mound wider than high; large, bright green foliage all
year. Pink flowers, in medium-sized truss. Mezitt, cross 1963.

```
                -fortunei--Sir Charles Butler 1/4
          -Mrs. A. T. de la Mare-
MARY                         -maximum 1/8
LUCILLE-          -Halopeanum-
          -        -griersonianum 1/4  -griffithianum 5/32
          -Earl of  -        -hardy hybrid--unknown 3/16
          Donoughmore-        -                 -griffithianum
                    -unnamed-          -George-
                    hybrid-Mrs. L. A.- Hardy-catawbiense 1/32
                          Dunnett -
                          -unknown
```
5ft(1.5m) -10F(-23C) EM Flowers of heavy substance, slightly
fragrant, rose opal, with dark red blotch in trusses of 9-15.
Plant leafy, as broad as high, with dark green leaves 6in(15cm)
x 2in(5cm). Mr. & Mrs. Freeman Stephens, reg. 1975.

* *
```
                          -griffithianum 1/4
          -Loderi King George-
MARY MAYO-          -fortunei 1/4
          -        -fortunei ssp. discolor 1/4
          -Ostbo Y 3-    -dichroanthum 1/8
                    -Fabia-
                          -griersonianum 1/8
```
4ft(1.2m) -5F(-21C) M 4/3 Flowers a blend of pinks, throat
suffused brilliant yellow, to 4.5in(11.5cm) wide, frilled; truss
of 11. Leaves to 6.5in(16.5cm). Bovee, reg. 1962. P.A. 1960.
CARIOCA Parentage as above
4ft(1.2m) OF(-18C) ML Flowers to 4in(10cm) across, center of
cream blending into a wide border of purplish pink, upper petal
spotted dark reddish orange. Bovee, reg. 1963.
EXOTIC Parentage as above
5ft(1.5m) 5F(-15C) M 4/3 Red flowers blended yellow and pink
4.5in(11.5cm) broad; truss of 12. Bovee, reg. 1962. P.A. 1961.
GERTRUDE BOVEE Parentage as above
5ft(1.5m) -5F(-21C) ML 4/3 Very dark green leaves 8in
(20.3cm) long. Compact plant with large flowers ruffled, soft
cream, blushed pink, upper petal red spots. Bovee, reg. 1972.
ROMA SUN Parentage as above
6ft(1.8m)(24 yrs.) OF(-18C) M As broad as tall, medium green
leaves, bullate, 8.25in(21cm) long. Frilled, fragrant flowers,

yellowish pink, becoming light yellowish green, edges deep pink;
reverse fades from deep pink to light yellow. Flat truss of 10.
Bovee cross; Sorenson & Watson, reg. 1975.
SEÑORITA   Parentage as above
5ft(1.5m) -5F(-21C) ML Leaves 6in x 2in (15.2cm x 5cm). Ruffled flowers of lilac pink, yellowish pink in throat, upper lobe
spotted brown, 4in(10.2cm) across; trusses 14. The Bovees, reg.
1962.
* *

```
                -griersonianum 1/2
MARY McQUILKAN-                        -campylocarpum 1/4
                -Souvenir of W. C. Slocock-
                                       -unknown 1/4
```
Small flowers, white with throat stained port wine red, held in
lax trusses. Late midseason.   Sir James Horlick, reg. 1962.

```
                    -decorum 1/4
        -unnamed hybrid-
MARY OLERI-          -fortunei ssp. discolor 1/4
        -                -griersonianum 1/4
        -Tally Ho-
                    -facetum (eriogynum) 1/4
```
4ft(1.2m) -10F(-23C) M   Flowers of good substance, yellowish
white, pink shadings on opening, throat a light grayed yellow-
green, 4in(10.2cm) wide, 7 lobes; conical truss of 13. Fragrant
and floriferous. Plant rounded, wide as high, with leaves held
3 years.   Alfred A. Raustein, reg. 1983.

MARY ROXBURGHE   Described under SIR FREDERICK MOORE, q.v.

MARY SWAYTHLING   Described under GLADYS, q.v.

MARY TASKER   Described under AMBER GEM, q.v.

```
        -Tom Everett--unknown 1/2
MARY TODD-              -wardii 1/4
        -unnamed hybrid-    -fortunei 1/8
              -Fawn-    -dichroanthum 1/16
                   -Fabia-
                        -griersonianum 1/16
```
3ft(.9m) high x 4ft(1.2m) -5F(-21C) M   Very fragrant flowers,
openly funnel-shaped, 4.5in(11.5cm) wide, in trusses of 9-12, 7-
lobed, pale greenish yellow in bud, opening to pale yellow with
strong yellowish pink edging.   J. Todd, cross 1969; reg. 1986.

MARY TRANQUILLIA   Described under CATHY CARTER, q.v.

MARY WATERER   Parentage unknown
A parent of MARHAM. Bright rich pink flowers with paler center
and buff spots.   Knap Hill Nursery, 1955.

* *
```
                -catawbiense 1/4
        -Pink Twins-
MARY YATES-         -haematodes 1/4
        -                    -griffithianum 1/4
        -Leah Yates---Mars, selfed-
                             -unknown 1/4
```
4ft(1.2m) -10F(-23C) M   Flowers orchid pink, shading lighter
to center, throat lightly flushed pale yellow with a few small
gold spots, openly funnel-shaped, 2.5in(6.4cm) across, 7-lobed;
spherical trusses hold 10.   Plant twice as wide as high, decumbent branches.   Henry Yates cross; Maletta Yates, reg. 1977.
RAVELS   Parentage as above, except reversed
Flowers Neyron rose, darker veins, large lime green dorsal
blotch, in conical trusses of 12. Shrub wider than tall, dense,
medium green foliage.   H. Yates, cross; Mrs. Yates, reg. 1977.
SHAAZAM   Parentage: PINK TWINS x LEAH YATES
4.5ft(1.35m) -10F(-23C) ML Flowers Neyron rose with a yellow
blotch, 7-lobed in ball-shaped trusses of 10. Yates, reg. 1977.
SUNSET YATES   Parentage as MARY YATES, above
3.5ft(1m) -10F(-23C) ML   Flowers of heavy substance, 3.5in.
(8.3cm) wide, Neyron rose, shading paler, held in trusses of 15.
Plant broader than tall, arching branches.   Yates, reg. 1977.
YATES' RED   Parentage: LEAH YATES x PINK TWINS
4ft(1.2m) -5F(-21C) ML Sparkling cardinal red flowers shading
to magenta in throat, grayed purple blotch in conical trusses of
13-15. Plant wider than high; petioles reddish.   Yates, 1977.
* *

MARYKE   Described under MARGARET DUNN, q.v.

```
              -brachycarpum 1/4
    -unnamed-       -wardii 3/16
    - hybrid-Crest-           -fortunei ssp. discolor 3/32
    -          -Lady   -
MARYPAT-          Bessborough-campylocarpum Elatum Group
    -              -catawbiense var. album 1/8        3/32
    -    -unnamed-      -wardii
    - hybrid-Crest-           -fortunei ssp. discolor
    -Monte-          -Lady
    Carlo-          Bessborough-campylocarpum Elatum Group
    -          -aureum 1/8
        -unnamed-
              hybrid-campylocarpum 1/8
```
Flowers chartreuse green, with an eye of brilliant yellow-green
specks. Often a parent of Delp hybrids.   Weldon E. Delp.

```
              -fortunei 1/4
    -Ruby Bowman-       -griffithianum 1/8
MARZO-       -Lady Bligh-
    -ririei 1/2       -unknown 1/8
```
6ft(1.8m) 5F(-15C) VE Magenta flower buds open to spirea red,
fading to roseine purple, with a blotch of violet purple deep in
throat. Trusses 9in(23cm) broad, dome-shaped, hold 10-14 flowers. Upright, rounded plant as wide as tall; dark green leaves,
concave, 7in(17.8cm) long.   Dr. David Goheen, reg. 1982.

* *
```
                      -caucasicum 1/4
              -Boule de-       -catawbiense 1/8
MASS WITH CLASS---PINK CAMEO F2- Neige  -unnamed-
              -              hybrid-unknown 1/8
              -catawbiense, red form 1/2
```
Buds of lilac and purple, opening to flowers of strong reddish
purple and vivid purplish red; dorsal spots ruby red and Indian
lake; moderate reddish orange anthers.   W. Delp.
RACY   Parentage as above
Buds of chrysanthemum crimson and deep red, open to flowers of
vivid purplish red and deep purplish pink; a white flare; dorsal
spots lettuce green; dark red stigma.   W. Delp.
TRI-STATE   Parentage as above
Ruby red buds open to frilled flowers of vivid purplish red with
a white flare; dorsal spotting dark red. Medium-sized; hardy to
-15F(-26C).   W. Delp.
* *


```
        -griersonianum 1/2
MASTER DICK-           -arboreum 1/8
        -       -Doncaster-
        -The Don-       -unknown 1/8
              -griffithianum 1/4
```
Carmine scarlet, brownish speckling.   Crosfield.   A.M. 1936.

MASTER MARINER   Described under MARINER, q.v.

MASTER, THE   See THE MASTER

```
                      -maximum 1/4
        -unnamed hybrid-
        -              -vernicosum (18139) 1/4
MASTERBLEND-      -aureum (chrysanthum) 1/4
        -unnamed hybrid-
                      -maximum 1/4
```
Buds of strong purplish red open to flowers light purplish pink
lightly tinted with strong purplish red; dorsal spots ruby red;
throat of brownish orange and dark red. Good foliage. W. Delp.

```
Out of order                      -griffithianum 1/8
                   -Queen Wilhelmina-
        -Britannia-             -unknown 1/8
MAUD CORNING-       -Stanley Davies--unknown
        -Skyglow--unknown
```
5ft(1.5m) -15F(-26C) L   Flowers of pale purplish pink, with
edges of orchid pink and sap green throat, of good substance, 7
overlapping lobes, fragrant; lax trusses hold 8. Plant rounded,
branching well; narrowly elliptic leaves held 2 years. Charles
Dexter cross; Holden Arboretum raiser; P. Bristol, reg. 1983.

```
                              -maximum 1/4
                  -unnamed hybrid-
                  -                     -vernicosum (18139) 1/8
            -Masterblend-              -aureum (chrysanthum) 1/8
            -         -unnamed hybrid-
            -                         -maximum
            -                   -catawbiense var. album 1/16
            -             -            -catawbiense
            -       -Lodestar-   -Catawbiense-       3/64
MASTERFUL-  -           -Belle - Album   -unknown 3/64
            -           -        Heller-        -catawbiense
            -           -           -white cat. hyb.-
            -     -R.O.-                     -unknown
            -     -Delp-                 -catawbiense
            -     -    -          -Atrosanguineum-
            -     -    -     -Atrier-            -unknown
            -Dusty- -Mary-    -griersonianum 1/32
              Whiz- Belle-   -decorum 1/32
                 -        -Dechaem-
                 -              -haematodes 1/32
                 -          -fortunei 1/8
                 -Golden Star-
                          -wardii 1/8
```

Buds of ruby red and beetroot purple, open to flowers of rhodamine and phlox purples with pale purplish pinks; undersides of
Tyrian purple; dorsal spots deep red.   W. Delp.

* *
```
           -griersonianum 1/2
MATADOR-
           -strigillosum 1/2
```
4ft(1.2m) OF(-18C) EM 4/3   Tubular-shaped flowers, dark
orange-red, in truss of 8. Attractive hairy leaves. Lord Aberconway.   A.M. 1945.   F.C.C. 1946.
EXBURY MATADOR   Parentage as above
3ft(.9m) 15F(-9C) M 3/3 Dark green foliage, buff indumentum.
Orange-scarlet flowers. Rothschild.   Color illus. PB pl. 65.
* *

MATILDA   See GRANDMA MATILDA

MAUD CORNING   See previous column

MAUREEN   Described under CARLENE, q.v.

```
                  -griersonianum 1/4     -griffithianum 5/32
          -Anna Rose-                  -George-
          - Whitney -      -Pink  - Hardy-catawbiense 3/32
          -        -      -  Pearl-        -arboreum 1/32
          -    -Countess-      -Broughtonii-
          -     of Derby-             -unknown 11/32
MAUREEN-  -          -      -catawbiense
OSTLER-   -        -Cynthia-
          -             -griffithianum
          -                     -griffithianum
          -          -Queen Wilhelmina-
          -    -Britannia-            -unknown
          -Burgundy-    -Stanley Davies--unknown
          -             -ponticum 1/8
          -Purple Splendour-
                     -unknown
```
Flowers in trusses of 20-21, rose opal, with dark spotting on the
dorsal lobe. Medium-sized shrub.   A. G. Ostler, reg. 1984.

```
           -edgeworthii (bullatum) 1/2
MAURICE SKIPWORTH-
           -burmanicum 1/2
```
White flowers with faintest green tint, and yellow speckling at
base, in 5-flowered trusses.   M. Skipworth cross; Dunedin Rhododendron Group, NZ, reg. 1977.

```
                      -catawbiense v. album Glass--Catalgla
MAUVE         -Calsap-                             1/4
PLUSH---CALTWINS F2-    -Sappho--unknown 1/4
           -            -catawbiense 1/4
           -Pink Twins-
                     -haematodes 1/4
```
Buds of ruby red and strong purplish red; flowers strong reddish
purple and mallow purple; dorsal spots moderate orange.   Delp.

MAUVE SATCHEL   Described under JOAN LANGDON, q.v.

```
                              -yakushimanum 1/4
            -Orange Marmalade-       -wardii 1/8
            -            -Mrs. Lammot-     -souliei ? 1/16
MAVIS-         Copeland  -Virginia Scott-
DAVIS-      -dichroanthum 1/8           -unknown 1/8
     -  -Dido-
     -       -decorum 1/8      -griffithianum 5/32
     -Lem's-                -Beauty of-
     Cameo-  -Norman Gill- Tremough-arboreum 1/32
        -    -            -griffithianum
        -Anna-               -griffithianum
         -Jean Marie de Montague-
                         -unknown
```
28in(71cm) x 28in(6 yrs) 0F(-18C) M   Flowers in trusses of 10
to 12, of heavy substance, 5 or 6 wavy lobes, pale yellow, edged
moderate reddish orange; the reverse of same. Very floriferous.
Flat, elliptic, dull green leaves.   J. A. Davis, reg. 1988.

```
           -maximum, white form 1/2
MAX FETTERHOFF-               -griffithianum 1/8
            -            -unnamed hybrid-
            -Mrs. Furnivall-       -unknown 1/4
            -            -      -caucasicum 1/8
            -unnamed hybrid-
                     -unknown
```
5ft(1.5m) x 4ft(1.2m)(25 yrs) -20F(-29C) ML   Domed truss of 16
widely funnel-shaped flowers, light purplish pink, white center,
white dorsal blotch spotted bronze to vivid chartreuse. Leaves
dull green; sparse brownish hairs below. Fetterhoff, reg. 1989.

MAX MARSHLAND   Described under CORMID, q.v.

```
                      -caucasicum 1/4
           -Chevalier F. de Sauvage-
MAX SYE-              -hardy hybrid--unknown 3/4
      -unknown
```
4ft(1.2m) OF(-18C) ML 2/3 Flower dark red with black blotch;
C. Frets & Son, 1935.

* **
           -maximum 1/2
MAXDIS-
           -fortunei ssp. discolor 1/2
White flowers.   G. Nearing & J. Gable, before 1958.
WESTDALE   Parentage as above
6ft(1.8m) -5F(-21C) ML   Buds of purplish pink open to pale
and light purplish pink flowers with a slight twin flare of reddish brown; outside of each lobe with stripe of pink; spherical
trusses of 20. Plant as wide as tall.   J. Wister cross, Scott
Horticultural Foundation; Gertrude Wister, reg. 1980.
* *

MAXECAT   Described under RUSSELL HARMON, q.v.

```
                      -maximum 1/2
MAXHAEM SALMON or MAXHAEM YELLOW-
                   -haematodes 1/2
```
5ft(1.5m) -15F(-26C) ML 3/3 Salmon flowers, medium-sized, in
well-filled trusses. Floriferous. Fine, dark green foliage.
Haematodes pollen, "true form", from E. J. P. Magor, Cornwall.
Joseph B. Gable.   Color illus. LW pl. 47.

MAXIE   Described under ALBERT CLOSE

MAXIMUM ROSEUM   See PONTICUM ROSEUM

MAXIMUM WELLESLEYANUM   See WELLESLEYANUM

* *
           -strigillosum 1/2
MAXINE -   -forrestii Repens Group 1/4
CHILDERS-Elizabeth-
           -griersonianum 1/4
```
3ft(.9m)  -5F(-21C)  E  4/4  Flower cardinal red, widely funnel-
campanulate, 2.5in(6.4cm) wide, 5-lobed, of heavy substance;
trusses of 8-10.  Shrub well-branched, rounded, wider than tall;
olive green leaves, light orange-brown indumentum beneath; new
growth reddish bronze.   The entire plant reflects strigillosum.
Mrs. A. Childers cross; Phetteplace, reg. 1977.
MAXINE MARGARET   Parentage as above
2ft(.6m)  -15F(-26C)  E  Flowers currant red, 5 black nectaries,
widely funnel-campanulate, 2in(5cm) wide, 5-lobed, of heavy sub-
```

stance; trusses of 8-11. Plant broader than tall; foliage dark
green, 3.5in(8.9cm) long.   M. & A. Childers, reg. 1977.
* *

MAXWELL T. MASTERS   Parentage unknown
Flowers of rosy crimson. Parent of ARMISTICE DAY. A. Waterer,
before 1915.

* *
            -haematodes 1/2
MAY DAY-
            -griersonianum 1/2
3ft(.9m) 5F(-15C) EM 3/4   Brilliant orange-scarlet flowers,
funnel-shaped, in lax truss of 8. Vigorous habit, rapid growth,
broader than tall. Dark green leaves, tan indumentum.   Widely
grown in mild climates.   A. M. Williams. A.M. 1932. Color
illus. ARS J 37:2 (1983), p. 75; F p. 54.
BODNANT MAY DAY   Parentage as above
Deep scarlet flowers, scented. Lord Aberconway, 1939.
BORDE HILL MAY DAY   Cross made at Borde Hill by Clarke.
EXBURY MAY DAY   Parentage as above
Deeper red flowers, more compact than A.M. form. Pale buff in-
dumentum beneath foliage. Rothschild. Color illus. PB pl. 53.
* *
            -caucasicum 1/2
MAY FIRTH-
            -unknown 1/2
Large, pale pink flowers, held in loose trusses. Early. Knap
Hill, reg. 1962.

MAY JEFFERY   Parentage unknown
Flowers of cerise pink, spotted.   Knap Hill, reg. 1968.

MAY MOONLIGHT   Parentage unknown
Flowers yellowish pink; fragrant. Dexter cross; G. Wister, reg.
1984.

                -haematodes 1/4
            -May Day-
MAY MORN-   -griersonianum 1/4
            -beanianum, pink form 1/2
Funnel-shaped flowers, 2in(5cm) across, azalea pink, flushed on
edges with porcelain rose, and held in trusses of 8-10.   Lord
Aberconway. A.M. 1946.

                    -fortunei ssp. discolor 1/4
            -Cornish Loderi-
MAY PINK-   -griffithianum 1/2
        -                    -griffithianum
            -Loderi Sir Edmund-
                            -fortunei 1/4
Fuchsine pink flowers, shaded with light purple. Loder, 1946.
A.M. 1946.

            -fortunei 1/2
MAY QUEEN-
            -unknown 1/2
Flowers large, waxy, rich pink.   Sir E. Loder, 1926.

                -campylogynum Cremastum Group 1/4
            -Candi-
MAY SCHWARTZ-   -racemosum 1/4
            -tephropeplum 1/2
2ft(.6m) 5F(-15C) E Flowers fuchsine pink, the reverse darker
and streaked, 1.25in(3.2cm) across, 5 wavy lobes, of heavy substance; small terminal inflorescences of 4-6. Free-flowering.
Plant broader than tall; glossy, narrowly elliptic leaves 1.4in.
(3.4cm) long, scaly beneath. Robert W. Scott, reg. 1977.

* *
            -Corona--unknown 1/4
        -Bow Bells-
MAY SONG-   -williamsianum 1/4
    -                      -fortunei ssp. discolor 1/8
    -     -Lady Bessborough-
    -Day -   -campylocarpum Elatum Group 1/8
    Dream-
            -griersonianum 1/4
3ft(.9m) OF(-18C) M Flowers pale pink, reverse flushed deeper
pink, openly campanulate, to 3.5in(8.9cm) wide, ruffled; trusses
of 9-11. Plant compact. G. Grace cross; Bovee, reg. 1972.

BELL SONG   Parentage as above
3ft(.9m) OF(-18C) M   Ruffled flowers, in two shades of pink.
Plant habit spreading and bushy.   Bovee intro.
* *

MAY TEMPLAR   Described under BRITANNIA, q.v.

MAY TIME   Listed under ANNA H. HALL, q.v.

            -sperabile 1/2
MAY WINE-
            -elliottii 1/2
2.5ft(.75m) high x 3ft(.9m)(7 yrs) 5F(-15C) M   Domed truss of
15; strong red buds open to vivid red, wavy-edged flowers. Foliage held 3 years; scant indumentum. Whitney; Bulgin, reg. 1986.

            -sutchuenense 1/2
MAYA-
        -ririei 1/2
Flowers pale mauve within, spotted deep purple and blotched with
intense purple at base. The exterior of flowers, a deeper shade
of mauve. Magor, 1933.   A.M. 1940.

MAYBE   Described under GAY SONG, q.v.

                        -souliei 1/8
                    -Soulbut-
        -Vanessa Pastel-   -fortunei--Sir Chas. Butler 1/8
MAYCROSS-   -griersonianum 1/4
        -aberconwayi 1/2
Flowers in truss of 9, funnel-shaped, 5-lobed, white with medium
purplish red throat markings; outside marked with stronger pink.
Shrub 5ft(1.5m) x 4ft(1.2m); ovate leaves. J. May, reg. 1988.

MAYFAIR   Described under SAPPHIRE, q.v.

                    -racemosum 1/2
MAYFLOWER---CONESTOGA, selfed-
                    -minus Carolinianum Group 1/2
Pink flowers, blooming early; hardy to -20F(-29C). Joseph B.
Gable, reg. 1958.

                    -dichroanthum ssp. scyphocalyx 1/4
        -Reginald Farrer-
MAYGOLD-   -fortunei ssp. discolor 3/8
    -      -wardii 1/4
        -Crest-   -fortunei ssp. discolor
            -Lady Bessborough-
                    -campylocarpum Elatum Group 1/8
Funnel-shaped flowers, 3.7in(9.5cm) broad, light yellow-green to
pale greenish yellow, late in May; truss of 10. Oblong, bullate
leaves, recurved. Bush 5.8ft(1.75m). J. May, reg. 1988.

                -elliottii 1/4
        -Kilimanjaro-   -Moser's Maroon--unknown 1/8
    -            -Dusky Maid-
MAYKING-   -fortunei ssp. discolor 1/8
    -            -dichroanthum 1/4
        -Francis Hanger-   -griffithianum 1/8
                -Isabella-
                    -auriculatum 1/8
Deep pink, funnel-shaped flowers, 4.7in(12cm) wide, dorsal lobes
heavily spotted black, vivid red exterior; trusses of 15 in May.
Ovate leaves to 6.7in(17cm); bush 6.5ft(2m). J. May, reg. 1988.

                    -campylocarpum Elatum Group 1/16
            -Penjerrick-
        -Amaura-   -griffithianum 1/16
    -Eros-   -griersonianum 5/8
MAYROS-   -griersonianum
    -          -haematodes 1/4
        -May Day-
            -griersonianum
A red-flowered hybrid. Lord Aberconway, 1946.

MAY'S DELIGHT   Described under OAKTON, q.v.

            -mekongense var. melinanthum 1/2
MAY'S LEMON-
            -lutescens, FCC form 1/2
Light yellow-green, funnel-shaped flowers about 1in(2.7cm) wide,
slightly edged pink; truss of 7 in April. Small lanceolate fol-

iage; new growth bronze. Plant 19.5in(.5m) x 19.5in.   J. May, cross 1969; reg. 1988.

MAYSPARK   Described under GYPSY ROVER, q.v.

MEADOW POND--form of wardii L. & S. 15764
4ft(1.2m) -5F(-21C) M 4/3   Large primrose yellow flowers, heavily blotched in crimson purple. Crown Estate, Windsor, reg. 1964.   A.M. 1963.

```
                         -catawbiense 1/2
           -Mrs. C. S. Sargent-
MEADOWBROOK-                   -unknown (1/2)
           -              -catawbiense
           -Everestianum-
                         -unknown
```
5ft(1.5m) -15F(-26C) ML 3/3   Fair plant habit; grows as wide as tall. Medium-large foliage. Flowers vibrant pink, with a white blotch, green spots, frilled; conical trusses hold 22. P. Vossberg, reg. 1958.   A.E. 1973.

```
              -burmanicum 1/2
MEADOWGOLD-         -xanthostephanum 1/4
           -Lemon Mist-
                   -leucaspis 1/4
```
2.5ft(.75m) 15F(-9C) E 4/3   Flowers sulphur yellow, spotted upper lobe, tubular funnel-shaped, 1.5in(3.8cm) wide; terminal inflorescence up to 3 buds, each of 4-6 flowers. Plant rounded, wider than tall; dark green, glossy leaves, 1.5in(3.8cm) long, scales beneath, held 2 years.   Robert W. Scott, reg. 1976.

```
                -caucasicum 1/4
      -Boule de Neige-         -catawbiense 1/8
MEATH-           -unnamed hybrid-
      -                       -unknown 1/8
      -yakushimanum--Koichiro Wada 1/2
```
3ft(.9m) -5F(-21C) ML Flowers light mauve pink, darker at the edges, a light olive yellow dorsal blotch, openly funnel-shaped, to 3.75in(9.5cm) wide, 7 waxy lobes, very fragrant; spherical trusses of 9. Plant upright; leaves about 4.25in(10.8cm) long, retained 3 years.   Dr. W. A. Reese, reg. 1979.

MECCA   Described under COLONEL ROGERS, q.v.

```
                -arboreum 1/4
      -Red Admiral-
MEDEA-          -thomsonii 1/4
      -sutchuenense 1/2
```
A hybrid with red flowers.   E. J. P. Magor, intro. 1931.

```
        -dichroanthum ssp. scyphocalyx 1/2
MEDUSA-
        -griersonianum 1/2
```
3ft(.9m) -5F(-21C) M 3/3   Flowers Spanish orange shading on lobes to mandarin red, heavily speckled with light brown. Plant dense, compact; gray-green leaves with light woolly indumentum. Lord Aberconway, 1936.   Color illus. VV p. 111.

```
           -campylocarpum 1/2
MEG MERRILEES-
           -A. W. Hardy Hybrid--unknown 1/2
```
Flowers of apricot and yellow, with a red blotch; also, a creamy white form, shading to yellow.   Slocock, 1924.

```
              -catawbiense var. album Glass--Catalgla 1/4
      -Tony's-                    -catawbiense 1/8
      -Gift -       -Catawbiense Album-
      -    -Belle Heller-           -unknown 3/8
MEGAN-                   -             -catawbiense
      -              -white catawbiense hyb.-
      -        -Moser's Maroon--unknown    -unknown
      -unnamed hybrid-
                   -yakushimanum 1/4
```
Buds of strong reddish purple and deep purplish pink opening to white flowers edged in lilac and magnolia purples; dorsal spotting of chartreuse green; white filaments.   W. Delp.

```
         -yakushimanum 1/2
MEIKA KING-
         -unknown 1/2
```
Flowers held in compact trusses, cream, with frilled pink edges. Habit as yakushimanum.   S. M. King, reg. 1984.

```
                   -ponticum 3/8
        -Purple Splendour-
                   -unknown 9/16        -catawbiense 1/16
MELANIE-          -Parsons Grandiflorum-
 SHAW -      -America-          -unknown
      -Dorothy-      -dark red hybrid--unknown
       Amateis-          -ponticum
             -Purple Splendour-
                        -unknown
```
5ft(1.5m) -10F(-23C) ML Frilled flowers of deep purple with a black blotch, center suffused deep red, 2.5in(6.5cm) broad; ball truss of 14-18. Narrow, glossy, elliptical leaves to 4in(10cm); plant wider than tall.   J. Shaw cross; J. Leonard, reg. 1988.

* *
```
           -Marion (Cheal)--unknown 1/2
MELBA-          -fortunei--Sir Charles Butler 1/4
     -Van Nes Sensation-          -maximum 1/8
                        -Halopeanum-
                               -griffithianum 1/8
```
Flowers amaranth rose, fading to very light solferino purple in center. V. J. Boulter, reg. 1972.
BEAUT ONE   Parentage as above
Campanulate flowers, medium fuchsia purple fading to light amaranth rose; truss of 12-15.   Boulter, reg. 1983.
WINTER BEAUTY   Parentage as above
Rose purple flowers, conspicuous yellowish brown spotting on the upper lobe.   Boulter, reg. 1972.
YOU BEAUT   Parentage as above
Orchid pink flowers.   Boulter, reg. 1972.
* *

```
             -Diadema--unknown 5/8
      -Herme-          -catawbiense 1/8
      -    -Everestianum-
MELIDIOSO-          -unknown
      -          -dichroanthum ssp. scyphocalyx 1/4
      -unnamed hybrid-
                   -unknown
```
Truss of 15 flowers, 6-7 wavy-edged lobes, medium purplish pink, rims and outside deeper, 3 dorsal lobes marked in strong orange-yellows on pale greenish yellow. Elliptic, glossy leaves, thin brownish indumentum below. Bush 3.7ft(1.1m) x 4ft(1.2m); blooms late May-early June.   Hachmann, cross 1977; Stok; reg. 1988.

```
                 -thomsonii 1/4
      -Ascot Brilliant-
MELISSA-          -unknown 1/4
      -arboreum 1/2
```
Red flowers with darker red spotting.   E. J. P. Magor, 1932.

```
        -myrtifolium (kotschyi) 1/2
MELIZ-
        -unknown 1/2
```
1ft(.3m) 0F(-18C) ML Venetian pink flowers lightly spotted in currant red, open-campanulate, to 1in(2.5cm) wide; lax inflorescences of 1-4 trusses, each of 5-8 flowers. Plant rounded, wider than tall; elliptic leaves 1.25in(3.2cm) long, densely scaly beneath.   J. F. Caperci, reg. 1976.

* *
```
              -wardii 1/2
MELLOW GOLD-
              -campylocarpum 1/2
```
B. F. Lancaster cross, before 1958.
FALVIA   Parentage as above
Yellow flowers.   Lord Aberconway, 1931.
JUST DREAMIN'   Parentage as above, except reversed
Trusses of 16 flowers, medium primrose yellow with darker yellow center. G. Langdon, Australia, reg. 1980.
YELLOW DREAM   Parentage: campylocarpum X wardii
Trusses of 14 flowers of light Dresden yellow with center deeper yellow, spotted red. G. Langdon, reg. 1982.
* *

```
Out of order          -griffithianum 1/4
            -Loderi Venus-
MELODY-          -fortunei 1/4
            -          -thomsonii 1/4
            -General Sir John du Cane-
                        -fortunei ssp. discolor 1/4
```
A tall, shapely plant. Creamy pink flowers, held in well-packed trusses. Rothschild, 1950.

```
              -yakushimanum 3/8    -fortunei ssp. discolor
        -            -Lady Bess--                      3/64
      -unnamed-   -Day - borough -campylocarpum Elatum
      - hybrid-   -Dream-griersonianum 3/64        1/64
        -         -Gold-           -fortunei ssp. discolor
   -Cisa-    Mohur-Margaret Dunn-     -dichroanthum 1/64
   -    -             -Fabia-
   -    -      -yakushimanum       -griersonianum
MELLOW-  -Serendipity-
YELLOW-           -aureum 1/4      -Pygmalion--unknown
   -              -unnamed hybrid-                 1/16
   -         -Weldy-           -haematodes 1/16
   -       -     -yakushimanum, Exbury form 1/8
   -Robert Weldon-
             -Serendipity (as above)
```
Buds of brilliant greenish yellow and strong yellowish pink open
to primrose yellow flowers; a light yellow-green flare. Delp.

MELODY   See previous column

```
        -caucasicum 1/2
MELPOMENE-
        -unknown 1/2
```
4ft(1.2m) -10F(-23C) EM Very dark pink buds, opening to pale
pink with strong cerise red markings. T. J. Seidel cross, 1894.

```
        -dichroanthum 1/2
MELROSE-   -fortunei ssp. discolor 1/4
     -Avocet-
           -fortunei 1/4
```
Flowers of pink. Plant not highly rated at Exbury Rothschild,
intro. 1947.

```
              -catawbiense var. album Glass--Catalgla 1/4
     -Ice Cube-            -catawbiense var.
     -      -Belle -Catawbiense Album-       album 1/16
     -      Heller-            -unknown 3/8
MELUSINE-    -             -catawbiense
LA FEE -     -white catawbiense hybrid-      1/16
     -      -             -unknown
     -      -Essex Scarlet--unknown
     -Scarlet Wonder-
             -forrestii Repens Group 1/4
```
5ft(1.5m)(12 yrs) -20F(-28C) ML Flowers 3.5in(9cm) wide, wavy
edges, of light purplish pinks, heavily spotted deep red on dorsal lobes; tall conical truss of 14-20. Flat smooth leaves held
4 years; plant broad as tall. Brueckner, cross 1975; reg. 1988.

```
                    -griffithianum 3/32
               -George-
          -Pink - Hardy-catawbiense 3/32
          - Pearl-      -arboreum 1/32
     -Countess -Broughtonii-
     - of Derby-         -unknown 1/32
   -unnamed-    -catawbiense
   - hybrid-  -Cynthia-
   -    -          -griffithianum
MELVILLE-   -      -griffithianum 1/8
   -    -Loderi Venus-
   -         -fortunei 1/8
   -    -dichroanthum 1/4
   -Fabia-
        -griersonianum 1/4
```
Vivid red, tubular funnel-shaped flowers from buds of strong
red. Elliptic leaves, slight fawn indumentum. Shrub to 10ft
(3.0m). Mid-to-late June. Waterers Nurseries, reg. 1986.

MEMOIR   Parentage unknown
A parent of ARIEL. Flowers lilac white, with green spots. A.
Waterer, before 1915.

```
        -campylocarpum 1/2
MEMORIAL -     -wardii 1/4
KATE BAGG-    -             -griffithianum 1/32
     -Idealist-        -Kewense-
     -       -Aurora-       -fortunei 5/32
     -Naomi-    -thomsonii 1/16
           -fortunei
```
Medium-sized plant, with trusses of 12-18 flowers, bell-shaped,
clear Dresden yellow, fading primrose yellow; without markings.
Handsome foliage, much like IDEALIST.   R. Strauss, reg. 1964.
A.M. 1964.

MEMORY   Described under GIPSY KING, q.v.

```
              -dichroanthum 1/8
         -Fabia-
   -Erebus-    -griersonianum 3/8
MENIPPE-   -griersonianum
   -       -griffithianum 1/4
   -Loderi-
        -fortunei 1/4
```
A pink-flowered hybrid. Lord Aberconway, intro. 1941.

```
              -dichroanthum 1/8
       -Astarte-         -campylocarpum Elatum Group 1/16
   -Ouida-    -Penjerrick-
   -    -            -griffithianum  1/16
MERA-   -griersonianum
   -         -neriiflorum 1/4
   -F. C. Puddle-
        -griersonianum 1/2
```
Pale pink flowers. Lord Aberconway, 1946.

```
                        -wardii 1/2
       -Lemon Lodge--Prelude F2-
MEREDITH COLLIER-          -fortunei 1/4
     -     -wardii
     -Crest-        -fortunei ssp. discolor 1/8
          -Lady  -
             Bessborough-campylocarpum Elatum Gp. 1/8
```
6.5ft(2.0m) x 6.5ft -5F(-21C) Oct.-Nov. Buds burnt orange to
Mars orange; funnel-shaped flowers, about 5in(13cm) wide, light
to pale chartreuse green; trusses of 9. Foliage 5in(13cm) long,
ovate, hairless.   G. Collier (NZ), cross 1972; reg. 1988.

```
        -campylogynum, white form 1/2
MERGANSER-
        -luteiflorum 1/2
```
A dwarf plant under 10in(25cm) tall by 17in(44cm) wide, compact,
vigorous, very free-flowering; leaves to 1.4in(3.5cm) long, dull
dark green. Flowers primrose yellow, funnel-shaped, 1.25in(3.2
cm) wide; truss of 3. Cox, reg. 1981. H.C. Wisley Trials 1981.

```
             -Mrs. Tritton--unknown (1/2)
     -Louis Pasteur-
MERKUR-     -Viscount Powerscourt--unknown
        -williamsianum 1/2
```
Flowers delicate rose, deeper at edges, in large, loose umbels.
D. Hobbie, 1953.

* *
```
        -griersonianum 1/2
MERLE LEE---AZOR, selfed-
           -fortunei ssp. discolor 1/2
```
6ft(1.8m) 5F(-15C) ML Plant of spreading habit; foliage 6in.
(15cm) x 1.75in(4.5cm). Funnel-shaped flowers, 4in(10cm) broad,
of rhodamine pink. B. J. Esch, reg. 1958. P.A. 1954.
PINK MERMAID   Parentage as above
6ft(1.8m) 5F(-15C) L   Funnel-shaped flowers in trusses of 9,
dawn pink, edged China rose, deeper in tube. Esch. P.A. 1954.
* *

MERLEY CREAM   Parentage unknown
5ft(1.5m) -15F(-26C) M   A super-hardy Dexter! Flowers light
cream with a greenish blotch. Dexter. Color illus LW pl. 21.

```
        -arboreum 1/2
MERLIN-   -sperabile 1/4
     -Eupheno-
        -griersonianum 1/4
```
Red-flowered hybrid. Lord Aberconway, 1950.

MERMAID   Parentage unknown
A very tall, vigorous plant, broader than high; dull, dark green
foliage. Compact trusses, 9in(23cm) across, holding 8 flowers;
corolla light Neyron rose, darker at wavy margins, campanulate,
4in(10cm) wide.   W. C. Slocock, reg. 1958. A.M. 1962.

* *
```
        -caucasicum--Cunningham's Sulphur 1/2
MEROPS-
        -lacteum 1/2
```
Sulphur yellow flowers. Magor cross; shown by C. Ingram, 1939.
GUEPIER   Parentage as above

Small, round truss of 17 flowers, chartreuse green with slightly
darker shading on upper lobe. C. Ingram, reg. 1962. A.M. 1961.
* *

```
                     -dichroanthum
            -Fabia-
       -Jingle-        -griersonianum
MERRIE- Bells-            -campylocarpum Elatum Group
 BELLS-    -Ole Olson-
      -                    -fortunei ssp. discolor
       -lacteum 1/2
```
4ft(1.2m) 5F(-15C) M Buds currant red, flowers scarlet red,
tubular bell-shaped, 5-lobed, in lax trusses of 10. Plant habit
rounded, as wide as tall; leaves dull dark green. Britt Smith,
reg. 1980.

* *
```
    -Marion (Cheal)--unknown              -griffithianum 1/16
MERRY-                      -George Hardy-
 LASS-          -Mrs. L. A. Dunnett-      -catawbiense 1/16
    -Rodeo-                   -unknown 5/8
           -griersonianum 1/4
```
Trusses of 16 flowers, light Neyron rose spotted red with creamy
yellow center. G. Langdon, reg. 1980.
MIN LANGDON   Parentage as above
Similar to above with 17 flowers per truss. Langdon, reg. 1980.
* *

MERRY MAE WHITE   Parentage unknown
2.5ft(.75m) -10F(-23C) ML White flowers, 6-lobed with 2 small
purple rays; trusses of 11. Hardgrove cross; Royce, reg. 1978.

```
         -yakushimanum--Mist Maiden 1/2  -catawbiense 1/16
MERRY MAIDENS-                  -Atrosanguineum-
    -               -Atrier-              -unknown 1/16
     -Mary Belle-       -griersonianum 1/8
      -             -decorum 1/8
            -Dechaem-
                -haematodes 1/8
```
5ft(1.5m) x 5ft(11 yrs) -15F(-26C) ML   Flowers in trusses of
20-24, buds of strong purplish red open to strong purplish pink,
blotch light orange, scented; ball truss 8in(20.3cm) wide. Flat
elliptic leaves 6in(15cm) long. H. M. Harrington, reg. 1988.

```
                       -catawbiense 1/4
          -Mrs. C. S. Sargent-
          -               -unknown 5/8
MERVEILLE DE BOSKOOP-              -griffithianum
            -               -Queen Wilhelmina-   1/8
            -Britannia-              -unknown
                    -Stanley Davies--unknown
```
Compact truss of 18 flowers, Persian rose with dark brown spot-
ting on upper lobe. Felix & Dijkhuis, Boskoop, reg. 1966.

MERVYN SETTLE   Described under CAROLINE ALLBROOK, q.v.

```
               -ciliatum 1/8
       -Rosy Bell-
   -Lady Berry-       -glaucophyllum 1/8
   -       -           -cinnabarinum 1/4
META-        -Royal Flush-
   -                -maddenii 1/4
    -cinnabarinum Roylei Group 1/4
   -Ivy-          -cinnabarinum
      -Royal Flush-
            -maddenii
```
6.5ft(1.9m) 10F(-12C) M Clusters of 4 funnel-shaped flowers,
Indian pink shading darker, 3in(7.6cm) wide. Well-branched, upright plant; leaves about 3.5in(8.9cm) long, covered beneath
with yellow to golden brown scales; foliage has spicy fragrance.
Dr. Carl G. Heller, reg. 1980.

```
               -catawbiense 1/8
        -unnamed-
    -Altaclerense- hybrid-ponticum 1/8
METEOR-         -arboreum 1/4
    -catawbiense 1/2
```
Flowers rosy crimson. Standish & Noble, before 1850.

METEOR--form of barbatum
5ft(1.5m) 5F(-15C) E 4/4   A scarlet-flowered form of the
species. Leaves bristly or "bearded" (hence barbatum). Mature

plants with smooth, reddish plum-colored bark.   Slocock.

```
        -dichroanthum ssp. scyphocalyx Herpesticum Group 1/2
METIS-
    -griersonianum 1/2
```
A hybrid with orange-red flowers. Lord Aberconway, 1941.

METTERNIANUS--form of degronianum ssp. heptamereum (metternichii)
A pink form of this species selected by Koichiro Wada and much
used by Dietrich Hobbie for hybridizing. Reg. 1958.

```
                     -griffithianum 1/4
         -Mrs. E. C. Stirling-
MEVROUW P. A.-           -unknown 9/16  -ponticum 1/6
 COLIJN-                 -Michael Waterer-
          -           -Prometheus-
          -Madame de-      -Monitor--unknown
           Bruin -       -arboreum 1/8
             -Doncaster-
                   -unknown
```
4ft(1.2m) -10F(-23C) ML 3/3   Plant of compact habit; dark
green leaves, 4.5in(11.5cm) long. Clear pink flowers in conical
trusses. M. Koster & Sons, reg. 1958.

* *
```
     -lindleyi 1/2
MI AMOR-
     -nuttallii 1/2
```
6ft(1.8m) 15F(-9C) M 5/3   Open habit, with leaves dark green
above, gray-green underneath. Very large flowers, to 6in(15cm)
wide, bell-shaped, white with yellow throat; trusses of about 6.
Maurice H. Sumner, reg. 1962. C.A. 1969. A.M. 1975.
SOUTHERN CLOUD   Parentage: lindleyi x nuttallii
Trusses of 3 to 11 flowers, Neyron rose outside, salmon inside,
with Indian yellow base. Leaves 7.5in(19cm) long. A. Bramley,
cross before 1965; J. F. Wilson, reg. 1983.
FLORAL FETE   Parentage as above, except reversed
6.5ft(2m) x 5ft(1.5m) Mid-Oct.(NZ) Tubular funnel-shaped flow-
ers to 4in(10cm) wide, yellowish white to ivory and white, vivid
yellow throat, outside tinted strong purplish pink; truss of 10-
14. Bullate leaves; reddish scales. I. F. Gordon, reg. 1988.
JANE HARDY   Parentage: nuttallii x lindleyi
Flowers Chinese yellow in throat, fading creamy white to edges,
the latter flushed with magnolia purple. Trusses of 3-6. G. A.
Hardy, reg. 1981. P.C. 1981. A.M. 1987.
REUTHE'S REWARD   Parentage: nuttallii x lindleyi
Large flowers of creamy white with apricot blotch. Foliage like
lindleyi. Reuthe, reg. 1971.
* *

MICHAEL BEEKMAN   Described under JOAN THOMPSON, q.v.

```
                     -griffithianum 3/16
                -Mars-
        -Captain Jack-   -unknown 5/16
        -             -facetum (eriogynum) 1/4
MICHAEL GRAF-               -griffithianum
        -               -Queen Wilhelmina-
        -    -Britannia-              -unknown
        -Leo-       -Stanley Davies--unknown
           -elliottii 1/4
```
5ft(1.5m) x 3ft(.9m)(15 yrs) 0F(-18C) M Flower openly campan-
ulate, 15 per truss, vivid red with edges strong red, faint dorsal spots. Narrow elliptic leaves; moderate orange indumentum
when young. P. Holden, cross 1970; Carol A. Graf, reg. 1986.

```
          -catawbiense
MICHAEL RICE-          and possibly unknown hybrids
      -maximum
```
6ft(1.8m) -15F(-26C) E Buds deep purplish red open to flow-
ers of deep purplish pink, darker spots and edges, widely funnel shaped, 3in(7.6cm) across, 5 wavy lobes, of good substance.
Spherical trusses hold 15. Plant with stiff branches; glossy
olive green leaves held 3 years. W. D. Smith, reg. 1979.

```
          -ponticum 1/2
MICHAEL WATERER-
      -unknown 1/2
```
6ft(1.8m) -15F(-26C) ML 2/3   Flowers of magenta red, fading
to rosy crimson, funnel-shaped, in a profusion of well-packed
spherical trusses. Plant habit compact and good; medium green
leaves 4in(10.2cm) long. Easy to propagate. J. Waterer, 1894.

Color illus. JS p. 90; VV p. 23.

```
                              -catawbiense 3/16
              -Mrs. Chas. S. Sargent-
              -unnamed-                 -unknown 11/16
              - hybrid-                 -catawbiense
         -      -      -Parsons Grandiflorum-
MICHAEL STENNING-  -America-       -unknown
         -          -dark red hybrid--unknown
         -                         -thomsonii 1/8
         -        -Bagshot Ruby-
         -Princess Elizabeth-      -unknown
                   -unknown
```
5ft(1.5m)(7yrs) -25F(-32C) ML 5/3   Ball-shaped truss 5.5in.
(14cm) wide, of 12 flowers 3.5in(9cm) broad, vivid purplish red;
purplish red blotch is surrounded by a star-shaped white zone, a
very striking sight! Convex leaves. Hinerman cross; reg. 1988.

MICHAEL WATERER   See previous column


```
              -burmanicum 1/2
MICHAEL'S PRIDE-
              -dalhousiae 1/2
```
A plant for the cool greenhouse, with attractive bronze new fol-
iage. Lime green buds; large, waxy, creamy yellow flowers, tubular, to 5in(12.7cm) long, lily-shaped and fragrant. Charles
Michael, reg. 1964.


```
          -griersonianum 1/2
MICHELE-
          -Afghan--unknown 1/2
```
Plant of moderate size, rather loose growth habit. Red flowers
in well-shaped trusses, early midseason. Rothschild, 1947.

MICHELLE ILENA   Described under CINQUERO, q.v.

MICROSPLASH   Described under CUMULUS, q.v.

MICROTONES   Described under FROSTED PINK, q.v.


```
            -sinogrande 1/2
MIDDLEMARCH-
            -lacteum 1/2
```
A full, rounded truss of 18-20 flowers, 8-lobed, creamy white in
bud, opening to white with red dorsal blotch, light spotting in
upper throat. Corolla campanulate, 3.2in(8cm) wide, 8-lobed.
Leaves medium green, paler below, to 8in(20.3cm) long. Col. S.
R. Clarke raiser; R. N. S. Clarke, reg. 1980. A.M. 1980.

MIDGET--form of leucaspis
A dwarf, compact form of this species, 6in(15cm) high and 12in.
(30.4cm) wide in 8 years. White flowers, 1.5in(3.8cm) across,
with 10 black stamens. Bovee, reg. 1972.

* *
```
                    -griffithianum 1/16
                -Loderi-
         -Albatross-      -fortunei 1/16
      -Cup Day-          -fortunei ssp. discolor 1/8
      -      -      -elliottii 1/8
MIDNIGHT-  -Fusilier-
      -                 -griersonianum 1/8
      -                 -ponticum 1/4
      -Purple Splendour-
                    -unknown 1/4
```
5ft(1.5m) -5F(-21C) M 4/4   Flowers of soft red-purple with
heavy, very dark spotting on upper lobe and center; round truss
of 16. Dark green, glossy foliage. K. Van de Ven, reg. 1978.
Color illus. ARS Q 31:3 (1977), p. 171.
NIGHTWATCH Parentage as above
Similar to above; flowers more lavender and blooming about two
weeks later. Plant very vigorous. K. Van de Ven.
* *


```
                    -minus Carolinianum Group 1/2
         -Olga Mezitt-
MIDNIGHT RUBY-         -minus var. minus 1/4
         -                 -minus Carolinianum Group
         -P.J.M., deep purple form-
                         -dauricum 1/4
```
1.5ft(.45m)(8 yrs, cutting) -20F(-29C) M   Frilled flowers 1.5
in(4cm) wide, strong reddish purple with yellowish brown eye; 10

to 15 in ball trusses. Small, wavy-edged leaves, scaly beneath,
turn almost black, autumn through blooming. Dense bush as broad
as high; floriferous. E. Mezitt, cross 1973; Weston, reg. 1988.


```
          -maximum 1/2
MIDSUMMER-
          -unknown 1/2
```
5ft(1.5m) -15F(-26C) VL   Rosy pink flowers in compact trusses
of about 13. Foliage deep green; open plant. Waterer & Crisp.

MIDSUMMER SNOW   Described under JULY FRAGRANCE, q.v.

MID-WINTER--seedling of dauricum
4ft(1.2m) -20F(-29C) VE 4/3   Bright rose purple flowers with
5 spreading lobes in terminal clusters of 2-6. Semi-deciduous,
sometimes retaining its leaves through winter.   Crown Estate,
Windsor, reg. 1964. A.M. 1963. F.C.C. 1969.


```
        -griffithianum 3/4
MIKADO-           -thomsonii 1/4
      -Cornish Cross-
                -griffithianum
```
Pale rose flowers. Lord Aberconway, intro. 1950.

* *
```
        -Blue Peter--unknown 5/16
MIKEY-    -catawbiense var. album Glass--Catalgla 1/4
      -Ice Cube-                -catawbiense 1/16
      -              -Catawbiense Album-
          -Belle Heller-            -unknown
                   -catawbiense var. album 1/8
```
Buds of Bishop's violet open to flowers of very pale and strong
purples, with a flare of beetroot purple. Medium size; hardy to
-25F(-32C). W. Delp.
SCOTT HARRIS   Parentage as above
Buds of strong and light purples opening to flowers of phlox and
rose purples, a flare of ruby red; dorsal spots ruby red. Medium-sized plant; hardy to -15F(-26C). Delp.
* *


```
                    -thomsonii 1/16
              -Shilsonii-
         -Bella-       -barbatum 1/16
      -Rosefinch-      -griffithianum 3/8
MILADY-       -griersonianum 1/4
      -       -griffithianum
      -Loderi-
              -fortunei 1/4
```
Flowers deep rose pink. Rothschild, cross 1935; intro. 1950.


```
              -minus Carolinianum Group 1/2
MILDRED AMATEIS-
              -edgeworthii 1/2
```
3ft(.9m) -5F(-21C) M   White flowers, flushed pink.   Edmond
Amateis, reg. 1958.

MILDRED CROSS   Described under GUSTO, q.v.


```
                    -fortunei 3/8
         -Faggetter's Favourite-
MILDRED-              -unknown 3/8
FAWCETT-              -Corona--unknown
      -         -unnamed hybrid-
      -Mrs. Donald-      -griersonianum 1/8
      Graham  -      -griffithianum 1/8
              -Loderi-
                   -fortunei
```
6ft(1.8m) 5F(-15C) M   Leaves 6.25in x 2in(16cm x 5cm). Flow-
ers blush pink, with orange-pink blotch, held in large trusses.
Carl P. Fawcett, reg. 1962. P.A. 1960.


```
          -minus, compact form 1/2
MILESTONE-
          -dauricum var. sempervirens 1/2
```
2ft(.6m) x 2ft(7 yrs) -15F(-26C) EM   Small frilled flowers of
vivid purplish red, 3-10 per truss. Leaves with rusty, green,
scaly indumentum; dense habit. Mezitt cross; Weston, reg. 1988.

MILKMAID   Parentage unknown
A parent of NORFOLK CANDY, a hybrid by James Russell. Flowers
yellow, edged lilac with slight violet and brown speckling and
an olive brown flare. Plant habit upright and straggly. Blooms

late season.   Harry White, Sunningdale, before 1955.

```
        -insigne 1/2
MILL REEF-
        -griersonianum 1/2
```
4ft(1.2m) 5F(-15C) ML   Elongated foliage on a medium-sized
plant. Flowers reddish purple with darker red dorsal spotting.
A. F. George, Hydon, reg. 1972.

```
                -decorum 1/4
        -Decatros-           -catawbiense 1/8
MILLARD KEPNER-      -Atrosanguineum-
                                -unknown 1/8
        -yakushimanum 1/2
```
4ft(1.2m) -5F(-21C) EM   Flowers dark pink, fading to lighter
pink with lilac undertone, openly funnel-shaped, to 3.5in(8.9cm)
wide, 7 wavy lobes, very fragrant; spherical trusses of 15.
Plant upright; narrow dark green leaves 5.5in(14cm) long, held 3
years. F. W. Schumacher cross; Dr. M. E. Byrkit, reg. 1975.

```
        -racemosum 1/2
MILLICENT SCOTT-         -xanthostephanum 1/4
        -Saffron Queen-
                -burmanicum 1/4
```
2.5(.75m) 5F(-15C) E   Flowers buff-colored, up to 1in(2.5cm)
across, with light red markings, blooming along the branches and
at tips, in buds of up to 3 flowers. Well-branched plant, twice
as wide as high; small rounded dark green leaves, dense golden
brown scales. New growth bronze green. R. W. Scott, reg. 1977.

```
        -yakushimanum, F.C.C. form 1/2
MILLIE-             -soulei 1/8
-        -Soulbut-
-Vanessa-        -fortunei--Sir Charles Butler 1/8
        -griersonianum 1/4
```
3ft(.9m) -5F(-21C) M 3/3   Pure white, ruffled flowers, tinged
green on the exterior. Compact plant; leaves like yakushimanum.
Sun-tolerant. H. E. Greer intro.

MILLIE LOU   Parentage unknown
Color like SCINTILLATION in Van Veen's book, p. 32. "If I had
to have only one rhodo I would pick MILLIE LOU" --V. Hardy to
-15F(-26C). Ed Robbins cross.

MILTON HOLLARD   Described under JOAN THOMPSON, q.v.

```
        -catawbiense 1/2
MIMS-
        -Diadema--unknown 1/2
```
Flowers light purplish pink with yellow-green markings.   T. J.
R. Seidel, 1910.

```
                -campylocarpum 1/4
        -Anita-
MIMULUS-        -griersonianum 1/2
        -        -griersonianum
        -Rapture-
                -arboreum ssp. zeylanicum 1/4
```
Red flowers. Lord Aberconway, intro. 1950.

MIN LANGDON   Described under MERRY LASS, q.v.

* *
```
                        -catawbiense 1/8
                -Parsons Grandiflorum-
        -Nova Zembla-           -unknown 3/8
MINAS MAID-          -hardy red hybrid--unknown
        -yakushimanum 1/2
```
3ft(.9m) -15F(-26C) L   Flowers phlox pink, dorsal flecks of
ruby, openly funnel-shaped, 2.25in(5.7cm) wide, 5 wavy lobes;
ball-shaped trusses of 15.   Plant rounded, slightly wider than
tall; dark glossy leaves with a moderate amount of grayed brown
indumentum beneath.   G. S. Swain cross; Dr. D. L. Craig, reg.
1979.   Color illus. ARS Q 33:3 (1979), p. 170.
NORMAN BEHRING   NOVA ZEMBLA x yakushimanum--PINK PARASOL
1ft(.3m) -25F(-32C) L   Flowers of light mallow purple, darker
edges, yellow-green spotting; corolla openly funnel-shaped, 2.2
in(5.5cm) across, 5-lobed; dome-shaped truss of 18. Plant wider
than tall; leaves with grayed orange indumentum.   Rudy Behring,
cross 1974; reg. 1985.
PETER BEHRING   NOVA ZEMBLA x yakushimanum--MIST MAIDEN
3ft(.9m) x 2.5ft(.75m)(12 yrs) -25F(-32C) L   Openly funnel-

shaped flowers in truss of 14, vivid purplish red, deep greenish
yellow spotting, and strong purplish red ribs.   Small, narrowly
elliptic foliage, medium olive green.   Rudy Behring, reg. 1986.
* *

MINAURA   Described under P.J.M., q.v.

```
                -catawbiense var. album Glass--Catalgla 1/2
                -                         -catawbiense
        -Tony's Gift-     -Catawbiense Album-
                -Belle -               -unknown
MIND -          Heller-               -catawbiense
POWER-                -white catawbiense hyb.-
        -Catalgla (as above)           -unknown
-unnamed-              -fortunei ssp. discolor 1/8
     hybrid-unnamed hybrid-        -dichroanthum
                -Fabia-
                        -griersonianum
```
Buds of strong purplish red and strong reddish purple, open to
flowers of strong and light purple, a pale purple flare.   Delp.

```
                -fortunei ssp. discolor 1/4
        -Sir Frederick Moore-       -arboreum ssp. zeylanicum
MINERVA-           -St. Keverne-             1/8
-                        -griffithianum 1/8
        -elliottii 1/2
```
Tall plant with pink flowers, large trusses.   Rothschild, 1947.

MING   Described under CHAT, q.v.

```
                -dichroanthum ssp. scyphocalyx 1/4
        -Medusa-
MING TOY-      -griersonianum 1/4
        -wardii 1/4
        -Crest-             -fortunei ssp. discolor 1/8
        -Lady Bessborough-
                -campylocarpum Elatum Group 1/8
```
3ft(.9m) -10F(-23C) EM Trusses of 7-9 flowers, yellow, shad-
ed orange, and translucent. Plant as broad as tall, leaves 4in.
(10cm) long, held 2 years. Arthur & Maxine Childers, reg. 1977.

```
        -tephropeplum 1/2
MINI BELL-
        -unknown 1/2
```
Trusses of up to 35 flowers, brick red, with spotting on upper
petal.   Stanley Irvine cross; H. H. McCuaig, reg. 1974.

```
        -racemosum, apricot form 1/2
MINI BRITE-
        -keiskei 1/2
```
A blend of yellows and pinks, red spotting. Low plant. Delp.

MINI GOLD   Described under BALLY COTTON, q.v.

```
        -maximum 1/2
MINI WHITE-
        -aureum (chrysanthum) 1/2
```
Dwarf -25F(-32C) ML Plant compact; dark green, ovate leaves,
4in(10cm) long. Flowers pure white, funnel-campanulate, 1.75in.
(4.5cm) wide; trusses of 15.   B. C. Potter, reg. 1972.

```
        -keiskei--Yaku Fairy 1/2
MINI-SOL-
        -valentinianum, dwarf form 1/2
```
1ft(.3m) x 1.5ft(.45m) OF(-18C) E   Light yellow-green flowers
with brilliant yellow throat, in lax truss of 4. Leaves with
golden scales both sides. Bovees intro.; Childers, reg. 1989.

* *
```
        -Corona--unknown 1/2
MINNEHAHA-
        -souliei 1/2
```
Plant low and spreading. Flowers pink and waxy in a small loose
truss, early midseason; not large, but showy. Rothschild, 1947.
QUEEN MAB   Parentage as above
Compact trusses of 12 flowers, 2.5in(6.4cm), Tyrian rose. Les-
ter Brandt cross; reg. 1962.
* *

```
        -ponticum 1/2
MINNETONKA-
        -unknown 1/2
```

2.5ft(.75m) x 3ft(.9m) -25F(-32C) M   Lavender pink flowers,
spotted orange to lemon yellow, held in a small dome-shaped
truss of 15. H. Motzkau cross; Van Veen reg. 1990.

MINNIE   Parentage unknown
6ft(1.8m) -10F(-23C) M   Flowers flat-shaped, blush pink with
marks of orange and chocolate; trusses of 12-14. Standish and
Veitch, 1862.

```
              -forrestii Repens Group 1/2
MINSTREL-          -neriiflorum 1/4
      -Neriihaem-
                   -haematodes 1/4
```
Deep red flowers. Lord Aberconway, intro. 1950.

```
                 -decorum ? 1/4
         -Caroline-
MINT JULEP-      -brachycarpum ? 1/4
         -       -catawbiense var. album Glass--Catalgla 1/4
         -Calsap-
                -Sappho--unknown 1/4
```
Buds of light purplish pink open to very pale purple, speckled
with strong greenish yellow. Hardy to -15F(-26C). W. Delp.

```
                   -brachycarpum 1/4
       -unnamed hybrid-  -wardii 1/8
       -          -Crest-        -fortunei ssp. discolor
       -              -Lady Bess--             7/64
       -                 borough -campylocarpum Elatum Gp.
MINT   -          -yakushimanum                5/64
PATTIE-  -unnamed-          -Lady Bessborough (as above)
       -  - hybrid-   -Day -
       -  -       -   -Dream-griersonianum 3/64
       -  -       -Gold-           -fortunei ssp. discolor
       -Cisa-   Mohur-Margaret Dunn-  -dichroanthum 1/64
       -                        -Fabia-
       -           -yakushimanum 1/4    -griersonianum
       -Serendipity-
                   -aureum (chrysanthum) 1/8
```
Buds of claret rose, empire rose and primrose yellow, opening to
frilled flowers pale yellow-green with a flare of pale greenish
yellow; dorsal spots cardinal red. W. Delp.

MINTERNE APRICOT   Listed under FABIA, q.v.

MINTERNE BERRYROSE   See under BERRYROSE

MINTERNE CINNKEYS   Described under CINNKEYS, q.v.

MIRA   Parentage unknown
A parent of LEOPOLD and other hybrids by T. J. R. Seidel, before
1910.

```
      -beanianum 1/2
MIRA-
      -meddianum 1/2
```
Flowers deep red or reddish purple. J. B. Stevenson, 1951.

MIRAGE   Described under GRISELDA, q.v.

```
              -Corona--unknown 1/4
         -Bow Bells-
MIRA-MI LINDA-      -williamsianum 1/4
         -    -wardii 1/4
         -Hawk-          -fortunei ssp. discolor 1/8
              -Lady
              Bessborough-campylocarpum Elatum Group 1/8
```
5ft(1.5m) -5F(-21C) M   Plant of open habit; elliptic leaves,
rounded at base, 2.25in(5.7cm) long. Upright trusses of 9 flowers of apricot, shading to Chinese coral, about 2.5in(6.4cm)
across. A. R. Heineman, reg. 1966.

MIRELLE VERNIMB--form of hemitrichotum
2ft(.6m) -5F(-21C) EM Pink flowers, .75in(1.9cm) wide, 5-lob-
ed bud axillary with 2-3 flowers per bud near the ends of stems;
24 or more form compact trusses 2in(5cm) across. Plant with
narrow leaves 1in(2.5cm) long, dark green above, densely scaly
below. Bryan Vernimb selection; reg. 1969.

MISCHIEF   Described under GYPSY ROVER, q.v.

```
                   -griffithianum 3/4
MISS ADELAIDE CLOW-      -maximum 1/4
                   -Halopeanum-
                             -griffithianum
```
White, flushed pink, chocolate spots. Lowinsky. A.M. 1919.

MISS JACK   Described under JAN-DI-LYN, q.v.

```
                      -griffithianum 3/16
              -Loderi Venus-
              -           -fortunei 1/8
       -Cotton Candy-              -griffithianum
MISS -         -           -George Hardy-
KITTY-     -Marinus Koster-      -catawbiense 1/16
     -unknown             -unknown 5/8
```
5ft(1.5m) 0F(-18C) M 4/4   Very large conical trusses bearing
huge flowers of pastel pink, with dark maroon throat; fragrant.
Fred Minch.

```
                  -griffithianum 1/2
MISS NOREEN BEAMISH-
                  -unknown 1/2
```
Deep pink flowers. M. Koster & Sons, 1823.

MISS OLYMPIA   Described under OLYMPIC LADY, q.v.

```
              -griersonianum 3/4
       -Azma-
MISS PINK-    -fortunei 1/4
       -griersonianum
```
Exhibited by Bolitho, 1943.

```
          -decorum 1/2
MISS PRIM-
          -irroratum 1/2
```
4ft(1.2m) -5F(-21C) E 3/3   White flowers, brilliant yellow-
green blotch, to 4in(10.2cm) wide; trusses of about 15. Foliage
4in(10.2cm) long. R. Bovee, reg. 1962.

MISS STREET   See ALICE STREET

MISSION BELLS   Described under JAMES BARTO, q.v.

MIST   Described under EVENING, q.v.

MIST MAIDEN--form of yakushimanum
3ft(.9m) -20F(-29C) M 4/5 Slightly faster growing than other
forms of this species. Buds very deep pink, opening to appleblossom pink, then white; flowers openly funnel-shaped, 2.5in.
(6.4cm) across, of 5 wavy lobes; ball-shaped trusses hold 14-17.
Plant broad, well-branched; stems and winter buds gray. Leaves
typical of the species; 5.75in(14.6cm) long, with heavy grayed
orange indumentum; held 5 years. Francis Hanger, Exbury, seed;
David G. Leach raiser; reg. 1983. Color illus. VV p. 80.

```
          -fortunei ssp. discolor 1/2
MISTAKE-                     -griffithianum 1/8
       -          -George Hardy-
       -Pink Pearl-      -catawbiense 1/8
       -        -      -arboreum 1/8
              -Broughtonii-
                        -unknown 1/8
```
Flowers pale pink, suffused with rose madder. Brig. J. M. J.
Evans. A.M. 1956.

MISTRESS OF HARKWOOD   Described under DISCRETION, q.v.

```
                  -williamsianum 1/2
MISTY MOONLIGHT---KIMBERLY, selfed-
                        -fortunei 1/2
```
4ft(1.2m) -10F(-23C) EM 3/4   A vigorous variety which grows
into a compact plant. Foliage glossy green with reddish purple
petioles, deeply colored stems and buds. Abundantly fragrant
flowers open pale orchid. Harold E. Greer, intro. 1982.

```
          -unknown 3/4
MISTY MORN-       -ponticum 1/4
       -Purple Splendour-
                    -unknown
```
5ft(1.5m) -5F(-21C) M   Flowers purple violet, rays of olive
yellow, openly funnel-shaped, 3.5in(8.9cm) across, of 5 frilled
lobes; truss of 12-14. Plant wider than tall; elliptic leaves;

new growth bluish green.   Mrs. H. A. Frederick, Jr., reg. 1976.

```
                -yakushimanum 1/2                    -catawbiense
       -unnamed-                -Parsons Grandiflorum-       5/32
       - hybrid-        -America-              -unknown
       -        -              -dark red hybrid--unknown 8/32
       -      -Cindy Lou-                -griffithianum 1/32
MITCH-                          -Mars-
       -              -unnamed hybrid-  -unknown
       -                          -catawbiense var. rubrum
       -      -yakushimanum--Koichiro Wada         1/16
       -unnamed hybrid-              -catawbiense
                     -Henriette Sargent-
                                   -unknown
```

Buds Tyrian purple and rose Bengal; frilled flowers of pale purplish pink, tinted rose Bengal; dorsal spots yellow-green; indumented leaves; medium-sized bush, hardy to -15F(-26C). W. Delp.

MITZI   Described under DEL, q.v.

```
                                -griffithianum 1/16
                 -Queen Wilhelmina-
          -Britannia-                -unknown  13/16
       -Burgundy-       -Stanley Davies--unknown
       -      -              -ponticum 1/8
MOBUR-      -Purple Splendour-
       -                     -unknown
       -Moser's Maroon--unknown
```
5ft(1.5m) 10F(-12C) ML Flowers in truss of 15, dahlia purple,
spotted maroon.   Halfdan Lem cross; Dr. Paul Bowman, reg. 1962.

```
          -williamsianum 1/2
MOCHICHA BELL-
          -unknown 1/2
```
Trusses of 2-3 flowers, dog-rose pink outside, silvery pink inside. I. A. Hayes, cross 1969; reg. 1980.

```
                 -haematodes 1/4
             -Humming Bird-
MOCHICHA MOON-               -williamsianum 1/4
             -unknown 1/2
```
Trusses of 4-5 flowers, cream flushed pale pink. I. A. Hayes,
cross 1969; reg. 1980.

```
          -impeditum 1/2
MOERHEIM-
          -unknown 1/2
```
1ft(.3m) -15F(-26C) EM 3/4 Buds appear on very young plants;
flowers open a pretty shade of violet, about 1.25in(3.2cm) wide.
Small foliage turns maroon in the winter.   J. D. Ruys, Moerheim
Nursery, Netherlands, reg. 1966.

MOERHEIM JUBILEE   Described under ELISABETH HOBBIE, q.v.

```
          -williamsianum 1/2
MOERHEIM'S PINK-      -catawbiense 1/4
             -Genoveva-
                     -unknown 1/4
```
Plant compact, vigorous, broader than tall; height at 10 years
about 3.5ft(1m); leaves of dull, dark green, 2.25in(5.7cm) long.
Flowers very pale pink, deeper near edges, widely funnel-shaped,
to 3.5in(8.9cm) across; spherical trusses of 8. Free-flowering.
D. Hobbie cross; reg. 1973. A.M. 1972. Color illus. F p. 54.

MOERHERMII--form of impeditum
1ft(.3m) -10F(-23C) EM 4/4   Compact plant; attractive foliage. Lavender flowers larger than usual for this dwarf species.

```
          -dichroanthum 1/2
MOHAMET-      -griersonianum 1/4
       -Tally Ho-
             -facetum (eriogynum) 1/4
```
4ft(1.2m) 5F(-15C) ML   Large, bell-shaped flowers of bright
scarlet with frilled margins, large scarlet petaloid calyces;
loose trusses of 5-6. Plant of medium size, rather open; light
green leaves with fawn indumentum beneath. Clones grown in N.W.
United States are deep salmon pink and orange-red; these often
bloom in autumn. Rothschild. A.M. 1945.

MOHUR   Described under DREAM GIRL, q.v.

MOLIERE   Parentage unknown

Flowers of a dull rose red, with black spotting on the upper petal. M. Koster & Son. A.M. 1953.

```
                -griffithianum 1/4
          -Loderi-
MOLLIE COKER-      -fortunei 1/4
          -unknown 1/2
```
6ft(1.8m) 0F(-18C) M   Roseine pink flowers, with a purplish
red blotch. Mrs. R. J. Coker, NZ, reg. 1979.

```
                -forrestii Repens Group 1/4
          -Elizabeth-
MOLLY ANN-      -griersonianum 1/4
       -garden hybrid--unknown 1/2
```
3ft(.9m) -10F(-23C) EM 4/4   Dense, compact shrub, as wide as
high; shiny, dark, rounded leaves. Rosy crimson flower 2in(5cm)
wide, funnel-shaped, 5 wavy lobes, of good substance, long-lasting; lax truss of 7. Floriferous.   Mrs. L Freimann, reg. 1974.

MOLLY BUCKLEY Described under NAOMI, q.v.

```
                     -minus Carolinianum Group 1/8
                -P.J.M.-
          -Balta-      -dauricum 1/8
MOLLY FORDHAM-      -minus Carolinianum Group 1/4
             -minus Carolinianum Group, white form 1/2
```
4ft(1.2m) -20F(-29C) EM 4/4   Masses of nearly white, small,
beautiful trusses. Green, glossy foliage contrasts with reddish
and maroon of the others in this group.   Weston Nurseries.

MOLLY MILLER   Described under BAMBI, q.v.

```
          -yakushimanum--Koichiro Wada 1/2
MOLLY-                     -griffithianum 1/8
SMITH-      -unnamed hybrid-
       -Mrs. Furnival-      -unknown 1/4
       -              -      -caucasicum 1/8
       -              -unnamed hybrid-
```
4ft(1.2m) 0F(-18C) M White flowers with prominent blotch of
marigold orange, openly funnel-shaped, 2.5in(6.4cm) across, 5-
lobed; conical trusses of 12. Floriferous. Plant rounded, as
wide as tall; heavy, dark green leaves with gray-brown indumentum beneath, held 3-4 years.   Cecil S. Smith, reg. 1984.

MONACA LAD   Described under CALSAP, q.v.

MONACO   Described under BANGKOK, q.v.

```
          -forrestii Repens Group 1/2
       -                              -catawbiense
MONICA-                     -Atrosanguineum-       1/8
       -(probably) Dr. H.C. Dresselhuys-      -unknown 1/4
       -                     -      -arboreum 1/8
                             -Doncaster-
                                   -unknown
```
3.3ft(1m) x 3.3ft -5F(-21C) EM   Flowers in trusses of 4-7,
funnel-shaped, 5-lobed, vivid red with faint brown-red spots.
Dull green, elliptic to ovate foliage, to 3in(7.5cm) long. D.
Hobbie, cross pre-1960; Royal Boskoop Hort. Soc., reg. 1988.

```
                -cinnabarinum 1/2
MONICA WELLINGTON-
             -unknown 1/2
```
Trusses of 4-5 flowers, tubular funnel-shaped, 2in(5cm) across,
inside deep rose purple, the reverse rayed with bright magenta;
Elliptic leaves 2in(5cm) long, glossy green above, scaly below.
Mrs. Roza Stevenson cross; Hydon Nurseries, reg. 1980.

MONIQUE   Described under BURGUNDY, q.v.

```
       -thomsonii 1/2
MONK-
       -arboreum ssp. delavayi var. delavayi 1/2
```
Dark red flowers.   Sir James Horlick, 1934.

MONSIEUR GUILLEMOT   Parentage unknown
6ft(1.8m) -10F(-23C) L 3/3 Synonym MADAME GUILLEMOT. Upright, fairly compact plant; glossy dark green leaves, loved by
insects. Dark rose flowers in a compact truss. Moser.   Color
illus. VV p. 68.

MONSIEUR THIERS   Parentage unknown

A parent of J. H. VAN NES. Flowers light red.   J. Macoy.


```
          -Mrs. E. C. Stirling-
MONSTROUS-                -unknown 1/2
     -                    -smirnowii 1/4
     -unnamed hybrid-
                          -unknown
```
Flowers rose pink or lavender pink.   C. Waterer.   A.M. 1925.

MONTCHANIN   Described under BRANDYWINE, q.v.


```
                    -catawbiense var. album 1/4
     -unnamed hybrid-      -wardii 1/8
     -            -Crest-        -fortunei ssp. discolor
MONTE-               -Lady       -            1/16
CARLO-               Bessborough-campylocarpum Elatum 1/16
     -               -aureum 1/4
     -unnamed hybrid-
                    -campylocarpum 1/4
```
2.5ft(.75m) -10F(-23C) M 4/3   Ball-shaped trusses of 16 flo-
wers, pale empire yellow flushed orchid pink, faint blotch of
Naples yellow; corolla widely funnel-shaped, 2.25in(5.7cm) wide,
with 5 wavy lobes. Plant rounded, nearly as wide as tall; dark
yellow-green, glossy leaves.   D. Leach, cross 1966; reg. 1981.

MONTEGO   Described under JACQUELINE LOOYE, q.v.

MONTEREY   Pink sibling of PINK FLOURISH, q.v.

MONTREAL   Described under LADY BESSBOROUGH, q.v.


```
          -augustinii 1/2
MOOD INDIGO-
          -unknown 1/2
```
5ft(1.5m) OF(-18C) EM   Deep indigo blue flowers in a loose
truss. Dark, aromatic foliage, bronze in winter.   L. Brandt.


```
          -fortunei 1/2
MOON MIST-                            -wardii ? 1/4
          -Lackamas Cream--form of Chlorops-
                                     -vernicosum ? 1/4
```
Plant 3ft(.9m) tall by 3.5ft(1m)(10 years); elliptic leaves 4in.
(10cm) long. Campanulate flowers of Dresden yellow, darker in
throat, with mahogany rays, 3.5in(8.9cm) wide; graceful upright
trusses of 10-12. Midseason.   B. Lancaster, reg. 1965.


```
          -catawbiense var. album 1/2
MOON-                     -neriiflorum 1/8
MIST-          -unnamed hybrid-
     -unnamed hybrid-          -dichroanthum 1/8
                    -fortunei ssp. discolor 1/4
```
6ft(1.8m) -15F(-26C) ML 4/3   Very large, waxy, light yellow
flowers flushed pale pink, with a golden blotch.   David Leach,
intro. 1968.


```
          -wardii 1/2
MOON SHADOW-
          -unknown 1/2
```
Very light yellow deepening in center, 7-lobed. Leaves obovate,
glabrous, 2.75in(7cm) long.   Mrs. R. J. Coker, reg. 1982.

MOON SHOT   Described under JOE GABLE, q.v.


```
               -griffithianum 9/16
          -Kewense-
     -Aurora-      -fortunei 5/16
-Naomi-      -thomsonii 1/8
MOONBEAM-      -fortunei
     -griffithianum
```
4ft(1.2m) -5F(-21C) M   Flowers pale primrose yellow, held in
shapely trusses on a tall plant.   Rothschild, 1947.

MOONDANCER   Described under BUTTER BRICKLE, q.v.


```
          -griffithianum 1/4
     -Loderi Venus-
MOONGLOW-      -fortunei 1/4
     -                    -fortunei ssp. discolor 1/4
     -Lady Bessborough-
                         -campylocarpum Elatum Group 1/4
```
Tall plant, blooming in midseason. Pink flowers in well-shaped
trusses. Rothschild, 1946.


```
                    -wardii Litiense Group 1/4
          -Henry R. Yates-
MOONGLOW (Delp)-      -unknown 1/4
          -catawbiense var. album Glass--Catalgla 1/2
```
Buds of rhodamine purple open to flowers of pale purplish pink,
fading white, with a sulphur yellow flare; dorsal spots of vivid
yellow-green; white filaments.   W. Delp.

MOONLIGHT BAY   Parentage unknown
Fragrant, pale pink flowers suffused faint yellow in throat, unmarked. Effect apricot. Dexter cross; G. Wister, reg. 1980.


```
          -macabeanum 1/2
MOONLIGHT SONATA-
          -Pamela--unknown 1/2
```
Trusses of 24 very light yellow flowers, stained phlox pink with
a ruby red blotch. New Zealand Rhododendron Assoc. raiser; Mrs.
J. Kerr, reg. 1979.


```
               -griffithianum 1/4
     -Mars-
     -      -unknown 3/8
MOONLIGHT TANGO-          -fortunei ssp. discolor 1/8
     -      -Ladybird-
     -Diva-      -Corona--unknown
          -griersonianum 1/4
```
Tall, showy trusses of cardinal red flowers. A tall plant, with
leaves 5in(12.7cm) long; late season.   Henny, reg. 1965.

* *
```
          -augustinii ssp. chasmanthum 1/2
MOONRISE-                -cinnabarinum ssp. Roylei Group 1/4
          -Lady Chamberlain-          -cinnabarinum 1/8
                         -Royal Flush-
                         (orange form)-maddenii 1/8
```
Cream flowers, suffused pale lilac pink; 6-flowered truss. Gen.
Harrison, cross 1949; intro. 1955.
PORTRAIT   Parentage as above
Trusses of 6 flowers, each 2in(5cm) across, of pale oyster pink.
Gen. Harrison, reg. 1962.
* *


```
                         -campylocarpum 1/4
          -Souvenir of W. C. Slocock-
MOONRISE-                -unknown 1/4
          -                -griffithianum 1/4
          -Loderi King George-
                         -fortunei 1/4
```
Crossed, raised, & reg. by the A. A. Wrights, before 1958.

* *
```
                              -campylocarpum 1/8
               -unnamed hybrid-
               -               -unknown 1/4
          -Adriaan-                -griffithianum 1/16
          - Koster-          -George Hardy-
MOONSHINE-      -Mrs. Lindsay-          -catawbiense 1/16
          -          Smith-Duchess of Edinburgh--unknown
          -wardii Litiense Group 1/2
```
5ft(1.5m) OF(-18C) M   Compact trusses of 16 flowers, shallow-
rotate, primrose yellow, darker on upper lobe, throat stained
with a dark crimson blotch. F. Hanger, RHS, Wisley. A.M. 1952.
MOONSHINE BRIGHT   Parentage as above
Rich yellow flowers in trusses of 20-22.   Thin, glossy foliage.
RHS Garden, Wisley, 1952.
MOONSHINE GLOW   Parentage as above
Openly funnel-shaped flowers of a yellow near uranium green, in
truss of 9. Dull green leaves 4.25in(10.8cm) x 2.3in(7cm). RHS
Garden, Wisley. H.C. 1957.
MOONSHINE SUPREME   Parentage as above
Flowers in truss of 15, primrose yellow with darker staining on
upper lobes, broadly campanulate. RHS Garden, Wisley. A.M.
1953. Color illus. F p. 55.
* *


```
               -wardii 1/4
          -Jervis Bay-          -fortunei ssp. discolor 1/8
MOONSHINE-          -Lady Bessborough-
CRESCENT-                -campylocarpum Elatum Gp. 1/8
          -wardii Litiense Group 1/2
```
4ft(1.2m) OF(-18C) M   Not of MOONSHINE grex, according to the
International Registrar. Plant upright with dull green leaves.

Flowers primrose yellow, in a compact, domed truss of 14.   RHS
Garden, Wisley, reg. 1962.   A.M. Wisley Trials 1960.

```
                -campylocarpum 1/2
MOONSTONE-
                -williamsianum 1/2
```
3ft(.9m) -5F(-21C) EM 4/4   Compact, rounded shrub, wider
than tall; dense foliage of flat, smooth, oval leaves, 2.5in(6.4
cm) long. Orange rose buds open to pale, creamy yellow flowers,
lightly tinged pink, openly campanule, 2.5in(6.4cm) across;
lax trusses of 3-5.   J. C. Williams, 1933.   Color illus. ARS Q
31:3 (1977), p. 171; F p. 55; VV p. 85.

```
        -wardii
MOONTIDE-
        -Loder's White--See Loder's White, 2 possible diagrams
```
4ft(1.2m) OF(-18C) EM 3/2 Habit rather open but rounded, up-
right. Leaves flat, oblong, medium green, to 4in(10.2cm) long.
White flowers, funnel-shaped, over 3in(7.6cm) wide; full, domed
truss of about 16.   R. Henny, reg. 1958.   P.A. 1955.

```
                              -fortunei ssp. discolor 3/8
                -King of Shrubs-       -dichroanthum 1/16
        -Holy Moses-          -Fabia-
        -         -                -griersonianum 1/16
MOONWAX-      -Souvenir of Anthony Waterer--unknown 1/4
        -               -griffithianum 1/8
        -         -Loderi-
        -Albatross-      -fortunei 1/8
                         -fortunei ssp. discolor
```
5ft(1.5m) OF(-18C) M 5/4   Flowers 4in(10.2cm) wide, 7-lobed,
fragrant, Naples yellow center with light mauve edges, unmarked.
Dome-shaped trusses hof 12. Plant broader than tall; stiff, upright branches. Narrow elliptic leaves to 6.5in(16.5cm).   Lem
cross; L. L. Newcomb, reg. 1981.   C.A. 1983. Color illus. ARS
J 38:4 (1984), p. 171.

```
                -griffithianum 3/8
        -Isabella-
        -         -auriculatum 1/4
MORAWEN-                -griffithianum
                -Loderi-
        -Shepherd's-      -fortunei 1/4
         Delight  -       -fortunei
                -Luscombei-
                           -thomsonii 1/8
```
Phlox pink flowers with upper 3 petals slightly marked with dark
pink spots. Heneage-Vivian.   A.M. 1950.

```
        -morii 1/2
MORFAR-
        -oreodoxa var. fargesii 1/2
```
Pinkish white with crimson spots.   Collingwood Ingram, 1949.

```
                        -yakushimanum--Koichiro Wada 1/2
MORGENROT (MORNING RED)-        -griffithianum 1/4
                           -Spitfire-
                                   -unknown 1/4
```
3ft(.9m) -10F(-23C) M   Dark red buds, opening to spinel red
flowers, shading inside to light Neyron rose, 5-lobed, in truss
of 16-18. Rounded, compact bush; leaves oblanceolate-obovate,
hairy. Hachmann cross; G. Stück, reg. 1983.   Color illus. ARS
J 39:2 (1985), p. 63; WS, 1989, p. 157.

```
* * * * * * * * * * * * * * * * * * * * * * * * * * * *
                        -griffithianum 5/16
    -Loderi King George-
    -                -fortunei 5/16
MORIO-                -griffithianum
    -                -Loderi-
    -      -Albatross-      -fortunei
    -Cup Day-       -fortunei ssp. discolor 1/8
    -               -elliottii 1/8
                -Fusilier-
                        -griersonianum 1/8
```
Red buds opening to very pale, greenish white flowers; truss of
14-18. Rather straggly plant. K. Van de Ven cross; reg. 1972.
Color illus. Cox pl. 125.
SATIN GLOW   Parentage as above
6ft(1.8m) 5F(-15C) EM   Huge, deep pink, fragrant flowers, of
silky texture, in big open trusses. Large, medium green leaves;

held one year. Plant floriferous, open, upright.   Van de Ven,
Australia. Color illus. Cox pl. 166.
* *

MORNING CLOUD   Described under HYDON BALL, q.v.

```
                -dichroanthum 1/4
            -Fabia-
MORNING FROST-      -griersonianum 1/4
            -unnamed hybrid--unknown 1/4
```
3ft(.9m) 5F(-15C) M   White flowers flushed red-purple, with
greenish yellow spotting.   J. Waterer & Crisp, reg. 1972.

MORNING MAGIC   Described under HYDON BALL, q.v.

```
                -griffithianum 1/4
        -Sunrise-
MORNING STAR-      -griersonianum 1/4
            -williamsianum 1/2
```
Pale pink flowers. Lord Aberconway, 1942.

MORNING SUNSHINE   Parentage unknown
5ft(1.5m) OF(-18C) EM 4/3   Flowers primrose yellow, 7-lobed,
4in(10cm) wide, in rounded truss of 14.   Whitney cross; Sather,
reg. 1977. Color illus. Cox pl. 126.

MOROCCO--form of coriaceum
5ft(1.5m) 5F(-15C) EM 3/4   A species with long leaves, 9in.
(23cm) by 3.5in(9cm) wide, covered below with pale fawn indumentum. Trusses hold 16 to 20 white flowers, with a blotch of deep
crimson. Crown Estate, Windsor, reg. 1962.

MOROCCO (Leach)   See LUXOR, described under CONGO, q.v.

MORRELLVILLE   Described under FOXBERG, q.v.

```
                -campylocarpum 1/4
        -Gladys-
        -      -fortunei 5/16      -griffithianum 5/16
MORTIMER-                -Kewense-
        -         -Aurora-      -fortunei
        Yvonne Pearl-      -thomsonii 1/8
                         -griffithianum
```
5ft(1.5m) -5F(-21C) M   Large, heavy trusses of 12 flowers,
white, suffused yellow, crimson blotch in throat; corolla campanulate, 5in(12.7cm) wide, exterior stained pink. Leaf 5.5in.
(14cm) long. Crown Estate, Windsor, reg. 1965.   A.M. 1964.

```
        -elliottii 1/2
MORVAH-
        -wattii 1/2
```
Spherical trusses of 20 flowers, Turkey red with spotting on upper lobes. Sir E. Bolitho, reg. 1962. A.M. 1956. F.C.C. 1959.

```
            -ambiguum 1/2
MOSAIQUE-      -cinnabarinum 1/4
        -Cinnkeys-
                -keysii 1/4
```
Small flowers of pale yellow, bright red at base, with 5 narrow
lobes; trusses of about 12. Small, dense plant, blooming late
midseason. Rothschild. A.M. 1945.

MOSER'S MAROON   Parentage unknown
5ft(1.5m) -10F(-23C) ML 2/3   Parent of many hybrids. Growth
habit vigorous, rather sprawling; new foliage an attractive red.
Small tight truss of very small flowers, dark wine red, spotted
black. Moser & Fils.   A. M. 1932. Color illus. F p. 56.

MOTH   Described under SILVER RAY, q.v.

MOTHER ELENA---Vaartnou selection from thomsonii
8ft(2.4m) x 6ft(1.8m) 5F(-15C) EM   Openly campanulate flowers
2.75in(7cm) wide, of heavy substance, strong cardinal red; 8-12
per flat truss, 6in(15.2cm) wide. Glossy oblong leaves held 2-3
years; bush open, floriferous. H. Vaartnou raiser; reg. 1989.

```
        -hippophaeiodes 1/2
MOTHER GREER-
        -unknown 1/2
```
1.5ft(.45m) -15F(-26C) ML 4/4   Similar in shape to the blue
flowers of hippophaeiodes, but larger; plant much more compact.
Blooms later than most "blue" rhododendrons.   Harold Greer's

mother's cross; Greer, intro. 1982.   Color illus. HG p. 167.

MOTHER JUULA---Vaartnou selection from vernicosum
8ft(2.4m) x 6ft(1.8m)(20 yrs) OF(-18C) E   Ball truss of 10-15
flowers, widely funnel-campanulate, 3.5in(9cm) across, 7-lobed,
light Neyron rose; darker midstripes on outside of lobes. Dense
floriferous bush; flat leaves to 4in(10cm) Vaartnou, reg. 1989.

```
                                  -griffithianum 1/4
MOTHER               -George Hardy-
OF PEARL--sport of PINK PEARL-            -catawbiense 1/4
                                  -arboreum 1/4
                     -Broughtonii-
                                  -unknown 1/4
```
6ft(1.8m) -5F(-21C) M 4/3 Rich pink buds open delicate pink,
fading to pure white, faint brownish spots, pink stamens; large,
slightly fragrant flowers. Vigorous plant, good foliage.   John
Waterer, 1925.   A.M. 1930.   Color illus. JS p. 48; VV p. 104.

```
             -griffithianum (aucklandii) 1/2
MOTTLED AUCKLANDII-
             -unknown 1/2
```
Shell pink flowers.   R. Gill & Son.

```
        -pemakoense 1/2
MOUKOENSE-
        -moupinense 1/2
```
White flowers, flushed with pink.   Lester E. Brandt, 1953.

MOULIN ROUGE   Described under PERRI CUTTEN, q.v.

```
                          -fortunei--Sir Chas. Butler 1/4
              -Van Nes Sensation-       -maximum 1/8
MOUNT CLEARVIEW-          -Halopeanum-
              -Purple  -ponticum 1/4     -griffithianum 1/8
              Splendour-
                          -unknown 1/4
```
5ft(1.5m) OF(-18C) M Flowers of imperial purple with beetroot
purple throat, dark gray-purple dorsal spotting, openly funnel-
shaped, 4in(10.2cm) across; dome-shaped trusses of 14. Rounded
plant, wide as tall; leaves held 3 years.   Newcomb, reg. 1981.

MOUNT EVEREST--form of cinnabarinum
A tall, free-flowering form of this species, with small rounded
leaves; tubular-shaped red flowers with yellow edges.   Slocock.

MOUNT EVEREST   Described under LAMELLEN, q.v.

* *
```
              -fortunei 1/4
        -Fawn-    -dichroanthum 1/8
           -Fabia-
MOUNT HOOD-         -griersonianum 1/8
      -         -wardii 1/4
        -Crest-            -fortunei ssp. discolor 1/8
              -Lady Bessborough-
                          -campylocarpum Elatum 1/8
```
6ft(1.8m) -5F(-21C) M Fragrant flowers, white with chartreuse
shading in throat, 6-lobed, open campanulate, 3.5in(8.9cm) wide;
conical truss of 11-13. Branches moderately; gray-green foliage
5.5in(14cm) long.   Carl H. Phetteplace, reg. 1975.
KAYLA RAE   Parentage as above
3ft(.9m) OF(-18C) M   Trusses 7in(17.8cm) high, of 14 flowers,
7-lobed, crimson with cardinal red deep in throat. Plant wider
than high.   C. Phetteplace cross; A. Holmeide, reg. 1985.
SNOW CREST   Parentage as above
Buds of China rose open to white flowers, lightly tinged French
rose, 5- to 7-lobed, in trusses 8in(20cm) wide, of 9-11 flowers.
Plant as wide as tall.   Childers cross; reg. 1978.
* *
* *
```
                          -griffithianum 3/8
              -Queen Wilhelmina-
        -Britannia-          -unknown 3/8
MOUNT MAZAMA-        -Stanley Davies--unknown
      -         -griffithianum
        -Loderi-
              -fortunei 1/4
```
5ft(1.5m) OF(-18C) M 4/4   An unusual flower: fuchsia red,
spotted brighter red; dark red nectar pouches, and stripes on
the reverse. Corolla openly funnel-shaped, 4.5in(11.5cm) broad,
5 wavy lobes. Plant wider than tall; leaves held 2 years.   G.

Grace, cross c. 1955; Molly & Louis Grothaus, reg. 1980.
ELIZABETH MOUNT   Parentage as above
Trusses of 9 flowers, Tyrian red purple in bud, opening to rose
Bengal, shading to nearly white, blotch scarlet red, suffused
blackish brown. Embley Park cross; G. Mount, reg. 1982.
LODBRIT   Parentage as above
5ft(1.5m) -5F(-21C) L   Dark crimson buds; flowers open cherry
pink, finally fading to soft pale pink. A large plant.   Origin
unknown.
* *

MT. MITCHELL (Gable)--form of maximum or maximum x catawbiense
6ft(1.8m) -25F(-32C) VL 3/3 From the mountains of North Carolina; an erratic plant, flowers sometimes pink, sometimes red,
or lighter. An excess of red pigment may also produce streaked
stems, leaves.   Gable, reg. 1958.

MOUNT MITCHELL (Leach)--form of maximum
5ft(1.5m) -25F(-32C) VL 3/3 Buds of red, opening to flowers
suffused strong pink, with a yellowish green dorsal blotch, exterior stained red. Trusses hold 16. Foliage 6in(15.2cm) long.
W. Baldsiefen seed; Leach raiser; reg. 1965.

MOUNT RAINIER   See TICKLED PINK (FAWCETT)

MOUNT SIGA   Described under KULU, q.v.

MOUNT WILSON--yakushimanum, selfed
Flowers pale pink, fading to white with yellow spotting.   P. G.
Valder, Australia, reg. 1972.

* *
```
                          -griffithianum 1/2
              -Dorothea-
MOUNTAIN AURA-          -decorum 1/4
              -red hybrid--unknown 1/2
```
3ft(.9m) -15F(-26C) ML 4/4 Flower flax blue, a white center,
4in(10.2cm) wide; rounded truss 7in(17.8cm) across. Leaves 6in.
6in(15.2cm) long, half as wide.   G. Guy Nearing, reg. 1968.
MOUNTAIN GLOW   Parentage as above
Densely branching plant; oval leaves to 6in(15.2cm) long. Flowers reddish purple, 4in(10.2cm) across, held in trusses 6in(15.2
cm) wide.   Nearing, reg. 1968.
MOUNTAIN QUEEN   Parentage as above
4ft(1.2m) -15F(-26C) ML 4/4   Oval leaves, 7in(17.8cm) long.
Slightly fragrant flowers to 4in(10.2cm) across, rose-colored,
in round trusses.   Nearing, reg. 1968.
* *

```
              -wardii 1/4          -griffithianum 1/32
        -Idealist-        -Kewense-
        -       -Aurora-     -fortunei 5/32
        -       -Naomi-   -thomsonii 1/16
MOUNTAIN DEW-        -fortunei
        -             -fortunei ssp. discolor 1/8
        -       -Lady Bessborough-
        -             -campylocarpum Elatum 1/8
        -Jalisco-  -dichroanthum 1/8
              -Dido-
                    -decorum 1/8
```
5ft(1.5m) 5F(-15C) ML Sweetly fragrant, primrose yellow flow-
ers on an attractive bush.   Reuthe, reg. 1972.

```
                    -caucasicum 1/4
        -Boule de Neige-          -catawbiense 1/8
        -       -unnamed hybrid-
MOUNTAIN FLARE-          -unknown 1/8
        -       -griffithianum 1/4
        -Loderi King George-
                    -fortunei 1/4
```
6ft(1.8m) -15F(-26C) ML   Buds light jasper red opening pale
empire rose, with greenish to purplish spotting; flowers openly
funnel-shaped, 4.5in(11.5cm) wide, fragrant; spherical truss of
15. Plant as wide as high with stiff, upright branches; leaves
7in(17.8cm) long, held 2 years.   G. Guy Nearing, reg. 1973.

MOUNTAIN GLOW   Described under MOUNTAIN AURA, q.v.

MOUNTAIN QUEEN   Described under MOUNTAIN AURA, q.v.

MOUNTAIN STAR   Described under YAKU WARRIOR, q.v.

```
                    -Essex Scarlet--unknown 1/4
            -Beau Brummel-
MOUTON ROTHSCHILD-          -facetum (eriogynum) 1/4
            -elliottii 1/2
```
Red, waxy, bell-shaped flowers in conical trusses. Floriferous,
late-blooming. E. de Rothschild, reg. 1962. A.M. 1958.

```
        -cinnabarinum ssp. xanthocodon Concatenans Group 1/2
MOZART-
        -ambiguum 1/2
```
Pastel shades of yellows and pinks. J. Stevenson, intro. 1951.

```
                -griffithianum 1/2
MRS. A. C. KENRICK-
                -unknown 1/2
```
Flowers deep rose pink with darker spotting. M. Koster & Sons.
A.M. 1925.

MRS. A. J. HOLDEN   Described under CAROL AMELIA, q.v.

```
                -griffithianum 1/2
MRS. A. M. WILLIAMS-
                -unknown 1/2
```
A large, dense plant. Flowers of bright scarlet with a flare of
black spots, in rounded trusses. Otto Schulz cross; C. B. van
Nes, intro. 1896. A.M. 1926. A.M. Wisley Trials 1933. F.C.C.
Wisley Trials 1954.

```
                -arboreum 1/4
        -Doncaster-
MRS. A. R. BEDE-          -unknown 3/4
        -unknown
```
Very large trusses of rich rose scarlet flowers, with a pale in-
terior. Much admired at Chelsea show, 1923. M. Koster.

```
                -griffithianum 1/4
        -Loderi-
MRS. A. R. MCEWAN-          -fortunei 1/4
                -unknown 1/2
```
6ft(1.8m) -5F(-21C) EM 3/3   Habit compact and roundish; fol-
iage glossy green, waxy, and large, 7.5in(19cm) x 2.5in(6.4cm).
Flowers 5in(12.7cm) across, fuchsine pink to Persian rose, white
in throat; dome-shaped trusses. H. Ihrig cross; University of
Washington, intro. 1958. A.E. 1956.

* *
```
                -fortunei--Sir Charles Butler 1/2
MRS. A. T. DE LA MARE-          -maximum  1/4
                -Halopeanum-
                        -griffithianum 1/4
```
5ft(1.5m) -15F(-26C) M 3/3   Plant can take full exposure in
many climates. Buds blush pink opening to delicately fragrant,
large white flowers with green spots; large, dome-shaped trusses
hold 12-14. C. B. van Nes. A.M. 1958. Color illus. ARS Q 35:1
(1981), p. 11; JS p. 52; VV p. 66.
ADMIRAL PIET HEIN   Parentage as above
Rosy lilac flowers, with more fragrance than the above.   C. van
Nes. A. M. 1957. Color illus. JS p. 65.
VAN NES SENSATION   Parentage as above
5ft(1.5m) -5F(-21C) M 4/4   Very large dome-shaped trusses of
widely funnel-shaped flowers, light orchid pink with paler centers, 7-lobed, fragrant. Sturdy, compact plant with attractive
foliage. C. B. van Nes. Color illus. VV p. 5.
* *

MRS. ALFRED TAUBMAN   Described under NUBAR, q.v.

```
                        -griffithianum 1/16
                -Kewense-
            -Aurora-          -fortunei 5/16
    -Naomi Nautilus-          -thomsonii 1/8
MRS. ALICE-          -fortunei
 BLYSKAL  -catawbiense--Catanea 1/2
```
6ft(1.8m) -15F(-26C) M   Buds roseine purple, opening to very
light purple flowers, with a creamy white throat. Trusses of 12
to 17. Walter Blyskal raiser; Mrs. James Walton, reg. 1983.

```
        -fortunei 1/2
MRS. ANTHONY SEYS-
        -unknown 1/2
```
Flowers in loose trusses of 9-10, creamy white, suffused moderate purplish pink on inside, outside flushed light reddish pur-

ple, a small blotch of dark red. Plant 12ft(3.6m) x 10ft(3.0m).
Flowering season May. L. de Rothschild, reg. 1986. A.M. 1986.

```
        -fortunei 1/2
MRS. ANTHONY WATERER-
        -unknown 1/2
```
5ft(1.5m) -5F(-21C) ML   White flowers with a yellowish brown
flare. A tall-growing shrub. Waterer, before 1915.

MRS. ARTHUR EVANS   See MRS. ARTHUR FAWCUS

```
            -caucasicum 1/2
MRS. ARTHUR FAWCUS-          -griffithianum 1/4
            -Kewense-
                    -fortunei 1/4
```
Flowers of pale yellow. Knap Hill, 1946.

```
            -campylocarpum 1/2
MRS. ASHLEY SLOCOCK-
            -hardy hybrid--unknown 1/2
```
Medium height; cream flowers, suffused apricot. Slocock, 1933.

* *
```
                        -griffithianum 1/4
            -Dawn's Delight-
MRS. BERNICE BAKER-          -unknown 1/4
                    -fortunei 1/2
```
5ft(1.5m) -5F(-21C) M 4/4   Habit rather open; attractive
foliage. Rose pink flowers lighter at center, with pale midline
markings down 5 wavy lobes; large trusses. Larson, reg. 1958.
Color illus. VV p. 79.
MRS. FRANK S. BAKER   Parentage as above, except reversed
Pink flowers. Exhibited by Larson, 1942.
* *

```
                    -decorum 1/4
            -unnamed hybrid-
            -          -fortunei ssp. discolor 1/4
MRS. BETTY HAGER-          -Michael-ponticum 1/16
            -          -Waterer-
                -Prometheus-          -unknown 5/16
            -Madame de-          -Monitor--unknown
                Bruin   -          -arboreum 1/8
                    -Doncaster-
                            -unknown
```
4ft(1.2m) OF(-18C) M   Deep pink flowers with a red blotch and
dorsal spotting; spherical trusses of 15. Leaves to 5.5in(14cm)
long. A. Raustein, reg. 1974.

MRS. BETTY ROBERTSON   Described under ZUIDERZEE, q.v.

MRS. BUTLER   See SIR CHARLES BUTLER

```
        -souliei 1/2
MRS. BYRON SCOTT-
        -unknown 1/2
```
Flowers straw yellow. Seed from England; H. L. Larson raiser &
distributor; reg. 1958.

```
                -griffithianum 1/4
        -Princess Juliana-
MRS. C. B. VAN NES-          -unknown 3/4
        -Florence Sarah Smith--unknown
```
5ft(1.5m) OF(-18C) M 3/3   Rose red buds opening almost red,
fading to a pretty, soft pink. Plant of rather open habit, with
medium green, glossy leaves. C. B. van Nes, reg. 1958.   Color
illus. VV p. 112.

MRS. C. S. SARGENT   See MRS. CHARLES S. SARGENT

```
                        -maximum 1/8
                -Halopeanum-
            -Snow Queen-          -griffithianum 1/2
            -          -griffithianum
MRS. C. WHITNER-          -Loderi-
            -          -fortunei 3/8
            -          -griffithianum
            -Loderi Sir Edmund-
                            -fortunei
```
A large plant for the light woodlands. Large white flowers suf-
fused magenta with a darker basal stain, trumpet-shaped, in conical trusses of 15. Sir Giles Loder. A.M. 1963.

MRS. CALABASH   Parentage unknown
5ft(1.5m) OF(-18C) M   Lilac pink flowers over very nice foliage.   Halfdan Lem cross.

* *
                      -decorum 1/2
MRS. CARTER GLASS-
            -catawbiense var. album Glass--Catalgla 1/2
White flowers. Gable, reg. 1958. (Probably identical to MRS.
POWELL GLASS, a.k.a. as ANNE GLASS)
DECALGLA   Parentage as above, except reversed
4ft(1.2m) -15F(-26C) M   Round trusses to 6in(15cm) wide, hold
12 flowers, white, spotted green. Gray brown new growth; plant
well-branched. J. Gable cross; G. Nearing, reg. 1973.
MRS. POWELL GLASS Parentage: Catalgla x decorum
5ft(1.5m) -20F(-29C) ML 4/2   Synonym ANNE GLASS. Pure white
flowers held in a large, rather lax trusses, and framed by dark
green leaves. Gable, exhibited 1949; reg. 1958.
STOCKHOLM Parentage: Catalgla x decorum
5ft(1.5m) -20F(-29C) E 3/3   Flowers white with 2 dorsal rays
of strong greenish yellow, in spherical truss of 14. Bush wider
than tall. Seed from Hobbie; Leach raiser; reg. 1974.
* *

                          -griffithianum 1/4
              -Coombe Royal-
MRS. CHARLES E. PEARSON-   -unknown 1/2
              -                    -catawbiense
              -Catawbiense Grandiflorum-   1/4
                                  -unknown
6ft(1.8m) -5F(-21C) M 3/4   Vigorous plant, with lush deep
green foliage; tolerates heat and sun. Widely funnel-shaped
flowers of pale pinkish mauve, fading paler, with heavy chestnut
brown spotting; very large, conical trusses. M. Koster & Sons,
1909. A.M. 1933. F.C.C. Wisley Trials 1955. Color illus.
JS p. 67; VV p. 34.

                    -catawbiense 1/2
MRS. CHARLES S. SARGENT-
                    -unknown 1/2
6ft(1.8m) -25F(-32C) ML 3/3   Plant rounded, moderately compact. Flowers dark carmine rose with yellow spotting in throat,
wavy margins; compact, dome-shaped trusses. One of the best of
the "ironclads". A. Waterer, 1888. Color illus. VV p. 88.

MRS. DAVIES EVANS Parentage unknown
4ft(1.2m) -10F(-23C) L Vigorous plant of compact habit; free-
flowering. Imperial purple flowers, a white blotch and yellow
spots, funnel-shaped, with frilled margins; compact globular
trusses.   A. Waterer, before 1915.   A.M. Wisley Trials 1958.
Color illus. JS p. 107.

                          -Corona--unknown (1/4)
                -unnamed hybrid-
MRS. DONALD GRAHAM-   -griersonianum 1/4
              -        -griffithianum 1/4
                -Loderi-
                        -fortunei 1/4
6ft(1.8m) 5F(-15C) L 3/3   Flowers of Tyrian rose with spinel
red line on reverse of lobes; truss of 8-10. Leaves 7in(17.8cm)
x 2in(5cm); plant upright, rather open. Seed from Rose, of England; Endre Ostbo raiser. P.A. 1954. A.E. 1958.

                    -griffithianum 1/2
MRS. E. C. STIRLING-
                    -unknown 1/2
5ft(1.5m) -5F(-21C) M 4/4   Ruffled flowers, blush pink shaded in mauve, with long up-curved stamens. Floriferous and sun-
tolerant. Growth habit upright when young, later spreading and
open. J. Waterer. A.M. 1906. Color illus. JS p. 101; VV p.
11, p. 86.

                      -griersonianum 1/4
            -Jibuti-   -arboreum 1/8
              -        -Gill's Triumph-
MRS. EDDY-   -griffithianum 1/8
              -              -griersonianum 1/4
              -Gladys Rillstone-
                      -unknown 1/4
An Exbury hybrid with trusses of 15 flowers, of light spirea red
heavily speckled light ruby red, an eye of darkest red purple.
Edmund de Rothschild, cross 1952; reg. 1982.

                          -griffithianum 1/4
                -unnamed hybrid-
MRS. EDWIN HILLIER-   -unknown 3/4
                -Monsieur Thiers--unknown
Dark pink flowers. C. B. van Nes & Sons.

MRS. ELIZABETH TITCOMB   See ELIZABETH TITCOMB

                          -griffithianum 5/32
              -Kewense-
          -Aurora-   -fortunei 9/32
MRS. ENA- -thomsonii 10/32
  AGIUS -   -wardii 8/32
        -                     -griffithianum
        -Idealist-   -Kewense-
                -     -Aurora-   -fortunei
                -Naomi-   -thomsonii
                        -fortunei
Trusses hold 10 flowers of very light yellow-green. Edmund de
Rothschild, cross 1955; reg. 1982.

                              -griffithianum 1/8
                    -unnamed-
              -Mrs. Furnival- hybrid-unknown 1/4
              -        -   -caucasicum
MRS. ERNA HEYDERHOFF- -unnamed hybrid-   1/8
              -              -unknown
            -catawbiense var. album Glass--Catalgla 1/2
4ft(1.2m) -10F(-23C) ML   White flowers with prominent blotch
of cardinal red, pale pink margins; trusses of about 21. Plant
as broad as tall, with dark green, glossy leaves, held 3 years.
James P. Bevry cross; Henry Heyderhoff raiser; reg. 1965.

MRS. FRANK S. BAKER   Described under MRS. BERNICE BAKER, q.v.

              -fortunei 1/2
MRS. FRED PAUL-
              -unknown 1/2
Light pink flowers. F. Paul.

* + *
                      -griffithianum 1/4
              -unnamed hybrid-
MRS. FURNIVALL-   -unknown 1/2
              -        -caucasicum 1/4
              -unnamed hybrid-
                      -unknown
4ft(1.2m) -10F(-23C) ML 5/5   Considered one of the best.
Often a parent of other hybrids. Light rose pink flowers paler
at center, conspicuous sienna blotch, crimson markings, widely
funnel-shaped, held in dome-shaped trusses. Handsome, compact
plant; dark green leaves, 4in(10.2cm) long. A. Waterer, 1920.
A.M. Exbury Trials 1933. F.C.C. Wisley Trials 1948. A.G.M.
1969. Color illus. F p. 57; JS p. 41; VV front cover, p. 8.
Information about the siblings, and the corrected spelling of
"Furnivall", came from The RHS Rhododendron, Camellia & Magnol-
ia Group Bulletin, no. 41, Aug. 1989, p. (2).
CHINTZ Parentage as above
Soft pink flowers with ruby spots. A. Waterer, intro. c. 1931.
FERELITH   Parentage as above
Mauve flowers. Knap Hill, reg. 1963.
FURNIVALL'S DAUGHTER   Parentage as above
5ft(1.5m) -5F(-21C) M 5/4 Beautifully shaped conical trusses
of 15 flowers, pink with a cherry blotch. Plant upright, vigor-
ous; large rugose leaves, lively green. Knap Hill. H.C. 1957.
A.M. 1958. F.C.C. Wisley Trials 1961. Color illus. HG p. 85;
Cox pl. 64.
* *

                      -edgeworthii 3/4
MRS. G. REUTHE-   -edgeworthii
              -Fragrantissimum-
                        -formosum 1/4
G. Reuthe, 1935.

                      -griffithianum 1/4
              -Coombe Royal-
MRS. G. W. LEAK-   -unknown 1/2
              -                    -caucasicum 1/4
              -Chevalier Felix de Sauvage-
                                  -unknown
6ft(1.8m) OF(-18C) EM 4/3   Tall, vigorous plant with smooth
olive green leaves. Flowers of clear light pink with a striking

brownish red blotch, crimson markings; large, compact, conical trusses. Grows in sun or shade. M. Koster. F.C.C. Wisley Trials 1934. Color illus. F p. 56; JS 112; VV p. 26, 49.

MRS. GEORGE HUTHNANCE   Described under JOAN THOMPSON, q.v.

```
                -minus Carolinianum Group 1/2
MRS. GEORGE O. CLARK-
                -moupinense 1/2
```
Pink flowers. G. O. Clark.

```
                -griffithianum 1/2
MRS. GEORGE PAUL-
                -unknown 1/2
```
Flowers blush pink changing to white. A. Waterer.

```
                -decorum ? 1/4
          -Caroline-
MRS. H. R. YATES-        -brachycarpum ? 1/4
                -unknown 1/2
```
5ft(1.5m) -15F(-26C) M 3/4 Synonym CAROLINE CREAM. Flowers open pale mauve, fading to cream. Parent of YATES' BEST. J. B. Gable.

MRS. H. STOCKER   Parentage unknown
Flowers of brilliant scarlet with a maroon blotch. M. Koster & Sons, before 1923. A.M. 1948.

```
          -fortunei 1/2
MRS. H. T. KRUG-
          -unknown 1/2
```
6ft(1.8m) -15F(-26C) E Buds deep pink, opening heather pink, edges shading to very pale sap green; flowers of good substance, openly funnel-shaped, 4in(10.2cm) across, 7-lobed, in compact domed trusses of about 12. Plant upright, broader than tall; dark green leaves retained 3 years. Harold Krug, reg. 1980.

```
                  -griffithianum 1/4
          -Princess Juliana-
MRS. HAROLD TERRY-        -unknown 3/4
          -Florence Smith--unknown
```
Soft rose pink flowers. C. B. van Nes & Son. A.M. 1948.

```
                -decorum 1/4
          -unnamed hybrid-
MRS. HELEN-        -fortunei ssp. discolor 1/4
 DUNKER   -    -wardii 1/4
          -Crest-        -fortunei ssp. discolor 1/8
          -Lady-
          Bessborough-campylocarpum Elatum Group 1/8
```
2.5ft(.75m) -5F(-21C) M Fragrant white flowers of good substance, openly funnel-shaped, 3.5in(8.9cm) across, 7 wavy lobes; large dome-shaped trusses of 9. Free-flowering. Plant upright, rounded, as broad as tall; dark, glossy, yellowish green leaves. Alfred A. Raustein, reg. 1983.

```
                -yakushimanum 1/2
MRS. HELEN JACKSON-        -wardii ? 1/4
                -Chlorops-
                -vernicosum ? 1/4
```
4ft(1.2m) x 4ft(19 yrs) OF(-18C) EM Buds pale yellowish pink, flowers yellowish white, strong greenish yellow spots, 7-lobed; truss 7in(17.8cm) wide. Leaves with light tan indumentum. Compact, rounded plant. F. Bump cross; G. Kesterson, reg. 1986.

```
                -Mrs. J. J. Crosfield--unknown 3/4
MRS. HELEN KOSTER-        -catawbiense 1/4
          -Catawbiense Grandiflorum-
                -unknown
```
4ft(1.2m) -10F(-23C) ML 3/3 Flowers light orchid with a purplish red blotch. Foliage deep green. M. Koster & Sons. A different plant with this name has also been distributed: it opens to orchid and slowly turns white, with a yellow eye.

```
                -elliottii 1/4
          -Fusilier-
MRS. HELEN WEYERHAUSER-        -griersonianum 1/2
          -    -griersonianum
          -Jean-
                -decorum 1/4
```
Pink-flowered hybrid. H. L. Larson, 1952.

```
          -grande 1/2
MRS. HENRY AGNEW-
          -arboreum ssp. cinnamomeum var. album 1/2
```
Flowers white, fringed pink. Mangles, 1915.

```
          -arboreum ? 1/2
MRS. HENRY SHILSON-
          -barbatum ? 1/2
```
Rounded loose trusses of 15-16 white flowers, suffused light roseine purple. Narrow, elliptic leaves, to 4.5in(11cm) long, dark green above, silvery gray below. Samuel Smith raiser; Hon. H. E. Boscawen exhibitor. A.M. 1973.

MRS. HORACE FOGG   Described under LAKE OZETTE, q.v.

```
          -unnamed hybrid--unknown 1/2
          -        -griffithianum 1/16
MRS. HOWARD PHIPPS-        -Kewense-
          -    -Aurora-        -fortunei 5/16
          -Naomi-    -
          -        -thomsonii 1/8
                -fortunei
```
Flowers medium orchid pink, in compact trusses of 13, blooming midseason. When registered, plant was 5ft(1.5m) tall x 3ft(.9m) wide, compact; matte leaves to 7in(17.8cm) long. Howard Phipps, intro. 1958; reg. 1972.

MRS. INNES HAMILTON   Described under ALARIC HAMILTON, q.v.

MRS. J. C. WILLIAMS   Parentage unknown
7ft(2.1m) -15F(-26C) L 4/3 Ruffled white flowers with small blotch of dark red spots, funnel-shaped, to 2.5in(6.4cm) wide; compact ball-shaped trusses of 16-19. Floriferous. Plant upright, wider than high. A. Waterer. A.M. Wisley Trials 1960.

```
          -diaprepes 1/2
MRS. J. COMBER-
          -decorum 1/2
```
White flowers tinged yellow at the base. Messel. A.M. 1932.

MRS. J. G. MILLAIS   Parentage unknown
5ft(1.5m) 5F(-15C) ML 5/3 White flowers, tinted orchid on opening, with a very large golden blotch. Young plants heavily budded. Mature plant of good stature. A. Waterer, reg. 1958. Color illus. Rhododendrons 1990, back cover.

```
                -catawbiense 1/4
          -Carl Mette-
MRS. J. H. VAN NES-        -unknown 1/2
          -        -griffithianum 1/4
          -Princess Juliana-
                -unknown
```
Pink flowers, spotted. C. B. van Nes & Sons.

MRS. J. J. CROSFIELD   Parentage unknown
A parent of MRS. HELEN KOSTER. Flowers pale rose with a crimson blotch. M. Koster & Sons.

MRS. J. P. LADE   Parentage unknown
5ft(1.5m) -5F(-21C) L Mauve flowers, with a darker center. Compact-growing; free-flowering. A. Waterer, before 1900.

```
          -thomsonii 1/2
MRS. JAMES HORLICK-        -caucasicum 1/4
          -Dr. Stocker-
                -griffithianum 1/4
```
6ft(1.8m) OF(-18C) EM Flowers of soft salmon pink, in large trusses. Sir James Horlick, cross 1931; flowered 1941.

```
          -maximum, pink-flowered 1/2
MRS. JO PAVLICK-        -catawbiense
          -Kettledrum-
                -unknown
```
6ft(1.8m) x 5ft(1.5m)(26 yrs) -20F(-29C) ML Flowers in domed trusses of 14 to 17; buds strong purplish red, opening to strong purplish red with white stripe and white dorsal blotch; dark red spotting. W. Fetterhoff, reg. 1989.

```
          -macabeanum 1/2
MRS. JOAN ZINK-
          -sport of macabeanum 1/2
```

8ft(2.4m) x 8ft(20 yrs) 5F(-15C) E   Flowers in trusses of 20,
fragrant, openly campanulate, 8-lobed. Pink buds open pale yellow with purplish red spots in 3 lobes. H. Vaartnou, reg. 1989.

```
                 -maximum 1/2
MRS. JOHN CLUTTON-
                 -unknown 1/2
```
White with small yellow-green blotch. A. Waterer. F.C.C. 1865.

MRS. JOHN CRAWFORD   Described under AZOR, q.v.

MRS. JOHN MILLAIS   See MRS. J. G. MILLAIS

MRS. JOHN WATERER   Parentage unknown
6ft(1.8m) -5F(-21C) L Parentage may include catawbiense, ponticum and arboreum, says Cox. One of first late-flowering hybrids created; 18-flowered trusses, rosy crimson, dark crimson
spots. Vigorous, dense-growing. J. Waterer, before 1865.

MRS. KINGSMILL   Described under MRS. RANDALL DAVIDSON, q.v.

```
                     -griffithianum 1/4
               -George Hardy-
MRS. L. A. DUNNETT-          -catawbiense 1/4
               -unknown 1/2
```
Very late blooming; flowers of rosy pink, with lighter centers.
M. Koster & Sons, cross 1909.

```
                  -wardii 1/2
MRS. LAMMOT COPELAND-          -souliei ? 1/4
                  -Virginia Scott-
                              -unknown 1/4
```
5ft(1.5m) OF(-18C) L 4/3   Flowers clear yellow, campanulate,
3.5in(8.9cm) across, held in trusses of 15. Large foliage, dark
green. Fertilizer-sensitive. H. L. Larson, reg. 1971.

```
                            -catawbiense 1/4
                   -B. de Bruin-
MRS. LEOPOLD DE ROTHSCHILD-          -unknown 1/4
                   -griersonianum 1/2
```
5ft(1.5m) -5F(-21C) M   Compact plant of medium size, blooming
profusely. Flowers of light red to scarlet, with unusual near-
orange background, spotted fawn; the corolla is widely expanded.
Stiffly pointed, glossy green leaves. Rothschild. A.M. 1933.

```
                     -griffithianum 1/4
               -George Hardy-
MRS. LINDSAY SMITH-          -catawbiense 1/4
               -Duchess of Edinburgh--unknown 1/2
```
6ft(1.8m) OF(-18C) ML 3/2   Parentage as in the Register; in
the Rhododendron Yearbook, 1929, R. W. Wallace, of Tunbridge
Wells, said one of its parents is LODER'S WHITE. Large, flat
white flowers, lightly spotted red on upper lobe; large trusses.
Plant open, sometimes pendant; light green leaves. M. Koster,
1910. A.M. 1933.

MRS. LIONEL DE ROTHSCHILD   Parentage unknown
5ft(1.5m) OF(-18C) M 4/2   Not shown as grex in the Register,
and the color is called pink, but the clone sold in the Northwest (USA) has a white flower with a blotch of crimson spots; it
is rated above. Hillier's Manual calls it white, edged in apple
blossom pink; Slocock's catalog says it's white with red spots.
Plant is compact, with upright branches and large, firm trusses
of widely funnel-shaped flowers. A. Waterer. A.M. 1931.

```
                            -catawbiense 1/8
                 -unnamed hybrid-
       -Altaclerense-                -ponticum 1/8
MRS. LOUDON-          -arboreum 1/4
       -          -maximum 1/4
         -unnamed hybrid-
                      -unknown 1/4
```
Flowers carmine or light bright rose, with all petals spotted.
Standish & Noble, 1850.

```
                 -campylocarpum 1/2
MRS. MARY ASHLEY-
                 -unknown 1/2
```
4ft(1.2m) 5F(-15C) EM 3/3   Similar to UNIQUE, with salmon
pink flowers shaded cream, funnel-shaped, held in domed trusses.
Plant fairly compact; leaves medium green, oval, and 3in(7.6cm)
long. W. C. Slocock, reg. 1958.

```
                 -fortunei 1/2
MRS. MATTHEW ROSE-
                 -unknown 1/2
```
Pink flowers. Paul.

MRS. MESSEL--form of decorum
White flowers. Messel. A.M. 1923.

```
                 -catawbiense 1/2
MRS. MILNER-
                 -unknown 1/2
```
A parent of several Seidel hybrids: MIMS, PLUSCH, QUENDEL.
Crimson flowers. A. Waterer, before 1900.

```
                 -yakushimanum 1/2
MRS. MURIEL CARFRAE-
                 -unknown 1/2
```
2.5ft(.75m) -5F(-21C) M   Deep pink buds, flowers phlox pink,
widely funnel-campanulate, 2in(5cm) wide, 5 wavy lobes, of heavy
substance; conical trusses of 12-15. Plant broader than tall;
elliptic leaves, held 3 years. W. Berg cross; J. F. Caperci
raiser; Ken Trainer, reg. 1975.

MRS. P. D. WILLIAMS   Parentage unknown
5ft(1.5m) -10F(-23C) L 3/2   Flowers ivory white with a large
golden brown blotch, of medium size; compact, rounded trusses.
Young plant may sprawl, sturdier later; very dark green, smooth,
narrow leaves to 5.5in(14cm) long. A. Waterer. A.M. 1936.

* *
```
                            -catawbiense 1/4
                 -Atrosanguineum-
MRS. P. DEN OUDEN-          -unknown 1/2
               -          -arboreum 1/4
                 -Doncaster-
                         -unknown
```
5ft(1.5m) -15(-26C) M   Plant of compact habit. Flowers deep
crimson, in great profusion. H. den Ouden & Son, intro. 1925.
DOCTOR H. C. DRESSELHUYS   Parentage as above
6ft(1.8m) -15F(-26C) M 2/3   Flowers aniline red with lighter
blotch in tall trusses. Nice foliage but rather scant. H. den
Ouden, intro. 1920.
DOCTOR H. J. LOVINK   Parentage as above
Flowers much like the above. H. den Ouden, intro. 1929.
PROFESSOR F. BETTEX   Parentage as above, except reversed
Bright red flowers tinged purple; nice foliage. H. den Ouden,
intro. 1925; reg. 1958.
VAN DER HOOP   Parentage as above
6ft(1.8m) -10F(-23C) ML A parent of ROWLAN P. CARY. Flowers
deep pink with dark brown spots. H. den Ouden, intro. 1925.
* *

```
                            -griffithianum 1/8
                 -Loderi-
           -Albatross-          -fortunei 1/8
MRS. PAUL B. SMITH-          -fortunei ssp. discolor 1/4
           -Pygmalion--unknown 1/2
```
4ft(1.2m) -5F(-21C)   Opalescent pink, a red throat. Upright,
slightly open-growing; dark emerald foliage. Larson, reg. 1958.

```
                            -griffithianum 1/4
                 -Loderi-
MRS. PERCY MCLAREN-          -fortunei 1/4
                 -pink seedling--unknown 1/2
```
Flowers of pale shell pink, with frilled lobes. Dr. R. W. Med-
licott, NZ, reg. 1979.

MRS. PHILIP MARTINEAU   Parentage unknown
6ft(1.8m) -5F(-21C) L 4/2   Rose pink flowers fading lighter
with a pale yellow eye, held in large rounded trusses. Habit is
sprawling. Knap Hill. A.M. 1933. F.C.C. Wisley Trials 1936.

MRS. POWELL GLASS   Described under MRS. CARTER GLASS, q.v.

MRS. R. G. SHAW   Parentage unknown
A parent of BONFIRE. Flowers blush pink, with a dark eye. A.
Waterer, before 1915.

MRS. R. S. HOLFORD   Parentage unknown
5ft(1.5m) -15F(-26C) ML 2/2 Parent of FLARE and HYPATIA,
both Exbury hybrids. Rosy salmon flowers flushed strawberry,
lightly spotted with crimson, widely funnel-shaped, 2.5in(6.4cm)

across, frilly-edged, in large tight trusses. Plant rounded, medium to tall; medium green leaves. A. Waterer, 1866.

* *
```
                    -griffithianum 1/2
MRS. RANDALL DAVIDSON-
                    -campylocarpum 1/2
```
Several forms: white, creamy yellow, pink. Mangles, about 1884.
MRS. KINGSMILL   Parentage as above
Yellow flowers, fading to cream. Mangles. A.M. 1911.
MAIDEN'S BLUSH   Parentage as above
Pale cream flowers, pink margins. Loder.
* *

```
             -arboreum 1/2
MRS. RICHARD GILL-
             -campanulatum 1/2
```
6ft(1.8m) 0F(-18C) M   Flowers bright salmon rose; blood red splashes in throat. Grown in NZ. R. Gill & Son, early 1900s.

```
                            -arboreum 1/8
                      -Doncaster-
                 -unnamed-         -unknown 3/8
MRS. ROBERT W. WALLACE- hybrid-unknown
                 -              -griffithianum 1/4
                 -George Hardy-
                            -catawbiense 1/4
```
Pale pink flowers fading to white, heavily spotted scarlet crimson with rose tinted exterior. M. Koster cross, 1909.

```
             -ponticum 1/2
MRS. S. J. BEALE-
             -unknown 1/2
```
Lilac-colored flowers. M. Koster & Sons.

MRS. T. H. LOWINSKY   Exact parentage unknown: a combination of catawbiense, maximum, and ponticum
5ft(1.5m) -15F(-26C) L 4/4   According to Bean (Trees and Shrubs... v. 3, p. 879) this is not the same hybrid as MRS. TOM H. LOWINSKY, which received an A.M. in 1919. Mauve buds open to white flowers tinged mauve fading white with a huge striking orange-brown blotch, widely funnel-shaped and 3in(7.6cm) across; compact trusses of 14. Floriferous and vigorous. Dark green leaves about 4.5in(11.5cm) long. Waterer, before 1917. Color illus. HG p. 180; JS p. 66.

MRS. THISTLETON DYER   See MRS. W. T. THISTLETON-DYER

MRS. TOM AGNEW   Parentage unknown
6ft(1.8m) -5F(-21C) L   Mauve pink buds open to white flowers, conspicuous yellow-brown flare; trusses of 16. Heat-tolerant. J. Waterer, before 1877.

```
             -griffithianum 3/4
MRS. TOM H. LOWINSKY-         -maximum 1/4
             -Halopeanum-
                       -griffithianum
```
5ft(1.5m) -15F(-26C) EM 4/3   Sometimes confused with Mrs. T. H. LOWINSKY. Rounded and rather compact plant; very dark green, glossy leaves 6in(15.2cm) long, somewhat convex. Flowers open blush, fading white, with reddish brown blotch; rounded trusses. Heat-tolerant. A. Waterer cross; Lowinsky intro. A.M. 1919. Color illus. VV p. 81.

MRS. TRITTON   Parentage unknown
A parent of LOUIS PASTEUR. Flowers crimson with light center. J. Waterer.

```
             -campylocarpum 1/2
MRS. W. C. SLOCOCK-
             -unknown 1/2
```
4ft(1.2m) -5F(-21C) EM 3/4   A compact shrub with flowers of apricot pink, fading to buff. Slocock. A.M. 1929.

```
             -fortunei 1/2
MRS. W. R. COE-
             -unknown 1/2
```
6ft(1.8m) -5F(-21C) ML 3/4   Flower deep bright pink, crimson throat, over 4in(10.2cm) wide; very large, dome-shaped trusses. Glossy, dark green foliage. C. O. Dexter, 1925-42; reg. 1958. Color illus. ARS J 43:3 (1989), p. 126.

```
                            -griffithianum 1/4
                      -Princess Juliana-
MRS. W. R. DYKES-         -unknown 1/2
                 -           -catawbiense 1/4
                      -Carl Mette-
                            -unknown
```
5ft(1.5m) -10F(-23C) ML 3/3   Flowers strong rose red; foliage of matte citrus green. C. B. van Nes. (The 3 PRINSES JULIANA in the Register are azaleas.)

```
                      -fortunei 1/2
MRS. W. T. THISTLETON-DYER-
                      -unknown 1/2
```
Synonym MRS. THISTLETON DYER. Flowers soft pink. George Paul.

```
                      -maximum 1/4         -catawbiense 1/16
              -Standishii-          -unnamed-
MRS. WALTER-        -Altaclerense- hybrid-ponticum 1/16
 BURNS   -                       -arboreum 1/8
              -griffithianum 1/2
```
6ft(1.8m) 0F(-18C) EM 3/3   Plant vigorous and upright; dark green leaves. Pale pink flowers, margins darker, rose blotch. T. Lowinsky. A.M. 1931.

```
                                  -griffithianum 1/8
                      -Queen Wilhelmina-
                 -Earl of -          -unknown 3/8
MRS. WAYNE W. KEYES- Athlone-Stanley Davies--unknown
                      -fortunei 1/2
```
Deep red flowers. H. L. Larson, 1958.

```
             -fortunei 1/2
MRS. WEBLEY-
             -unknown 1/2
```
Flowers of light rose, spotted. Paul.

MRS. WILLIAM AGNEW   Parentage unknown
6ft(1.8m) -10F(-23C) L   Pink flowers deepening at edges with a yellow blotch; trusses of 16-18. J. Waterer, before 1875.

```
             -griffithianum 1/2
MRS. WILLIAM WATSON-
             -unknown 1/2
```
White flowers with violet spots. A. Waterer. A.M. 1925.

```
             -mucronulatum 1/2
MUCRAM-
             -ambiguum 1/2
```
Flowers lavender pink. Joseph B. Gable, before 1958.

MUCRONATUM   Parentage unknown
A parent of MARGOT, an azealodendron. Formerly mucronatum, considered a species, now a hybrid.

```
             -minus 1/2
MUGBY JUNCTION-
             -unknown 1/2
```
Pink flowers spotted brown in throat, 5-lobed, funnel-shaped, in trusses of 5-8. Leaves to 2.25in(5.7cm) long, densely covered with reddish brown scales beneath. Plant from Hydon Nursery; R. N. S. Clarke raiser; reg. 1984. A.M. 1984.

```
             -thomsonii 1/2
MULROY VANGUARD-         -venator 1/4
             -Vanguard-
                       -griersonianum 1/4
```
Flowers in trusses of 7-10, funnel-campanulate, 5-lobed, vivid red, dorsal lobes with dark nectar pouches. Shrub to 10ft(3.0m) Earl of Leitrim, cross before 1952; Mary Forrest, reg. 1985.

```
             -ciliatum 1/2
MULTIFLORUM-
             -virgatum 1/2
```
2ft(.6m) 10F(-12C) EM   Like the species virgatum; blush pink flowers held in twos all up the stems. Olive green leaves, long and narrow. Waterer, Sons & Crisp, reg. 1958.

```
             -ponticum 1/2
MULTIMACULATUM-
             -brachycarpum 1/2
```
5ft(1.5m) -25F(-32C) ML 2/3   Very hardy plant praised in the

19th century and still worth growing; white flowers, orange-red
spots.   J. Waterer, before 1860.   Color illus. in F. Street's
Hardy Rhododendrons pl. IVb.

```
         -maximum 1/2
MUM-
         -unknown 1/2
```
5ft(1.5m) -10F(-23C) L   White with lemon yellow eye; trusses
of 18. Compact bush, fast-growing. J. Waterer, 1897.

MUMTAZ-I-MAHAL   Extinct hybrid reg. by L. E. Brandt, 1966.

```
              -cinnabarinum ssp. cinnabarinum 1/2
MUNCASTER BELLS-
              -cinnabarinum ssp. xanthocodon Concatenans Gp. 1/2
```
Flowers apricot, up to 3in(7.6cm) long, tubular bell-shaped, in
loose trusses. Sir John Ramsden raiser; Sir William Pennington-
Ramsden, reg. 1965.

```
              -arboreum 1/2
MUNCASTER HYBRID-
              -unknown 1/2
```
Early blooming flowers of pinkish red, with a paler throat, and
spotted.   Sir John Ramsden.

```
                    -griffithianum 3/8
              -unnamed hybrid-
              -          -unknown 1/4
MUNCASTER ICICLE-         -griffithianum
              -          -Loderi-
              -Lodauric-         -fortunei 1/8
                    -auriculatum 1/4
```
Fragrant white flowers with a red throat, funnel-shaped, up to
4in(10.2cm) across, in large loose trusses.   Sir John Ramsden
raiser; Sir William Pennington-Ramsden, reg. 1965.

```
              -campanulatum 1/2
MUNCASTER MIST-
              -floribundum 1/2
```
4ft(1.2m) -5F(-21C) EM 4/4   A compact shrub with campanulate
flowers in conical trusses, blue with darker markings. Sir J.
Ramsden raiser; Sir William Pennington-Ramsden, reg. 1965.

```
              -orbiculare 1/2
MUNCASTER RUBY
              -thomsonii 1/2
```
Medium-sized rose pink flowers, campanulate.   Sir John Ramsden
raiser; Sir William Pennington-Ramsden, reg. 1965.

```
                 -cinnabarinum 1/2
MUNCASTER TRUMPET-
                 -maddenii 1/2
```
Tubular bell-shaped flowers in loose trusses, white with apricot
throat, to 3.5in(8.9cm) wide.   Sir J. Ramsden raiser; Sir William Pennington-Ramsden, reg. 1965.

```
                         -minus Carolinianum Gp., pink  1/2
MUNCHKIN---unnamed hybrid, F2-
                         -valentinianum 1/2
```
Frilled white, flushed pink; full, tight, rounded truss.   Delp.

MUNDAI   Described under JOAN BYE, q.v.

```
                 -neriiflorum 1/4
         -F. C. Puddle-
MUREUN-          -griersonianum 1/4
         -barbatum 1/2
```
Deep red flowers.   Lord Aberconway, intro. 1946.

MURIEL   Described under MANSELLII, q.v.

```
                 -cinnabarinum Roylei Group 1/2
MURIEL GIAUQUE-
                 -maddenii ssp. crassum 1/2
```
6ft(1.8m) x 6ft(10 yrs) 15F(-9C) ML Flowers 4in(10cm) across,
deep to strong pink, strong red spots on dorsal lobe; lax truss
8in(20.4cm) wide. Scaly leaves. Mrs. J. P. Evans, reg. 1989.

```
                 -griersonianum 1/4
         -Griercalyx-
MURIEL HOLMAN-         -megacalyx 1/4
         -maddenii 1/2
```

Tremayne, exhibited 1941.

```
                    -griffithianum
              -Loderi-
MURIEL MESSEL-      -fortunei
              -Loder's White, q.v. for 2 possible parentage
                                               diagrams
```
Buds bright pink; flowers delicate pink to white.   Messel.
A.M. 1929.

```
* * * * * * * * * * * * * * * * * * * * * * * * * * * * *
                              -griffithianum 5/16
                    -Beauty of Tremough-
              -Norman Gill-         -arboreum 1/16
         -Anna-         -griffithianum
         -    -         -griffithianum
MURIEL-   -Jean Marie de Montague-
PEARCE-         -unknown 1/8
      -    -elliottii 1/4
         -Fusilier-
              -griersonianum 1/4
```
6ft(1.8m) 10F(-12C) EM   Plant upright, well-branched; dark
green leaves, narrowly elliptic, 4in(10.2cm) long, held 2 years.
Flowers shaded rose madder, much red spotting on upper 3 lobes,
openly funnel-shaped, 3.5in(8.9cm) wide; conical trusses of 14-
15.   Halfdan Lem cross; Owen Pearce, reg. 1973.
RED OLYMPIA   Parentage as above
5ft(1.5m) 5F(-15C) M 5/3 Cardinal red flowers open to lighter flowers spotted black, reverse medium red, openly cup-shaped,
4.25in(10.8cm) across. Leaves 7.5in(18.5cm) long, held 3 years.
Lem cross; L. J. Pearce, reg. 1975.
* *

```
         -Marion (Cheal)--unknown 3/4
MURRABA-         -ponticum 1/4
         -Purple Splendour-
                    -unknown
```
Deep mallow purple, shading lighter.   V. J. Boulter, reg. 1972.

```
                              -catawbiense 1/16
                    -Parsons Grandiflorum-
              -Nova -         -unknown
         -unnamed-Zembla-dark red hybrid--unknown
         - hybrid-    -griffithianum 1/8
         -    -Mars-
MUSTAFA-         -unknown
         -              -griffithianum
         -         -Mars-
         -unnamed hybrid-         -unknown
                    -yakushimanum--Koichiro Wada
```
2.5ft(.75m) x 3ft(.9m) -10F(-23C) ML Truss of 11-15 flowers,
vivid purplish red fading inward to white, faint dorsal spots of
greenish yellow; scurfy indumentum. Hachmann; Stück, reg. 1988.

```
         -fortunei 1/2
MUTTER EMMA-
         -unknown 1/2
```
Truss of 12 flowers, bright spirea red shading lighter, heavily
spotted with oxblood red.   B. Leendertz, W. Germany, reg. 1976.

```
                    -decorum 1/4
         -Decsoul-
MUY LINDO-    -souliei 1/4
         -         -griffithianum 1/4
         -Isabella-
                    -auriculatum 1/4
```
Flushed pink buds opening to white flowers, fragrant, funnel-
campanulate, 5.5in(14cm) across, 7-8 lobes; elongated trusses of
14-18. Large shrub. Ingram, cross 1952; reg. 1963. A.M. 1969.

MY DELIGHT---macabeanum, selfed
10ft(3m) x 10ft(22 yrs) 5F(-15C) E   Truss of 25-35 flowers,
7-lobed, light greenish yellow to pale yellow-green; red-purple
spotted rays. Orange-yellow indumentum.   Vaartnou, reg. 1989.

```
                         -xanthostephanum 1/8
              -Saffron Queen-
         -Owen Pearce-         -burmanicum 3/8
MY GUY-         -burmanicum
      -    -lindleyi 1/4
      -Mi Amor-
              -nuttallii 1/4
```

4ft(1.2m) x 3ft(.9m)(13 yrs)   tested only to 40F E Fragrant flowers, 5 frilled lobes, white without markings; lax truss 9in. (23cm) wide, of 7-13. M. & F. Sumner, reg. 1985.

```
                  -veitchianum 1/2
MY LADY---FORSTERIANUM, selfed-
                  -edgeworthii 1/2
```
2.5ft(.75m) 15F(-10C) E 4/3 Compact plant, as wide as high; glossy dark green leaves, bullate, 3in(7.6cm) long. Flowers white, blushed pink with a pale yellow throat, very open-rotate, 2.5in(6.4cm) wide, held in open trusses.   Mr. & Mrs. Maurice Sumner, intro. 1967; reg. 1972.

MY PET Parentage unknown
2ft(.6m) 0F(-18C) EM 3/3 Attractive dwarf; masses of yellow flowers with small red blotches. Whitney cross; Sathers, reg. 1976.

```
            -carneum 1/2
MY PRETTY ONE-
            -moupinense 1/2
```
2ft(.6m) 5F(-15C) VE 3/4 Rambling dwarf shrub with mahogany-colored bark, peeling at all seasons. Flowers apple blossom pink fading off-white, shallow trumpet-shaped, to 3.5in(8.9cm) wide, in trusses of 3. Del W. James cross; A. A. Childers, reg. 1965.

```
        -Nigrescens--unknown
MYRTE-
        -Mira--unknown
```
MIRA by Stevenson was not available at this date. Purple violet flowers with reddish brown markings. Seidel, cross 1910.

```
          -minus 1/2
MYRTIFOLIUM-
          -hirsutum 1/2
```
3ft(.9m) -15F(-26C) L 3/5 Broadly dome-shaped shrub; tolerant of heat and sun. Small foliage deep bronze red in winter, rich dark green in summer. Purplish rose flowers, spotted crimson, in terminal racemes. Late. Origin unknown; shown 1917. Color illus. HG p. 87.

```
          -Campylogynum Myrtilloides Group 1/2
MYRTLE BELLS-
          -glaucophyllum  1/2
```
Small flowers in clusters of 5-8, bell-shaped, 5-lobed, deep violet purple, red purple spotting in upper throat. H. E. Hawden cross; R. Strauss exhibited; reg. 1970. P.C. 1969.

```
                  -arboreum ssp. nilagiricum 1/8
        -Noyo Chief-
  -Rubicon-            -unknown 5/16
  -       -            -elliottii 3/8
MYRTLE-   -Kilimanjaro-          -Moser's Maroon--unknown
MANSON-             -Dusky Maid-
  -                          -fortunei ssp. discolor
  -           -elliottii
  -Kilimanjaro-          -Moser's Maroon--unknown
              -Dusky Maid-
                          -fortunei ssp. discolor 3/16
```
Trusses of 25 flowers 2.75in(7cm) wide, deep blood red with dark spotting. Leaves narrowly elliptic, glabrous. R. C. Gordon, reg. 1984.

```
          -thomsonii 1/4
  -Barclayi-            -arboreum 1/8
MYSTIC-   -Glory of Penjerrick-
  -                     -griffithianum  1/8
  -williamsianum 1/2
```
3ft(.9m) 5F(-15C) EM Very clear pink flowers. Gen. Harrison, cross 1950; intro. 1957.

```
          -smirnowii 1/8
        -Oh My!-
  -unnamed-     -yakushimanum 1/8      -catawbiense 1/16
  - hybrid-            -Parsons Grandiflorum-
MYSTIQUE-   -Nova Zembla-          -unknown 3/16
  -                 -dark red hybrid--unknown
  -yakushimanum, dwarf form 1/2
```
Buds of ruby red and strong purplish red opening to frilled flowers of strong purplish red; indumented foliage. W. Delp.

```
N
```

```
      -racemosum 1/2
NAHANNI-
      -lapponicum 1/2
```
3.5ft(1m) x 2.7ft(.8m)(16 yrs) -20F(-29C) M Flowers medium cyclamen purple shading to imperial purple, 1in(2.5cm) broad, 5-lobed; ball trusses of 16-20. Scaly leaves, to 1.2in(3cm) long. Lapponicum c. w. in Great Slave Lake area, N.W. Can.; the Indian name means far away (place). Dr. J. Brueckner cross; reg. 1989. Color illus. ARS J 44:2 (1990), p. 79.

```
             -fortunei ssp. discolor 1/2
NAMU-            -griersonianum 1/4
  -Mrs. Horace Fogg-         -griffithianum 1/8
              -Loderi Venus-
                         -fortunei 1/8
```
6ft(1.8m) -15F(-26C) M 4/4 Large trusses of 13-14 flowers, 6 or 7-lobed, roseine purple. H. L. Larson, reg. 1983.

NAN Described under LADY HOLLAND, q.v.

* *
```
          -fortunei 1/2
NANCEGLOS-
          -elliottii 1/2
```
A grex by Bolitho.   1945.
STELLABY Parentage as above
Misprinted in IRR, 1958 as SHELLABY.   RHS Garden, Wisley, 1954.
* *

```
                -smirnowii 1/4
        -unnamed hybrid-
NANCY BEHRING-         -fortunei 1/4
        -yakushimanum--Mist Maiden 1/2
```
3.5ft(1m) -20F(-29C) M Fragrant flowers, very light Neyron rose with pea green spotting in throat, openly funnel-shaped, 2.3in(6cm) wide, 5 frilled lobes; conical trusses of 14. Upright plant, well-branched and broad; dark yellow-green leaves held 3 years. R. Behring, reg. 1983.

```
                        -caucasicum 1/8
            -Cunningham's White-
      -Holden-          -ponticum, white 1/8
      -     -          -catawbiense 1/8
NANCY CAROL-    -red hybrid-
  -              -unknown 1/8
  -              -fortunei 1/4
  -Bob Peters Special-
                -unknown 1/4
```
3.5ft(1.05) x 3.5ft -15F(-23C) M Flowers 7-lobed, moderately fragrant, 15 per truss, deep pink flowers from darker buds, double flare on dorsal lobe. Plant of dense habit. Ray Carter, cross 1976; R. K. Peters, reg. 1986.

NANCY EVANS Described under BUTTER BRICKLE, q.v.

```
          -cinnabarinum ssp. xanthocodon Concatenans Group 1/2
NANCY  -
FORTESCUE-Lady Alice Fitzwilliam--unknown 1/2
```
Truss holds 11-13 flowers, rich chrome yellow. L. S. Fortescue cross; Keith Wiley, reg. for Fortescue Garden Trust, 1980.

NANCY LEE LUND Parentage unknown
5ft(1.5m) x 6.5ft(2.0m) -5F(-21C) EM Flowers in trusses of 12-15, light greenish yellow with 2 red spots on upper lobe. Leaves held 3 years. W. Whitney cross; F. Watters, reg. 1989.

```
          -pemakoense 1/2
NANCY READ-   -racemosum 1/4
        -Racil-
            -ciliatum 1/4
```
Light pink flowers. H. L. Larson, 1953.

NANCY SUE Parentage unknown
Flowers of magenta rose with gold spots. Stephens, reg. 1975.

```
                        -catawbiense 1/4
        -Catawbiense Grandiflorum-
NANCY'S BOUQUET-          -unknown 1/4
        -yakushimanum--Pink Parasol 1/2
```
3ft(.9m) x 1.5ft(.45m)(15 yrs) -25F(-32C) ML   Trusses of 13

flowers, openly funnel-campanulate, light purple with light
spots on upper lobe. Leaves held 3 years.   Behring, reg. 1989.

NANETTE   Parentage unknown
Flowers blush pink, dark blotch.   W. C. Slocock.   A.M. 1933.

```
                          -forrestii Repens Group 1/4
              -Elizabeth-
NANIE GARRETT-         -griersonianum 1/4
              -arboreum 1/2
```
Claret rose flowers in trusses of 18.   D. Dosser, reg. 1980.

NANKI POO   See AMANDA JOAN YOUNG

```
      -smirnowii 1/2
NANSEN-
      -unknown 1/2
```
Pale lilac rose flowers.   M. Koster & Sons.

NANUM--form of hanceanum Nanum Group
1ft(.3m) 5F(-15C) EM 4/4   Numerous dwarf plants bear the
label "var. nanum"; this one with small leaves and bright yellow
flowers. Compact, dome-shaped plant.   Origin unknown.

* *
```
                     -griffithianum 1/8
              -Kewense-
      -Aurora-         -fortunei 5/8
NAOMI-        -thomsonii 1/4
      -fortunei
```
5ft(1.5m) -5F(-21C) M 4/3   Large, sturdy, well-filled shrub,
producing an abundance of sweetly scented flowers of tender pink
with yellow undertones, a ray of faint brown, widely open, 7-
lobed, in big, rounded trusses.   Handsome foliage of rich green,
rounded at both ends.   Parent of many fine hybrids. This grex,
named after his youngest daughter, was the finest L. de Rothschild raised, and his favorite. Rothschild, 1926. A.M. 1933.
EXBURY NAOMI   Parentage as above
5ft(1.5m) -5F(-21C) M 4/4   Richly textured flowers of pink,
with shadings of yellow and apricot.   Medium compact shrub;
leaves 7in x 3in (17.8cm x 7.6cm), both ends rounded.
Rothschild, 1926. H.C. Wisley Trials 1968. A.M. 1933. Color
illus. ARS J 36:4 (1982), p. 135; PB pl. 12, 64.
MOLLY BUCKLEY   Parentage as above
Flowers bright orchid pink, speckled brownish orange.   L. de
Rothschild, reg. 1962.
NAOMI ASTARTE   Parentage as above
5ft(1.5m) -10F(-23C) M 4/4   Shrub of fairly compact habit;
leaves 7in(17.9cm) long and rounded at both ends. Flowers light
pink, shading to a soft yellow toward center and deeper yellow
in throat. Rothschild. Color illus. ARS Q 27:3 (1973), p. 171.
NAOMI CARISSIMA   Parentage as above
6ft(1.8m) -10F(-23C) EM 2/3   Flowers are pale pink, flushed
creamy white. Rothschild. Color illus. PB pl. 64.
NAOMI EARLY DAWN   Parentage as above
6ft(1.8m) -10F(-23C) EM 3/3   Pale pink flowers. Rothschild.
Color illus. JS p. 91.
NAOMI EXBURY   See EXBURY NAOMI
NAOMI GLOW   Parentage as above
6ft(1.8m) -10F(-23C) EM 4/4 Large flowers glowing deep pink,
darker in throat, in dome-shaped trusses. The only NAOMI of one
clear, single color. Rothschild. Color illus. F p. 58; PB pl.
64; VV p. 63.
NAOMI HOPE   Parentage as above
6ft(1.8m) -10F(-23C) EM 4/3 Flowers pink, tinged with mauve.
Rothschild. Color illus. PB pl. 64.
NAOMI NAUTILUS   Parentage as above
6ft(1.8m) -5F(-21C) M 4/4   Flowers rose, flushed pale orange
with a soft greenish yellow throat. One of the best of the
NAOMI group. Rothschild. A.M. 1938.
NAOMI NEREID   Parentage as above
6ft(1.8m) -10F(-23C) EM 4/4   Very fine foliage like NAOMI
NAUTILUS. Crimson and lavender flowers. Rothschild. Color
illus. PB pl. 13.
NAOMI PINK BEAUTY   Parentage as above
6ft(1.8m) -10F(-23C) EM 4/4 Flower satiny pink. Rothschild.
Color illus. PB pl. 64.
NAOMI PIXIE   Parentage as above
6ft(1.8m) -10F(-23C) EM 4/4   Habit rather compact. Large
flowers of bright pink with rich crimson stain in throat, held
in dome-shaped truss. Long-lasting flowers. Rothschild. Color

illus. ARS Q 27:3 (1973), p. 170.
NAOMI STELLA MARIS   Parentage as above
6ft(1.8m) -10F(-23C) EM 4/4 Flowers slightly larger, trusses
fuller, and leaves longer than in other clones. Flowers buff,
shaded lilac pink. Rothschild. F.C.C. Wisley Trials 1939.
PARIS   Parentage as above
6ft(1.8) -5F(-21C) M 3/3   Of good habit, nearly as broad as
tall and may grow to 20ft(6m).   Dark green foliage covers the
plant from ground up.   Flowers light purplish rose, 3in(7.6cm)
across; loose truss of 10-12. Mr. Barber called it "...perhaps
finest in this distinguished company". Rothschild, reg. 1969.
* *
```
              -Alstroemerioides--unknown
NAPOLEON BAUMANN-
              -unknown
```
6ft(1.8m) OF(-18C) ML   Now in commerce perhaps only in AUS
where it's grown mainly for its sun-tolerance. Light rose pink,
spotted crimson, in small trusses.   Baumann of Belgium, 1867.

```
                  -fortunei ssp. discolor 1/4
      -Margaret Dunn-    -dichroanthum 1/8
      -          -Fabia-
NARANJA-               -griersonianum 3/8
      -          -griersonianum
      -Tally Ho-
              -facetum (eriogynum) 1/4
```
Flowers vermilion to jasper red.   Lester E. Brandt, reg. 1963.

```
                  -augustinii 1/4
      -Blue Diamond-      -intricatum 1/8
NASCA BLOSSOM-        -Intrifast-
              -unknown 1/2     -fastigiatum 1/8
```
3ft(.9m) -5F(-21C) EM   Truss of 5-6 flowers, pale rose-tinged
purple; upper lobe spotted orange-brown. I. A. Hayes, reg. 1982.

```
                  -Loder's White, q.v. for 2 possible
              -C.I.S.-    -dichroanthum      parentages
      -Big Sam-      -Fabia-
      -                 -griersonianum 1/16
      -          -unnamed hybrid--unknown
NASELLE-         -dichroanthum
      -   -Dido-
      -          -decorum               -griffithianum
      -Lem's-                -Beauty of Tremough-
      Cameo-   -Norman Gill-          -arboreum
      -   -          -griffithianum
          -Anna-               -griffithianum
              -Jean Marie de Montague-
                           -unknown
```
4ft(1.2m) high x 5ft(1.5m) 10F(-12C) EM Flowers to 4in(10cm)
wide, 15 per lax truss, 6-lobed, China rose, shading to maize
yellow, burnt orange spotting; trusses 7in(17.8cm) across. New
growth pale maroon; leaf elliptic, parsley green, 4.5in(11.4cm)
long. BIG SAM is a sibling of NASELLE. J. Elliott, reg. 1987.

```
      -maximum 1/2
NASSAU RED-
      -unknown 1/2
```
A selected form or hybrid of maximum. Flowers bright rose pink.

NASTURTIUM   Described under EAST KNOYLE, q.v.

```
              -Marion--unknown 3/4
NATALIE MURRAY-               -caucasicum 1/4
              -Christmas Cheer-
                           -unknown
```
Light pink funnel-shaped flowers, paler at center, with yellow-
green spotting on dorsal lobe; trusses of 15-20. V. J. Boulter,
cross 1975; F. Boulter, reg. 1986.

NATHAN HALE   Parentage unknown
5ft(1.5m) -5F(-21C) ML Much fragrance; 7-lobed flowers, rose-
colored, with a dark rose patch; globular truss.   Dexter cross;
Mrs. H. C. Schlaikjer, reg. 1973.

```
              -haematodes 1/4
      -Hummingbird-
NATHANIEL-        -williamsianum 1/4
      -          -forrestii Repens Group 1/4
      -Elizabeth-
              -griersonianum 1/4
```

A hybrid from British Columbia. Cherry red flowers in trusses of six. Robert C. Rhodes, reg. 1979.

```
            -calophytum 1/2
NAUSICAA-                   -arboreum 1/4
            -Gill's Triumph-
                           -griffithianum 1/4
```
A hybrid introduced by E. J. P. Magor.

```
* * * * * * * * * * * * * * * * * * * * * * * * * *
        -aureum (chrysanthum) 1/2          -neriiflorum 1/16
NEALA-                          -Nereid-
    -            -Phyllis Ballard-      -dichroanthum 1/16
    -Dead Ringer-              -fortunei ssp. discolor 1/8
            -catawbiense--Clark's White 1/4
```
Buds of amber yellow and brick red open to barium yellow; dorsal spotting of vivid yellow-green. W. Delp.
SULTRY PEACH   Parentage as above
Buds of strong pink open to a mix of strong pink, moderate pink, and pale pink. Plant size low; hardiness -15F(-26C). Delp.
```
* * * * * * * * * * * * * * * * * * * * * * * * * *
```

NEAPOLITAN   Described under LITTLE PUDDING, q.v.

```
                        -catawbiense 1/4
            -unnamed hybrid-    -dichroanthum
            -              -Fabia-
        -Ginny-                 -griersonianum
        - Mae - -yakushimanum 1/8    -fortunei ssp. discolor
        -   -Si-        -Lady Bess-
        -   Si-   -Day - borough  -campylocarpum Elatum Gp.
        -    -Gold -Dream-griersonianum 7/64          1/64
        -    Mohur-            -fortunei ssp. discolor 5/64
NEATO -           -Margaret Dunn-    -dichroanthum 9/64
(Delp)-                     -Fabia-
        -                       -griersonianum
        -          -catawbiense var. album Glass--Catalgla 1/8
        -   -Tony's-               -catawbiense
        - - Gift -   -Catawbiense Album-
        -      -Belle -     -unknown 1/16
    -unnamed-   Heller-            -catawbiense
    hybrid-       -white catawbiense sdl.
        -          -maximum 1/16     -unknown
        -   -Russell-
        -Serenata- Harmon-catawbiense
        -          -dichroanthum
            -unnamed-    -fortunei ssp. discolor
            hybrid-unnamed-
                    hybrid-campylocarpum 1/32
```
Buds of moderate red, moderate reddish orange and moderate yellowish pink; flowers open to peach and moderate yellowish pink, with a pale yellow flare and dark red dorsal spots; throat brilliant greenish yellow. W. Delp.

```
            -campanulatum 1/2
NEAT-O (Goheen)-
            -yakushimanum--Koichiro Wada 1/2
```
3ft(.9m) 5F(-15C) EM 4/5   Buds Neyron rose, opening lighter, shading to very pale rose in throat, spotted Neyron rose; flowers campanulate, 1.25in(3.2cm) broad; of good substance, 5 wavy lobes; globular truss of 20-25. Plant rounded, as wide as tall; leaves held 3-4 years, heavy grayed orange indumentum beneath. grayed white tomentum on new growth. Goheen, reg. 1983.

NEBULA   Described under HAD, q.v.

```
                    -Corona--unknown 1/8
                -Coronis-    -griffithianum 1/16
        -unnamed hybrid-    -Loderi-
        -          -        -fortunei 1/6
NECTARINE-         -griersonianum 3/8
        -          -fortunei ssp. discolor 1/4
        -Margaret Dunn-    -dichroanthum 1/8
                    -Fabia-
                        -griersonianum
```
4ft(1.2m) OF(-18C) M 4/3   An unusual, orange-colored flower of lovely tones. Leaves long and narrow, dull olive green. L. E. Brandt, reg. 1958.

```
        -dichroanthum 1/2
NEDA-
    -caucasicum--Cunningham's Sulphur 1/2
```

Orange flowers, flushed pink.   Lord Aberconway, 1933.

```
        -griersonianum 1/2
NEHRU       -barbatum 1/4
    -Huntsman-
            -campylocarpum Elatum Group 1/4
```
Showy trusses of rich scarlet flowers on a tall, upright plant. Blooms early to midseason.   Rothschild, 1946.

```
        -unnamed peach-colored hybrid--unknown 9/16
NELDA-    -Dido-          -dichroanthum 1/8
PEACH-    -   -decorum 1/8          -griffithianum 5/32
    -Lem's-              -Beauty of-
    Cameo-   -Norman Gill- Tremough-arboreum 1/32
        -   -              -griffithianum
        -Anna-              -griffithianum
            -Jean Marie de Montague-
                        -unknown
```
2ft(.6m) x 2.5ft(.75m)(8 yrs) OF(-18C) M Flowers openly funnel-shaped, 4in(10cm) broad, 14 per truss, 7-lobed. Buds strong yellowish pink open to light yellowish pink; trusses 7in(17.3cm) wide; elliptic leaves. W. Robertson cross; J. Davis, reg. 1988.

```
                -decorum 1/4
        -unnamed hybrid-
NELLE S. -          -fortunei ssp. discolor 1/4
BAREFIELD-    -lacteum 1/4
    -unnamed-
    hybrid-    -griffithianum 1/8
            -Loderi-
                -fortunei 1/8
```
6ft(1.8m) 5F(-15C) L   Spinel red buds opening light Neyron rose, mimosa yellow throat with grayed orange spotting, reverse lighter rose; flowers openly funnel-shaped, 5in(12.7cm) across, 7-lobed; large spherical trusses of 10-12. Plant habit rounded, erect; narrow medium green leaves, 8.5in(21.6cm) long, held two years. Grady E. Barefield, intro. 1973; reg. 1983.

```
        -occidentale azalea 1/2
NELLIE-
    -rhododendron--unknown 1/2
```
Azaleodendron.   White flowers with large yellow blotch, funnel-shaped, 2.5in(6.4cm) wide, wavy recurved lobes; rounded trusses of about 12. Semi-deciduous; narrow leaves to 4in(10.2cm) long. Harry White, Sunningdale.

NEON LIGHT   Parentage unknown
A parent of CALLIGHT.

```
        -catawbiense var. album 1/2
NEPAL-          -wightii 1/4
    -unnamed hybrid-
            -fortunei 1/4
```
6ft(1.8m) -25F(-32C) M 4/4   Rose pink buds opening to large white flowers. Handsome plant in all seasons, with large foliage. Ultimately an imposing shrub 15 feet tall.   Leach, 1972.

NEPAL--form of cinnabarinum L S & H 21283
5ft(1.5m) 5F(-15C) EM-VL 4/4 Trusses of 4-8 tubular flowers, 1.25in(3.2cm) across by 2in(5cm) long, of soft aureolin yellow, deepening near base to medium rhodonite red. Oblanceolate foliage, scaly below.   Ludlow, Sherriff & Hicks collectors; J. B. Stevenson raiser; Hydon, reg. 1977. A.M. 1977.

NEPAL--form of niveum
5ft(1.5m) 5F(-15C) M 3/3 A large shrub; young shoots covered with light tan indumentum. Tight trusses of rich purple, campanulate flowers. Origin unknown. F.C.C. 1979.

NEPTUNE   Described under EULO, q.v.

```
        -neriiflorum 1/2
NEREID-
    -dichroanthum 1/2
```
2ft(.6m) OF(-18C) ML 3/4   Named for a Greek sea nymph. Parent of PHYLLIS BALLARD, BLONDIE. Compact plant with small, dark green, oblong leaves. Flowers of peachy salmon pink with faint orange spotting, waxy, bell-shaped, and 1in(2.5cm) across; 8 per lax truss. Grown from wild-collected seed of dichroanthum. E. F. Wilding, intro. 1934.

```
                    -dichroanthum ssp. apodectum 1/2
NERIIAPO-
          -neriiflorum 1/2
Flowers orange-red.   E. J. P. Magor, 1929.


                    -arboreum 1/2
NERIIARB-
          -neriiflorum 1/2
Flowers of clear red, with slight spotting of a darker red.   E.
J. P. Magor, 1928.


                    -neriiflorum 1/2
NERIIHAEM-
          -haematodes 1/2
Waxy flowers, blood red, and unspotted.   E. J. P. Magor, 1927.


                         -arboreum 1/4
          -Choremia
NERISSA-            -haematodes 1/2
-                   -neriiflorum 1/4
          -Neriihaem-
                    -haematodes
A Bodnant hybrid with blood red flowers.  Lord Aberconway, 1945.


NESTOR   Described under SHILSONII, q.v.
```

* *

```
          -fortunei 1/2
NESTUCCA-
          -yakushimanum 1/2
3ft(.9m) -10F(-23C) M 4/3    White flowers, brown traces in
throat, 5in(12.7cm) wide, dome-shaped truss of 14.  Plant com-
pact, rigid, wider than high; dark green leaves to 5in(12.7cm).
F. Hanger cross; Cecil Smith, intro. 1960.  P.A. 1950.
LITTLE WHITE DOVE   Parentage as above
3ft(.9m) 5F(-15C) M 4/4   Light rose pink buds, white flowers,
of heavy substance; truss of 12.  Dense plant; glossy dark green
leaves held 3 years.  Lancaster cross; J. Elliott, reg. 1974.
```

* *

```
                              -griffithianum 1/8
               -George Hardy-
     -Mrs. L. A. Dunnett-            -catawbiense 1/8
NETTY KOSTER-             -unknown 1/2
-                         -griersonianum 1/4
     -unnamed hybrid-
                    -unknown
Openly funnel-shaped flowers, crimson with darker spots on upper
petal.  M. Koster & Sons.   A.M. 1945.


     -williamsianum 1/2
NEVADO-
     -arboreum ssp. cinnamomeum var. album--Sir Chas. Lemon 1/2
4ft(1.2m) x 4ft.  OF(-18C) EM  Snow white flowers in profusion,
on loose domed trusses.  Plant rounded; foliage circular, dark
green.  NEVADO means "snowy".  Dr. David Goheen, reg. 1990.


               -Dexter hybrid--unknown 13/16
     -Janet Blair-
NEW   -          -unknown          -catawbiense 1/16
BEGINNING-          -Parsons Grandi-
-          -America-  florum        -unknown
     -Dorothy-       -dark red hybrid--unknown
     Amateis          -ponticum 1/8
          -Purple Splendour-
                    -unknown
1.5ft(.45m) x 1ft(.3m)(8 yrs) -15F(-26C) ML  Flower 3in(7.6cm)
wide, 7-lobed, light purple with moderate yellow and deep orange
-yellow spotting, frilled; truss of 15.  Plant upright; elliptic
foliage, glossy dark green, held 3 years.  Behring, reg. 1989.


NEW COMET   Described under EMERALD ISLE, q.v.


               -catawbiense album 3/8
     -Lodestar-
NEW   -          -catawbiense var. album
ELEGANCE-  -Belle Heller-            -catawbiense 1/16
          -          -white cat. hyb.-
     -Rona Pink, Dexter hybrid--unknown   -unknown 9/16
Bud of strong and light purple open to flowers of rose and phlox
purple, with strong purple on exterior; dorsal spotting of vivid
greenish yellow.  Dr. D Hinerman cross; W. Delp raiser.
```

* *

```
          -yakushimanum 1/2
NEW HOPE-  -elliottii 1/4
     -Kiev-      -thomsonii 1/8
          -Robert Fox-          -arboreum 1/16
               -Glory of  -
               Penjerrick-griffithianum 1/16
3ft(.9m)  -5F(-21C) EM  Flowers of dark pink fading lighter to
center, darker pink spotting on upper lobe,  funnel-shaped, 3.25
in(8.3cm) across, reverse dark pink; trusses of 10. Plant round-
ed, as wide as high; felted fawn indumentum underneath.    Bovee
cross; Charles Herbert, reg. 1976.
BUCKLEBURY   Parentage as above
6.3ft(1.9m) x 9.8ft(2.9m)(24 yrs.) ML   Campanulate, 5-lobed,
pale mauve flowers, 2.3in(6cm) wide, dorsal throat rose red; 13-
14 per truss. Obovate dark green leaves with dense woolly brown
indumentum.  Crown Estate, reg. 1986.   A.M. 1986.
```

* *

```
                    -campylocarpum 1/4
     -Mrs. W. C. Slocock-
NEW MOON-          -unknown 1/4
     -fortunei 1/2
Cream buds tinged mauve pink; white flowers tinged primrose yel-
low.  W. C. Slocock.  A.M. Wisley Trials 1953.


               -unnamed hybrid (67-LL-6)--unknown 3/4
NEW ORLEANS-      -Newburyport Belle (Fowle 19)--unknown
          -Casanova-          -catawbiense var. rubrum 1/8
               -Good Hope-
                         -wardii 1/8
4.5ft(1.4m) x 4ft(1.2m)  -20F(-29C) M 4/5   Buds of moderate
yellowish pink, open light barium yellow, deeper in the center,
with fine dorsal spotting of reddish brown; flower 5-lobed, 2in.
(5cm) wide; trusses of 16.   D. G. Leach, cross 1976; reg. 1985.


                         -minus Carolinianum Group 1/8
                    -P.J.M.-
          -unnamed hybrid, F2-    -dauricum Sempervirens 1/8
NEW   -          -unknown 1/2
PATRIOT-          -mucronulatum, pink form 1/4
     -unnamed hybrid-
               -unknown
3ft(.9m) x 3ft  -20F(-29C) EM   Trusses of 8 flowers extending
down stems 2in(5cm); buds deep red to strong purplish red, open-
ing vivid purplish red.  Mezitt, cross 1979; Weston, reg. 1989.


               -griersonianum 1/2
NEW PLYMOUTH CITY-
               -grande 1/2
7ft(2.1m) x 7ft(15 yrs)  15F(-9C) Oct.  Trusses of 20 flowers,
tubular campanulate, 5-lobed, rose madder in bud, opening light-
er rose, to blush pink in throat and outside of tube.  Dense,
compact habit with light brown indumentum on large leaves.   L.
Jury cross; S. J. & E. R. Rowe, reg. 1988.


NEW ROMANCE   Described under LAKE LABISH, q.v.


NEW WINE   Described under BLUE RHAPSODY, q.v.
```

* *

```
NEWBURYPORT BELLE   Parentage unknown
4ft(1.2m)  -15F(-26C) ML  Synonym FOWLE NO. 19.  Light purplish
pink flower, much yellow and green spotting gives effect of gold
blotch; domed truss of 16.  Free-flowering, well-branched plant.
Dexter cross; H. Fowle raiser; Scott Hort. Found., reg. 1985.
NEWBURYPORT BEAUTY   Parentage unknown
Synonym FOWLE NO. 18.  This hybrid and the above crossed by D.
Leach to create RIO and NORMANDY, q.v.  Flowers lavender pink.
Dexter and Fowle.
NEWBURYPORT CHARM   Parentage unknown
Synonym FOWLE NO. 20.  Flowers pale lavender and frilled, with a
pinkish purple edge; later fades white. This group of 3 is pre-
sumed to have same or similar parentage.  Dexter and Fowle.
```

* *

```
This entry out of order.
          -catawbiense 1/2
NEWPORT-
          -unknown 1/2
5ft(1.5m)  -10F(-23C)  ML   Flowers of an unusual plum purple,
held in very tight trusses.  Plant habit rather open; fine fol-
```

iage. "May have been grown from seed from North Cemetery," (In Butler)--Pride. Warren Stokes, Butler, PA, raiser; reg. 1958.

```
                                  -griffithianum 7/32
                         -Beauty of-
                    -Norman- Tremough-arboreum 1/32
                      - Gill -
                -Anna-        -griffithianum
                -    -                          -griffithianum
        -Pink    -   -Jean Marie de Montague-
        -Walloper-  -                    -unknown 3/16
NEWCOMB'S-      -                         -griffithianum
SWEERHEART-         -           -George Hardy-
          -        -Marinus Koster-        -catawbiense 1/16
          -decorum 1/2           -red hybrid--unknown
```
4ft(1.2m) 0F(-18C) M Flowers of light pinkish mauve darkening with age to orchid pink and edged in solferino purple, blotched in roseine purple; corolla openly funnel-shaped, 4in(10cm) wide, 6-lobed, fragrant. Ball-shaped truss of 11. Plant broader than tall.   L. L. Newcomb, reg. 1981.   C.A. 1983.   Color illus. Cox pl. 131.

NEZ PERCE CHIEF   See THE CHIEF

```
    -ponticum 1/2
NICHOLAS-
    -unknown 1/2
```
5ft(1.5m) -10F(-23C) ML 4/2 Polished dark green, pointed leaves suggest ponticum as a parent. Flowers of petunia purple, paler towards center, throat and center of upper segment white, spotted green; corolla openly funnel-shaped, 3.3in(8cm) wide. Trusses of about 19, closely packed, on a broad, tall shrub. E. de Rothschild, reg. 1965.   A.M. 1965.   Color illus. PB pl. 56.

NICHOLAS VAARTNOU--selection from rex
10ft(3.0m) x 6ft(1.8m)(20 yrs) 5F(-15C) E Flowers of heavy substance, openly campanulate, very pale purple to nearly white. Leaves held 4 years, 12in(.3m) x 4in(10.2cm); fawn-colored felt-like indumentum beneath. H. Vaartnou raiser; reg. 1990.

NICOLINE Described under BLINKLICHT, q.v.

```
    -wardii 1/2
NIGEL MARSHALL-
    -unknown 1/2
```
Light yellow flowers. National Trust, Mount Stewart, reg. 1983.

NIGHT EDITOR--form of russatum
4ft(1.2m) 5F(-15C) E 3/4   Upright plant, stiff branches; leaves narrowly elliptic, 2in(5cm) long, revolute, scaly. Spectrum violet flowers, edged and spotted with violet, openly funnel-shaped, 1.5in(3.8cm) wide, 5-lobed; small spherical truss of 6-7. Betty Sheedy, reg. 1981.

```
        -Blue Steel--impeditum 1/2
NIGHT SKY-           -russatum 1/4
        -Russautinii-
                 -augustinii 1/4
```
Trusses of 5 flowers, deep violet blue, paler in throat. Lanceolate leaves, sparsely scaly. J. P. C. Russell, reg. 1983.

```
        -decorum 1/2
NIGHTINGALE-           -ponticum 1/4
        -Purple Splendour-
                  -unknown 1/4
```
6ft(1.8M) -5F(-21C) ML Very large truss; flower light purple with darker shades and a dark red blotch. Plant of dense habit. Large shrub. G. Reuthe, reg. 1985.

NIGHTWATCH Described under MIDNIGHT, q.v.

NIGRESCENS   Parentage unknown
A parent of MYRTE, a hybrid by Seidel. Flowers dark plum color. A. Waterer, before 1871.

Out of order
```
    -irroratum--POLKA DOT 1/2
NIMROD-
    -calophytum 1/2
```
6ft(1.8m) -5F(-21C) EM   Long broad leaves of calophytum and tubular bell-shaped flowers of irroratum. Delicate pink blossoms, heavily spotted brown, in many large, well-filled trusses.

E. de Rothschild, reg. 1964.   A.M. 1987.

```
              -catawbiense var. album 1/2
    -unnamed-     -wardii 1/4
    - hybrid-Crest-          -fortunei ssp. discolor 1/16
    -          -Lady -
NIKKO-         Bessborough-campylocarpum Elatum Group 1/16
    -                -catawbiense var. album
    -     -Ivory Tower-     -wardii
    -unnamed-     -unnamed hybrid-
      hybrid-                  -fortunei 1/16
    -                -catawbiense var. album
    -unnamed hybrid-     -wardii
              -unnamed hybrid-
                   -decorum 1/16
```
5ft(1.5m) -15(-26C) M   Brick red buds open to primrose yellow flowers, darker in throat, widely funnel-campanulate, 3.2in(8cm) wide, 5-6 lobed; dome-shaped trusses of 14.   Rounded habit, wider than tall; dark yellow-green, narrow leaves, 4.75in(12cm) long, held 1-2 years. David G. Leach, reg. 1983.

* *
```
    -catawbiense var. album 1/2
NILE-
    -wardii L S & T 5679  1/2
```
6ft(1.8m) -20F(-29C) EM 3/3   Synonym SAHARA. Primrose yellow flowers with dorsal blotch of currant red, good substance, 3in(7.6cm) across, widely funnel-shaped; spherical trusses of 13-14. Plant rounded, broad as tall; glossy fresh green foliage retained 2 years. David G. Leach, intro. 1973; reg. 1983.
GOOD HOPE   Parentage as above
6ft(1.8m) -20F(-29C) EM 4/4   Buds jasper red open to canary yellow flowers, about 13 in trusses 6in(15cm) across.   Plant wide as tall, glossy green leaves. Leach, intro. 1976; reg. 1982. Color illus. ARS J 36:1 (1982), p. 3.
* *

                         -maximum 1/8
                  -Halopeanum-
        -Snow Queen-   -griffithianum 1/2
        -              -griffithianum
NIMBUS-   -Loderi-
        -          -fortunei 1/8
        -          -fortunei ssp. discolor 1/4
        -Cornish Loderi-
                 -griffithianum
```
6ft(1.8m) 5F(-15C) ML  Plant broader than tall, of vigorous, upright habit; leaves of medium dull green, to 7.5in(19cm) long. Creamy buds, flushed dawn pink,  opening white blushed pale pink and fading white, funnel-shaped, 4in(10cm) across, wavy margins; compact, spherical truss, 8-flowered.   Knap Hill.  A.M. 1965. F.C.C. Wisley Trials 1967.

NIMROD  See previous column

```
    -fortunei 1/2
NINA-
    -unknown 1/2
```
5ft(1.5m) -20F(-29C) M   Fragrant flowers, spirea red, heavy ruby red blotch circling the throat; trusses 10-flowered.  Plant twice as broad as tall; leaves  5in(12.7cm) x 2.5in(6.4cm).   Of uncertain origin.  E. T. Wytovich, reg. 1979.

```
        -fortunei ssp. discolor 1/2
NINETTE-
    -makinoi 1/2
```
Clear, pale pink flowers.   J. B. Stevenson, 1936.

NINOTSCHKA   Described under YAKU WARRIOR, q.v.

NIOBE   See KATE GREENAWAY

```
    -wardii 1/2
NIPPON-
    -Seidel hybrid--unknown 1/2
```
4ft(1.2m) -10F(-23C) M   Pollen parent may be a seedling of CUNNINGHAM'S WHITE.  Flat, yellow flowers with red blotch.  Compact, upright shrub.  Hobbie.   Color illus. WS, 1989, p. 48.
```

```
                        -griffithianum 1/16
                    -Loderi-
              -Albatross-      -fortunei 1/4
        -Cup Day-          -fortunei ssp. discolor 1/16
        -         -          -elliottii 1/16
    -Midnight-       -Fusilier-
    -         -           -griersonianum 1/16
    -         -           -ponticum 1/8
    -         -Purple Splendour-
NIRITA-              -unknown 1/8
    -                   -griffithianum
    -             -Kewense-
    -         -Aurora-      -fortunei
    -     -Naomi-      -fortunei
    -Carita-      -fortunei
        -campylocarpum 1/4
```
Flowers in trusses of 15, campanulate, white, spotted with vivid
reddish orange. Bush 2ft(.6m) high. K. van de Ven, reg. 1984.

```
        -decorum 1/2
NISSEQOGUE-
        -Pygmalion--unknown 1/2
```
3ft(.9m) -5F(-21C) M   Buds dark spirea red, flowers lighter
red with dorsal spotting of gray-brown in throat, widely funnel-
campanulate, 3in(7.6cm) wide, of good substance; dome-shaped
truss of 10. Plant well-branched, as broad as tall; glossy dark
leaves held 3 years. A. A. Raustein, reg. 1983.

```
                    -fortunei, cream form 1/8
            -Mary Garrison-
        -             -vernicosum (R 18139) 3/8
        -unnamed-                 -catawbiense 1/32
        - hybrid-      -Atrosanguineum-
        -         -Atrier-       -unknown 1/32
        -     -Mary -griersonianum 1/16
NO FRILLS-    Belle-    -decorum 1/16
BEAUTY -         -Dechaem-
    -                 -haematodes 1/16
    -              -maximum 1/4
        -unnamed hybrid-
                -vernicosum (R 18139)
```
Buds of jasper red and azalea pink open to flowers pale yellow
and shell pink; throat of vivid reddish orange.   W. Delp.

```
        -Boule de Neige Improved -caucasicum 1/4
        -(Boule de Neige, selfed)-          -catawbiense 1/8
        -                 -hardy hybrid-
NO WAY-                      -unknown 1/8
        -     -flavidum 1/4
    -unnamed-      -cinnabarinum Roylei Group 1/8
      hybrid-Lady    -
        -Rosebery-          -cinnabarinum 1/16
            -Royal Flush-
            (Pink form)-maddenii 1/16
```
A rare cross of lepidote and elepidote. Pale yellow flowers, a
red blotch. Hardy to at least -15F(-26C).   D. Hinerman cross;
W. Delp raiser.

NO WONDER   Described under BORN FREE, q.v.

```
        -yakushimanum 1/2            -griffithianum 1/16
NOBLE  -            -George Hardy-
MOUNTAIN-   -Mrs. L. A. Dunnett-      -catawbiense 1/16
        -Rodeo-          -unknown 1/8
            -griersonianum 1/4
```
15in(38cm) high x 20in(50.8cm)(6 yrs) 0F(-18C) M   Flowers in
truss of 15, 5-lobed, frilled edges, moderate purplish pink with
heavy dark red spotting.   Peste cross; S. Johnston, reg. 1986.

```
            -forrestii Repens Group 1/4
        -Elizabeth-
NOBLE PEARL-      -griersonianum 1/4
        -Kew Pearl--unknown 1/2
```
5ft(1.5m) 5F(-15C) EM Loose trusses, salmon pink. Considered
a fine early-flowering pink in Australia. K. van de Ven.

* *
```
        -caucasicum 1/2
NOBLEANUM-
        -arboreum 1/2
```
4ft(1.2m) -10F(-23C) E 2/2 Early and showy. Brilliant rosy
scarlet buds, opening rich rose flushed white inside, a few

crimson spots, widely funnel-shaped; compact trusses.   Slow-
growing shrub; leaves dark green, plastered buff indumentum.
One of the earliest man-made hybrids. A. Waterer, Knap Hill,
about 1832-1835. A.G.M. 1926.   Color illus. Cox. pl. 132.
HANDSWORTH SCARLET   Parentage may be same as above
5ft(1.5m) -5F(-21C) E Tight, red trusses holding 16 flowers.
Fisher & Sibray, before 1928.
NOBLEANUM ALBUM   Parentage as above
4ft(1.2m) -10F(-23C) E 2/2 White flowers. Knap Hill.
NOBLEANUM COCCINEUM   Parentage as above
5ft(1.5m) 0F(-18C) VE 2/2 A large, conical shrub with bell-
shaped, deep rose flowers, some basal spotting of dark crimson.
A. Waterer, 1835.
NOBLEANUM LAMELLEN   Parentage as above
Deep red flowers. Hybrid by E. J. P. Magor, intro. 1932.
NOBLEANUM SILBERAAD'S EARLY   Parentage as above
Flowers pale rose and pure white. Very early. Knap Hill.
NOBLEANUM VENUSTUM   Parentage as above
5ft(1.5m) 0F(-18C) VE 2/2 Dense, leafy bush; broad, rounded.
Compact truss of funnel-shaped flowers shining rose pink, medium
size. In England it flowers in late winter, even in a mild De-
cember. Raised by William Smith near Kingston, Surrey, in 1829.
A.G.M. 1969. A.M. 1973.
SUN OF AUSTERLITZ   Parentage may be same as above
Flowers crimson, shading to pale rose with light black spotting.
T. Methven, 1868.
* *

```
                            -ponticum 1/8
                    -unnamed hybrid-
            -Altaclerense-      -catawbiense 1/8
NOBLEANUM BICOLOR-      -arboreum 1/4
            -catawbiense 1/2
```
Flowers deep rose with white throat.   Standish & Noble, 1850.

```
            -smirnowii 1/4
    -unnamed hybrid-
NOBUE-      -catawbiense 1/4
    -     -yakushimanum 1/4      -fortunei ssp. discolor 3/32
    -unnamed-          -Lady Bess- -
      hybrid-    -Day - borough  -campylocarpum Elatum Group
        -Gold-Dream-griersonianum 3/32          1/32
        Mohur-        -fortunei ssp. discolor
        -Margaret Dunn-      -dichroanthum 1/32
                    -Fabia-
                    -griersonianum
```
Flowers of various shades of pink. Medium-sized plant; hardy to
-15F(-26C).   W. Delp.

```
            -griersonianum 1/4
    -Laura    -      -thomsonii 1/8
    -Aberconway-Barclayi-      -arboreum 1/16
NOCTURNE-          -Glory of -
    -              Penjerrick-griffithianum 5/16
    -       -griffithianum
    -Loderi-
        -fortunei 1/4
```
A red-flowered hybrid. Lord Aberconway, 1950.

```
                -catawbiense 1/4
        -red catawbiense hybrid-
NODDING BELLS-      -unknown 1/4
    -          -forrestii Repens Group 1/4
    -unnamed hybrid-
            -griersonianum 1/4
```
2ft(.6m) -10F(-23C) EM   A spreading bush with outer branches
arching downward. Cherry red flowers, openly campanulate. Some
fall blossoms. E. Amateis.

```
                -caucasicum 1/4
        -Dr. Stocker-
NOELE BOULTER-      -griffithianum 1/4
    -      -arboreum 1/4
    -Cornubia-      -thomsonii 1/8
        -Shilsonii-
            -barbatum 1/8
```
6ft(1.8m) 5F(-15C) E   An upright shrub with 10-14 flowers per
truss, Neyron rose in bud, stained ruby red in throat. Flower
color not given in the published registration.   V. J. Boulter,
Australia, reg. 1963.

```
            -Marion (Cheal)--unknown 5/8
NOILA-        -diaprepes 1/4
    -Lilac Time-                    -ponticum 1/8
              -Purple Splendour-
                        -unknown
```
Fuchsine pink flowers, heavily spotted with yellow on the upper
lobes. V. J. Boulter, reg. 1965.

```
        -cinnabarinum Roylei Group 1/2
NONESUCH-
        -maddenii 1/2
```
Flowers of pale apricot, fading cream.   Adams-Acton, 1942.

```
        -Marion (Cheal)--unknown 1/2
NOOROOK-
        -neriiflorum 1/2
```
3ft(.9m) OF(-18C) E   Flowers of Delft rose, 15-20 per truss,
overall light spotting, edged reddish scarlet.   Boulter, AUS,
reg. 1972.

```
                        -maximum 1/4
            -unnamed hybrid-
NORBITONENSE AUREUM-            -ponticum 1/4
            -azalea molle 1/2
```
Azaleodendron. Synonym SMITHII AUREUM. Flowers soft tawny yel-
low with darker markings, in a rhododendron-like truss, blooming
late. Plant habit neat, compact.   W. Smith of Norbiton, 1830.

```
                        -maximum 1/4
            -unnamed hybrid-
NORBITONENSE BROUGHTONIANUM-        -ponticum 1/4
            -azalea molle 1/2
```
Azaleodendron. Synonym BROUGHTONII AUREUM. Flowers soft yellow
with orange-yellow spots, about 2.5in(6.4cm) wide; small round
trusses. Foliage rough-textured, rather sparse.   Origin not
known; W. Smith of Norbiton, raiser c. 1830.   F.C.C. 1935.
Color illus. VV p. 129.

* *
```
        -Essex Scarlet--unknown 1/2
NORDERNCY-
        -williamsianum 1/2
```
Flowers deep rose.   Dietrich Hobbie, 1947.
OUDIJK'S SENSATION   Parentage as above
4ft(1.2m) -10F(-23C) EM 3/3   Loose trusses of 5-7 flowers,
bright Tyrian rose, darker pink margins. Dense shrub; leaves
cordate, sharply pointed.   Hobbie cross; Le Feber, reg. 1965.
Gold Medal Boskoop 1958, 1961.   Gold Medal Rotterdam 1960.
Color illus. WS, 1989, p. 28.
RED BELLS   Parentage as above
Bell-shaped, purplish red flowers in trusses of 6.   Compact
plant habit; ovate leaves, dark green. Hobbie cross; reg. 1969.
* *

```
            -catawbiense 1/4
        -unnamed hybrid-
NOREASTER-            -unknown 3/4
        -unknown
```
3ft(.9m) x 3ft(8yrs) -20F(-29C) ML Yellowish white flower 1.5
in(3.8cm) wide, funnel-shaped; ball truss of 13-18. Glossy elliptic leaf; dense, floriferous bush. Mezitt; Weston, reg. 1988.

```
            -Milkmaid--unknown 1/2
NORFOLK CANDY-        -dichroanthum 5/16
            -Marmora-        -fortunei ssp. discolor 1/8
                -Margaret Dunn-        -dichroanthum
                        -Fabia-
                            -griersonianum 1/16
```
Very light Chinese yellow flowers, with an orange-brown blotch.
J. Russell, reg. 1972.

Out of order
```
            -unnamed hybrid--unknown 1/2
NORMA HODGE-        -dichroanthum 1/4
        -Fabia-
            -griersonianum 1/4
```
A hybrid from British Columbia. Flowers of empire rose, with a
basal blotch of grayed red to Turkey red, radiating in a spotted
flare of Delft rose on 4 upper petals; trusses of 8. E. Langton
cross; R. C. Rhodes, reg. 1979.

```
                        -fortunei ssp. discolor 3/8
            -Roberte-
                        -campylocarpum Elatum Gp. 3/16
        -Coromandel-            -fortunei--Sir Charles
        -                -Soulbut-        Butler 1/32
    -Malabar-        -Vanessa-        -souliei 1/32
    -        -            -griersonianum 5/32
    -        -dichroanthum 7/32
    -    -Marmora-        -fortunei ssp. discolor
NORFOLK-        -Margaret Dunn-        -dichroanthum
JOHNNY-                -Fabia-
    -                    -griersonianum
    -        -fortunei ssp. discolor
    -    -Belle-
    -Spanish-    -campylocarpum Elatum Group
    Galleon-        -fortunei ssp. discolor
        -Margaret-        -dichroanthum
          Dunn  -Fabia-
                    -griersonianum
```
Trusses of 9-10 flowers 2in(5cm) across, 6-lobed, bright canary
yellow, dorsal spotting of rich crimson, deeper in throat.   At
27 years height was 5ft(1.5m).   J. P. C. Russell, reg. 1983.

NORLEN   Described under YAKU WARRIOR, q.v.

NORMA HODGE   See previous column

NORMAN BEHRING   Described under MINAS MAID, q.v.

```
        -calophytum 1/2
NORMAN COLVILLE-
        -rex ssp. arizelum 1/2
```
White flowers with blotch of dark grayed violet, widely funnel-
campanulate, 2in(5cm) wide/long, 5-lobed; rounded truss of 16 to
18. Leaf narrowly elliptic, dark green; brown felted indumentum
beneath. N. R. Colville cross; Mrs. Norman Colville, reg. 1979.
w.M. 1979.

```
                -griffithianum 3/4
        -Beauty of Tremough-
NORMAN GILL-        -arboreum 1/4
        -griffithianum
```
6ft(1.8m) 5F(-15C) ML 5/3   Very large flowers, white with a
red basal blotch, held in tall trusses.   Plant habit vigorous,
sturdy; leaf 5in(12.7cm) long. Grows best in partial shade. R.
Gill & Son. A.M. 1922.   A.M. Exbury Trial 1936.

```
            -fortunei ssp. discolor 1/2
NORMAN SHAW-        -catawbiense 1/4
        -B. de Bruin-
            -unknown 1/4
```
5ft(1.5m) -5F(-21C) L   A tall but compact hybrid, with phlox
pink flowers held in shapely trusses. Rothschild. A.M. 1926.

* *
```
        -Newburyport Beauty--unknown
NORMANDY-                    (Dexter hybrids)
        -Newburyport Belle (Fowle 19)--unknown
```
3.5ft(1.05m) -20F(-29C) M 4/4   Flowers strong, bright rose
pink, deeper on edges, dorsal spots of tangerine orange, openly
funnel-shaped, 2.8in(7.4cm) across, with 5-6 wavy lobes. Plant
rounded, broader than tall; elliptic dark foliage, held 2 years.
D. G. Leach, cross 1968; reg. 1983.
RIO   Parentage as above
3ft(.9m) -20F(-29C) M   Salmon pink flowers with yellow throat
in globular trusses of 16.   Plant much wider than tall; leaves
glossy, yellowish green, held 2 years. D. G. Leach, reg. 1983.
* *

```
                        -griffithianum 1/8
                -Coombe Royal-
        -Mrs. G. W. Leak-        -unknown 1/4
        -            -            -caucasicum
NORRIE KING-            -Chevalier Felix de Sauvage-        1/8
                            -unknown
        -decorum, pink form 1/2
```
6ft(1.8m) OF(-18C) EM Fuchsine pink with large maroon flare;
broad trusses of 12-15 flowers. S. King, Australia, reg. 1984.

NORSEMAN Parentage unknown, possibly hybrid of LEM'S RED LODERI
5ft(1.5m) -5F(-21C) M 4/3   Fluorescent rose pink. Foliage
dull green, cup-shaped. H. Lem cross; J. Elliott, reg. 1974.

```
                    -yakushimanum 1/2
NORTH CLIFF-                        -griffithianum 1/4
             -Jean Marie de Montague-
                                   -unknown 1/4
```
15in(38cm) high x 20in(50.8cm)(6 yrs) OF(-18C) M   Flowers
widely funnel-campanulate, wavy-edged, light purplish pink with
wide rim of strong purplish pink, strong red dorsal spots; truss
of 12. Broadly elliptic leaves, woolly yellow indumentum. Bush
well-branched. F. Peste, cross 1979; S. P. Johnston, reg. 1986.

NORTHERN LIGHTS   See ARCTIC GLOW

```
                               -minus Carolinianum Group 1/4
            -Laetevirens (Wilsonii)-
NORTHERN ROSE-                     -ferrugineum 1/4
            -mucronulatum--Cornell Pink 1/2
```
3ft(.9m) -20F(-29C) VE Flowers slightly darker pink than COR-
NELL PINK. A slow-growing semi-dwarf, with long pointed leaves.
Dr. R. Ticknor cross; Bovees Nursery intro.

```
                 -venator 1/2
NORTHERN ROVER-          -arboreum 1/4
                -Doncaster-
                        -unknown 1/4
```
Blood red flowers. Thacker, 1942.

NORTHERN STAR   Described under GIPSY MOTH, q.v.

NOSEGAY   Parentage unknown
5ft(1.5m) OF(-18C) M   Clear rose scarlet, with frilled lobes.
Compact plant; grown in New Zealand.   Origin unknown.

NOT TOO BEE   See WEE BEE

NOVA ZEMBLA   Described under AMERICA, q. v.

* *
```
               -arboreum ssp. nilagiricum ? 1/4
         -Noyo Chief-
NOYO BRAVE-         -unknown 1/4
          -yakushimanum--Koichiro Wada 1/2
```
2.5ft(.75m) OF(-18C) EM 4/4   Leaves 5in(12.7cm) x 2in(5cm).
Flowers 2.5in(6.4cm) wide, mandarin red fading with age, a very
small red blotch. Ball-shaped truss of 22.   Cecil Smith, reg.
1978.   Color illus. Cox pl. 134; Greer catalog, 1990, pl. 13.
FRANGO   Parentage as above, except reversed
5ft(1.5m) 5F(-15C) EM   Slightly fragrant flowers, empire rose
with orange spotting in trusses 5.5in(14cm) wide, 14-18 flowers.
Leaves held 4 years; beige indumentum. Dr. Goheen, reg. 1982.
NOYO MAIDEN   Parentage: yakushimanum--K. Wada x NOYO CHIEF
3ft(.9m) 5F(-15C) EM Plant broader than tall, leaves heavily
indumented, held 3 years. Clear pink buds open to white flowers
with no markings; round trusses of 15-19.   C. Smith, reg. 1983.
* *

```
          -arboreum ssp. nilagiricum ? 1/2
NOYO CHIEF-
          -unknown 1/2
```
4ft(1.2m) 5F(-15C) M 4/5   Formerly called a form of arboreum
kingianum.   Outstanding foliage of parsley green, very glossy,
deeply ribbed, 7in(17.8cm) long, plastered fawn tomentum below.
Flower a clear rose red, broadly campanulate, 2.5in(6.4cm) wide,
in compact trusses of 16.   Originated at Reuthe Nursery, England; L. E. Brandt raiser; Dr. & Mrs. P. J. Bowman, reg. 1966.
C.A. 1971.   Color illus. ARS J 44:1 (1990), p. 26; VV p. 29.

NOYO MAIDEN   Described under NOYO BRAVE, q.v.

* *
```
          -catawbiense var. album 1/2
NUANCE-                         -neriiflorum 1/8
                   -unnamed hybrid-
       -unnamed hybrid-         -dichroanthum 1/8
                        -fortunei ssp. discolor 1/4
```
5ft(1.5m) -15F(-26C) ML 4/4 Flowers pale orange-yellow, mar-
gins broadly suffused strong purplish pink, strong greenish yellow spotting; openly funnel shaped, 2.75in(7cm) wide, heavy substance; dome-shaped trusses of 14. Plant rounded, wide as tall;
elliptic medium green leaves held 2 years. Leach, intro. 1968;
reg. 1973.   Color illus. LW pl. 99.
BALI   Parentage as above
6ft(1.8m)   -15F(-26C) ML 4/4 Wide trusses of 14-17 flowers,

delicate pale pink, suffused yellow. Rounded plant, spreading
1.5 times wider than tall. Leach intro. 1974; reg. 1983. Color
illus. HG p. 86.
* *
* *
```
                             -griffithianum 1/8
                 -Kewense-
       -Aurora-         -fortunei 1/8
NUBAR-       -thomsonii 1/4
       -campylocarpum 1/2
```
Buds colored light rhodonite red open to very pale yellow-green,
deepening to light chartreuse green, with center speckles of the
deepest claret rose.   Edmund de Rothschild, reg. 1981.
MRS. ALFRED TAUBMAN   Parentage as above
Flowers in trusses of 12, 5-lobed, medium grayed purple, turning
pale yellowish pink, with empire rose shading and veining, later
fading to Egyptian buff.   L. de Rothschild, reg. 1984.
* *

NUBELLE   Described under HAD, q.v.

```
                  -williamsianum 1/4
            -Cowslip-
NUGGET-           -wardii 1/4
        -chamaethomsonii var. chamaethauma 1/2
```
Trusses of 8 flowers, empire yellow, flushed peach.   Lester E.
Brandt, reg. 1962.

```
                       -griffithianum 1/4
            -unnamed hybrid-
NUNEHAM PARK-           -unknown 3/4
            -Martin Hope Sutton--unknown
```
Red flowers.   C. B. van Nes & Sons, before 1922.

NUTBERGER   See BILL MASSEY

```
            -nuttallii 1/2
NUTCRACKER-
            -maddenii (polyandrum), pink form 1/2
```
Trusses of 7 flowers, tubular campanulate, to 4.4in(11cm) broad,
5-lobed, creamy white with deep yellow throat, strongly scented.
Leaves elliptic, dark green, densely scaly below. G. A. Hardy,
reg. 1984.   A.M. 1984.

NUTHATCH   Parentage unknown
Flowers azalea pink, bell-shaped.   Henny, reg. 1965.

NUTMEG   Described under ARTHUR OSBORN, q.v.

NUTMEGACALYX--form of megacalyx
4ft(1.2m) 15F(-9C) EM-L 4/3   Named by Kingdon Ward for its
fragrance, usually likened to nutmeg. Very large flowers, pure
white flushed pink. Too tender to grow outdoors even in London.
Shown by Adm. Heneage-Vivian of Clyne Park, Swansea. A.M. 1937.

```
            -forrestii Repens Group 1/2
NYMPH-                 -dichroanthum 1/8
      -    -Astarte-          -campylocarpum Elatum Group 1/16
      -Largo-       -Penjerrick-
      -                 -griffithianum 1/16
            -neriiflorum Euchaites Group 1/4
```
1ft(.3m) 5F(-15C) E 3/3   Dwarf of spreading habit, with dark
green leaves and deep red flowers.   Lord Aberconway, 1946.

                              O

* *
```
                              -catawbiense 1/8
             -Parsons Grandiflorum-
      -America-                 -unknown 3/8
OAKTON-      -dark red hybrid--unknown
      -yakushimanum 1/2
```
5ft(1.5m) -10F(-23C) M   Buds medium magenta open phlox pink,
striking pink pistil; waxy flowers 2.5in(6.4cm) wide, in domed
truss of 13. Plant taller than broad; white indumentum on new
growth. Schumacher cross; G. Ring III, reg, 1983.
ANKA HEINJE   Parentage as above, but reversed; seed parent is
Koichiro Wada form.   Flowers medium to light rose Bengal, with
yellow markings; truss of 16-20. Greenish brown calyx, 1in(2.5
cm) long. Leaves have brownish tomentum below.   Heinje cross;
D. Heinje Baumschulen, reg. 1986.

GEN SCHMIDT   Parentage as OAKTON, above
Buds cardinal and strong reds; flowers blend French rose, Neyron
rose, strong and spirea reds; cardinal red dorsal spotting. Bush
medium-sized ; hardy to -15F(-26C).   W. Delp.
MAY'S DELIGHT   Parentage as OAKTON, above
4ft(1.2m) -15F(-26C) M 3/4   Round, compact truss of flowers,
red in bud, fading to long-lasting pink. Plant wider than tall,
with thin plastered indumentum.   W. Delp, intro. 1965.
VINEBLUSH   Parentage as OAKTON, above
3.3ft(1.0m) x 3.3ft(24 yrs) -15F(-26C) ML Flowers in truss of
11; deep pink buds open to deep purplish pink, fading to lighter
pink then white. Dense habit; glossy elliptic leaves.   R. Forster cross; Al Smith named; Hort. Res. Inst. of Ont., reg. 1987.
VINEMARK   Parentage as OAKTON, above
6ft(1.8m) x 3.3ft(1.0m)(19 yrs) -15F(-26C) ML   Trusses of 20
flowers, wavy-edged, margins, light purple buds open to light
purple flowers of heavy substance with deeper colored flare.
Dense growth habit.   Origin as VINEBLUSH, above; reg. 1987.
* *

* *
            -fortunei 1/4
      -Fawn-   -dichroanthum 3/8
      -    -Fabia-
OASIS-   -griersonianum 1/8
      -    -dichroanthum
      -Dido-
            -decorum 1/4
Flower barium yellow, overlaid coral pink, widely funnel-shaped,
4in(10cm) wide; truss of 9.   Del James, intro. 1959; reg. 1972.
SEPTEMBER SONG   Parentage: Dido x Fawn
4ft(1.2m) OF(-18C) M 4/4 Compact growing, wider than tall;
foliage olive green. Flowers a medium orange. Sets flower buds
when young. Phetteplace cross; H. Greer, intro. 1988.   Color
illus. HG p. 168.
WARM SPRING   Parentage: Dido x Fawn
Medium-sized, compact plant with flowers Indian yellow, flushed
pink, trusses of 8-10. Del James, reg. 1962.
* *

OBERBÜRGERMEISTER JANSSEN (MAYOR JOHNSON)   Parentage unknown
Parentage possibly MAYDAY x GOLDSWORTH ORANGE, q.v.
4ft(1.2m) -5F(-21C) ML Large flower, trumpet-shaped, scarlet;
in full trusses. Plant spreading, wider than tall; matte green
foliage. J. Bruns, cross 1952.

OBERSCHLESIEN   Described under KING'S RIDE, q.v.

            -thomsonii 1/2
      -Barclayi-   -arboreum 1/8
      -    -Glory of Penjerrick-
OBERON-   -griffithianum 1/8
      -          -thomsonii
      -Thomwilliams-
            -williamsianum 1/4
A hybrid with flowers of deep rose.   Lord Aberconway, 1950.

OBOVATUM--form of lepidotum
1.5ft(.45m)   -5F(-21C)   EM 3/3 This form of the species has
large leaves and greenish yellow flowers.   Slocock Nurseries.

                        -intricatum 1/8
            -Intrifast-
      -Blue Diamond-   -fastigiatum 1/8
      -          -augustinii 3/8
OCEANLAKE-   -impeditum 3/8
      -    -Blue Tit-
      -Sapphire-   -augustinii
            -impeditum
2.5ft(.75m) -5F(-21C) EM 3/3 Deep violet blue flowers, flattened, 1in(2.5cm) wide, in truss of 8. Dense foliage about 1in.
(2.5cm) long. Sun-tolerant. Blooms later than other blues and
flowers last longer. Arthur Wright, Sr. & Jr., reg. 1966.

OCELOT--form of parmulatum K W 5875
3ft(.9m) 5F(-15C) EM 3/4   Loose trusses of 3-6 flowers, very
light sap green, each lobe with a deeper colored central band,
throat heavily spotted reddish purple; corolla tubular-campanulate, 2.2in(5.5cm) across.   Kingdon Ward collector; E. J. P.
Magor raiser; Gen. Harrison, reg. 1977.   A.M. 1977.

                                    -griffithianum 1/8
            -Loderi King George-
      -Akbar-   -fortunei 1/8
OCTAVIA-   -fortunei ssp. discolor 1/4
      -griersonianum 1/2
Plant medium-sized with good growth habit. Red flowers in well-
packed trusses. Blooms late midseason. Rothschild, 1947.

            -dichroanthum 1/2
OCTOPUS-
      -kyawii 1/2
Low and widely spreading plant. Orange flowers in loose trusses
in late season. Rothschild, 1950.

ODD BALL   Described under OH-TOO, q.v.

                  -wardii 1/4   -griffithianum 3/32
      -Idealist-   -Kewense-
      -    -Aurora-   -fortunei 5/32
      -    -Naomi-   -thomsonii 1/16
ODEE -   -fortunei   -griffithianum
WRIGHT-   -George Hardy-
      -          -Mrs. Lindsay-   -catawbiense 1/16
      -Mrs. Betty- Smith   -Duchess of Edinburgh--unknown
        Robertson-   -campylocarpum 1/8
            -unnamed hybrid-
                  -unknown 1/4
4ft(1.2m) -5F(-21C) M 5/4   Compact plant; waxy green leaves
3.5in(8.9cm) long. Peach buds opening chartreuse, carmine red
spotting in throat; flower 4.5in(11.5cm) wide, slightly ruffled,
in trusses of 12-15. A. O. Wright, Sr. & Jr., reg. 1965. P.A.
1966.   Color illus. Cox pl. 135; K p. 117; VV p. 75.

            -ponticum 1/2
ODORATUM-
      -azalea periclymenoides (nudiflorum) 1/2
4ft(1.2m) -15F(-26C) ML 2/3 An azaleodendron with fragrant,
orchid lilac flowers. Thompson's Nursery, before 1875.

                        -campylocarpum Elatum Group 1/16
                  -Penjerrick-
      -Amaura-   -griffithianum 1/16
      -Eros-   -griersonianum 5/8
OEDIPUS-   -griersonianum
      -          -facetum (eriogynum) 1/4
      -Jacquetta-
            -griersonianum
A scarlet-flowered hybrid.   Lord Aberconway, 1941.

                  -smirnowii 1/4
      -unnamed hybrid-
      -          -yakushimanum 1/4
OH JOYCE-   -maximum 1/4
      -          -Midsummer-
      -Joyce Lyn-   -unknown 1/8
      -                -maximum
            -unnamed hybrid-
                  -wardii 1/8
Medium-sized bush, hardy to -15F(-26C); wide pale peach flow-
ers, pink-tinged ruffled edges, a few gold dorsal spots. Delp.

OH! KITTY   Parentage unknown
4ft(1.2m) x 4ft(14 yrs) OF(-18C) M   Buds strong currant red,
opening strong pink with currant red throat; flowers funnel-
shaped, 5-7in(12.5-18cm) across, of 5 wavy lobes, very fragrant;
17 in domed truss 10in(25cm) wide and 15in(38cm) tall.   Leaves
elliptic, convex. Fred Minch, cross 1973; reg. 1988.

OH MY! Described under YAKU FRILLS, q.v.

OH WHOA! Described under KNOCKOUT, q.v.

            -yakushimanum 1/2
OHIO PINK-
      -unknown 1/2
3ft(.9m) -20F(-29C) ML Dome-shaped truss with 12-13 flowers,
deep purplish pink, with a paler blotch spotted olive brown,
widely funnel-campanulate, 2.5in(6.4cm) across, slightly fragrant. Plant wider than high; glossy, olive green leaves, new
growth with light brown tomentose.   John Ford raiser; Secrest
Arboretum, reg. 1984.
OHIO PINK BLUSH   Parentage as above

2.5ft(.75m) -15F(-26C) ML Flowers very pale purplish pink,
light purple shading at edges, sparse strong yellow spotting in
throat, widely funnel-shaped, 2.5in(6.4cm) wide, frilled,
slightly fragrant; domed trusses of 7-13. Plant rounded, broad;
slight tan indumentum below.   Ford raiser; Secrest, reg. 1984.
OHIO PINK GLO   Parentage as above
4ft(1.2m) -15F(-26C) ML Flowers strong purplish pink with reverse strong purplish red, widely funnel-campanulate, 2in(5cm)
across, with 5 wavy lobes; trusses of 15-18. Slightly fragrant.
Plant upright; leaves held 2 years, light brown tomentum on new
foliage.   J. Ford raiser; Secrest Arboretum, reg. 1984.
OHIO WHITE   Parentage as above
3ft(.9m) -15F(-26C) ML White flowers with small, vivid yellow
blotch in throat, widely funnel-campanulate, frilled, 2in(5cm)
wide; 8-10 in domed truss. Plant rounded, broad; brown tomentum
on new leaves.   John Ford raiser; Secrest Arboretum, reg. 1984.
SECREST PINK   Parentage as above.
2.5ft(.75m) -15F(-26C) M   Plant about twice as wide as tall;
dull olive leaves held 2 years. New growth has light brown tomentum. Strong purplish red buds open light purplish pink, with
a small dark blotch; flowers 2.5in(6.5cm) broad; truss of 11-17.
J. Ford raiser; Secrest Arboretum, reg. 1984.
* *

* *
            -wightii 1/4
       -China-
OH-TOO-   -fortunei 1/4
   -        -wardii 1/4
       -Goldbug-   -dichroanthum 1/8
            -Fabia-
                -griersonianum 1/8
4ft(1.2m) -5F(-21C) ML 4/3 Interesting multicolored flowers.
Red-purple buds open to rhodonite red, maturing to buttercup
yellow, with a salmon pink throat and heavy spotting of currant
red; mature flowers edged in rhodonite red; lax trusses of 14.
Plant rounded, as wide as high. W. Elliott cross; Whitney raiser; Sather, reg. 1975.   Color ill. ARS Q 30:4 (1976), p. 239.
ODD BALL   Parentage as above
5ft(1.5m) 10F(-12C) E Cardinal red buds open to brick red
flowers edged jasper red, much spotting of bright guardsman red;
7 wavy lobes; spots and nectaries terracotta. Lax truss of 12.
Well-branched plant, broad as tall.   Walter Elliott, reg. 1981.
* *

OKI ISLAND--form of degronianum ssp. heptamereum (metternichii)
"One of the best wild forms of this species in Japan. A fine
foliaged plant with rose-colored flower and a neat habit." From
catalog of Glendoick Gardens (P. Cox).

                        -fortunei ssp. discolor 1/8
            -Norman Shaw-   -catawbiense 1/16
    -Bellerophon-   -B. de Bruin-
    -        -   -unknown 1/16
OKLAHOMA-   -facetum (eriogynum) 1/2
    -        -griersonianum 1/4
    -Tally Ho-
            -facetum (eriogynum)
6ft(1.8m) 5F(-15C) VL   Currant red flowers, lightly spotted
darker red, with black anthers and stigma; large trusses of 22.
L. de Rothschild cross; Maj. A. E. Hardy intro.   A.M. 1975.

OLAN RAGAN   Parentage unknown; elepidote
6ft(1.8m) x 6ft(18 yrs) -10F(-23C) ML Flowers widely funnel-
shaped, 4in(10cm) across, pale lemon yellow with dark ruby red
dorsal ray; ball trusses of 12. Glossy leaves held 3 years. W.
A. Ragan, cross 1969; reg. 1988.

            -griffithianum 1/8
        -Mars-
     -Vulcan-   -unknown 1/8
OLD COPPER-   -griersonianum 1/2
    -        -dichroanthum 1/4
       -Fabia-
            -griersonianum
5ft(1.5m) -5F(-21F) L 4/4 Blossoms of a unique copper color.
Large campanulate flowers held in loose truss; long, dark green
leaves on an upright plant. Attractive hybrid; heat-tolerant.
Theodore Van Veen, Sr., reg. 1958.   Color illus. VV p. 15.

            -catawbiense 1/2
OLD PORT-
    -unknown 1/2
5ft(1.5m) -15F(-26C) M 3/3 Two hybrids grown under the name
OLD PORT. The above has flowers dark wine red or plum, blackish
crimson markings, glossy leaves like catawbiense. Plant medium-
sized, of dense habit. The other may be a ponticum cross, deeper wine purple, without blotches, glossy smooth foliage. Both
are vigorous and sturdy. A. Waterer, 1865. Col. ill. JS p. 80.

            -griersonianum 1/4
       -Azor-
OLD SPICE-   -fortunei 1/4
       -decorum 1/2
4ft(1.2m) -5F(-21C) ML 3/3 A vigorous plant; leaves to 7in.
(17.8cm) x 2in(5cm). Fragrant flowers of phlox pink, shading to
apricot, openly campanulate, 3.5in(9cm) wide, and held in truss
of 12.   Benjamin Lancaster, reg. 1963.

            -fortunei ssp. discolor 1/2
OLDENBURG-
    -williamsianum 1/2
5ft(1.5m) -10F(-23C) M   Small, pale pink flowers on long pedicels, in loose trusses. Large, compact plant; foliage bronze
when young. Cox reports flowers as too few. D. Hobbie, 1923.

            -catawbiense 1/2
OLDEWIG-
    -unknown 1/2
Ruby red flowers with lighter center and reddish brown markings
on light background. T. J. R. Seidel, intro. 1912.

OLE OLSON   Described under LADY BESSBOROUGH, q.v.

            -griersonianum 1/2
OLEANDA-   -arboreum 1/4
    -Doncaster-
            -unknown 1/4
Compact trusses hold 8-10 flowers, each 3in(7.6cm) across, col-
ored claret rose, blooming in late season. M. Haworth-Booth,
Farall Nurseries, reg. 1968.

* *
                        -griffithianum 1/8
                -George Hardy-
     -Mrs. Lindsay Smith-   -catawbiense 1/8
OLGA-   -Duchess of Edinburgh--unknown 1/4
    -      -dichroanthum 1/4
    -Dido-
       -decorum 1/4
3ft(.9m) -10F(-23C) ML Trusses of 12 flowers, openly funnel-
shaped, very light Chinese yellow, flushed azalea pink towards
margins, flecked orange-red. Slocock, reg. 1982.   A.M. Wisley
Trials 1986.
ARTHUR WARREN   Parentage as above except reversed
Loose, open-topped truss of 10-12 flowers, funnel-shaped, frilled, orange with wide red edging, yellow-orange spotting. Bush
medium-sized; leaf oblanceolate.   Slocock Nurseries, reg. 1985.
* *
* *
            -minus Carolinianum Group 1/2
OLGA MEZITT-
       -minus var. minus 1/2
NOTE: Parentage given as registered; Cox reports a possible
different parentage: minus Compacta x mucronulatum
3ft(.9m) -15F(-26C) EM 4/3 Clear phlox pink flowers, openly
funnel-shaped, 1.5in(3.8cm) across, 5-lobed; small dome-shaped
trusses cover the bush; buds very hardy. Upright, well-branched
bush; shiny leaves 2in(5cm) long, bright green in summer, mahogany in winter.   Edmund V. Mezitt; Weston Nurseries, reg. 1983.
AGLO   Parentage as above, except reversed
3ft(.9m) -15F(-26C) EM 4/4 Spell OLGA backwards--and you
have AGLO. Lighter pink than the above, and with reddish eye.
Sun-tolerant.   Mezitt.
* *
* *
            -griffithianum 1/4
        -Mars-
OLIN O. DOBBS-   -unknown 1/2
    -        -ponticum 1/4
    -Purple Splendour-
            -unknown

4ft(1.2m) -15F(-26C) M 5/3 Waxy flowers of deep reddish purple, brown spotting, openly funnel-shaped, 2.5in(6.4cm) across,
of heavy substance, 5-lobed; dome-shaped truss of 12-15. Plant
upright; 5in(12.7cm) leaves, held 3 years. O. O. Dobbs cross;
H. E. Greer, reg. 1979. Color illus. HG p. 117.
IRRESISTIBLE IMPULSE Parentage as above
5ft(1.5m) -15F(-26C) ML 4/4 Large trusses of deep red-purple
cover the plant; arge, dark purple blotch on upper lobe. Flowers when very young. Leathery leaves, deep green. Dobbs cross;
Greer, intro. 1982. Color illus. HG p. 116.
* *

OLINDA PRIDE Described under APRICOT ICE, q.v.

OLINDA SUNSET Described under AUSTRALIAN CAMEO, q.v.

```
        -moupinense 1/2
OLIVE-
        -dauricum 1/2
```
4ft(1.2m) -15F(-26C) VE 3/3 Flower orchid pink, darker spots
scattered over the base of the upper lobe; blossoms held singly
or in twos. Stirling Maxwell. A.M. 1942.

OLIVE JUDSON Described under VIRTUE, q.v.

```
                              -griffithianum
                   -George-        1/16
               -Betty Wormald- Hardy-catawbiense 1/16
        -Scandinavia-         -red hybrid--unknown
-unnamed-          -         -George Hardy (as above)
- hybrid, F2     -Hugh Koster-      -arboreum 1/32
-         -         -Doncaster-
OLIVE-   -catawbiense--       -unknown 11/32
SMITH-    La Bar's White 1/4
-         -catawbiense v. album Glass--Catalgla 1/4
   -Calsap-
      -Sappho--unknown
```
2.5ft(.75m) x 1.5ft(.45m)(5 yrs) -15F(-26C) ML Flowers of
heavy substance, openly funnel-shaped, 5 wavy-edged lobes, very
light purple with prominent, heavily spotted, deep purplish red
flare on dorsal lobe. Trusses hold 16. Al Smith, reg. 1989.

```
        -griffithianum 1/4
   -Loderi-
OLIVER-   -fortunei 1/4
   -unknown 1/2
```
Deep pink flowers. Messell. A.M. 1933.

```
        -griersonianum 1/2
OLIVER CROMWELL-
        -unknown
```
3ft(.9m) -10F(-23C) M Abundant orange-red flowers. Reuthe.

```
           -catawbiense 1/4
   -Charles Dickens-
OLIVER TWIST-        -unknown 1/4
   -yakushimanum 1/2
```
Semi-dwarf plant, as wide as tall; leathery leaves, matted with
tan indumentum. Globe-shaped truss of 20 flowers, clear fuchsine pink, ruffled, 2.5in(6.4cm) across. Midseason. At 5 years
plant was 16in(40.6cm) tall and wide. Lancaster, reg. 1969.

```
        -catawbiense, dwarf red form 1/2
OLLIE-
        -brachycarpum 1/2
```
Buds of roseine purple, opening to flowers of various shades of
same, a white flare; chartreuse green dorsal spots. Delp.

* *
```
        -Pacific Queen--unknown 1/2
OLWEN'S DREAM-
        -wardii 1/2
```
Flowers in truss of 7, funnel-shaped, of 7 reflexed lobes, carmine merging to scarlet. Hairless elliptic foliage, 4.7in(12cm)
long. Mid-Novovember, NZ. Mr. & Mrs. L. A. Grant, reg. 1988.
ORCHARD ROAD Parentage as above
Funnel-shaped flowers in trusses of 9, funnel-shaped, 7-lobed,
edges solferino purple, merging to pastel mauve. Foliage like
the above, a bit longer. Late Oct.-Nov. The Grants, reg. 1988.
* *

```
                    -fortunei ssp. discolor 1/8
        -Lady Bessborough-
   -Day Dream-          -campylocarpum Elatum Group 1/8
OLYMPIA-          -griersonianum 1/4
        -elliottii 1/2
```
Shrub of average size and good growth habit; deep green foliage.
Flowers brilliant red, fragrant, in large, well-shaped trusses,
in midseason. A tender child of elliottii. Rothschild, 1947.

```
        -dichroanthum 1/4
   -Fabia-
OLYMPIC BLONDIE-   -griersonianum 1/4
   -unknown 1/2
```
An additional 9 clones named from this cross, listed below. Roy
W. Clark.

OLYMPIC BRAVE	OLYMPIC CHINOOK	OLYMPIC KNIGHT
OLYMPIC BROWNIE	OLYMPIC HOSE-IN-HOSE	OLYMPIC MAID
OLYMPIC CHIMES	OLYMPIC HUNTER	OLYMPIC MISS

OLYMPIC KNIGHT Parentage as above
5ft(1.5m) 5F(-15C) M 3/3 Dark red flowers, prominent blackish red blotch. Good foliage. Clark, reg. 1958. P.A. 1960.

* *
```
                    -griffithianum 1/4
        -Loderi King George-
OLYMPIC LADY-          -fortunei 1/4
        -williamsianum 1/2
```
3ft(.9m) -5F(-21C) EM 4/4 Cup-shaped flowers, opening pale
pink, fading white, 4in(10.2cm) wide; lax truss of 7-8. Plant
compact, broader than tall, and covered with flowers. E. Ostbo
cross; R. W. Clark, reg. 1958. A.M. 1977.
MISS OLYMPIA Parentage as above
4ft(1.2m) OF(-18C) EM 4/4 Flowers to 4in(10cm) wide, blush
pink, throat deeper. E. Ostbo cross; R. W. Clark, reg. 1962.
WHITE OLYMPIC LADY Parentage as above
4ft(1.2m) OF(-18C) E 4/4 Low, spreading plant, wider than
tall. Large white flowers faintly blushed pink in lax trusses
of 14. Ostbo cross; Clark, reg. 1958. P.A. 1960. A.M. 1977.
* *

```
                    -griersonianum 1/2
OLYMPIC QUINAULT-
                    -unknown 1/2
```
Layritz Nursery cross; Roy W. Clark intro.

OLYMPIC SUNSET Described under WALT ELLIOTT, q.v.

```
                    -Moser's Maroon--unknown 1/4
        -Romany Chai-
OLYMPIC SWEETHEART-          -griersonianum 1/4
        -fortunei ssp. discolor 1/2
```
A hybrid by Roy W. Clark.

OLYMPIC TRIUMPH Parentage unknown; elepidote
5ft(1.5m) x 4ft(1.2m)(18 yrs) -10F(-23C) ML Trusses of 14.
Flowers of heavy substance, 7 wavy-edged lobes, from deep pink
buds. Corolla strong purplish pink at margins, shading to deep
purplish pink in throat; some red dorsal spots and rays. Narrow
oblong leaves, flat, wavy-edged. W. A. & Joan Ragan, reg. 1988.

OLYMPIC VICKI REINE See VICKI REINE

```
        -catacosmum 1/2
OMAR-
        -beanianum 1/2
```
Deep red flowers. J. B. Stevenson, cross 1939; intro. 1951.

```
        -catawbiense ? 1/2
OMEGA-
        -unknown rose-colored hybrid 1/2
```
5ft(1.5m) -20F(-29C) ML Light ruby red with red-brown or yellow-green markings on a light background. Seidel, 1912.

OMO--form of hyperythrum
3ft(.9m) -15F(-26C) EM 3/4 Loose, rounded trusses of 8-10
white flowers, 5-lobed, funnel-campanulate. Glossy, dark green
leaves to 5.25in(13.3cm) long. Ingram, reg. 1976. A.M. 1976.

```
* * * * * * * * * * * * * * * * * * * * * * * * * * *
                     -dichroanthum 1/8
           -Dido-
           -    -decorum 1/8          -griffithianum
      -Lem's-               -Beauty of-      7/32
      -Cameo-   -Norman Gill- Tremough-arboreum 1/32
      -    -Anna-            -griffithianum
ONE THOUSAND-         -              -griffithianum
  BUTTERFLIES-    -Jean Marie de Montague-
             -                    -unknown 1/2
             -         -Jan Dekens--unknown
        -Pink   -                -griffithianum
      Petticoats-      -Queen    -
                  -Britannia- Wilhelmina-unknown
                   -Stanley Davies--unknown
```
5ft(1.5m) OF(-18C) ML 5/4   Flowers of Neyron rose, shading
paler within; cardinal red blotch and flare, of butterfly shape.
Plant upright, well-branched, about as wide as tall; foliage of
dark yellowish green, held 3 years.   John G. Lofthouse, cross
1975; reg. 1981.   Color illus. ARS J 36:2 (1983), p. 118; Cox,
pl. 136.
EXCALIBUR   Parentage as above
5ft(1.5m) OF(-18C) M   Trusses 7.5in(19cm) tall, cone-shaped,
with 28-32 flowers of rose Bengal, centers lighter. Plant upright, with stiff branches.   Lofthouse, reg. 1983.
VIENNENSE WALTZ   Parentage as above
5ft(1.5m) OF(-18C) M   Buds rhodonite red opening to fragrant
flowers of light red with orange brown spotting, 6- to 7-lobed.
Trusses 9in(23cm) wide, holding 34 flowers, densely packed. Bush
3/4 as wide as tall.   J. Lofthouse cross; reg. 1984.
* *

```
                   -fortunei ssp. discolor 1/4
     -Golden Belle-   -dichroanthum 1/4
     -            -Fabia-
     -                  -griersonianum 1/8
OOH GINA-      -dichroanthum
     -    -Dido-
     -    -    -decorum 1/8
     -Lem's-               -griffithianum 5/32

      Cameo-        -Beauty of-
         -    -Norman- Tremough-arboreum 1/32
         -    - Gill -
         -Anna-    -griffithianum
         -              -griffithianum
         -Jean Marie de Montague-
                   -unknown 1/16
```
4ft(1.2m) OF(-18C) ML 4/4 Flowers orient red shading to cam-
ellia rose, blotch of cardinal red, openly funnel-shaped, 3.5in.
(8.9cm) wide, 7-lobed; 15-flowered trusses. Slightly fragrant,
floriferous. Plant rounded, broader than tall; spinach green
leaves retained 3-4 years.   C. R. Burlingame, reg. 1983.

OOH-LA-LA   Described under PIROUETTE, q.v.

OPAL FAWCETT   Parentage unknown
5ft(1.5m) OF(-18C) M 4/4   Leaves quite large. Flowers very
pale pink, fading to white, up to 3.5in(9cm) across, of 5 lobes,
slightly fragrant; truss of 16. E. Ostbo cross; C. P. Fawcett,
reg. 1958.   A.E. 1958.

```
              -maximum 1/2
        -unnamed hybrid-
OPALESCENCE-        -yakushimanum 1/4
     -               -maximum
     -unnamed hybrid-
                   -wardii 1/4
```
Buds spinel red and yellowish white, open to pale yellow-green
flowers, dorsal spots vivid yellow-green, throat pea green; medium orange-yellow stigma. W. Delp.

```
          -davidsonianum, Exbury pink form 1/2
OPEN DAWN-           -ciliatum 1/4
     -Countess of Haddington-
                   -dalhousiae 1/4
```
Buds of rose opal flushed cream, opening to camellia rose flow-
ers, fading white with a pink flush, a dorsal flare of greenish
yellow spots; fragrant. Oblong leaves with brown scales. R. C.
Gordon, reg. 1984.

```
                   -yunnanense 1/2
OPENWOOD-
     -unknown 1/2
```
Flowers of mauve lavender, speckled red.   Knap Hill, reg. 1962.

OPHIR   A clone of the grex DREAM GIRL, q.v.

* *
```
              -thomsonii ssp. thomsonii 1/2
OPORTO-
     -sanguineum ssp. sanguineum var. haemaleum 1/2
```
Loose trusses of 5-7 flowers, colored between cardinal red and
oxblood red. Corolla campanulate, 2in(5cm) across, 5-lobed, and
waxy in appearance.   Collingwood Ingram, reg. 1968. A.M. 1967.
BLACK PRINCE'S RUBY   Parentage as above
3ft(.9m) 1OF(-12C) E 4/3   Buds black-red open to currant red
flowers of heavy, waxy substance; openly campanulate with 5 wavy
veins; lax trusses of 5.   Nelson, cross 1965; Short, reg. 1977.
* *

ORANGE BELLS   See ORANGE MARMALADE

ORANGE BILL--cinnabarinum ssp. xanthocodon Concatenans Group
A compact plant, with beautiful apricot orange flowers and fine
foliage.   Kingdon Ward first saw it in the Himalayas.

ORANGE CROSS   See FRED HAMILTON

```
                   -ciliatum 1/16
              -Rosy Bell-
        -Lady -       -glaucophyllum 1/16
     -unnamed-Berry-         -cinnabarinum 3/16
     - hybrid-   -Royal Flush-
ORANGE -    -         -maddenii 3/16
DELIGHT-    -cinnabarinum ssp. xanthocodon 1/4
     -          -cinnabarinum Roylei Group 1/4
     -Lady Rosebery-       -cinnabarinum
              -Royal Flush-
                   -maddenii
```
7ft(2.1m) 1OF(-12C) M Funnel-shaped flowers in clusters of 6,
nasturtium orange; corolla 2in(5cm) wide and long, 5-lobed.
Plant well-branched, upright, half as broad as tall; glossy,
knobbed leaves, scaly beneath, held 3 years. Foliage with spicy
fragrance.   Dr. Carl G. Heller, cross 1967; reg. 1980.

```
                   -neriiflorum 1/16
              -Nereid-
        -unnamed-    -dichroanthum 1/16
        - hybrid-
     -Blondie-    -fortunei ssp. discolor 1/8
     -    -       -maximum 1/8
ORANGE HONEY-    -Russell Harmon-
     -              -catawbiense 1/8
     -catawbiense var. album Glass--Catalgla 1/2
```
5ft(1.5m) -2OF(-29C) L Flowers of salmon pink, like those of
MARY BELLE, in 18-flowered trusses. Plant habit rather open;
attractive foliage. Orlando S. Pride, 1977.

* *
```
              -yakushimanum 1/2
ORANGE MARMALADE-       -wardii 1/4
     -Mrs. Lammot-       -souliei ? 1/8
      Copeland -Virginia Scott-
                   -unknown 1/8
```
3ft(.9m) -5F(-21C) M 4/4   Turkey red buds open to rich amber
yellow flowers, flushed salmon pink; lax trusses hold 10-12; corolla campanulate, 2.5in(6.4cm) wide, of good substance, and 5-
lobed. Plant broad as tall. Larson cross; J. Davis, reg. 1983.
GOLDEN WEDDING   Parentage as above
2ft(.6m) OF(-18C) M 4/4 Brick red buds open to chrome yellow
flowers, 7-lobed; trusses of 10-14. Dwarf plant, wide as tall;
dark green leaves.   Larson cross; J. A. Davis, reg. 1984.
YELLOW PIPPIN   Parentage as above, except reversed
4ft(1.2m) -5F(-21C) M 3/3   Flowers open carmine red, fading
light aureolin yellow, center sulphur yellow, spotted chartreuse
green. Trusses of 12.   H. L. Larson, reg. 1983.
* *
```
                   -dichroanthum ssp. scyphocalyx 1/4
        -unnamed hybrid-
ORANGENGOLD-       -unknown 3/4
     -unknown
```

Flowers in loose, flat-topped trusses of 8-13, 5 wavy-edged lobes, yellowish orange with brown markings, outside light orange, edges of orange-pink. Silvery white indumentum beneath leaves. Shrub 3ft(.9m) x 4ft(1.2m)(17 yrs). J. Wieting cross; Walter Schhmalscheidt, reg. 1987.

```
                                      -catawbiense 1/16
                        -Parsons Grandi--
                  -Nova  - florum         -unknown 11/16
        -Hachmann's - Zembla-dark red hybrid--unknown
        - Feuerschein-      -griffithianum 1/8
                      -Mars-
ORATORIUM-            -unknown
        -                      -arboreum 1/8
        -              -Doncaster-
        -Thunderstorn-        -unknown
                      -unknown
```
3ft(.9m) x 4ft(1.2m) -15F(-26C) ML   Flowers in trusses of 11-15, openly funnel-shaped, dark red with white filaments. Plant habit dense, compact. Hachmann, cross 1967; Stück, reg. 1988.

```
        -fortunei ssp. discolor Houlstonii Group 1/2
ORBHOULST-
        -orbiculare 1/2
```
Pink flowers.   Origin uncertain.   A.M. 1932.

```
        -arboreum 1/2
ORBICARB-
        -orbiculare 1/2
```
Plant with brilliant red flowers, darker at base. Magor, 1936.

ORCHARD   Described under SCARLET KING, q.v.

```
                      -wardii 3/8
                -Crest-          -fortunei ssp. discolor 3/16
        -Honey Glow-  -Lady Bess--
ORCHARD-        -      borough  -campylocarpum Elatum Group
  GOLD  -        -unknown 1/4                  3/16
        -Crest (as above)
```
Funnel-shaped flowers, 7 deeply indented lobes, 3.5in(9cm) wide, uranium green, deeper towards center; trusses of 10. Elliptical leaves 4.5in(11.5cm) long. Flowers late Oct. to early Nov., NZ. Mrs. G. Grant, cross 1976; Mr. & Mrs. L. A. Grant, reg. 1988.

ORCHARD ROAD   Described under OLWEN'S DREAM, q.v.

OREGON EXPRESSIONS   Described under BURGUNDY BUTTERFLY, q.v.

```
        -azalea occidentale 1/2
OREGON QUEEN-
        -macrophyllum 1/2
```
5ft(1.5m) -10F(-23C) ML 2/3 An azaleodendron with light pink flowers, originating in those areas of Oregon where these two species are common. A natural hybrid. In The Register of 1958.

```
                -griersonianum 1/4
        -Gladys Rillstone-
OREGONIA-        -unknown
        -griersonianum 1/2
```
5ft(1.5m) 5F(-15C) LM   Plant of medium size and good habit. Deep, rich pink; shapely trusses.   Rothschild, 1947.

```
* * * * * * * * * * * * * * * * * * * * * * * * * * *
        -oreotrephes 1/2
OREOAUG-
        -augustinii 1/2
```
Light lilac with greenish brown spots.   E. J. P. Magor, 1932.
EUTERPE   Parentage as above
Rose-colored flowers.   Reuthe, 1941.
```
* * * * * * * * * * * * * * * * * * * * * * * * * * *
```

```
        -oreotrephes 1/2
OREOCINN-
        -cinnabarinum 1/2
```
Violet rose flowers with two lines of brownish pink inside; another form has flowers of soft apricot. Beautiful new foliage of an unusual blue-green, the color retained all summer.   E. J. P. Magor, 1926.   Color illus. ARS J 39:3 (1985), p. 150.

```
        -oreotrephes 1/2
OREOROYLE-
        -cinnabarinum Roylei Group 1/2
```

Parentage shown is only what is suggested by the name. A parent of two Bodnant hybrids: FLORESCENT, ROVER.

```
              -thomsonii 1/4
        -Shilsonii-
ORESTES-        -barbatum 1/4
        -griersonianum 1/2
```
A tall plant with large, dark scarlet flowers.   Lord Aberconway, intro. 1941.

ORGANDIE   Described under ICARUS, q.v.

```
                -neriiflorum 1/4
        -F. C. Puddle-
        -        -griersonianum 1/4
ORIANA-          -griffithianum 1/8
        -    -Loderi-
        -Coreta-      -fortunei 1/8
              -arboretum ssp. zeylanicum 1/4
```
Red flowers.   Lord Aberconway, 1946.

```
                -Duchess of Cornwall--unknown 1/2
ORIENT EXPRESS-
                -calophytum 1/2
```
Trusses are rounded and firm, holding up to 20 flowers, white flushed ruby red with a blotch of deeper ruby red in the throat. Corolla widely funnel-campanulate, 2.5in(6.4cm) across, 5-lobed. Long, dark green foliage, with a light coat of brown indumentum beneath.   R. N. S. Clarke, reg. 1979.   A.M. RHS 1979.

ORIFLAMME   Described under LADY CHAMBERLAIN, q.v.

ORIGINAL--form of caucasicum var. album
Pinkish white; variegated foliage.   Standish & Noble, 1850.

```
        -griersonianum 1/2
        -                              -griffithianum 1/8
ORION-        -Mrs. E. C. Stirling-
        -                    -unknown 9/32
        -Madame P. A.-                      -ponticum
          Colijn          -Michael Waterer-    1/32
                -      -Prometheus-      -unknown
              -Madame  -      -Monitor--unknown
               de Bruin-      -arboreum 1/16
                    -Doncaster-
                          -unknown
```
Introduced by Reuthe Nurseries.

```
        -fortunei ssp. discolor 1/2
ORION-        -fortunei 1/4
        -H. M. Arderne-
              -unknown 1/4
```
Flowers rose pink with red eye.   Waterer, Sons & Crisp, 1920.

```
                -neriiflorum 1/8
        -F. C. Puddle-
        -Phoebus-        -griersonianum 1/8
ORION-        -haematodes 1/4
        -        -griffithianum 1/4
        -Loderi-
              -fortunei 1/4
```
Rose pink flowers with a dark eye.   Lord Aberconway, 1950.

```
        -azalea viscosum 1/2
ORNATUM-
        -ponticum 1/2
```
3ft(.9m) -20F(-29C) ML   Azaleodendron. Dark scarlet flowers; another form, sulphur yellow with orange spots.   Gowan, 1832.

```
                -neriiflorum 1/8
              -Nereid-
        -Euryalus-      -dichroanthum 1/8
ORTEGA-        -griersonianum 1/2
        -        -griffithianum 1/4
        -Sunrise-
              -griersonianum
```
Pale rose flowers.   Lord Aberconway, 1941.

```
        -williamsianum 1/2
OSMAR-
        -unknown 1/2
```
5ft x 5ft(1.5m) -10F(-23C) EM   Loose trusses of 4-8 campanu-

late flowers, lilac and light pink, to 3.2in(8cm) wide. Foliage
deep green, recurved, almost orbicular.   Raised in UK pre-1965;
van Gelderen, de Wilde int.; Royal Boskoop Hrt. Soc., reg. 1988.

* *
                      -dichroanthum 1/4
            -Fabia-
OSTBO'S COPPER-   -griersonianum 1/4
-                          -campylocarpum 1/4
            -Mrs. W. C. Slocock-
                           -unknown 1/4
Copper red flowers.   Endre Ostbo, reg. 1958.
OSTBO'S LOW YELLOW   Parentage probably as above
3ft(.9m) OF(-18C) M 4/4 Buds apricot pink. Loose trusses of
creamy yellow flowers, 4.5in(11.5cm) wide. Foliage to 4in(10cm)
long. E. Ostbo, reg. 1960.   PA 1960.   Color illus. HG p. 98.
** *

                                      -ponticum 1/16
                          -Michael Waterer-
                 -Prometheus-   -unknown 5/16
        -Madame de-   -Monitor--unknown
        - Bruin   -   -arboreum 1/8
OSTFRIESLAND-   -Doncaster-
        -                  -unknown
        -forrestii Repens Group 1/2
3ft(.9m) OF(-18C) M 4/4 Scarlet red flowers.   Hobbie, 1949.

              -sanguineum ssp. didymum 1/4
        -Carmen-
        -       -forrestii Repens Group 1/4
OTHELLO-   -griffithianum 1/16
-                       -unnamed hybrid-
-        -Armistice Day-   -unknown 3/16
-unnamed-   -Maxwell T. Masters--unknown
        hybrid-griersonianum 1/4
Lester E. Brandt, intro. 1954.

OTHELLO (Aberconway)   Described under THE MOOR, q.v.

              -dichroanthum 1/4
        -Fabia-
-       -griersonianum 1/4
OTIS HYDE-   -griffithianum 1/8
-                -Loderi-
-Exbury Albatross-   -fortunei 1/8
                 -fortunei ssp. discolor 1/4
6ft(1.8m) 5F(-15C) ML   Bell-shaped flowers held in trusses of
12, rhodonite red with streaks of currant red; orange tint overall.   H. L. Larson, reg. 1965.

OTTAWA   Described under LADY BESSBOROUGH, q.v.

              -campylocarpum 1/4
        -Butterfly-   -catawbiense 1/8
OTTO HOMDAHL-   -Mrs. Milner-
        -ponticum 1/2   -unknown 1/8
4ft(1.2m) -5F(-21C) ML   Flowers openly funnel-shaped, 3in.
(7.6cm) across, of deep creamy yellow, crimson flecks on upper
lobes; rounded trusses of 15-18.   Plant compact; leaves 4in.
(10cm) long, with dark maroon petioles.   I. Owen Ostbo, 1969.

OUDIJK'S FAVORITE   Described under BLUE DIAMOND, q.v.

OUDIJK'S SENSATION   Described under NORDERNEY, q.v.

              -dichroanthum 1/4
        -Astarte-   -campylocarpum Elatum Group 1/8
OUIDA-   -Penjerrick-
        -          -griffithianum 1/8
-griersonianum 1/2
Flowers flushed pink rose, darker at base.   Lord Aberconway,
cross 1930.   A.M. 1936.

              -calophytum 1/2
OUR KATE-
        -macabeanum 1/2
First flowered 15 years after sowing seed.   Beautiful flowers,
openly campanulate, very light pink flushed deeper pink on margins, with sparkling ruby throat; large, impressive lax trusses

of 20. Shrub is a still-growing tree of 15ft(4.5m) and should
become much taller; leaves 11in(28cm) x 4in(10cm), loosely indumented below. Named for Lionel de Rothschild's eldest daughter.
E. de Rothschild, reg. 1963.   A.M. 1963.

                          -dichroanthum 1/2
OURO PURO---FRANCIS HANGER, F2-   -griffithianum 1/4
                      -Isabella-
                          -auriculatum 1/4
"Pure gold" in Portuguese.   Reported in Kraxberger as extinct,
but grown by David Balint and Clint Smith (State of Washington).
Flowers chrome yellow, flattened, 4.5in(11.5cm) wide, 7-lobed;
lax truss of 9. Plant medium-sized. L. E. Brandt, reg. 1965.

* *
                          -maximum 1/2
                -Midsummer-
        -unnamed-   -unknown 3/8
        - hybrid-   -maximum
            -Adele's Yellow-
OUTLINER-   -wardii 1/8
-                          -maximum
        -Ruddy Red Max (Clark Adams)-
                          -unknown

Buds of rose Bengal, rhodamine and phlox purples, light purplish
pink, opening to white flowers edged in vivid purplish red and
rhodamine pink. Trusses of 27 flowers.   W. Delp.
ROSY GLOW   Parentage as above
Buds deep red and strong purplish red; flowers of pale purplish
pink, deep red and strong purplish red.   W. Delp.
* *

                -catawbiense var. album Glass--Catalgla 1/4
        -Tony's-   -catawbiense 1/8
        - Gift-   -Catawbiense Album-
        -     -Belle Heller-   -unknown 3/8
OVATION-   -   -catawbiense
        -                -white hybrid-
        -                  -unknown
        -          -griffithianum 1/4
        -Lady Bligh-
                -unknown
Flowers pale purplish (phlox) pink; dorsal spotting of cardinal
red. Tall, well-branched plant.   Weldon Delp.

* *
                          -xanthostephanum 1/4
                -Saffron Queen-
OWEN PEARCE-   -burmanicum 3/4
                -burmanicum
4ft(1.2m) 20F(-7C) EM   Buds of sulphur yellow, opening lighter
yellow; flowers rotate, 2in(5cm) in diameter, in open trusses.
Plant habit compact; leaves 3in(7.6cm) long. Sumner, reg. 1972.
SAFFRON PRINCE   Parentage as above
Trusses of 8 flowers, brilliant yellow-green in bud, opening to
brilliant greenish yellow. Rounded plant, leaves held 3 years.
Mr. & Mrs. Maurice Sumner, cross 1962; reg. 1985.
* *

              -souliei 1/2
OXENDEN-
        -calophytum 1/2
Flowers in trusses of 10-11, 7-lobed, broadly campanulate; buds
moderate purplish pink opening white with yellow-green blotch in
throat; fragrant. Hairless, oblanceolate leaves. Plant 6ft(1.9
m) x 6ft(15 yrs); early May. G. Hardy; reg. 1988.   A.M. 1988.

              -williamsianum 1/2
OXLIP-
        -wardii Litiense Group 1/2
Buds of deep rose pink opening pale pink, fading white. Small
dainty bells in loose clusters, blooming early.   Very floriferous. Medium-sized, compact plant, with foliage like williamsianum. Rothschild, 1947.

OZ   Described under WIZARD, q.v.

P

* *
         -minus Carolinianum Group 1/2
P. J. M.-
         -dauricum Sempervirens Group 1/2
4ft(1.2m) -25F(-32C) E 4/4   Cold-hardy and heat-tolerant.
Small rounded leaves, green in summer, mahogany-colored in winter; aromatic. Flowers early, a bright lavender pink. Several
selected forms exist.   P. J. Mezitt, cross 1939; intro. 1959;
reg. 1987 as a group.   Color ill. Cox pl. 145; HG p. 116.
P. J. MEZITT   Parentage as above
Name as used in Britain, but not a selected clone.   Medium rosy
purple, slight throat markings deeper color, openly campanulate,
1.75in(4.5cm) wide; small truss of 4-9. Elliptic leaves, to 2.5
in(6.5cm), scaly beneath, aromatic, bronze and purple in winter.
Weston Nurseries, USA, raiser; Crown Estate, Windsor, exhibitor.
A.M. 1972.   Color illus. JS p. 56-57.
ALFREDA WIACZEK   Parentage: minus Carolinianum Gp. x dauricum
2.5ft(.75m) x 3ft(.9m) -15F(-26C) EM   Vivid reddish purple in
bud, opening strong reddish purple with white center, in a ball
truss of 6-12.   Leaf small, scaly, medium olive green; dark red
in winter.   G. D. Lewis, reg. 1987.
BEATRICE HYDE   Parentage as above (both parents, white forms)
4ft(1.2m) x 2ft(.6m) -5F(-21C) EM   White flowers widely funnel-shaped, 1in(2.5cm) x 1in., smooth edges, 14 per spherical
truss. Small leaves, scaly below.   R. Murcott, reg. 1987.
BELLVALE   Parentage as above (dauricum, white form)
3ft(.9m) -25F(-32C) EM   Leaves held 2 years, a rich, coppery
purple in autumn. Flowers light pink with mauve flare, of heavy
subsstance.   W. Baldsiefen, reg. 1973.
BLACK SATIN   Parentage: P. J. M. F2
3ft x 3ft(.9m) -20F(-29C) M   Tubular funnel-shaped flowers,
1.25in(3cm) across, of strong reddish purple; truss of 5, 2.5in.
(6.5cm) wide, 10 per branch.   Small, aromatic foliage, dark mahogany after bloom.   Mezitt cross; Weston Nurseries, reg. 1988.
DUTCHMAN JOE   Parentage as P. J. M.
2.5ft(.75m) -20F(-29C) EM   Terminal flower clusters of 1-4
trusses, each 3-5 flowers; color mauve paling to center. Plant
well-branched; leaves held 1 year.   W. Fetterhoff, reg. 1981.
P.J.M. ELITE   Same parentage as P. J. M.
One of several forms of this grex distributed by Wooton Nurseries.   Flowers a deeper pink; winter foliage bronze mahogany.
Weston intro. 1975; reg. 1987.
MINAURA   Parentage as P. J. M.
3ft(.9m) -20F(-29C) E   Leaves smaller than P. J. M., turning
dark mahogany in winter; flowers lavender pink. Mezitt; Weston.
P.J.M. REGAL   Parentage as P. J. M.
5ft(1.5m) x 4ft(1.2m) -30F(-35C) EM Flowers in small trusses
of 10-15, strong reddish purple. Blooms after VICTOR.   Weston,
reg.   1987.
P.J.M. VICTOR   Parentage as P. J. M.
Like others in this grex, but flowers a week earlier; smaller
foliage.   Weston Nurseries, intro. 1970; reg. 1987.
* *
* *
```
                            -catawbiense var. album 1/16
                        -                   -catawbiense
              -Lodestar-      -Cat. Album-          3/64
              -        -Belle -        -unknown 3/64
              -        Heller-              -catawbiense
              -              -white cat. hyb.-
          -R.O.-                           -unknown
          -Delp-                      -catawbiense
          -    -          -Atrosanguineum-
          -    -    -Atrier-            -unknown
      -un. -    -Mary -      -griersonianum 1/32
      -hyb.-    Belle-      -decorum 1/32
      -    -        -Dechaem-
PACESETTER-    -              -haematodes 1/32
      -    -vernicosum 18139 1/4
      -              -neriiflorum 1/8
      -        -Nereid-
      -unnamed hybrid-      -dichroanthum 1/8
                      -fortunei ssp. discolor 1/4
```
Buds blend brilliant to light greenish yellow and open to light
greenish yellow flowers.   Weldon Delp.
PEACH DELIGHT   Parentage as above
Buds strong purplish red to light purplish pink, open to yellow-
ish white flowers, edged red.   Delp.
WELL-SUITED   Parentage as above

Buds deep to moderate reddish lilac purple; flowers frilled, of
greenish yellow to yellow-green spots   on 3 dorsal lobes; light
purple anthers.   Delp.   Color illus. ARS J 43:1 (1989), p. 2.
* *
```
                            -griffithianum 1/4
              -Loderi Venus-
PACIFIC GLOW-            -fortunei 1/4
              -strigillosum 1/2
```
5ft(1.5m) 10F(-12C) E 4/4   Flowers of clear, unmarked pink
with darker throat, openly funnel-shaped, 3.25in(8.3cm) wide, 6-
lobed; ball-shaped trusses of 15-17.   Floriferous.   Plant compact, rounded, as wide as tall; leaves dull green, with moderate
brown indumentum.   Larson cross; Evelyn Jack, reg. 1979.   Color
illus. ARS Q 34:1 (1980), p. 35.

PACIFIC GOLD   Described under SPUN GOLD, q.v.

```
                      -fortunei ssp. discolor 1/4
          -King of Shrubs-      -dichroanthum 5/16
          -              -Fabia-
PACIFIC -                  -griersonianum 3/16
PRINCESS-        -fortunei 1/8
      -      -Fawn-        -dichroanthum
  -unnamed-      -Fabia-
      hybrid-              -griersonianum
      -        -dichroanthum
          -Dido-
              -decorum 1/8
```
Orient pink flowers with centers of orange buff.   Leaves to 4.75
in(12cm) long.   Hybridizer in the U.S. unknown;   Mrs. R. J. Coker, NZ, reg. 1982.

PACIFIC QUEEN   Parentage unknown
Flowers jasper red.   Mrs. R. J. Coker, reg. 1980.

```
                      -griffithianum 1/4
          -Loderi King George-
PACIFIC RIM-            -fortunei 1/4
          -macabeanum 1/2
```
Orchid pink buds opening to very light salmon flowers, 8-lobed,
with conspicuous brown anthers.   Leaves 6.8in(17.5cm) long.   H.
L. Larson, reg. 1982.

```
                      -neriiflorum 1/8
              -Nereid-
          -Peach Lady-      -dichroanthum 1/8
PACIFIC-        -fortunei ssp. discolor 1/4
SUNSET -                  -griffithianum 1/8
      -        -Loderi King George-
      -Malemute-            -fortunei 1/8
          -unnamed orange hybrid by Lem--unknown 1/4
```
4ft(1.2m) x 5ft(1.5m)(9 yrs) 10F(-12C) M Carmine flowers shad-
ing to yellow ochre in throat, with brick red spotting on dorsal
lobe; 6 wavy-edged lobes; lax trusses 7in(17.8cm) wide. Narrowly
oblong leaves to 6in(15.2cm).   J. Elliott, cross 1978; reg. 1989.

```
          -wardii 1/2
PAGE BOY-            -campylocarpum 1/4
      -Mrs. W. C. Slocock-
                  -unknown 1/4
```
A round and compact shrub, with trusses holding up to 13 flowers
colored cream, touched with pink.   Gen. Harrison, reg. 1965.

```
              -calophytum 1/4
          -Calrose-
PAGEANT-        -griersonianum 1/4
      -        -griffithianum 1/4
          -Loderi-
              -fortunei 1/4
```
A hybrid with pale pink flowers.   Lord Aberconway, intro. 1950.

PAINTED DOLL   Described under BIG SHOT, q.v.

PAINTED SKIES   Described under SIERRA SUNSET, q.v.

```
                           -catawbiense 1/4
                -Mrs. C. S. Sargent-
            -Meadowbrook-              -unknown 1/4
            -                          -catawbiense
PAINTED STAR-              -Everestianum-
            -                          -unknown
            -     -campylocarpum 1/4
            -Anita-
                  -griersonianum 1/4
5ft(1.5m)  -5F(-21C)  ML   Cream-colored flowers, with a reddish
throat.  Donald Hardgrove, reg. 1958.


                -catawbiense 1/2
PALE PERFECTION-
                -unknown 1/2
5ft(1.5m)  -15F(-26C)  ML  2/4  Narrow, medium-sized leaves on a
plant twice as broad as tall.  Flowers rose-colored, with a dis-
tinctive dark blotch, to 2.5in(6.4cm) across; trusses of about
13.  Richard Wyman cross; R. Ticknor, intro. & reg. 1967.
```

* *

```
                      -griffithianum 1/4
          -Loderi King George-
PALL MALL-            -fortunei 1/4
          -          -dichroanthum ssp. scyphocalyx 1/4
          -Socrianum-

                      -griffithianum 1/4
6ft(1.8m) OF(-18C)  M     Trusses of 10-12 flowers of deep pink,
with darker edges of rose red.  Mrs. Roza Stevenson cross;  Hy-
don Nurseries, reg. 1976.
PICCADILLY   Parentage as above
Trusses of 8-10 flowers, of good substance, bright pink.  Mrs.
Roza Stevenson raiser; Hydon Nurseries, reg. 1976.
```

* *

```
              -williamsianum 1/4
        -Pallida-
PALLA-        -griffithianum 1/4
      -griersonianum 1/2
Flowers of Neyron rose.   Lord Aberconway, intro. 1942.


              -davidsonianum 1/2
PALLESCENS-
              -racemosum 1/2
A natural hybrid.  Small shrub; scaly leaves; terminal inflores-
cence of pale pink, margins white or carmine.   Origin unknown.
A.M. 1933.


              -williamsianum 1/2
PALLIDA-
        -griffithianum 1/2
White flowers, flushed pink.   Lord Aberconway, 1933.


PALMA--form of parmulatum K W 5875
3ft(.9m)  5F(-15C)  EM  3/3   Truss of 3-7; flowers tubular-cam-
panulate, very light greenish white,  with deeper central bands,
heavy spotting.  Foliage oblong-ovate, glabrous.  Kingdon Ward
collector; Lord Aberconway raiser; reg. 1983.   A.M. 1983.


                    -fortunei 1/4
        -Ruby F. Bowman-           -griffithianum 1/8
PALOMA-            -Lady Bligh-
        -floccigerum 1/2          -unknown 1/8
6ft(1.8m) OF(-18C)  M   Dome-shaped trusses, 6in(15cm) across,
of 14-16 flowers,  Venetian pink with margins dawn pink,  dorsal
spotting of guardsman red.  Flowers openly campanulate, 2.5in.
(6.4cm) across, 5-lobed, of good substance.  Plant about half as
wide as tall;  leaves 5.5in(14cm) long, held 3 years.  Dr. D. W.
Goheen, cross 1966; reg. 1986; Dr. L. Bulgin, intro. 1983.


PAMELA   Parentage unknown
A parent of MOONLIGHT SONATA. Flowers deep blush.     Standish &
Noble, before 1860.


                 -griffithianum 1/2
PAMELA FIELDING-
                 -red hybrid--unknown 1/2
Flowers scarlet to white blush,  with the exterior carmine pink;
margins pale cerise.  C. B. van Nes & Sons, before 1922.
```

```
                -fortunei 1/2
PAMELA-LOUISE-
             -unknown 1/2
5ft(1.5m) -10F(-23C)  M  Flowers lilac pink, and fragrant.  Hy-
don Nurseries, reg. 1975.


                      -thomsonii 1/4
          -unnamed hybrid-
          -           -unknown 1/2
PAMELA LOVE-              -griffithianum 1/8
          -          -Loderi-
          -unnamed hybrid-    -fortunei 1/8
          -               -unknown
6ft(1.8m) OF(-18C)  E   Flat-topped truss 6in(15cm) across with
funnel-shaped flowers, rose Bengal.   M. V. Love, reg. 1965.


              -smirnowii 1/4
      -Oh My!-
      -     -yakushimanum 1/4
PANA-           -griffithianum 1/8
      -Mars-
    -Red Brave-  -unknown 1/8        -catawbiense 1/16
    -          -Parsons Grandiflorum-
       -America-              -unknown 3/16
              -dark red hybrid--unknown
Buds spinel red, cardinal red; flowers of red and white.   Delp.
```

* *

```
                      -dichroanthum 1/8
            -Goldsworth Orange-
      -Champagne-              -fortunei ssp. discolor 1/4
PANACHE-      -griersonianum 1/4
      -      -wardii 1/4
      -Crest-          -fortunei ssp. discolor
          -Lady Bessborough-
                      -campylocarpum Elatum Group 1/8
5ft(1.5m)  -5F(-21C)  M  Flowers of pale yellowish pink, flushed
pale yellow to strong red.  Ovate foliage, recurved margins, 5.5
in(12.5cm)  Knoll Gardens intr.; J. May, cross 1970; reg. 1987.
ENID MAY   Parentage as above
Flowers in truss of 11, funnel-shaped, 6/7-lobed,  pale yellow-
green, light green-yellow outside.  May, cross 1970; reg. 1988.
LUCKY BREAK   Parentage as above
Buds strong red and vivid reddish orange, opening  strong  red,
rims of lobes light orange and brilliant yellow.  Compact shrub,
wider than tall.  Mr. & Mrs. R. Drayson, cross 1976; reg. 1987.
SUNRISE OVER HARKWOOD   Parentage as above
Truss of 10-13 flowers;  buds vivid reddish orange,  opening
brilliant yellow, spotted deep-to-strong greenish yellow.  Olive
green leaves, lanceolate.  Mr. & Mrs. R. Drayson, reg. 1987.
```
* *

```
                       -catawbiense 3/16
             -Parsons
       -America-Grandiflorum-unknown 3/8
       -     -
     -FANFARE-     -dark red hybrid--unknown
     -     -          -catawbiense
PANAMA-     -Kettledrum-
     -           -unknown
     -     -Catalgla--catawbiense var. album Glass 1/4
     -unnamed-          -dichroanthum 1/16
       hybrid-          -unnamed hybrid-
       -unnamed-          -griersonianum 1/16
         hybrid-     -fortunei ssp. discolor 1/16
          -unnamed hybrid-
                 -Corona--unknown
5ft(1.5m) -15F(-26C)  ML  3/2  Cardinal red flowers with 5 wavy
lobes, spotted darker red, held in dome-shaped trusses of 10-13.
Plant twice as broad as tall;  leaves dark yellow-green.   D. G.
Leach cross, 1962; intro. 1976, later withdrawn; reg. 1983.


              -dichroanthum 1/4
      -Fabia-
PANDORA-      -griersonianum 1/4
      -facetum (eriogynum) 1/2
Light rose, veined white, chocolate spots.   Aberconway, 1941.


          -dichroanthum 1/2
PANIA-
      -unknown 1/2
4ft(1.2m)  EM     Pale salmon flowers; compact, spreading plant.
```

New Zealand Rhododendron Association introduced.

* *
```
        -G. A. Sims--unknown 1/2
PANOPLY-
        -facetum (eriogynum) 1/2
```
Flowers rose claret with darker spots on upper petals.   Col. S.
R. Clarke.   A.M. 1942.
RED CHIEF   Parentage as above
Red-flowered hybrid by Sir Giles Loder, 1948.
* *

PANTAGRUEL--form of diaprepes
6ft(1.8m) 5F(-15C) L 3/3   Flowers white, with green flush at
base. G. Gorer, reg. 1972.

PANTHER   Listed with CORONET, q.v.

PAPAYA PUNCH   Described under PINEAPPLE DELIGHT, q.v.

PAPILLON--form of augustinii ssp. rubrum (bergii) F 25914
Flowers strongly flushed mallow purple, paler towards rim, upper
corolla spotted medium purplish red, widely funnel-shaped, 2in.
(5cm) across; clusters of 5-7.   Leaves 2.5in(6.5cm) long, both
surfaces lightly scaly. G. Forrest collector; Col. S. R. Clark
raiser; R. N. S. Clarke exhibitor; reg. 1978.   A.M. 1978.

PAPRIKA SPICED   Described under PINEAPPLE DELIGHT. q.v.

```
                       -yakushimanum 1/4
            -unnamed hybrid-
PARDLESTONE-             -decorum 1/4
        -                       -dichroanthum
        -Goldsworth Orange-
                        -fortunei ssp. discolor
```
Flowers very pale lemon. G. D. Waterer, Knap Hill, reg. 1985.

```
                       -arboreum 5/32
            -Cardinal-     -thomsonii 1/16
     -Red Ensign-      -Barclayi-
     -          -griersonianum  -           -arboreum
PARAGON-          1/4   -Glory of  -
     -    -griffithianum      Penjerrick-
     -Loderi-                      -griffithianum
            -fortunei 1/4                     9/32
```
Rose-colored flowers. Lord Aberconway, intro. 1950.

PARICUTIN   Described under FOREST FIRE, q.v.

PARIS   Described under NAOMI, q.v.

* *
```
        -valentinianum 1/2
PARISIENNE-
        -burmanicum 1/2
```
3ft(.9m) 15F(-9C) EM 2/2   Dense habit, a maximum height of
4ft(1.2m). Many small loose trusses, slightly fragrant yellow
flowers, blooming in April at Exbury.   Rothschild, 1947.
GOLDFINGER   Parentage as above, except reversed
3ft(.9m) 15F(-9C) EM 2/2   Lax truss of 4, primrose yellow,
each flower 3in(7.6cm) broad. Foliage dark olive green, densely
scaly. A plant for the cool greenhouse.   Sir Giles Loder, reg.
1965.   A.M. 1965.
* *

PARKER'S PINK   Parentage unknown
5ft(1.5m) -25F(-32C) ML 3/2   Flowers of bright deep pink
heavily spotted dark red, fading to white in throat, 3.5in
(8.9cm) across, fragrant; 12-flowered trusses. Plant as broad
as tall, branching well; leaves held 2 years.   Dexter cross;
John Parker and Paul Vossberg raisers; reg. 1973.   A.E. 1973.
Color illus. ARS Q 25:3 (1971), cover; Cox pl. 137; LW pl. 3.

```
              -Loder's White, q.v. for 2 possible
        -C.I.S.-    parentages
        -          -dichroanthum
        -     -Fabia-
PARKER'S-          -griersonianum
TRIUMPH -             -decorum
        -     -unnamed hybrid-
        -Clara  -           -fortunei ssp. discolor
        Raustein-          -wardii
        -             -unnamed-
        -unnamed hybrid- hybrid-dichroanthum
                        -fortunei
```
3.5ft(1.05m) x 3.5ft(12 yrs) -10F(-23C) M   Flowers broadly
funnel-campanulate, 10 per truss, strong reddish orange buds,
open light orange-yellow. Rounded plant, well-branched; leaves
with slight indumentum. E. Parker cross; Raustein, reg. 1986.

PARKSIDE--form of charitopes
1ft(.3m) -5F(-21C) M 3/3   Flowers orchid pink, suffused and
heavily spotted with darker red purples, campanulate, 1.5in
(3.8cm) across, 5-lobed, clusters of 3-5. Leaves 2.25in(5.7cm)
long, dark green above, scaly beneath. Collector unknown; Crown
Estate, Windsor, reg. 1979. A.M. 1979.

PARKSIDE (Crown Lands)   See under PEREGRINE

```
              -catawbiense 1/2
PARSONS GLORIOSUM-
              -unknown 1/2
```
5ft(1.5m) -25F(-32C) ML 2/2   Old and hardy. Plant upright,
compact; deep green leaves 6in(15.2cm) long. Flowers orchid
lavender shaded pink, held in compact conical trusses. Samuel
Parsons, intro. c. 1850, Long Island, NY; also, A. Waterer in
England.   Color illus. VV p. 74.

```
              -catawbiense 1/2
PARSONS GRANDIFLORUM-
              -unknown 1/2
```
5ft(1.5m) -25F(-32C) ML 2/3   Habit and foliage rated fair;
the purplish rose flowers are more attractive than the above
ratings indicate; long-lasting.   S. Parsons, before 1875;
A. Waterer, distributor.

```
                       -Queen      -griffithianum
              -Britannia-Wilhelmina-      11/32
                   -Leo-     -          -unknown 9/32
                   -         -Stanley Davies--unknown
        -Whitney -  -elliottii 1/8
        -Late Red-      -Queen      -griffithianum
        -             -Wilhelmina-
PARTY GIRL-    -Britannia-        -unknown
        -             -Stanley Davies--unknown
        -             -griffithianum
        -Loderi King George-
                       -fortunei 1/4
```
6ft(1.8m) 5F(-15C) L   Flowers light spirea red, Neyron rose
margins, grayed orange in throat, fragrant, 4in(10.2cm) wide, 6-
lobed; 12 per truss. Plant rounded, broader than tall; glossy,
narrow leaves 6.5in(16.5cm) long. Fred Peste, reg. 1983.

* *
```
                       -dichroanthum 1/8
              -Dido-
        -          -decorum 1/8    -arboreum 1/32
        -Lem's Cameo-        -Beauty of-
        -            -Norman- Tremough-
        -            -  - Gill -        -griffithianum 9/32
PARTY -     -Anna-    -griffithianum
PACKAGE-    -                   -griffithianum
        -            -Jean Marie de Montague-
        -            -fortunei 1/4       -unknown
        -Ruby F. Bowman-      -griffithianum
                       -Lady Bligh-
                       -unknown
```
5ft(1.5m) 0F(-18C) M   Crimson buds open carmine rose, fading
lighter, with star-shaped stain deep in throat, widely funnel-
shaped, 4in(10.2cm) across, with 7 wavy and frilled lobes; conical trusses hold 15. Plant upright, as broad as tall; foliage
held 1.5 years; new growth bronze, dark red petioles.   J. G.
Lofthouse, cross 1976; reg. 1984.
CHARISMA   Parentage as above
Flowers rose and lavender, wide wavy edges.   Won show award of

Best New Hybrid, 1984.   Lofthouse.
* *
* *
```
                              -griffithianum 1/8
                     -unnamed hybrid-
         -Mrs. Furnivall-                 -unknown 1/4
         -                   -             -caucasicum 1/8
PARTY PINK-                -unnamed hybrid-
         -                                 -unknown
         -catawbiense var. album 1/2
```
5ft(1.5m) -20F(-29C) M 5/5   Flowers 3in(7.6cm) wide, openly
funnel-shaped, purplish pink shading lighter in the center, with
a bronze dorsal flare. Ball-shaped truss 6in(15cm) across, 18-
flowered. Plant broad, branching well, leaves widely elliptic,
held 3 years. D. G. Leach, reg. 1973. C.A. 1981. A.E. 1982.
S.P.A. 1983.   Col. ill. ARS J 38:2 (1984), cover; Cox pl. 138.
CYPRUS   Parentage as above
3ft(.9m) -20F(-29C) ML 4/4   Synonym CAPRI. Flowers 3.25in
(8.3cm) across, funnel-shaped, white with bold ochre blotch, in
large round truss of 20. Plant broader than tall; leaves held 3
years.   D. G. Leach, reg. 1983. C.A. 1982. A.E. 1983.
PERSIA   Parentage as above
5ft(1.5m) -20F(-29C) ML 4/4   Purple buds open to lighter
flowers of good substance, bold spotting of light olive green,
in truss 6.75in(17cm) across. Plant conical, spreading broad as
tall.   Leach, reg. 1982.   Color ill. ARS J 36:1 (1982), cover.
* *
```
                 -catawbiense 3/8
         -Caractacus-
         -              -unknown 7/16
PASSION-                -griffithianum 1/8
       -        -George Hardy-
       -Hugh   -             -catawbiense
       Koster-                    -arboreum 1/16
       -                -Doncaster-
       -unnamed hybrid-          -unknown
       -                            -unknown
```
7ft(2.1m) x 7ft. -15F(-26C) ML   Flowers in truss of 14-16, of
vivid purplish red, white in throat, dorsal lobe marked moderate
reddish orange. Hachmann, cross 1959; Stück, reg. 1988.

PASTEL   See VANESSA PASTEL

* *
```
                 -catawbiense, red form 1/4
         -unnamed hybrid-
PASTEL STAR-          -fortunei ssp. discolor 1/4
        -    -griersonianum 1/4
           -Azor-
              -fortunei ssp. discolor 1/4
```
A hybrid by Donald Hardgove, 1955.
STARRY EYED   Parentage as above
Pink flowers, blotched red. Hardgrove, intro. 1955; reg. 1958.
* *
```
                         -decorum 1/8
              -unnamed hybrid-
         -unnamed-           -fortunei ssp. discolor 1/8
         - hybrid-    -fortunei 1/8
         -     -unnamed-         -wardii 1/16
PASTOR DUNKER-      hybrid-unnamed hybrid-
         -                        -dichroanthum 1/16
         -                     -griffithianum 1/4
         -Jean Marie de Montague-
                         -unknown 1/4
```
3ft(.9m) OF(-18C) M   Flowers of heavy substance, 3in(7.6cm)
across, fragrant, pink, throat faint yellow, 15 per truss.
Plant semi-dwarf, broader than high; leaves 5in(12.7cm) x 2in(5
cm), held 3 years. A. A. Raustein, reg. 1979.

PATRICIA--form of campylogynum Charopaeum Group, selfed
1ft(.3m) 5F(-15C) ML 3/3   Small, rounded, dark green leaves,
paler beneath. Flowers magnolia purple, 1.25in(3.2cm) across.
J. F. Caperci, reg. 1962.
```
                              -dichroanthum 1/8
                    -Goldsworth-
         -Champagne (Tortoiseshell)- Orange   -fort. ssp. discolor
PATRICIA-                     -griersonianum 1/2        1/8
  CLARK -          -forrestii Repens Group 1/4
        -Elizabeth-
                  -griersonianum
```

Flowers in trusses of 7-10, open campanulate, 5-lobed, white,
with mustard yellow dorsal blotch.   A.J. Clark, cross 1979; J.
W. Clark, reg. 1984.
```
                         -thomsonii 1/4
         -General Sir John du Cane-
PATRICIA-              -fortunei ssp. discolor 1/4
HAREWOOD-           -griffithianum 1/4
         -Loderi King George-
                    -fortunei 1/4
```
Heather pink flowers suffused darker externally, held in trusses
of 10-11.   Geoffrey Hall cross; Lord Harewood, reg. 1979.
```
              -macabeanum 1/4
         -unnamed-              -griffithianum 1/8
         - hybrid-Loderi King George-
PATRICIA LEE-              -fortunei 1/8
         -     -wardii 1/4
           -Crest-          -fortunei ssp. discolor 1/8
              -Lady Bessborough-
                    -campylocarpum Elatum Gp. 1/8
```
2ft(.6m) -5F(-21C) EM   Plant twice as wide as tall; foliage
moss green, to 4.75in(12cm) long, held 1 year. Fragrant flowers, yellow with green tinge, widely funnel-campanulate, 3.5in.
(8.9cm) across, 7-lobed, held in trusses of 10. C. Phetteplace
cross; R. C. Sparks, reg. 1980.
```
              -yakushimanum 1/2
PATRICIA'S DAY-
              -dwarf yellow hybrid from Windsor--unknown 1/2
```
3ft(.9m) OF(-18C) M   Flowers of soft lavender, deeper veining
of pinkish lavender.   John Waterer, Sons & Crisp, reg. 1975.
```
              -Yaku Fairy--keiskei 1/2
PATTY BEE-
         -fletcherianum 1/2
```
1.5ft(.45m) -10F(-23C) EM 4/4   Flowers clear yellow, 5 wavy
lobes, openly funnel-shaped, to 2in(5cm) across, in lax trusses
of 6. Plant broader than tall, well-branched; small dark green
leaves, held 2 years.   Sun- and heat-tolerant. W. Berg cross,
1970; reg. 1977. A.E. 1984.   A.M. Wisley Trials 1989.   Col.
illus. ARS J 38:2 (1984), p. 103; Cox pl. 139; HG p. 76.

PAUL DETLEFSEN   Described under REDWAX, q.v.
```
              -Margaret--unknown 1/4
         -Glamour-
PAUL LINCKE-      -griersonianum 1/4
         -strigillosum 1/2
```
4ft(1.2m) 5F(-15C) E 4/3   Foliage like strigillosum, but
wider. Campanulate flowers of currant red, 2.5in(6.4cm) across,
in tight, upstanding trusses.   C. S. Seabrook, reg. 1965.
```
                              -catawbiense 1/4
                    -Catawbiense Album-
         -Belle Heller-          -unknown 1/4
         -    -                       -catawbiense
PAUL MAUNEY-      -white catawbiense hybrid-
         -                          -unknown
         -yakushimanum--Koichiro Wada 1/2
```
2ft(.6m) x 5ft(1.5m) -15F(-26C) M   Flowers in flattened ball
truss, 7-lobed, white in bud, open white, with yellow to brownish orange dorsal spotting. A. Angelili, cross 1969; D. S. Kellam, Jr., reg. 1989.

PAUL MOLINARI   Described under KIMBERLY ANNE, q.v.
```
         -Dexter No. 1035
PAUL R. BOSLEY-
         -unknown
```
Medium pink flowers with a red blotch, in rounded trusses; long
dark green recurved foliage. Paul Bosley, Sr.
```
         -maximum 1/2
PAUL VOSSBERG-
         -thomsonii 1/2
```
4ft(1.2m) -10F(-23C) L 3/4 Openly funnel-shaped flowers cardinal red with dark garnet blotch, 2.5in(6.4cm) wide with 5 wavy
lobes; spherical trusses of 13-15. Plant rounded, as broad as
tall, well-branched; spinach green leaves to 5.5in(14cm) long.
Mrs. J. F. Knippenberg, intro. 1975; reg. 1984.

PAULA   Parentage unknown; elepidote
2.5ft(.75m) x 2.5ft(7 yrs) -20F(-29C) ML Flowers 16 to 20 per
truss, tubular funnel-shaped, light yellowish pink in bud, opening to pale yellow. Dense growth habit; elliptic, convex foliage, to 4in(10cm) long. E. Mezitt cross; Weston, reg. 1988.

```
                               -fortunei ssp. discolor 1/8
                  -Norman Shaw-          -catawbiense 1/16
        -Bellerophon-        -B. de Bruin-
PAULETTE-                              -unknown 1/16
        -          -facetum (eriogynum) 1/4
        -kyawii 1/2
```
Shrub of average size and good growth habit; deep green foliage.
Bright crimson flowers in well-filled trusses, blooming late. A
rather tender plant. Rothschild, 1950.

PAULINE   Parentage unknown
Funnel-shaped crimson flowers with a striking dark eye. Plant
of medium height. T. Lowinsky raiser; Lionel de Rothschild
intro. A.M. 1933. A.M. Wisley Trials 1957.


```
          -fortunei 1/2
PAULINE BRALIT-
          -catawbiense, low white form 1/2
```
3ft(.9m) -10F(-23C) M   Rhodonite red buds opening to fragrant
white flowers, shading light pink at 2 dorsal lobe edges, with 3
grayed orange rays in throat. Flowers of good substance, openly
funnel-shaped, 2.5in(6.4cm) wide, in ball-shaped trusses of 11.
Upright, well-branched; leaves of heavy texture, held 2 years.
Mezitt, cross 1958; intro. 1965; reg. 1983.

* *
```
                         -fortunei 3/16
                    -Koster's Choice-
              -unnamed-          -unknown 1/32
              - hybrid-    -griffithianum
          -Palmer-    -Loderi-
      -unnamed-     -          -fortunei
      - hybrid-      -wardii (croceum) 1/8
      -        -            -griffithianum 5/32
PAWHUSKA-    -Loderi King George-
      -                   -fortunei
      -        -catawbiense 1/4
      -Madame Masson-
                 -ponticum 1/4
```
5ft(1.5m) -5F(-21C) ML 4/4 Beautiful white trusses; a plant
with large glossy foliage. Tom & Emma Bowhan.
SUGAR AND SPICE   Parentage as above
5ft(1.5m) -5F(-21C) ML 4/4 Creamy white flowers with a gold-
den brown blotch on upper lobe. Leaves dark, slender. Bowhan.
Color illus. HG p. 180.
* *

PEACE   Described under LEMON BILL, q.v.

PEACH   Listed under RADIANCE, q.v.

PEACH BRANDY   Described under ALWAYS ADMIRED

PEACH DELIGHT   Described under PACESETTER, q.v.

PEACH LADY   Described under CORAL, q.v.


```
          -Apricot No. 3--unknown 1/2
PEACH LODERI-          -griffithianum 1/4
          -Loderi King George-
                    -fortunei 1/4
```
Flat-topped trusses of 11 trumpet-shaped flowers, apricot pink,
spotted maroon in throat. Plant grew to 2.5ft(.75m) in 7 years,
with leaves 6in(15.2cm) long. Rollin G. Wyrens, reg. 1965.

PEACH NUGGET   Described under COURT JESTER, q.v.

PEACH PARFAIT   Described under BANGKOK, q.v.


```
                        -arboreum 1/16
                 -Doncaster-
          -Belvedere-    -unknown 1/16
      -unnamed-    -dichroanthum 1/4
      - hybrid-    -dichroanthum
      -    -Jasper-          -fortunei ssp. discolor
PEACH SATIN-          -Lady           3/16
      -      Bessborough-campylocarpum Elatum Gp.
      -           -griffithianum 1/8          1/16
      -    -Angelo-
      -Mary Drennen-    -fortunei ssp. discolor
                 -wardii 1/4
```
4ft(1.2m) OF(-18C) L 4/4 Leaves have deep veining. Flowers
apricot, with an orange glow. Larson cross; Clint Smith intro.


```
                      -Lady   -fortunei ssp. discolor
                 -Bess-  -                     1/32
           -Jalisco-borough-campylocarpum Elatum
      -unnamed-    -    -dichroanthum          1/32
      - hybrid-    -Dido-           1/32
      -unnamed-    -        -decorum 9/32
      - hybrid-    -    -griffithianum 3/32
      -    -    -Loderi-
      -    -decorum    -fortunei 5/16
PEACH           -griffithianum
SURPRISE-          -George Hardy-
      -        -Mrs. Lindsay-          -catawbiense 1/32
      -     -Dot- Smith    -
      -unnamed-    -        -Duchess of Edinburgh--unknown
         hybrid-    -fortunei                   1/16
      -       -fortunei
          -Fawn-    -dichroanthum
             -Fabia-
                 -griersonianum 1/16
```
5ft(1.5m) -5F(-21C) M 4/4   Peachy, creamy flowers in pro-
fusion. Large flower buds, attractive red bud scales. Foliage
smooth, glossy, olive green. Greer, 1988. Col. ill. HG p. 168.


```
          -catawbiense var. album Glass--Catalgla 1/4
      -Gosh -          -decorum ? 1/16
      -Darn!-      -Caroline-
PEACH-    -Mrs. H. R. Yates-    -brachycarpum? 1/16
TREE -    -yakushimanum 1/4      -unknown 1/8
      -    -        -fortunei ssp. discolor 3/32
      -Si Si-    -Day -Lady Bess- -
      -    -Dream- borough  -campylocarpum Elatum Group
      -Gold -    -griersonianum 3/32          1/32
      Mohur-    -fortunei ssp. discolor
          -Margaret Dunn-    -dichroanthum 1/32
                   -Fabia-
                      -griersonianum
```
Buds of carrot red; flowers of carrot red and peach. W. Delp.

PEACHBLOW--possibly a form of hirtipes K W 5659
3ft(.9m) OF(-18C) E 3/3   Plant of compact habit; light green
leaves 3in(7.6cm) long, yellow midrib. Apricot flowers, fading
primrose yellow. Best in partial shade.   J. Barto raiser;
A. A. Wright intro.

PEACHES AND CREAM   Described under BLAZEN SUN, q.v.


```
                   -catawbiense 3/8
      -Mrs. C. S. Sargent-
PEARCE'S-          -unknown 1/2
AMERICAN-               -catawbiense
BEAUTY -          -Atrosanguineum-
      -Dr. H. C. Dresselhuys-          -unknown
          -          -arboreum 1/8
             -Doncaster-
                 -unknown
```
6ft(1.8m) -15F(-26C) VL Parentage is uncertain. Flowers of
good substance, 3in(7.6cm) wide, deep red, olive yellow spots;
ball-shaped trusses of 18. Plant as broad as tall, dark olive
leaves, 7in(17.8cm) long. A fine plant. R. A. Pearce, late
1930s; E. Watson, reg. 1983.


```
                 -dichroanthum 1/8
             -Dido-
      -Ice Cream-    -decorum 1/8
PEARL DIVER-    -fortunei ssp. discolor 1/4
      -Moser's Maroon--unknown 1/2
```

4ft(1.2m) -10F(-23C) M Compact trusses of 18-20 flowers, pink
with a yellow throat. A. F. George, Hydon, reg. 1966.

```
                -catawbiense var. album Glass--Catalgla 1/2
PEARLESCENT-           -fortunei ssp. discolor 1/4
              -Golden Belle-    -dichroanthum 1/8
                          -Fabia-
                              -griersonianum 1/8
```
Buds of spinel red and crimson, opening to flowers of poppy red,
coral pink, and orient pink; throat primrose yellow.   W. Delp.

```
                      -griffithianum 1/4
           -Halopeanum-
PEARLY QUEEN-          -maximun 1/4
           -unknown 1/2
```
Flowers in trusses of 14, 5-lobed, Neyron rose in bud, opening
blush with prominent rose veining, large crimson flare; strongly
scented. Pukeiti Rhod. Trust raiser; G. F. Smith, reg. 1984.

```
        -Loder's White (2 possible parentage diagrams--
PEDLINGE-              see LODER'S WHITE)
        -decorum (Wilson no. 1782)
```
Leaves 7.5in(19cm) x 3in(7.6cm), narrowly elliptic. White flow-
ers with a greenish flush, 7-lobed, held in full trusses of 10
to 12. Maj. A. E. Hardy, reg. 1967. A.M. 1967.

```
        -minus Carolinianum Group, pink form
PEE WEE-
        -pemakoense Patulum Group 1/2
```
Flowers a blend of various shades of purples. W. Delp.

```
                      -sanguineum ssp.didymum 1/8
               -Carmen-
        -unnamed-       -forrestii Elatum Group 1/8
        - hybrid-
PEEKABOO-            -campylocarpum 1/8
        -      -Moonstone-
        -              -williamsianum 1/8
        -elliottii 1/2
```
2ft(.6m) -5F(-21C) EM 3/4   An attractive compact plant with
lovely rounded leaves, spring green. Glowing, blood red, waxy,
campanulate, pendant flowers. Wm. Whitney cross. Color illus.
VV p. 6.

```
           -wardii 1/2              -griffithianum 1/8
PEEPING TOM-          -unnamed hybrid-
          -Mrs. Furnivall-       -unknown 1/4
          -              -caucasicum 1/8
                 -unnamed hybrid-
                       -unknown
```
4ft(1.2m) OF(-18C) M 4/3   White flowers, a deep plum purple
eye, shallow-campanulate, to 2.5in(6.4cm) across; compact truss
of 10-12. Plant rounded and rather compact; ovate leaves 3in.
(7.6cm) long. Arthur Wright, Sr. & Jr., reg. 1966.

PEETER'S PRIDE---selection from montroseanum
10ft(3.0m) x 9ft(2.7m)(25 yrs) -5F(-21C) VE Flowers in truss
of 25, 8 wavy-edged lobes; buds deep rose pink opening deep pink
to light yellowish pink; attractive leaves. Vaartou, reg. 1989.

PEGGY   Parentage unknown
Pink flowers. Waterer, Sons & Crisp. A.M. 1940.

```
                    -campylocarpum Elatum Group 1/4
              -Penjerrick-
              -         -griffithianum 3/8
PEGGY ABKHAZI-        -griffithianum
              -    -Kewense-
              -Aurora-    -fortunei 1/8
                   -thomsonii 1/4
```
12ft(3.6m) x 8ft(2.4m)(25 yrs) OF(-18C) M Flowers in trusses
of 5-8, apricot cream, edged pink, with small red center blotch
in throat. Albert de Mezey cross; W. A. Dale, reg. 1989.

```
                              -griffithianum 1/16
                   -George Hardy-
        -unknown (13/16) -Pink -         -catawbiense 1/16
PEGGY  -              -Pearl-        -arboreum 1/16
BANNIER-Antoon van Welie-    -Broughtonii-
                  -unknown       -unknown
```
5ft(1.5m) -5F(-21C) M 4/3 Large pyramidal trusses hold 20-22
fringed flowers, Tyrian rose. van Nes, reg. 1962. A.M. 1960.

```
                       -catawbiense 1/8
             -Parsons Grandiflorum-
        -America-              -unknown 7/8
PEGGY BLOUGH-     -dark red hybrid--unknown
        -Scintillation--unknown
```
Flowers of creamy pink. Hardy to -10F(-23C). R. W. Blough.

```
        -unnamed-catawbiense var. album 1/2
      - hybrid-   -wardii 1/4
      -     -Hawk-        -fortunei ssp.. discolor 1/8
PEKING-      -Lady -
      -     -Bessborough-campylocarpum Elatum Group 1/8
      -     -catawbiense var. album--La Bar's White
      -unnamed-   -wardii
         hybrid-Crest-        -fortunei ssp. discolor
             -Lady-
                -Bessborough-campylocarpum Elatum Group
```
5ft(1.5m) -15F(-26C) M 4/3 Buds strong yellowish pink, open-
ing brilliant greenish yellow, dorsal blotch and sparse spotting
of dark red. Flowers of heavy substance, openly funnel-shaped,
6-lobed; round truss of about 15. Upright, well-branched plant;
dark green, slightly concave leaves. D. Leach, reg. 1973. (Introduced; later withdrawn)

```
        -Glory of Keston--unknown 1/2
PELE-     -haematodes 1/4
     -Mandalay-
           -venator 1/4
```
Plant spreading, nearly as wide as tall; barbatum-type bark and
and foliage. Flowers Turkey red with dark nectaries, in trusses
of 23-25. Lester E. Brandt, reg. 1965.

```
           -catawbiense 1/2
PELOPIDAS-
           -unknown 1/2
```
5ft(1.5m) -15F(-26C) ML   Frilled flowers of rosy crimson with
brown spotting; trusses of 24. J. Waterer, 1865.

* *
```
                  -pemakoense 1/2
PEMATIT CAMBRIDGE-      -impeditum 1/4
                  -Blue Tit-
                       -augustinii 1/4
```
2ft(.6m) -10F(-23C) E 3/4   Plant compact and vigorous; deep
green leaves 1in(2.5cm) long. Flowers of light mineral violet,
slightly darker margins and throat, funnel-shaped, to 1.6in(4cm)
across; small globular trusses of 3-4. Very floriferous. G.
Reuthe, Fox Hill Nurseries, reg. 1981. H.C. Wisley Trials 1981.
PEMATIT OXFORD   Parentage as above
Similar to above, but a smaller plant, with flowers deep bluish
purple. Reuthe.
* *

PENALVERNE   Listed under RADIUM, q.v.

```
           -griersonianum 1/2
PENELOPE-        -facetum 1/4
        -Dragon Fly-
                -auriculatum 1/4
```
Red flowers with dark spotting. Waterer, Sons & Crisp, 1935.

PENGAER   Described under CORNISH CROSS, q.v.

```
                  -concinnum var. pseudoyanthinum 1/2
PENHEALE BLUE-
              -russatum 1/2
```
Semi-dwarf plant, broader than tall, vigorous, compact; glossy,
small dark leaves. Very compact trusses of 20 flowers, wisteria
blue flushed spinel red, 1in(2.5cm) across. Floriferous. Lt.-
Col. N. R. Colville, reg. 1975. A.M. 1974. F.C.C. 1981.

* *
```
             -campylocarpum Elatum Group 1/2
PENJERRICK-
           -griffithianum 1/2
```
6ft(1.8m) 15F(-9C) EM 4/3   Considered one of the most beau-
tiful of all hybrids; perfect, bell-shaped flowers may be white,
creamy yellow, or pink, some fragrant; several forms exist.
Large shrub, fine foliage, smooth coppery bark. Plant habit upright; leaves 5in(12.7cm) long. Samuel Smith, Head Gardener,
Penjerrick. A.M. 1923.   Color illus. Cox pl. 141.
WILLIAM FORTESCUE   Parentage as above, except reversed

Buds suffused light rose red, opening to flowers light greenish
white throughout. L. S. Fortescue, cross 1958; reg. 1981.
* *

```
        -orbiculare 1/2
PENLLYN-
        -griffithianum 1/2
```
Flowers of shell pink. Lord Aberconway, intro. 1933.

PENNY   See INDIAN PENNY

PENNYWISE   Described under YAKU WARRIOR, q.v.

```
            -campylocarpum 1/2
PENROSE ATKINSON-
            -unknown 1/2
```
Almond pink flowers shaded orange.   Slocock.

```
        -williamsianum 1/2
PENSIVE-
        -irroratum 1/2
```
Rounded shrub; cordate leaves. Flowers pale pink, lightly spotted, 2.75in(7cm) wide; truss of 11.   Gen. Harrison, reg. 1965.

PEPPERMINT STICK   Described under YAKU PICOTEE, q.v.

```
                    -dichroanthum 1/8
            -Fabia-
    -Goldbug-        -griersonianum 1/8
PEPPERPOT-      -wardii 1/4
        -unnamed orange hybrid by Lem--unknown 1/2
```
3ft(.9m) 5F(-10C) EM 4/3 Straw yellow heavily spotted jasper
red on dorsal lobes, lighter elsewhere, campanulate, 1.5in(3.8
cm) wide, 5-lobed; lax trusses of 8-10.   Plant rounded, as wide
as tall; leaves spinach green, held 3 years; new growth reddish
brown. James A. Elliott, reg. 1978.

```
                -neriiflorum 1/8
        -F. C. Puddle-
    -Ethel-        -griersonianum 1/8
PERA-     -forrestii Repens Group 1/4
    -       -campylocarpum Elatum Group 1/4
    -Penjerrick-
            -griffithianum 1/4
```
A hybrid with rose-colored flowers. Lord Aberconway, 1946.

PERA (Lem) Described under ROSE ELF, q.v.

PERCY WISEMAN   Described under BAMBI, q.v.

PERDITA   Described under HALCYONE, q.v.

* *
```
        -souliei 1/2
PEREGRINE-    -wardii 1/4
    -Hawk-        -fortunei ssp. discolor 1/8
        -Lady     -
            Bessborough-campylocarpum Elatum Group 1/8
```
From Crown Lands, 1951.
PARKSIDE   From above grex; named by Crown Lands.
PEREGRINE FLEDGLING   Same as above
SMEW   Parentage as above
Pink buds change to white flowers, suffused pink; truss of 6-8.
Crown Lands, reg. 1961. P.C. 1961.
* *

```
            -calophytum 1/4
        -Babylon-
PERFECTLY PINK-    -praevernum 1/4
        -unknown 1/2
```
6ft(1.8m) -5F(-21C) E 4/4 Very large trusses of soft pink
with ring of deep maroon red in center of flowers. Leaves 10in.
(25.5cm) long, heavy stems. Greer, 1988. Col. ill. HG p. 147.

```
    -fortunei 1/2
PERFUME-
    -unknown 1/2
```
5ft(1.5m) OF(-18C) M May be sibling of HEAVENLY SCENT. Flowers medium pink, faint red spotting on upper lobe. A delightful
spicy fragrance. Rounded, well-branched plant.   Best in partial shade.   W. E. Whitney; Anne & Ellie Sather intro.

PERKY   Described under YAKU PICOTEE, q.v.

PERLA ROSA   Described under PORTENT, q.v.

PERLE BRILLANTE   Parentage unknown
Flowers light red, small dots.   Koster, Boskoop, reg. 1969.
* *

```
                -yakushimanum 1/4
        -Bambi-        -dichroanthum 1/8
PERRI -    -Fabia Tangerine-
CUTTEN-            -griersonianum 1/8
        -arboreum 1/2
```
Flowers bright claret rose with an enlarged pink calyx.   R.
L. Cutten, AUS, reg. 1976.
FLOOR SHOW   Parentage as above
Trusses of 17 flowers, colored Delft rose.   Cutten, reg. 1981.
FROU FROU   Parentage as above
Soft claret rose, darker stripes, in truss of 22. Cutten, 1982.
MARGARET CUTTEN   Parentage as above
Bright scarlet red flowers in trusses of 21. Cutten, reg. 1981.
MOULIN ROUGE   Parentage as above
Turkey red flowers held in trusses of 16.   Cutten, reg. 1981.
SUE CUTTEN   Parentage as above
Light scarlet flowers. Cutten, reg. 1981.
* *

PERRY WOOD--seedling of faberi ssp. prattii W 3958
5ft(1.5m) OF(-18C) M 3/4   Leaves narrowly elliptic, to 8in.
(20.3cm) long, with light brown indumentum beneath. White flowers, strong flush of purplish red in throat, 2in(5cm) wide, 16-
18 per truss.   Collector Wilson; Maj. A. E. Hardy, reg. 1968.
A.M. 1967.   Color illus. Rhododendrons 1988-89, RHS fig. 11.

```
        -forrestii Repens Group 1/2
PERSEPHONE-
        -floccigerum 1/2
```
Flowers of orange-red.   Lord Aberconway, 1941.

```
                -souliei 1/8
            -Soulbut-
        -Vanessa-    -fortunei--Sir Charles Butler 1/8
PERSEUS-    -griersonianum 1/2
    -        -facetum (eriogynum) 1/4
        -Jacquetta-
            -griersonianum
```
Rosy salmon pink flowers.   Lord Aberconway, 1941.

* *
```
                -cinnabarinum Roylei Group 3/4
        -Lady Chamberlain-        -cinnabarinum 1/8
    -            -Royal Flush -
PERSEVERANCE-        (orange form)-
    -                -maddenii 1/8
        -cinnabarinum Roylei Group
```
Flowers apricot, fading to coral. Adams-Acton, 1942.
REVLON   Parentage as above, except reversed
6ft(1.8m) -5F(-21C) M 4/3   Tall, slender plant with glossy
leaves, densely scaly. Flowers like gleaming waxen trumpets, of
bright carmine red, in clusters of 7. Rothschild. A.M. 1957.
* *

PERSIA   Described under PARTY PINK, q.v.

PERSIL   Parentage unknown
Vigorous, upright, compact habit, with foliage 3in(7.6cm) long,
light glossy green. Truss globular-shaped, holding 20 flowers,
funnel-shaped, buttercup yellow with white blotch on upper lobe.
Knap Hill origin; W. C. Slocock raiser. H.C. 1966.

PERSIMMON   Described under GOLDEN HORN, q.v.

```
                            -griffithianum
                -Queen Wilhelmina-    1/16
            -Britannia-        -unknown 5/16
        -Purple-        -Stanley Davies--unknown
PESTE'S BLUE ICE- Lace -        -ponticum 1/8
    -        -Purple Splendour-
        -yakushimanum 1/2    -unknown
```
2.5ft(.75m) high x 3ft(.9m)(9 yrs) OF(-18C) M   Flowers in
domed trusses of 21, 5 very wavy lobes, buds deep purplish pink,
open very pale purple, light spotting of deep greenish yellow.
Well-branched plant. F. Peste cross; S. P. Johnston, reg. 1986.

```
                    -Loder's White, q.v. for 2 possible
            -C. I. S.- parentages
            -              -            -dichroanthum
PESTE'S FIRE-      -Fabia-
   LIGHT         -              -griersonianum
            -              -dichroanthum
            -Fabia-
                    -griersonianum
```
3ft(.9m) x 3ft OF(-18C) M   Flowers in lax trusses of 13, ob-
lique-campanulate with lobes rolled back towards stem, wavy
margins, buds of strong red, opening light yellowish pink and
strong red spotting. Sharon Peste Johnston, reg. 1986.

```
                    -Whitney hybrid (pink to yellow) 1/2
PESTE'S PINK-      -wardii 1/4
   -YELLOW     -Crest-              -fortunei ssp. discolor 1/8
                    -Lady Bessborough-
                          -campylocarpum Elatum Gp. 1/8
```
6ft(1.8m) x 6ft(13 yrs) OF(-18C) EM Flower buds moderate pur-
plish pink, opening to pale yellow, streaked moderate purplish
pink; later entire truss changes to pale greenish yellow. Plant
well-branched.   Fred Peste cross; S. P. Johnston, reg. 1986.

```
                    -Whitney Appleblossom--unknown 1/2
PESTE'S PRIDE-      -dichroanthum ssp. scyphocalyx 1/4
            -Medusa-
                    -griersonianum 1/4
```
5.5ft(1.65m) x 5.5ft(13 yrs) OF(-18C) M   Campanulate flowers,
16 per ball truss, light yellowish pink, edged in strong pink,
light yellow dorsal spots. Leaves moderate olive green, narrowly elliptic. F. Peste, cross 1972; S. P. Johnston, reg. 1986.

```
                          -Blue Peter--unknown 7/8
            -unnamed hybrid-              -ponticum 1/8
            -              -Purple Splendour-
PETER ALAN-                    -unknown
            -              -Blue Peter--unknown
            -Blue Perfecta (Girard)-
                          -seedling--unknown
```
4.5ft(1.35m) -15C(-26C) M 4/4 Purplish blue flowers in truss
5-6in(12.7-15cm) wide. Foliage deep green, glossy, heavy textured. Plant broad, upright. Peter Girard, cross 1972; intro.
1977. "Best Blue" award, 1982, Great Lakes Chapter, ARS.

PETER BARBER   See JALISCO JUBILANT
Name (PETER BARBER) removed from Register; invalid registration.

PETER BEHRING   Described under MINAS MAID, q.v.

* *
            -strigillosum 1/2
PETER FAULK-
            -unknown 1/2
3ft(.9m) 10F(-12C) E 4/3 Ball-shaped trusses of 16 flowers,
bright cherry red with scattered darker spots, funnel-shaped,
2.5in(6.4cm) wide, 5- to 7-lobed. Plant broader than tall; dark
green leaves with patchy tawny indumentum beneath.   Peter Faulk
cross; Arthur Hanson raiser; Allen P. Johnson, reg. 1981.
MRS. ROBERT W. WALLACE   Parentage as above
Freely produced, soft pink flowers that fade to white, spotted
with scarlet crimson. M. Koster, cross 1909.
* *

```
                          -griffithianum 1/4
            -George Hardy-
            -              -catawbiense 1/4
PETER KOSTER-                    -arboreum 1/8
            -              -Doncaster-
            -unnamed hybrid-              -unknown 3/8
                          -unknown
```
5ft(1.5m) -5F(-21C) ML 2/3   Flowers bright magenta red with
lighter margins, trumpet-shaped, held in solid trusses. Sturdy,
bushy plant; flat leaves. M. Koster & Sons, cross 1909.

PETER LO TRUGLIO Parentage unknown; lepidote
4ft(1.2m) -5F(-21C) EM Flowers in ball truss of 11, open funnel-campanulate, 5 wavy-edged lobes, deep pink. Truglio, cross
1969; R. Murcott, reg. 1987.

```
                    -griffithianum 1/4
            -Loderi-
   -Albatross-      -fortunei 1/4
PETIA-      -fortunei ssp. discolor 1/4
            -              -griersonianum 1/4
   -Sarita Loder-      -griffithianum
            -Loderi-
                    -fortunei
```
This cross of 2 well-known hybrids produced a truss of 12 flow-
ers, white flushed amaranth rose, corolla 4in(10cm) across.   F.
Hanger, RHS Garden, Wisley. A.M. 1962.

PETITE FLEUR   Described under HEART THROB, q.v.

```
                    -Blue Peter--unknown 9/16
   -John Dosser-              -arboreum 1/16
   -              -Doncaster-
   -              -Corry Koster-      -unknown
PETRA'S-                          -griffithianum
DEBUT -              -George Hardy-
   -                          -catawbiense 1/16
   -              -griffithianum 3/16
   -unnamed hybrid-
   -Mrs. Furnival-              -unknown
   -              -caucasicum 1/8
            -unnamed hybrid-
                    -unknown
```
Flowers in trusses of 16, funnel-shaped, strong purple, with a
flare of strong greenish yellow. Shrub 3.3ft(1m). D. J. Dosser, reg. 1985.

* *
            -pemakoense 1/2
PHALAROPE-
            -davidsonianum 1/2
3ft(.9m) -10F(-23C) E 3/4   Vigorous, upright, compact habit;
glossy leaves 1in(2.5cm) long; 5 flowers, openly funnel-shaped,
translucent white, slightly flushed mauve.   Very floriferous.
Peter A. Cox, reg. 1969.   P.C. 1968.   A.M. Wisley Trials 1983.
SNIPE   Parentage as above
2ft(.6m) -5F(-21C) EM 3/4 White flowers suffused and spotted
in light orchid pinks. Glossy, light green leaves, scaly. Cox,
reg. 1978. A.M. 1975.
* *

```
                          -souliei 1/16
                    -Soulbut-
            -Vanessa-      -fortunei--Sir Charles Butler 1/16
   -Eudora-      -griersonianum 1/2
   -              -facetum (eriogynum) 1/4
PHANTASY-              -dichroanthum 1/8
   -              -Fabia-
   -Erebus-      -griersonianum
            -griersonianum
```
A hybrid with red flowers. Lord Aberconway, 1942.

```
            -griffithianum 1/2
PHANTOM-
            -hybrid unknown 1/2
```
Shell pink buds opening to white flowers, with a wine red blotch
at the base. Mrs. R. J. Coker, reg. 1979.

PHANTOM ROCK--form of sanguineum ssp. sanguineum var. haemaleum
Trusses hold 4-6 flowers, 5-lobed, tubular-campanulate, ruby
red. Leaves are dark, glossy above, gray-felted beneath. J.
Rock collector; raised by Col. S. R. Clarke; shown by R. N. S.
Clarke, reg. 1981. F.C.C. 1981.

PHEASANT TAIL   Described under SPARKLER, q.v.

```
                    -dichroanthum 1/8
            -Astarte-              -campylocarpum Elatum Group 1/16
   -              -Penjerrick-
   -PHIDIAS-              -griffithianum 1/16
   -              -neriiflorum 1/8
PHICO-      -F. C. Puddle-
   -                    -griersonianum 1/8
   -              -williamsianum 1/4
   -Cowslip-
            -wardii 1/4
```
Flowers are cream-colored flushed pink. Lord Aberconway, 1941.

```
                    -dichroanthum 1/4
          -Astarte-          -campylocarpum Elatum Group 1/8
          -          -Penjerrick-
PHIDIAS-                     -griffithianum 1/8
-                     -neriiflorum 1/4
          -F. C. Puddle-
                    -griersonianum 1/4
Flowers are clear rich red.   Lord Aberconway.   A.M. 1938.
```

```
                              -griffithianum 1/8
                    -unnamed hybrid-
          -Mrs. Furnivall-          -unknown
PHILIP TRIPP-                     -caucasicum 1/8
-          -unnamed hybrid-
     -unknown 3/4               -unknown
```
3ft(.9m) x 4ft(1.2m)(15 yrs) OF(-18C) M Flowers in trusses of
12, vivid purplish red, with wide edging of deep purplish pink;
moderate orange spotting.   P. Holden cross; reg. 1989.

```
                    -griffithianum 1/4
          -Mrs. E. C. Stirling-
PHILIP WATERER-          -unknown 1/2
-          -maximum 1/4
          -unnamed hybrid-
               -unknown
```
Conical trusses of funnel-shaped flowers, soft rose with darker
veins; wavy edges.   J. Waterer, Sons & Crisp. A.M. 1924.

```
          -rex ssp. rex 1/2
PHILIPPA-          -griffithianum 1/4
     -Sincerity-
          -unknown 1/4
```
Trusses of about 12 flowers, tubular-campanulate, 7-lobed, light
purplish pink in bud, opening white, dorsal blotch of dark red.
Gen. Harrison, cross c. 1960; Mrs. C. G, Hopwood, reg. 1989.

```
          -yakushimanum 1/2
PHILIPPA DE PASS-
          -unknown 1/2
```
Flowers in trusses of 11, 5-lobed, light salmon, tinged claret
rose when young, grayed yellow-green markings. Leaves with
woolly indumentum when young.   L. de Rothschild, reg. 1984.

```
               -campylocarpum 1/4
          -Lady Primrose-
PHILLIPPA HOWELLS-          -unknown 1/4
               -griersonianum 1/2
```
Crimson buds; pink and yellow flowers.   A. Howells, reg. 1968.

PHILOMENE   Described under IVIZA, q.v.

```
                    -dichroanthum 1/8
          -Astarte-          -campylocarpum Elatum 1/16
          -          -Penjerrick-
     -Phidias-          -griffithianum 5/16
     -          -          -neriiflorum 1/8
PHISUN-     -F. C. Puddle-
     -          -griersonianum 3/8
     -griffithianum 5/16
     -Sunrise-
          -griersonianum
```
Rose-colored flowers.   Lord Aberconway, intro. 1946.

```
* * * * * * * * * * * * * * * * * * * * * * * * * *
          -neriiflorum 1/4
     -F. C. Puddle-
PHOEBUS-          -griersonianum 1/4
     -haematodes 1/2
```
Flowers scarlet blood red.   Lord Aberconway, intro. 1941.
DRAGON   A sibling of the above.
```
* * * * * * * * * * * * * * * * * * * * * * * * * *
```

```
                    -griffithianum 1/4
          -Dawn's Delight-
PHOENIX-          -unknown 1/4
     -          -griersonianum 1/4
     -Tally Ho-
          -facetum (eriogynum) 1/4
```
Plant of average size, and rather open habit. Fine trusses of
waxy red flowers, in midseason.   Rothschild, 1950.

```
               -campylocarpum 1/2
PHRYNE-          -griffithianum 1/4
     -Loderi-
          -fortunei 1/4
```
Cream-colored flowers.   Lord Aberconway, intro. 1933.
LADY HORLICK   Parentage as above
Trusses of 7 flowers, white, lightly fragrant, 6in(15cm) across.
Sir James Horlick, Isle of Gigha, reg. 1962.
```
* * * * * * * * * * * * * * * * * * * * * * * * * *
* * * * * * * * * * * * * * * * * * * * * * * * * *
```

```
          -fortunei 3/4
PHYLE DONEGAN-          -griffithianum 1/4
          -Loderi Superlative-
               -fortunei
```
Slightly fragrant flowers colored rose Bengal, spotted.   Plant
for the cool greenhouse.   R. L. Rowarth, reg. 1970. P.C. 1969.
MADGE BRAMLEY   Parentage as above, except reversed
Flowers in trusses of 9-10, broadly funnel-shaped, 7-lobed, of
strong purplish pink, fading to center. Shrub 6.5ft(2.0m); oblong leaves.   A. Bramley cross; P. & C. Deen & Sons, reg. 1988.
```
* * * * * * * * * * * * * * * * * * * * * * * * * *
```

```
          -catawbiense var. album--Powell Glass 1/2
PHYLLIS-
          -yakushimanum 1/2
```
2ft(.6m) -15F(-26C) ML   Flowers white, strong reddish purple
edging and shading, openly funnel-shaped, 2in(5cm) across, in a
ball-shaped truss of 13-16. Plant well-branched; glossy olive
green leaves held 3 years.   R. G. Shanklin, reg. 1983.

PHYLLIS BALLARD   Described under CORAL, q.v.

```
                              -griffithianum
                    -George Hardy-          1/16
          -Mrs. Lindsay Smith-          -catawbiense
          -          -Duchess of          5/16
          -Diane-          Edinburgh--unknown 1/2
          -          -campylocarpum 1/8
PHYLLIS-     -unnamed hybrid-
KORN -          -unknown
     -          -catawbiense
     -Gomer Waterer-
          -unknown
```
5ft(1.5m) -10F(-23C) M 4/4 White flowers with large currant
red blotch which fades primrose yellow, 4in(10cm) wide, 5-lobed,
of heavy substance; trusses hold 12. Plant upright, branching
well; nice glossy foliage. Robert Korn cross; W. J. Shranger,
reg. 1981.

```
          -spinuliferum 1/2
PIA LEHMANN-
          -veitchianum Cubittii Group 1/2
```
4ft(1.2m) 15F(-9C) EM Flower greenish white at base of tube,
pale yellow shading through white to rose pink edges, upper
throat spotted pink and yellow. Trusses of 2-4.   A. F. George,
Hydon, reg. 1978.

PICCADILLY   Described under PALL MALL, q.v.

PICCANINNY   Described under LIMERICK, q.v.

```
          -catawbiense var. album Glass--Catalgla 1/2
PICKERING-          -fortunei 1/4
          -unnamed hybrid-
               -campylocarpum 1/4
```
6ft(1.8m) -5F(-21C) ML Truss of 8-10 flowers, light rose with
deeper edges, 3 upper lobes pale yellow with darker spotting,
throat yellow; corolla widely campanulate, to 3in(7.6cm) wide.
Free-flowering. Plant slightly wider than tall; glossy leaves.
Charles   Herbert,   reg.   1977.

PICOTEE ROSEUM (PICOTEE ROSEA)   Parentage unknown
Bright rose flower, intense black blotch. Veitch. F.C.C. 1863.

PICOTEED BEAUTY   Described under DOUG KLUGH, q.v.

```
          -campanulatum 1/2
PICTUM-
          -maximum ? 1/2
```
Flowers white to pale lilac with dark spots.   J. Waterer, 1839.

PICTUM---form of caucasicum
Pictum means "blotched". Dark rose pink buds open to pale mauve
pink, frilled flowers, large blotch of dark reddish spots; domed
truss of 12. Long, dark, smooth leaves; plant to 3ft(.9m) high.
Color illus. JS p. 112.

```
                              -catawbiense 1/8
                      -unnamed-
              -Altaclerense- hybrid-ponticum 1/8
PICTURATUM-           -arboreum 1/4
                      -maximum 1/4
              -unnamed hybrid-
                      -unknown 1/4
```
Flowers of bright rose, spotted crimson or blush white, with a
chocolate blotch. A. Waterer; Standish & Noble, offered 1850.

```
                      -wardii 1/8
              -unnamed-              -neriiflorum 1/16
              - hybrid-F. C. Puddle-
                              -griersonianum 1/16
          -Virginia-                  -griffithianum
          -Richards-          -George-          1/32
          -     -       -Mrs. Lindsay- Hardy-catawbiense
PIECES OF-    -     - Smith -          1/32
  EIGHT -    -Mrs. Betty-      -Duchess of
          -   Robertson-       Edinburgh--unknown
       -unknown 5/8      -campylocarpum 1/16
                      -unnamed-
                      hybrid-
                              -unknown
```
5ft(1.5m) OF(-18C) EM Flowers 7-lobed, 4.5in(11.5cm) wide,
fragrant, of pale yellow, spotted orange; conical trusses of 10.
Plant rounded, as broad as tall; glossy medium green leaves held
2 years. Roy Kersey, reg. 1977.

PIECES OF GOLD   Parentage unknown
3ft(.9m) OF(-18C) EM   Large foliage; fragrant flowers, 4in.
(10cm) across, ivory colored; truss of 10. Mrs. H. Frederick,
Jr., reg. 1978.

PIED PIPER   See ARNOLD PIPER

PIERCE'S APRICOT   Parentage unknown
4ft(1.2m) OF(-18C) E 4/4 Deep reddish pink buds. Flowers of
flesh-toned apricot, but the top flowers on a truss stay strong
pink: the truss seems to hold two different flowers, an unusual
effect. L. J. Pierce cross (?); Greer intro.

```
                              -fortunei 1/4
              -Madame Fr. J. Chauvin-
PIERRE LAPLACE-              -unknown 1/4
              -williamsianum 1/2
```
Flowers delicate rose. Dietrich Hobbie, 1952.

```
              -caucasicum 1/2
PIERRE MOSER-
              -unknown 1/2
```
Star-shaped flowers of light pink, wavy-edged; rounded trusses,
on a very tall plant. Blooms early. Moser & Fils, 1914. Col-
or illus. F p. 59, JS p. 48.

```
              -keiskei 1/2
PIKELAND-
              -campylogynum, Tower Court form  1/2
```
1ft(.3m) -5F(-21C) EM Plant rounded, as wide as tall; leaves
2.25in(5.7cm) long, scaly below, held 3 years. Flower pale rose
with darker edges and spotting, 1.25in(3.2cm) across, 5-lobed;
inflorescence of about 6 trusses, each 6- to 7-flowered. Free-
flowering. Charles Herbert, reg. 1976.

```
              -fortunei 1/2
PILGRIM-           -arboreum 1/4
          -Gill's Triumph-
                  -griffithianum 1/4
```
5ft(1.5m) -5F(-21C) M 4/4 Sturdy open plant, size increases
rapidly; long, narrow, dark green leaves. Large rounded trusses
hold huge, trumpet-shaped flowers of rich clear pink, sparsely
marked darker. G. H. Johnstone. A.M. 1926. Color illus. F
p. 52; VV p. xii.

```
              -Mrs. J. G. Millais--unknown 1/2
PILLOW-    -yakushimanum 1/4    -fortunei ssp. discolor 3/32
 TALK -    -          -Lady Bess-
       -Si Si-   -Day - borough -campylocarpum Elatum Group
          -Gold -Dream-griersonainum 3/32          1/32
          Mohur-          -fortunei ssp. discolor
          -Margaret Dunn-    -dichroanthum 1/32
                      -Fabia-
                              -griersonianum
```
Buds of spirea red, open to flowers of yellowish white, lightly
edged in spirea red; dorsal spotting of spirea red. Al Smith
cross; W. Delp raiser.

```
                      -campylocarpum Elatum Group 1/16
              -Penjerrick-
          -Amaura-          -griffithianum 1/16
          -Eros-     -griersonianum 3/8
PIMPERNEL-    -griersonianum
          -arboreum 1/2
```
Flowers are deep red. Lord Aberconway, intro. 1950.

PINAFORE   Described under BARBARA, q.v.

PINEAPPLE   Parentage unknown
Parent of an Exbury hybrid, GEISHA.

* *
```
                              -dichroanthum 1/4
              -Goldworth Orange-
          -Hotei-          -fortunei ssp. discolor 1/4
          -     -          -souliei 1/8
          -     -unnamed hybrid-
PINEAPPLE-              -wardii 1/8
  DELIGHT -                  -griffithianum
          -              -Queen Wilhelmina-          1/16
          -     -Britannia-          -unknown 3/16
          -Tropicana-     -Stanley Davies--unknown
           (Brandt)-          -dichroanthum
              -Goldsworth Orange-
                      -fortunei ssp. discolor
```
4.5ft(1.35m) OF(-18C) M 5/4   Flowers amber yellow, shading
lighter at rims, throat lemon yellow, scant grayed yellow spots;
corolla widely funnel-shaped, of good substance, 4in(10cm) wide,
7-lobed; spherical trusses of 12-14. Plant rounded, as broad as
high; dark green, bullate leaves held 3 years. Dr. E. Brockenbrough, cross 1971; Greg Kesterson intro.; reg. 1983.
APRICOT FANTASY   Parentage as above
6ft(1.8m) -5F(-21C) ML 5/5 Fragrant flower 4in(10cm) across,
7-lobed; 16 per truss, about 7in(18cm) wide, light yellowish
pink, with throat light orange-yellow; vivid red spotting. Dr.
Brockenbrough cross; Jeanine Smith, reg. 1986.   Color illus.
ARS J 42:3 (1988), p. 179.
PAPAYA PUNCH   Parentage as above
4ft(1.2m) x 5ft(1.5m)(14 yrs) OF(-18C) EM Deep yellowish pink
in bud, opening to light yellowish pink, with wide edge of pale
orange-yellow; flares of yellow in all lobes; trusses of 13-15
flowers. E. Brockenbrough cross; G. H. Kesterson, reg. 1986.
Color illus. ARS J 43:2 (1989), p. 119.
PAPRIKA SPICED   Parentage as above
3ft(.9m) OF(-18C) M 5/3   Flowers a delicious mixture of
orange, peach, gold, and yellow, liberally peppered with paprika
red. Calyx also speckled. E. Brockenbrough cross; B. Nelson,
reg. 1985.   Color illus. ARS J 40:3 (1986), p. 179.
* *

PINES   Described under SCARLET KING, q.v.

PINK BABY--form of pumilum K W 6961
Has both single and double flowers of a delicate shell pink or
pinkish mauve. A rock garden dwarf plant growing to 1ft(.3m).
Name first used by Frank Kingdon Ward; exhibited by Lord Swaythling, Townhill Park. A M. 1935.

```
                      -griffithianum 1/4
              -unnamed hybrid-
PINK BEAUTY-          -unknown 1/4
          -          -catawbiense 1/4
          -John Walter-
                  -arboreum 1/4
```
Flowers pink to pale rose pink. C. B. van Nes, before 1922.

```
                -williamsianum 1/2                   -griffithianum
PINK BOUNTIFUL-                    -Queen    -         1/16
                    -Britannia-Wilhelmina-unknown 3/16
           -Linswegeanum-        -
                    -          -Stanley Davies--unknown
                    -forrestii Repens Group 1/4
```
3ft(.9m) OF(-18C) M 4/4 Bell-shaped flower, wine red, light-
er towards the center. Plant vigorous, compact; leaves medium
dull green. Hobbie cross; Slocock, reg. 1969.   A.M. 1975.

```
                -maximum 1/4
           -Halopeanum-
PINK BRIDE-          -griffithianum 3/4
           -griffithianum
```
A tall plant with bell-shaped flowers, blushed pale.   Loder.
A.M. 1931.

```
                -Poot--unknown 1/2
PINK BRIGHTNESS-
                -williamsianum 1/2
```
Trusses hold 7-9 flowers, 2.5in(6.4cm) long, pale pink outside,
phlox pink inside, darker edges. D. Hobbie raiser; Le Feber,
reg. 1965.

* *
```
                -caucasicum 1/4
           -Boule de Neige-              -catawbiense 5/8
PINK CAMEO-          -unnamed hybrid-
           -          -unknown 1/8
           -catawbiense, red form  (possibly hybrid)
```
5ft(1.5m) -20F(-29C) ML 3/3   Lovely flesh pink flowers with
a deeper pink blotch.   Extremely hardy hybrid with good-looking
foliage. Anthony M. Shammarello, intro. 1955; reg. 1958.
BESSE HOWELLS Parentage as above
4ft(1.2m) -20F(-29C) EM 3/4 Compact habit, dark green leaves
with very ruffled, burgundy red flowers, red blotch; globular
trusses. A. M. Shammarello, intro. 1961; reg. 1973. Color illus. HG p. 136.
LAVENDER QUEEN Parentage as above, except reversed
5ft(1.5m) -10F(-23C) M 2/3   Sturdy, bushy habit. Flowers
light bluish lavender, a faint brown blotch, in rounded trusses.
Very easy to propagate. Shammarello.
PINK FLATR Parentage as above
5ft(1.5m) -20F(-29C) ML 3/3   Bushy, compact plant; leathery
dark green leaves, 3.5in(9cm) long. Flowers pastel pink with
conspicuous red blotch. Shammarello, reg. 1973.
PRIZE Parentage as above
4ft(1.2m) -20F(-29C) ML 3/2 Flowers clear shrimp pink, yellowish brown blotch; spherical truss. Shammarello, intro. 1955.
SATIN Parentage as above
Flowers shrimp pink. Shammarello, before 1958.
SHAM'S JULIET Parentage as above
4.5ft(1.35m) -20F(-29C) ML 3/3   A compact plant with olive
green leaves. Flowers 2.5in(6.4cm) wide, of apple-blossom pink
with a brown blotch; conical trusses. Shammarello, reg. 1972.
SHAM'S PINK Parentage as above
4ft(1.2m) -20F(-29C) ML 3/2 Foliage pea green, medium-sized.
Rose pink flowers, darker at edges, light red blotch; in spherical trusses. Shammarello, reg. 1972.
TONY Parentage as above
4ft(1.2m) -20F(-29C) ML 4/3 Handsome low-growing hybrid with
crinkly foliage; bright cherry red flowers.   Shammarello, 1955.
* *

PINK CAROUSEL   Described under CHECKMATE, q.v.

                -Four Star Beauty--unknown 1/2
           -                    -neriiflorum 1/8
PINK CHAMPAGNE-unnamed hybrid F2-   -Nereid-
                    -Pink-   -dichroanthum 1/8
                    Mango-fortunei ssp. discolor 1/4
```
Buds of ruby red and magenta rose, open to flowers pale purplish
pink, rimmed with magenta rose; dorsal spots of brilliant green-
ish yellow; white filaments.   W. Delp.


* * * * * * * * * * * * * * * * * * * * * * * * * *
```
           -yakushimanum 1/2
PINK CHERUB-   -arboreum 1/4
           -Doncaster-
                -unknown 1/4
```
3ft(.9m) -5F(-21C) M 4/4   Plant compact, vigorous, 2.25ft
(.68m) high by 4.5ft(1.4m) wide;  Flowers white, flushed light

---

fuchsia purple, funnel-shaped, 2in(5cm) across;  spherical truss
of 15-20.   Waterer & Crisp, reg. 1968.  A.M. Wisley Trial 1968;
F.C.C. Wisley Trials 1988.
BASHFUL  Parentage as PINK CHERUB
3ft(.9m) -15F(-26C) E 3/3  Flowers of camellia rose, deeper
shades of rose, red-brown blotch.  Compact habit.  Waterer, reg.
1971.  A.M. Wisley Trials 1989.
HOPPY  Parentage as PINK CHERUB
3ft(.9m) -10F(-23C) M 4/4   White flowers with greenish speck-
ling; ball-shaped trusses of 18.  Vigorous, compact plant; dull
green foliage.  Waterer and Crisp, reg. 1972.   A.M. 1977.
SLEEPY  Parentage (yakushimanum x Doncaster, selfed)
3ft.9m) -10F(-23C) M 4/4  Compact habit.  Flowers light lav-
ender pink with brown blotch.  Waterer & Crisp, reg. 1971.
SNEEZY  Parentage as PINK CHERUB
3ft.9m) -10F(-23C) M 4/4    Compact habit.  Red buds open to
pink flowers, darker at edges, a deep red blotch.  Waterer, reg.
1971.  A.M. Wisley Trials 1986.
SUPER STAR  Parentage as PINK CHERUB
Pink flowers.   J. Bruns, W. Germany, reg. 1972.
* * * * * * * * * * * * * * * * * * * * * * * * * *


PINK CHIFFON--form of fortunei
6ft(1.8m) -5F(-21C) M 3/3  Flowers Tyrian rose on the edges,
lighter pink inside with reddish orange markings, fragrant, fun-
nel-campanulate, to 5in(12.7cm) wide; tall truss of 9-12.   Rock
collector; Ruth M. Hansen, reg. 1968.


PINK CLOUD   Parentage unknown
5ft(1.5m) -10F(-23C) EM   Medium pink with dull yellow blotch;
trusses of 16.  Scented.   Whitney cross; Sather, reg. 1976.


PINK CREPE   Described under CHERRY JUBILEE, q.v.

```
           -oreodoxa 1/2
PINK CREST-
           -thomsonii 1/2
```
Trusses hold 6-8 flowers, colored rose Bengal; narrowly elliptic
leaves 4.25in(10.8cm) long.   A. F. George cross; P. J. Urlwin-
Smith, reg. 1982.

```
           -arboreum 1/2
PINK DELIGHT-
           -unknown 1/2
```
Clear deep pink or white flowers, edged deep rose pink.   R. Gill
& Son.  A. M. 1926.   Color illus. ARS J 42:2 (1988), p. 87.


PINK DIVINITY   Described under CHERRY JUBILEE, q.v.

```
                -fortunei ssp. discolor 1/2
PINK DOMINO-
           -hardy hybrid--unknown 1/2
```
Carmine pink flowers, spotted yellow.   Waterer, Sons & Crisp.
A.M. 1925.

```
           -calostrotum 1/2
PINK DRIFT-
           -polycladum Scintillans Group 1/2
```
1.5ft(.45m) -10F(-23C) EM 4/4    Neat, compact habit; small,
strongly aromatic foliage of cinnamon bronze.  Flowers rich lav-
ender rose in tidy clusters.  H. White, Sunningdale, pre-1955.

```
                         -fortunei, cream form 1/8
                    -Mary Garrison-
           -unnamed-   -vernicosum 1/8   -catawbiense
           - hybrid-   -Atrosanguineum-   1/32
           -         -   -Atrier-   -unknown 1/32
           -         -Mary Belle-   -griersonianum 1/16
PINK -   -   -decorum 1/16
FANTASY-   -Dechaem-
           -                    -haematodes 1/16
           -                         -neriiflorum 1/16
           -                    -Nereid-
           -         -Phyllis Ballard-   -dichroanthum 1/16
           -unnamed-   -fortunei ssp. discolor 1/8
           hybrid-catawbiense Clark's White 1/4
```
Buds of ruby red, strong purplish red, and Tyrian purple; flow-
ers white, edged with Tyrian purple and rose Bengal.   W. Delp.


PINK FLAIR   Described under PINK CAMEO, q.v.
```

* *
```
                     -fortunei 3/4
          -Madame Fr. J. Chauvin-
PINK FLOSS-                      -unknown 1/4
          -fortunei
```
Pink with white throat; foliage matte green.   H. Larson, 1956.
MARY D. BLACK   Parentage as above, except reversed
Pink flowers with red blotch.   H. Larson, 1956.
* *

```
               -catawbiense var. album 1/2
PINK FLOURISH-                      -decorum 1/8
          -               -unnamed hybrid-
           -unnamed-               -griffithianum 1/8
            hybrid-               -catawbiense 1/8
               -unnamed hybrid-
                              -unknown 1/8
```
6ft(1.8m) -25F(-32C) M 3/3 Leaves 5in(12.7cm) long. Flowers
pale pink, edged brighter pink with small yellow-brown blotch,
3.5in(8.9cm) wide, 5-lobed; pyramidal trusses of 15.   Bloomed
after temperature of -32F(-36C). D. G. Leach, reg. 1962. Col-
or illus. ARS Q 25:2 (1971), p. 100.

```
               -racemosum 1/2
PINK FLUFF-
          -davidsonianum 1/2
```
3ft(.9m) 5F(-15C) EM 4/3   Very similar to the selected form
of davidsonianum, RUTH LYONS, but more compact in growth habit.
Flowers open light pink then turn very clear, deep pink, openly
funnel-shaped, 3.5in(8.9cm) wide; terminal cluster of 2-6 trusses, each 2- or 3-flowered.   H. E. Greer, reg. 1979.

```
                         -griffithianum 1/8
               -Mars-
          -unnamed hybrid-     -unknown 1/8
PINK FONDANT-          -catawbiense var. album--Catalgla 1/4
          -wardii 1/2
```
5ft(1.5m) -15F(-26C) ML Fine pink flowers, of excellent sub-
stance; very good foliage.   Gable cross; Pride, intro. 1970.

```
                         -griffithianum 1/4
               -Miss Noreen Beamish-
PINK FRAGRANCE-               -unknown 1/4
          -fortune ssp. discolor 1/2
```
Flowers shell pink.   Thacker, 1940.

PINK FRILLS   Described under JOAN THOMPSON, q.v.

PINK FROSTING   Listed under ANNA H. HALL, q.v.

PINK GHOST   Described under RENOIR, q.v.

```
          -yunnanense 1/2
PINK GIN-          -cinnabarinum Roylei Group 1/4
          -Lady   -               -cinnabarinum 1/8
          Rosebery-Royal Flush-
               (pink form)-
                         -maddenii 1/8
```
Trusses hold 4-5 flowers, 1.5in(3.8cm) by 1.5in, 5-lobed, light
solferino purple shading to peach in the center. E. G. Millais,
reg. 1981.   P.C. 1981.

```
          -catawbiense--Gable's Red 1/2
PINK GLOBE-               -griersonianum 1/4
          -unnamed hybrid-
                    -fortunei 1/4
```
6ft(1.8m) -15F(-26C) ML   Rosy pink flowers with a small car-
dinal red blotch, 3.5in(9cm) wide; ball-shaped trusses hold 12.
Plant upright, as broad as tall; leaves 6in(15cm) long; held 3
years. G. Guy Nearing, reg. 1973.

PINK GLORY (Lady Loder)   Described under WHITE GLORY, q.v.

```
                         -arboreum 1/4
               -Glory of Penjerrick-
PINK GLORY (Heneage-Vivian)-          -griffithianum 1/2
          -          -griffithianum
           -Loderi-
                    -fortunei 1/4
```
Heneage-Vivian, 1938.

* *
```
          -ANTOON VAN WELIE, q.v.
PINK GOLIATH-PROFESSOR J. H. ZAAYER, q.v.
          -ANNIE E. ENDTZ, q.v.
```
Three hybrids of PINK PEARL have been crossed, but the exact
combination is unknown. Firm trusses of 15 flowers, each flower
4in(10.2cm) across, pure deep pink with lighter blotch, greenish
yellow stripes. Plant habit spreading; hardy in normal winters;
good for forcing.   P. van Nes, reg. 1963.   Gold Medal Boskoop
1958.   Certificate First Class Boskoop 1959.   Gold Medal Rotterdam 1960.
RECORD   Parentage as above
Deep pink flowers with slightly darker veining, fading to a light
pink; large pyramidal trusses carry about 14.   P. van Nes, reg.
1962. A. M. Boskoop 1958.
VIRGO   Parentage as above
Fringed flowers 3.5in(8.9cm) across, light pink on opening, then
fading white, a large reddish brown, spotted blotch; tall trusses
hold 17-18.   P. van Nes, reg. 1962.   A. M. Boskoop 1959.
* *

```
               -souliei 1/2
PINK HALCYON-               -fortunei ssp. discolor 1/4
          -Lady Bessborough-
                    -campylocarpum Elatum Group 1/4
```
Flowers in trusses of 6-7, 6-lobed, strong to moderate purplish
pink in bud, opening white with variable flushing of light
purplish pink with moderate purplish red blotch in upper throat.
A. E. Hardy, cross c. 1967; G. A. Hardy, reg. 1988.

```
                              -catawbiense 1/2
                    -unnamed hybrid-
PINK HYDRANGEA---PINNACLE, selfed-          -unknown 1/2
          -               -catawbiense
                    -unnamed hybrid-
                              -unknown
```
Pink flowers in abundance.   Hardy to -25F(-32C).   Blough.

PINK ICE   See PINK SHERBET

```
          -catawbiense, red form  1/2
PINK ICING-          -catawbiense, white form 1/4
          -Catalode-               -griffithianum 1/8
               -Loderi King George-
                         -fortunei 1/8
```
5ft(1.5m) -15F(-26C) ML Good foliage; ruffled bright pink
flowers, fading to off-yellow. Orlando S. Pride, intro. 1950.
Color illus. ARS Q 34:3 (1980), p. 142.

```
                              -griffithianum 1/2
PINK JEANS   Sport of JEAN MARIE DE MONTAGUE-
                              -unknown 1/2
```
14in x 14(.36m)(3 yrs) -5F(-21C) M Flowers in domed truss of
8-10; buds strong red opening strong purplish red at rims, shading to yellowish white at center, strong red spotting on ventral
half, rose red star in throat. Briggs Nursery, reg. 1989. See
color illus. Greer catalog, 1990, pl. 9.

```
                    -fortunei 1/4
          -Fred   -               -fortunei ssp. discolor
          -Wynniatt-     -Lady Bessborough-          3/16
PINK      -     -Jalisco-          -campylocarpum Elatum
LEOPARD-     -     -dichroanthum 1/16          1/16
          -          -Dido-
          -               -decorum 1/16
          -          -elliottii 1/4
          -Kilimanjaro-     -Moser's Maroon--unknown 1/8
               -Dusky Maid-
                    -fortunei ssp. discolor
```
Flowers in trusses of 10, tubular-campanulate, 5-lobed, buds of
strong red, opening strong purplish red to strong pink with dark
red spotting. Bush 4ft(1.2m) high x 6.5ft(1.95m)(26 yrs). Foliage lanceolate, 3.5in(9cm) long. Drayson, reg. 1987.

```
          -minus var. chapmanii 1/2
PINK MAGIC-
          -ciliatum, pink form 1/2
```
2ft(.6m) -10F(-23C) M Flowers deep pink, slightly tubiform;
floriferous. Shrub twice as wide as high, with beautiful green
foliage. Dr. A. E. Kehr.

```
                 -yakushimanum--Pink Parasol 1/2
PINK MAIDEN-
                 -yakushimanum--Mist Maiden 1/2
```
Low, rounded, spreading plant; floriferous. Foliage indumented. Bright pink buds open blush pink, aging to white; round trusses. Peter Girard cross; C. Trautmann raiser.

PINK MANGO   Described under BLAZEN SUN, q.v.

PINK MANIA   Described under ZIPPETY, q.v.

PINK MARICEE   See LIZ ANN

PINK MERMAID   Described under MERLE LEE, q.v.

PINK PANTHER--form of mucronulatum, selfed
6ft(1.8m) -10F(-23C) VE   Dark red buds open to deep pink flowers with 5 wavy lobes, widely funnel-shaped. Leaves typical of this species, 2.25in(5.7cm) long. E. K. Egan cross; Dr. G. Lewis, reg. 1977. Color illus. ARS Q 31:3 (1977), p. 170; ARS J 37:2 (1983), p. 70.

PINK PARASOL--form of yakushimanum
3.5ft(1m) -20F(-29C) EM 4/5   Plant over twice as broad as tall; soft bluish green, flat foliage, to 4.25in(10.8cm) long, with heavy tan indumentum; held 4 years. Rich pink buds open to pale mauve pink flowers, roto-campanulate, 3in(7.6cm) broad, aging clear pink to white, an apple-blossom effect of elegance. See also MIST MAIDEN. F. Hanger, Exbury, seed; Leach selected/ raised/reg. 1968.

PINK PARFAIT   Parentage unknown
A pink-flowered azaleodendron. J. Senko, reg. 1962. P.A. 1961.

```
            -yakushimanum 1/2
PINK PASTEL-                         -caucasicum 3/16
           -             -Jacksonii-           -caucasicum
           -Goldsworth Yellow-         -Nobleanum-
                              -campylocarpum 1/4  -arboreum 1/16
```
Buds of magenta rose open to flowers of amaranth rose, solferino purple, pale purplish pink and white. W. Delp.

```
               -griffithianum 1/4
          -George Hardy-
PINK PEARL-            -catawbiense 1/4
          -             -arboreum 1/4
          -Broughtonii-
                       -unknown 1/4
```
6ft(1.8m) -5F(-21C) M 3/3 Often called the standard by which all pinks should be judged. Deep pink in bud, opens soft pink, fading to blush and paler at edges, with a ray of reddish brown spots; in large conical trusses. Plant strong-growing, rather bare at base; leaves 5in(12.7cm) long. Parent of many hybrids. J. Waterer. A.M. 1897. F.C.C. 1900. A.G.M. 1952. Col. ill. F p. 59; JS p. 102; VV p. 80.

```
          -callimorphum 1/2
PINK PEBBLE-
          -williamsianum 1/2
```
Clear pink flowers. Gen. Harrison, 1954. A.M. 1975.

PINK PERFECTION   Parentage uncertain, possibly griffithianum hybrid or PINK PEARL x CYNTHIA
5ft(1.5m) OF(-18C) ML Not to be confused with a vireya of the same name. Pale pink flowers, tinged lilac; rather open conical truss. Petioles reddish; leggy grower. R. Gill, Cornwall, before 1900. Color illus. JS p. 63.

```
          -Jan Dekens--unknown 7/8
PINK PETTICOATS-
          -                -griffithianum 1/8
          -       -Queen Wilhelmina-
          -Britannia-           -unknown
                    -Stanley Davies--unknown
```
5ft(1.5m) -5F(-21C) EM 4/4   Flowers China rose at margins, lighter at center, openly funnel-shaped, to 2.5in(6.4cm) across, frilled picotee edges; tall compact truss of about 32. Upright, dense plant, slightly wider than tall; leaves 8in(20.3cm) long. Lofthouse, reg. 1966. C.A. 1971. Color illus. VV p. 96.

```
                           -griersonianum 1/8
              -Sarita Loder-      -griffithianum 1/16
       -unnamed-            -Loderi-
PINK   - hybrid-                  -fortunei 1/16
PRELUDE-      -calophytum 1/4
       -
       -macabeanum 1/2
```
6ft(1.8m) 10F(-12C) VE   Pink buds opening to flowers of very pale purple, faintly tinged pink when aging, throat circled by grayed purple blotch; corolla 2.25in(5.7cm) wide, 6-lobed. Plant broad as tall; glossy leaves 10in(25cm) long with light indumentum, tinted orange new growth. Elsie Watson, reg. 1985.

PINK PRINCESS   See GAY PRINCESS

```
          -catawbiense var. album--Catalgla 1/2
PINK PUNCH-
          -fortunei F2 1/2
```
3ft(.9m) -10F(-23C) M Flowers pink fading to pale pink edges, with a flare of speckled gold, funnel-campanulate, 2.75in(7cm) wide, 5-lobed; pyramidal truss of 15. H. R. Yates, reg. 1971.

PINK QUEEN   Parentage unknown
A Knap Hill hybrid, reg. 1972. A.M. 1972.

```
                           -caucasicum 1/8
              -Cunningham's-
          -Rocket- White      -ponticum, white form 1/8
PINK ROCKET-      -catawbiense, red form 1/4
          -yakushimanum--Pink Parasol 1/2
```
9.8in(25cm) high x 19.2in(50cm)(13 yrs) -25F(-32C) M   Similar to Shammarello's ROCKET, except color differs, and the plant is dwarf. Flowers strong purplish pink, vivid purplish red spots. Elliptic foliage, greenish indumentum. R. Behring, reg. 1986.

```
            -fortunei 1/2
PINK ROSETTE-              -griffithianum 1/4
            -Mrs. E. C. Stirling-
                          -unknown 1/4
```
Pinkish white, suffused fuchsine pink. Evans.   A.M. 1956.

PINK SCALLOP   Described under SATIN DOLL, q.v.

```
            -griffithianum 1/2
PINK SHELL-         -fortunei 1/4
          -H. M. Arderne-
                  -unknown 1/4
```
Pale pink flowers. Lowinsky. A.M. 1923.

```
            -yakushimanum, Exbury form  1/2
PINK SHERBET-
            -unknown 1/2
```
3ft(.9m) OF(-18C) M Flowers spirea red, paler in throat, fading to near-white, in ball-shaped trusses of 8-12. Plant rounded, as broad as high; elliptic leaves held 3 years, heavy silver indumentum beneath. H. L. Larson cross; J. Davis, reg. 1983.

```
            -ciliatum 1/2
          -Cilpinense-
PINK SILK-         -moupinense 1/2
          -Cilpinense, as above, but selfed and reselfed
```
Clusters of 3 flowers, very light Neyron rose. A. Teese, 1981.

* *
```
            -racemosum 1/2
PINK SNOWFLAKES-
            -moupinense 1/2
```
2.5ft(.6m) OF(-18C) E 4/4   Buds red, opening to white flowers flushed soft pink, darker spotting, openly funnel-shaped, in terminal clusters. Plant broader than tall, with small, glossy leaves, bronze red when new. R. W. Scott, reg. 1969. Color illus. ARS Q 29:1 (1975), p. 35.
JODI   Parentage as above
2ft(.6m) OF(-18C) E 4/3   Small leaves; small flowers, pink, some spotting, blooming at branch tips in clusters of up to 6 buds, each 4 flowers. H. Lem cross; Mae Granston, reg. 1977.
* *
Out of order
PINK SPARKLER   Parentage unknown
4ft(1.2m) OF(-18C) EM Luminous pink buds open to long-lasting pink and white flowers; fragrant. Low, bushy. Dexter cross; Vermeulen intro.

```
                                -catawbiense 1/4
                       -Charles Dickens-
          -unnamed hybrid-              -unknown 1/4
          -              -              -catawbiense
PINK SOLACE-              -Atrosanguienum-
          -yakushimanum 1/2              -unknown
```
2.7ft(.8m) x 4ft(1.2m)(23 yrs) -20F(-29C) ML Ball truss of 12
broadly funnel-shaped flowers; vivid purplish red in bud, opening slightly paler, fading light orchid pink; pinkish white midrib streaks. Dull green, elliptic leaves, with yellow felt-like
indumentum beneath. W. Fetterhoff, reg. 1989.

PINK SPARKLER See previous column

```
          -catawbiense 1/2
PINK TWINS-
          -haematodes 1/2
```
4ft(1.2m) -15F(-26C) ML 4/3 Unusual flowers of light shrimp
pink, hose-in-hose, fleshy, in trusses of 15. Plant compact,
slow-growing, broader than tall; ovate elliptic leaves, emerald
green with yellow petioles. Joseph B. Gable. Color illus. ARS
Q 29:1 (1975), p. 35; LW pl. 56; VV p. 13.

PINK WALLOPER Described under WALLOPER, q.v.

PINK WONDER Described under OHIO PINK, q.v.

```
          -aberconwayi 1/2
PINKERTON-
          -unknown 1/2
```
Pink flowers. Knap Hill, reg. 1975.

```
                                        -catawbiense 1/4
                       -Mrs. C. S.-
          -Meadowbrook- Sargent -unknown 1/4
          -unnamed-    -              -catawbiense
          - hybrid-    -Everestianum-
PINKIE PRICE-          -              -unknown
          -          -fortunei 1/2
          -sibling of the above
```
6ft(1.8m) -10F(-23C) ML Flower deep purplish pink shading to
almost white with 2 green blotches, 3.75in((9.5cm) wide, in compact trusses of about 10. Leaves elliptic, 4.75in(12cm) long.
Howard P. Phipps, reg. 1973.

```
                    -catawbiense 1/2
          -unnamed hybrid-
PINNACLE-          -unknown 1/2
          -          -catawbiense 1/2
          -unnamed hybrid-
                    -unknown
```
6ft(1.8m) -20F(-29C) ML 4/3 Vibrant pink flowers with a del-
icate citron yellow blotch, held in conical trusses. A shapely
plant with good foliage. Bloomed after -28F(-34C), 1984 & 1985.
A. M. Shammarello, intro. 1955; reg. 1958. Color illus. ARS Q
27:2 (Spring 1973), cover; LW pl. 91; VV p. 85.

PINWHEEL Parentage unknown
Yellow flowers with gold centers. L. Henny, reg. 1964.

```
          -arboreum 1/2
PIONEER (Aberconway)-          -sanguineum ssp. didymum 1/4
          -Arthur Osborn-
                    -griersonianum 1/4
```
A hybrid with red flowers. Lord Aberconway, intro. 1942.

```
                    -racemosum 1/4
          -Conemaugh-
PIONEER (Gable)-          -mucronulatum 1/4
          -unknown 1/2
```
5ft(1.5m) -25F(-32C) VE 4/3   Parentage as in Leach. Very
early flowering, with a heavy blooming of mauve pink; flowers
1in(2.5cm) wide. Plant upright, multiple stems; small leaves,
semi-deciduous. Propagates easily.   J. Gable, 1952. Color
illus. LW pl. 38; VV p. 114.

```
          -Pioneer (Parentage as above)
PIONEER SILVERY PINK-
          -unknown
```
4ft(1.2m) -20F(-29C) E Clearer pink than PIONEER (Gable) and
blooms 2 weeks later. Red autumn foliage and heat-tolerant.
Hoogendoorn.

```
          -caucasicum 1/4
     -Dr. Stocker-
PIPALUK-          -griffithianum 1/4
     -williamsianum 1/2
```
3ft(.9m) -10F(-23C) E   Very floriferous. Flowers opening
slightly pink, turning white when fully open, each 3in(7.6cm)
across, held in trusses of 8. Gen. Harrison, reg. 1968.

```
          -lowndesii 1/2
PIPIT-                    a natural hybrid
     -lepidotum 1/2
```
1ft(.3m) 0F(-18C) EM 3/3 Small, flat-faced flowers of light
creamy pink; very small foliage. Difficult to grow. Seed from
Stainton, Sykes & Williams expedition, Nepal, 1954; P. A. Cox,
raiser; reg. 1971.

```
          -Small Fry---Epoch, F2--minus Carolinianum Gp. 5/8
PIPS- -          -minus Carolinianum Gp.
SQUEAK-          -unnamed hybrid-
     -Hi Tech-          -fastigiatum 1/8
     -          -minus Carolinianum, tetraploid 1/8
     -unnamed-          -intricatum 1/32
          hybrid-     -Intrifast-
          -Blue  -          -fastigiatum 1/32
          Diamond-augustinii 1/16
```
Buds dark purplish pink, open to light purple flowers, with dor-
sal spotting of light greenish yellow. W. Delp.

PIQUANTE Described under VALASPIS, q.v.

```
          -catawbiense 1/4
     -B. de Bruin-
PIRATE-          -unknown 1/4
     -meddianum 1/2
```
A tall plant. Well-formed trusses of deep red flowers, in mid-
season. Rothschild, 1940.

```
                              -fortunei ssp. discolor 3/16
               -King of Shrubs-          -dichroanthum 3/16
          -unnamed-          -Fabia-
          - hybrid-          -griersonianum 1/16
          -          -          -fortunei 1/16
     -Coral-    -Fawn-    -dichroanthum
     -Queen-    -          -Fabia-
PIRIANDA-    -          -griersonianum
BLUSH -    -dichroanthum
     -    -Dido-
     -          -decorum 1/8
     -    -wardii 1/4
     -Crest-          -fortunei ssp. discolor
          -Lady Bessborough-
                    -campylocarpum Elatum Group 1/8
```
Flowers in trusses of 13-15, funnel-shaped, 7-lobed, yellowish
white, a reddish green flare on dorsal lobe.   Shrub 7ft(2.1m)
H. Ansell, cross 1976; Mrs. G. Ansell, reg. 1987.

```
                              -fortunei ssp. discolor 1/8
          -Lady Bessborough-
     -Jalisco-          -campylocarpum Elatum Group
PIRIANDA -    -          -dichroanthum 1/8          1/8
CHESTNUT-    -Dido-
FLARE -    -          -decorum 1/8
     -yakushimanum 1/2
```
Flowers strong pink with moderate orange flare on dorsal lobes;
trusses of 18-20. Shrub 3ft(.9m) x 3ft. H. Ansell, cross 1976;
Mrs. G. Ansell, reg. 1987.

```
               -Mrs. P. D. Williams--unknown 1/2
PIRIANDA GREEN FLARE-          -fortunei ssp. discolor 1/4
          -Margaret Dunn-          -dichroanthum 1/8
                    -Fabia-
                    -griersonianum 1/8
```
About 17 flowers per truss, funnel-shaped, 7-lobed, light
purplish pink, shading to pale purplish pink with a strong
greenish yellow flare on dorsal lobe.   Plant 4ft(1.2m) x 3ft
(.9m). H. Ansell, cross 1978; Mrs. G. Ansell, reg. 1987.

```
          -johnstoneanum 1/2
PIRIANDA HARVEY-          -chrysodoron 1/4
          -Chrysomanicum-
                    -burmanicum 1/4
```
Flowers in trusses of 7-8, light greenish yellow, 5-lobed;

5ft(1.5m) tall. H. Ansell cross; Mrs. G. Ansell, reg. 1987.

```
            -yakushimanum 3/4
PIRIANDA-        -yakushimanum
  LILAC -unnamed-                   -haematodes 1/16
        hybrid-        -May Day-
            -Dainty-        -griersonianum 1/8
            -          -forrestii Repens Group 1/16
                -Elizabeth-
                    -griersonianum
```
Flowers in trusses of 20, funnel-shaped, 5-lobed, very pale pur-
ple. Leaves with very light brown indumentum. H. Ansell, cross
1973; Mrs. G. Ansell, reg. 1987.

```
                -leucaspis 1/4
            -Bric-à-Brac-
            -            -moupinense 1/4
PIRIANDA PINK-              -ciliatum 1/8
            -          -Cilpinense-
            -unnamed hybrid-      -moupinense 1/8
                -unknown 1/4
```
Registration description of parentage: (Bric-à-Brac x seedling
from Cilpinense g.).   Flowers 2-3 per truss, funnel-shaped, 5-
lobed, wide margins of light cardinal red to deep purplish pink,
white center. Shrub 3.3ft(1m) tall; red bark. H. Ansell, cross
1975; Mrs. G. Ansell, reg. 1987.

* *

```
        -yakushimanum--Koichiro Wada 1/2
PIROUETTE-        -Jan Dekens--unknown 7/16
        -Pink   -                      -griffithianum
        Petticoats-        -Queen Wilhelmina-    1/16
            -Britannia-          -unknown
                    -Stanley Davies--unknown
```
4ft(1.2m) -10F(-23C) M 4/4   Large, ball-shaped trusses of 28
frilled flowers, flecked pink, fading to white. Compact plant.
Best in open shade.   John G. Lofthouse, reg. 1973. Best Of The
Show award, Vancouver, 1981.
BARRY RODGERS   Parentage (yakushimanum X Pink Petticoats)
3ft(.9m) OF(-18C) M Plant low, wider than tall; leaves held 1
year. Flowers pale purplish pink, stronger edging. Large truss
of 24.   Fred Peste cross; Sharon Peste Johnston, reg. 1986.
OOH-LA-LA   Parentage as BARRY RODGERS above
1.5ft(.45m) OF(-18C) ML   Synonym HOT PANTS. Flowers of 6
frilled lobes open Neyron rose, fades white, yellow flare, openly funnel-shaped, 3in(7.6cm) wide; spherical trusses of 22-26.
Plant broad as tall, decumbent branches. Leaves held 3 years;
new growth, pale gray-green tomentose. J. Lofthouse, reg. 1981.
* *

        -forrestii Repens Group 1/2
PIXIE-
    -dichroanthum ssp. apodectum 1/2
```
A hybrid with orange-red flowers.  Lord Aberconway, intro. 1941.

PIZZAZZ   Described under INNER SPIRIT, q.v.

PJM   See P. J. M. at beginning of Ps

PLAINEYE   Described under GREEN EYE, q.v.

```
                    -griffithianum 3/16
                -George-
            -Pink - Hardy-catawbiense 3/16
            -Pearl-   -arboreum 1/16
        -Countess-   -Broughtonii-
        -of Derby-   -unknown 1/16
    -Trude-   -catawbiense
PLATINUM-Webster-   -Cynthia-
  PEARL- -   -   -griffithianum
        -        -Countess of Derby (as above)
        -fortunei ssp. discolor 1/2
```
6ft(1.8m)  10F(-23C) ML  4/4    Strong-growing plant, forming
many very large buds. Pearl pink flowers, a dark rose blotch at
base; corolla rather open and ruffled.  Long, leek green leaves;
sturdy stems.  H. E. Greer, intro. 1982.  Color illus. HG p. 77.

PLEASANT   Listed under EXMINSTER, q.v.

PLEASANT DREAM   Parentage unknown
6ft(1.8m)  OF(-18C)  L  3/3   Pink, ruffled flowers 5in(12.6cm)
wide and fragrant; small orange blotch.  Truss of 10.   Whitney

cross; Sather, reg. 1975.

```
        -dichroanthum 1/2
PLEIADES-
        -dichroanthum ssp. scyphocalyx 1/2
```
Flowers orange with red.   Reuthe, 1941.

```
                            -catawbiense
                -Parsons Grandiflorum-   5/16
            -America-   -unknown
            -        -dark red hybrid--unknown 16/32
        -Vivacious-   -griersonianum 1/8
        -        -   -arboreum 1/32
        -    -Dr. Ross-   -Doncaster-
PLUM BEAUTY-   -Borde-   -unknown
        -            Hill-   -griffithianum
        -                -Mrs. A. M.-   1/32
        -    -catawbiense   Williams-unknown
        -Old Port-
            -unknown
```
Buds of ruby red opening to flowers of ruby red and deep to
moderate red; dorsal spots ruby red.   Al Smith cross; W.
Delp raiser.

PLUM BEAUTIFUL   Described under BLUE RHAPSODY, q.v.

PLUM WARNER--form of campylogynum Myrtilloides Group
1ft(.3m)  -10F(-23C)  M  3/4  Named by Kingdon Ward.  Form of
campylogynum with small plum-colored flowers, bell-shaped, like
"sculptured wax."  A rock garden plant.  A pink form received an
A.M. 1925; rose magenta form, F.C.C. 1945, both from Exbury.

* * * * * * * * * * * * * * * * * * * * * * * * * *

```
            -catawbiense 3/4
    -Mrs. Milner-
PLÜSCH-   -unknown 1/4
    -catawbiense
```
Ruby red flowers, faint reddish brown markings.  Seidel, 1913.
ERICH   Parentage as above
Purplish crimson flowers with ochre spots.   Seidel, 1903.
BIBBER   Parentage as above
Carmine red, sometimes called ruby red.   Seidel
GRANAT   Parentage as above
Flowers carmine red with faint brown markings.   Seidel, 1905.
* * * * * * * * * * * * * * * * * * * * * * * * * *

POET'S LAWN--form of hodgsonii
5ft(1.5m)  10F(-12C)  EM  3/4  Makes a large shrub or small tree
with 25 flowers in compact, rounded trusses of white, shaded in
rhodamine  purple.  Foliage 12in(30.4cm) long,  with thin brown
tomentum.   Crown Estate, Windsor, reg. 1964.  A.M. 1964.

POINT DEFIANCE   Described under WALLOPER, q.v.

POINT FOSDICK   Parentage unknown; possibly williamsianum hybrid
4ft(1.2m)  OF(-18C)  EM  4/4   New foliage bronze, with flowers
deep purplish red.  Plant compact.  Larson.

```
        -diaprepes 1/2
POLAR BEAR-
        -auriculatum 1/2
```
6ft(1.8m)  -5F(-21C)  L  3/3    Large flowers, trumpet-shaped,
white, with a light green throat, and  a lily-like fragrance,
held in large, rather loose trusses.  Plant vigorous, eventually
wider than high; under woodland conditions may reach 30ft(9m).
Handsome, heavily veined leaves, to 7in(17.8cm) long.  J. B.
Stevenson, 1926.  F.C.C. 1946.

* * * * * * * * * * * * * * * * * * * * * * * * * *

```
            -sanguineum ssp. didymum 1/4
        -Red Cap-
POLAR CAP-   -facetum (eriogynum) 1/4
        -            -diaprepes 1/4
        -Polar Bear-
            -auriculatum 1/4
```
Loose trusses of 7 flowers, funnel-campanulate, spinel red, some
faint darker markings.  Leaves dark green, sparsely covered with
brown woolly indumentum.  Urlwin-Smith, reg. 1974.  A.M. 1974.
POLAR CREST   Parentage as above
Trusses of about 9 flowers, the inner corolla spirea red, barred
crimson, rim flushed crimson.  P. J. Urlwin-Smith, reg. 1979.
POLAR DAWN   Parentage as above
```

Flower color carmine.   P. J. Urlwin-Smith, reg. 1974.
POLAR GLOW   Parentage as above
Trusses of 7 funnel-campanulate flowers, color very light Neyron
rose, heavily stained deep Neyron rose. Leaves narrowly elliptic, dark green above, underneath sparsely covered with brown
woolly indumentum. Urlwin-Smith, reg. 1974. P.C. 1974.
* *

```
            -smirnowii 1/2
POLAR STAR-           -arboreum 1/4
            -Doncaster-
                     -unknown 1/4
```
Red flowers.   M. Koster & Sons, cross 1902.

```
                   -diaprepes 1/4
            -Polar Bear-
POLAR SUN-           -auriculatum 1/4
            -facetum 1/2
```
Pink flowers.   Lord Digby cross, 1939; intro. 1955.

POLARIS   See HACHMANN'S POLARIS

```
                              -catawbiense 1/8
                  -Lee's Dark Purple-
            -Turkana-                 -unknown 1/2
POLARNACHT-           -ponticum 3/8
            -Purple Splendour-
                     -unknown
```
2.7ft(.8m) x 4ft(1.2m) -10F(-23C) ML Trusses of 12-14 funnel-
shaped flowers, wavy-edged, to 3in(7.5cm) broad; beetroot purple
throughout, dorsal lobe spotted deep red. Dark elliptic leaves
to 5.3in(13.5cm) long. Hachmann, cross 1976; Stück, reg. 1988.

POLKA DOT--form of irroratum
5ft(1.5m) 5F(-15C) EM 4/3 White flowers suffused pink and
heavily spotted deep purple. Rothschild.   A.M. 1957.   Color
illus. Rhododendrons 1990 (RHS) fig. 11.

```
                 -dichroanthum ssp. scyphocalyx 1/8
            -Socrianum-
      -unnamed-           -griffithianum 1/8
    - hybrid-    -wardii 3/8
POLLY -      -Rima-
CLARKE-           -decorum 1/8
      -    -wardii
      -Crest-           -fortunei ssp. discolor 1/8
           -Lady        -
         Bessborough-campylocarpum Elatum Group 1/8
```
5ft(1.5m) 5F(-15C) M Flowers light, soft yellow, from deeper
yellow buds. Trusses of 10.   A. F. George, Hydon, reg. 1978.

POLLY PEACHUM   See EMILY MANGLES

POLYNESIAN SUNSET   Parentage unknown
5ft(1.5m) OF(-18C) L 4/2 Currant red buds open to brick red
flowers, in trusses of 10-12, slowly fading through shades of
orange and salmon pink. Leaves twisted, rather pale. Whitney
cross; Sather, reg. 1976.

```
            -maddenii (polyandrum) 1/2
POLYROY-
            -cinnabarinum Roylei Group 1/2
```
Flowers of apricot and red. Late season.   Sir John Ramsden.

```
            -grande 1/2
POMO PRINCESS-
            -arboreum 1/2
```
6ft(1.8m) 15F(-9C) VE   Parentage uncertain, but probably as
shown above. Trusses of 13 flowers, carmine red fading lighter
to white in throat. Corolla widely funnel-campanulate, 2in(5cm)
across, of 10 wavy lobes. Plant broad, with leaves having brown
indumentum.   Seed from RHS, Wisley; J. S. Druecker & E. R. German, raisers; reg. 1978.

```
            -ponticum 1/2
PONTICUM ROSEUM-
            -maximum 1/2
```
Synonym MAXIMUM ROSEUM.   A tall, very hardy plant with flowers
pinkish lilac; long narrow leaves.   Origin unknown; propagated
and distributed by O. S. Pride and others in Pennsylvania.

POOT   Parentage unknown

A parent of PINK BRIGHTNESS. Red flowers.   Dietrich Hobbie.

```
                  -forrestii Repens Group 1/4
            -Elizabeth-
POPACATAPETL-           -griersonianum 1/4
            -Compactum Multiflorum--unknown 1/2
```
3ft(.9m) -5F(-21C) E 3/3 Flowers of Delft rose, upper seg-
ments spotted chrysanthemum crimson, funnel-shaped, 5in(12.7cm)
wide; 5-7 in open dome-shaped trusses. Plant very floriferous,
vigorous, broader than high.   Reuthe, reg. 1981. H.C. 1981.

```
            -aureum (chrysanthum) 1/2
POPCORN PUFF-
            -catawbiense var. album Glass 1/2
```
Buds of solferino purple and pale purplish pink opening to white
flowers with sap green dorsal spots. W. Delp.

```
                  -griffithianum 1/8
            -Loderi-
      -Lodauric-    -fortunei 1/8
POPEYE-      -auriculatum 1/4
      -           -ponticum 1/4
      -Purple Splendour-
                  -unknown 1/4
```
6ft(1.8m) -10F(-23C) ML   Flowers open dark mauve, fading to
white, with a large eye of deep purple. Vigorous plant; leaves
deep cedar green, of heavy texture. Mossman cross; Greer intro.

```
                  -maximum 1/4
            -Russell Harmon-
POPPINJAY-           -catawbiense 1/4
      -      -dichroanthum 1/4
      -Jasper-           -fortunei ssp. discolor 1/8
           -Lady Bessborough-
                  -campylocarpum Elatum Group 1/8
```
5ft(1.5m) -15F(-26C) VL 4/3   Buds of strong red opening to
flowers of strong orange, openly campanulate, 2.75in(7cm) wide,
of unusually heavy substance; ball-shaped trusses of 17. Plant
50% broader than tall, rather open; elliptic, undulant leaves of
dull dark green. Leach, reg. 1972.

```
                              -catawbiense
                 -Parsons Grandi--           1/8
            -America-  florum  -unknown 1/2
      -           -dark red hybrid--unknown
PORTAGE ROAD---CINDY LOU F2-           -griffithianum 1/8
      -           -Mars-
      -unnamed-           -unknown
            hybrid-catawbiense var. rubrum 1/4
```
Buds of ruby red and deep purplish red open to flowers of deep
purplish red; dorsal spotting dark greenish yellow.   W. Delp.

* *
```
            -mucronulatum 1/2
PORTENT-
            -ciliatum 1/2
```
White flowers.   David G. Leach, 1955.
PERLA ROSA   Parentage as above
Trusses of 1-5 buds, each with 2-3 flowers, soft lilac pink.
Research Station for Arboriculture, reg. 1982.
* *

```
            -neriiflorum Euchaites Group 1/2
PORTIA-
            -strigillosum 1/2
```
Flowers dark crimson scarlet, faintly spotted within.   Lord
Aberconway. A.M. 1935. F.C.C. 1947.

PORTRAIT   Described under MOONRISE, q.v.

```
            -cinnabarinum Roylei Group 1/2
POSTLING-
            -cinnabarinum Blandfordiiflorum Group 1/2
```
5ft(1.5m) 5F(-15C) EM-VL 4/4   The crossing of two forms of
the same species makes another species form, not a hybrid. Maj.
A. E. Hardy, reg. 1975. A.M. 1975.

```
      -yakushimanum 1/2
POSY-           -arboreum ssp. nilagiricum 1/8
      -           -Noyo Chief-
      -College Pink-           -unknown 3/8
            -unknown
```

Trusses of 22 flowers, rose pink fading to rose madder then to Neyron rose. Red spotting on upper lobe. R. C. Gordon, reg. 1982.

```
                    -yakushimanum 1/4     -fortunei ssp. discolor
                    -          -Lady Bess--                 1/8
          -unnamed-    -Day - borough -campylocarpum Elatum
          - hybrid-    -Dream-griersonianum              3/32
          -       -Gold -            -fortunei ssp. discolor
        -Cisa-    Mohur-Margaret Dunn-     -dichroanthum 1/64
        -         -yakushimanum  -Fabia-
POT OF- -Serendipity-                -griersonianum 1/64
GOLD  -          -aureum (chrysanthum) 1/8
      -        -Ostbo's Yellow--unknown 1/4
      -unnamed hybrid-    -wardii 1/8
                    -Crest-
                         -Lady Bessborough (as above)
```
Buds a blend of currant red, Delft rose, and chartreuse green; frilled flowers of primrose yellow; throat of light yellow-green and Delft rose; stigma currant red. W. Delp.

```
                -haematodes 1/4
          -Thor-    -dichroanthum 1/8
POTLATCH- -Felis-
        -        -facetum (eriogynum) 1/8
        -unknown 1/2
```
3ft(.9m) 5F(-15C) M 3/4 Small shrub, dense, thick foliage; leaves indumented. Large truss of bright scarlet. R. W. Clark.

```
        -maximum 1/2                 -griffithianum
        -          -wardii 1/8 -Kewense-        3/64
POTPOURRI-  -Idealist-  -Aurora-   -fortunei 5/64
        -     -      -Naomi-  -thomsonii 1/32
        -Odee -        -fortunei    -griffithianum
       Wright-              -Geo. Hardy-
                    -Mrs. Lindsay-      -catawbiense
          -Mrs. Betty- Smith  -Duchess of      1/32
          Robertson-        Edinburgh--unknown 1/8
          -                -campylocarpum 1/16
                    -unnamed hybrid-
                           -unknown
```
Buds moderate red open to flowers of barium yellow lightly edged deep pink; throat of cardinal red. W. Delp.

POW WOW Described under HIGHNOON, q.v.

POWDER MILL RUN Described under YAKU WARRIOR, q.v.

POWELL GLASS--white variant of catawbiense
5ft(1.5m) -15F(-26C) M 3/3   A fifth generation from seed, presumed to have stabilized so that seed from it would continue to produce pure white flowers.   Selected from seed of CATALGLA. Good foliage; vigorous, hardy plant. E. Amateis, reg. 1962.

```
* * * * * * * * * * * * * * * * * * * * * * * * * * *
                    -catawbiense var. album 1/8
                    -              -catawbiense
          -Lodestar-    -Catawbiense-        3/32
          -        -  - Album  -unknown 9/32
          -      -Belle -              -catawbiense
          -         Heller-Madame Carvalho-
        -R.O. Delp-                  -unknown
        -      -                  -catawbiense
        -      -            -Atrosanguineum-
        -      -    -Atrier-        -unknown
        -    -Mary -    -griersonianum 1/16
POWER BASE-    Belle-    -decorum 1/16
        -         -Dechaem-
        -      -              -haematodes 1/16
        -      -              -thomsonii 1/16
        -         -Bagshot Ruby-
        -    -Princess -        -unknown
        -Lanny - Elizabeth-unknown
          Pride-            -smirnowii 1/8
                    -unnamed hybrid-
                           -yakushimanum 1/8
```
Strong purplish red buds; flowers of moderate purplish pink, with specks of deep purplish red.   Weldon E. Delp. TIPSTER Buds strong purplish red, open reddish purple. Delp. WHIMZEE Ruby red in bud, opens to a blend of moderate to pale roseine purple, with strong ruby red dorsal spotting. Delp.
* *

```
          -ciliatum 1/2
PRAECOX-
        -dauricum 1/2
```
4ft(1.2m) -15F(-26C) E 3/3 Purple crimson buds open to rosy lilac flowers in clusters of 2-3, each 3-4 flowered, widely funnel-shaped, 2in(5cm) across.   Glossy dark leaves paler beneath, 2in(5cm) long.   Isaac Davies, 1861; shown by The Hon. H. E. Boscawen. Commended 1861. A.G.M. 1926; F.C.C. 1978.   Color illus. F p. 60; VV p. 120.

```
                         -valentinianum 1/8
                    -Eldorado-
          -unnamed hybrid-    -johnstoneanum 1/8
PRAIRIE GOLD-        -leucaspis 1/2
          -        -xanthostephanum 1/4
          -Lemon Mist-
                    -leucaspis
```
2ft(.6m) 15F(-9C) E 4/3   Yellow flowers, 1.5in(3.8cm) wide, terminal inflorescence of 1-3 trusses, each 3-4 flowered. Free-flowering. Plant twice as wide as tall, decumbent branches; gray-green leaves with minute white hairs, scaly beneath, 1.25in (3.2cm) long, held 1 year.   Robert W. Scott, reg. 1976.

```
                    -fortunei ssp. discolor 3/8
        -Lady -
        -Bessborough-campylocarpum Elatum Group 1/4
PRAWN-            -dichroanthum 1/8
        -        -Goldsworth-
        -Tortoiseshell- Orange  -fortunei ssp. discolor
        Wonder-
                    -griersonianum 1/4
```
A late-blooming hybrid with flowers colored salmon shrimp. W. C. Slocock, Goldsworth Nursery, reg. 1967.

```
* * * * * * * * * * * * * * * * * * * * * * * * * * *
          -wardii 1/2
PRELUDE-
        -fortunei 1/2
```
5ft(1.5m) -5F(-21C) M 4/3   The last cross made by Lionel de Rothschild, exhibited 9 years after his death.   Shrimp pink or coral buds opening creamy white, shading to primrose, openly cup shape; flattened globular trusses of 10. Plant compact, foliage like wardii, leathery, glossy deep green; the vigor of fortunei. Rothschild cross, 1942. A.M. 1951.
BENGT M. SCHALIN Parents: fortunei--Sir Chas. Butler x wardii Flowers bright yellow, red patches in throat.   D. Hobbie, 1952.
GOLDEN STAR Parentage as above, except reversed
5ft(1.5m) OF(-18C) ML 4/3   Flowers mimosa yellow, 3in(7.6cm) across with 7 wavy lobes; ball-shaped trusses of 7, 5in(12.5cm) wide. Free-flowering plant, as broad as tall. Elliptic leaves, held 2 years. Don Hardgrove cross; S. Burns, intro. 1966; reg. 1978.   Color ill. ARS Q 26:2 (1972), p. 106; ARS J 43:3 (1989), p. 126.
AMAZEMENT Parentage: fortunei x wardii
6ft(1.8m) -5F(-21C) ML Flowers 3in(7.6cm) wide, 7-lobed, very fragrant, yellow, up to 13 in ball-shaped trusses. Plant broad, well-branched. Hardgrove cross; Doris Royce, reg. 1978.
* *

```
                -maximum 1/2          -griffithianum 1/8
PRESIDENT KENNEDY-        -George Hardy-
                    -Pink Pearl-        -catawbiense 1/8
                    -        -arboreum 1/8
                         -Broughtonii-
                              -unknown 1/8
```
6ft(1.8m) -15F(-26C) ML   Truss of 20 flowers, pure white with blotch of pale greenish yellow. R. A. Fennichia, reg. 1965.

```
                    -catawbiense 1/2
PRESIDENT LINCOLN-
                    -unknown 1/2
```
6ft(1.8m) -25F(-32C) ML 2/3   Synonyms HERBERT PARSONS, BETSY PARSONS, BERTHA PARSONS. Not to be confused with ABRAHAM LIN- COLN. Very hardy and adaptable. Flowers of lavender pink with bronze blotch; tight, dome-shaped truss. S. Parsons, pre-1871.

Out of order
PRESIDENT ROOSEVELT Parentage unknown (Theodore, not FDR)
4ft(1.2m) OF(-18C) EM 4/4 Very nice variegated foliage, with frilled red flowers, white at centers. Plant from Holland, but may be of U.S.A. origin. Color illus. HG p. 138; JS p. 71.

```
                              -fortunei ssp. discolor
                        -Lady        -                  1/16
                              -Bessborough-campylocarpum Elatum Gp.
                 -Jalisco-         -dichroanthum 1/16          1/16
            -unnamed-        -Dido-
           - hybrid-              -decorum 1/16
PRESIDENT-          -yakushimanum 1/4
   POINT -                          -wardii ? 1/16
           -                 -Chlorops-
           -          -Lackamas-          -vernicosum ? 1/16
           -unnamed- Spice  -diaprepes 1/8
             hybrid-
                    -lacteum 1/4
```
3ft(.9m) 5F(-15C) M Spinel red buds open to flowers of very
light chrome yellow, 3in(7.6cm) wide, 7 wavy lobes, large dome-
shaped trusses of 14. Plant broader than high; leaves retained
3 years. Cecil Smith cross; Alice P. Smith raiser; reg. 1983.

PRESIDENT ROOSEVELT   See previous column

PRESIDENT VIGDIS   Described under MARGARET EINARSON, q.v.

```
         -maximum--Mt. Mitchell F2--Ruddy Red Max 1/2
PRETTY-                     -maximum 1/4
  PINK -            -Midsummer-
  -unnamed hybrid-          -unknown 1/8
         -                       -maximum
         -unnamed hybrid-
                            -wardii 1/8
```
Buds fuchsia purple and deep purplish pink open to flowers very
pale pinkish purple, edged with roseine purple. W. Delp.

```
                          -neriiflorum 1/16
                  -Nereid-
             -unnamed-        -dichroanthum 1/16
            - hybrid-
          -Blazen Sun-        -fortunei ssp. discolor 1/8
          -                        -maximun 1/8
PRIDE AND JOY-         -Russell Harmon-
          -                        -catawbiennnnnnnse 1/8
          -Jenny Lind--parentage unknown 1/2
```
Shades of orange and peach; very ruffled edges.   Pride cross.

```
                    -smirnowii 1/4
          -unnamed hybrid-          -fortunei ssp. discolor 1/8
PRIDE OF  -          -Lady -
DORCHESTER-          Bessborough-campylocarpum Elatum Gp.
          -yakushimanum--Koichiro Wada 1/2
```
2.5ft(.8m) x 2ft(.6m)(6 yrs) -15F(-26C) ML White flowers with
red throat, narrow speckled red flare, wavy-edged; ball truss of
14. Elliptic leaves; fawn indumentum. A. W. Smith, reg. 1989.

PRIDE OF GLENROSE   Parentage unknown
Large trusses of red flowers. W. E. Glennie, reg. 1980

PRIDE OF KINGS   Described under KING'S FAVOR, q.v.

PRIDE OF LEONARDSLEE   Described under LUSCOMBEI, q.v.

```
                  -racemosum 1/2
PRIDE Of SPLIT ROCK-
                  -unknown 1/2
```
Parentage is uncertain; may be a hardy form of racemosum. Flow-
ers bright pink, in racemes. Small leaves, dark mahogany red in
winter. Origin unknown, possibly N.W. Pennsylvania.

```
                 -dichroanthum 1/4
           -Dido-
    -Lem's -      -decorum 1/8          -griffithianum 7/32
    - Cameo-               -Beauty of-
    -         -Norman Gill- Tremough-arboreum 1/32
    -    -Anna-          -griffithianum
    -    -                     -griffithianum
PRIDENJOY-    -Jean Marie de Montague-
    -                         -unknown 1/4
    -                             -griffithianum
    -               -Queen Wilhelmina-
    -      -Britannia-          -unknown
    -Kubla Khan-      -Stanley Davies--unknown
    -               -dichroanthum
       -Goldsworth-
         Orange  -fortunei ssp. discolor 1/8
```

3ft(.9m) x 4.5ft(1.35m)(7 yrs) OF(-18C) E   Currant red buds
open pale yellow, flushed light shell pink, changing pale greenish yellow, dorsal lobe spotted jasper red, throat light yellow;
corolla 4.5in(11.5cm) wide, 7-lobed, scented; spherical trusses
of 23-28. Glossy, narrowly obovate leaves 6in(15.2cm) long; new
growth olive brown. L. Newcomb, cross 1979; reg. 1987.

```
                 -wardii 1/8
                                    -griffithianum 1/64
         -Idealist-          -Kewense-
         -         -Aurora-        -fortunei 5/64
   -unnamed-        -Naomi-        -
    - hybrid-          -      -thomsonii 1/32
    -            -      -fortunei
PRIMA-    -unknown 1/4
DONNA-            -fortunei ssp. discolor 1/8
    -Jalisco-     -Lady -
    -(selfed)-Bessborough-campylocarpum Elatum Group 1/8
    -          -dichroanthum 1/8
           -Dido-
                 -decorum 1/8
```
4ft(1.2m) 5F(-15C) M   Plant of compact habit, fine foliage.
Flowers chartreuse green, a brown blotch in the throat. John
Waterer, Sons & Crisp, reg. 1971.

```
               -degronianum ssp. heptamereum (metternichii)--
      -Rijneveld-      -griersonianum 1/8   Metternianus 1/4
      -           -unnamed-
PRIMEUR-        hybrid-unknown 3/8
      -          -Essex Scarlet--unknown
      -Scarlet Surprise-
                 -forrestii Repens Group 1/4
```
Trusses of 10-20 broadly funnel-shaped flowers 2in(5cm) wide, of
light red, with a red-purple blotch. Dark lanceolate leaves to
7.9in.(20cm); bush 9.8ft(2.9m) x 9.8ft. Blooms April-May.   A.
V. van Nes, cross c. 1960; Royal Boskoop Hort. Soc., reg 1988.

* *
```
          -irroratum 1/2
PRINCE ABKHAZI-
          -unknown 1/2
```
12ft(3.7m)(20 yrs) 5F(-15C) VE   Buds dark pink; flowers pale
lilac, 3 dorsal lobes spotted pinkish red, widely funnel-
campanulate, 3.5in(9cm) broad; 15-18 per spherical truss. New
growth reddish; leaves held 3 years. H. Vaartnou, reg. 1989.
PRINCESS ABKHAZI   Parentage as above
10ft(3m)(20 yrs) 5F(-15C) VE   Similar to the above. Flowers
2.5in(6.5cm) broad; all lobes uniformly and heavily spotted red.
Seed from University of British Columbia; Vaartnou, reg. 1989.
* *

```
          -caucasicum 1/2
PRINCE CAMILLE DE ROHAN-
          -unknown 1/2
```
5ft(1.5m) -15F(-26C) EM 3/3 Very ruffled flowers, light pink
with deep reddish pink blotch. Foliage slightly twisted, with
lighter green areas on leaves. Waelbrouck, cross 1855; J. Ver-
schhaffelt, intro. 1865. Color illus. JS p. 110.

PRINCE OF McKENZIE   Described under FAITH HENTY, q.v.

PRINCESS ALICE   Described under CAERHAYS PRINCESS ALICE, q.v.

```
          -hanceanum Nanum Group 1/2
PRINCESS ANNE-
          -keiskei 1/2
```
2ft(.6m) -5F(-21C) EM 4/4 Beautiful yellow flowers with a
faint greenish tint, campanulate, 2.75in(7cm) wide; truss of 8.
Plant of compact habit; very floriferous. Leaves change to various shades of bronze depending on climate. Reuthe, reg. 1974.
A.M. 1978. F.C.C. Wisley Trials 1983. Color illus. F p. 60.

```
               -thomsonii 1/4
          -Bagshot Ruby-
PRINCESS ELIZABETH-          -unknown 3/4
          -unknown
```
6ft(1.8m) -15F(-26C) ML 3/3 Upright plant, sparse branches
rather asymmetrical; dark leaves on thick reddish shoots, somewhat pendant and bullate. Deep crimson flowers, paler at base,
lightly spotted. Held in tall, conical trusses.   Waterer and
Crisp, 1928. A.M. 1933.

```
                  -ciliatum 1/2
PRINCESS HELENA-
                  -edgeworthii 1/2
```
Fragrant white flowers, tinged rose.   J. A. Henry, 1862.

```
                  -griffithianum 1/2
PRINCESS JULIANA-
                  -unknown 1/2
```
6ft(1.8m) 5F(-15C) EM 3/3   Buds vivid rose, opening to soft
rose pink, frilly flowers, fading white, in tight trusses. Vigorous, spreading plant; glossy dark leaves. Otto Schultz, cross
1890. A.M. 1910. Color illus. VV p. 26.

```
                  -dalhousiae 1/2
PRINCESS LEOPOLD-
                  -formosum 1/2
```
Flowers white, suffused rose.   J. A. Henry, 1862.

PRINCESS MARY OF CAMBRIDGE   Parentage unknown
5ft(1.5m) -25F(-32C) ML 3/3   Has been confused with MADAME
WAGNER, but not the same.   White with rose edges. Similar to
VINCENT VAN GOGH and RAINBOW only with tighter trusses, and more
hardy.   J. Waterer, before 1871.

```
                  -campylocarpum 1/2
PRINCESS OF ORANGE-                     -caucasicum 1/4
                  -Prince Camille de Rohan-
                                        -unknown 1/4
```
Shrub of neat, rounded habit. Funnel-shaped, waxy pink flowers,
with crimson markings and nectaries, crinkled margins, in loose
trusses. Early.   Veitch.

PRINCESS SONYA   Parentage unknown
Exhibited by G. Taylor, New South Wales, AUS. P.C. 1974.

```
                  -minus Carolinianum Group 1/2
              -Balta-         -minus Carolinianum Group
              -    -P. J. M.-
PRINCESS SUSAN-              -dauricum 1/4
              -                     -P. J. M. (as above)
              -white seedling, F2-
                                    -unknown 1/4
```
2ft(.6m) x 2ft -20F(20C) M   Flowers in a ball truss of 4-5,
5 wavy-edged lobes, deep reddish purple. Small leaves; mahogany
in winter, scaly when young.   Mezitt cross; Weston, reg. 1987.

PRINCESS WILLIAM OF WURTEMBERG   Parentage unknown
Flowers white, spotted crimson.   Veitch.   F.C.C. 1894.

PRINSES MARIJKE   Parentage unknown
Deep pink flowers, a lighter phlox pink inside; outside of petals rose madder.   Felix & Dijkhuis, 1948.   A.M. Boskoop 1948.

PRIZE   Described under PINK CAMEO, q.v.

PRODIGAL'S RETURN   Parentage unknown
4ft(1.2m) -5F(-21C) M 4/3 Clear, deep yellow flowers. Foliage glossy green, medium-long.   B. Nelson cross; Greer intro.

```
                      -catawbiense 1/4
                  -Everestianum-
PROFESSOR AMATEIS-            -unknown 1/4
              -      -fortunei--Sir Charles Butler 1/4
              -Van Nes -
              Sensation-            -maximum 1/8
                        -Halopeanum-
                                    -griffithianum 1/8
```
3ft(.9m) -15F(-26C) ML   Openly campanulate flowers, 3.5in.
(8.9cm) across, dawn pink, held in medium-sized trusses. Plant
broad as tall.   E. Amateis cross; Warren Baldsiefen; reg. 1972.

PROFESSOR F. BETTEX   Described under MRS. P. DEN OUDEN, q.v.

```
                             -griffithianum 1/8
                  -George Hardy-
              -Pink Pearl-        -catawbiense 1/8
              -        -          -arboreum 3/8
PROFESSOR HUGO-        -Broughtonii-
DE VRIES    -                     -unknown 3/8
            -            -arboreum
            -Doncaster-
                         -unknown
```

5ft(1.5m) -5F(-21C) ML 3/3   Very much like PINK PEARL, but
darker. Buds rich rose opening to lilac rose flowers with reddish brown ray, funnel-shaped, in large, conical trusses. Good
foliage.   L. J. Endtz & Co., reg. 1958; Maj. A. E. Hardy shown.
A.M. 1975.   Color illus. JS p. 36.

```
                           -griffithianum 1/8
                  -George Hardy-
              -Pink Pearl-        -catawbiense 3/8
              -          -        -arboreum 1/8
PROFESSOR J.-         -Broughtonii-
H. ZAAYER -                       -unknown 3/8
              -                   -catawbiense
              -red catawbiense hybrid-
                                  -unknown
```
5ft(1.5m) -5F(-21C) ML 3/2 Light red flowers in dome-shaped
trusses. Plant vigorous, very sprawly. Foliage large, twisted,
light green.   L. J. Endtz, 1958.

```
                  -fortunei 1/2
PROFUSION-
                  -unknown 1/2
```
Flowers rosy pink.   Paul.   A.M. 1896.

PROGRÈS   Parentage unknown; may be caucasicum hybrid
Synonym Le Progres.   Flowers light to darker rose pink, with a
purple blotch; truss of 9-12. Plant broad, compact; blooms very
early. Dark foliage. In Denmark, Germany, UK. Origin unknown.

```
                       -ponticum 1/4
              -Michael Waterer-
PROMETHEUS-             -unknown 3/4
              -Monitor--unknown
```
Scarlet crimson flowers.   C. Noble.

```
                  -strigillosum 1/2
PROMISE OF SPRING-
                  -arboreum 1/2
```
5ft(1.5m) 5F(-15C) VE 4/4   Flowers of fluorescent rose, on a
plant of medium size. Good foliage. Lofthouse, reg 1973.

```
              -saluenense ssp. chameunum Prostratum Group 1/2
PROSTIGIATUM-
              -fastigiatum 1/2
```
Deep purple flowers.   E. J. P. Magor.   A.M. 1924.

```
              -saluenense ssp. chameunum Prostratum Group 1/2
PROSTSAL-
              -saluenense 1/2
```
Flowers are pink violet, slightly spotted red.   Magor, 1926.

PROTOCOL   Described under GROOVY NO. TWO, q.v.

```
                      -Marion--unknown 17/32
              -Joan Langdon-
              -            -Sir Joseph Whitworth--unknown
              -                         -griffithianum 5/64
PROUD CIS-                 -Pink -        -George-griffithianum
              -           -Shell-Mrs. L. A.- Hardy-
              -     -Rosabel-  - Dunnett -        -catawbiense
              -unnamed-   -            -unknown    1/64
              hybrid-    -griersonianum 1/8
                  -arboreum 1/4
```
Truss of 17 flowers, bright Neyron rose.   G. Langdon, reg. 1982.

```
                      -catawbiense 5/16
              -Old Port-
PROUD       -       -unknown 7/16              -catawbiense
PERFORMER-                     -Parsons Grandi- -
              -           -America- florum      -unknown
              -unnamed hybrid-     -dark red hybrid--unknown
                          -yakushimanum 1/4
```
Buds of fuchsia purple open to flowers fuchsia purple and deep
purplish pink with dorsal spots deep greenish yellow.   Al Smith
cross; W. Delp raiser.

```
                  -forrestii Repens group 1/2
PRUHONICE-
                  -unknown 1/2
```
Raised in Czechoslovakia before 1975. Scarlet flowers, to 2in(5
cm) wide, funnel-shaped; truss of 8-10. Dark green leaves about
1.5in(4cm). Boot & Co., intro.; Royal Boskoop H. S., reg. 1988.

PSYCHE   Described under CAROLINE SPENCER, q.v.

```
        -leucaspis 1/2
PTARMIGAN-
        -orthocladum var. microleucum 1/2
```
1ft(.3m) -5F(-21C) EM 4/3   Pure white flowers, broadly funnel-shaped, 1in(2.5cm) across, in terminal clusters of several
trusses, each 2- or 3-flowered. Compact, spreading plant; foliage to 1in(2.5cm) long, densely scaly beneath. E. H. M. & P.
A. Cox, reg. 1965. F.C.C. 1965.

PUCK   Sibling of TWINKLES, q.v.

```
                        -griffithianum 3/8
        -Loderi King George-
        -                   -fortunei 1/2
PUGET SOUND-       -fortunei--Sir Charles Butler
        -Van Nes -
        -Sensation-          -maximum 1/0
                    -Halopeanum-
                        -griffithianum
```
6ft(1.8m) -5F(-21C) M 4/4   Very large, ruffled flowers, fra-
grant, pink with a slight tinge of lilac; tall, shapely trusses.
Vigorous plant habit; glossy dark leaves on rosy petioles.   Roy
W. Clark, reg. 1958.

PUKEITI--form of protistum var. giganteum
5ft(1.5m) 15F(-10C) E-EM 3/4   Trusses hold up to 30 flowers
of solferino purple, fading to fuchsia purple. Kingdon Ward,
collector, North Burma, 1953; G. F. Smith, reg. 1979.

```
        -catawbiense 5/8
PULCHELLUM-                     -catawbiense
        -             -unnamed hybrid-
        -Altaclerense-          -ponticum 1/8
                    -arboreum 1/4
```
Rosy pink flowers with a white throat.   Standish & Noble, 1850.

```
        -arboreum 1/2
PULCHERRIMUM-
        -caucasicum 1/2
```
White flowers.   J. Waterer, Sons & Crisp, 1835.

```
      -ferrugineum 1/2
PUNCTA-
      -minus var. minus 1/2
```
2ft(.6m) -15F(-26C) L Parentage is uncertain. Small clusters
of late-blooming pink flowers, partially concealed by new foliage. Aromatic, scaly leaves, much like LAETEVIRENS (WILSONII).
Origin unknown, before 1835.

```
        -maximum, selfed             -griffithianum
        -            -wardii 1/8 -Kewense-        3/128
  -unn.-   -Idealist-   -Aurora-       -fortunei 5/128
  -hyb.-   -          -Naomi-    -thomsonii 1/64
  -        -Odee -              -fortunei
  -        -Wright-                         -griff.
PURE AND-    -        -Mrs. Lindsay-      -Geo. Hardy-
SIMPLE -     -Mrs. Betty- Smith   -Duchess of    -cat.
  -           Robertson -        Edinburgh--unknown
  -          -unnamed-campylocarpum 1/32
  -                  hybrid-
  -                        -unknown
  -                  -maximum 1/2
  -Stokes Bronze Wings-
                  -catawbiense 17/64
```
Buds of shades of magenta rose opening to frilled white flowers;
dorsal spotting of strong yellow-green.   W. Delp.

PURE ELEGANCE   Described under CHECKMATE, q.v.

PUREST   Parentage unknown
2ft(.6m) -20F(-29C) EB 4/3   White flowers in profusion, on
an attractive plant of unknown origin.

PURITY   Described under FRAGRANTISSIMUM, q.v.

PURITY (Delp)   Described under BODY LANGUAGE, q.v.

```
                        -griffithianum 5/16
              -Beauty of-
            -Norman- Tremough-arboreum 1/16
            - Gill -
        -Anna-      -griffithianum
        -    -               -griffithianum
PURPLE-      -Jean Marie de Montague-
ANNA -              -unknown 1/8
        -      -campylocarpum Elatum Group 1/4
        -Ole Olson-
            -fortunei ssp. discolor 1/4
```
4ft(1.2m) 5F(-15C) L Flower funnel-shaped, 3.5in(8.9cm) wide,
5 wavy lobes, lilac purple with edging of violet purple; dome-
shaped trusses of 11-12. Plant rounded; elliptic, medium green
leaves 5.5in(14cm) long, held 3 years.   Barefield, cross 1961;
Mary Barefield, intro. 1976; reg. 1983.

```
          -ponticum 1/2
PURPLE ELEGANCE-
          -unknown 1/2
```
5ft(1.5m) -15F(-26C) ML 3/3   A hardy, rapid-growing, dense
hybrid that will stand sun. Showy purple-red flowers. Origin
unknown.

PURPLE EMPEROR--uniflorum var. imperator K W 6884
Named by F. Kingdon Ward. A tender, creeping plant for the rock
garden. Aromatic foliage; small flowers of bright purple. Exhibited by Lord Swaythling. A.M. 1934.

```
        -Moser's Maroon--unknown
PURPLE EMPEROR-
        -unknown
```
6ft(1.8m) -5F(-21C) ML 2/2 Tall plant of open habit. Leaves
5.5in(14cm) x 1.5in(3.6cm). Flowers dark purple, black dots on
upper petal. Propagates easily. Knap Hill. A.M. 1953.

PURPLE EYE   Described under GREEN EYE, q.v.

PURPLE FAKE--form of concinnum var. pseudoyanthinum
5ft(1.5m) -5F(-21C) M 4/3 Flowers orchid purple with crimson
spots, tubular campanulate, 2in(5cm) broad. Leaves 3in(7.6cm) x
2in(5cm).   See also CHIEF PAULINA. R. Henny, reg. 1962.

```
* * * * * * * * * * * * * * * * * * * * * * * * * * * * *
        -fastigiatum 1/2
PURPLE GEM-
        -minus Carolinianum Group 1/2
```
2ft(.6m) -20F(-29C) EM 3/4   Parentage may be the reverse of
above. Plant rounded; medium green, scaly leaves .75in(1.9cm)
long; new foliage a beautiful blue. Small flowers of light purple, brilliant purple in another form; many small trusses. Similar to RAMAPO, but not as dwarf. Joseph Gable cross; Nearing &
Hardgrove, in the 1950s; reg. 1958. Color illus. LW pl. 64.
RAMAPO   Parentage as above
2ft(.6m) -25F(-32C) 3/4   Leaves almost circular, 1in(2.5cm)
long, new growth dusty gray blue; in winter a deep metallic hue.
Flowers pinkish violet, in abundance. Nearing, exhibited 1940;
reg. 1958. Color illus VV p. 52.
* *
```

```
                        -griffithianum 9/32
                    -Loderi-
                -Albatross-   -fortunei 7/32
            -Cup Day-   -fortunei ssp. discolor 1/16
            -      -   -elliottii 1/16
        -Midnight-   -Fusilier-
        -      -   -griersonianum 1/16
        -      -   -ponticum 1/8
PURPLE-   -Purple Splendour-
GOWN -   -unknown 3/16
        -              -griffithianum
        -      -Pink Shell-   -fortunei
        -      -   -H. M Arderne-
        -Coronation Day-   -unknown
        -          -griffithianum
            -Loderi-
                -fortunei
```
Flowers in big trusses of 15, vivid purplish red, blotch of deep
purplish red.  Bush 3.3ft(1.0m) tall.  K. van de Ven, reg. 1986.
```

```
                   -unnamed hybrid--unknown 1/2
PURPLE HEART-                  -ponticum 1/2
           -Purple Splendour-
                       -unknown
```
5ft(1.5m) -5F(-21C) M   Flowers violet; a yellow green blotch
and markings. J. Waterer, Sons & Crisp, reg. 1972.

```
                                   -catawbiense 1/8
                   -Parsons Grandiflorum-
           -Nova Zembla-                -unknown 7/8
PURPLE JEWEL-        -red garden hybrid-unknown
           -unknown
```
6ft(1.8m) x 6ft(22 yrs) -10F(-23C) VL   Flowers in trusses of
12, medium purplish pink shading to nearly white in the throat;
prominent, dark red spotted blotch; trusses 5.5in(14cm) across.
Louis A. Hindla, reg. 1987.

```
                       -griffithianum 1/8
           -Queen Wilhelmina-
       -Britannia-                -unknown 5/8
PURPLE LACE-        -Stanley Davies--unknown
                       -ponticum 1/4
           -Purple Splendour-
                       -unknown
```
5ft(1.5m) -5F(-21C) ML 4/4   Parentage as in Van Veen. A
possible rival for PURPLE SPLENDOUR. Flowers fringed, deep
purple-red. Glossy green foliage. From Boskoop, via England;
reg. 1969. Color illus. VV p. 119.

```
                   -minus Carolinianum Group, pink form
PURPLE MAGIC---PEE WEE F2-                          1/2
                   -pemakoense Patulum Group 1/2
```
Frilled flowers in shades of lavenders and violets. W. Delp.

```
               -ponticum 1/4
           -Purple Splendour-
PURPLE OPAL-           -unknown 3/4
           -unknown
```
Trusses of 12-14 flowers, bell-shaped, rich purple violet.
Height about 3ft(.9m); elliptic leaves to 4in(10.2cm) long. V.
J. Boulter cross; reg. by F. Boulter, 1984.

PURPLE PEARL   Described under KICK-OFF, q.v.

PURPLE PILLOW--form of russatum
Low, compact form of this species. Leaves are small, glossy.
Flowers are amethyst violet, 1.25in(3.2cm) long. Many forms of
this species exist. Fa. J. Streng, Jr., Boskoop, reg. 1965.

```
               -ponticum 1/2
PURPLE SPLENDOUR-
               -unknown 1/2
```
5ft(1.5m) -10F(-23C) ML 4/3   King of the royal purples.
Large, ruffled flower, one of the darkest purples, and the black
blotch makes it seem even deeper; dome-shaped to spherical truss
of many flowers. Bush compact, sturdy; dark green leaves with
a depressed midrib. Easy to propagate; grows in sun or shade.
A. Waterer, pre-1900. A.M. 1931. A.G.M. 1969. Color illus.
F p. 60, 69; JS p. 47; VV p. 40.

PURPLE SUSY   Described under ANNA DELP, q.v.

```
                       -catawbiense 1/4
               -unnamed hybrid-
       -Pinnacle-              -unknown 1/4
       -        -             -catawbiense
PURPLOGIC-      -unnamed hybrid-
       -                      -unknown
       -               -dichroanthum 1/4
       -Goldsworth Orange-
                       -fortunei ssp. discolor 1/4
```
Buds of imperial purple opening to white flowers edged with
strong reddish purple and moderate purplish pink. W. Delp.

PURPURELLUM--form of cinnabarinum   L S & T 6349
Unusual plum purple, tubular-shaped flowers, on a slender shrub.
Attractive foliage. See also NEPAL.

```
               -catawbiense 1/2
PURPUREUM ELEGANS-
               -unknown 1/2
```
5ft(1.5m) -25F(-32C) ML 2/3   One of the old ironclads and

still considered a good plant, with blue-purple flowers and nice
foliage. H. Waterer, before 1850.   Color illus. VV p. 6.

```
                   -catawbiense 1/2
PURPUREUM GRANDIFLORUM-
                   -unknown 1/2
```
5ft(1.5m) -20F(-29C) ML 2/3 Good growth habit; large, convex
leaves. Flowers medium purple with golden orange blotch. H.
Waterer, before 1850.

PYGMALION   Parentage unknown
5ft(1.5m) -5F(-21C) ML 3/2 Crimson scarlet flowers, spotted
black. Foliage of dark olive green.   John Waterer, Sons &
Crisp. A.M. 1933.

```
               -campylocarpum 1/4
       -Moonstone-
PYGMY-         -williamsianum 1/4
       -         -sanguineum ssp. sanguineum var. didymoides 1/4
       -Carmen-
               -forrestii Repens Group 1/4
```
1ft(.3m) 0F(-18C) EM 4/3 A widely spreading dwarf plant, en-
tirely covered with dark red, bell-shaped flowers held in loose
trusses. Skonieczny.

```
               -arboreum 1/4
       -Doncaster-
PYRAMUS-       -unknown 1/4
       -         -griffithianum 1/4
       -Loderi-
               -fortunei 1/4
```
A hybrid intro. in 1933 by Lord Aberconway.

PYREX   Described under GROSCLAUDE, q.v.

```
               -thomsonii 1/2
       -Exminister-
PYROPE-        -campylocarpum 1/4
       -         -thomsonii
       -Cornish Cross-
               -griffithianum 1/4
```
A red-flowered hybrid. Lord Aberconway, 1932.

```
                       Q
```

```
               -souliei 1/4
       -Sulphur Yellow-
QUADROON-      -campylocarpum 1/4
       -griffithianum 1/2
```
A tall plant with good growth habit. Pale cream-colored flowers
in rather loose trusses. Rothschild, 1950.

```
               -catawbiense 1/2
QUADROONA -
(QUADRONA)-unknown 1/2
```
Flowers purplish red, a bronze blotch. J. Waterer, before 1874.

```
           -hyperythrum 1/2
QUAKER GIRL-            -griffithianum 1/8
       -          -Loderi-
       -Avalanche-       -fortunei 1/8
               -calophytum 1/4
```
A tall hybrid and a small species produced a medium-sized plant
of rather open growth habit, bearing large white flowers spotted
with green and held in good trusses. Rothschild, 1950.

QUALA-A-WA-LOO   Described under DR. RICHARD ANDERSON, q.v.

```
               -arboreum 1/4
       -Limbatum-
QUAPP-         -unknown 3/4
       -Diadema--unknown
```
Light purplish pink, light yellow markings. Seidel, 1914.

QUARRY WOOD-form of trichostomum Ledoides Group
2.5ft(.75m) -5F(-21C) M 4/3 White flowers flushed light rhodamine purple. Mrs. Martyn Simmons, reg. 1971. A.M. 1971.

QUARTZ-form of rex R 03800 or R 18234
6ft(1.8m) 5F(-15C) EM 3/4 Leaves 12in x 4in (30.4cm x 10cm),
covered beneath with brown tomentum. Flower 3in (7.6cm) across,
tubular bell-shaped, white with pinkish blue tinge and a crimson

blotch. Crown Estate, Windsor, reg. 1962.   A.M. 1955.


```
        -wardii 3/4
QUASAR-       -wardii
-             -                      -griffithianum 1/32
    -Idealist-          -Kewense-
    -      -Aurora-        -fortunei
    -Naomi-        -thomsonii 1/16
            -fortunei 5/32
```
5ft(1.5m) 10F(-12C) EM Deep shell pink buds opening to canary
yellow flowers, ruby red blotch in throat, 5-lobed, wavy, 2.75in
(7cm) wide; flattened trusses of 8.   Plant nearly as broad as
tall; elliptic yellow-green leaves held 3 years. H. A. Short,
cross 1970; reg. 1979.


```
        -leucaspis 1/2
QUAVER-
    -sulfureum 1/2
```
3ft(.9m) 5F(-15C) E 3/4   Creamy primrose yellow flowers,
widely funnel-campanulate, about 1in(2.5cm) wide, held loosely
in 4- to 6-flowered trusses. Very floriferous. Foliage dense,
woolly, deep green. Rothschild, 1950. A.M. 1968. Color illus.
F p. 62.


```
        -niveum 1/2
QUEEN ALEXANDRA-
        -grande (argenteum) 1/2
```
Cream-colored flowers tinged mauve.   Origin unknown.


```
        -yakushimanum 1/2
QUEEN ALICE-    -griffithianum 1/4
        -Alice-
        -unknown 1/4
```
4ft(1.2m) -5F(-21C) M   Large cherry red buds open to bright
pink. Attractive new growth.   Greer distributor.

* *
```
        -brachycarpum 1/4
    -unnamed hybrid-
QUEEN ANNE'S-       -catawbiense 1/4
-                          -fortunei 1/4
    -large white hybrid from Tyler Arboretum-
                        -unknown 1/4
```
5ft(1.5m) 0F(-18C) EM 4/4   Plant rounded, as wide as high;
olive green leaves held 2 years. Pale violet flowers fade fast
to clear white; no markings; corolla of heavy substance, 2.5in
(6.4cm) across; no stamens, fused and petaloid, .75in(1.9cm)
long. Many spherical trusses of 13 gardenia-like flowers. Dr.
H. T. Skinner, cross 1960; reg. 1979.   Color illus. ARS Q 33:4
(1979), p. 238; HG p. 149.
SAINT MARY'S   Parentage as above
6ft(1.8m) -10F(-23C) M   Lavender buds; fragrant flowers, pale
violet fading to pure white;   ball-shaped trusses of 9-13. Upright, tall plant, as broad as high; leaves 5in(12.7cm) long,
glossy olive green; best grown in sun.   Skinner cross of same
parents as above, but much earlier; Skinner, reg. 1979.
* *

        -dichroanthum 1/2
QUEEN BEE-
    -unknown 1/2
```
Compact plant 2ft(.6m) tall and 2.5ft(.75m) wide  when register-
ed.  Tubular bell-shaped flowers, 3in(7.6cm) long, burnt orange-
red, held in lax trusses of 6-7, terminal umbels.   Dr. William
Corbin, reg. 1962.


* * * * * * * * * * * * * * * * * * * * * * * * * * *
```
        -wardii 1/2   -griffithianum 1/32
    -Idealist-   -Kewense-
    -      -   -Aurora-   -fortunei 5/32
QUEEN   -   -Naomi-   -thomsonii 1/16
ELIZABETH II-   -fortunei
    -     -wardii
    -Crest-   -fortunei ssp. discolor 1/8
        -Lady   -
        Bessborough-campylocarpum Elatum Group 1/8
```
5ft(1.5m)  -10F(-23C)  M  Flowers of very pale chartreuse green,
openly funnel-shaped, 4.5in(11.5cm) across,  7-lobed, in trusses
of 12. Leaves 5.5in(14cm) x 2.5in(6.4cm).   Crown Estate, Wind-
sor, reg. 1967.  A.M. 1967.  F.C.C. 1974.
GRETCHEN GOSSLER   Parentage as above
5ft(1.5m)  -5F(-21C)  ML  4/3   Rounded plant, nearly as wide as

high,  olive green leaves.  Large flowers, yellowish green with
red blotch, in trusses of 12.  Phetteplace, reg. 1977.
LADY IN WAITING    Parentage as above
Flowers creamy yellow, strongly flushed light orange in bud, 7-
lobed, held in trusses of 11-12.   Crown Estate, Windsor Great
Park.  A.M. 1989.
QUEEN OF McKENZIE    Parentage as above, but colchicine treated
3ft(.9m)  -5F(-21C)  M     Flowers canary yellow with sulphur
yellow  throat  and garnet brown blotch,  the  reverse  marigold
orange;  flat truss of 9-11.  Phetteplace, reg. 1982.
* * * * * * * * * * * * * * * * * * * * * * * * * *


QUEEN MAB   Described under MINNEHAHA, q.v.


* * * * * * * * * * * * * * * * * * * * * * * * * * *
```
                        -griffithianum 1/16
            -George Hardy-
        -Pink Pearl-   -catawbiense 7/16
        -           -arboreum 1/16
    -Marion-   -Broughtonii-
    -      -   -unknown 7/16
    -      -   -catawbiense
QUEEN MARY-   -Catawbiense Grandiflorum-
    -               -unknown
    -           -catawbiense
    -Mrs. C. S. Sargent-
                -unknown
```
5ft(1.5m)  -15F(-26C)  M 3/4   Lovely rose pink flowers.  Plant
habit sturdy;  glossy, leather-like leaves.  Felix & Dijkhouis,
1950.  F.C.C. Boskoop 1948.   Color illus. VV p. 38.
GINA LOLLOBRIGIDA   Parentage as above
Flowers orchid purple, spotted brown, in compact trusses of 15.
Felix & Dijkhouis, Boskoop, reg. 1965.
* * * * * * * * * * * * * * * * * * * * * * * * * * *


QUEEN MOTHER   See THE QUEEN MOTHER


QUEEN NEFERTITI   Described under MARKEETA'S PRIZE, q.v.


```
        -Pink Bell--unknown 1/2
QUEEN O' THE MAY-
        -griersonianum 1/2
```
A parent of CHASTE.   White-flowered.   C. Smith; Hamilton, ex-
hibited before 1930.


```
        -meddianum 1/2
QUEEN OF HEARTS-
        -Moser's Maroon--unknown 1/2
```
6ft(1.8)  -5F(-21C)  ML  4/3  Deep red buds opening to glowing,
dark crimson flowers with white stamens, red calyx, and peppered
with small black spots on the upper lobes; domed trusses of 16.
Strongly veined dark leaves to 4.5in(11.5cm) long, thin pale in-
dumentum beneath.  A shrub of striking appearance; one of Lionel
de Rothschild's last crosses.  Rothschild.  A.M. 1949.  F.C.C.
1986.  Color illus. PB pl. 34.


QUEEN OF McKENZIE   Described under QUEEN ELIZABETH II, q.v.


```
QUEEN   -fortunei 1/2
SOURIYA-   -campylocarpum 1/4
    -unnamed hybrid-
            -unknown 1/4
```
6ft(1.8m)  -10F(-23C)  M   Sweetly fragrant flowers, pale ochre
edged with lilac, 7-lobed.   W. C. Slocock, 1937.  A.M. Wisley
Trials 1957.


```
                    -catawbiense 1/8
            -unnamed hybrid-
    -Altaclerense-   -ponticum 1/8
QUEEN VICTORIA-   -arboreum 1/4
    -unknown 1/2
```
Deep claret purple.   Standish & Noble, 1850.   F.C.C. 1882.


```
        -griffithianum 1/2
QUEEN WILHELMINA-
    -unknown 1/2
```
6ft(1.8m)  10F(-12C)  EM  4/3   Carmine buds open to very large,
deep rosy scarlet flowers, fading to rose pink, widely campanu-
late, in lax trusses. Plant stiffly branched.  O. Schulz, cross
1890; C. B. van Nes & Sons, intro. 1896.  Color ill. JS p. 109.
```

```
                    -souliei 1/2
QUEENS WOOD-
              -aberconwayi 1/2
```
White saucer-shaped flowers suffused a light red purple, with a
darker blotch; up to 8 in loose trusses. T. H. Findlay, Crown
Estate Commissioners, reg. 1972. A.M. 1972.

```
        -catawbiense 3/4
QUENDEL-          -catawbiense
    -Mrs. Milner-
                -unknown 1/4
```
Purplish red flowers, very dark brown markings. Seidel, 1914.

```
        -catawbiense 1/2
QUERELE-
      -unknown 1/2
```
Flowers of dark violet, a few markings. Seidel, intro. 1914.

```
        -Red Night--unknown 1/2
QUERIDA-
      -elliottii 1/2
```
Shining deep scarlet flowers, the reverse darker, widely campanulate, in tight trusses of about 16. A tall shrub; large, deep
green leaves. Edmund de Rothschild, 1950. A.M. 1952.

```
                -brachycarpum 1/4
      -unnamed-         -wardii 1/8
      - hybrid-Crest-          -fortunei ssp. discolor 1/16
      -           -Lady       -
QUEST-          Bessborough-campylocarpum Elatum Group 1/16
      -               -maximum 1/8
      -     -Opal-
      -unnamed-      -catawbiense 1/8
       hybrid-                 -caucasicum 3/32
      -          -Jacksonii-          -caucasicum
      -Goldsworth-          -Nobleanum-
          Yellow    -               -arboreum 1/32
                    -campylocarpum 1/8
```
Pale yellow flower (petaloid), speckled red; plant medium-sized.
W. Delp.

QUIET QUALITY   Parentage unknown
5ft(1.5m) -5F(-21C) M   Flowers light purplish pink, paling to
white in center, spotted yellowish green; frilled. Ball-shaped
truss of 9. Plant moderately branched; glossy foliage. Dexter
cross; Tyler Arboretum, reg. 1983.

QUINELLA   Described under VOODOO, q.v.

```
        -catawbiense 1/2
QUINTE-
      -unknown 1/2
```
Flower of lilac pink, lighter in throat, with greenish markings.
Seidel, cross 1906; intro. 1914.

```
        -ciliatum 1/2
QUIVER-
      -lutescens 1/2
```
A tender dwarf plant of small leaves, with cream-colored flowers
in small clusters. Floriferous. Rothschild, 1950.

                              R

```
                -catawbiense var. album 3/8
      -Lodestar-      -catawbiense var. album
      -     -Belle Heller-          -catawbiense
      -          -Madame Carvalho-          1/8
R. O. DELP-                    -unknown 1/8
      -                    -catawbiense
      -               -Atrosanguineum-
      -     -Atrier-          -unknown
      -Mary Belle-      -griersonianum 1/8
      -          -decorum 1/8
          -Dechaem-
                -haematodes 1/8
```
Flowers of peach, pink, and salmon. Plant of medium size; hardy
to -15F(-26C). Often a parent. Hinerman cross; W. Delp raiser.
Color illus. ARS J 43:1 (1989), p. 58.

```
        -chrysodoron 1/2
R. W. RYE-
      -johnstoneanum 1/2
```

4ft(1.2m) 10F(-12C) EM   Primrose yellow flowers, gradually
deepening in throat, pendulous, in trusses of 4. Lord Stair,
cross 1938; intro. 1951. A.M. 1951.

```
                        -catawbiense 1/8
            -Parsons Grandiflorum-
      -America-          -unknown 3/8
RACHTER-      -dark red hybrid--unknown
      -forrestii Repens Group 1/2
```
Scarlet red flowers. Dietrich Hobbie, 1947.

```
        -racemosum 1/2
RACIL-
      -ciliatum 1/2
```
3ft(.9m) -5F(-21C) E 3/2   Plant habit open when young, but
compact later; dark green foliage, 1.75in(4.5cm) long. Clusters
of 3-4 small, shell pink flowers cover the bush. Easily rooted.
Shown by N. S. Holland, 1937. Color illus. JS p. 51.

RACY   Described under MASS WITH CLASS, q.v.

```
* * * * * * * * * * * * * * * * * * * * * * * * * * * *
                    -souliei 1/8
            -Soulbut-
      -Vanessa-      -fortunei--Sir Chas. Butler
RADIANCE (Aberconway)-      -griersonianum 3/4          1/8
      -griersonianum
```
Deep rose pink flowers. Lord Aberconway, intro. 1936.
PEACH   Parentage as above
A hybrid by Trotter, 1946.
```
* * * * * * * * * * * * * * * * * * * * * * * * * * * *
```

RADIANCE (Konrad)   Described under ECSTASY, q.v.

```
            -smirnowii 1/4
      -Oh My!-
      -      -yakushimanum 1/4
RADIANT HEAT-          -sanguineum ssp. didymum 1/8
      -     -Carmen-
      -Little Gem-      forrestii Repens Group 1/8
                -elliottii (K W 7725) 1/4
```
Buds of currant red and vivid red. Frilled flowers of cardinal
red. W. Delp.

```
            -dichroanthum 1/4
      -Fabia-
RADIANT MORN-      -griersonianum 1/4
      -          -griffithianum 1/4
      -Sunrise-
            -griersonianum 1/4
```
Porcelain rose flowers, suffused geranium pink. Lord Abercon-
way. A.M. 1951.

```
        -calostrotum ssp. keleticum 1/2
RADIISTROTUM-
      -calostrotum ssp. calostrotum 1/2
```
2ft(.6m) -10F(-23C) ML Reported by Cox as one of the hardiest
of dwarf hybrids. Grown in W. Germany where it makes a creeping
bush, with flat-faced purple flowers. G. Arends.

```
* * * * * * * * * * * * * * * * * * * * * * * * * * * *
        -griersonianum 1/2
RADIUM-                    -griffithianum 1/8
      -          -Queen Wilhelmina-
      -Earl of Athlone-          -unknown 3/8
              -Stanley Davies--unknown
```
5ft(1.5m) 5F(-15C) ML 3/3 Rounded, loose trusses of geranium
scarlet flowers. Plant habit rather open; glossy leaves to 5in.
(12.7cm) long. Easily propagated. J. J. Crosfield, 1936.
PENALVERNE   Same cross as above, by Bolitho.
```
* * * * * * * * * * * * * * * * * * * * * * * * * * * *
```

```
        -calostrotum ssp. keleticum Radicans Group 1/2
RADMOSUM-
      -racemosum 1/2
```
Rosy mauve flowers. Thacker, exhibited 1946.

RAE BERRY--form of trichostomum
2.5ft(.75m) -5F(-21C) M 3/3 A deciduous shrub with straggly
habit; leaves fringed with hair. Flowers about 1in(2.5cm) long,
strong pink. Raiser Mrs. A. C. U. Berry; Bovees, reg. 1972.

```
                          -catawbiense 1/8
               -unnamed hybrid-
        -Altaclerense-                 -ponticum 1/8
RAEANUM-            -arboreum 1/4
     -                    -maximum 1/4
        -unnamed hybrid-
                          -unknown 1/4
Rosy crimson flowers with black spots.     Standish & Noble, 1859.
```

```
          -racemosum 1/2
RAEBURN-
          -tephropeplum 1/2
Flowers of light yellowish copper.    Collingwood Ingram, 1955.
```

RAE'S DELIGHT--form of degronianum
2ft(.6m) -10F(-23C) EM 4/3 Plant over twice as wide as tall,
compact, rounded; new growth has gray-brown indumentum. Roseine
purple flowers held in trusses of 12.   Seed from Japan; Mrs. A.
C. U. Berry raiser; Portland Chapter, ARS, reg. 1980.

RAGAN'S MARRIETTA   Parentage unknown; elepidote
8ft(2.4m) x 8ft(18 yrs) -10F(-23C) EM   Flowers of heavy substance, moderate fragrance, 4in(10cm) across, deep purplish pink
shading to white in centers of lobes. W. & J. Ragan, reg. 1989.

RAGAN'S PRIDE   Parentage unknown; elepidote
10ft(3.m) x 8ft(2.4m)(18 yrs) -10F(-23C) M Flowers in trusses
of 13, 7-lobed, buds strong purplish red open white with pink
blush edging, deep pink dorsal rays. W. & J. Ragan, reg. 1989.

```
           -griffithianum 1/2
RAGGED ROBIN-
           -unknown 1/2
Crimson cerise, fading lighter red.    J. Waterer, Sons & Crisp.
```

```
            -catawbiense var. album Glass--Catalgla 1/4
     -Tony's-                        -catawbiense 1/4
     -Gift -        -Catawbiense Album-
        -Belle Heller-              -unknown 1/8
RAGTIME-          -                      -catawbiense
     -                  -white catawbiense hyb.-
     -                       -maximum 1/8      -unknown
     -             -Russell Harmon-
     -Serenata-            -catawbiense
     -                     -dichroanthum 1/8
        -unnamed hybrid-      -fortunei ssp. discolor
                 -unnamed-               1/16
                 hybrid-campylocarpum 1/16
Buds of poppy red and coral pink open to flowers pale orange-
yellow and pale yellowish pink. Fragrant.  W. Delp.
```

RAIN OF GOLD   Parentage unknown
Fragrant flowers, pale yellow.   Frederick, reg. 1977.

```
       -Anthony Waterer hardy hybrid--unknown 1/2
RAINBOW-
       -griffithianum 1/2
6ft(1.8m) OF(-18C)  M 4/3   Upright plant, as wide as tall;
glossy leaves of slightly rough texture. Beautiful flowers with
deep pink edges and white centers. W. C. Slocock, 1928.   Color
illus. VV p. 94.
```

```
                -maximum 1/4
        -unnamed hybrid-
     -                  -vernicosum (R 18139) 1/4
RAINBOW-                   -neriiflorum 1/16
 BRIGHT-            -Nereid-
     -     -Phyllis Ballard-      -dichroanthum 1/16
     -unnamed-            -fortunei ssp. discolor 1/8
        hybrid-catawbiense--Clark's White 1/4
Buds of vivid purplish red open to flowers yellowish white edged
vivid purplish red; a flare of primrose yellow.   W. Delp.
```

RAINIER PINK   Parentage unknown
Flowers yellow, with pink on the reverse.   Jordan, reg. 1977.

```
       -neriiflorum Euchaites Group 1/2
RAJAH-
       -thomsonii 1/2
Flowers 5-lobed, 2.75in(7cm) across, of dark bright red, without
markings, held in trusses of 12.   Gen. Harrison, reg. 1962.
```

```
* * * * * * * * * * * * * * * * * * * * * * * * * * * * *
                         -catawbiense 1/8
            -Pink Twins-
        -Sunset-         -haematodes 1/8
        - Yates-                   -griffithianum 1/8
RALPH-     -Leah Yates--Mars, selfed-
 PAPE-                         -unknown 1/8
          -catawbiense var. album Glass--Catalgla 1/4
        -Pink Punch-
                    -fortunei 1/4
3ft(.9m)  -15F(-26C)  ML   Ball-shaped trusses of 13-17 flowers,
deep red with spirea red throat and faint olive spotting. Plant
twice as broad as high;  arching branches.   H. R. Yates, cross
1968; Mrs. Yates, reg. 1984.
YATES' VELVET GLOW   Parentage as above
2.5ft(.75m) -10F(-23C)  ML   Plant rounded, broader than tall.
Rose red flowers,  paler in center,  slight grayed crimson mark-
ings. Globular trusses of 22.   H. Yates cross; Mrs. Yates reg.
1984.
* * * * * * * * * * * * * * * * * * * * * * * * * * * * *
```

```
           -cerasinum, red form 1/2
RALPH PURNELL-       -arboreum 1/4
           -Doncaster-
                   -unknown 1/4
Dark red, 5-lobed, in compact truss of 20.   Thacker, reg. 1962.
```

RAMAPO   Described under PURPLE GEM, q.v.

```
                        -neriiflorum 1/8
            -F. C. Puddle-
        -Ethel-         -griersonianum 1/8
     -     -forrestii Repens Group 1/4
RAMILLIES-          -thomsonii 1/4
     -       -Shilsonii-
     -Redwing-        -barbatum 1/8
     -           -thomsonii
        -Barclayi-        -arboreum 1/16
            -Glory of  -
            Penjerrick-griffithianum 1/16
Blood red flowers.   Lord Aberconway, 1941.
```

```
               -barbatum 1/4
     -Huntsman-
RAMONA-        -campylocarpum Elatum Group 1/4
     -neriiflorum 1/2
6ft(1.8m) -15F(-26C)  ML   Flowers 2in(5cm) long, campanulate,
deep red, held in flat trusses.   Not to be confused with other
unregistered hybrids using this same name.   J. Ramsden raiser;
Sir William Pennington-Ramsden, Muncaster Castle, reg. 1965.
```

RAMSEY GOLD--form of keiskei
2ft(.6m) -10F(-23C) EM 4/4 A yellow-flowered selection by G.
Guy Nearing, after raising several generations of its seedlings.

RAMSEY TINSEL   Described under ELAM, q.v.

RANDOM HARVEST--fortunei ssp. discolor Houlstonii Group W 648A
5ft(1.5m) -5F(-21C) M 2/3 Trusses hold 10-12 flowers, white
tinged pink with some lettuce green in upper throat, funnel-
campanulate, 7- or 8-lobed.   Foliage dark green above, paler
beneath.   Wilson collector; R. N. Stephenson Clarke raiser;
reg. 1981. A.M. 1981.

```
                             -catawbiense 3/16
              -Parsons Grandiflorum-
        -America-          -unknown 1/2
     -Fanfare-    -dark red hybrid--unknown
     -          -catawbiense
RANGOON-    -Kettledrum-
     -           -unknown
     -      -forrestii Repens Group 1/4
     -Gertrud-              -ponticum 1/16
        Schäle-      -Michael Waterer-
           -Prometheus-          -unknown
               -Monitor--unknown
4ft(1.2m)  -15F(-26C)  EM 4/3   Plant twice as wide as tall at
maturity; elliptic, dark green leaves, about 3.75in(9.5cm) long,
retained 2 years.  Flowers medium to dark red, widely funnel-
shaped, 2in(5cm) across; dome-shaped trusses of 7-8.  Dark red
winter buds and leaf petioles.   David G. Leach, reg. 1973.
```

```
                  -griffithianum 1/2
RAOUL MILLAIS-
            -unknown 1/2
```
Very large trusses of salmon pink flowers with a pale center and
faintly spotted upper lobe. Fades lighter without changing hue.
M. Koster, before 1922.   A.M. 1935.

RAPHAEL (Waterer)   Parentage unknown
Large rosy crimson flowers, heavily spotted in chocolate.   John
Waterer. Cultivated by Methven, Edinburgh, about 1868.

RAPHAEL (Seidel) Parentage: probably a catawbiense cross
Flowers dark lilac or ruby, brown markings. Seidel, cross 1907.

RAPTURE   Described under GWILLT-KING, q.v.

```
                        -arboreum 1/8
            -Gill's Triumph-
    -Apache-                    -griffithianum 1/8
RASCAL-              -thomsonii 1/4
        -neriiflorum Euchaites Group 1/2
```
Deep red flowers. Gen. Harrison cross, 1947; intro. 1957.

RASPBERRY RIPPLE   Described under RENOIR, q.v.

```
                  -griffithianum 1/4
        -Mars-
RASPBERRY SHERBET-   -unknown 1/4
              -catawbiense--Catanea 1/2
```
6ft(1.8m) -15F(-26C) ML Flowers spirea red, with grayed white
blotch, widely funnel-campanulate, 2.75in(7cm) across, 5-lobed;
conical truss of 17-18. Upright plant habit; medium grass green
leaves retained 2 years. Walter J. Blyskal, reg. 1980.

RASPUTIN   Described under AZURRO, q.v.

RAVELS   Described under MARY YATES. q.v.

* *
```
   -fortunei 21/32
RAY-      -wardii 1/4
    -          -              -griffithianum 1/32
   -Idealist-           -Kewense-
    -         -Aurora-        -fortunei
      -Naomi-      -thomsonii 1/16
              -fortunei
```
5ft(1.5m) OF(-18C) M 3/3 Pale yellow flowers 4in(10cm) wide;
lax trusses of 10-12. D. James, reg. 1958. P.A. 1956.
ANCHORAGE   Parentage as above, except reversed
Truss of 9 flowers, very light yellow-green, darkening to chartreuse green eye, fading greenish white. Rothschild, reg. 1981.
* *
* *
```
                    -Pygmalion--unknown 1/8
            -unnamed hybrid-
      -Weldy-               -haematodes 1/8
RAY OF   -    -yakushimanum, Exbury form 1/4
SUNSHINE-
        -brachycarpum tigerstedtii 1/2
```
Buds of cardinal and strong reds open to flowers pale yellowish
pink, lightly tinted strong pink; a Dresden yellow flare. Delp.
SWEET WENDY   Parentage as above
Buds of strong and light purplish pinks, with pale orange-yellow
flare, dorsal spots currant red; stigma strong orange. W. Delp.
* *

```
            -campylocarpum 1/2
      -Unique-
RAYDEL-       -unknown 1/2
    -              -campylocarpum
    -Mrs. W. C. Slocock-
                    -unknown
```
6ft(1.8m) -10F(-23C) E   Mimosa yellow flowers, throat tinged
chartreuse, rims of Neyron rose, openly funnel-shaped, 2.5in(6.4
cm) wide; spherical truss of 12-14. Floriferous plant, as broad
as tall; elliptic leaves; new growth light green, red-tipped. D.
W. James, cross 1950; Amy Hitchcock, reg. 1980.

```
            -unnamed hybrid--unknown 1/2
RAYMOND WEAVER-
            -yakushimanum 1/2
```

3.5ft(1m) x (5.6ft)(1.7m)(20 yrs) -15F(-26C) ML Deep purplish
pink buds open white, large pale mustard blotch. Tight trusses,
dome-shaped, hold 13-15.
W. Fetterhoff, cross 1967; reg. 1989.

```
            -spinuliferum 1/2
RAZORBILL-
        -unknown 1/2
```
3ft(.9m) OF(-18C) EM 3/3   Flowers light rose pink, variable
darker pink overtones, small, tubular-shaped; conical, compact
truss of 12. Very floriferous, vigorous plant, wider than high;
dark green leaves 1.75in(4.5cm) long, hair-fringed, scaly underneath.   Cox, reg. 1976. A.M. 1981. F.C.C. 1983.   Color ill.
Cox pl. 152.

RAZZLE DAZZLE   Described under GREAT SCOTT, q.v.

REAL SCOOP   Described under ZIPPETY, q.v.

```
      -catawbiense 1/2
REBE-
    -smirnowii 1/2
```
Ruby red flowers, pale green markings. Seidel, intro. 1915.

* *
```
                        -catawbiense 1/8
            -Parsons Grandiflorum-
      -America-                    -unknown 3/8
RECHTER-        -dark red hybrid--unknown
        -forrestii Repens Group 1/2
```
Deep scarlet red.   D. Hobbie, 1947.
RED CARPET   Parentage as above
2ft(.6m) 10F(-12C) EM 3/4 Flower guardsman red, tinged black
around rims, shading to postoffice red in throat; veined darker.
Lax truss of 4. Plant much wider than high.   D. Hobbie, cross
1945; Walter Schmalscheidt, reg. 1983. F.C.C. Wisley Trials
1989. Color illus. WS, 1989, p. 17.
* *

```
            -arboreum 1/2
RED ADMIRAL-
        -thomsonii 1/2
```
6ft(1.8m) 10F(-23C) E   Early blooming, tall, tree-like plant
with campanulate flowers of glowing red.   Leaves held one year.
J. C. Williams, Caerhays Castle, c. 1947.

```
                  -smirnowii 1/8
            -Oh My!-
    -unnamed-       -yakushimanum 3/8
    - hybrid-               -sanguineum ssp. didymum 1/16
    -         -        -Carmen-
    -       -Little Gem-     -forrestii Repens Group 1/16
RED -                -elliottii (K W 7725) 1/8
ALERT-       -yakushimanum        -catawbiense
    -   -unn.-         -Parsons Grandi-
    -   -hyb.-   -America- florum      -unknown 1/8
    -     -Cindy-        -dark red hybrid--unknown
    -unn.-     Lou -          -griffithianum 1/64
    hyb.-              -Mars-
    -               -unn.-   -unknown
    -               hyb.-catawbiense var. rubrum 1/32
    -   -yakushimanum
    -unn.-                -catawbiense 5/64
      hyb.-Henriette Sargent-
                        -unknown
```
Buds of currant red open to flowers of vivid red; foliage indu-
mented. W. Delp.

```
            -grande 1/2
RED ARGENTEUM-
            -arboreum 1/2
```
A parent of DIOGENES. Exhibited in 1926.

RED BELLS   Described under NORDERNEY, q.v.

RED BRAVE   Described under ED'S RED, q.v.

```
                  -neriiflorum 1/4
            -F. C. Puddle-
RED BROCADE-            -griersonianum 1/4
            -arboreum 1/2
```
Deep red. Lord Aberconway, 1943.

* *
```
        -sanguineum ssp. didymum 1/2
RED CAP-
        -facetum (eriogynum) 1/2
```
3ft(.9m) 10F(-12C) VL Flowers late season, blood red or deep
plum red; loose truss. Foliage dark, glossy; a spreading plant,
sometimes compact. Compare ARTHUR OSBORN. Stevenson, 1935.
BORDE HILL RED CAP   Parentage as above
Red flowers with 7 per truss. Pedicels floccose. S. R. Clarke.
EXBURY RED CAP   Parentage as above
3ft(.9m) 5F(-15C) L 2/2 Flowers deep crimson.   Rothschild.
TOWNHILL RED CAP   Parentage as above
Flowers oxblood red, scarlet when back-lighted. Lord Swathling.
A.M. 1945.

* *

RED CARPET   Described under RECHTER, q.v.

RED CHIEF   Described under PANOPLY, q.v.

```
            -griersonianum 1/4
      -Tally Ho-
RED CLOUD-      -facetum (eriogynum) 1/4
      -Corona--unknown 1/2
```
5ft(1.5m) 5F(-15C) ML 3/3   Open habit; medium green leaves
to 6.5in(16.5cm). Flowers funnel-campanulate, 3.5in(9cm) broad,
claret rose to scarlet; domed truss of 18. Henny.   P.A. 1953.

RED COLLAR--form of edgeworthii K W 20840
4ft(1.2m) 15F(-9C) EM 4/4   Truss of 3-5 flowers, white suffused pink on 3 upper lobes and deeper on reverse, as a diffused
central band; throat lightly spotted yellow-orange. Frank Kingdon Ward collector; Sir Giles Loder, reg. 1981. F.C.C. 1981.

RED CREST   Described under FIRE PRINCE, q.v.

```
      -Moser's Maroon--unknown 1/2
RED CROSS-      -griersonianum  1/4
      -Tally Ho-
            -facetum (eriogynum) 1/4
```
Vigorous plant; large flowers of dark scarlet red.   Slocock.

```
        -arboreum 1/2
RED DAZZLE-
        -Ivery's Scarlet--unknown 1/2
```
Vivid red flowers with dark nectaries, deeper spotting in dorsal
throat, 1.8in(4.5cm) wide; truss of 37. Leaves elliptic-lanceo-
late; silvery plastered indumentum. Bush at 12 years, 6.5ft(1.9
m) x 3.2ft(.96m); Sept.-Oct., NZ. Hansen; The Rowes, reg. 1988.

```
                  -griffithianum 5/16
      -Jean Marie de Montague-
      -                -unknown 7/16
RED DELICIOUS-                  -griffithianum
      -              -Queen Wilhelmina-
      -   -Britannia-              -unknown
      -Leo-          -Stanley Davies--unknown
         -elliottii 1/4
```
5ft(1.5m) -5F(-21C) ML 4/4 Fire red flowers in rounded truss
of medium size. Dark, fir green leaves.   Greer, 1988. Color
illus. HG p. 170.

```
        -sanguineum ssp. sanguineum var. haemaleum 1/2
RED DEVIL-
        -sanguineum ssp. didymum 1/2
```
2ft(.6m) 0F(-18C) M 4/4 Two forms of the same species do not
make a hybrid. Blackish red flowers; compact habit. Fawcett.

* *

```
                                -catawbiense 1/16
                    -Parsons Grandiflorum-
            -America-              -unknown 3/8
            -        -dark red hybrid--unknown
      -Cindy Lou-              -griffithianum 3/16
      -        -        -Mars-
      -        -unnamed hybrid-   -unknown
RED DOG-                  -catawbiense var. rubrum 1/8
      -              -griffithianum
      -        -Mars-
      -Captain Jack-   -unknown
                  -facetum (eriogynum) 1/4
```

Buds of dark red and currant red, open to cardinal red flowers;
dorsal spots dark red. Hardy to -25F(-32C). W. Delp.
ROCK SOLID   Parentage as above
Strong reddish purple and deep purplish pink in bud, opening to
frilled flowers of light purple and strong purplish pink. Delp.
SOURCE BANK   Parentage as above
Buds of ruby red. Flowers magenta rose with a white flare, dor-
sal spotting of pale orange-yellow. W. Delp.
* *

RED DRAGON   Described under HECLA, q.v.

```
                -arboreum 5/16
      -Cardinal-      -thomsonii 1/8
      -        -Barclayi-      -arboreum
RED ENSIGN-          -Glory of      -
      -                Penjerrick-griffithianum 1/16
      -griersonianum 1/2
```
Flowers rose red.   Lord Aberconway, 1942.

```
                  -ponticum 1/2
            -Anah Kruschke-
RED EYE (Swenson)-      -unknown 1/2
            -        -ponticum
            -Purple Splendour-
                  -unknown
```
5ft(1.5m) -10F(-23C) ML 4/4   Dependable, sun-tolerant varie-
ty. Blooms young; propagates easily. Purplish red flowers with
a greenish gold eye slowly turning red. Plant rounded; glossy,
dense foliage. W. Swenson cross; Greer intro. 1982. Color ill.
HG p. 117.

RED EYE (K van de Ven)   See RED THROAT under FRECKLE PINK

```
        -catawbiense 1/2
RED FRILLED-
        -unknown 1/2
```
3.5ft(1m) -15F(-26C) M Flowers funnel-shaped, very light red-
purple, reverse of Tyrian rose, 5 wavy lobes. Conical truss of
12-15.   Plant 2/3 as wide as tall; dark green, glossy, elliptic
leaves, held 2 years. E. Mezitt, Weston Nurseries, reg. 1983.

```
                        -griffithianum 5/16
                  -Loderi-
            -Albatross-      -fortunei 1/4
      -Cup Day-      -fortunei ssp. discolor 1/8
      -        -        -elliottii 1/8
      -        -Fusilier-
RED GATE-          -griersonianum 1/8
      -                  -griffithianum
      -        -Pink Shell-        -fortunei
      -Coronation Day-      -H. M. Arderne-
      -              -griffithianum   -unknown 1/16
      -        -Loderi-
            -fortunei
```
Vivid purplish red flowers, funnel-shaped; truss of 10-13. El-
liptic leaf; plant 2.3ft(.69m) tall.   Dosser cross; reg. 1986.

RED GLOW   Described under GEM, q.v.

```
                  -thomsonii 1/2
      -Chanticleer-
      -        -facetum (eriogynum) 1/4
RED HACKLE-          -thomsonii
      -        -Shilsonii-
      -        -        -barbatum 1/8
      -Redwing-        -thomsonii
            -Barclayi-      -arboreum 1/16
                  -Glory of  -
                  Penjerrick-griffithianum 1/16
```
Deep red flowers.   Lord Aberconway, 1946.

RED HEAD   Described under ATRIER, q.v.

```
                        -griffithianum 1/8
                  -Queen Wilhelmina-
            -Britannia-              -unknown 3/8
RED HOT-        -Stanley Davies--unknown
      -        -forrestii Repens Group 1/4
      -Elizabeth-
            -griersonianum 1/4
```
Orient red, shaded mandarin red in throat.   Henny, reg. 1962.

```
                          -facetum (eriogynum) 1/16
                    -unnamed-
              -unnamed- hybrid-unknown 3/16
        -Dopey- hybrid-      -dichroanthum 1/8
        -     -      -Fabia-
        -     -            -griersonianum 1/8
        -     -            -yakushimanum 3/8
        -     -unnamed hybrid-             -dichroanthum
RED -              -Fabia Tangerine-
HOT -                        -griersonianum
NEWS-        -yakushimanum            -catawbiense
    -  -unnamed-            -Parsons Grandi-      5/64
    -  - hybrid-   -America- florum    -unknown
    -  -    -Cindy-      -dark red hybrid--unknown
    -  -    Lou -            -griffithianum 1/64
    -Mitch-            -Mars-
        -        -unnamed-   -unknown
        -            hybrid-catawbiense var. rubrum 1/32
        -    -yakushimanum
        -unnamed-              -catawbiense
            hybrid-Henriette Sargent-
                            -unknown
```
Buds of cardinal red and currant red opening to frilled flowers
of strong reds of various shades; dark red dorsal spots. Delp.

RED IMP--form of haematodes
A dwarf, compact plant with small leaves. Flowers medium red
outside, lighter inside. Midseason. Bovees, reg. 1962.

```
                                    -catawbiense
                        -Parsons Grandi-      5/32
                    -America- florum    -unknown
            -Vivacious-      -dark red hybrid--unknown 5/8
            -     -            -griersonianum -arboreum 1/64
            -     -Dr. Ross-      -Doncaster-
        -unnamed-            -Borde-      -unknown
        - hybrid-            Hill-      -griffithianum
        -     -            -Mrs.A.M.-      9/64
RED -      -            Williams-unknown
IMPULSE -      -Nova Zembla (parentage as America, above)
        -            -griffithianum
        -      -Mars-
        -unnamed-      -unknown
            hybrid-America (as above)
```
Deep red buds to cardinal red flowers; dorsal spotting of darker
red. Al Smith cross; W. Delp raiser.

```
                        -neriiflorum
                -F. C. Puddle-
            -Phoebus-      -griersonianum 1/8
RED LACQUER-      -haematodes 1/4
            -forrestii Repens Group 1/2
```
Dwarf, prostrate plant; elliptic leaves 2in(5cm) long. Campan-
ulate flowers of post office red, 1.7in(4.5cm) long, in clusters
of 5. Collingwood Ingram, reg. 1968. A.M. 1967.

* *
```
                -arboreum 1/8
            -Doncaster-
        -The Don-      -unknown 1/8
RED LAMP-      -griffithianum 1/4
        -facetum (eriogynum) 1/2
```
A hybrid by Crosfield, 1936.
INCHMERY Parentage as above
Waxy, deep pink flowers; tall plant. Late. Rothschild, 1941.
* *

```
                -griersonianum 1/4
            -Tally Ho-
RED LION-      -facetum (eriogynum) 1/4
        -catawbiense--GABLE'S RED 1/2
```
5ft(1.5m) -10F(-23C) L Upright, open plant; elliptic leaves
with thin, grayed indumentum, held 2 years. Guardsman red flowers, faintly spotted, 2in(5cm) across; in lax trusses of 10. G.
Guy Nearing, reg. 1973.

```
                -griffithianum 3/8
            -Loderi King George-
        -            -fortunei 1/4
RED LODERI-            -griffithianum
        -      -Queen Wilhelmina-
        -Earl of Athlone-      -unknown 3/8
            -Stanley Davies--unknown
```

Parent of HALFDAN LEM. Fred Rose cross; Halfdan Lem raiser.

```
                -elliottii 1/2
RED MAJESTY-
                -strigillosum 1/2
```
5ft(1.5m) 10F(-12C) E 4/3 Plant broader than tall; leaves to
8in(20.3cm) long. Flowers of currant red, heavily spotted,
campanulate, to 3in(7.6cm) wide, in rounded trusses of 10.   H.
L. Larson, reg. 1965.

```
                -elliottii 1/4
        -Fusilier-
RED MILL-      -griersonianum 1/4
        -Ruddy--unknown 1/2
```
Tall, compact plant; leaves 6in(15.2cm) long. Currant red flow-
ers, in trusses of 16. Marshall Lyons, reg. 1972.

RED OLYMPIA Described under MURIEL PEARCE, q.v.

* *
```
                    -dichroanthum 1/16
                -Fabia-
            -unnamed-      -griersonianum 1/16
        -unnamed- hybrid-haematodes 1/8
        - hybrid-            -griffithianum 5/16
RED -      -      -Queen Wilhelmina-
PAINT-      -Earl of-            -unknown 7/16
        -      Athlone-Stanley Davies--unknown
        -            -griffithianum
        -Jean Marie de Montague-
                    -unknown
```
4ft(1.2m) 0F(-18C) E   Plant upright, well-branched; narrow,
dark glossy leaves, 5in(12.7cm) long; held 4 years. Flowers of
clear bright red, openly funnel-shaped, 3in(7.6cm) wide; trusses
of 10-14. D. Goheen cross; C. McNew, reg. 1974.
JALIPEÑO Parentage as above
2.5ft(.75m) 5F(-15C) EM 4/3   Flowers bright red, dark brown
nectaries and spots; conical trusses of 16-18. Plant as wide as
high; leaves bullate, dark green. Dr. David Goheen, reg. 1977.
* *

RED PAISLEY Parentage unknown
Pink flowers with bright ruby red centers. Dexter cross.

* *
```
                    -williamsianum 1/4
                -Wilbar-      -thomsonii 1/8
            -      -Barclayi-      -arboreum 1/16
RED PANTALOONS-            -Glory of  -
            -            Penjerrick-griffithianum 1/16
            -chamaethomsonii var. chamaethauma 1/2
```
1.5ft(.45m) 15F(-9C) E   Hose-in-hose flowers of heavy sub-
stance, currant red; lax truss of about 4. Dwarf plant, rounded, as wide as tall, decumbent branches. Heller, reg. 1977.
ROSE PANTALOONS Parentage as above
Similar to above; flowers spinel red. Dr. C. Heller, reg. 1977.
* *

```
                    -Jan Dekens--unknown 13/16
            -Pink Petticoats-
        -            -Queen  -griffithianum
        -            -Britannia-Wilhelmina-      3/16
RED PETTICOATS-      -            -unknown
        -            -Stanley Davies--unknown
        -                  -griffithianum
        -      -Queen Wilhelmina-
        -Britannia-            -unknown
            -Stanley Davies--unknown
```
Excellent tight trusses of pure red, frilly flowers. Foliage of
average quality and quantity. John G. Lofthouse.

RED POLL See REDPOLL

```
                -dichroanthum 1/4
            -Golden Horn-
RED PUFF-      -elliottii 1/4
        -catawbiense var. album--Catanea 1/2
```
2ft(.6m) -15F(-26C) ML Red flowers 2in(5cm) across, speckled
darker red, in 16-flowered ball-shaped trusses 5in(12.7cm) wide.
Growth habit dwarf, decumbent; leaves in drooping rosettes, held
2 years. G. Guy Nearing, reg. 1973.

```
                  -griffithianum 3/8
          -Gill's Crimson-
RED QUEEN-           -unknown 1/4
        -           -thomsonii 1/4
        -Barclayi-          -arboreum 1/8
              -Glory of  -
             Penjerrick-griffithianum
```
Rounded trusses of 10 cardinal red flowers, openly funnel-cam-
panulate, 2.2in(5.5cm) wide, 5-lobed. Leaves to 6in(15cm) long,
of dull dark green, paler below.   The Second Lord Aberconway,
Bodnant, cross.   A.M. 1980.

```
                         -catawbiense 1/4
          -Atrosanguineum-
RED RIDING HOOD-         -unknown 1/4
          -griffithianum 1/2
```
Brilliant deep red flowers in large conical trusses, on a tall
shrub. Slocock Nurseries, 1933.

* *
```
       -maximum--Mount Mitchell (Leach) 1/2
       -              -griffithianum 1/8
RED RIVER-     -Mars-
       -       -     -unknown 9/32
       -unnamed-          -Parsons      -catawbiense 3/32
        hybrid-      -America- Grandiflorum-
        -        -     -                -unknown
          -Fanfare-        -dark red hybrid--unknown
                -                 -catawbiense
                   -Kettledrum-
                        -unknown
```
5ft(1.5m) -20F(-29C) L   Flowers bright red, shading pink to-
ward almost-white center, yellow dorsal flare lightly spotted in
yellow-green; pyramidal trusses of 16-19. Large rugose leaves,
undulate margins.   D. G. Leach, cross 1967; reg. 1984.
RED SEA   Parentage as above
5ft(1.5m) -25F(-32C) L   Flowers light red-purple shading rose
red to off-white in throat, widely funnel-shaped, 5- to 6-lobed;
upright trusses of 20. Plant broader than tall; dull green foliage, held 2 years. Leach, reg. 1984. (Intro., then withdrawn)
* *

RED ROCK   Described under GIBRALTAR, q.v.

```
                -arboreum 1/2
          -Red Admiral-
RED ROSELLA-         -thomsonii 3/8
         -        -arboreum--Blood Red
         -Cornubia-           -thomsonii
                -Shilsonii-
                     -barbatum 1/8
```
Flowers in trusses of 12-15, campanulate, frilly lobes of strong
red, fading paler red along midrib; black spots on dorsal lobes;
red calyx. Shrub to 7ft(2.1m). J. F. Wilson, reg. 1986.

RED ROVER   Described under ARGYLL, q.v.

```
              -thomsonii 1/4
       -Barclayi-          -arboreum 1/8
RED RUM-        -Glory of  -
       -      Penjerrick-griffithianum 1/8
       -forrestii Repens Group 1/2
```
2ft(.6m) OF(-18C) VE   Loose trusses of 4-5 flowers, scarlet
red, funnel campanulate, 2in(5cm) wide, 5-lobed. Leaves 3.3in.
(8.5cm) long, medium green, oblong. Crown Estate, Windsor, reg.
1974.   A.M. 1974.

RED SAILS   Described under FLADA W. BLOUGH, q.v.

RED SEA   Described under RED RIVER, q.v.

* *
```
              -griersonianum 3/4
          -Azor-
RED SNAPPER-     -fortunei ssp. discolor 1/4
          -griersonianum
```
Flowers pale geranium with darker edges. Plant of loose habit.
Rudolph Henny, cross 1946; intro. 1956; reg. 1958.
COLUMBIA SUNSET   Parentage as above, except reversed
5ft(1.5m) 5F(-15C) L   Red in bud, opening deep pink, darker
in center; truss holds about 14 flowers. Dark green leaves with
light fawn indumentum beneath. G. L. Baker, reg. 1968.

SAXA   Parentage as above, except reversed
Flowers of pale salmon rose.   Lord Aberconway, 1946.
* *

```
                         -griffithianum 1/8
               -George Hardy-
          -Mrs. Lindsay Smith-    -catawbiense 1/8
RED STAR-           -Duchess of Edinburgh--unknown
          -Moliere--unknown 3/4
```
Bright scarlet flowers in loose trusses.   M. Koster & Sons.

* *
```
                  -catawbiense 5/32
            -Blandyanum-          -catawbiense
            -        -     -unnamed-
          -Ascot     -    -Alta- - hybrid-
          -Brilliant-    clerense-     -ponticum 1/32
RED STAR-       -           -arboreum 1/16
        -     -thomsonii 3/4
        -thomsonii
```
Velvety crimson flowers, spotted black on upper petal.   Loder.
LEONARDSLEE FLAME   Parentage as above
Selected from the RED STAR grex by Sir Edmund Loder.
* *

RED TAPE   Described under HIGHNOON, q.v.

RED THROAT   Described under FRECKLE PINK, q.v.

```
                -griffithianum 1/8
          -Mars-
        -unnamed-  -unknown 7/16         -catawbiense 1/16
        - hybrid-       -Parsons Grandiflorum-
RED  -     -America-              -unknown
THUNDER-       -dark red hybrid--unknown
       -        -elliottii 1/4
       -Kilimanjaro-      -Moser's Maroon--unknown
                -Dusky Maid-
                      -fortunei ssp. discolor 1/8
```
Buds of currant red opening to flowers of Tyrian purple and rose
Bengal; dorsal spotting and throat of cardinal red.   Al Smith
cross; Weldon E. Delp raiser.

```
                -griffithianum 1/4
          -Mars-
RED TORCH-    -unknown 3/4
          -unknown
```
Trusses of 16-23 flowers, cardinal red with small black blotch.
Research Station for Woody Nursery Crops, Boskoop, reg. 1979.

RED VELOUR   Parentage unknown, possibly haematodes hybrid
3ft(.9m) 5F(-15C) M Nice buds open to bright velvet red flowers, spotted deeper; held in lax trusses. Very dark leaves on a
compact, well-branched plant. Whitney cross: The Sathers intro.

```
                -elliottii 1/4
          -Fusilier-
RED VELVET-      -griersonianum 1/4
          -williamsianum 1/2
```
2.5ft(.75m) OF(-18C) M 3/3   Plant broader than tall; leaves
4.5in(11.5cm) long. Flowers coral red, campanulate. An attractive plant, like an improved JOCK, q.v.   Larson, reg. 1964.

RED WALLOPER   Described under WALLOPER, q.v.

RED WAX   See REDWAX

REDBERTH   Described under YAKU WARRIOR, q.v.

REDDER YET   Parentage unknown
5ft(1.5m) -25F(-32C) ML   Possibly a seedling of AMERICA.
Leaves medium and narrow. Flowers red, 2.5in(6.5cm) across, in
rounded trusses of about 18. O. Pride, reg. 1979.

```
          -forrestii (close to forrestii ssp. papillatum) 1/2
REDPOLL-     -meddianum 1/4
        -Rocket-
              -strigillosum 1/4
```
2ft(.6m) OF(-18C) VE Bright ruby red flowers in trusses of 8.
Parentage confirmed by Hydon Nurseries. A. F. George, reg.
1974.   P.C. 1985.

```
              -dichroanthum 1/4
        -Dante-
   -      -facetum (eriogynum) 1/2
REDSKIN-                        -souliei 1/16
   -           -Soulbut-
   -      -Vanessa-         -fortunei--Sir Charles Butler 1/16
   -Eudora-           -griersonianum 1/8
       -facetum (eriogynum)
Scarlet flowers.  Lord Aberconway, 1950.
```

```
                    -fortunei ssp. discolor 1/4
       -Lady Bessborough-
   -                  -campylocarpum Elatum Group 1/4
REDSKIN CHIEF-
   -      -haematodes 1/4
      -May Day-
           -griersonianum 1/4
Red flowers.  Sunningdale Nurseries, 1955.
```

* *
```
      -haematodes 3/4
REDWAX-      -haematodes
    -May Day-
        -griersonianum 1/4
```
2.5ft(.75m) 5F(-15C) M 3/4 Flowers orient red and unspotted,
funnel-campanulate, 2.25in(5.7cm) wide, in loose trusses of 3-5.
Plant dense, spreading; dark green leaves, 3in(7.6cm) long with
heavy tan indumentum beneath. R. Henny, 1956. P.A. 1958.
EGBERT VAN ALSTYNE Parentage as above, except reversed
Orient red bell-shaped flowers, slightly larger than haematodes,
in open trusses. Compact, shapely plant. Seabrook, reg. 1968.
EMETT ADAMS Parentage: MAY DAY, dwarf form x haematodes
Blood red flowers, tubular-campanulate, in loose trusses of 6-8.
Heavily indumented, semi-dwarf, compact. Seabrook, reg. 1968.
HARRY VON TILZER Parentage same as EMETT ADAMS, above
Very small plant, compact and heavily indumented. Flowers blood
red, in loose trusses. C. S. Seabrook, reg. 1968.
PAUL DETLEFSEN Parentage same as EMETT ADAMS, above
Compact plant, to 2ft(.6m) in 10 years. Leaves dark and glossy,
indumented. Orient red flowers in loose truss. Seabrook, 1968.
STEPHEN FOSTER Parentage same as EMETT ADAMS, above
(Published registration: STEVEN FOSTER) Small plant with some
indumentum on dark green, glossy leaves. Flowers of blood red,
campanulate, in loose trusses. Seabrook, reg. 1968.
* *

```
                 -thomsonii 1/2
        -Shilsonii-
REDWING-      -barbatum 1/4
   -      -thomsonii
    -Barclayi-         -arboreum 1/8
        -Glory of  -
        -Penjerrick-griffithianum 1/8
```
Flowers pale rose, with a darker stripe down the center of each
lobe. Lord Aberconway. F.C.C. 1937.

```
                       -dichroanthum 1/16
            -Goldsworth-
       -Hotei- Orange  -fortunei s. discolor 1/16
   -      -           -souliei 1/16
   -      -unnamed hybrid-
   -Frilled-              -wardii 3/16
   -Petti- -    -Pink -Jan Dekens--unknown  -griffithianum
   -coats -    -Petti--Q. Wilhelmina-         1/64
   -      -unn.-coats -Britannia-         -unknown
REFLEC--   hyb.-         -Stanley Davies--unknown
  TIONS-      -wardii        -Pygmalion--unknown
   -      -unnamed hybrid-         11/64
   -      -Weldy-         -haematodes 1/16
   -unnamed-  -yakushimanum, Exbury form 1/8
    hybrid-         -yakushimanum 1/8
       -Serendipity-
           -aureum (chrysanthum) 1/8
```
Buds a blend of moderate red, moderate reddish orange, moderate
yellowish pink opening to yellowish white flowers lightly rimmed
in spinel red; dorsal spots moderate reddish orange. W. Delp.

```
   -minus Carolinianum Group 1/2
REGAL-
   -dauricum 1/2
```
4ft(1.2m) -25F(-32C) E 4/4   One of the selected forms of
P.J.M. propagated and distributed by Weston Nurseries.   Grows

4-7 inches per year. Blooms after VICTOR and before ELITE;
strong lavender pink flowers. Typical habit and foliage.

REGAL CROWN   Described under DUSTY WHIZ, q.v.

REGINALD CHILDS--form of uvarifolium
4ft(1.2m) 5F(-15C) E 4/4 White flower suffused light magenta
with a large blotch of bright cardinal red; trusses of about 20.
Foliage glossy dark green, ash gray plastered indumentum below.
RBG of Kew, from Wakehurst Pl., raiser; reg. 1977.   A.M. 1976.

```
            -dichroanthum ssp. scyphocalyx 1/2
REGINALD FARRER-
       -fortunei ssp. discolor 1/2
Apricot orange flowers.   Thacker, 1942.
```

```
          -dendricola Taronense Group 1/2
REINE LONG-      -ciliicalyx 1/4
     -Else Frye-
           -unknown 1/4
```
5ft(1.5m) 20F(-7C) EM Very fragrant, large, open white flow-
ers, streaked rose with a large yellow blotch, in loose trusses of 4-5.   Dr. Paul J. Bowman cross; E. H. Long, reg. 1964.

RELAXATION   Described under IRENE BAIN, q.v.

```
          -dichroanthum 1/4
    -Dante-
REMBRANDT-  -facetum (eriogynum) 1/4
   -      -griffithianum 1/4
    -Sunrise-
        -griersonianum 1/4
Scarlet flowers.  Lord Aberconway, 1950.
```

```
   -valentinianum 1/2
REMO-
   -lutescens 1/2
```
2.5ft(.75m) 10F(-12C) EM 3/2   Compact habit, narrow leaves,
as lutescens. Flowers in loose clusters as valentinianum; buds
of vivid lemon yellow, flowers bright yellow bells. For mild
climates. Stevenson, Tower Court, 1943. Color illus. F p. 82.

REMOTE CONTROL   Described under INNER SPIRIT, q.v.

```
   -forrestii Repens Group 1/2
REMUS-
   -beanianum 1/2
Carmine flowers.  Lord Aberconway, intro. 1946.
```

```
                 -griffithianum
       -Loderi King George-
   -              -fortunei
RENAISSANCE-              -griffithianum 3/8
   -      -George Hardy-
   -Peter -         -catawbiense 1/8
   -Koster-         -arboreum 1/16
       -unnamed-Doncaster-
          hybrid-         -unknown 3/16
           -unknown
Flowers light red.  J. Barto cross; Mrs. H. Fogg intr. pre-1958.
```

```
          -catawbiense 1/2
   -Annedore-
RENATA-      -unknown 1/2
   -      -catawbiense
   -Mrs. Milner-
       -unknown
Glowing dark purplish red flowers,  with very faint  brown mark-
ings.   T. J. R. Seidel, cross 1907; intro. 1915.
```

```
          -arboreum 1/2
RENDALL'S SCARLET-
       -ponticum 1/2
Bright red flowers.  Lord Aberconway, 1946.
```

```
                 -griffithianum 1/8
          -George Hardy-
       -Marinus Koster-         -catawbiense 1/8
RENDEZVOUS-         -red hybrid--unknown 1/4
       -yakushimanum--Koichiro Wada 1/2
```
4ft(1.2m) -10F(-23C) ML   Flowers spinel red fading to near-
white in throat, spotted cardinal red; truss of 17-24. Foliage

deep green, indumentum on upper surface.   Hachmann, cross 1968;
Stück, reg. 1985.

RENEE SHIREY   Described under BIG 'O', q.v.

```
          -elliottii 1/2
RENHAVEN-                  -dichroanthum 1/8
        -              -Fabia-
        -Umpqua Chief-       -griersonianum 1/4
               -        -griersonianum
               -Azor-
                       -fortunei ssp. discolor 1/8
```
4.5ft(1.35m) -5F(-21C) EM 4/3   Compact plant; dark, lanceo-
olate foliage to 6in(15.2cm) long. Flowers of glowing dark red,
lightly speckled, funnel-campanulate, 3in(7.6cm) wide; lax truss
of 6-8. Del James, reg. 1958. P.A. 1955.

* *

```
       -Pauline--unknown 1/2
RENOIR-
       -yakushimanum 1/2
```
3ft(.9m) -10F(-23C) M 3/3 Flower of Neyron rose with a white
throat, with crimson spots on upper lobe, deeply campanulate;
rounded trusses of 11. Floriferous plant. F. Hanger cross; RHS
Garden, Wisley, reg. 1963. A.M. 1961.
PINK GHOST Parentage as above, except reversed
White flowers flushed very pale pink, grayed orange spotting, in
spherical trusses of 15. RHS, Wisley, reg. 1973. A.M. 1972.
RASPBERRY RIPPLE Parentage: yakushimanum x PAULINE
White flowers lightly flushed pink towards the wide rose red
edges; upper lobe flecked dark purplish red; trusses of 16. RHS
Garden, Wisley, reg. 1982.
TELSTAR Parentage: PAULINE x yakushimanum
Flowers of rose madder, paling almost to white inside, the upper
throat oxblood red.   F. Hanger cross; RHS Garden, Wisley, reg.
1963. A.M. Wisley Trials 1966.
* *

```
       -forrestii Repens Group 1/2
REPARM-
       -parmulatum 1/2
```
Pale rose flowers. Lord Aberconway, intro. 1946.

REPLET   See RIPLET

* *

```
       -lacteum 1/2
REPOSE-
       -fortunei ssp. discolor 1/2
```
5ft(1.5m) -5F(-21C) EM 5/4   Much like lacteum, in size and
growth habit. Large, campanulate flowers, of creamy white,
flushed green, giving the effect of pale lemon; big truss of 18.
E. de Rothschild, intro. 1950; exhibited by Slocock. A.M. 1956.
Color illus. PB pl. 27.
DING DONG Parentage: fortunei ssp. discolor x lacteum
Silky white, campanulate flowers, pale yellow center.   Sir John
Bolitho, reg. 1962.   Color illus. ARS J 37:4 (1983), p. 186.
MARIANNE HARDY Parentage: lacteum x fortunei ssp. discolor
Creamy white flower with a blotch of yellowish orange in throat,
held in truss of 11-15. E. de Rothschild cross;   Maj. A. E. &
G. A. Hardy intro.; reg. 1982. F.C.C. 1982.
WELCOME STRANGER Parentage: lacteum x fortunei ssp. discolor
Flowers primrose yellow, mimosa yellow in throat, greenish red
markings on the upper lobes; campanulate, 7-lobed, 2.75in(7cm)
across; in large, flat-topped trusses. L. de Rothschild cross;
Maj. Hardy exhibitor; reg. 1977. A.M. 1977.
* *

```
       -facetum (eriogynum) 1/2
RETREAT-
       -Lowinsky hybrid--unknown 1/2
```
Tall plant of open habit. Red flowers shading to pink, in full
trusses. Rothschild, 1936.

```
            -Sappho--unknown
RETURN TO PARADISE-
            -unknown
```
5ft(1.5m) -10F(-23C) M Fragrant white flowers with golden tan
spotting, in dome-shaped truss of 16. Upright plant, over half
as wide as high. Foliage glossy yellowish green, held 2 years.
Mrs. Halsey A. Frederick, Jr., reg. 1978.

REUTHE'S PURPLE--form of lepidotum
1ft(.3m) OF(-18C) EM 4/4   Elliptic foliage to .8in(2cm) long,
densely scaly beneath, aromatic; flowers bright purple violet,
rotate-campanulate, to 1.5in(3.8cm) broad, in small clusters. A
Himalayan species.   Collector unknown; G. Reuthe raiser; reg.
1968. A.M. 1967.

REUTHE'S REWARD   Described under MI AMOR, q.v.

* *

```
       -forrestii Repens Group 1/2
RÊVE ROSE-
       -Corona--unknown 1/4
        -Bow Bells-
                 -williamsianum 1/4
```
2.5ft(.75m) -5F(-21C) EM 3/4   Beautiful little plant with
bright green leaves, 1.5in(3.8cm) long.   Small flowers, rose-
colored, in loose trusses of about 5.   L. E. Brandt, reg. 1958.
LORI EICHELSER Parentage as above
2ft(.6m) -5F(-21C) EM 4/4 Dense growth habit, twice as wide
as tall. Leaves deep jade green. Flowers campanulate, 2.5in.
(6.4cm) wide; trusses of 3-4 cover the small plant with cherry
pink bells. L. Brandt cross; K. Janeck, reg. 1967.
* *

```
            -griersonianum 1/2
REVELL'S RED-
            -unknown 1/2
```
Deep red flowers. Knap Hill Nursery, cross 1935; reg. 1963.

```
                -griffithianum 1/2
REV. R. W. CAREW HUNT-
                -unknown 1/2
```
Red flowers. O. Schulz, cross 1890; C. B. van Nes, intro. 1896.

```
         -auriculatum 1/2
REVERIE-          -arboreum ssp. zeylanicum 1/4
        -St. Keverne-
                 -griffithianum 1/4
```
A large, rather compact plant with large flowers, white blushed
pink, in late season. Rothschild, intro. 1950.

```
              -neriiflorum Euchaites Group 1/2
REVIEW ORDER-         -haematodes 1/4
             -May Day-
                    -griersonianum 1/4
```
Lax trusses of bell-shaped flowers, blood red with faint brown
spotting. Dense shrub; leaves with heavy tomentose underneath.
Lord Stair. A.M. 1954.

REVLON   Described under PERSEVERANCE, q.v.

```
                  -griersonianum 1/4
        -Dorinthia-          -haematodes 1/8
        -         -Hiraethlyn-
RHAPSODY-                -griffithianum 3/8
        -      -griffithianum
        -Loderi-
                -fortunei 1/4
```
Rose-colored flowers. Lord Aberconway, 1950.

RHODO ELITE   Described under HAD, q.v.

RHODOLAND'S SILVER MIST--form of yakushimanum
1.5ft(.45m) -20F(-29C) M   Plant twice as wide as high; shiny
foliage, 4in(10.2cm) long, heavy tan indumentum beneath; held 5
years. Flowers white, with greenish spots, tubular-campanulate,
2in(5cm) across, in flat trusses of 11 to 13. Arthur and Maxine
Childers collectors, Yakushima, Japan; reg. 1978.

* *

```
              -maximum 1/4
        -Fireking-       -forrestii Repens Group 1/8
        -      -Gertrud-                  -ponticum 1/32
RHODSOC-      -Schäle -       -Michael Waterer-
        -            -Prometheus-            -unknown 3/32
        -                   -Monitor--unknown
        -hyperythrum, Ex Gt. Britain 1/2
```
Buds of deep and strong purplish reds. Flowers of pale purplish
pink and white, edged in strong purplish red; W. E. Delp.
RHODWORKS Parentage as above
Buds rose Bengal and cardinal red opening to flowers pale pur-

plish pink edged with rose Bengal; trusses of 20.   W. Delp.
** *

RHODY ROMANCE   Described under WHIMSICAL, q.v.

RHONDA   Described under WINNING POST, q.v.

```
        -aperantum 1/2
RHYTHM-
        -forrestii Repens Group 1/2
```
Flowers deep red to pale rose.   Lord Aberconway, 1946.

RIA HARDIJZER   Described under HARDIJZER'S BEAUTY, q.v.

```
              -fortunei 1/2
RICHARD GILL-
              -thomsonii 1/2
```
Flowers of deep rose.   R. Gill & Son.   A.M. 1920.

RICHARD GREGORY   Described under LEONORE, q.v.

RICHARDS RED   Described under TIM CRAIG, q.v.

RICHIE   See RITCHIE

```
                  -dichroanthum 1/4
          -Golden Horn-
RICKSHAW-             -elliottii 1/4
      -               -fortunei ssp. discolor 1/4
          -Lady Bessborough-
                     -campylocarpum Elatum Group 1/4
```
5ft(1.5m) 5F(-15C) ML Bright flower, beige and orange, deeper
in throat; small double calyx. Well-filled, medium-sized truss
on a compact, medium-sized bush.   Rothschild.   P.C. 1958.

```
                      -souliei ? 1/8
              -Virginia Scott-
      -unnamed-              -unknown 1/8
      - hybrid-         -campylocarpum Elatum
      -          -Ole -              1/16
RIGGING SLINGER-   -Alice  -Olsen-fortunei ssp. discolor
      -         Franklin-                 1/16
      -              -Loderi   -griffithianum 1/16
      -                  King George-
          -yakushimanum 1/2       -fortunei 1/16
```
3ft(.9m) -5F(-21C) EM 4/4   Large, rounded trusses of rose
pink and cream. Compact habit, with heavily indumented foliage.
Larson cross; Clint Smith intro.

RIGHT ROYAL   Sibling of BETTY KING, q.v.

```
                      -smirnowii 1/8
              -unnamed hybrid-
      -                 -yakushimanum 1/8
  -Cherry Crisp-            -sanguineum ssp. didymum
  -           -         -Carmen-             1/16
RIGID-        -Little Gem-     -forrestii Repens Group 1/16
 RED -                 -elliottii (K W 7725) 1/8
    -                          -catawbiense
  -Bob     -yakushimanum 1/4 -Parsons Grand--     1/32
   As--unnamed-     -America- iflorum   -unknown 1/32
     hyb. F2-Cindy Lou-        -griffithianum 1/16
              -unnamed-Mars-unknown     1/16
                   hybrid-
                     -catawbiense var. rubrum 1/16
```
Buds of currant red and vivid red opening to frilled flowers of
cardinal red, currant red; contrasting white filaments.   Delp.

```
          -degronianum ssp. heptamereum--Metternianus 1/2
      -                    (metternichii)
RIJNEVELD-          -griersonianum 1/4
          -unnamed hybrid-
                   -unknown 1/4
```
Very hardy plant. Trusses of 6-10 flowers, coral pink, in early
midseason.   Dietrich Hobbie raiser; V. van Nes, reg. 1969.
Gold Medal, Boskoop 1966.

RIK   Described under MARY FLEMING, q.v.

RIMA   Described under ARTHUR SMITH, q.v.

```
              -catawbiense 1/4
      -Mrs. Milner-
RINALDO-        -unknown 1/4
      -smirnowii 1/2
```
Parent of GORLITZ, a German hybrid by Joh. Bruns.   Flowers ruby
red, markings of light green.   T. J. R. Seidel, intro. 1915.

```
                  -wardii 3/8
          -unnamed-     -dichroanthum ssp. scyphocalyx
        - hybrid-Medusa-               1/16
      -Darigold-        -griersonianum 3/16
      -        -        -fortunei ssp. discolor 1/8
      -        -Autumn Gold-
RING OF-          -griersonianum
 FIRE -     -wardii          -griffithianum 1/32
      -Idealist-        -Kewense-
      -     -Aurora-     -fortunei 5/32
          -Naomi-    -thomsonii 1/16
                  -fortunei
```
4ft(1.2m) 0F(-18C) ML 4/4 Very striking flower; yellow with
a narrow band of orange-red around the margins. Plant vigorous,
compact; dense foliage.   Willard & Margaret Thompson cross; H.
Greer, intro. 1984.   Color illus. Greer catalog, 1990, pl. 1.

RIO   Described under NORMANDY, q.v.

```
                  -dichroanthum 1/4
      -Goldsworth Orange-
      -          -fortunei ssp. discolor 1/4
RIPE-             -griffithianum 1/16
CORN-        -Kewense-
      -     -Aurora-     -fortunei 5/16
      -Exbury-    -thomsonii 1/8
        Naomi-fortunei
```
4ft(1.2m) -10F(-23C) M   The color is maize yellow, slightly
tinged with pink.   Slocock, reg. 1967.

```
          -forrestii Repens Group 1/2
RIPLET-          -campylocarpum Elatum Group 1/4
      -Letty Edwards-
                -fortunei 1/4
```
2ft(.6m) -5F(-21C) EM 4/4 Originally meant to be REPLET (re-
pens x LETTY). Low, spreading, heavy-stemmed plant; dark leaves
to 2.5in(6.4cm) long. Flowers crimson fading to salmon, 4in.
(10cm) wide; truss of 5-7. Another form has much yellow. Lem,
reg. 1963.   P.A. 1961.   A.M. Wisley Trials 1987. Color ill.
ARS Q 31:1 (1977), p. 35.

RITCHIE   Described under CALSAP, q.v.

RIVIERA BEAUTY--form of arboreum
Carmine pink flowers.   R. Gill & Son, before 1958.

RIVERSIDE   Described under FOXBERG, q.v.

ROAN MOUNTAIN---form of catawbiense (seed c.w. Roan Mountain NC)
5ft(1.5m) -25F(-32C) L   Flower truss of 16-20 flowers, deep
purplish red in bud, opening light purple with darker edges, a
white blotch flecked brilliant yellowish green.   Hardy species;
often a parent of extremely hardy hybrids. Dr. Homer E. Salley,
reg. 1988.   Color illus. ARS J 42:2 (1988), p. 91.

```
                  -cinnabarinum Roylei Group 1/2
ROBBIE EVANS-
            -yunnanense 1/2
```
3ft(.9m) x 3ft(5 yrs) 10F(-12C) EM   White flowers, aging to
very pale purple, outside strong purplish pink; lax truss 5.5in.
(14cm) wide. Elliptic leaves; tiny, rusty brown scales beneath.
J. P. Evans, NZ, cross in 1960s; Mrs. Evans, reg. 1988.

```
          -minus Carolinianum Group, pink form 1/2
ROBBY-    -mucronulatum 1/4
      -Mucram-
            -ambiguum 1/4
```
A compact plant, with white flowers larger than usual from this
parentage.   Weldon E. Delp, intro. 1965.

ROBERT ALLISON   Described under CADIS, q.v.

```
                -arboreum ssp. zeylanicum 1/2
ROBERT BALCH-
          -elliottii K W 19083  1/2
```
Trusses hold 10-16 flowers, currant red.   R. W. Balch cross;
Dunedin Rhododendron Group, reg. 1977.

ROBERT CROUX   Parentage unknown
5ft(1.5m) -10F(-23C) L Called a useful late red by Street and
Cox. Good plant habit; a vigorous grower. Croux & Fils, 1899.

ROBERT FORSYTHE   Described under DAVID FORSYTHE, q.v.


```
                -griffithianum 1/2
ROBERT FORTUNE-           -fortunei 1/4
             -H. M. Arderne-
                         -unknown 1/4
```
Flowers pink with crimson markings at base. A.M. 1922.

ROBERT FOX   Described under BARCLAYI, q.v.

ROBERT HINERMAN   PINNACLE x GOLDSWORTH ORANGE
Hardy to -25F(-32C). Bright red flowers. Hinerman, reg. 1990.


```
           -Everchoice--unknown
ROBERT HUBER-
          -unknown
```
4ft(1.2m) -5F(-21C) M   Probably a cross of 2 Dexter hybrids.
Dark pink buds opening to orchid pink flowers, with darker pink
edges, spotting of Spanish orange; spherical truss of about 14.
Plant upright, almost as broad as tall; glossy, yellowish green
foliage.   S. Everitt cross; Charles Herbert, reg. 1979.


```
          -lacteum 1/2
ROBERT KEIR-     -fortunei 1/4
         -Luscombei-
                  -thomsonii 1/4
```
5ft(1.5m) -5F(-21C) E   Flowers pale yellow, flushed pale pink
in throat and dark pink outside.   Stevenson, 1951.   A.M. 1957.

ROBERT LOHR BLOUGH---BOSLEY DEXTER 1005 F2--unknown
Sparkling pink flowers with yellow centers and wavy lobes. Hardy
to -25F(-32C). R. L. Blough.


```
               -haematodes 1/4
          -May Day-
ROBERT LOUIS-     -griersonianum 1/4
 STEVENSON -      -dichroanthum 1/4
     -      -                 -griffithianum 1/32
         -Jester-        -Kewense-
          -     -Aurora-        -fortunei
         -Naomi-      -thomsonii 1/16
                 -fortunei 5/32
```
2ft(.6m) OF(-18C) L 4/4   Plant habit open; leaves small, dark
green, very shiny, grooved at veins. Small, blood red flowers,
funnel-campanulate; loose trusses. Blooms later than most reds.
Cecil S. Seabrook, 1967.


```
          -calostrotum ssp. keleticum 1/2
ROBERT SELEGER-
          -unknown 1/2
```
1ft(.3m) -5F(-21C) EM 3/3   Low habit with tiny leaves, like
keleticum. Plant covered with rose purple flowers.   D. Hobbie.

ROBERT VERNE   Described under SIGRID, q.v.

ROBERT WELDON   Described under CUMULUS, q.v.


```
                -mauve seedling--unknown 1/4
          -A. Bedford-
          -          -ponticum 1/4
ROBERTA GAUVREAU-
          -              -griffithianum 1/8
          -         -Mars-
          -unnamed hybrid-  -unknown    -catawbiense 1/8
                     -Catawbiense Album-
                                 -unknown 1/4
```
39in(1m) x 39in(c.12yrs) ML Openly funnel-shaped flowers, of 5
wavy lobes, strong purplish red aging paler pink, blotch of medium purplish red; spherical truss of 12-16. Upright, semi-open
plant; dull green, elliptic foliage. L. Yavorsky, reg. 1987.

ROBERTE   Described under LADY BESSBOROUGH, q.v.


```
* * * * * * * * * * * * * * * * * * * * * * * * * * * * *
          -calophytum 1/2
ROBIN HOOD-
          -sutchenense 1/2
```
A parent of CAROL JEAN, SPELLBINDER. J. C. Williams, 1933.
ASSAYE   Parentage as above
White flowers, flushed pale magenta, ruby red blotch; big, heavy
trusses of 22.   J. C. Williams, reg. 1963.   A.M. 1963.
```
* * * * * * * * * * * * * * * * * * * * * * * * * * * * *
```


ROBIN LEACH   Described under APPLAUSE, q.v.

ROBINETTE   Parentage unknown
3ft(.9m) -5F(-21C) EM Rose-colored flowers with large colored
calyx. Attractive foliage; good habit, growing wider than tall.
Possibly James Elliott cross.


```
                -fortunei ssp. discolor Houlstonii Group 1/2
ROBIN REDBREAST-
                -orbiculare 1/2
```
4ft(1.2m) -5F(-21C) M   Scarlet buds open to rosy pink bells.
Foliage somewhat rounded.   Williams, 1933.


```
* * * * * * * * * * * * * * * * * * * * * * * * * * * * *
          -Marion--unknown 1/2
ROBYN (Cheal)-           -fortunei--Sir Charles Butler 1/4
          -Van Nes Sensation-  -maximum 1/8
                         -Halopeanum-
                                 -griffithianum 1/8
```
5ft(1.5m) -5F(-21C) EM Large, deep lilac flower; bushy habit.
One of the better Boulter hybrids distributed in Australia.
MELBA   Parentage as above
Pale pink flowers and curled foliage.   Boulter, 1972.
WINTER BEAUTY   Parentage as above
Bright mauve flowers with small buff yellow blotch. Boulter.
YOU BEAUT   Parentage as above
Deep lilac pink flower and vigorous grower. Boulter, c. 1972.
```
* * * * * * * * * * * * * * * * * * * * * * * * * * * * *
```


ROC   Described under FELICITY MAGOR, q.v.


```
                -griffithianum 1/4
          -Dorothea-
ROCHELLE-         -decorum 1/4
        -            -catawbiense 1/4
          -Kettledrum-
                  -unknown 1/4
```
4.5ft(1.35m) -10F(-23C) ML 4/4   Slightly fragrant flowers,
4in(10.2cm) across, rose-colored with a strawberry red blotch,
velvet-textured; 7-flowered trusses of unusual beauty.   G. Guy
Nearing, reg. 1970.   Color illus. HG p. 136; LW pl. 60.


```
                  -Pygmalion--unknown 1/8
          -unnamed hybrid-
          -Weldy-           -haematodes 1/8
ROCK OF AGES-     -yakushimanum, Exbury form 1/4
          -                 -maximum 1/4
          -Stokes Bronze Wings-
                         -catawbiense 1/4
```
Buds of strong reddish purple and phlox purple, open to frilled
flowers of pale purple, with a flare of beetroot purple; a white
throat; W. Delp.

ROCK ROSE--form of racemosum R 59578
Axillary flowers form a many-flowered raceme; color roseine purple fading to white in the throat, some greenish red and scarlet
spotting. Leaves aromatic, 1in(2.5cm) across.   J. B. Stevenson, reg. 1970.   A.M. 1970.

ROCK SOLID   Described under RED DOG, q.v.


```
          -meddianum 1/2
ROCKET-
       -strigillosum 1/2
```
Bell-shaped flowers, glowing blood red, in flat-topped trusses.
Early season. J. B. Stevenson, Tower Court. A.M. 1954.

ROCKET (Shammarello)   Described under CHEER, q.v.

```
                    -caucasicum 1/4
            -Dr. Stocker-
ROCKETFIRE-         -griffithianum 1/4
    -          -wardii 1/4
      -Hawk-          -fortunei ssp. discolor 1/8
            -Lady   -
              Bessborough-campylocarpum Elatum Group 1/8
```
Flowers sulphur yellow, in midseason. Dwarfish plant; leaves to
5.5in(14cm) long, dark green.   R. & L. Henny, reg. 1965.

* *

```
              -wardii 1/4
        -Crest-          -fortunei ssp. discolor 1/16
        -    -Lady   -
        -      Bessborough-campylocarpum Elatum Group 1/16
    -Yellow -        -wardii         -griffithianum
    - Rolls -   -Ideal-        -Kewense-          1/16
    - Royce-   - -ist-   -Aurora-     -fortunei 1/32
    -      -     -Naomi-   -thomsonii 1/32
    -    -Odee -        -fortunei
    -    Wright-                -griffithanum
    -      -         -Mrs.   -George-
ROCKHILL-      -      - Lindsay- Hardy-catawbiense
 IVORY -       -      - Smith -        1/64
 RUFFLES-      -Mrs. Betty-    -Duchess of Edinburgh
    -          Robertson-      --unknown 1/16
    -                -campylocarpum 1/32
    -              -unnamed-
    -              hybrid-unknown
    -        -fortunei 15/64
    -    -Fawn-    -dichroanthum 1/16
    -    -  -Fabia-
    -    -        -griersonianum 1/8
    -Skipper-      -griersonianum
    -    -Sarita-    -griffithianum
    -    - Loder-Loderi-
      -Penny-          -fortunei
        -        -wardii      -griffith...
        -Idealist-        -Kewense-
        -        -Aurora-    -fortunei
            -Naomi-      -thomsonii
                -fortunei
```
5ft(1.5m) 10F(-12C) E   Flowers 5in(12.7cm) across with 7 wavy
lobes, throat primrose yellow shading outward to yellowish white
with Turkey red spotting; truss 9in(23cm) across, of 15. Plant
broad, branching well, 3/4 as wide as tall; ivy green leaves retained 3 years.   James C. Brotherton, reg. 1983.
ROCKHILL PARKAY   Parentage as above
5ft(1.5m) 10F(-12C) E   Flowers 4.5in(11.5cm) across, 6-lobed,
sulphur yellow in throat, shading to creamy white, with a Turkey
red eye, in ball-shaped trusses of 15-17. Plant habit as above;
parsley green leaves.   Brotherton, reg. 1983.
ROCKHILL SUNDAY SUNRISE   Parentage as above
5ft(1.5m) 10F(-12C) E   Flowers 5in(12.7cm) across, 5-lobed,
primrose yellow with red blotch in throat. Upright plant with
stiff branches; ivy green leaves held 3 years. Brotherton, reg.
1983.
* *

```
        -maximum--Mt. Mitchell F2--Ruddy Red Max 1/2
ROCKY ROAD-          -yakushimanum 1/4
        -unnamed hybrid-
            -aureum (chrysanthum) 1/4
```
Deep red and ruby red buds, opening to pale purplish pink flower
edged strong purplish red; dorsal spots yellow green.   W. Delp.


```
        -catawbiense var. album Glass--Catalgla 1/2
ROCKY WHITE-
        -fortunei 1/2
```
5ft(1.5m) -10F(-23C) M   Fragrant white flowers without marks;
light lavender on opening; new growth copper color. C. Herbert.

ROCOCO   Described under BEAUFORT, q.v.

```
            -griffithianum 1/8
        -George Hardy-
    -Mrs. L. A. Dunnett-     -catawbiense 1/8
RODEO-          -unknown 1/4
    -griersonianum 1/2
```
6ft(1.8m) OF(-18C) ML   Parent of MERRY LASS. Red flower with
an orange flush.   Popular in Australia. M. Koster, 1958.


```
            -sanguineum ssp. didymum 1/2
RÖDHÄTTE-
        -williamsianum 1/2
```
3ft(.9m) -5F(-21C) ML 3/3   Blood red to deep rose flowers,
openly campanulate, suggesting elfin hats. Nice plant habit and
foliage.   Herbst, cross 1970.   Color illus. WS, 1989, p. 28.

ROGER CASH   Described under MARGARET EINARSON, q.v.

```
                -catawbiense 1/8
            -Parsons Grandiflorum-
    -Nova Zembla-          -unknown 5/8
ROLAND-     -hardy red hybrid--unknown
    -          -ponticum 1/4
    -Purple Splendour-
              -unknown
```
Flowers in trusses of 18-21, moderate purplish red with dark red
spotting. Rather glossy dark green leaves.   H. Hachmann, cross
1967; G. Stück, reg. 1984.

ROLAND COOPER--form of campanulatum
Leaves 6in(15.2cm) long, covered below with brown indumentum.
Flowers fragrant, white, spotted with crimson, held in trusses
of about 11.   R. E. Cooper collector; RBG, Edinburgh, raiser;
reg. 1965.   A.M. 1964.

```
        -yakushimanum 1/2
ROLY BARNSLEY-
        -rex 1/2
```
1ft(.3m) tall x 3ft(.9m)(13 yrs) -15F(-26C) M Flowers funnel-
shaped, 5-6 lobes of heavy substance, 2.5in(6.4cm) across, white
with medium ruby red flare, darker spotting on dorsal lobe; flat
truss of 13. Elliptic, concave leaves to 5in(12.7cm), felt-like
hairs below, white to fawn; held 3 years.   Behring, reg. 1989.

ROMA SUN   Described under MARY MAYO, q.v.

ROMALA   See under BARCLAYI, q.v.

ROMAN POTTERY   Described under FABIA, q.v.

```
        -elliottii 1/2
ROMANCE-          -facetum (eriogynum) 1/4
        -Jacquetta-
              -griersonianum 1/4
```
Leaves 9in(23cm) x 3in(7.6cm), with woolly beige indumentum be-
neath. Tight trusses of 12-14 flowers, each 3in(7.6cm) wide, of
geranium red, darker at the base, speckled cardinal red inside.
Lord Aberconway.   A.M. 1966.

* *
        -Moser's Maroon--unknown 1/2
ROMANY CHAL -
(GYPSY GIRL)-facetum (eriogynum) 1/2
6ft(1.8m) 5F(-15C) L 3/3   Upright, vigorous, tall plant; dark
green, recurved leaves to 6.5in(16.5cm) long, slight indumentum.
Bell-shaped flower of a rich, true, glowing red, faintly spotted
brown; very large round truss. Needs shade. Rothschild. A.M.
1932. F.C.C. 1937. Color illus. VV p. 58.
FARALL   Parentage as above
6ft(1.8m) 5F(-15C) ML 3/3   Selection by Haworth Booth, 1954.
* *

* *
        -Moser's Maroon--unknown 1/2
ROMANY CHI (GYPSY CHILDREN)-
            -griersonianum 1/2
5ft(1.5m) OF(-18C) ML   Upright, rather open plant, with large
dark green leaves. Flower of rich terracotta speckled brown, in
substantial trusses. Heat-tolerant. Rothschild.   A.M. 1932.
EMPIRE DAY   Parentage as above
Color red, otherwise similar to above. Knap Hill.   A.M. 1932.
* *

```
            -griffithianum 1/4
        -Loderi King George-
ROMA SUN-          -fortunei 1/4
        -Ostbo Y3--unknown 1/2
```
6ft(1.8m) OF(-18C) M   Leaves quite large; flowers large, ruf-
fled, fragrant, and yellowish pink. Edges deeper pink. Bovee,
reg. 1976.

```
                    -griersonianum 1/2
ROMANY RYE-         -souliei 1/4
          -Souldis-
                    -fortunei ssp. discolor 1/4
Trusses of deep blue, holding 9 flowers, each 4.5in(11.5cm)
wide and 3in(7.6cm) long.   Gen. Harrison, reg. 1962.


              -kyawii 1/2
ROMAREZ-
          -griersonianum 1/2
Late-blooming, dark red flowers.   J. B. Stevenson, cross 1932;
intro. 1953.  A.M. 1953.


                                      -arboreum 1/16
                    -Glory of Penjerrick-
          -Romala-                    -griffithianum 1/16
     -Coer-          -thomsonii 1/8
ROMARI-   -arboreum ssp. delavayi var. delavayi 1/4
          -meddianum 1/2
Red flowers.   J. B. Stevenson, cross 1939.


ROMBERGPARK   Described under RONSDORFER FRUHBLÜHENDE


                         -catawbiense 3/8
          -red catawbiense hybrid-
     -                   -unknown 5/8
ROMEO-                             -catawbiense
     -          -Parsons Grandiflorum-
     -America-                     -unknown
          -dark red hybrid--unknown
6ft(1.8m)  -20F(-29C)  ML  3/3   Tall, vigorous, shapely plant;
leathery dark leaves, 4in(10.2cm) long.  Flowers blood red with
darker blotch, funnel-shaped, 2.5in(5cm) across; globular truss-
es.  A. M. Shammarello, reg. 1972.


               -wardii (L and S 5679) 1/4
          -Inamorata-
ROMY-               -fortunei ssp. discolor 1/4
     -Mrs. J. G. Millais--unknown 1/2
6ft(1.8m) -5F(-21C)  L   Compact plant, spreading broader than
tall, very free-flowering with 13 per truss, primrose yellow.
E. G. Millais, reg. 1974.  H.C. 1974.
HIGH SUMMER   Parentage as above or reversed
Trusses of 8-10 flowers, very light yellow, shading to citrus
yellow in center.  E. G. Millais Nurseries, reg. 1981.  A.M.
Wisley Trials 1989.


RON LANGDON   Described under GLEN BRUCE, q.v.


                    -arboreum 1/4
          -Cornubia-            -thomsonii 1/8
RONA-          -Shilsonii-
     -                   -barbatum
     -barbatum 5/8
Deep red flowers.  Lord Aberconway, 1946.


                    -arboreum 1/4
          -Cornubia-            -thomsonii 3/8
RONA -         -Shilsonii-
MARTIN-             -barbatum 3/8
     -           -thomsonii
     -Shilsonii-
               -barbatum
Fine trusses of dark red flowers, medium-sized, in March.   Sir
James Horlick, Isle of Gigha, reg. 1962.


RONA PINK   Parentage unknown
5ft(1.5m) -5F(-21C)  E   Beautiful pink flowers.   Dexter cross;
Koenig intro.


          -hodgsonii 1/2
RONALD-
          -sinogrande 1/2
Heavy trusses of 30 flowers, white stained pink, with some vari-
able darker shading on the reverse.  The Gibsons, Glenarn, reg.
1958.  A.M. 1958.
```

```
* * * * * * * * * * * * * * * * * * * * * * * * * * * * *
               -Blue Peter--unknown 3/4
RONKONKOMA-               -ponticum 1/4
          -Purple Splendour-
                         -unknown
3ft(.9m)  -10F(-23C)  ML  Plant rounded, almost as wide as high;
leaves held 3 years.  Dark violet purple buds  open to  amethyst
violet  flowers,  darker edges and reverse,  3in(7.6cm)  across,
frilly, 5-lobed; spherical truss of 22.  A. Raustein, reg. 1977.
BLUE CROWN   Parentage as above, except reversed
Trusses of 20 flowers, spectrum violet, lighter center, blotched
medium grayed purple.  K. Van de Ven, reg. 1981.
BUMBLEBEE   Parentage as above, except reversed
Truss of 25-27 flowers, 5-lobed, phlox purple, large eye, maroon
and black, in center of dorsal lobe.  Ovate leaves, dark glossy
green.  Shrub 8.5ft(2.5m) in 20 years.   H. W. King, reg. 1984.
* * * * * * * * * * * * * * * * * * * * * * * * * * * * *


* * * * * * * * * * * * * * * * * * * * * * * * * * * * *
                         -oreodoxa 1/2
RONSDORFER FRÜHBLÜHENDE-        -arboreum 1/4
                    -Doncaster-
                              -unknown 1/4
Flowers rose to purple.  G. Arends, reg. 1958.
ROMBERGPARK   Parentage as above
Good habit with flowers of broad funnel-form, white outside,
pink toward base.  Early.  A. Arends cross; Böhlje, reg. 1969.
WESTFALENPARK   Parentage as above
Trusses of 15 broadly funnel-shaped flowers 5-7-lobed, deep pink
with brown throat markings.  G. Arends cross; Böhlje, reg. 1969.
* * * * * * * * * * * * * * * * * * * * * * * * * * * * *


               -griffithianum 1/2
     -Loderi-
ROSA BONHEUR-    -fortunei 1/4
     -               -thomsonii 1/4
     -Cornish Cross-
                    -griffithianum
Deep pink flowers.  Loder.


                         -Queen      -griffithianum 1/16
                    -Britannia-Wilhelmina-
          -Kluis Triumph-      -          -unknown 7/16
     -              -unknown  -Stanley Davies--unknown
ROSA PERLE-
          -makinoi 1/2
4ft(1.2m) -15F(-26C) ML   Flowers deep pink in small trusses.
Compact habit.  J. Bruns, reg. 1972.  Gold Medal, 1981.  Color
illus. WS, 1989, p. 83.


               -griffithianum 1/4
     -Pink Shell-          -fortunei 1/8
ROSABEL-    -H. M. Arderne-
     -               -unknown 1/8
     -griersonianum 1/2
Large, loose trusses of trumpet-shaped flowers, rose red in bud,
opening pale pink with darker veining, pale salmon pink with  a
dark eye when fully open.  A. Waterer, 1865.  A.M. 1936.


ROSALEA   Parentage unknown
5ft(1.5m)  5F(-21C)  E   Large flowers, light red, pale center.
Leaves held one year.   V. Boulter, before 1984.


          -yakushimanum 1/2
ROSALIE HALL-       -strigillosum 1/4
               -Double Winner-
                         -unknown 1/4
2ft(.6m) x 2ft  5F(-15C)  EM  Flowers widely funnel-campanulate,
19 per truss; 8 rose red, wavy lobes, fading to Neyron rose;
short, strong red rays in throat; reverse Neyron rose.  Dark
green, obovate leaves; heavy brown-orange indumentum.  Grayish
yellow-green new growth.   E. Newcomb cross; H. Hall, reg. 1988.


          -oreodoxa var. fargesii 1/2
ROSALIND-
          -thomsonii 1/2
Flowers of rose pink.  Lord Aberconway.  A.M. 1938.


                    -neriiflorum ssp. neriiflorum (phoenicodum) 1/2
ROSALIND OF ARDEN-
               -williamsianum 1/2
Flowers deep rose red.  Thacker, 1946.
```

```
                    -arboreum 1/4
            -Cornubia-          -thomsonii 1/8
            -      -Shilsonii-
ROSAMOND-                       -barbatum 1/8
        -       -griffithianum 1/4
            -Loderi-
                    -fortunei 1/4
Clear pink flowers.  Loder, 1934.
```

```
                        -griffithianum 1/4
                -George Hardy-
ROSAMUND MILLAIS-               -catawbiense 1/4
                -              -arboreum 1/4
                -Doncaster-
                        -unknown 1/4
Cerise, blotched purple.  M. Koster, 1922.  A.M. 1933.
```

```
            -caucasicum 1/2
ROSAMUNDII-
            -unknown 1/2
```
4ft(1.2m) -5F(-21C) VE 2/3   Often compared to CHRISTMAS
CHEER, this one blooms later, with pinker flowers and smoother
leaves. Blooming in March, the compact plant seems to be covered with rosy snowballs. Standish & Noble, mid-1800s. Color
illus. VV p. 130.

```
                    -griersonianum 1/4
        -Laura Aberconway-         -thomsonii 1/8
        -              -Barclayi-            -arboreum 1/16
ROSANITA-                     -Glory of  -
                             Penjerrick-griffithianum 1/16
        -yakushimanum 1/2
```
Trusses of 12 flowers, 5-lobed, light Neyron rose with a deeper
stripe down center of each lobe. Narrow leaves 5.5in(14cm) long
with woolly indumentum beneath. J. F. J. McQuire, reg. 1983.

```
            -Pygmalion--unknown 1/2
ROSE BARBARA-
            -yakushimanum 1/2
```
2.25ft(.68m) x 3.5ft(1m)(20 yrs) -25F(-32C) ML Buds of vivid
red open deep pink, with prominent purplish red dorsal spotting.
Domed trusses of 14 flowers. Dense habit; elliptic leaves with
slight plastered whitish indumentum. W. Fetterhoff, reg. 1989.

ROSE BAY--synonym maximum (not a selected form)

```
            -thomsonii 1/2
ROSE BEAUTY-
            -unknown 1/2
```
Flowers rosy pink with a few markings on upper lobe. R. Gill.

```
        -decorum 1/2
ROSE DU-        -maximum 1/4                -catawbiense
 BARRI -Standishii-           -unnamed hybrid-      1/16
            -Altaclerense-                -ponticum 1/16
                        -arboreum 1/8
```
Rose-colored flowers. Loder.

* *
```
        -racemosum 1/2
ROSE ELF-
        -pemakoense 1/2
```
1.5ft(.45m) 5F(-15C) E 3/4 White flowers blushed pink, campanulate. Plant compact, spreading; small, glossy, dark green
leaves. Floriferous; sun-tolerant.   B. Lancaster. P.A. 1954.
Color illus. VV p. 70.
LOIS   Parentage as above, except reversed
1.5ft(.45m) -5F(-21C) E 3/4 Flowers of soft purplish pink in
a profusion of terminal clusters. Well-branched plant, broader
than tall. H. E. Greer, intro. 1962; reg. 1980.
PERA   Parentage: pemakoense x racemosum
1ft(.3m) -5F(-21C) E 3/3   Prolific blooms of lilac pink, in
flat-topped trusses of 6. Vigorous plant. H. Lem, reg. 1958.
* *

```
                        -smirnowii 1/8
            -Goody Goody-
-unnamed-           -catawbiense 5/32
- hybrid- -yakushimanum 1/8    -fortunei ssp. discolor
-      -Si-          -Lady Bess--              3/64
-      Si-    -Day  - borough -campylocarpum Elatum Gp
-        -Gold-Dream-griersonianum            1/64
-          Mohur-            -fortunei ssp. discolor
ROSE -           -Margaret Dunn-   -dichroanthum 1/64
FANTASY-               -Fabia-
-                              -griersonianum 7/64
-                         -Queen Wil--griffithianum
-                -Britan-- helmina  -      3/64
-          -C.P.  - nia -         -unknown
-   -Anne Hard-Raffill-      -Stanley Davies--unknown.
-    - grove  -       -griersonianum
-unn.-     -Moser's Maroon--unknown 19/64
 hyb.-                    -catawbiense
-            -Parsons Grandiflorum-
-     -America-             -unknown
-Cindy-     -dark red hybrid--unknown
 Lou -          -griffithianum
-         -Mars-
-unnamed hybrid-    -unknown
                -catawbiense var. rubrum 1/16
```
Buds of moderate purplish red open to flowers of Tyrian purple,
rose Bengal, and vivid purplish red. W. Delp.

```
            -fortunei 1/2
ROSE HAINES-
            -unknown 1/2
```
5ft(1.5m) 0F(-18C) M   Flowers of heavy substance, 5-lobed,
frilled, cyclamen purple with sap green throat; in trusses of 9-
11. Upright plant, broader than tall, with dark green leaves.
C. English Jr. cross; C. R. Burlingame, intro. 1967; reg. 1977.

```
            -yakushimanum--Koichiro Wada 1/2
ROSE IMP-
            -unknown 1/2
```
Trusses of 12 flowers, light purplish pink with red flare in up-
per throat. Light tan indumentum on new foliage. Plant 1.7ft.
(.5m) at 10 years. Pukeiti Rhododendron Trust, reg. 1984.

* *
```
                -griersonianum 1/4
        -Tally Ho-
ROSE LANCASTER-        -facetum (eriogynum) 1/4
        -yakushimanum 1/2
```
4ft(1.2m) 5F(-15C) ML   Crimson buds, Neyron rose flowers of
heavy substance, 3in(7.6cm) across; ball-shaped trusses hold 18-
30. Plant rounded; leaves dark green with heavy tan indumentum.
B. Lancaster, cross 1962; Dr. David Goheen, reg. 1978.
TAKU   Parentage as above
4ft(1.2m) -5F(-21C) ML   Deep pink buds open medium pink, fade
to almost white. Much indumentum. G. Clark, intro. pre-1982.
* *

ROSE MANGLES   Described under ROYAL FLUSH, q.v.

```
            -griffithianum 1/2
ROSE NEWCOMB-
            -unknown 1/2
```
Flowers white with pink edges.   Mangles.

* *
```
                -griersonianum 1/4
        -Tally Ho-
ROSE OF CHINA-        -facetum (eriogynum) 1/4
        -fortunei ssp. discolor 1/2
```
4ft(1.2m) 0F(-18C) L 3/3 Plant upright, rounded; leaves 7in.
(17.8cm) long. Flowers clear China rose, campanulate, 4in(10cm)
wide, in trusses of 10-12. Sun-tolerant.   F. Rose cross; Lem
raiser; B. Lancaster intro.; reg. 1958.
BENGAL ROSE   Parentage as above
Flowers Bengal rose open bell-shaped, 4in(10cm) across, 12-15 in
upright truss. Vigorous, upright plant.   Lancaster, reg. 1963.
* *

```
                -fortunei ssp. discolor 1/2
ROSE PAGEANT-
            -Corona--unknown 1/2
```
6ft(1.8m) -5F(-21C) VL   Full, upright trusses of 12 flowers,

5-lobed, deep Neyron rose with white throat. Leaves 9in(23cm)
long.   Rudolph & Leona Henny, reg. 1965.

ROSE PANTALOONS   Described under RED PANTALOONS, q.v.

ROSE PERFECTION   Parentage unknown
A parent of SIDONA.   Deep red buds open clear pink.   R. Gill.

ROSE POINT   Described under BRICKDUST, q.v.

ROSE QUEEN   Parentage unknown
Flowers rose pink, tinged orange at base. Origin unknown. A.M.
1904.

ROSE RED   Parentage unknown
A parent of JACK LYONS.

```
                  -ciliicalyx 1/4
          -Else Frye
ROSE SCOTT-      -unknown 1/4
        -              -johnstoneanum 1/4
          -unnamed hybrid-
                          -veitchianum Cubittii Group 1/4
```
4ft(1.2m) E   Well-branched bush; glossy dark leaves, bullate,
3.5in(8.9cm) long.   White flowers blotched and marked in shades
of pink, 4.25in(10.8cm) wide, fragrant; trusses of 3-7. Floriferous. R. W. Scott, reg. 1977.

```
                -griersonianum 1/2
ROSE SPLENDOUR-          -ponticum 1/4
            -Purple Splendour-
                        -unknown 1/4
```
4ft(1.2m) OF(-18C) ML 4/3   Compact, upright, rounded plant;
dark green leaves with slight indumentum.   Flowers magenta rose
with eye of geranium lake, campanulate, 4in(10cm) wide; rounded
truss of 12. Sun-tolerant.   Lancaster, reg. 1958.

ROSEALIND   See ROSEALIND SLINGER

ROSEALIND SLINGER   Parentage unknown
Truss of 3-6 flowers, conical-campanulate, of 5 spreading lobes,
vivid purplish red in bud, opening strong purplish pink, outside
deeper; dark spotting. Very compact plant 4ft(1.2m) x 4ft. Elliptic leaf. Slieve Donard Nurs. intro.; E. Nelson, reg. 1987.

* *
```
                  -griffithianum 3/8
        -Loderi Venus-
        -               -fortunei 1/4
ROSEANN-                     -griffithianum
        -             -Queen Wilhelmina-
        -Britannia-           -unknown 3/8
                  -Stanley Davies--unknown
```
5ft(1.5m) 5F(-15C) M 4/4   Flowers 4.5in(11.5cm) across, me-
dium rose pink, lightly marked in throat; leaves 8.5in(21.6cm)
long, red petioles. Rudolph Henny, reg. 1958.   P.A. 1956.
EVELYN   Parentage as above, except reversed
Flowers blush pink and white. R. Henny, intro. 1956.
* *

ROSEBIRD--form of russatum
Known in New Zealand as russatum roseum. Trusses of 15-25 funnel-shaped flowers of deep purplish pink. Compact bush, 2.5ft.
(.75m) tall at registration; elliptic, scaly foliage. Dunedin
Rhododendron Group, reg. 1985.

ROSEBUD   See JANE HENNY

```
                    -thomsonii 1/8
              -Shilsonii-
        -Bella-        -barbatum 1/8
ROSEFINCH-    -griffithianum 1/4
        -griersonianum 1/2
```
Deep rose red, with bluish tinge. Lord Aberconway. A.M. 1938.

```
                -orbiculare 1/2
ROSEMARY CHIPP-   -griffithianum 1/4
            -Loderi-
                  -fortunei 1/4
```
Pale rose pink flowers. RBG, Kew. A.M. 1928.

```
                      -facetum (eriogynum) 3/4
ROSENKAVALIER-        -griersonianum 1/4
            -Tally Ho-
                  -facetum (eriogynum)
```
5ft(1.5m) 10F(-12C) L   Trusses of 15 flowers, scarlet with red
spotting on upper lobes, 4in(10cm) across. Leaves have fawn indumentum beneath. Needs partial shade.   Grown in New Zealand.
RHS Garden, Wisley, reg. 1961.   A.M. 1959.

ROSENOBLE--form of arboreum ssp. cinnamomeum var. roseum
Loose, rounded trusses of 16-18 flowers, 5-lobed, tubular-
campanulate, light roseine purple with darker veining. Leaves
to 8in(20.3cm); gray plastered indumentum.   Gill intro. 1910;
The Hon. H. E. Boscawen exhibited; reg. 1974. A.M. 1973.

```
                -catawbiense 1/2
ROSEUM ELEGANS-
                -unknown 1/2
```
6ft(1.8m) -25F(-32C) ML 2/4   A vigorous, fast-growing plant
with good foliage.   Flowers rose lilac, rather small, in dome-
shaped trusses. A very popular variety with many Eastern U.S.A.
nurserymen and landscapers. See also ENGLISH ROSEUM.   A. Waterer, before 1851.   Color ill. VV p. 105.

ROSEUM PINK   See ENGLISH ROSEUM

```
                -catawbiense 1/2
ROSEUM SUPERBUM-
                -unknown 1/2
```
6ft(1.8m) -20F(-29C) ML 2/3   Similar to ROSEUM ELEGANS, but
pinker flowers of purplish rose, on a full plant.   A. Waterer,
before 1865.   Color illus. VV p. 81.

ROSEVALLON--form of neriiflorum
2ft(.6m) 5F(-15C) EM   Bright red flowers on a plant with the
habit and leaf shape of neriiflorum, but has a striking purplish
red underleaf.   Selfed seed has reproduced this characteristic,
although plant registered as a hybrid of neriiflorum by Caerhays
Castle, Cornwall.   Crown Estate, Windsor, exhibitor; reg.
1975. A.M. 1975.

ROSEY BALL--form of rubiginosum
6ft(1.8m) -5F(-21C) EM   Flowers 5-lobed, 1.1in(3cm) wide,
strong purplish pink with red spots; spherical inflorescences of
several trusses of 6-8 flowers each. Plant upright, rather leggy; glossy olive green leaves, scaly beneath, held 2 years.   J.
Rock collector; Phetteplace raiser; reg. 1974.

```
        -decorum 1/2
ROSINA-            -wardii 1/4
LUKACH-    -Prelude-
      -unnamed-      -fortunei 1/8
        hybrid-   -wardii
            -Crest-      -fortunei ssp. discolor 1/16
                -Lady    -
              Bessborough-campylocarpum Elatum Group 1/16
```
3ft(.9m) OF(-18C) M Funnel-shaped flowers 2in(5cm) across, 5-
lobed, fragrant, primrose yellow, in truss of 8.   Upright plant,
nearly as broad as high; glossy yellow-green leaves 5.5in(14cm)
long, held 2 years.   Alfred A. Raustein, 1972; reg. 1983.

```
                  -catawbiense 1/2
      -Purpureum Elegans-
ROSLYN-              -unknown 1/2
      -          -catawbiense
      -Everestianum-
                  -unknown
```
6ft(1.8m) -10F(-23C) ML 4/3   Ruffled flowers, purplish vio-
let with paler center, 2.25in(6.4cm) wide, 5-lobed; about 12 per
spherical truss. Compact plant; dark green leaves held 2 years.
P. Vossburg, reg. 1972. A.E. 1973.

ROSS BIGLER   Parentage includes catawbiense, maximum
                and perhaps unknown hybrids.
6ft(1.8m) -15F(-26C) M   Flowers deep purplish pink with red-
purple blotch and edging, to 2.5in(6.4cm) across; trusses of 19.
Plant rounded, as wide as tall; leaves 4.5in(11.5cm) long, dull
olive green, held 2 years.   W. David Smith, reg. 1979.

ROSS L.   Parentage unknown
5ft(1.5m) -15F(-26C) E   Flowers brilliant pink, speckled with
dark red. Large foliage on plant of good habit.   Dexter cross.

Color illus. ARS J 43:4 (1989), p. 207.

```
                    -elliottii 1/4
            -Fusilier-
ROSS MAUD-        -griersonianum 1/4
        -        -campylocarpum 1/4
            -Unique-
                -unknown 1/4
Bright Neyron rose flowers.    A. Bramley, AUS, reg. 1975.
```

```
                        -catawbiense 1/4
                    -Omega-
            -unnamed hybrid-      -rose-colored hybrid--unknown 3/4
ROSSELLINI-         -                -catawbiense
        -            -Roseum Elegans-
            -Furnivall's            -unknown
            Daughter--unknown (may be Mrs. Furnivall, selfed)
```
4.7ft(1.4m) x 5ft(1.5m) -15F(-26C) ML   Flowers strong fuchsia
purple, shading roseine to white in throat, dorsal markings lettuce green, 3in(7.5cm) wide; compact truss of 13-16. Leaves recurved, almost ovate.   Hachmann, cross 1973; Stück, reg. 1988.

```
            -ciliatum 1/2
ROSY BELL-
            -glaucophyllum 1/2
```
2ft(.6m) -5F(-21C) VE 3/3   Plant of spreading habit, rather
open; pale green leaves, scaly on top, 2.5in(6.4cm) long. Rose
pink, bell-shaped flowers 1.5in(3.8cm) across; small trusses of
4-5. Flaky dark brown bark. Isaac Davies. A.M. 1894.

ROSY DREAM   Described under ANDRÉ, q.v.

```
            -griersonianum 1/2
ROSY FIDO-      -griffithianum 1/4
        -Loderi-
                -fortunei 1/4
Rose-colored flowers.   Sir James Horlick, 1930.
```

ROSY GLOW   Described under OUTLINER, q.v.

```
            -souliei 1/2
ROSY MORN-      -griffithianum 1/4
        -Loderi-
                -fortunei 1/4
```
Rich pink buds opening to pale salmon pink flowers with a darker
eye, saucer-shaped, in rounded trusses. Foliage like souliei.
Late season.   Credited to Rothschild in the Register; H. White,
Sunningdale, raiser. A.M. 1931. Color illus. PB pl. 55.

ROSY QUEEN   Same parentage as ASTEROID, q.v.

ROTHENBURG   Described under CITATION, q.v.

ROTHESAY   Parentage unknown
Flowers white with reverse blush.   R. W. Campbell, reg. 1977.

```
            -orbiculare 1/2
ROTUNDARB-
            -arboreum 1/2
Brilliant carmine, darker at base.   E. J. P. Magor, 1919.
```

```
        -Lowinsky hybrid--unknown 1/2
ROUGE-
        -elliottii 1/2
Very large flowers, very bright crimson, and very late blooming;
tall, tender offspring of elliottii. Rothschild.  A.M. 1950.
```

```
                        -arboreum 1/8
                    -Doncaster-
            -Professor -      -unknown 1/2
            - F. Bettex-          -catawbiense 1/8
ROUGE DE MAI-           -Atrosanguineum-
            -                    -unknown
            -                -caucasicum 1/4
            -Madame Jeanne Frets-
                            -unknown
```
Trusses of 20 flowers, China rose with dark brown blotch, 3.5in.
(8.9cm) wide. D. Hendriksen, reg. 1965. A.M. Boskoop 1961.

ROUGE ET NOIR--form of sperabile var. weihsiense K W 7124
Loose trusses hold 11 flowers, tubular-campanulate, deep crimson
with darker spotting in throat. Foliage has thin, fawn-colored,

woolly indumentum below. Plant 13ft(3.9m) at registration.   S.
R. Clarke raiser; R. N. S. Clarke, reg. 1985.   A.M. 1985.

```
                    -thomsonii 1/8
                -Bagshot Ruby-
        -Princess Elizabeth-      -unknown 9/16
        -                -unknown    -catawbiense
ROUGEMOUNT-         -Parsons Grandiflorum-        1/16
        -        -America-            -unknown
        -        -      -dark red hybrid--unknown
        -Cindy Lou-      -griffithianum 1/8
            -unnamed-      -Mars-
            hybrid-catawbiense var. rubrum 1/8
                        -unknown
```
Very large trusses of rose red. Hardy to -20F(-29C). Plant of
medium height; slightly open; average foliage.   Dr. Tom Ring.

ROUND WOOD--form of lanigerum (silvaticum) K W 6258
4ft(1.2m) 5F(-15C) EM 4/3 Small tree with oblong, lanceolate
leaves, dark green above with whitish indumentum below. Rounded, compact trusses of cherry red flowers. Crown Estate, Windsor, reg. 1951. A.M. 1951.

```
        -Oreoroyle--unknown 1/2
ROVER-          -cinnabarinum 1/4
        -Royal Flush-
                -maddenii 1/4
Flowers rose pink.   Lord Aberconway, 1946.
```

ROWALLAN SURPRISE   Parentage unknown
Flowers of spirea red.   D. Deans, reg. 1982.

```
                    -neriiflorum 1/8
                -Neriihaem-
            -Hebe-      -haematodes 1/8
ROWENA-    -williamsianum 1/4
        -          -griersonianum 1/4
        -Red Dragon-
                -thomsonii 1/4
Loose trusses  of funnel-shaped flowers,  salmon red, 3in(7.6cm)
```
across. Late midseason.   Sir John Ramsden cross; Sir William
Pennington-Ramsden, reg. 1965.

```
        -brachycarpum 1/2
ROWLAND-                    -catawbiense 1/8
P. CARY-          -Atrosanguineum-
        -Van der Hoop-          -unknown
        -                    -arboreum 1/8
                -Doncaster-
                        -unknown 1/4
```
6ft(1.8m) -20F(-29C) L   Buds dark pink, flowers blush pink
with light tan spotting, in spherical trusses of 19-20. Rounded
plant, as broad as tall; dark green leaves with thin brown indumentum; new growth silvery green. E. A. Cary, reg. 1974.

```
        -burmanicum 1/2
ROY HUDSON-
        -nuttallii 1/2
```
5ft(1.5m) 15F(-9C) EM   Well-branched plant; foliage olive
green, very scaly on upper surface, held 2-3 years. Fragrant
flowers, white with saffron yellow throat, 3.5in(8.9cm) wide;
terminal inflorescence of many buds, each 6-8 flowered.   H. W.
Kerrigan, reg. 1978.   Color illus. ARS J 39:3 (1985), p. 122.

```
            -griersonianum 1/4
        -Azor-
        -      -fortunei ssp. discolor 1/2
ROYAL ANNE-          -neriiflorum 1/8
        -          -Nereid-
        -unnamed-      -dichroanthum 1/8
        hybrid-fortunei ssp. discolor
Loose trusses of 8-10 flowers, buttercup yellow suffused vermil-
```
ion, spotted dull sap green.   E. J. Greig, Royston, 1962.

* *
```
                -cinnabarinum Roylei Group 3/4
        -Lady Rosebery-          -cinnabarinum 1/8
ROYAL -          -Royal Flush-
BEAUTY-                -maddenii 1/8
        -cinnabarinum Roylei Group
```
5ft(1.5m) 10F(-12C) 4/3   Flowers in various shades of red.
Lord Digby, intro. 1953.

CERNE   A named selection from above cross.   Lord Digby, 1954.
* *

```
                -elliottii 1/2
ROYAL BLOOD-
                -Rubens--unknown 1/2
```
4ft(1.2m) OF(-18C) L Exceptional truss of 36 flowers, cardi-
nal red with dark blood red spotting.   Francis Hanger, RHS
Garden, Wisley. A.M. 1954.

```
                    -cinnabarinum Roylei Group 1/4
            -Lady    -
            -Rosebery-           -cinnabarinum 1/8
ROYAL BLUSH-        -Royal Flush-
           -                    -maddenii 1/8
                -cinnabarinum Blandfloriiflorum Group 1/2
```
Flowers of crimson and gold.   Adams-Acton, 1935.

```
            -Essex Scarlet--unknown 1/4
         -unnamed-
ROYAL    - hybrid-facetum (eriogynum) 3/8
COACHMAN-              -griersonianum 1/8
         -    -Tally Ho-
         -unnamed-         -facetum (eriogynum)
           hybrid-         -neriiflorum Euchaites Group 1/8
                -Sunshine-
                    -beanianum 1/8
```
5ft(1.5m) 5F(-15C) ML Brilliant red flowers with darker spot-
ting over all petals.   J. Waterer, Sons & Crisp, reg. 1975.

```
            -Helene Schiffner--unknown 1/2
ROYAL DECREE-        -forrestii Repens Group 1/4
            -Elizabeth-
                -griersonianum 1/4
```
3ft(.9m) x 2.7ft(.8m) 10F(-12C) EM Buds strong purplish red;
flower center magenta rose, shading to medium beetroot purple at
rims, dorsal lobe light yellowish gray, edged and spotted moderate brown. Trusses of 15-18. L. Bulgin, cross 1979; reg. 1989.

```
                -facetum (eriogynum) 1/8
           -unnamed-         -dichroanthum 1/4
        -unnamed- hybrid-Fabia-
        - hybrid-              -griersonianum 1/4
        -     -         -haematodes 1/8
ROYAL   -    -May Day-
DRAGOON-         -griersonianum
        -                         -dichroanthum
        -         -Fabia Tangerine-
        -unnamed hybrid-           -griersonianum
                -         -griffithianum 1/8
                -Mars-
                    -unknown 1/8
```
5ft(1.5m) 5F(-15C) M   Dark blood red flowers.   J. Waterer,
Sons & Crisp, reg. 1975.

* *
```
            -cinnabarinum 1/2
ROYAL FLUSH-
            -maddenii 1/2
```
6ft(1.8m) 5F(-15C) M 4/4   Two forms, pink and yellow, both
flowers of heavy substance, tubular-campanulate, on a tall, upright plant, with dark green leaves and clusters of long waxy
trumpets.   Pink form has wide, rather flattened flowers of soft
pink; the yellow opens as champagne, tinged pink, changing to
cream, flushed pale yellow.   J. C. Williams, Caerhays Castle,
1930.   Color illus. ARS J 39:3 (1985), p. 151; HG p. 73.
CINNANDRUM Parents: cinnabarinum Roylei X maddenii (polyandrum)
Apricot and deep rose. Lord Aberconway.   A.M. 1937.
CINNANDRUM TANGERINE   Parentage as above
Deep rose outside; pale apricot within. Lord Aberconway. A.M.
1937.
FULL HOUSE   cinnabarinum Blandfordiiflorum Group x maddenii
Trumpet-shaped flowers, deep pink flushed rose.   G. Johnstone.
HETHERSETT   Parentage as ROYAL FLUSH, above
Trusses of 7 tubular-shaped flowers, sweetly fragrant, primrose
yellow fading to buff; the reverse tinged nasturtium orange. H.
Mangles cross; Mrs. Douglas Gordon, reg. 1962.   A.M. 1962.
ROSE MANGLES   Parentage as ROYAL FLUSH, above
A parent of COCK OF THE ROCK. Flowers rose pink.   Mangles.
SIRIUS Parentage: maddenii ssp. crassum x cinnabarinum Roylei
Bright pink. Reuthe cross; Maj. Hardy exhibitor. P.C. 1973.
* *

```
                                -catawbiense
                -Parsons Grandiflorum-        1/16
        -America-        -unknown 17/32
    -unnamed-        -dark red hybrid--unknown
    - hybrid-         -griffithianum 3/32
    -    -    -Mars-
-Purple-    -Blaze-    -unknown
- Susy -            -catawbiense var. rubrum 1/16
    -    -griffithianum
    -    -Mars-
ROYAL-    -Red  -    -unknown           -catawbiense
JELLY-    Brave-    -Parsons Grandiflorum-
    -    -America-           -unknown
    -         -dark red hybrid--unknown
    -         -catawbiense v. album Glass--Catalgla
    -Ritchie---unnamed  -                      1/4
        hybrid F2-Sappho--unknown
```
Buds of strong and deep purplish red; flowers of imperial purple
and strong reddish purple; flare of Dresden yellow. Dr. T. Ring
cross; W. Delp raiser.

```
            -Moser's Maroon--unknown 1/4
        -Romany Chai-
ROYAL MAIL-        -griersonianum 1/2
        -         -griersonianum
        -Tally Ho-
            -facetum (eriogynum) 1/4
```
A bushy plant with silvery young shoots, and scarlet flowers in
late season.   W. C. Slocock, 1940.

```
                -catawbiense 1/4
        -Catawbiense Boursault-
ROYAL MINT-        -unknown 1/4
        -    -wardii 1/4
        -China-
            -fortunei 1/4
```
4ft(1.2m) x 3ft(.9m)(12 yrs) -15F(-26C) ML Domed truss of 25
openly campanulate flowers 2.7in(7cm) wide, white suffused lilac
and fading pure white. Smooth, oblong leaves, 5.5in(14cm) long;
Bjarke Aunsbjorn cross; Thorvall Aunsbjorn, reg. 1989. (Denmark)

```
            -Kaiser Wilhelm--unknown 1/2
        -Homer-
ROYAL PINK-    -Agnes--unknown
        -williamsianum 1/2
```
3ft(.9m) -15F(-26C) M 4/4   Rounded, vigorous, compact plant;
good foliage of broadly elliptic leaves. Flowers to 3in(7.6cm),
openly funnel-shaped, pale fuchsine pink inside, the exterior of
darker rose. Tight spherical trusses. Dietrich Hobbie cross;
Le Feber reg. 1965.   Silver Medal, Boskoop 1958.   Gold Medal
Rotterdam 1960.   Color illus. HG p. 137.

ROYAL PURPLE (Standish & Noble)   Parentage unknown
5ft(1.5m) -15F(-26C) ML   3/3   Small, violet purple flowers
with an orange-yellow blotch; rounded truss of 12. Impressive,
large bush, well-shaped.   Standish & Noble, c. 1860.

ROYAL PURPLE (Whitney)   Parentage unknown
5ft(1.5m) -15F(-26C) ML 3/4   Attractive, deep shiny green
foliage. Flower rich purple with a bright yellow eye. Whitney.

```
            -Moser's Maroon--unknown
ROYAL STAR-
        -unknown
```
Full, well-rounded trusses of fine deep purple flowers, with a
very dark purple blotch. Plant medium-sized; foliage recurved.
Donald Hardgrove.

ROYAL WINDSOR   Described under ENGLEMERE, q.v.

ROYALE--form of orbiculare
Trusses of 8 flowers, 7-lobed, Persian rose. Leaves orbicular,
glabrous. Tall plant. Lady Adam Gordon, reg. 1983.

```
                -yunnanense 1/4
        -Yunncinn-
ROYALTY-        -cinnabarinum 1/2
        -         -cinnabarinum
        -Royal Flush-
            -maddenii 1/4
```
Loose, pendant trusses hold 4-6 flowers, signal red at base fad-
ing to Neyron rose, orange-red blotch in upper throat. Foliage

elliptic, 2.25in(5.7cm) long, densely covered with brown pitted
indumentum. Lord Aberconway, 1944.   A.M. 1968.

```
            -maddenii 1/2
ROYLMADD-
            -roylei var. magnificum ? 1/2
```
Flowers are carmine lake. E. J. P. Magor, 1920.

ROYSTON FESTIVAL   Described under LEONORE, q.v.

```
            -forrestii Repens Group 1/2
ROYSTON RED-
            -thomsonii 1/2
```
2.5ft(.75m) 0F(-18C) E 4/4   Very attractive bright blood red
flowers, showing color earlier than most "reds".   Harry White
cross; named by Alleyne Cook.

```
                 -auriculatum 1/2
ROYSTON   REVERIE-                    -dichroanthum    1/4
                 -Fabia-
                      -griersonianum 1/4
```
Trusses hold 8 flowers, light yellow with edges of light brick
red. E. J. & Mary Grieg cross; A. R. Cook, reg. 1981.

* *
```
                 -fortunei ssp. discolor 1/4
          -Last Rose-
          -                 -griersonianum 1/8
ROYSTON ROSE-    -Tally Ho-
          -                 -facetum (eriogynum) 1/8
          -auriculatum 1/2
```
Flowers of China rose; trusses of 15.   E. J. & M. Greig cross;
Alleyne R. Cook, reg. 1981.
ROYSTON SUMMERTIME Parentage as above, except reversed
Trusses of 10 white flowers with edges very light Neyron rose, a
flare of grayed red. Greig cross; A. R. Cook, reg. 1981.
* *

ROZA HARRISON   See ROZA STEVENSON

ROZA STEVENSON   Described under BRUNHILDE, q.v.

```
          -wardii 1/2
ROZAMARIE-           -campylocarpum Elatum Group 1/4
          -Penjerrick-
                    -griffithianum 1/4
```
Large loose trusses of bell-shaped flowers, clear yellow, bloom-
ing in midseason. Compact, medium-sized plant, with attractive
foliage. J. B. Stevenson, 1951.

```
                    -arboreum 1/8
          -Glory of Penjerrick-
    -Romala-                -griffithianum 1/8
ROZIE-    -thomsonii 1/4
    -fortunei ssp. discolor 1/2
```
Flowers of deep rose pink. J. B. Stevenson cross, c. 1919.

RUBAIYAT--form of arboreum
6ft(1.8m) 10F(-12C) E 3/4   Trusses 5in(12.7cm) wide, holding
21 bright red flowers which attracted attention to this tender,
tree-like species over 150 years ago; leaves 7in(17.8cm) long by
2in(5cm) wide, glossy, plastered with silvery indumentum below.
Edmund de Rothschild, reg. 1969.   A.M. 1968.

RUBENS   Parentage unknown
3ft(.9m) -5F(-21F) ML 3/2   A parent of ROYAL BLOOD. Flowers
deep rich red with white stamens, dark spotting on upper lobe;
tight, dome-shaped trusses.   Plant broader than tall; foliage
flat, leathery, 5in(12.7cm) long. A. Waterer, before 1865.

RUBESCENS   Parentage unknown
A parent of SIR RICHARD CARTON.   Red flowers.   Unknown origin.

```
                 -arboreum ssp. nilagiricum (kingianum) 1/4
       -Noyo Chief-
RUBICON-          -unknown 3/8
    -            -elliottii 1/4
    -Kilimanjaro-        -Moser's Maroon--unknown
                 -Dusky Maid-
                         -fortunei ssp. discolor 1/8
```
5ft(1.5m) 10F(-12C) EM 5/4   Trusses hold 17 or 18 flowers of
cardinal red, spotted black inside, on the upper lobes.   R. C.

Gordon, NZ, reg. 1979.   Color illus. HG p. 170; Cox pl. 160.

```
                             -catawbiense 1/8
                -Parsons Grandiflorum-
       -Nova Zembla-          -unknown 6/8
       -          -hardy red hybrid--unknown
RUBIKONDA-               -arboreum 1/8
       -          -Doncaster-
       -Thunderstorm-    -unknown
                  -unknown
```
3.7ft(1.1m) x 4.3ft(1.3m) -15F(-26C) ML Funnel-shaped flowers
about 2in(5cm) wide, medium ruby red, tinged vivid red-rose Bengal, 3 dorsal lobes marked dark grayed purple; contrasting white
stamens. Trusses of 12-17. Hachmann cross; Stück, reg. 1988.

```
            -sanguineum ssp. didymum 1/2
RUBINA-     -griersonianum 1/4
      -Tally Ho-
            -facetum (eriogynum) 1/4
```
Low, spreading plant; leaves with fawn indumentum beneath. Dark
red, trumpet-shaped flowers, in late summer.   Crosfield, 1938.

RUBRUM DAVIDIAN--form of augustinii
A form of this species with red flowers; blooms earlier in the
season than the typical species. (See Bean, Trees and Shrubs...
v. 3, p. 603)

```
                 -fortunei 1/2
RUBY F. BOWMAN-       -griffithianum 1/4
             -Lady Bligh-
                     -unknown 1/4
```
5ft(1.5m) -5F(-21C) M 4/4   Long-lasting, large trusses of 15,
rose pink, with flower centers shaded deeper pink, ruby red in
throat. Flat leaves 7in(17.8cm) long. Sun-tolerant.   Dr. Paul
Bowman, 1958.   P.A. 1951.   Color illus. VV p. 59.

```
                 -forrestii Repens Group 1/4
          -Charm-        -thomsonii 1/8
RUBY GEM-    -Shilsonii-
        -               -barbatum 1/8
        -haematodes 1/2
```
Deep red flowers. Lord Aberconway, 1943.

```
                        -sanguineum ssp. didymum 1/8
                   -Carmen-
         -unnamed-     -forrestii Repens Group 1/4
         - hybrid-          -forrestii Repens Group
RUBY HART-     -Elizabeth-
         -               -griersonianum 1/8
         -elliottii 1/2
```
2ft(.6m) 0F(-18C) EM 5/5 Dark red flowers 1.5in(3.8cm) wide,
in lax trusses of 7. Plant as broad as tall; dark green leaves,
gray-brown indumentum.   Whitney, cross c. 1956; Sathers, reg.
1976. A.M. 1988. Color illus. Cox pl. 161; VV p. 48.

```
                              -facetum (eriogynum) 1/8
                    -unnamed-
                    - hybrid-unknown 17/64
         -unnamed-      -dichroanthum 1/8
         - hybrid-Fabia-
     -Dopey-          -griersonianum 1/8
     -    -                -yakushimanum 1/8
     -    -unnamed hybrid-       -dichroanthum
     -              -Fabia Tangerine-
     -                         -griersonianum
     -                              -griffithianum
RUBY ICE-        -Jean Marie de Montague-       7/64
     -  -Fireman Jeff-              -unknown
     -  -    -        -haematodes 1/16
     -  -    -Grosclaude-
     -  -              -facetum (eriogynum)
     -Tom -                  -catawbiense 1/32
     Ring-        -Parsons Grandi-
     M.D.-  -America- florum      -unknown
     -    -unn.-    -dark red hybrid--unknown
     -    -hyb.-        -griffithianum
     -    -   -   -Mars-
     -Anna- -Blaze-      -catawbiense, red form 1/32
     Delp-      -Mars (as above)
     -       -unknown
         -Red Brave-
              -America (as above)
```

Buds of cardinal red opening to vivid red flowers, with dorsal
spots cardinal red; calyx empire rose.   W. Delp.

```
        -griersonianum 1/2
RUDDIGORE
        -arboreum ssp. delavayi var. delavayi 1/2
```
Scarlet flowers. Lord Aberconway, 1948.

RUDDY   Parentage unknown
A parent of RED MILL. Flowers deep red.   Origin unknown.

```
        -Little Red Riding Hood--unknown
RUDOLF FRIML-
        -unknown
```
6ft(1.8m) 5F(-15C) ML Light green, medium-sized leaves. Flowers solferino purple, funnel-shaped, 3.5in(8.9cm) across, held
tight trusses. Seabrook, reg. 1964.

```
            -dichroanthum 1/4
        -Fabia-
RUDOLPH'S ORANGE-     -griersonianum 1/4
        -                -orbiculare 1/4
        -Temple Belle-
                    -williamsianum 1/4
```
4ft(1.2m) OF(-18C) ML 3/3   Plant sturdy, wider than tall;
leaves 2.75in(7cm) long, held one year. Flowers openly campanulate, 2in(5cm) across, light orange shaded pink inside and out;
lax trusses of 6. R. Henny cross; J. F. Caperci, reg. 1977.

```
                            -griffithianum
                -Queen Wilhelmina-      1/8
            -Britannia-        -unknown 3/8
RUDY-LEONA---QUINELLA-     -Stanley Davies--unknown
    (selfed)-     -haematodes 1/4
            -May Day-
                -griersonianum 1/4
```
Broad plant, up to 3ft(.9m) high with leaves 6in x 2.5in (15cm x
6.4cm). Truss holds 6-10 flowers, dark currant red, semi-double
to double. Rudolph & Leona Henny, reg. 1969.

```
            -griersonianum 1/4
        -Azor-
RUDY'S CANDY-     -fortunei ssp. discolor 1/4
        -Corona--unknown 1/4
```
4ft(1.2m) OF(-18C) ML 3/3 Leaves 5.5in(14cm) long. Flower 3
in(7.6cm) wide, two-toned, deep pink outside, 6 or 7 lobes; tall
trusses of 13-17. Rudolph & Leona Henny, reg. 1970.

RUDY'S FAIRY TALE --
                -- See FAIRY TALE (Henny)
RUDY'S FAIRYTALE --

```
            -maximum 1/4
    -unnamed-
    - hybrid-vernicosum (R 18139) 1/4      -griffithianum
    -                    -Geo. Hardy-      1/32
RUFFLED-        -Mrs. Lindsay-     -catawbiense 1/16
 DREAM -        - Smith   -Duchess of Edinburgh--unk.
    -       -Harvest-        -campylocarpum 1/16
    -       - Moon  -unnamed hybrid-
    -unnamed-            -unknown 5/32
      hybrid-   -catawbiense var. album Glass--Catalgla 1/8
        -Ice -                -catawbiense
        Cube-        -Catawbiense Album-
            -Belle Heller-        -unknown
                -catawbiense var. album 1/16
```
Buds of strong purplish red open to frilled white flowers, edged
with mallow purple; dorsal spots moderate orange.   W. Delp.

RUFFLED RIDGE   Described under HAD, q.v.

```
        -Ben Moseley--unknown 3/4
RUFFLED RIM-        -catawbiense 1/4
        -Old Port-
            -unknown
```
Buds of strong purplish red and spirea red. Frilled flowers of
strong and light purple, with a flare of fuchsia purple and dark
red dorsal spotting. Al Smith cross; W. Delp raiser.

```
        -catawbiense 1/2
RUFFLES-
        -unknown 1/2
```

5ft(1.5m) -15F(-26C) ML 3/3 Ruffled flowers of light orchid
pink blooming later than most; apple green leaves held by straw-
colored petioles.   Origin unknown.

```
                -yakushimanum 1/4
        -Hydon Glow-     -griersonianum 1/8
        -        -Springbok-     -ponticum 1/16
        -                -unnamed-
RUFFLES -                 hybrid--unknown 1/8
AND FRILLS-        -dichroanthum 1/8
        -    -Dido-
        -    -        -decorum 1/8
        -Lem's-                -griffithianum
        Cameo-        -Beauty of Tremough-      5/32
        -        -Norman-        -arboreum 1/32
        -Anna- Gill -griffithianum
                -griffithianum
            -Jean Marie -
                de Montague-unknown
```
6ft(1.8m) -5F(-21C) M Flowers openly funnel-shaped, frilled,
6-lobed, fragrant, throat Naples yellow, shading through orient
pink at edges to jasper red in dorsal throat, with spotting; the
reverse suffused azalea pink. Domed truss of 12. Leaves heavy
textured, held 3 years; bronze when young. Wildfong, reg. 1984.

```
        -forrestii Repens Group 1/2
RUFUS-
        -sanguineum ssp. sanguineum var. sanguineum 1/2
```
Red flowers. Lord Aberconway, 1941.

RUSHMOOR   ((FABIA x discolor hybrid x griersonianum) x discolor
                hybrid x eriogynum)) x MAYDAY)
Above parentage incomplete, as published. Flowers light orchid
pink, deepening to phlox pink. J. Waterer & Crisp, reg. 1975.

```
        -russatum 1/2
RUSSAUTINII-
        -augustinii 1/2
```
5ft(1.5m) -10F(-23C) EM 4/3 Lepidote hybrid with small foliage like russatum. Flower truss of 2-5, close to augustinii in
size, slate blue with darker eye; blooms profusely at early age.
Sir John Ramsden, 1937.

* *
```
        -maximum 1/2
RUSSELL HARMON-
        -catawbiense 1/2
```
6ft(1.8m) -25F(-32C) L 4/3 Excellent, large, high trusses of
25 flowers, magenta pink. A little open but a good plant habit.
Difficult to propagate. May be a natural hybrid. Introduced by
La Bar's Rhododendron Nursery.
MAXECAT   Parentage as above
Pink flowers, blooming late; very hardy. J. Gable.
* *

```
            -catawbiense 1/2
RUSSELLIANUM-
            -arboreum 1/2
```
A large shrub or small tree, with rounded trusses of crimson red
flowers. Blooms early to midseason. Russell, 1831.

* *
```
            -arboreum 1/2
RUSSELLIANUM SUPERBUM-
            -unknown 1/2
```
Red flowers. T. Methven, 1868-69.
RUSSELLIANUM TIGRINUM   Parentage as above
Red flowers, spotted. T. Methven, 1868-69.
* *

RUSTIC MAID   Described under AMETHYST (Arends), q.v.

```
            -neriiflorum 1/8
        -F. C. Puddle-
    -Ethel-        -griersonianum 1/8
RUTH-    -forrestii Repens Group 1/4
    -        -thomsonii 1/4
    -Barclayi-            -arboreum 1/8
        -Glory of Penjerrick-
                -griffithianum 1/8
```

Blood red flowers.   Lord Aberconway, 1946.

```
                           -maximum 1/4
              -Marchioness of Lansdowne-
RUTH A. WEBER-                        -unknown 1/2
         -              -catawbiense 1/4
             -Old Port-
                   -unknown
```
4ft(1.2m) -5F(-21C) ML 3/3 Violet-colored flowers with light
purple spotting, 3.75in(9.5cm) across, 5-lobed; spherical truss
of 17. Floriferous. Upright plant; dark green leaves held 3
years.   Edwin O. Weber, reg. 1974.

```
              -yakushimanum 1/2
RUTH DAVIS-
         -degronianum ssp. heptamereum (metternichii) 1/2
```
2.5ft(.75m) -10F(-23C) M Cherry red buds open to white flow-
ers, reverse pink until fully open, held in ball-shaped trusses
of 17. Semi-dwarf plant, broader than tall with distinctive
winter foliage, glossy dark green.   Joseph Gable cross;   Ross
B. Davis, Jr., reg. 1978; reg. published 1988.

```
                  -wardii 1/4
          -Idealist-                    -griffithianum 1/32
         -         -           -Kewense-
RUTH -        -     -Aurora-    -fortunei
HANSEN-     -Naomi-    -thomsonii 1/16
       -          -fortunei 13/32
       -    -wightii 1/4
        -China-
            -fortunei
```
5ft(1.5m) OF(-18C) ML 4/3 Moderately compact plant, medium
green leaves 6in(15.2cm) long. Flowers primrose yellow, paler
at edges, to 4.5in(11.5cm) wide, 6-lobed, in conical trusses of
13.   Dr. Carl W. Phetteplace, reg. 1969.

RUTH LYONS--form of davidsonianum
5ft(1.5m) OF(-18C) M 4/3 An upright plant with leaves fold-
ing upwards from the midrib. Flowers bright pink, up to 1.25in.
(3.2cm) wide, in flat-topped truss of 6-7.   James Barto raiser;
M. G. Lyons, reg. 1962.   P.A. 1961.

```
           -peach-flowered hybrid--unknown 9/16
           -           -dichroanthum 1/8
RUTH MOTTLEY-    -Dido-
         -Lem's-    -decorum 1/8      -griffithianum 5/32
         -Cameo-            -Beauty of-
         -      -Norman- Tremough-arboreum 1/32
         -      - Gill -
         -Anna-     -griffithianum
         -       -                 -griffithianum
            -Jean Marie de Montague-
                          -unknown
```
3ft(.9m) x 2.5ft(.75m)(12 yrs) OF(-18C) M Domed truss of 12-
15 flowers, strong purplish pink at edges, paler at center; dorsal lobes spotted brilliant orange. Flat elliptic leaves to 5.5
in(14cm).   W. Robertson, cross 1975; J. A. Davis, reg. 1989.

RUTH WICK   Described under ANDRÉ, q.v.

```
* * * * * * * * * * * * * * * * * * * * * * * * * * * * *
                         -griffithianum 1/2
         -Loderi Pink Diamond-
         -                   -fortunei 1/4
RUTHELMA-              -thomsonii 1/4
         -Cornish Cross-
                      -griffithianum
```
Flowers of reddish pink. Sir E. Loder.
CORALIA   Parentage as above
Salmon-colored flowers. Sir E. Loder.
H. WHITNER   Parentage as above
Clear pink flowers. Sir E. Loder. A.M. 1935
* *

S

```
* * * * * * * * * * * * * * * * * * * * * * * * * * * * * *
                    -dichroanthum 1/4
            -Goldsworth Orange-
SABINE-                  -fortunei ssp. discolor 1/4
         -      -haematodes 1/4
         -May Day-
              -griersonianum 1/4
```
Rose Bengal; throat spotted Venetian pink. J. Bruns, reg. 1972.
ULRIKE   Parentage as above
Flowers bright claret rose, darker edges.   J. Bruns, reg. 1972.
* *

```
         -russatum 1/2
SACKO-        -impeditum 1/4
         -Moerheim-
              -unknown 1/4
```
2ft(.6m) -10F(-23C) M Bluish purple flowers; 5-7 in round-
ed trusses. Small dark leaves, slightly scaly; plant spreading
and compact. Recommended by Cox.   A. van Vliet, cross c.1970;
Royal Boskoop Hort. Soc., reg. 1988.   A.M. Boskoop 1977.

```
* * * * * * * * * * * * * * * * * * * * * * * * * * * * * *
            -Rose Perfection--unknown 1/2
SADONIA-
         -fortunei 1/2
```
Rose pink flowers.   Lord Aberconway cross, 1926; intro. 1933.

```
              -arboreum 3/4
         -Cornubia-        -thomsonii 1/8
SADY-      -Shilsonii-
         -               -barbatum 1/8
         -arboreum
```
Flowers similar to CORNUBIA, cardinal red, blooming from end of
May to Sept. in Victoria, Australia.   A. Bramley, reg. 1964.

SAE NO. 1   See SANDWICH APPLEBLOSSOM

```
                      -xanthostephanum 1/4
            -Saffron Queen-
SAFFRON PRINCE-        -burmanicum 3/4
              -burmanicum
```
3ft(.9m) x 2.5ft(.75m)(5 yrs) 40F E   Trusses of 8 flowers,
brilliant yellow-green in bud, opening to brilliant greenish
yellow, widely funnel-campanulate, 2in(5cm) across; floriferous.
Plant rounded; leaves 2.5in(6.4cm) long, held 3 years.   M. & F.
Sumner, reg. 1985.

```
              -xanthostephanum 1/2
SAFFRON QUEEN-
         -burmanicum 1/2
```
4.5ft(1.35m) 20(-7C) EM 4/3   Growth habit upright, open;
leaves glossy green, narrow, to 3in(7.6cm) long. Flowers sulphur yellow with dark spotting, 2.5in(6.4cm) wide; lax truss of
8-9. Charles Williams.   A.M. 1948.   Color ill. Cox pl. 162;
HG p. 76.

SAGAMORE BAYSIDE   Parentage unknown; Dexter hybrid
5ft(1.5m) -5F(-21C) M Light purplish pink flower, wavy edges,
yellow-green stripe down center; trusses of 9. Dull olive green
foliage; well-branched plant.   Tyler Arboretum, reg. 1982.

```
            -fortunei 1/2
SAGAMORE BRIDGE-
              -unknown 1/2
```
6ft(1.8m) -5F(-21C) M Flowers of purplish pink, flushed dull
yellow, heavy-textured; spherical trusses of about 14. Foliage
olive green; floriferous, broad, rounded plant.   Dexter cross;
intro. about 1950; Scott Horticultural Foundation, reg. 1980.

SAHARA   See NILE

SAIL WING   Described under JOHN CALLER, q.v.

SAINT BREWARD   Described under BLUE TIT, q.v.

```
                          -griffithianum 1/4
             -unnamed hybrid-
SAINT GEORGE-              -unknown 1/2
        -                 -fortunei 1/4
             -H. M. Arderne-
                          -unknown
```
Light crimson buds, opening paler, distinctly veined with pale
crimson.   Waterer, Sons & Crisp, 1932.   A.M. 1946.

```
                   -arboreum ssp. zeylanicum 1/2
SAINT KEVERNE-
             -griffithianum 1/2
```
Bright red flowers with a few dark brown dots.   P. D. Williams.
A.M. 1922.

```
             -augustinii 3/4
SAINT KEW-              -impeditum 1/4
        -Saint Breward-
                       -augustinii
```
Trusses of 11-13 clustered flowers, violet blue with traces of
darker shading at margins, 1.75in(4.5cm) wide. Narrow, pointed
leaves to 2in(5cm) long. Gen. Harrison, reg. 1970.   P.C. 1970.

```
                   -souliei 1/4
             -Souldis-
SAINT MABYN-              -fortunei ssp. discolor 1/4
             -unknown 1/2
```
Trusses of 10 flowers 4in(10.2cm) across, saucer-shaped, white
tinged yellow inside and palest pink outside, top petal spotted
red.   Gen. Harrison, cross 1921; reg. 1967.

SAINT MARY'S   Described under QUEEN ANNE'S, q.v.

SAINT MERRYN   Described under BLUE STAR, q.v.

```
             -russatum 1/2
SAINT MINVER-              -impeditum 1/4
        -Saint Breward-
                       -augustinii 1/4
```
3ft(.9m) -10F(-23C) E   Violet blue flowers; a low, compact
plant.   Gen. Harrison, reg. 1973.   F.C.C. Wisley Trials 1986.

SAINT TUDY   Described under BLUE TIT, q.v.

```
                          -intricatum 1/8
                   -Intrifast-
             -Blue Diamond-        -fastigiatum 1/8
SAINT WENN-              -augustinii 1/4
             -polycladum Scintillans Group 1/2
```
The flowers are mauve.   Gen. Harrison, reg. 1973.

* *
```
                   -campylocarpum Elatum Group 1/2
SAKI---LETTY EDWARDS, selfed-
                          -fortunei 1/2
```
5ft(1.5m) 0F(-18C) EM   Creamy, pastel pink flowers, held in a
tight truss. Rather open plant, light green leaves. V. Boulter
cross, Australia.
CHARLES BEGGS   Parentage as above
Tyrian rose flowers, lighter in center; trusses of 10-12. Foliage may be sun-damaged.   A. Bramley, Australia, reg. 1966.
* *

```
                          -haematodes 1/8
                   -Humming Bird-
             -Mochica Moon-        -williamsianum 1/8
SALINAR PRINCESS-         -unknown 1/4
             -aberconwayi 1/2
```
Trusses of 7 flowers, saucer-shaped, 6-lobed, 2.3in(7cm) across,
spotless white. Low plant, stiff but compact; elliptic leaves
2.3in(7cm) long. I. A. Hayes, reg. 1987.

SALLY FULLER   Described under FRAN LABERA, q.v.

```
             -fortunei 1/4
      -Duke of York-        -catawbiense 1/8
SALM-              -Scipio-
      -                    -unknown 1/8
      -venator 1/2
```
Bright red flowers.   Dietrich Hobbie, 1954.

```
                   -williamsianum 1/4
             -Jock-
SALMON JUBILEE-        -griersonianum 1/4
             -unknown 1/2
```
Soft scarlet buds open to salmon-colored flowers; truss holds 5
to 9. Lady Marion Philipps, Picton Castle, S. Wales, reg. 1977.

SALMON TROUT   Described under LADY CHAMBERLAIN, q.v.


```
                          -griffithianum 3/4
             -Queen Wilhelmina-
SALOME-              -unknown 1/4
             -griffithianum
```
Flowers of rose red.   Lord Aberconway, 1950.

```
             -griersonianum 1/2
SALTWOOD-              -maximum 1/4
             -Lady Clementine Mitford-
                          -unknown 1/4
```
Openly funnel-shaped flowers, 4.3in(11cm) wide, 7-lobed, of deep
Neyron rose, reverse carmine rose; loose trusses of 8-9. Leaves
6in(15cm) long, dark green above, pale below. Maj. A. E. Hardy,
reg. 1965.   A.M. 1965.

```
                   -sanguineum ssp. didymum 1/4
      -Arthur Osborn-
      -                 -griersonianum 1/4
SALUS-              -griffithianum 1/8
      -        -Loderi-
      -Coreta-        -fortunei 1/8
                   -arboreum ssp. zeylanicum 1/4
```
Flowers of deep red.   Lord Aberconway, 1941.

```
             -griffithianum 1/2
SALUTATION-
             -lacteum 1/2
```
Tall, attractive bush, rather tender, bearing large, well-filled
trusses of cream-colored flowers, midseason.   Rothschild, 1953.

SALUTE   Described under ELISABETH HOBBIE, q.v.

```
                          -catawbiense 1/2
             -Roseum Elegans-
      -              -unknown 1/2
SAM VACCARO-              -catawbiense
      -        -Purpureum Elegans-
      -Roslyn-              -unknown
      -              -catawbiense
             -Everestianum-
                          -unknown
```
3.5ft(1m)(21 yrs) -22F(-30C) ML Widely funnel-shaped flowers,
2.5in(6.5cm) wide, bluish white fading white, edged pale violet,
ruby blotch; truss of 12-15. Glossy, olive green leaves; plant
wider than tall.   Fetterhoff, reg. 1986.

```
                          -griffithianum 17/64
             -Loderi King-
      - George        -fortunei 9/64
      -Morio-              -griffithianum
      -        -        -Loderi-
      -        -        -Albatross-        -fortunei
      -Lockington-  -Cup-        -fortunei ssp. discolor
      - Pride    -   Day-        -elliottii 5/32        5/32
      -        -        -Fusilier-
      -        -              -griersonianum 5/32
SAMANTHA-        -              -griffithianum
SAWERS-        -Mrs. E. C. Stirling-
      -              -unknown 1/8
      -
      -Cup Day (as above)
```
Flowers in truss of 12-14, funnel-shaped, 5-lobed, outside deep
purplish pink, inside lighter pink, fading to cream at lobe center, purplish pink spotting. Shrub 4ft(1.2m) tall; narrow elliptic foliage, to 5in(12.5cm).   D. J. Dosser, Australia, cross
1980; reg. 1989.

```
                              -catawbiense 1/4
               -Mrs.C.S.Sargent-
       -unnamed hybrid-            -unknown 5/8
       -                   -America (as below)
SAMARSA-                      -griffithianum 1/8
       -                   -Mars-
       -unnamed hybrid-    -unknown          -catawbiense
                   -             -Parsons Grandiflorum-
                   -America-               -unknown
                              -dark red hybrid--unknown
```
Large flowers, clear pink. Hardy to -25F(-32C). R. L. Blough.

SAMISEN--yakushimanum, Exbury form selfed
3ft(.9m) -15F(-26C) ML Flower of good substance, light Neyron
rose, edges shading paler rose at base, widely campanulate, 1.75
in(4.5cm) broad; truss of 12-18. Plant well-branched, 50% wider
than tall; leaves with plastered rust indumentum, held 3 years.
See also BIG YAK. Ben Nelson seed; Mary L. Hill raiser, reg.
1984.

SAMMETGLUT (VELVET GLOW) Described under BLINKLICHT, q.v.

```
                        -catawbiense var. album 1/4
       -unnamed hybrid-
       -              -yakushimanum 1/4        -catawbiense
       -                   -Parsons Grandiflorum-   3/32
SAMOA-            -America-               -unknown
       -         -        -dark red hybrid--unknown 1/4
       -    -Fanfare-         -catawbiense
       -unnamed-    -Kettledrum-
         hybrid-         -unknown
              -         -forrestii Repens Group 1/8
              -Gertrud-            -ponticum 1/32
               Schäle-       -Michael Waterer-
                   -Prometheus-          -unknown
                         -Monitor--unknown
```
5ft(1.5m) x 7ft(2.1m)(24 yrs) -20F(-29C) EM 5/4 Vivid Tur-
key red flowers, faint dorsal spotting, 2.2in(5.3cm) across; 15
per truss; elliptic leaves, rough upper surface, tiny whit hairs
below. David G. Leach, cross 1962; reg. 1985.

```
       -azalea occidentale 1/2
SAMURAI-        -elliottii 1/4
       -Fusilier-
               -griersonianum 1/4
```
Azaleodendron. Trusses hold 28-30 flowers, Neyron rose with a
red throat. First bloomed 1963 from seeds planted in 1950. L.
E. Brandt, reg. 1969.

SANDLING Described under HALCYONE, q.v.

SANDRA Described under GOLDKRONE, q.v.

SANDWICH APPLEBLOSSOM Parentage unknown; elepidote
7ft(2.1m) x 7ft(15yrs) -10F(-23C) M Flowers in trusses of 14,
slightly fragrant, deep purplish pink at margins with strong
greenish yellow spots. Dense growth habit. See also DEXTER'S
APPLEBLOSSOM. Dexter cross; Heritage Plantation, reg. 1989.

```
       -sanguineum ssp. sanguineum var. sanguineum 1/2
SANGREAL-
       -griersonianum 1/2
```
Introduced by the Marquess of Headfort, 1937.

```
       -griersonianum 1/2
SANTA CLAUS-
       -unknown 1/2
```
Flowers a deep bright red. Gen. Harrison, reg. 1965.

SANTANA Described under YAKU WARRIOR, q.v.

SANTA'S WHISKERS Described under HEART TALK, q.v.

* *

```
           -impeditum 3/4
       -Blue Tit-
SAPPHIRE-        -augustinii 1/4
       -impeditum
```
2.5ft(.75m) -5F(-21C) EM 4/4 Spreading, rounded plant with
leaves .75in(1.9cm) long, tinged blue-green. Small light blue

to lavender blue flowers; floriferous; sun tolerant. Knap Hill
Nursery, before 1958. A.M. Wisley Trials 1967. Color illus.
ARS Q 31:3 (1977), p. 171; F p. 63; VV p. 70.
MAYFAIR Parentage as above
Dense plant with attractive foliage. Flowers as SAPPHIRE, open-
ing later. Knap Hill, reg. 1969.
* *

SAPPHO Parentage unknown; possibly maximum hybrid
6ft(1.8m) -10F(-23C) M 3/2 Often a parent. Buds of mauve
open to pure white flowers, with a conspicuous blotch of violet
overlaid with blackish purple. Medium-sized flowers, widely
funnel-shaped, held in large conical trusses. Plant habit open,
rather leggy; narrow, olive green leaves. SAPPHO was mentioned
in the earliest surviving nursery catalogue, dated 1847. A.
Waterer. A.G.M. 1969. A.M. 1974. Color illus. Cox pl. 165;
F p. 64; JS p. 67; VV p. 25, 106.

```
       -Sappho--unknown 1/2
SAPPHO'S CHOICE-
           -catawbiense--Catanea 1/2
```
3ft(.9m) 5F(-15C) M Flowers white with beetroot purple flare
of spotting in dorsal lobe, held in dome-shaped trusses of 17.
Flowers similar to those of SAPPHO, but plant habit superior and
spreads well: as broad as tall. Emil V. Bohnel cross; L. M.
Player raiser; reg. 1984.

SARAH HARDY Described under CONDOR, q.v.

SARAH JANE Described under HEATHER MOTH, q.v.

```
       -fortunei ssp. discolor 1/2
SARDIS-        -catawbiense 1/4
    -C. S. Sargent-
           -unknown 1/4
```
A parent of FIREDRAKE. RBG, Kew.

```
                   -griersonianum 3/8
       -Sarita Loder-    -griffithianum 1/0
       -            -Loderi-
SARITA COKER-            -fortunei 1/8
       -          -fortunei ssp. discolor 1/4
       -King of Shrubs-    -dichroanthum 1/8
           -Fabia-
               -griersonianum
```
Trusses of 10 flowers, 7-lobed, deep Neyron rose in bud, opening
lighter, with brighter red throat. Mrs. R. J. Coker cross; A.
G. Holmes intro.; Mrs. R. J. Coker, reg. 1983.

* *
```
           -griersonianum 1/2
SARITA LODER-    -griffithianum 1/4
       -Loderi-
           -fortunei 1/4
```
4ft(1.2m) 5F(-15C) ML 3/3 Dark crimson buds, opening to deep
rose or salmon flowers; loose truss. Plant upright, open; long,
pointed leaves. Col. G. H. Loder, High Beeches. A.M. 1934.
DENCOMBE Parentage as above
Flowers of shrimp pink. Col. Loder.
* *

```
       -sargentianum 1/2
SARLED-
       -trichostomum Ledoides Group 1/2
```
2ft(.6m) -10F(-23C) ML 4/3 Slow-growing, compact, dwarf lepidote. Rounded trusses of small tubular flowers, creamy white;
pink in bud, daphne-like. Hardy in Ontario. C. Ingram. A.M.
1974. Color illus. Rhod. Soc. of Can. Bull. 7:2 (1978), p. 15.

```
       -Blue Peter--unknown 1/2
SASHA-        -fortunei 1/4
   -unnamed hybrid-        -wardii 1/8
           -unnamed hybrid-
                   -dichroanthum 1/8
```
3ft(.9m) -5F(-21C) M Leaves 5in(12.9cm) x 2.5in(6.4cm), held
3 years. Flowers white, shading to medium reddish purple; truss
holds 14. A. A. Raustein, reg. 1980. Color illus. ARS J 36:3
(1982), p. 102.

```
              -minus Carolinianum Group, Delp's deep pink 1/4
     -unnamed-                    -racemosum 1/16
     - hybrid-         -Conemaugh-
SASSY -      -Pioneer (Gable)-        -mucronulatum 1/16
LASSIE-              -unknown 1/8
     -          -minus Carolinianum Group, tetraploid form
     -unnamed hybrid-                                   1/4
              -fastigiatum 1/4
```
Medium-sized lepidote. Flowers open vivid reddish purple; foli-
age to 2in(5cm), shiny grass green. but bronze in winter. Hardy
to -17F(-27C). W. Delp.

SATAN'S FURY   Described under COURT JESTER, q.v.

SATIN   Described under PINK CAMEO, q.v.

```
              -fortunei 37/64
     -Ray-        -wardii 1/8
     -   -      -              -griffithianum 5/64
     -  -Idealist-       -Kewense-
     -         -      -Aurora-      -fortunei
SATIN -      -Naomi-      -thomsonii 1/32
BOUQUET-         -fortunei
     -                   -griffithianum
     -              -George Hardy-
     -   -Mrs. Lindsay-      -catawbiense 1/16
     -Dot- Smith   -Duchess of Edinburgh--unknown 1/8
        -fortunei
```
4ft(1.2m) OF(-18C) ML   Light green foliage, 6in(15cm) long.
Flowers off-white with yellow-green centers, held in spherical
trusses of 10-12.   Arthur & Maxine Childers, reg. 1972.

```
          -yakushimanum--Koichiro Wada 1/2
SATIN CLOUD-
          -unknown 1/2
```
Plant 3ft(.9m) tall, at 10 years. Trusses of 12 or 13 flowers,
light purplish pink spotted red in throat. Thick tan indumentum
beneath young leaves. G. F. Smith, Pukeiti Rhododendron Trust,
reg. 1984.

* *
```
         -Bosley/Dexter 1005--unknown 1/2
SATIN DOLL-
         -catawbiense var. album Glass--Catalgla 1/2
```
Rose pink flowers with ruffled edges, contrasting white anthers.
Large domed trusses.   O. Pride cross; Dr. J. Browning raiser.
PINK SCALLOP   Parentage as above
Pink edges, light centers; striking blotch on upper lobe. White
stamens.   Pride cross; Browning raiser.
BALLET   Parentage as above
Pink flowers, a greenish blotch.   Pride cross; Browning raiser.
* *

SATIN GOLD   Described under CHICKAMAUGA, q.v.

```
              -souliei 1/16
         -Soulbut-
     -Vanessa-      -fortunei--Sir Charles Butler 3/16
  -Radiance-      -griersonianum
     -      -griersonianum 3/8
SATIRE-      -griffithianum 1/8
  -   -Loderi-
  -Coreta-      -fortunei
     -arboreum 1/4
```
Bright red flowers.   Lord Aberconway, 1950.

```
         -haematodes 1/4
     -Choremia-
SATYR-      -arboreum 1/4
  -strigillosum 1/2
```
Red flowers.   Lord Aberconway, 1941.

```
         -calophytum 1/2
SAUSALITO-      -griffithianum 1/4
     -Loderi Venus-
              -fortunei 1/4
```
6ft(1.8m) -5F(-21C) E 4/4   Light pink flowers, to 4in(10cm)
wide, with 1in(2.5cm) red blotch on dorsal lobe; reverse strong
pink. Trusses of 11-14. Bright green leaves 6in(15cm) long, on
a vigorous plant.   John Henny, reg. 1968.   P.A. 1967.

```
              -dichroanthum 1/16
         -unnamed hybrid-
     -unnamed-Calcutta-      -kyawii 1/16
     - hybrid-      -catawbiense var. album Glass-Catalgla
SAVANNA-      -catawbiense var. album Glass--Catalgla 3/8
     -      -Newburyport Belle (Fowle 19)--unknown
     -Casanova-      -catawbiense var. rubrum 1/8
              -Good Hope-
                   -wardii 1/8
```
2ft(.6m) x 3ft(.9m)(9 yrs) -20F(-29C) M 4/5   Buds of medium
yellowish pink; 18-20 flowers per truss, 5-lobed, 1.75in(4.5cm)
wide, pale Dresden yellow to light greenish yellow at center and
dorsal lobe, with vivid greenish yellow spotting. Elliptic foliage 4.3in(10.8cm) x 1.7in(4.2cm); reddish brown tomentum covers
buds of new growth and petioles.   Leach, cross 1976; reg. 1985.

SAVER   Described under JACQUELINE LOOYE, q.v.

SAXA   Described under RED SNAPPER, q.v.

```
                   -griffithianum 1/4
              -George Hardy-
         -Betty Wormald-      -catawbiense 1/4
         -      -red hybrid--unknown 3/8
SCANDINAVIA-      -griffithianum
         -George Hardy-
         -Hugh Koster-      -catawbiense
         -      -arboreum 1/8
              -Doncaster-
                   -unknown
```
3ft(.9m) OF(-18C) ML 3/2   Plant wider than tall; leaves 7in.
long, medium green. Funnel-shaped flowers of dark crimson, with
a black blotch. Large, dome-shaped trusses.   M. Koster & Sons.
A.M. 1950.

* *
```
              -griffithianum 3/8
         -Mars-
         -      -unknown 3/8
SCARLET BLAST-      -griffithianum
         -      -Mars-
         -unnamed hybrid-      -unknown
                   -catawbiense var. rubrum 1/4
```
5ft(1.5m) -20F(-29C) M 4/2   Plant rather open, broader than
tall; dark green convex, elliptic leaves. Flower rotate-campanulate, 2.6in(6.6cm) wide, dark red shading lighter, blotch light
pinkish yellow; firm pyramidal trusses of 17.   Intro. but later
withdrawn; D. G. Leach, reg. 1972.
INCA CHIEF   Parentage as above
5ft(1.5m) -20F(-29C) M 4/4   Strong purplish red, lighter center, blotch darker red; flower rotate-campanulate, to 3in(7.6cm)
wide; firm truss of 17-18. Plant as broad as tall; foliage 5in.
(12.5cm) long.   Not distributed. Leach, reg. 1972.
JAVA   Parentage as above
5ft(1.5m) -10F(-23C) ML 4/2 Cardinal red flower, Neyron rose
in throat, widely funnel-campanulate, 2.75in(7cm) across; domed
trusses of 17. Plant wider than tall; leaves held 2 years.   D.
G. Leach, cross 1958; reg. 1983.
* *


```
                   -catawbiense 1/2
              -unnamed red hybrid-
SCARLET GLOW-      -unknown 1/2
         -      -catawbiense
         -unnamed red hybrid-
                   -unknown
```
5ft(1.5m) -15F(-26C) ML 2/3 Brick red, funnel-shaped flower,
2.5in(6.4cm) across, in conical trusses of 15. Plant compact;
dark green leaves to 3.5in(9cm) long. Shammarello, reg. 1972.

* *
```
              -arboreum ssp. zeylanicum 1/4
         -Ilam Alarm-      -griffithianum 1/8
SCARLET KING-      -unnamed hybrid-
         -griersonianum 1/2      -unknown 1/8
```
5ft(1.5m) 5F(-15C) ML 4/3 Rich scarlet flowers on an attrac-
tive shrub; dark green foliage with white indumentum. Does well
in warm climates.   W. T. Stead, NZ, before 1947.
HOMESTEAD   Parentage as above
Flowers in truss of 16-18, cardinal red; deeper dorsal spotting.

Foliage with silvery indumentum below. G. Smith, reg. 1985.
ILAM RED GLOW   Parentage as above
Large Turkey red flowers; vigorous, tree-like plant. E. Stead
raiser; G. Smith, reg. 1986.
KAKA   Parentage as above
Turkey red flowers with darker spotting; needs shade. G. Smith,
reg. 1986.   Color illus. Cox pl. 91.
ORCHARD   Parentage as above
Scarlet flowers; medium-sized trusses. Good foliage on a rather
open plant. The original named clone.   Stead, before 1958.
PINES   Parentage as above
Turkey red with darker spotting. Popular. G. Smith, reg. 1986.
* *

```
                 -fortunei 1/4
         -Luscombei-
SCARLET LADY-        -thomsonii 1/4
         -haematodes 1/2
```
A parent of GLASGOW GLOW.   Stirling Maxwell, 1936.

```
            -neriiflorum 1/2
SCARLET NYMPH-
            -strigillosum 1/2
```
3ft(.9m) 5F(-15C) EM Rounded plant, broader than tall; leaves
4in(10.2cm) long, with loose brownish indumentum. Campanulate,
blood red flowers, 1.5in(3.8cm) wide, in rounded trusses. H. L.
Larson, reg. 1965.

SCARLET SURPRISE   Described under ELISABETH HOBBIE, q.v.

```
                -forrestii Repens Group 3/4
      -Elizabeth-
SCARLET-        -griersonianum 1/4
TANAGER-
      -forrestii Repens Group
```
Small shrub with intense scarlet flowers. C. Ingram, reg. 1970.

```
       -Pygmalion--unknown 49/64                -catawbiense
       -                     -Parsons Grandi-           1/32
       -           -America- florum     -unknown
       -    -unnamed-    -dark red hybrid--unknown
       -    - hybrid-            -griffithianum
SCARLET-   -Viet-    -         -Queen Wil-          3/64
TRUSS -    - Vet-    -Britannia- helmina-unknown
       -    -    -              -Stanley Davies--unknown
       -    -    -                     -catawbiense
       -    -    -         -Parsons Grandi-
       -    -    -America- florum     -unknown
      -Gary -  -unnamed-    -dark red hybrid
      Davis-   hybrid-    -griffithianum
       -        -Mars-
       -           -unknown      -thomsonii 1/32
       -              -Bagshot Ruby-
       -    -Princess -        -unknown
      -Lanny - Elizabeth-unknown
        Pride-          -smirnowii 1/16
              -unnamed hybrid-
                      -yakushimanum 1/16
```
Buds of dark red and currant red open to frilled flowers cardi-
nal red; dorsal spotting ruby red; white throat. W. Delp.

SCARLET WONDER Described under ELISABETH HOBBIE, q.v.

```
       -thomsonii 1/2
SCARLETT-              -griffithianum 1/8
 O'HARA-     -Queen Wilhelmina-
      -Langley-          -unknown 3/8
       Park -
            -Stanley Davies--unknown
```
Loose trusses of waxy red flowers on a handsome bush. Sir James
Horlick, cross 1932; exhibited 1942.

SCHAMENEK'S GLOW   Described under YAKU FRILLS. q.v.

```
       -catawbiense 1/2
SCHARNHORST-
       -unknown 1/2
```
A parent of GRAFIN KIRCHBACH. Flowers shade from dark ruby red
to purplish red, with dark brown markings; frilled.   T. J. R.
Seidel, cross c. 1908; intro. 1916.

```
          -arboreum 1/4
      -Doncaster-
SCHILLER-     -unknown 1/4
      -          -griffithianum 1/4
      -George Hardy-
              -catawbiense 1/4
```
Flowers light rose, fringed. M. Koster & Sons, cross 1909.

```
              -Mrs. J. G. Millais--unknown 5/8
SCHNEEBUKETT-           -caucasicum 1/8
(SNOW-     -      -Viola-
 BOUQUET) -Bismarck- -unknown
                -catawbiense 1/4
```
6ft(1.8m) -10F(-23C) ML Trusses hold 18-26 flowers, 5- to 6-
lobed, clear white blotched ruby red, about 3.2in(8cm) across.
Elliptic leaves to 6.4in(16cm). H. Hachmann, cross 1965; Stück,
reg. 1983. Color illus. WS, 1989, p. 140.

* *
```
             -catawbiense 1/4
SCHNEEKRONE-Humboldt-
 (SNOW-   -      -unknown 1/4
  CROWN) -yakushimanum--Koichiro Wada 1/2
```
Trusses hold 12-17 flowers, 5-lobed, opening light Neyron rose
fading to clear white with soft pink tinge, ruby red spotting.
Elliptic, hairy leaves.   H. Hachmann, cross 1968; Stück, reg.
1983. Color illus. Cox pl. 168; WS, 1989, p. 159.
LAMENTOSA   Parentage as above
2.5ft(.75m) x 5ft(1.5m) -15F(-26C) ML Flowers in truss of 11-
17, of very pale purple, flattened, exterior veined dark to medium purplish pink, a striking large blotch of dark red dorsally.
Hachmann cross; Stück, reg. 1988.   Col. ill. WS, 1989, p. 154.
* *

```
             -wardii 1/4
      -Babette-
      -        -yakushimanum--Koichiro Wada 1/4
SCHNEE- -        -Direktör              -fortunei 1/16
SPIEGEL -   -Hachmann's- E. Hjelm--fortunei hyb. F2-
(mirror)-unn.- Ornament -       -catawbiense    -unknown 3/8
      hyb.-       -Humboldt-       1/16
             -unknown
          -Furnivall's Daughter--unknown
```
2.7ft(.8m) x 3.7ft(1.1m) -10F(-26C) ML Flowers in trusses of
8-13, 5 wavy-edged lobes, white throughout, large basal spot in
dorsal throat of moderate purplish red to deep pink. Hachmann,
cross 1977; Stück, reg. 1988.   Color illus. WS, 1989, p. 141.

* *
```
           -Mrs. J. G. Millais--unknown 1/2
SCHNEEWOLKE-
(SNOWCLOUD)-yakushimanum--Koichiro Wada 1/2
```
White flowers, 5-lobed; trusses of 12-17. Hairy leaves, revo-
lute margins. Hardy to -13F(-24C).   Hachmann, cross 1968; G.
Stück, reg. 1983. Color illus. WS p. 160.
HACHMANN'S PORZELLAN (porcelain)   Parentage as above
Flowers in trusses of 15-17, pure white, conspicuously blotched
yellow-green. Leaves with dark reddish brown indumentum below.
Hachmann cross; G. Stück, reg. 1984.
* *

```
       -griffithianum 1/2
SCHUBERT-
       -unknown 1/2
```
Flower pale orchid, fringed, with a light blotch. Bushy, vigorous plant. M. Koster & Sons, before 1958.

```
          -catawbiense ? 1/2
SCHUYLKILL-              (Possibly a natural hybrid)
          -decorum ? 1/2
```
2.5ft(.75m) -5F(-21C) EM   Leaves 5.75in(14.6cm) long. Pink
flowers fading to creamy white, with some darker pink spotting;
a pink stripe down center of each lobe; rounded truss of 18. C.
Herbert, reg. 1977.

```
          -Mrs. J. G. Millais--unknown 1/2
SCHWANENSEE-
          -yakushimanum--Koichiro Wada 1/2
```
3.3ft(1.0m) x 6ft(1.8m) -15F(-26C) ML   Flowers in trusses of
10-12, 5 slightly wavy lobes of white, spotted strong greenish
yellow; leaves with brown indumentum below. H. Hachmann, cross
1970; Stück, reg. 1988.

SCINTILLATION   Parentage unknown
5ft(1.5m) -15F(-26C) M 4/5   Often a parent; distinctive, deep
green, shining leaves of waxy texture, on a shrub broader than
tall. Strong stems carry large trusses of about 15 flowers, of
pastel pink, flared golden bronze markings in throat. One of
the most popular of the Dexter hybrids.   Dexter cross, 1925-42;
Paul Vossberg raiser; reg. 1973. A.E. 1973. Color illus. ARS Q
29:3 (1975), p. 171; Cox pl. 169; VV p. 32, cover.

```
         -catawbiense 1/2
SCIPIO-
         -unknown 1/2
```
Purplish red flowers.   A. Waterer, before 1871.

SCOTT HARRIS   Described under MIKEY, q.v.

SEA MIST   Described under SEAGULL, q.v.

SEA SHELLS   Parentage unknown
3ft(.9m) OF(-18C) M 4/4   Coral pink flowers with creamy yellow center.   Origin unknown.

SEA SPRAY   Described under LINGOS, q.v.

SEAFOAM   See FAIRWEATHER

* *
```
             -griffithianum 1/4
         -Loderi-
SEAGULL-     -fortunei 1/4
         -sutchuenense 1/2
```
Loose trusses of 12 to 15 pure white flowers, speckled crimson.
Leaves dull green, light brown indumentum, 8.5in(21.6cm) x 3in.
(6.7cm).   Lady Loder, 1938.   A.M. 1938.   F.C.C. 1976.
SEA MIST   Parentage as above
Dark pink flowers.   Lady Loder.
SEAMEW   Parentage as above
Flowers pure white or pale pink.   Lady Loder.   A.M. 1940.
* *

SEALING WAX   Described under BLOOD ORANGE, q.v.

SEAMEW   Described under SEAGULL, q.v.

SEARCHLIGHT   Parentage unknown
A parent of AUTUMN BEAUTY, by F. Lovegrove, Australia.

```
         -campylocarpum 1/2
SEA-SHELL-
         -unknown 1/2
```
Flowers creamy yellow with a chocolate blotch.   W. C. Slocock.

```
         -Moser's Maroon--unknown 1/2
SEA-TAC-
         -williamsianum 1/2
```
3ft(.9m) OF(-18C) E   3/3   Leaf 2.5in x 1.5in (6.4cm x 3.8cm).
Dark grayed red buds; dark cardinal red flowers, 2.5in (6.4cm)
wide, in ball trusses of 7.   Floriferous, rounded plant; named
for Seattle-Tacoma Airport, WA.   H. Larson, reg. 1977.

```
                   -fortunei ssp. discolor 3/8
                -Ladybird-
             -Diva-    -Corona--unknown 1/8
SEATTLE GOLD-    -griersonianum 1/4
             -                -fortunei ssp. discolor
             -Lady Bessborough-
                        -campylocarpum Elatum Group 1/4
```
6ft(1.8m) OF(-18C) M 3/3   Plant of compact habit; long, slender
leaves. Flowers warm light yellow with brown markings, held in
compact trusses.   H. Lem cross; Don McClure, reg. 1958.

```
                 -lacteum 1/4
         -unnamed-              -griffithianum 1/16
SEATTLE- hybrid-      -Loderi-
 QUEEN -      -Lodauric-       -fortunei 1/16
         -                -auriculatum 1/8
         -campylocarpum 1/2
```
Ivory flowers.   H. Lem cross; D. McClure, intro. before 1958.

```
             -leucaspis 1/2
SEATTLE SPRINGTIME-
             -mucronulatum 1/2
```

3ft(.9m) 5F(-15C) E 3/2   Growth habit open; small leaves of
medium olive green. White flowers, flushed with amaranth rose,
1.25in(3.2cm) across.   B. O. Mulligan, intro. 1954.

SECOND ATTEMPT--form of callimorphum
3ft(.9m) -5F(-21C) M 3/4   Trusses of 4-5 flowers, white with
a large blotch of grayed purple, reverse flushed fuchsia purple.
Leaves broadly elliptic, 1.75in(4.5cm) long, dark glossy green.
Crown Estate, reg. 1980.   A.M. 1980.

SECOND HONEYMOON   Described under HONEYMOON, q.v.

SECREST PINK   Described under OHIO PINK, q.v.

```
                   -griersonianum 1/2
SECRETARY OF STATE-        -haematodes 1/4
                   -Grosclaude-
                          -facetum (eriogynum) 1/4
```
Large trusses of blood red flowers.   The Rt. Hon. Michael Noble
cross; Sir George Campbell, reg. 1965.

SEEMLY   Described under KITTY COLE, q.v.

```
                             -griffithianum 1/16
                      -George-
                  -Pink - Hardy-catawbiense 1/16
                  -Pearl-        -arboreum 3/16
         -Professor  -    -Broughtonii-
SEESTADT  -Hugo de Vries-          -unknown 3/16
BREMERHAVEN -        -arboreum
(SEAPORT...)-    -Doncaster-
         -insigne 1/2    -unknown
```
Trusses of 8-10 flowers, pink with a darker blotch, 2.75in(7cm)
across. Plant 5-6ft(1.5-1.8m) tall. Dark green, broadly elliptic leaves.   W. Bruns, cross 1961; Joh. Bruns, reg. 1985. Col-
or illus. WS, 1989, p. 84.

```
         -catawbiense 1/2
SEFTON-
         -unknown 1/2
```
4ft(1.2m) -20F(-29C) ML 3/2   Low, spreading, straggly growth
habit. Dark maroon flowers, spotted darker; trusses larger than
most catawbiense hybrids. A. Waterer, 1881.   Color illus. ARS
Q 26:4 (1972), cover.

```
         -cinnabarinum Blandfordiiflorum Group 1/2
SELIG-
         -maddenii (calophyllum) 1/2
```
Flowers pink, fading to salmon pink and orange on tube.   Lady
Loder, 1937.   F.C.C. 1937.

```
                      -yakushimanum (Larson No. 6) 1/2
SENATOR HENRY JACKSON-        -griersonianum 1/4
              -Mrs. Horace Fogg-         -griffithianum
                      -Loderi Venus-          1/8
                                 -fortunei 1/8
```
3ft(.9m) -5F(-21C) M 4/4 Yakushimanum-like indumented leaves
of lustrous deep green; pure white flowers; rounded trusses; a
handsome, insect-resistant shrub, and first distributed as CHINA
DOLL; the (duplicated) name was changed in 1985.   Larson cross;
Fisher intro.   Color illus. ARS J 23:1 (1989), p. 55.

```
         -keiskei 1/2
SENEGAL-
         -minus Carolinianum Group, white form 1/2
```
Flowers 4.5in(4cm) across, 5-lobed, pale greenish yellow, faint-
ly flushed pale orange on opening, soon aging uniformly yellow
to ivory; trusses of 7-8. Narrowly elliptic foliage, 2.3in(6cm)
long. Semi-dwarf; hardiness -15F(-26C).   Leach, reg. 1985.

```
         -Lackamas Blue--augustinii 3/4
SEÑORA-              -intricatum 1/8
MELDON-      -Intrifast-
         -Blue Diamond-      -fastigiatum 1/8
              -augustinii
```
5ft(1.5m) 5F(-15C) E   Wisteria blue flowers with a few green
spots, to 5in(12.7cm) wide, in terminal clusters; floriferous
and fragrant. Upright rounded plant, well-branched; small yellowish green leaves held 2-3 years.   Dr. D. Goheen, reg. 1982.

```
                -griffithianum 1/4
        -Loderi King George-
SEÑORITA-               -fortunei 1/4
        -Ostbo Y3--unknown 1/2
```
5ft(1.5m) -5F(-21C) ML Foliage 6in(15.2cm) x 2in(5cm). Ruf-
fled flowers, lilac pink, with yellowish pink throat, upper lobe
spotted brown, 4in(10cm) across; truss of 14. The Bovees, reg.
reg. 1962.

SEÑORITA CHERE   Described under YAKU WARRIOR, q.v.

```
                -sperabile 1/4
        -Eupheno-
SENTINEL-       -griersonianum 1/4
-               -thomsonii 1/4
  -Barclayi-            -arboreum 1/8
                -Glory of  -
                Penjerrick-griffithianum 1/8
```
Blood red flowers. Lord Aberconway, 1950.

SEPTEMBER SNOW   Described under COPELIA, q.v.

SEPTEMBER SONG   Described under OASIS, q.v.

```
        -Lady        -campylocarpum Elatum Group 1/8
             -Bessborough-
    -Jalisco-            -fortunei ssp. discolor 1/8
    -       -    -dichroanthum 1/8
    -       -Dido-
SERENA-        -decorum 1/8
    -           -souliei 1/8
    -       -Soulbut-
    -Vanessa-        -fortunei--Sir Charles Butler 1/8
        -griersonianum 1/4
```
Flowers of bright carmine pink, cherry at base of corolla; the
reverse is pale pink, suffused cherry.   Francis Hanger cross;
RHS Garden, Wisley.   A.M. 1956.

SERENADE--form of davidsonianum
6ft(1.8m) OF(-18C) EM 4/3 A tall shrub with dark green lanceolate foliage; flowers a very clear pink. Plant hardier than
the F.C.C. form of this species. Origin unknown.

SERENATA   Described under TAHITI, q.v.

```
        -yakushimanum 1/2
SERENDIPITY-
        -aureum (chrysanthum) 1/2
```
1ft(.3m) -25F(-32C) M Plant compact and spreading; dark green
leaves 2.75in(7cm) long. Flowers pale primrose, widely campanulate, 2.3in(6.4cm) wide; truss of 10. B. C. Potter, reg. 1972.

SERIN   Listed under ALBINO, q.v.

```
                        -catawbiense 1/16
             -Parsons Grandiflorum-
        -America-            -unknown 3/8
    -Cindy-      -dark red hybrid--unknown
    - Lou -              -griffithianum 1/16
    -       -        -Mars-
SERIOUS-    -unnamed hybrid-      -unknown
  PINK -                -catawbiense var. rubrum 1/8
    -           -catawbiense var. album Glass--Catalgla
    -       -Calsap-                             1/8
    -       -       -Sappho--unknown
    -Caltwins-        -catawbiense 1/8
        -Pink Twins-
            -haematodes 1/8
```
Buds of vivid and moderate purplish reds; flowers roseine purple
with a white flare; dorsal spots moderate orange. W. Delp.

SESAME--form of pachytrichum
6ft(1.8m) -5F(-21C) E 2/2   Grows over 10ft(3m) high. White
flowers, some tinged shades of solferino purple, campanulate, in
lax trusses of 8. Lord Aberconway, reg. 1963. A.M. 1963.

SESTERIANUM   Described under FRAGRANTISSIMUM, q.v.

```
    -spinuliferum 1/2
SETA-
    -moupinense 1/2
```
5ft(1.5m) 5F(-15C) E 4/3 Upright plant; small-leaved. Narrowly campanulate flowers, pink with a much paler base, the reverse darker pink, in umbels. Lord Aberconway, 1933. A.M.
1933.   F.C.C. 1960.   Color illus. ARS Q 35:3 (1981), p. 142;
Cox pl. 170.

SEVEN DEVILS--form of macrophyllum
5ft(1.5m) x 5ft -5F(-21C) ML 2/3 Flowers of deep wine red,
widely campanulate, in domed trusses of about 20. Leaves lanceolate.   Crosses with elepidotes; parent of SPARKLING BURGUNDY.
Williamm Magness collector, near Seven Devils Rd., Bandon, Ore.;
Dr. Frank Mossman intro.; reg. 1986.

```
                        -griffithianum 1/4
             -Loderi Sir Joseph Hooker-
SEVEN STARS-               -fortunei 1/4
             -yakushimanum 1/2
```
3ft(.9m) OF(-18C) M 4/4 Flowers white with dawn pink flush,
campanulate, 2in(5cm) wide; dome-shaped truss holds 15. Very
free-flowering. Plant vigorous, upright; matte green foliage.
Crown Estate, Windsor, reg. 1966. H.C. 1965.   A.M. 1967.
F.C.C. Wisley Trials 1974. Color illus. F p. 65; Cox pl. 171.

SEVENTH HEAVEN--form of sutchuenense (W 1232)
5ft(1.5m) -10F(-23C) VE 4/3 Trusses of 14-16 flowers, white
in throat, suffused lilac, numerous small ruby spots. Leaves to
9.25in(23cm) long, dark green.   E. H. Wilson, probable collector; R. N. Stephenson Clarke, reg. 1978.   A.M. 1978.

```
                        -griffithianum 1/8
             -Queen Wilhelmina-
    -Britannia-            -unknown 3/8
SEVENAC-       -Stanley Davies--unknown
    -hanceanum 1/2
```
3ft(.9m) -5F(-21C) EM One of the very few hybrids reported to
be a cross of a lepidote and an elepidote. A compact shrub with
scarlet red flowers. Hydon Nurseries.

SEVILLE   See MADRID

SHAAZAM   Described under MARY YATES, q.v.

```
                -elliottii 1/2
SHADOW SECRETARY-               -griersonianum 1/4
             -Sarita Loder-      -griffithianum 1/8
                      -Loderi-
                          -fortunei 1/8
```
Signal red flowers, in large racemose umbels of 17-18. Glabrous
leaves, 10in(25.4cm) x 2.5in(6.4cm).   The Rt. Hon. M. A. Noble
cross; Sir George Campbell, reg. 1966.

SHAH JEHAN   Described under DREAM GIRL, q.v.

```
                        -griffithianum 1/4
             -Mrs. E. C. Stirling-
SHAKESPEARE-              -unknown 3/4
             -Essex Scarlet--unknown
```
Bright rose pink flowers. M. Koster & Sons, 1916.

SHALIMAR   Parentage: Dexter hybrids, open pollinated
5ft(1.5m) -5F(-21C) ML   Large leaves; flowers 4.5in(11.5cm)
wide, 7-lobed, slightly fragrant, pale lavender pink; trusses of
12. Vossberg raiser; Schlarkjer, reg. 1974.

```
                            -griffithianum 3/8
                 -Beauty of Tremough-
             -Norman Gill-      -arboreum 1/8
    -Anna-        -griffithianum
    -    -            -griffithianum
    -    -Jean Marie de Montague-
SHALOM-              -unknown 7/16
    -                -griffithianum
    -        -George Hardy-
    -    -Pink -        -catawbiense 1/16
    -Antoon van-Pearl-    -arboreum
    Welie  -    -Broughtonii-
        -unknown    -unknown
```
5ft(1.5m) -5F(-21C) ML   Leaves 4.75in(12cm) long. Flowers
white, shaded rose, with darker rose flare, 3.5in(8.9cm) across.
Flattened trusses hold 16. Halfdan Lem cross; N. E. Hess, reg.
1974. C.A. 1973.

```
            -keiskei, dwarf form 1/2
SHAMROCK-
            -hanceanum Nanum Group 1/2
```
1.5ft(.45m) -5F(-21C) EM 4/4 Tubular funnel-shaped flowers,
1.25in(3cm) across by 1in(2.5cm) long, 5-lobed, of an unusual
chartreuse color with slight yellow spotting; small trusses hold
8-9. Plant well-branched, over twice as broad as high. Dr.
R. L. Ticknor, cross 1971; reg. 1978. Color illus. ARS Q 32:4
(1978), cover; K p. 128.

```
                      -unnamed-catawbiense 7/16
           -Pinnacle- hybrid-
           -         -          -unknown 5/16
           -         -unnamed-catawbiense
SHAM'S CANDY-      hybrid-
           -               -unknown
           -                        -caucasicum 1/8
           -         -Boule de Neige-      -catawbiense
           -Pink Cameo-          -unnamed-
           -                      hybrid-unknown
                      -catawbiense, red form 1/8
```
5ft(1.5m) -20F(-29C) ML 4/3 Synonym CANDY. Upright plant,
as broad as tall; glossy elliptic leaves, held 2 years. Flowers
strong purplish pink, with a yellow-green blotch, to 2.75in(7cm)
wide; conical trusses of 12. A. M. Shammarello, reg. 1975.

SHAM'S JULIET   Described under PINK CAMEO, q.v.

SHAM'S PINK   Described under PINK CAMEO, q.v.

SHAM'S RUBY   Described under FANFARE, q.v.

```
                      -unnamed-griffithianum 1/16
           -Mrs. Furnival-  hybrid-
           -         -          -unknown 5/8
           -unnamed-          -unnamed-caucasicum 1/16
           - hybrid-          hybrid-
SHANGHAI-  -                  -unknown
           -catawbiense var. album 1/4
           -unnamed mauve seedling, gold-blotched--unknown
```
6ft(1.8m) -10F(-23C) ML 4/3 Plant wider than tall, branching
moderately; medium green elliptic leaves, held 2 years. Flower
widely funnel-shaped, 3.75in(9.5cm) wide, white flushed pink on
perimeter of lobes, big blotch of strong orange-yellow; corolla
lobes recurved. Trusses spherical, about 18-flowered, 7.25in.
(18.5cm) across. Leach, reg. 1973. Color illus. HG p. 85.

```
                 -thomsonii 1/4
           -Gen. Sir John du Cane-
SHANGRI LA-          -fortunei ssp. discolor 1/4
           -griffithianum 1/2
```
Large white flower, flushed pink, in big compact truss. Erect,
vigorous bush; blooms late. Rothschild, reg. 1965. P.C. 1965.

```
           -soulei 1/2
SHARON-                -griffithianum 1/4
           -Loderi King George-
                      -fortunei 1/4
```
Flowers white, with a crimson blotch. Del James. P.A. 1955.

SHARON PESTE   Described under CAROLINE ALLBROOK, q.v.

```
                      -minus Carolinianum Group, pink form 1/4
           -unnamed hybrid-
SHARP      -              -calostrotum, rose form 1/4
IMPRESSION-
           -dauricum--Arctic Pearl 1/2
```
Medium-sized lepidote, hardy to -15F(-26C) with flowers lavender
and violet and gold spotted. W. Delp.

Out of order
```
                              -catawbiense
                 -Parsons Grandiflorum-    1/16
           -America-          -unknown
           -unnamed hybrid-      -dark red hybrid--unknown 11/16
SHENANDOAH-          -sutchuenense 1/4
           -unknown
```
5ft(1.5m) M -25F(-32C) Flowers in truss of 16, strong purplish
red, flushed strong purplish red on exterior, a bold dorsal
blotch and spotting of strong purplish red. Leach, reg. 1986.

```
                              -catawbiense
                 -Parsons Grandiflorum-    1/8
           -America-          -unknown 17/32
-Vivacious-      -dark red hybrid--unknown
-          -          -griersonianum 1/8
-    -Dr. Ross-          -arboreum 1/32
-    -          -Doncaster-
-    -Borde Hill-          -unknown
-          -          -griffithianum
-                -Mrs. A. M.-      1/8
SHARPIE-          -Williams -unknown
-                -Parsons  -catawbiense
-                -Grandiflorum-
-          -America-          -unknown
-    -unnamed-      -dark red hybrid--unknown
-    - hybrid-          -griffithianum
-    -          -Mars-
-Cindy Lou-    -Blaze-  -unknown
-                catawbiense, red form 1/16
-                -griffithianum
-          -Mars-
-Red Brave-  -unknown
           -America (as above)
```
Vivid red buds open to flowers of strong cardinal red, veined on
reverse in vivid red, stamens and pistil also vivid red. Plant
medium-sized, hardy to -15F(-26C). Weldon E. Delp.

SHARPSHOOTER   Described under CHASTITY, q.v.

SHAWME LAKE   Parentage unknown
5ft(1.5m) -5F(-21C) E   Large flowers of rose lavender, deeper
flare; lax trusses with bicolor effect. Dexter; named pre-1973.

SHEER DELIGHT   Described under MADHATTER, q.v.

```
                 -griffithianum 1/2
SHEFFIELD PARK-
                 -unknown 1/2
```
Pink flowers with scarlet crimson edges and crimson red exterior.
C. B. van Nes & Sons.

SHEFFIELD PARK ANGELO   Described under ANGELO, q.v.

SHEILA ANN   Parentage: Probably sanguineum x unknown
3ft(.9m) 5F(-15C) M 3/3 Flowers of very deep, dark red, with
attractive foliage. Caperci, reg. 1970.

```
* * * * * * * * * * * * * * * * * * * * * * * * * * * *
                 -elliottii 1/2
SHEILA MOORE-
                 -decorum 1/2
```
Rose pink flowers with darker spotting on upper lobes; 12-flow-
ered trusses. Lord Digby, 1948. A.M. 1948.
CERISETTE   Parentage as above
Fuchsine pink, scarlet band in throat. Lord Digby. A.M. 1954.
```
* * * * * * * * * * * * * * * * * * * * * * * * * * * *
```

```
                 -fortunei ssp. discolor 1/2
SHEILA OSBORN-          -griffithianum 1/4
           -Strategist-          -catawbiense 1/8
                      -John Waterer-
                                -unknown 1/8
```
Rose pink flowers. RBG, Kew, 1928. A.M. 1928.

SHELLABY   Name correction STELLABY; listed under NANCEGLOS, q.v.

SHENANDOAH   See previous column

```
                 -griffithianum 1/4
           -Loderi-
SHEPHERD'S DELIGHT-      -fortunei 1/2
           -              -fortunei
           -Luscombei-
                      -thomsonii 1/4
```
Introduced by Heneage-Vivian, Clyne Castle, Wales, 1927.

```
                 -Moser's Maroon--unknown 3/4
           -Grenadier-
SHEPWAY-          -elliottii 1/4
           -G. A. Sims--unknown
```
Firm, rounded trusses hold 15-17 flowers, dark red, shading to
lighter red to throat, darker spotting, 3in(7.6cm) wide. Leaves

dark green, with traces of brownish woolly indumentum.   Maj. A.
E. Hardy, reg. 1976.   A.M. 1976.

SHERILL   Described under AMBER GEM, q.v.


```
            -arboreum ssp. cinnamomeum var. album 1/2
SHERWOODEANUM-
            -catawbiense 1/2
```
Lilac rose flowers, heavily spotted.   J. Waterer, before 1865.

* *
```
         -thomsonii 1/2
SHILSONII-
         -barbatum 1/2
```
6ft(1.8m) 0F(-18C) VE Early-blooming, waxy, blood red flower,
markings dark brown. Rounded, symmetrical large shrub, or small
tree has reddish plum, barbatum-like bark; foliage as thomsonii.
R. Gill, before 1900.   A.M. 1900.   Color illus. Cox pl. 172.
NESTOR   Parentage as above, except reversed
Cardinal red flowers, a few darker markings in throat, 5-lobed,
13 per truss. Leaves elliptic, dark green.   Sir Edmund Loder
cross; The Hon. H. E. Boscawen, reg. 1969.   A.M. 1969.
* *
* *
```
        -yakushimanum, Exbury form 1/2
SHIRLEY-      -sanguineum ssp. sanguineum var. haemaleum 1/4
        -Thomaleum-
              -thomsonii 1/4
```
4ft(1.2m) x 3ft(.9m) 10F(-12C) M Flowers in trusses of 19, 7-
lobed, moderate to dark purplish pink buds open to pink, fading
rapidly to yellowish white. Pink and white trusses are present
at the same time. Leaves with yellowish white, felted indumentum. A. P. Johnson, reg. 1986.
LEONA MAUD   Parentage: yakushimanum x Thomaleum
2.5ft(.75m) high x 4ft(1.2m)(15 yrs) 0F(-18C) M   Buds strong
red; flowers 3in(7.6cm) across, 5-lobed, vivid purplish red with
deep red spotting; ball truss of 18. Well-branched bush; leaves
elliptic, with greenish indumentum. A. P. Johnson, reg. 1986.
* *
```
                 -dichroanthum
             -Fabia-
       -C. I. S.-    -griersonianum
       -        -
SHIRLEY -      -Loder's White, q.v. for 2 possible
CREELMAN-                      parentage diagrams
       -      -unnamed hybrid--unknown
       -Apricot-            -fortunei ssp. discolor
       Nectar -    -Lady
              -        -Bessborough-campylocarpum Elatum Group
                 -Jalisco-
                     -    -dichroanthum
                     -Dido-
                         -decorum
```
4ft(1.2m) 5F(-15C) M   Turkey red buds open to flowers spinel
red, 7-lobed, 3.25in(8.9cm) wide; spherical trusses hold 7-14.
Plant upright, as wide as tall; dark leaves, scant brown indumentum beneath. C. C. Barrow cross; Alice P. Smith, reg. 1983.

```
                               -griffithianum 1/16
                 -Queen Wilhelmina-
          -Britannia-            -unknown 5/16
          -           -Stanley Davies--unknown
          -Purple Lace-       -ponticum 1/8
SHIRLEY-         -Purple Splendour-
 PESTE -yakushimanum 1/2        -unknown
```
3ft(.9m) x 3ft 0F(-18C) M   Dome-shaped trusses of 17 flowers,
strong purplish red in bud, opening strong purplish pink, spotted dark red; strong purplish red rays down lobe exteriors. Elliptic leaves, glossy olive green, slight indumentum when young.
Fred Peste, cross 1976; Shirley Peste Johnston, reg. 1986.


```
          -strigillosum 1/2
SHIRLEY ROSE LENT-
          -praevernum 1/2
```
5ft(1.5m) 10F(-12C) VE   Plant rounded and well-branched; narrow, dark olive green leaves held 3 years; new growth reddish.
Deep pink flowers with a few darker spots, tubular-campanulate,
2.25in(5.7cm) across; spherical trusses of 13. B. Nelson cross;
Dr. C. G. Heller, reg. 1977.

SHIRLEY SCOTT   Described under JOAN BYE, q.v.

```
                  -dichroanthum 3/8
             -Fabia-
             -     -griersonianum 3/8
SHIRLEY-JEAN-    -dichroanthum
       -      -Fabia-
       -      -     -griersonianum
       -Otis-             -griffithianum 1/16
       Hyde-     -Loderi-
            -Albatross-    -fortunei 1/16
                      -fortunei ssp. discolor 1/8
```
Trusses of 6-7 flowers, 5-lobed, of bright azalea pink, heavily
spotted in yellow ochre; calyx also bright azalea pink. Leaves
about 4.8in(12.5cm) long. H. L. Larson, reg. 1982.


```
            -hippophaeoides Fimbriatum Group 1/2
SHOOTING STAR-
            -racemosum 1/2
```
3ft(.9m) -5F(-21C) E 3/3   Long spires of lavender pink cover
this fast-growing dwarf; must be trimmed back after blooming to
keep compactness. Leaves 3-4 times longer than wide. Does well
in open sun; young plants heavily budded. H. Greer, reg. 1989.


```
                 -caucasicum 1/8
             -Boule de-      -catawbiense 7/32
         -Besse - Neige -hardy hybrid-
         - Howells-            -unknown 25/64
         -      -             -catawbiense
         -      -unnamed red hybrid-
         -                -unknown
SHORT -                     -griffithianum 7/64
CIRCUIT-        -Jean Marie de Montague-
       -  -Fireman-            -unknown
       -  - Jeff -      -haematodes 1/16
       -  -    -Grosclaude-
       -Tom -        -facetum (eriogynum) 1/16
       Ring-                 -catawbiense
       M.D.-          -Parsons Grandi-
       =         America- florum    -unknown
       -  -unnamed-    -dark red hybrid--unknown
       -  - hybrid-       -griffithianum
       -Anna-          -Mars-
       Delp-    -Blaze-  -unknown
       -          -catawbiense var. rubrum 1/32
       -      -Mars (as above)      -catawbiense
       -Red Brave-      -Parsons Grandi-
            -America- florum    -unknown
                     -dark red hybrid--unknown
```
Cardinal red buds open to frilled flowers of cardinal red; dor-
sal spotting ruby red; white filaments. W. Delp.

* *
```
           -minus Carolinianum Group--Epoch 1/2
           -            -minus Carolinianum Group, tetraploid
SHORT STUFF-   -unnamed-                          1/8
           -   - hybrid-fastigiatum 3/16
           -Hi Tech-            -intricatum 1/16
           -         -Intrifast-
           -Blue Diamond-    -fastigiatum
                      -augustinii 1/8
```
A lepidote with strong and light purple buds opening to flowers
of same; greenish yellow dorsal spotting. W. Delp.
SHOWDOWN   Parentage as above
Flowers slightly frilled, moderate purplish pink. Delp.
SNAPPY   Parentage as above
Dark purplish pink in bud, opening to very pale purple. Delp.
SOFT SATIN   Parentage as above
Very pale purple in bud opening to frilled flowers of pale pur-
ple, with dark purplish pink anthers. W. Delp.
* *

SHORTOFF--dwarf form of maximum
3ft(.9m) -20F(-29C) VL Trusses 3in(7.6cm) wide by 4in(10.2cm)
high; white flowers, slight yellow-green dorsal spots, 5-lobed.
Plant 2/3 as broad as tall, 40% of the size of a typical species
(original plant about 8ft(2.4m) high, at 44 years), and flowers
later. Glossy, olive green leaves to 4in(10cm), slight orangey
indumentum; new growth tan tomentose. Collected on Shortoff Mt.
in North Carolina, USA; Henry Wright raiser; C. Towe, reg. 1985.

```
                        -campylocarpum 1/2
SHOT SILK-
                        -dichroanthum 1/2
A shrub of moderate height, with many flowers  of yellowish pink
and orange.  Blooms midseason.   Sir John Ramsden, 1933.


                   -yakushimanum, Exbury form 1/2
SHOW BOAT-          -decorum 1/4
           -Tumalo-                    -griffithianum 1/8
                   -Loderi King George-
                                       -fortunei 1/8
4ft(1.2m) -5F(-21C) M  4/4     Plant compact, rounded and well-
branched; olive green leaves with scant buff indumentum,  held 2
or 3 years. Pink buds;  white flowers with a small yellow-green
blotch, 7 wavy lobes, 2.75in(7cm) wide.  Phetteplace, reg. 1975.


SHOW DOWN   Described under SHORT STUFF, q.v.


SHOW-OFF (Wright)  Described under DOUBLOONS, q.v.


SHOWTIME   Described under ECSTASY, q.v.


SHOWOFF (Delp)  Described under GAY DAY, q.v.


SHRIMP GIRL   Described under BAMBI, q.v.


                       -yakushimanum 1/4
          -Shrimp Girl-           -dichroanthum 3/16
          -          -Fabia Tangerine-
          -          -           -griersonianum 1/4
SHRIMPFIELD-          -elliottii 1/8
          -     -Fusilier-
          -     -     -griersonianum
          -Winkfield-           -fortunei ssp. discolor
          -      -Lady  -              1/16
          -Jalisco-Bessborough-campylocarpum Elatum
               Elect -   -dichroanthum        1/16
                         -Dido-
                              -decorum 1/16
Flowers in truss of 18, 5 wavy lobes, vivid red at base outside
shading yellowish pink to cream;  inside cream, heavily flecked
crimson, 2 small blotches; long petaloid calyx, vivid red; obo-
vate leaves, thin fawn indumentum.  J. F. McQuire, reg. 1987.


     -yakushimanum 1/2
     -         -Lady      -fortunei ssp. discolor 3/16
SI SI-           -Bessborough-
     -    -Day -           -campylocarpum Elatum Group 1/16
     -Gold -Dream-griersonianum
     -Mohur-       -fortunei ssp. discolor
           -Margaret-      -dichroanthum 1/16
              Dunn  -Fabia-
                        -griersonianum 3/16
5ft(1.5m) -15F(-26C)  ML  4/3     Strong red buds open to strong
and light pinks; throat pale yellow with red blotch.  Plant vig-
orous, sturdy.  Weldon E. Delp.


SIAM  Described under ANNA H. HALL, q.v.


                    -ponticum 1/4
         -Purple Splendour-
SIBYLLE-            -unknown 1/4
GARRETT-            -fortunei 1/4
       -unnamed hybrid-         -wardii 1/8
                      -unnamed hybrid-
                                 -dichroanthum 1/8
3.5ft(1m) x 3.5ft(16 yrs) OF(-18C)  M  Buds of strong purplish
red; flowers light purple,  prominent dorsal dark purple blotch;
truss of 12, 6in(15.2cm) wide.  A. A. Raustein, reg. 1986.


SIDEKICK   Described under BOB DANIK, q.v.


SIDLAW--possibly a form of vernicosum
5ft(1.5m)  -15F(-26C)  M  2/3  Leaves 4in(10cm) long, dark green
above, paler below.  Trusses hold 9-12 flowers of white, flushed
light purple with darker veining; a large blotch of Indian lake.
E. H. M. & P. A. Cox, Glendoick Gardens, reg. 1969.   P.C. 1969.


     -Rose Perfection (R. Gill)--unknown 1/2
SIDONIA-
     -fortunei 1/2
Rose pink.  Lord Aberconway, 1933.
```

SIERRA BEAUTY   Described under CANADIAN BEAUTY, q.v.

* *

```
                      -wardii 1/4
            -Crest-          -fortunei ssp. discolor 1/8
SIERRA DEL ORO-    -Lady  -
              -          Bessborough-campylocarpum Elatum Group 1/8
              -lacteum 1/2
3ft(.9m) OF(-18C)  VE    Trusses lasting 4 weeks, to 7in(17.8cm)
across, of 15 light yellow flowers, with 5 wavy, reflexed lobes,
3.5in(8.9cm) wide.  Plant broader than tall; arching branches;
leaves held 1.5 years.  J. G. Lofthouse, reg. 1982.
SIERRA TREASURE   Parentage as above
5ft(1.5m)  OF(-18C)  E    Fragrant flowers 4.5in(11.5cm) across,
yellow with 3 maroon blotches in throat, 5 wavy, reflexed lobes.
Trusses  hold 13, 8in(20cm) wide.   Plant as broad as high; dark
green, concave leaves.  Lofthouse cross; Dr. Rhodes, reg. 1985.
```

* *

```
                    -yakushimanum 1/8
          -unnamed hybrid-     -dichroanthum 5/32
    -Sunup- -          -Fabia-
    -Sundown-           -griersonianum 3/32
    -         -                   -dichroanthum
    -         -          -Fabia-
    -         -  -unnamed-    -griersonianum
    -         -unnamed- hybrid-bureavii 1/16
    -         hybrid-  -wardii 1/16
SIERRA-          -Crest-       -fortunei ssp. discolor
  STARS-          -Lady    -             1/32
    -              Bessborough-campylocarpum Elatum Gp
    -              -dichroanthum            1/32
    -            -Dido-
    -            -  -decorum 1/16    -griffithianum
    -     -Lem's-        -Beauty of-         7/64
    -     -Cameo-  -Norman- Tremough-arboreum 1/64
    -     -       -  - Gill -griffithianum
    -1000        -Anna-           -griffith.
    -Butterflies-  -       -Jean Marie de Montague-
    -            -                       -unknown
    -            -Pink   -Jan Dekens--unknown 1/4
              Petticoats-      -Queen   -griffithianum
                       -Britannia- Wilhelmina-
                       -           -unknown
                       -Stanley Davies--unknown
2ft(.6m) x 2ft(6 yrs)  OF(-18C)  EM    Flowers in trusses of 11-
13, 5 wavy lobes, vivid red in bud, opening pale purplish pink,
with a wide edging of vivid red, throat deep pink.  Leaves with
light orange-brown indumentum below.  J. Lofthouse, reg. 1986.
```

SIERRA SUNRISE Described under CANADIAN BEAUTY, q.v.

* *

```
                   -yakushimanum 1/8
         -unnamed-          -dichroanthum 7/32
         - hybrid-Fabia (selfed)-
    -Sunup-  -          -griersonianum 3/32
    - Sundown-          -dichroanthum
    -         -         -Fabia-
    -         -  -unnamed-    -griersonianum
    -         -unnamed- hybrid-bureavii 1/16
    -         hybrid-
    -         -    -wardii 1/16
SIERRA-          -Crest-       -fortunei ssp. discolor
SUNSET-          -Lady    -             1/32
    -              Bessborough-campylocarpum Elatum
    -              -dichroanthum           Group 1/32
    -   -Dido-
    -   -    -decorum 1/8
    -Lem's-              -griffithianum 5/32
    Cameo-         -Beauty of-
    -     -Norman- Tremough-arboreum 1/32
    -     - Gill -
    -Anna-   -griffithianum
    -              -griffithianum
    -Jean Marie de Montague-
                       -unknown 1/16
4ft(1.2m) OF(-18C)  EM    Strong salmon buds open to carmine red
flowers, edged shell pink.  Plant compact, as broad as high with
deep green leaves, held 2.5 years.  J. G. Lofthouse, reg. 1984.
ENTICEMENT   Parentage as above
3ft(.9m) x 3ft(6 yrs)  OF(-18C)  M   Flowers in trusses of 9-12,
```

vivid red in bud, open pale purplish pink with edges deep pink;
orange-red spotting in throat.   Lofthouse, reg. 1986.
PAINTED SKIES   Parentage as above
2ft(.6m) x 1.5ft(.45m)(6 yrs) OF(-18C) EM Buds of strong pink
open to light yellowish pink, darkening into strong pink at rims
of lobes; 2 orange rays on dorsal lobe.   Lofthouse, reg. 1986.
* *

SIERRA TREASURE   Described under SIERRA DEL ORO, q.v.

SIESTA   Described under ANDRÉ, q.v.

SIGISMUND RUCKER   Parentage unknown
Late-blooming flowers of an unusual, rich cherry magenta, with a
black flare; medium-sized trusses.   A. Waterer.   F.C.C. 1872.

* *
```
                        -dichroanthum 1/4
            -Jasper-          -fortunei ssp. discolor 1/8
              -    -Lady  -
SIGMUND ROMBERG-     Bessborough-campylocarpum Elatum Gp. 1/8
           -         -haematodes 1/4
          -May Day-
                   -griersonianum 1/4
```
3ft(.9m)(9 yrs.)   Open habit. Campanulate, lemon yellow flowers
to 3in(7.6cm) wide; flat truss of 12-18.   Seabrook, reg. 1964.
GEORGE M. COHAN   Parentage as above, except reversed
Medium-sized, open plant with flowers azalea pink, base carrot
red; to 3in(7.6cm) across; open trusses.   Seabrook, reg. 1967.
* *

```
              -catawbiense 1/4
         -Atrosanguineum-
SIGNAL-          -unknown 1/4
 HORN -              -caucasicum 3/16
   -         -Jacksonii-          -caucasicum 1/16
   -Goldsworth-          -Nobleanum-
    Yellow          -arboreum
                -campylocarpum 1/4
```
5ft(1.5m) -15F(-26C) ML   Leaves 7in(17.8cm) x 2in(5cm). Flow-
ers rosy pink, with deeper pink edges, and a distinctive spotted
red blotch, to 2in(5cm) across; lax trusses of about 8.   G. Guy
Nearing, reg. 1973.

* *
```
                      -griffithianum 1/4
            -George Hardy-
       -Marinus Koster-          -catawbiense 1/8
SIGRID-          -red hybrid--unknown 1/4
  -          -fortunei 1/4
  -Pilgrim-          -arboreum 1/8
          -Gill's Triumph-
              -griffithianum
```
4.5ft(1.35m) 5F(-15C) L   Plant upright, moderately branched;
dark green leaves retained 2 years.   Pink flowers fading paler,
darker edges and reverse, of heavy substance; truss of 12, very
weather-resistant.   Sigrid Laxdall, cross 1963; reg. 1977.
AUNTY THORA Parentage as above
Buds Tyrian rose; flowers glowing pink, red blotch, 5-lobed; 12
per ball-shaped truss.   Broad, rounded plant; new stems are red.
Laxdall, reg. 1979.   Color illus. ARS Q 33:4 (1979), p. 239.
JEANNE YVONNE   Parentage as above
10ft(3.m) x 10ft(25 yrs) 5F(-15C) M   Buds of strong red opening deep pink, aging to white, in truss of 13. Flowers 4in(10cm)
wide, 6 wavy-edged lobes; long, pink-edged calyx. Elliptic foliage 6in(152cm) long.   S. Laxdall cross; D. Laxdall, reg. 1988.
JENICE COFFEY   Parentage as above
3ft(.9m) 10F(-12C) L   Trusses of 15 flowers, rose pink with
minor deep pink spots, star-shaped red mark in throat; deep pink
stripes down reverse. Leaves held 2 years. Laxdall, reg. 1979.
ROBERT VERNE   Parentage as above
5ft(1.5m) 10F(-12C) L   Flowers of heavy substance, Tyrian
rose, prominent maroon spotting. Plant upright, half as wide as
tall.   More compact when grown in sun. Laxdall, reg. 1979.
SOFUS ECKREM   Parentage as above
5ft(1.5m) 10F(-12C) L Phlox pink buds open to rose pink flowers, deeper rims, 4.5in(11.5cm) wide; conical trusses of 10-11.
Glossy dark leaves, 8in(20.3cm) long.   Laxdall, reg. 1979.
* *

```
                   -wardii 1/2
         -China-
SIGRID -          -fortunei 1/4
AUNSBJORN-     -wardii
         -Crest-          -fortunei ssp. discolor 1/8
              -Lady Bessborough-
                        -campylocarpum Elatum 1/8
```
3.3ft(1.0m) x 2.7ft(.8m) OF(-18C) ML   Flowers of heavy sub-
stance, saucer-shaped, 3.5in(8.9cm) wide, fragrant, 7-lobed, of
pale yellow fading to near-white; ball truss of 18.   Oblong foliage to 7.8in(20cm).   Thorvall Aunsbjorn, Denmark, reg. 1989.

```
                   -catawbiense 1/4
         -Humboldt-
SILBERGLANZ-          -unknown 1/4
         -yakushimanum--Koichiro Wada 1/2
```
3ft(.9m) x 5ft(1.5m) -10F(-23C) ML Funnel-campanulate flowers
in truss of 11-13, 5 wavy-edged lobes, white with faint dorsal
spots, pale yellow-green. Loose habit; glossy dark leaves, thin
brown indumentum.   Hachmann, cross 1968; Stück, reg. 1988.

```
                        -yakushimanum--Koichiro Wada 1/2
SILBERWOLKE (SILVER CLOUD)-          -catawbiense 1/4
              -Album Novum-
                   -unknown 1/4
```
3ft(.9m) -15F(-26C) ML   Flowers of very light purple, spotted
yellow-green, the reverse shaded darker; truss of 12-16. Hairy,
ovate leaves to 4in(10cm) long. Hachmann, cross 1963; G. Stück,
reg. 1983.   A.M. Boskoop 1982.   Color illus. WS, 1989, p. 159.

```
                   -degronianum 1/2
SILENT SURPRISE-
                   -aureum 1/2
```
Dwarf -25F(-32C) EM   A plant only 9in(23cm) high in 11 years,
but 25in(64cm) broad. Buds of pink, opening to primrose yellow
flowers, without markings, 2.25in(5.7cm) wide; dome-shaped truss
holds 7-9.   Leaves to 3in(7.6cm), retained 2-3 years.   B. C.
Potter, reg. 1983.

```
                        -catawbiense 1/8
              -Charles Dickens-
      -Dr. V. H. Rutgers-          -unknown 3/8
SILJA-          -Lord Roberts--unknown
      -viscidifolium 1/2
```
Cardinal red flowers held in trusses of 6-8.   Dietrich G.
Hobbie cross; B. Leendertz, reg. 1976.

```
         -leucaspis 1/2
SILKCAP-          -ciliatum 1/4
         -Cilpinense-
                   -moupinense 1/4
```
Pure white flowers.   Crown Lands, 1951.

```
                        -fortunei ssp. discolor
                   -Ladybird-
              -Diva-          -Corona--1/8
         -Seattle-     -griersonianum
        - Gold -          -fortunei ssp. discolor
     -unnamed-     -Lady Bessborough-
     - hybrid-          -campylocarpum Elatum 1/4
     -          -fortunei ssp. discolor
SILKY-     -Autumn Gold-     -dichroanthum
 GOLD-          -Fabia-
     -               -griersonianum
     -     -fortunei ssp. discolor
     -Bonito-     -fortunei
          -Luscombei-
                   -thomsonii
```
5ft(1.5m) OF(-18C) L 4/3   Very soft pastel hues of yellow
contrast with the rugged, deeply veined foliage. Larson cross;
Clint Smith intro.

```
         -caucasicum 1/2
SILVER BELLS-
         -williamsianum 1/2
```
2ft(.6m) -5F(-21C) E Flowers pure silvery white, bell-shaped,
ruffled, 2.5in(6.4cm) wide, in trusses of 6-7.   Leaves glossy
dark green, oval, 2.5in.(6.5cm) long; plant about twice as broad
as high.   B. Lancaster, reg. 1966.

```
                    -yakushimanum 1/4
              -unnamed hybrid-
SILVER DOCTOR-                -unknown 3/4
                  -yellow hybrid--unknown
White flowers tinged light red.   J. Waterer, Sons & Crisp, reg.
1975.


                   -campylocarpum 1/4
        -Mrs. W. C.-
     - Slocock  -unknown 5/16
SILVER -                       -griffithianum 1/4
JUBILEE-        -Pink Shell-          -fortunei 3/16
     -          -           -H. M. Ardenne-
    -Coronation Day-                 -unknown
        -                  -griffithianum
            -Loderi-
                 -fortunei
Flowers chartreuse green fading to pale greenish white, crimson
markings in the upper throat. Trusses hold 14.   A. F. George,
cross 1967; Hydon Nurseries, reg. 1978.


* * * * * * * * * * * * * * * * * * * * * * * * * * * * *
             -megeratum 1/2
SILVER RAY-
        -boothii Mishmiense Group 1/2
Orange flowers.   Lord Aberconway, 1950.
MOTH   Parentage as above
Flowers lemon yellow,  heavily spotted brown.  Lord Aberconway.
A.M. 1955.
* * * * * * * * * * * * * * * * * * * * * * * * * * * * *


                     -dichroanthum 1/8
              -Fabia-
         -unnamed-       -griersonianum 1/4
         - hybrid-       -fortunei ssp. discolor 3/16
         -     -unnamed-
SILVER -       hybrid-facetum (eriogynum) 1/8
SIXPENCE-              -fortunei ssp. discolor
       -          -unnamed-
       -     -unnamed- hybrid-unknown 1/16
     -unnamed- hybrid-
       hybrid-      -griersonianum
              -unnamed-    -wardii 1/8
              -unnamed-
              hybrid-yakushimanum 1/8
3ft(.9m) -5F(-21C) 5/4    White flowers,  blushed with empire
rose, spotted in yellow.  John Waterer, Sons & Crisp, reg. 1975.
A.M. Wisley Trials 1986.


                      -yakushimanum 1/8
              -unnamed-
            - hybrid-            -dichroanthum 3/32
            -      -Fabia, selfed-
      -Sunup- -                -griersonianum 3/32
      -Sundown-                -dichroanthum
      -     -           -Fabia-
      -     -    -unnamed hybrid-  -griersonianum
SILVER -   -unnamed-        -bureavii  1/16
TRUMPETS-   hybrid-   -wardii 1/16
       -          -Crest-       -fortunei ssp. discolor
       -          -Lady -           1/32
       -          Bessborough-campylocarpum Elatum
       -                              1/32
      -yellow Whitney hybrid--unknown 1/2
3ft(.9m) OF(-18C) M   Buds of plum red  open to trumpet-shaped
flowers, plum color fading to white with blotched throat.  Leafy
calyx, spotted as flower.  Trusses 9in(23cm) across, 7-10 flow-
ers.  Plant semi-dwarf with arching branches and dark green
leaves; as wide as tall.  Lofthouse, cross 1979; reg. 1984.


SILVER TWIST   Described under STAR SHINE, q.v.


               -edgeworthii 1/2
SILVER WEDDING-
               -veitchianum Cubittii Group 1/2
Loose clusters of 3 flowers, 5-lobed, 5in(12.7cm) across,  white
flushed with shades of cardinal red,  upper throat suffused  and
spotted grayed yellow.  Leaves 4.5in(11.5cm) long,  scaly below.
G. A. Hardy cross; Maj. A. E. Hardy, reg. 1968.   P.C. 1978.
```

```
              -myrtifolium 1/2
SILVERBURN-
          -telmateium 1/2
Lepidote hybrid. Flowers orchid purple, held in compact trusses
of 3-4.  J. N. J. Hartley, intro. 1951; reg. 1962.   A.M. 1958.


SILVIA--form of lanigerum (silvaticum)
4ft(1.2m) 5F(-15C) E 4/4    Crimson to pink flowers suffused
white, in large truss of 30, blooming very early.  Lance-shaped
leaves with gray-brown indumentum beneath.  Hambro.  A.M. 1954.


SIMITA   Described under FRED WYNNIATT, q.v.

SIMONA   Described under MAHARANI, q.v.


                   -dichroanthum 1/8
            -Astarte-         -campylocarpum 1/16
            -       -Penjerrick-
         -Solon-              -griffithianum 7/16
         -    -      -griffithianum
SIMPLICITY-    -Sunrise-
         -           -griersonianum 1/8
         -    -griffithianum
          -Loderi-
               -fortunei 1/4
Brilliant red flowers.  Lord Aberconway, 1950.


          -G. A. Sims--unknown 3/4
SIMSODOUR-           -ponticum 1/4
        -Purple Splendour-
                        -unknown
Deep,  rich  purple flowers,  with a black  blotch.   Col. G. H.
Loder, 1938.


         -concinnum 1/2
SINBAD-           -cinnabarinum Roylei Group 1/4
     -Lady       -
     -Chamberlain-         -cinnabarinum 1/8
             -Royal Flush-
                        -maddenii 1/8
Crown Lands, exhibited 1952.


          -griffithianum 1/2
SINCERITY-
         -unknown 1/2
Plant habit and  foliage similar  to griffithianum.  Flowers 5-
to 7-lobed, deep pink fading to near-white, 5in(12.7cm) across;
conical trusses hold 9.   Gen. Harrison, reg. 1965.


SINGAPORE   Described under FLAMENCO, q.v.


              -dichroanthum ssp. scyphocalyx 1/2
SIR ARTHUR -      -dichroanthum 1/4
CONAN DOYLE-Jasper-
              -Lady        -fortunei ssp. discolor 1/8
              -Bessborough-
                    -campylocarpum Elatum Group 1/8
A small, but not dwarf plant; bluish green rounded leaves.  Cam-
panulate flowers, Spanish orange with pink edges, unfading, 2.5
in(6.4cm) wide, in flat trusses of 8-10.  Seabrook, reg. 1967.


SIR CHARLES BUTLER--form of fortunei
Synonym MRS. BUTLER.   Pale mauve to delicate pearl rose.  Often
a parent.   G. Paul.


SIR CHARLES LEMON--form of arboreum ssp. cinnamomeum var. album
5ft(1.5m) 5F(-15C) EM 4/5    Considered a natural hybrid of
arboreum and  campanulatum  by plant explorer A. D. Shilling.
Very handsome foliage with bright cinnamon brown indumentum; the
new leaves unfold white.  Flowers ivory white,  faintly spotted
in the throat; large rounded trusses.   Lord Aberconway, intro.
1937; seed, Sir J. Hooker.   Color illus. Cox pl. 173; VV p. 52.


* * * * * * * * * * * * * * * * * * * * * * * * * * * * *
                   -fortunei ssp. discolor 1/2
SIR FREDERICK MOORE-      -arboreum ssp. zeylanicum 1/4
                  -Saint Keverne-
                        -griffithianum 1/4
6ft(1.8m) -5F(-21C) ML A large rhododendron, large trusses of
large flowers, clear pink and fragrant.  Named for the Director
of Glasnevin Botanic Gardens, Dublin.  Rothschild, 1935.  A.M.
1937.  F.C.C. Wisley Trials 1972.
```

CHARLOTTE DE ROTHSCHILD   Parentage as above
6ft(1.8m) -5F(-21C) ML   Flowers clear pink, spotted, campanulate, in truss of 14. L. de Rothschild, reg. 1962. A.M. 1958.
MARY ROXBURGHE   Parentage as above
Large spreading plant with large pink flowers, darker in throat, held in large trusses.   L. de Rothschild intro. 1954.   Color illus. PB pl. 26.
* *

SIR GEORGE SANSOM   Described under LACTCOMBEI, q.v.

```
                    -griffithianum 1/2
SIR ISAAC BALFOUR-
                    -unknown 1/2
```
Reddish pink.   Otto Schulz, raised c.1890; C. B. van Nes intro.

```
                                        -fortunei 1/4
          -Director E. Hjelm---fortunei hyb. F2-
          -                           -unknown 1/4
SIR ISAAC-                             -caucasicum 1/16
 BROCK   -              -Cunningham's White-
         -    -Rocket-               -ponticum, white 1/16
         -Monique-     -catawbiense, red form 1/8
         Behring-yakushimanum 1/4
```
3ft(.9m) x 3ft(8 yrs) -15F(-26C) ML   Deep purplish pink buds. Frilly heavy-textured flowers, light purplish pink, yellow flare and deep orange-yellow dorsal spotting, fragrant; domed truss of 11; flat elliptic leaves, held 3 years.   R. Behring, reg. 1989.

```
          -fortunei 1/2
SIR JAMES-
          -unknown 1/2
```
5ft(1.5m) -10F(-23C) M 3/3   Light pink flowers; floriferous. Medium green foliage.   Probably a Dexter hybrid. J. B. Gable.

SIR JAMIE DARLING   Described under FORTUNE, q.v.

```
                 -ponticum 1/2
SIR JOHN BROUGHTON-
                 -unknown 1/2
```
Light carmine red flowers.   Before 1867.

```
                -Corona--unknown 1/2
SIR JOHN RAMSDEN-
                -thomsonii 1/2
```
Above parentage as in Register, 1958. Hillier shows pollen parent either campylocarpum or wardii. Lax trusses hold 10 large flowers, carmine with pale pink margins. A large plant with a vigorous loose habit. Waterer, Sons & Crisp. A.M. 1926. A.M. Wisley Trials 1948. F.C.C. Wisley Trials 1955.

SIR JOSEPH WHITWORTH   Parentage unknown
A parent of JOAN LANGDON. Waterer.

```
                  -yakushimanum 1/4
       -China Doll-          -griersonianum 1/8
       -          -Mrs. Horace-          -griffithianum
SIR PHILLIP-      Fogg    -Loderi Venus-         1/16
 BENNETT  -                          -fortunei 1/16
          -unnamed hybrid--unknown 1/2
```
Truss of 14 flowers 3.5in(9cm) wide, 7-lobed; buds light orange, opening pale yellow, aging medium roseine purple with light orange buff center; outside suffused and striped phlox pink. Bush 1.7ft(.5m) x 2.7ft(.8m); elliptic foliage, 5.8in(15cm) long. R. Malone, cross 1980; N. Sullivan, reg. 1989.

```
                    -griffithianum 1/4
            -unnamed hybrid-
SIR RICHARD CARTON-       -unknown 3/4
            -Rubescens--unknown
```
Flowers of crimson scarlet with cream-colored stamens and style. C. B. van Nes & Sons.

```
             -arboreum 1/2
SIR ROBERT PEEL-
             -ponticum 1/2
```
6ft(1.8m) 5F(-15C) VE   Flowers of crimson, with a blue tinge. A vigorous plant, of good habit. Heat-tolerant. A street tree in New Zealand. Waterer, before 1871.

```
          -haematodes 1/4
     -Choremia-
SIREN-     -arboreum 1/4
     -griersonianum 1/2
```
5ft(1.5m) 10F(-12C) M   Bell-shaped, waxy, brilliant red flowers, with darker spotting; rounded truss. Dark, glossy foliage on a small shrub that blooms midseason. Lord Aberconway, 1942. A.M. 1942.

SIRIUS   Described under ROYAL FLUSH, q.v.

```
                                -catawbiense
                   -Parsons Grandi-        1/8
            -America- florum      -unknown 3/8
SIZZLER---unnamed hybrid F2-      -dark red hybrid--unknown
                                -yakushimanum 1/2
```
Cardinal red buds open to flowers of rose Bengal and vivid purplish red; dorsal spotting Tyrian purple.   W. Delp.

SKEETER HILL   Described under HI DRAMA, q.v.

SKERRYVORE MONARCH   Parentage unknown
5ft(1.5m) -5F(-21C) M   Watermelon pink, spotted greenish yellow. Dexter cross; Beinecke raiser; G. Wister, reg. 1981.

```
              -fortunei 25/64
       -Fawn-    -dichroanthum 1/8
       -   -Fabia-
       -       -griersonianum 1/4
SKIPPER-              -griersonianum
       -Sarita Loder-    -griffithianum 5/64
       -    -     -Loderi-
       -Indian-         -fortunei
        Penny-    -wardii 1/8    -griffithianum
          -Idealist-      -Kewense-
                  -    -Aurora-   -fortunei
                  -Naomi-   -thomsonii 1/32
                      -fortunei
```
5ft(1.5m) 0F(-18C) EM 5/3 Compact plant; leaves 6in(15.2cm) long. Flowers empire yellow, lighter at center, widely campanulate, to 5in(12.7in) wide; compact rounded trusses of 14.   Del James cross; C. Thompson, reg. 1972.

```
          -fortunei 1/2                -catawbiense 1/8
SKOKOMISH-                  -Atrosanguineum-
       -Dr. H. C. Dresselhuys-     -unknown 1/4
       -              -arboreum 1/8
                 -Doncaster-
                      -unknown
```
Parker, before 1958.

```
              -yakushimanum 1/4
      -unnamed hybrid-  -griffithianum 1/8
      -         -Mars-
SKOOKUM-         -unknown 1/2
      -              -catawbiense 1/8
      -     -Parsons Grandiflorum-
      -America-         -unknown
           -dark red hybrid--unknown
```
4ft(1.2m) x 4ft(15 yrs) -20F(-29C) M   Plant rounded and well-branched; flowers in dome-shaped trusses of 15, strong red with white filaments.   A similar sibling is named SKOOKUMCHUCK. Larson cross; Fred Minch raiser, reg. 1986.

SKYGLOW   Parentage unknown
5ft(1.5m) -5F(-21C) L 3/2   A parent of MAUD CORNING. Poor leaf color and growth habit. Fragrant flowers, 6-lobed, to 3in. (7.6cm) across, peach-colored, edged pink, with a pale greenish yellow blotch, in flattened trusses of 12.   Much like ASHES OF ROSES, q.v. Veitch of England raiser; C. Dexter intro. to USA; Heritage Plantation, reg. 1978. Color illus. LW pl. 18.

SLEEA--form of martinianum
Pink-flowered. From G. Reuthe; Mrs. Kenneth, of Argyll, reg. 1965. P.C. 1964.

SLEEPY   Described under PINK CHERUB, q.v.

SLIPPERY ROCK   Described under HAD, q.v.

```
              -sanguineum ssp. didymum 1/4
       -Carmen-
SMALL FRY-      -forrestii Repens Group 1/4
       -              -campylocarpum 1/4
       -Moonstone-
                     -williamsianum 1/4
```
2ft(.6m) OF(-18C) EM 3/4   Dark green foliage held by bright
red stems; flowers rose red.   Hill cross; Fisher intro.

```
          -pemakoense 1/2
SMALL GEM-
          -leucaspis 1/2
```
1.5ft(.45m) -5F(-21C) E 4/4   Both parents are evident, leucaspis in the flower, pemakoense in the plant. Buds heavily and
when very young. Opening buds are pink, flowers then turn white
with slight blush of soft pink; deep brown anthers. L. Frisbee.

SMALL WONDER   Described under FLAMENCO, q.v.

```
                           -Pygmalion--unknown 1/8
                 -unnamed-
                 -Weldy- hybrid-haematodes 1/32
         -unnamed-     -yakushimanum, Exbury form 1/16
         - hybrid-         -yakushimanum 1/4
         -       -Serendipity-
    -unn.-                 -aureum (chrysanthum) 3/16
    -hyb.-                 -neriiflorum 1/32
    -   -                 -Nereid-
    -   -     -Phyllis Ballard-     -dichroanthum 1/32
SMASHING-  -unnamed-          -fortunei ssp. discolor 1/16
    -     hybrid-catawbiense--Clark's White 1/8
    -            -yakushimanum
    -   -Serendipity-
    -   -         -aureum          -thomsonii 1/32
    -Indy-                  -Bagshot Ruby-
    Pink-   -Princess Elizabeth-          -unknown
    -Lanny-               -unknown
    Pride-            -smirnowii 1/16
         -unnamed hybrid-
                         -yakushimanum
```
Buds of currant red and cardinal red, opening to flowers of rose
Bengal and pale purplish pink; indumented foliage.   W. Delp.

SMEW   Described under PEREGRINE, q.v.

```
       -smirnowii 1/2
SMIRNAUCK-
       -griffithianum (aucklandii) 1/2
```
Pure white flowers. E. J. P. Magor, 1924.

```
         -arboreum 1/2
SMITHII ALBUM-
         -unknown 1/2
```
White flowers, spotted. See also BODDAERTIANUM.

SMITHII AUREUM   See NORBITONENSE AUREUM

SMOKE--form of augustinii
6ft(1.8m) -5F(-21C) EM 4/3   A beautiful clear blue form from
the Trewithen Garden.

```
                         -griffithianum
              -Queen Wilhelmina-          1/16
         -Britannia-          -unknown 13/16
    -Burgundy-     -Stanley Davies--unknown
    -        -          -ponticum 1/8
SMOKEY NO. 9-     -Purple Splendour-
    -                   -unknown
    -Moser's Maroon--unknown
```
6ft(1.8m) -5F(-21C) ML 4/3   Fir green leaves, heavily veined.
Leafy flower buds open to deep purple flowers, in full trusses.
Halfdan Lem.

* *

```
              -ponticum 3/8
    -Purple Splendour-
SMYRNA-         -unknown 3/8
    -          -campylocarpum 1/4
    -Constant Nymph-          -ponticum
              -Purple Splendour-
                        - unknown
```
Large lavender flowers, without markings. Knap Hill, reg. 1968.

BESS   Parentage as above or reversed
Lavender flowers. Donald Waterer cross; Knap Hill, reg. 1975.
* *

SNAPPY   Described under SHORT STUFF, q.v.

SNEEZY   Described under PINK CHERUB, q.v.

SNIPE   Described under PHALAROPE, q.v.

SNOW   Registered as WYNTERSET WHITE, q.v.

```
         -Loder's White, q.v. for 2 possible
SNOW BELLS-          parentage diagrams
       -williamsianum
```
1.5ft(.45m) OF(-18C) E   Plant broader than tall, dense; oval
leaves 2in(5cm) long. Flowers pure white, openly campanulate,
2.5in(6.4cm) wide; trusses of 5-7.   B. F. Lancaster, reg. 1968.

SNOW BIRD   See WHITE BIRD

```
          -arboreum 1/2
SNOW BUNTING-
          -sutchuenense 1/2
```
White flowers.   J. C. Williams.

```
         -souliei 1/2
SNOW CAP-                    -griffithianum 1/8
    -       -Loderi White Diamond-
    -unnamed-          -fortunei 1/8
    hybrid-
         -williamsianum 1/4
```
4ft(1.2m) -5F(21C) M 3/3   Shell pink buds opening to pure
white flowers without markings, 3.25in(8.3cm) wide, 7-lobed, in
truss of 7; floriferous. Plant rounded, as broad as tall; foliage held 3 years.   Whitney cross; G. & A. Sather, reg. 1976.

SNOW CREST   Described under MOUNT HOOD, q.v.

```
          -moupinense 1/2
SNOW FAIRY-
          -mucronulatum ? 1/2
```
Mrs. Roza M. Stevenson raiser.   P.C. 1957.

SNOW GOOSE   Described under ANNE GEORGE, q.v.

```
          -aureum (chrysanthum) 1/2
SNOW JOB-
          -maximum, white form, Jackson Center, Pa. 1/2
```
Buds of pale greenish yellow open to flowers pale yellow-green,
throat light greenish yellow; dorsal spots strong yellow-green.
W. Delp.

```
          -leucaspis 1/2
SNOW LADY-
          -ciliatum ? 1/2
```
2.5ft(.75m) 5F(-15C) E 4/5   Pure white, in bud and flower.
In W. G. Tucker collection; from Rothschild, as the species leucaspis.   P.A. 1955.   Color illus. Cox pl. 174.

```
          -dalhousiae 1/2
SNOW MANTLE-
    -          -edgeworthii 1/4
    -Fragrantissimum-
               -formosum 1/4
```
Trusses hold 3 flowers, white with a gold throat fading out. R.
C. Gordon, NZ, reg. 1982.

SNOW PEAK   Described under LOCKINGTON PRIDE, q.v.

```
               -maximum 1/4
         -Halopeanum-
SNOW QUEEN-          -griffithianum 1/2
    -       -griffithianum
    -Loderi-
         -fortunei 1/4
```
5ft(1.5m) 5F(-15C) M 4/2   Deep pink buds opening to large,
funnel-shaped, pure white flowers, with a tiny red basal blotch;
large, dome-shaped trusses. One of the best whites. Vigorous
plant of open habit; leaves to 8in(20.3in) long, won't withstand
sun. Sir Edmund Loder. A.M. 1934.   A.M. Wisley Trials 1946.
F.C.C. Wisley Trials 1970.

```
                -fortunei ssp. discolor 3/4
SNOW SHIMMER-            -maximum 1/4
            -unnamed hybrid-
                        -fortunei ssp. discolor
```
6ft(1.8m) -5F(-21C) L   Flowers 4in(10cm) wide, 7-lobed, very
fragrant, white with a pale yellow glow at center; ball-shaped
trusses of 10. Plant broader than tall; olive green leaves, new
growth greenish brown. John & Gertrude Wister, Scott Horticultural Found., reg. 1980. Color illus. ARS Q 34:3 (1980), cover.

```
            -leucaspis 1/4
        -Snow Lady-
SNOW SPRITE-        -ciliatum ? 1/4
        -moupinense 1/2
```
1ft(.3m) 5F(-15C) E   Plant as wide as high, more compact than
its parents. Glossy green leaves 1.5in(3.8cm) long. Pure white
5-lobed flowers, chocolate brown anthers, openly campanulate; 3-
5 per truss. B. F. Lancaster & R. Whalley, reg. 1969.

SNOW WHITE   Described under KEWENSE, q.v.

```
        -sutchuenense 1/2
SNOWBALL-            -griffithianum 1/4
        -Loderi Pink Diamond-
                        -fortunei 1/4
```
White flowers.   "Not from Leonardslee"--Sir Giles Loder.

```
                        -maximum 1/2
            -Stokes Bronze Wings-
SNOWBERRY BEAUTY-            -catawbiense 1/4
        -                -maximum 1/4
            -Adele's Yellow-
                        -wardii 1/4
```
Buds of fuchsia purple and deep purplish pink, opening to white
flowers; pea green dorsal spotting; anthers pale purple.   Delp.

```
        -griffithianum 1/2
SNOWDROP-
        -unknown 1/2
```
Pure white flowers. A parent of JOAN RAMSDEN.   Origin unknown.

SNOWFLAKE   Described under BRITE MITE, q.v.

```
        -yakushimanum 1/2
SNOWSTORM-        -Corona--unknown  5/16
        -Cary Ann-        -griffithianum 1/16
        -        -Mars-
            -Vulcan-    -unknown
                        -griersonianum 1/8
```
Pure white flowers, with rose spotting, a fine contrast to dark
green foliage. Plant vigorous, compact. Lofthouse, reg. 1973.

```
        -ririei 1/2
SNOWY RIVER-
        -niveum 1/2
```
Rounded trusses of 13-15 flowers, lilac with deeper veining and
flushing, 1.75in(4.5cm) wide. Leaves 6in(15.2cm) long, thinly
plastered fawn indumentum beneath.   The Second Lord Aberconway
cross; Lord Aberconway, reg. 1974.   A.M. 1974.

```
            -sanguineum ssp. sanguineum var. sanguineum 1/4
        -Sangreal-
SNUGBUG-        -griersonianum 1/4
        -tsariense 1/2
```
4ft(1.2m) -5F(-21C) M Openly funnel-shaped flower, 3in(7.6cm)
long, 5-lobed, opening cherry red, fading to carmine rose; truss
5in(12.7cm) wide. Leaves held 3 years.   Wildfong, reg. 1983.

```
                        -catawbiense 1/8
            -Catawbiense Album-
        -Wizard-            -unknown 1/8
        -        -dichroanthum 1/8
        -        -Fabia-
SO WHAT!-            -griersonianum 1/8
        -                -aureum (chrysanthum) 1/8
        -        -unnamed-
        -Candes-- hybrid-maximum 1/8        -neriiflorum 1/32
          cent  -            -Nereid-
            -        -Phyllis Bal--        -dichroanthum 1/32
            -unnamed- lard    -fortunei s. discolor 1/16
                hybrid-catawbiense--Clark's White 1/8
```
Spinel red buds opening to white flowers, edged with spinel red;

dorsal spotting of brilliant greenish yellow; throat chartreuse
green.   Jack Looye cross; Weldon Delp raiser.

```
        -dichroanthum ssp. scyphocalyx 1/2
SOCRIANUM-
        -griffithianum 1/2
```
A parent of BOW STREET, CHEAPSIDE, PALL MALL. Apricot-colored
flowers. J. B. Stevenson, 1951.

```
                            -fortunei ssp. discolor
                -Ladybird-            3/16
                -    -Diva--Corona--unknown 1/16
        -Seattle Gold-    -griersonianum 1/8
SOFT    -        -            -fortunei ssp. disc.
SATIN (Brandt)-        -Lady Bessborough-
            -yakushimanum 1/2        -campylo. Elatum 1/8
```
3ft(.9m) -5F(-21C) M 4/5 Cream-colored flowers with sheen of
satin. Compact plant, small dark leaves.   Brandt.

SOFT SATIN (Delp)   Described under SHORT STUFF, q.v.

SOFT SENSATION   Described under EASTER BUNNY, q.v.

```
        -yakushimanum 1/2
SOFT SHADOWS-
        -argyrophyllum 1/2
```
Trusses of 12-15 flowers, 5-lobed, carmine rose fading to pure
white. Leaves 3.5in(8.9cm) long, with fawn suede-like indumentum beneath.   F. M. Jury, NZ, reg. 1982.

SOFUS ECKREM   Described under SIGRID, q.v.

```
        -campylocarpum ssp. caloxanthum 1/2
SOLARIUM-            -caucasicum 1/8
        -    -Dr. Stocker-
        -Damaris-        -griffithianum 1/8
            -campylocarpum 1/4
```
Flowers clear yellow, spotted crimson.   Sunningdale, 1955.

SOLDIER PALMER   Described under SPARKLER, q.v.

```
            -dichroanthum 3/4
        -Dido-
SOLDIER SAM-    -decorum 1/4
        -dichroanthum
```
3ft(.9m) -10F(-23C) M   Flowers yellow-orange tinged red on
outside; trusses of 12. Prolific bloomer.   Reuthe, reg. 1985.

SOLENT QUEEN   Described under ANGELO, q.v.

SOLENT SNOW   Described under ANGELO, q.v.

SOLENT SWAN   Described under ANGELO, q.v.

SOLID IMPACT   Described under ACTIVE DUTY, q.v.

```
                        -griffithianum 1/4
        -Jean Marie de Montague-
SOLIDARITY-            -unknown 1/4
        -yakushimanum 1/2
```
3ft(.9m) -15F(-26C) M 4/4   Large trusses of deep pink flow-
ers, strong purplish red at margins, blending to light purplish
pink in throat. Plant dense and well-shaped.   H. A. Schannen,
cross 1969; reg. 1990. Color illus. Greer catalog, 1990, pl. 8.

```
* * * * * * * * * * * * * * * * * * * * * * * * * * * *
                        -griffithianum 1/8
            -Queen Wilhelmina-
        -Britannia-            -unknown 3/8
SOLITUDE-        -Stanley Davies--unknown
        -        -elliottii 1/4
        -Fusilier-
            -griersonianum 1/4
```
4ft(1.2m) 0F(-18C) ML 3/3   Glowing red flowers, with dark
spotting. Long recurved leaves like FUSILIER. Vigorous plant.
Rudolph Henny, before 1958.
BRITALIER   Parentage as above
4ft(1.2m) -5F(-21C) L 4/4 A fine late-blooming red. Davis.
* *

```
            -dichroanthum 1/4
    -Astarte-        -campylocarpum Elatum Group 1/8
    -        -Penjerrick-
SOLON-                -griffithianum 3/8
    -        -griffithianum
    -Sunrise-
            -griersonianum 1/4
```
Pale rose flowers. Lord Aberconway, 1941.

SOLVEIG   Listed under FABIA, q.v.

```
                -ponticum 1/4
    -Purple Splendour-
SONATA-            -unknown 1/4
    -dichroanthum 1/2
```
3ft(.9m) OF(-18C) L 3/3 Orange flowers, edged with burgundy.
Sun-tolerant plant; very dense foliage. G. Reuthe, 1949. H.C.
Wisley Trials 1959. Color illus. Cox pl. 175; JS p. 92.

SONATINE   Described under YAKU WARRIOR, q.v.

* *
```
        -russatum 1/2
SONGBIRD-        -impeditum 1/4
        -Blue Tit-
                -augustinii 1/4
```
3ft(.9m) -5F(-21C) EM 4/4   Clusters of violet blue, bell-
shaped flowers. Plant habit strong and tidy; small, glossy foliage. Sir James Horlick, 1954. A.M. 1957. Color illus. Cox
pl. 176; F p. 64.
SONGSTER   Parentage as above
A small, compact shrub, covered with small blue flowers. Blooms
early. Sir James Horlick, 1957.
* *

```
    -wardii 1/2
SONIA-                -arboreum ssp. cinnamomeum var. album
    -        -unnamed-                                1/8
    -Constance- hybrid-griffithianum 1/8
    -
            -auriculatum 1/4
```
Ivory white flowers.   Possibly Rothschild; not registered.

SONIC RAY   Described under COURT JESTER, q.v.

```
                -maximum 1/4
        -Opal (Delp)-
        -            -catawbiense 1/4
SONIC WAVES-                    -caucasicum 3/16
        -            -Jacksonii-        -caucasicum
        -Goldsworth Yellow-        -Nobleanum-
                    -cammpylocarpum 1/4 -arboreum 1/16
```
Buds of magnolia purple open to mallow purple flowers; dorsal
spots strong greenish yellow. W. Delp.

```
        -caucasicum 1/2
SOPHIA GRAY-
        -unknown 1/2
```
A parent of BUXUM, GIPSY MAID. Fimbriated pink flowers, spotted
with burnt umber. M. Koster & Sons, before 1922.

```
        -yakushimanum 1/2
SOPHIE PESTE-        -dichroanthum ssp. scyphocalyx 1/4
        -medusa-
                -griersonianum 1/4
```
15in(.38m) high x 18in(.46m)(6 yrs) OF(-18C) M   Flowers in
domed trusses of 15, strong purplish red in bud, opening pale
purplish pink with deep purplish pink edges. Young leaves with
moderate orange-yellow indumentum; well-branched, dwarf plant.
Fred Peste cross; S. P. Johnston, reg. 1986.

```
        -souliei 1/2
SOULARB-
        -arboreum 1/2
```
A deep cherry red flower. E. J. P. Magor, 1926.

```
        -souliei 1/2
SOULBUT-
        -fortunei--Sir Charles Butler 1/2
```
White tinged pink, broad crimson spotting. E. J. P. Magor, 1926.

* *
```
        -souliei 1/2
SOULDIS-
        -fortunei ssp. discolor 1/2
```
Large flowers of blush pink fading to off-white, with a small
crimson basal blotch, saucer-shaped, in loose trusses on a tall
plant. Mid- to late-season. E. J. P. Magor, 1927. P.A. 1954.
ENDRE OSTBO   Parentage as above
6ft(1.8m) OF(-18C) ML 3/3   Flowers pale blush pink, fringed
darker pink, spotted red, saucer-shaped, to 4in(10cm) wide; lax
trusses of about 9. Endre Ostbo, reg. 1962. P.A. 1954.
EXBURY SOULDIS   Parentage as above
This form tall but compact. Pink buds opening to white flowers,
with notched petals and crimson blotch. Rothschild. A.M. 1948.
* *

```
        -souliei 1/2
SOULKEW-        -griffithianum 1/4
        -Kewense-
                -fortunei 1/4
```
Flowers are blush white, pink outside. E. J. P. Magor, 1926.

```
        -souliei 1/2
SOULKING-
        -arboreum ssp. zeylanicum 1/2
```
Crimson pink flowers. E. J. P. Magor, 1926.

SOURCE BANK Described under RED DOG, q.v.

```
                -fortunei ssp. discolor 1/4
        -unnamed hybrid-
        -                -decorum 1/4
SOUTHERN-                        -griffithianum 1/32
  BELLE -                -Kewense-
        -        -Aurora-        -fortunei
        -    -Naomi-        -thomsonii 1/16
        -Carita-        -fortunei 5/32
                -campylocarpum 1/4
```
5ft(1.5m) 5F(-15C) ML   Jasper red buds open to fragrant flow-
ers, primrose yellow fading to light Naples yellow; domed truss
6.5in(16.5cm) across, of 11 flowers. Plant 3/4 as wide as tall;
leaves 5in(12.7cm) long. G. E. Barefield, cross 1959; M. Barefield, reg. 1981.

SOUTHERN CLOUD   Described under MI AMOR, q.v.

SOUTHERN CROSS   Described under GIPSY MOTH, q.v.

```
        -minus var. chapmanii 1/2
SOUTHLAND-
        -keiskei, prostrate form 1/2
```
1.5ft(.45m) -10F(-23C) M   Flowers salmon-colored. Plant very
floriferous, wider than tall; very compact growth.   A. E. Kehr.

SOUVENIR DE ANTHONY WATERER   Parentage unknown
4ft(1.2m) -10F(-23C) L   May be a maximum hybrid. Salmon red,
with an orange-yellow eye. Waterer. (Two hybrids of almost the
same name and description, are listed in 1959 I.R.R.)

```
                -arboreum 1/4
SOUVENIR DE -Doncaster-
D. A. KOSTER-        -unknown 3/4
            -Charles Waterer--unknown
```
5ft(1.5m) -5F(-21C) ML   A profusion of dark scarlet flowers,
with dark spotting. D. A. Koster raiser; Wezelenberg intro.
A.M. 1922.

```
                    -griffithianum 1/8
            -George Hardy-
        -Pink -        -catawbiense 3/8
        -Pearl-        -arboreum 3/8
SOUVENIR DE -    -Broughtonii-
DR. S. ENDTZ-            -unknown 1/8
        -            -catawbiense
        -John Walter-
                -arboreum
```
6ft(1.8m) -10F(23C) M   Buds of rose, opening to flowers of
rich, pink marked with a crimson ray, widely funnel-shaped, 3.25
in(8.3cm) wide; domed trusses of 15-17. Plant vigorous, broader
than tall; dark green leaf 6.5in(16.5cm) long. L. J. Endtz, of
Boskoop. A.M. 1924. A.G.M. 1969. F.C.C. Wisley Trials 1970.
Color illus. F p. 64; JS p. 42.

```
                -griffithianum 1/2
SOUVENIR DE MADAME-
  J. H. VAN NES    -unknown 1/2
Scarlet flowers.   O. Schulz, raiser 1890; C. B. van Nes & Sons,
intro. 1896.


SOUVENIR OF ANTHONY WATERER   Parentage unknown
6ft(1.8m)  -10F(-23C) M   A parent of several hybrids.  Flowers
dark rosy red or salmon, yellow blotch.   A. Waterer.


                -campylocarpum 1/2
SOUVENIR OF W. C. SLOCOCK-
                -unknown 1/2
4ft(1.2m)  -5F(-21C) M  3/3   Similar to UNIQUE.  Plant compact
and attractive.  Buds of deep apricot pink opening pale primrose
yellow, lightly flushed apricot,  and pink on reverse;  rounded
trusses.  Medium green leaves, with a slight twist.   Slocock.
A.M. 1935.   Color illus. F p. 65; VV p. 14.


                -fortunei ssp. discolor 1/2
          -Belle-
          -        -campylocarpum Elatum Group 1/4
SPANISH GALLEON-
          -                   -fortunei ssp. discolor
          -Margaret Dunn-     -dichroanthum 1/8
                        -Fabia-
                             -griersonianum 1/8
Flowers of butter yellow.  Sunningdale Nurseries, 1955.


SPANISH GLORY   Described under CORAL ISLAND, q.v.


                -fortunei ssp. discolor 1/4
        -Evening Glow-    -dichroanthum 1/8
        -             -Fabia-
        -                  -griersonianum 1/8
SPANISH LADY-                              -griffithianum
        -               -Queen Wilhelmina-       1/16
        -           -Britannia-           -unknown 5/16
        -Lamplighter-        -Stanley Davies--unknown
        -                               -fortunei 1/8
              -Madame Fr. J. Chauvin-
                               -unknown
5ft(1.5m)  -5F(-21C)  ML  4/4  Flowers warm reddish orange, with
a golden glow.  Long, narrow pine green leaves.  Vigorous plant.
Harold and Morna Stockman cross.   Greer, intro. 1988.


                -fortunei 1/4
        -Pilgrim-
        -          -arboreum 1/8
        -       -Gill's Triumph-
SPARKLE PLENTY-          -griffithianum 1/8
        -        -sanguineum ssp. didymum 1/8
        -Red Cap-
                -facetum (eriogynum) 1/4
Flowers light yellow to white with vermilion spots, held in tall
trusses.  Medium, upright growth habit.  Henny, reg. 1964.


* * * * * * * * * * * * * * * * * * * * * * * * * * * * * *
                -facetum (eriogynum) 1/8
          -unnamed-
          - hybrid-unknown 5/16
      -unnamed-    -dichroanthum 1/8
      - hybrid-Fabia-
SPARKLER-              -griersonianum 1/8
      -      -yakushimanum 1/4
      -unnamed-                      -griffithianum 1/16
       hybrid-       -Queen Wilhelmina-
          -Britannia-           -unknown
                    -Stanley Davies--unknown
3ft(.9m)  OF(-18C) ML    Plant of compact habit.  Large flowers
of rich bright red,  non-fading and floriferous.   J. Waterer,
Sons & Crisp, reg. 1971.
BORDERER   Parentage as above
Flower of China rose, deepening at margins.  Waterer, reg. 1975.
PHEASANT TAIL   Parentage as above
3ft(.9m)  OF(-18C) M   Rose pink flowers, lighter center.  Wat-
erer, Sons & Crisp, reg. 1975.
SOLDIER PALMER   Parentage as above
3ft(.9m)  OF(-18C) M  Compact plant; flowers brick red, spotted
red.   John Waterer, Sons & Crisp, reg. 1975.
TOLKIEN   Parentage as above
Small, upright trusses of  rather small cardinal red flowers, on
a dense, upright plant; leaves pointed.  Holds color better than
```

```
SPARKLER--Cox.  P. Wiseman, cross 1958; D. E. Mayers, reg. 1985.
* * * * * * * * * * * * * * * * * * * * * * * * * * * * * *

                -ponticum 1/4
          -Purple Splendour-
SPARKLING BURGUNDY-       -unknown 1/4
          -macrophyllum--Seven Devils 1/2
5ft(1.5m)  10F(-12C)  M  Flowers openly funnel-shaped, 2in(10cm)
wide,  soft lilac purple throat with touch of white,  some aster
violet spotting.  Trusses dome-shaped, 17-flowered.  Plant habit
open, upright; ivy green leaves, retained 3 years.   Dr. Frank
Mossman cross, 1973; J. Brotherton, reg. 1983.


* * * * * * * * * * * * * * * * * * * * * * * * * * * * * *
          -fortunei ssp. discolor 1/2
SPARKLING JEWEL-       -fortunei 1/4
          -unnamed hybrid-
                    -unknown 1/4
6ft(1.8m)  -5F(-21C)  ML  Very fragrant flowers, white with pale
yellow-green spotting,  openly funnel-shaped,  4in(10cm) across,
7-lobed.  Ball-shaped trusses hold 11.  Plant upright, branching
moderately; leaves held 2 years.   John & Gertrude Wister, Scott
Horticultural Foundation, reg. 1980.
SUNLIT SNOW   Parentage as above
6FT(1.8m)  OF(-18C)  L    Fragrant flowers, funnel-shaped, 4in.
(10cm) across, light purplish pink to bright yellow-green in the
throat; flat truss of 9.  Plant broader than tall.  John & Ger-
trude Wister, reg. 1981.
* * * * * * * * * * * * * * * * * * * * * * * * * * * * * *


SPATTER PAINT--form of irroratum
5ft(1.5m)  5F(-15C)  VE   Venetian pink flowers with heavy spot-
ting over most of corolla.  Campanulate flowers 2in(5cm) across,
5-lobed; flattened trusses of 13.  Upright, well-branched plant;
handsome foliage, leaves held 4 years; new growth of red bracts.
Seed from the Rock, 1948 Expedition;  J. Henny  and C. C. Smith
raisers; Meldon Kraxberger, reg. 1979.   Color illus HG p. 35.


SPECIAL IMPACT   Described under ACTIVE DUTY, q.v.


SPECIAL SPARKLE   Described under ACTIVE DUTY


     -fortunei ssp. discolor 1/2
SPECTRA-
     -unknown 1/2
Flowers flushed pink, fading to white.  Blooms late season.  E.
Ostbo; C. P. Fawcett, reg. 1962.


                -maximum 1/4
        -Russell Harmon-          (natural hybrid)
SPELLBINDER-          -catawbiense 1/4
        -          -calophytum 1/4
        -Robin Hood-
                -sutchuenense 1/4
6ft(1.8m)  -15F(-26C)  E  3/4  Flowers of heavy substance, clear
frosty pink,  dorsal spotting of deep purple red,  widely campan-
ulate, 3.5in(8.9cm) wide;  globular trusses of 16.  Floriferous.
Plant well-branched, rounded; densely furnished with glossy fol-
iage of unusual size, 9.5in(24cm) long.  Bush spreads to 15 feet
across.  David G. Leach, reg. 1975.


SPHINX   Parentage unknown
Deep pink flowers; dark red blotch.  Luenenschloss, reg. 1965.


SPICED HONEY   Described under JEANNE CHURCH, q.v.


     -scabrifolium var. spiciferum 1/2
SPICIL-     -ciliatum 1/4
     -Cilpinense-
              -moupinense 1/4
4ft(1.2m)  OF(-18C)  VE   Flowers light roseine purple fading to
very light mallow purple, held in small clusters;  long-lasting,
long blooming period.  A compact plant with reddish stems.  Hy-
bridizer unknown;  H. G. Rutland intro.;  Dunedin Rhododendron
Group, NZ, reg. 1980.


          -fortunei 1/2
SPICY NUTMEG-
          -unknown 1/2
Flowers 5- to 7-lobed, pinkish lilac, with dorsal rays and spot-
ting of medium Indian lake; very fragrant.  Narrow elliptic fol-
iage to 6in(15cm) long.  Plant 7.6ft(2.4m) at 13 years.   M. E.
```

Hall, cross 1970; E. J. Brown, reg. 1984.

```
* * * * * * * * * * * * * * * * * * * * * * * * * * * * * *
        -spinuliferum 1/2
SPINBUR-
        - burmanicum 1/2
```
A cross by Lord Stair, 1950.
LOCHINCH SPINBUR   Parentage as above
A loose-growing plant with long leaves, scaly beneath. Tubular-
shaped flowers of light yellow, stained pink, in loose trusses.
Lord Stair. A.M. 1957.
```
* * * * * * * * * * * * * * * * * * * * * * * * * * * * * *
        -maximum--Mt. Mitchell F2--Ruddy Red Max 1/2
SPIN-OFF-              -aureum (chrysanthum) 1/4
        -unnamed hybrid-
                      -maximum 1/4
```
Buds of strong purplish red. White flowers, heavily edged with
strong purplish red and mallow purple; dorsal spots of beetroot
purple and deep greenish yellow; white filaments. W. Delp.

```
* * * * * * * * * * * * * * * * * * * * * * * * * * * * * *
        -spinuliferum 1/2
SPINULOSUM-
        -racemosum 1/2
```
4ft(1.2m) 5F(-15C) E 4/3 Light pink buds and dark pink flow-
ers make attractive two-tone effect. Flowers narrowly campanulate with protruding anthers, grow along stems, in pompom-like
small trusses. Long growth of racemosum. RBG, Kew. A.M. 1944.
EXBURY SPINULOSUM   Parentage as above
Small flowers, orange-red tubes 1in(2.5cm) long, in clusters.
Narrow leaves, dark green, glossy. Rothschild. A.M. 1948.
KATHRYN REBOUL   Parentage as above
3ft(.9m) -5F(-21C) EM   Small leaves; flowers only 1in(2.5cm)
across; pale yellow with salmon pink blushing, in trusses of 14.
Don Hardgrove cross; Adele Reboul, reg. 1975.
```
* * * * * * * * * * * * * * * * * * * * * * * * * * * * * *
                              -catawbiense
        -Parsons Grandiflorum-          1/8
        -Nova Zembla-              -unknown 3/8
SPIRIT OF LEONARDO-       -dark red hybrid--unknown
        -fortunei, hardy selection 1/2
```
16in(40.6cm) x 12in(30.5cm)(14 yrs) -20F(-29C) M   Buds strong
purplish red, opening pale purplish pink, with strong purplish
red rims, deep purplish red flare; truss of 11. Glossy elliptic
foliage.   Clay's Nurseries intro.; Rudy Behring, reg. 1986.

```
        -griffithianum ? 1/2
SPITFIRE-                May include MRS. R.S. HOLFORD, q.v.
        -unknown 1/2
```
6ft(1.8m) 0F(-18C) ML   Tall, compact shrub with fine growth
habit; good foliage. Flowers deep chrysanthemum crimson with
a dark brown blotch. Considered one of the best late reds. A.
Kluis, 1946.

SPLASHY VISION   Described under CRYSTAL YELLOW, q.v.

```
        -catawbiense--La Bar's White 1/2
SPOTMAGIC---unnamed hybrid F2-        -fortunei 1/4
        -unnamed hyb.-
                      -wardii (croceum) 1/4
```
Buds of strong purplish red opening to very pale purple flowers,
edged with vivid reddish purple; dark red dorsal spotting. Al
Smith cross; W. Delp raiser..

```
        -triflorum 1/2
SPRING DANCE-
        -unknown 1/2
```
4ft(1.2m) 5F(-15C) VE   Similar to the species triflorum.
Clusters of small, pale lavender flowers. Blooms with PRAECOX.
Popular in NZ--Cox.   J. Barto raiser; The Bovees, reg. 1962.

```
                      -catawbiense 1/2
        -unnamed hybrid-
SPRING DAWN-            -unknown 1/2
        -              -catawbiense
        -Mrs. Charles S. Sargent-
                      -unknown
```
5ft(1.5m) -20F(-29C) EM 3/3 Flowers strong rosy pink with a
warm golden yellow blotch. Shammarello. Color illus. Cox pl.
177; LW pl. 83; VV p. 73.

```
                              -minus Carolinianum Group 1/4
        -Laetevirens (Wilsoni)-
SPRING DELIGHT-               -ferrugineum 1/4
        -unknown 1/2
```
2ft(.6m) -20F(-29C) EM   Synonym A.M.S. Plant well-branched,
wider than tall; olive green leaves held 2 years. Flowers pale
pale purplish pink fading to white with a light olive brown spot
in dorsal throat, 1.5in(3.8cm) wide, 5 wavy-edged lobes.   A. M.
Shammarello, intro. 1979; reg. 1981.   Color illus. in Flower &
Garden, Dec.-Jan. issue, 1981.

SPRING FIESTA   Described under GLEN BRUCE, q.v.

```
        -unknown (Lapponicum ?) 1/2
SPRING FLING-
        -russatum 1/2
```
2.5ft(.75m) -10F(-23C) E 4/3   An abundance of dark electric
blue flowers. Growth habit compact; small, deep green foliage,
reddish bronze in winter. H. E. Greer, intro. 1982.

SPRING FROLIC   Described under ANNA H. HALL, q.v.

SPRING GLORY   Described under CHEER, q.v.

```
                              -griffithianum 1/16
              -George Hardy-
        -Pink Pearl-        -catawbiense 7/16
        -              -arboreum 1/16
        -Marion-       -Broughtonii-
        -              -unknown 7/16
        -              -catawbiense
SPRING GLOW-    -Catawbiense Grandiflorum-
        -                      -unknown
        -              -catawbiense
        -Mrs. C. S. Sargent-
                      -unknown
```
Compact trusses of 16 flowers, each 3.5in(9cm) across, magenta
with brown spotting. Fa. Felix & Dijkhuis, reg. 1966.   Flora
Nova, Silver Medal, Boskoop, 1958.

SPRING MAGIC   Described under ELISABETH HOBBIE, q.v.

SPRING PARADE   Described under CHEER, q.v.

```
        -aureum (chrysanthum) 1/2
SPRING SNOW-
        -degronianum ssp. heptamereum (metternichii) 1/2
```
2.5ft(.75m) -5F(-21C) E   Plant rounded, about twice as wide as
tall; leaves 2.5in(6.4cm) long, with thin tan indumentum. Light
pink buds, opening white. Unmarked flowers 2in(5cm) across, in
truss of 7-10.   Crossed at University of Washington Arboretum;
Brian Mulligan, reg. 1978.

```
                      -racemosum 1/4
        -unnamed hybrid-
SPRING SONG-          -keiskei 3/4
        -keiskei
```
2.5ft(.75m) -10F(-23C) EM   Light yellow flowers, aging to sal-
mon apricot.   D. Hardgrove, exhibited 1951; reg. 1958.

SPRING SONNET--form of vernicosum   R 59625
5ft(1.5m) -15F(-26C) M 3/3   Loose truss of 6-11 white flowers, with sparse ruby spotting in throat, reverse tinged rose,
2.75in(7cm) wide, 7-lobed. Upper surface of leaves waxy (vernicosum = varnished).   J. Rock collector; Lord Aberconway intro.;
reg. 1976. A.M. 1976.

```
        -williamsianum 1/2
SPRING SUN-
        -unknown 1/2
```
3ft(.9m) 0F(-18C) ML 3/3   Compact plant habit, with rounded
leaves as williamsianum. Flowers light yellow.   Hobbie intro.

```
        -griersonianum 1/2
SPRINGBOK-          -ponticum 1/4
        -unnamed hybrid-
                      -unknown 1/4
```
4ft(1.2m) 0F(-18C) ML   An open-growing plant with large truss
of about 18 flowers, vivid carmine pink, spotted crimson.   A.
F. George, reg. 1964.

```
                    -griersonianum 3/8
              -Azor-
       -Umpqua Chief-    -fortunei ssp. discolor 1/8
       -           -      -dichroanthum 1/4
SPRINGFIELD-           -Fabia-
       -                   -griersonianum
       -     -fortunei 1/4
       -Fawn-    -dichroanthum
              -Fabia-
                    -griersonianum
```
5ft(1.5m) 5F(-15C) L 5/3   Flower of orange-pink, with slight
crimson dorsal spotting and ring at base of throat, to 4in(10cm)
wide; flat truss of about 11.   Plant upright; fir green foliage
4in(10.2cm) long.   Del James cross; H. Greer, reg. 1979. Color
illus. ARS Q 33:4 (1979), p. 239; HG p. 181; K p. 116.

SPRINGTIME (Klupenger)   See WILLIAMS

```
              -praevernum 1/2
SPRINGTIME-
              -arboreum ssp. cinnamomeum var. album  1/2
```
White flowers shading to pale greenish yellow in throat.   Gill,
1945. A.M. 1945.

* *
```
                         -wardii 1/2
       -Mrs. Lammot Copeland-            -souliei ? 1/8
       -                    -Virginia Scott-
SPUN GOLD-                        -unknown 1/8
       -                   -griffithianum 1/8
       -          -Angelo-
       -Mary Drennen-    -fortunei ssp. discolor 1/8
              -wardii
```
3ft(.9m) OF(-18C) ML Amber yellow flowers with small red dor-
sal spots, openly campanulate, 3in(7.6cm) across; lax trusses of
12-14. Upright plant, broad as tall, well-branched; matte green
leaves.   Larson cross; W. Robertson, intro. 1980; reg. 1983.
BUTTERED POPCORN   Parentage as above
4ft(1.2m) -5F(-21C) L 4/3   Yellow flower with 2 rays of brown
converging on a dark eye.   Light green leaves.   Larson cross;
Clint Smith intro.
DINY DEE   Parentage as above
3ft(.9m) OF(-18C) M 4/4   Lemon yellow flowers open from buds
of orange in trusses 6in(15cm) across, of 9-12. Color changes
with age to deep gold. Plant as wide as high, deep green leaves
held 2 years.   H. Larson cross; J. Davies, reg. 1986.
HAZEL FISHER   Parentage as above
4ft(1.2m) -5F(-21C) L 5/4   Unusual flowers of yellow, lavender, and apricot with dark eye; leaf dark green.   Larson cross;
Clint Smith intro.   Col. ill. ARS J 44:1 Winter (1990), p. 59.
HJALMAR L. LARSON   Parentage as above
3ft(.9m) -10F(-23C) M 5/4   Edges and reverse of flowers pale
brick red, inside lemon yellow, upper lobe spotted scarlet red.
Leaves elliptic, glabrous.   Larson cross; Mrs. L. Hodgson, reg.
1982.
LEMON MARMALADE   Parentage as above
4ft(1.2m) -10F(-23C) L 4/4   Clear yellow flowers late in season.   Larson cross; Clint Smith intro.
PACIFIC GOLD   Parentage as above
4ft(1.2m) OF(-18C) M   Bright orange-red buds open to funnel-
shaped flowers, aureolin yellow with pale yellow margins, 3in.
(7.6cm) across, 5 wavy lobes; dome-shaped truss of 8-12. Plant
as wide as high; new growth mahogany green.   Larson cross; Mrs.
J. A. Davis, reg. 1986.
SPECIAL NOTE: All the hybrids described in this group probably
have the same parentage, but registration records show the male
parent to be an "unnamed, late-flowering yellow" for SPUN GOLD,
DINY DEE, PACIFIC GOLD, and HJALMAR L. LARSON.
* *

Out of order
       -fortunei 1/2
STACIA-   -catawbiense 1/4
       -Everestianum-
                    -unknown 1/4
```
5ft(1.5m)  -15F(-26C) ML   Plant wider than tall; spinach green
leaves, 5.8in(15cm) long, held 2 years. Fragrant flowers about
3.25in(8.3cm) across, cobalt violet, paler in the throat, faint
blotch of uranium green; spherical truss of 12.   Druecker cross;
E. German, reg. 1976.

```
              -brachycarpum 21/64   -wardii? 3/32
    -Dated Yellow-   -Chlorops-
    -        -unnamed hybrid-   -vernicosum? 1/16
    -                   -aureum (chrysanthum) 1/8
    -              -catawbiense v. album--Catalgla 1/16
    -        -Gosh -   -decorum?
SQUIRT-   -Darn!-   -Caroline-   1/64
    -     -Sweet-   -Mrs.H.R.Yates-   -brachycarpum?
    -     - Lulu-   -unknown 3/32
    -     -   -   -neriiflorum 1/64
    -     -   -   -Nereid-
    -     -unn.-Phyllis Bal--   -dichroanthum 1/64
   -Jenny--   hyb.-   lard -fortunei s. discolor 3/64
    poo -   -catawbiense--Clark's White 1/16
    -      -brachycarpum
    -    -unn-   -wardii
    -   -hyb-Crest-   -fortunei ssp.
    -    -   -Lady Bess- discolor
   -unn.-   borough -campylocarpum Elatum 1/64
   hyb.-   -catawbiense 1/64
    -              -Parsons Grandi-
    -    -America- florum   -unknown
   -Cindy-   -dark red hybrid--unknown
    Lou -   -griffithianum 1/64
    -              -Mars-
    -unnamed-   -unknown
         hybrid-catawbiense var. rubrum 1/32
```
Buds of jasper red and azalea pink, opening to pale pink flowers
lightly tinted pale purplish pink, undersides of strong purplish
red; throat strong yellow-green.   W. Delp.


STACIA   See previous column

```
              -williamsianum 1/2
STADT ESSEN-   -Mrs. Tritton--unknown
       -Louis Pasteur-
                    -Viscount Powerscourt--unknown
```
4ft(1.2m) -10F(-23C) ML     Clear pink flowers and deep green
foliage. One of the better-looking williamsianum hybrids.   D.
Hobbie intro. 1978.   Color illus. WS, 1989, p. 30.

```
                    -campylocarpum Elatum Group 1/4
         -Letty Edwards-
STADT WESTERSTEDE-   -fortunei 1/4
   (THE CITY...)   -   -wardii 1/4
         -unnamed hybrid-
                    -unknown 1/4
```
Trusses of 10-13 flowers,  5-lobed, light yellow  with a divided
red basal blotch.   J. Böhlje, cross 1966; Walter Schmalscheidt,
reg. 1984.   Color illus. WS, 1989, p. 104.


STAN KUBAS   Parentage unknown
3ft(.9m) OF(-18C) EM   Vibrant red campanulate flowers in neat
clusters, on a free-flowering, rounded plant. Narrow dense fol-
iage.   Kubas.

```
       -griffithianum 1/2
STANDISHI-
       -unknown 1/2
```
Flowers white, with red spots.   Veitch.

```
       -maximum 1/2   -catawbiense 1/8
STANDISHII-   -unnamed hybrid-
       -Altaclerense-   -ponticum 1/8
                    -arboreum 1/4
```
Violet crimson flowers, black spots.   Standish & Noble, 1850.

```
              -elliottii 1/4
         -Fusilier-
         -        -griersonianum 1/4
STANFORD-   -fortunei ssp. discolor 1/8
         -Lady Bessborough-
    -Jalisco-   -campylocarpum
    Goshawk-   Elatum Group (1/8)
         -    -dichroanthum 1/8
         -Dido-+
              -decorum 1/8
```
Cross and intro. by Maj. A. E. Hardy.   A.M. 1975.


STANLEY   Described under FORTUNE, q.v.


STANLEY DAVIES   Parentage unknown
```

4ft(1.2m) -10F(-23C) ML 4/4 A parent of BRITANNIA and many
other hybrids. Fiery red flowers with black markings, held in
compact truss of 16. Broadly dome-shaped, densely leafy plant,
slow-growing; midrib markedly sunken.   Davies of Ormskirk,
England, 1890.

```
            -glaucophyllum 1/2
STANLEY PERRY-
            -trichostomum Radinum Group 1/2
```
Frilled flowers, 5-lobed, .75in(2cm) across, old rose color,
held in trusses of 10.   Thacker of Warwickshire, reg. 1962.

```
            -yakushimanum 1/2
STANLEY RIVLIN-          -elliottii 1/4
            -Royal Blood-
                        -Rubens--unknown 1/4
```
3ft(.9m) OF(-18C) M Buds cardinal red opening paler red, out-
side heavily flushed spirea red, the interior spotted with crimson.   A. F. George, Hydon Nurseries, reg. 1972.

STANWAY   Described under FRED WYNNIATT, q.v.

STAR OF SPRING   Parentage unknown
5ft(1.5m) -5F(-21C) EM Flowers 6-lobed, of clear pink fading
white, spotted red, 3.5in(9cm) across; truss of about 13.   Medium to large foliage. D. Hardgrove cross; Royce, reg. 1979.

* *
```
            -augustinii 1/2
STAR SAPPHIRE-
            -minus Carolinianum Group 1/2
```
3ft(.9m) -5F(-21C) EM   Large bluish flowers on an upright-
growing plant. D. Hardgrove, before 1958.
TERRY HERBERT   Parentage as above, except reversed
4ft(1.2m) -5F(-21C) EM   Small foliage; flowers 2in(5cm) wide
clear orchid without markings, in terminal inflorescence to 5
buds, of up to 12 flowers each. C. Herbert, reg. 1977.
* *
* *
```
          -yakushimanum 1/2
    -unnamed-                    -griffithianum 3/16
    - hybrid-       -Queen Wilhelmina-
STAR -    -Britannia-           -unknown 3/16
SHINE-              -Stanley Davies--unknown
     -                   -griffithianum
     -            -Loderi-
    -unnamed hybrid-    -fortunei 1/8
                   -yakushimanum
```
Plant of compact habit; flowers amaranth rose.   John Waterer,
Sons & Crisp, reg. 1971. A.M. 1977.
SILVER TWIST   Parentage as above
Flowers creamy white. Waterer, Sons & Crisp, reg. 1975.
* *

```
      -davidsonianum, Exbury form 1/2
STAR TREK-
      -Ruth Lyons--davidsonianum 1/2
```
3ft(.9m) -15F(-26C) E 4/3 Crossing 2 forms of a same species
creates another form, not a hybrid.   Terminal spherical inflorescence, 4in(10.2cm) wide, of 3-5 trusses, each with 3-4 purple
flowers. Plant as broad as tall; glossy, dark green leaves,
2.25in(5.7cm) long.   Arthur A. Childers, reg. 1977.

```
        -yakushimanum 1/2
STARBRIGHT-          -griffithianum 1/4
        -Lady Bligh-
                -unknown 1/2
```
3ft).9m) -15F(-26C) M 4/4   Pink buds open to star-shaped,
white flowers. Plant habit as yakushimanum. Phetteplace cross;
Greer, intro. 1988.
```
                -griffithianum 1/8
               -Mars-
          -Vulcan-   -unknown 5/8
STARBRIGHT (Shapiro)-   -griersonianum 1/4
          -Slocock 24--unknown
```
Flowers white with red margins.   Shapiro. Color illus. ARS J
42:2 (1988), p. 63.

```
      -Moser's Maroon--unknown 3/4
STARBURST-
          -ponticum 1/4
      -Purple Splendour-
              -unknown
```

6ft(1.8m) 5F(-15C) L 4/3   Flower has gold blotch surrounded
by white on a background of deep reddish purple. Plant upright,
open; deep green leaves on red petioles.   Greer, intro. 1982.

STARCROSS   Described under GIPSY MOTH, q.v.

STARDANCER   Described under BUTTER BRICKLE, q.v.

STARDUST (DELP)   Described under DUSTY WHIZ, q.v.

STARDUST (FAWCETT)   Described under TICKLED PINK, q.v.

```
        -griffithianum 1/2
STARFISH-
        -unknown 1/2
```
5ft(1.5m) OF(-18C) ML Flower soft pink shading to white, and
it really is starfish-shaped. Plant of medium height. Waterer,
Sons, & Crisp, before 1922.   Color illus. JS p. 45.

STARGLIDER   Described under BLOODLINE, q.v.

```
              -fortunei ssp. discolor
          -Ladybird-
      -Diva-        -Corona--unknown 1/8
STARLET-    -griersonianum 1/4
      -williamsianum 1/2
```
2.5ft(.75m) 5F(-15C) EM 4/4 Elliptic-ovate leaves 3in(7.6cm)
long. Flowers funnel-rotate, 4in(10cm) across, rose madder to
crimson; loose truss of 5-6. H. Lem cross; C. P. Fawcett, reg.
1964. P.A. 1963.

* *
```
          -minus Carolinianum Group 1/2
STARLIGHT-
          -leucaspis 1/2
```
White flowers. Donald Hardgrove, 1953.
EIDER   Parentage as above
1.5ft(.45m) -5F(-21C) EM 4/4 Dwarf, compact, spreading plant
with matte green leaves 2.25in(5.7cm) long. Small white flowers
in little snowball trusses of 6-8. Cox, reg. 1981. A.M. 1981.
* *

STARRY EYED   Described under PASTEL STAR, q.v.

STARRY NIGHT   See GLETSCHERNACHT

```
      -catawbiense 1/2
STELLA-
      -unknown 1/2
```
5ft(1.5m) -10F(-23C) ML Synonym STELLA WATERER. Flower lilac
rose, spotted dark chocolate. A. Waterer. F.C.C. 1865.

```
        -forrestii Repens Group ? 1/2
STEPHANIE-
        -griersonianum ? 1/2
```
2ft(.6m) OF(-18C) M 3/3 Compact, small-leaved plant. Clear
light red flowers. W. Whitney cross; Sather, reg. 1976.

```
          -williamsianum 1/2
STEPHANIE WILSON-
          -unknown 1/2
```
Trusses hold 9 flowers, pale seafoam green fading to very light
Neyron rose. Edmund de Rothschild, intro. 1979; reg. 1982.

```
                    -griffithianum 1/8
                -Queen Wilhelmina-
          -Britannia-        -unknown 3/8
STEPHEN-        -Stanley Davies--unknown
 CLARKE-        -fortunei ssp. discolor 1/4
      -Autumn Gold-    -dichroanthum 1/8
              -Fabia-
                  -griersonianum 1/8
```
4.ft(1.2m) -5F(-21C) M 4/3 Carmine buds open to coral pink
flowers with edges Neyron rose, fading to empire yellow; trusses
hold about 11. Plant upright, wider than tall; foliage held 3
years. Mrs. J. H. Clarke cross; S. Clarke, reg. 1981.

STEVEN FOSTER   See STEPHEN FOSTER, described under REDWAX, q.v.

```
                Parentage includes catawbiense, maximum, and
STEWART MANVILLE   perhaps unknown hybrids
```
7ft(2.1m) -15F(-26C) ML Upright, spreading plant; leaves med-

ium olive green, held 2 years. Flowers of medium purplish red,
spotted with deep greenish yellow, 3in(7.6cm) across, 5-lobed;
spherical truss of 14. Floriferous. W. David Smith, reg. 1980.

STINGRAY   Described under CHECKMATE, q.v.

```
               -unknown garden hybrid 1/2
STOCKHOLM (Bruns)-
               -williamsianum 1/2
```
Flowers of delicate pink.   Joh. Bruns, about 1942.

STOCKHOLM   Described under MRS. CARTER GLASS, q.v.

```
               -maximum 1/2
STOKES BRONZE WINGS-
               -catawbiense 1/2
```
Flowers reddish purple, with brownish orange flare and spotting.
Parent of many Delp hybrids. Warren Stokes cross. Color illus.
ARS J 42:4 (1988), p. 186.

STONEHURST--form of lanigerum (silvaticum)
Flowers a light shade of cherry red, campanulate, 2.5in(6.4cm)
wide; tight globular trusses of 35. Plant typical of species;
thick indumentum beneath. R. Strauss, reg. 1961. A.M. 1961.

```
          -griersonianum 1/2
STOPLIGHT-        -arboreum 1/4
     -Cornubia-          -thomsonii 1/8
               -Shilsonii-
                         -barbatum 1/8
```
6ft(1.8m) 10F(-12C) EM 4/2 Oblong leaves 5.5in(15.5cm) long.
Flowers of geranium red, faintly blotched, funnel-campanulate,
3.5in(8.9cm) wide, 5-lobed; 13 per truss.   R. Henny, reg. 1958.
P.A. 1951. (One of the first plants to receive the ARS award)

```
          -griffithianum 1/2
STRATEGIST-        -catawbiense 1/4
     -John Waterer-
                  -unknown 1/4
```
Broad, bright green foliage. Well-shaped, blush pink flowers,
deep rose at margins, pale yellow spots in throat; tall conical
trusses. A large, late-blooming plant.   J. Waterer.

STRAWBERRIES AND CREAM   Described under CARY'S CREAM, q.v.

```
          -Pygmalion--unknown 1/2
STRAWBERRY SUPREME-
          -yakushimanum 1/2
```
2ft(.6m) high x 3ft(.9m) -15F(-26C) ML   Widely funnel-shaped
flowers in dome-shaped trusses of 14, bright red with a grayed
purple dorsal blotch. Dense, spreading bush; narrow elliptical
leaf, plastered tan hairs below. Fetterhoff cross; reg. 1989.

```
          -caucasicum 1/2
STRAWBERRY SWIRL-        -caucasicum 1/4
          -Nobleanum-
                    -arboreum 1/4
```
4ft(1.2m) -15F(-26C) EM   Attractive blend of rose hues with a
darker blotch, and pink stripes on reverse.   Origin unknown.

```
          -aberconwayi 1/2
STREATLEY-
          -yakushimanum 1/2
```
White flowers shaded with rosy pink, some light red spotting and
red margins, 3.5in(8.9cm) wide; lax trusses of 9. Magenta buds
contrast nicely with the open flowers.   Crown Estate, Windsor,
reg. 1964. A.M. 1964.

```
                    -yakushimanum 3/4
          -unnamed hybrid-     -griffithianum 1/8
          -              -Mars-
STUNNING ARRAY-                 -unknown 1/8
          -                    -yakushimanum, Delp-selected
          -modified yakushimanum-
                               -yakushimanum, Exbury form
```
Buds of strong purplish red. Flowers light purplish pink, edged
strong purplish red; dorsal spots spirea red.   W. Delp.

```
     -edgeworthii 1/2
SUAVE-
     -bullatum (sic) 1/2
5ft(1.5m) 10F(-12C)  EM  4/3    An old hybrid still in cultiva-
```

tion. Flowers campanulate, pure white; reverse pink, shading to
white.   Emil Liebig, before 1863.

```
               -catawbiense var. album Glass--Catalgla 1/4
          -Tony's-                -catawbiense 1/8
          - Gift -     -Catawbiense Album-
          -    -Belle -          -unknown 1/8
SUBTLE BEAUTY-     Heller-          -catawbiense
          -              -white catawbiense hyb.-
          -                        -unknown
          -     -valentinianum 1/4
          -Eldorado-
               -johnstoneanum 1/4
```
Flowers very pale purple with a flare of brilliant yellow green.
Tall plant. W. Delp.

SUCCESS   Described under CUP DAY, q.v.

```
               -catawbiense, red form 1/4
     -unnamed-          -forrestii Repens Group 1/8
     - hybrid-Elizabeth-
     -               -griersonianum 1/8
SUDAN-                         -catawbiense 3/16
     -          -Parsons Grandiflorum-
     -     -America-          -unknown 5/16
     -Fanfare-     -dark red hybrid--unknown
     -          -catawbiense
          -Kettledrum-
               -unknown
```
4ft(1.2m) -15F(26C) M 4/3   Flowers cherry red, blotched very
light mimosa yellow, 5-lobed, openly funnel-shaped, to 2.25in.
(5.7cm) wide; domed truss of 14. Plant wider than tall, decumbent branches; leaves dark yellowish green, 4in(10cm) long, held
2 years. David G. Leach, intro. 1976; reg. 1983.

SUDS   Described under CUMULUS, q.v.

```
               -griffithianum 1/2
SUE---Loderi King George, selfed-
               -fortunei 1/2
```
6ft(1.8m) OF(-18C) M 5/3 Beautiful shrub with all the Loderi
characteristics. Very tall, narrow trusses of deep pink, fragrant flowers, 5in(12.7cm) wide.   Del James, reg. 1958.

SUE CUTTEN   Described under PERRI CUTTEN, q.v.

```
          -fortunei 1/2
SUE GORDON-
          -unknown 1/2
```
Trusses of 11, fuchsia purple.   Lady Adam Gordon, reg. 1981.

SUE LISSENDEN   Described under CORMID, q.v.

```
     -haematodes 1/2
SUEDE-
     -bureavii 1/2
3ft(.9m) -10F(-23C)  M  5/3   Red flowers  fading to deep rose,
with brown speckles in throat.   G. A. Judson, reg. 1973.
```

```
               -griffithianum
     -Loderi Sue--Loderi King George, F2-        1/4
SUELLEN-     -fortunei          -fortunei 1/2
     -Fawn-          -dichroanthum 1/8
     -     -Fabia-
          -griersonianum 1/8
```
8ft(2.4m) x 10ft(3m)(25 yrs) OF(-18C) M Flowers very fragrant,
7 wavy lobes, light purplish pink; truss of 9. Leaf to 7.5in(19
cm), held 1 year; plant of broad habit.   Childers, reg. 1988.

SUGAR AND SPICE   Described under PAWHUSKA, q.v.

```
          -decorum 1/2
SUGAR DADDY-
          -unknown 1/2
5ft(1.5m)  OF(-18C)  EM   Plant habit upright, stiff.  Flower of
amaranth rose, fading white, a green blotch in throat; compact,
rounded trusses.   John Waterer, Sons & Crisp, reg. 1971.
```

```
               -catawbiense var. album Glass--
          -unnamed hybrid-          Catalgla 1/4
SUGAR FROSTING-        -fortunei 1/4
          -decorum, McLaren form 1/2
```

5ft(1.5m) x 8ft(2.4m)(12 yrs) M   Flowers in trusses of 10-14,
openly funnel-shaped, 7 wavy-edged lobes, white, extremely fragrant. George Ring III, cross 1972; A. R. Brooks, reg. 1985.

```
                            -griffithianum 3/16
                  -George Hardy-
                      -Pink -      -catawbiense 3/16
              -Countess-Pearl-     -arboreum 1/16
              -of Derby-     -Broughtonii-
      -Trude -        -          -unknown 3/16
      -Webster-       -      -catawbiense
      -        -      -Cynthia-
SUGAR-          -          -griffithianum
PINK-      -Countess of Derby (as above)
    -           -fortunei 1/8
    -      -Fawn-      -dichroanthum 1/16
    -unnamed-    -Fabia-
      hybrid-      -griersonianum 3/16
                -Pink Bell   unknown
          -Queen o' the May-
                      -griersonianum
```
6ft(1.8m) -5F(-21C) M 4/4   Flowers cotton candy pink, deep-
er in the throat, with light brown spotting; corolla 5in(12.7cm)
across; about 12 per truss, which may be 1ft(.3m) tall. Heavy,
smooth, deep green leaves, 7.5in(19cm) long; a vigorous, upright
plant. H. Greer, reg. 1979.   Color illus. ARS Q 28:1 (1974),
p. 34; HG p. 75; K p. 73.

```
                  -campylocarpum 1/4
            -Moonstone-
SUGAR PLUM-      -williamsianum 1/4
      -          -wardii 1/4
            -Caroline Grace-
                  -unknown 1/4
```
3ft(.9m) OF(-18C) EM 3/3   Deep pink flowers, widely funnel-
shaped, to 3in(7.6cm) wide; lax trusses of 5-8. A dense, small-
leaved plant. Arthur Wright, Sr. & Jr., 1964.

```
        -sulfureum 1/2
SULFMEG-
        -megeratum 1/2
```
Lepidote hybrid.   Flowers pale sulphur yellow, held in clusters
of 2-3. E. J. P. Magor, cross 1924; intro. 1940. A.M. 1940.

* *
```
          -souliei 1/2
SULPHUR YELLOW-
          -campylocarpum 1/2
```
J. C. Williams cross. Exhibited by Lord Swaythling, 1939.
TOWNHILL SULPHUR YELLOW   Parentage as above
Selection by Lord Swaythling, 1939.
* *

SULTRY PEACH   Described under NEALA, q.v.

```
                      -catawbiense 1/8
            -Parsons Grandiflorum-
      -America-            -unknown 9/16
SUMATRA-      -dark red hybrid--unknown
    -      -forrestii Repens Group 1/4
      -Gertrud-            -ponticum 1/16
        Schäle-      -Michael Waterer-
            -Prometheus-            -unknown
                  -Monitor--unknown
```
2ft(.6m) -15F(-26C) M 4/5 Dome-shaped trusses of 8-10 cardi-
nal red flowers, 2.6in(6.5cm) across, openly funnel-shaped, with
5 wavy lobes. Plant over twice as wide as high; very dense foliage of yellow-green, 3in(7.6cm) long. Leach, intro. 1973; reg.
1983. Col. ill. ARS J 36:1 (1982), p. 3; Cox pl. 178; HG p. 88.

SUMMER FLAME   Parentage unknown
Conical-campanulate flowers, wider than long, pale pinky red, 5
nectar pouches at base; trusses of 10. Pedicels, calyx, corolla
base with dense white hairs. Donard Nurs.; E. Nelson reg. 1988.

Out of order
```
        -maximum 1/2
SUMMER ROSE-            -Moser's Maroon--unknown 1/4
      -Romany Chai-
            -griersonianum 1/4
```
5ft(1.5m) -10F(-23C) VL   Flowers deep pink, with dark reddish
purple spotting on dorsal lobes, widely funnel-shaped, 2.5in(6.4

cm) wide, 5-lobed; globular truss of 8-12. Plant upright, wider
than tall; narrowly elliptic leaves, with thin tan indumentum;
new growth with silvery gray tomentose, new stems red.   Dr. R.
Ticknor cross; E. Mezitt, Weston Nurseries, reg. 1980.

```
                -maximum 1/4
      -Summer Snow-            -ungernii 1/8
      -      -unnamed hybrid, selfed-
SUMMER GLOW-                  -auriculatum 1/8
      -      -griffithianum 3/16
      -    -Mars-
      -Scarlet-   -unknown    -griffithianum
        Blast -          -Mars-
            -unnamed hybrid-    -unknown 3/16
                  -red catawbiense 1/8
```
7ft(2.1m)(14 yrs) -15F(-26C) VL 5/5   Flowers of vivid rose
Bengal shading to pale purplish pink at center, dorsal spotting
of light orange-yellow, exterior of bright Tyrian purple; pedicels dark red, very small pink calyx. Truss of 13. Leaves narrowly elliptic, 6.25in(16cm) long, on a wider-than-tall plant.
Leach, cross 1971; reg. 1985.

SUMMER ROSE   See previous column

SUMMER SCANDAL   Parentage unknown
Pink flowers with deeper pink edges.   Kersey cross; Frederick,
reg. 1976.

```
                -auriculatum 1/4
        -unnamed hybrid-
SUMMER SEQUEL-            -fortunei ssp. discolor 1/4
            -catawbiense var. album Glass--Catalgla 1/2
```
7ft(2.1m)(22 yrs) -15F(-26C) VL   Truss of 16-17 flowers, pale
purplish pink, lobe edges and reverse darker pink; dorsal blotch
and spotting, strong greenish yellow; corolla 3.3in(8.5cm) wide.
David G. Leach, reg. 1984.

```
            -maximum 1/2
SUMMER SNOW-            -ungernii 1/4
      -unnamed hybrid, selfed-
                  -auriculatum 1/4
```
6ft(1.8m) -15F(-26C) VL 4/2   White flowers with small rayed
dorsal blotch strong greenish yellow, funnel-campanulate, 4in.
(10cm) wide, dome-shaped, rather loose truss of about 11. Flowers not obscured by new growth. Vigorous plant, as wide as tall
and becomes tree-like; leaves variable, to 9.5in(24cm) long. D.
G. Leach, reg. 1970.

```
            -maximum 1/4
      -Summer Snow-            -ungernii 1/8
      -      -unnamed hybrid, selfed-
SUMMER SOLACE-            -auriculatum 1/8
      -      -catawbiense var. album--Catalgla 1/2
```
4.5ft(1.35m) x 4.5ft(17 yrs/seed) -15F(-26C) VL 3/5 Truss of
16-20 white flowers, bold yellow-green spotting; narrowly elliptic leaf 8in(20cm) long, bright glossy green. Leach, reg. 1985.

```
                        -smirnowii 1/32
                  -unnamed hybrid-
            -unnamed-            -griersonianum 9/32
            -      - hybrid-catawbiense, white form 1/16
            -unnamed-            -fortunei ssp. discolor 1/8
      -unnamed- hybrid-unnamed hybrid-
      - hybrid-            -Corona--unknown 13/64
SUMMER-      -griersonianum
  SONG -      -maximum 1/8
      -      -unnamed-            -dichroanthum 1/16
      -      - hybrid-Goldsworth-
      -unnamed-            Orange   -fortunei ssp. discolor
        hybrid-            -Parsons      -catawbiense 1/32
        -      -America- Grandiflorum-
      -unnamed-            -unknown
        hybrid-      -red hybrid--unknown
            -            -forrestii Repens Gp. 1/16
            -Gertrud Schäle-      -Michael-ponticum
                  -      -Waterer-
                  -Prometheus-      -unknown
                        -Monitor--unknown
```
Corolla of pale purplish pink with a deep greenish yellow dorsal
blotch, 5-lobed, 2.4in(6cm) broad, small ivory calyx; trusses of
20. Hairless oblanceolate leaves, 6.7in(17cm) x 2in(5cm). Mid-
July flowering.   David G. Leach, cross 1975; reg. 1986.

```
                -maximum 1/4
        -Summer-          -ungernii 1/8
        - Snow -unnamed hybrid-
        -                        -auriculatum 1/8
SUMMER -                       -griffithianum 1/16
SPLENDOR-              -unnamed-
        -        -Mrs. Furnival- hybrid-unknown 1/8
        -              -         -          -caucasicum
        -Party Pink-        -unnamed hybrid-  1/16
        -                              -unknown
            -catawbiense var. album 1/4
```
6.2ft(1.9m)(16 yrs) -15F(26C) VL Heather pink buds opening to
orchid pink flowers, paler in throat, with bold dorsal blotch of
orange buff, 3.25in(8.3cm) wide; 13 per truss. Elliptic foliage
5.75in(14.6cm) long. David G. Leach, reg. 1984.

```
                -maximum 1/2
SUMMER SUMMIT-          -auriculatum 1/4
        -unnamed hybrid-
        -              -fortunei ssp. discolor 1/4
```
11.3ft(3.4m)(26 yrs) -20F(-29C) VL   Phlox pink buds, opening
to white flowers flushed orchid pink at base and exterior, aging
white, with dark olive yellow dorsal spotting; corolla about 2.5
in(6.4cm) wide. Dense foliage of elliptic leaves to 6in(15.2cm)
long, dark green.   David G. Leach, reg. 1984.

```
            -wardii 1/2
SUMMER'S DAWN-
        -garden hybrid--unknown 1/2
```
Yellow flowers.   Collingwood Ingram, exhibited 1936.

SUMMERTIME--form of maximum
6ft(1.8m) -25F(-32C) L   White flowers suffused roseine purple
with upper throat yellow-green, in trusses of 22-24. Tall-growing plant with leaves 5.5in(14cm) long, dark green.   Collector
unknown; Crown Estate, Windsor, reg. 1974.   A.M. 1974.

SUMMIT GOLD   Described under BALLY COTTON, q.v.

```
                    -smirnowii 1/8
                -Oh My!-
            -        -yakushimanum 1/8   -catawbiense
    -unnamed hybrid-              -Atrosanguineum-
    -              -Atrier-           -unknown
    -              -Mary -   -griersonianum
    -              Belle-    -decorum
SUN -                 -Dechaem-
BREEZES-                      -haematodes     -griffith.
    -                            -Queen    -
    -                 -Britannia- Wilhelmina-unknown
    -        -C.P. Raffill-       -Stanley Davies
    -Anne  -             -griersonianum
      Hardgrove-Moser's Maroon--unknown
```
Light yellow flowers edged with deep pink; throat strong green-
ish yellow; calyx light yellow. W. Delp.

```
                -campylocarpum ssp. caloxanthum 1/4
            -Solarium-              -caucasicum 1/16
    -        -        -Dr. Stocker-
SUN CHARIOT-    -Damaris-          -griffithianum 1/16
    -                    -campylocarpum 1/8
        -wardii 1/2
```
Yellow flowers.   L. de Rothschild raiser; Waterer, Sons & Crisp
intro.; Sunningdale exhibited, 1955.

SUN DEVIL   Parentage unknown; elepidote
3ft(.9m) x 4ft(1.2m) 5F(-15C) M   Synonym SUNDANCE. Flowers
in lax trusses of 9-10, 6-lobed; buds deep pink opening to light
yellowish pink, rimmed in medium yellowish pink.   Pale orange-
yellow indumentum beneath leaves; dull, green, convex, elliptic
leaves, 4.5in(11.4cm) long.   W. Whitney cross; Dr. Otis Burris
raiser; L. Bulgin, reg. 1989.

```
            -Nereid
    -King of Jordan-Tally Ho
SUN FLAME-          -fortunei ssp. discolor
    -Whitney hybrid--unknown
```
2.5ft(.75m) -5F(-21C) M (Exact combination of the parentage of
King of Jordan is uncertain.) Trusses of 9-13 fragrant flowers,
7-lobed, throat mimosa yellow shading to orient pink at edges.
Plant much broader than tall, with yellow-green leaves 5.5in(14
cm) long; retained 3 years. Mrs. Bernice I. Jordan, reg. 1977.

```
        -Parker's Pink--unknown 1/2
        -            -decorum 1/8
SUN GLEAM-    -unnamed hybrid-
        -Clara  -          -fortunei ssp. discolor 1/8
        Raustein-              -wardii 1/16
        -              -unnamed hybrid-
        -unnamed-              -dichroanthum 1/16
        hybrid-
            -fortunei 1/8
```
2ft(.6m) -5F(-21C) M Cardinal red buds open to white flowers,
edged light red, exterior rose Bengal, 5 wavy to frilled lobes;
spherical trusses of 12. Plant rounded, as wide as tall; leaves
4.5in(11.5cm) long, held 3 years.   A. A. Raustein, reg. 1983.

SUN OF AUSTERLITZ   Described under NOBLEANUM, q.v.

```
            -wardii 1/4
        -Crest-          -fortunei ssp. discolor 1/4
        -    -Lady Bessborough-
SUNBEAM-              -campylocarpum Elatum Group 1/8
        -                  -dichroanthum 1/8
        -        -Goldsworth Orange-
        -Tortoiseshell-          -fortunei ssp. discolor
        Champagne  -griersonianum 1/4
```
5ft(1.5m) -10F(-23C) L   Deep yellow flowers, green stamens;
held in large, rounded trusses.   Origin unknown.

SUNDANCE   See SUN DEVIL

```
        -augustinii, Tower Court form 1/2
SUNDARI-
    -trichanthum, Tower Court form 1/2
```
5ft(1.5m) -5F(-21C) EM   Plant upright, well-branched; narrow
elliptic leaves, 3.35in(8.3cm) long, scaly beneath; held 2 to 3
years. Frilled flowers, widely funnel-shaped, zygomorphic, 2.5
in(6.5cm) across, violet with a pale center, light yellow-green
spots in throat; trusses of 4-5.   H. A. Short, reg. 1977.

```
                -griersonianum 1/2
    -Dorinthia-          -haematodes 1/8
    -        -Hiraethlyn-
SUNDOR-              -griffithianum 3/8
    -        -griffithianum
    -Sunrise-
        -griersonianum
```
Flowers scarlet salmon.   Lord Aberconway, 1946.

```
                -griffithianum 3/4
    -Loderi Pink Diamond-
SUNKIST-              -fortunei 1/4
    -griffithianum
```
White flowers, suffused pink.   Loder.

SUNLIT SNOW   Described under SPARKLING JEWEL, q.v.

SUNNINGDALE---form of hippophaeoides (HABA SHAN form)
3ft(.9m) -25F(-32C) E 4/3 Deep lavender blue flowers .75in.
(2cm) wide, 11 per dense truss, opening slowly over a long period. Small, gray-green, aromatic leaves. G. Forrest collector;
Sunningdale Nurseries raiser.   A.G.M. 1925.

```
            -dichroanthum 3/8
        -Golden Horn-
SUNNINGDALE-          -elliottii 1/4
    APRICOT  -          -fortunei ssp. discolor 1/4
        -Margaret Dunn-    -dichroanthum
            -Fabia-
                -griersonianum 1/8
```
Apricot-colored flowers.   Sunningdale Nurseries raiser; Hamil-
ton Smith, exhibited 1955.

SUNNINGDALE BLUE---form of impeditum
1ft(.3m) -15F(-26C) EM 4/4 Plant very dwarf, with flowers of
pale violet blue. Young foliage blue-green.   Sunningdale.

SUNNY DAY   Parentage unknown
4ft(1.2m) x 4ft 0F(-18C) EM Primrose yellow flowers, 6 lobed,
12 per truss; red spotting. Whitney cross; Sather, reg. 1985.

```
                -caucasicum 1/2      -fortunei ssp. discolor 1/4
SUNNY SIDE UP-              -Ole Olson-
            -Lem's Goal-          -campylocarpum 1/8
                     -griersonianum 1/8
                  -Azor-
                       -fortunei ssp. discolor
```
Buds of pale yellowish pink and poppy red open to large frilled
flowers, yellowish white; dorsal spots chartreuse green.   Delp.

```
         -griffithianum 1/2
SUNRISE-
         -griersonianum 1/2
```
6ft(1.8m) 5F(-15C) ML 4/2   Large flowers opening deep pink,
fading with age to white except margins and base. Plant as wide
as tall; medium green, dull leaves, 6.5in(16.5cm) long.   Several
forms exist.   Lord Aberconway, 1933.   F.C.C. 1942.

SUNRISE OVER HARKWOOD   Described under PANACHE, q.v.

SUNRISE SERENADE   Described under BUTTER BRICKLE, q.v.

SUNRISE-SUNSET   See SUNUP-SUNDOWN

```
                    -griffithianum 1/2
       -Queen Wilhelmina-
SUNSET-              -unknown 1/4
     -         -griffithianum
     -Loderi-
              -fortunei 1/4
```
Flowers of pale yellow shaded pink, or white flushed pale pink.
G. Loder, exhibited 1931.   A.M. 1931.

SUNSET (Henny)   Described under HIGHNOON, q.v.

* *
```
             -griersonianum 1/2
SUNSET LAKE-             -arboreum 1/4
             -unnamed hybrid-
                         -decorum 1/4
```
Trusses of 8-12 flowers, light crimson to crimson lake with deep
red throat. Oswald Blumhardt, NZ, reg. 1974.
SUNSET QUEEN   Parentage as above
Large loose trusses of rich coral rose.   Blumhardt, reg. 1974.
* *

SUNSET OVER HARKWOOD   Described under PANACHE, q.v.

SUNSET QUEEN   Described under SUNSET LAKE, above.

SUNSET YATES   Described under MARY YATES, q.v.

```
         -neriiflorum Euchaites Group 1/2
SUNSHINE-
         -beanianum 1/2
```
Bright, dark red flowers.   Gen. Harrison, 1955.

```
                  -campylocarpum Elatum Group 1/4
            -Ole Olson-
      -Alice  -       -fortunei ssp. discolor 1/4
      -Franklin-          -griffithianum 1/8
SUNSPRAY-       -Loderi King George-
      -                     -fortunei 1/8
      -        -wardii 1/4
      -Crest-             -fortunei ssp. discolor
            -Lady Bessborough-
                          -campylocarpum Elatum Group
```
6ft(1.8m) -5F(-21C) M 5/3   Flowers funnel-campanulate, 5in.
(12.7cm) broad, with 6 wavy lobes, pale primrose yellow edges,
deeper at center and throat; flat trusses of 9-10. Glossy, dark
green leaves on an upright plant, taller than broad, moderately
branched. W. J. Swenson raiser; H. E. Greer, reg. 1979. Color
illus. HG p. 76.

```
                -catawbiense var. album Glass--Catalgla
      -unnamed hybrid-          -dichroanthum      1/4
SUNSTRUCK-          -Goldsworth Orange-
      -            -yakushimanum 1/4  -fortunei s. discolor
      -Serendipity-                              1/8
                  -aureum (chrysanthum) 1/4
```
Buds of ruby red and strong purplish red, opening to pale purple
flowers, star-shaped, edged heavily with strong reddish purple
and deep purplish pink; a light greenish yellow flare. W. Delp.

SUNTE ROCK--form of praestans (coryphaeum) R 59480
5ft(1.5m) -5F(-21C) EM 3/4   Flowers of 6-8 lobes, 2.5in.
(6.4cm) across, of transparent white streaked rose red, upper
throat blotched ruby red. Oblanceolate leaves to 12in(30.5cm)
long; plastered, silvery brown indumentum beneath.   Rock collector; Geoffrey Gorer raiser; reg. 1970.   P.C. 1969.

```
              -sutchuenense 1/2
SUNTE ROSE--form of Geraldii-
              -praevernum 1/2
```
Flowers light rhodamine purple, with a reddish purple blotch and
spotting in upper throat. G. Gorer, reg. 1971.   A.M. 1971.

```
              -yakushimanum 1/4
     -unnamed-      -dichroanthum 3/16
     - hybrid-Fabia-
SUNUP -           -griersonianum 3/16
 SUNDOWN-      -Fabia (as above)
     -      -unnamed-
     -unnamed- hybrid-bureavii 1/8
      hybrid-    -wardii 1/8
           -Crest-          -fortunei ssp. discolor 1/16
                -Lady    -
                 Bessborough-campylocarpum 1/16
```
2.5ft(.75m) 0F(-18C) E   Blood red buds open to flowers empire
rose fading to shell pink, in trusses 6in(15cm) across, of 8-10
flowers. Semi-dwarf plant, compact, spreading much broader than
tall. J. G. Lofthouse, cross 1975; reg. 1982.

```
                       -griffithianum
            -Queen Wilhelmina-        1/16
         -Britannia-        -unknown 3/16
    -Linswegeanum-      -Stanley Davies--unknown
SUOMI-         -forrestii Repens Group 1/4
    -degronianum ssp. heptamereum (metternichii)--Metternianus
3ft(.9m)  -5F(-21C)  VE  3/3  Red flowers.  Hobbie, 1953.    1/2
```

* *
```
       -wardii 5/8
SUPER-             -souliei 1/8
BOWL -    -Rosy Morn-       -griffithianum 1/16
   -Zelia  -       -Loderi-
    Plumecocq-              -fortunei 1/16
       -       -wardii
       -Crest-        -fortunei ssp. discolor 1/16
            -Lady   -
             Bessborough-campylocarpum Elatum Gp. 1/16
```
3ft(.9m) x 2ft(.6m)(9 yrs) -5F(-21C) ML Flower brilliant yel-
low with deep pink throat in flat truss of 9-12; corolla rotate-
campanulate, 3.5in(9cm) across, 7-lobed. Hairless, ovate leaves
4.3in(11cm) x 2.4in(6cm).   B. Aunsbjorn, reg. 1988.
WARDZEL   Parentage as above
3ft(.9m) x 2ft(.6m) -5F(-21C) ML   Vivid greenish yellow flowers; flat truss of 9-14; leaves as above. Aunsbjorn, reg. 1988.
* *

SUPER JAY   Described under DR. RICHARD ANDERSON, q.v.

```
                      -maximum 1/4
        -Stokes Bronze Wings-
SUPER Q. T.-              -catawbiense 1/4
        -             -fortunei 1/4
        -Donna Hardgrove-       -wardii 1/8
                     -unnamed hybrid-
                          -dichroanthum 1/8
```
Moderate and strong purplish red and ruby red buds. Flowers of
roseine purple; a deep red flare, dark red dorsal spots.   Delp.

```
                          -catawbiense
        -Parsons Grandi-        1/32
     -America- florum      -unknown 3/8
     -Cindy-      -dark red hybrid--unknown
     - Lou -          -griffithianum 1/32
    -unnamed-    -         -Mars-
    - hybrid-  -unnamed hybrid-    -unknown
    -       -             -catawbiense var. rubrum
    -       -             -dichroanthum 1/8    1/16
SUPER SLICK-   -Goldsworth Orange-
    -                 -fortunei ssp. discolor 1/8
    -   -catawbiense var. album Glass--Catalgla 1/4
    -Calsap-
       -Sappho--unknown
```

Buds of vivid red and ruby red opening to flowers of strong purplish red; dorsal spotting of ruby red across 3 lobes. W. Delp.

SUPER STAR   Described under PINK CHERUB, q.v.

SUPERBISSIMUM   Parentage unknown
Dwarf plant with large, white, fragrant flowers. Veitch, before
1839. F.C.C. 1897.

```
                    -dichroanthum 1/8
              -Goldsworth-
        -Hotei- Orange   -fortunei ssp. discolor 1/8
        -          -               -souliei 1/8
SUPERGOLD-    -unnamed hybrid-
        -                       -wardii 1/8
        -        -lacteum 1/4
        -Joanita-
                 -campylocarpum ssp. caloxanthum 1/4
```
5ft(1.5m) OF(-18C) EM   Spherical trusses of 15 flowers, 5- to
6-lobed, medium orange-yellow with small red-orange blotch, 2.5
in(6.4cm) across. Plant upright with stiff branches, as wide as
tall; floriferous. Dark, glossy, convex foliage, 3.5in(8.9cm),
long.   John Lofthouse, cross 1974; reg. 1983.

* *
```
        -falconeri 1/2
SURPRISE-
        -thomsonii 1/2
```
Flowers of mauve, with a black blotch. J. Waterer, before 1867;
Loder, exhibited 1937.
FALTHO   Parentage as above
Rose madder flowers, faint spotting on upper lobes, and dark red
basal spotting. Loder. A.M. 1954.
J. E. HARRIS   Parentage as above
From a cross by J. G. E. Harris, 1940.
SURPRISE PACKET   Same cross as above by Digby, 1953.
* *

SURPRISE PACKET   See under SURPRISE, above

SURRENDER   Described under GOLDEN YEARS, q.v.

SURREY HEATH   Described under VENETIAN CHIMES, q.v.

```
                         -catawbiense 1/4
           -Mrs. Charles S. Sargent-
SURVIVOR-                     -unknown 1/4
           -fortunei, hardy form 1/2
```
Buds of beetroot purple and strong purplish red, open to flowers
of strong purplish red and moderate purplish pink; dorsal spots
of light olive green; strong purplish red stigma.   W. Delp.

```
      -campanulatum 1/2
SUSAN-
      -fortunei 1/2
```
6ft(1.8m) -5F(-21C) M 4/4   Large, bushy plant with excellent
foliage; glossy, dark green, flat leaves 5.5in(14cm) long. Rosy
lavender buds opening cool lilac blue, paler toward center, and
spotted maroon on upper lobe; large loose trusses. Grows fast.
J. C. Williams raiser, Caerhays Castle; Slocock intro. A.M.
1930.   A.M. Wisley Trials 1948.   F.C.C. Wisley Trials 1954.
Color illus. Cox pl. 180; F. p. 66; JS p. 64; VV p. 49.

SUSAN KAY   Described under ADELE'S YELLOW, q.v.

* *
             -Loder's White, q.v. for 2 possible parentage diagrams.
SUSAN LONSDALE-
             -Kew Pearl--unknown
White flowers, tinged light spirea red, heavily spotted on all
lobe with Indian lake. H. D. Rose, Australia, reg. 1973.
WARBURTON   Parentage as above
Very much like the above. Rose, reg. 1973.
* *

```
             -nuttallii 1/2
SUSANNAH HURLEY-
             -megacalyx 1/2
```
A cool greenhouse plant. Large, tubular-shaped, white flowers,
suffused yellow deep in throat, reverse slightly tinged pink;
trusses of 3-5. G. A. Hardy. F.C.C. 1989.

```
                 -haematodes 1/2
SUSSEX BONFIRE-          -thomsonii
              -Cornish Cross-
                        -griffithianum 1/4
```
Deep blood red flowers with darker calyx. Matures at 5ft(1.5m).
Loder of Leonardslee. A.M. 1934.

SUSY   Described under ANNA DELP, q.v.

```
          -barbatum 1/2
SUTCHBARB-
          -sutchuenense 1/2
```
An introduction by E. J. P. Magor, 1936.

```
                    -catawbiense 1/4
           -Camich-          -ponticum 1/8
           -      -Michael Waterer-
SUZY BELL-                   -unknown 1/8
        -        -forrestii Repens Group 1/4
        -Elizabeth-
                  -griersonianum 1/4
```
1.5ft(.45m) -5F(-21C) M   Synonym TINKER BELL. Flowers openly
campanulate, 2in(5cm) wide, of Tyrian purple, without markings;
lax trusses of 7-9. Floriferous. Plant wider than tall, with
arching branches; leaves to 3.5in(8.9cm) long; held 2 years; new
growth bronze, tan tomentum.   J. B. Gable & H. Yates raisers;
Mrs. Maletta Yates, reg. 1980.

SWALLOWFIELD   Described under BRADFIELD, q.v.

```
                          -ponticum 1/4
            -Purple Splendour-
SWAMP BEAUTY-             -unknown 1/4
           -                 -griffithianum 1/4
           -Loderi Superlative-
                             -fortunei 1/4
```
5ft(1.5m) 10F(-12C) ML   4/4   Flowers open funnel-shaped, 4in.
(10cm) wide, of 5-6 wavy lobes, roseine purple with maroon spotting, shading to white in throat, large maroon blotch.   Trusses
7in(17.8cm) wide, ball-shaped, 18-flowered. Upright bush, about
as wide as tall; leaves held 2 years. J. A. Elliott, reg. 1983.
Color illus. Cox pl. 181.

SWAN LAKE   Described under BLANC-MANGE, q.v.

SWAN SONG   Described under CANDIED APPLE, q.v.

SWANSDOWN   Described under LODESTAR, q.v.

SWEET BAY--form of trichostomum Radinum Group
Trusses of 25 flowers, deeply lobed, color Tyrian rose suffused
white, giving a pleasing pink effect. Leaves 1.5in(3.8cm) long,
underside densely scaly.   Crown Estate, Windsor, reg. 1963.
A.M. 1960.

```
               -yakushimanum 1/4
         -Tols-
SWEET  -      -catawbiense 1/4
DESTINY-      -lacteum 1/4
       -Joanita-
               -campylocarpum ssp. caloxanthum 1/4
```
Buds of strong red and moderate pink, open to frilly flowers
of pale to moderate pink; dorsal spots moderate red.   Delp.

```
                                -thomsonii 1/16
                    -Bagshot Ruby-
            -Princess Elizabeth-      -unknown 15/32
  -unnamed-                  -unknown
  - hybrid-       -smirnowii 1/8
  -       -unnamed-
  -       hybrid-yakushimanum 1/8      -catawbiense 1/16
SWEET-                      -Parsons Grandi-
JENNY-       -America- florum    -unknown
  -      -unnamed-       -dark red hybrid--unknown
  -      -hybrid -        -griffithianum 3/32
  -      -        -Mars-
  -unnamed-      -Blaze-   -unknown
   hybrid-         -catawbiense, red form 1/16
  -            -Mars (as above)
      -Red Brave-
            -America (as above)
```
Buds of currant red and cardinal red open to frilled flowers of

vivid red; dorsal spotting ruby red.   W. Delp.

```
                    -catawbiense var. album Glass--Catalgla 1/4
        -Gosh Darn!-                          -decorum? 1/16
        -            -              -Caroline-
        -            -Mrs. H. R. Yates-        -brachycarpum? 1/16
SWEET-                              -unknown 1/8
   LULU-                            -neriiflorum 1/16
        -                   -Nereid-
        -unnamed-Phyllis Ballard-        -dichroanthum 1/16
           hybrid-                -fortunei ssp. discolor 1/8
                    -catawbiense--Clark's White 1/4
```
Buds of deep pink and moderate red open to flowers moderate yel-
lowish pink, with dorsal spots of strong orange; throat Chinese
yellow. Medium-sized plant.   W. Delp.

```
                          -catawbiense
                    -Pink Twins-
            -Shaazam-              -haematodes
            -            -                    -griffithianum
        -Earlene-        -Leah Yates--Mars F2-
SWEET -                               -unknown
MEDLEY-         -yakushimanum--Koichiro Wada
        -              -maximum
        -Adele's Yellow-
                    -wardii
```
Buds of rose Bengal opening pale purplish pink; flowers edged
with vivid purplish red; a flare of pale yellow-green. W. Delp.

```
            -ponticum 1/2
SWEET SIMPLICITY-
            -unknown 1/2
```
5ft(1.5m) -5F(-21C) ML 2/3 Bushy plant, almost round; leaves
5in(12.7cm) long, glossy dark green. Deep pink buds, opening to
ruffled flowers flushed white, edged in pink, 2.5in(6.4cm) wide;
rounded, well-filled trusses.   J. Waterer, Sons & Crisp, 1922.
A.M. Wisley Trials 1970.

```
            -Jan Dekens--unknown
SWEET SIXTEEN-
            -unknown
```
5ft(1.5m) -5F(-21C) M 4/3   Flowers of orchid pink, a deeper
pink picotee edging, 4.75in(12cm) across; about 12 in spherical
trusses. Plant covered with large, curled leaves. Difficult to
propagate. William Whitney cross; Sathers, 1976.   Color ill.
ARS Q 30:4 (1976) p. 238.

```
                    -facetum 1/4
        -unnamed hybrid-     -dichroanthum 1/4
        -                -Fabia-
SWEET SUE-                     -griersonianum 1/4
        -              -yakushimanum 1/4
        -unnamed hybrid-               -dichroanthum
                -Fabia Tangerine-
                          -griersonianum
```
2.5ft(.75m) 0F(-18C) ML   From pink buds, campanulate flowers
2.8in(7cm) wide, very pale pink, heavily flushed crimson to carmine, edges lighter, sparse spotting of scarlet red; domed truss
of 11. Dull green leaves 4.25in(11cm) long. Vigorous, upright,
floriferous bush, wider than high. Waterer, Sons & Crisp, 1972.
H.C. Wisley Trials 1982.

SWEET VIOLET   Described under GUSTO, q.v.

SWEET WENDY   Described under RAY OF SUNSHINE, q.v.

```
                -williamsianum 1/4
            -Cowslip-
SWEETIE PIE-        -wardii 1/4
            -forrestii Repens Group 1/2
```
Loose trusses of 6 flowers of pale cream flushed pink. Compact,
dwarf plant; leaves about 1in(2.5cm) long, rounded, dark green.
Early season.   D. W. James, reg. 1962.

SWEN   Described under YAKU WARRIOR, q.v.

SWINHOE--form of floribundum
6ft(1.8m) 10F(-12C) M 3/3   Leaves crinkled above, with woolly indumentum beneath.   Lax trusses of about 8 large flowers,
purple with a crimson blotch in the throat, and frilled margins.
Edmund de Rothschild, reg. 1963.   A.M. 1963.

```
            -edgeworthii 1/2
SYLVANIA-
        -formosum var. inequale 1/2
```
Trusses of 3-6 flowers, funnel-shaped, up to 4.8in(12cm) across,
white with small yellow-orange blotch; strongly fragrant. Foliage glossy green above, scaly below.   J. S. Basford raise Brodick Castle; G. A. Hardy, reg. 1984.   F.C.C. 1984.

```
                    -Monsieur Thiers--unknown 1/2
            -J. H. van Nes-
SYLVIA V. KNIGHT-            -griffithianum 1/4
        -            -Corona--unknown
            -Bow Bells-
                    -williamsianum 1/4
```
5ft(1.5m) 10F(-12C) EM   Plant upright, well-branched; leaves
4.5in(11.5cm) long, elliptic, dark olive, held 1-2 years. Flowers openly campanulate, 3.75in(9.5cm) wide, of spinel red, white
flare on each lobe, small red dorsal blotch; truss of 18. Bruce
Briggs cross; E. L. Knight, reg. 1979.

```
                    -sanguineum ssp. didymum 1/4
        -Arthur Osborn-
SYMPHONY-          -griersonianum 1/2
        -              -neriiflorum ssp. neriiflorum 1/4
        -F. C. Puddle-
                    -griersonianum
```
Red flowers.   Lord Aberconway, 1941.

```
            -arboreum ssp. cinnamomeum var. album 1/2
SYONENSE-
        -catawbiense 1/2
```
Delicate pink, spotted crimson. Iveson, 1849.   Knightian Medal.

```
              -catawbiense var. album Glass--Catalgla 1/2
TANTRAMAR-           -forrestii Repens Group 1/4
         -Treasure-
                    -williamsianum 1/4
```
3ft x 3ft(.9m)(19 yrs) -20F(-29C) M Flowers in lax trusses of
7, shades of strong purplish red on the edges, center, and outside. Dense habit; leaves held 3 years. R. Behring, reg. 1989.
Color illus. ARS J 44:2 (1990), p. 78.

TANYOSHO   Described under MARDI GRAS, q.v.

```
            -griersonianum 1/2
    -Rapture-
TARA-       -arboreum ssp. zeylanicum 1/4
    -           -griersonianum
    -Tally Ho-
            -facetum (eriogynum) 1/4
```
A shapely free-flowering bush; leaves 5.5in(14cm) long. Flowers
funnel-campanulate, 2.25in(5.7cm) long by 1.5in(3.8cm) wide, of
soft Turkey red, lightly spotted; compact trusses hold 17. Gen.
Harrison, reg. 1962. A.M. 1964.

TARANTELLA   Described under ERATO, q.v.

```
      -falconeri 1/2
TARANTO-
      -falconeri ssp. eximium 1/2
```
Two forms of the same species, crossed by Admiral A. W. Heneage-
Vivian, Clyne Castle, Wales. Intro. 1940.

```
       -catacosmum 1/2
TASCO-
       -griersonianum 1/2
```
Plant about 5ft(1.5m) tall and broad; floriferous. Leaves have
cinnamon brown indumentum below. Lax trusses hold about 6 widely campanulate flowers of deep scarlet, with extended calyces.
E. de Rothschild, 1966.   P.C. RHS 1967.   Color ill. PB pl. 9.

```
                    -catawbiense 1/16
        -Nova  -Parsons Grandiflorum-
        -Zembla-              -unknown 7/16
  -unnamed-    -hardy red hybrid--unknown
  - hybrid-  -griffithianum 1/4
  -        -Mars-
TATJANA-       -unknown
  -                 -griffithianum
  -          -Mars-
  -unnamed hybrid-   -unknown
            -yakushimanum--Koichiro Wada 1/4
```
4ft(1.2m) -10F(-23C) ML Trusses of 14-16 flowers, strong pur-
plish red, paling from edges to centers. Dark green leaves have
woolly indumentum beneath. Hachmann, cross 1969; G. Stück, reg.
1984.   Color illus. WS, 1989, p. 162.

TATOOSH   See ROSEANN

TAURUS   Described under GRACE SEABROOK, q.v.

```
               -wardii ?
      -Chlorops-
TEA TIME-       -vernicosum ?
     -          -Loder's White, q.v. (2 possible parentages)
      -C. I. S.-      -dichroanthum
                 -Fabia-
                    -griersonianum
```
2.5ft(.75m) high x 3ft(.9m)(21 yrs) OF(-18C) ML   Lax, domed
trusses 7in(17.8cm) wide with 13 flowers; 7-lobed, hose-in-hose,
moderate purplish pink with strong purplish red markings. Foliage held 1 year; new growth bronze.   Childers, reg. 1988.

```
   -brachyanthum ssp. hypolepidotum 1/2
TEAL-
   -fletcherianum 1/2
```
3ft(.9m) OF(-18C) M 4/4   Widely campanulate flowers held in
truss of 5-8, clear light yellow. Leaves narrowly elliptic, to
2.25in (5.7cm) long. Reddish peeling bark.   P. Cox, reg. 1977.
A.M. 1977.   Color illus. HG p. 76.

TEATICKET   Parentage unknown
6ft(1.8m) -5F(-21C) E Light bluish pink flowers with yellow-
green spots in throat. Dexter, cross before 1942.

```
              -Loder's White, q.v. for 2 possible diagrams
        -C. I. S.-    -dichroanthum
                 -Fabia-
TED DRAKE-        -griersonianum
      -    -wardii
        -Crest-         -fortunei ssp. discolor 1/4
           -Lady Bessborough-
                          -campylocarpum Elatum Group
```
5ft(1.5m) 10F(-12C) ML   Plant upright, well-branched; glossy,
dark yellow-green leaves, 5in(12.7cm) long. Barium yellow flowers with brick red rays in throat, reverse tinged scarlet. Lobe
tips cut off, making a circular hoop-skirt effect; spherical
trusses of 10-13.   Phetteplace cross; E. F. Drake raiser; Diane
A. Lux, reg. 1981.

```
            -griersonianum 1/2
TED GREIG-          -campylocarpum 1/4
     -unnamed hybrid-
                -fortunei ssp. discolor 1/4
```
A slender shrub of 5ft(1.5m) at 10 years; truss of 9-10 flowers,
geranium lake, lighter on the exterior of corolla and margins.
Royston Nursery, before 1962; reg. 1965.

TED WATERER   Parentage unknown
Flowers of blush lilac, in compact trusses.   J. Waterer, before
1922. A.M. 1925.

```
                        -ponticum 1/4
            -Purple Splendour-
     -                   -unknown 3/8
TED'S ORCHID SUNSET-          -Corona--unknown
     -             -unnamed hybrid-
           -Mrs. Donald-          -griersonianum 1/8
             Graham    -    -griffithianum 1/8
                    -Loderi-
                          -fortunei 1/8
```
5ft(1.5m) -5F(-21C) M 4/3   Orchid flowers with a deep bronze
center. Bronze green leaves, on reddish petioles, held 2 years.
Upright, spreading plant.   Fawcett.   Color illus. HG p. 117.

```
                       -griffithianum 9/32
        -Jean Marie de Montague-
     -                   -unknown 1/4
     -                     -griffithianum
TELL TAYLOR-         -Kewense-
     -         -Aurora-      -fortunei 5/32
     -    -Naomi-    -thomsonii 1/16
     -Carita-    -fortunei
        -campylocarpum 1/4
```
A very large open plant with very large, glossy leaves. Crimson
flowers, funnel-shaped, 3.5in(8.9cm) wide; rather tight trusses.
Midseason.   C. S. Seabrook, reg. 1965.

TELSTAR   Described under RENOIR, q.v.

```
         -griffithianum 1/4
     -Mars-
TEMPEST-  -unknown 1/4
     -    -dichroanthum 1/4
     -Fabia-
         -griersonianum 1/4
```
5ft(1.5m) -5F(-21C) L 4/3   Flowers of fine bright red, about
3in(7.6cm) broad, in loose trusses of 8-10.   Wright, reg. 1963.

```
         -orbiculare 1/2
TEMPLE BELLE-
         -williamsianum 1/2
```
3ft(.9m) -5F(-21C) EM 3/4   Plant neat, rounded, compact.
Campanulate flowers, rich rose pink, in small loose truss; pest
resistant. RBG, Kew, 1916.   Color illus. F p. 34, 67.

```
                   -fortunei ssp. discolor 1/4
          -Lady Bessborough-
     -Jalisco-         -campylocarpum Elatum Group 1/4
     -       -    -dichroanthum 1/8
TEMPLE-    -Dido-
GOLD -       -decorum 1/8
     -    -wardii 1/4
        -Crest-         -fortunei ssp. discolor
          -Lady      -
          -Bessborough-campylocarpum Elatum Group
```
Bright yellow flowers and calyces. Mrs. M. Temple, reg. 1985.

```
            -Lady        -fortunei ssp. discolor 1/8
         -Day  -Bessborough-
         -Dream-          -campylocarpum Elatum 1/8
TEMPTATION-    -
         -          -griersonianum 1/4
         -unknown 1/2
```
4ft(1.2m) -5F(-21C) ML 3/3   Flowers of creamy peach, with the
centers darker peach. Leaves dull green, recurved, twisted. Red
bud scales give color all winter.   J. E. Eichelser.

```
         -catawbiense var. album--La Bar's White 1/2
         -                -campylocarpum Elatum Group 1/8
TENNESSEE-    -Ole Olson-
         -unnamed-        -fortunei ssp. discolor 1/8
           hybrid-  -dichroanthum 1/8
                -Fabia-
                -griersonianum 1/8
```
Buds of strong purplish pink open to light purplish pink flowers
that change to pale yellowish pink; a bold dorsal blotch of red.
Smooth, elliptic foliage.   D. G. Leach, cross 1959; reg. 1986.

```
         -dichroanthum 1/4
      -Fabia-
TENSING-    -griersonianum 1/2
      -        -Moser's Maroon--unknown 1/4
      -Romany Chai-
            -griersonianum
```
3ft(.9m) -10F(-23C) L   Narrowly campanulate flowers of cam-
ellia rose, shading to a tinge of orange in the throat, in large
trusses.   Francis Hanger cross; RHS Garden, Wisley. A.M. 1953.

```
      -yakushimanum 1/2
TEQUILA-            -arboreum 1/8
SUNRISE-      -Doncaster-
      -Borde Hill-    -unknown 1/4
         -            -griffithianum 1/8
         -Mrs. A. M. Williams-
            -unknown
```
Compact, globular trusses hold 13 flowers, openly funnel-shaped,
strong purplish pink, flushed very pale pink at base, bases of
dorsal lobes flushed and spotted bright red. Plant height 7.5ft
(2.3m) at registration.   Francis Hanger cross; Royal Horticultural Society, reg. 1985.   A.M. 1985.
Another hybrid of the same name by Jos. Davis, (ORANGE MARMALADE
x LEM'S CAMEO) is distributed in the Northwest U.S. These flowers are deep yellow with orange tones.

TERRY HERBERT   Described under STAR SAPPHIRE, q.v.

```
* * * * * * * * * * * * * * * * * * * * * * * * * *
         -ciliatum 1/4
      -Praecox-
TESSA-    -dauricum 1/4
      -moupinense 1/2
```
4ft(1.2m) -5F(-21C) E 3/3   Lilac pink flower, a ray of crim-
son spots, 2in(5cm) broad, in loose, flattened umbels. Vigorous
plant with reddish bronze bark; small emerald green leaves with
convex edges.   J. B. Stevenson. A.M. 1935. A.G.M. 1969. Col-
or illus. JS p. 98.
TESSA BIANCA   Parentage as above, or may be reversed
3ft(.9m) -5F(-21C) E 4/4   White flowers, flushed pale pink,
the throat tinged light yellow. Plant habit compact. Possibly
TESSA improved. Lester Brandt, reg. 1965.
TESSA ROZA   Parentage as TESSA, above
4ft(1.2m) OF(-18C) E 4/3   A slightly deeper pink than TESSA,
spotted with deep carmine. J. B. Stevenson. A.M. 1953.
```
* * * * * * * * * * * * * * * * * * * * * * * * * *
         -campylocarpum 1/2
THACKER'S SULPHUR-
            -caucasicum--Cunningham's Sulphur 1/2
```
Compact trusses of 15 flowers, bell-shaped, 5-7 lobes, sulphur
yellow with blotch of red.   T. C. Thacker, 1940; reg. 1962.

```
            -neriiflorum 1/8
         -Nereid-
      -Euryalus-    -dichroanthum 1/8
THAIS-      -griersonianum 1/4
      -      -griffithianum 1/4
      -Loderi-
            -fortunei 1/4
```
Pale pink flowers.   Lord Aberconway, 1941.

```
* * * * * * * * * * * * * * * * * * * * * * * * * * *
            -ciliatum 1/2
THALIA (Brandt)-
            -ciliicalyx 1/2
```
A hybrid by Lester E. Brandt, 1954.
TACOMA MAIDEN   Parentage as above
3ft(.9m) 10F(-12C) E   Pure white, fragrant flowers in April.
Open habit.   Brandt cross; C. P. Fawcett intro.; reg. 1961.
```
* * * * * * * * * * * * * * * * * * * * * * * * * *
```

```
               -catawbiense 5/32
         -Blandyanum-            -catawbiense
         -         -unnamed-
      -Ascot    -Alta-  - hybrid-
      -Brilliant-  clerense-    -ponticum 1/32
THALIA-            -arboreum 1/16
(Magor)-    -thomsonii 1/4
      -griffithianum 1/2
```
A flower of mauve rose, with a large crimson blotch and spots.
E. J. P. Magor, reg. 1958.

```
            -smirnowii 1/8
         -unnamed hybrid-
         -            -yakushimanum 1/4
      -Cherry Crisp-    -sanguineum ssp. didymum 1/16
      -      -Carmen-
      -      -Little-    -forrestii Repens Group 1/16
THANKS-     Gem -elliottii (K W 7725) 1/8
MOMS -                  -catawbiense 1/16
      -            -Parsons Grandiflorum-
      -      -America-            -unknown 1/4
      -  -unnamed-    -dark red hybrid--unknown
      -Tim  - hybrid-yakushimanum
      Craig-      -America (as above)
         -Frank Moniz-  -griffithianum 1/16
            -Mars-
               -unknown
```
Buds of cardinal red open to star-shaped, white frilled flowers,
edged strong red; dorsal spots light greenish yellow.   W. Delp.

THATCHER'S RED   Parentage unknown
Very large flowers, tubular funnel-shaped, vivid red, with
darker spots; prominent red calyx. Leaves have thick indumentum
of brownish orange. Shrub to 2.5ft(.75m).   New Zealand season,
Oct.-Nov. Mrs. V. F. Thatcher, reg. 1986.

THE BRIDE--form of caucasicum var. album, selfed
6ft(1.8m) -15F(-26C) ML 2/3   An old selected form, with white
flowers blotched yellow; a good growth habit. Standish & Noble,
before 1850.   F.C.C. 1871.

THE BRIDGE   Parentage unknown
Trusses of 14-15 flowers, spinel red.   Mr. & Mrs. A. G. Holmes,
reg. 1979.

```
            -Moser's Maroon--unknown 1/4
         -Romany Chal-
THE CHIEF-      -facetum 1/4
         -elliottii 1/2
```
6ft(1.8m) OF(-18C) ML   Synonym NEZ PERCE CHIEF. A tall plant
of open habit; elliptic leaves 8.5in(21cm) long. Dome-shaped
trusses of 16 oxblood red flowers, campanulate-recurved, 3.75in.
(9.5cm) across. Arthur & Maxine Childers, reg. 1972.

```
         -glaucophyllum 1/2
THE CLOWN-
         -unknown 1/2
```
Trusses of 3-9 flowers, white flushed brownish red, with dark
spotting in upper throat.   Origin unknown; acquired from G.
Reuthe; R. N. S. Clarke, reg. 1982.   A.M. 1982.


```
* * * * * * * * * * * * * * * * * * * * * * * * * * *
         -arboreum 1/4
      -Doncaster-
THE DON-    -unknown 1/4
      -griffithianum 1/2
```
Considered a fine plant with flowers of strawberry red fading to
pink. Height medium to tall.   T. Lowinsky. A.M. 1920.
DON ERNESTO   Parentage as above, except reversed

Trusses of rich, rosy scarlet.   Lowinsky.   A.M. 1920.
DONA TIZIA   Parentage as DON ERNESTO
Flowers pale pink fading to white, deeper pink outside.   Bright
red pedicels.   Lowinsky.   A.M. 1921.
DONNA ANITA   Parentage as DON ERNESTO
Shell pink flowers.   Lowinsky.   A.M. 1920.
DONNA FLORENZA   Parentage as DON ERNESTO
Flowers of deep rich rose.   Lowinsky.   A.M. 1920.
* *

```
               -falconeri 1/4
          -Muriel-
THE DOWAGER-        -grande 1/4
          -arboreum 1/2
```
Tight round trusses of 24-26 flowers, widely funnel-campanulate,
margins very pale orchid pink, corolla suffused with tints of
purplish pink, lightly spotted, 2in(5cm) across.   Narrow leaves
9.5in(24.3cm) long, silver-gray indumentum below.   Dowager Lady
Loder raiser; Miss E. Godman exhibitor.   A.M. 1968.

```
              -griffithianum 1/4
        -Loderi-
THE DREAM-        -fortunei 1/4
        -unknown 1/2
```
Truss holds about 10 flowers of rhodamine pink, shading lighter.
Mrs. R. J. Coker, cross 1957; reg. 1979.

```
          -catawbiense, red form; possibly hybrid
THE GENERAL-
          -catawbiense, red form;  possibly hybrid
```
5ft(1.5m) -20F(-29C) ML 3/3 Crimson flowers with a dark red
blotch; upright trusses. Dark green leaves. Shammarello, 1955.

* *
```
                                    -griffithianum 1/2
THE HONORABLE JEAN MARIE DE MONTAGUE-
                                    -unknown 1/2
```
5ft(1.5m) -5F(-21C) M 4/4 Often called "Jean Marie" or "Jean
Marie de Montague", but first named JOYCE MONTAGUE.   The red by
which all newly introduced reds are judged.   Large, bright scarlet flowers, in dome-shaped trusses of 10-14.   Budding on very
young plants.   Bush compact, spreading; dense, thick, sun-tolerant foliage, deep emerald green,   C. B. van Nes & Sons, before
1950.   A.M. Wisley Trials 1989.   Color illus. HG p. 135; JS p.
74; VV p. 21.
THE HONORABLE JEAN MARIE DE MONTAGUE PINK SPORT   Parentage above
5ft(1.5m) -5F(-21C) M 4/4 Similar to THE HONORABLE JEAN MARIE
except flowers are bright pink instead of red; handsome dark foliage. Origin unknown. Greer, intro. 1989.
* *

```
                    -catawbiense, red form 1/4
          -unnamed hybrid-
THE MASTER-              -unknown 1/4
          -              -caucasicum 1/4
          -Cunningham's White-
                        -ponticum, white form 1/4
Rose pink flowers.    A. M. Shammarello, exhibited 1955.
```

```
                -wightii 1/4
        -China-
THE MASTER-        -fortunei 1/2
        -              -campylocarpum Elatum Group 1/4
        -Letty Edwards-
                      -fortunei
```
5ft(1.5m) -10F(-23C) M 4/4 Large pink flowers with dark red
basal blotch; very large globular trusses of 14. Vigorous, upright plant, broader than tall; dull, dark green leaves, 8.5in.
(21.6cm) long. Slocock, 1948. A.M. Wisley Trials 1966.

* *
```
                       -sanguineum ssp. didymum 1/4
          -Arthur Osborn-
THE MOOR-              -griersonianum 1/4
          -facetum (eriogynum) 1/2
```
Red flowers. Lord Aberconway, 1941.
OTHELLO   Parentage as above
Cardinal red flowers.   Lord Aberconway, 1941.
TREMEER   Parentage as above
Named for its place of origin in Cornwall. Gen. Harrison, 1953.
* *

* *
```
              -souliei 1/4
          -Halcyone-
THE QUEEN-        -Lady        -fortunei ssp. discolor 1/8
 MOTHER -        -Bessborough-
        -                      -campylocarpum Elatum Group 1/8
        -aberconwayi 1/2
```
3ft(.9m) -10F(-23C) M 4/4   Trusses of 9-10 flowers, magenta
rose paling to light rhodamine purple.   Leaves 3.25in(8.3cm)
long, dark green. Crown Estate, Windsor, reg. 1968. A.M. 1968.
WOODSIDE   Parentage as above
Pink and white flowers.   Crown Estate, reg. 1968. P.C. 1968.
* *

```
          -ponticum 1/2
THE REBEL-
          -unknown
```
5ft(1.5m) -15F(-26C) ML 4/3   Flowers of deep reddish purple
with showy white stamens. Martin Wapler named; Greer intro.

```
              -catawbiense, white form 1/2
THE VIRGIN-        -oreodoxa var. fargesii 1/4
          -unnamed hybrid-
                          -unknown 1/4
```
White flowers.   Abbott, before 1958.

THE WARRIOR   Parentage unknown
5ft(1.5m) -10F(-23C) ML   Flowers of light crimson red, tinged
blue, and spotted.   J. Waterer, intro. 1867.

```
                -campylocarpum Elatum Group 3/8
     -Penjerrick-
THEALE-        -griffithianum 1/4
      -        -wardii 1/4
      -Crest-        -fortunei ssp. discolor 1/8
            -Lady        -
            -Bessborough-campylocarpum Elatum Group
```
Open trusses of 10 flowers, primrose yellow with slight flush of
cardinal red in throat, widely campanulate, 2.25in(5.7cm) wide.
Crown Estate, Windsor, reg. 1967. A. M. 1966.

THELMA   Described under DARLENE, q.v.

* *
```
                 -Moser's Maroon--unknown 1/4
      -Romany Chal-
THERESA-        -facetum (eriogynum) 1/4
       -griersonianum 1/2
```
Stavordale, exhibited 1950.
FESTIVAL   Parentage as above
Red-flowered hybrid by Stavordale, 1950. Color illus. F. p. 45.
* *

```
          -moupinense 1/2
THICKET-
          -seinghkuense 1/2
```
Truss of 3-4 flowers, chartreuse green, with the throat spotted
Spanish orange. Crown Estate, Windsor, reg. 1961. P.C. 1960.

THIMBLE--seedling of campylogynum Cremastum Group
1ft(.3m) -10F(-23C) EM 3/4   Leaves covered with brown scaly
indumentum. Bell-shaped flowers, clusters of 1-3, 5-lobed, salmon pink. Collector unknown; C. Ingram, reg. 1967. A.M. 1966.

```
          -Furnivall's Daughter, parents as MRS. FURNIVALL, q.v.
THIRD   -        -wardii
NILLENNIUM-Crest-        -fortunei ssp. discolor
                -Lady Bess--
                borough  -campylocarpum Elatum Gp.
```
2.7ft(.8m) x 2.3ft(.7m) -5F(-21C) ML Saucer-shaped flowers, 7-
lobed, 4.4in(11cm) wide, strong dawn pink, fading to faint salmon; ball truss of 12. Smooth, oblong leaves, 5.5in(14cm) long;
plant spreading, floriferous.   T. Aunsbjorn cross; reg. 1989.

```
          -thomsonii 1/2
THOMADEN-
          -adenogynum 1/2
```
An introduction by E. J. P. Magor, 1927.

```
          -sanguineum ssp. sanguineum var. haemaleum 1/2
THOMALEUM-
          -thomsonii 1/2
```

Dark crimson flowers.   Collingwood Ingram, reg. 1958.

```
            -forrestii Repens Group 1/2
THOMAS CHURCH-     -campylocarpum 1/4
            -Moonstone-
                   -williamsianum 1/4
```
Dwarf plant 3ft(.9m) by 3ft. with leaves 2in(5cm) long. Trusses
hold 5 flowers, light orpiment (golden) orange when open, darker in bud.   Lester E. Brandt, reg. 1968.

```
            -thomsonii 1/2
THOMDETON-              -adenogynum 1/4
        -Xenosporum (detonsum)-
                       -unknown 1/4
```
An introduction by E. J. P. Magor, 1941.

```
          -thomsonii 1/2
THOMKING-                -griffithianum 1/4
        -Mrs. Randall Davidson-
                       -campylocarpum, Hooker's form 1/4
```
An introduction by E. J. P. Magor, reg. 1958.

* *
```
          -thomsonii 1/2
THOMWILLIAMS-
          -williamsianum 1/2
```
2ft(.6m) -5F(-21C) EM 3/4   Deepest rose pink, waxy flowers,
in loose trusses of about 6. Foliage like williamsianum; dense,
rounded habit. Sun-tolerant.   E. J. P. Magor, intro. 1927.
BODNANT THOMWILLIAMS   Parentage as above
Waxy, clear rose magenta flowers.   Lord Aberconway.   A.M. 1935.
CHERRY BRIGHT   Parentage as above
1.5ft(.45m) OF(-18C) M 3/3   Very bright cherry red flowers,
7-8 per truss. Cordate leaves.   B. F. Lancaster, reg. 1964.
CURRANT BELLS   Parentage as above
2ft(.6m) 5F(-15C) EM   Currant red flowers, bell-shaped, in
trusses of 9. Plant wider than tall, dense; dark green foliage.
B. F. Lancaster, reg. 1967.
* *
```
```
          -haematodes 1/2
THOR-   -dichroanthum 1/4
      -Felis-
            -facetum (eriogynum) 1/4
```
3ft(.9m)  5F(-15C)  M  4/4   Parentage may be reversed.  Flowers
of geranium lake, with large calyces. A compact plant; foliage
indumented.   L. Brandt, reg. 1963.   Color illus. Cox pl. 83.

THORON HOLLARD   Described under JOAN THOMPSON, q.v.

```
        -oreodoxa var. fargesii 1/2
THROSTLE-
        -morii 1/2
```
Hybrid by Collingwood Ingram.   P.C. 1970.

```
                      -fortunei ssp. discolor 1/4
      -Lady Bessborough-
-                      -campylocarpum Elatum Group 1/4
THROSTLE-
-                     -souliei 1/8
-      -Soulbut-
-Vanessa-   -fortunei 1/8
         -griersonianum 1/4
```
A hybrid by Mrs. M. Rabbets, Ringwood, Hants., England.   P.C.
1960.

* * * * * * * * * * * * * * * * * * * * * * * * * * *
```
                    -haematodes 1/2
THUMBELINA---MAY DAY, selfed
                    -griersonianum 1/2
```
2.5ft(.75m)  5F(-15C)  M    Leaves 2in x 1in(5cm x 2.5cm); loose,
open-growing plant. Flowers small, bell-shaped, deep rose, with
flounced calyx; 8-9 per truss.   Tressa McMurry, reg. 1965.
TINKERBELL   Parentage as above
Low-growing plant, compact but spreading, 2ft(.6m) tall by
3ft(.9m) in 8 years. Flowers rose pink, openly bell-shaped, in
trusses of 8-9. Blooms in midseason. Tressa McMurry, reg. 1965.
* * * * * * * * * * * * * * * * * * * * * * * * * * *

THUNDER   Seedling from P. J. M. group, selfed
3ft(.9m) x 2ft(.6m)  -20F(-29C)  M  Strong purplish red flowers,
3-5 per truss, 5 wavy lobes; ball-shaped  trusses  2.5in(6.4cm)
```

wide. Foliage dark mahogany; dense habit. Mezitt cross; Weston
Nurseries, reg. 1987.

```
          -ponticum ? 1/2
THUNDERHEAD-
          -unknown 1/2
```
5ft(1.5m) -15F(-26C) ML 3/3 Dull green, slightly curved foliage. Flowers of deep purple, much like PURPLE SPLENDOUR, but
lacking the blotch.   Roy W. Clark.

```
               -arboreum 1/4
        -Doncaster-
THUNDERSTORM-   -unknown 3/4
        -unknown
```
4ft(1.2m) -10F(-23C) M   Blood red, waxy flowers speckled with
darker red, white stamens; domed trusses hold about 18. Foliage
dark, glossy.   Slocock, cross 1930.   A.M. Wisley Trials 1955.

```
        -Sappho--unknown 1/2
TIANA-
        -yakushimanum, Exbury form 1/2
```
5.5ft(1.65m) high x 8ft(2.4m)(12 yrs) -5F(-21C) M   Flowers in
flat trusses of 13, white with dark red butterfly-shaped blotch.
Upright, open growth. R. Murcott cross; W. Brack, reg. 1989.

```
             -decorum ? 1/4
      -Golden Jubilee-
TIARA-               -unknown 1/4
-                    -griffithianum 1/4
      -Loderi King George-
                    -fortunei 1/4
```
4ft(1.2m) 5F(-15C) E   Fragrant white flowers with chartreuse
green throat, in compact, erect trusses. Light green leaves to
9in x 4in (23cm 10cm).   M. V. Love, reg. 1965.

```
                 -caucasicum 1/8
          -Viola-
     -Bismarck-    -unknown 1/8
TIBET-    -catawbiense 1/4
     -williamsianum 1/2
```
Plant medium low, compact; ovate leaves 3in(7.6cm) long, on
red petioles. Flowers pinkish in bud, white in full bloom.
Hobbie cross; Gebr. Boer, reg. 1969.   Gold Medal Boskoop 1966.
Color illus. WS, 1989, p. 31.

TICKLED PINK (Delp) Described under LOOK OUT, q.v.

* *
```
                   -campylocarpum ? 1/4
          -Unique-
-                  -unknown 1/4
TICKLED PINK-   -wardii 1/4
          -Crest-               -fortunei ssp. discolor 1/8
                  Lady Bessborough-
                               -campylocarpum Elatum Gp. 1/8
```
4ft(1.2m) OF(-18C) EM   Flowers creamy yellow and pink with
peach edges, darkening with age; rounded trusses. Foliage wavy,
twisting, as in UNIQUE.   C. Fawcett, intro. c. 1983.
EASTER PARADE   Parentage as above
Pale yellow flowers.   C. Fawcett.
MOUNT RANIER   Parentage as above
3ft(.9m) -5F(-21C) EM 3/3 Trusses of ivory cream flowers;
foliage dark emerald green; plant upright-growing.   Fawcett,
1980.
STARDUST   Parentage as above
Primrose yellow with glossy foliage; open-growing.   C. Fawcett.
* *

TICKLEY   Described under FAISA, q.v.

```
                    -griffithianum 1/4
        -Jean Marie de Montague-
TICK-TOCK-          -unknown 1/4
        -williamsianum 1/2
```
Rose pink flowers, funnel-campanulate, in rounded trusses of 10.
Low, compact plant; leaves 2.75in(7cm) long.   H. E. Greer, reg.
1963.

* *
```
       -dichroanthum 1/2
TIDBIT-
       -wardii 1/2
```

3ft(.9m) 5F(-15C) M 3/4   A vigorous plant, wider than high,
straggly; dark green, glossy, pointed leaves 3.25in(8.3cm) long.
Flowers first flushed cherry red, turning straw yellow and deep-
ening with age, campanulate, 2in(5cm) wide; trusses of 6 to 7;
free-flowering. R. Henny, reg. 1958.   P.A. 1957. H.C. 1977.
Color illus. VV p. 95.
CALLAGOLD   Parentage as above
Dwarf 5F(-15C) L   Reddish flowers, capped amber gold, 1.5in
(3.8cm) wide. Leaves to 3in(7.6cm).   R. Henny, reg. 1964.
CRACKERJACK   Parentage as above
Dwarf 5F(-15C) ML   Campanulate flowers of empire yellow 2.5in
(6.7cm) wide, 8-10 per truss. R. Henny, reg. 1965.
ELLA   Parentage as above
4ft(1.2m) 10F(-12C) ML 4/3 Apricot copper buds open to orange
to yellow; flowers, flat, 3in(7.6cm) across; truss of 7. Leaves
held 3 years; likes some shade, roots easily. Henny, reg. 1958.
WARDANTHUM   An early selection of the above cross by Stevenson.
* *

```
                 -dichroanthum 1/4
         -Tidbit-
  -         -wardii 1/2        -griffithianum 1/32
TIDDLYWINKS-      -wardii     -Kewense-
         -Idealist-   -Aurora-     -fortunei 5/32
                -Naomi-    -thomsonii 1/16
                      -fortunei
```
4ft(1.2m) OF(-18C) M 4/4 Flowers of deep lemon yellow with a
giant calyx, giving a hose-in-hose effect. Foliage glossy, deep
Irish green. Thompson, 1988. Color illus. HG p. 149.

```
         -yunnanense (chartophyllum) 1/2
TIEPOLO-           -ciliatum 1/8
  -         -Praecox-
  -Clodion-       -dauricum 1/8
            -cinnabarinum Roylei Group 1/4
```
Magenta flowers. G. M. Adams-Acton, 1934.

```
                     -racemosum 1/8
                -Conemaugh-
  -Anna    -Pioneer-    -micronulatum 1/0
TIFFANY-Baldsiefen-    -unknown 1/4
  -          -Pioneer (as above)
         -keiskei 1/2
```
2.5ft(.75m) -15F(-26C) M 3/3   Attractive dwarf. Star-shaped
reflexed flowers primarily pink with mixture of apricot and yellow in throat, semi-double. Pointed leaves. Warren Baldsiefen,
reg. 1972. Color illus. HG p. 137.

```
        -dichroanthum 1/2
TIGER-          -fortunei 1/8
  -        -Luscombei-
  -Cremorne-        -thomsonii 1/8
         -campylocarpum 1/4
```
3ft(.9m) -10(-23C) M   Shrub vigorous and compact, as broad as
high; medium green leaves 3in(7.6cm) long. Yellow flowers tinted orange-red, heavy spotting of grayed purple on upper segment,
2.75in(7cm) wide. Loose, flat truss of 4-6. Reuthe, reg. 1971.
H.C. Wisley Trials 1970.

TIGER SPLENDOUR   Described under CAROLINE ALLBROOK, q.v.

TIGHT END   Described under BODY LANGUAGE, q.v.

```
         -dichroanthum 1/4
      -Dido-
TILEHURST-   -decorum 1/4
         -griersonianum 1/4
      -Sarita-   -griffithianum 1/8
      Loder -Loderi-
              -fortunei 1/8
```
Compact, but not tight, trusses of 10-12 flowers, porcelain rose
shading to carmine rose at tip of lobe, flushed and mottled col-
oring; corolla 2.5in(6.4cm) wide. Narrowly ovate leaves to 5in.
(12.7cm) long. Crown Estate, Windsor, reg. 1967. P.C. 1966.
Color illus. ARS J 37:2 (1983), p. 67.

* *
```
                      -catawbiense 1/8
              -Parsons Grandiflorum-
         -America-          -unknown 1/2
      -unnamed-     -dark red hybrid--unknown
      - hybrid-yakushimanum 1/4
TIM CRAIG-      -griffithianum 1/8
              -Mars-
      -Frank-   -unknown          -catawbiense
      Moniz-    -Parsons Grandiflorum-
         -America-          -unknown
                -dark red hybrid--unknown
```
Deep red buds open to strong red flowers with touches of red and
white in the throat; white stamens. Weldon E. Delp.
CHARMER   Parentage as above
Cardinal red in bud opening to cardinal and strong reds; dorsal
spots cardinal red; throat white and cardinal red. Delp.
BLOODSHOT   Parentage as above
A blend of cardinal and currant reds in bud; flowers of currant,
cardinal and spirea reds, with dark red spotting on three dorsal
lobes, yellowish white anthers. Delp.
BRUCE STAFF   Parentage as above
Buds of cardinal red and currant red open to flowers of cardinal
red and guardsman red; dorsal spots deep red. Delp.
CALYPSO (Delp)   Parentage as above
Cardinal red buds open to a blend of cardinal and vivid red with
darker red dorsal spots; throat white and cardinal red. Delp.
HEATARAMA   Parentage as above
Dark cardinal red in bud with lighter red flowers; dark cardinal
red dorsal spotting. Delp.
RICHARD'S RED   Parentage as above
Vivid and currant reds in bud; flowers a blend of the same reds,
with dark red dorsal spots. Delp.
VIGOROUS PINK   Parentage unknown
Buds of cardinal and deep red open to a blend of vivid purplish
red and pale purplish pink, with ruby red dorsal spotting. Very
full trusses. Delp.
* *

```
              -griffithianum 5/32
         -Mars-
  -Vulcan-    -unknown 7/32
  -         -griersonianum 1/2
TIM -          -griersonianum
FLINT-      -Azor-
  -unnamed-    -fortunei ssp. discolor 1/8
      hybrid-          -Queen   -griffithianum
      -         -Britannia-Wilhelmina-
      -C. P. Raffill-     -     -unknown
              -         -Stanley Davies--unknown
                 -griersonianum
```
5ft(1.5m) 5F(-15C) ML   Fragrant flowers, color between Turkey
red and currant red, 2.6in(6.6cm) wide, fragrant, 5- or 6-lobed;
spherical truss of 11. Rounded plant, nearly as broad as tall;
leaves with light golden brown indumentum, held 3 years. Grady
Barefield cross; Mary Barefield, reg. 1981.

TIMOTHY JAMES   Described under BAMBI, q.v.

```
              -fortunei ssp. discolor 1/4
      -Disca-          -decorum? 1/8
  -         -Caroline-
TIN LIZZIE-          -brachycarpum? 1/8   -catawbiense 1/16
  -              -Parsons Grandiflorum-
  -      -America-          -unknown 5/16
  -Dorothy-      -dark red hybrid--unknown
  Amateis-          -ponticum 1/8
         -Purple Splendour-
                -unknown
```
Flowers strong purplish pink with throat moderate orange. Delp.

```
         -yakushimanum--Koichiro Wada 1/2
TINA -                -griffithianum
HEINJE-          -Queen Wilhelmina-       1/16
  -         -Britannia-          -unknown 7/16
  -Kluis Sensation-    -Stanley Davies--unknown
              -unknown
```
Intense red in bud, opening to dark pink and red with a dark red
eye; flowers in trusses of 14-15. Compact habit. Blooms late
May-early June. Heinje, reg. 1986. Color illus. WS, p. 112.

```
              -Westbury--unknown 3/8          -catawbiense 1/8
      -Wheatley-              -Mrs. C. S. Sargent-
TINA      -Meadowbrook-              -unknown
LOUISE-       -              -catawbiense
  -              -Everestianum-
      -yakushimanum 1/2              -unknown
```
22in(.56m) x 28in(.7m)(7 yrs) -5F(-21C) M   Ball trusses of 12
flowers 2.5in(6.5cm) wide, 7 wavy-edged lobes, lightly fragrant;
corolla white, central streaks light spinel red. Leaves smooth,
elliptic; bush dense, very floriferous. R. L. Means; reg. 1989.

```
          -wardii Litiense Group 1/2
TINA MARIE-     -wardii 1/4
      -Crest-              -fortunei ssp. discolor 1/8
            -Lady Bessborough-
                  -campylocarpum Elatum Group 1/8
```
5ft(1.5m) high x 6ft(1.8m) OF(-18C) M   Openly funnel-shaped
flowers, 6-10 per truss, 5-7 lobes of light yellow-green with
brilliant yellow-green throat. Flat trusses, 7in(17.8cm) wide.
Walt Elliott, cross 1974; Art Tracy, reg. 1986.

TINICUM   Parentage unknown.
Flowers 7-lobed, broadly funnel-shaped, pale pink with brilliant
chartreuse throat. Leaves to 5.3in(13cm). Bush 6.5ft(1.95m) at
36 years. Seed from the Everitt Estate, NY; J. Wister and Scott
Hort. Found. raisers; Scott Horticultural Foundation, reg. 1988.

```
        -catawbiense 5/8
TINKER HILL-                    -decorum 1/8
  -                -unnamed hybrid-
      -Lavender Charm-        -griffithianum 1/8
      -              -catawbiense
          -Purpureum Elegans-
                  -unknown 1/8
```
5ft(1.5m) -5F(-21C) EM   Plant upright, well-branched; leaves
glossy, dark yellow-green, 4.25in(10.8cm) long. Magenta buds,
opening to Neyron rose flowers with ruby red blotch and dorsal
spotting, 4in(10.2cm) wide, fragrant, 7-lobed; spherical trusses
of 13.   Charles Herbert, reg. 1977.

TINKERBELL   Described under THUMBELINA, q.v.

```
        -maximum 1/2
TINTORETTO-
        -unknown 1/2
```
Flowers light pink with a reddish blotch.   C. Frets & Son.

```
                      -fortunei ssp. discolor 1/8
              -Lady Bessborough-
    -Jalisco Elect-        -campylocarpum Elatum Gp. 1/8
  -          -dichroanthum 3/16
TIOGA-        -Dido-
  -            -decorum 1/8
  -          -fortunei 3/16
  -      -Fawn-    -dichroanthum
  -unnamed-    -Fabia-
    hybrid-          -griersonianum 3/16
        -          -griersonianum
          -Sarita Loder-    -griffithianum 1/16
                -Loderi-
                    -fortunei
```
5ft(1.5m) 5F(-15C) ML   Plant well-branched, willowy, broader
than tall; leaves 4in(10cm) long, dark green, retained 3 years.
Flowers primrose yellow, lightly spotted reddish brown, to 4in.
(10.2cm) across, 7-lobed, in lax trusses of 8; free-blooming.
Del James cross; W. V. Joslin, reg. 1974.

TIPSTER   Described under POWER BASE, q.v.

```
      -griffithianum 3/4
TIP-THE-WINK-    -griffithianum
      -Kewense-
          -fortunei 1/4
```
6ft(1.8m) OF(-18C) M 5/3   No additional information located
about this hybrid by Col. G. H. Loder, High Beeches. Closely
related to the Loderi hybrids, by Sir Edmund Loder of Leonardslee. F.C.C. 1936.

```
            -fortunei ssp. discolor 1/4
      -Beckyann-
TISH-      -campylocarpum 1/4
  -          -fortunei, Gable's cream form 1/4
  -unnamed      hybrid-
            -vernicosum R 18133 1/4
```
4ft(1.2m) -5F(-21C) ML An upright plant, as broad as tall;
glossy leaves 5.5in(14cm) long. Flowers 3.25in(8.3cm) wide,
Naples yellow, deeper in throat, unmarked, fragrant, 6-lobed;
spherical truss of 10.   H. Yates cross; Mrs. Yates, reg. 1976.

```
          -facetum (eriogynum) 1/4
      -unnamed hybrid-        -dichroanthum 1/4
  -        -Fabia Tangerine-
TITIAN-              -griersonianum 1/4
BEAUTY-      -yakushimanum 1/4
      -unnamed hybrid-      -dichroanthum
            -Fabia Tangerine-
                  -griersonianum
```
3ft(.9m) OF(-18C) M 3/3   Plant has neat, erect, compact hab-
it, with small foliage. Flowers of Turkey red.   John Waterer,
Sons & Crisp, reg. 1971.   Color illus. Cox pl. 184.

TITNESS ALADDIN   Described under ALADDIN, q.v.

```
          -griersonianum 1/2
TITNESS BEAUTY-    -griffithianum 1/4
      -Loderi-
          -fortunei 1/4
```
Sir James Horlick, 1937.

```
                        -griffithianum
                  -George Hardy-        7/16
            -Pink -      -catawbiense 3/16
            -Pearl-    -arboreum 1/16
      -Countess of-    -Broughtonii-
      - Derby    -            -unknown 1/16
      -      -        -catawbiense
TITNESS BELLE-      -Cynthia-
      -            -griffithianum
      -      -griffithianum
      -Loderi-
          -fortunei 1/4
```
Large flowers of deep rose, fading pink, in large trusses.   Sir
James Horlick, cross 1930; intro. 1942.

```
                -catawbiense 9/64
            -Blandy-          -catawbiense
          - anum -      -unnamed-
      -Ascot      -Alta-  - hybrid-
      -Brilliant-    clerense-    -ponticum
      -      -        -arboreum    1/64
    -J. G. -      -thomsonii 1/8
    -Millais-      -griffithianum 5/16
    -      -    -George-
      -Pink - Hardy-catawbiense
TITNESS-    Pearl-    -arboreum 3/32
CRIMSON-    -Broughtonii-
  -          -unknown (1/16)
  -      -griffithianum
  -Loderi-
          -fortunei 1/4
```
Early-flowering, glowing deep red blossoms, in trusses of 11-12.
Sir James Horlick, reg. 1962.

```
            -griffithianum 1/4
      -Loderi-
TITNESS DELIGHT-    -fortunei 1/4
        -unknown 1/2
```
Bell-shaped flowers in trusses of 11, light pink fading white,
and slightly scented.   Sir James Horlick, reg. 1962.

```
          -barbatum 1/2
TITNESS PARK-
        -calophytum 1/2
```
Trusses of 18 flowers, varying shades of phlox pink, with chocolate blotch in throat, some chocolate spotting.   Sir J. Horlick
cross; Crown Estate exhibitor. A.M. 1954.   F.C.C. 1974.

```
                        -thomsonii 1/4
                -Shilsonii-
TITNESS PERFECTION-    -barbatum 1/4
                -praevernum 1/2
```
An early flowering hybrid, rose pink with a deep throat.   Sir
James Horlick, reg. 1962.

```
                        -thomsonii 1/4
                -Shilsonii-
TITNESS PINK-          -barbatum 1/4
                -sutchuenense 1/2
```
Early-flowering, deep rosy pink.   Sir J. Horlick, reg. 1962.

```
                        -griffithianum 1/4
                -Loderi-
TITNESS SAUCY-        -fortunei 1/4
                -unknown 1/2
```
Trusses of 12 flowers, each 3in(7.6cm) across, slightly scented,
apple blossom pink fading to white. Midseason.   Sir James Horlick, reg. 1962.

```
                        -dichroanthum 1/4
                -Fabia-
TITNESS SCARLET-       -griersonianum 1/4
                -neriiflorum 1/2
```
Loose trusses of dark reddish orange scarlet flowers. Midseaon.
Sir James Horlick, reg. 1962.

* *
```
                -basilicum 1/2
TITNESS TRIUMPH-
                -montroseanum (mollyanum) 1/2
```
Pink flowers.   Sir James Horlick, cross 1939; intro. 1956.
TITNESS VICTORY   Parentage as above
Compact trusses of white flowers, lightly tinted mauve. Blooms
early season.   Sir James Horlick, reg. 1962.
* *

```
                -wightii 1/2
TITTENHURST-
                barbatum 1/2
```
Primrose yellow flowers.   Exhibited by G. White.   A.M. 1933.

```
                -Corona--unknown 1/2
TITTENHURST BELLE-
                -griffithianum 1/2
```
Flowers rose pink. T. Lowinsky.   A.M. 1925.

TOASTMASTER   Parentage unknown; Dexter hybrid
8ft(2.4m) high x 11ft(3.3m)(40 yrs) -5F(-21C) M Buds of deep
purplish pink, opening to flowers 4in(10.2cm) across, of pale
purplish pink, very fragrant. Truss 7in(17.8cm) high, with 6-7
flowers.   Named by John Wister; Swarthmore College, reg. 1985.

* *
```
                -elliottii 1/4
        -Fusilier-
TOD B.  -        -griersonianum 1/4
GALLOWAY-    -dichroanthum 1/4
        -Jasper-              -fortunei ssp. discolor 1/8
                -Lady Bessborough-
                        -campylocarpum Elatum Group 1/8
```
Medium-sized plant, open, rather flat and spreading; light green
leaves.   Flowers of varying light pink and yellow shades, showy
double calyx; flat truss of 8-12.   C. S. Seabrook, reg. 1965.
CECIL S. SEABROOK Parentage as above
Flowers buttercup yellow, fading to orange buff, 22 in a flat
truss. Dark green leaves, with beige indumentum. Plant resembles FUSILIER.   Seabrook, reg. 1967.
* *

TODMORDEN   Described under ACCLAIM, q.v.

Out of order
```
                -griffithianum 1/4
        -Mars-
TOKATEE-    -unknown 1/4
        -williamsianum 1/2
```
2.5ft(.75m) OF(-18C) EM Plant rounded, twice as wide as high;
small leaves held 4 years. Deep pink flowers, very pale at lobe
centers and throat, lightly spotted rose, 2.75in(7cm) across;

lax trusses of 7.   B. F. Lancaster cross; L. C. Grothaus, reg.
1975.   C.A. 1972.

```
                -dichroanthum 7/32
        -Dido-
        -    -decorum 3/16
    -Lem's-                -griffithianum 5/32
    -Cameo-        -Beauty of-
    -    -    -Norman- Tremough-arboreum 1/32
    -    -    - Gill -
    -    -Anna-    -griffithianum
    -    -        -griffithianum
    -    -Jean Marie -
TOFINO-    de Montague-unknown 1/16
    -                    -fortunei ssp. discolor 5/32
    -        -Lady
    -    -Jalisco-Bessborough-campylocarpum Elatum Gp. 3/32
    -    -    -    -dichroanthum
    -    -    -Dido-
    -unnamed-        -decorum
    hybrid-        -wardii 1/16
    -        -Crest-        -fortunei ssp. discolor
    -        -    -Lady     -
    -unnamed-    Bessborough-campylocarpum Elatum Gp
    hybrid-
    -            -fortunei ssp. discolor
    -King of Shrubs-    -dichroanthum ssp.
            -Fabia-
                -griersonianum 1/32
```
6ft(1.8m) OF(-18C) ML   Red buds open to light Dresden yellow
flowers, Neyron rose markings, 4in(10.2cm) wide; dome-shaped
trusses of 15-16. Plant upright, about as broad as tall; glossy
convex leaves, dark yellow-green, heavy-textured, held 2 years.
John Lofthouse, reg. 1983.

TOKATEE   See previous column

```
                -boothii ? 1/2
TOLCARNE-
                -unknown 1/2
```
Light yellow-green flowers, held in trusses of 4-5.   Of unknown
origin; intro. by Heaton Rutland c. 1968; Dunedin Rhododendron
Group, NZ, reg. 1981.

```
                -facetum 1/4
    -unnamed hybrid-    -dichroanthum 1/8
    -            -Fabia-
TOLKIEN-            -griersonianum 1/8
    -        -yakushimanum 1/4
    -unnamed-                -griffithianum 1/16
        hybrid-        -Queen Wilhelmina-
        -Britannia-        -unknown 3/16
                -Stanley Davies--unknown
```
Plant has growth habit of yakushimanum. Cardinal red flowers.
P. Wiseman, cross 1958; D. E. Mayers, reg. 1985.   A.M. Wisley
Trials 1988.

```
                -griersonianum 1/4
    -Sarita Loder-    -griffithianum 1/8
    -        -Loderi-
TOLO-            -fortunei 1/4
    -        -lacteum 1/4
    -unnamed hybrid-    -campylocarpum 1/8
            -Mary Swathling-
                -fortunei
```
A hybrid by Del W. James, before 1958.

```
                -yakushimanum 1/2
TOLS-
                -catawbiense 1/2
```
A parent of BLOODLINE and other Delp hybrids. Buds magenta,
opening to pale purplish pink edged a vivid purplish red. W. L.
Tolstead.

TOLTUE Parentage unknown; elepidote
10ft(3.0m) x 8ft(2.4m)(18 yrs) -5F(-21C) L Flowers 5in(12.7cm)
across, 7-lobed, white, lightly flushed in pale purplish pink,
greenish yellow throat; domed truss 9in(23cm) wide x 7in(17.3cm)
high. Upright, open growth habit.   W. & J. Ragan, reg. 1989.

```
                            -souliei ? 1/8
                    -Virginia-
            -unnamed- Scott  -unknown (1/8)
            - hybrid-        -Ole  -campylocarpum Elatum
            -       -Alice -Olson-              Group 1/16
TOM                 -  Franklin- -fortunei ssp. discolor 1/16
ETHRINGTON-         -                -griffithianum 1/16
            -               -Loderi  -
            -                   King George-fortunei 1/16
            -yakushimanum 1/2
```
5ft(1.5m) 10F(-12C) E   Upright plant, moderately branched;
elliptic leaves 5in(12.7cm) long, held 3 years. Rosy buds opening to fragrant primrose yellow flowers, unmarked, 3.75in(9.5cm)
wide, 8-lobed; dome-shaped truss of 12. H. Larson, reg. 1979.

TOM EVERETT Parentage unknown
5ft(1.5m) -10F(-23C) M   Strong purplish red buds open deep
purplish pink fading to near-white; domed truss of 11 scented
flowers. Compact, slow-growing plant.   C. Dexter cross; Scott
Hort. Foundation, reg. 1985.

TOM KOENIG   Described under MARY FLEMING, q.v.

```
                              -griffithianum 7/32
                -Jean Marie de Montague-
            -Fireman-               -unknown 13/32
            - Jeff -         -haematodes 1/8
            -    -Grosclaude-
            -               -facetum (eriogynum) 1/8
TOM         -                       -catawbiense 1/16
RING, M.D. -         -Parsons    -
            -       -America- Grandiflorum-unknown
            -  -unnamed-      -dark red hybrid--unknown
            -  - hybrid-              -griffithianum
            -  -            -Mars-
          -Anna-      -Blaze- -unknown
          Delp-       -catawbiense var. rubrum 1/16
            -         -griffithianum
            -   -Mars-
            -Red -    -unknown
            Brave-America (as above)
```
Buds of currant red open to flowers of vivid red, fully hose-in-
hose. Tall plant. Dr. Tom Ring cross; W. Delp raiser.

TOM SPRING-SMYTH--form of dalhousiae T.S.S. 32
Collected by Tom Spring-Smyth. Introduced as a cool greenhouse
plant. Maj. E. Hardy, reg. 1974. A.M. 1974.

```
                              -arboreum 1/16
                    -Doncaster-
            -unnamed-         -unknown
            - hybrid-         -neriiflorum 1/16
            -        -Nereid-
          -Witch Doctor-      -dichroanthum 1/16
            -        -        -griffithianum 1/16
TOM STIELER-    -     -Mars-
            -        -Vulcan- -unknown
            -unknown 5/8      -griersonianum 1/8
```
4ft(1.2m) x 2.5ft(.75m)(15 yrs) 0F(-18C) M Flowers in trusses
of 12, 5-lobed, strong red buds open strong purplish pink with
heavy dark red spotting and brownish orange part way up each
petal. New growth light reddish brown. P. Holden, reg. 1986.

```
              -griffithianum 1/4
          -Mars-
TOM THUMB-  -unknown 1/4
       -         -catawbiense, red form 1/4
       -Cathaem no. 1-
              -haematodes 1/4
```
2.5ft(.75m) -15F(-26C) M 4/4 Very slow-growing plant with a
distinctive leaf, indented at midsection. Flowers of good,
clear red, a few small pale markings at base, widely funnel-
shaped, 5-lobed (joined most of length); rounded trusses of 10-
12. Joseph B. Gable cross. Color illus. LW pl. 52.

```
          -sanguineum ssp. didymum 1/2
TOM THUMB-
          -thomsonii 1/2
```
At 25 years shrub was 3ft(.9m) high. Umbels of 4 flowers borne
low on plant, beneath the leaves. Flowers tubular-campanulate,
deep crimson, 1.5in(3.8cm) long; obovate leaves to 2.75in(7cm).
E. J. P. Magor cross; Maj. E. W. M. Magor, reg. 1962.

```
                        -arboreum 1/4
                    -Doncaster-
TOM WILLIS FLEMMING-    -unknown 3/4
                    -unknown
Deep red flowers.  W. C. Slocock.
```

```
                    -haematodes 1/4
          -Choremia-
TOMAHAWK-        -arboreum 1/4
          -hookeri 1/2
Blood red flowers.  Lord Aberconway, 1950.
```

```
                              -dichroanthum 1/8
                    -Goldsworth Orange-
          -Tortoiseshell Wonder-      -fortunei 1/8
TOMBOLA-              -griersonianum 1/2
       -        -Moser's Maroon--unknown 1/4
       -Romany Chai-
              -griersonianum
```
The trusses hold up to 16 flowers, bright reddish pink, blotched
with orangey brown.   Research Station for Woody Nursery Crops,
Boskoop, reg. 1979.

TOMBOY   Described under HAD, q.v.

```
                -dichroanthum 1/4
          -unnamed hybrid-
TOMEKA-         -griersonianum 1/4
       -decorum 1/2
```
5ft(1.5m) 10F(-12C) M 4/3 Flowers vermilion with an orange
glow, red veins, dorsal spots, and nectaries. Lax trusses of
5lo to 9 flowers. Leaves long, narrow. Del James, cross 1964;
Hadley Osborn, reg. 1979.

* *
```
                    -griffithianum 1/4
                -Mars-
TOMMIE--TOM THUMB, selfed-    -unknown 1/4
                    -catawbiense, red form 1/4
                -Cathaem no. 1-
                    -haematodes 1/4
```
Semi-dwarf -10F(-23C) M 3/4   Flowers red, pink, or pinkish
salmon. Named forms include: BONNIE, LITTLE BONNIE, MARY YATES,
(Gable), and the TOMMIES NO. 1 to NO. 12. Joseph B. Gable.
TOMMIE NO. 2   Parentage as above
Semi-dwarf -10F(-23C) M 4/3 Bi-color flowers. In the LW
photograph, soft salmon red with cream centers of the 5 divided
lobes, upper lobe spotted darker; rather small flattened trusses
of 6-7. The ARS picture shows white flowers with wide pink marg-
gins with pale spotting, 5 joined lobes, very rounded trusses of
about 12. Who has whom? Joseph B. Gable. Color illus. ARS
J 36:1 (1982), p. 10; LW pl. 49.
* *

```
                -neriiflorum 1/4
          -Daphne-         -arboreum 1/8
TOMYRIS-        -Red Admiral-
          -thomsonii    -thomsonii 5/8
```
Claret red, bell-shaped flowers of good substance, held in loose
trusses of 5-7. E. J. P. Magor cross; named and reg. by Maj. E.
W. M. Magor, 1963.

```
          -decorum 1/2
TONY-
          -unknown 1/2
White flowers.  Lt. Col. L. C. R. Messel.  A.M. 1930.
```

TONY (Shammarello) Described under PINK CAMEO, q.v.

TONY SHILLING--form of arboreum ssp. cinnamomeum var. roseum
Trusses of 25 flowers, medium rose pink, spotted and streaked
crimson. RBG, Kew, Wakehurst Place, reg. 1974. F.C.C. 1974.

```
          -catawbiense var. album Glass--Catalgla 1/2
TONY'S GIFT-              -catawbiense 1/4
       -        -Catawbiense Album-
       -Belle Heller-        -unknown 1/4
       -              -catawbiense
          -white catawbiense hybrid-
                    -unknown
```
A tall plant, hardy to -25F(-32C). Flowers white with a yellow-
green blotch. A. M. Shammarello cross; Weldon Delp raiser.

```
                  -campylogynum Charopeum Group--Patricia 1/2
TOO BEE-
         -keiskei--Yaku Fairy 1/2
```
1ft(.3m) -10F(-23C) EM Venetian pink flowers with claret rose
spotting, 5 wavy-frilled lobes, 1.5in(3.8cm) wide, in clusters
of 3-5; floriferous. Bush is twice as broad as high, rounded;
small, elliptic, convex leaves, held 2 years. Berg, cross 1972;
reg. 1983. A.E. 1989. A.M. 1988. Color illus. ARS J 44:1
(1990), p. 2.

```
                          -dichroanthum 1/8
                -Fabia-
       -Hello Dolly-    -griersonianum 1/8
       -              -smirnowii 1/4
TOO LIPS-          -catawbiense var. album Glass--Catalgla
       -     -Calsap-                           1/8
       -Caltwins-    -Sappho--unknown 1/8
       -              -catawbiense 1/8
                -Pink Twins-
                          -haematodes 1/8
```
Buds of strong red open to flowers of deep and strong pinks;
dorsal spotting vivid yellow-green. W. Delp.

```
       -arboreum--Bennett's Arboreum 1/2
TOOLANGI-           -arboreum ssp. zeylanicum 1/8
   RUBY -    -Ilam Alarm-          -griffithianum 1/16
     -Scarlet-      -unnamed hybrid-
       King -griersonianum 1/4        -unknown 1/16
```
Flowers in trusses of 28-30, tubular campanulate, strong red
with darker spots on 2 two lobes. Bush 6.5ft(2.0m) tall. H.
van de Ven, cross 1981; Toolangi Nursery, reg. 1988.

```
                    -dichroanthum 1/8
                -Goldsworth-
                - Orange   -fortunei ssp. discolor 1/8
       -Hotei ? -          -souliei 1/8
TOP BANANA-      -unnamed hybrid-
       -                  -wardii 1/8
       -unknown 1/2
```
3ft(.9m) 5F(-15C) EM Brick red buds opening to empire yellow
flowers, unmarked, openly funnel-shaped, 2.5in(6.4cm) wide, 6-
lobed; spherical truss of 17. Plant upright, taller than broad;
glossy dark leaves, held 2 years. William Whitney; Anne Sather
intro.; reg. 1985. Color illus. ARS J 38:3 (1984), p. 115.

TOP DOG Described under CHECKMATE, q.v.

TOP HAT Parentage unknown
4ft(1.2m) -5F(-21C) EM 4/3 Similar to HIGH GOLD, but foliage
less glossy. Bright yellow flowers on plant of nice, compact
habit. Whitney cross; Briggs intro.

```
                                      -catawbiense
TOP                          -Sefton-         1/4
NOTCH---DAVID HARRIS, F2---unnamed hybrid, F2-  -unknown 1/2
                             -Purple  -ponticum
                             Splendour-         1/4
                                      -unknown
```
Buds of dark red open to frilled flowers violet purple and deep
red; dorsal spots on 3 lobes dark red; throat white. W. Delp.

```
                -griffithianum 1/4
       -Loderi King George-
TOPAZ-             -fortunei 1/2
       -                  -fortunei
       -Faggetter's Favourite-
                          -unknown 1/4
```
Trusses of 7-10 flowers in early season, phlox pink on exterior,
white interior. Upright, tall plant; foliage 7in(17.8cm) x 2.5
in(6.4cm). Henny, intro. 1963; reg. 1972.

TOPAZ (NZ Rhod. Assoc.) See KIMBOLTON YELLOW

TOPPER Described under FREE REIGN, q.v.

```
                          -griffithianum 1/4
                -George-
TOPSVOORT--sport of PINK PEARL- Hardy-catawbiense 1/4
   PEARL         -        -arboreum 1/4
                -Broughtonii-
                          -unknown (1/4)
```
6ft(1.8m) -5F(-21C) EM 4/3   Similar to PINK PEARL, q.v.

This has large, pale pink flowers, with notched lobes, mauve red
frilled edges. Topsvoort Nursery, Holland, intro. 1935. Color
illus. HG p. 87.

TOPSY Parentage unknown: elepidote
3ft(.9m) x 3.5ft(1.05m) M Truss of 11 flowers, funnel-campanulate, 6 wavy-edged lobes of pale purplish pink. J. May, reg.
1988.

```
                          -griffithianum 1/4
             -Queen Wilhelmina-
       -Britannia-         -unknown 3/8
TORCH-      -Stanley Davies--unknown
       -            -griersonianum 1/4
       -Sarita Loder-    -griffithianum
                    -Loderi-
                          -fortunei 1/8
```
6ft(1.8m) -5F(-21C) M   Flowers of rosy orange, the throat a
deeper color; blotch of dark brown. W. Slocock.

```
             -sanguineum ssp. didymum 1/4
       -Arthur Osborn-
TOREADOR-    -griersonianum 3/4
       -griersonianum
```
Dark red flowers turn glowing bright scarlet with back-lighting.
Trusses of 7-8. Lord Aberconway, 1941. A. M. 1942.

```
                                -griffithianum 1/32
                    -Queen    -
             -Britannia-Wilhelmina-unknown 3/32
          -Wilgen's-    -Stanley Davies--unknown
          - Ruby  -    -catawbiense 1/16
       -unnamed-    -John Walter-
       - hybrid-          -arboreum 1/16
       -         -haematodes 1/4
TORNADO-    -May Day-
       -          -griersonianum 1/4
       -            -haematodes
       -     -May Day-
       -Billy Budd-    -griersonianum
                 -elliottii 1/8
```
Currant red flowers, in trusses of 9-14. Research Station for
Woody Nursery Crops, Boskoop, reg. 1979.

```
                    -sanguineum ssp. didymum 1/8
          -Arthur Osborn-
       -Toreador-         -griersonianum 5/8
TORSUN-    -griersonianum
       -         -griffithianum 1/4
       -Sunrise-
                 -griersonianum
```
Rose red flowers. Lord Aberconway, 1945.

* *
```
                                -dichroanthum 1/4
             -Goldsworth Orange-
TORTOISESHELL-         -fortunei ssp. discolor 1/4
             -griersonianum 1/2
```
White, pale yellow center. Slocock, 1946. Col. ill. JS p. 49.
CHAMPAGNE Parentage as above
4ft(1.2m) 5F(-15C) ML 4/3 Plant broader than tall, rather
open. Unusual creamy apricot flowers; trusses of 14. Slocock,
1946. H.C. 1962. A.M. Wisley Trials 1967. Color, Cox pl. 186.
TORTOISESHELL ORANGE Parentage as above
4ft(1.2m) -5F(-21C) ML 4/3 Large flowers of deep clear
orange, mid- to late season. Plant upright; long slender
leaves. Slocock Nurseries, 1945.
TORTOISESHELL SALOME Parentage as above
4ft(1.2m) -5F(-21C) ML 4/3 Large flowers of biscuit, shaded pink. Sometimes called BISCUIT. Slocock, 1946.
TORTOISESHELL SCARLET Parentage as above
4ft(1.2m) -5F(-21C) ML 4/3 Similar to others in this grex,
but with orange scarlet flowers. Slocock, 1946.
TORTOISESHELL WONDER Parentage as above
4ft(1.2m) -5F(-21C) ML 4/3 Flowers a blend of orange salmon
with salmon pink. W. C. Slocock. A. M. 1947.
* *

```
                        -degronianum ssp. heptamereum (metter-
     -First Step, selfed-          nichii)--METTERIANUS 1/8
TOSCA-            -arboreum 1/4
     -                -griersonianum 1/4
     -Vulcan's Flame-     -griffithianum 1/4
                     -Mars-
                          -unknown 1/8
```
A heat-resistant hybrid. Ruffled flowers warm rosy pink at mar-
gins, turning lighter toward the center; a long, white, recurved
pistil. Attractive medium green foliage.   Koichiro Wada, 1962.
Color illus. ARS J 37:4 (1983), p. 194.

```
                          -griffithianum 1/16
                    -Kewense-
               -Aurora-      -fortunei 5/16
     -Exbury Naomi-     -thomsonii 1/8
TOSCA-          -fortunei
     -wardii Litiense Group 1/2
```
Rounded trusses of 10 flowers, shallowly campanulate, 3.75in(9.5
cm) wide, opening primrose yellow from buds of pale pink. F.
Hanger cross, RHS Garden, Wisley; reg. 1962.   A.M. 1959.

```
          -ferrugineum 1/2
TOTTENHAM-
          -unknown 1/2
```
2ft(.6m) -10F(-23C) ML 3/3   Pale pink tubular flowers, held
in loose trusses of 10. Foliage very dark green, densely covered beneath with brown scales; yellow petioles.   Moerheim.

```
            -agastum 1/2
TOUCH OF CLASS-      -griersonianum 1/4
            -Tally Ho-
                     -facetum (eriogynum) 1/4
```
Flower buds are deep jasper red, opening a lighter shade of red.
Mrs. R. J. Coker, reg. 1980.

TOUCH OF GOLD   Parentage unknown
Large, fragrant flowers of pale peach with blotch of golden
chartreuse; truss of 7.   Frederick, reg. 1963.

```
             -griffithianum 1/2
TOUCHSTONE-
             -unknown 1/2
```
Large loose trusses of very large, bell-shaped flowers, mottled
deep pink.   J. J. Crossfield, Embley Park. A.M. 1937. F.C.C.
1939.   Color illus. ARS J 36:4 (1982), p. 139.

```
          -minus Carolinianum Group, white form 1/2
TOW HEAD-
          -ludlowii 1/2  (Pollen from Cox)
```
1ft(.3m) -15F(-26C) EM 4/4   Plant twice as broad as tall;
leaves 1.75in(4.5cm) long, glossy, and scaly on both surfaces.
Flowers brilliant greenish yellow with orange-yellow spotting on
dorsal lobe, 1.5in(3cm) wide, 5 per bud; blooms before new foliage appears. David G. Leach, reg. 1968.

TOWARDII   Described under BLANDYANUM, q.v.

```
                          -catawbiense 1/4
TOWER OF          -Atrosanguineum-
POWER---Dr. H. C. Dresselhuys, F2-     -unknown 1/2
          -          -arboreum 1/4
               -Doncaster-
                          -unknown
```
Buds vivid reddish purple opening to flowers vivid reddish pur-
ple; a white flare; dorsal spots brilliant yellow-green. Delp.

```
                          -griffithianum 1/16
                    -Queen Wilhelmina-       1/16
               -Britannia-          -unknown 3/16
     -C. P. Raffill-      -Stanley Davies--unknown
     -                -griersonianum 3/8
TOWHEE-               -sanguineum ssp. didymum 1/8
     -          -Red Cap-
     -unnamed-      -facetum (eriogynum) 1/4
      hybrid-      -griersonianum
               -Tally Ho-
                     -facetum (eriogynum)
```
4.5ft(1.35m) 5F(-15C) ML 3/3   Leaves 4.5in x 1.5in (11.5cm
x 3.8cm).   Bright scarlet red, waxy flowers, 3.5in(8.9cm)
across, in open-topped trusses of 10.   Del W. James, reg. 1968.
P.A. 1956.

TOWNHILL ALBATROSS   Described under ALBATROSS, q.v.

TOWNHILL CREMORNE   Described under CREMORNE, q.v.

TOWNHILL DAMARIS   Listed under DAMARIS, q.v.

TOWNHILL RED CAP   Described under RED CAP, q.v.

TOWNHILL SULPHUR YELLOW   Listed under SULPHUR YELLOW, q.v.

```
          -Blue Peter--unknown 1/2
TRACI SUZANNE-            -griffithianum 1/4
          -Loderi King George-
                          -fortunei 1/4
```
6ft(1.8m) 5F(-15C) L   Plant rounded, with willowy branches;
narrow leaves 6in(15.2cm) long, held 3 years. Buds light cyclamen purple, opening pale orchid spotted green on upper lobe;
flower to 3.5in(8.9cm) wide, fragrant, in spherical truss of 12.
Floriferous.   E. L. Kaiser cross; Mrs. Mae Granston, reg. 1977.

```
          -yakushimanum 1/2
TRACIGO-
          -sperabile 1/2
```
3ft(.9m) 5F(-15C) M 3/3 Plant upright and rounded, wider
than tall; dark green leaves, grayed orange indumentum beneath,
held 4 years. Flowers of good substance, 2in(5cm) across; many
dome-shaped trusses of 12-15 produce a delightful apple blossom
effect with bright red buds, flower exteriors pink, white inter-
iors.   Dr. David Goheen, reg. 1983.

```
                          -campylocarpum Elatum Group 1/16
                    -Penjerrick-
               -Amaura-      -griffithianum 1/16
          -Eros-      -griersonianum 3/8
TRAFALGAR-      -griersonianum
          -          -fortunei 1/4
          -Luscombei-
                     -thomsonii ssp. thomsonii 1/4
```
Rose pink flowers.   Lord Aberconway, 1950.

```
                          -griffithianum 1/8
                    -unnamed hybrid-
          -Mrs. Furnivall-          -unknown 3/4
TRAIL BLAZER-      -          -caucasicum 1/8
          -          -unnamed hybrid-
          -Sappho--unknown          -unknown
```
5ft(1.5m) -10F(-23C) M 4/4   Flowers resemble MRS. FURNIVALL,
pink with a striking blotch, but here the blotch is ruby red;
flowers openly funnel-shaped, 3in(7.6cm) wide, in globular
trusses of 19. Vigorous plant, twice as wide as tall; glossy
dark leaves held 3 years.   A. A. Wright, Sr. & Jr., reg. 1979.

```
* * * * * * * * * * * * * * * * * * * * * * * * * * * *
          -Corona--unknown 5/8
TRANQUILITY-          -griffithianum 1/6
     -          -Mars-
     -Vulcan-      -unknown
                     -griersonianum 1/4
```
Cross by A. A. Wright, Jr. & Sr., reg. 1958.
CARY ANN   Parentage as above
3ft(.9m) 5F(-15C) M 3/4   Flowers coral red, trumpet-shaped;
conical trusses of 17. Good, dark green foliage.   Tolerant of
full sun. Wright Sr. & Jr., reg. 1962. P.A. 1961 Color illus.
VV p. 25.
```
* * * * * * * * * * * * * * * * * * * * * * * * * * * *
```

```
                          -cinnabarinum 1/4
               -Royal Flush, cream form-
TRANSIT GOLD-          -maddenii 1/4
               -cinnabarinum ssp. xanthocodon 1/2
```
8ft(2.4m) x 4ft(1.2m)(25 yrs) OF(-18C) E Flowers tubular fun-
nel-shaped, medium grayish yellow, 1.4in(3.5cm) across, of heavy
substance; lax trusses of 4-7. Oblong leaves 2.5in(6.4cm) long;
scaly below. Dr. S. Holland cross; W. Dale, reg. 1989. (British
Columbia) Color illus. ARS J 43:1 (1989), p. 31.

```
          -unknown 1/2
TRAVIS L.-            -griffithianum 1/8
     -          -Loderi-
     -Albatross-      -fortunei 1/8
               -fortunei ssp. discolor 1/4
```
4ft(1.2m) -5(-21C) EM   Upright plant habit, arching branch-

es; long, narrow leaves, smooth and dark green.   Flowers about 4.5in(11.5cm) across, of ivory white with pale greenish white blotches, 7 wavy lobes; globular trusses of 8-12.   Clifford Cannon, reg. 1981.

```
            -forrestii Repens Group 1/2
TREASURE-
        -williamsianum 1/2
```
2ft(.6m) -5F(-21C) EM 3/4   A mounded shrub, with gnarled branches; neat, rounded dark green leaves, bronze when young. Nodding campanulate flowers of deep rose, 2in(5cm) across.   J. J. Crosfield, 1937.

```
            -arboreum, blood red form 1/2
TREBAH GEM-
          -griffithianum 1/2
```
Soft pink flowers.   R. Gill & Son.

TRELAWNY   Described under DUKE OF CORNWALL, q.v.

```
                    -griffithianum 3/8
        -Loderi Pink Diamond-
-                       -fortunei 3/8
TRELEAN-          -griffithianum
-       -Kewense-
-Aurora-      -fortunei
        -thomsonii 1/4
```
13ft(4m) 5F(-15C) M   Flowers in trusses of 12, 8-lobed, deep red in bud, opening white flushed light purplish pink. G. T. Witherwick, reg. 1989.

```
        -bureavii 1/2
TRELEAN -
BURDOOLA-          -griersonianum 1/8
-       -Matador-
-               -strigillosum 1/8  -arboreum 1/32
-Bandoola-              -Doncaster-
-               -The Don-        -unknown 1/32
    -Red Lamp-      -griffithianum 1/16
            -facetum 1/8
```
3.3ft(1m) 5F(-15C) M   Flowers in trusses of about 6, 5-lobed, deep red in bud, opening vivid red to deep pink with dark spotting in dorsal throat.   G. T. Witherwick, reg. 1989.

```
        -diaprepes 1/2
TRELEAN QUITE SOMETHING-
            -unknown 1/2
```
Flowers in trusses of about 12, 6 to 7-lobed, tipped pink in bud, opening white; unmarked. G. T. Witherwick, reg. 1989.

TREETOPS   Described under BEAUTY OF TREMOUGH, q.v.

TREMEER   Described under THE MOOR, q.v.

```
                -smirnowii 1/8
            -Oh My!-
-unnamed-      -yakushimanum 1/8
- hybrid-aureum (chrysanthum) 1/4
-           -catawbiense var. album Glass--Catalgla 1/8
TRENDLINE-      -                   -decorum? 1/32
-       -Gosh -              -Caroline-
-       -Darn!-Mrs. H. R. Yates-      -brachycarpum?
-Sweet-            -unknown 1/16    1/32
    Lulu-            -neriiflorum 1/16
-               -Nereid-
    -Phyllis Ballard-      -dichroanthum 1/16
                -fortunei ssp. discolor 1/8
```
Buds of light and strong purples open to frilled flowers very pale purple with dorsal spots moderate reddish orange.   Delp.

```
        -azalea occidentale 1/2
TRESSA MCMURRY-
        -ponticum 1/2
```
3ft(.9m) 0F(-18C) ML Azaleodendron. Plant upright, as wide as tall with dark green, narrow leaves 3in(7.6cm) long. Widely funnel-campanulate flowers 1.5in(3.8cm) wide and long, fuchsine pink with a sienna blotch; flat trusses of 10-18. Floriferous. Mrs. T. McMurry, reg. 1977.

TRETAWN   Described under ARBCALO, q.v.

```
* * * * * * * * * * * * * * * * * * * * * * * * * * * * * * * *
                -cinnabarinum Blandfordiiflorum 1/4
        -Full House-
TREWITHEN-      -maddenii 1/4
 ORANGE -
            -cinnabarinum ssp. xanthocodon Concatenans Group 1/2
```
4ft(1.2m) 5F(-15C) M 4/3   Loose, tubular-shaped, deep orange-brown flowers in pendant trusses. Erect plant; sea green foliage. G. H. Johnstone, Trewithen. F.C.C. 1950.
GEORGE JOHNSON   Parentage as above
Flowers bright nasturtium orange in loose trusses of 7-9.   Aromatic leaves, indumented.   Shown by C. Ingram.   A.M. 1967.
```
* * * * * * * * * * * * * * * * * * * * * * * * * * * * * *
```

TRIANGLE--form of cinnabarinum ssp. tamaense K W 21003
Flowers axillary, in loose clusters of 24-26, flushed with purple shades, white deep in throat. Leaves dull dark green, 2in x 1.25in (5cm x 3cm), lightly scaly. F. Kingdon Ward collector; Maj. A. E. Hardy raiser; reg. 1978.   P.C. 1978.

TRIANON Described under FRED WYNNIATT, q.v.

```
    -triflorum 1/2
TRIAUR-
    -xanthostephanum 1/2
```
A yellow-flowered hybrid by E. J. P. Magor, 1920.

TRIDENT   Described under FIRETAIL, q.v.

TRILBY   Described under BRITANNIA, q.v.

```
            -unnamed-dichroanthum ssp. scyphocalyx 1/8
        -Calcutta- hybrid-
-       -       -kyawii 1/8
TRINIDAD-      -catawbiense var. album Glass--Catalgla 1/4
-           -maximum  1/8
-       -Russell Harmon-
-Tahiti-          -catawbiense 1/8
-           -dichroanthum 1/8
    -unnamed-      -fortunei ssp. discolor 1/16
        hybrid-unnamed-
                hybrid-campylocarpum
```
4ft(1.2m) -20F(-29C) ML   Spherical trusses hold 14 flowers, sharply defined bright cherry red corolla perimeter, with ivory center, and sparse grayed yellow dorsal spotting, 2.75in(7cm) across.   Plant broader than tall; dark green leaves held 3 years. Leach, reg. 1982. Color illus. Cox pl. 187.

```
        -catawbiense, white form--Powell Glass, selfed 1/2
TRINITY-
    -yakushimanum 1/2
```
2.5ft(7.5m) -25F(-32C) ML Plant about as wide as tall; leaves held 3 years; new growth has thin orange-tan indumentum. Flower white with faint green dorsal spotting, shaded pink on edges and reverse on opening, 2.75in(7cm) across, slightly fragrant; globular trusses of 14.   Orlando S. Pride, reg. 1979.

TRIPOLI   Parentage unknown
5ft(1.5m) -10F(-23C) EM   Flowers of bright red. High foliage density. Dexter cross.   Color ill. ARS J 43:4 (1989), p. 207.

```
        -dichroanthum 1/2
TRISTAN THACKER-
        -G. A. Sims--unknown 1/2
```
Flowers salmon orange.   Thacker, 1944.

```
    -yakushimanum 1/2
TRISTAR-      -haematodes 1/4
    -Choremia-
        -arboreum 1/4
```
Flowers in trusses of 15, 5-lobed, deep yellowish pink, with crimson nectar pouches and white splashes in throat. Color does not fade. Leaves with woolly indumentum, at first white, fading to fawn.   J. F. McQuire, reg. 1986.

TRI-STATE   Described under MASS WITH CLASS, q.v.

```
    -thomsonii 3/4
TROAS-          -thomsonii
    -Cornish Cross-
            -griffithianum 1/4
```
Early-blooming crimson flowers in larger trusses than thomsonii,

but not as large as those of CORNISH CROSS. Foliage resembles
thomsonii, slightly larger.   Sir John Ramsden, 1942.

```
              -neriiflorum 1/4
       -F. C. Puddle-
TROJAN-        -griersonianum 1/4
       -       -thomsonii 1/4
       -Shilsonii-
              -barbatum 1/4
```

Dark red flowers.   Lord Aberconway, 1950.

TROPICANA (Brandt) Described under KUBLA KHAN, q.v.

```
           -Lady Alice Fitzwilliam--unknown 1/2
TROPICANA-
           -maddenii ssp. crassum 1/2
```
White waxy flowers, strongly fragrant, larger and opening wider
than the species maddenii ssp. crassum. Quite hardy. Michael
Haworth-Booth, reg. 1963.

```
                          -sanguineum ssp. didymum 1/8
              -Arthur Osborn-
       -Toreador-          -griersonianum 3/8
TROUBADOUR-        -griersonianum
       -arboreum 1/2
```
Blood red flowers.   Lord Aberconway, 1950.

```
                       -griffithianum 3/8
              -George Hardy-
         -Pink -          -catawbiense 3/8
       -Countess-Pearl-     -arboreum 1/8
       -of Derby-      -Broughtonii-
TRUDE -       -          -unknown 1/8
WEBSTER-       -    -catawbiense
       -        -Cynthia-
       -selfed      -griffithianum
```
5ft(1.5m) -10F(-23C) M 5/4 Parentage published in Kraxberger
was incorrect. First plant to be given the Superior Plant Award
by the ARS. Extra-large, upright trusses of 14; flowers a clear
shade of pink, upper lobe spotted, 5in(12.7cm) wide, 5-lobed.
Leaves of medium green, glossy, about 7in(17.8cm) long, a slight
twist. Harold E. Greer, reg. 1961.   S.P.A. 1971. Color illus.
Greer Cat. 1990, pl. 11; ARS Q 31:2 (1977), cover; Cox pl. 188.

TRUE LOVE   See HONEY DEW

TRUE TREASURE   Parentage unknown
5ft(1.5m) OF(-18C) ML   Rose pink, frilled flowers, centered
maroon blotch. Less hardy than many Dexters. C. Dexter cross.

* *
```
              -arboreum 1/8
       -Doncaster-
   -Belvedere-      -unknown 1/8
TRULA-      -dichroanthum 1/2
   -      -dichroanthum
   -Jasper-          -fortunei ssp. discolor 1/8
       -Lady Bessborough-
              -campylocarpum Elatum Group 1/8
```
5ft(1.5m) 10F(-12C) ML 4/3 Plant well-branched, as broad as
tall; dark green leaves, narrowly elliptic, 4.5in(11.5cm) long;
held 3 years. Flowers medium yellowish orange, green spotting,
edging and exterior jasper red, 3in(7.6cm) across; 6 wavy lobes;
in ball-shaped trusses of 10. H. L. Larson, reg. 1979.
KAY KIRSTEN   Parentage as above, except reversed
4ft(1.2m) -5F(-21C) M 4/3 Satin amber ball trusses; foliage
very smooth, 5.25in(13.3cm) long. Larson, reg. 1982.
* *


```
           -yakushimanum 1/4
       -White Wedding-
TRULY FAIR-          -makinoi 1/4
       -War Paint--elliottii 1/2
```
2.5ft(.75) OF(-18C) M Flowers open pink and fade white, heavy
brownish spotting and flare, 1.75in(4.5cm) wide, frilled, 5-
lobed. Floriferous. Plant vigorous,
much broader than tall; elliptic, pointed leaves with heavy
felt-like indumentum. John G. Lofthouse cross, 1969; reg. 1981.

```
                       -catawbiense 3/8
           -unnamed red hybrid-
       -unnamed-          -unknown 5/16
   - hybrid-       -griersonianum 1/8
       -       -unnamed-          -Moser's Maroon--unknown
TRUMPETER-       hybrid-Romany Chal-
       -                   -facetum 1/16
       -             -griffithianum 1/8
       -             -Mars-
   -unnamed hybrid-   -unknown
                 -catawbiense var. rubrum
```
5ft(1.5m) -10F(-23C) L 4/2   Funnel-shaped flowers, 2.25in
(5.7cm) wide, of heavy substance, strong red with dorsal spotting of dark red; trusses of 10-15. Plant much wider than tall;
light green, elliptic leaves held 3 years. D. Leach, reg. 1973.

```
                 -campylocarpum 1/4
       -Mrs. W. C. Slocock-
TRUTH-          -unknown 1/4
       -       -decorum 1/4
   -unnamed hybrid-
          -griffithianum 1/4
```
Trusses hold up to 12 flowers, each 4.5in(11.5cm) wide by 2.5in.
(6.4cm) long; pale pink buds, opening to a white corolla. Gen.
Harrison, reg. 1962.

TUESDAY'S CHILD   Parentage unknown
6.5ft(2m) x 4ft(1.2m)(12 yrs) 5F(-15C) E   Flowers in trusses
of 8-10, open funnel-shaped, 5 flat lobes, strong purplish pink
in bud, opening pale purplish pink, unmarked. Evergreen shrub.
A. A. Childers cross; Mrs. M. Kraxberger, reg. 1985.

```
       -Dexter's Honeydew--unknown 1/2
TUFFET-
       -campylocarpum (Gable's 20-60) 1/2
```
Very compact, spreading, floriferous plant; small glossy leaves.
Light pink flowers, 3.7in(9.5cm) wide; truss of about 7. Blooms
late April in North Carolina .   V. & C. R. Haag.

```
              -edgeworthii (bullatum) 1/4
   -unnamed hybrid-
TUI-          -unknown 3/4
   -unknown
```
Trusses of 3-5 flowers, sulphur yellow in bud opening white with
red flush and a yellow flare. G. F. Smith, Pukeiti Rhododendron
Trust, NZ; intro. & reg. 1979.

```
       -decorum 1/2
TUMALO-          -griffithianum 1/4
       -Loderi King George-
              -fortunei 1/4
```
5ft(1.5m) OF(-18C) M 4/3 Plant compact and spreading; leaves
light green 6.5in(16.5cm) long. Fragrant, ruffled white flowers
green at base, suffused pale chartreuse on opening, 5-6in(12.7-
15.2cm) wide; large rounded trusses. Blooms so heavily, partial
disbudding may be needed. D. W. James, reg. 1958. P.A. 1955.

```
              -yakushimanum 3/8      -fortunei. ssp.
       -unnamed-          -Lady    - discolor 3/64
       - hybrid-      -Day -Bessborough-campylocarpum
       -          -Gold -Dream-griersonianum  Elatum Gp. 1/64
       -          -Mohur-     -fortunei ssp. discolor
   -Cisa-          -Margaret-     -dichroanthum 1/64
   - -          Dunn  -Fabia-
   - -                   -griersonianum 3/64
TUMBLING-   -          -yakushimanum
ANGELS -   -Serendipity-
       -          -aureum (chrysanthum) 3/8
       -             -smirnowii 1/8
       -          -unnamed hybrid-
       -             -yakushimanum
   -unnamed hybrid-
          -aureum (chrysanthum)
```
Cardinal red buds open to frilly flowers, pale purplish pink and
vivid purplish red; throat pale yellow-green, deep red.   Delp.

```
              -brachycarpum 1/4
   -unnamed-      -wardii 1/8
TUNNEL- hybrid-Crest-          -fortunei ssp. discolor 1/16
VISION-   -    -Lady    -
   -    -      Bessborough-campylocarpum Elatum Gp. 1/16
   -aureum (chrysanthum) 1/2
```
Buds of brilliant yellow-green open to flowers sap green; dorsal

spotting brilliant yellow-green.   W. Delp.

```
        -nuttallii 1/2
TUPARE-
        -lindleyi 1/2
```
Flowers in trusses of 4-6, tubular campanulate with deep
indentations, buds creamy pink, opening white, with a deep
yellow basal blotch. Strongly and sweetly scented. Purplish
green new growth and peeling mahogany bark. Late Oct-Nov season, New Zealand. E. F. Stead, cross pre-1950; Sir R. Matthews
raiser; G. F. Smith, reg. 1986.

```
                 -catawbiense 1/4
        -Lee's Dark Purple-
TURKANA-             -unknown 1/2
      -                  -ponticum 1/4
        -Purple Splendour-
                         -unknown
```
3ft(.9m) x 4ft(1.2m) -15F(-26C) ML Flowers in trusses of 11-
14, 5-lobed, moderate purplish red and deep purplish red, dorsal
lobe marked dark red. Hachmann, cross 1964; Stück, reg. 1988.

TURKISH DELIGHT   Parentage unknown
4ft(1.2m) -20F(-29C) 3/3 Large pink flowers on an attractive
medium-sized, somewhat open plant. Hybridizer not known.


```
                              -catawbiense 1/8
             -Parsons Grandiflorum-
      -America-                    -unknown 3/8
TUSACARORA-        -dark red hybrid--unknown
         -maximum 1/2
```
7ft(2.1m)(15 yrs) -20F(-29C) L Flowers in trusses of 10, open
funnel-campanulate, 5-lobed, moderate red with strong red spots
on dorsal lobes. Finkelstein cross; C. G. Heller, reg. 1984.


```
                     -griffithianum
             -George Hardy-
     -Mrs. Lindsay Smith-        -catawbiense
     -                  -Duchess of Edinburgh--unknown
TUTU-           -dichroanthum
     -     -Fabia-
     -C.I.S.-     -griersonianum
```
-Loder's White, q.v. for 2 possible parentage diagrams
3ft(.9m) 5F(-15C) ML Plant compact, as wide as tall; elliptic
leaves, about 7in(18cm) long, light green. Flowers 4in(10cm) a-
cross, pale buff shading to delicate empire yellow; rather loose,
spherical trusses of 8-9. Edwin K. Parker, reg. 1971.


```
           -yakushimanum 1/4   -fortunei ssp. discolor
       -Si-        -Lady Bess--            3/64
       -Si-    -Day - borough -campylocarpum Elatum Gp.
       -  -Gold-Dream-griersonianum        1/64
 -unnamed- Mohur-        -fortunei ssp. discolor
 - hybrid-     -Margaret Dunn-      -dichroanthum 1/64
 -       -              -Fabia-
 -       -          -yakushimanum  -griersonianum 7/64
 -        -Serendipity-
 -              -aureum 1/8           -griffithianum
TUTU-               -Queen Wil--          1/16
LOU-          -Britannia- helmina -unknown 5/16
 -        -Anne  -C. P.  -      -Stanley Davies--unknown
 -        -Hard- -Raffill-griersonianum
 -        -grove -
 -              -Moser's Maroon--unknown   -catawbiense
 -Enchanter-              -Parsons Grandi-    1/32
 -       -           -America- florum  -unknown
 -       -   -unnamed-     -dark red hybrid--unknown
 -       - - hybrid-        -griffithianum
 -Anna-      -      -Mars-
 Delp-     -Blaze- -unknown
 -                  -catawbiense, red form 1/32
 -             -Mars (as above)
          -Red Brave-
                  -America (as above)
```
Buds of vivid purplish red opening to frilled white flowers
edged with strong purplish red and light purplish pink; dorsal
spotting currant red; stigma moderate orange.   W. Delp.

```
                     -fortunei 1/4
    -unnamed hybrid, selfed-  -griffithianum 1/8
    -               -Alice-
    -                    -unknown 1/8
TWILIGHT-                -fortunei ssp. discolor 1/8
PINK -     -Lady
    -          -Bessborough-campylocarpum Elatum Gp 1/8
    -    -Jalisco-
    -    -     -   -dichroanthum 3/16
 -Comstock-   -Dido-
    -             -decorum 1/16
    -        -dichroanthum
    -Jasper-        -fortunei ssp. discolor
       -Lady
          -Bessborough-campylocarpum Elatum Group
```
4ft(1.2m) -5F(-21C) M 4/4   Plant of compact, rounded habit,
with dense, apple green foliage. The large calyx gives the appearance of a double. Color is a warm pink that seems to glow
at twilight. Greer, intro. 1982.   Color illus. HG p. 73.

```
              -dichroanthum 1/4        -griffithianum 1/32
     -Whitney's-            -George-
    - Orange -    -Mrs. Lindsay- Hardy-catawbiense 1/32
    -      -Diane- Smith   -Duchess of Edinburgh--unk
TWILIGHTER-       -            -campylocarpum 1/16
    -            -unnamed hybrid-
    -                      -unknown 1/8
    -catawbiense var. album Glass--Catalgla 1/2
```
Buds of Tyrian purple open to pale purplish pink edged vivid
purplish red, a pale yellow flare; spotting pale yellow. Delp.

```
        -racemosum 1/2
TWINKLES-
        -scabrifolium var. spiciferum 1/2
```
4ft(1.2m) OF(-18C) EM 3/2   Growth habit vigorous; decumbent
tendency responds well to pruning. Small, dark green leaves are
gray beneath. Abundance of small, light pink flowers appear all
along the stems.   Another clone, PUCK, is not described in this
book. A. A. Wright, Jr. & Sr., reg. 1958.

```
              -catawbiense 1/4
       -Pink Twins-
      -         -haematodes 1/4
TWINS CANDY-             -griffithianum 1/4
      -          -Loderi Venus-
      -Cotton Candy-      -fortunei 1/8
          -Marinus-griffithianum
             Koster-
                  -unknown 1/8
```
5ft(1.5m) -5F(-21C) EM Plant upright, rounded; glossy leaves
5in(12.7cm) long. Flowers 4in(10cm) wide, 7-lobed, vibrant pink
shading paler at center, the upper 2 lobes spotted cardinal red.
Ball-shaped trusses of about 18. Charles Herbert, reg. 1978.

```
        -minus Carolinianum Group 1/2
TWISTER-
        -dauricum 1/2
```
Blooms with P.J.M.; colors of flowers and winter foliage closely
resemble P.J.M. Small, pointed leaves have an unusual twist.
Plant well-branched, of good growth habit, and very hardy.   Dr.
G. David Lewis.

```
                  -griffithianum 1/2
      -Loderi King George-
TWO KINGS-            -fortunei 1/4
     -           -griffithianum
       -King George-
              -unknown 1/4
```
Trusses hold 12-13 flowers, white, flushed with shades of rhod-
amine pink. Col. G. H. Loder cross; The Hon. H. E. Boscawen,
reg. 1982.

```
            -griersonianum 1/4
     -Esquire-
     -      -unknown 1/4
TYEE-    -wardii 1/4
     -                   -griffithianum 1/32
     -Idealist-    -Kewense-
     -        -Aurora-    -fortunei 5/32
      -Naomi-  -thomsonii 1/10
          -fortunei
```
5ft(1.5m) 5F(-15C) ML 3/3 Primrose yellow flowers, uranium

green throat, 4in(10.2cm) across, in lax trusses of 11. Leaves
4in x 1.5in (10.2cm x 4cm). D. W. James, reg. 1960. A.E. 1960.

```
                -nuttallii 1/2
TYERMANNII-
                -formosum 1/2
```
5ft(1.5m) 20F(-7C) M   Large lax trusses; large flowers, lily-
shaped, tinged outside with green and brown, aging to pure white,
much yellow in throat; sweetly fragrant. Dark, glossy green foliage; main trunk of this handsome plant has rich brownish bark.
Tyermann cross. F.C.C. 1925.

```
                    -griersonianum 1/4
        -Karkov-                -arboreum 1/8
        -            -Red Admiral-
TZIGANE-                         -thomsonii 1/8
        -                               -griffithianum 1/8
        -                       -King George-
        -Gipsy King-                    -unknown 1/8
                        -haematodes 1/4
```
Crimson flowers with a much enlarged crimson calyx, for a hose-
in-hose effect, held in shapely trusses of about 11. Leaves are
sharply pointed, to 8in(20.3cm) long, with thin fawn indumentum.
Plant of good habit, rather spreading; blooms early midseason.
Rothschild, intro. 1955.

U

ULRIKE   Described under SABINE, q.v.

ULTRASLEEK   Described under BEDAZZLED, q.v.

UMPQUA CHIEF   Described under GOLDEN GLOW, q.v.

```
        -ungerii 1/2
UNGERIO-
        -facetum  (eriogynum) 1/2
```
An introduction by E. J. P. Magor, 1933.

```
        -campylocarpum 1/2
UNIQUE-
        -unknown 1/2  (Possibly GOLDSWORTH YELLOW, q.v.)
```
4ft(1.2m) -5F(-21C) EM 3/5   Leaves clover green, glossy, ob-
long; a dense, rounded plant. Bright pink buds open to buttery
cream flowers on rose red pedicels; young flowers may be flushed
pink. With some shade does well in warm climates. W. Slocock.
A.M. 1934. F.C.C. Wisley Trials 1935. Color illus. F p. 67,
JS p. 79; V.V. p. 61-62.

UNKNOWN WARRIOR   Described under BRITANNIA, q.v.

UP FRONT   Parentage unknown
Flowers of pink and white.   Dexter cross.

```
                                -griffithianum
                -Queen Wilhelmina-        1/8
        -Earl of Athlone-               -unknown 3/8
URSULA SIEMS-           -Stanley Davies--unknown
                -forrestii Repens Group 1/2
```
Flowers intense scarlet carmine, translucent, of good sub-
stance, in umbels of 6-10.   Dietrich Hobbie, 1951.

V

```
                    -caucasicum 1/4
        -Boule de Neige-                -catawbiense 1/8
        -               -unnamed hybrid-
        -                               -unknown 1/8
VADA BELLE-             -wardii 1/8
        -       -               -griffithianum
        -   -Idealist-      -Kewense-           5/6
        -   -       -   -Aurora-        -fortunei 9/64
        -Yellow-    -Naomi-     -thomsonii 1/32
        Creek-          -fortunei
        -               -griersonianum 1/8
        -Sarita Loder-      -griffithianum
                        -Loderi-
                            -fortunei
```
1.75ft(.53m) -15F(-26C) M   Flowers light primrose yellow with
blotch and some spotting of yellow-green, widely funnel-shaped,
about 2in(5cm) wide; ball-shaped trusses of 9-12. Plant broader
than tall; glossy leaves, held 2 years.   W. Fetterhoff, cross
1960; reg. 1981.

* *
```
                -valentinianum 1/2
VALASPIS-
                -leucaspis 1/2
```
3ft(.9m) 10F(-12C) VE 3/4   A semi-dwarf of spreading habit.
Loose trusses hold 4-5 widely campanulate flowers of pale yellow
(another form bright yellow).   Small, hairy leaves, bronze when
young.   Lord Aberconway. A.M. 1935.
PIQUANTE   Parentage as above
Flowers 2in(5cm) across, pale yellow, darker in center; trusses
of 3.   Gen. Harrison, reg. 1962.
* *

```
                -souliei 1/4
        -Latona-
VALDA-          -dichroanthum 1/4
        -haematodes 1/2
```
Flowers rosy red.   Lord Aberconway, 1941.

VALEWOOD PINK   Parentage unknown
Flowers shell pink with darker margins.   Mangles. A.M. 1934.

```
                -dichroanthum 1/4
        -Astarte-                -campylocarpum Elatum Group 1/4
VALIANT-        -Penjerrick-
        -                       -griffithianum
        -haematodes ssp. chaetomallum 1/2
```
Red flowers.   Lord Aberconway, 1946.

VALLERIE KAY   Described under MARY JANE, q.v.

* *
```
                -Essex Scarlet--unknown 1/2
VALLEY CREEK-
                -fortunei 1/2
```
6ft(1.8m) -5F(-21C) ML   An upright plant with stiff branches;
narrowly elliptic leaves 6.75in(17cm) long, held 3 years. Deep
rosy pink flowers, a dark blotch, 3.5in(9cm) wide, 5 to 7-lobed,
slightly fragrant, in flat truss of 10.   J. Gable cross; Charles
Herbert, reg. 1976.
ACCOLADE   Parentage as above
6ft x 5ft (1.8 x 1.5m)(30 yrs) OF(-18C) M   Purplish red in
bud, opening white suffused strong purplish pink.   Ben & Marion
Shapiro, reg. 1989.   Color illus. ARS J 42:2 (1988), cover.
CUM LAUDE   Parentage as above
6ft(1.8m) x 7ft(2.1m)(30 yrs) OF(-18C) M Dark red buds; flowers strong heather pink, paling to a white center, 2 dorsal rays
and all-over sparse spotting of strong magenta rose, 5-7 slightly wavy-edged lobes, 3.5in(9cm) wide; domed truss of 14-15. Upright, floriferous plant.   B. & M. Shapiro, reg. 1989.
FORTUNE COOKIE   Parentage as above
6ft x 6ft(1.8m)(29 yrs) OF(-18C)   Very fragrant flowers in
trusses of 13-15, strong purplish red in bud opening to moderate
purplish pink with a strong yellow-orange dorsal flare. B. & M.
Shapiro, reg. 1989.
GREAT FORTUNE   Parentage as above
5ft(1.5m) x 7ft(2.1m)(30 yrs) OF(-18C) M Flowers in trusses
of 12-14, 6-lobed, buds vivid purplish red, open with purplish
pink margins shading to white centers.   Shapiro, reg. 1989.
LISSOME   Parentage as above
8ft(2.4m) x 6ft(1.8m)(30 yrs) OF(-18C) M Flowers in trusses
of 14-15, 7-lobed, deep purplish pink, shading lighter in
streaks to throat, deep red spotting.   Shapiro, reg. 1989.
* *

```
                        -catawbiense 1/4
        -Atrosanguineum-
VALLEY FORGE-           -unknown 1/4
        -               -fortunei 1/4
        -unnamed hybrid-
                        -williamsianum 1/4
```
6ft(1.8m) -5F(-21C) ML   Flowers medium spinel red, spotted in
cardinal red, heavily on dorsal lobe, 3.8in(9.5cm) wide, 7-lobed;
trusses of 15-18. Plant upright, rounded, well-branched; glossy
leaves 6in(15.2cm) long.   Charles Herbert, reg. 1976.
```
                -azalea occidentale 1/2
VALLEY SUNRISE-         -ponticum 1/4
        -Purple Splendour-
                        -unknown 1/4
```
4ft(1.2m) -5F(-21C) ML 4/3   Azaleodendron. Flowers have a
sensational orange blotch, glowing against an orchid background.
Ticknor cross; Greer, intro. 1983.   Color illus. HG p. 116.

```
                 -moupinense 1/2
VALPINENSE-
                 -valentinianum 1/2
Flower buds are deep primrose yellow, opening a lighter yellow.
Lord Aberconway.   A.M. 1943.
```

```
                              -griffithianum 1/8
                 -Queen Wilhelmina-
      -Britannia-                 -unknown 3/8
VAMPIRE-          -Stanley Davies--unknown
      -            -dichroanthum 1/4
      -Fabia-
                 -griersonianum 1/4
Red flowers.  A. A. Wright, Sr. & Jr., reg. 1958.   P.A. 1951.
```

VAN   Described under ANNA ROSE WHITNEY, q.v.

```
                       -catawbiense 1/4
           -Charles Dickens-
VAN DEN BROEKE-            -unknown 3/4
           -Lord Roberts--unknown
Crimson flowers.   H. den Ouden & Sons, cross 1912; intro. 1925.
```

VAN DER HOOP   Described under MRS. P. DEN OUDEN, q.v.

```
                    -thomsonii 1/4
         -Chanticleer-
VAN HUYSUM-          -facetum (eriogynum) 1/4
         -            -ponticum 1/4
         -Purple Splendour-
                    -unknown 1/4
Deep red flowers.  G. M. Adams-Acton, 1935; reg. 1958.
```

VAN NES GLORY   Described under BRITANNIA, q.v.

VAN NES SENSATION   Described under MRS. A. T. DE LA MARE, q.v.

```
            -griersonianum 1/2
VAN VEEN-
         -Pygmalion--unknown 1/2
6ft(1.8m)  -5F(-21C)  ML  3/2  Flowers of rich, clear, dark red,
3in(7.6cm) across, in rounded trusses of 7.  Plant habit rather
open; long, dark green leaves.   T. Van Veen, Sr., intro. 1956.
Color illus. VV p. vi.
```

```
                         -catawbiense 1/4
           -Charles Dickens-
VAN WEERDEN POELMAN-         -unknown 3/4
           -Lord Roberts--unknown
5ft(1.5m)  -15F(-26C)  ML  Crimson flowers.  H. den Ouden cross;
intro. 1925; reg. 1958.
```

```
                       -dichroanthum 1/4
             -Goldsworth-
      -Hotei- Orange   -fortunei ssp. discolor 3/16
      -     -               -souliei 1/8
      -     -unnamed hybrid-
VANCOUVER USA-          -wardii 1/4
      -          -wardii
      -    -Crest-          -fortunei ssp. discolor
      -unnamed-   -Lady    -            1/16
        hybrid-   Bessborough-campylocarpum Elatum Gp.
                   -              -dichroanthum          1/16
                  -Roman Pottery-
                       -griersonianum 1/8
3.5ft(1.0m) high x 5ft(1.5m)  5F(-15C)  M  Spreading habit,
dense growth; flowers in trusses of 18-20, strong pink with pale
orange-yellow throat and prominent pinkish red spotting;
reverse strong pink.  Lofthouse, cross 1977; R. W. Cavender,
reg. 1988.  Best New Hybrid award, Portland Ch., ARS, 1987.
```

```
* * * * * * * * * * * * * * * * * * * * * * * * * * * * *
            -souliei 1/4
       -Soulbut-
VANESSA-        -fortunei--Sir Charles Butler 1/4
       -griersonianum 1/2
5ft(1.5m)  5F(-15C)  ML  Flowers soft pink, spotted carmine at
the base, in handsome trusses.  Spreading, shapely, slow-grow-
ing bush; foliage glossy dark green.  Lord Aberconway, cross
1924; intro. 1929.  F.C.C. 1929.
VANESSA PASTEL   Parentage as above
5ft(1.5m)  5F(-15C)  ML  3/3   Buds open brick red, changing to
```

apricot to deep cream with darker bronze yellow in throat, exterior of orange buff suffused rose pink, pale peach. A much
pinker form also exists. Flowers to 4.5in(10.8cm), 5-lobed, 8
per truss. Plant rather upright; pointed moss green leaves 5in
(12.7cm) long. Lord Aberconway, cross 1930. A.M. 1946. F.C.C.
Wisley Trials 1971.   Color illus. ARS J 37:2 (1983), p. 67; Cox
pl. 190.

```
* * * * * * * * * * * * * * * * * * * * * * * * * * * * *
            -venator 1/2
VANGUARD-
            -griersonianum 1/2
3ft(.9m)  15F(-9C)  EM  3/2  Plant bushy, broader than tall;
dark green leaves, 5.5in(14cm) long.  Bright scarlet red flowers
in lax trusses.  Blooms at an early age; floriferous.  Lord
Headfort, Co. Meath, IRE., 1940.
```

```
                    -souliei 1/8
         -Soulbut-
      -Vanessa-        -Sir Charles Butler--fortunei 1/8
VANITY-      -griersonianum 1/4
      -      -dichroanthum 1/4
      -Dante-
             -facetum (eriogynum) 1/4
Flowers of scarlet.  Lord Aberconway, intro. 1946.
```

```
         -griffithianum 1/2
VANITY-
         -hardy hybrid--unknown 1/2
Flowers open pale pink, fading to pearly white, narrow edging of
rose madder, funnel-shaped, 4in(10.2cm) across; trusses hold 11.
Vigorous, upright plant; glossy leaves to 7in(18cm) long.  Very
free-flowering.  Slocock, reg. 1962.  H.C. 1962.
```

VANITY FAIR   Described under EUDORA, q.v.

```
                     -maximum 1/4
           -Midsummer-
           -            -unknown 5/16
VANITY FAIR (Delp's)-             -griffithianum 1/16
         -                 -Mars-
         -         -Vulcan-    -unknown
         -Old Copper-      -griersonianum 1/4
         -               -dichroanthum 1/8
                     -Fabia-
                          -griersonianum
Flowers open white edged with deep purplish pink; throat
greenish bronze.  W. Delp.
```

```
        -thomsonii 1/2
VANTOM-
        -Van Nes hybrid--unknown 1/2
Pink flowers.  Exhibited 1938; reg. 1958.
```

```
                    -souliei 1/8
         -Soulbut-
      -Vanessa-        -fortunei--Sir Charles Butler 1/8
VANVEN-      -griersonianum 1/4
      -venator 1/2
Deep red flowers.  Lord Aberconway, intro. 1946; reg. 1958.
```

```
VARIEGATUM---form of ferrugineum
2ft(.6m)  -15F(-26C)  M  3/4    Leaves have a thin, creamy white
border; new growth has rust-colored scales.  Flowers rose or rose
scarlet, held in clusters of 6-12.  Plant slow-growing and dwarf.
Bean, v. III, p. 660.
```

```
VARIEGATUM---form of ponticum
4ft(1.2m)  -10F(-23C)  L  2/3  Lavender flowers with variegated
foliage.  A vigorous plant from Ireland; distributed by The Rho-
dodendron Species Foundation, Federal Way, WA.
```

```
                     -sanguineum ssp. didymum 1/4
          -Carmen-
VARNA-           -forrestii Repens Group 1/4
       -williamsianum 1/2
Yellow flowers flushed with rose.  Lord Aberconway, intro. 1946;
reg. 1958.
```

```
        -aperantum 1/2
VASCO-
        -stewartianum 1/2
```

Red flowers.   Lord Aberconway, intro. 1946; reg. 1958.

* *
```
               -cataubiense--Compactum 1/2
VATER BÖHLJE-
               -williamsianum 1/2
```
4ft(1.2m) -10F(-23C) EM Rose lilac flowers on compact, round-
ed mound of green. D. Hobbie cross; G. Böhlje, intro. 1970.
Color illus. WS, 1989, p. 31.
GRAND PRÉ   Parentage as above
Flowers phlox pink in loose trusses; plant compact, very small
leaves. D. Craig of Nova Scotia intro.
* *

```
          -cataubiense 1/2
VAUBAN-
          -unknown 1/2
```
Mauve with a bronze yellow blotch.   A. Waterer, reg. 1958.

```
               -cataubiense var. album 1/4
        -Moon MIst-                     -neriiflorum 1/16
        -          -unnamed hybrid-
VEE VEE-    -unnamed hybrid-            -dichroanthum 3/16
-                       -fortunei ssp. discolor 1/8
-                  -maximum 1/4
        -unnamed hybrid-    -dichroanthum
                      -Fabia-
                           -griersonianum 1/8
```
3ft(.9m) x 6.5ft(2.0m)(13 yrs) -15F(-26C) VL 5/5 Flower pale
yellow-green with broad perimeter band of light purplish pink
and bold dorsal blotch of brilliant yellow; trusses of 20-24.
Flower and vegatative buds awned.   David G. Leach, reg. 1985.

```
          -impeditum 1/2
VEESPRITE-
          -racemosum 1/2
```
1.5ft(.45m) -10F(-23C) EM Very small leaves, .75in(2cm)
x .5in(1.3cm); flowers also very small, .75in(2cm) across, Persian rose, in terminal clusters of 3-5 flowers each. R. Forster, Hort. Research Inst. of Ontario, Canada, reg. 1968.

```
          -dichroanthum 1/4
     -Fabia-
VEGA-     -griersonianum 1/4
     -haematodes 1/2
```
Scarlet flowers.   Lord Aberconway, 1941.

VELDTSTAR   Described under GIPSY MOTH, q.v.

```
          -wardii 3/4
     -Prelude-
VELLUM-   -fortunei 1/4
     -wardii
```
Very light chartreuse; trusses of 6.   Rothschild, reg. 1980.

```
                        -griffithianum 1/8
               -unnamed hybrid-
        -Pink Beauty-           -unknown 1/8
        -          -              -cataubiense 1/8
VELMA ROZETTA-          -John Walter-
        -                    -arboreum 1/8
        -               -griersonianum 3/8
        -unnamed hybrid-   -griersonianum
                      -Azor-
                           -fortunei ssp. discolor 1/8
```
Hybrid by William Whitney, before 1958.

```
          -venator 1/2
VENAPENS-
          -forrestii Repens Group 1/2
```
Dwarf plant with deep red flowers in midseason. Ramsden, 1948.

```
          -venator 1/2
VENCO-          -griffithianum 1/8
     -     -Loderi-
     -Coreta-    -fortunei 1/8
          -arboreum ssp. zeylanicum 1/4
```
Crimson scarlet flowers. Lord Aberconway, 1946.

* *
```
               -facetum (eriogynum) 1/4
        -unnamed hybrid-    -dichroanthum 1/8
VENETIAN-          -Fabia-
CHIMES -               -griersonianum 1/8
-               -yakushimanum 1/4
        -unnamed hybrid-          -Queen     -griffithianum 1/16
                      -Britannia-Wilhelmina-
                                 -unknown 3/16
                           -Stanley Davies--unknown
```
2ft(.6m) OF(-18C) M 4/3 Plant vigorous, compact, wider than
high; leaves to 4in(10.2cm) long. Flowers campanulate, 4.5in
(11.5cm) across, carmine rose with dark spotting; ball-shaped
trusses of 11.   John Waterer & Crisp, reg. 1971.   A.M. 1979.
SURREY HEATH   Parentage as above (as registered)
3ft(.9m) OF(-18C) M 4/4   John Street says parentage is yakushimanum x Britannia. Flower rose pink with lighter center;
tight-growing plant. Waterer & Crisp, reg. 1975.   Color illus.
JS p. 42.
* *

```
                    -unnamed-griffithianum 3/16
                    - hybrid-
               -Mrs. Furnivall-     -unknown 1/4
               -          -          -caucasicum 1/16
        -Party Pink-          -unnamed hybrid-
VENICE-          -cataubiense var. album 1/4          -unknown
-               -yakushimanum 1/4
        -unnamed hybrid-    -griffithianum
                      -Mars-
                           -unknown
```
4ft(1.2m) -20F(-29C) ML   Flowers delicate pale pink, flushed
darker, faint dorsal spotting of yellow, openly funnel-shaped,
3.25in(8.3cm) wide; spherical truss of 22.   Plant rounded, wide
as tall; leaves held 2-3 years.   Leach, cross 1965; reg. 1983.

```
                    -campylocarpum Elatum Group 1/8
               -Penjerrick-
        -Amaura-          -griffithianum 1/8
VENUS-          -griersonianum 1/4
        -facetum (eriogynum) 1/2
```
Flowers bright red or salmon red.   Lord Aberconway, 1936.

```
                    -wardii 1/8
               -unnamed-          -neriiflorum 1/16
               - hybrid-F. C. Puddle-
               -               -griersonianum 3/32
        -Virginia-               -griffithianum
        -Richards-               -George-
        -          -          -Mrs. Lindsay- Hardy-cataubiense 1/32
        -          -          - Smith          -
VERA  -     -Mrs. Betty-          -Duchess of Edinburgh
ELLIOTT-          Robertson-               --unknown
-               -          -campylocarpum 1/16
-                    -unnamed-
        -fortunei 1/2     hybrid-unknown 1/8
```
6ft(1.8m) OF(-18C) ML Rose-colored flowers, lightly spotted
orange-red, 7-lobed, 4.5in(11.5cm) across, held in trusses of up
to 10. Leaves 6.5in x 2.5in (16.5cm x 6.4cm).   Walter Elliott,
cross 1955; reg. 1977.

```
                    -griffithianum 1/8
               -Loderi-
        -Albatross-     -fortunei 1/8
VERA HAWKINS-     -fortunei ssp. discolor 1/4
        -     -dichroanthum 1/4
        -Fabia-
               -griersonianum 1/4
```
6ft(1.8m) 5F(-15C) ML Flowers of porcelain rose, veined with
rose, dark orange spots with an overlay of pale yellow on upper
petal, to a deep red in throat.   Flowers 4in(10cm) across, campanulate, in trusses of 12. Plant broader than tall; leaves 6in
(15.2cm) long.   H. L. Larson, reg. 1965.

VERNA CARTER   Described under MARY JANE, q.v.

```
                    -fortunei ssp. discolor 1/4
          -Lady        -
VERNA     -Bessborough-campylocarpum Elatum Group 1/4
PHETTEPLACE-
          -yakushimanum, Exbury form 1/2
```

6ft(1.8m) -5F(-21C) ML 4/2 Plant rounded, as broad as tall;
olive green leaves, 5in(12.7cm) long. Flowers 3.5in(9cm) wide,
ivory shaded pink with vivid red dorsal blotch, the reverse pink
diffusing through corolla; globular trusses of 13-15. Dr. Carl
H. Phetteplace, reg. 1975.

VERNUS   Described under CHEER, q.v.

```
                -campylocarpum 1/2
VERONICA MILNER-          -neriiflorum 1/4)
                -Little Ben-
                         -forrestii Repens Group 1/4
```
Rose madder flowers.   E. J. Greig, Royston Nursery, reg. 1962.

```
                -campylocarpum 1/2
VERROCCHIO-
                -neriiflorum 1/2
```
Amber-colored flowers.   G. M. Adams-Acton, 1936.

```
                                        -griffithianum
                        -George-        7/16
                        -Pink Pearl- Hardy-catawbiense 3/16
        -Trude  -Countess -      -          -arboreum 1/16
        -Webster- of Derby-      -Broughtonii-
        -         (selfed)-                  -unknown 5/16
VERY BERRY-             -             -catawbiense
        -             -Cynthia-
        -                         -griffithianum
        -                         -griffithianum
        -Jean Marie de Montague-unknown
```
6ft(1.8m) -10F(-23C) ML 4/4   Tall, cone-shaped truss of rose
red; leaves 10in(25.5cm) long. Greer, intro. 1988. Color illus.
HG, back cover.

```
        -pseudochrysanthum 1/2
VERYAN BAY-
        -williamsianum 1/2
```
A dense, rounded shrub, with almost-circular sea green leaves
and many large, clear pink flowers; early midseason. Unknown.

```
        -williamsianum 1/2
VESPER BELLS-
        -albertsenianum 1/2
```
1ft(.3m) ? E   Rose Bengal buds open to lighter rose bell-
shaped flowers, 3in(7.6cm) wide, in truss of 6-9. Plant twice
as broad as tall, dense; oval leaves. B. Lancaster, reg. 1967.

```
                        -ponticum 1/8
                -Michael Waterer-
        -Prometheus-            -unknown 3/8
VESTA-          -Monitor--unknown
        -williamsianum 1/2
```
Flowers of deep rose.   Dietrich Hobbie, 1949; reg. 1958.

VESTA   Parentage unknown
White flowers.   Standish & Noble pre-1860; reg. 1958.

```
        -catawbiense, white form 1/2
VESTALE-
        -unknown 1/2
```
White flowers.   David G. Leach, intro. 1954; reg. 1958.

```
        -griersonianum 1/2
VESTRIS-
        -orbiculare 1/2
```
Deep rose flowers.   Lord Aberconway, cross 1929; intro. 1946;
reg. 1958.

```
        -catawbiense 1/2
VESUVIUS-
        -arboreum 1/2
```
Synonym GRAND ARAB. Flowers bright orange scarlet, shaded violet
on upper segment. J. Waterer, before 1867; reg. 1958.

```
        -griersonianum 3/4
VESUVIUS-       -Moser's Maroon--unknown 1/4
        -Romany Chai-
                -griersonianum
```
Flowers brilliant vermilion red, unspotted; well-shaped trusses
of 12-15. Small, compact plant with foliage like griersonianum.
Very late, hardier than most late reds. Sunningdale, reg. 1958.

```
                -soulei 1/16
        -Soulbut-
        -Vanessa-       -fortunei--Sir Charles Butler 1/16
-Etna-         -griersonianum 1/4
-             -dichroanthum 1/8
VETA-  -Fabia-
-             -griersonianum
-venator 1/2
```
Rose-colored flowers.   Lord Aberconway, 1946.

* *
```
        -diaprepes 1/2
VIBRANT-
        -wardii 1/2
```
Trusses of 14 flowers, 4in(10.2cm) wide, saucer-shaped, 6-7
frilled lobes, greenish white and without marks. Young foliage
bronze. Gen. Harrison, reg. 1962.
VIGIL   Parentage as above, except reversed
Trusses of 15 flowers, each 3.5in(9cm) across, saucer-shaped, 7-
lobed, colored cream, basal spots. Gen. Harrison, reg. 1962.
* *

```
        -impeditum 1/2
VIBRANT VIOLET-
        -augustinii, Tower Court form
```
3ft(.9m) OF(-18C) E   Very bright violet flowers and small,
pointed, dark green leaves.   Fujioka, reg. 1986.

```
                        -griffithianum 1/8
                -unnamed hybrid-
        -Mrs. Furnival-        -unknown 3/4
        -             -         -caucasicum 1/8
VICKE LEE-      -unnamed hybrid-
        -                     -unknown
        -Corona--unknown
```
4ft(1.2m) x 6ft(1.8m) OF(-18C) ML Strong purplish red flowers
with heavy spotting of moderate purplish red; trusses of 20.
Dense growth habit. W. Elliott cross; R. Tracy, reg. 1988.

VICKI REINE   Parentage unknown
5ft(1.5m) -5F(-21C) ML 4/3 Flower bicolor, deep rose red on
margins, fading white in throat, rose exterior, to 4.5in(11.5cm)
across; trusses of about 12. Plant as wide as high; dark green,
deeply veined leaves, 7.5in(19cm) long. Roy Clark, reg. 1963.
C.A. 1971.   Color illus. HG p. 73.

```
                        -griffithianum 1/4
                -Pink Shell-    -fortunei
        -             -H. M. Arderne-
        -Coronation Day-        -unknown
VICTOR -       -         -griffithianum
BOULTER-       -Loderi-
        -             -fortunei 3/16
        -unknown 9/16
```
Trusses of 12-14 flowers, funnel-shaped, magenta rose with ruby
red blotch, the reverse darker magenta. Plant 4ft(1.2m) at registration; elliptic leaves 3.5in(8.9cm) long.   V. J. Boulter
cross; F. Boulter, reg. 1983.

VICTOR FREDERICK   Parentage unknown
6ft(1.8m) 5F(-15C) M   Large foliage; large flowers to 5in
(13cm) across, a very bright red with a darker red blotch all
around the throat; truss of 17. H. Lem cross; J. Sinclair, reg.
1974.

```
                        -griersonianum 1/4
                -Mrs. Horace Fogg-      -griffithianum 1/8
VICTOR HERBERT-        -Loderi-
        -             Venus-fortunei 1/8
        -strigillosum 1/2
```
Crimson, campanulate flowers, 3in(7.6cm) across; flat trusses of
12-15. Plant at 9 years 3.5ft(1m) tall, 4ft(1.2m) wide; foliage
like strigillosum, but broader. Early.   Seabrook, reg. 1964.

```
                        -campylocarpum 3/4
                -Moonstone-
VICTORIA DE ROTHSCHILD-        -williamsianum 1/4
                -campylocarpum
```
Trusses of 5 to 7 flowers, light yellow with greenish tinge. E.
de Rothschild, reg. 1980.

```
* * * * * * * * * * * * * * * * * * * * * * * * *
              -dalhousiae 1/2
VICTORIANUM-
              -nuttallii 1/2
4ft(1.2m)  20F(-7C)  EM  5/2  Erect plant, may be leggy.  Creamy
yellow in bud, opening pure white, in lax trusses of 5.  Pince,
before 1871 or Cuvelier, 1879; reg. 1958.
CREAM TRUMPET    Parentage as above
White flowers with large orange blotch, funnel-campanulate, in
trusses of 3-4.  RBG, Edinburgh, reg. 1962.  F.C.C. 1958.
EDINENSE    Parentage as above, except reversed
White flowers, stained yellow at base.    Origin unknown; reg.
1958.
* * * * * * * * * * * * * * * * * * * * * * * * *


              -low white hybrid--unknown
VICTORIA'S CONSORT-
              -white hybrid with yellow center--unknown
4ft(1.2m) x 3ft(.9m)(7 yrs)  -20F(-29C)  ML      An elepidote;
flowers in trusses of 11-14, deep purplish pink buds open to
yellowish white flowers with light greenish yellow eye.  Ball
truss 6in(15.2cm) across.  E. Mezitt cross; Weston, reg. 1988.


       -wardii ? 1/2
VIDA-                   -decorum ? 1/4
     -unnamed hybrid-
                        -unknown 1/4
6ft(1.8m)  0F(-18C)  ML  4/3   Buds of orange-yellow open clear
deep yellow, unmarked.  Steinmetz cross; Childers, reg. 1965.


VIENNA    Described under IDEALIST, q.v.


                        -decorum ? 1/8
                 -Caroline-
            -Robert Allison-      -brachycarpum ? 1/8
VIENNA WOODS-               -fortunei ssp. discolor 1/4
            -fortunei--Sir Charles Butler 1/2
5ft(1.5m) x 5ft(13 yrs)  -5F(-21C)  Flowers moderately fragrant,
heavy substance, 10-12 per truss, 7-lobed, deep purplish pink
buds open to very pale purple flowers.  Flat truss, 7in(17.8cm)
wide.  Dense habit.  E. Walbrecht cross; R. Brooks, reg. 1987.


VIENNESE WALTZ    Described under ONE THOUSAND BUTTERFLIES, q.v.


* * * * * * * * * * * * * * * * * * * * * * * * *
                           -catawbiense 1/8
                 -Parsons Grandiflorum-
         -America-                   -unknown 11/16
   -unnamed-      -dark red hybrid--unknown
   - hybrid-                  -griffithianum 3/16
   -       -      -Queen Wilhelmina-
VIET VET-   -Britannia-           -unknown
   -                 -Stanley Davies--unknown
   -             -America (as above)
   -unnamed hybrid-   -griffithianum
                 -Mars-
                     -unknown
Deep red buds open to flowers of strong red  with white throats.
Plant of medium size; hardy to -15F(-26C).    Weldon E. Delp.
BILLY BOY    Parentage as above
Buds of deep red open to spirea red with a brilliant greenish
yellow flare; dorsal spots deep greenish yellow.  W. E. Delp.
* * * * * * * * * * * * * * * * * * * * * * * * *


VIGIL    Described under VIBRANT, q.v.


VIGOROUS PINK    Described under TIM CRAIG, q.v.


              -dichroanthum 1/8
       -Astarte-          -campylocarpum Elatum Group 1/16
   -Solon-         -Penjerrick-
   -       -          -griffithianum 3/16
   -       -griffithianum
VIKING-   -Sunrise-
   -              -griersonianum 1/8
   -           -thomsonii 1/4
   -Chanticleer-
              -facetum (eriogynum) 1/4
Flowers rosy red.    Lord Aberconway, 1950.


VIKING LADY    Parentage unknown
Flowers of light mimosa yellow.  Loeb, reg. 1971.
```

```
VIN ROSÉ--form of cinnabarinum Roylei Group
5ft(1.5m)  5F(-15C)  M  3/3    Pendulous flowers,  open-tubular,
waxy,  plum crimson.  A slender,  upright plant.   Crown Estate,
Windsor, reg. 1962.    A. M. 1953.


       -yakushimanum 1/2        -fortunei ssp. discolor
VIN -            -Lady Bess--               1/16
ROSÉ-     -Jalisco- borough -campylocarpum Elatum Group
   -          -     -dichroanthum 1/16         1/16
   -unnamed-     -Dido-
       hybrid-           -decorum 1/16
   -                 -elliottii 1/8
              -Fusilier-
                 -griersonianum 1/8
John Waterer, Sons and Crisp, 1975.


                 -griffithianum 1/4
       -Lady Bligh-
VIN ROSÉ-           -unknown 1/4
       -aberconwayi 1/2
Cecil Smith cross.


VINCENT VAN GOGH    Parentage unknown
5ft(1.5m)  -10F(-23C)  M  4/3  Parent of DOROTHY PESTE ANDERSEN.
Bright cerise red flowers, striped white.    M. Koster & Sons,
intro. 1939; reg. 1958.


                   -decorum ? 1/8
              -Caroline-
         -Robert Allison-   -brachycarpum ? 1/8
VINEBELLE-          -fortunei ssp. discolor 1/4
         -yakushimanum 1/2
6.5ft(2.0m) x 6.5ft(22 yrs)  -10F(-23C)  ML  Flowers in trusses
of 12-14, 5 wavy lobes, moderate purplish pink buds, opening to
white, with olive green spotting.  Leaves with plastered tan in-
dumentum.  R. Forster cross; Hort. Res. Inst. of Ont. raiser; A.
W. Smith, reg. 1986.


                      -George-griffithianum
              -Betty  - Hardy-          1/8
              - Wormald-      -catawb. 1/8
         -Scandinavia-       -red hybrid--unknown
         -              -Hugh -George Hardy (as above)
VINEBLANC--unnamed       Koster-      -arboreum 1/16
         hybrid F2-           -Doncaster-
         -                  -unknown 3/16
              -catawbiense var. album--La Bar's White 1/2
6ft(1.8m) x 5ft(1.5m)(22 yrs)  -10F(-23C)  ML  Flowers in domed
trusses of 14, yellowish white, 5 wavy-edged lobes.  R. Forster
cross; Al Smith, Hort. Research Institute of Ontario, reg. 1989.


VINEBLUSH    Described under OAKTON, q.v.


       -smirnowii 1/2
VINEBROOK-          -fortunei ssp. discolor 1/4
       -Lady Bessborough-
                 -campylocarpum Elatum Group 1/4
6.5ft(2.0m) x 3.25ft(1.0m)(25 yrs)  -15F(-26C)  ML    Flowers in
ball trusses of 15, 5 wavy lobes, white with strong purplish red
flares and light spotting.  Slight felted indumentum underside
of leaves.  R. Forster cross; Hort.  Res. Inst. of Ont. raiser;
A. W. Smith reg. 1986.


              -catawbiense--La Bar's White 1/8
       -unnamed hybrid-
       -unnamed-           -fortunei 1/8
VINECREST- hybrid-wardii (croceum) 1/4
       -wardii Litiense Group 1/2
3.5ft(1.0m) x 3.5ft(13 yrs)  -15F(-26C)  M   Flower buds peach-
colored open to light greenish yellow with small red-brown rays.
Trusses of 12 flowers.  Leaves moderate olive green.  Ken Begg
cross;  Hort. Res. Inst. of Ont. raiser; A. W. Smith, reg. 1986.
Color illus. ARS J 43:4 1989, p. 215.


Out of order
VINEMAX    Parentage unknown
8ft(2.4m) x 5ft(1.5m)(22 yrs)  -10F(-23C)  VL  Flowers in domed
trusses of 18, buds moderate deep purplish red opening deep
purplish pink with strong greenish yellow spotting.  R. Forster
raiser; Al Smith, Horticultural Research Inst. of Ontario, reg. 1989.
```

```
* * * * * * * * * * * * * * * * * * * * * * * * * * *
                          -griffithianum
                -George Hardy-            1/8
          -Betty Wormald-        -catawbiense 1/8
    -Scandinavia-        -red hybrid--unknown 3/16
    -                    -George Hardy (as above)
    -        -Hugh Koster-        -arboreum 1/16
VINEDALE-            -Doncaster-
    -                        -unknown
    -                -catawbiense var. album Glass--Catalgla
    -unnamed hybrid-                          1/4
                -fortunei 1/4
7ft(2.1m) x 4ft(1.2m)(25 yrs)  -15F(-26C)  M  Flowers in trusses
of 13, open funnel-shaped, 6 wavy lobes, light purplish pink,
with light yellow dorsal spotting; scented.  R. Forster cross;
Hort. Res. Inst. of Ont. raiser; A. W. Smith, reg. 1985.
VINELAND FRAGRANCE    Parentage as above
5ft(1.5m) x 4ft(1.2m)  -20F(-29C)  M  Flowers in trusses of 12,
light purplish pink, throat strong purplish pink, very wide edge
of very pale purple, 4 rays of moderate reddish orange.  Very
fragrant.    Same origin as VINEDALE, above.  Reg. 1985.
* * * * * * * * * * * * * * * * * * * * * * * * * * *

VINEMARK    Described under OAKTON, q.v.

VINEMAX    See previous column

                          -catawbiense 3/32
                -Carl Mette-
          -Hassan-        -unknown 1/32
    -unnamed-        -catawbiense
    -unnamed- hybrid-        -dichroanthum ssp. scyphocalyx
    - hybrid-        -unnamed-                    1/16
VINEMOUNT-    -        hybrid-kyawii 1/16
    -        -catawbiense var. album Glass--Catalgla 1/4
    -catawbiense var. album--La Bar's White 1/2
4ft(1.2m) x 3.5ft(1.0m)(18 yrs)  -15F(-26C)  ML   Open funnel-
shaped flowers in trusses of 14, vivid reddish purple, with a
pale yellow dorsal blotch.  R. Forster cross; Hort. Res. Inst.
of Ont. raiser; A. W. Smith, reg. 1986.

VINEROUGE    Described under ED'S RED, q.v.

VINESTAR    Described under MARY FLEMING, q.v.

                -catawbiense 3/16
          -Kettledrum-
    -Sham's Ruby-        -unknown 5/16        -catawbiense
    -            -        -Parsons Grandiflorum-
VINEWOOD-        -America-                -unknown
    -                        -dark red hybrid--unknown
    -williamsianum 1/2
2.5ft(.75m) x 2.5ft(23 yrs)  -15F(-26C)  M  Flowers in ball
truss of 6, moderate purplish pink, reverse deep purplish pink.
R. Forster cross; H.R.I.O., Vineland, Ont., intro.; A. W. Smith,
reg. 1989.

VINTAGE ROSE    Described under CHELSEA SEVENTY, q.v.

                -campanulatum 1/4
    -Madame Nauen-
VIOLA-        -unknown 1/4
    -            -catawbiense 1/4
    -unnamed hybrid-
                -ponticum 1/4
Parentage as in Walter Schmalscheidt; listed in the Register as
a caucasicum hybrid. A parent of ALBERT, BISMARCK, and  TIBET.
Flower porcelain white. T. J. R. Seidel, cross 1872; reg. 1958.

                -ponticum 1/2
VIOLET GOSE-        -sutchuenense 1/4
    -Geraldii-
                -praevernum 1/4
Flowers of mauve to pansy violet, in trusses of 17, early mid-
season.  Compact plant, 4ft(1.2m) in 10 years; leathery, dark
green leaves.   Melvin V. Love, reg. 1965.

                -caucasicum 1/2
VIOLET PARSONS-
                -thomsonii 1/2
Profuse trusses of salmon pink or peach pink flowers.    Plant of
moderate size.   Offered by Slocock.  Reg. 1958.
```

```
VIRGIN--form of catawbiense
Pure white flowers in small- to medium-sized trusses.  Plant up-
right, broad, slow-growing; foliage medium.    Weston Nurseries.

VIRGIN, THE        See THE VIRGIN

VIRGINIA ANDERSON    Described under KRISTIN, q.v.

                -neriiflorum 1/2
VIRGINIA CARLYON-
                -thomsonii 1/2
Dense, hemispherical trusses of about 12 flowers, 5-lobed, of
strong red, without markings.    Mrs. G. Carlyon, reg. 1985.

VIRGINIA DELITO    Described under ALICE SWIFT, q.v.

                -yakushimanum--Koichiro Wada 1/4
          -Kristin-        -corona--unknown 3/8
    -        -Bow Bells-
VIRGINIA DELP-        -williamsianum 1/8
          -catawbiense var. album Glass--Catalgla 1/4
    -Calsap-
                -Sappho--unknown
2ft(.6m) x 2.5ft(.75m)  -15F(-26C)  ML  Light purple shading to
very pale purple at center, large blotch moderate yellow. Tall,
conical truss 6in(15.2cm) x 6in.    Al W. Smith, reg. 1989..

                -maximum  1/8
          -Maxecat-
    -unnamed-        -catawbiense 1/8
    - hybrid-        -dichroanthum 1/8
    -        -Jasper-            -fortunei ssp. discolor
VIRGINIA-        -unnamed hybrid-            1/16
LEACH -            -campylocarpum 1/16
    -            -catawbiense var. album 1/4
    -unnamed hybrid-
                -griersonianum  1/4
4ft(1.2m)  -15F(-26C)  ML  4/3  Flowers of vibrant greenish yel-
low edged in strong purplish pink, dorsal lobe deeper yellow,  a
faint blotch of orange-brown  spots.  Flowers openly funnel-
shaped, 3in(7.6cm) wide, partially hose-in-hose; pyramidal
trusses hold 18.  Shrub wider than tall; dark green leaves
4.5in(11.5cm) long.  D. G. Leach, reg. 1972.   Not distributed.

* * * * * * * * * * * * * * * * * * * * * * * * * * *
                -wardii 1/4
    -unnamed-                -neriiflorum  1/8
    - hybrid-F. C. Puddle-
VIRGINIA-            -griersonianum 1/8
RICHARDS-            -George-griffithianum 1/16
    -        -Mrs. Lindsay- Hardy-
    -Mrs. Betty- Smith        -catawbiense 1/16
    Robertson-        -Duchess of Edinburgh--unknown
    -            -campylocarpum 1/8            1/4
                -unnamed-
                hybrid-unknown
4ft(1.2m)  -OF(-18C)  M  4/4   Flowers open pale yellow with a
pink blush and crimson blotch, fading to Chinese yellow; garden
effect is peach or apricot.  Flowers 4.5in(11.5cm) wide,  in
trusses of 12. Plant compact, with dark glossy foliage.  Other
forms exist.  William Whitney, intro. 1965; Sathers, reg. 1976.
A.M.  Wisley Trials 1985.   Color illus. ARS J 31:3 (1984),  p.
115; VV p. 2; Cox pl. 191.
LEVERETT RICHARDS    Parentage as above
4ft(1.2m) OF(-18C)  M  4/4  More yellow than sibling above, but
similar in multiple color tones of pink and apricot.  Whitney.
* * * * * * * * * * * * * * * * * * * * * * * * * * *

                -souliei ? 1/2
VIRGINIA SCOTT-
                -unknown 1/2
Yellow flowers.  H. L. Larson.

                -ciliatum 1/4
          -Countess of Haddington-
VIRGINIA-            -dalhousiae 1/4
STEWART-
                -nuttallii 1/2
5ft(1.5m)  25F(-3C)  EM  Plant upright, wider than tall; glossy,
dark, elliptic leaves, scaly beneath, 4in(10.2cm) long.  Very
fragrant white flowers, with a quickly fading yellow stain in
```

the throat, about 3.5in(8.9cm) wide, in flat trusses of 7.   H. W. Kerrigan cross; Coulter Stewart, reg. 1975.

VIRGO   Described under PINK GOLIATH, q.v.

* *
```
                  -oreotrephes 1/2
VIRTUE-              -cinnabarinum Roylei Group 1/4
     -Lady Chamberlain-           -cinnabarinum 1/8
                      -Royal Flush -
                      (orange form)-maddenii 1/8
```
Mauve flowers, 2.25in(5.7cm) across, held in trusses of about 6. Gen. Harrison, reg. 1962.
OLIVE JUDSON   Parentage as above
Flowers rosy carmine with darker markings in the throat. G. A. Judson cross; reg. 1973.
* *

```
             -racemosum 1/2
VISCOUNT-
 LINLEY -ciliatum 1/2
```
Similar to RACIL, in color and shape of truss.   Alfred Bramley, reg. 1963.

VISCOUNT POWERCOURT   Parentage unknown
A parent of LOUIS PASTEUR. Purplish red flowers, striking black blotch.   J. Waterer, before 1888. A.M. 1906

VISCOUNTESS ELVEDEN   Parentage unknown
Flowers pink with average foliage. Named for the head of the Guinness family. Grown in NZ, see Cox. W. Slocock intro.

```
                              -griffithianum
                -George Hardy-          1/16
     -Mrs. Lindsay Smith-        -catawbiense 1/16
   -Diane-           -Duchess of Edinburgh--unknown
VISCY-   -unnamed hybrid-    -campylocarpum 1/8
 -                   -unknown 1/4
 -viscidifolium 1/2
```
5ft(1.5m) -10F(-23C) ML In English the name would be WHISKY. Flowers orange and yellow with dark red spotting. Large glossy foliage, insect-resistant. Unusual plant, worth growing. D. Hobbie intro.   Color illus. Cox pl. 192; WS, 1989, p. 53.

```
           -brachycarpum 1/4      -wardii ? 3/16
   -Dated Yellow-        -Chlorops-
   -           -unnamed hybrid-   -vernicosum ? 1/16
VISION-              -aureum (chrysanthum) 1/8
QUEST -              -maximum 1/4
   -         -Midsummer-
   -unnamed hybrid-       -unknown 1/8
   -                -maximum
           -unnamed hybrid-
                   -wardii
```
Buds of fuchsia purple and ruby red open to pale purplish pink edged with fuchsia purple; white flare. Medium size. W. Delp.

```
           -fortunei 3/8
     -Mary Cowan-
     -           -diaprepes 1/4
VISTOSO-            -griffithianum 1/8
     -       -Loderi-
     -Avalanche-      -fortunei
           -calophytum 1/4
```
6ft(1.8m) OF(-18C) M   Trusses 10in(25cm) wide, of 12-14 fragrant flowers, empire rose with darker spotting, openly funnel-campanulate, 5.5in (14cm) wide, of 7 wavy lobes. Plant upright, half as broad as high; dark green leaves held 3 years.   Dr. D. Goheen, cross 1962; reg. 1985; Dr. L. Bulgin intro.

```
           -maximum 1/4
   -unnamed hybrid-
   -       -vernicosum (18139) 1/4
VITAMAX-                -neriiflorum 1/16
   -             -Nereid-
   -       -Phyllis Ballard-   -dichroanthum 1/16
   -unnamed hybrid-        -fortunei ssp. discolor 1/8
           -catawbiense--Clark's White 1/4
```
Buds of ruby red open to flowers of strong purplish red and strong purplish pink; throat of ruby red and strong purplish red. Tall plant. W. Delp.

```
            -catawbiense 1/8
        -Parsons Grandiflorum-
   -America-          -unknown (1/2)
VIVACIOUS-   -dark red hybrid--unknown
   -      -griersonianum 1/4   -arboreum 1/16
   -Dr. Ross-        -Doncaster-
      -Borde Hill-        -unknown
              -griffithianum 1/16
               -Mrs. A. M.-
              Williams -unknown
```
4ft(1.2m) -5F(-21C) ML 4/4 Flowers of heavy substance, 2.5in (6.4cm) wide, shaded medium cardinal red; spherical trusses of 10 or more. Plant rounded, broader than tall; medium green, elliptic leaves held 2 years.   Ray Forster cross; Horticultural Research Institute, Ont., reg. 1975.   Color illus. HG p. 170.

VIVIA WARD   Parentage unknown
Flowers of solferino purple with a deep reddish purple flare in throat; trusses of 12. A. G. Holmes, reg. 1982.

```
                    -catawbiense 1/8
        -Altaclerense-       -ponticum 1/8
VIVID-      -arboreum 1/4
   -        -maximum 1/4
   -unnamed hybrid-
   -        -unknown 1/4
```
Flowers rose or bright purplish rose.   Standish & Noble, 1850.

VIVID-0 See ESTACADA

VOLCANO   Parentage unknown
Medium-sized plant, compact. Flowers small, dark red. Found growing in AUS, see Cox. Origin unknown.

VOLKER   Described under BOB BOVEE, q.v.

```
              -campylocarpum Elatum Group 1/16
        -Penjerrick-
     -Amaura-       -griffithianum 5/16
   -Eros-    -griersonianum 3/8
VOLTAIRE-   -griersonianum
   -      -griffithianum
   -Loderi-
      -fortunei 1/4
```
Flowers red or pink.   Lord Aberconway, 1950.

```
          -Scintillation--unknown 9/16
   -               -catawbiense 1/16
VOLUPTUOUS-      -Atrosanguineum-
   -      -Atrier-       -unknown
   -Mary Belle-   -griersonianum 1/8
           -decorum 1/4
```
5ft(1.5m)(11 yrs) -5F(-21C) ML   Scented flowers, 7 wavy-edged lobes, 4in(10cm) wide, purplish pink edges, star-shaped centers, cardinal red throat, dorsal spotting of deep crimson; truss of 18. Upright dense plant; glossy oblong leaves to 5.5in(14cm), held 3 years.   W. Brack, cross 1976; reg. 1989.

```
                 -griffithianum 1/8
           -George Hardy-
   -Mrs. Lindsay Smith-   -catawbiense 1/8
VONDEL-      -Duchess of Edinburgh--unknown 1/2
   -          -campylocarpum 1/4
   -unnamed hybrid-
          -unknown
```
Pale yellow flowers.   M. Koster & Sons.

* *
```
                 -griffithianum 1/8
        -Queen Wilhelmina-
   -Britannia-       -unknown 3/8
VOODOO-    -Stanley Davies--unknown
   -      -haematodes 1/4
   -May Day-
      -griersonianum 1/4
```
5ft(1.5m) 5F(-15C) ML 3/3 Flowers funnel-campanulate, 2.5in (6.4cm) wide, rose red shading to cardinal red in throat; trusses of 10-12. Semi-dwarf plant; leaves 4.5in(11.5cm) long, recurved margins, tan indumentum beneath.   Rudolph Henny, reg. 1958. P.A. 1952.
QUINELLA   Parentage as above
3ft(.9) OF(-18C) M 3/3   Flowers geranium red; appear double

with the calyx as large as the flower. Leaves dull green, rather narrow. R. Henny, reg. 1958.
* *

VOSSBERG'S BUFF Parentage unknown; elepidote
3.6 x 5.5ft(1.1 x 1.6m)(25 yrs) -5F(-21C) ML Heavy, fragrant flowers, 7-lobed, 3.3in(8.5cm) wide, Egyptian buff, sparse blood red dorsal spotting, light yellow-green throat; ball truss of 12 -14; smooth shiny leaves to 4.7in(12cm). Hardgrove or Vossberg cross, 1963; Vossberg & Conners raisers; E. Conners, reg. 1988.

* *
```
         -griffithianum 1/4
   -Mars-
VULCAN-   -unknown 1/4
         -griersonianum 1/2
```
5ft(1.5m) -15F(-26C) ML 4/4 Often a parent. Registered as a clone, but several forms are known. Bright, fire red flowers, with dark green, pointed leaves; a rounded plant. Waterer, Sons & Crisp, 1938. A. M. Wisley Trials 1957. Color illus. VV p. 12.
VULCAN'S FLAME Parentage as above, except reversed
5ft(1.5m) -15F(-26C) ML 4/4 Very like VULCAN, but may be a bit more hardy. Bright red flowers, to 3in(7.6cm) wide; trusses of 12-15. Vigorous, rather compact plant; leaves deep yew green with red petioles. Appropriately, it does well in hot climates. B. F. Lancaster, reg. 1958. Color illus. VV p. 100.
* *
```
                  -griersonianum 1/4
      -Vulcan's Flame-   -griffithianum 1/8
VULCAN'S BELLS-          -Mars-
      -                  -unknown 1/8
      -williamsianum 1/2
```
2ft(.6m) OF(-18C) M 3/4 Plant a sturdy mound, broader than high, densely foliaged; oval leaves, dark green, about 2.5in(6.4 cm) long. Flowers of clear rose red, openly campanulate, 2.5in (6.4cm) wide. B. F. Lancaster, reg. 1967.

VULCAN'S FLAME Described under VULCAN, q.v.

ᵂ
```
      -haematodes 1/2
W. F. H.-        -griersonianum 1/4
      -Tally Ho-
                -facetum (eriogynum) 1/4
```
3ft(.9m) 5F(-15C) EM A small plant with funnel-shaped, waxy flowers of brilliant scarlet in lax trusses. Named after W. F. Hamilton, head gardener at Pylewell Park, Hampshire. W. I. Whitaker, intro. 1941.


```
      -griffithianum 1/2
W. H. FORSTER-
      -unknown 1/2
```
Bright red flowers. Hybridizer unknown; reg. 1958.

* *
```
         -griffithianum 1/4
   -Loderi-
W. LEITH-   -fortunei 1/4
   -decorum 1/2
```
Flowers of ivory, tinged faint greenish yellow, lobes recurved; upright trusses. A sturdy, erect plant; large foliage. Named after the Head Gardener, Clyne Castle, Swansea. Adm. Heneage-Vivian, Wales, reg. 1958. Loder Cup, 1934. A. M. 1935.
WHITE ENSIGN Parentage as above, except reversed
Adm. Heneage-Vivian, exhibited 1937; reg. 1958.
* *


```
         -fastigiatum 1/2
WACHTUNG---sport of RAMAPO-
         -minus Carolinianum Group 1/2
```
A parent of MATILDA. Leon Yavorsky.

WAKEHURST--form of rubiginosum
6ft(1.8m) OF(-18C) EM 3/3 Campanulate flowers 2in(5cm) across, mallow purple with crimson spots on upper lobe, in truss of 25. Sir Henry Price, reg 1952. A. M. 1960.

* *
```
                           -griffithianum 7/16
               -Beauty of Tremough-
   -Norman Gill-            -arboreum 1/16
-Anna-         -griffithianum
-    -                      -griffithianum
-    -Jean Marie de Montague-
WALLOPER-                   -unknown 3/8
-                           -griffithianum
-              -George Hardy-
-Marinus Koster-            -catawbiense 1/8
               -red hybrid--unknown
```
6ft(1.8m) -5F(-21C) M 5/4 Flowers deep pink, in huge truss. Large, vigorous plant, heavily foliaged; new growth red. Named forms described below; unnamed forms also exist. Lem cross.
ARNOLD PIPER Parentage as above
6ft(1.8m) -5F(-21C) M 4/4 Synonym PIED PIPER. Currant red buds; flowers 5in(12.7cm) wide, rose red, grayed purple blotch, in truss of 15. Elliptic leaves held 3 years, brownish green new growth Lem cross; A. Piper raiser; Lofthouse, reg. 1981.
LEM'S MONARCH Parentage as above
Synonym PINK WALLOPER. Huge trusses of perfect, satin pink flowers. Attractive large foliage on a strong-stemmed plant. Lem. C.A. 1971.
POINT DEFIANCE Parentage as above
6ft(1.8m) -5F(-21C) M 5/5 Large flowers of heavy substance, 4.5in(11.5cm) wide, white, edged red on all lobes without blotch; tall, compact trusses of 17. Tall, vigorous plant; leaves 7.25in(18.5cm) long, dark matte green. Lem cross; Tacoma Park Dept., reg. 1970.
RED WALLOPER Parentage as above
6ft(1.8m) -5F(-21C) M 4/4 Deep rose red in bud, opening slowly through shades of pink to a beautiful pastel pink. Matures as strong plant, large stature, handsome foliage. Lem.
* *


```
         -griersonianum 1/2
WALLUSKI CHIEF-
         -macrophyllum 1/2
```
Flowers of soft rose red with darker specks, 3in(7.6cm) across, campanulate; trusses of 15. Upright, rounded plant, 6ft(1.8m) at 10 years; leaves 7in(17.8cm) long. G. L. Baker, reg. 1965.

WALLY (VALLYA) Described under LLENROC, q.v.


```
         -fortunei--Lu Shan 1/2
WALLY ZEGLAT-
         -unknown 1/2
```
Large plant with lacy flowers, deep rose purple fading lighter, brown speckled blotch. Blooms midseason. W. Zeglat raiser; J. G. Lofthouse, reg. 1973. Best of Show, Vancouver, 1970.

* *
```
                  -wardii 1/2
         -Crest-        -fortunei ssp. discolor 3/16
         -    -Lady-
         -    Bessborough-campylocarpum Elatum 3/16
-Lemon-                            -griffith.
-Custard-                 -George-    1/64
-    -                -Mrs. Lindsay- Hardy-
-    -               - Smith   -   -cat. 1/64
-    -    -Mrs. Betty-      -Duchess of
WALT -    -Robertson-       Edinburgh--unk.
ELLIOTT- -unnamed-
-    -  hybrid-      -unnamed-campylocarpum 1/32
-    -          -         hybrid-
-    -    -wardii      -unknown 1/16
-Crest (as above)
```
6ft(1.8m) OF(-18C) M Fragrant flower, funnel-shaped, 6-lobed, Naples yellow, edged in light Venetian pink, 5in(12.7cm) wide; lax trusses of 7-10. W. Elliott, cross 1969; reg. 1982.
GOLD INCENSE Parentage as above
6ft(1.8m) 5F(-15C) M 4/4 Very fragrant flowers, buttercup yellow, edges light Neyron rose, in large truss of 14-18. Plant wide as tall. W. Elliott cross; F. Peste raiser; reg. 1983.
OLYMPIC SUNSET Parentage as above
10ft(3.0m) x 8ft(2.4m)(15 yrs) OF(-18C) ML Fragrant flowers in trusses of 7-9, 7-lobed, moderate yellowish pink suffused with light yellow on 3 lobes. W. Elliott, reg. 1989.
* *

```
                    -catawbiense 1/4
          -John Walter-
WALTDIS-              -arboreum 1/4
          -fortunei ssp. discolor 1/2
```
Large flowers of deep clear rose, slightly fragrant; large tight
umbels. Dietrich Hobbie, intro. 1952.

WALTER CURTIS   Parentage includes catawbiense, maximum and
                     and perhaps unknown hybrids
7ft(2.1m) -15F(-26C) M   Upright, spreading plant; olive green
leaves, slightly hairy, a thin brown indumentum beneath. Flowers medium purplish pink, with brilliant yellow-green spotting,
3in(7.6cm) wide, 5-lobed; spherical trusses of 18. Floriferous.
W. David Smith, reg.1979.

WALTER HUNNEWELL   Parentage unknown
5ft(1.5m) -10F(-23C) ML   White   flowers, 14-16 per truss;
edges almost ruby red, reverse Indian lake.   Red-stemmed new
growth. W. Hunnewell cross; Weston, reg. 1984.

WALTER MAYNARD---form of ciliicalyx
4ft(1.2m) 15F(-10C) M 4/3 Trusses hold 3-4 white flowers, a
stripe of soft red-purple from base to rim of each lobe fading
to edges, upper throat flushed yellow-green, 3.3in(8.5cm) wide.
Glossy, dark green leaves, 3.5in(8.9cm) long, scales underneath.
Geoffrey Gorer, Sunte House, exhibited.   A. M. 1975.

```
                             -wardii 1/2
              -unnamed hybrid-
              -                 -wardii (astrocalyx) 1/4
WALTER SCHMALSCHEIDT-                      -campylocarpum
              -             -Koster's Cream-             1/8
              -Linsweger Gold-          -unknown 1/8
                             -wardii
```
Tubular funnel-shaped flowers of clear, rich yellow, unfading.
Broad, upright, compact bush; glossy, dark green foliage.   Hans
Robenek, cross c. 1977.   Color illus. WS, 1989, p. 64.

```
                     -minus Carolinianum Group 3/4
          -Laetevirens (Wilsoni)-
WALTHAM-              -ferrugineum 1/4
          -minus Carolinianum Group
```
2.5ft(.75m) -25F(-32C) M 3/4   A low, compact plant, growing
2-4in(5-10cm) per year; small, dark green foliage.   Clear pink,
delicate flowers; many small trusses.   Dr. R. Ticknor cross; E.
Mezitt, Weston Nurseries, intro.   Color illus. HG p. 137.

WANSBECK   Parentage unknown
Flowers light purplish pink with an orange-red blotch.   RHS,
Wisley raiser; reg. 1972.

```
          -dichroanthum 1/2
       -Fabia-
WANTAGE-       -griersonianum 1/4
       -       -dichroanthum
       -Dido-
          -decorum 1/4
```
Two feet (.6m) high and 6ft(1.8m) wide in 16 years; narrowly el-
liptic leaves 4.5in(11.5cm) long. Flowers widely funnel-campanulate, 2in(5cm) across, rowan berry red, held loosely in trusses
of 6-8. Crown Estate, Windsor, reg. 1971. P.C. 1970.

```
          -griffithianum 1/4
       -Mars-
WAR DANCE-   -unknown 3/4
       -Pygmalion--unknown
```
4ft(1.2m) -10F(-23C) M Trusses of 17-21 flowers, bright cur-
rant red, with black dorsal blotch and spotting, to 2.75in(7cm)
across, with 5 wavy lobes. Plant much broader than high; dark
green leaves 5in(12.7cm) long.   M. E. Hall, cross 1970; E. J.
Brown, reg. 1979.

```
                    -griersonianum 1/8
          -Tally Ho-
    -unnamed-       -facetum (eriogynum) 1/8
    - hybrid-               -griffithianum 3/16
WAR -      -        -Queen Wilhelmina-
LORD-      -Britannia-          -unknown 9/16
    -              -
    -                   -Stanley Davies--unknown
    -Britannia (as above)
```
Handsome flowers of deep red in May. Knap Hill, reg. 1967.

WAR PAINT--form of elliottii
Crimson scarlet flowers.   Selected by Del James. P.A. 1956.

WARBURTON   Described under SUSAN LONSDALE, q.v.

WARDANTHUM   Listed under TIDBIT, q.v.

```
                     -griffithianum 3/8
          -Tip-the-Wink-      -griffithianum
WARDEN WINK_           -Kewense-
          -                    -fortunei 1/8
          -wardii 1/2
```
Shown by Mr. Mansfield, Gardener to Col. G. Loder, High Beeches,
1939.

WARDIAN CREAM--selection of wardii or wardii hybrid
Flower light yellowish cream.   Ben Nelson raiser, Seattle area.

WAREHAM   Parentage unknown
5ft(1.5m) -5F(-21C) M   Purplish pink flowers, small yellowish
green spotting; truss of about 13. A rounded plant with yellow-
green leaves. Fragrant.   Dexter cross; Tyler Arb., reg. 1980.

WARDZEL   Described under SUPER BOWL, q.v.

* *
```
                          -fortunei ssp. discolor 1/4
             -Lady Bessborough-
       -Jalisco-            -campylocarpum Elatum Group 1/4
       -          -dichroanthum 1/8
WARFIELD-    -Dido-
       -          -decorum 1/8
       -    -wardii 1/4
       -Crest-           -fortunei ssp. discolor
             -Lady Bessborough-
                  -campylocarpum Elatum Group
```
Flowers very light primrose yellow, deeper in center and throat,
marked in currant red, widely funnel-campanulate, to 3.75in(9.5
cm) across; 10-12 in rounded trusses. Leaves 5.5in(14cm) long.
Crown Estate, Windsor, reg. 1971. A.M. 1970.
BUTTERSTEEP Parentage as above
Flowers barium yellow with a small blotch of currant red, 7-
lobed, in loose trusses of 12-14.   Pale green elliptic leaves
4in(10cm) long.   Crown Estate, reg. 1972.   A.M. 1971.
* *

```
                     -Moser's Maroon--unknown (1/2)
          -Romany Chal-
WARLOCK-            -facetum (eriogynum) 1/4
       -                -ponticum 1/4
       -Purple Splendour-
                     -unknown
```
5ft(1.5m) OF(-18C) L 4/3   Plant broader than tall, with de-
cumbent branches; leaves dark green, to 5.5in(14cm) long, held 3
years; new growth maroon. Flowers of 5 waxy lobes, 3.5in(8.9cm)
across, dark reddish purple, black dorsal blotch and spotting;
flat trusses of 14.   C. Bledsoe raiser; D. Bledsoe, reg. 1975.

```
                     -dichroanthum 1/4
          -unnamed hybrid-
WARM GLOW-           -unknown 3/4
          -Vida--unknown
```
3ft(.9m) OF(-18C) ML 4/4   Campanulate flowers, 2.5in(6.4cm)
wide, pale orange, darker in throat, slight dark red spotting,
reddish orange outside; lax trusses of 12. Plant wide as tall;
elliptic leaves 4.25in(10.8cm) long.   Greer, reg. 1979.   Color
illus. HG p. 169.

```
              -dichroanthum 3/8
       -Dido-
WARM  -   -decorum 1/4
SPRING-   -fortunei 1/4
       -Fawn-     -dichroanthum
              -Fabia-
                  -griersonianum 1/8
```
Plant of medium size and compactness; leaves 8in(20.3cm) long.
Rounded trusses of 8-10 flowers, Indian yellow flushed pink, 4in
(10.2cm) long.   Del W. James, reg. 1962.

```
                                    -thomsonii 1/16
                        -Bagshot Ruby-
            -Princess Elizabeth-          unknown 1/2
        -Wendy-              -unknown
       - Lyn -          -smirnowii 1/8
       -       -unnamed hybrid-
WARM WINNER-                  -yakushimanum 1/8
       -          -griffithianum 1/8
       -       -Mars-
      -unnamed-    -unknown            -catawbiense 1/16
       hybrid-       -Parsons Grandiflorum-
          -America-              -unknown
                    -dark red hybrid--unknown
```
Buds dark red and strong red opening to strong and deep red;
deep yellowish pink filaments; dark red stigma. W. Delp.

WARWICK   Parentage unknown
5ft(1.5m) -20F(-29C) EM Pale mauve pink flowers in full truss
and fragrant. Leaves tend to droop, partially concealing flowers. C. O. Dexter cross.


```
                    -griersonianum 5/16
              -unnamed-              -haematodes 9/32
             - hybrid-    -Choremia-
       -unnamed-      -Siren-          -arboreum 1/32
       - hybrid-    -          -griersonianum
WATER      -      -dichroanthum 1/8
CRICKET-      -Fabia-
       -              -griersonianum
       -          -haematodes
       -Grosclaude-
              -facetum (eriogynum) 1/4
```
4ft(1.2m) OF(-18C) M   White flowers, flushed rose where the
petals meet. J. Waterer & Crisp, reg. 1975.


```
              -ferrugineum 1/2
WATERER'S HYBRIDIUM-
              -unknown 1/2
```
Rose pink flowers. Waterer.


```
        -cinnabarinum 1/2
WATERFALL-
        -maddenii ssp. crassum, Cooper's form 1/2
```
Inner corolla of flower is very light orchid pink, darkening in
the throat to bright rhodamine pink. Lord Aberconway, Bodnant,
reg. 1972. A. M. 1971.

WAXEN BELL--form of campanulatum
Leaves 3in(7.6cm) long, orange-brown indumentum below. Flowers
in loose trusses of 13, phlox purple, spotted with dark purple.
RBG, Edinburgh, reg. 1966. A. M. 1965.


```
            -griffithianum 1/4
       -Loderi-
WAXEYE-     -fortunei 1/4
       -unknown 1/2
```
Trusses of 12-13 flowers, white with a very light green flare.
Mr. & Mrs. A. G. Holmes, NZ, reg. 1979.


```
                -dichroanthum 1/8
          -Astarte-          -campylocarpum Elatum Gp. 1/16
      -Phidias-    -Penjerrick-
      -       -              -griffithianum 1/16
      -       -          -neriiflorum 1/8
WAYFARER-    -F. C. Puddle-
      -              -griersonianum 1/8
      -          -thomsonii 1/4
      -Chanticleer-
              -facetum (eriogynum) 1/4
```
Red flowers. Lord Aberconway, intro. 1950.


```
        -calophytum 1/2
WAYFORD-          -arboreum 1/4
      -Gill's Triumph-
              -griffithianum 1/4
```
A plant of magnificent foliage--elliptic leaves 13in x 4.5in
(33cm x 11.5cm), with sparse gray tomentum beneath. Trusses
large, heavy, of about 24 openly campanulate flowers, white with
dark crimson outside, 3in(7.6cm) across. E. J. P. Magor cross;
Crown Estate, Windsor exhibited. A.M. 1957. F.C.C. 1976.

WAYNE PINK   Parentage unknown

6ft(1.8m) -10F(-23C) ML   Flowers spirea red, 3.5in(9cm) wide;
large trusses of about 22. Leaves 7in(18cm) long. C. O. Dexter
cross; Knippenberg, reg. 1967.


```
                       -maximum 1/4
        -Lady Clementine Mitford-
WEBER'S PRIDE-          -unknown 1/2
        -          -catawbiense 1/4
        -Kate Waterer-
                -unknown
```
5ft(1.5m) -5F(-21C) M 3/3 Flowers of rhodamine purple with
orange blotches, saucer-shaped, 3.25in(8.3cm) across, in trusses
of 17. Upright, well-branched plant; bright green leaves, held
3 years. E. O. Weber, reg. 1974.


```
            -keiskei (as var. cordifolium) 1/2
WEB'S SPECIAL-
            -keiskei, dwarf form 1/2
```
7in(17.3cm) high x 2ft(.6m)(12 yrs) OF(-18C) EM Pale greenish
yellow flowers with deep greenish yellow spotting in trusses
3.5in(9cm) across. W. Berg, cross 1972; B. M. Smith, reg. 1989.


```
                -catawbiense 1/8
       -Harrisville---Newport F4-
       -              -unknown 1/8
WED-              -caucasicum 3/16
       -          -Jacksonii-          -caucasicum
       -Goldsworth Yellow-          -Nobleanum-
       -              -          -arboreum 1/16
              -campylocarpum 1/4
```
Buds of strong, light and pale purplish pinks open to flowers of
pale purplish pink, edged Neyron rose, primrose yellow flare;
dorsal spots of strong yellow-green; white filaments.   W. Delp.


```
                -ponticum 3/8
          -Purple Splendour-
WEDDING CAKE-          -unknown 3/8
       -          -fortunei 1/4
       -unknown hybrid-
              -Purple Splendour (as above)
```
5ft(1.5m) x 5.5ft(1.65m) OF(-18C) ML Flowers in trusses of
12-13, white with light purplish pink margins and a brilliant
greenish yellow flare. Ben and Marion Shapiro, reg. 1989.


```
              -veitchianum 1/2
WEDDING GOWN-
              -burmanicum 1/2
```
Funnel-shaped flowers in trusses of 5-7, yellowish white,
slightly yellow in throat and on dorsal lobe. Plant 5ft(1.5m)
tall. K. van de Ven, reg. 1986.


```
        -campylogynum Charopaeum Group--Patricia 1/2
WEE BEE-
        -keiskei--Yaku Fairy 1/2
```
1.5ft(.45m) high x 2.5ft(.75m)(13 yrs) 5F(-15C) EM   Funnel-
shaped flowers, 3-5 per lax truss, 5 wavy lobes, vivid red
shading to strong pink in throat, strong red rays down each
lobe; buds deep yellowish pink. Dwarf plant, well-branched. W.
E. Berg, reg. 1987. A.E. 1989.


```
        -minus Carolinianum Group, white compact form, F2 1/2
WEE LOVE-
        -keiskei 1/2
```
10in(25.4cm) high x 39in(1.0m)(13 yrs) -22F(-30C) M Greenish
yellow buds open to creamy white, wavy-edged lobes; 4-16 flowers
of 1-2 buds of 2-10 flowers, per domed truss. Small glossy foliage; brown scales below. W. Fetterhoff, cross 1972; reg. 1988.


```
        -minus Carolinianum Group--Epoch 1/2
       -          -minus Carolinianum Group--Delp's Pink 1/8
WEE   -unnamed-          -racemosum 1/32
SQUIRT-   - hybrid-      -Conemaugh-
       -Mini-    -Pioneer-          -mucronulatum 1/32
       Mode-          -unknown 1/16
       -              -minus Carolinianum Group (tetraploid) 1/8
       -unnamed-
              hybrid-fastigiatum 1/8
```
Buds from strong to pale purplish pink, opening to white edged
light purplish pink; dorsal spots strong yellow-green. W. Delp.

WEGA   See PSYCHE, under CAROLINE SPENCER

WELCOME STRANGER   Described under REPOSE, q.v.

WELDON'S GIFT   Described under ATOMIC BLAST, q.v.

```
                    -Pygmalion--unknown 1/4
        -unnamed hybrid-
WELDY-                  -haematodes 1/4
        -yakushimanum (Exbury form) 1/2
```
Flowers of frilled pink, fading to ivory, with white filaments.
Plant medium-sized; hardy to -15F(-26C). Kehr cross; W. Delp.

```
                            -campylocarpum Elatum Group 1/16
            -Penjerrick-
        -Amaura-              -griffithianum 1/16
    -Eros-        -griersonianum 3/8
WELKIN-   -griersonianum
    -haematodes 1/2
```
Trusses of about 4 flowers, varying in color from geranium lake
to Delft rose. Lord Aberconway.   A. M. 1946. F. C. C. 1951.

```
                -maximum 1/2
WELLESLEYANUM-
                -catawbiense 1/2
```
Synonym MAXIMUM WELLESLEYANUM. Flowers white, tinged light rose.
A. Waterer, 1880.

```
            -fortunei 1/2
WELLFLEET-
            -decorum 1/2
```
Dexter hybrid; parent of ACCLAIM, ARONIMINK, TODMORDEN, and
others.

WELL-SUITED   Described under PACESETTER, q.v.

* *
```
            -decorum 1/2
WELSHPOOL-
            -yakushimanum--Koichiro Wada 1/2
```
3ft(.9m) -5F(-21C) M   Plant upright, half as broad as tall;
leaves held 3 years, light tan indumentum.   Fragrant flowers,
white with faint yellow dorsal blotch and spots, 6-lobed; globular trusses of 10. Floriferous. Dr. Whildin Reese, reg. 1977.
JANE REDFORD   Parentage: yakushimanum x decorum
Truss of 9-13 flowers, 7-lobed, Neyron rose buds, opening white,
flushed lighter red externally (especially on mid-ribs) with
spots of citron green in throat. Leaves oblong to oblanceolate.
Knap Hill Nurseries cross; Ray Redford, reg. 1983.
TANANA   Parentage: decorum x yakushimanum, Exbury form, selfed
2.5ft(.75m) -10F(-23C) M Trusses of 12-15 flowers, white with
yellowish green spots, slightly fragrant, 7-lobed. Plant wider
than tall; leaves held 4 years. Childers, cross 1963; reg. 1979.
* *
```
            -Dexter hybrid--unknown
    -Janet Blair-
WEMROCK-            -unknown
    -white seedling--unknown
```
2ft(.6m) high x 3.5ft(1.m) -10F(-23C) M Flowers in trusses of
12, 5-lobed, pale yellow to pale orange-yellow with strong
orange-yellow flare and strong pink edging. Trusses 6in(15.2cm)
wide. Anna Gray named; Leon Yavorsky, cross 1976; reg. 1986.

```
            -thomsonii 1/4
    -Cornish Cross-
WENDY-            -griffithianum 1/4
    -williamsianum 1/2
```
4ft(1.2m) 5F(-15C) EM 3/3   Rounded leaves and cherry-colored
flowers; a showy display.   Lester E. Brandt, reg. 1962.

```
            -forrestii Repens Group 1/4
        -Elizabeth-
WENDY LONSDALE-        -griersonianum 1/4
        -neriiflorum Euchaites Group 1/2
```
Flowers of cherry red. H. D. Rose, Australia, reg. 1973.

WENDY LYN   Described under LANNY PRIDE, q.v.

* *
```
                -haematodes 1/4
        -Humming Bird-
WERRINGTON-            -williamsianum 1/4
        -forrestii Repens Group 1/2
```

Williams, intro. 1953.
LITTLE BIRDIE   Parentage as above, except reversed
Dwarf plant with blood red flowers.   Rudolph Henny, reg. 1958.
LITTLE BOBBIE   Parentage as above, except reversed
Another dwarf selection by Henny.
LITTLE JANET   Parentage as above, except reversed
Dwarf plant with red flowers. Henny, reg. 1958.
LITTLE PATTY   Parentage as Werrington, above
Orient red flowers, held in trusses of 4-5. Henny, reg. 1962.
* *

```
                    -catawbiense 1/8
            -Charles Dickens-
    -Dr. V. H. Rutgers-        -unknown 3/8
WESER-            -Lord Roberts--unknown
    -williamsianum 1/2
```
Rose-colored flowers. Dietrich Hobbie, 1951.

WESLEY HAYES   Parentage unknown
Flowers yellowish white.   Mrs. Wesley Hayes, reg. 1972.

```
                        -dichroanthum ssp. scyphocalyx 1/4
        -Reginald Farrer-
WESSEX WONDER-          -fortunei ssp. discolor 3/8
        -        -wardii 1/4
        -Crest-        -fortunei ssp. discolor
        -Lady  -
            Bessborough-campylocarpum Elatum Gp. 1/8
```
Funnel-shaped flowers, 3.7in(9.5cm) wide, 7-lobed, pale yellow-
green, striped rhodonite red between lobes; truss of 7. Smooth
ovate-obovate leaves. Plant 4.5ft(1.3m) x 3.5ft(1m), blooming
late in May.   J. May, cross 1968; reg. 1988.

WESTBURY   Parentage unknown
4ft(1.2m) -10F(-23C) M   Fragrant and frilled flowers of light
purplish pink, edges darker, two greenish yellow rays in throat.
Slow-growing, spreading.   Dexter cross; Vossberg raiser; Tyler
Arboretum, reg. 1982.   Color illus. Cox pl. 194.

WESTBY   Described under FLADA W. BLOUGH, q.v.

WESTDALE   Described under MAXDIS, q.v.

WESTFALENPARK   Described under RONSDORFER FRUHBLUHENDE, q.v.

WESTHAVEN--form of aberconwayi
4ft(1.2m) -5F(-21C) M   A plant of open, spreading habit, as
wide as tall; dark green foliage, 3in(7.6cm) long, flat and saucer-shaped; held 4 years. White flowers with a few maroon spots
held in trusses of 15.   Thomas J. McGuire, reg. 1972.

WESTON   Parentage unknown
5ft(1.5m) -10F(-23C) ML   Rose-colored flowers with golden
spotting, reverse darker; 10 per truss. Leaves 4.5in x 1.5in
(11.5cm x 3.8cm).   Dexter cross; Mezitt, reg. 1979.

```
                    -P.J.M. (double-flowered sdl.)
        -unnamed hybrid-
WESTON'S CRESCENDO-        -minus Carolinianum Group
        -unknown
```
2.5ft(.75m) high x 3.5ft(1.05m) M Deep pink buds open moderate
purplish red maturing to pale orange yellow.   Leaves held 2
years, rusty brown scales. Mezitt cross; Weston, reg. 1989.

```
                -minus Carolinianum Group 1/4
        -P.J.M.-
WESTON'S PINK DIAMOND-        -dauricum var. sempervirens 1/4
        -mucronulatum--Cornell Pink 1/2
```
5ft(1.5m) -15F(-26C) E   Rose Bengal buds open to flat,
saucer-shaped flowers, light fuchsia purple, in ball-shaped
trusses of 8-12.   Upright plant, well branched, 2/3 as broad as
high with leaves glossy yellow-green, retained 1 year. Mezitt,
cross 1964; Weston Nurseries, intro. 1977; reg. 1983.

```
            -fortunei ssp. discolor 1/2
WESTWARD HO-
            -hardy hybrid--unknown 1/2
```
Deep pink flowers, crimson in the throat. Slocock, 1932.

WEWEI   Described under DUKE OF CORNWALL, q.v.

```
                    -fortunei ssp. discolor 1/4
        -Sir Frederick-          -arboreum ssp. zeylanicum 1/8
WEYBRIDGE- Moore      -St. Keverne-
       -                       -griffithianum 1/8
       -yakushimanum 1/2
```
Plant of low, spreading habit, vigorous and compact; leaves 4.5
in(11.5cm) long, glossy dark green. Flowers pale pink, margins
almost white, the reverse near Tyrian rose, 2.3in(6cm) across;
spherical trusses of 12.   Francis Hanger cross, RHS Garden,
Wisley; reg. 1965. H.C. Wisley Trials 1964.

WFH See W. F. H., filed at start of W's

* *
```
        -Westbury--unknown 3/4        -catawbiense 1/4
WHEATLEY-        -Mrs. C. S. Sargent-
    -Meadowbrook-                     -unknown
            -                         -catawbiense
               -Everestianum-
                          -unknown
```
6ft(1.8m) -15F(-26C) M 3/4   Fragrant rose pink flowers with
yellow-green rays in throat; 3.25in(8.3cm) wide, frilled; ball
truss of 16. Plant broad as high, well-branched; leaves 7in
(17.8cm) long, held 2 years. H. Phipps cross; Paul Vossberg,
reg. 1972. A.E. 1973. Color illus. ARS Q 26:2 (1972), cover.
BROOKVILLE Parentage as above
5ft(1.5m) -10F(-23C) ML 3/3   Delicate pink, shaded white,
with deeper flare and gold throat, frilled. Good foliage;
prefers some shade. H. Phipps cross; intro. 1959.
* *

WHEELER DEALER Described under CALSAP, q.v.

WHIMSEY Described under FINESSE, q.v.

* *
```
        -yakushimanum 1/4        -fortunei ssp. discolor
        -               -Lady                       3/32
    -Si Si-   -Day -Bessborough-campylocarpum Elatum
    -          -Dream-                              1/32
    -     -Gold -    -griersonianum 3/32
    -     Mohur-       -fortunei ssp. discolor
WHIMSICAL-        -Margaret Dunn-    -dichroanthum 1/32
    -                        -Fabia-
    -                               -griersonianum
    -              -smirnowii 1/4
    -unnamed hybrid-
                 -catawbiense 1/4
```
Flowers mallow purple edged with strong purplish pink; dorsal
spotting of deep red; throat vivid yellow-green. W. Delp.
RHODY ROMANCE Parentage as above
Buds of spirea red and white open to large frilled white flowers
with pale yellow dorsal spotting; throat pale greenish yellow;
anthers pale orange yellow; stigma strong yellowish pink. Delp.
* *

WHIMZEE Described under POWER BASE, q.v.

WHIPPED CREAM Parentage unknown
White flowers. Mrs. R. J. Coker, reg. 1980.

WHIRLIGIG---maximum (Gable's curly leaf form) F2
4ft x 4ft(1.2m)(17 yrs) -20F(-29C) VL   Flowers in domed
trusses of 15-24, buds deep purplish pink opening pale purplish
pink with brilliant yellow-green spotting over a brilliant yellow-green blotch. G. D. Lewis, reg. 1989.

```
                        -griffithianum 1/8
             -unnamed hybrid-
      -Mrs. Furnivall-         -unknown 1/2
      -          -               -caucasicum 1/8
WHIRLIGIG-        -unnamed hybrid-
  (Delp) -                       -unknown
      -    -catawbiense var. album Glass--Catalgla 1/4
      -Calsap-
          -Sappho--unknown
```
Buds of moderate purplish pink and very pale purple open to
white, frilled flowers; dorsal spots of deep red and strong purplish red on 3 lobes; white filaments. Al Smith cross; W. Delp
raiser.

WHIRLWIND Described under HAD, q.v.

WHIRLYBIRD Described under EASTER BUNNY, q.v.

```
               -williamsianum 1/2
WHISPERINGROSE-        -forrestii Repens Group 1/4
             -Elizabeth-
                       -griersonianum 1/4
```
3ft(.9m) OF(-18C) EM 4/4   Compact plant; foliage small and
rounded with red petioles. Campanulate flowers, carnation rose.
Floriferous. Buds young. H. E. Greer, intro. 1982. Color
illus. HG p. 97; Cox pl. 196.

WHISTLE PUNK Described under GYPSY ROVER, q.v.

```
                -maximum 1/4
      -Fireking-        -forrestii Repens Group 1/8
      -     -Gertrud-                   -ponticum
      -     -Schäle -    -Michael Waterer-  1/32
      -          -Prometheus-          -unknown
WHISTLE-                -Monitor--unknown
  STOP -                        -catawbiense 1/16
      -          -Parsons Grandiflorum-
      -     -America-                   -unknown 11/32
      -          -dark red hybrid--unknown
      -Cindy Lou-              -griffithianum 1/16
      -               -Mars-
        -unnamed hybrid-   -unknown
                     -catawbiense var. rubrum 1/8
```
Buds of ruby and cardinal reds opening to frilled flowers of
cardinal and strong reds; vivid purplish red filaments. Delp.

```
                  -yakushimanum
       -Serendipity-
WHISTLER-      -aureum (chrysanthum)
       -sutchuenense var. geraldi
```
Buds of strong red and deep moderate pink open to white flowers
with throats of ruby red and deep purplish red. W. Delp.

```
                   -campylocarpum
          -Albino-
          -     -Loder's White, q.v. for 2 possible parentage
WHITE BEAUTY-    diagrams
          -                 -griffithianum
          -Loder's Pink Diamond-
                             -fortunei
```
Pure white flowers, 12 to a truss. Origin unknown. A.M. 1945.

WHITE BIRD Described under YAKU DUCHESS, q.v.

```
                  -campanulatum 1/2
WHITE CAMPANULA-
                  -unknown 1/2
```
4ft(1.2m) -5F(-21C) M 3/4   White flowers of good substance.
Exceptional foliage. Origin unknown, possibly Hillier Nursery.

```
            -fortunei or griffithianum 1/2
WHITE CLOUD-
            -hardy hybrid--unknown 1/2
```
5ft(1.5m) OF(-18C) M Propagated in large numbers by tissue
culture. Large flowers of pure white, held in big flat trusses.
Slocock, intro. 1934.

```
         -Scintillation--unknown 13/16
WHITE  -        -griffithianum 1/8
COLOSSUS-  -Mars-
    -unnamed-  -unknown            -catawbiense 1/16
     hybrid-        -Parsons Grandiflorum-
           -America-               -unknown
              -dark red hybrid--unknown
```
5ft(1.5m) x 5ft -10F(23C) ML   Dome truss 7in(17.8cm) wide, 7-
lobed white flowers from pink buds, moderate orange-yellow
markings. Upright, spreading habit. A. W. Smith, reg. 1989.

```
           -wardii 1/4
     -Crest-          -fortunei ssp. discolor 1/8
     -    -Lady Bessborough-
WHITE CREST-         -campylocarpum Elatum Group 1/8
     -
     -hyperythrum 1/2
```
Pink in bud, opening white. Raised at Exbury Gardens; grown by
Brig. C. E. Lucas Phillips; reg. 1970.

        -low, white hybrid--unknown
WHITE DIMPLES-
      -white hybrid, yellow center--unknown
3ft(.9m) x 2ft(.6m)(7 yrs) -20F(-29C) ML   Flowers in trusses
of 20, 5 wavy lobes; strong purplish pink buds open to yellowish
white. Ball trusses 6in(15.2cm) broad. Dense habit; very floriferous. E. Mezitt cross; Weston Nurseries, reg. 1987.

              -aureum (chrysanthum) 1/4
        -unnamed hybrid-
WHITE DOVE-   -maximum 1/4
      -catawbiense var. album Glass--Catalgla 1/2
Buds of light yellow-green and pale greenish yellow opening to
white flowers with vivid yellow-green dorsal spots. W. Delp.

        -scopulorum 1/2
WHITE DOVES-
      -formosum var. inaequale 1/2
White flowers with a yellow-green mark in the throat; trusses of
4. F. M. Jury, reg. 1982.

WHITE ENSIGN   Described under W. LEITH, q.v.

           -minus Carolinianum Group 1/4
        -unnamed hybrid-
WHITE FELICITY-   -dauricum--Arctic Pearl 3/4
      -dauricum--Arctic Pearl
3.5ft(1.0m) x 2ft(.6m)(9 yrs) -25F(-32C) EM   Flowers in
trusses of 9 (several 2-3-flowered clusters), 5 wavy lobes, pure
white with yellow anthers. Leaves with scaly indumentum. D. W.
Paden, reg. 1987.

WHITE FLARE   Described under CAROLINE ALLBROOK, q.v.

* *
      -irroratum 1/2
WHITE GLORY-   -griffithianum 1/4
     -Loderi-
       -fortunei 1/4
Large funnel-shaped flowers in loose trusses of 15-18; cream-
colored buds opening white. Early season. Dowager Lady Loder.
A.M. 1937.
PINK GLORY   Parentage as above
Tall plant; trumpet-shaped flowers, blush pink and stained rose
madder. Lady Loder. A.M. Wisley Trials 1940.
* *

WHITE GOLD   Described under GREAT SCOTT, q.v.

      -yakushimanum 1/2
WHITE GULL-
      -unknown 1/2
3ft(.9m) -5F(-21C) ML Plant rounded, wider than tall; glossy,
convex leaves with tan indumentum, held 3 years; new growth
tomentose. Buds of light pink open to frilled white flowers with
faint touch of pink at edges, chartreuse green dorsal spotting,
2.75in(7cm); spherical trusses of 20. C. Herbert, reg. 1979.

WHITE LACE--form of racemosum
4ft(1.2m) -5F(-21C) EM 4/3   Pure white, with no pink tinge.
P. A. Cox, reg. 1974. A.M. 1974.

* *
       -maximum 1/4
     -Halopeanum-
WHITE LADY-   -griffithianum 1/2
 -         -griffithianum
    -Loderi Pink Diamond-
          -fortunei 1/4
Pure white flowers. Sir E. Loder.
LEONARDSLEE GERTRUDE   Parentage as above
Both of the above have pure white flowers. Sir Edmund Loder.
* *

      -calophytum 1/2
WHITE -   -caucasicum 3/16
MUSTANG-   -Jacksonii-   -caucasicum
  -Goldsworth-   -Nobleanum-
    Yellow -   -arboreum 1/16
       -campylocarpum 1/4

Synonym DEBUTANTE. Plant 7ft(2.1m) tall when registered; leaves
10in(25.4cm) long. Flowers to 3.5in(9cm) across, white blotched
dawn pink. Very early.   Rudolph & Leona Henny, reg. 1964.

WHITE NES LODERI   See EMILY ALLISON

WHITE OLYMPIC LADY   Described under OLYMPIC LADY, q.v.

WHITE PEARL   See HALOPEANUM

       -williamsianum 3/4   -griffithianum
WHITE PIPPIN-   -Loderi King George-   1/8
      -White Olympic Lady-   -fortunei 1/8
           -williamsianum
Truss of 7 flowers, 5-lobed, light greenish-white, 2.5in(6.4cm)
across. Leaves rounded-elliptic, 2in x 1.2in (5cm x 3cm).   H.
L. Larson, reg. 1983.

WHITE PLAINS--form of alutaceum var. iodes.
3ft(.9m) -10F(-23C) EM 3/4   Truss of 17-18 flowers, 5-lobed,
funnel-campanulate, white with the reverse shading to light sap
green. Leaves dull green, underneath heavily felted with rust-
colored indumentum. George Forrest collector; Col. S. R. Clarke
raiser; R. N. S. Clarke, reg. 1978. A.M. 1978.

        -fortunei ssp. discolor 1/2
WHITE QUEEN-
      -campylocarpum 1/2
5ft(1.5in) -5F(-21C) ML Leaves 6.5in x 3in) (16.5cm x 7.6cm).
Flowers 4in(10.2cm) across, white spotted deep chocolate on
upper petal, 7-lobed, in trusses of 10.   C. Herbert, reg. 1967.

WHITE ROBE   Described under BUNTING, q.v.

WHITE SAILS   Parentage unknown
Pure white flowers. Mrs. R. J. Coker, reg. 1980.

      -Corry Koster--unknown 1/2
WHITE SAMITE-   -griffithianum 1/4
     -Loderi-
       -fortunei 1/4
White flowers. A.M. 1932.

      -dauricum, white form 1/2
WHITE SURPRISE-
       -mucronulatum, white form 1/2
3.5ft(1.05m) x 2.5ft(.75m) -15F(-26C) EM   Flowers greenish
white with strong greenish yellow spotting. Open growth habit;
leaves scaly below, turn brilliant yellow in fall. Mehlquist,
cross 1973; J. Shaw raiser; J. Leonard, reg. 1988.

      -decorum 1/2   -griffithianum 1/8
WHITE SWAN-   -George Hardy-
 -Pink Pearl-   -catawbiense 1/8
       -      -arboreum 1/8
       -Broughtonii-
        -unknown (1/8)
6ft(1.8m) -5F(-21C) M 4/3   Extra large and perfectly formed
trusses of satin white flowers, a green basal blotch. Plant upright, rather compact; dusty green, concave leaves, to 6in(15cm)
long. John Waterer, Sons & Crisp. A. M. 1937. F.C.C. 1957.

WHITE VELVET--form of yakushimanum
2ft(.6m) -5F(-21C) M   Pink buds opening to light pink, fading white, tan specks on upper lobe; flowers slightly fragrant,
2in(5cm) wide; trusses hold 16. Plant broader than tall; leaves
dark green with tan indumentum, held 3 years.   Seed from Japan,
Edgar Greer; Cyril H. Ward, intro. and reg. 1974.

     -Loder's White, q.v. for 2 possible parentage diagrams
WHITE WAY-   -griffithianum
 -        -George Hardy-
  -Mrs. Lindsay Smith-   -catawbiense
        -Duchess of Edinburgh--unknown
White flowers with a faint yellow blotch. Lord Digby, 1952.
A.M. 1952.

      -yakushimanum, Exbury form 1/2
WHITE WEDDING-
       -makinoi 1/2
2ft(.6m) -5F(-21C) M   Plant 10in(25cm) high by 14in(35.5cm)
completely covered by open trusses at 2.5 years; small, heavily

indumented leaves. Frilled flowers, opening pink, fading white, the upper lobe speckled, 2.5in(6.4cm); 14 per compact truss with 3 to a terminal inflorescence.   John G. Lofthouse, reg. 1971.

```
                        -edgeworthii (bullatum) 1/2
WHITE WINGS-
            -ciliicalyx 1/2
```
Very large flowers in neat trusses of 4-5, pure white with yellow flare, sweetly fragrant. A compact plant with large foliage, like edgeworthii. Scrase-Dickins. A. M. 1939.

```
                              -Pygmalion--unknown 1/16
                 -unnamed hybrid-
          -Weldy-             -haematodes 1/16
     -unnamed- -yakushimanum, Exbury form 1/8
     - hybrid-            -yakushimanum 1/4
WHITE -        -Serendipity-
WONDER-                  -aureum (chrysanthum) 3/8
     -                     -smirnowii 1/8
                 -unnamed hybrid-
     -unnamed hybrid-            -yakushimanum
                 -aureum (chrysanthum)
```
Buds a blend of pale purplish pink, strong and light purplish pinks opening to white frilled flowers with dorsal spots of light yellow-green. Indumented foliage. W. Delp.

WHITEBAIT--form of sargentianum, white form
1ft(.3m) -5F(-21C) EM 3/4 Very slow-growing dwarf with shiny leaves and small creamy yellow flowers. E. H. M. & P. A. Cox. A.M. 1966.

WHITE'S CUNNINGHAM'S SULPHUR   See CUNNINGHAM'S SULPHUR

WHITE'S FAVOURITE--form of dichroanthum F 6761
Trusses of 4-5 flowers, 5-lobed, orange-red with edges deeper, 1.25in(3.2cm) wide. Lanceolate leaves 3.5in(8.9cm) long; young leaves with silky gray indumentum. Plant about 5ft(1.5m) tall. Harry White raiser, Sunningdale; J. P. C. Russell, reg. 1983.

```
              -catawbiense var. album Glass--Catalgla 1/2
WHITEWATER  -      -fortunei 1/4         -decorum 1/16
NORTH CAROLINA- -        -unnamed hybrid-
        -unnamed-      -           -griersonianum 1/10
          hybrid-Madonna-   -           -catawbiense
                   -       -Parsons  -     1/32
                   -America- Grandiflorum-unknown 3/32
                       -dark red hybrid--unknown
```
10ft(3.0m) x 12ft(3.6m)(25 yrs) -20F(-29C) M   Flowers white with large sap green dorsal blotch in throat; tall truss of 13. Well-branched plant.   V. and C. R. Haag cross; reg. 1988.

```
              -Pauline--unknown 1/2
        -Grenadine-
WHITMOOR-     -griersonianum 1/4
     -           -elliottii 1/4
        -Royal Blood-
                -Rubens--unknown
```
Flowers of medium cardinal red, spotted in upper throat.   Crown Estate, Windsor, reg, 1972. A.M. 1971.

WHITNEY APPLEBLOSSOM   Parentage unknown
4ft(1.2m) 5F(-15C) M   Medium pink flowers, resembling appleblossoms, upper lobe spotted gold and red. A rounded plant with deep green leaves.   Whitney cross; Sathers intro.

WHITNEY BUFF   Parentage unknown
5ft(1.5m) -5F(-21C) M   Flowers of creamy buff in large trusses. Whitney cross; Sathers intro.

WHITNEY DWARF RED   Parentage unknown
3ft(.9m) OF(-18C) EM 4/4   Low-growing with shiny green foliage. Red buds, red flowers. Whitney cross; Sathers intro.

```
                            -griffithianum 3/16
                 -Queen Wilhelmina-
            -Britannia-      -unknown 9/16
        -Leo-       -Stanley Davies--unknown
WHITNEY -    -elliottii 1/4
LATE RED-                 -griffithianum
        -         -Queen Wilhelmina-
        -Britannia-              -unknown
                   -Stanley Davies--unknown
```

A parent of PARTY GIRL.   William Whitney cross.

WHITNEY PURPLE   Possible ponticum hybrid
5ft(1.5m) -10F(-23C) ML 3/3 Dark red in bud opening strong purplish red with prominent dorsal blotch of dark grayish purple. Much like one form of OLD PORT. Whitney cross; Sather, reg. 1987.

WHITNEY'S GEORGEANNE   Parentage unknown
3ft(.9m) 5F(-15C) ML 3/3 Trusses of salmon orange; leaves small, narrow. Whitney cross; Sathers intro.

WHITNEY'S LATE ORANGE   Parentage unknown
4t(1.2m) -5F(-21C) L 4/3 Parents may be dichroanthum and late-blooming fortunei. Flowers unmarked Spanish orange, in full trusses; sharply pointed, mistletoe green foliage, on well-shaped, up-right plant. W. Whitney cross; Sathers intro.

WHITNEY'S LATE YELLOW   See MARY DRENNEN

WHITNEY'S ORANGE   Parentage unknown, when registered in 1976;
               1985 Whitney catalog: dichroanthum x Diane.
3ft(.9m) OF(-18C) ML 4/3 Light orange flowers, with a darker blotch, spotted and edged in red; spherical trusses of about 15. Another form: deeper orange, unmarked.   Whitney cross; Sather, reg. 1976.

WHITTENTON   Parentage unknown
6FT(1.8m) -15F(-26C) M   Flowers light purplish pink on a vigorous plant. Dexter cross; Willard raiser; J. Wells, reg. 1980.

```
* * * * * * * * * * * * * * * * * * * * * * * * * * * * * *
                          -thomsonii 1/8
              -Bagshot Ruby-
         -Princess Elizabeth-      -unknown 3/8
WHIZETTE-               -unknown
         -maximum, white form, Jackson Center, PA 1/2
```
Flowers of deep and strong pink; deep pink calyx. W. Delp.
WILD CARD   Parentage as above
Buds of strong red open to pale pink (French rose), edged strong purplish red. Plant medium-sized; hardy to -15F(-26C).   Delp.
```
* * * * * * * * * * * * * * * * * * * * * * * * * * * * * *
```

```
                        -catawbiense 3/32
                 -unnamed-
          -Boule de- hybrid-unknown 11/16
          - Rose F2-      -caucasicum 1/16
          -      -Boule de-      -catawbiense
          -      Neige -unnamed-
     -Carolyn Dana-       hybrid-unknown
     - Lewis  -                -thomsonii
     -        -      -Bagshot Ruby-     1/32
     -        -Princess -          -unknown
WHOOPEE!-    -Lanny- Elizabeth-unknown
        -     Pride-      -smirnowii 1/16
        -        -unnamed hybrid-
        -                  -yakushimanum 1/16
     -Dexter's Brick Red Orange--unknown
```
Spirea red in bud opening to frilled flowers deep, moderate, and pale purplish pink, a deep purplish red flare; dorsal spots of deep purplish red; white throat; white anthers. W. Delp.

```
                         -catawbiense 3/32
               -unknown hybrid-
          -Boule de -         -unknown 3/8
          - Rose F2-      -caucasicum 1/16
          -       -Boule de Neige-      -catawbiense
     -Carolyn-               -unnamed-
     - Dana -                 hybrid-unknown
     - Lewis-                  -thomsonii 3/32
     -                   -Bagshot-
WHOOPEE -      -Princess - Ruby -unknown
DING -      -Lanny Pride- Elizabeth-unknown
     -          -          -smirnowii 3/16
     -          -unnamed hybrid-
     -                  -yakushimanum 3/16
     -Lanny Pride (as above)
```
Buds of cardinal and currant red opening to large frilled flowers of cardinal and currant red; dorsal spots dark red; white throat. W. Delp.

WIANNO   Parentage unknown

5ft(1.5m) -5F(-21C) M Buds reddish purple open to flowers of
moderate to light purplish pink in trusses of 8-10. Dexter
cross; Willard raiser; Tyler Arboretum, reg. 1980.

WICKATUNK   Described under LLENROC, q.v.

```
            -yakushimanum 1/2
WICKHAM'S FANCY-
            -unnamed hybrid--unknown 1/2
```
White flowers, slightly tinted with pink.   John Waterer, Sons
& Crisp, reg. 1975.

* *
```
                -dichroanthum
           -Fabia-
     -C. I. S.-        -griersonianum
     -          -Loder's White, q.v. for 2 possible
WICKIUP-                            parentage diagrams
     -          -fortunei ssp. discolor
     -Argosy-
                -auriculatum 1/2
```
5ft(1.5m) 5F(-15C) M 4/3   Beautiful multi-colored flowers,
orange, apricot, and lemon yellow, a touch of cherry red in the
throat. Attractive plant and foliage.   J. A. Elliott cross.
WICKIUP'S SISTER   Parentage as above
Similar to above with more yellow and habit more upright. J. A.
Elliott.
* *
```
                          -smirnowii 1/8
                 -unnamed hybrid-
                 -          -yakushimanum 1/8
      -Oh Joyce-
      -          -          -maximum 1/8
      -          -Midsummer-
      -    -Joyce Lyn-      -unknown 3/16
      -          -          -maximum
WIDE RECEIVER-           -Adele's Yellow-
      -          -          -wardii 1/16
      -          -          -catawbiense 1/8
      -    -Catawbiense Album-
      -Wizard-           -unknown
           -          -dichroanthum 1/8
           -Fabia-
                 -griersonianum 1/8
```
Buds of deep purplish red opening to white edged with strong
purplish red and strong purplish pink; vivid red stigma. Delp.

```
                          -ponticum 1/16
                   -Michael-
              -Prometheus-Waterer-unknown 5/16
              -          -
     -Madame de Bruin-   -Monitor-unknown
     -          -          -arboreum 1/8
WIEKHOFF-          -Doncaster-
     -                    -unknown
        -williamsianum 1/2
```
Deep rose flowers. Dietrich Hobbie, intro. 1947.

```
        -minus Carolinianum Group 1/2
WIGEON-
        -calostrotum--Gigha 1/2
```
2ft(.6m) -10F(-23C) M 3/3   Deep lavender pink flowers,
deeper spotting on upper lobes, short red stamens; rounded
trusses. Propagated in large numbers by tissue culture.   P.
Cox, cross 1971; reg. 1982.   A.M. Wisley Trials 1987.   Color
illus. Cox pl. 197.
* *
```
        -williamsianum 1/2
WILBAR-        -thomsonii 1/4
     -Barclayi-             -arboreum 1/8
        -Glory of Penjerrick-
                          -griffithianum 1/8
```
4ft(1.2m) 5F(-15C) E 3/3   Dark pink flowers. Plant low and
compact, spreading wider than tall; dark green, ovate leaves.
Lord Aberconway, intro. 1946.

```
                          -griffithianum 1/4
          -Jean Marie de Montague-
WILD AFFAIR-              -unknown 3/4
          -Moser's Maroon--unknown
```
6ft(1.8m) -5F(-21C) ML 4/3   Bright red flowers, light yellow

blotch. Large leaves of deep fir green. Plant growth vigorous,
rather open. Greer, 1982. Color il. Greer cat. 1990, pl. 14.

```
                -smirnowii 1/8
            -Oh My!-
       -unnamed hybrid-   -yakushimanum 1/8
WILD AND-           -aureum (chrysanthum) 1/4
WACKY   -          -fortunei 1/4
      -Margaret Dunn-     -dichroanthum 1/8
            -Fabia-
                -griersonianum 1/8
```
Buds of cardinal and strong reds open to frilled flowers of
strong, light and pale pinks; throat of brilliant greenish
yellow and cardinal red. W. Delp.

WILD CARD   Described under WHIZETTE, q.v.

```
        -yakushimanum 1/2
                          -sanguineum ssp. didymum 1/8
WILD ONE-             -Carmen-
      -Little Gem-    -forrestii Repens Group 1/8
            -elliottii 1/4
```
Buds a blend of currant red and cardinal red opening to flowers
moderate pink edged cardinal red; foliage indumented. W. Delp.

WILD WEALTH--form of yakushimanum
3ft(.9m) tall x 5ft(1.5m)(25 yrs) -10F(-23C) M   Pale purplish
pink buds open to white flowers with pale yellow blotch, flushed
green, wavy-edged, widely funnel-campanulate, 3.5in(8.8cm) wide.
Domed truss of 12. Oblong convex leaves 3in(7.6cm) long; bright
white indumentum aging to tan. Seed collected wild on Yakushima
by Dr.T. Rokujo, 1961; Mrs. M. L. B. Hill, reg. 1987.

```
                          -dichroanthum 1/8
          -Astarte-        -campylocarpum Elatum Group
          -          -Penjerrick-              1/16
     -Phidias-        -
     -          -          -griffithianum 1/16
WILFRED-          -neriiflorum 1/8
     -          -F. C. Puddle-
     -                    -griersonianum 1/8
     -williamsianum 1/2
```
The flower is pink. Lord Aberconway, intro. 1946.

```
                          -griffithianum 1/8
                 -Queen Wilhelmina-
          -Britannia-        -unknown 3/8
WILGEN'S RUBY-        -Stanley Davies--unknown
          -          -catawbiense 1/4
          -John Walter-
                -arboreum 1/4
```
5ft(1.5m) -15F(-26C) ML 4/3   Flowers very deep red with a
brown blotch. Attractive foliage; hardy, compact plant.   A.
C. van Wilgen. F.C.C. Boskoop 1951. Color illus. VV p. 125;
Cox pl. 198; JS p. 34.

```
          -Wilgen's Ruby--unknown 1/2
WILGEN'S SURPRISE-
          -williamsianum 1/2
```
Trusses 4.5in(11.5cm) wide, 7-8 flowers of light China rose with
a deeper rose throat. A vigorous plant, much broader than tall;
dull, light green leaves, 3in(7.6cm) long.   Van Wilgen's Nurseries. H. C. 1974.

WILLARD   Parentage unknown
5ft(1.5m) -10F(-23C) M   Strong purplish red flowers with
purplish red throat in ball-shaped truss of 12.   Plant wider
than tall, yellow-green foliage. Dexter cross; Willard raiser;
J. Wells, intro. 1959; Tyler Arboretum, reg. 1980.

WILLBRIT Described under BRITANNIA'S BELLS, q.v.

```
        -griffithianum 1/2
WILLEM VOGT-
        -unknown 1/2
```
Red flowers. C. B. van Nes & Sons.

```
        -williamsianum 1/2
WILLETT-        -campylocarpum Elatum Group 1/4
      -Letty Edwards-
                -fortunei 1/4
```
23F(-5C) ML 4/5   "Best yellow of all" in Australia. Form,

habit, and foliage of williamsianum. Pale yellow, 5-8 flowers
per truss. Bramley cross.

```
                    -catawbiense 1/2
WILLIAM AUSTIN-
                    -unknown 1/2
```
Dark purple crimson flowers, spotted.   J. Waterer, before 1915.

WILLIAM BEAN   Described under ATOMIC BLAST, q.v.

WILLIAM DOWNING   Parentage unknown
Flowers of rich purplish brown with a large, intense blotch, in
mid-season. Good dark foliage on a medium-sized, floriferous
plant. Hardy in New Zealand.   Standish & Noble, before 1870.

```
                            -catawbiense 1/4
                -English Roseum-
WILLIAM FETTERHOFF-          -unknown 1/4
                -yakushimanum 1/2
```
Compact plant with flowers of nonfading clear light pink. Hardy
to -15F(-26C).   Fetterhoff cross; O. S. Pride, intro. 1975.

WILLIAM FORTESCUE   Described under PENJERRICK, q.v.

```
                -campylocarpum 1/4
        -Gladys-
WILLIAM-        -fortunei 3/8
 KING -                  -griffithianum 1/8
    -             -Loderi-
    -Ilam Cream-          -fortunei
                    -unknown 1/4
```
Flowers primrose yellow. Shrub 7ft(2.1m) tall at registration.
Mrs. L. M. King cross, 1958; S. M. King, reg. 1985.

WILLIAM MONTGOMERY   Described under ATRIER, q.v.

```
                    -dichroanthum 3/8
        -Roman Pottery-
    -                   -griersonianum 1/4
WILLIAM-                          -dichroanthum
 MOSS -             -Goldsworth-
   -              - Orange    -fortunei ssp. discolor 1/8
   -Golden Fleece-             -griffithianum 5/32
   -                         -Kewense-
   -            -Aurora-          -fortunei 1/32
        -Yvonne-          -
             -             -thomsonii 1/16
                    -griffithianum
```
Flowers azalea pink to shrimp pink, in trusses of 7-11. William
Moss, reg. 1974.

WILLIAM P. CARY   Described under CARY'S CREAM, q.v.

```
                    -arboreum 1/8
            -Doncaster-
        -Belvedere-         -unknown 1/8
WILLIAM-        -dichroanthum 1/2
PATTMAN-        -dichroanthum
        -Fabia-
            -griersonianum 1/4
```
Salmon orange flowers, 5-lobed, held in trusses of 10. That-
cher, reg. 1962.

WILLIAM ROGERS COE   Parentage unknown
5ft(1.5m) -5F(-21C) M   Flowers pink and white. Dexter cross.

```
                    -dichroanthum 1/2
WILLIAM W. DRYSDALE-         -griersonianum 1/8
                -unnamed-Azor-
                    hybrid-  -fortunei ssp. discolor 1/8
                    -unknown 1/4
```
Orange-colored flowers. Thacker, 1944.

```
                        -catawbiense 5/32
            -Blanayanum-               -catawbiense
        -            -          -unnamed-
    -Ascot   -         -Alta-  - hybrid-
    -Brilliant-         clerense-         -ponticum 1/32
WILLIAM-         -          -arboreum 1/16
WATSON -          -thomsonii 1/4
        -griffithianum 1/2
```
Flowers reddish outside, shell pink inside.   Gill. A.M. 1925.


```
            -nuttallii 1/2
WILLIAM WRIGHT SMITH-
            -veitchianum 1/2
```
These bell-shaped flowers are 5.5in(14cm) across, white with a
distinct orange tinge, and frilled lobes.   RBG, Edinburgh, reg.
1962. F.C.C. 1960.

WILLIAMS   Parentage unknown
5ft(1.5m) -10F(-23C) L 4/3   Syn. SPRINGTIME. Much like MRS.
FURNIVALL, but blooms later.   Klupenger Nursery intro.

```
            -arboreum 1/2
WILLIAMSONII-
            -azalea, molle 1/2
```
Azaleodendron.   Flowers almost white, tinted pale lilac. B. S.
Williams & Son.   A. M. 1890.

```
                        -thomsonii 1/16
                    -Cornish Cross-
            -unnamed-         -griffithianum 3/16
        -Harold- hybrid-wardii 1/8
        - Heal-          -griffithianum
WILLY-NILLY-    -Loderi King-
        -        George  -fortunei 1/8
        -williamsianum 1/2
```
Creamy white flowers.   Collingwood Ingram, reg. 1972.

```
        -ciliatum 1/2
WILSONI-
        -glaucophyllum 1/2
```
Two hybrids are known by this name; the other WILSONI is registered as LAETEVIRENS, q.v. Pale rose flowers.   Origin unknown.

```
            -souliei 1/2
WIN PAUL-         -fortunei ssp. discolor 1/8
    -    -Ladybird-
    -Diva-         -Corona--unknown 1/8
        -griersonianum 1/4
```
4.5ft(1.35m) 0F(-18C) EM   Plant as broad as tall; leaves 5in.
(12.7cm) long. Flowers campanulate, 3.5in(8.9cm) wide, deep
purplish pink with paler center and brick red spots; small round
trusses.   H. L. Larson, reg. 1972.

WINDBEAM   Described under WYANOKIE, q.v.

```
                -maximum 1/4
        -unnamed hybrid-
WINDFLOWER-         -yakushimanum 1/4
        -maximum, white form from Jackson Center, PA 1/2
```
White flower with dorsal spots of brilliant yellow-green. Delp.

```
            -minus,  Caroliniananum Group, white form 1/2
WINDLE BROOK-         -ciliatum 1/4
            -Cilpinense-
                -moupinense 1/4
```
Yellowish white flowers with pale green spots. Crown Estate
Commissioners, reg. 1971. P.C. 1971.

WINDLES   Described under MANOR HILL, q.v.

```
                        -griffithianum 1/8
                    -Queen Wilhelmina-
                -Britannia-         -unknown 5/8
WINDLESHAM SCARLET-     -Stanley Davies--unknown
            -         -arboreum 1/4
                -Doncaster-
                    -unknown
```
4-5ft(1.2-1.5m) -5F(-21C) ML   Compact, domed trusses of 12-16
flowers, cardinal red with black spots. Vigorous, compact, floriferous plant; dull, dark leaves 6.5in(16.5cm) long.   Fromow
Nurseries, reg. 1969. A.M. Wisley Trials 1968. F.C.C. Wisley
Trials 1971.

```
        -ponticum ? 1/2
WINDSOR LAD-
        -unknown 1/2
```
4.5ft(1.35m) -10F(-23C) ML 4/3   Blush lilac flowers, with a
bold golden eye; compact trusses of 16. Narrow foliage of medium length, on a well-shaped plant. Knap Hill Nurseries.   Color
illus. JS p. 85. (Named for a Derby winner?)

WINDSWEPT   See next column

WINIFRED DRAKE   Parentage unknown
Orange pink. Drake cross; Zimmerman raiser; Lux, reg. 1981.

WINIFRED KENNA   Parentage unknown
Orchid flowers with purple blotch.   Loeb, reg. 1966.

```
                  -formosum 1/2
WINIFRED MERSON-
                  -burmanicum 1/2
```
Uranium green in bud, opening to white flowers with chrome yel-
low flush.   T. Lelliott, AUS, reg. 1967.

WINIFRED MURRAY--form of cephalanthum
2ft(.6m) -5F(-21C) M 4/3 Loose truss of 8 flowers, tubular-
shaped, .25in(.64cm) across, Neyron rose fading to white.
Leaves up to .5in(1.3cm) long, densely covered with flaky brown
scales. Mrs. K. Dryden, reg. 1979. A.M. 1979.

```
                                    -neriiflorum 1/32
                         -Nereid-
              -Phyllis Ballard-    -dichroanthum 1/32
          -unnamed-               -fortunei ssp. discolor
    -unnamed- hybrid-catawbiense--Clark's White 1/8    1/16
    - hybrid-Dexter hybrid, pale yellow 1/4
    -                              -catawbiense
                         -Parsons Grandiflorum-    3/32
WINDSWEPT-         -America-              -unknown
          -AA 17-        -dark red hybrid--unknown 5/32
    -       -       -        -catawbiense
    -Matthew-    -Ann Rutledge-
      Weldon-            -unknown
    -                        -caucasicum 3/32
    -            -Jacksonii      -caucasicum
    -Goldsworth-        -Nobleanum-
      Yellow  -            -arboreum 1/32
              -campylocarpum 1/8
```
Buds are 3 shades of spirea red opening to frilled flowers yel-
lowish white, throat deep red and chartreuse green.   W. Delp.

```
          -griffithianum 1/4
    -Loderi-
WINK-      -fortunei 1/4
    -          -campylocarpum 1/4
    -Mrs. Mary Ashley-
              -unknown 1/4
```
Pink flowers.   Rudolph Henny, reg. 1962. P.A. 1960.

```
          -elliottii 1/4
    -Fusilier-
    -          -griersonianum 1/4
WINKFIELD-      -Lady        -fortunei ssp. discolor 1/8
    -          -Bessborough-
    -Jalisco-        -campylocarpum Elatum 1/8
      Elect -    -dichroanthum 1/8
              -Dido-
                  -decorum 1/8
```
Pinkish yellow flowers, upper lobes stained mandarin red on the
reverse with throat tinged and spotted crimson.   Crown Estate,
Windsor, reg. 1962, A M. 1958.

WINNECONNET   Parentage unknown
6ft(1.8m) -10F(-23C) M   Floriferous plant; flowers pale purplish pink, edged deeper pink, fragrant; trusses hold about 10.
C. O. Dexter cross; Williard raiser; James Wells, reg. 1980.

```
                  -catawbiense var. album--Catalgla 1/8
          -Gosh-                -decorum ? 1/32
          -Darn-        -Caroline-
    -Ginny's-    -Mrs.H.R.Yates-    -brachycarpum ? 1/32
    -Delight-            -unknown 1/16
    -        -        -fortunei 1/8
WINNING-    -Donna    -        -wardii 3/16
  COLORS-        Hardgrove-unnamed hybrid-
    -                        -dichroanthum 1/16
    -                -maximum 1/4
    -      -Stokes Bronze Wings-
    -unnamed-            -catawbiense 1/8
      hybrid-        -maximum
          -Adele's Yellow-
                  -wardii
```
Buds of cardinal red open to flowers of strong, light and pale
purplish pinks, throat of brilliant greenish yellow and strong

yellow-green. Anthers grayish red-orange.   W. Delp.

```
                  -catawbiense var. album 3/8
          -Lodestar-        -catawbiense var. album
          -        -Belle Heller-        -catawbiense
          -                -Madame Carvalho-
WINNING ONE-                    -unknown 1/8
          -                -catawbiense 1/8
          -        -Atrosanguineum-
          -    -Atrier-        -unknown
          -Mary -    -griersonianum 1/8
          Belle-    -decorum 1/8
              -Dechaem-
                  -haematodes 1/8
```
Pale apricot flowers, flushed rose; with yellow throat.
Hinerman cross; Delp raiser.

* *
```
          -Marion (Cheal)--unknown
WINNING-            -griffithianum 1/4
  POST -    -Pink Shell-        -fortunei 3/16
  -Coronation-        -H. M. Arderne-
      Day  -            -unknown 9/16
          -    -griffithianum
              -Loderi-
                  -fortunei
```
Truss of 12, bright rose Bengal. Boulter, Australia, reg. 1978.
RHONDA   Parentage as above
Flowers in trusses of 12-15, funnel-shaped, 5-lobed, vivid
purplish red with a strong purplish red flare in throat. 6.5ft
(2.0m) tall. V. J. Boulter raiser; F. R. Waghorn, reg. 1988.
* *

WINNING WAYS Parentage unknown
4ft(1.2m) OF(-18C) EM A red-flowered hybrid by C. O. Dexter.
Tyler Arboreum, reg. 1983.

```
              -haematodes 1/4
    -Humming Bird-
WINSOME-        -williamsianum 1/4
    -griersonianum 1/2
```
3ft(.9m) OF(-18C) EM 4/4 Buds remain reddish all winter,
open into rosy cerise flowers in great abundance. Compact plant
with small pointed leaves. Lord Aberconway, 1939. A.M. 1950.

WINTER BEAUTY   Described under MELBA, q.v.

WINTER BRIGHTNESS--form of mucronulatum
5ft(1.5m) -15F(-26C) VE 3/3 Rich purplish red flowers 1.5in
(3.8cm) across on a deciduous plant. Leaves 3in x 1.5in (7.6cm
x 3.8cm). Crown Estate, Windsor, reg. 1962. F.C.C. 1957.

WINTER FAVOURITE   Parentage unknown
A parent of DENISE.

```
                  -leucaspis 1/4
          -Bric-a-brac-
WINTER LIGHTS-        -moupinense 1/4
          -scopulorum 1/2
```
5ft(1.5m) x 3ft(.9m)(11 yrs) 15F(-9C) VE   Flowers in lax
trusses of 3-4, white with a vivid yellow dorsal blotch. Leaves
deep green with dark red scales below. Wm. Moyles, reg. 1986.

```
                  -williamsianum 1/4
          -Kimberly-
WINTER SNOW-        -fortunei 1/4
          -aberconwayi
```
4ft(1.2m) -10F(-23C) EM   Snowy white trusses in abundance.
Small leaf only slightly longer than wide. Greer, intro. 1988.
Color illus. HG p. 149.

```
                  -catawbiense--La Bar's White
              -unnamed-            1/16
          -unnamed- hybrid-fortunei 1/16
      -Vinecrest- hybrid-wardii 1/4
WINTER  -    -wardii Litiense Group 1/4
WONDERLAND-        -smirnowii 1/8
          -unnamed hybrid-
      -unnamed-        -yakushimanum 1/8
        hybrid-        -maximum 1/8
          -Adele's Yellow-
                  -wardii
```

Buds of strong purplish red open to frilled white flowers with throat of strong purplish red; filaments white. Al Smith cross; Delp raiser.

```
        -mucronulatum 1/2
WINTERSET-
        -unknown 1/2
```
6ft(1.8m) -15F(-26C) VE   Foliage typical of the species; semi-deciduous. Flowers pink, with a yellow-green flare, 2.75in(7cm) wide, in small truss of 4-5. Floriferous.   Dr. E. Brockenbrough raiser; reg. 1976.   C.A. 1975.

WINTERSET WHITE   See WYNTERSET WHITE

```
        -yakushimanum 1/2
WISHMOOR-
        -wardii Litiense Group 1/2
```
3ft(.9m) -5F(-21C) M   Tight, round trusses of 13 flowers, 7-lobed, bell-shaped, orange-red in bud opening very light prim-rose yellow.   Leaves 4in(10cm) long, light indumentum below. Crown Estate, Windsor, reg. 1972.   A.M. 1972; F.C.C. 1987.

```
        -williamsianum 1/2
WISP-
        -irroratum--Spatter Paint 1/2
```
4ft(1.2m) OF(-18C) E 4/4 Fast-growing and compact plant with bronze-colored new growth; leaves mature to a deep fir green. Flowers candy cane pink with darker spotting over entire flower. R. Landregan cross; B. Sheedy raiser; T. Skei, reg. 1987.

WISSAHICKON   Described under ACCLAIM, q.v.

WISTFUL   Described under GYPSY ROVER, q.v.

WITCHERY   Described under CAPTAIN JACK, q.v.

```
                        -arboreum 1/8
                -Doncaster-
        -               -unknown 1/4
     -unnamed-          -neriiflorum 1/8
     - hybrid-Nereid-
WITCH -                 -dichroanthum 1/8
DOCTOR-         - griffithianum 1/8
        -       -Mars-
        -Vulcan-        -unknown
                -griersonianum 1/4
```
4ft(1.2n) OF(-18C) ML 3/3 Heavy spotting over the entire flower. Cardinal red with exceptionally large calyx. Foliage deep fir green.   H. Lem cross; James Elliott, reg. 1974.

```
* * * * * * * * * * * * * * * * * * * * * * * * * * * *
                        -catawbiense 1/4
                -Catawbiense Album-
WIZARD-                 -unknown 1/4
        -       -dichroanthum 1/4
        -Fabia-
                -griersonianum 1/4
```
4ft(1.2m) -10F(-23C) ML 4/3   Flowers apricot and buff with edges of old rose, yellow streaks flaring from throat, large calyx of apricot; trusses hold 14-20. Leaves 5.5in(14cm) long, sharply pointed.   Halfdan Lem, reg. 1962.   A.E. 1959.
OZ   Parentage as above
3ft(.9m) 5F(-15C) M   Flowers carmine rose at edges, shading through lemon yellow to Naples yellow in throat, spotted orange on dorsal lobe; dome-shaped trusses of 11-15. Plant broad as tall, well-branched. Lem cross; Barefield, reg. 1980.
* *

```
                -griffithianum 1/4
        -Alice-
WONDERLAND-     -unknown 1/4
        -auriculatum 1/2
```
Funnel-shaped flowers held in compact trusses of 12, each 3.5in(9cm) across, creamy pink in bud, opening white with a yellowish tinge.   Slocock, reg. 1962.   A.M. Wisley Trials 1958.

```
        -brachyanthum ssp. hypolepidotum 1/2
WOODCHAT-
        -ludlowii 1/2
```
2ft(.6m) OF(-18C) ML   Deep chartreuse yellow, bell-shaped

flowers on long stalks in trusses of 3.   Cox, reg. 1982.   H.C. 1982.

```
                -forrestii Repens Group 1/4
        -Elizabeth-
WOODCOCK-       -griersonianum 1/4
        -hyperythrum 1/2
```
3ft(.9m) -10F(-23C) EM 3/4 Flowers rosy red. Leaves elon-gated; growth compact. RHS Garden, Wisley, reg. 1972. P.C. 1971. A.M. Wisley Trials 1986.

```
                -yakushimanum 1/4
        -unnamed-              -griffithianum 1/16
        - hybrid-       -Queen -
        -       -Britannia-Wilhelmina-unknown 3/16
WOODPECKER-             -Stanley Davies--unknown
        -       -griersonianum 1/4
        -unnamed-       -Lady   -fortunei ssp. discolor
         hybrid-        -Bessborough-           1/16
        -Jalisco-               -campylocarpum Elatum Gp.
         Elect -                               1/16
        -               -dichroanthum 1/16
                -Dido-
                        -decorum 1/16
```
Plant of stiff habit with flowers primrose yellow, fading paler towards edges. Brown blotch in throat.   John Waterer, Sons & Crisp, reg. 1971.

WOODSIDE   Described under THE QUEEN MOTHER, q.v.

```
        -peach-colored hybrid--unknown 9/16
        -       -dichroanthum 1/8
WOODY-  -Dido-
PEACH-  -       -decorum 1/8         -griffithianum 5/32
        -Lem's-         -Beauty of-
        Cameo-  -Norman Gill- Tremough-arboreum 1/32
        -Anna-          -griffithianum  -griffithianum
                -The Hon. Jean Marie de Montague-
                                -unknown
```
3ft(.9m) x 3ft(.9m)(8 yrs) OF(-18C) E   Ball trusses of 12-15; flowers 3.5in(9cm) broad, 5-6 wavy lobes, light orange-yellow to light yellowish pink, with vivid red throat and dorsal spot-ting; buds strong pink. Flat elliptic leaves of dull green, 4.5 in(11.5cm) long.   W. Robertson cross; J. A. Davis, reg. 1987.

```
        -ludlowii 1/2
WREN-
        -keiskei--Yaku Fairy 1/2
```
1ft(.3m) OF(-18C) EM 4/4   Flowers 5-lobed, of clear yellow. Leaves shiny, deep green, scaly below. Habit prostrate, but mound-forming.   Peter A. Cox, cross 1971; reg. 1984.   Color illus. ARS J. 44:1 Winter 1990, p. 2.

WYANDANCH PINK   Parentage unknown
5ft(1.5m) -10F(-23C) M   Flowers bright pink with light spot-ting. Leaves very large, glossy and veined. Slow to set flower buds, but worth waiting for.   Dexter cross.

```
* * * * * * * * * * * * * * * * * * * * * * * * * * * *
                -minus Carolinianum Group 1/4
        -Conestoga-
WYANOKIE-       -racemosum 1/4
        -unknown 1/2
```
3ft(.9m) -15F(-26C) M 3/4   Abundance of small white flowers on a small-leaved bush.   G. Guy Nearing, before 1958.   Color illus. LW pl. 63.
WINDBEAM   Parentage as above
4ft(1.2m) -25F(-32C) EM 4/3   Various forms exist: apricot, pink, or white flower 1in(2.5cm) wide. Small, aromatic foliage; plant half as wide as tall, straggly habit. Nearing, reg. 1958. A.E. 1973.   Color illus. LW pl. 61, 62; VV p. 40; Cox pl. 199.
* *

WYNTERSET WHITE   Parentage unknown
7ft(2.1m) -20F(-29C) EM   Synonyms SNOW, KORDUS WHITE. Flow-ers open as light lavender, aging to greenish white. Red bud scales in winter.   Named by Jay Murray; Wynterset Nurseries, reg. 1990.

X

X-ACTLY GREAT   Described under DOUBLE DARE, q.v.

```
         -cinnabarinum ssp. xanthocodon 1/2
XANROY-
    -cinnabarinum Roylei Group 1/2
Orange-red flowers.   Lord Aberconway, 1946.


                      -adenogynum 1/4
    -Xenosporum (detonsum)-
XENARB-                  -unknown 1/4
    -arboreum 1/2
Flowers are deep cherry color.   E. J. P. Magor, 1926.


       -Helene Schiffner--unknown 1/2
XENIA-
    -fortunei--Sir Charles Butler 1/2
White flowers, crimson lines at base.   Lowinsky.  A.M. 1919.


       -fortunei 1/2
XENOPHILE-     -griersonianum 1/4
    -Tally Ho-
             -facetum (eriogynum) 1/4
Flowers are widely funnel-campanulate, magenta with staining of
darker shade and heavy spotting of deep crimson, held in truss-
es of 12.   R. Strauss, reg. 1964.  A.M. 1964.


              -adenogynum 1/2
XENOSPORUM (detonsum)-
              -unknown 1/2
XENOSPORUM was an old name for  detonsum, formerly called a
species but now considered a hybrid of adenogynum.


XEROX   Parentage unknown
5ft(1.5m)  -5F(-21C)  M   Flowers pink and white.  Dexter cross.
```

                              Y

```
YAKDAY   Described under IRENE BAIN, q.v.


YAKU ANGEL--form of yakushimanum
2.5ft(.75m) -15F(-26C) M   Buds light purplish pink opening to
white flowers with light brown spotting.  Trusses hold 13 to 17.
Dwarf plant, spreading twice as wide as tall; deep green foliage
retained 3 years; new growth with white tomentose.   E. V. Allen
selected; H. E. Greer intro.; reg. 1976.  C.A. 1975.


YAKU CORONET   Described under ELEANOR BEE, q.v


              -wardii ? 1/4
    -Lackamas Cream--Chlorops-
YAKU CREAM-           -vernicosum ? 1/4
    -yakushimanum--Koichiro Wada 1/2
2ft(.6m)  -10F(-23C)  M    Plant a bushy mound, wider than tall;
dark green leaves  4in(10.2cm) long. Mimosa yellow flowers turn
primrose yellow, 2in(5cm) across, campanulate, 6-lobed. Trusses
hold 12.  Benjamin F. Lancaster, reg. 1968.
```

* *

```
              -smirnowii 1/8
    -unnamed-      -Parsons     -catawbiense 1/32
    - hybrid-     -Grandiflorum-
    -King Tut-    -America-         -unknown 3/32
YAKU      -            -dark red hybrid--unknown
DUCHESS-    -catawbiense (red form) 1/4
    -yakushimanum--Koichiro Wada 1/2
4ft(1.2m) -15F(-26C)  M  4/4   Red buds open to flowers of deep
pink with a lighter blotch, unspotted, aging paler pink, 2.25in.
(5.7cm) wide, reverse deep purplish pink; spherical truss of 15.
Medium-sized, indumented leaves.    This cross produced a "Royal
Family" of 6.   A. M. Shammarello, cross 1961; reg. 1977.
JANE MARTIN   Parentage as above
1ft(.3m) x 2ft(.6m)  -10F(-23C)  M   Strong red buds open white
at center, strong pink margins; trusses of 12-16.  Dense growth
habit, spreading.  O. S. Pride cross; E.T. Connors raiser; A. S.
Martin, reg. 1988.  Best Tubbed Plant award, Princeton Ch. 1988.
WHITE BIRD   Parentage as above
2.5ft(.75m)  -25F(-32C)  ML Dwarf plant, as wide as tall; young
leaves have much orange-brown indumentum. Pink buds open white.
Ball-shaped trusses of 14.   O. S. Pride, reg. 1979.
YAKU DUKE   Parentage as above
3ft(.9m) -15F(-26C)  M  4/4     Plant upright, wider than high,
arching branches; narrow olive green leaves,  dark orange-yellow
indumentum; new growth has silvery tomentose.  Flowers open pur-
```

```
plish pink with soft pink throat, aging paler,  tubular funnel-
shaped; spherical trusses of 14.   Shammarello, reg. 1977.
YAKU KING   Parentage as above
3ft(.9m)  -15F(-26C) M 4/4  Strong red buds open to flowers of
deep pink, blotched paler pink, and fading lighter; reverse deep
purplish pink, 2.25in(5.7cm) across;  ball-shaped trusses of 18.
Medium-sized, indumented leaves.   Shammarello, reg. 1977.
YAKU PRINCE   Parentage as above
3ft(.9m)  -15F(-26C) M 4/4   Plant upright and rounded; narrow
olive green leaves with dark orange-yellow indumentum.  Flowers
2.5in((6.4cm) wide, open strong purplish pink with paler blotch,
dark red-orange spotting; exterior strong purplish pink.    Ball-
shaped trusses of 14.    Shammarello, reg. 1979.   Color illus.
ARS Q 27:1 (1973), p. 35;  LW pl. 89.
YAKU PRINCESS   Parentage as above
3ft(.9m)  -15F(-26C) M 4/4   Leaves 3.75in(9.5cm) long, indu-
mented.  Flowers of apple blossom pink with a blush pink blotch
and greenish spots, fading paler; spherical trusses of about 15.
Shammarello, reg. 1977.
YAKU QUEEN   Parentage as above
3ft(.9m)  -15F(-26C) M 4/4   Leaves medium-sized, indumented.
Flowers pale pink with a dim yellow blotch, fading white;  about
16 per truss.  Shammarello, reg. 1977.  C.A. 1981.
```

* *

```
YAKU FAIRY--form of keiskei
1ft(.3m) -10F(-23C)  EM 4/4   Differs only in height and habit
from the type, being very slow-growing and prostrate.  Widely
funnel-shaped, clear yellow flowers, 1.75in(4.5cm) across; small
trusses of 3-5.  Red-tinged new growth.   B. N. Starling,  reg.
1971.  A.M. 1970.


YAKU FANTASIA   Described under ELEANOR BEE, q.v.
```

* *

```
         -smirnowii 1/2
YAKU FRILLS-
         -yakushimanum--Koichiro Wada 1/2
3ft(.9m)  -10F(-23C) ML 4/4  Plant mound-shaped, broader than
high; dark leaves with heavy tan indumentum.  Pink buds open to
frilled white flowers, 2.5in(6.4cm) wide; ball-shaped trusses of
12.  B. F. Lancaster, reg. 1969.
CRETE   Parentage: smirnowii x yakushimanum
7ft(2.1m)  -15F(-26C)  M 4/5 Magenta rose buds open to flowers
light mallow purple, a few ochre spots, aging to white; in dome-
shaped  trusses of 12.  Plant broader than tall; leaves held  4
years, heavily indumented.    Lancaster cross; Leach, reg. 1982.
HEINRICH PEIFFER   (smirnowii x yakushimanum--MIST MAIDEN)
1ft(.3m) x 2ft(.6m)(15 yrs)  -25F(-32C)  ML   Buds of deep pur-
plish pink,  opening lighter, with golden green spotting on dor-
sal lobes, tips, and outside edging.  Leaves heavily indumented;
held 4 years.   Rudy Behring, reg. 1986.
OH MY!   Parentage: smirnowii x yakushimanum
Buds of roseine purple,  opening to light rhodomine purple, fad-
ing to white.  Open-faced flowers; indumented foliage.  Hardy
to -15F(-26C).   Weldon Delp.
SCHAMENEK'S GLOW   Parentage: yakushimanum x smirnowii
3ft(.9m)  -10F(-23C)  ML 4/4   Well-branched plant, wider than
tall; dark glossy leaves have heavy fawn indumentum.  Flowers of
pale pink to white, with a chartreuse blotch;  spherical trusses
of 12.   Joan Schamanek cross; Marie Tietjens, reg. 1976.
```

* *

```
                      -wardii ? 1/8
              -Chlorops-
    -Lackamas Spice-     -vernicosum ? 1/8
YAKU INCENSE-     -diaprepes 1/4
    -yakushimanum 1/2
4ft(1.2m) 5F(-21C)  M  3/3   White flowers with a slight blush
and yellow-green spotting.  No indumentum.   Lancaster.


YAKU KING   Described under YAKU DUCHESS, q.v.
```

* *

```
         -Moser's Maroon--unknown 1/2
YAKU PICOTEE-
         -yakushimanum--Koichiro Wada  1/2
2.5ft(.75m)  -10F(-23C)  M 4/4   Plant wide as high; elliptic,
recurved, dark leaves with matted indumentum beneath.  Flowers
rose Bengal, white at center, rotate-campanulate, 2.75in(7cm)
wide; ball-shaped truss of 15.   B. F. Lancaster, reg. 1969.
LAURAGO   Parentage: MOSER'S MAROON x yakushimanum
```

4ft(1.2m) 5F(-15C) M Flowers of Neyron rose, dark olive green
dorsal spotting, fragrant; conical trusses of 16-18. Plant wide
as tall; leaves have golden buff indumentum. Goheen, reg. 1983.
PEPPERMINT STICK   Parentage: MOSER'S MAROON x yakushimanum
2.5ft(.75m) OF(-18C) ML   Plant wider than tall; narrow leaves
6in(15cm) long, held 4 years. White flowers, rose-rimmed, star-
shaped center; 21 flowers per truss. Benj. Lancaster cross; T.
McGuire, reg. 1973. C.A. 1974.
PERKY   Parentage: MOSER'S MAROON x yakushimanum
Flowers in trusses of 13, 5 wavy-edged lobes, white, with strong
purplish red to pink on edges and reverse; yellow blotch. Plant
2.5ft(.75m). J. May, reg. 1987.
* *

YAKU PRINCE   Described under YAKU DUCHESS, q.v.

YAKU PRINCESS   Described under YAKU DUCHESS, q.v.

YAKU QUEEN   Described under YAKU DUCHESS, q.v.

YAKU SENSATION   Described under ELEANOR BEE, q.v.

```
                      -griersonianum 1/4
            -Rose Splendour-                -ponticum 1/8
YAKU SPLENDOR-              -Purple Splendour-
            -                         -unknown 1/8
            -yakushimanum--Koichiro Wada 1/2
```
1.5ft(.45m) -10F(-23C) M   Globe-shaped dwarf plant as wide as
high, with indumented foliage. Truss of 18 flowers, phlox pink,
paler inside, ruffled, 5-lobed. B. F. Lancaster, reg. 1968.

```
                      -griffithianum 1/8
                -Mars-
            -Vulcan's Flame-   -unknown 1/8
YAKU SUNRISE-              -griersonianum 1/4
            -yakushimanum--Koichiro Wada 1/2
```
2ft(.6m) -10F(-23C) M 4/4 Openly campanulate flowers of rose
madder, edges and the reverse darker, 2.75in(7cm) wide, 5-lobed;
compact trusses of 10. Plant 50% broader than high; deep green,
slightly recurved leaves to 3in(7.6cm) long. B. F. Lancaster,
reg. 1967.

* *
```
                -griffithianum 1/4
            -Mars-
YAKU WARRIOR-       -unknown 1/4
            -yakushimanum 1/2
```
1.5ft(.45m) -10F(-23C) M   Trusses of 18 flowers, Tyrian rose,
lighter center, campanulate, 2in(5cm) wide. Plant broader than
high; recurved leaves, thin indumentum. Lancaster, reg. 1968.
CRIMSON STAIN   Parentage as above
3ft(.9m) -15F(-26C) ML   Purplish red buds open to flowers of
diffused white, then white, with margins purplish red. Corolla
3in(7.6cm) across; ball truss of 14. Leaves olive green, lightly indumented. A. F. Serbin & R. G. Shanklin, reg. 1983.
NORLEN   Parentage as above
5ft(1.5m) -20F(-29C) M   Flowers azalea pink, with peppermint
stripes center of lobes on opening, then fading white, 5 frilled
lobes; truss of 20. Plant broad as tall. H. Hall, reg. 1980.

REDBERTH   Parentage as above, except yakushimanum--Koichiro Wada
3ft(.9m) -5F(-21C) ML Plant upright and well-branched; leaves
variable in size and shape, to 6in(15cm) long. Flowers strong
red, 3in(7.6cm) wide; trusses of 20. Dr. W. Reese, reg. 1976.
BAGOLY'S BEAUTY   Parentage as REDBERTH above
3ft(.9m) -10F(-23C) M   Rose red buds open to flowers roseine
purple; ball truss of 16. Elliptic leaves, pale beige indumentum; plant broad. Bagoly, cross 1966; Marie Tietjens, reg. 1986.
CONNIE YATES   Parentage as REDBERTH, above
3ft(.9m) -10F(-23C) ML 4/4   Flowers 2.5in(6.3cm) wide, dark
pink with white blaze, golden spots; 14-flowered truss. Leaves
medium. Mrs. Yates, reg. 1977. Color illus. LW pl. 103.
CRASWELL   Parentage as REDBERTH, above
3.5ft(1m) -5F(-21C) M Openly funnel-shaped, carmine red flowers, 2in(5cm) across, in trusses of 14. Upright plant, as broad
as tall; leaves held 3 years. Dr. W. Reese, reg. 1977.
EGGERT ROHWER   Parentage as REDBERTH, above
3ft(.9m) x 4ft(1.2m)(12 yrs) -10F(-23C) ML Flowers in trusses
of 14-16, 5 wavy-edged lobes, strong purplish red at the edges,
otherwise strong purplish pink, shading to white in throat, unmarked. H. Hachmann cross; G. Stück, reg. 1988.

EMANUELA   Parentage as REDBERTH, above
2ft(.6m) x 4ft(1.2m) -10F(-23C) ML Funnel-campanulate flowers
of white with strong Neyron rose rims and exterior, dorsal markings of orange buff; truss of 12-16.   Petals very weatherproof.
Dark oblong leaves, recurved rims. Compact bush. Hachmann,
cross 1968; Stück, reg. 1988. Color ill. WS, 1989, p. 148.
FANTASTICA   Parentage as REDBERTH above
Flowers of strong Neyron rose, shading to white in throat, light
spotting of citron green, about 2in(5cm) wide. Elliptic leaves,
to 4.3in(11cm) long, woolly beneath. H. Hachmann, cross 1968;
G. Stück. reg. 1985.   Color illus. ARS J 39:2 (1985), p. 62;
WS, 1989, p. 150.
HACHMANN'S MARLIS   Parentage as REDBERTH, above
2.7ft(.8m) x 4.6ft(1.4m) -10F(-23C) ML   Flowers to 3in(7.5cm)
broad, deep purplish pink lobe margins and exterior, inside white
with medium grayed red dorsal markings; large rounded truss of 14
-17. Elliptic leaves to 5.25in(13.5cm); thin whitish indumentum
beneath. Hachmann, cross 1970; G. Stück, reg. 1988.
HACHMANN'S ROSABELLA   Parentage as REDBERTH, above
3.5ft(1m) x 4ft(1.2m) -10F(-23C) ML Tight truss of 15-18 funnel-shaped flowers, 2.4in(6cm) wide, wavy-edged, strong purplish
red paling almost white in throat, strong yellow-green markings
on dorsal lobe; conspicuous pale yellow anthers. Glossy foliage
of mid-dark green. Hachmann, cross 1973; Stück, reg. 1988.
HACHMANN'S ROSENELFE   Parentage as REDBERTH, above
2ft(.6m) x 3.4ft(1.1m) -10F(-23C) ML Flowers in trusses of 9-
11; buds strong purplish red, opening deep purplish pink; dorsal
lobes are blotched white. Hachmann, cross 1970; Stück, reg.
1988.
KANTILENE   Parentage as REDBERTH, above
3ft(.9m) x 4ft(1.2m) -10F(-23C) ML   Compact trusses of 15-19;
flowers deep purplish pink edged in vivid purplish red; dorsally
spotted white. Compact plant; leaf edges recurved. Hachmann,
cross 1968; G. Stück, reg. 1988. Color illus. WS, 1989, p. 153.
MOUNTAIN STAR   Parentage as REDBERTH, above
Parentage from John Street, 1987. Trusses hold 18-20 flowers,
rose pink, with pale centers and a red-speckled dorsal blotch.
Frederick Street, reg. 1962. A. M. Wisley Trials 1989. Color
illus. JS p. 44.
NINOTSCHKA   Parentage as REDBERTH, above
2ft(.6m) x 3.5ft(1m) -10F(-23C) ML Funnel-campanulate flowers
in trusses of 15-20. Strong purplish red buds and exterior; the
inside strong purplish pink, unmarked, wavy-edged; elliptic foliage, thin brown indumentum. Hachmann cross; Stück, reg. 1988.
PENNYWISE   Parentage as REDBERTH, above
4ft(1.2m) -5F(-21C) ML Cardinal red buds open to carmine rose
flowers, 5 frilled lobes, truss of 17. Plant taller than wide,
leaves held 3 years. Dr. W. Reese, reg. 1977.
SANTANA   Parentage as REDBERTH
3ft(.9m) x 4ft(1.2m) -10F(-23C) L   Flowers in trusses of 11-
14, strong purplish pink, shading white at center, dorsal lobe
spotted medium orange on white base. Buds strong purplish red.
Hans Hachmann, cross 1968; Stück, reg. 1988.
SONATINE   Parentage as REDBERTH, q.v.
2.5ft(.75m) x 4ft(1.2m) -10F(-23C) ML   Flowers in trusses of
12-15, of vivid purplish red, shading to white in throat, dorsal
marks of strong yellow-green. Hachmann cross; Stück, reg. 1988.
Color illus. WS, 1989, p. 160.

POWDER MILL RUN   Parentage: yakushimanum X MARS
3ft(.9m) -5F(-21C) ML   Leaves long and narrow. Flowers deep
pink, shading to white in center; ball-shaped truss of about 24.
Bagoly cross; C. Herbert, reg. 1976.
AVIVA ANN   Parentage as POWDER MILL RUN, above
4.5ft(1.35m)(17yrs) -17F(-27C) ML Flowers of heavy substance,
wavy margins, trusses of 15-19, 6.5in(16.5cm) across. Buds deep
purplish pink opening pale purplish pink, deeper at rims. Plant
dense, twice as broad as tall. A. R. Brooks, reg. 1986.
SEÑORITA CHERE   Parentage as POWDER MILL RUN, above
4ft(1.2m) -15F M 4/4 Red buds open to rose flowers, in very
tight trusses. Plant compact, with heavy green leaves. Attractive the year around. Greer cross; Boltman, intro. 1988.
SWEN   Parentage as POWDER MILL RUN, above
4ft(1.2m) -10F(-23C) M Flowers of heavy substance, of Tyrian
purple, lighter at center, white flare, funnel-shaped, 2.75in(7
cm) wide; ball truss of 15. Plant as broad as high; leaves have
reddish brown indumentum. Willard Swenson cross; Childers,
reg. 1978.
* *

YAKUSHI MAIDEN   Described under GYPSY ROVER, q.v.

```
                  -cinnabarinum Roylei Group 1/4
       -Lady Chamberlain-            -cinnabarinum 3/8
       -                    -Royal  Flush-
YAMA-                    (orange form)-maddenii 1/8
       -              -yunnanense 1/4
       -Yunncinn-
                  -cinnabarinum
Yellow-tinged, plum-colored flowers.   Lord Aberconway, 1946.
```

```
                  -campylocarpum 1/4
       -Letty Edwards-
YAMINA-                    -fortunei 3/4
       -fortunei
Flowers uranium green, feathered red on the upper lobe.     A. J.
Teese, Australia, reg. 1964.
```

YANGTZE BEND--form of uvarifolium F 10639
4ft(1.2m) 5F(-15C) EM 3/2 Leaves 9in(23cm) long, with plastered whitish indumentum below.   Rose pink flowers blotched and
spotted in Indian lake red, 2.5in(6.4cm) across, funnel-campanulate; large compact trusses of 26.   RBG, Edinburgh, reg. 1966.
A.M. 1965.

```
            -yakushimanum 1/2
YASHMAK-
            -campylocarpum 1/2
Flowers moderate purplish pink with blotching and spotting of deep
currant red.   Collingwood Ingram, reg. 1972.
```

```
                  -catawbiense (red form) 1/2
YATES' ALBINO-    -griffithianum 1/4
                  -Mars-
                        -unknown 1/4
4ft(1.2m) -10F(-23C) ML  Rounded plant, as wide as tall, with
arching branches; leaves apple green 5.25in(13.3cm) long, held 2
years. Lax trusses of about 11 white flowers, 2.7in(7cm) broad,
blotch of medium apple green.  Mrs. Yates, reg. 1976.
```

* *

```
                        -decorum ? 1/8
                  -Caroline-
            -Mrs. H. R.-        -brachycarpum ? 1/8
            - Yates    -unknown 1/4
YATES' BEST-
            -yakushimanum--Koichiro Wada 1/2
```
3ft(.9m) -15F(-26C) ML   Buds of rose opening to small pink
flowers, fading to white, of heavy substance; ball-shaped truss
of 12. Rounded plant as wide as high, arching branches; medium-
sized leaves, brownish indumentum.   H. Yates, cross 1962; Mrs.
Yates, reg. 1977.
YATES' SECOND BEST   Parentage as above
3ft(.9m) -15F(-26C) ML Plant rounded, wider than tall; glossy
leaves 4.75in(12cm) long, grayed orange indumentum below; new
growth has orange-brown tomentum. Buds rose, opening to frilled
pink flowers, aging white, yellow dorsal spotting. Ball trusses
of 11. H. Yates cross; Mrs. Yates, reg. 1977.
* *

```
                        -catawbiense 1/4
            -Mrs. Charles S. Sargent-
YATES' HAZEL-                 -unknown 1/4
            -vernicosum 1/2
```
5ft(1.5m) -20F(-29C) ML Flower of heavy substance, 3in(7.6cm)
across, 6-lobed, of rhodamine pink with grayed yellow blotch;
spherical trusses hold 12. Plant upright, as wide as tall; foliage 5.5in(14cm) long, elliptic. Mrs. Yates, reg. 1977.

```
                        -catawbiense, red form 1/8
            -unnamed hybrid-    -griffithianum 1/16
            -                    -Mars-
      -unnamed-              -unknown 1/4
      - hybrid-              -thomsonii 1/16
      -     -             -Bagshot Ruby-
YATES'-     -Princess-          -unknown
IRENE -     Elizabeth-unknown
      -                    -catawbiense v. album Glass--Catalgla
      -     -unnamed hybrid-                            1/8
      -     -          -fortunei 1/8
      -Big-          -decorum ? 1/16
      Savage-    -Caroline-
            -Cadis-       -brachycarpum ? 1/16
                  -fortunei ssp. discolor 1/8
```

4.5ft(1.35m) x 2ft(.6m)(11 yrs) -5F(-21C) ML   Flowers in conical trusses of 18 to 20, strong purplish red; truss 6in(15.2cm)
wide. Upright, dense growth; floriferous.   M. Yates cross; C.
Yates, reg. 1989.

```
                        -griersonianum 1/8
            -Vulcan's Flame-       -griffithianum 3/16
      -Joe Kruson-            -Mars-
YATES'-    -Mars (as above)    -unknown 7/16
MONICA-                   -catawbiense 1/4
      -Red Pond (Stokes)-
                  -unknown
```
2.3ft(6.9m) x 3.6ft(1.08m)(17 yrs) -25F(-32C) ML Flowers wavy-
edged, strong red, funnel-shaped, 2.5in(6.4cm) wide; ball truss
of 16. Dull green, elliptic leaves 5in(12.7cm) long. Floriferous. H. Yates, cross 1970; C. Yates, reg. 1988.

```
                        -catawbiense 1/4
            -Catawbiense Grandiflorum-
YATES' PURPLE-               -unknown 1/2
            -                 -ponticum 1/4
            -Purple Splendour-
                  -unknown
```
3ft(.9m) -5F(-21C) ML   Imperial purple flowers fading light-
er, with plum purple blotch and spotting, to 2.5in(6.4cm) wide;
dome-shaped trusses of 10-13. Broad, upright plant; elliptical
leaves held 2 years. Yates cross, 1965; Mrs. Yates, reg. 1979.

YATES' RED   Described under MARY YATES, q.v.

YATES' SECOND BEST   Described under YATES' BEST, q.v.

```
                  -Catalgla--catawbiense var. album Glass 1/4
      -unnamed-        -wardii 3/8
      - hybrid-unnamed-
YATES' TREENA-        hybrid-unknown 1/8
      -        -wardii
      -unnamed-
            hybrid-yakushimanum 1/4
```
3ft(.9m) -10F(-23C) ML   Buds of rose, shaded yellow, open to
canary yellow flowers, with dorsal rays of burgundy spots, to 3
in(7.6cm) across, 5 wavy-frilled lobes, domed truss of 12 to 14.
Upright, well-branched plant, wider than tall; cyprus green foliage to 4in(10.2cm), held 2 years. H. Yates cross; Mrs. Yates,
reg. 1984.

YATES' VELVET CHARM   Described under RALPH PAPE, q.v.

```
            -catawbiense var. album Glass--Catalgla 1/4
      -unnamed-
YATES' YELLOW- hybrid-wardii 1/4          -decorum ? 1/16
RIBBONS    -                 -Caroline-
      -       -Mrs. H. R. Yates-     -brachycarpum ? 1/16
      -Yates'-            -unknown 1/8
      Best -yakushimanum--Koichiro Wada 1/4
```
3.5ft(1.05m) x 2.5ft(.75m)(11 yrs) -15F(-26C) L Buds of deep
pink open to widely campanulate flowers of pale greenish yellow,
throat slightly darker; lax ball trusses of 16. Plant upright;
leaves held 3 years. M. Yates cross; C. Yates, reg. 1989.

```
                        -catawbiense 1/2
YEARS OF PEACE---MRS. C. S. SARGENT, selfed-
                        -unknown 1/2
```
5ft(1.5m) -15F(-26C) M   Formerly known as JOHN FOSTER DULLES.
Hardy, sun-tolerant flowers of pink, sparsely spotted on upper
petals, 3in(7.6cm) broad, in dome-shaped trusses of 6-10. Plant
vigorous and upright, with glossy, dark green foliage.   E. J.
Mezitt, Weston Nurseries, reg. 1981.

```
                  -yakushimanum 1/4
            -Serendipity-
YELLGREN ICE-        -aureum (chrysanthum) 1/4
            -Pygmy Red--unknown 1/2
```
Buds of moderate reddish orange and pale greenish yellow opening
to flowers pale greenish yellow; dorsal spots strong yellow-
green; throat light greenish yellow.   W. Delp.

```
            -Cunningham's Sulphur--form of caucasicum ? 1/2
YELLOW BELLS-        -campylocarpum 1/4
            -Moonstone-
                  -williamsianum 1/4
```
2ft(.6m) -5F(-21C) E   Glossy, waxen leaves 2.5in(6.4cm) long

on a shrub as wide as tall. Bell-shaped, ruffled, chrome yellow
flowers 1.5in(3.8cm) across, in trusses of 10-12.   Don Newkirk
cross; B. F. Lancaster intro.; reg. 1967.

* *
```
              -Ostbo's Yellow--unknown 3/4
YELLOW BELLY-      -brachycarpum 1/4
           -Bristol Cream-
                          -unknown
```
Buds of cardinal red open to frilled flowers yellowish white;
light greenish yellow flare; dorsal spots strong yellow-green.
W. Delp.
ZOOT SUIT Parentage as above
Buds of strong reds, deep pinks and light greenish yellows open
to flowers of pale yellow-green edged with deep pink.   W. Delp.
* *

YELLOW BUNTING--form of fletcherianum
2.5ft(.75m) 5F(-15C) EM 4/4   Form is typical of the species
with primrose yellow flowers 1.75in(4.5cm) wide, foliage of warm
russet in winter. Compact shrub with oblong-lanceolate leaves,
2in(5cm) long. Formerly known as "Rock's valentinianum", its
correct status was determined by H. H. Davidian. Raised from a
cutting of plant at RBG, Edinburgh, by E. H. & P. A. Cox, reg.
1965. A.M. 1964.

```
                  -brachycarpum 1/8
         -unn.-      -wardii 3/32
         -hyb.-Crest-          -fortunei ssp. discolor 7/64
-unn.-      -Lady
-hyb.-          Bessborough-campylocarpum Elatum Gp. 3/64
 -   -                   -catawbiense var. album 1/16
 -   -   -unnamed-      -wardii
 -   -   -hybrid -Crest-
YELLOW-   -Monte-          -Lady Bessborough (as above)
CHERUB-    Carlo-      -aureum (chrysanthum) 3/16
 -        -unnamed hybrid-
 -                      -campylocarpum 1/16
 -                  -aureum (chrysanthum)
 -        -unnamed hybrid-
 -        -          -maximum 1/8
 -unnamed-              -neriiflorum 1/32
  hybrid-          -Nereid-
 -          -Phyllis Ballard-      -dichroanthum 1/32
 -        -unnamed-      -fortunei ssp. discolor
            hybrid-
                -catawbiense var. album--Clark's White 1/8
```
Jasper red and azalea pink buds open to flowers of light green-
ish yellow, with strong greenish yellow dorsal spotting; reverse
of petals veined with strong red.   Weldon Delp.

YELLOW CREEK   Described under INDIAN PENNY, q.v.

```
              -catawbiense var. album Glass--Catalgla 1/8
         -Gosh-          -decorum ? 1/8
         -Darn-      -Caroline-
-All -   -Mrs. H. R. Yates-      -brachycarpum 1/8
-East-          -unknown 1/8
 -   -          -Mrs. H. R. Yates (as above)
 -   -unnamed hybrid-
YELLOW-          -wardii 1/8
CRAZE-          -dichroanthum 1/8
 -              -Fabia-
 -      -unnamed hybrid-      -griersonianum 1/8
 -      -          -yakushimanum 1/8
-Fairweather-          -dichroanthum
 -              -Fabia-
         -Hello Dolly-      -griersonianum
                  -smirnowii 1/8
```
Buds of currant and vivid red, yellowish pink and primrose
yellow, open to pale yellow-green; primrose yellow on underside
of petals; strong greenish yellow dorsal spots.   W. Delp.

YELLOW DATE   Described under BETTY WHITE, q.v.

YELLOW DREAM   Described under MELLOW GOLD, q.v.

```
                  -minus Carolinianum Group 1/8
              -Conestoga-
         -Wyanokie-      -racemosum 1/8
YELLOW EYE-      -unknown 3/4
         -unknown
```

4ft(1.2m) -20F(-28C) EM   Large, cream-colored flowers with a
striking yellow flare: garden effect yellow; spherical trusses
on an upright, vigorous plant. New growth reddish. G. G. Nearing cross; Dr. A. Fitzburgh raiser.

YELLOW FELLOW--form of mekongense K W 406
4ft(1.2m) 5F(-15C) M 2/2   A deciduous shrub, with immature
leaves, hairy and densely scaly. Fine yellow flowers held in
groups of 3-5. Kingdon Ward collector; Col. S. R. Clarke raiser; R. N. S. Clarke, reg. 1979. A.M. 1979.

```
                  -racemosum 1/4
     -Mary Fleming-
YELLOW-          -keiskei 1/4
FEVER -          -keiskei, dwarf form 1/4
     -Banana Boat-
                  -dauricum--Arctic Pearl 1/4
```
2.5ft(.75m) high x 3ft(.9m) -10F(-23C) Flowers light greenish
yellow, tinged light pink changing to light greenish yellow,
heavily tinged moderate purplish pink. Leaves scaly both sides,
dull green. Dense habit. G. D. Lewis, cross 1976; reg. 1988.

YELLOW GARLAND--form of xanthostephanum F 21707
4ft(1.2m) 15F(-10C) EM 3/3   Plant may grow to 9ft(2.7m);
leaves 1.5in(3.8cm) long, silvery beneath. Flowers aureolin
yellow, 1in(2.5cm) wide, campanulate; trusses hold 4-8. Color
may vary between plants. G. Forrest collector; Crown Estate,
Windsor, reg. 1962. A.M. 1961.

YELLOW GATE   Parentage unknown; elepidote
5.5ft(1.65m) high x 8ft(2.4m)(25 yrs) Flowers in flat truss
of 12, open light yellow-green from buds deep purplish pink.
Growth habit spreading, very dense. Cowles cross; Heritage
Plantation of Sandwich, reg. 1989.

* *
```
                          -dichroanthum 3/16
                  -Goldsworth-
         -Tortoiseshell- Orange  -fortunei ssp. discolor
         - Wonder  -              1/8
         -              -griersonianum 3/16
   -Apricot-              -griffithianum 3/16
   - Gold -          -Loderi-
   -   -   -Albatross-      -fortunei 1/32
   -   -Cup-      -fortunei ssp. discolor
   -   Day-      -elliottii 1/16
YELLOW-   -Fusilier-
GOLD -          -griersonianum
   -          -dichroanthum
   -   -Dido-
   -   -   -decorum 1/8          -griffithianum
   -Lem's-          -Beauty of-
    Cameo-      -Norman Gill- Tremough-arboreum 1/32
      -Anna-      -          -griffithianum
         -Jean Marie de Montague-      -griffithianum
                      -unknown 1/16
```
Flowers 13-15 per truss, funnel-shaped, 5-lobed, light yellowish
pink. Shrub 3.5ft(1m) x 3.5ft. K. van de Ven, Australia, cross
1979; Olinda Nursery, reg. 1986.
MARIA'S CHOICE   Parentage as above
Flowers are double, funnel-shaped, light yellow; lobes moderate
yellowish pink. Trusses of 15-18. Shrub 3.5ft(1.0m).   K. van
de Ven, reg. 1986.
* *

```
                  -sulfureum 1/2
YELLOW HAMMER-
              -flavidum 1/2
```
4ft(1.2m) 5F(-15C) EM 4/3 Very deep yellow flowers, .5in
(1.27cm) wide, tubular campanulate; 3-flowered trusses. Very
floriferous; may bloom again in autumn. Plant upright, open;
small, light green, scaly leaves. One of few yellows that does
well in sunny locations. J. C. Williams, about 1931; reg. 1958.
Color illus. Cox pl. 201; JS p. 81.

YELLOW JACKET   Described under DEL, q.v.

YELLOW PAGES   Parentage unknown
4ft(1.2m) x 6ft(1.8m)(15 yrs) 0F(-18C) M   Flowers in domed
trusses of 13-15, 5 wavy-edged lobes, brilliant yellow fading
lighter. Many characteristics of lacteum. Wm. Whitney cross.

1973; Briggs Nursery, reg. 1989.

YELLOW PETTICOATS   Described under FRILLED PETTICOATS, q.v.

YELLOW PIPPIN   Described under ORANGE MARMALADE, q.v.

```
                      -wardii 3/8
              -Crest-            -fortunei ssp. discolor 1/8
              -    -Lady Bessborough-
              -                  -campylocarpum Elatum 1/8
YELLOW ROLLS-       -wardii           -griffithianum
  ROYCE      -    -Idealist-      -Kewense-        3/64
             -    -      -Aurora-      -fortunei 5/64
            -Odee -    -Naomi-    -thomsonii 1/32
            Wright-         -fortunei
                 -                  -George-griffithianum
                 -        -Mrs. Lindsay- Hardy-
                 -        -  Smith   -    -catawbiense
                 -Mrs. Betty-     Duchess of      1/32
                   Robertson-         Edinburgh--unknown
                       -           -campylocarpum      1/8
                       -unnamed-           1/16
                       hybrid-unknown
Rich yellow contrasts with bright green.  Geo. Clarke cross.
```

```
                      -wardii 1/8      -griffithianum
              -Idealist-          -Kewense-      9/128
              -     -      -Aurora-      -fortunei
         -unnamed-     -Naomi-    -thomsonii 1/64
         - hybrid-              -fortunei
         -      -    -wardii
        -unnamed-    -Hawk-      -fortunei ssp. discolor
        - hybrid-          -Lady Bess-
        -      -          borough-campylocarpum Elatum 5/32
        -      -    -campylocarpum 1/8
YELLOW-       -Phyrne-      -griffithianum
  SALLY-       -Loderi-
        -               -fortunei 13/128
        -               -fortunei ssp. discolor 5/32
        -    -Lady Bessborough-
        -Jalisco-             -campylocarpum Elatum Group
             -    -dichroanthum 1/8
             -Dido-
                 -decorum 1/8
Very light yellow, tinged pale rose.  Waterer, Crisp, reg. 1975.
```

* *
```
                   -aberconwayi 1/2
YELLOW-unnamed hybrid-      -yakushimanum--Koichiro Wada 1/4
SAUCER  (selfed)    -unnamed-
                    hybrid-      -dichroanthum 1/8
                      -Fabia-
                          -griersonianum 1/8
```
4ft(1.2m) OF(-18C) M   Newly opened flowers mottled flame
orange, turning aureolin yellow with lemon yellow throat, small
red dorsal spot; corolla of good substance, rather flat, 3in.
(7.6cm) wide; truss of 8. Broad plant.   C. Smith, reg. 1982.
GRANDMA'S SAUCER   Parentage as above.
3ft(.9m) -5F(-21C) M 3/3   Sibling to the above. Flattened
flowers of deep yellow. Open habit; small leaves. Cross 1972.
* *

YELLOW SPRING   Described under MARY FLEMING, q.v.

* *
```
                      -maximum 1/4
              -unnamed hybrid-
              -            -vernicosum (18139) 1/8
     -Masterblend-        -aureum (chrysanthum) 3/16
     -        -unnamed hybrid-
     -                    -maximum
YELLOW -        -brachycarpum 1/8
STREAKER-    -unnamed-    -wardii 3/32
     -    - hybrid-Crest-        -fortunei ssp. discolor
     -    -          -Lady            3/64
     -Marypat-      Bessborough-campylocarpum Elatum
     -        -catawbiense v. album      3/64
     -    -unnamed-            1/16
     -Monte- hybrid-Crest (as above)
     Carlo-    -aureum (chrysanthum)
         -unnamed-
         hybrid-campylocarpum 1/16
```

Flowers creamy yellow with light greenish yellow throat. Delp.
HANGUP   Parentage as above
Buds of deep red and strong purplish red open to flowers light
purplish pink, lightly edged with strong purplish red; throat of
light yellow and deep red.   W. Delp.
* *

```
         -dichroanthum ssp. scyphocalyx 1/2
YELLOW-    -aureum (chrysanthum) 1/4
 WOLF -unnamed-        -sanguineum ssp. didymum 1/16
      hybrid-    -Rubina-    -griersonianum 3/32
         -      -    -Tally Ho-
         -unnamed-        -facetum (eriogynum) 1/32
         hybrid-dichroanthum 1/16
         -Fabia-
             -griersonianum
```
Semi-dwarf plant 2ft(.6m) tall; dark green leaves to 3in(7.6cm)
long, paler below. Fire red buds; flowers orange buff, stained
peach on edges and reverse, 2in(5cm) wide. Flat trusses of 5-7.
J. A. Witt, University of Washington Arboretum, reg. 1977.

```
         -forrestii Repens Group 1/2
YEOMAN-    -haematodes 1/4
     -Choremia-
         -arboreum 1/4
```
1.5ft(.45m) OF(-18C) EM 3/3   A small sturdy plant with small
deep green leaves; many bright red, waxy, bell-shaped flowers.
Lord Aberconway. A.M. 1947.

```
                      -Pygmalion--unknown
              -unnamed hybrid-        1/16
              -Weldy-      -haematodes 1/16
     -unnamed hybrid-    -yakushimanum, Exbury form 1/8
YIPPEE!-        -maximum, Jackson Center, PA, white form
     -aureum (chrysanthum) 1/2            1/4
```
Buds a mixture of light yellowish pink, pale orange-yellow, can-
ary yellow and pale greenish yellow, opening to a very frilled
yellowish white flower, with a throat of light yellow-green and
pale greenish yellow. Flowers 7-lobed.   W. Delp.

YO YO   Parentage unknown
1.5ft(.45m) -5F(-21C) EM 3/4   Small foliage; flowers are red
with dull purple spotting; flat trusses hold 8.   Whitney cross;
Sather, reg. 1976.

```
             -souliei 1/16
         -Soulbut-
     -Vanessa-    -Sir Charles Butler--fortunei
     -Eudora-    -                    1/16
YOLANDE-    -    -griersonianum 1/8
     -    -facetum (eriogynum) 1/4
     -dichroanthum ssp. scyphocalyx 1/2
```
A hybrid with rose-colored flowers.   Lord Aberconway, 1941.

* *
```
                      -catawbiense
              -Parsons Grandiflorum-    3/16
         -America-            -unknown
         -        -dark red hybrid--unknown 5/16
     -AA 17-        -catawbiense
YOO      -    -Ann Rutledge-
HOO!---MATTHEW -     .     -unknown
  WELDON F2-            -caucasicum 3/16
     -        -Jacksonii-    -caucasicum
     -Goldsworth-    -Nobleanum-
         Yellow  -campylocarpum 1/4 -arboreum 1/16
```
Buds blend ruby red, deep purplish red, and strong purplish red,
opening to frilled flowers of moderate and strong purplish red,
deep and pale purplish pinks. Dorsal spots ruby red.   W. Delp.
DOUBLE TAKE   Parentage as above
Buds of China rose and spirea red open to frilled white flowers,
with light yellowish green flare; dorsal spotting vivid yellow-
green and moderate reddish orange; magenta rose anthers.   Delp.
* *

YOU BEAUT   Described under MELBA, q.v.

YOU BETCHA!   Described under INNER SPIRIT, q.v.

```
                   -cinnabarinum Roylei Group 1/4
         -Lady Chamberlain-
YOUNG    -                     -cinnabarinum 1/8
CHAMBERLAIN-            -Royal Flush-
         -yunnanense 1/2            -
                                   -maddenii 1/8
```
Trusses of 7-9 flowers, 3in(7.6cm) wide, 5-lobed, white suffused
pink with slight brown spotting on reverse; truss pendant, like
LADY CHAMBERLAIN. Elliptical leaves, 3.3in(8.5cm) long. D. B.
Fox, reg. 1983.

```
                        -smirnowii 1/4
         -unnamed hybrid-            -fortunei ssp. discolor 1/8
YOURS-              -Lady        -
TRULY-             Bessborough-campylocarpum Elatum Group 1/8
     -yakushimanum--Ken Janeck 1/2
```
Buds a blend of strong and vivid purplish reds, deep and strong
purplish pink opening to frilled flowers of pale purplish pink;
strong greenish yellow dorsal spots. Foliage indumented. Al
Smith cross; W. Delp raiser.

YOUTHFUL SIN   Described under YUNNCINN, q.v.

YO-YO   Parentage unknown
1.5ft(.45m) -5F(-21C) EM 3/4   Red flowers, to 1.25in(3cm)
across, dorsal lobe spotted dull purple; flat trusses hold about
8. Small leaves.   William Whitney cross; A. Sather, reg. 1976.

```
         -cinnabarinum 3/4
YUCABA-           -yunnanense 1/4
      -Yunncinn-
                 -cinnabarinum
```
Plum-colored flowers.   Lord Aberconway, 1946.

YUCONDUS--form of erythrocalyx F 21741; now called a hybrid,
          perhaps of wardii X selense
4ft(1.2m) -5F(-21C) E-M 2/3   Small trusses of flowers deep
Neyron rose in bud, fading when open to almost white, variably
stained and suffused by light rose pinks, broadly funnel-campanulate, 2in(5cm) wide. Elliptic, dark green leaves tend to conceal flowers. G. Forrest collector; Col. S. R. Clarke raiser;
R. N. S. Clarke, reg. 1979.   A.M. 1979.

YUKON   Described under HUDSON BAY, q.v.

YUM YUM--form of tsariense L & S 2858
2ft(.6m) OF(-18C) M 3/5   Plant compact; leaves 1.5in(3.8cm)
long, with persistent cinnamon brown indumentum beneath. Carmine
buds open to white flowers, blushed phlox pink, 1.75in(3.8cm)
wide, in trusses of 3-4. Ludlow & Sherriff collectors; Mrs.
R. M. Harrison, reg. 1965.   A.M. 1964.

* *
         -yunnanense 1/2
YUNNCINN-
         -cinnabarinum 1/2
Flowers violet rose, darker on outside; interior reddish brown.
J. C. Williams also made this cross, earlier.   E. J. P. Magor,
intro. 1924.
YOUTHFUL SIN   Parentage as above, except reversed
Flower rhodamine purple. Lord Aberconway, reg. 1962. A.M. 1960
* *

YUPPIE POWER   Described under ALMOND CREAM, q.v.

* *
         -griffithianum 5/8
         -Kewense-
     -Aurora-   -fortunei 1/8
YVONNE-   -thomsonii 1/4
      -griffithianum
```
6ft(1.8m) 5F(-15C) EM 3/3 A tall, compact bush; flat trusses
of very large flowers, widely funnel-shaped, white blushed pink,
having a translucent quality. One of the earliest crosses, LR
112, it was rediscovered after World War II.   Rothschild, 1925.
YVONNE DAWN   Parentage as above
6ft(1.8m) 5F(-15C) M 3/3   Latest to flower and the finest of
this grex. Very large flowers, of heavy substance, flesh pink
fading almost white with age.   L. de Rothschild.
YVONNE OPALINE   Parentage as above
6ft(1.8m) 5F(-15C) M 3/3   Very large, openly funnel-shaped
flowers. Buds of deep pink open to flowers pale rose inside,

deeper rose reverse.   Rothschild. A.M. 1931. Color illus. ARS
J 36:4 (1982), p. 135.
YVONNE PEARL   Parentage as above
6ft(1.8m) 5F(-15C) M 3/3   Similar to others of this group.
Flowers of good substance, pale pearly pink.   Rothschild, 1925.
YVONNE PRIDE   Parentage as above
6ft(1.8m) 5F(-15C) M 3/3   Flowers like very large funnels, 5
in(12.7cm) wide, pale pink fading almost white.   Tall, compact
plant. Rothschild. A.M. 1948.
* * * * * * * * * * * * * * * * * * * * * * * * * * * * *

YVONNE DAVIES   Described under CORMID, q.v.

                            Z

```
              -concinnum 1/4
      -Daphne-
ZAMPA-   -augustinii 1/4
      -               -neriiflorum 1/4
      -F. C. Puddle-
                   -griersonianum 1/4
```
A red-flowered hybrid.   Lord Aberconway, 1941.

```
         -dichroanthum 1/2
ZANNA-
     -catawbiense var. compactum ? 1/2
```
Orange-pink flowers.   Haworth-Booth, reg. 1962.

```
         -catacosmum 1/2
ZARIE-
     -meddianum 1/2
```
Red flowers.   J. B. Stevenson cross, 1939; intro. 1951.

```
                   -souliei 1/4
         -Rosy Morn-   -griffithianum 1/8
ZELIA   -   -Loderi-
PLUMECOCQ-   -fortunei 1/8
         -       -wardii 1/4
         -Crest-   -fortunei ssp. discolor 1/8
                -Lady Bessborough-
                         -campylocarpum Elatum Group 1/8
```
Large, open, saucer-like flowers of yellow with a pink blush, on
tall, handsome trusses.   Foliage and plant habit like CREST; the
flowers resemble souliei.   Named after Mme. Plumecocq, sponsor,
the Valenciennes International Flower Show, 1962.   E. de Roth-
schild, reg. 1968.   Color illus. ARS J (1982), p. 139.

ZELLA   Parentage unknown
A parent of SARAH HARDY.   Large, LODERI-type flowers, pale shell
pink, fading later; well-shaped, compact trusses.   Collingwood
Ingram, reg. 1964.   P.C. 1964.

```
                          -griffithianum 1/4
              -George Hardy-
      -Mrs. Lindsay Smith-   -catawbiense 1/8
      -              -Duchess of Edinburgh--unknown 1/4
ZELLINDO-   -griffithianum
      -        -Isabella-
      -Muy Lindo-   -auriculatum 1/8
      -              -decorum 1/8
        -unnamed hybrid-
                      -souliei 1/8
```
No colors or other description given in published registration.
Collingwood Ingram,  reg. 1972.

```
                       -campylocarpum Elatum Group 1/16
              -Penjerrick-
      -Amaura-   -griffithianum 1/16
      -Eros-   -griersonianum 5/8
ZENOBIA-   -griersonianum
      -            -sanguineum ssp. didymum 1/4
      -Arthur Osborn-
                 -griersonianum
```
A hybrid with deep red flowers. Lord Aberconway, 1941.

```
                       -caucasicum 1/8
              -Boule de Neige-   -catawbiense
      -Besse Howells-   -unnamed hybrid- 7/16
ZESTY-   -catawbiense, red form   -unknown 3/16
     -      -haematodes 1/4
     -China Boy-   -catawbiense
            -red catawbiense hybrid-
                          -unknown
```
```

Buds of ruby red and strong and vivid purplish reds open to
frilled flowers strong and vivid purplish red, deep and pale
purplish pinks; ruby red dorsal spots. W. Delp.

```
                  -smirnowii 1/4
     -unknown hybrid-
ZIP-                  -bureavii 1/4
TIP-    -yakushimanum 1/4
    -Bob-                              -catawbiense 1/32
    As-              -Parsons Grandiflorum-
      -       -America-              -unknown 1/8
      -Cindy-     -dark red hybrid--unknown
     Lou -              -griffithianum 1/32
          -              -Mars-
          -unnamed hybrid-   -unknown
                  -catawbiense var. rubrum 1/16
```

Buds of dark red and strong purplish red opening to a very pale
purple star edged in strong purplish red and strong reddish purple; greenish yellow spots.   Al Smith cross; W. Delp raiser.

* *
```
                  -catawbiense 1/2
ZIPPETY---SEFTON F2-
                  -unknown 1/2
```
Frilled flower rose red, white flare, dark maroon blotch. Delp.
PINK MANIA   Parentage as above
Buds of strong purplish red and strong reddish purple; flowers
strong reddish purple and mallow purple; dorsal spots ruby red
on 3 lobes. W. Delp.
REAL SCOOP   Parentage as above
Buds of dark red and deep red open to frilled flowers of light
reddish purple and moderate purplish pink; a white flare; ruby
red dorsal spots on 3 lobes. W. Delp.
* *

ZOË GRAVES   Parentage unknown; elepidote
10ft(3.0m) x 6ft(1.8m)(25 yrs) -15F(-26C) M   Broadly funnel-
shaped flowers of 7 wavy-edged lobes, 3.3in(8cm) wide, light
rose purple with deep purplish pink rims, a dark red blotch;
domed truss of 10. Dull green convex leaves.   C. Dexter cross;
Winterthur Museum & Gardens, reg. 1987.

ZOOT SUIT   Described under YELLOW BELLY, q.v.

```
    -souliei 1/2
ZORA-
    -wardii var. puralbum 1/2
```
White flowers.   J. B. Stevenson, cross 1934; intro. 1951.

```
          -yakushimanum--Koichiro Wada 1/4
     -Frango-          -arboreum ssp. nilagiricum 1/8
     -        -Noyo Chief-
ZORBA-          -unknown 1/8
     -      -yakushimanum 1/4
     -Tracigo-
          -sperabile 1/4
```
3ft(.9m) x 5ft(1.5m)(15 yrs) 5F(-15C) EM   Flowers in lax
trusses of 10-12 with 5 very wavy-edged lobes, vivid red in
bud, opening deep pink outside and pale purplish pink
inside. L. W. Bulgin intro.; D. W. Goheen cross; reg. 1989.

* *
```
                  -griffithianum 1/8
          -George Hardy-
     -Mrs. Lindsay Smith-          -catawbiense 1/8
ZUIDERZEE  -          -Duchess of Edinburgh--unknown 1/2
(ZUYDERZEE)-          -campylocarpum 1/4
     -unnamed hybrid-
          -unknown
```
3ft(.9m) 5F(-15C) M 3/3   Grex named for sea off north Hol-
land. Compact shrub, wider than tall; leaves very light green,
and easy to burn. Pale yellow campanulate flowers, spotted with
red. Shade required. M. Koster. A.M. 1936.
ADRIAAN KOSTER   Parentage as above
4ft(1.2m) -5F(-21C) M   Flowers of creamy white with a yellow
center, overlaid with red spotting; compact trusses. Vigorous
plant; veined leaves.   A parent of MOONSHINE, q.v. M. Koster,
1920. A.M. 1935.
DIANE   Parentage as above
6ft(1.8m) -5F(-21C) EM 3/2   Crowded trusses of 8 to 10 large
cream yellow flowers flushed primrose yellow. Upright, vigorous

plant; prefers shade. Glossy green leaves. A parent of PHILLIS
KORN, ROTHENBERG, VISCY. M. Koster, 1920. A.M. Wisley Trials
1948.   Color illus. JS p. 88.
GREENFINCH Parentage as above.   C. Ingram cross, 1945.
HARVEST MOON Parentage as above
4ft(1.2m) -5F(-21C) M 3/3   Interesting foliage, 4in(10.2cm)
long, glossy yellowish green, heavily textured. Flowers of pale
lemon or creamy yellow, reddish flare; compact trusses of 10-12.
A parent of SIMONA, q.v. M. Koster. A.M. 1948. Color illus.
F p. 47; JS p. 105; VV p. 102.
JERSEY CREAM   Parentage as above
Compact, rounded trusses of funnel-shaped, cream-colored flowers
with crimson marks. J. J. Crosfield. A.M. 1939.
MRS. BETTY ROBERTSON   Parentage as above
4ft(1.2m) -5F(-21C) M 3/3   Medium-sized, creamy yellow flowers, red blotch; dome-shaped trusses. Compact, spreading plant;
rough-textured leaves 4in(10cm) long.   Parent of VIRGINIA RICH-
ARDS, ODEE WRIGHT. M. Koster. Color ill. JS p. 49; VV p. 114.
* *

```
                         -arboreum 1/8
               -Glory of Penjerrick-
     -Robert Fox-          -griffithianum 1/8
ZYXYA-          -thomsonii 1/4
     -          -forrestii Repens Group 1/4
     -Elizabeth-
               -griersonianum 1/4
```
3ft(.9m) 5F(-15C) E   Narrowly ovate leaves 4in(10.2cm) long.
Flowers widely funnel-campanulate, 3in(7.6cm) broad, clear blood
red, in trusses of 5-7. Gen. Harrison, reg. 1966. A.M. 1966.

REVISED NAME	FORMER NAME	REVISED NAME	FORMER NAME
aberconwayi	aberconwayi	cinnabarinum ssp. tamaense	tamaense
adenogynum	adenogynum	cinnabarinum ssp. xanthocodon	xanthocodon
adenogynum Adenophorum Group	adenophorum	Concatenans Group	concatenans
adenopodum	adenopodum	concinnum	concinnum
agastum	agastum	coriaceum	coriaceum
albertsenianum	albertsenianum	coryanum	coryanum
alutaceum var. iodes	iodes	crinigerum var. crinigerum	crinigerum var. crinigerum
alutaceum var. russotinctum	russotinctum	cuffeanum	cuffeanum
ambiguum	ambiguum	dalhousiae var. dalhousiae	dalhousiae
annae Laxiflorum Group	laxiflorum	dauricum	dauricum var. dauricum
anthopogon ssp. anthopogon	anthopogon var. anthopogon	davidsonianum	davidsonianum
ssp. hypenanthum	hypenanthum	decorum	decorum
aperantum	aperantum	degronianum	
araiophyllum	araiophyllum	ssp. heptamereum	metternichii
arboreum ssp. arboreum	arboreum ssp. arboreum	dendricola Taronense Group	taronense
arboreum ssp. cinnamomeum	arboreum ssp. arboreum	diaprepes	diaprepes
var. album	var. album	dichroanthum ssp. dichroanthum	dichroanthum ssp. dichroanthum
var. cinnamomeum	var. cinnamomeum	ssp. apodectum	ssp. apodectum
var. roseum	var. roseum	dichroanthum ssp. scyphocalyx	dichroanthum ssp. scyphocalyx
arboreum ssp. delavayi		Herpesticum Group	ssp. herpesticum
var. delavayi	delavayi	diphrocalyx	diphrocalyx
arboreum ssp. nilagiricum	arboreum ssp. nilagiricum	eclecteum var. eclecteum	eclecteum var. eclecteum
arboreum ssp. zeylanicum	zeylanicum	edgeworthii	edgeworthii (bullatum)
argyrophyllum	argyrophyllum	elliottii	elliottii
ssp. argyrophyllum	var. argyrophyllum	eudoxum var. eudoxum	eudoxum ssp. eudoxum
argyrophyllum ssp. hypoglaucum	hypoglaucum	faberi ssp. prattii	prattii
argyrophyllum ssp. nankingense	argyrophyllum var. nankingense	facetum (eriogynum)	facetum (eriogynum)
augustinii ssp. augustinii	augustinii var. augustinii	falconeri ssp. eximium	eximium
augustinii ssp. chasmanthum	augustinii var. chasmanthum	falconeri ssp. falconeri	falconeri
augustinii ssp. rubrum	bergii	fastigiatum	fastigiatum
aureum var. aureum	aureum	ferrugineum	ferrugineum
auriculatum	auriculatum	flavidum var. flavidum	flavidum var. flavidum
auritum	auritum	fletcheranum (fletcherianum)	fletcheranum (fletcherianum)
barbatum	barbatum	floccigerum ssp. floccigerum	floccigerum var. floccigerum
basilicum	basilicum	floribundum	floribundum
beanianum	beanianum	formosum var. formosum	formosum
beesianum	beesianum	Iteophyllum Group	iteophyllum
boothii Mishmiense Group	mishmiense	formosum var. inaequale	inaequale
brachyanthum ssp. brachyanthum	brachyanthum var. brachyanthum	forrestii ssp. forrestii	forrestii var. forrestii
brachyanthum ssp. hypolepidotum	brachyanthum var. hypolepidotum	Repens Group	var. repens
brachycarpum ssp. brachycarpum	brachycarpum	forrestii ssp. papilliatum	var. tumescens
bureavii	bureavii	fortunei ssp. discolor	discolor
burmanicum	burmanicum	Houlstonii Group	houlstonii
callimorphum ssp. callimorphum	callimorphum	fortunei ssp. fortunei	fortunei
calophytum var. calophytum	calophytum	fulgens	fulgens
calostrotum ssp. calostrotum	calostrotum	fulvum	fulvum
calostrotum ssp. keleticum		glaucophyllum	glaucophyllum
Radicans Group	radicans	var. glaucophyllum	var. glaucophyllum
campanulatum ssp. campanulatum	campanulatum var. campanulatum	glischrum ssp. rude	rude
campylocarpum ssp. caloxanthum	caloxanthum	grande	grande
campylocarpum ssp. campy-	campylocarpum var. campy-	griersonianum	griersonianum
locarpum	locarpum	griffithianum	griffithianum
Elatum Group	var. elatum	haematodes ssp. chaetomallum	chaetomallum var. chaetomallum
campylogynum	campylogynum var. campylogynum	haematodes ssp. haematodes	haematodes
campylogynum Charopaeum Group	var. charopaeum	hanceanum	hanceanum var. hanceanum
campylogynum Cremastum Group	var. cremastum	Nanum Group	var. nanum
campylogynum Myrtilloides Group	var. myrtilloides	heliolepis var. heliolepis	heliolepis
carneum	carneum	hemitrichotum	hemitrichotum
catacosmum	catacosmum	hemsleyanum	hemsleyanum
catawbiense	catawbiense	hippophaeoides var.	
caucasicum	caucasicum	hippophaeoides	hippophaeoides
cephalanthum ssp. cephalanthum	cephalanthum var. cephalanthum	Fimbriatum Group	fimbriatum
cerasinum	cerasinum	hirsutum	hirsutum
chamaethomsonii var. chamae-	chamaethomsonii var. chamae-	hirtipes	hirtipes
thomsonii	thomsonii	hodgsonii	hodgsonii
var. chamaethauma	var. chamaethauma	hookeri	hookeri
charitopes ssp. charitopes	charitopes	hyperythrum	hyperythrum
charitopes ssp. tsangpoense	tsangpoense var. tsangpoense	impeditum	impeditum
Curvistylum Group	var. curvistylum	insigne	insigne
chrysodoron	chrysodoron	intricatum	intricatum
ciliatum	ciliatum	irroratum ssp. irroratum	irroratum
ciliicalyx	ciliicalyx	japonicum var. japonicum	metternichii
cinnabarinum ssp. cinnabarinum	cinnabarinum var. cinnabarinum	japonicum var. pentamerum	degronianum
Blandfordiiflorum Group	var. blandfordiiflorum	johnstoneanum	johnstoneanum
Roylei Group	var. roylei	keiskei	keiskei

REVISED NAME	FORMER NAME	REVISED NAME	FORMER NAME
keysii	keysii var. keysii	ririei	ririei
kyawii	kyawii	roxieanum var. roxieanum	roxieanum var. roxieanum
lacteum	lacteum	rubiginosum	rubiginosum
lanigerum	lanigerum	rubiginosum Desquamatum Group	desquamatum
lepidotum	lepidotum	rufum	rufum
leucaspis	leucaspis	rupicola var. chryseum	chryseum
lindleyi	lindleyi	rupicola var rupicola	rupicola
lowndesii	lowndesii	russatum	russatum
ludlowii	ludlowii	saluenense ssp. chameunum	
luteiflorum	luteiflorum	Prostratum Group	prostratum
lutescens	lutescens	saluenense ssp. saluenense	saluenense
macabeanum	macabeanum	sanguineun ssp. sanguineum	
macrophyllum	macrophyllum	var. sanguineum	sanguineum ssp. sanguineum
maculiferum ssp. anhweiense	anhweiense	sanguineum ssp. sanguineum	
maddenii ssp. crassum	crassum	var. didymoides	ssp. consanguineum
maddenii ssp. maddenii	maddenii	var. didymoides	ssp. didymoides
maddenii ssp. maddenii	polyandrum	ssp. didymum	ssp. didymum
magnificum	magnificum	var. haemaleum	ssp. haemaleum
makinoi	makinoi	sargentianum	sargentianum
mallotum	mallotum	scabrifolium var. spiciferum	spiciferum
martinianum	martinianum	scopulorum	scopulorum
maximum	maximum	searsiae	searsiae
meddianum var. meddianum	meddianum var. meddianum	seinghkuense	seinghkuense
var. atrokermesinum	var. atrokermesinum	selense ssp. selense	selense var. selense
megacalyx	megacalyx	sidereum	sidereum
megeratum	megeratum	sinogrande	sinogrande var. sinogrande
mekongense var. mekongense	mekongense	smirnowii	smirnowii
Viridescens Group	viridescens	smithii	smithii
mekongense var. melinanthum	melinanthum	souliei	souliei
micranthum	micranthum	sperabile var. sperabile	sperabile var. sperabile
microgynum Gymnocarpum Group	gymnocarpum	spinuliferum	spinuliferum
minus var. chapmanii	chapmanii	stewartianum	stewartianum var. stewartianum
minus var. minus	minus	strigillosum	strigillosum
Carolinianum Group	carolinianum var. carolinianum	sulfureum	sulfureum
mollicomum	mollicomum var. mollicomum	sutchuenense	sutchuenense var. sutchuenense
montroseanum	montroseanum	taggianum	taggianum
morii	morii	telmateium	telmateium
moupinense	moupinense	temenium var. gilvum	
mucronulatum	mucronulatum var. mucronulatum	Chrysanthum Group	temenium var. chrysanthum
myrtifolium	myrtifolium	tephropeplum	tephropeplum
neriiflorum ssp. neriiflorum	neriiflorum ssp. neriiflorum	thayeranum	thayeranum
Euchaites Group	ssp. euchaites	thomsonii ssp. thomsonii	thomsonii var. thomsonii
nivale ssp. nivale		traillianum var. dictyotum	dictyotum
niveum	niveum	trichanthum	trichanthum
nuttallii	nuttallii	trichocladum	trichocladum
orbiculare ssp. orbiculare	orbiculare	trichostomum	trichostomum var. trichostomum
oreodoxa var. fargesii	erubescens	Ledoides Group	var. ledoides
oreodoxa var. fargesii	fargesii	Radinum Group	var. radinum
oreodoxa var. oreodoxa	oreodoxa	triflorum	triflorum var. triflorum
oreotrephes	oreotrephes	tsariense	tsariense
orthocladum var. microleucum	microleucum	ungernii	ungernii
pachytrichum	pachytrichum	uniflorum var. imperator	imperator
parmulatum	parmulatum	uvariifolium	uvariifolium var. uvariifolium
pemakoense	pemokoense	valentinianum	valentinianum
pemakoense Patulum Group	patulum	veitchianum	veitchianum
phaeochrysum var. phaeochrysum	dryophyllum	Cubittii Group	cubittii
phaeochrysum var. phaeochrysum	phaeochrysum	venator	venator
pocophorum var. pocophorum	pocophorum	vernicosum	vernicosum
polycladum	compactum	vesiculiferum	vesiculiferum
polycladum	polycladum	virgatum ssp. oleifolium	oleifolium
Scintillans Group	scintillans	virgatum ssp. virgatum	virgatum
polylepis	polylepis	viscidifolium	viscidifolium
ponticum	ponticum	wardii var. puralbum	puralbum
praestans	praestans	wardii var. wardii	wardii
praevernum	praevernum	Litiense Group	litiense
principis Vellereum Group	vellereum	wasonii	wasonii var. rhododactylum
protistum var. giganteum	giganteum	wattii	wattii
pruniflorum	tsangpoense var. pruniflorum	wightii	wightii
pseudochrysanthum	pseudochrysanthum	williamsianum	williamsianum
pubescens	pubescens	xanthostephanum	xanthostephanum
pumilum	pumilum	yakushimanum ssp. yakushimanum	yakushimanum
racemosum	racemosum	yungningense	yungningense
recurvoides	recurvoides	yunnanense	yunnanense
rex ssp. arizelum	arizelum	Hormophorum Group	hormophorum
rex ssp. fictolacteum	fictolacteum	zaleucum	zaleucum
rigidum	rigidum		

Aberconway, The Rt. Hon. Lord, Bodnant, Tal-y-Cafn, Colwyn Bay,
  Clwyd, North Wales, UK
Acland, Cuthbert (d.) Stagshaw, Ambleside, Cumbria, UK
Adams-Acton, G. M. (d.) Beach House, Cooden Beach, Sussex, UK
Allen, Mr. & Mrs. E. F., Felcourt, Copcock, Ipswich, Suffolk, UK
Amateis, Edmond (d.) Brewster, NY
Anderson, A. & S., 220 Mulberry Way, Franklin Lakes, NJ 07417
Anderson, Edw. 2903 Huntington Pl., Longview, WA 98632
Anne, Countess of Rosse, Nymans, Handcross, W. Sussex, UK
Ansell, Mrs. G., Hacketts Rd., Olinda, Victoria, AUS
Archibold, Bruce & Valerie, Starveacre, Dalwood, Axminister,
  Devon, UK EX13 7HH
Arends, G. (d.) Wuppertal, W. Germany
Arsen, F., 13 Vermont St., Lindenhurst, Long Island, NY 11757
Arthur H. Scott Horticultural Foundation,
  Swarthmore College, Swarthmore, PA 19081
Aunsbjorn, Thorvall, Drivvejen 31, Randers 8900, Denmark
Austin, Ray, Washougal, WA
Australian Rhododendron Society, Box 21, Olinda 3788,
  Victoria, AUS

Bacher, John (1883-1961) Portland, OR
Bagoly, Lewis, 700 Terphanny Lane, Strafford, PA 19087
Bahnson, E. R., 2725 Windsor Rd., Winston-Salem, NC 27104
Bailey, J. & J. E., 8536 NE 26th, Bellevue, WA 98004
Bain, Mrs. Irene, Glenview, Rd. 1, Napier, NZ
Baker, George L. (d.) Astoria, OR
Balch, R. W., Dunedin, NZ
Baldanza, Samuel (d.) Benton Harbor, MI
Baldsiefen, Warren (d. 1974) Bellvale, NY
Baldwin, M., Mountain Highway, Boronia, Victoria, AUS
Balint, David M., 6410 NE 17th Ave., Vancouver, WA 98665
Banks, W. L. & R. A., Hergest Croft, Kington, Herefordshire, UK
Barber, Peter N., Otterwood Gate, Exbury Rd.,
  Beaulieu, Brockenhurst, Hampshire, UK
Barefield, Grady E. (d.) and Mary W. (d.) Seattle, WA
Barto, James E. (1881-1940) Eugene, OR
Basford, J. S., Brodick Castle, Isle of Arran, Scotland, UK
Becales, Joseph, 36 Ivy Lane, Glen Mills, PA 19342
Beekman, J., Sassafras, Victoria, AUS
Behring, R., 108 Dunvegan Rd, St. Catharines, ONT, Can. L2P 3T5
Bell, Gwen, 5242 - 37th Ave. SW, Seattle, WA 98126
Benmore---See Younger Botanic Garden
Berg, Warren E., Rt 1, Wren Ct., Port Ludlow, WA 98365
Berry Botanic Garden, 11501 SW Summerville, Portland, OR 97219
Bertin (Originator of R. Madame Masson, 1849)
Biltmore Gardens, Ashville, NC
Black, Michael, Green Bank, Grasmere, Cumbria, UK
Bledsoe, D. (d.) Snohomish, WA
Blough, R. L., Krings St., Rt. 3, Box 58, Johnstown, PA 15904
Blumhardt, Oswald, Rd. 9, Koromiko Nurseries, Whangarei, NZ
Blyskal, W. J., Box 134, Cherry Valley, NY 13320
Bodnant---See Aberconway
Bohlje, G. D., Westerstede, Ger.
Bolitho, Lt. Col. Sir Edward H. W. (d.) Trengwainton,
  Penzance, Cornwall, UK
Bond, John D., Crown Estate, Windsor Great Park, Windsor, UK
Borde Hill---See Clarke, R. N. Stephenson
Boscawen, Hon. H. E. & Anne, High Beeches, Handcross, Sussex, UK
Bosley, Sr., Paul (d.) Mentor, OH
Boulter, F., Everest Crescent, Olinda, Victoria, AUS
Boulter, V. J. & Sons, Olinda, Victoria, AUS
Bovee, Robert M. (d.) Portland, OR
Bowers, Clement Gray (d.) Binghamton, NY
Bowman, Dr. & Mrs. Paul J., Box 495, Fort Bragg, CA 95437
Braadfladt, H. J., 447 Excelsior Rd., Eureka, CA 95501
Brack, Werner, RFD, 202 Steep Bank Rd., St. James, NY 11780
Bramley, Alfred, Perrins Creek Rd., Kallista, Victoria, AUS
Brandt, Lester E. (d.) Tacoma, WA
Brechtbill's Nursery, Eugene, OR
Briggs, Dr. Ben T. Briggs, 825 Grant St, Shelton, WA 98584
Briggs, Bruce, 4407 Henderson Blvd., Olympia, WA 98501
Brockenbrough, Dr. E. C., 3630 Hunts Point, Bellevue, WA 98004
Brodick Castle Gardens, Isle of Arran, Scotland, UK
Brooks, A. R., 225 Holden Wood Rd., Concord, MA 01742
Brooks, J. Judson, Shields Lane, Sewickley, PA 15143
Brotherton, J. C., 20620 NE Freedom Rd., Battleground, WA 98604

Brown, Edward J., County St., Rt. 5, Lakeville, MA 02346
Browne of Upway, Victoria, AUS
Browning, Dr. J. R. & Blanche, 1133 McCully Dr., Pittsburgh,
  PA 15235
Brueckner, Dr. J., 1436 Carmen, Mississauga, ONT, Can. L5G 3Z1
Bruns, Joh., Bad Zwischenahn, W. Germany
Brydon, P. H., 3025 Oakcrest Dr. NW., Salem, OR 97304
Brykit, Dr. Max E., 28 W. Potomac St., Williamsport, MD 21795
Buckland Monachorum--See Fortescue Garden Trust
Bulgin, Lansing W., Rt. 3, Box 233, Sherwood, OR 97140
Burlingame, C. R., Rt. 3, Box 1068, Hoquiam, WA 98335
Burns, Mrs. C., Ridge Rd., Muttontown, Syosset, L.I., NY 11791
Butler, Mr. & Mrs. M. K., 17427 Clover Rd., Bothell, WA 98011
Byls, J., Ghent, Belgium (Raised arboreum hybrids, 1860-75)

Caerhays Castle---See Williams, John Charles
Campbell, B. W., 209 Waireka Rd., Ravensbourne, Dunedin, NZ
Campbell, Sir Ilay, Inveraray, Argyll, Scotland, UK PA32 8YA
Cannon, Clifford, 2705 Cain Rd., Olympia, WA 98501
Caperci, James F., (d. 1987) Kent, WA
Carlyon, Miss G., Tregrehan, Par, Cornwall, UK
Cary, Edward A., 246 Boston Pike, Shrewsbury, MA 01545
Cavendish, Hugh, Holker Hall, Grange-Over-Sands, Cumbria, UK
Chamberlain, D. F., Royal Botanic Garden, Edinburgh, Scot., UK
Childers, Arthur A., Rhodoland Nursery, Vida, OR 97488
Childers, Maxine, 46451 McKenzie Highway, Vida, OR 97488
Christie, Sylvester (d.) Blackhills, Scotland, UK
Clark, Roy W., 2101 Olympia Ave., Olympia, WA 98506
Clarke, R. N. Stephenson, (1925-1987) Borde Hill, Sussex, UK
Clarke, Col. S. R. (d.) Borde Hill, Haywards Heath, Sussex, UK
Clarke, Dr. Harold J., 9750 Edwards Dr., Sun City, AZ 85351
Clarke, Steve, Clarke Nurseries, Long Beach, WA 98631
Clyne, Mrs. J. S., 38A Seddon St., Highfield, Timarau, NZ
Coe, William R. (d.) Oyster Bay, NY
Coker, Mrs. R. J., 129 Ilam Rd., Christchurch, NZ
Collier, G., Titoki Point, R.D. 1, Taihape, NZ
Collinson, Peter (Introduced maximum to Britain, 1736)
Colville, Col. N. R. (d.) Penheale Manor, Launceston,
  Cornwall, UK
Colville, Mrs. N. R., Penheale Manor, Launceston, Cornwall, UK
Connelly, E. E., 5 Humphrey Pl., Oakland, CA 94610
Connors, E. T., 42 Woodlane Rd., Jackson, NJ 08527
Consolini, Anthony (d.) Sandwich, MA (Gardener to C. O. Dexter)
Cook, Alleyne R., 2117 Larson, North Vancouver, BC, Can.
Cooper, Roland Edgar (1890-1962) Collector
Coplen, M. G. (d.) Rockville, MD
Corbin, Dr. W. L. 522, SW Yamhill, Portland, OR 97204
Core, William, Silvercreek, WA
Corsock--See Ingall, Peter
Cottage Gardens Inc., 4992 Middle Ridge Rd., Perry, OH 44081
Cowles, John C., 745 Washington St., Wellesley, MA 02181
Cox, Kenneth, Glendoick Gardens, Perth, Scotland, UK
Cox, Peter A., Glendoick Gardens, Perth, Scotland, UK
Craig, Dr. D. L., Research Station, Kentville, NS, Can.
Crosfield, J. J. (d.) Embley Park, Romsey, Hampshire, UK
Crown Estate Commissioners, The Great Park, Windsor,
  Berkshire, UK
Crystal Springs Rhodendron Garden, Portland, OR
Cullen, J., Royal Botanic Garden, Edinburgh, Scotland, UK
Cutten, R. L., Ferny Creek, Victoria, Australia

Dale, W. A., 1894 Chinook Pl., Sidney, BC, Canada V8L 3V7
Davies, Isaac (d.) Ormskirk, Lancashire, UK
Davis, J. A., 1323 - 132nd Ave., E., Sumner, WA 98390
Davidian, H. H., Royal Botanic Garden, Edinburgh, Scot., UK
Davis, Ross B., Jr., 404 Conestoga Rd., Wayne, PA 19087
Davis, Mrs. T., Sassafras, Victoria, AUS
Deans, James, Homebush, Christchurch, NZ
de Belder, R., Kalmthout, Belgium
de Longchamp, Roger, 540 Mt. Elam Rd., Fitchburg, MA 01420
Deen, P. & C., Kallista, Victoria, AUS
Delp, Weldon E., Box 434, Harrisville, PA 16038
Del's Lane County Nursery, Eugene, OR 97401
Dexter, Charles O. (1862-1943) Sandwich, MA
Digby, Captain, The Lord, Minterne, Dorchester, Dorset, UK
Dosser, D. J., George St., Warburton East, Victoria, AUS
Dougall, Capt. Maitland (d.) Woodham, Woking, Surrey, UK

Drake, Messers. Jack...Inshriach Alpine Plant Nursery, Aviemore,
   Invernesshire PH22 1QS, Scotland, UK
Drewry, James H. (d.) Fort Bragg, CA
Druecker, John S., Box 511, Fort Bragg, CA 95437
Drayson, R.J.R., Wimborne, Dorset, BH21 6RP, England, UK
Dryden, Mrs. K., 30 Sheering Lower Rd., Sawbridgeworth,
   Hertfordshire, UK
Dunedin Rhododendron Group, 43 Teignmouth St., Abbotsford, Green
   Island, Otago, NZ

Edinburgh---See Royal Botanic Garden, Edinburgh, Scotland, UK
Egan, Ernest K., 40 Pease Rd., Woodbridge, New Haven, CT 06519
Eichelser, John (d.) Olympia, WA
Elliott, James A., Rt. 4, Box 544, Astoria, OR 97103
Elliott, Jeffrey, 234 Withells Rd., Christchurch 4, NZ
Elliott, Walter, 700 James Dr., Shelton, WA 98584
Embley Park--See Crosfield, J. J.
Endtz, L. J. & Co., Boskoop, Holland (Later named Blaauw & Co.)
Evans, Bert (Head Gardener at Penjerrick, 1935-1970)
Evans, Mrs. J. B., Golden Bank, Redruth, Cornwall, UK
Evans, Mrs. J. P., 70 Lincolnshire Dr., Oakland, CA 94618
Evelyn, Dr. Trevor & Sandra, 3470 Stephenson Pt. Rd., Nanaimo,
   BC, Canada, V9T 1K2
Everitt, Samuel A. (d.) Halesite, Huntington, Long Island, NY
Exbury Gardens---See Rothschild
Experimental Station, Boskoop, Holland

Farrer, Reginald (1880-1920) Plant Explorer
Fawcett, Carl P., 8616 19th St. W., Tacoma, WA 98466
Felcourt--See Allen, E. F.
Felix and Dijkhuis, Boskoop, Holland
Fennichia, Richard A., 712 Bay Rd., West Webster, NY 14580
Fetterhoff, William F., 5279 Richland Rd., Gibsonia, PA 15044
Findlay, Hope (d.) Windsor Great Park, Windsor, England, UK
Ford, Mrs. John E., 2770 Meadow Brook Dr., Wooster, OH 44691
Forster, R. Ray, Horticultural Research Institute of Ontario,
   Vineland Station, ON, Can.
Fortescue, L. S. (d. 1981) Garden House, Buckland Monachorum,
   Yelverton, Devon, UK
Fortescue Garden Trust, Garden House, Buckland Monachorum,
   Yelverton, Devon, UK
Fortune, Robert (1812-80) Plant Explorer
Fowler, R. J., 153 Chinquapin Lane, Waynesville, NC 28786
Fox, Barclay (1873-1930) Son of Robert Fox,
   Penjerrick, Cornwall, UK
Fox, D. B., Bullwood Nurs., 54 Woodlands Rd., Hockley, Essex, UK
Foxhill Nurseries--See Reuthe, E. W.
Fraser, George (d.) Vancouver, BC, Can.
Frederick, Mrs. Halsey A., Jr., 530 Fisher's Rd., Bryn Mawr, PA
Freimann, Mrs. LeVern, 1907 38th St., Bellingham, WA 88225
Frets, C., Boskoop, Holland
Fromow, W., Windlesham, Surrey, UK
Frye, Else (d.) Seattle, WA
Fuller, Henry & Selma, The Shores, 1700 3rd Ave. W., Brandon, FL

Gable, Caroline, Stewartstown, PA, 17363
Gable, Joseph B. (1886-1972) Stewartstown, PA
Gatke, R. M. (d.) Salem, OR
Genista Gardens, Olinda, Victoria, Australia
George, A. F., Hydon Nurs., Hydon Heath, Godalming, Surrey, UK
German, Eugene R., Box 454, Fort Bragg, CA 95437
Gibson, A. C. (d.) and J. F. (d.) Glenarn, Rhu, Dumbartonshire,
   Scotland, UK
Gigha, Isle of---See Horlick, Sir James N.
Gill, Richard & Sons (before 1900) Penryn, Cornwall, UK
Gillies, George, Supt., Marshall Field Estate, Oyster Bay, NY
Gillis, Jeanie, Horticulturist, Heritage Plantation,
   Sandwich, MA 02563
Girard, Sr., Mrs. Peter, 6839 N. Ridge E., Geneva, OH 44041
Girard, Sr., Peter (d) Geneva, OH
Glenarn---See Gibson, A. C.
Glendoick Gardens---See Cox, Peter
Glenkinglas, The Rt. Hon. The Lord, Strone House, Cairndow,
   Argyll, Scotland, UK
Glennie, W. E., Glenrose, Blicks Rd., R. D. 2, Blenheim, NZ
Godsall, Robert, Head Gardener, Muncaster Castle,
   Ravenglass, Cumbria, UK
Goheen, Dr. David, Box 826, Camas, WA 98607

Golden, Albert, 117 Parker Ave., San Francisco, CA 94118
Goodrich, Col. & Mrs. R. H., 10015 Saddle Rd., Vienna, VA 22180
Gordon, Lady Adam, Hethersett, Littleworth Cross,
   Seale, Surrey, UK GU10 1JL
Gordon, R. C., Ben Moi, Utiku RD 4, Taihape, NZ
Gorer, Geoffrey, Sunte House, Haywards Heath, Sussex, UK
Gowen, J. R. (d.) Gardener to the Earl of Carnarvon, Highclere
   Castle, Newbury, Berkshire, UK
Grace, George (1897-1974) Portland, OR
Grange, The---See Ingram, Capt. Collingwood
Granston, Mrs. Mae K., 14346 Bear Creek Rd. NE., Woodinville,
   WA 98072
Grant, C. A., Kapunatiki, Orton Rd., Temuka, NZ
Grant, Mr. & Mrs. L. A., Kapunatiki, Orton R.D. 26, Temuka, NZ
Greer, Edgar (1895-1972) Eugene, OR
Greer, Mr. & Mrs. Harold E., Greer Gardens, 1280 Goodpasture
   Island Rd., Eugene, OR 97401
Gregory, R. M. (d.) Werrington Pk., Launceston, Cornwall, UK
Greig, Mrs. E. J., Royston Nursery, Royston, BC, Can.
Griebnow, Paul, 805 Fairview Ave. SE., Salem, OR 97302
Griswold, Mrs. W. O., Kirkland, WA 98033
Grothaus, Mr. & Mrs. Lewis C., 12373 SW., Boones Ferry Rd.,
   Lake Oswego, OR 97034
Gustafson, Dr. Richard, 28 Wood Hollow, Lawrenceville, NJ 08648
Guttormsen, W. L., 1233 SE. First St., Canby, OR 97013

Haag, Charles & Velma, Rt. 1, Box 89, Brevard, NC 28712
Hachmann, Hans, Brunnenstrasse 68,
   2202 Barmstedtin Holstein, Germany
Hall, G., Harewood House, Leeds, Yorkshire, UK
Hall, H., 7204 - 184th St., Snohomish, WA 98290
Hall, Maurice, 135 Norlen Park, Bridgewater, MA 02324
Hamilton, Cdr. I., Christchurch Rd., Virginia Water, Surrey, UK
Hancock, M. L. (d.) Mississauga, ON, Can.
Hanger, Francis (d.) Former Curator, RHS Gardens, Wisley, Surrey
Hansen, Ruth, 3514 N. Russett St., Portland, OR 97217
Hardgrove, Donald L. (d.) Merrick, Long Island, NY
Hardijzer, W. H., The Nurseries, Boskoop, Holland
Hardy, Maj. A. E., Sandling Park, Hythe, Kent, UK
Hardy, G. A., Hillhurst Farm, Hythe, Kent, UK CT21 3HU
Harewood, Lord, Harewood House, Leeds, Yorkshire, UK LS17 9LF
Harewood House Gardens---See Hall, Geoffrey
Harrison, Maj. Gen. E. G. W. W., (1893-1987)
Harrison, Mrs. Roza (d.) Tremeer, St. Tudy, Cornwall, UK
Haverfield, J. Warburton, Victoria, AUS
Haworth-Booth, Michael, Farall Nurseries, Roundhurst Haslemere,
   Surrey, UK
Hayes, I. A., 2 Wellman Croft, Selly Oak, Birmingham, UK B17 0TN
Hayes, Mrs. Wesley, Centrewood Waimate, Box 29, S. Canterbury NZ
Headfort, Marquess of (d.) Headfort, Kells Co., Meath, Eire
Heinje Baumschulen, D., Hauptstrasse 39, Postf. 1221 D-2905
   Edewecht, W. Germany
Heller, Dr. Carl G. (d.) Poulsbo, WA 98370
Heneage-Vivian, Adm. A. W. (d.) Clyne Castle, Swansea, Wales, UK
Henny, John, 8529 67th Ave. NE., Brooks, OR 97305
Henny, Mrs. Leona, 8991 75th Ave. NE., Rt. 6, Brooks, OR 97305
Henny, Rudolph (1909-1963) Brooks, OR
Henry, Mrs. I., 6 Gordon Rd., RD 22, Stratford, NZ
Herbert, Charles (d.) Phoenixville, PA
Heritage Plantation, Sandwich, MA (Formerly C. O. Dexter estate)
Hess, Nathaniel E., Sloanes Court, Sands Point, NY 11050
Heyderhoff, Henry, 348 Glen Wild Ave., Bloomingdale, NJ 07403
High Beeches--See Boscawen, The Hon. H. E.
High Beeches Gardens Conservation Trust, The, Handscross, West
   Sussex, UK RH17 6HQ
Hill, Mrs., M. L. B., 1106 Greenhill Ave., Wilmington, DE 19805
Hillberg, F. J., 37 Wiltshire, North Yate, Avon, England, UK
Hillier & Sons, Winchester, Hants., UK
Hilscher, S., 4449 - 140th St., Bellevue, WA 98006
Hindla, Louis A., 986 Church St., Bohemia, NY 11716
Hinerman, Dr. D. L., 6800 Scio Church Rd., Ann Arbor, MI 48103
Hitchcock, Amy M., 1040 Ferry St., Eugene, OR 97401
Hobbie, Dietrich, (1899-1985) Oldenburg, W. Ger.
Hodgson, Mrs. Lillian, Vancouver, BC, Can.
Holden Arboretum, Sperry Rd., Mentor, OH 44060
Holden, Mrs. John, Rt. 4, Box 188, Shelton, WA 98584
Hollard, Bernard, Kaponga, Taranki, NZ
Holman, Nigel T., Chyverton, Zelah, Truro, Cornwall, UK

Holmeade, A., 507 Carl Way, Aberdeen, WA 98520
Holmes, Mrs. A. G., Rakaia, NZ
Holmes, A. Graham, Holmeslee, Rakaia, Canterbury NZ
Hooftman, Hugo T., Boskoop, Holland
Hopwood, Mrs. C. G., Tremeer, St. Tudy, Bodmin, Cornwall, UK
Horlick, Sir James N. (d.) Isle of Gigha, Argyll, Scotland, UK
Horsley, D. A., 7441 Tracyton Blvd., NW, Bremerton, WA 98310
Horticultural Research Inst., Vineland Sta., ONT, Can. LOR 2ED
Howard, Heman A., Box 197, South Wellfleet, MA 02663
Howells, A., Dickens Lane, Olinda, Victoria, AUS
Hughes, J. Hollis, Rt. 3, Box 264, Warrior, AL 35180
Huthnance, G., Carrington Rd., New Plymouth, NZ
Hydon Nurs., Clock Barn Lane, Hydon Heath, Godalming, Surrey, UK

Ihrig, Herbert (d.) Seattle, WA
Ingall, Peter (1899-1984) Corsock House, Castle Douglas, Scot.
Ingram, Capt. Collingwood (d. 1981) Cranbrook, Kent, UK
Institute of Ornamental Plant Growing, Caritasstraat 21,
  B-9230-Melle, Belgium

Jack, Evelyn, Univ. of British Columbia, Vancouver, BC, Can.
James, Delbert W. (1894-1963) Eugene, OR
James, Mrs. Ray, (d.) Eugene, OR
Jarvis, Bernard R., 26924 Meridian E., Graham, WA 98338
Johnson, Allen P., 9370 SE. Cornell Rd., Port Orchard, WA 98366
Johnson, S. Peste, 1005 Turner, Shelton, WA 98584
Johnstone, Miss E. G., Little Glendoe, 43 Tolearne Ave., Maori
  Hill, Dunedin, NZ
Johnstone, Maj. G. H. (d.) Trewithen, Grampound Rd., Cornwall, UK
Jordan, Bernice I., 1009 7th Ave. N., Tumwater, WA 98502
Jordan, E. W., 121 Boundary Rd., Oakville, New So. Wales 2765, AUS
Joslin, W. V., Rt. 4, Box 338, Coos Bay, OR 97420
Jury, F. M., Tikorangi, Waitara, NZ
Jury, L. E., New Plymouth, NZ

Keeley, Mrs. J. E., 33 June St., Timaru, NZ
Kehr, Dr. A. E., 240 Tranquility Pl., Hendersonville, NC
Kellam, Jr., D. S., 2225 Carmel Rd., Charlotte, NC 28226
Kennedy, John F., Park, New Ross, Ireland
Kenneth, Mrs. K. L., Tighnabruaich, Ardrishaig, Argyll, Scot.
Kerr, Mrs. J. M., 253 Memorial Ave., Christchurch 5, NZ
Kerrigan, Howard W., 24249 2nd St., Hayward, CA 94541
Kerrigan, R., 24146 Old River Rd., Junction City, OR 97448
Kew, Royal Botanic Gardens, Richmond, Surrey, UK
Kilboggett--See Maskell, Sidney
King, S. M., 30 Devon Rd., Wanganui, NZ
Kingdon Ward, Frank (1885-1958) Explorer and author
Kluis, Anthony, Boskoop, Holland (Later moved to USA)
Klupenger, Joseph, Rt. 2, Box 118, Aurora, OR 97002
Knap Hill Nurseries, Woking, Surrey, UK
Knight, Edgar L. (d.) Shelton, WA
Knight, Frank P. (1903-1985)
Knippenberg, Mrs. J. F., Laurelwood Gardens, 736 Pines Lake
  Drive W., Pines Lake, Wayne, NJ 07470
Koenig, Thomas W., 22 Rona St., Interlaken, NJ 07712
Konrad, Dr. Mark G., 437 Maple Lane, Sewickley, PA 15143
Korn, Robert 3700 NE. 9th Court, Renton, WA 98055
Korth, Allan C., 1465 38th Ave., Santa Cruz, CA 95060
Koster, D. A., Boskoop, Holland
Koster, M. & Sons, Boskoop, Holland
Koster, P. M., Bridgeton, NJ (Formerly of Boskoop)
Kraxberger, Mrs. M., 8450 Oleson Rd., Portland, OR 97223
Krug, H., 225 NW. 97th Ave., Portland, OR 97229
Kruschke, Franz (d.) Clackamas, OR

La Bar's Rhododendron Nursery (formerly), Stroudsburg, PA
Lamellen---See Magor, Maj. E. Walter M.
Lancaster, Benjamin F. (1892-1970) Camas, WA
Langdon, G., The Basin, 1405 Mountain Hwy., Victoria, AUS
Larson, Hjalmar L. (1897-1983) Tacoma, WA
Lawson, J. G., Alpine Nursery, Aviemore, Inverness-shire, Scot.
Lawton, Lloyd H., 3941 Main Rd., Tiverton, RI 02878
Laxdall, Mrs. Sigrid, 3023 W. Alderwood, Bellingham, WA 98225
Leach, Dr. David G., 1894 Hubbard Rd., North Madison, OH 44057
Leendertz, B., Baumschule 'Heilmannshof' Krefeld-Traar, W. Ger.
Leith, W. (d.) Head Gardener, Glyne Castle, Swansea, UK
Lelliott, T., 15 Owen St., Boronia, Victoria, AUS
Lem, Halfdan (1886-1969) Seattle, WA

Leonard, J., 14 Gully Lane, RFD 1, E. Sandwich, MA 02537
Leonardslee--See Loder, Sir Giles
Lewis, Don & Carolyn Dana, 2250 Glendaloch, Ann Arbor, MI 48104
Lewis, Dr. G. David, 52 Glenwood Rd., Rt. 1, Colts Neck, NJ
Lingholm--See Rochdale, Viscount
Linington, Mr. & Mrs. E. J., 11 Tamatt Crescent, Vancouver,
  BC, Can. V6N 2C8
Lochinch--See Stair, Lord
Lock, Surgeon Capt. J. A. N., Lower Coombe Royal,
  Kingsbridge, Devon, UK
Lockhart, R. D., 25 Rubislaw Den N., Aberdeen, Scot., UK
Loder, Sir Edmund (d.) Leonardslee
Loder, Col. G. H. (d.) High Beeches
Loder, Gerald (d.) Wakehurst Place
Loder, Sir Giles, Bt., Ockenden House, Cuckfield, Sussex, UK
Lofthouse, John G., 6649 Osler Ave., Vancouver, BC, Can.
Longwood Gardens, Kennett Square, PA 19348
Lowinsky, T. (d.) Tittenhurst, Sunninghill, Berkshire, UK
Luenenschloss, Carl, 11 Brook Terrace, Fair Haven, NJ 07701
Lux, Mrs. V. A., Jr., 1680 Monroe St., Port Townsend, WA 98368
Lyons, Marshall W. (d.) Eugene, OR
Lyons, Ruth (d.) Renton, WA

McClure, Donald K., 4032 NE 95th St., Seattle, WA 98115
McClure, W., Lawrence Ct., The Patch, Victoria, AUS
McCuaig, Mr. & Mrs. H. H., 5759 Newton Wynd, Vancouver, BC, Can.
McDonald, Bea, 422 Rt. 130, RFD 2, Sandwich, MA 02563
McDonald, Dr. Sandra, Box 268, Hampton, VA 23669
MacEwen, Brig. Gen. D. (d.) Corsock House (See Ingall)
McGuinness, P. J., 14 Court St., West Haven, Conn 06516
McGuire, Thomas J., 9210 SW Westhaven Dr., Portland, OR 97225
Mackenzie, Mrs. Elizabeth, Hill Cottage, Fressingfield,
  By Diss, Norfolk, UK
McLaren, Henry (1879-1953) Bodnant (Later Lord Aberconway)
McLaren, Ruth, Agate Pass Garden, Box 288, Suquamish, WA
McLaughlin, C. A., Dunedin, NZ
McNew, Charles C., 2710 Mt. Brynion Rd., Kelso, WA 98626
McQuire, J. F. J., Botany Hill, Farnham, Surrey, UK GU10 1LZ
Magor, Maj. E. Walter M., Lamellen, St. Tudy, Cornwall, UK
Magor, Edward J. P. (1874 1941) Lamollon, St. Tudy, Cornwall, UK
Malland, L., 12643 NE 70th Place., Kirkland, WA 98033
Maloney, Francis, 3636 Corliss Ave. N., Seattle, WA 98103
Manenica, Mrs. Victor, 310 Hemlock Park Rd., Aberdeen, WA 98520
Mangles, Miss Clara (1846-1931) Littleworth, England
Mangles, James Henry (1832-1884) Valewood, England
Manten, H., Heideweg 53, 4170 Geldern 1, West Germany
Martin, A. S., 3993 Huntington Pike, Huntington Valley, PA 19006
Martin, Dr. Louis G., 19 Lansdowne Rd., Toledo, OH 43623
Maskell, Sidney, Kilbogget, Ireland
Mauritsen, Richard, 8812-S-218th St., Kent, WA 98031
Maxwell, Sir John Stirling, Pollock House, Glasgow, Scotland, UK
May, J., Wimborne Botanical Gardens, Dorset, UK
Mayers, Dan E., Loth Lorien, Wadhurst, Sussex, UK TN5 6PN
Medlicott, Dr. R. W., Ashburn Hall, Dunedin, NZ
Mehlquist, Dr. Gustav A. L., 51 Brady Ln., Storrs, CT 06268
Messel, Lt. Col. L. C. R. (d.) Nymans, Handcross, Sussex, UK
Methven, T. (Before 1871) Edinburgh, Scotland, UK
Mezitt, Edmund V., (d.) Hopkinton, MA
Mezitt, P. J. M. (d.) Hopkinton, MA
Mezitt, R. Wayne, 25 Phipps St., Hopkinton, MA 01748
Mezitt, Wally B., 15 Phipps St., Hopkinton, MA 01748
Michael, Charles (d.) Head Gardener to The Rt. Hon. Chas. W.
  Williams, Caerhays Castle, Gorran, Cornwall, UK
Millais, E. G., Crosswater Farm, Churt, Farnham, Surrey, UK
Miller, Robert F., Star Route, Box 82, New Hope, PA 18938
Minch, Fred & Jeanne, 4329 Chrisella Rd., Puyallup, WA 98372
Morris Arboretum, University of Pennsylvania, 9414 Meadowbrook
  Ave., Philadelphia, PA 19118
Moser et Fils, Versailles, France
Moss, William, Bryn Derwen Caerwys, Mold, Clwyd, Wales, UK
Mossman, Dr. Frank D., 1200 W. 39th St., Vancouver, WA 98660
Mount Stewart, Newtownards, County Down, North Ireland, UK
Moyles, W., 4243 Norton Ave., Oakland, CA 94602
Moynier, William A., 2701 Malcolm Ave., Los Angeles, CA 90064
Mraw, L. B., 48 Shelbourne Dr., Trenton, NJ 08638
Mulligan, Brian O., 11632 106th Ave. NE., Kirkland, WA 98033
Muncaster Castle---See Pennington-Ramsden, Sir William
Murcott, Richard, Linden Lane, East Norwich, NY 11732

Murray, Robt. & Jay, 21 Squire Terrace, Colts Neck, NJ 07722

Nearing, G. Guy (1890-1986) Mahwah, NJ
Nelson, Milton R., 5409 NW Lincoln Ave., Vancouver, WA 98663
Nelson, E. C., Botanic Gardens, Glasnevin, Dublin 9, Ireland
Newcomb, E. F. & L., 18432 Snohomish Ave., Snohomish, WA 98290
Noble, Charles (d. before 1870)
Noble, Rt. Hon.--See Glenkinglas, The Rt. Hon.
Nymans Garden--See Anne, Countess of Rosse

Osborn, A. Hadley, Filoli, Canada Rd., Woodside, CA
O'Shannassy, J., McGowans Rd., Donvale, Victoria 3111, AUS
Ostbo, Endre (1884-1958) Seattle, WA
Ostler, A. G., Stratford, NZ

Paden, Donald, 2112 Race St., Urbana, Ill.
Pandrea, Joseph, 4516 S. 8th St., Tacoma, WA 98405
Parker, Edwin K., Rt. 2, Box 35, Astoria, OR 97103
Parsons, Samuel B. (1819-1906) Flushing, Long Island, NY
Penheale Manor---See Colville, Mrs. Norman
Penjerrick---See Fox, Barclay
Pennington-Ramsden, Sir William, Muncaster Castle
  Ravenglass, Cumberland, UK
Perry, Mr. & Mrs. Matahiwi, Masterton, NZ
Peste, Fred, (1909-1985) Shelton, WA
Peters, R. K., Box 142, Bendersville, PA 17306
Phetteplace, Dr. Carl H. (d.) Leaburg, OR
Philipps, Lady Marion, Picton Castle, Dyfed, South Wales, UK
Phipps, Howard, Post Rd., Westbury, Long Island, NY 11590
Pierce, Lawrence J., 900 University St., Apt. 11B, Seattle, WA
Pot, Julian (d.) Chesterfield, OH
Potter, Basil C., 167 Lampman Ave., Port Ewen, NY 12466
Price, Sir Henry (d.) Wakehurst, Sussex, UK
Pride, Orlando S. (1905-1983) Butler, PA
Prizeman, G. J. N., Farnham Lane, Haslemere, Surrey, UK
Prycl, Otto, Rt. 1, New Stanton, PA 15672
Puddle, F. C., Former Curator, Bodnant, Tal-y-Cafn,
  Colwyn Bay, Clwyd, North Wales, UK
Puddle, F. C., Jr., Curator, Bodnant, Tal-y-Cafn,
  Colwny Bay, Clwyd, North Wales, UK
Pukeiti Rhododendron Trust, RD 4, New Plymouth, NZ
Putney, Florence, Box 288, Suquamish, WA 98392

Rabbetts, Mrs. M., Rockford, Ringwood, Hants., UK
Ragan, W. & J., 11224, W. Lake Joy Dr., Carnation, WA 98014
Ramsden, Sir John (d.) Bulstrode Park & Muncaster Castle
Ranier Mountain Alpine Gardens, Seattle, WA
Raper, A., The Patch, Victoria, AUS
Raustein, A. A., 230 Union Ave., Holbrook, NY 11741
Rawinsky, G. B., Primrose Hill Nursery, Surrey, UK
Reboul, Adele, Box 373, St. James, Long Island, NY 11780
Redford, Ray, 39 Rectory Rd., Farnborough, Hants., UK GU 14 7BT
Reese, Dr. W. A., Redbarn Nursery, Box 215, Pennsburg, PA 18073
Reid, G. Albert, Rt. 1, Box 243, Blackman Rd., Bargintown,
  Linwood, NJ 08221
Reiley, H. E., 10210 Pine Tree Rd., Woodsborough, MD 21798
Research Station for Woody Nursery Crops, Boskoop, Holland
Reuthe, G., Foxhill Nurseries, Jackass Lane, Keston, Kent, UK
Reeves, Melvin, Box 369, Yamhill, OR 97148
Rhodes, Dr. Robert C., Maple Ridge, BC, Can.
Ring, George W., 11400 Valley Rd., Fairfax, VA 22033
Ring, Tom, MD., 57460 Hospital Rd., Bellaire, OH 43906
Rochdale, Viscount, Lingholm, Keswick, Cumbria, UK
Rock, Joseph Francis (1884-1962) Plant Explorer
Rosenthal, J., 86- 52 Pinto St., Holliswoods, NY 11423
Ross, Mrs. Henry, Ross Estate, Brewster, NY
Rothschild, Edmund de, Exbury Gardens, Southhampton, Hants., UK
Rothschild, Lionel de (1882-1942) Founder of Exbury Gardens
Rouse, J. L., U. of Melbourne, Parkville, Victoria, 3052, AUS
Rowarth, R. L., 22 Bayview Ave., Upway, Victoria, AUS
Rowe, S. J. & E. R., Huthnance Nurseries, 527 Carrington Rd.,
  R.D. 1, New Plymouth, NZ
Royal Boskoop Horticultural Society, c/o D. M. van Gelderen,
  Rijnveld 72, 2771 XS Boskoop, Holland
Royal Botanic Garden, Edinburgh, Scotland, UK
Royal Botanic Garden, Kew, Richmond, Surrey, UK
Royal Horticultural Society's Garden, Wisley, Ripley, Woking,
  Surrey, UK

Royce, Mrs. Doris, Basket Neck Nursery, Box E, Remsenburg, NY
Royston Nursery, Royston, BC, Can.
Russell, J. P. C., The Dairies, Castle Howard, Yorkshire, UK
Rutherford, Mrs. Jean, Kelso, WA
Ruys, J. D., Moerheim Nursery, Dedemsvaart, Holland
Rye, R. H., Gardener to Earl of Stair, Lochinch. (1921-56)

Salley, Dr. Homer E., Box 315, Grand Rapids, OHIO 43522
Sampson, D., Scotsford Rd., Broad Oak, Heathfield, Sussex, UK
Sandling Park---See Hardy, Maj. A. E.
Sangster, Ralph, 64 Strabane Ave, Box Hill N, Melbourne 3129 AUS
Sather, Mrs. Anne, & Miss Ellie, Box F., Brinnon, WA 98360
Saunders, Palmer F., 3030 Gilham Rd., Eugene, OR 97401
Schamanek, John (d.) Philadelphia, PA
Schannen, H. A., Box 2061, Princeton, NJ 08540
Schilling, A. D., Wakehurst Place Gardens, Ardingly, Haywards
  Heath, Sussex, UK
Schlaikjer, Mrs. H, C., Box 193, Halesite, Long Island, NY 11743
Schmalscheidt, Walter, Ziegelhof-Strasse 85, 2900 Oldenberg,
  Germany
Schmick, H., Im Grund 6, D-2056 Glinde, West Germany
Schram, Brian, 1180 Center St., Fenwick, ONT. Canada LQS ICO
Schroeder, Dr. H. Roland (d.) Evansville, IN
Schrope, Ned W., Rt. 2, Hegins, PA 17938
Schultz, Otto, Head Gardener, Royal Porcelain Factory,
  Berlin, Germany (1890)
Schumacher, F. W., Spring Hill Rd., East Sandwich, MA 02537
Scott, Arthur H., Horticultural Foundation, Swarthmore, PA 19081
Scott, Robert W., 9 Beverly Ct., Berkeley, CA 94707
Scrase-Dickins, C. R. (d.) Coolhurst, Horsham, Sussex, UK
Seabrook, Cecil S. (d.) Tacoma, WA
Seidel, T. J. (d.) Dresden, E. Ger.
Senko, Joseph F., Box 506, Cornelius, OR 97113
Shammarello, A. M. (1903-1982) South Euclid, OH
Shanklin, R., Apt. 526, 10100 Hillview Rd., Pensacola, FL 32514
Shapiro, Ben & Marion, 64 North Dr., East Brunswick, NJ 08816
Sheedy, Betty, 4335 SW. Twombly, Portland, OR 97201
Sherriff, George (1898-1982) Plant Explorer
Shilling, A. D., Wakehurst Place Gardens, Ardingly, Sussex, UK
Short, Howard A., A-11 350 Grow Ave., Bainbridge Island, WA
Shrauger, W. J., 140 Karr, Hoquiam, WA 98550
Sinclair, J. E., 617 NW. 175th St., Seattle, WA 98177
Skei, T., 05831 Mercer Lake Rd., Florence, OR 97439
Skinner, Dr. Henry T. (1907-1984) Hendersonville, NC
Slocock, M. O., Slocock Nursery, Woking, Surrey, UK
Slocock, Walter C., Goldsworth Nursery, Woking, Surrey, UK
Slonecker, H. J., 15200 SE. Woodland Way, Milwaukie, OR 97267
Slootjes, G. H., Boskoop, Holland
Smith, A. P., 21505 President Point Rd., NE, Kingston, WA 98346
Smith, A. W. (d. 1989) Niagara Falls, ONT, Canada
Smith, Britt M., 25809 124th Ave. SE., Kent, WA 98031
Smith, Cecil C., 5065 Ray Bell Rd. NE., St. Paul, OR 97137
Smith, Dr. Eric Ernest, Epsom, Surrey, UK
Smith, Graham F., Rd. 4, Taranaki, New Plymouth, NZ
Smith, J. P., 16833 NE 172nd Pl., Woodinville, WA 98072
Smith, Samuel, Head Gardener at Penjerrick, 1889-1935
Smith, W. David, Box 3250, Rd. 3, Spring Grove, PA 17362
Smith, William, Norbiton Common, Kingston, Surrey, UK
Snell, G. L. S., 970 Mountain Hwy., Boronia, Victoria, AUS
Snow's Ride Nurseries, Windlesham, Surrey, UK
Sorenson & Watson, 1737 S. W. Coronado, Portland, OR 97219
Spady, Dr. H. A., 9460 Sunnyview Rd. NE., Salem, OR 97301
Sparks, Robert C., 1107 W. Harvard Ave., Shelton, WA 98584
Spring-Smyth, T. LeM, 14 Derwent Rd., New Milton, Hants., UK
Stair, Lord, Lochinch, Stranraer, Wigtownshire, Scotland, UK
Standish & Noble, Nurs. owners before 1857, Windlesham, Surrey
Stanton, Donald B., Wollongong, N.S.W., AUS
Stanton, Ernest N., 21803 W. River Rd., Grosse Isle, MI 48138
Starling, B. N., Little Marles Cottage, Severs Green, Epping
  Upland, Essex, UK
Stead, L. Roland, Waterford, Amberley, North Canterbury, NZ
Stephens, J. Freeman, 896 Marine Dr., Bellingham, WA
Stevenson, John Barr (d.) Tower Court
Stevenson, Mrs. Roza---See Harrison, Mrs. Roza
Stewart, Coulter, 155 Broadmoor Ct., San Anselmo, CA
Stokes, Warren E., (1892-1969) Butler, PA
Strauss, R., Stonehurst, Ardingly, Sussex, UK
Street, Frederick J., Heathermead Nurs., Woking, Surrey, UK

Strutt, E. A., Galloway House, Wigtown, Scot., UK
Strybing Arbor., 9th Ave. & Lincoln Way, San Francisco, CA 94122
Stück, G., Hasselkamp 10, D-2300 Kronshagen/Keil, W. Ger.
Sullivan, N., P.O. Box 606, Burnie, Tasmania 7320, AUS
Sullivan, Peter, 221 Rickland Ave., San Francisco, CA 94110
Sumner, M. H., 350 Edgehill Way, San Francisco, CA 94127
Sunningdale Nurseries, Windlesham, Surrey, UK
Sunrise Rhododendron Gardens, Bainbridge Island, WA 98110
Sunte House---See Gorer, Geoffrey
Sutton, P., 6 Mark Pl., Queanbeyan, New South Wales 2620, AUS
Swain, George S., Agriculture Research Sta., NS, Can.
Swaythling, The Lord (d.) Bridley Manor, Worplesdon, Surrey, UK
Swenson, Willard J., 1005 Irvington Dr., Eugene, OR 97404
Swift, D. G., 164 Fleetwood Dr., Saunderstown, RI 02874

Tacoma Metropolitan Pk., Point Defiance Rhod. Garden, Tacoma, WA
Tasker, H. R., Ashburton, NZ
Taylor, G., Burbank Seed Farms, Wyong 2259, N.S.Wales, AUS
Teese, A. J., Moore's Road, Monbulk, Victoria, AUS
Temple, Mrs. M., Koromako, The Downs, Rd. 21, Geraldine, NZ
Thacker, T. C., Knowle Nurseries, Warwick, Birmingham, UK
Ticknor, Dr. Robert L., 844 N. Holly St., Canby, OR 97013
Tietjen, W. D., 52 Reeves Ave., Guilford, CT 06437
Tietjens, Marie, 1064 Wagon Rd., Blue Bell, PA 19422
Tighnabrauaich, Ardrishaig, Argyll, Scotland, UK
Todd, J., Box 1320, Lenoir, NC 28645
Tolstead, Dr. W. L., Elkins College, Elkins, W VA 26241
Towe, L. C., Box 212, Walhalla, SC 29691
Tower Court---See Stevenson, John Barr
Tracy, A., Box 214, Shelton, WA 98584
Trainor, Kenneth, 10502 32nd Ave., Seattle, WA
Trautmann, C., 3318 Mowbray Lane, Cincinnati, OH 45226
Tremeer--See Harrison, Maj. Gen. E. G. W. W.
Trewithen, St. Austell, Cornwall, UK
Tuomala, Carl, 20451 Lyta Way, Fort Bragg, CA 95437
Tyler, John J., Arboretum, Box 216, Painter Rd., Lima, PA 19037

University of Washington Arboretum, Seattle, WA
Urwin-Smith, P. J., The Glade, Ascot, Berkshire, UK

Van de Ven, K., Monbulk Rd., Olinda, Victoria, Australia
van den Akker, C. A., Boskoop, Holland
van Gelderen, D. M., Boskoop, Holland
van Houtte, Louis (1810-1876) Belgium
van Nes, Adr. Boskoop, Holland
van Nes, C. B., Boskoop, Holland
van Nes, P., Boskoop, Holland
van Nes, Vuyk, Boskoop, Holland
Van Veen, Allen, 750 NW. 107th Ave., Portland, OR 97229
Van Veen, Theodore, Jr., 4201 SE. Franklin, Portland OR, 97206
Van Veen, Theodore, Sr. (1881-1961) Portland, OR
van Wilgen Nurseries, Boskoop, Holland
Vaartnou, H., 2950 Lansdowne Rd., Victoria, BC, Can. V8R 3R2
Veitch, Sir Harry James (1840-1924) London, England
Vernimb, Bryan, Rt. 2, Box 250, Howell, NJ 07731
Verschaffelt, Ambrose (1825-1886) Ghent, Belgium
Vossberg, Paul (d.) Westbury, Long Island, NY

Wada, Koichiro (1907-1981) Hakoneya Nursery, Yokohama, Japan
Waghorn, F. R., 60 Dunloe Ave., Box Hill North, Victoria, AUS
Wakehurst Place, Ardingly, Sussex, UK (Ext. of Kew Gardens)
Walker, Mrs. S., Fernhill, Sandyford Co., Dublin, Ireland
Wallace, Robert (d. 1934) Tunbridge Wells, Kent, UK
Waldman, P., 211, Burrs Lane, Dix Hills, NY 11746
Walters, Dr. & Mrs. L. Gordon, RD 4, Butler, PA 16001
Walton, Mrs. J. R., 33 Sycamore Dr., Upper Saddle River, NJ
Ward--See Kingdon Ward, Frank
Ward, Cyril H., 3111 NE. 49th St., Vancouver, WA 98663
Warren, Mrs. P. J., Dunedin, NZ
Waterer, Anthony (1853-97) Knap Hill, Woking, Surrey, UK
Waterer, Anthony, Jr. (d. 1924) Knap Hill, Woking, Surrey, UK
Waterer, F. Gomer (d.) Bagshot, Surrey, UK
Waterer, Hosea (d.) Owner of Knap Hill, 1842-53
Waterer, G. D., Kilve, Bridgewater, Somerset, UK TA5 1SQ
Waterer, John, Sons & Crisp, Bagshot, Surrey, UK
Watson, Elsie M., 11530 Holmes Pt. Dr. NE., Kirkland, WA 98033
Watters, F. E., 205 Gray Ave., Shelton, WA 98584
Watts, Lynden, 14450 NE 15th Pl., Bellevue, WA 98007

Weber, Edwin O., 14964 18th St. SW., Seattle, WA 98166
Wells, James S., 474 Nut Swamp Rd., Red Bank, NJ 07701
Weston Nurseries, E. Main St., Hopkinton, MA 01748
Whitaker, W. I., Pylewell Park, Lymington, Hampshire, UK
White, G. Harry, Manager, Sunningdale Nurseries (1897-1936)
 Windlesham, Surrey, UK
Whitney, William E. (1894-1973) Brinnon, WA
Wick, Robert H., 8611 Fernwood NE., Olympia, WA 98506
Wildfong, Milton, Mission, BC, Can.
Wilding, Eustace Henry, Wexham Place, Stoke Poges,
 Buckinghamshire, UK
Wiley, K., The Garden House, Monachorum,
 Buckland Monachorum, Yelverton, Devon, UK
Williams, A. M., Werrington Park, Launceston, Cornwall, UK
Williams, Charles, Caerhays Castle, Gorran, Cornwall, UK
Williams, John Charles (d. 1939) Caerhays Castle
Williams, F. Julian, Caerhays Castle, Gorran, Cornwall, UK
Williams, Michael, Lanarth, St. Keverne, Cornwall, UK
Williams, Percival D. (d.) Lanarth, St. Keverne, Cornwall, UK
Williams, V., Arden, Toolangi, Victoria, AUS
Wilson, Dr. Ernest Henry (d.) Plant Explorer
Windsor Great Park--See Crown Estate
Winterthur Museum and Gardens, Winterthur, DE 19735
Wisley--See Royal Horticultural Society's Garden
Wister, John C. (d.) Swarthmore, PA
Wister, Mrs. J. (Gertrude) 735 Harvard Av., Swarthmore, PA 19081
Withers, Dr. R. M., 10 Urquhart St, Hawthorn, Victoria 3122, AUS
Witherwick, G. T., Trelean, St.-Martin-in-Meneage, Truro,
 Cornwall, UK TR12 6BZ
Witt, Joseph A. (d. 1984) Seattle, WA
Woodlands Nursery Garden, Carroll Ave., Ferndown, Dorset, UK
Wright, Arthur A., Jr., 1285 SE. Township Rd., Canby, OR 97013
Wright, Arthur A., Sr. (d.) Milwaukie, OR
Wyatt, Vernon, E. 3230, Hwy. 106, Union, WA 98592
Wyrens, Dr. Rollin G., 17600 Marine Dr., Stanwood, WA
Wytovich, E. T., Buck Laurel Acres, 497 1st St., Port Carbon, PA
Urzesinski, C. J., 3010 Elm Lane, Middleton, WI 53562

Yates, Connie, Rt. 2, Box 268, Frostburg, MD 21532
Yates, Mrs. Henry (Maletta) (1912-1987) Frostburg, MD
Yavorsky, Leon, Bennett Rd., Freehold, N. J. 07728
Yeates, J. S., 51 Long Melford Rd., Palmerston North, NZ
Yelton, Dr. E. H., 330 W. Court St., Rutherfordton, NC 28139
Young, Howard, Chadd's Ford, PA 19317
Younger Botanic Garden, Benmore by Dunoon, Argyll, Scotland, UK
 (Extension of RBG, Edinburgh)

Zimmerman, Robert G., Rt. 1, Box 368, Chimacum, WA 98325

Bean, W. J. <u>Trees</u> <u>and</u> <u>Shrubs</u> <u>Hardy</u> <u>in</u> <u>the</u> <u>British</u> <u>Isles</u>, V. III, 8th. ed., M.
    Bean & John Murray (Publishers), London, 1976.

Bulgin, L. W., <u>Rhododendron</u> <u>Hybrids,</u> <u>A</u> <u>Compendium</u> <u>By</u> <u>Parent</u>, Ellanhurst
    Gardens, Sherwood, OR, 1986.

Chamberlain, D. F. <u>A</u> <u>Revision</u> <u>of</u> <u>Rhododendron,</u> <u>Notes</u> <u>from</u> <u>the</u> <u>Royal</u> <u>Botanic</u>
    <u>Garden</u>, Edinburgh, Vol. 39, No. 2, 1982.

Clarke, J. Harold, ed. <u>Rhododendron</u> <u>Information</u>, American Rhododendron Society,
    Portland, OR, 1980.

Cowles, Eveleth C. <u>The</u> <u>Dexter</u> <u>Estate:</u> <u>Its</u> <u>Gardens</u> <u>and</u> <u>Gardeners</u>, Massachusetts
    Chapter, American Rhododendron Society, 1980.

Cox   Cox, Peter & Kenneth. <u>Encyclopedia</u> <u>of</u> <u>Rhododendron</u> <u>Hybrids</u>, Timber Press,
        Portland, OR, 1988.

Cullen, J. A. <u>A</u> <u>Revision</u> <u>of</u> <u>Rhododendron,</u> <u>Notes</u> <u>from</u> <u>the</u> <u>Royal</u> <u>Botanic</u> <u>Garden</u>,
    Edinburgh, Vol. 39, No. 1, 1980.

Davidian, H. H. <u>The</u> <u>Rhododendron</u> <u>Species,</u> <u>V.</u> <u>1,</u> <u>Lepidotes</u>, Timber Press, Port-
    land, OR, 1982.

Davidian, H. H. <u>The</u> <u>Rhododendron</u> <u>Species,</u> <u>V.</u> <u>2,</u> <u>Elepidotes,</u> <u>Pt.</u> <u>I,,</u> Timber
    Press, Portland, OR, 1989.

F   Fairweather, Christopher. <u>Rhododendrons</u> <u>and</u> <u>Azaleas</u> <u>for</u> <u>Your</u> <u>Garden</u>, Floraprint,
        Calverton, Nottingham, England, 1980.

I.R.R. Fletcher, H. R., comp. <u>The</u> <u>International</u> <u>Rhododendron</u> <u>Register</u>, Royal Horticul-
        tural Society, Vincent Square, London, 1958.

HG   Greer, Harold E. <u>Greer's</u> <u>Guidebook</u> <u>to</u> <u>Available</u> <u>Rhododendron</u> <u>Species</u> <u>and</u>
        <u>Hybrids</u>, Offshoot Publications, Eugene, OR, 1988.

        <u>Hillier's</u> <u>Manual</u> <u>of</u> <u>Trees</u> <u>and</u> <u>Shrubs</u>, 5th ed., Hillier Nurseries, Ampfield
        House, Ampfield, Romsey, Hampshire, England, 1981.

        Huse, Robert D., & Kenneth L. Kelly. <u>A</u> <u>Contribution</u> <u>Toward</u> <u>Standardization</u> <u>of</u>
        <u>Color</u> <u>Names</u> <u>in</u> <u>Horticulture</u>, American Rhododendron Society, Portland, OR, 1985

        Kelly, Kenneth L., & Deane B. Judd. <u>Color:</u> <u>Universal</u> <u>Language</u> <u>and</u> <u>Dictionary</u> <u>of</u>
        <u>Names</u>, National Bureau of Standards, Washington, D. C., 1976.

K   Kraxberger, Meldon, ed. <u>American</u> <u>Rhododendron</u> <u>Hybrids</u>, American Rhododendron
        Society, Portland, OR, 1980.

        Leach, David G. <u>Rhododendrons</u> <u>of</u> <u>the</u> <u>World</u> <u>and</u> <u>How</u> <u>to</u> <u>Grow</u> <u>Them</u>, Charles
        Scribner's Sons, New York, 1961.

LW   Livingston, Philip A., & Franklin H. West, eds. <u>Hybrids</u> <u>and</u> <u>Hybridizers:</u> <u>Rhodo-</u>
        <u>dendrons</u> <u>and</u> <u>Azaleas</u> <u>for</u> <u>Eastern</u> <u>North</u> <u>America</u>, Harrowood Books, Newton Square
        PA, 1978.

        Murray, Jay & Robert. <u>Rhododendron</u> <u>and</u> <u>Azalea</u> <u>Names,</u> <u>A</u> <u>Database</u>
        <u>of</u> <u>Parentage</u>, Clover Springs Computer Services, Wickatunk, NJ, 1990.

        Nelson, Pat, comp., with Marlene Buffington, Nadine Henry. <u>Selected</u> <u>Rhododendron</u>
        <u>Glossary</u>, 3-D Publications, Graham, WA, 1982.

PB   Phillips, E. C. Lucas & Peter N. Barber. <u>The</u> <u>Rothschild</u> <u>Rhododendrons:</u> <u>A</u> <u>Record</u>
        <u>of</u> <u>the</u> <u>Gardens</u> <u>at</u> <u>Exbury</u>, rev. ed., Cassell, London, 1970.

        Rand, E. F., Jr. <u>The</u> <u>Rhododendron</u>, Hurd and Houghton, 1876.

        Royal Horticultural Society. <u>Royal</u> <u>Horticultural</u> <u>Society</u> <u>Color</u> <u>Chart</u>, The So-
        ciety, Vincent Square, London, 1966.

RHS   Royal Horticultural Society. <u>Rhododendron</u> <u>Species</u> <u>in</u> <u>Cultivation;</u> <u>The</u> <u>Rhododen-</u>
        <u>dron</u> <u>Handbook</u>, The Society, Vincent Square, London, 1980.

        Royal Horticultural Society, Rhododendron Group. <u>The</u> <u>Rhododendron</u> <u>Handbook,</u> <u>Part</u>
        <u>Two,</u> <u>Rhododendron</u> <u>Hybrids</u>, The Society, Vincent Square, London, 1969.

        Salley, H. E. & Greer, H. E. <u>Rhododendron</u> <u>Hybrids:</u> <u>A</u> <u>Guide</u> <u>to</u> <u>Their</u> <u>Origins</u>,
        Timber Press, Portland, OR, 1986.

WS   Schmalscheidt, Walter. <u>Rhododendron-und</u> <u>Azaleenzüchtung</u> <u>in</u> <u>Deutschland</u>, Garten-
        bild Heinz Hansmann Gmbh & Co. KG, 3260 Rintein 1.

        Street, Frederick. <u>Hardy</u> <u>Rhododendrons</u>, Collins, London, 1954.

JS   Street, John.   <u>Rhododendrons</u>, Globe Pequot Press, Chester, Conn., 1987.

VV   Van Veen, Ted. <u>Rhododendrons</u> <u>in</u> <u>America</u>, rev. ed., Binford & Mort, Portland, OR,
        1980.

        PERIODICALS AND YEARBOOKS:

ARS   American Rhododendron Society. <u>Quarterly</u> <u>Bulletin</u> 1958-1981. Portland, OR.
                                       <u>Journal</u>, 1982-90.

RHS   Royal Horticultural Society. <u>Rhododendron</u> <u>Year</u> <u>Book</u> 1958-1971. Vincent Square,
        London.

                                     <u>Rhododendrons</u>, 1972/73.

                                     <u>Rhododendrons</u> <u>with</u> <u>Magnolias</u> <u>and</u> <u>Camellias</u>, 1974-90

        Catalogs and price lists of rhododendron nurseries.

ALEX DER'S LOCKINGTON (Lockington Pride x Coronation Day) White. D. J. Dosser.

AMIGO-TWO (Amigo x (aberconwayi x elliottii War Paint) Purplish red. D. W. Goheen.

ARGENTINA ([white catawbiense x yakushimanum] X [Fanfare x Gertrud Schale]) Purplish red. Leach.

ARMINIUS (America x yakushimanum) X unknown Deep pink, red blotch. Rudy Behring.

BARNSDALE DEERBANK (Antonio x Barnsdale Pink) Purplish pink. T. H. N. White.

BARNSDALE GLADE (Antonio x Barnsdale Pink) Purplish pink. T. H. N. White.

BARNSDALE PINK (Naomi grex hybrid) Purplish pink. T. H. N. White.

BELLRINGER (Parentage unknown) Greenish yellow, reddish brown flare. Don S. Kellam, Jr.

BORN WINNER ([maximum x yakushimanum] X Adele's Yellow) Purplish red. W. E. Delp.

BORNEO (white catawbiense X [dichroanthum ssp. apodectum x Loderi White Diamond] Pale yellow. Leach.

BOSKOOP CONCORDE (Antoon van Welie x Max Sye) Rich pink. A. van Nes.

BOTANY BRIDE (yakushimanum x Hydon Dawn) Deep purplish pink. J. F. J. McQuire.

BRITTANY (Bowie x dwarf keiskei) Yellowish pink. D. G. Leach.

BUTTERHORN (Eldorado x dalhousiae var. rhabdotum) Primrose yellow. R. W. Scott.

CARYS (yunnanense x Lady Chamberlain) Light purple; purplish red flare. A. J. B. Edwards.

CHARLIE HERBERT (Captain Jack x yakushimanum Exbury form) Purplish pink. C. & E. Rahn.

CHECKMATE (Sport of PJM Victor) Strong reddish purple. Weston Nurseries.

CHIEF PAT KANIM (Parentage unknown) Purple and white. W. & J. Ragan.

CHINA CLIPPER (Skipper x China) Greenish yellow. Mrs. George Clarke.

CHORUS LINE (Lem's Cameo x Pink Petticoats) Purplish red. John G. Lofthouse.

CLARK'S CHINA DOLL (Skipper x China) Purplish pink. Mrs. George Clarke.

CLARK'S GOLDEN GATE (Parentage unknown) Purplish red. Mrs. George Clarke.

CONNECTICUT YANKEE (Possible catawbiense hybrid) Dark greenish yellow. G. A. L. Mehlquist.

CRAYON (Dad's Killer x Purple Splendour) Light purple, deep red spotting. Steve Mauritsen.

CREOLE BELLE (Vulcan x Harvest Moon) Purplish red, deep red flare. W. & M. Thompson.

CRISTOBEL MAUDE (yakushimanum x Torch) Pale purplish pink, strong red eye. A. F. George.

DAVID LAM (Sunup-Sundown x Lem's Cameo) Light pink, spotted deep yellowish pink. Lofthouse.

DESERT ORCHID (yakushimanum x The Master) Pale purplish pink, fading white. A. F. George.

DONVALE GEM (yakushimanum x arboreum) X arboreum Strong purplish pink. J. A. O'Shannassy.

DORIS GRISWOLD ([Fabia x bureavii] X Jean Marie de Montague) Purplish pink. Linda Malland.

DOTTED SWISS (R. O. Delp x Fiery Orange) Light purple, greenish yellow flare. W. E. Delp.

ELIN (yakushimanum x Britannia) Light purple/vivid purplish red. A. J. B. Edwards.

FIRESTORM (Vulcan x Chocolate Soldier) Deep red. Mark H. Brand.

FORT BRAGG CENTENNIAL (Form of maddenii ssp. crassum) Yellowish white. Eleanor Philp.

FRAN'S SONG [(yakushimanum x Fabia) x CIS] X (Fawn x Indian Penny) Pale yellow. R. E. Burns.

FRYE BUTT (Dad's Killer x Purple Splendour) Purplish pink. Steve Mauritsen.

GUILFORD (Parentage unknown) Purplish pink, strong purplish pink margins. W. D. Tietjen.

HAMPSHIRE BELLE (Parentage unknown) Deep purplish pink. E. W. George.

HAY LEE (Marion seedling x Marion seedling) Strong purplish pink. D. J. Dosser.

HELEN MARIE (Pink Pearl x Loderi King George) Bright rose pink. Lord Harewood.

HELGOLAND (Scandinavia x yakushimanum 'Hanano-ego') W. Schmalscheidt.

HYDON BEN (yakushimanum x Billy Budd) Strong red. A. F. George.

HYDON GOLD (New Comet x Crest) Light greenish yellow. A. F. George.

HYDON PEARL (yakushimanum x The Master) Light purplish pink. A. F. George.

JANE STENNING (Calsap x Besse Howells) Dark red, black blotch. D. L. Hinerman.

JEDA (Butter Brickle x [Sunup-Sundown x Whitney hybrid]) Pale orange yellow. J. G. Lofthouse.

JOANNA STENNING ([America x Mars] X Pink Mango) Purplish red, white blotch. D. L. Hinerman.

LEMON PIE (Parentage unknown) Light greenish yellow, unmarked. Mrs. George Clarke.

LEMON TART (Parentage unknown) Yellow-green, purplish red blotch. Mrs. George Clarke.

LEON'S BICOLORED (Catawbiense Album x Mars) Reddish purple, white center. Leon Yavorsky.

LITTLE BETH (Parentage unknown) Very pale purple. Mrs. George Clarke.
LOFTHOUSE'S LEGACY (Butter Brickle x Viennese Waltz) Light orange yellow. John G. Lofthouse
LYNSEY ANN (soulei x ?soulei) Strong purplish pink. S. Hilscher.
MARGO REYNOLDS (yakushimanum x Mars) Purplish pink, white center. Leon Yavorsky.
MARIA STENNING (Janet Blair x Calsap) Light purple, reddish purple marks. D. L. Hinerman.
MARIO PAGLIARINI (fortunei x unknown) Very pale purple. John J. McGuire.
MICHAEL BEHRING (wardii x brachycarpum ssp. tigerstedii) Pale purplish pink. Rudy Behring.
MIDNIGHT SUN (catawbiense hybrid x catawbiense hybrid) Purple, white blotch. Stokes/Pyycl.
MIKE DAVIS (yakushimanum hyb. x Lem's Cameo) Light purplish pink. Joe A. Davis.
MISTY LILAC (Catalgla x Mrs. Tom H. Lowinsky) Pale purple, yellow blotch. Rudy Behring.
MONICA ROSE (thomsonii x unknown) Deep rose pink. Mrs. M. R. Thorpe.
MOSSMAN'S FRECKLES (Cavalcade x yakushimanum) Deep red, outside shell pink. Ernie Metcalfe.
NICOLA NEWMAN (Cornubia x sutchuenense) Reddish purple. A. Stephenson Clark.
PEACH PERFECTION (Butter Brickle x [Sunup-Sundown x Whitney hybrid]) Strong red and yellowish pink. John G. Lofthouse.
PEGGY ZABEL (Parentage unknown) Yellowish white. Bohle/Briggs Nursery.
PENTLAND (Selection from oreotrephes) Strong reddish purple. P. A. Cox.
PILLAR BOX (Grosclaude x Tally Ho) Vivid red, not fading. J. F. J. McQuire.
PLUM PERFECT (Julia Grothaus x Purple Splendour) Purplish pink, dark red blotch. Julia G. Vea.
RAINBOW'S END (Butter Brickle x [Fabia selfed x Lem's Early Orange]) Red-yellow to light orange. John G. Lofthouse.
RAVENNA (Scarlet Blast X [(white catawbiense x yakushimanum) x (Fanfare x Gertrud Schale)] Strong red. D. G. Leach.
RED POND (America x Kettledrum) Strong purplish red. W. Stokes/O. Prycl.
RING OF FIRE (Darigold x Idealist) Yellow, edged strong red. W. & M. Thompson.
ROLLIE (A. Bedford x fragrant pink hybrid) Pale purple to pale orange yellow. Rollie Mulkey.
SABRINA ADLER (ciliicalyx x moupinense) White, light red spotting. R. W. Scott.
SEB (yakushimanum x Popacatepetl) Deep purplish pink, fading white. J. F. J. McQuire.
SILVER SKIES (yakushimanum 'Koichiro Wada' x Medusa) Pale pink. F. Fujioka.
SOUTHERN SKIES (Sunup-Sundown x Lem's Cameo) Yellowish pink. John G. Lofthouse.
STOKES BRONZE WINGS (maximum x catawbiense) Light purple, greenish yellow flare. Stokes/Delp.
STONELAW (edgeworthii x burmanicum) White, flushed purplish pink. Dunedin Rhod. Group.
SUNSET BAY (Odee Wright x Malemute) Primrose yellow, pink blush. J. A. Elliott.
TABASCO (yakushimanum x Noyo Chief) X Escataba Vivid red. D. W. Goheen.
TEAR DROP (minus var. minus Carolinianum Group, Delp's tetraplid form x fastigiatum) Vivid and light purple. W. E. Delp.
TOP GUN (Parentage unknown) Peony purple, black spotting. Wright's Nursery.
TRELEAN LAVENDER GIRL (Naomi Nautilus x unknown) Very pale purple. G. T. Witherwick.
TRELEAN VISION (yakushimanum x bureavii) White, suffused purplish pink. G. T. Witherwick.
UNIQUE MARMALADE (Orange Marmalade x Unique) Deep pink to light orange. Joe A. Davis.
VICTORIA HALLETT (strigillosum x arboreum) Strong red. High Beeches Conservation Trust.
WAIREKA (Lovelock x ciliatum) Pale yellow green, brilliant yellow blotch. W. B. Campbell.
WANNA BEE (yakushimanum x Jiminy Cricket) Pale purplish pink. Warren Berg.
WAY AHEAD (Cary Ann x Mars) China rose, white center. Wright's Nursery.
WHIDBEY ISLAND (niveum x rex) Light purple, edged vivid violet. Meerkerk R. Gardens.
WINNING COLORS (Purple Lace x yakushimanum, Whitney's dwarf form) Shell pink, white center. Susan K. Metcalfe.
WISP OF GLORY (Parentage unknown) Purplish pink, edged purplish red. Mrs. George Clarke.
WOJNAR'S PURPLE (Parentage unknown) Reddish purple, dark purple flare. Wojnar/Mehlquist.
WOOD'S COLT (aberconwayii x unknown) Pale purple/purplish pink. Pauline Newberry/Eleanor Philp.
YELLOW ROLLS ROYCE (Crest x Odee Wright) Brilliant greenish yellow. G. Clark cross; H. Spady.